The American Experiment

The American Experiment

A HISTORY OF THE UNITED STATES

SECOND EDITION

VOLUME II: SINCE 1865

STEVEN M. GILLON

UNIVERSITY OF OKLAHOMA

CATHY D. MATSON

UNIVERSITY OF DELAWARE

HOUGHTON MIFFLIN COMPANY   BOSTON NEW YORK

Vice President and Publisher: Charles Hartford
Senior Sponsoring Editor: Sally Constable
Development Editor: Jan Fitter
Editorial Assistant: Arianne Vanni
Project Editor: Reba Libby
Senior Art and Design Coordinator: Jill Haber Atkins
Senior Photo Editor: Jennifer Meyer Dare
Senior Composition Buyer: Sarah Ambrose
Senior Designer: Henry Rachlin
Manufacturing Coordinator: Carrie Wagner
Senior Marketing Manager: Sandra McGuire
Marketing Assistant: Molly Parke

Cover image: An Incident in Contemporary American Life, mural by Mitchell Jamieson, Commemorating Marian Anderson's concert on the steps of Lincoln Memorial, 1943.
Courtesy of the U.S. General Services Administration, Fine Arts Collection.

Text credits are on page A-30, which constitutes an extension of the copyright page.

Printed in the U.S.A.

Library of Congress Catalog Card Number: 2003110168

Instructor's exam copy ISBN: 0-618-59587-2
For orders use student text ISBN: 0-618-42951-4

2 3 4 5 6 7 8 9-QT-08 07 06 05 04

Brief Contents

CONTENTS

17   Conquering the West, 1862–1900   655

18   The Industrial Experiment, 1865–1900   696

19   The New Urban Nation, 1865–1900

22   The Experiment in American Empire, 1865–1917

25   "Fear Itself": Crash, Depression, and the New Deal, 1929–1938   969

26   War and Society, 1933–1945 1010

27   The Cold War, 1945–1952 1053

32   America After the Cold War, 1988–2000   1262

Epilogue: The Challenges of the New Century

MAPS AND GRAPHS

PREFACE

America's written history began more than five hundred years ago with the encounters of Native Americans, Europeans, and Africans who struggled to bend nature to their needs and understand or overwhelm each other in countless ways. As this richly textured history unfolded, scholars also created many twists and turns in our understanding of this past. During the last quarter of the nineteenth century, historians in the United States emphasized the roles of political and intellectual leaders, as well as institutions and diplomacy. "History is past politics and politics are present history," declared Henry B. Adams, a founding member of the American Historical Association (AHA), in 1884.

Challenges to this perspective arose by the turn of the twentieth century, as when Carl Becker, in his own presidential address to the AHA, referred to "everyman" in the widest possible terms as "his own historian." But not until the 1960s did scholars pioneer fresh methods in writing "New History" that emphasized narrating the past "from the bottom up"; they found "patterns of intimate personal behavior" that revealed the lives of people who had remained hidden from our understanding of the past. The New History represented a dramatic turn away from the traditional ways of representing our past. It forced scholars to recognize that our history was shaped by the interaction of a variety of groups and cultures that had been excluded from older narratives. It also highlighted the importance of culture, and often stressed the role of conflict over consensus in telling the story of America's past. While it expanded our understanding of the enormous diversity of the American experiment, the New History often struggled to find a unified narrative that captured the drama and excitement of the past.

The American Experiment combines the best of both approaches by finding common ground between political and cultural approaches to history. It expands our histories beyond the realm of elite actors and powerful institutions to include the far wider arenas of public and private culture. While paying close attention to politics and political culture it appreciates how race, class, and gender have shaped our nation's history. It also recognizes the need for synthesis in historical writing, but without neglecting the threads of individual experiences in the larger fabric of American history.

APPROACH

Drawing on the best of these new directions, this book narrates the broad contours of change at the imperial or national level, and, at the same time, explains the lives of people in diverse communities who lived sometimes ordinary, sometimes extraordinary, lives. We believe that it is equally important to study how institutions emerged, rulers ruled, and economies developed, as it is to explain everyday work, family life, and different customs.

We have chosen the title *The American Experiment* to underscore our belief that North America's past can be best understood as an ongoing struggle of various competing experiences of individuals, communities, and polities. These experiences were contested and continually reshaped for almost two centuries in the crucibles of Native American villages, European settlements, and African-American communities. The American Revolution tested and extended the ideals that lay behind such experiences during struggles for what was perceived to be liberty and equality. The unresolved tension between ideals and social realities would emerge as a central theme of American history for the next two centuries. The nation experimented with different approaches and strategies as it struggled—and continues to struggle— to reconcile its broad belief in individual liberty and equality with the reality of racial discrimination, class conflict, and gender inequality. The same tension has shaped America's relationship to the world, especially since the late nineteenth century, as the nation's leaders have attempted to balance the ideal of spreading democracy and supporting human rights with the realities of global military power. In the widest sense, this is how the American experiment unfolded.

THEMES

This book's four central themes highlight these ideals and realities on many levels. The first theme focuses on competing views of the proper role of government. For generations, colonists, then independent Americans, debated just what degree of control a central government should have over their everyday lives, what kinds of powers should be given to governing bodies, and what kinds of leaders should rule. But when scholars recount this story, too often they have focused primarily on charting the growth in the size and scope of central governing powers and the achievements of national political and intellectual leaders. This kind of narrative cannot fully explain how, in reality, American political culture has been characterized by competing views of the proper role of government, including but not limited to the persistence of conservative attitudes about limited government, as well as widespread belief in the centrality of self-help and individualism in the face of growing national government.

A second theme addresses issues of identity. What qualities do Americans believe define them best? The answers, we believe, change over time. Our history has been defined by the shifting struggles among ethnic, religious, regional, class, and racial groups to shape both the multiplicity of particular identities and a sequence of unifying images about being "American." Being "colonists" suggested to thousands of settlers that they were politically subordinate, as well as culturally and economically dependent, on the imperial center. But settlers often paid more attention to religious backgrounds, local social status, or their identity as residents of one locale. Post-Revolutionary Americans embarked on an intense struggle to make—or make over—their identity. They often spoke and wrote about "the nation," but the term meant different things to different parts of the population. For most of our history, American identity has been defined in racial terms, as African-Americans underwent the unsettling transformations of slavery, struggled for emancipation, and later demanded the rights of citizenship. But especially in recent decades, it has included the attempts of other disenfranchised groups—

Hispanics, Asians, women, and homosexuals—to challenge the dominant structure and force a reluctant acceptance of their unique contributions to American society.

Third, our book explores how we can use the concept of "culture" to explore the variety of regional, ethnic, market, political, racial, and other environments in which Americans construct their lives. From the start, colonists sometimes willingly, sometimes unwittingly blended characteristics of European and African cultures with the Indian cultures and natural environment in which they settled. Long before the American Revolution, the continent's amazingly heterogeneous population was undergoing rapid changes, continually negotiating accommodation of its cultural differences, and sometimes facing bloody conflicts over them. By the beginning of the twentieth century, new instruments of mass culture produced intense conflict between local cultures and a shifting but recognizable national culture. We ask, has a distinctive *American* culture emerged? If so, when and how? If not, how shall we understand the multiplicity of cultures under the umbrella polity we call America?

Finally, our book examines America's ambivalent relationship to the outside world. Enormous changes in the relations among world nations have occurred as we evolved from a knot of English colonies into a world superpower. Along the way, Americans have often measured their collective success in comparison to the condition of other world peoples, but in an important sense, we have not completely abandoned the isolationist streak that has been so much a part of our past. Indeed, even during the period of America's rise to world power, our leaders were driven more by a desire to remake the world in our image than by a need to join the international community of nations. In the pages that follow, we have asked how Americans explained their place in the world at various turning points in their own evolution.

FEATURES

Our focus on themes and use of "experiment" as a motif for understanding the American past structure our narrative and give students an organizing framework. The narrative seeks to link significant events through American history with important concepts and historians' interpretations as they are reflected in current scholarship. We have also included numerous revealing quotations and vivid anecdotes. Among the special features that our book offers are chapter-opening vignettes that illustrate one or more of the chapter's central themes, followed by an introductory paragraph and a series of focus questions that guide students' reading and thinking. In addition to a chronology and a brief conclusion, each chapter also includes a "Competing Voices" section that provides students and teachers with the opportunity to examine primary sources. Two short excerpts that represent differing viewpoints about a common issue are framed with headnotes, paragraphs of background context, and guiding questions that help students become familiar with the tools of working historians.

NEW TO THE SECOND EDITION

Several chapter-opening vignettes have been replaced in this second edition, in response to our own experiences and feedback from instructors using the book. In addition, to help draw students into the vignette and its message, we now open each chapter with an inviting quotation from the vignette narrative. Focus questions at the start of chapters have been reviewed, and in many cases refined, based on feedback we have received. A number of new documents have been selected for the "Competing Voices" section of each chapter, based both on shifts in historical interpretations in recent years and on the effectiveness of these new selections in classrooms, as tested by both the authors and by students and teachers who have used the book.

In addition to the features we have retained from the first edition, we have added a new feature entitled "Competing Interpretations" following eight chapters. Each of these essays summarizes a major turning point of historical interpretation over decades of scholarly investigation. Among multiple benefits for students, "Competing Interpretations" will

—introduce students to an essential dimension of how historians work and interpret the past.

—help students develop critical reading and thinking skills for analyzing historical argument.

—bring students a deeper understanding of a significant "problem" in American history.

The four essays appearing in volume I were written by Cathy Matson. For volume II, Steve Gillon is grateful to **Professor David Wrobel** of the University of Nevada at Las Vegas for composing the four new essays. In fact, it was David, a scholar of the American West, who as a user of *The American Experiment* suggested this new feature.

In producing this second edition of *The American Experiment* we have revised the narrative of both volumes in several important respects. We have, in the first place, scrutinized our presentation of the past with respect to accuracy, interpretation, and style in every chapter and introduced myriad line-by-line, paragraph-by-paragraph emendations. Second, we have introduced new wording and quotations to further explain central historical developments, and we have added entirely new sections of material that elaborate the themes of America's place in a shifting world context, especially as it is reflected in emerging global studies scholarship.

Readers will also notice that *The American Experiment* has been redesigned in appearance. We believe the new format makes the text more inviting, while better highlighting pedagogical and structural guideposts. A number of new maps have been added, especially in volume I, and many maps have been enhanced for clarity and appearance. The bibliographical essays have been reviewed closely and revised to reflect the appearance of significant new scholarship.

STUDY AND TEACHING AIDS

Supplements Available with *The American Experiment*, Second Edition

The **Houghton Mifflin History Companion** is a collection of web site and CD resources designed as an easy-to-use complement to *The American Experience*. It is organized according to the chapters in the text and has four parts—the **Instructor**

Companion web site, the **Instructor Companion CD-ROM**, the **Student Study Companion**, and the **Student Research Companion.**

The History Companion

- The **Instructor Companion web site** features the Instructor's Resource Manual by J. Kent McGaughy of Houston Community College Northwest, primary sources with instructor notes, hundreds of maps, images, audio and video clips, and PowerPoint and flash slides for classroom presentation.

- The **Instructor Companion CD-ROM** includes all the material on the web site and offers additional audio and video clips for classroom use, the Test Bank by D. Antonio Cantu of Ball State University in Word and **HMTesting**, a computerized version of the test bank with a flexible test-editing program with a comprehensive gradebook function.

- The **Student Study Companion** by D. Antonio Cantu of Ball State University is a free, online study guide to accompany *The American Experiment.* The Study Companion contains a variety of tutorial resources including ACE practice tests with feedback, annotated links to history sites, chronology exercises, flashcards, and other interactive activities.

- The **Student Research Companion** is a free, online tool with a wealth of interactive maps and primary sources. Students can use the maps for research, classroom assignments, or review of their geography skills. Primary sources provide a real-world introduction to historical evidence. The sources include headnotes that provide pertinent background information and questions that students can answer and e-mail to their instructors.

BLACKBOARD/WEBCT CD-ROM

Rand McNally Atlas, free with text

Please contact your local Houghton Mifflin sales representative for more information about these learning and teaching tools, WebCT and Blackboard cartridges, and the transparencies for United States history.

ACKNOWLEDGMENTS

We are deeply grateful to the key people at Houghton Mifflin who have helped us usher this second edition through revision and production, including Sally Constable, our senior history editor, and Sandy McGuire, senior marketing manager. Jan Fitter, our indefatigable development editor, has improved every page of this book not only with her matchless ability to wield the English language, but also with her deep understanding of American history. At different stages of work on this edition, Rosemary Jaffe and Reba Libby, our project editors, worked tirelessly to make sure all the pieces, large and small, fell into place. Many thanks to our photo researcher Lisa Jelly Smith and our art editor Penny Peters; we hope they will agree that this second edition provides our students with superior visual representations of American history. We also wish to thank Kisha Mitchell, editorial assistant at Houghton Mifflin, as well as Kathy Brown and Charlie Hartford. Cathy Matson also deeply appreciates the many helpful comments of reviewers, teaching assistants, and students who criticized and inspired myriad aspects of volume I over the years. Steve Gillon owes a debt of gratitude to Heather Clemmer of the University of Oklahoma. A talented writer and editor, Heather has helped in every stage of this book's development.

Writing a textbook for the survey in American History is an enormous undertaking, and we wish to acknowledge our deep appreciation for the help of our colleagues who reviewed portions of the book in its various stages of revision:

Todd Estes, *Oakland University*

Lisa C. Tolbert, *University of North Carolina Greensboro*

Pat Ledbetter

Jonathan Lee

Kevin F. Decker, *SUNY Plattsburgh*

Dr. Reid S. Derr, *East Georgia College*

Thomas F. Ciani, *Raritan Valley Community College*

Thomas D. Veve, *Dalton State College*

David M. Wrobel, *University of Nevada Las Vegas*

James L. Moses, Ph.D., *Assistant Professor of History, Arkansas Tech University*

H. Warren Gardner, *University of Texas of the Permian Basin*

Edward R. Crowther, *Adams State College*

Marcia Brawner Vaughn, *Murray State University*

Charles Levine, *Mesa Community College*

Michael Kennedy, *University of Michigan—Flint*

Carl H. Moneyhon, *University of Arkansas at Little Rock*

Elisabeth Evans Wray, *History Department, School of Arts and Sciences & Liberal Arts Program, School of Continuing Studies, University of Richmond*

Thomas A. Castillo, *University of Maryland, College Park*

David P. Kilroy, *Wheeling Jesuit University*

Todd Forsyth Carney, *Southern Oregon University*

Alan Bearman, *Washburn University*

Richard J. Moss, *Colby College*

Stephen Tallackson, *Instructor, Purdue University—Calumet*

Holly Baggett, *Southwest Missouri State University*

Robert Glen Findley, *Assistant Professor of History and Government at Odessa College*

David J. Voelker, *University of Wisconsin—Green Bay*

Dr. Leonard D. Ortiz, *Baker University*

Dr. James Myers, *Professor of History, Odessa College*

Dr. Danton Kostandarithes

Professor Gary D. McElhany, Ph.D., *Southwestern Assemblies of God University*

Anna Bates, *Aquinas College*

Howard Smead, *University of Maryland, College Park*

Martin T. Olliff, *Assistant Professor of History, Troy University*

Terri Diane Halperin, *University of Richmond*

Dr. John K. Derden, *East Georgia*

Steven M. Gillon

Cathy D. Matson

Reconstruction and the New South

1864–1900

The experiments of the Reconstruction Era (1863–1877) brought intense struggles between groups with competing notions of government power, individual rights, and race relations.

The opening act of *Our American Cousin* had already begun when the president's carriage pulled up to Ford's Theater in Washington on April 14, 1865. At 8:25 P.M. President Lincoln, accompanied by his wife Mary and a young couple, Major Henry Rathbone and Clara Harris, quietly made his way to the presidential box, which overlooked the stage. Someone in the theater spotted Lincoln, and within minutes the packed crowd of 1,675 was giving the president an enthusiastic standing ovation. The actors joined in while the band struck up "Hail to the Chief."

Lincoln settled into his black walnut rocking chair; Mrs. Lincoln sat on his right. The guard who had been sitting outside the door leading to the president's box had decided to go across the street to meet some friends. It proved to be a fatal mistake. During the third act, John Wilkes Booth, a deranged actor and Confederate sympathizer, dashed into the president's box, pulled a small pistol from his pocket, and placed it within six inches of Lincoln's head. As he cried out, "Sic semper tyrannus!" ("Thus be it ever to tyrants!"), Booth pulled the trigger. The president slumped forward in his chair. Booth jumped out of the haze of blue gun smoke brandishing a dagger. While Mary embraced her husband, Major Rathbone wrestled with the attacker. Booth escaped Rathbone's grasp by slashing his arm to the bone. Then he leaped from the box, only to catch his spur on a flag adorning its rail and crash to the stage.

The president lay mortally wounded. The bullet had struck behind his left ear, tunneled through his brain, and lodged behind his right eye. Four soldiers and two doctors carried him to a small privately owned house across the street. An observer recorded the scene in his diary: "The quaint sufferer lay extended diagonally across the bed, which was not long enough for him. . . . His slow, full respiration lifted the

[bed] clothes with each breath he took. His features were calm and striking." The physicians gathered around the bed knew that Lincoln could not survive his wound. Mary, overcome with grief, refused to accept his fate. "Love, live but one moment to speak to me once—to speak to our children," she cried. Lincoln never spoke again. The following morning, April 15, at 7:22 A.M. Abraham Lincoln, the sixteenth president of the United States, took his last breath. "Now he belongs to the ages," whispered Secretary of War Edwin Stanton.

Union troops engaged in a massive manhunt to find Lincoln's killer. They tracked him down in a barn in Virginia and killed him in a blaze of gunfire. His last words were, "Tell mother I die for my country. I thought I did for the best." Investigators quickly discovered that Booth had not acted alone. On the same night that Booth shot Lincoln, his accomplices planned attacks on Vice President Andrew Johnson and Secretary of State William Seward. Johnson escaped unharmed, but Seward suffered severe stab wounds. A military tribunal convicted eight people of conspiracy to kill the president. Despite often flimsy evidence, four were hanged.

The bullet that killed Lincoln also changed the direction of Reconstruction, the government policy toward the defeated South. Lincoln's death removed a masterful politician, emboldened those seeking to impose a punitive peace on the South, and elevated to the presidency a man unprepared for the bitter political debates that followed. The experiments of the Reconstruction Era (1863–1877) brought intense struggles between groups with competing notions of government power, individual rights, and race relations. President Johnson, believing he was following Lincoln's plan for a quick "restoration" of the Union, rigidly supported states' rights, leniency toward the former rebels, and noninterference in attempts to restrict the rights of the freed people. Radical Republicans, who included former abolitionists and freed slaves, challenged Johnson's program and were able to seize control of Reconstruction policy in 1866. Wielding the power of the national government, they hoped to punish unrepentant planters, ensure the political and economic rights of the former slaves, and solidify the Republican Party's control of the South.

African-Americans were central players in the Republican effort to "reconstruct" southern society. Freed from the bonds of slavery, they moved to strengthen old institutions such as the family and church, to create new political institutions, and to secure economic independence. Despite important gains, black experiments in freedom were soon frustrated by white Democrats who clamored for the "redemption" of the defeated South. Using violence and intimidation, "Redeemers" successfully fought to recreate the white-dominated social order that had existed before the war. In the face of determined southern Democrats and internal divisions in the North, the Republicans backed away from their commitment to Reconstruction, leaving the experiment incomplete. The "New South" that emerged from war and Reconstruction had changed in significant ways, but for many African-Americans it bore striking similarities to the South of old.

- Why did President Johnson and congressional Republicans divide over Reconstruction policy?

- What did the Radical Republicans hope to accomplish, and what role did government play in their methods?

CHRONOLOGY

1863	Lincoln issues Proclamation of Amnesty and Reconstruction
1864	Radical Republicans pass Wade-Davis Bill
1865	Lincoln assassinated; Johnson becomes president Freedmen's Bureau created Southern states pass Black Codes House forms the Joint Committee on Reconstruction Thirteenth Amendment passed and ratified; prohibits slavery
1866	Fourteenth Amendment passed; establishes citizenship for blacks Fifteenth Amendment passed; gives black males the vote Republicans sweep off-year elections
1867	First Reconstruction Act Tenure of Office Act
1868	Johnson impeached and acquitted Fourteenth Amendment ratified Grant elected president
1869	National Woman Suffrage Association and American Woman Suffrage Association founded
1870	Fifteenth Amendment ratified Ku Klux Klan launches terrorist campaign First Enforcement Act
1871	Last of southern states rejoin the Union Ku Klux Klan Act
1872	Liberal Republicans nominate Greeley for president Grant reelected president Crédit Mobilier, "salary grab," and Whiskey Ring scandals uncovered General Amnesty Act
1873	Panic of 1873 begins Colfax Massacre
1875	Civil Rights Act of 1875
1876	Presidential election is disputed
1877	Compromise of 1877; Hayes becomes president
1880	Harris publishes *Uncle Remus*
1884	Twains publishes *The Adventures of Huckleberry Finn*
1895	Booker T. Washington's "Atlanta Compromise"
1896	*Plessy* v. *Ferguson* establishes "separate-but-equal" doctrine

- How did African-Americans respond to freedom and political participation? How did southern whites react to black participation?

- Why has Reconstruction been called "America's unfinished revolution"?

- How did the New South reflect the failure of Reconstruction? How different was it from the Old South?

This chapter will address these questions.

PRESIDENTIAL RECONSTRUCTION: THE FIRST EXPERIMENT, 1864–1866

The North's victory had ended the Civil War, but the battle for the peace had just begun. Congressional Republicans and the White House clashed even before the war ended over a central question: how much authority did the federal government have to impose conditions on the defeated states of the South? Lincoln had experimented with a lenient plan for returning the rebel states to the Union, but his assassination strengthened the hands of those Republicans who supported harsher measures. The difficult task of formulating a new policy fell to Vice President Andrew Johnson, a man ill equipped for the difficult challenges ahead.

The Legacy of Battle

The war had devastated southern society. The countryside, said one observer, "looked for many miles like a broad black streak of ruin and desolation." Most major cities were gutted by fire. A northern visitor called Charleston a place of "vacant houses, of widowed women, of rotting wharves, of deserted warehouses, of weed-wild gardens, of miles of grass-grown streets, of acres of pitiful and voiceless barrenness."

More than just razing cities, the Civil War shattered an entire generation of young men in the South. In Alabama 29 percent of the 122,000 men who bore arms died. One-third of Florida's 15,000 soldiers failed to return. An estimated 23 percent of South Carolina's white male population of arms-bearing age were killed or wounded. Many who survived were maimed in battle. In 1866 the state of Mississippi spent a fifth of its revenues on artificial arms and legs for Confederate veterans.

The war ruined the South's economic life. The region's best agricultural lands lay barren. It would take more than a decade for the staples of the southern economy—cotton, tobacco, and sugar—to recover from the wartime devastation. Union forces destroyed or dismantled most factories and tore up long stretches of railroad. According to some estimates, the South's per capita wealth in 1865 was only about half what it had been in 1860. All Confederate money was worthless. Most unsettling of all the changes the war had brought to the economy of Southern whites was the end of slavery. Slave property, which was estimated at over $2 billion in 1860, disappeared.

In contrast, the North emerged from battle with new prosperity and power. The Republicans who dominated the wartime Congress enacted a uniform system of banking and a transcontinental railroad. They also fueled the North's economy through generous appropriations for internal improvements. Railroads thrived by carrying troops and supplies; the meatpacking and textile industries soared in

The Ruins of Richmond
Burned-out shells of buildings were all that remained of the Richmond business district in April 1865. Confederate troops, not wanting supplies to fall into the hands of the Union army, had actually set many of the fires as they fled. The ruins are indicative of the total devastation of the South at the war's end. The massive rebuilding effort was just one of the monumental tasks facing the nation during Reconstruction. *(Getty Images)*

response to demands from troops for food and uniforms. The per capita wealth of the North doubled between 1860 and 1870. The number of manufactures increased by 80 percent, and property values increased from $10 billion to over $25 billion. In 1870 the per capita wealth of New York State was more than twice that of all eleven ex-Confederate states combined.

The war also ravaged the political landscape in America. War-born hostility shaped the competition between the two parties long after the war had ended. Republicans depended on hatred of southern rebels to cement their biracial coalition. "The Democratic party," proclaimed Indiana governor Oliver P. Morton, "may be described as a common sewer and loathsome receptacle, into which is emptied every element of treason, North and South." Democrats appealed to their natural constituency of former slave owners by charging that Republicans were the defenders of economic privilege and political centralization and a threat to individual liberty. Stressing the potent message of white supremacy also drove an ideological wedge between freed slaves and poor whites.

The war had a long-term impact on the sectional balance of power in the nation. Before 1861 the slave states had achieved an extraordinary degree of power in the national government. In 1861 the United States had lived under the Constitution for seventy-two years. During forty-nine of those years, the country's president had been a southerner—and a slaveholder. After the Civil War, a century passed before another resident of the Deep South was elected president. However, southern whites continued to exercise considerable influence in national politics. When the Democratic Party won control of the House of Representatives in 1874, northern and southern party members joined forces to frustrate Republican law-makers, beginning a twenty-year partisan stalemate in Congress. The war gave birth to the modern American state, dominated by a national government far more powerful than anything the nation had known previously. The federal budget for 1865 exceeded $1 billion (twenty times the budget for 1860); with its new army of clerks, tax collectors, and other officials, the federal government became the nation's largest employer. The increased size and scope of government found expression in language: northerners replaced references to the country as a "union" of separate states with a new emphasis on a singular, consolidated "nation."

The presence of nearly 3.5 million former slaves represented the most dramatic legacy of the war. The black abolitionist Frederick Douglass observed that the for-mer slave "was turned loose, naked, hungry, and destitute to the open sky." The new challenges that freedom presented forced experimentation by black and white. What labor system would replace slavery? Was freedom enough, or would blacks achieve equality and obtain the right to vote?

Lincoln's Plan for Union Though not committed to any single plan for Reconstruction, Lincoln favored a lenient and conciliatory policy toward the South, as he made clear in 1863. Lincoln hoped that a charitable approach would produce defections from the southern cause and hasten the war's end. Beyond outlawing slavery, he offered no protection for freed slaves. He also insisted that the ultimate authority for Reconstruction of the states rested with the president, not Congress. Since the Union was "constitutionally indestructible," Lincoln argued that the southern states had never officially left the Union but had merely engaged in military rebellion. Therefore, Lincoln's power as commander-in-chief gave him control over the defeated states in the South.

In December 1863 Lincoln issued a Proclamation of Amnesty and Reconstruc-tion declaring that southern states could organize new governments after 10 per-cent of those who had voted in 1860 pledged their loyalty to the Union and accepted the Union's wartime acts outlawing slavery. Each state would then con-vene a constitutional convention and elect new representatives to Congress. Lin-coln offered a general amnesty to all Confederate citizens except high-ranking civil and military officials. His plan did not extend the right to vote to freed people. Car-rying out his policy, the president recognized reconstituted civil governments in Louisiana and Arkansas in 1864 and in Tennessee in February 1865.

Many congressional Republicans argued that by declaring war on the Union, the Confederate states had broken their constitutional ties and were "conquered provinces" subject to the authority of Congress. The most strenuous criticism came from a group of Radical Republicans. Most Radicals had antebellum ties to aboli-tionist reform and believed that it was the national government's responsibility to guarantee political rights and economic opportunity to the freed people in the South. Led by Senator Charles Sumner of Massachusetts and Representative Thad-deus Stevens of Pennsylvania, the Radicals wanted the North to impose a more puni-tive peace settlement. They planned to reshape southern society by confiscating southern plantations and redistributing the land to freed slaves and white southern-ers who had remained loyal to the Union. The North must, Stevens contended, "revolutionize Southern institutions, habits, and manners . . . or all our blood and treasure have been spent in vain."

In 1864 the Radicals challenged Lincoln by passing their own, more stringent peace plan. The Wade-Davis Bill, sponsored by Senator Benjamin Wade of Ohio and Representative Henry Winter Davis of Maryland, required 50 percent of white male citizens to declare their allegiance before a state could be readmitted to the Union. Moreover, only those southerners who pledged—through the so-called ironclad oath—that they had never voluntarily borne arms against the Union could vote or serve in the state constitutional conventions. The bill also required the state conventions to abolish slavery.

Lincoln killed the bill with a pocket veto, meaning that he "pocketed" it and did not sign it within the required ten days after the adjournment of Congress. The authors of the bill denounced Lincoln's action in the Wade-Davis Manifesto. Lincoln had to understand, they warned, that "the authority of Congress is paramount and must be respected." Flexing its muscle, Congress refused to seat the delegates from states that applied for readmission under Lincoln's plan.

The vast majority of congressional Republicans fell somewhere between Lincoln and the Radicals. Like the president, these so-called moderates wanted a quick end to the war and a speedy restoration of the Union. They showed little interest in Radical plans for social and economic Reconstruction. Many wanted to keep former Confederate leaders from returning to power and hoped to provide a minimum of political rights for freed people. The former slave, argued Lyman Trumbull, will "be tyrannized over, abused, and virtually reenslaved without some legislation by the nation for his protection." But the critical question was, how much protection? All Republicans shared a determination to solidify their party's power in the North and extend their influence in the South. Hostility toward former rebels and political expediency, more than reformist zeal, shaped their approach to the South.

Behind the scenes, Lincoln was working to find common ground among his fellow Republicans. In March 1865 the president and Congress agreed on the creation of the Bureau of Refugees, Freedmen, and Abandoned Lands (Freedmen's Bureau) to provide "such issues of provisions, clothing, and fuel" as might be needed to relieve "destitute and suffering refugees and freedmen and their wives and children." Over the next few years, the bureau built schools, paid teachers, and established a network of courts that allowed freed people to file suit against white people.

Lincoln, a masterful politician, might have maintained a congressional majority behind a fairly moderate program. Three days before his death, in the last speech he ever delivered, Lincoln suggested that he might support freedmen's suffrage, beginning with those who had served in the Union army. Whether Lincoln and his party could have forged a unified approach to Reconstruction is one of the great unanswered questions of American history.

Restoration Under Johnson

A few hours after Lincoln's death, Vice President Andrew Johnson of Tennessee was sworn in as president. Johnson rose from humble origins. His father, a porter and janitor, died when Andrew was three. Working as a tailor's apprentice at the age of ten, Johnson taught himself how to read and eventually started his own tailor shop. After prospering in business, he decided to enter politics. A Democrat, Johnson modeled himself after his hero, Andrew Jackson, who had fought for "common people" against powerful interests. "I am for the people," he declared as he rose from state assemblyman to U.S. senator. During the war, Johnson refused to support secession; and, after Federal forces captured Nashville, Lincoln appointed him as Tennessee's military governor. Many Republicans believed that Johnson, a southern Democrat who had remained loyal to the Union, could help unify the nation. In 1864 party leaders nominated him to serve as Lincoln's vice president.

Once in office, Johnson tried to continue Lincoln's lenient policy while also appeasing the Radicals. Like Lincoln, he insisted that the president held authority over Reconstruction policy, and he was more interested in "restoring" the Union than in "reconstructing" southern society. Unlike Lincoln, however, Johnson was a vain man consumed by deep suspicions and insecurities. He was ill suited for the delicate compromising and negotiating that would be necessary to maintain the Republican coalition. Moreover, Johnson was openly hostile to former slaves and deeply skeptical of Radical plans to provide freedmen with political rights. "This is a country for white men," the president said in 1865, "and by God, as long as I am President, it shall be a government for white men." Initially, he kept Radicals off balance with his strong denunciations of Confederate leaders. "Treason is a crime and crime must be punished. Treason must be made infamous and traitors must be impoverished," he declared. The president's rhetoric resulted from his populist hostility toward powerful southern planters, but Radicals interpreted it as support for their agenda. "Johnson, we have faith in you," Radical leader Ben Wade of Ohio remarked after visiting the new president. "By the gods, there will be no trouble now in running the government."

During the summer of 1865 Johnson executed his own plan of restoration. He appointed a provisional governor for each of the former Confederate states (except those states that had begun Reconstruction under Lincoln) and instructed the governors to convene constitutional conventions. The president insisted that the new constitutions revoke their ordinances of secession, repudiate the Confederate debt, and ratify the Thirteenth Amendment, which declared that "neither slavery nor involuntary servitude, except as punishment for crime . . . , shall exist within the United States."

Johnson also took a lenient approach to former rebels. He offered "amnesty and pardon, with restoration of all rights of property" to almost all southerners who took an oath of allegiance to the Constitution and the Union. Those ex-Confederates who were excluded from amnesty could personally petition Johnson for a pardon. The president approved nearly 90 percent of the petitions. By October 1865 ten of the eleven rebel states claimed to have passed Johnson's test for readmission to the Union. The Thirteenth Amendment was ratified in December. Satisfied with the South's progress, Johnson told Congress in December that the "restoration" of the Union was virtually complete.

Initially, most Republicans supported the outlines of Johnson's policy. Moderates wanted to strengthen some provisions but agreed that the federal government could not guarantee suffrage or civil rights for African-Americans. Radicals, though calling for stronger protections for blacks, hoped southern leaders would respond

Taking the Oath of Allegiance   Under President Johnson's Reconstruction plan, most Southern men could receive amnesty and a pardon for their previous Confederate service by swearing their allegiance to the Constitution and the Union before military officials. The plan expedited the process of readmitting southern states, but proved to be too lenient. The new state constitutions did not protect the freed slaves' civil rights and paved the way for the "Black Codes." Despite their oath of allegiance, many southern voters elected former Confederate leaders, including Confederate Vice President Alexander Stephens, to high-ranking political positions. (The South: A Tour of its Battle-Fields and Ruined Cities *by John Trowbridge, 1866.*)

favorably to the president's policy and offer the vote to some African-Americans. Over the next few months, however, Republican support for the president's policy faded as evidence mounted of both southern defiance and increasing discrimination against the freed people.

Southern leaders were in no mood for compromise or conciliation; they were committed to restoring the old racial order. The delegates who met to form the new governments in the South showed contempt for northern Reconstruction plans, rejecting even Johnson's benign policy. In fact, the "restoration" government looked much like the old Confederate government. Many of the conventions approved of constitutions that limited suffrage to whites. The provisional governor of Alabama declared that "the State affairs of Alabama must be guided and controlled by the superior intelligence of the white man." Southern voters defiantly elected to Congress the former vice president of the Confederacy, Georgia's Alexander Stephens, four Confederate generals, eight colonels, six cabinet members, and a host of other rebels.

All of the newly constituted state governments passed a series of stringent laws called "Black Codes." The codes varied from state to state, but all were designed to restrict the economic opportunities of freedmen and prevent former slaves from leaving plantations. Local officials who caught freedmen off the plantation without a current labor contract (renewed yearly) arrested and charged them with vagrancy, a crime that carried a fine, imprisonment, or involuntary servitude. Some states tried to prevent African-Americans from owning land. Other laws excluded African-Americans from juries and prohibited interracial marriages. Edmund Rhett of South Carolina summed up the purpose of the Black Codes: "The general interest both of the white man and of the negroes requires that he should be kept as near to the condition of slavery as possible, and as far from the condition of the white man as is practicable."

The President Versus Congress Southern resistance angered Radicals and many moderates in Congress. When the Thirty-ninth Congress convened in December 1865, moderates and Radicals refused to allow the newly elected representatives from former Confederate states to take their seats. Immediately after the House of Representatives turned the southerners away, Thaddeus Stevens called for the appointment of a special Joint Committee of Fifteen on Reconstruction "to inquire into the conditions of the States which formed the so-called Confederate States of America." Radicals quickly seized control of the committee, which consisted of nine House members and six senators.

After public hearings that revealed evidence of violence against freed slaves, the committee recommended congressional passage of new legislation to protect them. In January 1866 Congress voted to extend the life of the Freedmen's Bureau and enlarge its powers. In February Johnson issued a stinging veto message. The following month Congress passed a civil rights bill that extended the authority of federal courts to protect blacks. Again Johnson angrily vetoed the measure.

Why did Johnson assume a confrontational posture? There is no doubt that he sincerely believed both bills to be unconstitutional. The civil rights bill, he declared in his veto message, represented a stride "toward centralization and the concentration of all legislative power in the National Government." Political considerations were just as important. Johnson hoped that by forcing a confrontation he could isolate the Radicals from moderate Republicans. He refused to believe that moderates would break with him over the issue of freed people's rights. Ultimately, he hoped to build a new coalition that would include Democrats in the North and South, and a small number of moderate and conservative Republicans in the North.

But Johnson seriously miscalculated the lines of division within the party. In the words of the *New York Herald*, the president's actions were "a windfall, a godsend. He [Johnson] gave them Johnson to fight instead of fighting among themselves." The Senate vote to override his veto of the Freedmen's Bureau bill should have given him pause. Though the bill fell two votes short, thirty of thirty-eight Republicans voted in favor. In April moderates joined with the Radicals to override the presidential veto and enacted the Civil Rights Act of 1866. Despite all their differences, Radicals and moderates now shared a common disdain for the president and his Reconstruction policies, which rewarded rebels and made disaffection respectable in the South. "I have tried hard to save Johnson," observed moderate William Fessenden, "but I am afraid he is beyond hope."

A number of violent incidents in the South strengthened the Radicals' resolve to protect the rights of the freed people. In May a mob composed of white policemen and firemen invaded a black neighborhood in South Memphis, Tennessee. Before the riot ended, forty-eight people, all but two black, were dead; five black women had been raped; and hundreds of homes, churches, and schools had been torched. Three months later, in New Orleans, opponents of Radical Reconstruction went on a violent rampage when the Reconstruction governor attempted to reconvene the 1864 constitutional convention to reduce the growing power of former Confederates and to enfranchise blacks. The mob killed thirty-four blacks and three white Radicals. "It was not a riot," declared the military commander of the region. "It was an absolute massacre by the police." Radicals blamed Johnson's lenient policies for the outbreak. "Witness Memphis, witness Orleans," cried Sumner. "Who can doubt that the President is the author of these tragedies?"

Most people did not go as far as Sumner in blaming the president for the riots, but the violence undermined Johnson's claim that southern blacks did not need federal protection. In July Radicals and moderates joined forces again to pass the Freedmen's Bureau bill over a second veto. By overriding two presidential vetoes, Congress asserted its control over Reconstruction.

CONGRESSIONAL RECONSTRUCTION: THE RADICAL EXPERIMENT, 1866–1870

Commanding a clear majority in Congress, Radicals sent the Fourteenth and Fifteenth Amendments to the states. They designed the amendments to protect the rights of freed people and to strengthen the Republican Party's position in the South. They specifically excluded women from the protections of both amendments, angering women's suffrage supporters and creating deep divisions within the movement. Republican efforts to safeguard their gains by limiting the president's power resulted in the nation's first presidential impeachment trial.

Citizenship, Equal Protection, and the Franchise

In June 1866 the coalition of moderates and Radicals passed the Fourteenth Amendment to the Constitution. The amendment was the first national effort to define American citizenship. It declared that "all persons born or naturalized in the United States" were "citizens of the United States and of the State wherein they reside" and were guaranteed "equal protection" and "due process" under the law. The amendment reflected the growing consensus among Republicans that national legislation was necessary to force the South to deal fairly with blacks. By asserting that the national government played a role in guaranteeing individual rights, Republicans instituted a significant shift in the relationship between the federal government and the people. The amendment also established an important foundation for future challenges to the states' rights doctrine.

The amendment was a compromise measure designed to enhance the Republican Party's power. At the insistence of many moderates, it stopped short of enfranchising black men. But Radicals added a provision requiring a reduction in the representation in Congress of any state that denied adult males the vote. Either way the Republicans won control of Southern political affairs. Southern states would either extend the franchise to black voters, thus increasing the number of likely Republicans, or they would lose seats in Congress. The amendment also included a Radical demand that former Confederate leaders be prevented from holding federal or state offices; but moderates added a clause giving Congress the authority to override the disqualification in individual cases.

To take effect, the amendment had to be ratified by three-quarters of the states, and it became the central campaign issue during the fall 1866 congressional elections. Johnson denounced the amendment and urged southern states not to ratify it. Interpreting the elections as a referendum on the Fourteenth Amendment and his Reconstruction policy, the president planned an unprecedented campaign tour—called "a swing around the circle"—that took him from Washington to Chicago and St. Louis and back. He hoped the trip would exploit public sentiment against extending political rights to blacks and focus anger on Republican leaders. Instead, it further eroded support for presidential Reconstruction within his own party. Johnson alienated many moderate Republicans with his description of Radicals as "factious, domineering, tyrannical" men. "Why not hang Thad Stevens and Wendell Phillips?" he shouted to an audience in Cleveland.

Republicans skillfully focused the campaign on Johnson's support for the disloyal South. They successfully employed the tactic of "waving the bloody shirt" to remind northern voters of the thousands of family members and friends who died at the hands of southern armies. Viewing themselves as the defenders of the Union, Republicans held Johnson and the South responsible for thwarting Reconstruction.

On election night the voters appeared to repudiate the president. The Republicans won a three-to-one majority in both houses of Congress and gained control of the governorship and legislature in every northern state as well as in West Virginia, Missouri, and Tennessee. "This is the most decisive and emphatic victory ever seen in American politics," exclaimed the Radical journal, *The Nation*.

The moderate Republicans interpreted the election results as a clear call for Radical Reconstruction. Congress moved rapidly and, on March 2, 1867, adopted the First Reconstruction Act; supplementary acts followed in 1867 and 1868. These acts reversed presidential restoration and established new requirements for southern states to gain entry into the Union.

The First Reconstruction Act declared that "no legal government" existed in the South. It divided the South (with the exception of Tennessee, which had ratified the Fourteenth Amendment) into five military districts, each under the command of a Union general (see map on page 623). To be considered reconstructed, the law required southern states to call new constitutional conventions with all male citizens eligible to vote. The convention delegates then had to draft and approve state constitutions that guaranteed black suffrage. Finally, after the newly elected legislatures ratified the Fourteenth Amendment, the states would be accepted into the Union. During 1868 six states—North Carolina, South Carolina, Florida, Alabama, Louisiana, and Arkansas—met the requirements and were readmitted.

The new plan was far tougher than Johnson's policy, but many Radicals wanted to go farther. They pressed for federal support for black schools and the disfranchisement of ex-Confederate leaders. A few Radicals called for the distribution of land to former slaves. Thaddeus Stevens advocated confiscating millions of acres of

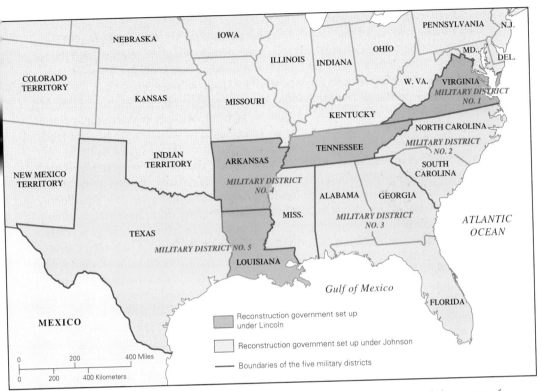

Military Reconstruction Districts   The Military Reconstruction Act shifted the power of Reconstruction from the president to Congress by invalidating the governments set up by Lincoln and Johnson. The act divided the ten states into five military districts in which commanding officers were given control of protecting the "rights of persons and property." Once state constitutional conventions framed new constitutions that guaranteed freedmen the right to vote and the state legislature ratified the Fourteenth Amendment, Congress would readmit them as a state and permit representation in Congress.

land from the "chief rebels" in the South and giving 40 acres to every adult male freedman. "How can republican institutions, free schools, free churches, free social intercourse exist," he asked, in a "community" of wealthy planters and "serfs"? (See Competing Voices, page 652.)

Stevens was right in recognizing that without large-scale redistribution of land, blacks had little hope of achieving economic independence. But the Republicans failed to develop a systematic land distribution program. As Union armies occupied parts of the South during the war, Union commanders had developed a variety of plans for dealing with confiscated lands. General William T. Sherman set aside the Sea Islands off Georgia's coast and land in South Carolina for African-American refugees who burdened his army. Each family received 40 acres of land and the loan of army mules. By the summer of 1865 some forty thousand freed people had settled on "Sherman's land." In October, however, Johnson ordered Sea Island blacks to work out arrangements with the legal owners of the land. Angry blacks protested: "Why do you take away our lands? You take them from Us who have always been true, always true to the Government! You give them to our all-time enemies! That is not right!" When some of the Sea Islanders refused to deal with the white owners, Union soldiers forced them to leave or work for their old masters.

In 1866 Republicans tried to address the land problem by passing the Southern Homestead Act, which set aside 44 million acres of land for freedmen and loyal whites. But most freed people and many whites lacked the resources to buy the land or purchase the tools needed to work it. For Republicans, even many Radicals, the idea of land reform was too extreme. Despite their support for federally imposed Reconstruction, most Republicans clung to nineteenth-century notions of individualism and limited government. The federal government could guarantee equality of opportunity, but it could not confiscate private property to redress past wrongs. Doing so, most believed, would require an extraordinary expansion of federal power and result in a clear violation of individual liberty. "A division of rich men's lands amongst the landless," argued *The Nation*, "would give a shock to our whole social and political system from which it would hardly recover without the loss of liberty."

Radicals may have been uncomfortable with land reform, but suffrage was at the heart of the Radical plan for Reconstruction. Most Radicals believed that once blacks had political rights, social and economic benefits would follow. To safeguard black votes, Republicans framed the Fifteenth Amendment. Section 1 forbade states to deny their citizens the right to vote on the grounds of "race, color, or previous condition of servitude." Section 2 gave Congress power to enforce the amendment by appropriate legislation.

The Republican authors carefully designed the Fifteenth Amendment to further their political ambitions. Like the Fourteenth Amendment, it was the result of compromises between moderates and Radicals. The amendment extended the vote to blacks, but it did not guarantee universal manhood suffrage, from which Republicans had little to gain. Republicans wanted to prevent former Confederates—most of whom were Democrats—from voting. Nor did the amendment, as Radicals proposed, prohibit the use of poll taxes and other methods to restrict black voting. Mainstream Republicans wanted to preserve voting restrictions against immigrants in the North, whom they considered unworthy of suffrage. Massachusetts and Connecticut used literacy tests to deny the vote to recent European immigrants. California used them to prevent Chinese immigrants from voting.

Ratification of the amendment in March 1870 produced widespread Republican jubilation. Frederick Douglass announced that blacks now would "breathe a new atmosphere, have a new earth beneath, and a new sky above." White and black men marched in a large parade through Washington, D.C., waving banners that read "The Nation's second birth" and "the fifteenth amendment, Uncle Sam's bleaching powder."

Reconstruction and Women's Suffrage

The debates over the Fourteenth and Fifteenth Amendments represented a turning point in the struggle for women's suffrage. Nineteenth-century feminists had been closely tied to the antislavery cause, and many male abolitionists had been active in the movement for women's rights. During the war, feminists had put aside the suffrage issue to support the Union cause in abolishing slavery. Once the war ended, feminist leaders hoped to refocus public attention on the question of women's suffrage.

Potential allies, however, saw little political reward in extending the franchise to women. Most Republicans believed that black male votes were the key to gaining control of the southern states. Former abolitionists who had supported women's suffrage in the past worried that pushing the issue now would distract attention from the most important question: political and economic rights for former slaves. As Wendell Phillips admonished women leaders, "One question at a time. This hour belongs to the Negro."

Instead of supporting their former suffragist allies, Republicans sanctioned the denial of women's suffrage. The Fourteenth Amendment, in fact, wrote the term *male* into the Constitution for the first time. Disappointed feminists accepted defeat at the federal level and focused on the reform of state constitutions. In 1866 Elizabeth Cady Stanton, Susan B. Anthony, and Lucy Stone created the Equal Rights Association to lobby and petition for the removal of racial and sexual restrictions at the state level, but their efforts were unsuccessful. As Republican men withdrew funding and support, many feminist leaders felt betrayed, convinced, as Stanton declared, that woman "must not put her trust in man" in seeking her own rights. "Standing alone, we learned our power," Stanton and Anthony wrote later. "Woman must lead the way to her own enfranchisement and work out her own salvation."

Angry with their former allies, Stanton and Anthony campaigned against ratification of the Fifteenth Amendment. Ratification, Anthony charged, would create an "aristocracy of sex." They employed racist and elitist arguments in opposing the new amendment. Stanton argued that black men should not be elevated over "women of wealth, education, virtue, and refinement." In 1869 she urged her followers to support women's suffrage "if you do not wish the lower orders of Chinese, Africans, Germans and Irish, with the low ideas of womanhood to make laws for you and your daughters." That same year, these radicals formed the all-female National Woman Suffrage Association (NWSA).

Another group of feminists led by Lucy Stone broke with Stanton and supported the amendment, conceding that this was "the Negro's hour." Women, they contended, could afford to wait for the vote. Their goal was to maintain an alliance with Republicans in the hope of enlisting Republican support for women's suffrage after Reconstruction issues had been settled. To advance their cause, they formed the moderate American Woman Suffrage Association (AWSA), which focused on achieving suffrage at the state level. This disagreement over strategy would divide the women's movement for a generation to come.

The Impeachment of a President

Fearing that Johnson would subvert its plans for the South, Congress passed several laws in March 1867 aimed at limiting his presidential power. The Tenure of Office Act, the most important of the new restrictions, required the president to seek Senate approval before removing any officeholder who had been previously approved by the Senate. In this way, congressional leaders could protect

Republican appointees, such as Secretary of War Edwin M. Stanton, who openly collaborated with the Radicals. In August 1867 Johnson suspended Stanton and, as required by the Tenure of Office Act, asked for Senate approval. When the Senate refused, Johnson had Stanton physically expelled from his office and appointed Union General Ulysses S. Grant as interim secretary of war.

On February 24 the House of Representatives, seizing on Johnson's violation of the Tenure of Office Act, voted to impeach the president. It charged him with eleven counts of "high crimes and misdemeanors." Of the eleven articles of impeachment, the first eight related to Johnson's "illegal" dismissal of Stanton. Article X accused Johnson of bringing Congress into disgrace by "inflammatory and scandalous harangues" and of degrading his office "to the great scandal of all good citizens."

The trial in the Senate, which the Constitution empowers to act as a court in impeachment cases, opened on March 5, 1868, and continued until May 26, with Chief Justice Salmon P. Chase presiding. To remove the president from office, two-thirds of the Senate—thirty-six of fifty-four senators—needed to vote for impeachment. On the first day of the trial, Radical Benjamin Butler of Massachusetts presented the charges against the president. "This man by murder most foul succeeded to the Presidency, and is the elect of an assassin to that high office, and not of the people," he charged. "We are about to remove him from the office he has disgraced by the sure, safe, and constitutional means of impeachment."

The president's attorney, Henry Stanbery, argued that Stanton was not protected by the Tenure of Office Act because he had been appointed by Lincoln. And in any case, Johnson's removal of Stanton was not a criminal act but a test of the legality of a law that was probably unconstitutional.

As the case came to an end, it was obvious that the vote would be close. "There is an intensity of anxiety here, greater than I ever saw during the war," Representative James Garfield wrote two hours before the vote. At the last moment, seven moderate Republicans broke ranks, voting for acquittal along with twelve Democrats. The conviction of the president failed by one vote. The moderates agreed that Johnson had broken the law, but they believed that the violation did not warrant removal from office, fearing that such a move would establish a dangerous precedent and weaken the presidency.

THE RADICAL EXPERIMENT IN THE SOUTH, 1865–1872

With military Reconstruction in place, the Republican Party emerged as the dominant force in southern politics. It controlled the state conventions, wrote the new constitutions, and controlled the new governments. At the same time, millions of African-Americans took advantage of their freedom to strengthen traditional institutions, especially the family and the church. But their hopes for economic independence were frustrated by a new labor system that trapped them between freedom and slavery. Despite political domination, the white South struggled to maintain its own social structure and cultural identity, including distinctions of class and race.

The Southern Republicans

The southern Republican Party was an uneasy coalition of three distinct groups. African-Americans formed the largest group of the Republican rank and file. In five states—Alabama, Florida, South Carolina, Mississippi, and Louisiana—blacks constituted a majority of registered voters in 1867. In three others—Georgia, Virginia, and North Carolina—they accounted for nearly half the registered voters. The number of African-Americans who held office during Reconstruction never reflected their share of the electorate. No state elected a black governor; only a few selected black judges. In only one state—South Carolina—did blacks have a majority in the legislature. But blacks did win a number of important political positions throughout the South. Over six hundred blacks, many of them former slaves, served in state legislatures during Republican rule. Sixteen African-Americans served in the U.S. House of Representatives in the Reconstruction era. In 1870 Mississippi's Hiram Revels became the first African-American member of the U.S. Senate.

African Americans also found more-informal ways to engage in politics and support the Republican Party. Churches and congregations, mixing spiritual and secular messages, served as places to discuss and debate political issues. In many parts of the South, African-Americans joined the Union League to further the cause of Reconstruction. Founded in Ohio in 1862 to build support for the war, the Union League followed the Federal army as it swept through the South. It organized local councils in rural communities to educate newly enfranchised blacks about the "duties of American citizenship." Although only men could join the Union League, women often participated in public rallies and meetings. A second group of Republicans included a diverse lot whom critics called "carpetbaggers," Northerners who supposedly came South with all their belongings packed into a single carpet-covered traveling bag. In 1871 a Democratic congressman described a carpetbagger as an "office seeker from the North who came here seeking office by the negroes, by arraying their political passions and prejudices against the white people of the community." In fact, carpetbaggers included northern businessmen, former Freedmen Bureau agents who had invested money in the region, and Union army veterans who stayed in the South after the war. Most combined a desire for personal gain with a commitment to reform the South by introducing northern ideas and institutions. They made up only a sixth of the delegates to the state conventions, but carpetbaggers held more than half the Republican governorships in the South and almost half its seats in Congress.

The third group consisted of white southerners who resented the planter elite and believed that Republican policies would favor them over the wealthy landowners. They included southern Unionists, small-town merchants, and rural farmers. Democrats called them "scalawags," an ancient Scots-Irish term for small, worthless animals. To Democrats, a scalawag was "the local leper of the community," even more hated than the carpetbagger. "We can appreciate a man who lived north, and even fought against us," declared a former North Carolina governor, "but a traitor to his own home cannot be trusted or respected."

It was a fragile coalition. Class differences divided the business-minded carpetbaggers and poor scalawags. With a more limited vision of state power, scalawags opposed high taxes to fund the reformist social programs endorsed by carpetbaggers.

But race remained the issue with the greatest potential for shattering the Republican coalition in the South. Black demands for political rights and economic independence clashed with the deeply held racial attitudes of most scalawags. "[O]ur people are more radical against rebels than in favor of negroes," declared a scalawag leader.

The Republican Program

Although fragile, the coalition of southern Republicans had a profound impact on public life in the South. Under Republican rule, all the southern states rejoined the Union between 1868 and 1871. In states where the Republican coalition remained unified—South Carolina, Louisiana, and Florida—Reconstruction governments remained in power for as many as nine years. In other states, such as Virginia, they ruled for only a few months.

Republicans hoped to remake southern society in the free-labor image of the North. The new Republican regimes expanded democracy. They repealed Black Codes, modernized state constitutions, extended the right to vote, and made more offices elective. The "fundamental theme" of the South Carolina constitution was "a raceless and classless democracy." Reconstruction administrations guaranteed the political and civil rights of African-American men. They could now serve on juries, school boards, and city councils; hold public office; and work as police officers. To ensure these rights, many state legislatures passed tough antidiscrimination laws. A South Carolina law, for example, levied a fine of $1,000 or a year's imprisonment for owners of businesses that practiced discrimination.

Believing that education was the foundation for a democracy, many Republican governments established their states' first public school systems. An 1869 Louisiana law prescribed universal free schooling "without distinction of race, color, or previous condition." In practice, however, whites stayed away from schools that admitted blacks. When the Reconstruction government forced the University of South Carolina to admit African-Americans in 1873, nearly all whites withdrew. Two years later the university was 90 percent black. Few African-Americans objected to the segregation. For now, they agreed with the abolitionist Frederick Douglass, who accepted that separate schools were "infinitely superior" to no schools at all.

African-Americans eagerly embraced the expanded educational opportunities. Throughout the South, African-Americans raised money to build schoolhouses and pay teachers. A Mississippi farmer vowed, "If I never does do nothing more, I shall give my children a chance to go to school, for I consider education next best thing to liberty." By 1869 the Freedmen's Bureau was supervising nearly three thousand schools serving over 150,000 students throughout the South. Over half the roughly 3,300 teachers in these schools were African-Americans. Between 1865 and 1867 northern philanthropists founded Howard, Atlanta, Fisk, Morehouse, and other black universities in the South.

In most cases, however, the efforts to improve education were overwhelmed by crowded facilities and limited resources. Often African-American and poor white children had to skip school so they could help their families by working in the fields. Between 1865 and 1870 only 5 percent of black children in Georgia attended school regularly; for whites, the figure was 20 percent.

The new Republican governments embarked on ambitious programs to rebuild and expand the South's infrastructure, which had been destroyed during the war.

They paved new roads and subsidized manufacturing. Believing that transportation was the key to southern industrial development, Republicans poured enormous energy into rebuilding and expanding the region's railroad system. Between 1868 and 1872 the South added over 3,000 new miles of track. State governments also spent more money than ever before on public institutions such as orphanages and asylums.

Paying for rebuilding the devastated South proved troublesome. Like their northern counterparts, southern states used general property taxes to pay for the expanded services. By levying taxes on personal property as well as real estate, the states hoped to force wealthy planters to bear much of the burden. But despite higher taxes, spending outpaced revenues, producing large deficits. Between 1868 and 1872 the deficits of Louisiana and South Carolina almost doubled, and between 1868 and 1874 that of Alabama tripled.

Corruption compounded the revenue problem. In South Carolina, for example, the state maintained a restaurant and barroom for the legislators at a cost of $125,000 for one session. White southerners pounced on the stories of corruption in Republican governments, claiming it proved that blacks were incapable of self-government. Southern black officials were no more corrupt than their white coun-

Sharecropping in Georgia Lacking the skills required of other industries and unable to finance the purchase of land, many African-Americans worked the fields of wealthy Southern whites. Cotton remained king of the Southern economy after the Civil War and black sharecroppers hoped that cultivation of this crop would eventually provide them with an opportunity to become their own landholders. However, blacks found themselves at the mercy of creditors and the international cotton market, making it virtually impossible to escape the fields and forcing the entire family into a perpetual state of economic servitude. *(Corbis)*

terparts, and the Democratic urban machines in the North probably stole more public money than the Republican regimes in the South. Southern critics ignored the evidence because they were not really concerned with corruption. What they objected to was African-Americans gaining and exercising political power.

The Meaning of Freedom   A black Baptist minister, Henry M. Turner, stressed that freedom meant the enjoyment of "our rights in common with other men." The newly freed slaves sought countless ways to challenge the authority whites had exercised over their lives. Freedmen acquired belongings—dogs, guns, and liquor—that had been forbidden under slavery, and they abandoned the old expressions of humility—tipping a hat, stepping aside, casting eyes low. They dressed as they pleased. As slaves, they often had no surnames. Freedom provided the opportunity to assume the last name of a prominent person. Free to travel for the first time, many former slaves packed their meager belongings and left the plantation.

For many, freedom provided the cherished opportunity to reunite with family members. "In their eyes," wrote a Freedmen's Bureau agent, "the work of emancipation was incomplete until the families which had been dispersed by slavery were reunited." Parents reunited with each other and with children who had been taken in by planters and overseers. Thousands of African-American couples who had lived together under slavery flocked to churches to have their relationships sanctioned by marriage. By 1870 the majority of African-Americans lived in two-parent families.

Freedom changed gender relations within the black family. Slavery had imposed a rough equality on men and women: both were forced to work long hours in the fields. But freedom allowed them to define separate spheres. Initially, men continued to work in the fields, while many women wanted to stay home and attend to the family. Some wives, however, asserted their independence by opening individual bank accounts, refusing to pay off their husbands' debts, and filing complaints of abuse. In most cases, though, economic necessity ended the hopes of independence or domesticity by forcing women back into the fields. According to one former slave, women "do double duty, a man's share in the field, and a woman's part at home. They do any kind of field work, even ploughing, and at home the cooking, washing, milking, and gardening."

African-Americans pooled their resources to buy land and build their own churches. During slavery, southern Protestant churches had relegated blacks to second-class status, forcing them to sit in the back rows and preventing them from participating in many church functions. By 1877 the great majority of black southerners had withdrawn from white-dominated congregations and founded, then filled, their own churches. The new churches, and the ministers who led them, played key roles in the social, political, and religious lives of the parishioners.

Sharecropping   For many African-Americans, economic independence was the most powerful expression of freedom. "All I want is to get to own four or five acres of land, that I can build me a little house on and call my home," a Mississippi black said. Without large-scale redistribution of land, however, few former slaves realized their dream of landownership. Instead,

Abyssinian Baptist Church
African-Americans demonstrated their preference for autonomy in religious matters by founding their own churches. Their withdrawal from mixed congregations of every denomination was in part a response to the poor treatment they received from white church members. In these churches, seating was segregated and black members were usually barred from church government. Religion had historically been crucial to African-American identity, and these independent churches soon became the most important institutions in their communities. *(Library of Congress.)*

they were forced to hire out as farm laborers. At first, most freedmen signed contracts with white landowners and worked in gangs, laboring long hours under white supervisors much as they had in slavery. What the freed people wanted, a Georgia planter observed, was "to get away from all overseers, to hire or purchase land, and work for themselves." The desire to gain a degree of autonomy led many freed people to abandon the contract labor system in favor of tenant farming. As a South Carolina freedman put it, "If a man got to go cross the river, and he can't get a boat, he take a log. If I can't own the land, I'll hire or lease land, but I won't contract."

The most widely used form of tenant farming was known as sharecropping (see map on page 632). Under this scheme, former plantation owners subdivided their land into farms of 30 to 50 acres, which they leased to workers. The tenants were given seed, fertilizer, farm implements, and food and clothing to take care of their families and grow a cash crop, usually cotton. In return, the landlord took a share of the crop (hence "sharecropping") at harvest time. At first, freed people were enthusiastic about sharecropping. The system provided workers with a sense of freedom, and many saw it as a first step toward independence. It allowed families to work the fields together, and the reward, usually a half-share of the crop, exceeded the small wages they had received under the old system. While thousands of poor white farmers became sharecroppers, the vast majority were black.

Rather than being a step toward independence, however, sharecropping trapped many African-Americans in a new system of labor that was neither slave nor free. Because of a chronic shortage of capital and banking institutions, sharecroppers turned to local merchants, who developed the crop-lien system. Under

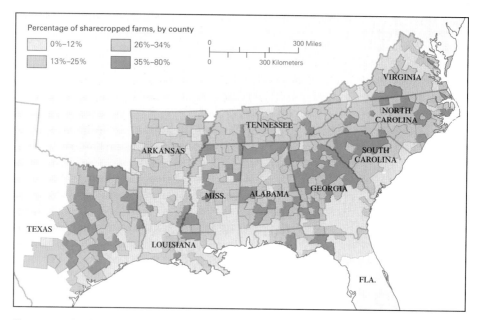

Sharecropping in the South by County, 1880   The depression of the 1870s increased the number of southern blacks and whites who worked land they did not own but leased through sharecropping. In 1880, the areas with the heaviest concentration of sharecropping were found in regions dominated by cotton production, cutting across South Carolina to eastern Texas. Continued deflation of crop prices and the depression of the 1890s sent tenancy rates soaring even higher, especially in the Deep South.

this system, the merchants, who were often also the landowners, provided loans to sharecroppers and tenant farmers in exchange for liens, or claims, on the year's cotton crop. As the only available creditors, merchants and planters could charge usurious interest rates and mark up prices. "It's owed before it's growed," complained many tenant farmers. With half their crop owed to the landowner and half, or often more, owed to the merchant, sharecroppers fell into debt they could not escape. Those who sought better conditions elsewhere found few options. Migrating north was not feasible; most northern businessmen refused to hire black workers. Some Southern blacks fled west, including thousands who migrated to Kansas in the 1860s to escape Southern "oppression and bondage." Most freedmen searching for better lives remained in the South, migrating to new cities or plantations, but rarely improving their lot.

In effect, an informal system of debt peonage, in which increasing debt denied economic opportunities to black families, replaced the formal structure of slavery. A black laborer described his unenviable condition: "I signed a contract—that is, I made my mark for one year. The Captain was to give me $3.50 a week, and furnish me a little house on the plantation. . . ." A year later, he found himself in debt to the planter, so he signed another contract, this one for ten years. During this time, he was "compelled" to buy his food, clothing, and other supplies from the plantation store. At the end of his contract, he tried to leave the plantation but was told he owed $165 and consequently found himself reduced to a "lifetime slave."

PRESIDENT GRANT AND THE DIVIDED NORTH, 1868–1876

In 1868 Republicans looked to Civil War hero Ulysses Grant to lead the party. But Grant proved to be a weak leader, and reports of scandals soon eroded support for his administration. The revolt of "Liberal Republicans" in 1872 revealed the depth of disaffection with Grant and the growing divisions among Republicans in the North. Concerned by the intrusive federal role in Reconstruction, northern liberals hoped to end the government's interventionist experiment in the South. The persistent debate about the "money question" underscored the uncertainty Americans felt about federal power and began to set battle lines between the eastern business establishment and rural America.

Ulysses Grant and the "Spoilsmen"

By the time of the Republican national convention in 1868, the most popular man in the country was General Ulysses S. Grant, whose troops had destroyed General Robert E. Lee's Confederate army in Virginia, effectively ending the Civil War. Months before the election, Republicans were forming Grant clubs. "No man ever had a better chance to be a great magistrate than he," noted an observer. It was no surprise that Republicans nominated Grant on the first ballot at their convention in Chicago.

The campaign exposed the political tensions produced by the Civil War and Reconstruction. The Democrats, who met in New York on July 4, picked Horatio Seymour, former governor of New York, as their candidate. The Democratic platform blasted the Republicans for subjecting the nation, "in time of profound peace, to military despotism and negro supremacy." The Republicans once again "waved the bloody shirt," reminding voters that they had saved the Union and charging that Democrats were the party of rebellion.

Grant carried the Republicans to victory on election day, winning 214 electoral votes to Seymour's 80 and carrying twenty-six states to Seymour's eight. The popular vote did not match his resounding victory in the electoral college. He won by only 306,592 votes (3,013,421 to 2,706,829). In fact, Grant's victory was made possible by the 450,000 votes cast by the freed people in the southern states under military occupation. In Congress, the Democrats picked up a few seats, but Republicans retained their large majorities in both the House and Senate.

Grant's success on the battlefield did not translate into effectiveness in the White House. The growth in federal power and the close relationship between government and business provided elected officials with ample opportunity for personal gain. With a few exceptions, Grant appointed greedy men who could not resist the temptation. These "spoilsmen" tainted the Grant administration with scandal. In 1869 the president's brother-in-law gave in to temptation by joining the crafty financier Jay Gould in an effort to corner the gold market. In 1872 a congressional committee confirmed newspaper reports of widespread bribery of prominent Republican officials by Union Pacific Railroad promoters, who were trying to cover up a phony construction company, called Crédit Mobilier, through which they diverted profits into their own pockets. That same year greedy congressmen pushed through a bill doubling the president's salary and increasing the salary of congressmen by 50 percent, retroactive to 1870, thus granting each member $5,000 in back salary. The press vehemently protested the "salary grab," and public indignation forced Congress to repeal the law in 1874.

The most dramatic scandal, which reached into the White House itself, involved the so-called Whiskey Ring, a network of large whiskey distillers and Treasury agents, led by a Grant appointee and former Union general, who defrauded the Internal Revenue Service of $4 million in taxes. Worst of all, Grant's private secretary, Orville E. Babcock, was involved in the duplicity. There is no evidence that Grant knew about the fraud, but his poor choice of associates earned him widespread public censure.

The Liberal Revolt

As early as 1870 a small but vocal group of distinguished Republicans had become disaffected with Grant's administration. These self-proclaimed "Liberal Republicans" were a mixed lot, though most were educated middle-class reformers who believed in limited government and rule by an enlightened elite. The Liberals wanted people like themselves to replace the party hacks who dominated the Grant administration. As a result, they made the creation of a civil service system, based on merit rather than political appointments, the centerpiece of their campaign.

In keeping with their belief in limited government, the Liberal Republicans also supported amnesty for all former Confederates and removal of troops from the South. Many saw the "southern question" as a distraction that enabled party spoilsmen to retain the allegiance of voters by "waving the bloody shirt," while avoiding the more important issues of civil service reform and effective government. Reformers had abolished slavery, the Liberals argued; now it was up to African-Americans themselves to make the most of their new opportunities.

In 1872 the Liberal Republicans organized a national convention that produced a platform criticizing the parent party's southern policy and advocating civil service reform. For president they nominated Horace Greeley, the eccentric editor of the *New York Tribune* and a longtime champion of reform. The choice stunned many veteran political observers, who believed that Greeley had little chance of beating Grant. One reporter gibed that there had been "too much brains and not enough whiskey" at the convention.

A month after Greeley's nomination, the regular Republicans met in Philadelphia and chose Grant for reelection on the first ballot. Despite his declining popularity and new revelations of scandal, Grant was still a powerful political force, enjoying support from southern Republicans, business interests, and Radicals. Above all, he still evoked the glory of his Civil War victory at Appomattox. The Republicans adopted a platform paying lip service to civil service, but taking a strong stand in favor of political and civil rights for all citizens in every part of the country.

Democrats realized that they had a lot to gain by joining forces with the disaffected Liberal Republicans. "Anything to Beat Grant" became their slogan. That meant that Democrats had to support Greeley, who had been a severe critic of the Democratic Party. The choice between Grant and Greeley, moaned Georgia's Alexander Stephens, was a choice between "hemlock and strychnine." At their convention in Baltimore, Democrats overlooked their differences and nominated Greeley.

In the election of 1872 Grant won 56 percent of the popular vote, a larger percentage than in 1868. Grant carried thirty-one states and took 286 of the 349 electoral votes. His popular vote margin (3,596,745 to 2,843,446) was the highest since Andrew Jackson's in 1828. But the election also revealed the extent of southern disaffection with Radical Reconstruction. In the South, the Republicans could muster only 50.1 percent of the popular vote.

The Money Question

Continuing revelations of corruption and persistent arguments about "the money question"— federal monetary policy—dominated Grant's second term in office. To help finance the Civil War, Congress had issued almost $450 million in so-called greenbacks—paper currency that was not backed by either gold or silver. The inflation of the money supply led to a steep increase in prices and shook public faith in the government. When the war ended, the government proposed to call in greenbacks for payment in gold or silver.

In general, restricting the money supply hurt debtors and helped creditors. People who had borrowed money when the currency was inflated would have to repay loans when fewer dollars were in circulation. Conversely, creditors who had loaned inflated dollars would receive payment in currency worth more since there was less of it. The debate, however, was never that simple, since not everyone viewed the issue in terms of economic self-interest. Eastern business interests tended to see the debate over paper currency in religious terms: Government had a moral obligation to back its currency in gold; failure to do so was sinful. In addition to fear over falling farm prices, hatred of the eastern establishment—the "money power"— drove many farmers to favor inflated money.

The conflicting and complicated views on the currency cut across party lines. Despite disagreement within his own party, Grant sided with the advocates of hard money, endorsing payment of the national debt in gold as a point of national honor. The president's support for hard money could not have come at a worse time. In 1873 the bankruptcy of the Northern Pacific Railroad set off the Panic of 1873—a steep economic depression that lasted six years. By 1876 eighteen thousand businesses were bankrupt, and nearly 15 percent of the labor force was unemployed. In 1878 alone, more than ten thousand businesses failed. Those who managed to hold on to their jobs suffered painful wage cuts.

Many people, believing that Grant's tight, or contracted, money policy contributed to the depression, increased their calls to print more greenbacks. In 1874 the Democrats and a handful of Republicans succeeded in passing a bill that increased the number of greenbacks in circulation, but Grant vetoed it. The following year, Republicans passed the Specie Resumption Act, which called for redeeming all greenbacks by 1879 and replacing them with certificates backed by gold. The legislation satisfied creditors, but it failed to calm the fears of small farmers and debtors, who worried that any money standard tied to gold would be too restrictive.

As the nation emerged from depression in 1879, the clamor for "easy money" subsided. It would resurface more persistently in the 1890s.

THE FAILURE OF RECONSTRUCTION, 1870–1877

By the mid-1870s a number of forces conspired to produce the downfall of Radical Reconstruction. In the South the persistent tradition of individual rights and local control, combined with a belief in white supremacy, allowed the Democrats to topple a number of Republican state governments. A host of influences—disillusionment with government corruption, fears of a Democratic resurgence, economic strains, and general weariness—convinced northerners it was time to abandon their experiment. In a series of decisions the Supreme Court signaled the North's retreat. The "Compromise of 1877," which resolved a disputed presidential election, marked the end of Reconstruction.

The South Redeemed

Former large slave owners were the bitterest opponents of the Republican program in the South. The Republican effort to expand political and economic opportunities for African-Americans threatened their vested interest in controlling agricultural labor and their power and status in southern society. In response, they staged a massive counterrevolution to "redeem" the South by regaining control of southern state governments.

Initially, some Democrats tried to woo black voters away from the Republicans with moderate appeals on racial and economic questions. When their appeals fell on deaf ears, they launched an ideological attack designed to unify southern whites and stir up fear and uncertainty among blacks and their allies.

In making their case against Republican rule, the Redeemers tapped into values that had deep roots in American political culture. They claimed that the Republican Party favored centralized power and special privilege rather than local rule and individual rights. "The principle of the Union is no longer justice, but force," declared a prominent white southerner. Most of all, however, the Redeemer appeal rested on the South's social and cultural foundation of racism and white supremacy. Alabama's State Conservative Committee designated January 30, 1868, as a day of fasting and prayer to deliver the people of the state "from the horrors of negro domination." Mississippi Democrats condemned the black members of the state's Radical constitutional convention as "destitute alike of the moral and intellectual qualifications required of electors in all civilized communities."

For Democrats, playing "the race card" served two purposes. First, the appeal to racial pride lured poor whites away from the Republicans and prevented the formation of a biracial, class-based coalition. "I may be poor and my manners may be crude, but I am a white man," declared a disgruntled scalawag. "That I am poor is not as important as that I am a white man; and no Negro is ever going to forget that he is not a white man."

Second, Democrats hoped to frighten blacks and Republican whites into avoiding voting and other political action. Throughout the Deep South, planters and their supporters organized secret societies to terrorize blacks and Republicans. The Ku Klux Klan emerged as the most powerful of the new terrorist groups. In 1865 a social circle of young men in Pulaski, Tennessee, organized themselves as the "Invisible Empire of the South." New chapters of the secret lodge quickly formed in other states. Klan members, who included poor farmers as well as middle-class professionals, donned ghostly white robes and indulged in ghoulish rituals. Their intention was to frighten their victims into thinking they were the avenging ghosts of the Confederate dead.

After 1870 the Ku Klux Klan fought an ongoing terrorist campaign against Reconstruction governments and local leaders. Acting as a guerrilla army for those who sought the restoration of white supremacy, Klansmen whipped and killed Republican politicians, burned black schools and churches, and attacked Republican Party gatherings. In some communities, Klan members paraded through the streets carrying coffins bearing the names of prominent Radicals and labeled "Dead, damned and delivered." In the bloodiest episode, Klan members murdered nearly a hundred African-Americans in Colfax, Louisiana, on Easter Sunday 1873.

In response to the racial terrorism, Congress passed three Enforcement Acts in 1870 and 1871. The first prohibited state officials from interfering with a citizen's right to vote. A second act created federal election marshals to oversee congressional elections. In April 1871 Congress passed the Ku Klux Klan Act, which outlawed the Klan and any other conspiratorial group that sought to deprive individuals of their Constitutional rights. It also empowered the president to suspend *habeas corpus* and to use federal troops to suppress "armed combinations."

The legislation restricted Klan activities, but it could not stem the Democratic resurgence in the South. Democrats redeemed Tennessee, Virginia, North Carolina, and Georgia from Radical rule between 1869 and 1871; Texas followed in 1873, and Arkansas in 1874. In 1875 a notorious campaign of terror and intimidation against black voters allowed the Democrats to seize control of Mississippi. The Democratic slogan became "Carry the election peaceably if we can, forcibly if we must." Republicans fearful of violence stayed away from the polls. "The Republicans are paralyzed through fear and will not act," the anguished carpetbag governor of Mississippi wrote to his wife. "Why should I fight a hopeless battle . . . when no possible good to the Negro or anybody else would result?"

The Republican Retreat

At the national level, too, a number of forces were pushing the Republican Party to abandon its Reconstruction experiment. First, the idealism that had once informed Republican efforts had long since faded. Many party leaders felt that "waving the bloody shirt" was counterproductive. Republicans now sought reconciliation, not confrontation, with the South. In May 1872 Congress passed a General Amnesty Act that, with some exceptions, allowed Confederate leaders to vote and to hold public office.

Second, Republicans realized that they were paying a heavy political price for their southern policies and receiving little benefit from them. Divided among themselves, Republicans watched their congressional majorities dwindle in the wake of a dramatic Democratic resurgence. In 1874 the Democrats gained a majority in the House of Representatives for the first time since 1856. "The election is not merely a victory but a revolution," declared a New York news-paper.

The Panic of 1873 outweighed Reconstruction as a factor in the Republican defeat, but the election's implications for Reconstruction policy were clear. Northern voters were tired of dealing with the "southern question" and the "Negro question." "The truth is our people are tired out with the worn out cry of 'Southern outrages'!!" a weary Republican cried. "Hard times and heavy taxes make them wish the 'ever lasting nigger' were in hell or Africa."

Third, northerners increasingly accepted the southern view of African-Americans as people inferior in intelligence and morality who required the paternal protection of the superior white race. Negative stereotypes in northern newspapers depicted blacks as ignorant, lazy, and dishonest, incapable of exercising the same rights as whites. "They [blacks] plunder, and glory in it," one northern journalist summed up; "they steal, and defy you to prove it." Even loyal administration supporters were convinced that Reconstruction was organized theft. The *New York Times* called the South Carolina legislature "a gang of thieves," its government "a sort of grand orgie."

Fourth, serious strains emerged within Republican ranks in the South. Race played a central role in fracturing the always fragile southern Republican Party. Poor whites were never willing to concede political equality to blacks. Republicans found it difficult to satisfy their black constituents' demands for equality without alienating whites. White Republicans were also divided among themselves. Scalawags resented carpetbaggers, who they believed had seized offices that should have gone to native whites. Meanwhile, in state after state, Democrats skillfully exploited deepening fiscal problems by blaming Republicans for excessive spending and sharp tax increases.

These pressures proved too much for most Republicans. With support for Reconstruction unraveling, Radical pleas for new measures to protect the political and civil rights of African-Americans fell on deaf ears. The one exception was the Civil Rights Act of 1875, passed in the closing hours of the Republican-controlled Congress. The law guaranteed persons of every race "the full and equal treatment" of all public facilities such as hotels, theaters, and railroads.

However, several Supreme Court decisions involving the Fourteenth and Fifteenth Amendments undermined protection of black rights. In the so-called *Slaughterhouse Cases* of 1873, the Court offered a narrow definition of the Fourteenth Amendment by distinguishing between national and state citizenship. The amendment, the justices declared, guaranteed only those rights dependent on national citizenship. What were those rights? Most were of little concern to freed people: access to courts and navigable waterways and the ability to run for federal office, travel to the seat of government, and be protected on the high seas and abroad. By giving the states primary authority over citizens' rights, the courts weakened civil rights enforcement. In 1876 the Court decided, in *United States v. Cruikshank*, that a mob attack on blacks trying to vote did not violate the Fourteenth Amendment. In 1883 the Court reaffirmed its limited view of the Constitution in *United States v. Harris*, finding that the lynching of four black prisoners did not represent an infringement of their Fourteenth Amendment rights.

The Compromise of 1877

Republican leaders approached the 1876 presidential campaign with foreboding. "My God, it is ruin!" exclaimed Republican James G. Blaine. In an effort to distance themselves from the scandals of the Grant administration, party leaders turned to Ohio Governor Rutherford B. Hayes. Not only did Hayes hail from an electoral-vote–rich state, but he had also earned a reputation for honesty, possessed an honorable Civil War record, and supported civil service reform. He had articulated a moderate stance on Reconstruction, which Republicans hoped would appeal to conservative Republicans and moderate Democrats.

The Colfax Massacre, 1873   Throughout Reconstruction, freed slaves faced the threat of violence from whites who resented any alteration of the social order. The killing of nearly one hundred blacks in Colfax, Louisiana, was the bloodiest of these incidents. Blacks had taken up positions around the Colfax courthouse to protect Republican officers threatened by conservative whites seeking to reclaim the state by force. A white mob attacked the black defenders and not until President Grant ordered federal troops to the area was peace restored. Although three whites were ultimately convicted in a federal court of the Colfax deaths, the Supreme Court overturned the verdicts in *U.S.* v. *Cruikshank*. The Court argued that under the Fourteenth Amendment, the federal government could prosecute only states, not individuals, for civil rights violations. *(Frank & Marie-Therese Wood Print Collections, Alexandria, VA.)*

Signaling that they planned to make the Grant scandals a central theme of their campaign to gain the presidency, the Democrats nominated Governor Samuel J. Tilden of New York, a well-known corruption fighter. At their June convention in St. Louis, gleeful Democrats chanted "Tilden and Reform" and passed a platform promising to save the nation from "a corrupt centralism which has honeycombed the offices of the Federal government itself with incapacity, waste, and fraud."

On election night, it appeared that the Democrats had regained the White House for the first time since before the Civil War. Tilden received 51 percent of the popular vote (4,284,020) to Hayes's 48 percent (4,036,572). But Republicans charged that Democrats won the elections in three southern states—Louisiana, South Carolina, and Florida—by fraud and intimidation. Both sides claimed the electoral votes in those states (see map below).

When Congress reconvened in January it confronted an unprecedented situation: three states with two different sets of electoral votes. If Congress accepted all the Republican votes, Hayes would have a one-vote electoral majority. The Constitution did not cover such a scenario, and as weeks passed without a solution, people feared that the impasse could escalate into a major national crisis.

On January 29, 1877, Congress set up a fifteen-member Joint Electoral Commission to resolve the dispute. The committee was made up of seven Democrats and seven Republicans, with the swing vote going to an independent member of the Supreme Court, Justice David Davis. But Davis withdrew from the Court and the commission. With no Democrats or any other independents on the Court, a

The Election of 1876   Without any clear issues in 1876, Democrats and their presidential nominee Samuel J. Tilden emphasized the corruption that had hampered Grant's administration, while Republican nominee Rutherford B. Hayes linked the Democratic Party to the Confederacy. Early election returns showed Tilden ahead in the popular and electoral vote, but Republicans disputed the results in Louisiana, Florida, and South Carolina while Democrats countered with a claim to one electoral vote in Oregon. Ultimately, the Joint Electoral Commission gave all twenty electoral votes to Hayes.

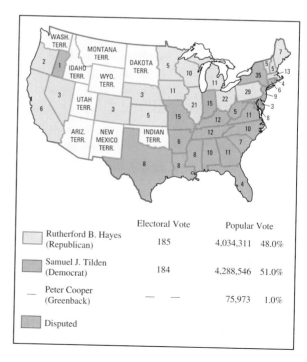

	Electoral Vote	Popular Vote	
Rutherford B. Hayes (Republican)	185	4,034,311	48.0%
Samuel J. Tilden (Democrat)	184	4,288,546	51.0%
Peter Cooper (Greenback)	— —	75,973	1.0%
Disputed			

Republican named Joseph P. Bradley took Davis's seat on the commission. Not surprisingly, the commission voted eight to seven along straight partisan lines and gave the election to Hayes.

Congress still had to approve the results, and the Democrats were threatening to filibuster. On February 26, 1877, prominent Ohio Republicans and powerful southern Democrats met at the Wormley House hotel in Washington, where they reached an informal agreement, later called the Compromise of 1877. The Republicans promised that Hayes would withdraw the last federal troops from Louisiana, Florida, and South Carolina; include at least one southerner in his cabinet; provide federal subsidies for southern internal improvements; and give conservatives control of political patronage. In return, the Democrats promised to support Hayes's election and to accept the Reconstruction amendments. On March 2, 1877, only two days before the scheduled inauguration, the House voted to accept the commission's report and declared Hayes elected by an electoral vote of 185 to 184.

Hayes's election signaled the formal end of the Reconstruction era. In his first month in office, the new president appointed a southern Democrat to his cabinet and ordered federal troops back to their southern barracks, symbolically ending their interference in local politics. In a speech in Atlanta in the fall of 1877 Hayes told former slaves that their "rights and interests would be safer" if southern whites were "let alone by the general government."

THE NEW SOUTH, 1870–1900

At the end of Reconstruction, southern propagandists filled the newspapers with calls for economic experimentation to create a "New South." They wanted the South to abandon its old agrarian ways and transform itself into a bustling center of commerce and industry. Despite the development of new factories and the rise of a few large cities, southern society, steeped in white supremacy, remained economically dependent on cheap labor and King Cotton. This burden prevented the South from making major gains. Culturally, southerners remained deeply tied to the past at the same time that they experimented with new forms of artistic expression. For many African-Americans, the New South looked much like the old. Southern leaders developed a number of ingenious methods to limit black voting, and they imposed a rigid system of segregation.

Visions of Industry   In the early 1880s boosters of the New South told everyone who would listen about the profound changes transforming the region. Led by Henry Grady, editor of the *Atlanta Constitution*, propagandists promised to remake the southern economy in the image of the North, claiming that a society of machines and factories was needed to replace the old agrarian order. Henry Watterson, a Louisville editor and orator, urged that "the ambition of the South is to out-Yankee the Yankee." The first step, however, was to convince southerners of the need for change. "Beyond all question," insisted a Richmond journal, "we have been on the wrong track and should take a new departure."

The clearest evidence of change was the rise of cities. People from every level of rural society left the countryside for towns. "The towns are being recruited by those too poor to be able to live in the country, as well as by those too rich to be willing to live there," observed a reporter. Atlanta, which had only fourteen thousand residents at the close of the Civil War, had a population close to forty thousand in 1880 and ninety thousand two decades later. Birmingham, Alabama, saw its population grow from three thousand in 1880 to thirty-eight thousand in 1900.

The spirit of the New South penetrated the halls of statehouses and governors' mansions. Many state legislatures tried luring northern bankers and capitalists with attractive investment opportunities. William H. Harrison, Jr., a prominent New South spokesman, maintained that no foreign country offered "such tempting inducements to the capitalist for profitable investments" as did the New South. In 1877 five southern states repealed laws reserving land for private homebuilders so that they might entice investors to exploit their coal, iron, and timber resources.

With the aid of new investment, southern industries such as textiles, iron, and lumber experienced a boom. The South's textile mills boasted the latest and most sophisticated machinery. By 1890 textile spindles, which doubled the output per worker, appeared in 90 percent of southern mills, compared with only 70 percent of New England mills. Jefferson County, the home of Birmingham, had only twenty-two factories in 1870; thirty years later it had five hundred. By the late 1880s southern pig iron production had surpassed the total output of the entire country in 1860. By 1910 the South was producing almost half of all lumber milled in the United States. The lumber industry claimed one in five southern manufacturing workers. "Never before has the lumber business been so active," a paper proudly reported in 1882.

To make their new factories accessible to northern markets, many states built new railroad tracks. Between 1880 and 1890 track mileage more than doubled, going from 16,605 to 39,108 miles. On May 30, 1886, work crews throughout the South pushed thousands of miles of track three inches closer together to create a uniform national railroad system. The change helped railroads expand the development of the South's landlocked mineral resources, particularly the iron mines of Tennessee, Virginia, and Alabama. By 1898 Birmingham was the largest shipping point for pig iron in the country and the third largest in the world.

King Cotton and the Crop-Lien System

Proponents of the New South exaggerated the amount of change that had actually taken place. Although new industries and signs of progress abounded, the South continued to lag far behind the prosperous North. In 1860 the South housed 17 percent of the country's manufacturing; by 1904 it had only 15 percent. Despite the growth of cities, most people in the South continued to live in rural areas. The 1890 census showed that only 3.9 percent of North Carolinians and 5.9 percent of Alabamans were considered urban.

The economy of the postwar South remained tied to agriculture. The spread of the crop-lien system as the South's main form of agricultural credit forced more and more farmers, both white and black, into growing cash crops—crops that could earn the most money on the open market. Cotton, which yielded more value per acre than any other crop, was the crop of choice. By 1880 nearly three-quarters of the African-American farmers and about one-third of the white farmers in the cot-

Virginia Coalfields   After the war, the South lagged far behind the North in economic development. Closing the gap became a major goal for Southerners who supported Henry Grady's vision of the New South. The discovery of coalfields in Virginia in 1873 provided a major impetus for railroad construction and buoyed the region's economy. Although the South made great strides toward a more diversified economy, southern industry still accounted for only 10 percent of the United States' industrial capacity by 1900. (*Virgina Historical Society.*)

ton states were sharecroppers or tenants. The number of cotton mills in the South rose from 161 in 1880 to 400 in 1900. In 1880 there were 45 mills in the United States producing 7 million gallons of cottonseed oil annually for export; by 1900 there were 357, all but 4 in the South.

The South's dependence on a single crop had many unforeseen consequences. For one thing, it made the South less self-sufficient, since many farmers plowed over land that had been used to grow food and replaced the food crops with cotton. By 1880 the South was not growing enough food to feed its people. The near total dominance of King Cotton also inhibited economic growth across the region. As more and more farmers turned to cotton growing as the fastest way to obtain credit, expanding production depressed prices. Competition from new cotton centers in the world market, notably Egypt and India, furthered the downward spiral. The decline in cotton prices dragged the rest of the southern economy down with it. By the 1890s per capita wealth in the South equaled only one-third that of the East, Midwest, or Far West.

Declining cotton prices produced a grim desperation in the South and only increased suspicion and hostility toward the North. In 1879 the *New York Tribune* showed little sympathy: "Fifteen years have gone over the South and she still sits crushed, wretched, busy displaying and bemoaning her wounds."

The Culture of the New South

Paralleling the contrast between industrial boosterism and continued dependence on agriculture, cultural trends pulled the South in different directions. On the one hand, a wave of nostalgia swept across the region as whites honored Civil War soldiers. The movement began as a defense of the "Lost Cause" in the 1860s, then evolved into a nostalgic celebration of old soldiers. Caught up in the "cult of the Confederacy," many white southerners joined the United Confederate Veterans and the United Daughters of the Confederacy, which raised funds for the erection of new monuments. Nine thousand whites of all ages dragged a new statue of Robert E. Lee to its site in Richmond in 1890. Over a hundred thousand people attended the unveiling three weeks later. The region's natives revered Decoration Day, when they carried spring flowers to the graves of the soldiers killed during the war.

At the same time that many white southerners were celebrating the past, southern fiction writers were questioning the relevance of the values and customs that had shaped their society. These writers attempted to explain their region to northern readers while challenging prevailing notions of race and gender. In *Uncle Remus: His Songs and Sayings* (1880), Joel Chandler Harris allowed a former black slave to tell stories in which the weak could outwit the strong. The success of Harris's book convinced Mark Twain, America's most visible and successful man of letters, to take another look at the South. In 1881 Twain took a boat trip down the Mississippi to reacquaint himself with a region he had previously explored in *Tom Sawyer* (1876). He was shocked by what he witnessed. The New South, Twain declared, was "a solemn, depressing, pathetic spectacle." His impressions created the backdrop for his greatest work, *The Adventures of Huckleberry Finn*, published in 1884. Among other things, the book explored the enormous distance between the South's perception of itself as a bastion of civilization and its real status as an impoverished and violent place.

Women writers played prominent roles in shaping the literature of the New South. Ruth McEnery Stuart's short stories about white women in fictional Simpkinsville portrayed females as active agents and men as ineffectual and absent. Kate Chopin juxtaposed the conventions of Protestant America with what she saw as more honest and healthier European standards of sexual behavior. Her book *The Awakening*, published in 1899, created such an outcry that it was pulled from library and bookstore shelves. The leading woman writer of the New South was Ellen Glasgow. Her most famous novel, *The Deliverance*, became the second-best-selling book in America in 1904. It told the story of young people of the South achieving success, but only after overcoming the suffocating burden of southern customs.

Music emerged as the most powerful force for cultural innovation in the New South. Music appealed to people of every description. Musical instruments were among the first mass-produced commodities southerners bought. Cheap banjos were mass-produced in the 1880s, and guitars in the 1890s. Students of both races were eager to learn formal music. Instructors taught classical music and voice throughout the towns and cities of the South. Bouncy popular music filled parlors, stages, tents, and streets. Every town of any size had an "opera house" that hosted traveling performers. In 1891 a band tournament in Troy, Alabama, drew four thousand visitors and ten brass bands from nearby towns.

In every other aspect of southern society racial distinctions were hardening, but culturally the line between white and black music was blurring. In cities throughout the South, the polyrhythms and improvisation of African music blended with traditional European styles. Much of the experimentation took place in New Orleans, which contained one of the largest concentrations of musicians in the South. The city attracted black and white musicians who trained together, played in the same bands and nightclubs, exchanged ideas, and borrowed styles.

The Triumph of White Supremacy   The Redeemers who gained power in the South ousted, state by state, the carpetbag rule of the Reconstruction era. Some Redeemers gained power by compromising with their opponents; others conquered by brute force. They were a mixed group that included the scions of the old planter class as well as new business leaders. They were united by what they opposed: biracial coalitions and the use of state power as an agent of change.

Free of interference from the North, Redeemer governments in the South waged an aggressive assault on African-Americans. Democrats regained control of state governments and imposed sweeping changes, slashing social programs, lowering taxes, and placing a premium on restoring social stability. Education programs were especially hard hit. Public schools closed in some parts of Maryland in 1871. In 1872 only a third of Tennessee's counties levied school taxes; only about 28 percent of the state's children attended school. "Schools are not a necessity," declared the governor of Virginia.

All former Confederate states changed their constitutions to create methods by which they could exclude the black vote. The Mississippi constitution of 1890 set the pattern. It required a poll tax of $2 from prospective voters at registration. To vote, men had to present their receipts at the polls. Anyone who mislaid his receipt forfeited his vote. Other states included literacy tests that required prospective voters to be "able to read the Constitution, or to understand the Constitution when read." Since white Democratic registrars interpreted the ability to read or understand, officials could use these ordinances to discriminate in favor of poor illiterate whites and against black citizens, literate or not. Louisiana adopted the "grandfather clause," which limited the franchise to anyone who had a grandfather on the electoral roll in 1867, before the Fifteenth Amendment that gave freedmen the right to vote had been enacted.

The results of these various efforts to eliminate the black vote were dramatic. Louisiana, for example, had 130,334 registered black voters in 1896. Eight years later there were only 1,342. In Alabama 181,000 black voters were registered in 1890; in 1900, 3,000. In the South as a whole, black voter participation fell by 62 percent in the 1890s. In 1900 Ben ("Pitchfork") Tillman of South Carolina boasted on the floor of the Senate, "We have done our best. We have scratched our heads to find out how we could eliminate the last one of them. We stuffed ballot boxes. We shot them. We are not ashamed of it."

Along with disfranchising blacks, southern lawmakers gave informal segregation in public facilities the force of law. Until the 1880s the South had established a system of segregation by custom. Schools, hospitals, parks, courthouses, hotels, and restaurants were separated by race. Social custom reinforced the distance between the races. Whites never addressed black men they did not know as "mister," but rather as "boy," "Jack," or "George." Black women were never called "Mrs.," but rather "aunt" or by their first name. According to custom, the two races did not shake hands, walk together, or fraternize in public. Black men removed their hats in public places reserved for whites, whereas whites did not remove their hats even in black homes.

While some blacks resisted the exclusion from white-owned hotels and restaurants, they could usually find accommodations in black-run businesses. Travel was a different story, for members of both races had to use the same railroads. When middle-class blacks carrying first-class tickets refused to be consigned to second-class seating, southern whites developed "separate but equal" railcars. These new restrictions—called "Jim Crow laws" after a minstrel song of 1830 that presented blacks as childlike and inferior—made it legally as well as socially impossible for blacks and whites to mingle. The laws were soon extended to libraries, hotels, restaurants, hospitals, prisons, theaters, parks, and playgrounds. Blacks and whites used separate bathrooms and separate toilets, and were even buried in separate cemeteries.

The Supreme Court, which had already made discrimination by individuals and businesses legal, now allowed state governments to make segregation part of the fabric of American life. In *Plessy* v. *Ferguson* (1896), the Court upheld, by a seven to one majority, a Louisiana law that required railroads to provide "equal but separate accommodations for the white and colored races." The Court ruled that the Fourteenth Amendment applied only to political rights and did not extend to "social equality." Legislatures were thus free to pass laws that maintained "the customs and traditions of the people." Justice Henry B. Brown of Michigan, speaking for the majority, ruled with racist candor, "If one race be inferior to the other socially, the Constitution of the United States cannot put them upon the same plane." A year later the judges endorsed segregated public schools as a means to prevent "commingling of the two races upon terms unsatisfactory to either." The justices also upheld the poll taxes and literacy tests used by state officials to disfranchise blacks.

Growing Democratic power emboldened whites to resort to violence without fear of reprisal. Between 1889 and 1898 blacks suffered 187 lynchings a year in the United States, four-fifths of them in the South. Southern newspapers reported the hangings in graphic detail to stimulate and attract white readers and to intimidate blacks. In many cases, victims' eyes were gouged out and their fingers, toes, and genitals were cut off before they were doused with flammable liquids and burned alive. Afterwards, cheering mobs would drag the charred bodies through town. Despite the horrific nature of these executions, spectators traveled long distances to watch; some combed through the charred remains for souvenirs or had their photos taken with mutilated corpses.

Democratic restoration also led to the expansion of the convict lease system. In 1876 three Georgia companies contracted to lease the state's convicts for twenty

Lynching Victims   After federal troops pulled out of the South, racial violence gradually reached epidemic proportions, with white southerners lynching thousands of African-Americans before the century's end. The victims, deemed "uppity" by whites, were usually singled out for being too assertive or successful, or for refusing to show the proper deference to whites. These four Kentucky sharecroppers were guilty of being sympathetic toward a black man who had killed his white employer in self-defense. One of the bodies bears the message, "Let white people alone or you will go the same way." *(Gilman Paper Company Collection.)*

years in return for annual payments of $25,000. The convicts were assigned to labor camps in which brutal and degrading conditions prevailed, and overseers forced them to toil from sunrise to sunset, disciplined by the rod and the whip.

Occasionally, blacks resisted the repression by organizing in their local communities. When a sheriff arrested a black man in McIntosh County, Georgia, and threatened lynching, local blacks mobilized a network of sentinels around the jailhouse and rang the nearby church bell to alert residents. The accused man was eventually tried and acquitted. Most of the time, however, black protests were limited to appeals to the professed paternalism of whites.

The most prominent voice belonged to Booker T. Washington. Born in 1856 to a slave woman and her white master, whose identity he never knew, Washington later attended the Hampton Institute in Virginia, a black school established and run by northern whites. In 1881 Washington helped organize the Tuskegee Institute, a state vocational school for blacks. He gained national prominence in 1895 when white organizers invited him to speak at Atlanta's Cotton States and International Exposition—the first time in southern history that a black man had been asked to address whites at such an important event. In a speech that became known as the "Atlanta Compromise," Washington told his segregated audience that blacks should put aside their ambitions for political power and social equality and instead focus on developing useful vocational skills. "It is at the bottom of life we must begin, and not at the top," he said. Political and social equality would proceed naturally once blacks had proven their economic value. "Dignify and glorify common labor," he urged. "Agitation of questions of racial equality is the extremist folly." To both races, he advised cooperation and mutual respect. Washington's message of accommodation was almost universally popular with whites. Blacks were more ambivalent. Southern blacks who favored gradual nonconfrontational change embraced his philosophy, but some northern black leaders complained that Washington had compromised too much.

For the freed people whose aspirations had been raised by Republican rule, "redemption" was demoralizing. No one could deny the enormous changes that had transformed American society over the previous two decades: slavery had been abolished and the federal government assumed the power to protect individual rights. African-Americans created political and social institutions that had not existed before Reconstruction. But as the African-American leader W. E. B. Du Bois observed, "The slave went free; stood a brief moment in the sun; then moved back again toward slavery." Reconstruction had failed to provide blacks with either economic independence or political rights. For many African-Americans, the long road to freedom had just begun.

CONCLUSION

The question of how to deal with the defeated South divided the North at the end of the war. Radicals, who passionately opposed slavery, took an expansive view of federal power, believing that the national government had the right to reshape southern society by breaking up the old plantation system and guaranteeing political and economic rights to the freed people. President Johnson, on the other hand, supported states' rights, opposed the expansion of federal power, and favored a lenient policy toward the former Confederate states. Politics also played a role in the conflicting experiments. Radicals hoped that former slaves would form the foundation of a powerful Republican Party in the South. Johnson, on the other hand, planned to use opposition to Reconstruction to build a new national coalition of moderate Democrats and Republicans.

The president's disdain for compromise and negotiation complicated his relationship with Congress and allowed the Radicals to seize control of Reconstruction policy in 1866. Once in power, the Radicals passed the Fourteenth and Fifteenth Amendments to the Constitution. Republican regimes in the South expanded democracy, built biracial public schools, and embarked on an ambitious public works program. The Radical experiment, however, quickly unraveled, confronted by a rejuvenated Democratic Party in the South that was willing to use violence and intimidation to regain power. A severe depression, widespread charges of corruption, and concerns about government power divided the northern Republican Party. The Compromise of 1877 signaled the Republicans' retreat from Reconstruction. The Republicans had destroyed the slave system, but their experiment in securing basic economic and political rights for African-Americans remained incomplete.

African-Americans played a central role in defining the new meaning of freedom in the South. Their experiments cast aside old forms of deference to whites, built up community institutions, and restored ties among family members separated by slavery. Economic independence, however, remained elusive. By 1880 nearly 75 percent of black southerners were working as sharecroppers.

Propagandists of the New South hoped to remake the southern economy in the image of the North, but southern realities limited economic experimentation. The region remained predominately rural and agricultural, tied to a single crop. Culturally, many whites celebrated the past at the same time that others questioned the underpinnings of southern society. No ambiguity, however, obscured the way the white South exercised power. The white Redeemer governments moved aggressively to limit the rights of African-Americans, prevented them from voting, and imposed a formal system of segregation that would dominate southern life well into the next century. Most northerners accepted the redemption of the South by whites and turned their attention westward, to the conquest of the frontier.

Annotated Suggested Readings

Eric Foner's *Reconstruction: America's Unfinished Revolution, 1863–1877* (1988) is an impressive synthesis of recent scholarship on all aspects of Reconstruction, with the experience of the freedmen as the central theme. *The Era of Reconstruction, 1865–1877* (1965) by Kenneth Stampp is the classic revisionist work on the period. James McPherson's *Ordeal by Fire: The Civil War and Reconstruction* (1967) includes a basic overview of the events and politics of the time.

Reconstruction during Lincoln's tenure is treated by Peyton McCrary in *Abraham Lincoln and Reconstruction: The Louisiana Experiment* (1978). Louis Gerteis demonstrates the haphazard nature of wartime Reconstruction through an examination of the government's dealings with the former slaves in *From Contraband to Freedman: Federal Policy Toward Southern Blacks, 1861–1865* (1973). Historians have been very critical of Lincoln's successor. Eric McKitrick leads off the barrage of criticism historians have heaped on Johnson with *Andrew Johnson and Reconstruction* (1966). Other critical accounts include *Andrew Johnson and the Uses of Constitutional Power* (1980) by James Sefton; and Hans Trefousse, *Impeachment of a President: Andrew Johnson and Reconstruction* (1975). In *Reunion Without Compromise: The South and Reconstruction, 1865–1868* (1973), Michael Perman contends that Johnson encouraged southern defiance by giving the South too much choice and that this stubbornness doomed presidential Reconstruction. Donald Nieman, *To Set the Law in Motion: The Freedmen's Bureau and the Legal Rights of Blacks, 1865–1868* (1979), examines Johnson's role in the failure of the Freedmen's Bureau to adequately defend the rights of blacks. Dan Carter's *When the War Was Over: The Failure of Self-Reconstruction in the South, 1865–1867* (1985) contrasts with most of these works, portraying the southern white leaders during presidential Reconstruction not as reactionary and ardent secessionists but as cautious conservatives.

The rise of the Radical Republicans is discussed in Edward L. Gambill's *Conservative Ordeal: Northern Democrats and Reconstruction, 1865–1868* (1981). Michael Les Benedict, *A Compromise of Principle: Congressional Republicans and Reconstruction* (1974), looks at the inner workings of the Republican Party. In *An American Crisis: Congress and Reconstruction, 1865–1867* (1963), W. R. Brock maintains that Radicals had early and widespread popular support.

The collapse of congressional Reconstruction is the subject of William Gillette in *Retreat from Reconstruction, 1869–1879* (1979). David Montgomery, *Beyond Equality: Labor and the Radical Republicans, 1862–1872* (1967), argues that the Radicals foundered on the issue of class, not race. Heather Cox Richardson makes a similar argument in *Death of Reconstruction: Race, Labor, and Politics in the Post-Civil War North* (2001). Ian Polakoff discusses the official end of Reconstruction in *The Politics of Inertia: The Election of 1876 and the End of Reconstruction* (1973). Roy Morris, Jr., *Fraud of the Century: Rutherford B. Hayes, Samuel Tilden and the Stolen Election of 1876* (2003), carefully recreates the story of the election and presents evidence that Republican fraud in the South denied Tilden his presidency.

In *A More Perfect Union: The Impact of the Civil War and Reconstruction on the Constitution* (1973), Harold Hyman demonstrates how the crises of war and reunion transformed the Constitution. Stanley Kutler examines the Supreme Court during this period in *The Judicial Power and Reconstruction Politics* (1968), countering the image of the Court as a foe of congressional Reconstruction. In *Emancipation and Equal Rights: Politics and Constitutionalism in the Civil War Era* (1978), Herman Belz evaluates Reconstruction from a constitutional perspective and judges it a success.

For discussion of northern political life in general during congressional Reconstruction, *The Press Gang: Newspapers and Politics, 1865–1878* (1994) by Mark Wahlgren Summers is an entertaining and insightful read. Brooks Simpson examines Grant's stance toward Reconstruction and his transition from soldier to politician in *Let Us Have Peace: Ulysses S. Grant and the Politics of War and Reconstruction, 1861–1868* (1991). Alexander Keyssar offers an excellent analysis of the impact of reconstruction on suffrage in *The Right to Vote: The Contested History of Democracy in the United States* (2000).

Willie Lee Rose's *Rehearsal for Reconstruction: The Port Royal Experiment* (1964) is perhaps the best examination of wartime Reconstruction in action. Leon Litwack's *Been in the Storm So Long: The Aftermath of Slavery* (1979) and Joel Williamson's *After Slavery: The Negro in South Carolina During Reconstruction* (1966) also discuss the former slaves' response to emancipation. Jacqueline Jones, *Labor of Love, Labor of Sorrow* (1986), examines the gender dimension of race relations in the postwar South.

There are numerous studies on the South during congressional Reconstruction. In *The Road to Redemption: Southern Politics, 1869–1879* (1984), Michael Perman shows how division within each party in the South led to a merger of moderate factions by the end of Reconstruction. Steven Hahn examines the Reconstruction origins of southern populism in *The Roots of Southern Populism: Yeoman Farmers and the Transformation of the Georgia Upcountry, 1850–1890* (1983). James Roark studies the impact of emancipation and Reconstruction on the former slaveholders in *Masters Without Slaves: Southern Planters in the Civil War and Reconstruction* (1977).

The African-American experience during congressional Reconstruction is covered by W. E. B. Du Bois's still-classic *Black Reconstruction in America* (1935). More recently, Thomas Holt's *Black Over White: Negro Political Leadership in South Carolina During Reconstruction* (1977) and Edmund L. Drago's *Black Politicians and Reconstruction in Georgia* (1982) examine the experience of blacks in Reconstruction governments. Steven Hahn focuses on the black struggle for political and economic power in the rural south in his masterful *A Nation Under Feet* (2003).

The role of southern violence in the demise of Reconstruction is discussed in *White Terror: The Ku Klux Klan Conspiracy and Southern Reconstruction* (1967) by Allen Trelease; and *But There Was No Peace: The Role of Violence in the Politics of Reconstruction* (1984) by George Rable. Philip Dray's *At the Hands of Persons Unknown: The Lynching of Black America* (2002) describes not only the horrific crimes, but also the culture of lynching that emerged in the South and those who fought against it.

C. Vann Woodward's classic *Origins of the New South, 1877–1913* (1951) is still a valuable treatment, focusing on the rise of a business-oriented middle class in the South after the Civil War. Jonathan Weiner offers a different take in *Social Origins of the New South,*

1860–1885 (1978). Edward Ayers offers an insightful analysis in *The Promise of the New South: Life After Reconstruction* (1992). On the Lost Cause, see Gaines Foster's *The Ghosts of the Confederacy* (1989). Robert Kenzer examines the role of blacks in the economy of the urban South in *Enterprising Southerners* (1997). David Blight details the success of southern mythmaking in *Race and Reunion: The Civil War in American Memory* (2002).

The rise of Jim Crow is also discussed by C. Vann Woodward in another classic, *The Strange Career of Jim Crow* (1955). Michael Klarman traces the long history of legalized segregation in *From Jim Crow to Civil Rights* (2004). Leon Litwack's *Trouble in Mind: Black Southerners in the Age of Jim Crow* (1998) is a comprehensive and moving account of the trials of African-Americans in the post-Reconstruction South. The perpetuation of black poverty after slavery is the subject of Jay Mandle's *Not Slave, Not Free: The African American Economic Experience Since the Civil War* (1992).

The istory ompanion

The Boundaries of Congressional Reconstruction

A Southern Critique of the Reconstruction Acts

Benjamin H. Hill, a former Confederate senator, gave this speech in Atlanta on July 16, 1867. He was responding to the passage in March of the Reconstruction Acts, which imposed military rule across the former Confederacy. His seething anger is directed at Congress, which he believed had overstepped its legal boundaries with its ambitious plan for transforming the South.

The people of the North honestly love the Constitution, but the leaders there hate it and intend to destroy it. . . .

By carrying out these measures you disfranchise your own people. Suppose we concede, for argument, that it is right to enfranchise all the negroes; if this be right, by what principle of law or morals do we disfranchise the white people? . . . In the face of the fact that a republican government can rest upon and be perpetuated only by the virtue and intelligence of the people, you propose to exclude the most intelligent from participating in the government forever! . . .

But you say that you are in favor of going into the Union, because if you do not your property will be confiscated. . . . I am ashamed to talk or use arguments about confiscation in time of peace! It is a war power, not known to international law except as a war power, to be used only in time of war, upon an enemy's goods! Confiscation in time of peace is neither more nor less than robbery! . . .

These bills propose at every step to abrogate the Constitution—trample upon the State and its laws—to blot out every hope—to perjure every man who accepts them, with every principle of honor, justice, and safety disregarded, trampled upon, and despised—all to perpetuate the power of their wicked authors. . . . That which is now proposed is *force*. It is proposed by men who do not live in this State, and whose agents do not live here; and it is sought to be accomplished by military power, but under the pretense of your sanction—not to please yourselves, but them. . . .

This whole scheme is in violation of all the issues of the war . . . and all the terms of surrender. More than a hundred thousand men abandoned Lee's army because they were assured that if they laid down their arms they would be in the Union again with all their rights as before. . . . The people—the soldiers of the United States—were then willing to fulfill the obligation; but the politicians intended to deceive you. . . .

My colored friends, will you receive a word of admonition? Of all the people, you will most need the protection of the law. . . . Do you believe that the man who is faithless to the Constitution will be faithful to you? . . . They promise you lands, and teach you to hate the Southern people, whom you have known always and who never deceived you. Are you foolish enough to believe you can get another man's land for nothing, and that the white people will give up their land without resistance?

If you get up strife between your race and the white race, do you not know you must perish? . . . You can have no safety in the Constitution and no peace except by cultivating relations of kindness with those who are fixed here, who need your services, and who are willing to protect you.

Thaddeus Stevens Proposes Land Reform

Pennsylvania Congressman Thaddeus Stevens was perhaps the most Radical of the Republicans. In his view, the Reconstruction Acts did not go far enough. He envisioned a complete overhaul of southern institutions and real political and economic opportunity for the freed slaves. On March 19, 1867, in the midst of the debate over the Reconstruction Acts, he introduced a land reform bill that would have given each freedman household 40 acres of land.

The cause of the war was slavery. We have liberated the slaves. It is our duty to protect them, and provide for them while they are unable to provide for themselves. . . .

Have we not a right, if we chose to go to that extent, to indemnify ourselves for the expenses and damage caused by the war? We might make the property of the enemy pay the $4,000,000,000 which we have expended, as well as the damages inflicted on loyal men by confiscation and invasion, which might reach $1,000,000,000 more. This bill is merciful, asking less than one tenth of our just claims. . . .

The first section orders the confiscation of all the property belonging to the State governments, and the national government which made war upon us, and which we have conquered. . . .

The fourth section provides first that out of the lands thus confiscated each liberated slave who is a male adult, or the head of a family, shall have assigned to him a homestead of forty acres of land (with $100 to build a dwelling), which shall be held for them by trustees during their pupilage. Let us consider whether this is a just and politic provision.

Whatever may be the fate of the rest of the bill I must earnestly pray that this may not be defeated. On its success, in my judgment, depends not only the happiness and respectability of the colored race, but their very existence. Homesteads to them are far more valuable than the immediate right of suffrage, though both are their due.

Four million persons have just been freed from a condition of dependence, wholly unacquainted with business transactions, kept systematically in ignorance of all their rights and of the common elements of education, without which none of any race are competent to earn an honest living, to guard against the frauds which will always be practiced on the ignorant, or to judge of the most judicious manner of applying their labor. But few of them are mechanics, and none of them skilled manufacturers. They must necessarily, therefore, be the servants and the victims of others unless they are made in some measure independent of their wiser neighbors. . . .

Make them independent of the old masters so that they may not be compelled to work for them upon unfair terms, which can only be done by giving them a small tract of land to cultivate for themselves, and you remove all this danger. You also elevate the character of the freedman. Nothing is so likely to make a man a good citizen as to make him a freeholder. Nothing will so multiply the productions of the South as to divide it into small farms. Nothing will make men so industrious and moral as to let them feel that they are above want and are the owners of the soil which they till. . . .

I do not speak of their fidelity and services in this bloody war. I put it on the mere score of lawful earnings. They and their ancestors have toiled, not for years, but for ages, without one farthing of recompense. They have earned for their masters this very land and much more. . . .

Congress is dictating the terms of peace. . . . This bill is very merciful toward a cruel, outlawed belligerent, who, when their armies were dispersed, would gladly have compromised if their lives were saved.

Thaddeus Stevens, long an advocate for African-American rights, was a leader of both the Radical Republicans and the House of Representatives as a whole, admired even by those who were enraged by his strident style and unorthodox views. He and his fellow Radical Republicans saw in Reconstruction a "golden moment" not only to ensure the equality of blacks under the law, but also to foment real change in the South through the destruction of the plantation system and the transformation of the freed slaves into self-sufficient and upwardly mobile small farmers. On more than one occasion, Stevens introduced plans for the redistribution of southern land, at one time going as far as to advocate the seizure of wealthy southerners' property by the federal government. Stevens's plans exemplified innovative social and political thinking, which not only included economic opportunity for the former slaves and the restructuring of southern society, but also envisioned using the federal government in unprecedented ways to accomplish these ends.

Stevens's ambitious ideas challenged existing views of federal power, which suggested that government could ensure legal, but not economic, equality of all its citizens. Even the Reconstruction Acts, which did pass into law, pressed the boundaries of federal power, as southerners were quick to point out. White southerners protested against the federal government's occupation of southern soil, its imposition of martial law, and its insistence on setting the terms of the states' readmission to the Union. After declaring they could secede from the Union, the southern states now claimed they had never left and should not be treated as a conquered nation. Southerners felt they should be able to form new governments quickly, with little federal interference and with minimal impact on southern institutions and traditions.

QUESTIONS FOR ANALYSIS

1. Why does Hill call congressional Reconstruction unconstitutional? Do his claims have any merit? Explain.

2. What is Hill's advice to the freed slaves? Do you think he is sincere?

3. Summarize the provisions of Stevens's bill. How does he justify Congress's right to enact it?

4. What reasons does Stevens give to support the necessity of land reform?

5. Based on the chapter and these selections, how do you think our society might be different today had Reconstruction gone farther? How would it be the same?

17

Conquering the West

1862–1900

"We tried to run, but they shot us like we were buffalo."

Late in 1888 in western Nevada a Paiute Indian named Wovoka had a vision of the future that predicted a return to the past—to a time before the white man had stolen the Indians' lands, forced them onto reservations, and slaughtered the buffalo that sustained them. "My brothers, I bring to you the promise of a day," he preached, "when the red men of the prairie will rule the world." To hasten the day of salvation, he taught, Indians must dance in a large circle. If their faith was strong enough, the old world of their ancestors would return and the white man would vanish. Word quickly spread across the Plains and the Great Basin about the messiah and his "Ghost Dance."

The new ritual terrified many whites. Missionaries condemned the "heathen" Native American religious practice, claiming it kept Indians from becoming "civilized." The press, always hungry for a sensational news story, began writing about "hostile" Sioux. Army officials worried that the mysterious dancing would lead to unrest. "Indians are dancing in the snow and are wild and crazy," a nervous agent at Pine Ridge Reservation in South Dakota wired to Washington. "We need protection and we need it now."

The War Department responded by dispatching army troops to the Indian reservation to arrest the Ghost Dance "fomenters of disturbances." The army was convinced that the Sioux chief Sitting Bull was the "high priest and leading apostle of this latest absurdity." On the morning of December 15, 1890, U.S.-trained Indian policemen at the Sioux's Standing Rock Reservation in South Dakota burst into Sitting Bull's house to arrest him. A group of the chief's armed and angry supporters confronted the policemen. One of them, Bear That Catches, pulled a gun from under his blanket and shot one of the officials. A hail of bullets followed, leaving Sitting Bull, eight of his followers, and six policemen dead.

The news of Sitting Bull's fate alarmed Big Foot, the aging chief of another band of Sioux, who fled with his people into the wilderness. On December 28, five days after starting south to Pine Ridge to join other chiefs for a meeting, Big Foot surrendered to the Seventh Cavalry. The soldiers escorted Big Foot, along with the 120 men and 230 women and children traveling with him, to a camp near a frozen creek called Wounded Knee, where the Indians pitched their tepees in a low hollow. The soldiers— a total of about 500—camped on a rise just to the north.

"The following morning there was a bugle call," remembered an Indian named Dewey Beard. Surrounded by mounted soldiers, the Indians were ordered to assemble at the center of camp and turn over their weapons. Big Foot advised his men to give up old, damaged guns but to hide the good ones. Realizing the deception, the cavalry commander intensified his search, ordering his men to move from tepee to tepee. As the tension built, the medicine man, Yellow Bird, began dancing and chanting Ghost Dance songs, urging the young braves to be firm. "Do not fear," he shouted, "but let your hearts be strong." Suddenly, one Indian, Black Coyote, pulled a rifle from under his blanket and held it over his head. Two soldiers grabbed him and struggled for the gun. It went off, firing overhead. Several braves grabbed rifles and aimed at the cavalry. "By God, they have broken!" an officer shouted. The Indians fired, and at about the same moment came the command "Fire! Fire on them!"

The cavalry's superior firepower quickly overwhelmed the Indians. "We tried to run, but they shot us like we were buffalo," said Louise Weasel Bear. The actual

Arapaho Ghost Dance   The Ghost Dance came from the teachings of the Paiute medicine man, Wovoka, who believed it would renew Native American culture and lead to an age of peace and prosperity. This positive message, and the dance, spread from the Great Basin east onto the Plains. Wounded Knee brought an end to the Ghost Dance for the Sioux in 1890, but other tribes of the Northern Great Plains, including the Arapaho, continued to perform the dance. Because of its sensitive nature, Native Americans generally refused to allow whites to witness or record the dance, but a number of artists created their own interpretation of the spiritual ritual. *(Corbis.)*

CHRONOLOGY

1851	Treaty of Fort Laramie
1862	Pacific Railroad Act Homestead Act
1864	Massacre at Sand Creek
1866	Fetterman massacre
1867	Treaty of Medicine Lodge Creek Abilene established as major cattle depot
1868	Battle of the Washita Second Treaty of Fort Laramie
1869	Transcontinental Railroad completed
1872	Yellowstone National Park founded
1873	Timber Culture Act
1874	Red River War Women's National Indian Association founded Glidden invents barbed wire
1876	Battle of Little Bighorn
1877	Desert Land Act
1878	Timber and Stone Act
1879	Exodusters migrate to Kansas
1881	Jackson publishes *A Century of Dishonor*
1882	Congress prohibits Chinese immigration
1887	Dawes Act
1890	Wounded Knee massacre
1891	Forest Reserve Act
1892	Miners' strike at Coeur d'Alene Sierra Club founded
1893	Turner's frontier thesis
1903	*The Great Train Robbery*

fighting lasted only a few minutes, but it killed 250 Native Americans. "Dead and wounded women and children and little babies were scattered all along there where they had been trying to run away," Black Elk reported. "The soldiers had followed them along the gulch, as they ran, and murdered them in there."

The massacre at Wounded Knee represented the end of the most violent phase of America's westward expansion—Indian suppression. For the previous three decades, with the help of a generous government land policy, millions of people—native-born, foreign immigrants, and Mexicans—had flooded into the West. Some mined for gold; some raised cattle; and still others turned to farming. Despite their differences, those who settled in the West shared a thirst for new opportunities and a reckless attitude toward the land and its native inhabitants.

Americans in the West undertook social and economic experiments in keeping with the nation's traditions. By the end of the century the West had taken on some of the characteristics of the industrial East. Large business interests dominated the economic landscape; mining camps and temporary cow towns had grown into thriving communities. As the "frontier" disappeared, Americans transformed the idea of the West into a national mirror that reflected their view of themselves as a nation of rugged individuals who had tamed a savage empire.

- What role did the federal government play in settling the West?

- How and why did westward expansion devastate Native American society and culture?

- How did migrants to the West approach the environment and its resources? In what ways did western enterprise reflect that in the East?

- What cultural attitudes and racial stereotypes did the settlers bring with them, and how did these assumptions shape the societies they created in the West?

- Why did Americans transform the West into a cultural symbol of rugged individualism? In what ways was this image accurate or inaccurate?

This chapter will address these questions.

THE WESTWARD EXPERIMENT

While the debate over Reconstruction drew attention to the ravaged South, the prospect of prosperity lured people West. The generation after the Civil War witnessed the most extensive movement of population in American history. This migration included immigrants from China and Europe, African-Americans from the South, Hispanics from the Southwest, and small farmers from the East. Despite their diverse backgrounds, millions who experimented with relocation searched for the same thing: opportunity. Promoting their quests were a government eager to give public lands to private developers and railroad executives hungry to attract business. The combination created a recipe for unprecedented expansion.

The New Migrants   "The wagons are going in our direction by the hundreds," observed Uriah Wesley Oblinger in 1872. A former Union army veteran and farmer from Indiana, Oblinger had grown tired of working for other people and decided to establish a homestead of his own in Nebraska. In motive and action, Oblinger was part of one of the greatest migrations in history. During the last four decades of the nineteenth century, more than 2 million people flooded into the American West. Together, they added 190 million acres of cultivated lands to the country's inventory, an area equal to Great Britain and France combined.

Before the Civil War, most settlers had skipped over the center of the nation and headed directly to California or Oregon. Most of the new migrants, however, settled on the Great Plains, the semiarid region that extended from Montana and the Dakotas south to Texas. This vast area made up one-fifth of the United States. Rainfall averaged less than fifteen inches per year, and the soil produced scarce trees to harvest for lumber to build homes. A few migrants ventured farther west to the rough High Plains—including present-day Montana, Wyoming, Colorado, New Mexico, and Arizona—that rolled into the Rocky Mountains. Sandwiched between the Rockies to the east and the Cascade and Sierra Nevada Mountains to the west was the Great Basin of Idaho and Utah. In other words, what people referred to as "the West" was a diverse region containing many discrete locations and unique features.

The American West was not the only frontier open for settlement. In the 1880s European migrants flooded the Canadian Great Plains, lured by government promises of free land. The search for fertile farmland also prompted land rushes in New Zealand and Argentina, while reports of gold in Australia and diamonds in South Africa attracted global migrants in search of elusive wealth. Each frontier developed in its own unique fashion, but in each region the quest for prosperity encouraged mobility and often produced violent clashes with native populations.

A very large minority of those who took part in the American migration were born outside the United States. In Nebraska 25 percent of the 123,000 people living in the new state in 1870 were foreign-born. In the same census immigrants made up between 20 and 30 percent of the populations of South Dakota, Montana, Wyoming, and Colorado. In 1890 in North Dakota the figure was 45 percent, higher than in any other state in the country. In the northern Plains states large numbers of Norwegians, Swedes, Germans, Irish, and Canadians set up communities. Between 1876 and 1890 more than 200,000 Chinese arrived at West Coast ports on steamships. The Chinese migrants were mostly men who were planning to work away from home temporarily. They were illiterate or had very little schooling, but they dreamed of new possibilities inspired by stories of the "Golden Mountain."

Far to the south Hispanic settlers, many immigrating from Mexico, spread from the frontier in New Mexico throughout the Southwest and as far north as Colorado. They were aided by the U.S. Army, which subdued the Navajo and Apache Indians who had prevented expansion in the region. Peasants and tradesmen looking for new trading opportunities pioneered the new settlements. By 1900 as many as a hundred thousand Mexican immigrants were living in southern Texas, Arizona, New Mexico, and southern California.

The majority of new migrants, however, were native-born. Between 1870 and 1900 over 2.5 million native-born Americans moved west. Among them were a small number of African-Americans. In 1879, following brutal murders and general repression during the election campaigns of 1878 in the South, African-Americans known as the Exodusters left their homes in Louisiana, Mississippi, and Texas to establish new and freer lives in Kansas. As many as twenty-six thousand may have left the South for Kansas and Kansas City, Missouri, in 1879–1880.

Native-born migrants to the West shared a number of characteristics. First, those who planned to establish farms believed that their seeds and farm animals would adapt best if they moved horizontally, staying on the same latitude as their home state. Settlers from Mississippi, for example, were likely to move to Texas, while those from Illinois settled in Nebraska. Second, since it cost money to move and establish a farm, most of the new migrants were relatively prosperous farmers, merchants, and professionals. Third, migrants who moved to work in mines, cut timber, or raise livestock tended to be overwhelmingly male, while family settlements predominated in farm communities. Fourth, the stream ebbed and flowed depending on fluctuations in the economy, increasing during boom times and decreasing in times of depression. Finally, the settlers tended to be restless people who moved more than once.

For all new migrants, both foreign and native, moving West offered the prospect of a better life. "Hardly anything else was talked about," observed writer Hamlin Garland about his Iowa neighbors. "Every man who could sell out had gone west or was going." A popular saying had arisen: "If hell lay to the west, Americans would cross heaven to get there." It was a sentiment shared by whites, blacks, Europeans, Mexicans, and Chinese. "All I know," a Chinese immigrant later recalled, "was that [travelers to the Golden Mountain] who came back were always rich." When asked his motives for coming, a black migrant to Kansas in the 1870s answered: opportunity. "That's what white men go to new countries for isn't it? You do not tell them to stay back because they are poor."

Railroad companies, young western states, and land speculators encouraged migration to the West because settlement drove up land prices and created a population of potential consumers. New states, needing the revenue from the sale of land to fund schools, hired promotional bureaus to lure new settlers. Land speculators advertised their western holdings with handbills, pamphlets, and newspaper stories. Promoters often exaggerated the fertility of the West, claiming that development had transformed the environment. A succession of unusually wet years in the 1870s and 1880s convinced many people that "rain follows the plow."

Personal contact with family members out West or neighbors who returned for visits often provided another incentive to go west. Ephraim G. Fairchild, a resident of Jones County, Iowa, in 1857 wrote to a relative, "I think that I can plough and harrow out hear without being nocked and jerked about with the stones as I allways have been in Jersey . . . if father and Mother and the rest of the family was out here . . . they would make a living easier than they can in Jersey."

The Homestead Act of 1862

Except during the Civil War, the federal government rarely touched the lives of most Americans during the nineteenth century. That was not the case in the West, however, where the national government shaped every aspect of settlement. In 1862 Congress launched one of its boldest attempts to lure migrants west by passing the Homestead Act. The new law allowed any citizen (or any immigrant who had taken the first step toward becoming a citizen) to claim 160 acres of land simply by paying a fee of $10. If he "lived upon or cultivated" the land for five years, the land became his, free and forever. If the homesteader did not want to wait five years, he could pay for the land at $1.25 an acre and own it outright after six months.

The Republican architects of the Homestead Act believed that free land in the West would help ordinary white Americans achieve independence, keeping the United States free of the dependent relations of either an industrial society such as Europe's or a slave society as the South had been. Proponents, who called the act "the greatest democratic measure of all history," believed that it would create a class of prosperous farmers who would form the economic and political backbone of the nation. The *New York Tribune* claimed that the legislation would diminish "the number of paupers and idlers and increase the proportion of working, independent, self-subsisting farmers in the land evermore."

Though it played an important role in the settlement of the West, the Homestead Act fell short of its framers' intention of awarding most western land to small farmers. Instead, the legislation allowed wealthy speculators to obtain immense tracts of land. The speculators hired men to stake out claims and then deed the land over to their employers. Few prospective homesteaders could afford to compete with speculators; they lacked the money to pack up their belongings, travel west, and buy the machinery necessary to start a farm. In addition, eastern lawmakers with little understanding of the unique conditions in the West had designed the legislation. A 160-acre parcel was ideal for a farm in the East, but in the West it was too small for grazing or dry farming and too large for irrigated farming. Despite these problems, many individual families did establish homesteads in the West. By the end of 1895, for example, over 430,000 settlers filed homesteads in Kansas, Nebraska, and the Dakotas.

Over the next few years Congress passed a number of other measures to encourage movement west. In each case, though, instead of helping struggling

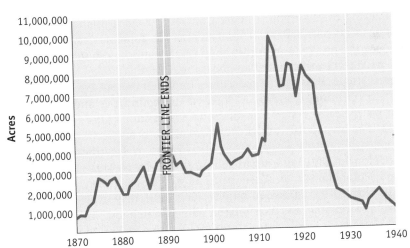

Public Land to Homestead Despite the end of the frontier line in 1890, the number of homesteads carved from public lands continued to rise well into the twentieth century. Note the dramatic jump during the 1910s when America provided food for Europe during World War I and the precipitous decline as agriculture prices dropped in the 1920s, bottoming out just as the nation entered the Great Depression.

young farmers, the legislation aided land speculators who used the poorly written laws to seize large holdings. In 1873 came the Timber Culture Act, which allowed a homesteader (or a rancher or speculator) to claim an additional 160 acres if he would plant trees on 40 of the acres. In 1877 Congress passed the Desert Land Act, which allowed an individual to claim 640 acres of land if he would begin irrigation. In most cases, no water existed, and nearly 95 percent of the claims were estimated to be fraudulent. Under the Timber and Stone Act of 1878, any citizen or immigrant could purchase up to 160 acres of western forest for $2.50 an acre. This measure enabled lumber companies to obtain thousands of acres by hiring dummy applicants whom they marched in gangs to the land offices.

The national government exercised a direct and powerful influence in the region. As new areas of the West opened, they were organized as territories under the control of Congress and the president. In 1860 almost one-third of the area of the United States was divided into territories. The president selected the governor and judges in each territory. Congress set budgets and oversaw the activities of territorial governments. Political connections were often more important than qualifications when it came to making appointments. "You pledged us that we should have good men and good lawyers sent to us as judges, and we get to constitute our Supreme Court an ass, a knave, and a drunkard," a Dakota resident complained to the U.S. attorney general.

While it avoided active involvement in the affairs of local territories, Congress was occasionally capable of forceful intervention. Its attacks on the Mormon practice of polygamy (having more than one wife) were a good example. Following a Supreme Court decision in 1878 ruling the practice illegal (*United States* v. *Reynolds*), Congress passed legislation imposing heavy fines and imprisonment on anyone convicted of practicing polygamy. In 1887 Washington increased the pressure by directly attacking the Mormon Church: Congress passed legislation forbidding it from holding assets over $50,000. Four days after the Supreme Court ruled the law constitutional, the president of the Mormon Church announced that by divine revelation he had been instructed to ban polygamy.

Congress also established the procedures for statehood. After residents of a territory signed a petition, Congress established the boundaries and authorized an election of delegates to a state constitutional convention. After the constitution had been ratified by popular vote, the territory officially applied for statehood, and Congress voted to approve or deny the petition. Kansas used these procedures to enter the Union in 1861, and it was soon followed by Nevada (1864), Nebraska (1867), and Colorado (1876). Then partisan struggles between Democrats and Republicans blocked the admission of new states until 1889, when North Dakota, South Dakota, Montana, and Washington gained statehood. After Utah banned polygamy, Congress approved the territory's statehood petition in 1896. The process of establishing states in the West was completed early in the next century when Oklahoma (1907) and Arizona and New Mexico (1912) joined the Union.

The Railroad and Western Expansion

The federal government also lured migrants West by providing privately owned railroad companies with financial assistance. In 1862 Congress passed the Pacific Railroad Act, which pledged the nation to building a train link between

East and West. Through this law, the government provided two companies with economic incentives, including land and cash loans, to construct the first transcontinental railroad. The Central Pacific started building eastward from Sacramento in January 1863, and the Union Pacific began laying track westward from Omaha, Nebraska, by the end of the year. In May 1869 the two work gangs met at Promontory Point, Utah, just east of the Great Salt Lake. The Union Pacific's Engine No. 119 and the Central Pacific's Jupiter "kissed amid a shower of champagne," joining the nation across a "desert" that an earlier generation had believed would never be settled.

Five days later the two companies began regular service. Whereas the wagon trip to Oregon along the Overland Trail had taken six to eight weeks, the rail journey took one week. Once a day the Pacific Express would head west from Omaha for Sacramento. And once a day eastbound passengers would board the Atlantic Express in Sacramento for a run of about 2,000 miles to Omaha. During the next fifteen years, three more routes were opened across the Rockies.

The railroads launched a massive campaign to attract settlers to live along their tracks and provide business for their freight trains. "You can lay track to the Garden of Eden," said a railroad executive, "but what good is it if the only inhabitants are Adam and Eve?" Railroad land departments organized excursions for newspapermen, sent agents abroad to attract immigrants, and distributed handbills describing the "millions of acres" of fertile lands available for purchase. In 1874 an office set up by Union Pacific promoter General Grenville Dodge spent $105,000 to advertise its lands in 2,311 newspapers and magazines. As added incentive, the railroads provided easy credit terms and special passenger rates for prospective settlers. The promotional efforts brought dramatic results: the 1870 population of Kansas had been 364,000; in 1887 more than a million and a half people lived there.

THE ASSAULT ON NATIVE AMERICAN CULTURES

The new migrants showed little regard for the Native American communities that existed in the West. Believing Native Americans to be racially inferior, the settlers subdued, sometimes brutally, Indians who blocked their path to the region's rich natural resources. Many Indians, dependent on resources that white incursion disrupted or destroyed, struggled to preserve their communities and their lifestyles. By the end of the century their experiment in resistance had failed. The new migrants had established their hold over the land and overwhelmed the rich native cultures of the West.

The Plains Indians   In 1865 approximately a quarter of a million Native Americans lived in the western half of the country. Some were eastern tribes, such as the Cherokee, Creek, and Shawnee, who had been forced west by the federal government. In the Southwest were the Pueblo Indians, sophisticated farmers who lived in huge apartment complexes of adobe or stone. The Ute, Shoshone, and Nez Percé settled throughout the central and northern Rocky Mountains. Nearly two-thirds of the Native Americans, however, lived on the Great Plains. Included among the Plains tribes to the northwest were the Blackfoot of Idaho and Montana. The central Plains were home to the Cheyenne, Crow, and Arapaho, while the Kiowa, Apache, and Comanche roamed present-day Texas and New Mexico. The Sioux (or Lakota) of present-day Minnesota and North and South Dakota were the dominant power on the northern Great Plains.

The Plains Indians were a diverse group, and simple generalizations are not easy. Tribes spoke different languages. Some practiced sedentary farming, while others were seminomadic hunters. Most tribes, which sometimes boasted populations in the thousands, were subdivided into smaller bands of three to five hundred men and women. Each band had a governing council, though most members participated in decision making. In most tribes the men hunted, traded, and supervised the bands' religious life. Women were responsible for raising children, preparing meals, and growing and gathering vegetables and wild fruits, though there were exceptions to these generalizations.

Native American views of the environment were strikingly different from those of the white settlers. Although beliefs varied, Indians tended to imbue the nonhu-

Family of Bannocks in Idaho, 1872 By the nineteenth century, the Northern Paiute-speaking Bannocks had migrated east from Oregon into the Snake River valley of Idaho. There they found large buffalo herds and ample tall grass for their horses. By the 1850s, whites traveling the Oregon trail and Mormons settling in Utah had begun depleting the number of buffalo and the Bannocks retaliated with raids on those passing through. This brought the tribe in conflict with the U.S. Army and as with many tribes in the late 1860s, the Bannocks signed a treaty which moved them onto the Fort Hall Reservation with the Shoshones. On the reservation, Bannock families attempted to live as they always had, but dwindling resources made them increasingly dependent on the U.S. government. *(Corbis.)*

man world with a spiritual dimension: plants and animals were conscious beings endowed with symbolic and religious meaning. Indians tried to exploit available resources without upsetting the balance that sustained human and nonhuman alike. No Indian thought of himself as owning a piece of the land. He might own his horses, his weapons, and his tepee, but the land itself was the "property" of the whole tribe, to be used communally and protected from other tribes. Whites, on the other hand, believed that God had created the land and its resources for human domination and development. They thought that progress depended on individual ownership of land and mastery over its resources. Indians were mystified by the white man's emphasis on individualism and private property. "The White man knows how to make everything," said Sioux leader Sitting Bull, "but he does not know how to distribute it" (see Competing Voices, page 691).

The proliferation of horses escaping northward from the Spanish Southwest in the sixteenth century transformed Indian life on the Plains. Until the arrival of the horse, Indian tribes depended on dogs to carry supplies. The Indian work dog could carry about fifty pounds on its back and pull another seventy-five pounds. A horse, by comparison, could carry two hundred pounds and pull another three hundred pounds for 10 to 12 miles a day. Trained from an early age to ride horses, Indians became effective hunters and fighters. "A Comanche on his feet is out of his element," observed western explorer George Catlin, "but the moment he lays his hands upon his horse . . . he gracefully flies away like a different being."

The horse was a mixed blessing to most tribes. By allowing Indians to cover more territory, horses promoted economic conflict and warfare between tribes. The growing horse population also upset the delicate grassland ecology. The horse aided the Plains Indians in the activity that became central to their survival and their culture: hunting buffalo. Before the horse, Indians had stalked buffalo on foot—a slow process that limited the number of animals they could kill. On horseback, however, braves could surround and kill dozens of buffalo in a few minutes. Ironically, the more lethal methods of killing, combined with drought and disease, decimated the bison herds and threatened the foundation of Indian society.

Then in the 1860s the coming of the railroads sounded the death knell for the buffalo. Like the Indians, eastern manufacturers had learned to turn stiff buffalo hides into soft leather for shoes, cushions, and belts, and the railroads transported the product to eastern markets. Not content to be freight carriers, the railroads offered buffalo excursions for professional hunters and church groups, allowing them to blast away from the windows of the train. Between 1872 and 1874 commercial and sport hunters killed over 4 million buffalo. The slaughter of more than 13 million buffalo by 1883 represented a crushing victory in the white man's war on the Plains Indians.

The Indian Wars

Before the 1850s Americans named the land west of the Mississippi "Indian Country," relocated eastern tribes to the region, and prohibited white settlement. The idea of a permanent Indian country fell victim to American expansionism. As steamboats churned up the Missouri and Conestoga wagons rolled across the Plains, whites killed livestock and destroyed Indian crops. Many Indians resented the encroachments on their land, and the chances of violent conflict rose.

In 1851, fearing that Indian antipathy toward the intruders might burst into open warfare, the Department of Indian Affairs decided to divide Indian lands into small, well-defined tribal territories, or reservations. In the Treaty of Fort Laramie, representatives of the northern Plains tribes agreed to stay within a defined territory and vowed not to harass wagons traveling designated paths. In return, the government offered $50,000 worth of supplies every year for fifty years and promised quick punishment of any whites who trespassed on Indian lands. Two years later the government negotiated a similar treaty with the southern Plains Indians. Together the treaties created northern and southern "Indian colonies" divided by an American corridor.

The treaties failed to resolve the conflict, as boundaries proved difficult to enforce. White settlers continued to usurp Indian lands, and many Indians refused to accept the new boundaries. In the late 1850s and early 1860s miners and other settlers moved into Colorado, running stagecoaches across Cheyenne hunting grounds. In 1864, after a series of violent clashes, Cheyenne and Apache warriors accepted the invitation of the territorial governor to gather at Sand Creek in southeastern Colorado. Promised safe passage by the governor, Chief Black Kettle led his community of seven hundred followers to the site.

Early on the morning of November 29, 1864, a group of Colorado militia led by Colonel John M. Chivington surrounded Black Kettle's people. "Kill and scalp all, big and little," Chivington told his men. Black Kettle tried to convince the soldiers of his peaceful intent by raising a white flag, but Chivington ignored the gesture. In the slaughter that followed, ninety-eight Cheyenne women and children and a handful of older men died. Chivington's soldiers scalped and mutilated the Indian corpses, gathering grisly trophies to take back to Denver. The white public applauded the slaughter at Sand Creek. The *Rocky Mountain News* called it a "brilliant feat of arms." The army, however, was appalled by Chivington's slaughter of unarmed women and children. General Nelson A. Miles called the massacre the "foulest and most unjustified crime in the annals of America."

Following the attack the central Plains exploded into war. Cheyenne runners carried war pipes to the Lakota, Arapaho, and Cheyenne camps. "We have now raised the battle ax until death," declared one chief. By early 1865 warrior bands had retaliated for Chivington's attack by burning stagecoaches, pulling down telegraph wires, and looting ranches along the South Platte River. In 1866 the Teton Sioux ambushed and killed Captain William J. Fetterman and his seventy-nine soldiers in Wyoming. "All this country is ruined," concluded an army major. "There can be no such thing as peace in the future."

The army cried out for vengeance against the Indians after the Fetterman massacre. "We must act with vindictive earnestness against the Sioux, even to their extermination, men, women, and children," declared Civil War hero William T. Sherman, who now commanded the army in the war against the Indians. But officials in the Interior Department, who remained in control of Indian policy, had a different idea. In 1867 they formed a peace delegation to end the war with the tribes by pursuing "the hitherto untried policy of conquering with kindness."

The result of the peace overture was the Treaty of Medicine Lodge Creek (1867). According to the agreement, the southern Plains tribes—Cheyenne, Arapaho,

Kiowa, and Comanche—agreed to relocate away from white settlement and onto reservations in western Oklahoma. In return, the government promised to provide food and supplies for thirty years and establish schools. The following year a handful of northern tribes signed a second Treaty of Fort Laramie, agreeing to remain on a reservation that encompassed all of present-day South Dakota, including the Black Hills, which many Sioux regarded as a sacred dwelling place of spirits. For its part, the government recognized the Sioux's right to buffalo outside the reservation "so long as buffalo may range there in numbers sufficient to justify the chase." Many Indian chiefs, however, refused to move to the new reservations. "I don't want to settle," declared a Kiowa chief. "I love to roam over the prairies."

It took the concerted effort of the army to coerce the Indians onto the reservations. On November 27, 1868, Lieutenant Colonel George Custer and his men killed over a hundred Cheyenne, including Black Kettle, in a surprise attack on a Cheyenne village. Still, bands of Kiowa, Comanche, and southern Cheyenne continued to leave the reservation to hunt and conduct raids into Texas. Following the "Red River War" in 1874 the army forced the Indians back onto their reservations and, in 1875, sent many of their leaders to prison in Florida. Only then did conflict on the southern Plains subside (see the map on page 668).

White expansion remained the chief obstacle to lasting peace. In 1874 reports circulated that the Black Hills were rich in gold. By the middle of 1875 thousands of white prospectors were illegally digging and panning in the area. The Sioux protested the invasion of their territory and the violation of sacred ground. The government offered to lease the Black Hills or to pay $6 million if the Indians were willing to sell the land. "You should bow to the wishes of the Government which supports you," an official told the chiefs. "Gold is useless to you, and there will be fighting unless you give it up." When the tribes refused, the government imposed what it considered a fair price for the land, ordered Indians to move, and in the spring of 1876 made ready to force them onto the reservation.

Sitting Bull, leader of the Hunkpapa Sioux, prepared to meet the white troops. "We must stand together or they will kill us separately," he said. "These soldiers have come shooting; they want war. All right, we'll give it to them." He sent couriers to every Sioux, Cheyenne, and Arapaho camp, summoning them to a rendezvous on the Little Bighorn River. In June more than three thousand Indians joined Sitting Bull in defiance of the government's orders to cede the Black Hills. "There were more Indians . . . ," a Cheyenne woman named Kate Big Head noted, "than I ever saw anywhere together."

The U.S. Army's Seventh Cavalry, led by Colonel George Custer, was not far behind. Custer, a West Point graduate who finished last in his class, was a superb horseman with a commanding presence and a flair for the dramatic. He also burned with ambition and was determined to make his mark. On June 25, 1876, Custer recklessly advanced on what he thought was a minor Indian encampment. Instead, it turned out to be the main Sioux force. The Sioux warriors surrounded and slaughtered Custer and his men, including several Indian scouts, in the greatest Native American victory of the Plains wars.

If Little Bighorn was a disaster for the army, it also sealed the fate of the Indians. After the deaths of Custer and his soldiers, the national mood hardened. "Who

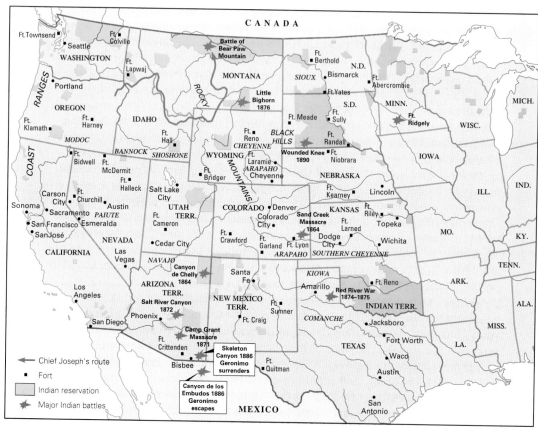

Western Indian Wars and Reservations, 1860–1890   As more white Americans moved west, clashes with Native Americans intensified. At Sand Creek and Camp Grant, Native Americans suffered heavy casualties when whites attacked villages, while in the Red River War and Battle of Fort Ridgely tribes retaliated against unfair treatment by whites. Treaties moved tribes from their traditional hunting grounds onto reservations which limited their mobility and often lacked the natural resources they required to sustain their way of life. Some tribal leaders, including Chief Joseph of the Nez Percé and Geronimo of the Chiricahua Apache, chose to defy the boundaries of the reservation and suffered the consequences.

slew Custer?" asked the *New York Herald*. "The celebrated peace policy . . . which feeds, clothes, and takes care of their noncombatant force while men are killing our troops." The army sent fresh troops to crush Indian resistance once and for all. Companies of cavalry were expanded from sixty-four to one hundred men each, and recruits hurried to join up as "Custer's Avengers." That winter, soldiers swept across Sioux lands without mercy, slaying warriors, destroying villages, burning food supplies, and leaving women and children homeless in terrible cold. Though fighting between the army and the Native American tribes flared periodically for fifteen years, there was never again a real war, nor a battle on the scale of the Little Bighorn.

Why did Indian resistance fail? First, the army had many technological advantages over the Indians. Telegraph communications and railroads enabled the troops to be quickly concentrated and deployed. Second, the soldiers were better armed. In 1873 the frontier forces received their first standardized arms issue, the single-action Colt revolver and the new Springfield rifle and carbine—all employing powerful .45-caliber ammunition. The Springfields were single-shot weapons, but they were more accurate and less prone to misfires. Their range of up to 3,500 yards often kept Indians at distances that rendered their less powerful repeating weapons or bows and arrows useless. Third, in addition to advantages in communications and firepower, the army skillfully exploited tribal rivalries to prevent the Indians from concentrating their power against a common enemy. Plains warriors from pacified nations—Pawnee, Crow, and Arikara—scouted for the army and welcomed the chance to seek revenge against their perpetual, powerful enemies, the Sioux and Cheyenne.

"Reforming" the Indians

"This civilization may not be the best possible," declared a government official in 1889 about the white world, "but it is the best the Indians can get. They cannot escape it, and must either conform to it or be crushed by it." Already demoralized by their confinement on reservations, Indians confronted a wholesale assault on their culture and community organization in the 1880s. Dictated by government policy, this assault was an experiment in converting the Indians to white civilization—to make them "walk the white man's road," as Sitting Bull put it.

Ethnocentric reformers led the assault on Native American cultures. Clergymen, social workers, and government officials were committed to assimilating Indians into American culture. These reformers capitalized on the outrage provoked by best-selling books such as Helen Hunt Jackson's *Century of Dishonor* (1881), which exposed American duplicity and corruption in dealing with the Indians. The reform spirit energized organizations such as the Women's National Indian Association (WNIA), founded in 1874, and its offshoot, the Indian Rights Association. The government furthered this assimilation by allowing reformers to take Indian children as young as five from their families and put them in boarding schools, where they were taught to abandon old ways and become members of a "new social order." In the schools and on the reservations, reform programs forced Indians to abandon their language, their customs, and their faith. The goal, declared a reformer, was to "kill the Indian and save the man."

Land reform was the centerpiece of the assimilation advocates' effort. They believed that the key to civilizing Indians was to convert them into individual landowners. As long as Indians owned their lands in common, Massachusetts senator Henry Dawes contended, they would lack "selfishness," which was "at the bottom of civilization." To break the Indians' old communal concept of land, the reformers proposed that reservations be divided into lots and given to the Indians in "severalty"; that is, the Indians were to be treated as "several" or separate individuals. According to one supporter of the plan, the breakup of the reservations and the sale of "surplus" lands to whites would teach Indians the "habits of thrift and industry" and the pride of proprietorship. "The aggressive and enterprising Anglo-Saxons" would set up their farms "side by side" with Indian farms, and "in a little while contact alone" would lead Indians to emulate the work ethic of their white neighbors.

re Entering School
Sioux. 97

Seven little Indians in four different stages
of civilization.

"Seven Little Indians in Four Different Stages of Civilization"   White philanthropists, believing that white civilization's westward trek would destroy the Indian if it did not include him, began a concerted effort to assimilate Native Americans into white culture and society. Educating Indian children at boarding schools, completely cut off from their family traditions, was one means to this end. White teachers gave students Christian names, dressed them in "proper" clothing, and inculcated them with white Protestant values. These seven children, probably students at such a school, have been outfitted to demonstrate the progressive stages of the "civilization" process. Ironically, these reformers did as much as Indian removal itself to destroy Native American culture. *(Courtesy of the Fogg Art Museum, Harvard University Art Museums. On deposit from the Carpenter Center for the Visual Arts.)*

This view became policy in 1887 when Congress passed the Dawes General Allotment Act, which supporters claimed would serve as "a mighty pulverizing engine for breaking up the tribal mass." The law provided varying amounts of land for all tribal members, with the maximum amount, 160 acres of farmland or 320 acres of grazing land, being allotted to a head of a family. Once each family had received its allotment, the government would sell the remaining land as "surplus," which could be purchased by white homesteaders. "The Indian may now become a free man," noted a partisan, "free from the thraldom of the tribe; free from the domination of the reservation system; free to enter into the body of our citizens."

This conversion of Indians into individual landowners was marked at "last-arrow" pageants. On these occasions, the government ordered the Indians to attend a large assembly on the reservation. Dressed in traditional tribal costume and carrying a bow and arrow, each Indian was individually summoned from a tepee and told to shoot an arrow. He then retreated to the tepee and reemerged wearing "civilized" clothing, symbolizing a crossing from the savage to the civilized world. Standing before a plow, a white official sealed the transition: "Take the handle of this plow, this act means that you have chosen to live the life of the white man—and the white man lives by work." At the close of the ceremony, each allottee was given an American flag and a purse with the instruction, "This purse will always say to you that the money you gain from your labor must be wisely kept."

The reformers failed to achieve their goals, and their good intentions forced Native Americans to pay a heavy price. White grafters moved in quickly; Indians were persuaded to adopt white "guardians" for their tracts, and these guardians robbed them of their land. U.S. agents who supervised the allotment procedure were sympathetic to western economic interests and settlers. In most cases, they assigned the most arid acreage to Indians and sold the best land as surplus. In 1881 Indians held 155 million acres of land. By 1890 this figure had declined to 104 million acres, and by 1900 it had dwindled to 77 million acres.

EXPERIMENTS IN RESOURCE EXPLOITATION

The migrants who traveled in search of wealth viewed the West and its resources as limitless. Over the next few decades they aggressively extracted minerals from mountains, rounded up cattle for slaughter, harvested crops for the market, and cut trees for production. Few of the hardy individualists who discovered the gold, herded the cattle, or staked out the farms reaped great wealth from their ventures. In time large investors muscled out the small entrepreneurs and captured most of the profit. By the end of the century a small group of critics had begun challenging the notion that the West had limitless resources. The West, it turned out, was not as different from the East as many people had believed.

The Mining Frontier   Mining was a powerful magnet attracting people to the West. The discovery of gold in the foothills of the Sierra Nevada Mountains had triggered the California gold rush of 1848. By the mid-1850s, as opportunity for making a quick fortune in California declined, prospectors spread across the West. For decades mining represented the largest nonagricultural source of jobs in the region. The lure of riches drew large numbers of foreign immigrants to the West. In most mining camps, between one-quarter and one-half of the population was foreign-born. In 1859 news of fresh strikes near Pike's Peak in Colorado and in the Carson River valley of Nevada set off wild migrations. A hundred thousand miners had arrived in Pike's Peak country by June 1859, many in covered wagons inscribed "Pike's Peak or Bust!" While prospectors were gathering around Pike's Peak, a couple of adventurous miners discovered the Comstock Lode on the slopes of Mount Davidson, near Gold Hill, Nevada. Comstock became the great success story of western mining. The biggest strike came in 1873, when a team of miners hit a seam of gold and silver more than 54 feet wide, the richest discovery in the history of mining. Between 1859 and 1879 miners extracted $306 million worth of gold and silver from the Comstock Lode.

During the 1860s and 1870s veins of gold brought thousands of miners to Washington, Idaho, Colorado, Montana, and the Dakotas. To collect the gold, the prospectors used a simple process called placer mining—washing the dirt from a stream in a pan or sluice. The water carried off the lighter silt and pebbles, leaving the heavy grains of gold in the bottom. Prospectors occasionally found as much as $8,000 worth of gold in a day, but the initial discoveries played out quickly.

As the placers gave out, a great deal of gold remained, but it was locked in quartz or buried deep in the earth. Mining became an expensive business, far beyond the reach of independent prospectors. Tapping veins of gold or silver required powerful machinery to move vast quantities of dirt and sand and huge mills to crush the ore. Hydraulic mining, which depended on large-scale reservoirs and elaborate flumes delivering massive volumes of water at high pressure, devastated streambeds and created mountains of rubble.

As hard-rock mining supplanted placer operations, more miners became laborers who were paid by the day or week to work underground in difficult and dangerous conditions. By 1880 a census showed 2,770 men working below ground at the Comstock Lode. They suffered in underground temperatures that sometimes soared

Hydraulic Mining   The discovery of vast quantities of natural resources lured prospectors to the West, but most of the ore lay beneath the ground so miners turned to using pressurized water jets to mine gold. Such techniques, aimed at fast profit, devastated the environment. Hydraulic mining clogged rivers and streams with residue, resulting in flooding and mudslides that ruined countless acres of potential farmland.   *(Corbis.)*

above one hundred degrees. Poor ventilation often led to headaches and dizziness, while long-term exposure to quartz dust and lead produced fatal lung diseases. Miners had to contend with misfired dynamite, cave-ins, and fires. For a time, so many accidents occurred that a worker died every week. In the late 1870s accidents disabled one of thirty miners and killed one of eighty. Overall, as many as 7,500 men died digging out silver and gold on the western mining frontier, and perhaps 20,000 more were maimed.

The threatening working conditions in the mines produced angry, and frequently violent, confrontations between workers and mine owners. The mining corporations and their managers often inspired the rise of trade unionism by refusing even to discuss basic issues with their employees, importing "scabs" to replace striking workers, calling for the National Guard to suppress strikers, and seeking injunctions to terminate strikes. In 1892 miners struck at Coeur d'Alene, Idaho, demanding recognition for their union. When angry miners destroyed mill property, the governor declared marshal law, sent in six companies of the Idaho National Guard, and crushed the strike. Such powerful allies gave mine owners the upper hand in labor disputes, but did not prevent the union movement from spreading.

Cattle Kingdom   The grasslands of the West offered another way to get rich: cattle ranching. Early in the sixteenth century the Spanish began importing European cattle into America. Over the years the cattle multiplied. Some escaped and became wild, especially in southern Texas, where they bred with cattle brought by American settlers. The result was the Texas longhorn, a breed that multiplied rapidly and lived easily on the land. Nearly 5 million were roaming the southern Plains by the mid-nineteenth century.

After the Civil War the demand for meat increased. The federal government purchased more than fifty thousand head of western cattle every year to feed Indian tribes living on reservations. The invention of refrigerated train cars allowed cattle ranchers to ship their beef to cities in the East and Midwest. In New York City a three-year-old steer brought $80; in Illinois a steer brought $40. This rising demand combined with plentiful supply in the West offered great opportunity for enterprising cattle ranchers. There was one small problem: a tick barely the size of a pinhead rode along on Texas cattle. The tick carried the Texas fever, which, though it had no effect on cattle, killed most other forms of livestock, causing fearful farmers in Missouri to block Texas cattlemen from bringing their herds north.

In 1867 an Illinois entrepreneur named Joseph G. McCoy came up with a solution to the problem: he would lead his cattle up the Chisholm Trail through Oklahoma, a westerly route that avoided farmlands. He established a shipping point for cattle at the small town of Abilene, Kansas, where the Kansas Pacific Railroad crossed Mud Creek. When he first visited Abilene in 1867, McCoy described it as a "small, dead place, consisting of about one dozen log huts." He paid $2,400 for a town site and its 480 acres. Within sixty days he had transformed the village of Abilene into a well-equipped cattle town, with a shipping yard to accommodate three thousand head, a barn, an office, and "a good three story hotel."

By 1870 drovers were moving thousands of cattle northward, sometimes for distances as long as 1,500 miles. By 1880 more than 6 million cattle had been driven to the rails. The cow towns and the trails followed as the railroads moved west. In

Kansas new towns sprouted up in Ellsworth, Wichita, Caldwell, and Dodge City. As homesteaders filled the southern and central Plains and as ranching depleted grazing, cattle drivers sought the unexploited grasslands farther west and north, taking them to Ogallala, Nebraska; Cheyenne, Wyoming; and Miles City, Montana (see map below).

The long drives north from Texas to the cow towns marked the heyday of the American cowboy. The number of cowboys who rode the cattle trails totaled no more than forty thousand. They were surprisingly young—their average age was only twenty-four. About one in every six or seven was Mexican. In fact, it was Mexicans, not Americans, who in the eighteenth century had originated the cowboy's trade and almost all of its tools, from big hats and kerchiefs to tooled leather saddles and boots. African-Americans, many of whom had learned to ride and rope while serving as slaves on Texas ranches, made up a similar proportion of cowboys. This diverse group had one thing in common: they were all wage laborers who drove someone else's cattle to market.

By the mid-1880s cattle represented by far the biggest business in the Old West—with perhaps no more than three dozen people controlling more than 20 million acres of U.S. soil. Attracted by the prospect of huge profits, eastern investors included the varied likes of William Rockefeller, William K. Vanderbilt, and a wealthy New Yorker and future president named Theodore Roosevelt. Along with the eastern investors came a host of money-heavy Europeans who had learned of huge profits to be made in cattle. They bought large tracts of land and mass-

Cattle Trails   As the railroad and farming settlements moved west, so did the great cattle trails. Starting their journey in southern Texas, cowboys drove their herds through sparsely populated territories to meet up with the ever-expanding railroad system. Towns that emerged along the rail line, like Abilene, Dodge City, and Cheyenne, became centers for the livestock industry and provided entertainment and lodging for restless cowboys.

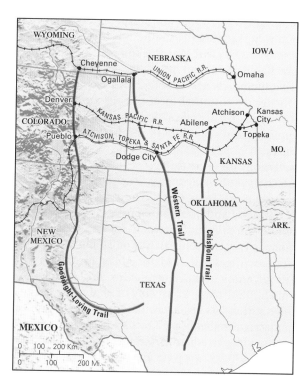

produced cattle for eastern consumers. The most impressive operation was the XIT Ranch in the panhandle of Texas. Extending for 200 miles, the ranch occupied parts of ten counties and employed as many as 150 cowboys who rode 1,000 horses, herded 150,000 head of cattle, and branded 35,000 calves a year.

The boom, however, was short-lived. Overgrazing destroyed the grass that cattle needed. Severe weather on the southern ranges in the winter of 1885 killed nearly 85 percent of the herds. The following winter temperatures that dropped to forty-five degrees below zero killed between 40 and 50 percent of cattle on the northern Plains. The cattle business recovered, but it took different directions. Outside capital, so plentiful in the boom years, dried up. Many ranchers turned to sheep raising. Sheep needed less water and grazed on shrubs that cattle would not touch. By 1900 sheep had replaced cattle as the leading industry in both Wyoming and Montana.

Cultivating the Land

With migration into the Plains bringing vast new lands under the plow, farmers had to develop new methods for dealing with the harsh environment. For one thing, they needed fencing material to protect their lands from herds of cattle. In 1874 Illinois farmer Joseph F. Glidden solved the problem by inventing barbed wire, which was cheaper and could cover more area than traditional fencing. Within ten years barbed wire was a standard feature on farms across the country.

A second problem was the harsh climate, especially the lack of rainfall, and the punishing physical labor required to plant and harvest crops. Some farmers used windmills to pump water from underground wells. Farmers also developed "dry farming" techniques, which slowed evaporation by covering the soil with a blanket of dust. Many experimented with drought-resistant crops that could withstand the severe Plains winters. As the century progressed technological improvements cut the amount of labor required to plant and harvest. Between 1850 and 1900 farm machinery reduced the cost of producing leading crops by about half.

During the 1880s worldwide overproduction that depressed crop prices combined with bad weather on the Plains to wipe out thousands of western farmers. Many small farmers remained on their homesteads, but they were increasingly frustrated with their failing economic prospects. A Minnesota girl described her family's plight to the governor: "We have no money now nothing to sell to get any more clothes with as the grasshoppers destroyed all of our crops what few we had for we have not much land broke yet. . . . We . . . almost perish here sometimes with the cold."

Poor harvests and falling prices failed to dampen the enthusiasm for new farm settlements. Land speculators lobbied Congress to open up Indian Territory in present-day Oklahoma to white settlement. In 1889 Congress sided with the speculators over the heated objections of the fifty-five tribes that called the area home. The government officially opened the land to the rush of would-be owners at noon on April 22, 1889, but many settlers—called "sooners"—had illegally entered the territory beforehand and established claims on the best land. By nightfall hopeful homesteaders had laid claim to 1.2 million acres of land.

In a brief period of time, the small farmer, like the enterprising individual miner and cattle rancher, was replaced by large business interests. By the late nineteenth century huge bonanza farms dominated the nation's agricultural landscape, underscoring the increasing influence of corporations. The growth of agribusiness was most visible in California. In 1871 reformer Henry George described California as "not a country of farms but a country of plantations and estates." Statistics supported his observations. By 1900 nearly two-thirds of the state's farms covered 1,000 acres or more. California was not alone. By 1900 the average farm in the Dakotas measured 7,000 acres.

Despite the hardships of Plains farming, the region became the breadbasket of America in the decades after the Civil War. Farm output more than tripled between 1860 and 1900. Vast wheat fields stretched across Minnesota, the Dakotas, Montana, and eastern Colorado. Railroads allowed farmers to participate in a national marketplace. California sent fruit, wine, and wheat to eastern markets. By 1890 American farmers were participating in a global economy, exporting large amounts of wheat and other crops. To an Austrian observer the surplus seemed "the greatest event of modern times."

Timber and the Origins of Conservation

Demand for lumber and timber from the mining industry and growing towns and cities led to the opening of forestry operations in the West. Between 1850 and 1860 California's population soared from 93,000 to 379,000. San Francisco, which saw its population explode from 2,000 to 55,000 between 1849 and 1855, was at the heart of the demand. Six times in the eighteen months between December 1849 and June 1851, the boom town burned to the ground; each time it was rebuilt, a process that consumed millions of trees.

The great forests of the Northwest covered thousands of square miles and contained a host of majestic trees. The Douglas fir, which ranged southward from British Columbia to western Oregon, reached heights of 250 feet and diameters of 10 feet. The coastal redwood, which extended from Oregon south to Monterey, California, towered 350 feet and had diameters of 15 feet. The redwood's inland cousin, the Sierra redwood, contained enough wood to build forty five-room houses. Entrepreneurs from other timber-producing states such as Maine, Michigan, and Wisconsin marveled at the size of the trees and recognized the potential profit from harvesting the timber. The development of railroads opened the area to timber operators, allowing them to ship lumber to markets in the East. In 1900 Frederick Weyerhaeuser inaugurated the era of lumber giants when he bought 900,000 acres of prime land in the Pacific Northwest.

The firms recruited "homeless, womenless" lumberjacks from New England and the Midwest to work in the forests and mills. The work proved hard and dangerous. On average, one logger died every day from 1870 to 1910. The greatest threat to both loggers and the industry came from fire. In 1902 fires raged from Canada to California for seven days. The flames destroyed almost three-quarters of a million acres.

The depletion of the nation's forests by loggers led a few critics to question the popular view of the West as an area of limitless resources. In 1879, in his widely read *Progress and Poverty*, the reformer Henry George challenged the government's policy of giving away publicly owned natural resources to individuals and corporations seeking to enrich themselves. People have a right to what they produce them-

The Lumber Industry   In the Pacific Northwest, the lumber industry was the way to make a profit quickly. Like mining and commercial farming, it too had devastating environmental consequences, as no regulations were yet in place to protect what should have been a renewable resource. In this photograph, a team of oxen hauls logs out of a forest in Washington State.   *(Darius Kinsey Collection, Whatcom Museum of History & Art.)*

selves, he wrote, "but man has another right, declared by the fact of his existence— the right to use so much of the free gifts of nature as may be necessary to supply all the wants of that existence, and which he may use without interfering with the equal rights of anyone else; and to this he has a title as against all the world."

By the 1870s some government officials were beginning to exhibit concern over the consequences of indiscriminate land use and resource exploitation. In 1872 Congress set aside the first major reservation of federal land when it created 2-million-acre Yellowstone National Park to be a "pleasuring ground for the people" in perpetuity. But at the time, the creation of Yellowstone Park was an isolated event rather than a reversal of the practice of giving away federal resources to private interests.

Concern about the environment inspired a small but dedicated group of activists. John Muir, a bearded, mystical Scotsman, emerged as the most eloquent and effective advocate for protecting the environment. People, he argued, should honor and safeguard the wilderness. "Climb the mountains and get their good tidings," he wrote. "Nature's peace will flow into you as the sunshine into the trees. Muir was a driving force behind the Forest Reserve Act of 1891, which gave the president authority to set aside portions of the federal domain. The government quickly withdrew from potential sale 13 million acres to set up fifteen forest reserves. Six years later, President Grover Cleveland created another thirteen reserves totaling over 21 million acres. In 1892 Muir helped found the Sierra Club, which devoted itself to "preserving the forests and other natural features of the Sierra Nevada Mountains."

SOCIETY IN THE WEST: EXPERIMENT AND IMITATION

Many people who traveled west planned to start new lives amid the boundless opportunity they expected. In most cases, however, they struggled to recreate a society they had known before they migrated. Settlers from the eastern United States and Europe not only brought familiar institutions and old values to their experiments in community building, but also incorporated racial attitudes that dismissed minority cultures as inferior. The Indians were the greatest victims of these racial attitudes, but other minority groups in the West, most notably people of Chinese and Hispanic heritage, suffered as well.

Western Towns and Cities

Few new western towns were lucky enough to attract the full array of skills and talents that contributed to the convenience and comfort of life in the East. There were, for instance, few qualified doctors or schoolteachers. Still, any community that hoped to grow beyond infancy needed a range of services. Typically, one of the first citizens of any community was the editor of the local newspaper, hired by the town's promoters. His function was not so much to report on local events as to sing the praises of the community to prospective settlers. A hotel—to accommodate future townspeople as well as transients—was generally among the first structures in new towns. Saloonkeepers were particularly numerous in towns whose prime visitors were cowboys or miners. Abilene, Kansas, boasted eleven saloons to welcome trail-parched cowboys. No town was complete without a blacksmith to shoe horses and oxen, sharpen plows, and repair wagons. Perhaps the most indispensable townsman of all was the merchant who ran the cornerstone of a new town's commercial life—the general store.

Western towns offered an impressive slate of entertainment to tired and lonely residents. Local tastes differed, but certain types of entertainment were popular virtually everywhere. When John Robinson's Great World Exposition rolled into western communities, all hearts thrilled to its triumphant parade of "31 Chariots, 4 Steam Organs, 60 Cages, 8 Bands and 2 Calliopes." Boxing matches, usually held in saloons, were popular. An 1867 prizefight in Cheyenne between John Hardey and John Shannessy for a purse of $1,000 ran 126 rounds. Each round lasted until one man was knocked down, at which point the boxers rested for thirty seconds.

Gambling was the frontier's favorite pastime. To assuage the rigors, loneliness, and boredom of life, people bet not only on poker and dice but also on a dozen other games of chance. It was easy to find wagers at a dogfight or cockfight, a battle between bulls and bears, or a horse race or boxing match. In San Francisco nearly a thousand gambling halls sprouted within a few years of the discovery of gold. Inside the gilded walls of one of these sumptuous palaces, wrote British diarist J. D.

Bortwick, "Nothing was heard but a slight hum of voices, and the constant clinking of money."

Along with gambling and drinking, prostitution was central to the early social life of largely male camps and towns. In 1860, 2,306 men and only 30 women—mostly prostitutes—were living in the Comstock Lode towns of Gold Hill and Virginia City. A decade later, when the population was more gender balanced, at least one in twelve women was a prostitute. A Seattle writer expressed the common western attitude that while eastern vice was "silent, muffle-footed, velvet-gloved, masqued-faced," the western variety went about "openly, unclad, unpolished, open-handed."

Western towns were frequently rough and violent places. "I have seen many fast towns," one seasoned cowboy declared, "but Abilene beat them all." A local merchant characterized the town as a "seething, roaring, flaming hell." In cow towns, drunkenness and fistfights were common, but many cattle towns outlawed the carrying of handguns within the city limits and established police forces to patrol the streets and enforce the ordinances. No cattle town ever buried more than five murder victims during a single year, despite the presence, on both sides of the law, of gunfighters like Doc Holliday, John Wesley Hardin, Bat Masterson, and Wyatt Earp. Fistfights escalated into gunfights far more often in mining towns because few passed gun-control laws. The mining town of Bodie, California, was a good example. During its boom years Bodie had twenty-nine killings, which converted to an annual homicide rate of 116 per 100,000 population. No eastern city in the 1880s had a crime rate remotely close to that.

Middle-class women led the effort to "civilize" the boisterous cattle and mining towns by establishing schools, churches, and charity associations that often checked male-inspired disorder and created family-oriented communities. The white women who left their homes to live in the West carried with them prevailing notions of domesticity, which suggested that women represented the moral foundation of the family and society. An honorable woman "is a missionary of virtue, morality, happiness and peace to a circle of careworn, troubled, and often, alas, demoralized men," Eliza Farnham noted in her influential 1856 book, *California, Indoors and Out*. As expected, white women living in western towns led the efforts for moral reform, attacking prostitution, liquor, gambling, and crime.

Joining women reformers in their efforts were Protestant missionaries who saw the salvation of the West as part of their patriotic and Christian duty. Many people welcomed churches in their towns as a sign of civility and stability, even if they rejected the message preached from the pulpit. A church, editorialized the *Albuquerque Morning Democrat* in 1893, "does as much to build up a town as a school, a railroad, or a fair." In mining towns and cattle towns ministers tried to pass laws promoting temperance, limiting public activities on Sundays, and restricting gambling. Most of the measures failed, but by focusing public attention on the problems, ministers and their allies gradually succeeded in confining prostitution and gambling to specific areas of town.

Perhaps because of the forbidding terrain and harsh climate, most residents in the West settled into cities. According to the 1880 census the West contained twenty-four cities with populations of eight thousand or more. Nine of those cities—Dallas, Denver, Kansas City, Lincoln, Los Angeles, Omaha, Portland, Salt Lake City, and Topeka—doubled their populations during the decade. Los Angeles grew by over 350 percent. Denver saw its population grow seven times during the 1870s and then triple again by 1890. In the West, only San Francisco and Omaha had more residents than Denver. In most cases, boosters attracted migrants by promoting the uniqueness of western life at the same time that developers and planners tried to recreate the style and architecture of existing cities.

The Hardships of Farm Life

Since trees were in short supply on the Plains, the log cabin that had been the usual first home of settlers farther east in earlier periods yielded to the sod house and dugout in the West. These dim dwellings allowed little light or air to enter. Unless they were walled and plastered, they were also damp and dirty. As one Nebraska girl put it, "There was running water in our sod house. It ran through the roof." Settlers shared their homes with mice, centipedes, spiders, and snakes that crawled out of the walls. One such dugout in Nickolls County, Nebraska, housed six family members in a single room of 9 by 12 feet furnished with a bed, a stove, a table, and several boxes. In 1876 nine-tenths of the settlers of Butler County, Nebraska, lived in houses made of dirt.

Climate presented a new challenge for western settlers. In addition to being dry, the interior West was hotter in the summer, colder in the winter, and windier at virtually any time than the eastern states. Glendive, Montana, recorded a 164-degree range in temperatures in 1893, from a summer high of 117 degrees to a winter low of 47 degrees below zero. The winters brought blizzards, some lasting for days, and east of the Rockies the summers brought tornadoes.

And then there were the grasshoppers. In a bad year, such as 1874, grasshoppers swarmed onto the northern prairies in such numbers that farmers mistook them for storm clouds massing on the horizon. The insects fell from the skies like hail until they lay four- to six-inches deep on the ground. A Wichita newspaper reported in 1878 that the grasshoppers devoured "everything green, stripping the foliage off the bark and from the tender twigs of the fruit trees, destroying every plant that is good for food or pleasant to the eyes, that man has planted."

The grueling conditions were especially difficult for farm women. Unmarried women might find jobs as teachers, seamstresses, and domestic servants, but for most married women work revolved around the family: cooking meals, taking care of children, and maintaining the house. Girls and women occasionally helped on the farm, but gender boundaries remained clear. "I could help the boys with the plowing or trapping," recalled Susie Crockett of Oklahoma, but "they would never help me with the sewing." Men socialized with other farm or ranch workers, but women were often isolated at home. At times the isolation and loneliness could overwhelm women: "I was alone all the daylight hours with the cattle, and all around me the prairie was dying. The sound of death was in the wind that never stopped blowing across the whitening grass, or rustling the dead weeds at the edges of the fields," wrote Grace Snyder, a farmer's wife in Custer County, Missouri. "As long as I live I'll never see such a lonely country," a woman said of the Texas plains; and a Nebraska woman sighed, "These unbounded prairies have such an air of desolation, and the stillness is very oppressive."

Farm women also had to contend with endless chores. As late as the 1920s a typical farm wife could expect to devote nine hours a day to such chores as cleaning, sewing, laundering, and preparing food. She spent an additional two hours a day cleaning the barn and chicken coop, milking the cows, caring for poultry, and gardening. Childbirth was perhaps the greatest trial of all, since it often took place without either a midwife or a doctor in attendance. One woman remarked that farm wives were "not much better than slaves. It is a weary, monotonous round of cooking and washing and mending and as a result the insane asylum is 1/3d filled with wives of farmers."

Racism in the West: The Chinese

During the 1860s twenty-four thousand Chinese—two-thirds of the Chinese population in America—worked in the California mines. As mining profits began to decrease in California, the Chinese left the gold fields, and thousands joined other Chinese migrants to work on the transcontinental railroad. Then, after the completion of the Central Pacific line in 1869, many Chinese workers flocked to cities. By 1900 nearly half the Chinese population of California lived in urban areas, with San Francisco's Chinese neighborhood emerging as the largest community.

In 1868 an observer noted that San Francisco's Chinatown was a thriving and colorful community "made up of stores catering to the Chinese only," where residents strolled the streets "in their native costumes, with queues down their backs." In addition, Chinatown boasted a host of organizations and associations. Locals established temples for worship and formed district associations to find shelter and jobs for new arrivals. Other groups settled disputes among community members and provided educational and health services. For recreation, residents attended the local theater, which featured an all-Chinese cast and orchestra.

Though successful in creating flourishing communities, the Chinese found their lives circumscribed in many ways. Only Native Americans suffered more racial violence than the Chinese. Most whites tolerated Chinese workers when jobs were plentiful or when they took the arduous and unappealing task of building railroads. When Chinese workers moved into the cities, however, they competed against white workers for desirable positions. Anti-coolie clubs, which began springing up in California during the late 1860s and blossomed in the 1870s, sought laws against employing Chinese workers and organized economic boycotts of Chinese-made goods. Protests soon became violent; economic depression led to anti-Chinese riots by unemployed white workers throughout California. The racial unrest spread across the region. In Rock Springs, Wyoming, whites murdered twenty-eight Chinese. In Seattle angry whites rounded up Chinese, placed them in boats, and forced them out to sea.

Thus by the early 1870s anti-Chinese agitation had become an almost irresistible way for politicians to attract the votes of white workers. The new California constitution of 1879 denied the vote to the Chinese and forbade their employment on any state or local public works project. In 1882 Congress suspended Chinese immigration for ten years. Later legislation extended the ban. Such discrimination and immigration restriction served to drastically reduce the total Chinese population in the United States. Many migrants returned to China, and new migrants could not enter to replace them. The Chinese population of California fell by at least one-third between 1890 and 1900.

Those Chinese who remained found themselves concentrated in low-wage jobs, segregated within individual industries, and paid less than white workers—if they could find work at all. Many were forced into self-employment. By 1890 there were 6,400 Chinese laundry workers in California, representing 69 percent of the state's launderers. In 1900 one out of four employed Chinese men worked in a laundry.

The Hispanic Heritage in the Southwest

The wave of white settlement transformed Hispanic communities scattered across Texas, New Mexico, Arizona, and California. While a small Hispanic elite, the *Ricos*, profited by aligning itself with the encroaching Anglos, most Hispanics suffered.

Throughout the Southwest, white settlers, lawyers, and politicians cheated Hispanics out of their lands. In 1848 the U.S. government had promised *Californios* (Hispanic residents of California) U.S. citizenship and the "free enjoyment of their liberty and property." Despite the promise, *Californios* working in the gold rush mines were forced to pay the Foreign Miners Tax. As white immigrants flooded into California, they squatted on large *Californio* ranches, killing livestock and laying claim to the land. The government eventually upheld most Hispanic land claims, but not before long and expensive litigation had drained the owners penniless. Hispanics, "who at one time had been the richest landowners," a group of *Californio* ranchers complained in 1859, "today find themselves without a foot of ground, living as objects of charity." The story was similar in New Mexico, where businessmen and politicians swindled over 2 million acres of land from the original residents. An observer noted that "by 1860 the Anglos had gotten control, by fair means or foul, of nearly every ranch worth having north of the Nueces."

The persistent waves of white migration after the Civil War challenged Hispanics' traditional life in the Southwest. The coming of the railroads created a new national trading system that destroyed the local markets and independent farms that had formed the backbone of the region's economy. Hispanics found themselves, along with migrants from Mexico, thrust into a racially divided labor system. On Texas cattle ranches, for example, the managers were Anglo while the cowhands were Mexican. In New Mexico gold mines, Mexicans executed the dangerous manual work while Anglo workers operated the machines. In Los Angeles 75 percent of Mexican workers were employed in unskilled and low-paying jobs, compared with 30 percent of the Anglos. Even when Mexicans did the same work as Anglos, they were paid less, a fact "largely accounted for by discrimination against the Mexicans in payment of wages," a congressional investigation reported.

In many areas, Hispanics fought to preserve control of their societies. In New Mexico, the only territory in which Spanish-speaking residents represented a clear majority, angry *Hispanos* (as they were called there) organized themselves as a masked night-riding outfit known from their costume as *Las Gorras Blancas* (the White Caps). In 1889 and 1890, with perhaps seven hundred men joining the raids, they cut Anglos' fences, burned their haystacks, and occasionally torched their barns and houses. In most areas, however, the tide of Anglo migrants simply over-

Mexican-American Mine Workers, Southwest, 1890s   The southwestern United States, part of Mexico before 1848, had been home to a large Hispanic population for centuries. The growth of economic enterprise—mining, ranching, farming—in the late nineteenth century instigated a new wave of Mexican immigration just before 1900. The earlier Hispanic community suffered from growing attacks on their land and political influence, while new immigrants looking for work found employment only in the lowest paying sectors, like mining. Both groups faced racial discrimination by whites pouring into the region.   *(Wyoming Division of Cultural Resources.)*

ran Hispanic communities. In 1845 only seven thousand Anglos lived in California; by 1900 their numbers had swelled to nearly 1.5 million.

The influx of Anglos eroded Hispanic political influence. Santa Barbara's experience illustrated the process. For years the most important center of Spanish and Mexican culture in California, Santa Barbara had a class of vigorous and well-to-do ranchero families who were accustomed to ruling themselves. As late as 1867 Spanish-surnamed voters composed nearly 63 percent of the electorate in the city and nearly as much in the county. By 1873 the proportion of Spanish-surnamed voters had shrunk to about 34 percent in the city and county. In Los Angeles the figure fell from more than three-fourths of the city's population in 1850 to 19 percent in 1880.

THE WEST AND THE AMERICAN IMAGINATION

Americans came to view the disappearing frontier as a proving ground for the American experiment. By the end of the nineteenth century the West had assumed many of the characteristics of the East. Yet in the popular imagination, the West emerged as a symbol of traditional American values of rugged individualism, limited government, and social progress.

"The Myth of the Garden"   As the frontier faded in the face of technology and change, twentieth-century Americans clung to what historian Henry Nash Smith described as "The Myth of the Garden." According to this notion, the West was an agrarian Eden where free land and honest toil produced virtuous citizens. The myth served a clear purpose: it transformed the West into a symbol of American character. "All the associations called up by the spoken word, the West," wrote novelist Hamlin Garland in 1891, "were fabulous, mythic, hopeful." The myth reinforced America's perception of itself as a land of rugged individuals, as a civilization with a mission to remake the world—or in this case the continent—in its own image, and as a society unencumbered by oppressive government.

The myth found its fullest expression in popular culture. The first "westerns" were dime novels, which by the 1860s were selling in editions of fifty thousand or more. In

Valley of the Yosemite   Albert Bierstadt (1830–1902), a German immigrant raised in Massachusetts, first traveled west in 1859 to study the landscape of the Colorado and Wyoming territories. Bierstadt, recognizing the growing interest of easterners in images of the frontier, made a total of three trips to the west, compiling sketches he would later turn into monumental portraits in his New York studio. This portrait, first sketched by the artist during his 1864 tour of Yosemite Valley in the Sierra Nevada Mountains, captures the essence of "The Myth of the Garden" with its towering cliffs, tranquil waters, and spiritual light which envelops the scenery.   *(© Burstein Collection/Corbis.)*

1887 Edward L. Wheeler created the most memorable western hero: Deadwood Dick. Young and handsome, Dick used his daring horsemanship and finely tuned shooting skills to fight against powerful villains. Such a hero, observed a historian, "confirmed Americans in the traditional belief that obstacles were to be overcome by the courageous, virile, and determined stand of the individual as an individual."

Other popular writers joined in the celebration of the West. In the 1880s, in his widely read, multivolume *The Winning of the West,* a young Theodore Roosevelt described the West as a land of strong, virtuous, hardworking people who were extending civilization into "barbarian" territory. The conquest of the West by English-speaking people, he wrote, was "the great, epic feat in the history of our race." The West embodied all the qualities that Roosevelt admired in America. "No man can really understand our country, and appreciate what it really is and what it promised," he wrote, "unless he has the fullest and closest sympathy with the ideals and aspirations of the West."

For the American public, nothing brought the mythic West more directly into their lives than the Wild West shows. From among fifty or more traveling shows, the one that popularized the American West most successfully was Buffalo Bill's "Wild West and Congress of Rough Riders." By the time William Cody got around to opening his "Wild West, Rocky Mountain, and Prairie Exhibition" in 1883, he already enjoyed wide fame as Buffalo Bill. A well-known scout for the frontier army, Cody assumed celebrity stature during the 1870s thanks to the literary vision of Edward Zane Carroll Judson, who used the pen name Ned Buntline.

Cody's shows accommodated twenty thousand people and presented "actual scenes, genuine characters" from the West. Native Americans in flowing headdress and carrying elegantly feathered sticks rode bareback into the arena on stunning painted horses. The Sioux leader Sitting Bull joined the show as a living, breathing exhibit, riding around the arena on horseback to a serenade of boos and catcalls. The cowboys, who wore spotless ten-gallon hats and furry chaps, bore little resemblance to typical sweat-stained ranch hands. Cody brought Americans the perfect frontierswoman in the person of Annie Oakley. Her remarkable marksmanship set her apart from effete eastern ladies, but her genteel appearance and stylish costumes revealed her to be a "true" woman.

One of the most popular performances reenacted "Custer's Massacre," culminating with Cody standing head bowed in a spotlight on the darkened battlefield. Mark Twain was delighted: "Genuine . . . down to its smallest details." The show made $100,000 in 1885 and did far better the following season, when it drew a million people during its run on New York's Staten Island and another million during a winter stand in the city's Madison Square Garden.

The End of the Frontier

In 1893 historian Frederick Jackson Turner added a scholarly dimension to the popularization of the western myth. The superintendent of the 1890 census noted that he could no longer locate a continuous frontier line beyond which population thinned out to fewer than two per square mile. "Up to and including 1880," he reported, "the country had a frontier of settlement, but at present the unsettled area has been so broken into by isolated bodies of settlement that there can hardly be said to be a frontier line." The report provided the inspiration for Turner's provocative frontier thesis, which he first presented in a paper titled, "The Significance of the Frontier in American History." Turner argued that, more than anything else, the frontier concept had shaped the American character. "The existence of an area of free land," Turner wrote, "its continuous recession, and the advance of American settlement westward, explain American development." The frontier, he argued, separated America from Europe because it allowed individualism and democracy to develop. Turner concluded: "Four centuries from the discovery of America, at the end of a hundred years under the Constitution, the frontier has gone and with its going has closed the first period of American history." Turner's "frontier thesis" not only traced America's democratic frontier past; it also raised questions about what the closing of that frontier meant for America's future.

Scholars criticized Turner for ignoring European influences on American culture and for espousing a crude form of environmental determinism, but his writing reflected a widespread concern about the fading frontier. The same worries inspired popular artists and writers to romanticize the Old West. Magazines such as *Cosmopolitan, Ladies' Home Journal, Collier's Red Book,* and the *Saturday Evening Post* depended on a dozen or more western illustrators for the art accompanying western fiction pieces. One of the most notable, William H. D. Koerner, turned out more than twenty-four hundred illustrations, approximately six hundred of which depicted western themes. He, like other artists, depicted westerners as individuals of character, refinement, and integrity.

For most of the twentieth century, movies and, later, television played the central role in perpetuating the myth of the West. Beginning with *The Great Train Robbery* (1903), a trailblazer in cinematic storytelling that ran for a full nine minutes, movie producers transformed the western into a set formula. The key ingredient was a noble cowboy, usually a youthful bachelor who, against great odds, made up his mind to right a wrong. Along the way he was forced to fight villainous characters: desperate Indians, corrupt cattle ranchers, or heartless outlaws.

Thus a diverse group of writers, artists, and scholars presented Americans with an engaging but distorted view of the past. The celebration of rugged individualism failed to acknowledge the role the government had played in every step of western development. The view of the frontier as the westward-moving source of America's democratic politics exaggerated the homogenizing effect of the frontier environment and failed to account for the persistence of racial, class, and gender differences. In most of these scenarios, Native Americans appeared as noble savages whose disappearance documented the cultural superiority of white society. Hispanics were depicted as docile peasants, ferocious bandits, or sensual fandango dancers. The contributions of African-Americans, Asians, and women were ignored altogether.

The popular portrayals of the West may have failed to capture the diversity and complexity of the region, but they offered powerful reinforcement to America's perception of itself as a land of individual freedom and unbounded opportunity—beliefs that would be sorely tested in the years ahead.

CONCLUSION

Following the Civil War new migrants traveled west across America in search of a better life, just as migrants sought opportunity on frontiers in other parts of the world. In America the federal government played a central role in making the westward experiment possible. Washington passed laws that offered Americans an economic incentive to settle the West and develop its resources. The Homestead Act and subsequent laws succeeded in attracting hundreds of thousands of settlers, but contrary to the intentions of the authors, the laws tended to benefit land speculators more than independent farmers. The federal government's presence in the region went beyond passing laws: it organized each territory, selected the governor and judges, set budgets, and established procedures for statehood.

The forced removal of Native Americans represented the most visible demonstration of federal power in the West. New immigrants to the region came from diverse backgrounds, but they shared the desire to possess and harness the West's natural resources. They disregarded existing treaties guaranteeing Indian land rights and ignored Native American cultural traditions, which rejected private ownership of land and imbued nature with symbolic and religious meaning. When the new and old cultures clashed, the national government used its superior technology and firepower to suppress the Indians. Having defeated the Indians in battle, the government continued the experiment in suppression by joining with reformers to destroy their culture. The Dawes Act forced Indians to adopt "Western" notions of land management, while reformers worked to "civilize" the Indians, forcing them to abandon their culture, language, and traditions.

With the Indians out of the way, farmers, miners, and ranchers moved aggressively to exploit the region's natural resources. In each case, however, large industries replaced small ventures, imposing an industrial order similar to that in the East. Conservationists such as John Muir challenged the widespread idea that the West was a land of limitless resources, but theirs were often lonely voices.

Like the economy, the new society that emerged in the West also replicated older cultural values. Reflecting traditional notions of domesticity, middle-class women often led the effort to civilize tough mining and cattle towns. Along with spearheading crusades for moral reform, they founded schools, churches, and charity associations designed to foster a family-centered environment. Racial stereotypes and discrimination migrated to the region with the majority of settlers. Chinese immigrants who sought opportunity in the West were often victims of racial violence. In 1882 Congress responded to the violence by eliminating the target: banning Chinese immigration. In California and New Mexico, wealthy Hispanic landowners found themselves defrauded of millions of acres of land. At the same time the Anglo majority relegated working-class Hispanics to the lowest-paying jobs.

Ironically, Americans transformed the West into a powerful symbol of individualism and self-help, a place where the American experiment could achieve its full potential. Dime novels, popular Wild West shows, and later motion pictures reaffirmed America's view of itself as a nation of rugged individuals who conquered the Indians and civilized a wild continent. The portrayals often ignored the role of government and usually neglected the contributions of women, African-Americans, Hispanics, and Asians. But the popular view of the West revealed the power of myth and the persistence of Americans' deeply held attitudes about themselves and the world around them. This romantic view of frontier life bolstered hopes in the future of the American experiment at a time when traditional ideas of American individualism faced significant challenges wrought by industrialization.

Annotated Suggested Readings

The history of the American West has received considerable attention in the last two decades. A good overview can be found in Rodman W. Paul's *The Far West and the Great Plains in Transition, 1859–1908* (rev. ed., 1998). Clyde A. Milner II, Carol A. O'Connor, and Martha A. Sandweiss, eds., *The Oxford History of the American West* (1994), offer twenty-three thoughtful essays on the western experience. Another collection of essays, *Historians and the American West* (1983), edited by Michael P. Malone, reflects the diversity of the western peoples from the prehistoric Indians to the metropolis of the twentieth century. An excellent survey of the American West that has stood the test of time is R. A. Billington and Martin Ridge's *Westward Expansion: A History of the American Frontier* (6th ed., 2001). Walter Nugent, *Into the West: The Story of Its People* (1999), is the best demographic overview.

The last two decades have seen a number of historians reject Turner's frontier thesis, a move toward what many are calling the "New Western History." Leading this attack against the past is Patricia Nelson Limerick's *The Legacy of Conquest: The Unbroken Past of the American West* (1987). In *"It's Your Misfortune and None of My Own": A New History of the American West* (1990), Richard White examines the interaction between different racial and ethnic groups as they and the federal government sought to prosper from the region's natural resources. A rejection of Turner's image of the isolated frontier serves as the foundation for William Cronon's *Nature's Metropolis: Chicago and the Great West* (1991). Cronon, along with George Miles and Jay Gitlin, edited *Under an Open Sky: Rethinking America's Western Past* (1992), which explores the role of the West in American history through such issues as the environment, race relations, and regional identity. Robert Hine and John Mack Faragher's *The American West: A New Interpretive History* (2000) synthesizes the last thirty years of research in an overall survey of the West.

Historians have produced numerous works on the role of women in the West. Two books edited by Susan Armitage and Elizabeth Jameson are among the best: *The Women's West* (1987) and *Writing the Range: Race, Class, and Culture in the Women's West* (1997). Other works, such as Glenda Riley's *The Female Frontier: A Comparative View of Women on the Prairie and Plains (1988)*, have provided detailed descriptions of particular aspects of women's lives and occupations in the West. Anne Butler explains why women became prostitutes in western cities in *Daughters of Joy, Sisters of Misery* (1985). Paula Petrik's *No Step Backward: Women and Family on the Rocky Mountain Mining Frontier, 1865–1900* (1987) traces the transformation of women as they sought to advance their economic opportunities and social equality. In other western towns, women joined forces in the home mission movement to improve conditions for all women, as addressed in Peggy

Pascoe's work, *Relations of Rescue: The Search for Female Moral Authority in the American West, 1874–1939* (1990).

The impact of African-Americans in the West has also slowly become the focus of historical analysis. William L. Katz's breakthrough work, *The Black West* (3rd ed., 1987), tells the history of blacks who, despite their omission from most historical accounts, participated in every stage of frontier development—from fur trapper to cowboy. The role of black soldiers in the West after the Civil War is the focus of Monroe L. Billington's *New Mexico's Buffalo Soldiers, 1866–1900* (1991). The migration of freedmen from the South serves as the backdrop for Nell Irvin Painter's *Exodusters: Black Migration to Kansas After Reconstruction* (1992).

Other minority groups, including the Hispanic and Chinese communities, have also found voices in a number of works. In *Chicanos in a Changing Society: From Mexican Pueblos to American Barrios in Santa Barbara and Southern California, 1848–1930* (1996), Albert Camarillo traces the loss of power by urban Mexican-Americans as whites moved onto their land. Sarah Deutsch has also depicted the transformation of Hispanic life in *No Separate Refuge: Culture, Class, and Gender on the Anglo-Hispanic Frontier in the Overland Trail* (1979). In *A Chinaman's Chance: The Chinese on the Rocky Mountain Mining Frontier* (1997), Liping Zhu demonstrates the ways that Chinese immigrants adapted to their environment in the Rocky Mountains. *Chinese on the American Frontier* (2001), edited by Arif Dirlik and Malcolm Yeung, expresses the interaction of Chinese and whites in western communities.

The last thirty years has also seen a massive influx of books on the impact of white expansion on Native Americans. Wilcomb E. Washburn's *The Indian in America* (1975) serves as a good introduction. James Wilson utilizes oral traditions and archeological discoveries to recreate Native American life in his general survey, *The Earth Shall Weep* (1999). Robert Utley, *The Indian Frontier of the American West, 1846–1890* (1984), provides a synthesis of the hostilities created as Native Americans fought the reservation system. The image of Indians is examined in Robert Berkhofer's *The White Man's Indian: Images of the American Indian from Columbus to the Present* (1978); and Francis Paul Prucha's *The Great Father: The United States Government and the American Indians* (1984). Andrew Isenberg's *The Destruction of the Bison* (2000) traces the history of the buffalo and their importance to Native Americans and white entrepreneurs.

The impact of federal policy on Indians in the West has proven to be a fertile topic for historians. Richard White's *The Roots of Dependency: Subsistence, Environment, and Social Change Among the Choctaws, Pawnees, and Navajos* (1983) compares the experiences of three tribes over several centuries as whites forced them to abandon independence and economic self-sufficiency. In *The Dispossession of the American Indian, 1887–1934* (1991), Janet A. McDonnell argues that government projects proved disastrous to the Native Americans.

Henry Nash Smith was the first to analyze a number of American beliefs about the West in his work *Virgin Land: The American West as Symbol and Myth* (1950). William H. Goetzmann and William N. Goetzmann examine the impact of visual images of the West on Americans in *The West of the Imagination* (1986). Martha Sandweiss looks at the importance of photography in *Print the Legend: Photography and the American West* (2004). David Wrobel examines the role of promoters in shaping images of the west in *Promised Lands: Promotion, Memory, and the Creation of the American West* (2002). In *Wilderness and the American Mind* (4th ed., 2001), Roderick Nash traces the history of American's preoccupation with nature. William Cronon's edited collection, *Uncommon*

Ground: Rethinking the Human Place in Nature (1995), includes a number of provocative essays. The image of the West as a garden ultimately led to the creation of national parks, the focus of Albert Runte's *National Parks: The American Experience* (1979). Jules David Prown et al. examine western art in *Discovered Lands, Invented Pasts*. Richard Slotkin addresses the enduring hold of the west on the popular imagination in *Gunfighter Nation* (1998) and *Regeneration Through Violence* (2000).

The **istory** **ompanion**

Native Americans, Whites, and the Land

Dawes General Allotment Act

Responding to critics of the government's reservation policy who believed that Indians would become civilized only when they became landowners, Congress passed the Dawes Act in 1887.

Be it enacted by the Senate and House of Representatives of the United States of America in Congress assembled, That in all cases where any tribe or band of Indians has been, or shall hereafter be, located upon any reservation created for their use . . . the President of the United States be, and he hereby is, authorized, whenever in his opinion any reservation or any part thereof of such Indians is advantageous for agricultural and grazing purposes, to cause said reservation, or any part thereof, to be surveyed, or resurveyed if necessary, and to allot the lands in said reservation in severalty to any Indian located thereon in quantities as follows:

To each head of a family, one-quarter of a section;

To each single person over eighteen years of age, one-eighth of a section;

To each orphan child under eighteen years of age, one-eighth of a section; and

To each other single person under eighteen years now living, or who may be born prior to the date of the order of the President directing an allotment of the lands embraced in any reservation, one-sixteenth of a section. . . .

That upon the approval of the allotments provided for in this act by the Secretary of the Interior, he shall cause patents to issue therefor in the name of the allottees, which patents shall be of the legal effect, and declare that the United States does and will hold the land thus allotted, for the period of twenty-five years, in trust for the sole use and benefit of the Indian to whom such allotment shall have been made, or, in case of his decease, of his heirs according to the laws of the State or Territory where such land is located, and that at the expiration of said period the United States will convey the same by patent to said Indian, or his heirs as aforesaid, in fee, discharged of said trust and free of all charge or incumbrance whatsoever. . . .

That upon the completion of said allotments and the patenting of the lands to said allottees, each and every number of the respective bands or tribes of Indians to whom allotments have been made shall have the benefit of and be subject to the laws, both civil and criminal, of the State or Territory in which they may reside; and no Territory shall pass or enforce any law denying any such Indian within its jurisdiction the equal protection of the law. And every Indian born within the territorial limits of the United States to whom allotments shall have been made . . . and every Indian born within the territorial limits of the United States who has voluntarily taken up, within said limits, his residence separate and apart from any tribe of Indians therein, and has adopted the habits of civilized life, is hereby declared to be a citizen of the United States, and is entitled to all the rights, privileges, and immunities of such citizens. . . .

691

Native Americans and Landownership

In these two selections, Chief Joseph of the Nez Percé and a group of Hopi chiefs try to explain their people's attitude toward and usage of their land, in hopes of averting more government interference. The Hopi were specifically addressing the Dawes Act of 1887, which subdivided Indian lands into individual titles, a concept foreign both to the Hopi traditional land tenure system and to their concept of farming. Chief Joseph speaks eight years after peacefully resisting an illegal treaty to cede Nez Percé land. In 1877 his people were finally captured and forced onto a reservation.

(*Chief Joseph, 1871*) The Earth was created by the assistance of the sun, and it should be left as it was. . . . The country was made without lines of demarcation, and it is no man's business to divide it. . . . I see whites all over the country gaining wealth, and see their desire to give us lands which are worthless. . . . The earth and myself are of one mind. The measure of the land and the measure of our bodies are the same. Say to us if you can say it, that you were sent by the Creative Power to talk to us. Perhaps you think the Creator sent you here to dispose of us as you see fit. If I thought you were sent by the Creator I might be induced to think you had a right to dispose of me. Do not misunderstand me, but understand me fully with reference to my affection for the land. I never said the land was mine to do with as I chose. The one who has the right to dispose of it is the one who has created it. I claim a right to live on my land, and accord you the privilege to live on yours.

(Hopi Petition, 1894) According to the number of children a woman has, fields for them are assigned to her, from some of the lands of her family group, and her husband takes care of them. Hence our fields are numerous but small, and several belonging to the same family may be close together, or they may be miles apart, because arable localities are not continuous. There are other reasons for the irregularity in size and situation of our family lands, as interrupted sequence of inheritance cause by extinction of families, but chiefly owing to the following condition, and to which we especially invite your attention.

In the Spring and Summer there usually comes from the Southwest a succession of gales, oftentimes strong enough to blow away the sandy soil from the face of some of our fields, and to expose the underlying clay, which is hard, and sour, and barren; and as the sand is the only fertile land, when it moves, the planters must follow it, and other fields must be provided in place of those which have been devastated. Sometimes generations pass away and these barren spots remain, while in other instances, after a few years, the winds have again restored the desirable sand upon them. In such event its fertility is disclosed by the nature of the grass and shrubs that grow upon it. If these are promising, a number of us united to clear off the land and make it again fit for planting, when it may be given back to its former owner, or if a long time has elapsed, to other heirs, or it may be given to some person of the same family group, more in need of a planting place. . . .

The American is our elder brother, and in everything he can teach us, except in the method of growing corn in these waterless sand valleys, and in that we are sure we can teach him.

Historically, white culture has viewed its environment as a commodity for human use and consumption. Most white settlers viewed the Great Plains as an endless source of economic opportunity, whether in mining, ranching, or farming. Despite warnings from scientists such as John Wesley Powell that the climate was too hot and dry for growing cash crops, thousands of families moved west, encouraged by the promise of free land and profit and lured by railroad companies and land speculators eager to develop the area and make a buck themselves.

Indian use of the land was far different from that of whites because of the cultural significance they gave to their environment. Although each tribe's culture was unique, all Native American cultures gave the land a spiritual significance. They tried to live in harmony with the land, believing that the human world and the natural world shared a larger consciousness. While the Indians also manipulated their environments, using burning to discourage certain species and cultivate others, their cultural beliefs placed limits on the use of nature. Indian culture produced a more communal economy, conservative hunting practices, and subsistence and migratory farming practices that protected the soil from overuse and erosion.

Instead of considering that Indians might have something to teach whites about the limits of their environment, the U.S. government sought to eradicate Indian culture in order to make way for white destiny. The decimation of the buffalo, the restriction of Indians to small reservations, and finally the attempted conversion of Indians into commercial farmers through the Dawes Act all ultimately opened more land for white use. White use was often abuse, as when white Plains farmers employed techniques such as deep plowing and irrigation in an effort to counter the natural tendencies of the local environment. The result was soil erosion, cycles of drought, and general ecological instability that culminated in the Dust Bowl of the 1930s.

QUESTIONS FOR ANALYSIS

1. What do the terms *severalty* and *in trust* mean, and what was their impact on reservation life?

2. What incentive does the government provide Native Americans who remain on their allotted plots of land?

3. What difference does Chief Joseph see in the white and Indian relationships with the land?

4. Does Chief Joseph claim ownership of the land? Why?

5. Why does the traditional Hopi land system not include permanent, continuous farms?

6. In what ways is Hopi farming and landholding communal rather than individualistic?

7. Does the Dawes Act fail to take into consideration Native American culture?

The West and America

The western frontier was very much a part of the American imagination before 1893. But in that year Frederick Jackson Turner presented his "The Significance of the Frontier in American History" and gave the story academic legitimacy. Turner argued that the frontier had molded a distinct American character, marked by individualism and self-reliance, democracy, and nationalism, thereby creating an exceptional nation.

That Turner declared the frontier to be closed did not stop American popular culture from emphasizing the positive aspects of the frontier's significance as represented by rugged western frontier characters like Buffalo Bill Cody and, later, western movie heroes such as John Wayne. The American West increasingly came to be viewed in the late nineteenth and early twentieth centuries as the most American part of the United States, the great source of American uniqueness or exceptionalism. Turner's students went on to popularize his frontier thesis and defend it against critics. Indeed, the Turnerian approach dominated U.S. history textbooks in the early twentieth century and became the commonly accepted explanation for American development.

But like all complex historical matters, the public memory of the western frontier and the historical scholarship on the topic were not always in perfect alignment. By the early 1930s, and especially after Turner's death in 1932, historians began to critique the frontier thesis. They argued that there was no substantive evidence to support his claims that the frontier had made the United States more democratic, individualistic, or nationalistic and emphasized that the frontier thesis ignored the contributions of immigrants and the role of cities in American development. Furthermore, the frontier individualism that Turner had pointed to did not seem the most desirable trait for a country mired in a devastating economic depression, one that demanded cooperative efforts, not competition.

The criticism of the Turner thesis continued in the post–World War II years. Henry Nash Smith's influential book, *Virgin Land: The American West as Symbol and Myth* (1950), emphasized the centrality of western American mythology to the American national consciousness and thus treated the nation's creation story as a mythic construction, not as the matter-of-fact story that Turner and his followers told. Also, starting in the mid-1950s, Earl Pomeroy questioned the distinctiveness of the American West, arguing that the region's political, economic, and cultural systems were more imitative of those in the eastern United States than innovative.

But as most professional scholars became increasingly critical of the Turnerian explanation for American development, middle school, high school, and college students were still, in the middle third of the twentieth century, reading American history textbooks incorporating Turner's frontier thesis. The most influential of these works was Ray Allen Billington's *Westward Expansion*, which first appeared in 1949 and has appeared in five subsequent editions since. Generations of Americans have been exposed to Turner's frontier thesis through Billington's book.

By the late 1970s, however, historians increasingly began to reassess the story of the American West. Many of these scholars had come of age during a particularly tumultuous and disillusioning time in American history—one marked by Vietnam, Watergate, violent resistance to civil rights, and a growing environmental consciousness. These scholars rejected the colorful, romantic, triumphal, white male-centered western history and focused instead on the dire consequences of America's westward expansion, particularly for peoples of color and for the western environment.

The new approach was labeled the New Western History, and Patricia Nelson Limerick became the movement's leading spokesperson. In her influential book, *The Legacy of Conquest: The Unbroken Past of the American West* (1987), Limerick rejected the frontier thesis, with its emphasis on white westward movement, and focused instead on the convergence of many races and cultures in the West. She also rejected the notion of the end of the frontier in 1890 and explored the West's twentieth-century history and the continuities between the past and present.

The result of this paradigm shift in western history, Elliott West suggested in 1990, was "A Longer, Grimmer, But More Interesting Story," one marked by increased attention to the twentieth-century West, the history of the environment, and the experiences of peoples of color and women. From the mid-1980s to the early 1990s, that story was told in a group of influential works by historians including Donald Worster, William Cronon, and Richard White, in addition to Limerick.

Sensing a good story, the print media played up the conflict between the Old and the New Western History, focusing particularly on the theme of a generational divide among scholars. One reporter dubbed the debate the "gunfight at the politically OK corral." Some scholars argued that the New Western Historians painted a western past that was too bleak. The western writer Larry McMurtry, for example, referred to the new western revisionism as "failure studies" and criticized Limerick and others for emphasizing too heavily the grim, dark, and depressing aspects of western history. These scholarly debates over the western past have captured the public imagination because the West occupies such a central place in the American national consciousness. Remembering a triumphal frontier story of national development is surely comforting for many Americans; it is a story to be proud of. The scholarly questioning of that story can seem like a direct attack on the national heritage.

Recently, scholarship has appeared that views the West not as a part of an exceptional American frontier process or as a distinct region but within a broader global context. In the late 1980s Walter Nugent examined the American West in relation to other frontiers and empires in the late nineteenth century. Limerick, in the late 1990s, urged western historians to "go global" in their scholarship and parallel the West with other regions of the world. Historians could, for example, compare the U.S. government's conquest and subsequent treatment of Native American peoples with other colonizing countries' treatment of other indigenous peoples. An excellent example of this new global approach to the western American past is Gunther Peck's study *Reinventing Free Labor: Padrones and Immigrant Workers in the North American West, 1880–1923* (2000). Peck examined Mexican, Greek, and Italian labor in the West, which he defined transnationally to include Mexico and western Canada. Such studies tend to deexceptionalize the West, to view it as more similar to than different from other places around the world. When and whether the public will embrace this latest version of the story of the West remains to be seen.

18

The Industrial Experiment

1865–1900

The rise of big business, the emergence of a national (and global) economy, and the changing nature of work fundamentally altered the way Americans earned a living.

On the evening of July 16, 1877, a train crew working for the Baltimore and Ohio Railroad abandoned a train in the Martinsburg, West Virginia, depot. Railroad employees then uncoupled the engines of the train and ran them into the roundhouse. They told officials that no trains would leave the station until their demands for better wages were met. Police, unable to remove the workers and their families and friends who joined them, pulled back for the night. Thus began the Great Railway Strike of 1877, the culmination of years of frustration on the part of industrial employees. Suffering from the fourth year of an economic depression, workers faced uncertain employment. In March 1877 the heads of the nation's four largest railroads had announced a 10 percent cut in worker salaries. In June the Baltimore and Ohio had cut wages an additional 10 percent, and when workers tried to unionize, the B & O promptly fired the leaders. Lacking organization, the strike that began on July 16 was spontaneous, as was the reaction of workers around the country. One Martinsburg striker explained the necessity of action: "Strike and live! Bread we must have! Remain and perish! . . . Therefore let the clashing of arms be heard, let the fiery elements be poured out if they think it right, but in heed to our right and in defense of our families, we shall conquer or we shall die!"

The violence began the next day. When the Martinsburg militia tried to take the engines out of the roundhouse, a striker shot a militiaman, and the militia responded by killing the striker. The mob immediately overwhelmed the militia, forcing a retreat. Soon six hundred freight cars piled up in Martinsburg.

West Virginia's governor and the president of the B & O wired President Rutherford Hayes, requesting federal troops to "protect the law abiding people of the State against domestic violence, and to maintain supremacy of the law." Hayes ordered three hundred troops to Martinsburg, but the strike had already spread, fueled by workers' outrage at the use of federal force in a domestic labor dispute. Fearing unrest, the mayor of Baltimore ordered the militia, made up mostly of industrial employees, to assemble at the armory. A crowd gathered, angry that fellow workers would assist in the suppression of the strike, and stoned the militia when they tried to emerge from the armory. The militia responded with gunfire, killing ten.

When word of the strike reached Pittsburgh, Pennsylvania Railroad workers halted all trains. The local militia, many of whom had friends and relatives in the crowd, refused to remove the strikers, so the governor sent in six hundred Philadelphia militiamen. The "outsiders" were met by strikers throwing bricks and coal, leading the militia to fire into the crowd, killing twenty in five minutes. The mob scattered, but returned later that evening, six thousand strong, to torch the trains in the depot. Before order was restored, the strikers had destroyed one hundred engines and two thousand cars.

The strike spread to other industrial centers, including Chicago, East St. Louis, and Houston, Texas. In southern communities, strikes often began with protests by black workers who earned significantly less than white workers and were the first fired when cutbacks occurred. San Francisco workers who gathered to express sympathy for the eastern strikers acted out their frustration with working conditions and low wages by attacking Chinese workers and setting fire to lumberyards.

In the end, facing federal regulars, special police squads, and armed company patrols, workers failed to maintain control of the ground they conquered. But the strike did show that unity among workers of different occupations was possible. It also made the country aware that labor kept America running, as two-thirds of the nation's railroads stood idle during the height of the strike. For Samuel Gompers, founder of the American Federation of Labor, the strike of 1877 "sounded a ringing message of hope to us all." However, the strike also proved that action could be deadly, claiming almost one hundred lives in two weeks. The Great Railroad Strike also made clear to many workers that as long as they acted without a centralized plan or leadership, significant changes in their working conditions would remain elusive.

The Great Railroad Strike illustrated a changing relationship between Americans and the nation's economy. Little had prepared the country for the enormous economic experimentation that would transform American life in the last half of the nineteenth century. The rise of big business, the emergence of a national and global economy, and the changing nature of work fundamentally altered the way Americans earned a living. The wrenching impact of industrialization led to new experiments in regulating business and organizing unions to protect workers' interests. Whether or not they favored the changes taking place around them, most Americans would have agreed with Harvard historian Henry Adams: "My country in 1900," he wrote, "is something totally different from my own country in 1860. I am wholly a stranger in it. Neither I, nor anyone else, understands it."

- How did advances in technology, marketing, and transportation—particularly the railroads—spur industrial expansion after the Civil War?

- How did American cultural values sanction competition? What methods did business managers use to limit competition, and how did government respond?

- Who were the working people of industrializing America, and what conditions and attitudes did they encounter?

- How did organized labor respond to the new environment? Why weren't organizing efforts more successful?

This chapter will address these questions.

THE SETTING FOR INDUSTRIAL EXPANSION, 1865–1889

In 1889 economist David A. Wells announced, "An almost total revolution has taken place, and is yet in progress, in every branch and in every relation of the world's industrial and commercial system." Wells was observing the "Second Industrial Revolution." Unlike the "First Industrial Revolution," which started in Britain in the late eighteenth century, this revolution emerged in Germany and the United States during the 1870s. Whether in Berlin or Pittsburgh, however, the economic transformation shared common features: a growing population; the development of new inventions; the expansion of the railroads; and the emergence of a national marketplace that kindled consumer demand. This favorable environment invited entrepreneurs and government to launch ambitious experiments in harnessing the nation's industrial potential.

Technological Innovation

A writer looking back in 1896 insisted that the period after the Civil War was "an epoch of invention and progress unique in the history of the world. . . . It has been," he noted, "a gigantic tidal wave of human ingenuity and resource." There was certainly much to crow about: between 1790 and 1860 the U.S. Patent Office recorded 36,000 patents; during the 1890s alone, it registered 234,956.

After the Civil War, in every branch of industry and manufacturing, new inventions raised productivity and lowered the cost of finished products. Specialized machines gradually replaced hand operations in textile manufacturing, shoemaking, and metalworking operations. The invention of the typewriter (1867), the cash register (1879), and the adding machine (1891) allowed businesspeople to work more efficiently.

Among the most enduring inventions were those that enhanced the quality of life in America. The flush toilet, invented in England in the 1870s, appeared in America during the 1880s. The tin can allowed producers to preserve food for long periods of time; people could now eat vegetables and fruits out of season and store meat and milk conveniently in the home. Railroad refrigeration cars enabled growers to ship produce long distances. By the end of the century the urban middle class could eat fresh lettuce, strawberries, and grapes as well as beef and pork shipped from farms in the South and West.

Innovations in communication allowed organizations to operate on a national scale. By 1880 Western Union, which controlled 80 percent of the country's telegraph lines, operated nearly 200,000 miles of telegraph routes from coast to coast. Transat-

CHRONOLOGY

1859	Darwin publishes *The Origin of Species*
1866	National Labor Union created
1867	Invention of the typewriter Introduction of Pullman sleeping car
1869	First transcontinental rail line completed Great Atlantic and Pacific Tea Company (A&P) opened African-Americans form the Colored National Labor Union Knights of Labor organized
1872	Ward starts first successful mail-order business
1873	Financial panic leads to depression
1876	Bell patents the telephone
1877	Great Railway Strike sweeps nation Edison invents the phonograph
1879	Invention of the cash register Edison successfully tests his electric light bulb George publishes *Progress and Poverty*
1881	Standard Oil Trust formed
1884	Knights win victory against Union Pacific Railroad
1886	Westinghouse develops first alternating current system Sears, Roebuck, and Company founded Haymarket Square bombing American Federation of Labor formed
1887	Interstate Commerce Act
1888	Bellamy publishes *Looking Backward*
1889	Carnegie publishes "The Gospel of Wealth"
1890	Sherman Antitrust Act
1901	United States Steel Corporation organized

lantic cable lines, first laid by British and American crews in 1858, enabled Americans to transmit messages to Europe in a matter of hours, rather than waiting the twelve days it would take a letter to arrive by steamship. Within twenty years 107,000 miles of undersea cable connected Americans to Europe, Northern Africa, India, and China. After Alexander Graham Bell transmitted the first words over wire in March 1876, demand for the telephone grew quickly. By 1880 fifty thousand telephones were in use in the United States, including one in the White House, and fifty-five cities had local service. In 1885 the Bell interests organized the American Telephone and Telegraph Company, and by 1900 the number of telephones had increased to 1.5 million.

From the standpoint of industrial output, perhaps the most significant breakthrough took place in the production of steel. Manufacturers and builders preferred steel over iron because of its increased strength and durability. After the Civil War, two new processes—the Bessemer and the open hearth—led to furnaces large and hot enough to melt the wrought iron needed to produce large quantities of steel. In 1860 the United States produced 13,000 tons of steel. By 1879 American furnaces were turning out over a million tons a year. By 1910 the United States was making over 28 million tons and was by far the top producer of steel in the world. In 1880 only nine companies could produce more than 100,000 tons a year. By the early 1890s several companies exceeded 250,000 tons, and two produced over 1 million tons a year.

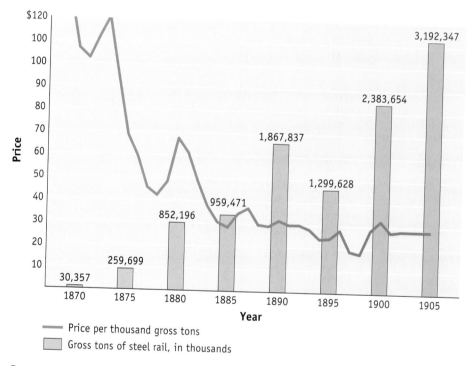

Bessemer Steel Rail Production, 1867–1907   Except for during the depression of the 1890s, steel rail production rose consistently throughout the late nineteenth century. Englishman Henry Bessemer's invention in the 1850s made the production of steel from iron possible in large quantities and the discovery of new iron ore deposits in the upper Midwest after the Civil War paved the way for American production. Railroads jumped on the chance to replace iron rails with the stronger, more flexible steel, especially as the price of a thousand gross tons dropped dramatically—from over $100 in 1870 to a low of $18 in 1898.

Thomas Edison and the "Invention Business"

Leading the advances in technology were a group of independent inventors such as Thomas Edison, William Stanley (induction coil, a transmitter for alternating current), and Wilbur and Orville Wright (internal-combustion engine airplane). Free from organizational entanglements, they worked in small labs with a handful of assistants on problems of their own choosing. In the absence of adequate theory, they resorted to experimentation. "No experiments are useless," Edison snapped when told he carried out too many. While their passion lay in creation, the inventors often formed alliances with capitalists to create companies to manufacture and sell their patented inventions, but they distanced themselves from day-to-day managerial responsibilities.

Thomas Edison was the most prolific inventor of his day. During his lifetime he registered 1,328 patents, and a host of new industries grew from his innovations. In

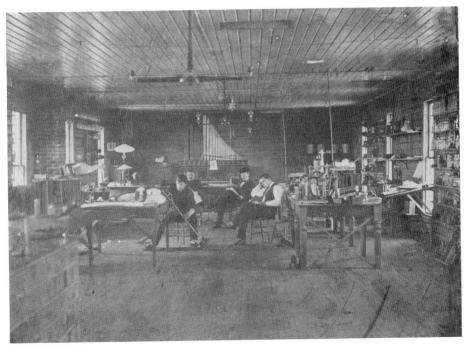

Edison's Menlo Park Lab In 1876, Thomas Edison, the most prolific inventor of the post–Civil War era, moved his work into a two-story structure built by his father in Menlo Park, New Jersey. Edison referred to the place as the "invention factory" and for five years Edison worked nonstop in the lab with approximately twenty-five assistants. His staff came from around the world and included scientists, mathematicians, and carpenters who provided the skills needed to turn Edison's ideas into reality, along with accountants and bookkeepers who kept track of the money needed to run the business. In 1882, Edison moved much of the laboratory's equipment and library to New York City so he could manage both the creation of new devices and monitor the progress of Edison Electric Illuminating Company. *(Corbis)*

1876 Edison, who was not yet thirty years old, set up shop in Menlo Park, New Jersey, and went into the full-time "invention business." Before settling into his new lab, Edison proposed as a goal "a minor invention every ten days and a big thing every six months or so." Over the next few years "the Wizard of Menlo Park" produced a stream of new creations including the phonograph, Dictaphone, mimeograph, dynamo, and methods to extend electric transmission. His discovery of the phonograph sparked the idea for motion pictures. "It should be possible," he wrote in his notebook, "to devise an apparatus to do for the eye what the phonograph was designed to do for the ear."

Edison's most noteworthy breakthrough came in 1879 when he successfully tested the first incandescent electric light bulb. In the hunt for an ideal filament, Edison claimed to have tested "no fewer than 6,000 vegetable growths" before stumbling on a strip of tungsten. In 1882 the Edison Electric Illuminating Company (which merged with other companies making light bulbs to form Edison General Electric Company in 1888) began to supply current to four hundred lights servicing eighty-five customers in New York City.

Because he used direct current, Edison's lighting system was limited to a radius of about two miles. In 1886 George Westinghouse, who founded the Westinghouse Electric Company, developed the first alternating current system, which allowed transmission of electricity over longer distances. Two years later Nikola Tesla, a Croatian immigrant, discovered a way to convert alternating current into power that could drive machines and, together with Ohio engineer Charles Brush, enabled factories to use electrical power.

The Railroads

Railroads played a crucial role in America's Industrial Revolution both by consuming industrial output and by helping to develop a powerful national economy. By 1890 railroads crisscrossed the nation, linking raw materials in the West to factories, markets, and consumers in the East. The nation was laced with 35,000 miles of railroad in 1865; by 1900, 200,000 miles were in operation—more than in all of Europe (see map on page 703). The surge in railroad construction spurred the expansion of other industries, especially steel, stone, and lumber. In 1882, for example, the railroads purchased nearly 90 percent of all steel produced in the United States.

At the same time, technological improvements—the invention of the air brake (1869) and the automatic car coupler (1873), and the introduction of the Pullman sleeping car (1867)—made rail travel safer and more comfortable. Between 1877 and 1890 the volume of railroad freight rose from 231 million tons to 691 million tons, and passenger traffic swelled from 180 million to 520 million miles.

Railroad expansion required huge investments of capital. Government—federal, state, and local—provided cash loans totaling over $150 million. State and local governments also granted the railroads tax exemptions. The federal government contributed 134 million acres of public land, and states added another 48.9 million acres. Together, the gifts of public lands, comprising an area larger than the United Kingdom, Spain, and Belgium combined, were valued at between

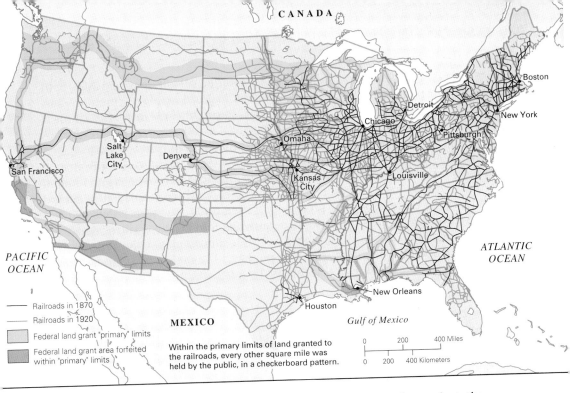

Railroads and Railroad Land Grants, 1870–1920 Setting a national precedent, the Pacific Railroad Bill of 1862 provided federal land grants to railroad companies in order to facilitate improved transportation. After the completion of the first transcontinental line in 1869, other railroad companies joined in the quest to link regions by rail. Thanks to the ever-dropping price of steel and government support, new railroads sprung up across the country—from short lines that connected the rural areas of the Midwest to the long trunk lines that interconnected the developing territories of the Far West to markets in the East.

$130 million and $500 million. The demands for extraordinary amounts of private capital to finance the railroads led to the centralization of America's money and investment markets on Wall Street. Railroads listed their stocks and bonds on the New York Stock Exchange to attract investors from across the country and from Europe. The modern investment house grew up to sell the new securities.

The private capital required to develop this industry also produced the nation's first big businessmen, often referred to as "robber barons" for their cutthroat business dealings. Jay Gould, one of the most successful, used the Panic of 1873 to accumulate small rail lines that faced bankruptcy. By 1880 Gould and his partners had monopolized much of the nations' central and western lines, charging high rates to clients who had no alternative to Gould's railroads. Meanwhile, Gould inflated the stock of his companies and siphoned profits for use in his own business ventures rather than putting them back into the railroads for maintenance and improvements. Gould admitted shortly before his death in 1892 that he was "the most hated man in America" for his business activities, but he died worth more than an estimated $100 million.

In size and complexity, the railroads dwarfed all other enterprises, both private and public. In 1891 the Pennsylvania Railroad employed more workers than the largest government agency (the Post Office). Since the railroads extended over thousands of miles and involved a complicated system of planning and coordination, executives pioneered the development of new managerial methods that would spread to other industries. Railroads were the first to develop a central controller's office to handle financial transactions and modern accounting practices to measure performance, set rates, and tabulate detailed statistics about every aspect of production. Time-study engineers calculated the most efficient way for workers to do a particular job. Quality-control inspectors reviewed the finished work. To keep track of the burgeoning white-collar empire of managers and supervisors, railroads produced the first organizational charts, with clearly defined lines of authority to guarantee the smooth running of the corporation.

The New Consumer Society

Improved transportation contributed to major changes in American shopping habits. In the early nineteenth century, when most Americans lived in villages and on farms, people bought items they needed from general stores, which sold almost everything. By the late nineteenth century, large department stores and chain stores were eclipsing the general store, especially in larger towns and in cities of the upper Midwest and northern Atlantic states. Bypassing middlemen, they bought directly from manufacturers and, since they purchased large quantities of goods, negotiated volume discounts that they passed on to their customers in the form of low prices. Unlike general stores or smaller shops, they delivered goods to consumers' homes, guaranteed quality, and accepted returns from dissatisfied customers.

Every major city had one or more leading department stores. Shoppers in New York strolled down the aisles of A. T. Stewart and Macy's. Bargain hunters in Philadelphia flocked to Wanamaker's and Gimbel's. Chicagoans spent many Saturday afternoons browsing at Marshall Field's and Carson, Pirie, Scott. By the end of the century, most urban department stores featured restrooms, lunch counters, nurseries for children, complaint and credit counters, and offices.

The chain store complemented the department store in the transformation of shopping. The first chain was the Great Atlantic and Pacific Tea Company (A&P), which opened in 1869. By 1876 A&P boasted a network of sixty-seven grocery stores. Frank Winfield Woolworth opened his first "five-and ten-cent store" in Lancaster, Pennsylvania, in 1879. By 1910 he was operating over a thousand stores nationwide. Other chains—Grand Union, Kroger, and Jewel Tea—changed the way Americans shopped for groceries.

The expanding consumer culture reached rural areas through mail-order catalogs that offered a host of consumer products, from clothing to cutlery. Aaron Montgomery Ward established the first successful mail-order business in 1872. Sears, Roebuck, and Company, founded in 1886, offered stiff competition with its lavishly illustrated catalog. From the Sears catalog, consumers could order

Macy's Department Store   Technological innovation and the revolution in transportation in the late nineteenth century permitted the mass marketing of goods in settings such as the department store. This photograph of the Macy's food section displays the abundance and variety of goods that lured in the consumer. The department store was more than a convenience; it was a wonder that turned shopping into an adventure, particularly for American women, who increasingly became the target demographic for retailers. Women, like this Macy's clerk, were also a strong presence behind the counter at department stores.   *(Museum of the City of New York.)*

everything from watches to stoves to thimbles. When asked by his Sunday School teacher where the Ten Commandments came from, a boy from rural Idaho replied, "From Sears, Roebuck, where else?" By the 1890s the Ward's catalog contained ten thousand products.

Retailers turned to professional advertisers to reach a vast pool of ready customers. By 1900 American advertisers spent $95 million a year, which marked a tenfold increase from 1865. "Goods suitable for the millionaire at prices in reach of the millions," Macy's boasted to potential buyers. In addition to traditional formats—handbills, circulars, and posters—advertisers took special advantage of growing urban newspapers. Department stores bought full-page advertisements in the metropolitan dailies and promoted featured merchandise in Sunday supplements. Rather than simply informing customers of products, advertisers tried to persuade people to purchase a particular brand. Outdoor advertising also assumed a new scale. In every city, by the turn of the century, mammoth electric signs glowed aside and atop buildings.

The rise of department and chain stores planted the seeds of a new culture of consumption that would flower in the years after World War I. By 1910 many stores contained over a hundred separate departments under one roof, selling staples, liquor, name-brand pianos, and even lion and panther cubs. "It speaks to us," observed a merchant of the vast array of new consumer goods, "only of ourselves, our pleasures, our life. It does not say, 'Pray, obey, sacrifice thyself, respect the King, fear thy master.' It whispers, 'Amuse thyself, take care of yourself.' Is not this the natural and logical effect of an age of individualism?"

The department store stood as an imposing symbol of another important change that was transforming American society: the forging of a global economy. While the railroad knitted together local economies into a national market, innovations in steamboat technology—the screw propeller, steel hulls, more powerful engines—linked national markets into a global network. The expanding global economy provided consumers with a greater variety of imported products: Egyptian cotton, Australian wool, and Chinese silks. But it also produced more competition and greater uncertainty, especially for American farmers and workers.

THE NEW INDUSTRIAL ORDER

A new generation of industrial experimenters, including Andrew Carnegie, John D. Rockefeller, and J. Pierpont Morgan, devised new methods for managing the rapidly changing industrial order. Entrepreneurs embraced a cultural foundation that glorified competition, limited government, and individual achievement, as popularized by writers such as Carnegie and Horatio Alger, who fostered a "Gospel of Success." But at the same time the industrial titans praised competition as bringing the fittest to the fore, they worked to control prices and corral competition. Their efforts raised new questions about the role that government should play in regulating industry.

Managing the New Industrial Empire   To coordinate their vast industrial empires, business leaders created the modern corporation. A number of features distinguished the modern corporation from older forms of business organization. The first differences concerned the nature of ownership. Traditional business enterprises had been owned by one individual or a small number of people bound by ties of kinship and marriage. The owners also managed the business, overseeing day-to-day operations. In contrast, ownership of the modern corporation was spread over a large number of stockholders who, in turn, hired professional managers to run the business.

The law gave legal sanction to this new arrangement. In the 1880s a number of states adopted incorporation laws to encourage commerce and industry. Under these laws stockholders could share in the profits of the company, but their risk would be limited to the amount of money they invested. The Supreme Court gave corporations broad protection under the Fourteenth Amendment, claiming that states could not deny corporations equal protection under the law or deprive them of their rights without due process.

Over time, corporations developed new management techniques to streamline their operations and maximize their efficiency, following the example set by the railroads. Corporations created layers of managers to implement long-range plans and oversee the daily affairs of their far-flung operations. Managers created formalized procedures and devised organizational charts with clearly defined lines of authority to guarantee the smooth running of the corporation. One by-product of these changes was that relations between owners and workers, and even among managers, became distant and impersonal.

Along with producing a clear organizational structure, corporations devised new ways to consolidate their control over the market. One method was vertical integration, whereby a company attempted to control the entire production and distribution process for its products, from extracting raw materials, to creating the product, to transporting the finished product to retailers. Gustavus Swift used vertical integration to establish dominance over the meatpacking industry. By the 1890s Chicago-based Swift and Company had integrated forward, moving closer to consumers, by purchasing refrigerated railcars to ship the meat to markets in the East and hiring wagons to deliver the goods to butcher shops. At the same time, the company integrated backward, closer to the raw materials, by raising its own cattle.

A second method of seizing control of the market was horizontal integration, which took place when companies limited competition by taking over firms engaged in similar activities (see figure on page 708). The railroads pioneered the use of "pools" to establish control over the market. To avoid cutthroat competition, railroad executives entered into voluntary agreements to divide traffic and artificially inflate rates. Since they were not legally enforceable, the agreements rarely worked for long, but that did not stop other industries eager to limit competition and guarantee profits from following suit.

Titans of Industry: Carnegie, Rockefeller, and Morgan

During the 1880s and 1890s Andrew Carnegie applied the idea of vertical integration to dominate the steel industry. Born in Scotland, Carnegie emigrated to the United States with his impoverished parents in 1848. He gradually climbed the American industrial pyramid, starting out as a messenger boy in a Pittsburgh telegraph office. In 1873, at the age of thirty-eight, he used money earned from investments to build the giant J. Edgar Thomson Steel Works in Pittsburgh. Mingling the Puritan doctrine of stewardship with ruthless business practices, Carnegie managed to keep his prices low and drive competitors out of business. To guarantee adequate supplies, he acquired sources of iron ore for pig iron to produce his steel, and of coke and coal to fire the furnaces, and he developed a fleet of steamships and a railroad for transporting the raw materials directly to his mills. "From the moment these crude stuffs were dug out of the earth until they flowed in a stream of liquid steel in the ladles," noted a contemporary, "there was never a price, profit, or royalty paid to an outsider."

While Carnegie championed the benefits of vertical integration, a young merchant from Cleveland, John D. Rockefeller, used horizontal integration to build the Standard Oil Company into one of the titans of corporate business. Born in 1839 in upstate New York, Rockefeller settled in Ohio and invested in an oil refinery during the Civil War. Over the next decade he consolidated his control over the oil industry. He managed to reduce costs and drive the competition out of business by keeping wages low, paying meticulous attention to detail, and negotiating secret deals with

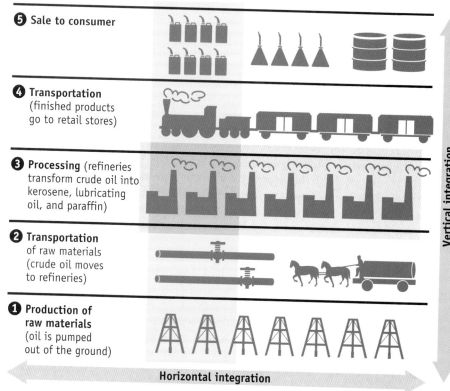

5 Sale to consumer

4 Transportation
(finished products
go to retail stores)

3 Processing (refineries
transform crude oil into
kerosene, lubricating
oil, and paraffin)

2 Transportation
of raw materials
(crude oil moves
to refineries)

1 Production of
raw materials
(oil is pumped
out of the ground)

Vertical integration

Horizontal integration

● Steps in petroleum production/distribution

Vertical and Horizontal Integration of the Petroleum Industry   Prior to the dominance of Standard Oil Company, many different companies specialized in certain aspects of petroleum production. Some companies produced only the raw materials, while railroad companies did nothing but transport the products, and independent merchants sold the product to consumers. John D. Rockefeller entered the petroleum business by building a refinery (step 3 on the graph) and then expanded his company to include other processing plants, thereby creating horizontal integration. Rockefeller gradually extended the reach of Standard Oil vertically by acquiring oil leases and oil wells (step 1), then pipelines (step 2), followed by the establishment of advantageous contracts with railroads (step 4), and ultimately purchasing retail stores (step 5).

the railroads. In 1871, for example, he joined with other refiners to form a secret pool, called the South Improvement Company, that negotiated massive rebates with railroad agents. A rebate was a secret agreement in which the railroad reduced freight rates in return for the privileged customer's promise to ship large volumes. The pool existed for only a few months before it was exposed, but during that time Standard bought twenty-one of the twenty-six refineries in Cleveland. Like Carnegie, Rockefeller also practiced vertical integration, making his own barrels, building his own storage warehouses, and manufacturing his own chemicals. Rockefeller's success was staggering. In 1870 he had controlled 10 percent of the refined petroleum produced in the country; by the end of the decade he produced 90 percent.

Confronted with the need to coordinate his expansive financial empire and to regulate production levels and prices to assure steady profits, Rockefeller created a novel business organization, the trust. Ohio law prohibited corporations from owning plants in other states or from owning stock in out-of-state corporations. In 1881 Rockefeller used a loophole in the law to establish the Standard Oil Trust, which consisted of nine trustees empowered "to hold, control, and manage" Standard's numerous assets, including oil interests outside the state. The trust allowed Rockefeller to exert greater control over the Standard empire, centralize the management and decision-making process, and adjust quickly to changing circumstances. During the 1890s, with trusts under attack from Congress and the courts, Rockefeller developed another ingenious method of industrial consolidation, the holding company. In these large-scale mergers, holding companies bought the stock of member companies and thereby established direct, formal control over their operations.

Rockefeller's example inspired other manufacturers to follow his lead. Between 1880 and 1904 the nation experienced 318 mergers affecting four-fifths of the nation's manufacturing industries. By 1904 the two thousand largest business firms in the United States made up less than 1 percent of the nation's businesses but controlled 40 percent of the economy. By 1900 James Buchanan Duke's American Tobacco Company, one of the few large manufacturers based in the South, was producing half the smoking tobacco, 62 percent of the chewing tobacco, and 93 percent of cigarettes made in the United States. Henry O. Havemeyer's "Sugar Trust" employed twenty-five thousand of the thirty thousand refinery workers in the country. The U.S. Steel Corporation, organized in 1901 as the first billion-dollar corporation, controlled 60 percent of the industry. A congressional committee reported in 1888 that "the number of combinations and trusts formed and forming in this country is . . . very large. . . . New ones are constantly forming and . . . old ones are constantly extending their relations."

The merger movement gave birth to a new type of businessman, the broker who raised the money to permit business expansion. In the late nineteenth century many American corporations wanted to grow but lacked money to purchase new equipment and expand production. They searched for investors who, for a share of the profits, would loan them money for expansion. J. Pierpont Morgan emerged as the most famous investment banker of his age. By channeling European capital into the United States, Morgan facilitated the union between finance and industry. In return, he demanded a measure of control over the corporations he helped create. He successfully managed the reorganization of several railroads and raised the money for the creation of the U.S. Steel Corporation. A congressional committee in 1912 reported that the House of Morgan held 341 directorships in 112 corporations that controlled over $22 billion in assets, more than the assessed value of all property in the twenty-two states and territories west of the Mississippi River.

| **A Business Culture** | Americans' deeply ingrained faith in concepts of individual liberty and limited government, articulated soon after the nation's founding by Thomas Jefferson and his supporters, |

reinforced and supported the activities of the nation's business leaders. Against this background, the convergence of three different streams of thought—laissez-faire, Social Darwinism, and the gospel of success—created a powerful incentive for growth.

The eighteenth-century Scottish thinker Adam Smith, a professor of logic and moral philosophy at the University of Glasgow, was the father of the doctrine of laissez-faire. In 1776 Smith published his monumental work on political economy, *The Wealth of Nations*, which argued that the free market, guided by a self-correcting "Invisible Hand" and unencumbered by government regulation, would guarantee economic growth. Smith considered self-interest the prime motivation for human behavior and the free market the most efficient method for realizing that self-interest. The public interest, he reasoned, would be served through the widespread private pursuit of self-interest.

Nearly a century later Smith's ideas found support from an unlikely source: naturalist Charles Darwin. After a four-year voyage around the world observing flora and fauna, Darwin developed a radical new theory of evolution. In a groundbreaking book, *The Origin of Species* (1859), Darwin concluded that plant and animal species had evolved over thousands of years. Species that evolved and adapted to changing environments survived; species that did not successfully adapt became extinct. Nature, he argued, had established clear rules that guided the competition among and within species, allowing for the survival of the fittest.

Many people tried to extend Darwin's findings to human development, and their speculations led to what has been called Social Darwinism. The free enterprise system, as they conceived it, gave everyone an equal chance for survival and riches. The English philosopher Herbert Spencer, who coined the term *survival of the fittest*, argued that competition was natural and served the public interest. William Graham Sumner, a professor of political economy at Yale, emerged as the most influential Social Darwinist in America. Just as natural laws governed the working of the universe, he believed, so did natural laws determine man's social and economic behavior. It was foolish for governments to attempt to change or ameliorate these forces. To take power or money away from millionaires, Sumner scoffed, was "like killing off our generals in war." It was "absurd," he wrote, to pass laws permitting society's "worst members" to survive, or to "sit down with a slate and pencil to plan out a new social world."

The Gospel of Success and Its Critics

The gospel of success had always been an important part of American culture. The Puritans had preached that the possession of worldly goods was a sign of grace, and writers such as Benjamin Franklin made wealth a virtue. By the late nineteenth century Americans seemed consumed with the secrets of material success. Periodicals and manuals, many of them written by Protestant clergy, emphasized that financial gain was not incompatible with Christian teaching, and that hard work and thrift were essential for both earthly success and eternal salvation. "Work has sometimes been called worship, and the dusty, smoky workshop a temple," observed a popular writer, "because there man glorifies the great Architect by imitating him in providing for the wants of his creatures." Two writers—Andrew Carnegie and Horatio Alger—added new force to this appealing belief.

In 1889 industrialist Andrew Carnegie wrote a widely circulated article, "The Gospel of Wealth," that celebrated the benefits of better goods and lower prices that resulted from competition. Carnegie argued that "our wonderful material development" outweighed the harsh costs of competition. The concentration of wealth in the hands of a few leading industrialists, he concluded, was "not only beneficial but essential to the future of the race." Those most fit would bring order and efficiency out of the chaos of rapid industrialization. Unlike most other industrialists, Carnegie also insisted that the rich were obligated to spend some of their wealth to benefit their "poorer brethren."

In fiction, by far the most popular writer of success stories was Horatio Alger. His novelettes, which bore such titles as *Work and Win, Do and Dare,* and *Risen from the Ranks,* sold 20 million copies by the end of the century. Book after book told the tale of rags to riches, the journey from poverty to fame and fortune. Alger's typical hero was a boy of about fifteen who possessed the predictable virtues of honesty, sobriety, and a commitment to work hard. These qualities were instrumental in each success story, but accident or chance also played roles.

Not everyone accepted the new business culture. In 1888 Edward Bellamy, the son of a Baptist minister, published his best-selling *Looking Backward,* which envisioned a utopian socialist society. In Bellamy's utopia, the government owned the means of production and distributed wealth equally among all citizens. Competition was irrelevant. He denounced "the imbecility of the system of private enterprise" and the callousness of industrialists who "maim and slaughter [their] workers by thousands." Though *Looking Backward* inspired the creation of hundreds of Bellamy discussion clubs, it never translated its condemnation of capitalist society into a successful reform movement.

In *Progress and Poverty* (1879) Henry George joined Bellamy in offering a biting critique of the emerging industrial order. George objected to the crass materialism and the growing disparity between rich and poor, which he believed resulted from inflated land prices. Wealth in the industrial era, he argued, was created not by productive labor, but by speculation. He proposed a simple solution to the problem: a "single tax" of 100 percent on the profits from selling land. *Progress and Poverty* sold over 3 million copies and sparked the formation of Land and Labor Clubs to promote the single-tax idea.

George's and Bellamy's radical rhetoric reflected their loyalty to traditional values and their indignation that the promise of American life was not being fulfilled. However, neither challenged deeply held American notions about limited government. George, claiming that the state should "clear the ways, and then let things alone," believed that the single tax would result in a smaller government closer to "the ideal of Jeffersonian democracy." He embraced capitalism, opposed income taxes, and viewed labor unions as a temporary evil. Bellamy believed that irrational competition, not the nature of capitalism itself, was to blame for most social problems. Citizens of his utopian state would experience "far less interference of any sort with personal liberty."

Regulating the Trusts   Public reaction to the consolidation of American business was confused and uncertain. Americans enjoyed the benefits of the rising industrial order—new products were flooding the market, and prices of most items were actually declining.

Though often exaggerated, the rags to riches stories of a few industrialists struck many Americans as proof that anyone could achieve the American Dream of success. Critics, however, complained that the trusts destroyed competition, stifled individual opportunity, and undermined the foundation of the free enterprise system. "If the tendency to combination is irresistible, control of it is imperative," warned Henry Demarest Lloyd, a Chicago lawyer, journalist, and author.

Struggling with these contradictory attitudes, Americans moved to address some of the abuses committed by big business. Not surprisingly, they turned first to the railroads. By 1875 many states had established regulatory commissions to supervise railroads within their borders. The courts, however, often took a conservative view of state regulation, and most of the commissions proved ineffective. By the mid-1880s Congress was being pushed to regulate by those—such as farm organizations and oilmen in the Pennsylvania fields—who felt discriminated against by the railroads' high rural rates and preferential treatment of powerful customers. In January 1887 Congress passed the Interstate Commerce Act. Attacking the monopolistic and competitive evils connected with the railroads and declaring that rates must be "reasonable and just," the act created a five-man commission empowered to use the federal courts to enforce decisions.

Public outcry against the trusts continued to swell. The 1888 Republican platform declared "opposition to all combinations of capital, organized in trusts or otherwise, to control arbitrarily the conditions of trade among our citizens." The Democrats attacked "trusts and combinations . . . which . . . rob the body of our citizens by depriving them of the benefits of natural competition." Congress responded to the pressure in 1890 by passing, with only one dissenting voice in either house, the Sherman Antitrust Act. The law declared illegal "every contract, combination in the form of trust or otherwise, or conspiracy, in restraint of trade or commerce among the several States, or with foreign nations." Any individual who was "injured in his business or property" by corporations violating the act was authorized to sue for triple damages.

Neither the Interstate Commerce Act nor the Sherman Antitrust Act had any measurable impact on the trend toward consolidation. The laws were poorly drafted, reflecting the divided loyalties of most lawmakers, who opposed government interference in the marketplace but wanted to be responsive to public sentiment. In the end, the two measures turned enforcement over to the courts, which looked skeptically on government power. Both laws, however, established important precedents for federal regulation of industry, and both would become powerful weapons in the hands of an activist government in the next century.

In many ways, the trust represented a rational adjustment to the challenge of production and distribution in an expanding national market. Despite their many abuses, trusts provided central coordination over the specialized functions of the new industrial organizations, which reflected a larger social trend. As the leader of an organized charity movement observed, "We live in an atmosphere of organization. . . . Men are learning the disadvantages of isolated action. Whether or not we approve of trusts and trades-unions and similar combinations, and whatever their motives, they rest on a foundation which is sound alike from the business and religious standpoint: namely, the principle of union and co-operation."

THE CHANGING WORLD OF WORK, 1870–1900

The Industrial Revolution fundamentally altered the nature of work in America. Laboring in large factories forced workers to discard an older style of work and adjust to the monotony of repeating their task over and over. Along with the nature of work, the composition of the work force changed as well.

The Factory System   Before the Civil War the United States was an overwhelmingly agricultural nation. About 60 percent of all workers toiled on farms, versus about 30 percent involved in nonagricultural pursuits. By the end of the century those numbers had reversed. Growing urban areas in the Northeast and Midwest saw their manufacturing work forces quadruple, from 1.5 million workers in 1860 to nearly 6 million in 1900.

Workers not only moved from agriculture to manufacturing; they also labored in large factories rather than small shops. "Of the nearly three millions of people employed in the mechanical industries of this country, at least four-fifths are working under the factory system," a statistician estimated in 1880. In the South, where cotton mills and tobacco factories were the largest industrial employers, the average factory work force doubled between 1870 and 1900. The Cambria Iron Works in Johnstown, Pennsylvania, employed a thousand workers in 1860; by the end of the century that number had swelled to nearly ten thousand. In many cities, huge factories employing thousands of workers became commonplace. By 1910 General Electric employed fifteen thousand workers at its plant in Schenectady, New York, as did the Pullman Car Company and International Harvester in Chicago.

Finally, workers who had been self-employed now depended on someone else to pay their wages. In 1860 as many people were self-employed as earned wages. By 1900 two of every three Americans relied on wages. The transformation from small shop production to factory wage earner robbed many workers of their sense of independence. "They no longer carried the keys of the workshop, for workshops, tools and keys belonged not to them, but to their master," observed union leader Terence Powderly.

Managers searching for new ways to organize and control the workplace placed their faith in so-called scientific management. Pioneered by an engineer named Frederick W. Taylor, scientific management imposed a new level of regimentation on factory life. Taylor suggested that companies could lower costs and increase profits by subdividing manufacturing into small tasks. He used a stopwatch to dissect the "millions of different operations" that workers performed. With these time-motion studies, he was able to determine the simplest, and cheapest, way of performing each job.

Taylor's system of scientific management eventually resulted in the standardization of work procedures that made many factory tasks painfully monotonous. "The different branches of the trade are divided and subdivided so that one man may make just a particular part of a machine and may not know anything whatever about another part of the same machine," machinist John Morrison told a Senate committee in 1883. At a Boston meeting of working women in 1869, Aurora Phelps described the consequences for women in the garment industry:

When I was younger girls were taught full trades. They made pants, coats, overcoats, and then they learned to cut. Now one stitches the seam, another makes the button-holes, and another puts the buttons on, and when the poor girl stitches up the seams and finds her work slack she goes from shop to shop, perhaps for weeks, before she can find the same kind of work.

The factory system also burdened workers with a tighter system of discipline. Employers often forbade singing, drinking, joking, smoking, or conversation on the job. Foremen imposed fines for even minor infractions. Many companies denied immigrant workers time to celebrate their holidays and holy days. Companies enamored of the rigors of scientific management abolished older work patterns, which saw periods of heavy work followed by leisurely breaks, and institutionalized a continual pace of work synchronized with machines. "In the factory there is no chance to read," complained one man, "and the noise and hum of machinery prevent general conversation, even when the rules and discipline do not positively forbid it."

Dreams of Social Mobility

There is conflicting evidence about whether workers experienced a higher standard of living during these years. Industrialization and the development of a national consumer marketplace actually led to a measurable drop in wholesale prices for most goods. The biggest plunge came in the price of food. A cut of meat that cost a dollar in 1870 sold for only seventy-eight cents in 1880. As a result, between 1880 and 1914 real wages of the average worker rose about $7 a year. But such figures can be deceptive. The earnings of skilled workers—machinists, engineers, carpenters, printers—improved much more than did those of unskilled workers. The average annual wage for manufacturing workers in 1900 was $435, or $8.37 a week. However, unskilled workers were paid only ten cents an hour on average, about $5.50 a week. Regional variations were also pronounced. In 1880 workers in the South earned about 30 percent less than their counterparts in the East and Midwest.

Despite some general figures showing progress, large numbers of workers remained desperately poor. An 1883 study of working conditions in Illinois estimated that 25 percent of the state's workers, both skilled and unskilled, "fail to make a living." Job insecurity plagued most workers. Periodic depressions ravaged the American worker in 1873–1878, 1883–1885, and 1893–1897. In his book *Poverty* (1904), social scientist Robert Hunter claimed that unemployment was the most common cause of poverty in America. "The annual wages of more than one workman in every four," he observed, "suffered considerable decrease by reason of a period of enforced idleness, extending in some cases over several months."

The harsh reality of the new industrial order clashed with the popular image of rags-to-riches social mobility. "A man here may be a common laborer," a business leader expounded in typical fashion in 1883, "but if he has the right material in him there is no reason why he should not occupy the best place in the nation." The fragmentary evidence from the period suggests otherwise. A handful of unskilled workers managed to join the ranks of the semiskilled, but few reached middle-class status. The poor improved their condition over time, but often by putting the entire family to work. With a few exceptions, the leaders of industry came from established families of old American stock.

Not surprisingly, contemporary accounts of worker attitudes are filled with expressions of resentment toward the new industrial system. Workers resisted many of the new work restrictions and requirements by forming cooperative alliances and organizing wildcat strikes. But most felt helpless against the onslaught of industrialization. "That a deep-rooted feeling of discontent pervades the masses, none can deny," Terence Powderly wrote in 1885. Two years later, after surveying working-class opinion in his state, a government official in Connecticut commented on "the feeling of bitterness which so frequently manifests itself in their utterances," their "distrust of employers," and their palpable "discontent and unrest."

The New Working People

Changes in the composition of the work force were just as dramatic as the changes in the nature of work. Immigrants, lured to the United States by low fares on steamships and industrial agents who recruited in rural European regions, filled many of the new factory jobs. "Not every foreigner is a workingman," a Chicago clergyman observed, "but in the cities, at least, it may almost be said that every workingman is a foreigner." In 1870 nearly one-third of all workers in manufacturing jobs were foreign-born. As a result of the subdivision of factory tasks, most work did not require the laborer to have previous training. Employers, therefore, could save money by seeking employees who lacked the skills needed to find better-paying jobs. Recent migrants, unable to speak English and lacking artisan skills, had to accept any employment offered.

Native workers often resented the new migrants, fearing they would depress wages by agreeing to work for less money. An ironworker in Wisconsin complained, "Immigrants work for almost nothing and seem to be able to live on wind—something which I can not do." Another worker charged that immigrants bring "wages down below the breadline." The animosity was further fueled by the new workers' ethnicity, which led native-born Americans to consider them inferior, a subject discussed in the next chapter.

The new factory system also pulled a greater number of women into the workplace. Between 1870 and 1900 the number of women working outside the home nearly tripled. By the turn of the century 5 million American women were earning wages, nearly a quarter through manufacturing jobs. Three of four women workers were under twenty-five; most were either recent immigrants or the daughters of immigrant parents. Most saw work as a means of supporting their families, not as an act of personal liberation. The head of the Massachusetts Bureau of Labor reported in 1882 that "a family of workers can always live well, but the man with a family of small children to support, unless his wife works also, has a small chance of living properly."

When employed in factories, women tended to occupy jobs that were viewed as natural extensions of household activity. About half worked in the garment industry, making gloves, hats, and stockings. A government study in the 1880s found that the average weekly wage for a woman working in a major city was $5.24, but weekly expenses for a self-supporting woman were about $5.51. Women were excluded from skilled work and from the professions. Only 5 of the nation's 40,736 lawyers, 67 of 43,874 clergy, and 525 of 62,383 doctors were women in 1870.

The fastest-growing sector of women's employment was in clerical positions as typists and bookkeepers. In 1870 women made up only 3 percent of office workers;

twenty years later they held 17 percent of clerical jobs in the United States. These working "girls" tended to be white, native-born single women, eighteen to twenty-four years old. Corporations and the federal government led the way in hiring women to fill clerical positions. "No invention has opened for women so broad and easy an avenue to profitable and suitable employment as the Type-Writer," E. Remington and Sons, a major manufacturer of the machines, declared in 1875. Department stores also hired women as salesclerks. In 1870 "saleswomen" were too few to be counted in census records. By 1900 they numbered over 142,000.

The dominant view was that a woman did not require a "living wage" because, as one investigator reported, "it is expected that she has men to support her." The

Women Typesetters, 1883   The new economy expanded the number of unskilled and semi-skilled jobs, thus facilitating the entrance of a greater number of women into the work force. With the burgeoning demand for newspapers and printed materials after the Civil War, printing companies hired women to do traditionally male jobs, like typesetting. Fearing that women might work through strikes conducted by their male counterparts, the International Typographical Union began accepting women membership in 1869 and elected a woman as their corresponding secretary the following year, the first woman to hold an office in a national union. While it is unknown whether the women in this picture, working at a press in Kansas, were part of the ITU, they were most likely native-born women who were expected to quit their jobs once they married. *(Kansas State Historical Society.)*

vast majority of Americans firmly believed that a woman's place was in the home, "queen of a little house—no matter how humble—where there are children rolling on the floor." Since many employers assumed that women entered the work force for "pin money" "to decorate themselves beyond their needs and station," they assumed they could pay them less money than they paid men. Unions were often hostile to female workers. "Wherever she goes," a labor official declared in 1900, "she is reducing [man's] wages, and wherever large numbers of women are employed in any occupation, the point will be reached where women get as much as a man by making man's wages as low as a woman's."

The era witnessed another addition to the industrial work force: children. Not only did children work for less pay than adults, but they could work inside delicate machinery where adults could not reach. The number of working children in non-agricultural positions tripled between 1870 and 1900. In 1900 one out of every ten girls and one out of every five boys between the ages of ten and fifteen held jobs. In the South children provided a pool of cheap labor for the region's cotton and woolen mills. In Paterson, New Jersey, about half of all boys and girls aged eleven to fourteen had jobs. In a Chicago candy factory children worked eighty-two hours a

The Hazards of Child Labor The working-class family usually required several of its members' labor in order to make ends meet. Over half a million children under the age of sixteen worked long hours and in dangerous conditions in factories around the nation. Children's poorer coordination and more exuberant natures made them particularly susceptible to injury on the job. This fourteen-year-old in Cincinnati lost his arm to a veneering saw in a box factory. *(University of Maryland Baltimore County.)*

week during the Christmas season. "Poor, puny, weak little children," complained a female spinner in one of Rhode Island's mills, "are kept at work the entire year without intermission of even a month for schooling. The overseers are to them not over kind and sometimes do not hesitate to make them perform more work than the miserable little wretched beings possibly can."

Throughout this period, nearly 75 percent of African-Americans lived in the South and were engaged in agricultural work. The handful who found jobs in the manufacturing sector labored in low-paying, menial occupations. In 1870 Atlanta blacks held over three-fourths of their city's unskilled jobs. Whites moved into comparatively well-paid jobs in cotton mills, while blacks marched off to work in flour mills and tobacco factories. "In this city it is the negroes who do the hard work," admitted a man from Nashville. Even when working at the same job, blacks received lower wages than whites. In 1870 white hands at the Atlanta Rolling Mill earned three dollars a day while blacks received one dollar.

THE HOUSE OF LABOR

In an 1871 address entitled "The Foundation of the Labor Movement," Wendell Phillips, an abolitionist and labor reformer from Massachusetts, enumerated what the workers of America wanted: "short hours, better education, cooperation in the end and, in the meantime, a political movement that will concentrate the thought of the country on this thing." However, organized labor achieved only limited success in focusing the attention of the nation on "this thing." Organizers needed to unite a work force that was deeply divided by geography, race, ethnicity, level of skill, and gender. Initially, labor attempted to challenge the foundation of the industrial order. The rise of the American Federation of Labor (AFL), however, signaled a new experiment in accommodating the industrial system and working within it to achieve incremental reforms.

The Origins of Industrial Unionism

In seeking to form national unions, nineteenth-century labor leaders faced a number of obstacles. First, business leaders opposed unions so vehemently that they were willing to use force to prevent their formation, and they could depend on the courts to favor capital against labor. Second, faith in social mobility and individualism had limited the development of class solidarity among workers in America. After surveying textile workers, officials with the Massachusetts Bureau of the Statistics of Labor reported that most laborers supported unions "in the abstract," but considered local organizations "simply vehicles for the fomentation of incipient riots and disorderly conduct." Finally, the diversity of the work force militated against feelings of labor solidarity. The high proportion of immigrants created divisions by language, ethnic origin, and religion, and both native-born and immigrant laborers refused to associate with blacks. These differences made it easy for employers to play one group off against the other.

The new industrial order, however, provided workers with powerful incentives to unionize. Struggles with employers over wages and working conditions, and especially over reducing the workday to eight hours, inspired union organization in a number of trades. Workers drew on a rich ideological tradition to justify their efforts. Native-born workers tapped into the egalitarian ideals of the American Revolution. At the same time, many immigrants, especially those from Germany, Ireland, and Britain, brought with them more radical notions of class solidarity. The International Workingmen's Association, founded by German immigrants in 1868, set as its goal "the abolition of all class rule."

In 1866 workers took the first steps toward forming a national labor organization when several craft unions and reform groups met in Baltimore to create the National Labor Union (NLU). Claiming three hundred thousand members by the early 1870s, the organization supported a range of causes including temperance, women's rights, and the establishment of cooperatives to bring the "wealth of the land" into "the hands of those who produce it," thus ending "wage slavery." Its central demand, however, was the adoption of a national eight-hour-day law for all workers.

Seeking wide labor support, many NLU leaders supported admitting African-Americans and women. If "workingmen of the white race do not conciliate the blacks, the black vote will be cast against them," observed NLU founder William Sylvis. But most member unions refused to admit blacks, and in 1869 African-American workers, calling their exclusion "an insult to God and injury to us, and disgrace to humanity," formed the separate Colored National Labor Union (CNLU). Most male workers also opposed admission of women to the NLU, claiming that they did not belong in the workplace and their presence depressed male wages.

The depression that began with the Panic of 1873 and continued for more than five consecutive years decimated the NLU. Thousands of workers lost their jobs, and unemployment in cities such as New York ran as high as 33 percent. "The sufferings of the working classes are daily increasing," wrote a harried worker. "Famine has broken into the home of many of us, and is at the door of all." More concerned with survival and relief than with passage of an eight-hour law, industrial workers abandoned their newly formed unions in droves. In New York City, for example, union membership plummeted from forty-five thousand in 1873 to five thousand in 1877.

Union membership declined, but industrial activism increased. The Panic of 1873 ushered in a period of labor strife and turmoil. A wave of railroad strikes swept the nation. When the four railroad barons met to cut wages in March 1877, their purpose was clear: "The great principle upon which we joined to act was to earn more and to spend less," they declared. The outcome was the Great Railway Strike ignited in Martinsburg. As we have seen, in the short run, labor suffered a humiliating defeat: management refused to accept their demands; many demonstrators ended up in jail; and public opinion turned decidedly hostile to the increasingly violent protests. But the confrontation also focused national attention on the legitimate concerns of workers. Determined to avoid future confrontations, railroad executives devoted more time and resources to labor relations.

The Knights of Labor

The Noble Order of the Knights of Labor, a trade union of Philadelphia garment cutters, seized the faltering banner of national unionism. After the strikes of 1877, union leader Uriah S. Stephens promised to organize workers into one "great brotherhood." Trade unions, he complained, were "too narrow in their ideas and too circumscribed in their field of operations." In 1879 the Knights chose Terence V. Powderly as their "Grand Master Workman." Under Powderly's leadership, the Knights opened their ranks to unskilled workers, blacks, immigrants, and women. The Knights demanded the eight-hour day, equal pay for women, and the abolition of child labor, but they rejected the notions that workers constituted a permanent class and that the interests of labor and capital were incompatible. They opposed strikes as "acts of private warfare" and instead emphasized cooperation between labor and management.

With the Knights leading the charge, the labor movement gained new ground. Another economic depression, accompanied by drastic wage cuts, hit in the early 1880s. This time, however, the labor movement capitalized on discontent to achieve spectacular growth. In 1884 militant local unions affiliated with the Knights struck and won a victory against the Union Pacific Railroad. The following year they scored a greater triumph against Southwestern Railroad. Powderly opposed both strikes, but in the wake of the victories against two of the most powerful corporations in America, workers across the country jumped on the bandwagon. By 1886 the Noble Order boasted fifteen thousand local assemblies representing between seven hundred thousand and 1 million members. Nearly 10 percent of the country's nonagricultural work force claimed membership.

Among the workers joining the Knights were large numbers of African-Americans and women. "The colored people of the South are flocking to us," a Knights organizer bragged in the 1880s. In Alabama, West Virginia, and Tennessee, African-American coal miners formed the backbone of the Knights. In 1884, after some initial hesitation, Powderly declared that "women should be admitted on equality with men." By the end of the decade, women made up nearly 10 percent of Knights membership. The organization took a very different approach, however, to Chinese immigrants. Reflecting the prejudice of many white workers, the Knights barred Chinese workers from joining and lobbied for passage of legislation prohibiting Chinese immigration. On the West Coast, which had the country's largest Chinese community, the Knights placed a "white" label on union products.

In 1886 the powerful Knights faced perhaps their greatest challenge when the giant McCormick reaper works locked out its employees in February and reopened the following month with nonunion labor. When police killed two unionists in a May 3 rally, a group of anarchists, who preached the violent overthrow of the capitalist system, called a meeting for the following day "to denounce the latest atrocious act of the police." They chose to meet at the cavernous Haymarket Square—a plaza near downtown Chicago. Rain kept the crowd small—it peaked at perhaps 1,200—and only 330 remained near the end of the rally when a force of 180 policemen arrived and ordered the protesters to disperse. As the police moved in, someone threw a bomb. After the explosion, the police regrouped and charged the crowd, firing guns and swinging clubs. When it ended, a policeman lay dead and 60 people were injured. A local reporter described the scene at Haymarket as one of "wild carnage."

Overnight the shock waves of the Haymarket bombing swept across the country. An outraged middle-class public denounced the anarchist workers as "vipers" and "curs," "hyenas" and "serpents." "The only good anarchist is a dead anarchist," a Cincinnati newspaper judged. Eventually, eight men were tried for the bombing. Despite flimsy evidence, all were convicted. Four were hanged; one committed suicide in jail. In 1893 Illinois governor Peter Altgeld pardoned the three surviving anarchists, claiming that prosecutors never produced evidence of guilt and that the trial had been unfair.

Haymarket broke the momentum of direct labor resistance to the new industrial order for nearly a decade. Though the Knights repudiated the anarchists and had not been involved in the incident, a business propaganda campaign linked trade unionism with anarchy. "The explosion of the bomb on the Haymarket square abruptly ended [the movement]," a government official in Illinois reported. In the second half of 1886 employers locked out some hundred thousand workers. The Knights, helpless to protect their members, lost them in droves. From a peak of 1 million supporters in 1886, membership slipped to five hundred thousand the following year.

The American Federation of Labor (AFL)

The Haymarket incident lent momentum to more conservative trade unionists who objected to the Knights' ambitious social agenda. They believed that the Knights expended too much energy talking about brotherhood and cooperation and not enough fighting for tangible benefits for working people (see Competing Voices, page 727). In December 1886 trade union

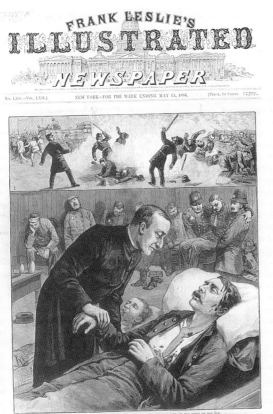

Haymarket Scene from the Cover of *Frank Leslie's Illustrated Newspaper* The bloody incident in Haymarket Square was devastating for labor's public image. Though the protest was initially a peaceful one and the origins of the bomb remain a mystery, the press portrayed the event as a one-sided attack on police. Notice that the crowd on the left side of the top frame is shown fleeing the scene heavily armed with swords. For middle-class Americans, the popularized version of the events was a disturbing commentary on the radical and violent potential of organized labor. *(Library of Congress.)*

representatives met in Columbus, Ohio, and organized the American Federation of Labor. As its name implied, the AFL was a loose federation of skilled trades—cigar makers, ironworkers, carpenters, and others—linked through an executive council to lobby for prolabor national legislation and to offer assistance during strikes.

The new organization reflected the philosophy of Samuel Gompers, who served as president from 1886 until his death in 1924. Born in London in 1850, Gompers emigrated to the United States in 1863 and rose through the ranks of the cigar makers' union. He believed in "pure and simple" unionism, which rejected sweeping assaults on the existing economic system and concentrated on winning concrete benefits: higher wages, shorter hours, and better working conditions. By rejecting the more ambitious political agenda of the Knights and by focusing on bread-and-butter issues of immediate concern to workers, Gompers signaled labor's acceptance of the new wage-labor system and organizers' desire to work within that system. He claimed that his philosophy could be summed up in one word: "More."

Under Gompers's leadership, AFL membership swelled from 140,000 in 1886 to nearly 1 million by 1900. Consisting largely of workers in skilled trades, the AFL made little effort to recruit semiskilled workers in mass-production industries. After a brief and halfhearted attempt, the federation abandoned its efforts to unionize women. The AFL denied that women needed to work for wages. "In our time, and at least in our country, generally speaking," Gompers said in 1905, "there is no necessity of the wife contributing to the support of the family by working." The AFL believed that "the man is the provider" and that women working away from home "bring forth weak children."

Despite the success of the AFL, only a small fraction of American workers belonged to unions. In 1900 only about 1 million of 27.6 million workers were unionized. Most workers were concerned with getting and keeping jobs, not with union organizing. The growing power of big business would continue to test the resolve of American workers, exposing the strengths and limitations of the AFL's brand of unionism.

CONCLUSION

Following the Civil War, the United States began an experiment in industrialization that in a few decades would transform America's economy and society. Economic and technological innovation, including revolutionary improvements in national and global transportation and communications, created a climate in which the nation's vast resources could be harnessed for their industrial potential.

The railroads served as a powerful engine driving America's Industrial Revolution. Construction of thousands of miles of new track linked manufacturers with both resources and consumers, forging a national marketplace and leading to new methods of stimulating and satisfying consumer demand. Other industries expanded operations to meet the railroads' insatiable demands for steel, lumber, and other materials to build track and assemble cars. Finally, railroad managers pioneered the use of new methods for coordinating large organizations, while ruthless businessmen like Jay Gould accumulated vast networks of rail lines.

Although they lionized competition, industrialists took measures to control it. Railroads were the first to experiment with practices designed to limit competition and ensure profits. Their methods of organizing "pools," based on voluntary agreements among industry representatives, seemed primitive compared to the trusts and holding companies that John D. Rockefeller created to seize control of the oil industry. Rockefeller was so successful that dozens of other industrialists followed his example. In the resulting wave of mergers, a handful of powerful business leaders consolidated markets and gained greater control of whole industries.

The American tradition of individual liberty and limited government meshed easily with economic and social doctrines that emphasized competition and individual achievement. In this cultural climate, many Americans accepted the idea that wealth was the just reward for successful competition. Andrew Carnegie extended this idea, arguing that the concentration of wealth and industry among a few proven industrial leaders would benefit society as a whole. Many critics, however, pointed out that the rise of monopoly often strangled the American tradition of individual freedom.

The consolidation experiment confronted the federal government with new questions and new challenges. After some initial hesitation, Washington decided that government had a role to play in limiting the power of trusts and protecting competition in the marketplace. The federal government took its first tentative steps toward regulation with passage of the Interstate Commerce Act (1887), which regulated the railroads, and the Sherman Antitrust Act (1890), which declared trusts illegal. In the short run, neither law had much impact. In the long run, however, these early experiments provided the legal and administrative scaffolding for government regulation in the twentieth century.

American workers experienced the full force of industrialization's impact. By the end of the century the majority of American workers earned wages by toiling in immense, impersonal factories. Management's fascination with principles of scientific management, standardization of work procedures, and tougher discipline contributed to a workplace that was often tedious, repetitive, and dangerous. Many of the new industrial workers were immigrants, and differences in backgrounds often created tension among working people. Families' needs to make a living also forced women and children to join the work force in large numbers. In most cases, they labored under difficult conditions for lower wages than their adult male counterparts.

Workers resisted the hardship of industrialization by forming cooperative alliances, organizing wildcat strikes, and joining unions. In these early years of the labor movement, union organizers faced two central questions: Should working people challenge the foundation of the new industrial order or focus solely on labor issues? And should unions attempt to organize all workers or concentrate on skilled workers who possessed the most power? Both the National Labor Union and the Knights of Labor hoped to build a broad-based reform movement of skilled and unskilled workers to challenge the new industrial order. The American Federation of Labor (AFL), which emerged in 1886 after the decline of the Knights, instead focused on the bread-and-butter issues that were of most concern to its skilled membership. By the end of the century the AFL and its brand of national unionism had emerged as the dominant force in American labor.

Most American workers, however, remained unorganized. Unionizing efforts confronted resistance from business, the courts, and most non–working-class Americans. Workers themselves remained divided by ethnic differences and thought less about joining unions than about their own day-to-day well-being in the new industrial society.

Annotated Suggested Readings

The best recent survey of the economic transformations occurring in the late nineteenth century United States is Walter Licht's *Industrializing America* (1995). *Scale and Scope: The Dynamics of Industrial Capitalism* (1990), by Alfred D. Chandler, Jr., also examines the changes in technology, marketing, and management vital to the growth of industrialization. Maury Klein's *The Flowering of the Third America* (1992) provides a general overview of inventions, the factory system, communication, and the growing class inequality. For an older economic history, see Edward C. Kirkland's *Industry Comes of Age* (1961).

The social impact of technology and the role of culture as an impetus to innovation are the focus of a number of works. Alan I. Marcus and Howard P. Segal's *Technology in America* (1989) traces the impact of American culture on new technology. Carolyn Marvin, *When Old Technologies Were New* (1988), shows how technology reshaped social relations and altered Americans' perception of the world. Focusing on the city of Chicago, Harold L. Platt's *The Electric City* (1991) examines how electricity changed the city itself and how its inhabitants adapted to new machines. Thomas J. Misa traces the production and use of steel in *A Nation of Steel* (1995).

Arguably America's greatest inventor, Thomas Edison is the topic of a number of historical works. Neil Baldwin provides an excellent biography as well as vivid descriptions and drawings of Edison's inventions in *Edison: Inventing the Century* (1995). David E. Nye argues in *Electrifying America* (1990) that Edison's greatest invention was in the production, distribution, and marketing of electricity. Andre Millard's *Edison and the Business of Innovation* (1990) examines how Edison laid the foundation for new industries.

A number of books address the importance of the railroad industry in shaping continued economic growth in the late nineteenth century. David Howard Bains offers the most comprehensive account in *Empire Express: Building the First Transcontinental Railroad* (1999). Also valuable are *The North American Railroad* (1995) by James E. Vance, Jr., and Albro Martin's *Railroads Triumphant* (1992). The unique relationship between the railroads and urbanization is the focus of John R. Stilgoe's *Metropolitan Corridor* (1983). For the life cycle of the railroad worker from recruitment to retirement, see Walter Licht's *Working for the Railroad* (1983).

Editors T. J. Jackson Lears and Richard W. Fox chronicle the rise of America's consumer culture in a series of essays entitled *The Culture of Consumption* (1983). William Leach explores the origins of the consumer culture in *Land of Desire: Merchants, Power, and the Rise of a New American Culture* (1994). Susan Porter Benson looks at the role of department stores in *Counter Cultures* (1986). Stephen Fox's *The Mirror Makers* (1984) and Daniel Pope's *The Making of Modern Advertising* (1983) focus on the development of advertising. The role of businessmen who helped advertisers create mass markets is the subject of Susan Strasser's *Satisfaction Guaranteed: The Making of the American Mass Market* (1989). The impact of the mass market changed the diets of most Americans, according to *Revolution at the Table* (1988) by Harvey A. Levenstein.

The modern business culture that emerged in the last half of the nineteenth century is a topic touched upon by a number of historians. In *Power and Morality* (1980), Saul Engelbourg argues that business ethics improved as a result of publicity and regulation. The ways in which corporate organizations reshaped American culture are analyzed in Alan Trachtenberg's *The Incorporation of America* (1982) and *Colossus: How the Corporation Changed America* (2001). Conflicting versions of America's work ethic serve as the foundation of Daniel T. Rodgers's look at labor conditions and the morality of work in *The Work Ethic in Industrial America* (1978). A number of prominent individuals who rejected the changes in business and work ethics are examined in John L. Thomas's *Alternative America: Henry George, Edward Bellamy, Henry Demarest Lloyd and the Adversary Tradition* (1983).

The management systems developed to operate the new industrial empires are examined in Alfred D. Chandler's *The Visible Hand* (1977). The reasons for business consolidation and the economic impact of these mergers form the framework for Naomi R. Lamoreaux's *The Great Merger Movement in American Business* (1985). Joanne Yates examines how managers implemented new ideas in *Control Through Communication* (1989). Oliver Zunz's *Making America Corporate* (1990) analyzes the relationship between middle-class professionals and the new work culture they created.

Historians have written numerous biographies of the intriguing men behind the rise of big business. Ron Chernow's *The House of Morgan* (1990) examines the creative ways in which the Morgan family made its money. One of the best biographies on John D. Rockefeller, Sr., which seeks to depict the complexities of the oil giant's life rather than presenting the familiar one-dimensional robber baron image, is Ron Chernow's *Titan* (1998). Focusing on Andrew Carnegie's business contributions is Harold Livesay's *Andrew Carnegie and the Rise of Big Business* (2nd ed., 2000).

The changing nature of work and the culture surrounding work are the focus of David Montgomery's *The Fall of the House of Labor* (1987). The changing relationship between employees and employers, intensified by the efficient managerial practices of Frederick W. Taylor, is the topic of Daniel Nelson's *Managers and Workers* (1979). Joshua Rosenbloom looks at industrialization's impact on labor markets in *Looking for Work, Searching for Workers* (2002). Herbert G. Gutman's *Work, Culture, and Society in Industrializing America* (1976) examines the social and cultural values that industrial employees brought to the factory that shaped the nature of their work.

The impact of industrialization on the working class, especially on women, is a common subject for labor and social historians. Melvyn Dubofsky, *Industrialism and the American Worker, 1865–1920* (3rd ed., 1996) remains a standard work. For essays on working women's views on industrial and domestic labor, see Sarah Eisenstein's *Give Us Bread, Give Us Roses* (1983). Alice Kessler-Harris's *Out to Work* (1982) surveys the transformation in women's paid and domestic work. The growing number of women in office jobs is the theme of Margery Davies's *Woman's Place Is at the Typewriter* (1982). Susan E. Kennedy's *If All We Did Was to Weep at Home* (1979) looks at the temporary nature of women's work outside the home and working-class attempts to mirror the middle-class cult of domesticity. For a more recent study of working-class men and women, see the essays in *Work Engendered: Toward a New History of American Labor* (1991), edited by Ava Baron.

Other works have examined the life of the working class both inside the factory and within the home. Herbert Gutman's *Power and Culture* (1987) presents essays concerning nineteenth-century wage earners, immigrants, and freed slaves. In *The Shadow of the Mills* (1989), S. J. Kleinberg describes the familial and individual costs of industrialization on workers in Pittsburgh. Peter R. Shergold compares the living standards of workers in Pittsburgh and Birmingham, England, in *Working Class Life* (1982).

Numerous works deal with the formation of unions to combat the worst aspects of industrialization. Several focus on the rise and fall of the Knights of Labor, among them Robert E. Weir's *Beyond Labor's Veil* (1996). Kim Voss's *The Making of American Exceptionalism* (1993) analyzes the Knights of Labor in the context of union radicalism and its decline as a result of employer counteroffenses. The differences between the Knights of Labor and the American Federation of Labor are explored in Gerald N. Grob's *Workers and Utopia* (1961). A balanced study of Samuel Gompers and his role in shaping the American Federation of Labor is Harold Livesay's *Samuel Gompers and Organized Labor in America* (1978). Attempts by women to unionize are examined in Barbara Mayer Wertheimer's *We Were There* (1977) and Susan Levine's *Labor's True Woman* (1984). The relationship between black factory workers and the unions is described in William H. Harris's *The Harder We Run: Black Workers Since the Civil War* (1982).

The ⓗistory ⓒompanion

Organized Labor

The Constitution of the Knights of Labor

The Knights of Labor, under the leadership of Terence Powderly, adopted its constitution at its 1878 convention in Reading, Pennsylvania. The document expresses the Knights' broad vision for organizing all workers and reforming society as a whole.

The recent alarming development and aggression of aggregated wealth which, unless checked, will invariably lead to the pauperization and hopeless degradation of the toiling masses, render it imperative, if we desire to enjoy the blessings of life, that a check should be placed upon its power and upon unjust accumulation, and a system adopted which will secure to the laborer the fruits of his toil; and as this much-desired object can only be accomplished by the thorough unification of labor, and the united efforts of those who obey the divine injunction that "In the sweat of thy brow shalt thou eat bread," we have formed the [Knights of Labor] with a view of securing the organization and direction, by cooperative effort, of the power of the industrial classes; and we submit to the world the objects sought to be accomplished by our organization, calling upon all who believe in securing "the greatest good to the greatest number" to aid and assist us:—

I. To bring within the folds of organization every department of productive industry, making knowledge a standpoint for action, and industrial and moral worth, not wealth, the true standard of individual and national greatness.

II. To secure to the toilers a proper share of the wealth that they create; more of the leisure that rightfully belongs to them; more societary advantages; more of the benefits, privileges, and emoluments of the world. . . .

IV. The establishment of cooperative institutions, productive and distributive.

V. The reserving of the public lands—the heritage of the people—for the actual settler; —not another acre for railroads or speculators.

VI. The abrogation of all laws that do not bear equally upon capital and labor. . . .

X. The substitution of arbitration for strikes, whenever and wherever employers and employes [sic] are willing to meet on equitable grounds.

XI. The prohibition of employment of children in workshops, mines and factories before attaining their fourteenth year. . . .

XIII. To secure for both sexes equal pay for equal work.

XIV. The reduction of the hours of labor to eight per day. . . .

It is intended by the Knights of Labor to supersede the wage system by a system of industrial cooperation, productive and distributive.

Samuel Gompers on the American Federation of Labor

In the first selection, Gompers, a founding member of the AFL and its first president, recounts the formation of the organization out of the conflicting aims of the Knights of Labor and the trade unions. The second selection is from Gompers's testimony before the Senate Education and Labor Committee in August 1883. He explains why he supports strikes and believes that arbitration will not succeed until workers achieve economic and organizational power.

After my initiation of the [Knights of Labor] in the seventies, I heard of it now and then but never as a substitute for trade unions. With the eighties, when it abandoned complete secrecy, it grew much more rapidly. . . .

[F]riction [soon began] developing over K. of L. encroachments on trade union functions. The two movements were inherently different. Trade unions endeavored to organize for collective responsibility persons with common trade problems. They sought economic betterment in order to place in the hands of wage-earners the means to wider opportunities. The Knights of Labor was a social or fraternal organization. It was based upon a principle of cooperation and its purpose was reform. . . .

The struggle between the trade unions and the K. of L. was at high tide when I assumed the task of making the American Federation of Labor something more than a paper organization. . . .

My earliest official efforts were concentrated in promoting stability of labor organizations. This had to be done by making the idea an inseparable part of the thought and habits of trade unionists by establishing a business basis for unionism and then driving home the fallacy of low dues. Cheap unionism cannot maintain effective economic activity. Sustained office work and paid union officials for administrative work have become the general practice since the Federation was organized. A big service of the Federation has been in crystallizing and unifying labor thought and practice. . . .

Economic betterment—today, tomorrow, home and shop—was the foundation upon which trade unions have been built. Economic power is the basis upon which may be developed power in other fields. It is the foundation of organized society. Whoever or whatever controls economic power directs and shapes development for the group or the nation. Because I early grasped this fundamental truth, I was never deluded or led astray by rosy theory or fascinating plan that did not square with my fundamental.

While I am in the labor movement and take a stand opposed to strikes whenever they can be avoided, I have no sympathy with, nor can I endorse or echo, the statement of many men who are too ready to condemn strikes. Strikes have their evils but they have their good points also, and with proper management, with proper organization, strikes do generally result to the advantage of labor, and in very few instances do they result in injury to the workingmen, whether organized or unorganized. . . .

Strikes ought to be, and in well-organized trades unions they are, the last means which workingmen resort to to protect themselves against the almost never satisfied greed of the employers. Besides this, the strike is, in many instances, the only remedy within our reach as long as legislation is entirely indifferent to the interests of labor.

By the late 1870s industrialization had drawn clear battle lines between labor and capital, and the former seemed to be losing the war. An economic depression had settled over the country, hitting those at the bottom of the socioeconomic ladder the hardest and eroding what little force workers possessed in the face of increasing corporate power. As the independent artisan gave way to the assembly line, workers increasingly felt like cogs in the industrial machine, stripped of their autonomy.

The apparent solution to the dilemma of the industrial worker was to confront organized capital with organized labor. The Knights of Labor was the first relatively successful attempt at assembling workers in a national body. But under Terence Powderly, the Knights became a reform movement that sought to bind together all the "productive classes"—workers and farmers, regardless of skill, sex, or race, and even some employers—to build a society that embodied economic cooperation, equality of opportunity, and the virtues of hard work. The Knights worked not just for broad economic change but also pressed government for political and moral reforms, such as women's suffrage and the prohibition of alcohol.

Samuel Gompers found the Knights' high ideals and pursuit of broad reform impractical. Whereas Powderly glossed over class conflict, Gompers insisted that workers and their employers had fundamentally different interests. Unless wage workers organized separately and defended themselves, they would be exploited. While the Knights disapproved of strikes, Gompers believed that until workers could improve their overall economic position, strikes were often "the only means whereby the rightful demands of labor can be secured." He accepted that the industrial order was here to stay; workers must now fight for what they might realistically achieve, the bread-and-butter issues, instead of sweeping reform. He also more clearly understood that only a tightly controlled organization of skilled workers could challenge corporate power. Progress for a select group of laborers was better than no progress at all.

The Knights of Labor and the American Federation of Labor represented two different conceptions of modern America. One remained optimistic that the industrial order could be reconciled to traditional values and molded into a cooperative society; the other recognized that industrialization had divided the parties into opposing camps in a cutthroat battle for economic gain. The AFL achieved its goals by limiting them, and the Knights died out with the last vestiges of an older America.

QUESTIONS FOR ANALYSIS

1. What are the aims of the Knights of Labor?

2. What primary methods does their constitution propose for achieving them?

3. What does the slogan "the greatest good to the greatest number" say about the Knights' values?

4. What are the aims of the AFL?

5. What are the methods Gompers proposes?

6. What does Gompers's endorsement of striking say about his view of American society?

7. Can you think of any recent issues over which idealists and pragmatists divided in seeking similar goals?

19

The New Urban Nation

1865–1910

"From the other end of the earth from where I came,
America was a land of living hope, woven of dreams,
aflame with longing and desire."

Like the millions of other immigrants who left their homelands and traveled to America around the turn of the century, Anzia Yezierska longed for a better life. "From the other end of the earth from where I came," she recalled, "America was a land of living hope, woven of dreams, aflame with longing and desire." Born in Poland in the 1880s, Yezierska traveled to America with her poor parents and eight siblings, arriving in New York sometime in the early 1890s. Like many other Jews from eastern Europe, she and her family settled into a crowded tenement apartment on Manhattan's Lower East Side.

Over the next few years Yezierska survived by working long hours in a local sweatshop. "While the morning was still dark I walked into a dark basement," she remembered. "And darkness met me when I turned out of the basement." In addition to the challenge of making enough money to pay rent and buy food, Yezierska struggled to assimilate to American society. She enrolled in English classes and joined a local women's association, but she still felt estranged from America. "Between my soul and the American soul were worlds of difference that no words could bridge over," she reflected. But one day she had a revelation: "I saw that it was the glory of America that it was not yet finished," she realized. "And I, the last comer, had her share to give, small or great, to the making of America."

Newcomers who flooded American cities at the end of the nineteenth century presented the nation with new challenges and great opportunities. Industrialization and migration were intrinsically linked. As immigrants crowded into a handful of cities where unskilled factory positions were available, local governments were overwhelmed by a host of new problems: crowded living arrangements, poor sanitation, intense poverty. When established institutions proved unresponsive, many immigrants turned to neighborhood social institutions and powerful political machines to help ease the transition to their new lives. The presence of so many new migrants combined with industrial development and innovations in transportation altered the size and shape of American cities. Immigrants also created a dynamic urban culture, a "democracy of amusement" that would transform the cultural landscape in America. Not everyone welcomed urbanization and its social experiments. The last quarter of the nineteenth century witnessed a potent backlash against immigrants and the emerging urban culture.

- What impact did the flood of new immigrants have on urban life in the last quarter of the nineteenth century?

- How did changes in transportation and improvements in technology influence the geography of the city?

- How did urban life influence American culture and identity?

- Why did many middle-class Protestants find the city threatening, and what did they do about it?

This chapter will address these questions.

THE BIRTH OF THE MODERN CITY

"We live in the age of great cities," the Reverend Samuel Lane Loomis informed his seminary students in 1886. "Each successive year finds a stronger and more irresistible current sweeping in toward the centres of life." The entire Western world was swept up in the current. In 1850, 25 percent of French citizens were living in cities; by 1911 it was 44 percent. Germany saw an increase from 30 percent to 60 percent. The most dramatic transformation, however, took place in the United States. "The age of great cities" created new opportunities, but it also produced unprecedented problems of congestion, sanitation, crime, and vice that vexed public officials. Urban political bosses undertook some public safety and sanitation measures while lining their own pockets, but improvements seldom reached the working-class bulk of city populations.

City People: Migrants and Immigrants

The number of people living in the United States tripled between 1860 and 1920, from 31 million to over 105 million. During that same period, however, the number of people living in American cities increased ninefold, from 6 to 54 million (see figure on page 732). In 1860 only New York, Philadelphia, and Brooklyn had more than 250,000 residents. By 1890 eleven cities, all except San Francisco located in the East and upper Midwest, had surpassed that size. By 1900 almost 40 percent of Americans lived in cities, and the 1920 census showed that for the first time more than half the U.S. population resided in urban communities. "We cannot all live in cities," a newspaper commented, "yet nearly all seem determined to do so." Some of the figures are astonishing: Between 1860 and 1920 New York's population exploded from 800,000 to 5.5 million. Chicago, the second-most-populous city, grew from 100,000 to 2.7 million. A flood of migrants transformed Los Angeles from a sleepy town of 5,700 in 1870 to a thriving metropolis of over 600,000 by 1920.

Many new city residents were rural laborers pushed off the land by economic hardship and drawn to the city by the prospect of jobs and a better life. Mechanization not only reduced the number of people necessary to harvest crops but also flooded the market with surplus product, which in turn led to lower prices and a declining quality of life for many farmers. A less tangible but important lure for migrants was the glitter of city life. Rural people accustomed to the social and cultural isolation of farms were dazzled by the excitement of the shops, theaters, restaurants, churches, and department stores of the urban scene. Kansas City, noted a rural migrant, was a "gilded metropolis" filled with "marvels," a veritable "round of joy." As a result, between 1870 and 1920, 11 million Americans left the farm for the city.

Rural southern blacks also fed the migratory stream into northern industrial cities. Between 1900 and 1920 nearly 750,000 African-Americans fled the discrimination and terrorism of the South and traveled north in search of greater freedom and new economic opportunities. In 1900 thirty-two cities reported more than 10,000 African-American inhabitants. By 1920 almost 85 percent of blacks living outside the South lived in urban areas. The black populations of New York, Philadelphia, and Chicago surpassed 100,000.

Despite their native-born status, African-Americans who sought industrial employment ran up against exclusion by employers who preferred to hire from the mass of European immigrants flooding the country. Cheaper and better transportation made the great tide of immigration possible, but dissatisfaction with conditions

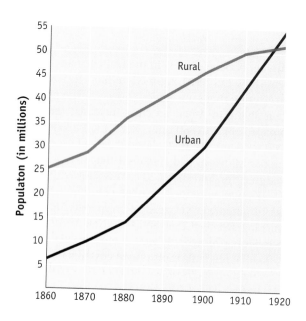

Rural and Urban Population, 1860–1920   Thanks to natural increase and immigration, the American population rose dramatically between 1860 and 1920. Railroad hubs, trade centers, and towns conveniently located near natural resources were transformed into major metropolitan areas as people sought better job opportunities. While cities along the East Coast remained the most heavily populated in the nation, urban centers across the country, including Omaha, Denver, and Portland, could boast that they were home to over 100,000 people by 1920. That year's census report indicated that for the first time more American lived in areas considered "urban" than in rural regions.

CHRONOLOGY

1862	Morrill Act gives land to states for colleges
1868	First women's club, Sorosis, established
1869	Boss Tweed gains control of New York's political machine
1871	The Great Chicago Fire
1873	First cable cars operate in San Francisco
1874	Women's Christian Temperance Union (WCTU) organized Chautauqua education program launched
1876	National League of Professional Baseball Clubs organized
1880	Salvation Army begins work in New York
1882	Chinese Exclusion Act
1883	Pulitzer buys *New York World*
1884	Twain publishes *The Adventures of Huckleberry Finn*
1885	Safety bicycle invented
1887	Members of the St. Louis Browns refuse to play an all-black baseball club American Protection Association founded
1888	First electric trolley line completed in Richmond, Virginia
1891	Basketball invented
1895	Anti-Saloon League formed Coney Island amusement park opens in Brooklyn
1896	First motion picture shown in New York's Koster and Bial Theatre
1897	First subway constructed in Boston
1900	Proportion of Americans living in cities nears 40 percent
1902	Macy's opens in New York
1913	Woolworth Building completed in New York

at home, plus expectations of better opportunities in America, sparked most decisions to leave. Overpopulation, unemployment, famine, and chronic and epidemic diseases drove many from their homelands as part of the largest global migration in history. In other cases, new agricultural techniques led landlords to consolidate their lands and farming operations, thereby evicting long-time tenants. Government policies pushed others to leave. In eastern Europe, especially in Russia, the official persecution of minorities led millions of Jewish families to emigrate. While they were pushed by many different forces, nearly all the new immigrants were pulled by the demand for unskilled labor. America's emerging industrial empire required a large pool of cheap labor. Speculators and steamship lines eager to promote business advertised exaggerated tales of an America whose streets were "paved with gold." Although jobs proved disappointing, most immigrants remained in the United States. However, a considerable number, approximately 30 percent, returned to Europe, unable to establish themselves in America or preferring to use what they had earned in the United States to create a better life in their home country.

Whether residents were permanent or temporary, immigration figures were staggering. During the forty years before the Civil War, 5 million immigrants poured into the United States to seek their fortunes. From 1860 to 1900 almost 14 million arrived. In 1882 alone nearly 789,000 people came. By 1890 about 15 percent of the population, 9 million people, were foreign-born. In the first decade of the new century, almost 6.3 million immigrants entered the United States—more than 1.3 million in 1907 alone. In that year, Ellis Island, which opened in 1892 and quickly became America's busiest immigration station, processed an average of 5,000 new immigrants a day.

The first wave of immigrants came ashore in the mid-1800s and hailed from Britain and Ireland, Germany, and Scandinavia. Irish and Germans were the largest groups. Also between 1850 and 1882, more than three hundred thousand Chinese entered the United States, settling mostly in the West. Then the pattern slowly began to change. By 1890 Irish, English, Germans, and Scandinavians made up only 60 percent of all immigrants, while "new immigrants" from southern and eastern Europe (Italy, Poland, Russia, Austria, Hungary, Greece, Turkey, and Syria) made up most of the rest. Italian Catholics, followed by Slavs and eastern European Jews, were the most numerous. Between 1876 and 1930 more than 5 million Italians and 2 million Jews settled in the United States. The Slavic groups—which included Russians, Ukrainians, Slovaks, Slovenes, Poles, Croatians, Serbs, and Bulgarians—accounted for about 4 million new arrivals (see figure on page 735).

Except in the South, immigrants dominated the populations of the nation's major cities. Most of the new urban residents settled in the nation's industrial core, which stretched south from Massachusetts to Maryland and westward to Illinois, southern Wisconsin, and eastern Missouri. By 1920 this region claimed sixteen of the twenty-five largest cities, and nine of the top ten. In 1920 more than 80 percent of all Irish, Russian, Italian, and Polish immigrants lived in cities, and nearly two-thirds of all immigrants resided in urban areas. Nearly 90 percent of Chicagoans were first- or second-generation immigrants by 1880. In New York, Milwaukee, Detroit, and St. Louis, the figure was about 80 percent. New York City, where most immigrants arrived and many stayed, was home to more Italians than lived in Naples, more Germans than lived in Hamburg, and twice as many Irish as lived in Dublin. In 1916, 72 percent of people living in San Francisco spoke a foreign language.

Immigrant Communities   Ethnic groups frequently traveled to the United States in a series of migratory chains made up of relatives and friends, often from the same neighborhood or village in the old country. Relatives and friends who had emigrated sent back instructions on where to make steamship and railroad connections, advice on where to live and work, and

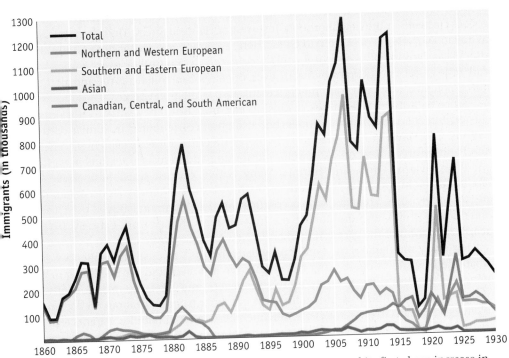

Immigration, 1860–1930   In the 1880s, America experienced its first sharp increase in immigration since the Civil War as a result of new jobs created by industrialization and unsatisfactory conditions in Europe. In the last decades of the nineteenth century the United States also saw a shift in the national origin of immigrants as the number of people from southern and eastern Europe climbed, surpassing the number of northern and western European immigrants after 1895. The overall immigration rate peaked in the early twentieth century before dropping dramatically at the start of World War I. The resumption of immigration after the war directly influenced the passage of the Immigration Act of 1924.

money for the passage to America. More than half of the Italians who settled in Cleveland before World War I, for example, came from a handful of villages in southern Italy.

Once in America, immigrants tried to recreate their sense of community, forming urban enclaves with a wide range of support institutions and associations. New York's Lower East Side, Boston's North End, Chicago's West Side, and Los Angeles's east-side *barrio* were home to close-knit concentrations of immigrants. These domains provided newcomers with supportive communities and familiar customs as they adjusted to the strangeness of American urban society. Journalist Jacob Riis claimed that a map of New York City in 1890 "coloured to designate nationality, would show more stripes than on the skin of a zebra, and more colours than any rainbow." Czech immigrants living in the Pilsen district on Chicago's West Side attended church services conducted in Czech, ate at Czech restaurants, and read Czech-language newspapers. Not far away, near the corner of Halstead and Maxwell Streets, more than

90 percent of the residents were Jewish, as evidenced by the forty Orthodox synagogues clustered in the neighborhood. Just west of Halstead Street, Yiddish gave way to Italian and, a few blocks later, to Greek. Here, according to a visitor, "practically all stores bear signs in both Greek and English, coffee houses flourish on every corner, in dark little grocery stores one sees black olives, dried ink-fish, tomato paste, and all the queer, nameless roots and condiments which are so familiar in Greece."

Since they depended on ties of kinship and friendship, new arrivals not only clustered in the same neighborhoods, but also often concentrated in similar occupations. The Slavic groups were heavily represented in Chicago's slaughterhouses and Pennsylvania's steel mills, as well as in mining and industrial regions in western Pennsylvania, Ohio, and Illinois. Many Greeks opened small businesses. A reporter noted in 1904 that "practically every busy corner in Chicago is occupied by a Greek candy store." Italians, who accounted for more common laborers than any other ethnic group, also dominated the fruit business in New York City. By 1916 nearly 70 percent of the garment workers in New York City were Jews.

For many immigrants the family provided a bulwark against the challenges of urban life. The strains of adapting to a strange environment and the need to earn a living forced family members to mute differences and stress cooperation. The nuclear family remained the model for most immigrants. In 1905 about 95 percent of Jews and Italians in New York City were members of intact families. Parents exercised considerable power over the career paths of their children, often forcing boys and girls to leave school early to work. Among unskilled German immigrants in Detroit, 66 percent of young men and 43 percent of teenage girls worked outside the home. "When you work, you understand, you used to bring your pay home and give it to your parents," recalled an immigrant. "And whatever they feel they want to give you, they decide. There was no disagreement." Girls faced the added responsibility of performing household chores and caring for younger siblings. While children worked outside the home, married women focused their attention on their roles as wives, mothers, and homemakers. A survey of immigrant families in Chicago in 1900 revealed that only 2 percent of wives worked outside the home.

For many newcomers, the traditions and rituals of the church served as the critical cultural link to the Old World. Immigrants who may never have attended services in the old country joined churches and synagogues for social as well as spiritual support. Churches celebrated important events—births, deaths, and weddings—and fellow church members offered assistance during times of unemployment. Many religious institutions established social services such as welfare organizations, hospitals, and orphanages. In many communities, incoming Catholic ethnic groups clashed with established church authorities, insisting that priests conduct services in parishioners' native languages and that churches honor distinctive cultural practices and local patron saints of immigrants' former villages. German, Polish, and Irish Catholics, for example, organized their own parishes and built separate church buildings. Jewish immigrants from eastern Europe, who objected to the more liberal German-American Reform Judaism, formed their own Orthodox synagogues.

In addition, most newcomers created mutual aid societies to provide financial security and cultural autonomy. Usually organized by men from the same town in the old country, the societies collected modest dues from their members to bankroll a fund for aiding needy families. By 1910 seven thousand such aid societies were serving nearly two-thirds of Polish immigrants in America. Many immigrant groups set up loan societies to help budding entrepreneurs. Jews founded thousands of free-loan societies, while Chinese communities aided small businesses through the *woi*, a family loan society. Though founded to provide social insurance, societies often evolved into male social clubs.

The saloon also played a central role for immigrants in the modern city. A 1900 survey of Chicago found over five hundred saloons serving the 120,000 working-class residents of the stockyards district. The nearby middle-class neighborhood of Hyde Park contained only twenty-one drinking establishments for its 65,000 residents. In saloons patrons enjoyed a break from the harsh demands of everyday life. They played cards, discussed politics, exchanged tips on jobs, and held union or fraternal meetings. Saloons provided the only free public toilets in the city, and many offered their customers free lunch and newspapers. Many saloonkeepers also cashed checks and loaned money to regulars.

The Transportation Revolution

The influx of new immigrants coincided with dramatic changes in transportation. Before 1825 no city in America possessed a mass-transit system, so the physical expansion of the city was limited to walking distances, usually about 2 miles from the city center. As a result, the "walking city" was compact and congested. Most of the city's inhabitants—African-Americans, immigrants, and native-born white workers—clustered near the waterfront in houses and tenements. Wealthy people established separate neighborhoods, but they too lived in the city center, close to their places of business. Owners, managers, and workers not only lived near one another, but they also set up residences close to their common places of work.

Innovations in urban mass transit revolutionized the nature of the walking city. In the 1830s many cities began experimenting with the horse-drawn omnibus. The omnibus, which traveled over a fixed route and charged a daily fare of between six and twelve cents, became a standard feature in large cities by the 1850s. In 1853 New York operated seven hundred twelve-passenger omnibuses that transported 120,000 passengers a day. The carriages were often crowded, and the ride was noisy and bumpy. "Modern martyrdom may be succinctly defined as riding in a New York omnibus," the *New York Herald* complained in 1864. In the mid-1850s many cities switched to the horse railway, in which omnibuses rolled on rails. By the mid-1880s more than three hundred cities were operating 525 horsecar lines, which offered a faster and smoother ride than the older omnibus. In 1873 San Francisco introduced the cable car, which was pulled by an underground chain and was especially useful in hilly cities. By the mid-1890s residents rolled along some 626 miles of cable-car track in over twenty American cities, led by Chicago's more than 86 miles of track.

The electrification of the street railways, however, represented the most significant innovation in urban transportation in the nineteenth century. Electric streetcars, or trolleys, were faster, were more reliable, and covered greater distances than either horsecars or cable-car systems. By 1900 most cities had replaced their horse-powered cars with new electric streetcars. In 1890, for example, Pittsburgh had 13 miles of electrified track carrying 46.3 million passengers. By 1902 the steel city boasted 470 miles of track that transported 168.6 million riders. Nationwide that year trolleys carried more than 2 billion urban passengers on 22,000 miles of electrified track. Electrification also allowed engineers to develop mass-transit systems above and below the ground. In the 1880s Brooklyn, Boston, Philadelphia, Kansas City, and Chicago built elevated lines. In 1897 Boston became the first city to construct a subway system, with New York (1904) and Philadelphia (1908) not far behind.

Mass transit, especially the electric trolley, fundamentally altered the social and economic fabric of American metropolitan areas by extending the outer reach of urban settlement. In 1850 Boston extended about 2 miles outward from city hall. By 1900 it had spread more than 6 miles. Initially streetcar lines were built to existing areas on the fringe of the city, which allowed small towns to develop into large communities. In 1886 President Grover Cleveland purchased a country house in the underdeveloped outskirts northwest of Georgetown in Washington, D.C. Within a few

Electric Cars of New Orleans   In nineteenth-century urban transportation, nothing transformed the urban landscape like the electric streetcar. Rail lines and their electric wires lined the streets of downtown districts, as seen in this picture of Canal Street in 1890, and stretched out in each direction toward the urban fringe where "streetcar suburbs" developed. Major thoroughfares were often crowded and dangerous as pedestrians, horse-drawn wagons, trolleys, and later automobiles shared the streets together. This congesti   led many cities, like New York and Boston, to construct underground transportatic   stems.   *(Library of Congress.)*

years, however, a trolley line transformed the area into the booming community of Cleveland Park. In city after city, the homeowners moved along the trolley tracks.

For the white middle class, the suburbs offered the best of both worlds: easy access to the business district but safe distance from downtown congestion, dirt, and crime. Advertisers and land developers played to both concerns with claims like, "Those who wish to secure a quiet home sufficiently remote from the city to be out of its turbulence and yet within a convenient business distance had better seek out North New York." The appeals seemed to work. Between 1900 and 1915 the population of Manhattan increased by 16 percent, but the population of the borough of Queens surged 160 percent.

As mass transit made the suburbs accessible to the middle class, new construction techniques made single-family homes affordable. The balloon-frame house, introduced in the 1830s, used an inexpensive interior wood frame joined by nails, which required fewer workers and simpler tools than older homes, with their exterior masonry walls and complicated joints. The new structure put single-unit homes within financial reach of middle-income families and fueled the exodus to the suburbs.

Historian Kenneth Jackson claims that the rise of suburbs "represented the most fundamental realignment of urban structure in the 4,500-year past of cities on this planet." As the wealthy and the middle class abandoned the central district of the city as a place of residence, they left behind the poor and racial minorities. The process of suburbanization, which would intensify later in the century, led to a widening physical and social gap between rich and poor and a hardening of racial division in America.

City Neighborhoods   With the physical expansion of the city and the rise of suburbs, urban areas developed distinctive identities. Downtown business and shopping districts provided the economic nucleus of modern cities. To attract a largely middle-class female clientele, retailers clustered together large department stores designed to make shopping both convenient and pleasant. Manhattan located its finest stores along Broadway and Fifth and Sixth Avenues. In Chicago shoppers and tourists could wander up and down State Street, peering in the windows at the cornucopia of consumer goods. New York's Macy's store, offering twenty-three and a half acres of consumer goods, a restaurant, and elaborate floor displays, opened its doors in 1902. Five years later Marshall Field opened a similar shopping emporium in Chicago. Luxury hotels sprouted to accommodate business travelers and wealthy shoppers. A newspaper noted in 1897 that guests at New York City's Astoria Hotel "will be lodged and fed amid surroundings as gorgeous as those of king's palaces."

Demand for more space for managing, marketing, and financing the new industrial corporations and their products combined with technological innovation to push cities upward as well as outward. The church spire had dominated the skyline of preindustrial cities, but after the 1850s the invention of the elevator and the use of iron, rather than masonry, for structural support enabled the construction of buildings more than a few stories in height. As the Bessemer process made steel cheaper, architects began using the material to construct strong skeletons for their buildings, providing more open space on each floor and allowing the structure to rise still higher into the sky. By the early twentieth century the skyscraper, or "cloudscraper" as contemporaries sometimes called it, had altered the urban skyline. Skyscrapers turned streets in New York into caverns. The Woolworth Building, completed in 1913, stood fifty-five stories high, soared 760 feet into the air, and ranked as the tallest building in the world until surpassed by the Chrysler Building (1929) and then the Empire State Building (1931).

A cluster of diverse neighborhoods ringed the central business district, their residents' standings in the social hierarchy measured by their distance from the city's growing industrial plants. The jewel in every city's crown was the area of large mansions and manicured grounds that housed its wealthiest citizens and separated them from the most congested and factory-adulterated parts of town. In New York the barons of American industry—Astors, Goulds, Fricks, Whitneys, and Carnegies—lined Fifth Avenue. Boston's economic elite preferred Back Bay, while Philadelphia's most prominent families chose Rittenhouse Square. Mining magnate William Clark's New York mansion contained 130 rooms, and the Whitney residence, just a few blocks away, included a seventeenth-century ballroom and eleven marble bathtubs.

Although opulent mansions were out of their reach, members of the new urban middle class earned enough money to purchase houses in the suburbs or rent comfortable apartments. The Industrial Revolution had swelled the ranks of the middle class, which now included a variety of managerial, technical, clerical, and public service workers in addition to the traditional professionals and businesspeople. The number of white-collar workers increased from 374,433 in 1870 to 3.2 million in 1910.

Living conditions were least comfortable for the city's poor and working-class residents. Lacking the money to commute daily by trolley, they had to live packed in close to the factories and mills, often the most polluted areas of the city. In 1890 in New York, 1 million people, two-thirds of the population, were packed into thirty-two thousand tenement buildings. Conditions were particularly bad on the Lower East Side, the section of Manhattan east of Third Avenue and south of Fourteenth Street. As historian Kenneth Jackson has noted, the Lower East Side at the turn of the century had "the highest recorded density of population in world history." Some parts of Chicago had three times as many people as the most crowded parts of Tokyo and Calcutta.

Urban tenement houses were generally congested and filthy. The first tenement house of record was erected on Water Street in New York City in 1833. By 1867 more than eighteen thousand shabby tenements had sprung up in the city. Built on long but narrow lots of 15 by 100 feet, most tenements were four to six stories in height, with four separate apartments on each floor. Since many tenants shared apartments, a single building would often house as many as 150 people. The tenement, Lewis Mumford wrote in *Sticks and Stones* (1924), "raised bad housing into an art." Residents crammed into tiny rooms barely 8 feet wide, with poor ventilation and no heat, bathrooms, or kitchens. A New York housing inspector investigating odors emanating from a tenement found the "entire cellar floor covered with a putrid slime; imbedded therein were various kinds of organic matter in every stage of decomposition, together with dead cats, dead rats, and the skeleton remains of several small animals."

Most cities also contained vice districts and skid row neighborhoods, which served as home to prostitutes, gamblers, pimps, and society's outcasts. Most of

Chicago's gambling houses, dance halls, pawnshops, and brothels were concentrated in the Levee. New York's Tenderloin, San Francisco's Barbary Coast, and New Orleans's Storyville were among the best-known red-light districts. Within a few miles of the gilded quarters of the wealthy, the city's poorest residents lived in cheap lodging-house slums, with five-cent-a-night flophouses. A middle-class observer who spent a night in Chicago's skid row claimed that "the animalism and despicable foulness and filth made one almost despair of mankind." Chicago estimated its transient down-and-out population at thirty thousand, and every major city counted thousands who endured similar hardship.

Still, the makeup of urban neighborhoods changed constantly. In a ten-year period between 1905 and 1915 nearly two-thirds of the Jews living on New York's Lower East Side left, migrating to other, less-congested parts of the city. In urban neighborhoods across the country, Italians were giving way to Greeks, Irish to Poles, and Germans to Czechs. In most cities, however, racism prevented African-Americans from participating in this ritual of residential mobility. In 1908 the white residents of Chicago's fashionable Hyde Park organized to prevent blacks from moving into their neighborhood. "The districts which are now white must remain white,"

Chicago Tenement Scene   Tenements housed many families in crowded and unsanitary conditions. Residents slept, ate, cooked, cleaned, and sometimes worked in a few small, cramped rooms they shared with their extended families, and even boarders. This picture of a mother and two of her children suggests the multitude of tasks performed in a single room and the lack of space in which to live and raise a family.   *(Chicago Historical Society.)*

pronounced a local leader. Within a few years, a number of cities—Baltimore, Louisville, Atlanta, Richmond, Dallas, and New Orleans—passed laws making it illegal for blacks to move into white neighborhoods. In 1917 the Supreme Court declared residential segregation ordinances unconstitutional, but most cities found informal methods to achieve the same end.

The Urban Environment   Urban residents were assaulted daily by the stench of human and animal waste and the noise of clattering cable cars and trolleys. Journalist H. L. Mencken recalled that his hometown of Baltimore smelled "like a billion polecats." One reason was horse manure. In a city such as Milwaukee, a horse population of 12,500 deposited up to 133 tons of manure every day. In 1900 health officials in Rochester, New York, estimated that if they stacked all the manure produced by the city's 15,000 horses in a single day, it would rise 175 feet in the air, cover an acre of land, and breed 16 billion flies.

Another source of odor was the privy, "a single one of which," noted a city health official, "may render life in a whole neighborhood almost unendurable in the summer." In 1877 Philadelphia had 82,000 cesspools. The census of 1880 reported that the soil of New Orleans was saturated "very largely with the oozings of foul privy vaults." A middle-class visitor to a city slum wrote, "Look up, look down, turn this way, turn that—there is no prospect but the unkempt and the disorderly, the slovenly and the grim; filth everywhere, trampled on the sidewalks, lying in windows, collected in the eddies of doorsteps."

Most cities simply dumped what little waste they collected in the nearest body of water. New York, Boston, and Chicago installed underground sewers to carry wastes into nearby oceans or lakes. By 1916 New York City was dumping nearly 500 million gallons of raw sewage a day into the Hudson and East Rivers. In most cases, the polluted waters also served as the main source for the city's drinking water. In 1870 no city had a filtration system, and by 1900 only 6 percent of the urban population received filtered water. Pittsburgh waited until its death rate from typhoid fever reached four times the national average before constructing a public filter system.

Other infectious diseases, too, found breeding grounds in squalid city neighborhoods. Two thousand Philadelphians died from smallpox in 1870. Other cities, including Chicago, Boston, Baltimore, and Washington, suffered similar epidemics. The problem was especially acute in southern cities, which could not depend on the winter chill to kill vermin and retard the putrefaction of garbage. In just one year, 1873, Memphis suffered three major epidemics—yellow fever, smallpox, and cholera—that infected one-fourth of the city's population and killed thousands. "The deaths grew daily more numerous," claimed a witness; "funerals blocked the way."

Since most cities lacked building codes or professional fire departments, the threat of fire was as great as the risk of fever. Successive fires in the 1870s took enormous tolls of life and property. Fire swept through Boston's business district in 1872 and destroyed hundreds of buildings. Chicago survived the most spectacular fire of the century. The 1871 inferno destroyed over seventeen thousand buildings and left 150,000 people homeless. Personal ads appeared in the paper as people tried to find loved ones: "Henry Schneider, baby, in blue poland waist, red skirt, has white hair. Lost."

The influx of millions of immigrants combined with intense poverty to produce soaring crime rates. "Crime was never so bold, so frequent, and so safe as it is this winter," complained a frustrated New Yorker in 1870. "We breathe an atmosphere of highway robbery, burglary, and murder. Few criminals are caught, and fewer punished." The nation's homicide rate nearly tripled in the 1880s, much of the increase coming in the cities. Gangs of urban youths, frustrated by privation, roamed the streets. The Hayes Valley gang terrorized residents of San Francisco, while the Baxter Street Dudes, the Daybreak Boys, and the Alley Gang menaced New Yorkers. In 1900 the *Chicago Tribune* estimated that murders and homicides nationally had climbed from 1,266 in 1881 to 7,340 in 1898, or from about 25 per million people to over 107 per million.

Many cities responded to the new problems by creating housing commissions, professional firefighting and police forces, and regulatory codes designed to improve the quality of urban life. In the 1880s and 1890s the widespread recognition of the germ theory of disease led many state and municipal boards to enact new measures to protect public health. Building codes required firewalls and professional firefighting departments. City governments purchased steam engines and pumping machinery to battle blazes. Despite the notable progress, a strong tradition of privatism and a reluctance to assert municipal authority limited the effort to respond to the growing public need for a clean, safe environment. In most cities, landlords who wanted sewer and water in their buildings, for example, had to pay for the connections from the street, passing the costs onto already hard-pressed residents. Occupants of crowded buildings in poor neighborhoods who needed better sanitation the most were the least likely to be able to afford it.

City Politics

The growth of the American city presented unprecedented problems for urban government, which remained weak and fragmented. *Harper's Weekly* noted in 1857 that New York City had become "a huge semi-barbarous metropolis . . . not well-governed and not ill-governed, but simply not governed at all." State legislators viewed cities as a source of patronage, not real power. Most mayors were figureheads. To fill the vacuum in urban government, a new political phenomenon arose: the urban machine. The machine, a political party with grassroots organization, provided urban residents with services in return for support of machine candidates in local elections. Once entrenched in elected office, these men rewarded the leaders of the machine, called bosses, with government contracts and control of the city, which they often divided into districts, or wards.

The machine bosses and their ward supporters served an important function in urban life. The machine provided urban residents with jobs, legal assistance, food, and welfare. They greeted immigrants as they arrived at the docks, helped workers who had lost their jobs, and intervened with the police when their constituents ran afoul of the law. If a family's breadwinner was injured or died, the bosses donated food and clothing. During cold winters they made sure families had coal to heat their tenement apartments. They organized picnics for poor children and donated money to hospitals and orphanages. "There's got to be in every ward somebody that any bloke can come to—no matter what he's done—and get help," said a

Boston ward leader. "Help, you understand; none of your law and justice, but help." Bosses won the favor of city businessmen by selecting local firms to build streets and sewers, granting franchises for operating utilities, and choosing printers, banks, and other small firms to receive municipal contracts. Businessmen paid kickbacks to the boss for the privilege of receiving city business.

In return, the bosses expected, and usually received, the votes of those benefiting from their efforts. Leaving nothing to chance, however, the local machine developed numerous techniques for cheating at the polls. These included padding registration lists with phony names and addresses. In Philadelphia the list of voters once included a boy of four and his dog. Machines employed gangs of men whose motto was "vote early and often." In any election, several precincts might record more votes than there were residents. One voter who claimed to be an Episcopal bishop, William Croswell Doane, had an argument at the polls. "Come off," scolded an election official. "You're not Bishop Doane." The man retorted, "The hell I ain't, you bastard!"

William M. Tweed, head of the famed Tweed Ring in New York, may have been the best known of the bosses. Tweed rose through the ranks of New York's dominant Tammany Hall political machine, serving in turn as city alderman, member of Congress, and New York State assemblyman. By 1867 he held seventeen different city offices simultaneously and controlled twelve thousand patronage jobs. During a reign of barely a dozen years, Tweed milked New York City out of millions of dollars. In 1870 the city spent more than $12 million on a new courthouse, including $7,500 for thermostats and $41,190 for brooms. A similar courthouse in Brooklyn cost only $800,000. A small portion of the ring's graft trickled down to the poor, helping struggling families and supporting local institutions, but most of the money ended up in the pockets of party officials. By 1871 Tweed, worth $12 million, owned an expansive apartment on Fifth Avenue and an estate in Connecticut. His empire collapsed that same year when he was arrested and convicted of 104 counts of fraud and bribery. He died in prison a few years later.

Tweed may have been the most notorious of the political bosses, but many other local political leaders used similar methods. In Washington, D.C., in the 1870s Alexander R. Shepherd embarked on an ambitious $20 million public works program, laying sewers, paving streets, and building bridges. The initiative improved urban life, but it also provided an opportunity for extensive corruption that made Boss Shepherd a wealthy man. Many cities followed the Tweed model by concentrating power in the hands of a single boss, but in Chicago and Boston individual ward leaders carved out their own empires, refusing to relinquish power to a citywide leader.

NEW EXPERIMENTS IN CULTURE

The concentration of millions of people from different backgrounds into a relatively small space produced a dynamic new urban culture. In their search for shared experiences, city people turned to a new "democracy of amusement." Spectator sports, vaudeville, and theater helped foster a sense of community for urban residents. The democracy of amusement, however, remained an exclusively white experiment from which African-Americans were systematically excluded. The new culture also found expression in the arts, as writers and artists displayed a new

Who Stole the People's Money   Thomas Nast, a *Harper's Weekly* illustrator, depicted the Tammany Hall political machine in 1870 as information regarding the New York County Courthouse over-expenditures came to light. William Tweed, the well-dressed man holding his hat in the left of the cartoon, points the finger of blame for the courthouse scandal on the companies hired to build and furnish the courthouse—including the plasterer who was paid $133,187 for two days' work and the furniture contractor who received $179,729 for three tables and forty chairs. In turn, no one wants to take the blame for the gross misappropriation of city funds, right down to every "Tom, Dick, and Harry," but public outcry resulted in the conviction and imprisonment of Tweed and several of his associates.   *(Harper's Weekly, 1871.)*

emphasis on realism. Amid the cultural experimentation, many women, taking advantage of new opportunities, challenged traditional notions of womanhood.

A Democracy of Amusement

Just when the city was becoming more sharply divided by race and class, a new culture of shared amusement emerged to blur some of the lines. The enormous expansion of cities, the growing demand for leisure-time activities among workers, and the widespread use of electricity brought people of diverse backgrounds together in a new world of "public" amusement.

The vaudeville house was the most popular of the new forms of entertainment. "The vaudeville theatre," wrote actor Edwin Milton Royle in *Scribner's Magazine* in 1899, "is an American invention. There is nothing like it anywhere else in the world." During its heyday, about one in seven Americans attended a show at least once a week. At one time New York had thirty-seven vaudeville houses, Philadelphia thirty, and Chicago twenty-two.

Because the theater was open six days a week, from noon to midnight, and charged only ten cents for admission, vaudeville operators had to design programs that appealed to a diverse audience. A 1911 survey of "public recreation" in San Francisco reported that vaudeville audiences were not "predominantly 'rich' or 'poor'," but "fair-to-do" and "struggling." The shows typically opened with a trained animal routine or a dance number. Comic skits followed, ridiculing the trials of urban life. After further musical numbers and acts by ventriloquists, jugglers, strongmen, and magicians, the curtain came down following a "flash" finale such as flying trapeze artists.

According to *Theatre Magazine*, vaudeville's popularity revealed that city residents were taking their "amusement seriously." But more serious theater also drew crowds. Middle-class Americans flocked to live theater for drama, musical comedy, and revues of every kind. New York captured the lead in theatrical excellence early in the nineteenth century with houses in the Bowery, Astor Place, and Union Square. Between 1890 and 1900 the combined seating capacity of New York City's theaters more than doubled. By the turn of the century New York had more theaters than any city in the world. A British visitor in 1912 was astonished to find "nearly twice as many first-class theaters in New York as in London." Other major cities—Chicago, Boston, San Francisco, New Orleans—built lavish theaters. A city's well-to-do also used these new theaters to house musical genres that suited their cultural tastes, particularly operas, symphonies, and ballets.

Millions of Americans traveled to amusement parks to escape the rigors of everyday urban life. In 1870 amusement parks were unheard of in America; by 1900 they were a standard feature in every major city. The most famous was New York's Coney Island, where for only a few dollars a family could enjoy exciting mechanized rides such as the roller coaster in Steeplechase Park. Most parks offered a complement of mechanized rides, dance halls, pavilions, and ballrooms where men and women could mingle. "The men like it because it gives them a chance to hug the girls," observed the owner of a Coney Island funhouse, and "the girls like it because it gives them a chance to get hugged."

African-Americans were systematically excluded from equal participation in the new democracy of entertainment. One black vaudeville performer recalled that "colored people could buy seats only in the peanut gallery." American entertainment helped build a sense of community among white urbanites by highlighting their differences from blacks. Entertainers used humor and insult to reinforce the wall that separated the races. Building on the tradition of blackface minstrelsy popular before the Civil War, white songwriters, illustrators, promoters, and performers produced a flood of "darky shows" and "coon songs." More than six hundred "coon songs" were published during the 1890s; one, titled "If the Man in the Moon Were a Coon," sold upward of 3 million copies.

Spectator Sports   City dwellers, confined to monotonous work in factories or sedentary work in offices and stores, craved new forms of physical recreation. Cycling and roller-skating crazes swept the country, and lately introduced sports such as golf, lawn tennis, and ice hockey appealed to the upper and middle classes, while basketball, which required little equipment and could be played on urban playgrounds, emerged as the preferred sport of working-class communities.

But while many Americans participated in sports new and old, far more people joined in as spectators at elite and professional events. Boxing attracted large city crowds. During the 1880s John L. Sullivan, the "Boston Strong Boy," traveled around the country offering to pay opponents who could go four rounds with him. In 1892 Sullivan lost to James J. Corbett in the first championship bout in which the fighters were required to wear padded gloves. While working-class communities embraced basketball and boxing, the middle and upper-middle classes adopted football. The annual Thanksgiving Day game between Princeton and Yale—the two best college teams in the nation—marked the beginning of New York's winter social season.

Baseball emerged as the most popular new urban sport. Baseball in its modern form had appeared during the 1840s when a group of wealthy New Yorkers organized the Knickerbocker Club. In 1862 in Brooklyn, William H. Cammeyer built the first enclosed baseball field in the country, but it was not until 1869 that teams began to charge admission and pay players. In 1876 eight teams—New York, Philadelphia, Hartford, Boston, Chicago, Louisville, Cincinnati, and St. Louis—came together to form the National League of Professional Baseball Clubs. By the late 1880s annual attendance at National League games had reached 8 million. Men and boys tried to emulate the professionals in vacant lots and on empty streets.

Baseball grabbed America's imagination. "As an amusement enterprise, baseball today is scarcely second to theater," a fan noted in 1910. The game's rules imposed a sense of order on chaotic urban society, while the expanse of greenery appeared to bring the countryside into the metropolis. Many people believed that the shared cultural experience at the ballpark would erode class differences. Reformer Jane Addams wrote of the "outburst of kindly feeling" after a home run in a ballpark and asked, "Does not this contain a suggestion of the undoubted power of a public recreation to bring together all classes of a community in the modern city unhappily so full of devices for keeping men apart?"

Baseball may have blurred class distinctions in the city, but it reinforced racial differences. Integrated teams were fairly common in the North in the late 1870s, and by the middle of the next decade blacks were playing with whites at the highest levels of organized baseball—the major and minor leagues. But then in 1887 all but two members of the St. Louis Browns refused to play an exhibition game against an all-black club. Rather than face a full-scale revolt, the major league owners shook hands on a "gentleman's agreement" to sign no more blacks. From the mid-1880s to the 1940s no black ballplayers, other than those who passed for Indian or Cuban, played in the major or minor leagues. African-Americans who came to the ballpark as spectators suffered similar indignities. Even in ballparks where "Negro" teams played against one another, seating was segregated. The vast majority of black fans stayed away from the major and minor leagues.

The Metropolitan Press

Technological innovations in printing and manufacturing newspapers combined with a growing public need for information to create a new form of journalism—a journalism of exposure. The invention of the steam press and the use of paper made of wood pulp, rather than more expensive cloth, allowed printers to

Choosing Sides   Americans increasingly turned to sports to fill their leisure time. Whether active participants or interested spectators, people were especially drawn to baseball. The first professional league was founded in 1876, but community baseball clubs had begun years before. Baseball appealed to all classes—from urban youths, who could play a game of baseball in any empty neighborhood lot, to middle-class suburban boys like the ones in this picture, in the process of determining who would pick the first player. *(National Baseball Hall of Fame.)*

produce more copy at lower cost. For most of the nineteenth century newspapers had limited circulation, were often mouthpieces for political parties, and ignored local events, preferring instead to focus on national or state issues. After the Civil War, newspapers attracted readers with human interest stories and investigative articles that exposed the scandals and injustices of contemporary society. The new style of journalism filled a pressing need as city residents tried to make sense of the bewildering events around them. Ambitious publishers, such as Joseph Pulitzer, who acquired the *New York World* in 1883, and William Randolph Hearst, who purchased the *San Francisco Call* in 1887, were eager to tap into the growing urban market.

Newspapers expanded coverage of urban affairs, increased in size, and added special features. Papers adopted a new format, with separate sections for sports, financial news, book notices, and theater reviews. Publishers also tried to reach out to non–English-speaking immigrants by publishing cartoons and comic strips. Since advertisers believed that women exercised control over family income, newspapers scrambled to attract female readers. The *World* added stories on fashion and etiquette, along with guidance on attaining beauty and "advice letters" on family issues. At the end of the decade the *Philadelphia Inquirer* devoted a section of its Sunday edition to "women's topics," which included a series on "The Art of Dressing."

In 1840 readers could choose from 138 daily and 1,141 weekly newspapers in the United States. By 1900 publishers were turning out 2,190 dailies and more than 15,813 weeklies. The United States published more newspapers than the rest of the world combined. In addition to the changes in mass-circulation newspapers, many immigrant communities issued their own foreign-language papers, which allowed newcomers to adjust to life in America while simultaneously asserting their cultural autonomy. By 1917 there were 1,323 foreign-language newspapers in the United States, including 522 in German, 103 in Italian, 84 in Spanish, and 17 in Japanese. The Yiddish-language *Jewish Daily Forward* was the most popular immigrant newspaper in the country, selling 175,000 copies daily.

Literature and the Arts

The new social environment influenced artistic developments in America as well. In contrast to the midcentury artists and writers who had celebrated a romanticized view of America's landscape and people, late-century works highlighted the darker aspects of American life. "Let fiction cease to lie about life," novelist William Dean Howells wrote; "let it portray men and women as they are." Howells applied this new realism with characters forced to contend with the corrupting influences of money and power.

Mark Twain, the pen name of Samuel Langhorne Clemens, gave a distinctive and very American style to realism in fiction. The first major American author to be born west of the Mississippi, Clemens added local color to his writings by drawing on his experiences as a river pilot and a newspaper reporter in the Mississippi Valley region. His most famous book, *The Adventures of Huckleberry Finn*, provided a critical examination of the existing social order in America. Floating down the Mississippi on a raft, Huck and his black friend Jim try to outrun what Twain contemptuously called "sivilization": a society filled with corruption, petty materialism, and hypocrisy. After witnessing a mob tar and feather a local con man, Huck concluded, "It was enough to make a body ashamed of the human race. . . . I never seen anything so disgusting."

Other writers, deeply influenced by Social Darwinism, developed a style of literary naturalism. Like the realists, these writers preached fidelity to the details of contemporary life, but they informed their novels with a tone of pessimistic determinism. Writers such as Frank Norris, Theodore Dreiser, and Stephen Crane viewed life as a relentless struggle in which powerful social forces determined an individual's fate. In *The Octopus* (1901) Norris wrote about a predatory railroad that destroyed wheat growers in the nation's heartland. Dreiser's powerful *Sister Carrie* (1900) traces the downward journey of an innocent country girl who, corrupted by urban pleasures, becomes a prostitute.

The same fascination with urban realism influenced artists who tried to capture the frenetic pace and harsh reality of city life. The key figure in this new artistic realism was Robert Henri, who used his position as head of the Pennsylvania Academy of Fine Arts to train an entire generation of artists later to be dubbed the Ashcan school. Heeding Henri's call for "making pictures from life," his students searched for authenticity in everyday events and people. George Luks used the backdrop of crowded tenements and shops on New York's Lower East Side for his depiction of *Hester Street* (1905). George Bellows celebrated the raw energy of urban life in *Cliff Dwellers* (1913), a depiction of slum life in crowded Manhattan.

Challenging Domesticity The growing independence of middle-class women was one of the most noticeable expressions of the new urban culture. The nineteenth-century "cult of domesticity" stressed that a woman's proper place was in the home, providing for the moral, spiritual,

George Wesley Bellows' *Cliff Dwellers* George Bellows, born in Columbus, Ohio, in 1882, was part of a generation of artists in the late nineteenth and early twentieth centuries who sought to depict the realities of urban life. While Bellows at times painted rural communities, his most well-known works depict New York City, including gritty scenes of boxers in the ring, the city's bustling street activity, and portraits of the working class. A critic of this type of artistic work, unimpressed with art that focused on the dynamics of the street, the tenement building, and the alley referred to artists like Bellows as members of the Ashcan school, a label that continues to be used to describe this artistic movement. *(Los Angeles County Museum of Art, Los Angeles County Fund Photograph © 2004 Museum Associates/LACMA.)*

and physical well-being of her family. During the last half of the nineteenth century, a number of changes provided American women with the opportunity to challenge traditional notions of gender roles.

In 1800 the average white woman had seven children; by 1900 the figure had fallen below four, reflecting that women were beginning to attain control over their sex lives. "Woman must have the courage to assert the right to her own body as the instrument of reason and conscience," observed feminist Lucinda Chandler. Another very tangible indicator of women's changing relationship to men was the substantial rise in the divorce rate. In 1880 one in every twenty-one marriages ended in divorce. By 1900 the rate had climbed to one in twelve.

Since they spent less time caring for children, middle-class white women had more options to receive an education and seek professional employment. Between 1870 and 1900 eighteen thousand women received college degrees. Nationally, the percentage of colleges admitting women jumped from 30 percent to 71 percent. A number of all-women's colleges opened their doors, including Vassar, Bryn Mawr, Smith, and Wellesley. At these schools, noted the president of Bryn Mawr, "everything exists for women students and is theirs by right not by favor." Education gave many women the self-confidence to break with the Victorian ideal of passive womanhood and pursue the professions. In 1890 women made up only 17 percent of the work force, but they held 36 percent of all "professional" positions. However, traditional male professions such as law, medicine, and the ministry resisted woman entrants, and colleges steered women toward a handful of occupations, such as teaching, nursing, library science, and social work.

Career women argued that their maternal skills and sensibilities made them especially well-suited to address certain important public issues—schooling the young, tending to the poor, and improving the health of women and children. "The home does not stop at the street door," noted the dean of women at the University of Chicago in 1911. "It is as wide as the world into which the individual steps forth. The determination of the character of that world and the preservation of those interests which she has safeguarded in the home, constitute the real duty resting upon women."

Educated middle-class white women created female-dominated institutions allowing women to learn from one another and work toward common goals. The women's club movement began in 1868 with the formation of Sorosis, established by journalists and other career women. The club described itself as "an order which shall render the female sex helpful to each other and actively benevolent in the world." By 1892 the General Federation of Women's Clubs, an umbrella organization established that year, boasted 495 affiliates and 100,000 members. By 1900 women's club rosters had swelled to 160,000. One woman writer declared, "We have art clubs, book clubs, dramatic clubs, poetry clubs. We have sewing circles, philanthropic organizations, scientific, literary, religious, athletic, musical, and decorative art societies." Devoted to "self-culture," women's clubs often read and reported on "great literature" and organized cultural events. In their own way, they were important training grounds for public activity. Clubwomen learned to speak in public, to prepare and present reports, and to raise and manage money.

African-American women, barred from participation in the white clubs, formed their own associations. Like their white counterparts, members ran day nurseries, reading programs, and welfare projects, but they also concerned themselves with race-specific issues such as antilynching campaigns. Josephine Ruffin, who formed Boston's New Era Club for black women, described her mission as "the moral education of the race with which we are identified." She set out to improve "home training" of children, provide racial leadership, and demonstrate that black women could forge "an army of organized women for purity and mental worth."

Victorian constraints on women loosened further at the end of the century when a bicycling vogue swept urban America. Men and women joined in and were pedaling over 10 million bicycles by 1900. To ride a bike, women had to wear divided skirts and simple undergarments. Over time the bicycle contributed to a new image of women as physically active and independent. The "Gibson Girl," the creation of magazine illustrator Dana Gibson, became a popular icon of the new woman. Pictures showed the self-sufficient Gibson Girl relishing her freedom, playing tennis, swinging a golf club, and riding a bicycle.

Nanni Helen Burroughs   Nannie Burroughs, holding the banner, exemplified the reformist spirit of her age as an activist for women and African-Americans. Burroughs founded the Women's Industrial Club and was the first president of the National Training School for Women and Girls in Washington, D.C. Both organizations sought to educate young women in the domestic sciences and in technical skills. She also supported efforts to encourage racial pride and black history, advocated equal rights for women, and co-founded the Women's Convention, an auxiliary of the National Baptist Convention, U.S.A., sponsor of this picture. *(Library of Congress.)*

THE PERSISTENCE OF PIETY

The new urban culture seemed threatening to many old-stock Protestant Americans, who feared the erosion of their traditional values. Many members of the American middle class, their ranks expanded by the growing number of salaried employees, organized to defend the dominant values rooted in the nation's rural past. Reformers preached about the need for cultural refinement, created private societies, and tried to convert urban residents to Protestantism. When persuasion and preaching failed, they turned to coercion. They enacted obscenity laws, banned entertainment on Sundays, and boarded up saloons. But while some focused on such reformist experiments, other Americans, fearful of the waves of poor foreigners arriving on America's shores, fought to limit immigration.

Defending "American" Culture

Most of the cultural and political battles of the late nineteenth century pitted native-born Protestant values against the culture of the immigrant city. City residents, a New Jersey educator declared in 1879, knew "little, or positively nothing . . . of moral duties, or of any higher pleasures than beer-drinking and spirit-drinking, and the grossest sensual indulgence. . . . [T]hey eat, drink, breed, work, and die."

White Protestants frequently expressed fear that millions of foreigners would dilute the native American racial stock. "It is scarcely probable that by taking the dregs of Europe," social scientist Richard Mayo Smith wrote in 1890, "we shall produce a people of high social intelligence and morality." Newspaper editorials assailed the "invasion of venomous reptiles" and "long-haired, wild-eyed, bad-smelling, atheistic, reckless foreign wretches, who never did an honest hour's work in their lives." Others saw immigrants as direct threats to their jobs.

No one articulated the nativist position more forcefully than the Reverend Josiah Strong. In his popular and influential book, *Our Country: Its Possible Future and Its Present Crisis* (1885), Strong stated flatly that "the typical immigrant is a European peasant, whose horizon has been narrow, whose moral and religious training has been meager or false, and whose ideas of life are low." Immigration, he added, "not only furnishes the greater portion of our criminals, it is also seriously affecting the morals of the native population."

Many people worried that immigrant women would have more children than native-born Protestants, allowing "the ignorant, the low-lived and the alien" to take over the country by sheer numbers. To encourage population growth among the American-born, reformers opposed birth control and divorce. Between 1860 and 1890 forty states and territories enacted antiabortion statutes. At the same time, they tightened divorce statutes to discourage marital separation. In most states, divorce laws were rewritten around the concept of "fault" or moral wrongdoing. To obtain a divorce, it had to be shown that one party had transgressed seriously against the other.

The middle-class reaction to the new urban culture took many forms. On one front, prominent spokesmen tried to instill a code of manners that would model respectable values. Good manners, including proper etiquette in all social occasions, especially dining and entertaining, became an important badge of status. Americans published more than 150 etiquette manuals between 1830 and 1910. Etiquette writers taught Americans who wished to be respectable and successful how to observe the dictates of decorum, including frequent bathing and conventional grooming. They expressed a persistent concern with instituting an American code of manners that would tame the excesses of democracy. "Brutes feed. The best barbarian only eats. Only the cultured man can dine."

On a larger scale, reformers founded museums, art galleries, libraries, and other institutions designed to inculcate appreciation for the respectable arts. In the 1870s New York, Boston, Chicago, and Philadelphia constructed museums of fine arts. In the 1890s workers completed construction of the Boston Public Library, the New York Public Library, and the Library of Congress. By 1900 more than nine thousand public libraries enlightened the country.

A broader effect on urban geography came from the City Beautiful movement, which sought to reform the urban landscape to inspire civic loyalty and reduce vice among working-class residents. This movement called for city planning and architectural cohesion in public buildings, and it emphasized the importance of public parks built to serve as green oases where urban dwellers could escape to a more natural, more "American" landscape. The rise of the city represented a profound crisis in American life. It challenged the deeply ingrained Jeffersonian vision of independent farmers living on and occupying the land. "The life of great cities," Henry George warned in 1898, "is not the natural life of man." To remedy the problem, architects such as Frederick Law Olmsted envisioned large public parks as a way to bring rural beauty to the modern city, to create a psychological sense of freedom, and to provide moral uplift to urban life. In the 1850s Olmsted helped design New York's Central Park, the first major public park in the United States. "No one who has closely observed the conduct of the people who visit [Central] Park," Olmsted declared in 1870, "can doubt that it exercises a distinctly harmonizing and refining influence upon the most unfortunate and most lawless classes of the city,—an influence favorable to courtesy, self-control, and temperance." By 1870 as many as one hundred thousand people visited the park daily.

Looking inward as well as outward, middle-class spokesmen organized private meeting places to escape the pressures of everyday life and reinvigorate their faith. In 1874 John Vincent, a Methodist clergyman, and Lewis Miller, an Ohio businessman, started a summer program at Chautauqua Lake in New York's scenic Allegheny Mountains to train Sunday School teachers. The Chautauqua Literary and Scientific Circle promoted "habits of reading and study in nature, art, science, and in secular and sacred literature, in connection with the routine of daily life." In addition to instruction, the assembly offered recreation on the lake and lectures on topics other than religious themes. Chautauqua grew to be one of Victorian America's most popular middle-class resorts. By the 1890s more than two hundred thousand people participated in similar programs organized around the country.

Finally, American Protestants engaged in an aggressive campaign to recruit new members. The swelling numbers of Catholics and Jews in the nation's cities convinced many church leaders of the need to extend their influence in urban areas. A number of Protestant denominations founded urban missions, which combined lively preaching with charity work. The Salvation Army, founded in England in 1873 by Methodist minister William Booth and established in New York in 1880, proved the most successful of the Protestant urban initiatives, claiming seven hundred branches in cities across the United States by 1900. Another familiar technique for reaching urban residents was the revival. In 1875 Dwight L. Moody conducted highly publicized Protestant revivals in Brooklyn, Philadelphia, New York, Chicago, and other cities. With financial backing from wealthy supporters and a mesmerizing speaking style, Moody drew thousands of middle-class followers to his rallies, where he preached the "three R's" of the gospel: "Ruin by sin, Redemption by Christ, and Regeneration by the Holy Ghost." The efforts of Protestant preachers produced a dramatic increase in church membership—from 4.5 million in 1860 to 12.5 million in 1890.

Not all Protestant reformers chose to work through the church. Many middle-class Americans turned to the charity organization movement, an ostensibly "secular" initiative designed to improve the "moral character" of urban residents. Participants in the charity movement believed that poverty and vice resulted from individual failing, not from a lack of opportunity. "Misery and suffering," chided an organization handbook, "are the inevitable results of idleness, filth, and vice." In most cases, poverty's roots lay in "the characters of the poor themselves." The solution was "the moral elevation of the poor." The key, argued a movement leader, was to promote "the personal intercourse of the wealthier citizens with the poor," by sending a "friendly visitor"—usually a middle-class woman—to meet with slum families each week. The visitor's purpose was to use "the moral support of true friendship" to embed in the poor a "new desire to live rightly."

The Purity Crusades

Reformers' efforts to help immigrants voluntarily adopt middle-class values of temperance and domesticity soon evolved into legislative coercion. The purity movement, which included Protestant clergy, former abolitionists, and women's rights activists, launched an assault on the vice districts, which they viewed as seedbeds for prostitution. They pressured city officials to form special commissions to investigate the vice problem. A Chicago commission called prostitution "the greatest curse which today rests upon mankind." By 1913 city police had shut down entire red-light districts in forty-seven cities. Suppression, noted a Minneapolis reformer, represented "the only sane and safe method of correcting the depraved passions of the human heart."

By the mid-1880s the attack on prostitution had evolved into a broad crusade for social purity. Reformers took aim at the many manifestations of urban culture—vaudeville, theaters, college football, dance halls, and amusement parks. A reformer who visited a dance hall later reported with alarm, "I saw one of the women smoking cigarettes, most of the younger couples were hugging and kissing, [and] there was a general mingling of men and women at the different tables." Many American cities and towns passed ordinances that promoted religious observance on Sunday by banning all business activities. Between 1886 and 1895 the social purity campaign succeeded in raising the age of consent for sex from as low as ten years in some states to between fourteen and eighteen in twenty-nine states.

Many reformers believed that any attempt to purify the social environment required the legal suppression of unwholesome influences. Anthony Comstock, the founder of the New York Society for the Suppression of Vice, emerged as the most powerful spokesman for censorship. In 1873 he wrote and helped steer through Congress the so-called Comstock Law, which banned from the mails any matter "designed to incite lust." As special agent to the postmaster general, he saw to it that the law was rigorously enforced, and he was quick to halt distribution of any publication containing advertisements for contraceptives. In a single decade Comstock confiscated an estimated fourteen tons of books and about one and a half million circulars, poems, and pictures.

No reform, however, attracted more middle-class support than the assault on that bastion of male working-class culture, the saloon. Reformers had long been concerned with temperance, but before the Civil War they had attacked drinking primarily as an individual rather than a social problem. Most of their activities focused on reforming individual drinkers, not on eliminating alcohol altogether through institutional change. By 1870, however, middle-class Protestant women, working through the Women's Christian Temperance Union (1874) and the Anti-Saloon League (1895), organized a national crusade against alcohol.

All efforts to "improve" or "better" urban residents and their culture reflected opposition to immigrants and their cultural and religious practices. Many Americans, however, felt the answer rested not in reforming immigrants, but in restricting their numbers and their rights. This nativism found expression in private groups that opposed immigrants and often took direct action against them. The American Protection Association (APA), a secret organization founded in 1887, led the anti-immigrant campaign. The APA attracted support from workers threatened by competition from Irish laborers, and from native-born Americans worried about Catholic conspiracies. Its members pledged "to strike the shackles and chains of blind obedience to the Roman Catholic church from the hampered and bound consciences of a priest-ridden and church-oppressed people." The APA intimidated Catholic political candidates with hints of violence. In 1894 a group of Boston patricians formed the Immigration Restriction League, a tenacious political lobbying group that advocated literacy tests for all immigrants in an effort to drastically limit the number allowed into the country.

The Chinese suffered the sharpest nativist attacks. Starting in the 1850s businessmen lured thousands of Chinese to fill jobs in western mines and railroad construction, and by 1880 more than seventy-five thousand Chinese lived in California, making up about 9 percent of the state's population. As nonwhites and non-Christians, Chinese immigrants frightened Americans. Steadily growing discrimination and prosecution culminated in the Chinese Exclusion Act of 1882, by which Congress suspended Chinese immigration (see page 681).

Public Education   By 1890 most cities and states with large immigrant populations mandated compulsory schooling between certain ages (usually eight to fourteen). As a result, attendance in public schools increased from 6.9 million in 1870 to 17.8 million in 1910, and the number of public schools mushroomed from five hundred to ten thousand. Many cities created kindergarten programs for preschool children and expanded high school from three to four years. City schools also initiated night school programs to help older immigrants learn English and vocational skills. By 1900 nearly a dozen states required schools to provide students with free textbooks.

Supporters argued that public schools would help immigrants abandon old ways and assimilate into American society. The superintendent of New York's system claimed that a school should be "a melting pot which converts the children of the immigrants of all races and languages into sturdy, independent American citizens." In 1903 a writer noted that kindergartens presented the "earliest opportunity to catch the little Russian, the little Italian, the little German, Pole, Syrian, and the rest and begin to make good American citizens of them." Advocates of public education also saw schools as a vehicle for maintaining social order. In addition to the traditional curriculum, students learned the value of good citizenship, patriotism, and respect for authority.

Immigrant communities usually embraced the opportunity to receive free education. In 1914 nearly all elementary-age Jewish children in New York City attended public schools. Families often chose to violate compulsory attendance laws, however, because they depended on the earnings of their school-aged children. In New York fewer than 33 percent of German children and only 25 percent of Italians attended high school, compared with 60 percent of native-born white children. In Chicago less than 10 percent of Italian and Polish children advanced beyond the sixth grade in 1910.

Many immigrants, worried that public schools threatened their cultural traditions or their religious values, established private or church schools. By 1900, in cities with large Catholic populations, between 20 and 40 percent of school-age children, nearly a million in all, were enrolled in parochial schools. By 1914 California's Japanese community had established thirty-one schools to teach the Japanese language. German immigrants took a different approach, pressuring public schools themselves to teach German. By 1900 nearly 25 percent of public high school students in the United States studied German. School districts in St. Louis and Buffalo, both with large German populations, offered bilingual instruction in German and English.

The increasing numbers of Americans attending secondary school produced greater demand for higher education. As a result of the Morrill Act of 1862, all but a handful of states had founded land-grant colleges by the end of the century. At the same time, large donations from wealthy industrialists led to the creation of Vanderbilt (1873), Johns Hopkins at Baltimore (1876), Stanford (1893), and others. In 1892 John D. Rockefeller revived the faltering University of Chicago with a $34 million gift. By 1900 five hundred colleges and universities served 232,000 undergraduates and 5,700 graduate students.

Leading universities experimented with curriculum changes, adding new subjects such as economics, political science, and modern languages to the standard offerings of Latin, Greek, mathematics, rhetoric, and theology. Private and public universities created graduate programs in numerous scholarly disciplines and added professional schools in medicine, law, architecture, engineering, business, and education. While academic quality and standards varied greatly, a British observer noted approvingly in 1888 that the United States possessed "not less than fifteen and perhaps even twenty seats of learning fit to be ranked beside the universities of Germany, France and England."

CONCLUSION

In the last quarter of the nineteenth century millions of migrants from Europe and from rural areas in the North and South transformed American cities. The diversity of newcomers and their experiments in adaptation contributed to the multicultural flavor of urban life. In an effort to maintain an older sense of community, they formed ethnic enclaves and created a variety of support institutions and associations. Cities became collections of distinct neighborhoods, each with its own dialect, cuisine, and religious institutions. In most cities the demands for public services—decent housing, clean water, sanitation, fire protection—overwhelmed local officials. When established institutions failed to address their needs, many immigrants turned to representatives of powerful local political machines such as Boss Tweed's Tammany Hall in New York.

While immigrants transformed the city's environment, a revolution in transportation helped recast the urban landscape. A series of advances in mass transit, beginning with the horse-drawn omnibus and culminating with the electric street trolley, expanded the distance that people could live from the city center and still commute to work. As people spread out from the city core, urban space became more specialized and more segregated. Downtowns rose skyward with the advent of steel high-rise construction and emerged as centers for shopping and business. The city's wealthiest citizens clustered in one neighborhood, the poor and working class in another, and the middle class began moving to the suburbs.

Ironically, while mass transit was pushing city residents apart, a new urban culture was pulling them together. Public amusements—vaudeville shows, theater performances, and amusement parks—created a social environment in which the city's diverse population could share a common experience. City dwellers embraced spectator sports and came together in huge numbers to watch basketball, football, and baseball. The new "public" culture was for whites only, however. African-Americans were barred from participation in major sporting events and forced to enter vaudeville houses through the back door. In an effort to reach the mass of city residents, newspapers expanded their coverage of local affairs and included special features to attract readers. Writers and artists, often using the city as a backdrop, developed new methods and styles to capture the harsh reality of industrializing America. Middle-class women challenged older notions of domesticity and gained more control over their sex lives. Increasing numbers attended college and entered professions such as teaching, nursing, and social work.

Not everyone welcomed the changes swirling around them. Many middle-class Protestants feared that immigrants were intellectually and morally inferior to native-born white Americans and viewed cities as breeding grounds for vice, corruption, and poverty. Protestant reformers tried to uplift the new urban culture by teaching cultural refinement and by building libraries, museums, and public parks. Church members organized rallies to convert the largely Catholic and Jewish newcomers, while "secular" reformers embraced charity work. When persuasion failed, reformers resorted to coercion, using state power to forbid prostitution, censor sexually explicit materials, and ban alcohol. Some nativist groups took direct action to limit immigrants' political rights and lobbied for immigration restriction. Many states adopted mandatory school attendance laws, hoping that public education could hasten the assimilation process.

The emotional cultural debates pitting native-born Protestants against immigrants dashed Americans' expectations of a peaceful period of unity following the Civil War. Americans who looked to their political leaders for experiments to address the pressing problems of industrialism and to ameliorate the intense social conflicts were sorely disappointed.

Annotated Suggested Readings

Several surveys on urban history trace the growth of American cities in the late nineteenth century, as seen in Raymond A. Mohl's *The New City: Urban America in the Industrial Age, 1860–1920* (1985). Other books, including Howard P. Chudacoff's *The Evolution of American Urban Society* (rev. ed., 1994) and Eric H. Monkkonen's *America Becomes Urban* (1988), emphasize the dynamic mobility of people and the impact of changing government services and transportation on the urban community. In *The Other Bostonians: Poverty and Progress in the American Metropolis, 1880–1970* (1973), Stephan Thernstrom studies the persistent mobility of Boston's residents as each generation slowly bettered its socioeconomic situation. Howard P. Chudacoff explores urban mobility in *Mobile Americans: Residential and Social Mobility in Omaha, 1880–1920* (1972) and the development of the urban bachelor life in *The Age of the Bachelor* (1999).

Migrants from rural parts of the United States included an increasing number of southern blacks in the late nineteenth century. William H. Harris's *The Harder We Run* (1982) analyzes the racism African-Americans faced in northern industries and their efforts to adapt to an urban way of life. In *Black Migration and Poverty* (1979), Elizabeth Pleck discusses the limited opportunities open to African-Americans in Boston. James Borchert's *Alley Life in Washington* (1980) sees both change and continuity in the lives of urban African-Americans.

Numerous historians have focused their attention on the rising flood of immigrants into American cities—for example, Alan M. Kraut in *The Huddled Masses* (1982). Walter T. K. Nugent's *Crossings: The Great TransAtlantic Migrations* (1992) analyzes the reasons people decided to leave Europe, focusing on the growing populations and declining opportunities in their homelands. *The Transplanted* (1985) by John Bodnar describes how immigrants adapted to their new surroundings in American cities and attempted to maintain control of their lives.

Many more historians narrow their work to include only certain groups of immigrants. Josef F. Barton's *Peasants and Strangers* (1975) compares the adjustments made to life in Cleveland by the city's Italian, Rumanian, and Slovak populations. In *World of Our Fathers* (1976), Irving Howe tells the story of eastern European Jews and the culture they brought with them. Placing the Italian experience in Chicago into a larger context of urbanization, Humbert S. Nelli's *Italians in Chicago* (1970) describes the impact of ethnic divisions between northern and southern Italians. Ronald Takaki's *Strangers from a Different Shore* (1989) investigates the adaptations of Asian immigrants. Essays compiled by Sucheng Chan in *Entry Denied* (1991) look at the way these new migrants handled social and legal exclusion.

The nativist backlash to immigration is best analyzed in John Higham's *Strangers in the Land* (1955). David Ward's *Poverty, Ethnicity, and the American City* (1989) analyzes native-born Americans' fear of immigrants. Leonard Dinnerstein and David M. Reimers examine the impact of nativist pressure on the deterioration of immigrants' native heritage in *Ethnic Americans* (1982).

A number of works describe the expansion of the city and the impact of the transportation revolution on an urban population. The evolution of transportation in the nineteenth century, as evidenced in the changes to public transportation in New York, Boston, and Philadelphia, is recorded in Charles W. Cheape's *Moving the Masses* (1980). Kenneth T. Jackson analyzes the rise of the suburbs in *Crabgrass Frontier* (1985).

Eric H. Monkkonen's *Police in Urban America* (1981) covers the history of America's police forces. Alan M. Kraut's *Silent Travelers: Germs, Genes, and the "Immigrant Menace"* (1994) examines Americans' fear of diseases brought by foreigners and the innovations made in public health care and government initiative to stave off this threat. Health concerns and the desire to better conditions for all residents led to the emergence of sanitary engineers, as described in Martin V. Melosi's *Garbage in the Cities* (1981). Stanley K. Schultz's *Constructing Urban Culture* (1989) discusses the work of not only sanitary engineers, but also judges, architects, and novelists whose ideas concerning better urban living sparked the rise of city planning.

A general study of city politics is a work edited by Alexander B. Callow, *The City Boss in America* (1976). An interesting study of five big city bosses is John M. Allswang's *Bosses, Machines, and Urban Voters* (rev. ed., 1986). Despite the corruption in urban politics, Jon C. Teaford argues in *The Unheralded Triumph* (1984) that city governments provided numerous benefits through public services.

The rise in urban entertainment and its connection to the working class are the focus of several works. Kathy Peiss's *Cheap Amusements* (1986) looks at working women's attempts to escape from domestic restraints through the dance halls, parks, and clubs they visited. David Nasaw's *Going Out: The Rise and Fall of Public Amusements* (1999) provides useful background on a host of new forms of urban entertainment. The voice of the working class could also be found in vaudeville shows, as described by Robert V. Snyder in *The Voice of the City: Vaudeville and Popular Culture in New York City* (1989) and in John Kasson's *Amusing the Million: Coney Island at the Turn of the Century* (1978). Class struggle is evident in Roy Rosenzweig's *Eight Hours for What We Will* (1983). Gunther P. Barth finds that some city institutions promoted commonalities among all citizens in *City People: The Rise of Modern City Culture in Nineteenth Century America* (1980).

The emergence of professional and collegiate sports in the late nineteenth century is well documented in Stephan A. Riess's *City Games* (1989). A broader survey of the history of sports in America, from pre-Columbian games to modern athletic events, is Allen Guttmann's *A Whole New Ball Game* (1988). The adaptation of professional sports to the college model and the role of Harvard and Yale in setting the pace of collegiate sports are examined in Ronald A. Smith's *Sports and Freedom* (1988).

The changing image of women and the rising independence of the New Woman are the themes of Martha Banta's *Imaging American Women* (1987). Sheila M. Rothman's *Woman's Proper Place* (1978) describes the changes in technology and education that helped alter women's activities and social roles. In *The Rise of the New Woman* (2003), Jean Matthews examines how these new opportunities prepared women to fight for equality. Linda W. Rosenzweig's *The Anchor of My Life* (1993) explores the relationship between Victorian mothers and their New Women daughters.

The attempt of upper-class reformers to control the lives of all city residents in order to quell their own fears of social and moral disorder is the subject of Paul Boyer's *Urban*

Masses and Moral Order in America (1978). Sven Beckert looks at the power of urban elites in his influential *The Monied Metropolis: New York City and the Consolidation of the American Bourgeoisie, 1850–1896* (2003). John F. Kasson's *Rudeness and Civility* (1991) looks at the evolution of manners as the cruder colonial times gave way to structured rules of behavior and dress. In *The New Urban Landscape* (1986), David Schuyler describes the upper classes' vision of a more pastoral urban environment and their application of professional planning to upgrade the city. The monumental efforts to establish city planning in New York are described in Keith Revell's *Building Gotham* (2003).

Efforts to reform working-class people by controlling their behavior are the focus of David J. Pivar's *Purity Crusade* (1973) and Joel Schwartz's *Fighting Poverty with Virtue* (2000). Nicola Kay Beisel's *Imperiled Innocents: Anthony Comstock and Family Reproduction in Victorian America* (1997) looks at Comstock's work as part of a larger effort by the upper classes to impose their beliefs on others. The work of women in these moral reform movements and their growing desire for the vote as a means of social control are the subjects of Lori Ginzberg's *Women and the Work of Benevolence* (1991).

The education of native-born and foreign-born city dwellers is the subject of several works, such as David B. Tyack's *The One Best System* (1974), which looks at the power relationships and ethnic blocs at the heart of urban education. Lawrence A. Cremin's *American Education: The Metropolitan Experience* (1988) looks at education as a variety of institutions, from schools to cinemas, that transmit knowledge, values, attitudes, and skills to the young. Also useful is David Nasaw's *Schooled to Order* (1979). The higher education of the upper class produced our modern emphasis on professionalism, as seen in Burton J. Bledstein's *The Culture of Professionalism: The Middle Class and the Development of Higher Education in America* (1976).

The **H**istory **C**ompanion

Immigration and American Identity

Francis A. Walker, "Restriction of Immigration"

Calls for immigration restriction escalated during the 1890s. In 1894 a group in Boston formed the Immigration Restriction League (IRL) to pressure Congress and the White House to pass legislation requiring a literacy test for all immigrants. Francis A. Walker, a leading member of the league, published an article in the *Atlantic Monthly* that outlined the worries about the rising tide of immigrants.

Let us now inquire what are the changes in our general conditions which seem to demand a revision of the opinion and policy heretofore held regarding immigration. Three of these are subjective, affecting our capability of easily and safely taking care of a large and tumultuous access of foreigners; the fourth is objective, and concerns the character of the immigration now directed upon our shores. . . .

First, we have the important fact of the complete exhaustion of the free public lands of the United States. . . . .A second change in our national condition, which importantly affects our capability of taking care of large numbers of ignorant and unskilled foreigners, is the fall of agricultural prices which has gone on steadily since 1873. . . . There has been a great reduction in the cost of producing crops in some favored regions . . . but there has been no reduction in the cost of producing crops upon the ordinary American farm at all corresponding to the reduction in the price of the produce. It is a necessary consequence of this that the ability to employ a large number of uneducated and unskilled hands in agriculture has greatly diminished.

Still a third cause which may be indicated, perhaps more important than either of those thus far mentioned, is found in the fact that we have now a labor problem. . . . No longer is it a matter of course that every industrious and temperate man can find work in the United States. And it is to be remembered that, of all nations, we are the one which is least qualified to deal with a labor problem. We have not the machinery, we have not the army, we have not the police, we have not the traditions and instincts, for dealing with such a matter, as the great railroad and other strikes of the last few years have shown.

I have spoken of three changes in the national condition, all subjective, which greatly affect our capability of dealing with a large and tumultuous immigration. There is a fourth, which is objective. It concerns the character of the foreigners now resorting to our shores. Fifty, even thirty years ago, there was a rightful presumption regarding the average immigrant that he was among the most enterprising, thrifty, alert, adventurous, and courageous of the community from which he came. . . . Today the presumption is completely reversed. So thoroughly has the continent of Europe been crossed by railways, so effectively has the business of emigration there been exploited, so much have the rates of railroad fares and ocean passage been reduced, that it is now among the least thrifty and prosperous members of any European community that the emigration agent finds his best recruiting-ground.

Finally, the present situation is most menacing to our peace and political safety. In all the social and industrial disorders of this country since 1877, the foreign elements have proved themselves the ready tools of demagogues in defying the law, in destroying property, and in working violence. . . . There may be those who can contemplate the addition to our population of vast numbers of persons having no inherited instincts of self-government and respect for law; knowing no restraint upon their own passions but the club of the policeman or the bayonet of the soldier; forming communities, by the tens of thousands, in which only foreign tongues are spoken, and into which can steal no influence from our free institutions and from popular discussion.

Congressman Robert H. Clancy, "An 'Un-American Bill'"

Public anxiety about rising numbers of immigrants peaked after World War I. In 1921 Congress passed the Quota Act, which established limits on future immigration based on a nationality's percentage of the population in 1910. Three years later Congress debated the Immigration Act of 1924 (Johnson-Reed Act). The law passed with only six dissenting votes. One of those dissenting votes was cast by Detroit Republican Congressman Robert H. Clancy, who defended the "Americanism" of his Jewish, Italian, and Polish constituents.

Since the foundations of the American commonwealth were laid in colonial times over 300 years ago, vigorous complaint and more or less bitter persecution have been aimed at newcomers to our shores. Also the congressional reports of about 1840 are full of abuse of English, Scotch, Welsh immigrants as paupers, criminals, and so forth.

Old citizens in Detroit of Irish and German descent have told me of the fierce tirades and propaganda directed against the great waves of Irish and Germans who came over from 1840 on for a few decades to escape civil, racial, and religious persecution in their native lands.

The "Know-Nothings," lineal ancestors of the Ku-Klux Klan, bitterly denounced the Irish and Germans as mongrels, scum, foreigners, and a menace to our institutions, much as other great branches of the Caucasian race of glorious history and antecedents are berated to-day. All are riff-raff, unassimilables, "foreign devils," swine not fit to associate with the great chosen people—a form of national pride and hallucination as old as the division of races and nations.

But today it is the Italians, Spanish, Poles, Jews, Greeks, Russians, Balkanians, and so forth, who are the racial lepers. And it is eminently fitting and proper that so many Members of this House with names as Irish as Paddy's pig, are taking the floor these days to attack once more as their kind has attacked for seven bloody centuries the fearful fallacy of chosen peoples and inferior peoples. The fearful fallacy is that one is made to rule and the other to be abominated. . . .

We have many American citizens of Jewish descent in Detroit, tens of thousands of them—active in every profession and every walk of life. They are particularly active in charities and merchandising. One of our greatest judges, if not the greatest, is a Jew. Surely no fair-minded person with a knowledge of the facts can say the Jews of Detroit are a menace to the city's or the country's well-being. . . . Forty or fifty thousand Italian-Americans live in my district in Detroit. They are found in all walks and classes of life—common hard labor, the trades, business, law, medicine, dentistry, art, literature, banking, and so forth. . . . They rapidly become Americanized, build homes, and make themselves into good citizens. . . . They do the hard work that the native-born American dislikes. Rapidly they rise in life and join the so-called middle and upper classes. . . .

The Polish-Americans are as industrious and as frugal and as loyal to our institutions as any class of people who have come to the shores of this country in the past 300 years. They are essentially home builders, and they have come to this country to stay. They learn the English language as quickly as possible, and take pride in the rapidity with which they become assimilated and adopt our institutions.

The foreign born of my district writhe under the charge of being called "hyphenates." The people of my own family were all hyphenates—English-Americans, German-Americans, Irish-Americans. . . . To me real Americanism and the American flag are the product of the blood of men and of the tears of women and children of a different type than the rampant "Americanizers" of to-day.

Between 1865 and 1914 more than 25 million immigrants arrived in America. Since they could not afford to buy land, most settled in cities. By 1900, for example, immigrants and their children made up 80 percent of the residents of New York City. The massive influx produced anxiety among many native-born Americans who feared that newer immigrants from southern and eastern Europe would have a difficult time assimilating into American society. For more than three decades the nation engaged in a spirited debate about whether to limit the number of new immigrants allowed in the country. The debate, which culminated in the passage of restrictive legislation in the 1920s, touched on questions central to the issue of American identity. What does it mean to be an American? Does being an American mean speaking the same language, worshiping the same god, accepting the same political values? Americans were debating those questions at the beginning of the twentieth century. They were still debating them at the beginning of the twenty-first century.

QUESTIONS FOR ANALYSIS

1. Why does Walker believe that the new immigrants cannot become good Americans?

2. How does he see globalization and the communications revolution impacting immigration?

3. Do you see any similarities between Walker's argument and those used today against immigration?

4. How do you explain Clancy's assertion that America, itself a land of immigrants, has always greeted "newcomers" with "bitter persecution"? How could members of Congress who were the children of immigrants vote to restrict new immigrants?

5. How is Clancy's definition of "Americanism" different from Walker's definition?

20

State and Society

1877–1900

*The money issue "was not a contest between persons,"
Bryan said. . . . It represented a clash between "the common
people" and "the encroachments of organized wealth."*

he twenty thousand Democrats packed into the sweltering Chicago Coliseum were restless. They had come to select a candidate to lead them in the 1896 presidential campaign, and now they eagerly awaited the arrival of William Jennings Bryan. The delegates were a contentious group, deeply divided over national policy. Desperate farmers from the South and West favored an inflationary policy of "free silver," which would allow the use of plentiful silver for money. Conservative interests in the East wanted to reassure business leaders by maintaining support for the gold standard.

At the youthful age of thirty-six, Bryan had already developed a reputation as the most powerful orator of his time. His magnetic voice and evangelical style earned him numerous titles: the "Nebraska Cyclone," "Knight of the West," the "Boy Orator of the Platte," and the "Silver-tongued Orator." Born in a small farming town in southern Illinois, Bryan moved to Lincoln, Nebraska, and won election to Congress in 1890. A tall, powerfully built man with a thick mane of black hair, he viewed politics through a moral prism as a proving ground on which the forces of good and evil did battle. He possessed unbounded faith in the wisdom of common people, steadfastly opposed privilege and monopoly, and longed to return the nation to its Jeffersonian roots.

Bryan felt faint in the minutes before he ascended the podium, but once he took the stage, the jitters passed. For the next forty minutes he mesmerized the audience. "His wonderful voice filled the auditorium," recalled a delegate. The money issue "was not a contest between persons," Bryan said, but "a question of principle." It represented a clash between "the common people" and "the encroachments of organized wealth." Bryan posed the fundamental question of the campaign: "Upon which side will the Democratic party fight; upon the side of 'the idle holders of capital' or upon the side of 'the struggling masses'?" As his captive audience sat in stunned silence, Bryan moved to his dramatic close. In response to those who advocated a gold standard, Bryan vowed, "You shall not press down upon the brow of labor this crown of thorns, you shall not crucify mankind upon a cross of gold." To add dramatic effect to his metaphor, Bryan stretched out his arms and tilted his head as if he were hanging from a cross.

Bryan's speech electrified the convention hall. For nearly an hour, delegates carried him on their shoulders. Many supporters were so moved by Bryan's eloquence that they slumped in their seats and wept. One reporter called Bryan "a young David with his sling, who had come to slay the giants that oppressed the people." The following day delegates nominated Bryan for president.

The 1896 presidential campaign, which pitted Bryan against Republican William McKinley, was one of the most exciting elections in American history. It also marked a turning point in American politics. The previous twenty years had been characterized by a stubborn stalemate that produced mediocre leaders and meager legislation. Fearful of offending potential voters, neither party strayed far from the political center. But in 1896, for the first time since the Civil War, serious issues divided the parties. A crippling economic depression combined with the rise of a powerful agrarian protest movement, which provided the backbone of Bryan's campaign, upset the political balance and led many to demand new experiments in national politics. The Populists offered a compelling vision of government that contrasted sharply with prevailing views of both parties. In nominating the controversial Bryan, the Democrats abandoned an incumbent president, Grover Cleveland, and embraced an inflationary monetary policy. In nominating McKinley and championing the conservative "gold standard," Republicans set up the election as a contest over national policy. The 1896 election would mark the end of the Gilded Age and its inconclusive national politics.

- Why did the national government fail to grapple with the pressing issues facing Americans during the Gilded Age?

- What were the roots of the farmers' discontent?

- How did different groups of Americans view the crisis of the 1890s?

- What attitudes toward government were at odds in the 1896 election?

This chapter will address these questions.

THE POLITICS OF STALEMATE

In 1873 Mark Twain and Charles Dudley Warner created an enduring label for politics in post-Reconstruction America when they wrote a novel entitled *The Gilded Age*. Like the book's fictitious characters, American politicians during this period seemed more interested in gaining office than in addressing issues or experimenting to solve problems. Locked in political stalemate and reluctant to alienate potential voters in close elections, they nominated similar candidates and avoided controversial questions. During the Gilded Age, heated debates over tariffs, patronage, and money replaced the passionate clashes over slavery and states' rights of the Civil War era.

CHRONOLOGY

1873	Twain and Warner publish *The Gilded Age* Congress demonetizes silver
1877	Hayes becomes president Great Railway Strike *Munn* v. *Illinois* affirms state regulation of railroads
1880	Garfield elected president
1881	Garfield assassinated; Arthur becomes president
1883	Pendleton Civil Service Act
1884	Cleveland elected president
1886	National Alliance Exchange system established
1888	Harrison elected president
1890	"Billion Dollar Congress" Sherman Antitrust Act passed McKinley Tariff passed Sherman Silver Purchase Act passed
1892	Populist Party wins over a million votes Homestead strike Cleveland elected president
1893	Panic of 1893
1894	Coxey's Army marches on Washington Pullman strike Congress repeals Sherman Silver Purchase Act
1895	*Pollock* v. *Farmers Loan and Trust* strikes down income tax
1896	McKinley elected president Populists "fuse" with Democrats
1897	Dingley Tariff
1900	Gold Standard Act

The Failure of Politics The two decades following Reconstruction represent one of the least memorable periods in American political history. Between Abraham Lincoln and Theodore Roosevelt, the United States produced no memorable leaders. How often do we hear the name of a single president between 1877 and 1901? Southern writer Thomas Wolfe referred to the Gilded Age presidents as "the lost Americans: their gravely vacant and bewhiskered faces mixed, melted, swam together. . . . Which had the whiskers, which had the burnsides: which was which?"

Even contemporaries poked fun at the inferior and uninspiring efforts of the men in public life during these years. "The period," complained the Harvard historian Henry Adams, "was poor in purpose and barren in results." He went further, suggesting, "One might search the whole list of Congress, Judiciary, and Executive during the twenty-five years and find little but damaged reputations."

Why was the period so lackluster in political style and content? For one thing, Americans emerging from the turmoil of Civil War and Reconstruction had grown weary of heated debates over emotional issues. Assaulted by the forces of industrialization, immigration, and urbanization, Americans searched for stability and order in their politics, not idealism and passion. But stability required politicians to avoid great issues and divisive debates and to focus instead on building powerful organizations. Patronage replaced ideology as the glue that bonded the parties together. British observer James Bryce said the two major parties "were like two bottles. Each bore a label denoting the kind of liquor it contained, but each was empty."

Equilibrium stemmed from another unique feature of Gilded Age politics: the parties were evenly balanced in numbers, and neither was able to gain the upper hand. Henry Adams observed that though "no real principle divides us, . . . some queer mechanical balance holds the two parties even." In the years between 1872 and 1896, no president won a majority of the popular vote. In the presidential contest of 1880 the Republicans won 48.5 percent of the popular vote, the Democrats 48.1 percent. After that election, Republicans held 147 seats in the House and Democrats 135. Each party had 37 representatives in the Senate. As a consequence of the divided electorate, no president between 1877 and 1897 served with a majority of his party in control of both houses of Congress for a full term.

Because of the tight competition, party leaders searched for bland candidates who would not alienate powerful voting blocs. Both parties vied for control of a handful of "swing" states—Connecticut, New Jersey, New York, Indiana, Ohio, and Illinois—whose electoral votes would determine election outcomes. The ideal presidential candidate during the Gilded Age resided in a critical state, had fought for the Union during the Civil War, and had avoided taking controversial positions.

There were real differences between Democrats and Republicans, but internal conflicts often obscured ideological divisions, preventing either party from speaking with a unified voice. The Republican Party after 1880 reflected the continuing loyalties that grew out of the Civil War. Based in the Northeast and Midwest, it celebrated its legacy as the party of Lincoln that had freed the slaves and saved the Union. More willing than Democrats to advocate federal activism, Republicans promoted economic growth through land grants, subsidies to railroads, and protective tariffs. In the North Republicans "waved the bloody shirt," symbolically invoking the memory of fallen Union soldiers by labeling Democrats the "party of treason" responsible for the war between the states and unworthy of governing. "Not every Democrat was a Rebel," they reminded voters, "but every rebel was a Democrat." The appeal was especially persuasive with the 1 million surviving veterans of the Civil War who were organized into a powerful lobby called the Grand Army of the Republic (GAR), which urged its members to "vote as you shot." Not surprisingly, Republicans nominated a Union veteran as president in eight of nine presidential contests between 1868 and 1900. With grateful memories of emancipation and Reconstruction, African-Americans too voted for the party of Lincoln.

Divided among themselves, Republicans were often unable to present a united front. The most pronounced divisions were between "Stalwarts," who claimed to stand firm in their opposition to Hayes's Reconstruction policy, and "Half Breeds," a label Stalwarts gave their adversaries, whom they considered phony Republicans. The *Cincinnati Commercial* observed, "The Republican party in Congress is composed of factions in such deadly antagonism to each other that the hate among them is more intense than that given the Democrats." The Stalwarts were led by state bosses such as Senator Roscoe Conkling of New York, who was known for his arrogant manner, flair for fine clothes, and passion for political intrigue. Politics "is a rotten business," he declared. "Nothing counts except to win." Having built a powerful political machine in New York on the back of political patronage, Conkling opposed reform efforts that would diminish his fiefdom. He summed up his political philosophy in a sentence: "I do not know how to belong to a party a little." James G. Blaine of Maine, leader of the Half-Breeds, emerged as Conkling's chief challenger for control of the party. A consummate politician, Blaine, whom his supporters called "the plumed knight from Maine," never forgot a name or a face and was capable of arousing the party faithful with his inspiring oratory. The Half-Breeds believed that their appeal rested on issues, not patronage. They wanted to build a coalition based on calls for economic nationalism and political reform.

Like the Republicans, the Democrats were divided into rival, often regional, camps. In the South Democrats waved their own bloody shirt to maintain the support of the provincial Protestant farmers who had fought for the Confederacy and viewed northern Republicans as the real traitors. A second wing of the Democratic Party consisted of urban political machines and their loyal immigrant constituency. What united the disparate factions was a common commitment to the antimonopoly rhetoric that had begun with Andrew Jackson in the 1820s. Democrats promoted states' rights and a decentralized, limited government. "Local self-government," the party's 1872 platform declared, "will guard the rights of all citizens more securely than any centralized power." Democrats also shared a belief in white supremacy. In the South their racial views translated into efforts to disfranchise blacks; in parts of the West they fought to deny citizenship to Chinese immigrants.

Important issues divided the parties, but a new generation of political leaders was determined to soften their ideological identities. Republicans often muted their support for centralized government in an effort to appeal to more conservative voters. The Kansas Republican Party platform declared that "the powers of the general government having been stretched to an unhealthy extent, to meet the crisis of civil war and reconstruction, [they] should now be restored to their normal action." For their part, Democrats tried to win over key swing voters by downplaying their Civil War support for slavery and states' rights. In Ohio the Democratic platform proposed a "New Departure," calling on the party to "accept the material and legitimate results of the war."

Many people, dismayed with both the Democrats and Republicans, turned to third parties. Though they advocated different causes and appealed to different voters, all third-party challengers drew scores of supporters from both mainline parties. A national Prohibition candidate ran for president in every election after 1872. Antimonopoly parties sprang up in eleven states during the mid-seventies. In 1878 the

Greenback Party, which called for an expansion of the currency, won more than a million votes. In 1892 angry farmers in the West and South created the Populist Party.

However, ethnic and religious issues, not questions of economic policy, frequently determined election outcomes. In the North and West Republicans wooed Protestants of British descent or established American stock by promising to maintain high moral standards, which usually meant support for Sunday-closing laws, English-only public schools, and prohibition of alcohol. The Republican message attracted the support of "pietistic" religious groups—Methodist, Baptist, Congregational, and Presbyterian—that defined sin broadly and felt obliged to impose those standards widely. Outside the South Democrats captured the allegiance of Irish Catholics and other urban immigrants by targeting ethnic groups. They appealed to "liturgical" religious faiths—Catholics, German Lutherans, and Episcopalians—that defined sin narrowly and opposed using government power to enforce proper behavior. As one Chicago Democrat explained, "A Republican is a man who wants you to go to church every Sunday. A Democrat says if a man wants to have a glass of beer on Sunday he can have it."

Ironically, despite the mediocre candidates and dull debates, parties played a central role in the political life of Gilded Age Americans, providing a sense of national attachment and group identity. Election campaigns were elaborate and festive affairs, filled with colorful parades and mass rallies. Novelist Brand Whitlock described a typical parade: "the smell of saltpeter, the snorts of horses, the shouts of men, the red and white ripple of the flags that went careering by in smoke and flame." If the spirited rallies were not enough to motivate voters, the parties provided other, more tangible incentives. Before the 1890s the parties controlled the voting process. Voters filled out party-distinctive "slip tickets" in full view of party officials before depositing their votes in the ballot box. The system encouraged straight-ticket voting and widespread corruption. Parties hired operatives to get people to the polls and then paid them for their votes. The standard rate for a Pennsylvania congressional race was said to be $30 plus room and board.

The combination of passion and organization produced the highest percentages of voter turnout in American history (see figure on page 771). In some states outside the South it soared above 80 percent. In 1888, for example, Ohio registered a 94 percent turnout and Indiana 95 percent. Iowa, where 99 percent of voters went to the polls in 1868, set an all-time U.S. record. Of course, the universe of eligible voters remained small. Women could not vote. Whites in many areas in the South were experimenting successfully with new methods such as the poll tax to restrict black suffrage (see page 645). Their counterparts in the North used similar methods to discourage recent immigrants from voting. Despite these restrictions, the United States had more legal voters than any other democracy—11 million in 1880. About 1.8 million males of voting age—14 percent of the total—could not vote. In comparison, 40 percent of the adult male population was denied the ballot in Britain.

The Limits of National Government

With the exception of Reconstruction and western land development, the federal government remained largely invisible to most citizens. "An American may," James Bryce observed, "through a long life, never be reminded of the federal government, except

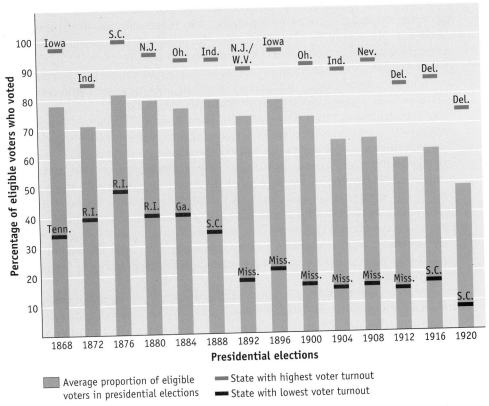

Voter Turnout in Presidential Elections, 1868–1920 The average proportion of eligible voters in presidential elections, indicated by the bar, remained around 80 percent during the post–Civil War era, beginning a gradual decline after 1896. While the gap between the state with the highest average voter turnout (shown above the bar) and the lowest average voter turnout (shown below the bar) varied, it is interesting to note the impact of Mississippi's constitution of 1890 and of the efforts of other former Confederate states to exclude black voters. *(From American Politics in the Gilded Age, 1868–1900 by Robert W. Cherny. Copyright © 1997 by Harlan Davidson, Inc. Used by Permission)*

when he votes at presidential and congressional elections, lodges a complaint against the post-office, and opens his trunks for a custom-house official on the pier at New York when he returns from a tour in Europe." Despite its growth during the Civil War, the national government was relatively small, employing only nine thousand nonmilitary personnel, of whom six thousand were stationed in Washington. The federal budget, which in the last year of the Civil War had ballooned to $1.3 billion, dropped to $242 million by 1886. With the exception of the Post Office, which accounted for half of all civilian federal employees, and the Pension Office, which disbursed benefits to Union veterans and their families, the federal government had little direct impact on the daily lives of most Americans.

In Washington, Congress replaced the president as the focus of political power. The impeachment of Andrew Johnson (see page 625) had shifted the balance of power away from the chief executive. Grant had deferred to Congress in making appointments and in developing legislation, and subsequent presidents tended to follow suit. The prevailing wisdom was that the president should execute the laws, not propose new legislation. Senator John Sherman of Ohio framed the situation clearly: "The executive department of a republic like ours should be subordinate to the legislative department." In any case, no Gilded Age president could command majorities in Congress to push through innovative legislation.

Industrialization forced Congress to protect America's economic interests by creating a favorable environment for business growth through such efforts as regulating the money supply and tariffs, but Congress lacked the will or the resources to govern effectively. An unruly institution, Congress chafed against rules that, in the words of one congressman, were designed "to disturb legislators and obstruct legislation." The Senate, which was known as the Millionaire's Club, became the home of powerful party leaders who felt little loyalty to the institution or to the president. Since senators were still elected by state legislatures, it was easy for wealthy men to "buy" a Senate seat. Each senator, observed one member, "kept his own orbit and shone in his sphere, within which he tolerated no intrusion from the President or from anybody else."

The states and counties, not the federal government, did most of the governing. Most states funded schools and prisons and provided homes for disabled Civil War veterans. By the 1880s many states had created commissions to oversee railroads and to regulate social and economic activities—chartering corporations, granting divorces, licensing saloons. Most state constitutions specified that the legislature should be in session only a few months a year. As a result, most people looked to local authorities for nearly all government services. City and town governments built and maintained roads, established boards to manage the public schools, and collected property taxes.

The Issues: Patronage, Money, and Tariffs

In previous decades Americans had debated the momentous issues of freedom and slavery. Gilded Age elections frequently turned on questions of patronage. Beginning in the 1830s winning candidates for national office instituted the spoils system, rewarding supporters and contributors with government jobs. The spoils system made party loyalty, not qualifications and competence, the chief criterion for public office. President Benjamin Harrison estimated that during the first eighteen months of his term he had spent four to six hours a day dealing with job seekers. Throughout the period party leaders, who expected to be able to fill party posts and other positions with loyal followers regardless of their qualifications, battled with reformers who charged that patronage bred corruption and wasted money.

The second issue that animated political discussions concerned the money supply. During the Civil War the government had issued $450 million in greenbacks—paper money not backed by gold or silver. For the next two decades Americans debated whether to print more paper money or to remove it from circulation entirely. The dispute raged through the 1870s and led to the formation of the Greenback Party. Just as the battle over greenbacks began to subside, a new fight

"A Presidential Conjurer"   Although he built his political career on patronage, including a lucrative position as New York's customs collector, Chester A. Arthur spent his years as president working for civil service reform. Despite Arthur's personal convictions, many people believed that the president would have to bow to pressures within his Republican Party to maintain the spoils system. In this cartoon by Joseph Keppler, Arthur is the magician, pulling political appointments out of his hat in order to satisfy politicians, while reserving a table full of "tricks" for future use. (Puck *October 12, 1881, University of California at Berkeley, Bancroft Library.)*

erupted over silver-backed money. Since 1837 the nation's money supply had been tied to the value of gold and silver. Congress had set the ratio at sixteen to one, meaning that one ounce of gold was worth sixteen ounces of silver. By 1873 so little silver remained in circulation that Congress stopped coining it and citizens could no longer use it as legal tender to pay public or private debts. But the resulting contraction of the money supply led to a steep economic slide and provoked renewed calls for some form of silver coinage.

On one side of the divide were debt-ridden farmers in the South and West. They believed that the amount of money in circulation determined the level of activity in the economy. The more paper money the government printed, the more business activity and the more prosperity for everyone. An expanded money supply allowed farmers to charge higher prices for their products and to pay back loans with inflated dollars. On the other side, bankers and businessmen, who held loans and owned property that would decline in value if the money supply expanded, wanted to maintain the status quo. They developed great reverence for the gold standard, whereby all money printed had to be backed by gold reserves, which unlike silver were limited and thereby had a stable, consistent value. Business interests often found unlikely allies in urban workers who feared higher prices for food and other essentials. Over the next twenty years, as the two sides struggled over this contentious issue, the mundane question of the money supply took on moral implications that went beyond simple economics. For many people, the debate over the money supply translated into a battle between rural, agricultural interests of the South and West and urban industrial and banking interests of the Northeast.

Finally, Americans debated the wisdom of maintaining high tariffs on imported products. The tariff issue was as old as the republic, but it assumed a new importance following the Civil War. During the war the government raised tariff rates to protect American industry—which paid heavy taxes to support the war effort—against competition from foreign companies. At the end of the war the government dropped the taxes but kept the tariff, giving American producers a protected market in which to sell their goods. Since they faced little competition, America's expanding and industrializing manufacturers raised their prices and amassed record profits. At the same time, the Treasury Department was building a sizable bank account from tariff revenues. During the 1880s the Treasury surplus averaged over $100 million a year. This surplus stood as a continual temptation to legislators, who wanted to spend it on pork-barrel projects in their home districts. Businessmen, who gravitated toward the Republican Party, strongly supported continued high tariffs. Over time, Democrats, responding to the pleas of western farmers suffering from the high prices of consumables, called for reduced tariff rates.

NATIONAL POLITICS FROM HAYES TO HARRISON, 1877–1890

Questions of patronage and civil service dominated the Republican administrations of Rutherford Hayes, James Garfield, and Chester Arthur. In 1884 the Democrats regained the White House. Although the new president, Grover Cleveland, differed little from his Republican predecessors on most issues, his bruising battles over pension benefits, patronage, and the tariff left him vulnerable to Republican attacks. Four years later Benjamin Harrison, the Republican candidate, took advantage of Cleveland's liabilities to win election. High tariffs remained safe in the hands of Harrison, but the "Billion Dollar Congress" during his term depleted the Treasury with its reckless spending.

Republicans in Power: Hayes, Garfield, and Arthur

Rutherford B. Hayes tried to bring a new integrity to the White House in the wake of the corruption that had marred the Grant administration. His wife, the first college-educated First Lady, added to the new tone by refusing to serve alcohol in the White House, leading newspapers to derisively call her Lemonade Lucy. Visitors accustomed to free drinks complained that in the Hayes White House "the water flowed like wine."

His tainted election victory in 1876 (see page 641) prevented Hayes from becoming a strong president. In addition, Democrats controlled the House throughout his administration and the Senate for the last two years. The president's limited view of executive power contributed to his ineffectiveness. He proposed little legislation designed to deal with pressing economic and social problems. Hayes supported the return to the gold standard instigated by the Specie Resumption Act as the only remedy for the decade's economic slump. He vetoed the Bland-Allison bill, which allowed for a limited amount of silver to be coined annually. However, facing pressure from western mining interests and silver supporters, Congress overrode Hayes's veto. Hayes also had no policy for dealing with the first great industrial conflict in American history—the railway strike that began on the Baltimore and Ohio Railroads in July 1877 (see page 719). Only at the request of four state governors did Hayes send federal troops to intervene in the strike and restore order. He angered labor further when he vetoed a bill in 1879 to restrict Chinese immigration. Labor unions on the West Coast had pushed for the restrictions, claiming that Chinese "coolie" immigrants were stealing jobs from American workers.

Hayes did make a systematic effort to attack one controversial issue: patronage and corruption in government. He called for civil service reform in his inaugural address, and in June 1877 he challenged Conkling's machine by issuing an executive order forbidding federal officeholders "to take part in the management of political organizations, caucuses, conventions, or election campaigns." In October, after Congress was in recess, Hayes fired two leading members of Conkling's machine—customs collector Chester A. Arthur and naval officer Alonzo Cornell—after an investigation accused them of fraud. An irate Conkling fired back, blocking Senate confirmation of the president's replacements for the two officials. Hayes won the battle of wills when Congress eventually approved the new replacements, thus underscoring that the president, not party leaders, controlled the most important federal appointments.

Since Hayes had announced at the start of his term that he would not seek reelection, Republicans scrambled to find a new candidate in 1880. Each of the party's factions pushed its candidate: Stalwarts rallied around a third term for Grant; Half-Breeds supported Blaine; Independents favored John Sherman. When it became clear that none of the rivals would receive enough votes for nomination at the party convention, delegates turned to a compromise candidate, James A. Garfield. A former president of Hiram College in Ohio, Garfield won election to the Ohio Senate in 1859. He rose quickly through the party ranks and emerged as one of the leading members of Congress. A self-taught scholar, Garfield could speak both German and French and write Latin with one hand and Greek with the other at the same time. To appease the Stalwarts, delegates offered the vice presidency to Chester A. Arthur—the New York customs official and Conkling henchman whom Hayes had dismissed from office!

The Democrats tried a new tactic by adopting the Republican strategy of nominating a Civil War hero, General Winfield Scott Hancock. In keeping with the tone of Gilded Age politics, both candidates ignored important issues and focused on personalities. The Republicans emphasized Garfield's log-cabin roots and mocked Hancock for his lack of political experience, publishing a book entitled *Record of the Statesmanship and Achievements of General Winfield Scott Hancock*. The book was filled with blank pages. The Democrats responded by tying Garfield to the Crédit Mobilier scandal (see page 634).

On election day Garfield eked out a narrow victory. Only 39,213 votes out of the 9 million cast separated winner and loser. Garfield's margin in the electoral college was more commanding: 214 to 155. Though the campaign was uninspiring, 79.4 percent of eligible voters turned out on election day (see map on page 776).

Battles over patronage consumed the early months of Garfield's administration. Conkling had helped the Republicans win New York, and now he expected his reward: control over all patronage positions in the state. Garfield rejected Conkling's claim and forced the issue by withdrawing all appointments from the Senate until Conkling backed down. When his fellow senators abandoned him, Conkling resigned his seat. The president did not have much time to savor his victory. On July 2, 1881, just four months after taking the oath of office, President Garfield was shot and killed by a deranged office seeker named Charles Guiteau. "I am a Stalwart and Arthur is President now," Guiteau shouted as he pulled the trigger. Garfield was incapacitated for two months before dying on September 19.

Garfield's death elevated Stalwart leader Chester Arthur to the presidency. "Chet Arthur, President of the United States?" one of his friends exclaimed. "Good God!" To everyone's surprise, however, Arthur sided with advocates of civil service and tariff reform, and against Conkling. He skillfully used public sentiment, aroused by the Garfield assassination, to encourage congressional efforts to enact the first national civil service law. The Pendleton Civil Service Act, passed in January 1883, set up an independent three-member Civil Service Commission to provide "open competitive examinations for testing the fitness of applications for the public service now classified or to be classified." The law listed only 14 percent of federal jobs as "classified services," but it gave the president the power to enlarge the classified services at his dis-

Consistently Democratic

Twice Democratic, once Republican

Once Democratic, twice Republican

Consistently Republican

Territories—Not voting for president

Voting in Presidential Elections of 1880, 1884, 1888   The impact of the Civil War was still evident in the partisan politics of the 1880s. Most states that fought for the Union remained consistently behind the Republican Party, while the former Confederate states held firm to the Democratic Party and garnered support from Border States as well. In both the 1884 and 1888 election, the shifting alliances of New York, in addition to Indiana in 1888, proved the deciding factor in closely contested presidential races.

cretion. By 1901 the law covered 44 percent of all federal employees and served as a model for most state and local governments. In 1882 Arthur supported the recommendation of a congressional commission to reduce the tariff, but House Republicans watered down the proposal, and the bill Arthur eventually signed—dismissed as the "Mongrel Tariff"—provided for only a small reduction in rates.

Arthur accomplished more than anyone would have predicted, but he won few friends. His vigorous prosecution of the so-called Star Route Frauds, a scheme to win contracts for postal routes, angered old political cronies who hoped to profit from the plot. Arthur's liberal use of the presidential veto angered many groups that hoped to benefit from government spending. In 1882 he rejected a wasteful $18 million river and harbors bill and the Chinese Exclusion Act. Congress overrode both vetoes, but Arthur had established his independence from party bosses.

In November 1882 the public registered its disapproval of Arthur and the Republicans in the midterm elections. Democrats made major gains, picking up a total of thirty-six seats in the key electoral vote states of New York, Ohio, Pennsylvania, Michigan, and Missouri. The *New York Tribune* understood the election's significance: "this result makes President Arthur an absolute impossibility as a future candidate."

The Election of 1884

The presidential election of 1884 was one of the dirtiest campaigns in U.S. history. "Party contests," cried the *Nation*, "have never before reached so low a depth of degradation in this . . . country." Henry Adams told a friend, "We are all swearing at each other like demons."

The Republicans dumped Arthur and turned to James G. Blaine, one of the party's most capable and experienced leaders. Though popular with party regulars, Blaine was shadowed by suggestions that he once profited from shady deals with the Union Pacific. The rumors were nearly a decade old and had been investigated by a congressional committee, which found no proof that Blaine had broken the law. The controversy gained new life on September 15 when the *Boston Journal* released letters Blaine had written in 1876 to a railroad attorney. In a cover letter Blaine pleaded with the attorney to sign a statement clearing him of any misdeeds. Blaine signed off with a warning: "Burn this letter!"

High-minded reformers in the Republican Party refused to support a Blaine-headed ticket. The *Nation's* editor, E. L. Godkin, remarked that Blaine had "wallowed in spoils like a rhinoceros in an African pool." The editor of the *New York Sun* labeled Godkin and his fellow reformers Mugwumps, ironically adapting an Algonquian word meaning a great chieftain to ridicule a reformer as a political fence-sitter whose "mug" was on one side of the fence and "wump" on the other. The Mugwumps cultivated a style of independence and moral rectitude that disdained the ordinary demands of partisan politics. Most were old-stock Americans, educated at elite universities, who rejected the crass political gamesmanship of partisan politics. Since many were prominent educators and journalists, they used their positions to influence public opinion. But their contempt for the general public prevented them from building a mass political movement.

The presence of the Mugwumps on the political scene convinced the Democrats that they could seize the moral high ground by nominating a principled opponent. For that role they selected New York Governor Grover Cleveland, who had attracted national attention for battling graft and corruption as mayor of Buffalo, New York. In 1882 he won the governorship, and over the next two years his attacks on New York's Tammany Hall organization (see page 744) earned him the nickname "Grover the Good."

Cleveland, too, was forced to defend himself against withering assaults on his character. On July 21 the *Buffalo Evening Telegraph* published a piece headlined "A Terrible Tale: A Dark Chapter in a Public Man's History." The story revealed that Cleveland had, some ten years earlier, fathered an illegitimate child. Though disappointed by the blemish on his private life, the Mugwumps threw their support behind Cleveland.

The 1884 Presidential Campaign   The fight for the White House between James G. Blaine and Grover Cleveland focused more on the personal integrity of the two nominees than on political issues. Democrats repeatedly accused Blaine of corrupt dealings with big business, while portraying their candidate as "Grover the Good" for his attacks on Tammany Hall. However, Cleveland, a bachelor, faced allegations that he was the father of an illegitimate son born to a Buffalo, New York, widow. Republicans attacked Cleveland for the indiscretion, but Cleveland was able to lessen the political fallout by acknowledging the boy was his, despite lingering questions regarding the boy's actual paternity. (Puck *1884,* *Granger Collection.*)

The scandals produced some of the most colorful campaign slogans in American politics. "Blaine, Blaine, James G. Blaine, the continental liar from the state of Maine," Democrats chanted. Republicans countered with "Ma, ma, where's my pa?" To which Democrats responded, "Gone to the White House, ha, ha, ha!"

The race appeared to be a dead heat going into the final weeks. As with most of the elections during this period, the outcome hinged on New York's thirty-six electoral votes. Blaine had made inroads into the powerful Irish-American community and threatened to carry the state. Then on October 29, Blaine's "Black Wednesday," the candidate made a serious mistake that probably cost him the election. When Blaine attended a morning meeting of Protestant ministers, a preacher welcomed him with a reference to Democrats as the party of "Rum, Romanism, and Rebellion." Blaine, perhaps failing to catch the implied insult to Catholics, let the slur pass without objection. Within hours Democrats flooded the city with handbills repeating the remark.

The episode undoubtedly helped Cleveland win a narrow victory. Blaine lost New York by only a little more than 1,100 votes, and the votes of that state proved to be decisive in the electoral college, where the margin was 37 votes (Cleveland's 219 versus Blaine's 182). Nationally, only about 29,000 votes of the 10 million cast separated Cleveland and Blaine.

Grover Cleveland: A Democrat in the White House

Cleveland became the first Democrat to occupy the White House since the Civil War. He was also the first president to be married in the White House and the first to father a child while president. (His daughter Ruth became the inspiration for the Baby Ruth candy bar.) The change in power, however, did not signal a change in governing strategy. Cleveland embraced the prevailing belief that the federal government should refrain from meddling in people's lives and in the economy. The proper role for the president, he believed, should be to restrain Congress from granting special privileges to some groups at the expense of others. "Though the people support the government the government should not support the people," Cleveland asserted. In his inaugural address, which he recited from memory, he promised to adhere to "business principles," and his cabinet consisted of conservatives and business-minded Democrats from the East and South.

Cleveland's fiscal conservatism led to a number of costly political confrontations. Believing that "public office is a public trust," Cleveland vetoed pork-barrel bills for rivers and harbors. In 1887 he vetoed a general pension bill for Civil War veterans, claiming that it was unnecessary and wasteful. The decision may have reflected sound economic policy, but as a Democrat without a war record Cleveland was vulnerable to partisan charges that he was pro-South and unpatriotic. The Grand Army of the Republic blistered Cleveland for his decision, and the intense public reaction forced the president to retreat. By the end of his term Cleveland had vetoed three times as many bills as all his predecessors combined.

The president's record on civil service was mixed enough to alienate both reformers and spoilsmen. He filled three-quarters of unclassified federal offices with Democrats, including all internal revenue collectors and nearly all the heads of customhouses. But at the same time Cleveland increased by two-thirds the number of jobs classified as civil service.

Cleveland's vocal opposition to high tariffs angered many businessmen. In 1887 he devoted his entire annual message to Congress on arguments for tariff reduction. Calling tariffs "vicious, inequitable, and illogical," he predicted "financial convulsion and widespread disaster" if the high rates continued. The president claimed that the existing tariff presented two problems: it made the Treasury a "hoarding place for money needlessly withdrawn from trade and the people's needs," creating a large federal budget surplus that tempted Congress to spend money on wasteful projects, and it encouraged monopoly and high prices by eliminating foreign competition. Given his views of presidential power, however, Cleveland exercised little leadership, leaving it to Congress to develop legislation. In the end, Senate Republicans blocked Democratic efforts to adjust the tariff.

The Election of 1888

Cleveland had made many enemies during his four years as president, but the Democrats renominated him to head the ticket in 1888. Republicans searched for a candidate who would not offend voters and who would allow the campaign to focus on Cleveland's record. They found their man on the seventh ballot when they nominated former senator and outspoken protectionist Benjamin Harrison of Indiana, grandson of former president William Henry Harrison. A man of intelligence and integrity, Harrison lacked personal warmth and charm. "Harrison sweats ice water," declared a critic. The nominee promised to conduct a high-minded campaign focused on "great principles," not personalities. The Republican platform accepted the protective tariff as the chief "great principle" and also promised generous pensions to veterans. For all their professions of principle, Republicans were not above using dirty tricks in the campaign. Cleveland spent much of his time battling false rumors, including one that he had beaten his wife.

A last-minute campaign trick left Cleveland on the defensive. A Republican posing as an English immigrant had written to a British minister asking advice on how to vote. The minister took the bait and replied: "Would you do England a service by voting for Cleveland and against the Republican system of tariff." Gleeful Republicans published the letter on October 24. As planned, the minister's reply provoked a storm of protest against foreign intervention on the president's behalf.

With Cleveland busy fending off groundless rumors, Harrison and the Republicans raised over $4 million—the largest campaign fund to date—from business leaders worried about falling tariff rates. John Wanamaker, a Philadelphia merchant and chief Republican fundraiser, put matters bluntly in a letter to leading businessmen: "We want money and we want it quick." Campaign leaders used the contributions to purchase millions of pamphlets, flyers, and handbills and to pay speakers to travel around the country drumming up support for Harrison.

Despite the Republicans' vigorous efforts and Cleveland's troubles, the outcome was very close. Cleveland won the popular vote by a margin of nearly 100,000: 5,537,857 to 5,447,129. But Harrison, victorious in the key states of Indiana and New York, carried the electoral college by 233 to 168. When his campaign manager arrived in Indianapolis to congratulate Harrison on his victory, the president-elect exclaimed,

"Providence has given us the victory." The cynical adviser was stunned that the pious Harrison gave God more credit than his operatives. "Think of the man!" he ranted to a journalist. "He ought to know that Providence hadn't a damn thing to do with it." Harrison would never know, he charged, "how close a number of men were compelled to approach the gates of the penitentiary to make him president."

Harrison and the Billion Dollar Majority

Not only had Republicans laid claim to the White House in 1888; they also secured majorities in the House and the Senate. Taking advantage of the opportunity, they passed some of the most significant legislation enacted in the entire period. The Sherman Silver Purchase Act, passed to mollify the western wing of the party, increased the amount of silver to be purchased by the Treasury, but not necessarily coined and circulated, to 4.5 million ounces a month. The McKinley Tariff raised duties to their highest level. Not all Republican initiatives succeeded, however. House Republicans tried to pass a federal election bill that would have guaranteed the voting rights of blacks in the South. Democrats, who condemned the legislation as a "force bill" to restore "Negro rule," succeeded in filibustering it to death.

Of the legislation to emerge from the Republican Congress, the Sherman Antitrust Act eventually proved to be one of the most important. The first attempt to regulate big business, it imposed stiff penalties on "every contract, combination in the form of trust or otherwise, or conspiracy, in restraint of trade or commerce." The Senate approved the act by fifty-two to one, and the House passed it without a dissenting vote (see page 712).

Harrison and the Republicans did not stop at legislative initiatives. They also rewarded their supporters by raiding the Treasury surplus. To serve as commissioner of pensions, the president appointed a past GAR commander who, soon after taking office, exulted, "God help the surplus!" Congress assisted his efforts to provide "an appropriation for every old comrade who needs it" by passing the Dependent Pension Act of 1890. Within five years the number of pensioners grew from 676,000 to nearly a million, and federal pension expenditures ballooned from $80 million to $159 million. Rivers and harbors expenditures also reached new highs, and the Republicans returned federal taxes paid by northern states during the Civil War. Such lavish spending quite properly earned the label "Billion Dollar Congress" for the 1890 session.

Voters punished the extravagant Republicans in the midterm election of 1890, rewarding the Democrats with sixty-six congressional seats and control of the House of Representatives. This voter response represented more than just a stinging rebuke of the Billion Dollar Congress. In many key states, religious and ethnic groups revolted against the Republican Party's affection for restrictive social legislation such as prohibition. Most of all, the election revealed the growing political activism of farmers in the South and West.

AGRARIAN REVOLT, 1880–1892

Few groups suffered more in the new industrial system than America's farmers. Frustrated with falling prices and high costs, the farmers fought back. By the 1880s they had formed a powerful new movement of Farmers' Alliances in the West and South. Realizing that most of the farmers' needs were beyond the power of the state governments, Alliance members developed a national program, seeking new forms of federal intervention. The Alliance platform stressed a number of bold proposals, and the experiment in political activism created a new sense of solidarity among farmers. In 1892, after scoring impressive victories in the 1890 election, Alliance members formed the Populist Party.

The Farmers' Discontent
Since the early days of the republic the American farmer had symbolized independence and self-sufficiency in a society that revered these qualities. "Those who labor in the earth," Thomas Jefferson once wrote, "are the chosen people of God." Farmers, however, confronted a paradox: though an emblem of self-reliance, they prospered or struggled at the whim of uncontrollable forces. Foremost among those forces was the weather, but the new industrial order, which integrated farmers into an international market, introduced a host of other factors. Farmers suddenly found themselves depending on an impersonal system that they could not understand, let alone control.

As a result of the emergence of a new global economy, American farmers had to contend with competition from countries such as Russia and Argentina, which expanded their wheat production to capture a part of the U.S. market. Most of all, farmers became victims of their own success. They produced such an overabundance of wheat and cotton that supply outpaced demand, producing lower prices. The average price of American wheat fell from $1.05 per bushel in 1866 to 67 cents in 1895. Corn dropped from 43.1 to 29.7 cents a bushel, and cotton from 15.1 to 5.8 cents a pound. The price of corn dropped so low that farmers in Kansas burned it in place of coal. Ironically, as commodity prices dropped, farmers had to cultivate more wheat or cotton to try to raise the same amount of money. The result was a vicious cycle of surpluses, price declines, and debt (see figure on page 783).

Frustration increased in the heartland as farmers watched everyone else benefit from their labors—railroad and grain storage operators who charged exorbitant rates, consumers who bought their product at low costs, machinery salesmen who sold new equipment at tariff-protected prices. Farmers, on the other hand, saw a dramatic decline in their quality of life. As one exasperated speaker put it, "The farmer fed all other men and lived himself upon scraps."

Farmers searching for an explanation for their plight saw the railroads as the chief villain. Farmers felt victimized by the high railroad rates that prevailed in farm regions having no alternative forms of transportation. On long hauls the rates were low because of competition; on local hauls, for which there was no competition, the rates were disproportionately high. It cost Minnesota farmers more to ship their grain to St. Paul or Minneapolis than to New York. The railroads also favored the big shipper, who had leverage to negotiate lower prices, over the small shipper.

A second target of farmers' complaints were grain elevator operators. The elevators were giant storage bins located next to railroad tracks, from which grain was loaded onto trains. Western railroads forced farmers to sell their grain to local ele-

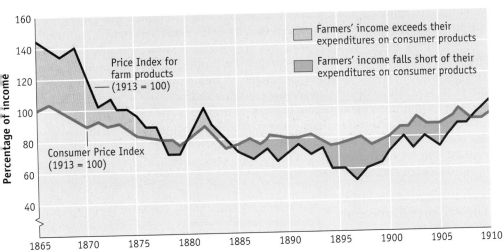

Consumer Prices and Farm Product Prices, 1865–1910   Farm prices, on a steady decline after the Civil War, remained above consumer expenditures until the late 1870s. As consumer prices began to level in the 1880s, farm prices continued their downward trend, leading farmers to spend more on consumer items they needed than on the farm goods they produced.

vator operators or use their services for a fee. The operators were supposed to pay for the grain according to market rates. However, especially in the remote West, unscrupulous operators exploited farmers by offering less than the standard price. Since the elevator operators had a monopoly on access to railroads, farmers could not negotiate better prices or sell their crops to other bidders.

Already by the mid-1860s some farmers had begun to organize to share their grievances and pool their resources. In 1867 Oliver Hudson Kelley, a clerk in the Department of Agriculture, founded the National Grange of the Patrons of Husbandry. Initially, the Granges functioned as social groups, sponsoring picnics, dances, lectures—anything to break up the loneliness of farm life. By 1875 Granges had attracted eight hundred thousand members in twenty thousand locals throughout the Midwest, South, and Southwest, and had become more activist. The Granges tried to lower the cost of consumer goods by appointing agents to negotiate directly with manufacturers, cutting out middlemen. In 1872 Montgomery Ward, the first company to sell goods by catalog, was founded specifically to do business with Grangers. The Granges also founded or acquired mills, elevators, and plants for production and insurance companies and banks for finance.

To deal with their chief adversary—the railroads—Grange members focused on state regulation, seeking and obtaining laws to establish the maximum rates that railroads and elevators could charge. When states did pass new regulations, business groups often resisted, and many of the cases ended up before the Supreme Court. In *Munn* v. *Illinois* (1877), the most important, the justices upheld the right of Illinois to regulate private property so long as it was "devoted to a public use." But the case was not the victory it seemed. The Court ruled that state commissions had the power to regulate local rates, but not long-haul rates. Railroads responded by raising the long-distance rates to compensate for the lost revenue on local rates. Later decisions limited regulation of railroads by ruling that states did not have the power to determine rates of carriers that crossed state lines.

The Grange movement ran out of steam at the end of the 1870s. In some states, Grangers victory in the *Munn* case convinced farmers that the battle with monopolies had been won. In other states, the railroads used fear and intimidation to discourage farmers from organizing. Everywhere, inexperience and mismanagement plagued Grange efforts to develop into a powerful economic force.

The Alliance Movement of the 1880s

At the end of the 1880s, amid another slump in prices for farm products, a host of organizations blended into the national Alliance Movement. Initially, the movement developed distinct branches in the South and Midwest. In the Plains many Grange members formed the Northwestern Alliance. In the South farmers organized in Texas to form the Southern Alliance. A Colored Farmers' Alliance for blacks grew up alongside the Southern Alliance, which was a whites-only organization. Most estimates place the Colored Farmers' Alliance membership at about 250,000—a remarkable accomplishment when white violence was a common response to blacks' attempts to organize.

In 1886 Dr. Charles W. Macune, an energetic and inspiring leader, expanded the southern network of local chapters, or suballiances, into a national system of state Alliance Exchanges. The Alliances established an elaborate system for reaching farmers in isolated areas. Each created its own press supported by hundreds of local papers that reached millions of readers each week. Between 1887 and 1891 the Alliances sent lecturers into forty-three states and territories to recruit members and encourage cooperation. The farm movement's vibrant leaders excited audiences. In Kansas, Mary Elizabeth Lease captured the popular imagination by telling audiences of farmers "to raise less corn and more hell." An Irish-American raised in Pennsylvania, Lease had lost her father and two brothers in the Civil War. After the war she moved to Kansas and became one of the state's first female lawyers; from that foundation she advanced to leadership in the Alliance.

Lease's high profile underscored the Alliance effort to expand its coalition to include women, working people, and African-Americans. Novelist Hamlin Garland observed, "No other movement in history—not even the anti-slavery cause—appealed to the woman like this movement here in Kansas." Not all Alliance groups allowed women to assume leadership roles, but overall the movement expanded the opportunities available to women. Hoping to build a partnership of the "producing classes," the Alliances also advocated the eight-hour workday and government support of labor unions' right to bargain collectively. At the same time, Georgia's Tom Watson, one of the most respected of the Southern Alliance leaders, appealed to black tenant farmers and sharecroppers to join with their white counterparts in ousting the white political elite. "You are made to hate each other," he informed black and white farmers, "because upon that hatred is rested the keystone of this arch of financial despotism which enslaves you both." Despite the egalitarian rhetoric, however, racial differences often prevented poor southern whites and blacks from working together for a common cause. "[We] believe this is a white man's government, and we should rule this country," noted a Georgia farmer. When black Arkansas cotton pickers organized a work stoppage in 1891, white farmers lynched at least fifteen strikers.

In 1889 the Alliances met in St. Louis to develop a national program. Their platform called for breaking up the concentrated power of railroads, grain buyers, and banks. "The fruits of the toil of millions are boldly stolen to build up colossal fortunes for a few, unprecedented in the history of mankind," they complained. Their solution was to call for government ownership of the railroads and banks. "We believe the time has come," the Alliances' Populist Party proclaimed in 1892, "when the railroad companies will either own the people or the people must own the railroads." Their platform called for inflation of the money supply by printing more greenbacks, minting silver, or both. In addition, they advocated structural changes to make government more responsive to the public: the initiative and referendum (which permitted voters to propose legislation through petitions and to void laws passed by the legislature), the secret ballot, and popular election of U.S. senators (who were still chosen by state legislatures).

The centerpiece of their program was Macune's subtreasury plan, which called for the creation of federal subtreasury offices, near warehouses or elevators, in which farmers could store their nonperishable crops. Subtreasuries would guarantee 80 percent of the value of the stored commodities. This arrangement would allow farmers to market their produce at any time of the year, providing them with leverage to bargain for the highest price for their crops.

Members of the Farmers' Alliance tapped into deep currents in American culture to articulate a powerful critique of the emerging industrial order. Evangelical Protestantism inspired the soul of the agrarian protest movement. Alliance members viewed themselves as missionaries restoring the message of Christianity to American life. Their rhetoric rang with religious imagery, and their rallies resembled religious camp meetings. "The battle is between God's people and the worshippers of the golden calf," proclaimed a Kansas farmer. Deeply rooted fears of concentrated wealth and power fed into the farmers' protest. Alliance supporters, soon to be called Populists, combined two powerful—and often conflicting—strands in American political thought. Like many Democrats since the days of Andrew Jackson, Populists identified themselves with the interests of the "common man" in their struggle against the power brokers of the new industrial order. On the other hand, like the Republicans of their time, they believed that a powerful federal government should play a role in protecting the public welfare. To these existing ideas they added a commitment to increased public participation in the decision-making process and a disdain for traditional political parties.

In 1890 Alliance members decided to enter national politics. Farmers in the Midwest clamored for a third party to challenge both the Democrats and the Republicans. In the South farmers tried to capture control of the powerful

Democratic Party. Though the midwestern and southern strategies varied, the results were the same: farm candidates scored impressive victories. The Plains farm movement, organized as the People's Party in Kansas, won control of the state legislature, elected five congressmen, and filled a Senate seat. In Nebraska Populists took two of the three congressional seats and seized control of both houses of the legislature. The Southern Alliance, which in many communities quietly courted black votes by promising to support political (not social) equality, elected four pro-Alliance governors, captured the legislature in seven states, and sent forty-four congressmen and several senators to Washington.

The Populist Party, 1892

Inspired by their victories, Alliance leaders laid the groundwork for a national third party to challenge the Democrats and Republicans. The People's Party of America opened its convention on July 4, 1892, in Omaha, Nebraska. "It was a religious revival," reported one observer, "a crusade, a pentecost of politics in which a tongue of flame sat upon every man, and each spoke as the spirit gave him utterance." The Populists presented a long list of reforms, including the popular election of senators, a graduated income tax, antitrust legislation, and public ownership of the railroads. The central issue was a proposal to increase the amount of money in circulation by adopting the free and unlimited coinage of silver at a ratio of sixteen ounces of silver to one ounce of gold.

For president the Populists nominated General James Baird Weaver, a former Union general and Greenback Party candidate in 1884. Large and enthusiastic crowds responded to Weaver's Populist message in the Midwest. At many campaign stops the forceful Mary Lease joined Weaver and stirred up crowds, claiming that the government "is no longer a government of the people, by the people, and for the people, but a government of Wall Street, by Wall Street, and for Wall Street." It was a different story in the South, where many white farmers opposed the Populists' racial egalitarianism and remained wedded to the Democratic Party. Lease said that on one southern campaign stop so many people threw eggs at Weaver that he looked like "a regular walking omelet."

While Weaver and the Populists struggled to build a new party, the Democrats and Republicans offered a replay of the 1888 election. Republicans nominated Harrison on the first ballot and approved a platform that attributed "the prosperous conditions of our country" to the "wise revenue legislation" of their party, exemplified by the McKinley Tariff. The Democrats selected former President Grover Cleveland and passed a platform denouncing "Republican protection as a fraud, a robbery, of the great majority of the American people for the benefit of the few."

The new Populist Party made an impressive debut on election day, but it was not substantial enough to derail the major parties. Weaver earned 1,029,846 votes and 22 electoral votes, and Populist candidates won five Senate seats, eleven congressional races, and three governorships. The party drew most of its support from among struggling farmers and laborers in the Midwest, the Rocky Mountain states, and the South. Capitalizing on the disenchantment with Republicans that voters had expressed in the 1890 midterm elections, Cleveland achieved a decisive victory, winning 277 electoral votes to Harrison's 145. He drew about 373,000 more popular votes than his Republican challenger (5,555,426 to 5,182,690), becoming the only president to serve two nonconsecutive terms. For the first time since the Civil War, the Democrats won a majority in both Houses of Congress (see map on page 788).

Despite the Populists' impressive showing in the election, troubling signs clouded the future of the party. Southern Democrats, believing that their party could not win the presidency without southern votes, indulged in bribery, stuffing ballot boxes, and fraudulent counting to maintain party loyalty and thwart Populist candidates. Fraud and intimidation peaked in Georgia, where the popular Tom Watson, seeking reelection to Congress, made a special effort to bring black tenant farmers into the Populist Party. "Watson ought to be killed and it ought to have been done long ago," the Democratic governor dared declare. Democratic operatives murdered as many as fifteen African-Americans. They shipped in more cooperative blacks from across state lines to swell Democratic vote totals. The vote recorded in Watson's home district was double the number of legal voters. The tactics succeeded; Watson lost the election.

Populist Party Button

Thomas E. Watson became one of the first politicians in Georgia to support the Farmers' Alliance, insisting that farmers needed "its advocates and champions in positions of power and importance." In 1890, Watson won election to the House of Representatives on the Alliances' St. Louis platform, but lost his bid for re-election in 1892. Watson opposed the fusion of the Populist and Democratic parties in 1896, but accepted his party's nomination for vice president. Populist Party campaign buttons either depicted Watson with Bryan or, showing the factionalism within the party, with Watson alone as the Populist Party's presidential candidate. *(From "The Encyclopedia of Political Buttons", 1985. Hake's Americana, York, PA.)*

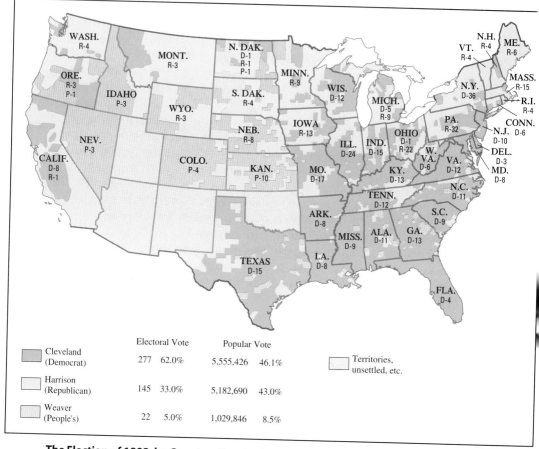

		Electoral Vote		Popular Vote	
Cleveland (Democrat)		277	62.0%	5,555,426	46.1%
Harrison (Republican)		145	33.0%	5,182,690	43.0%
Weaver (People's)		22	5.0%	1,029,846	8.5%

Territories, unsettled, etc.

The Election of 1892, by County   Despite limited success in the electoral college, the People's Party candidate, James B. Weaver of Iowa, received over one million votes. While most of Weaver's votes were from the farmers of the West, the People's Party made inroads into the Democratic-dominated South as shown by the number of counties that voted for Weaver.

THE CRISIS OF THE 1890S

Leaving office in 1893 President Harrison boasted, "There has never been a time in our history when work was so abundant, or when wages were so high." Yet within a few months the United States plunged into a deep depression. The economic downturn that President Cleveland inherited created widespread fears of social unrest. Armies of unemployed people descended on Washington in search of relief, asking for an unprecedented experiment in intervention by the national government. Workers, who had to endure steep wage cuts, joined in thousands of strikes, not a few of which resulted in violence. While such activism convinced many people that U.S. society was unraveling, President Cleveland focused his energy on returning the nation to the gold standard. His failure to reverse the depression produced a huge Republican victory in the 1894 midterm election and set the stage for the 1896 presidential election.

The Depression of 1893

The new industrial order created an interdependent economy: a crisis in one sector of the economy sent shock waves rippling throughout the nation. Thus, as the agricultural expansion ended in the late 1880s, many railroad companies found themselves overextended and unable to meet their obligations. The bankruptcy of the Philadelphia and Reading Railroad in spring 1893 started a chain reaction that resulted in the deepest depression to that date. By the summer a number of other railroads had also failed, including the Erie, the Northern Pacific, the Union Pacific, and the Santa Fe. By August, a quarter of all U.S. railroads, which operated forty thousand miles of track and represented $2.5 billion in capital, were bankrupt.

As railroad construction ceased, the demand for steel dropped, forcing dozens of companies out of business. Overextended banks, already suffering from the withdrawal of European investments as a result of economic weakness abroad, failed—nearly five hundred in 1893. Cash-poor banks called in their loans, and individuals and firms that could not repay went bankrupt. The wave of bank failures flooded Wall Street with panic selling as stock prices reached all-time lows. On May 5, 1893—"Industrial Black Friday"—the market suffered a dramatic drop. At the same time, the demand for gold produced a dangerous drain on Treasury reserves, which sank below the $100 million mark. A business journal noted in August that "never before has there been such a sudden and striking cessation of industrial activity."

The depression, which lingered for four years, created widespread suffering. As companies folded, the numbers of laid-off workers multiplied. By 1894 nearly 3 million workers were idle. By the end of the year, at least one worker in five was out of work. "Men died like flies under the strain," Henry Adams observed, "and Boston grew suddenly old, haggard, and thin."

Since most people believed that assisting the poor was a private matter, the burden of relief fell most heavily on local charities, benevolent societies, churches, labor unions, and ward bosses. But these groups were overwhelmed by the demand for services. Over a hundred thousand homeless people roamed the streets of Chicago. "Famine is in our midst," declared the head of the city's relief efforts. At one point Chicago saloons were handing out free lunches to an estimated sixty thousand people a day. A Washington, D.C., newspaper reported "a vast army of unemployed, and men pleading for food who have never before been compelled to seek aid."

Fear of social unrest gripped the entire country. "We are on the eve of a very dark night," a writer warned President Cleveland, "unless a return of commercial prosperity relieves popular discontent." Industrialist James J. Hill wrote the president, "Business is at a standstill and the people are becoming thoroughly aroused." The editors of *Railway Age* shared the fear of turmoil. "It is probably safe to say, that in no civilized country in this century," they wrote, "has society been so disorganized as it was in the United States during the first half of 1894."

Social Unrest: Coxey's Army and the Pullman Strike

For a brief period Americans seemed to have lost faith in democracy. In spring 1894 unemployed masses formed small "armies" that threatened to "invade" Washington to secure relief from the depression. It was the first time that so many protesters had called on the federal government to provide jobs for the unemployed. Altogether seventeen industrial armies marched on Washington, scaring the administration into thinking that they represented incipient rebellion across the country. The most famous march was led by "General" Jacob Coxey, a wealthy quarry owner from Ohio. Starting on Easter Sunday 1894, Coxey, accompanied by his wife and infant son, Legal Tender Coxey, led five hundred unemployed men, women, and children from Ohio to Washington. Coxey and his followers planned to present government leaders with "a petition with boots on" in support of a public works program of road building. The press covered the march as if it were a foreign invasion. "For every two sloggers in Coxey's ranks there was at least one reporter," recalled a journalist. When Coxey entered the Capitol grounds, a hundred mounted police officers routed the demonstrators and arrested Coxey for trespassing on the grass.

Violent labor strikes contributed to a growing fear of revolution. Even before the depression, rumblings of unrest rolled across the land. The Great Railway Strike of 1877 had ignited nearly two decades of labor violence. In 1892 labor disputes shook Andrew Carnegie's steel plant in Homestead, Pennsylvania. When workers objected to the company plan to reduce wages, manager Henry Clay Frick ordered a lockout, hired three hundred strikebreakers from the Pinkerton National Detective Agency, and built a barbed-wire fence around the plant to keep out workers.

Early on the morning of July 6 the strikebreakers tried to sneak into the plant on barges sailing down the Monongahela River from Youngstown. Workers, who had set up a twenty-four-hour watch, greeted their replacements with rocks, sticks, and gunfire. After an all-day battle the Pinkertons surrendered. Three Pinkertons and ten strikers died in the fighting. The strike dragged on through the summer. By October, with the help of eight thousand state militia troops, Frick had hired new workers and forced the strikers to accept a harsh new settlement. The strike left a legacy of bitterness and ended effective organizing in the steel industry for a half-century.

The depression added to labor's discontent as wages were cut, employees laid off, and factories closed. During the first year of the depression, 1,400 strikes sent more than half a million workers from their jobs. The worst walkout idled 170,000 coal miners in Pennsylvania and the Midwest, where strikers bombed mine shafts, dynamited coal trains, and fought state militia. For nearly two weeks in June 1894, fighting rocked coalfields in Illinois, Ohio, and Indiana.

While Coxey's Army was calling for government aid to the unemployed, the Pullman Palace Car Company was laying off a large portion of its workers. The number of employees fell from 5,500 in July 1893 to 3,300 in May 1894. Many of those who kept their jobs saw their wages reduced as much as 25 percent. The company did not, however, reduce the rent it charged workers in the model factory town in which most employees lived. In May 1894 workers went on strike when the company refused their requests for lower rents or higher wages. In June the Ameri-

Coxey's Army   The depression of 1893 caused tremendous economic turmoil, and by 1894, hundreds of disgruntled, unemployed laborers sought ways to protest their plight by confronting politicians in Washington, D.C. Jacob Coxey and the Army of the Commonweal of Christ left his home in Massillon, Ohio, on March 25, 1894, five hundred strong. Coxey had hoped another 100,000 disgruntled workers would join the march before they arrived in the capital on April 30, but those numbers never materialized. Nevertheless, Coxey's Army, seen in this photo, impressed spectators with its size and enthusiasm, and stirred fears of further labor unrest. *(Library of Congress.)*

can Railway Union (ARU) came to the assistance of the Pullman workers by voting to boycott all Pullman cars, which meant that union members would refuse to work on the trains of most railroads. Until the ARU was created in 1893, railroad workers were represented by separate unions of engineers, firemen, switchmen, and conductors. Under the dynamic leadership of Eugene Debs, an official of the locomotive firemen's union, the ARU forged a powerful alliance of all railroad workers, making it the largest single union in the nation, with more than 150,000 members. As a result of this solidarity, the strike spread rapidly, delaying the mail and tying up railroad traffic in the Chicago area.

The Chicago press reacted violently to the strike. The *Herald* openly supported the railroads, declaring, "If they yield one point it will show fatal weakness." The *Tribune* ran a series of stories branding Debs as a drunken tyrant whose "reckless" actions had endangered "the lives of thousands of Chicago citizens." No one opposed the strike more than U.S. Attorney General Richard Olney, who wired the federal attorney in Chicago: "I feel that the true way of dealing with the matter is by a force which is overwhelming and prevents any attempt at resistance." Under pressure from the business community and at the insistence of Olney, President Cleveland decided to put an end to the boycott. When the strikers ignored a court injunction, Cleveland exploded. "If it takes the entire army and navy to deliver a postcard in Chicago, that card will be delivered," he swore, and promptly dispatched two thousand troops to Chicago to "restore law and order."

The arrival of the troops on July 4 incited widespread protest and violence. Angry strikers burned railroad cars; reports estimated the damage to railroad property at $340,000. A *Chicago Evening Post* headline screamed, "Frenzied Mob Still Bent on Death and Destruction." After a few days, the federal troops restored order and helped crush the strike. At the same time Debs and other union leaders were arrested for violating the injunction and were sentenced to six months in jail.

Most people supported Cleveland's tactics, but a few critics complained. Illinois Governor John Peter Altgeld protested the president's use of federal troops without a request from the state, calling the order a "violation of a basic principle of our institutions." The government's decision to imprison Debs without a jury trial or conviction worried many people, even conservatives. However, with the fear of social unrest at a fever pitch, most people applauded Cleveland's use of force. Future president Theodore Roosevelt, then serving as a civil service commissioner, advised his fellow citizens that such radical sentiment could only be suppressed "by taking ten or a dozen of their leaders out, standing them against a wall and shooting them dead."

Depression Politics   Despite the army of unemployed and clear signs of social unrest, Cleveland clung to his conservative faith that government had no responsibility to assist those in distress. "While the people should patriotically and cheerfully support their Government," President Cleveland had explained at his inauguration, "its functions do not include the support of the people."

The causes of the depression may have been complex, but Cleveland was certain he had discovered the culprit: the collapse of the international monetary system. Equally convinced of the solution, he committed all the powers of his office to balancing the budget and returning the United States to the gold standard. To that end, Cleveland called Congress into special session in August to repeal the Sherman Silver Purchase Act. Western interests responded with a bill calling for free coinage of silver to increase the money supply. After a passionate, sometimes brilliant debate, Cleveland's forces carried the day. The voting revealed the sectional differences over the issue. Nearly all the votes in favor of the White House proposal came from the industrial East; almost all the votes in support of the free silver proposal came from the West.

Cleveland's action precipitated a run on gold reserves as people flooded into banks to redeem their silver certificates. Worried that the government would not have enough gold to support all the certificates, Cleveland turned to J. P. Morgan and a group of Wall Street bankers to provide backing for new government bonds. The syndicate bought the bonds at a discount and then sold them to the public for a hefty profit. The move did little to stop the drain on gold reserves, but it aroused public ire. It seemed to ordinary people that this was another tightfisted bargain in which wicked capitalists had profited. Critics complained that Cleveland was "now fastened by golden cords to a combination of the worst men in the world." Not until 1896, when the Treasury issued $100 million in bonds supported by public subscription, did the crisis pass.

Cleveland's depression policies angered millions of Americans, and his efforts to lower tariffs particularly alienated many of his business supporters. Shortly after assuming office, Cleveland endorsed congressional efforts to reduce tariffs. Senate Republicans, however, succeeded in adding nearly six hundred amendments to the original bill, which actually increased tariffs on many items even as it placed numerous raw materials on the "free" list. On August 28, 1894, the Wilson-Gorman Act became law over Cleveland's veto. Cleveland declared that "the livery of Democratic tariff reform has been stolen and worn in the service of Republican protection."

The most significant feature of the legislation had nothing to do with tariffs, however; it was a controversial federal income tax. Congress included the tax—a modest 2 percent on all incomes over $4,000—to cover the revenue lost by reducing some tariffs. Americans had experimented with the income tax during the Civil War, but outraged critics viewed the imposition of a permanent peacetime tax as a threat to American liberty. A divided Supreme Court agreed, and in *Pollock* v. *Farmers Loan and Trust* (1895), the Court struck down the tax. Speaking for the majority, Justice Stephen Field warned, "It will be but the stepping stone to others, larger and more sweeping, 'til our political contests will become a war of the poor against the rich; a war constantly growing in intensity and bitterness."

The public registered its dissatisfaction with Cleveland's response to the depression in the 1894 midterm elections. The Democratic Party suffered the greatest defeat in congressional history, losing 113 House seats. "The truth is," said one senator, "there was hardly an oasis left in the Democratic desert."

Despite the massive display of discontent with the Democrats, internal squabbling combined with resistance from the major parties kept Populist gains in the election to a minimum. Nationally, the Populists elected only four senators and four congressmen. In Kansas Republicans held a mock funeral to mark the death of the Populist challenge. With the Democrats confined to the South and the Populist advance fizzling, the Republicans reigned supreme. They had every reason to feel confident about the upcoming 1896 presidential election.

THE REPUBLICAN TRIUMPH: THE ELECTION OF 1896

The Democrats abandoned the beleaguered Cleveland in 1896, nominating the dynamic William Jennings Bryan who championed the "free silver" cause. The Democrats' change of heart left the Populists in a quandary: should they nominate their own candidate or form a coalition with the Democrats? After a bruising fight, they decided to endorse Bryan but select their own candidate, Georgia's Tom Watson, for vice president. When the Republicans nominated Ohio's

William McKinley, the 1896 campaign became a sectional clash over the "money question" and the national government's economic policy role. The outcome would end the political stalemate of the previous twenty years.

Democrats and Populists

Cleveland's decision to return to the gold standard produced serious strains in the Democratic Party between midwestern farmers who clamored for silver and eastern business interests who favored gold. The contending factions descended on the Democratic convention in Chicago to battle for the party's soul. "You ask us to endorse Cleveland's fidelity," "Pitchfork" Ben Tillman, the Democratic governor of South Carolina, shouted to Cleveland's supporters in the platform debate. "I say he has been faithful unto death, the death of the Democratic party."

The key moment in the proceedings came on the second day of debate, when Nebraska's William Jennings Bryan gave his "Cross of Gold" speech. Aroused by Bryan's passionate address, the pro-silver insurgents took control of the platform hearing. The party's platform, which adopted all of the insurgents' agenda, condemned "trafficking with banking syndicates," demanded free and unlimited coinage of both silver and gold at the legal ratio of sixteen to one, attacked the protective tariff, and denounced the Supreme Court for invalidating the income tax.

The next day Democrats nominated Bryan for president. To balance the ticket and calm the fears of the party's conservatives, the convention selected Arthur Sewall, a multimillionaire banker and shipbuilder from Maine, as his running mate. Gold Democrats, determined not to be crucified on a cross of silver, bolted the party and nominated Senator John M. Palmer of Illinois. The *New York World* observed, "The sceptre of political power has passed from the strong certain hands of the East to the feverish, headstrong mob of the West and South."

In embracing the silver issue, the Democratic Party had commandeered the centerpiece of the Populist program. As they gathered in St. Louis for their convention, Populist Party leaders debated how to respond to the changing political situation. Many midwestern Populist leaders believed they would be most effective if they joined forces with the Democrats. They wanted to endorse Bryan—in other words, create a "fusion" ticket. Congressman Jerry Simpson cautioned that if the Populists did not endorse Bryan, the party "would not contain a corporal's guard in November." Another party leader, rationalizing that Bryan was "more of a Populist than a Democrat," proclaimed "there was nothing left of the Democratic party at Chicago but the name."

Advocates for fusion ran into tough opposition. Southern Populists, who had fought a bitter war against an entrenched Democratic Party in their home states, rejected the idea. Tom Watson complained that merging with the Democrats would mean "we play minnow while they play trout; we play June bug while they play duck; we play Jonah while they play the whale." In the Midwest, memories of the Democratic Party's support for slavery and disunion dimmed hope for a fusion ticket. Kansas's Mary Elizabeth Lease angrily declared, "My father and brothers died on the field of battle defending the flag and the Union that the Democratic party, represented by Bryan . . . sought to destroy." Joining Watson and Lease were urban radicals who viewed the Populist Party as a vehicle for more radical changes in the industrial order. Free silver, they believed, was a diversion from the main task of building a new reform party. Predicted Minnesota's Ignatius Donnelly, "Narrow Populism to free silver alone and it will disappear in a rat hole."

After a long and rancorous debate, the convention adopted the fusionist strategy. The Populist Party endorsed Bryan as its presidential candidate but, in an effort to retain its separate identity, nominated its own candidate for vice president, Georgia's Tom Watson. The fusionist strategy ultimately demoralized and destroyed the party. Ignatius Donnelly complained afterward that "the Democrats raped our convention while our leaders held the struggling victim." By the time the campaign was over in the South, Thomas Watson admitted, "Our party, as a party, does not exist any more. Fusion has well nigh killed it. The sentiment is still there, but the confidence is gone."

The Election of 1896

The Republican convention lacked the excitement and drama that characterized both the Democratic and Populist gatherings. "There is no life in it," journalist William Allen White wrote. "The applause is hollow; the enthusiasm dreary and the delegates sit like hogs in a car and know nothing about anything." The party regulars nominated William McKinley of Ohio for president and Garret A. Hobart, a corporation lawyer, as vice president.

McKinley had served in the Union army during the Civil War before winning a seat in Congress in 1876. After losing his congressional seat in 1890, he served two terms as Ohio's governor. A calm, affable man, McKinley had earned a reputation as a political moderate who understood the need for compromise. "He was a small-town man with considerable sophistication," the historian H. Wayne Morgan has observed, "and a political success who never let power or fame turn his head." During his years in Congress, McKinley angered traditional Republicans by occasionally supporting silver measures. By 1896, however, McKinley had recanted his silver votes, and that shift, along with his strong support for high tariffs, had made him the favorite of party regulars.

The famous attorney Clarence Darrow described the 1896 presidential campaign as "the greatest battle of modern times." Between August and November Bryan traveled 18,000 miles by train, visited twenty-six states and more than 250 cities, and communed with millions of Americans—most of them struggling farmers and "common people" who traveled hundreds of miles to hear him speak. Bryan personified the spirit of democratic insurgency. Countless citizens who felt excluded from the new industrial order, especially struggling farmers, looked to Bryan for hope and inspiration. Novelist Willa Cather noted how "rugged, ragged men of the soil weep like children" when listening to him. Another observer noted that after his speeches hundreds of "the poor, the weak, the humble, the aged, the infirm" reached out "hard and wrinkled hands with crooked fingers and cracked knuckles to the young great orator, as if he were in very truth their promised redeemer from bondage." When he arrived in North Carolina, his followers ignited tar barrels along the tracks from Asheville to Raleigh to light his way.

In obvious contrast to Bryan, McKinley stayed at home in Canton, Ohio, speaking to groups of supporters from his front porch. When urged to challenge Bryan on the campaign trail, McKinley replied, "I might just as well put up a trapeze on my front lawn and compete with some professional athlete as go out speaking against Bryan." Strengthening McKinley's campaign, however, was a new breed of political boss. Under the watchful eye of Cleveland businessman Mark Hanna, the Republicans pioneered new methods of selling their candidate that would set the tone of political campaigns for the next century. They began by raising large sums of money. The Republican National Committee pulled in and paid out over $4 million—the most ever spent on a political campaign and ten times more than the opposition. Standard Oil alone spent $300,000 on the campaign—almost matching the entire Democratic war chest. Hanna marketed his candidate by organizing pro-McKinley speakers to support local candidates, mobilizing professional party workers, and hiring scholars and public relations experts to write pamphlets that addressed the concerns of specific groups. McKinley supporters unveiled a new campaign weapon—buttons with a pin attached to the back. As McKinley observed, "This is a year for press and pen."

While Bryan's silver crusade appealed to the Democrats' traditional base of struggling farmers and big-city machines, McKinley used his considerable resources to craft a broader message. Bryan's emphasis on higher crop prices and cheaper money proved unattractive to many urban workers, who desired low food prices and a stable currency that would preserve the real value of their wages. AFL president Samuel Gompers complained that Bryan showed little concern for the economic well-being

The 1896 Presidential Campaign   The election of 1896 pitted two very different politicians and personalities against each other. Republican nominee William McKinley conducted a front-porch campaign, receiving supporters at his home where he gave only well-rehearsed speeches. Carefully selected reporters in the crowd then circulated his speeches in newspapers across the country. William Jennings Bryan, the Democratic and Populist candidate, chose to run a more active campaign. Bryan's whistle-stop tour led him around the country by railroad. At each stop, Bryan gave impromptu speeches to the people of the community, often using the railcar platform as his podium. *(Nebraska State Historical Society.)*

of "the merchants and laborers of the industrial centres." The Republicans success-fully portrayed Bryan as a radical whose agenda would destroy capitalism while at the same time stressing McKinley's support for the protective tariff and the gold standard as keys to economic recovery. The *New York Tribune* denounced Bryan as a "wretched rattle-pated boy, posing in vapid vanity and mouthing resounding rottenness." The *Louisville Courier Journal* slammed the smooth-talking Democrat as "a dishonest dodger . . . a daring adventurer . . . a political faker."

The election produced tremendous public interest, with four of every five vot-ers going to the polls. Voter turnout in closely contested midwestern states reached as high as 95 percent. So many people cast ballots that Bryan received more votes than any previous presidential candidate in history and still lost the election! McKinley reaped the benefits of his campaign strategy, winning 7,102,246 popular votes to Bryan's 6,492,559. In the electoral college he collected 271 votes to Bryan's 176 (see map below).

The election accentuated the continuing sectional differences in America. Bryan, who carried twenty-one states, did not take one outside the South or east of the Mississippi. The twenty-two great industrial states of the North and East, plus Oregon, voted decisively for McKinley. Many urban voters, alienated by Bryan's evangelical Protestantism as well as his economic agenda, turned to the Republi-cans. For his part, McKinley downplayed potentially divisive moral issues, empha-sizing his tariff and gold policies, both of which were popular with workers. The appeal worked: of the eighty-two cities with populations of at least forty-five thou-sand, only a dozen supported Bryan, and seven of these were in the Solid South and two in the silver states. As a Kansas Republican noted, "McKinley won because the Republicans had persuaded the middle class, almost to a man, that a threat to the gold standard was a threat to their prosperity."

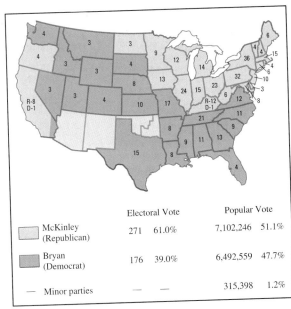

	Electoral Vote		Popular Vote	
McKinley (Republican)	271	61.0%	7,102,246	51.1%
Bryan (Democrat)	176	39.0%	6,492,559	47.7%
Minor parties	—	—	315,398	1.2%

The Election of 1896 With the People's Party endorsement, Democratic nominee William Jennings Bryan used his cam-paign to promote his silver cru-sade, appealing to farmers and the traditional Democratic base in the South. Meanwhile his opponent, William McKinley, conducted a "front porch" cam-paign, promising prosperity for all and remaining neutral on many of the moral issues Bryan emphasized in his movement. While Bryan won almost as many states as McKinley, Bryan failed to win the electoral-rich states of the North.

The McKinley Presidency

The 1896 election produced the first undisputed majority since 1872. It shattered the stalemate that had mired the parties since the Civil War. McKinley took advantage of the opportunity and planned to reassert the power of the presidency. He crisscrossed the nation to build public support for his policies, provided regular briefs to the Washington press corps, and installed telephone lines in the White House so that he could coordinate with executive departments.

His efforts allowed him to push key parts of the Republican agenda through Congress. In 1897 Congress passed the Dingley Tariff, which, along with reducing the number of items on the "free" list, raised rates to the highest level in American history. The Republicans passed the Gold Standard Act of 1900, which set the gold dollar as the sole standard of currency. To appease western interests, the act allowed for the creation of national banks in small towns, granting them authority to issue paper money. On both the tariff and the gold issues, Republicans displayed remarkable party unity—97 percent voted for the tariff and 100 percent for the gold act.

The reform spirit that drove the Populist crusade lost much of its steam after 1896. The Republican triumph left many farmers demoralized, while the gradual return of prosperity eased social tensions. As a result, McKinley felt little need to respond to the wide-ranging Populist agenda for regulation of industry and direct democracy. The dawn of the new century, however, would produce a new generation of progressive reformers determined to make such Populist ideas as direct election of senators and enforcement of antitrust legislation a reality.

CONCLUSION

During the Gilded Age, a new politics of stalemate replaced the experiments in activist Republican government of the Civil War and Reconstruction eras. With the bitter debates over slavery and federalism fading, Americans longed for political stability. The political parties, torn by internal rifts and vying for votes in a handful of key states, were unable to forge governing coalitions. In addition, the presidency lost much of its power following the impeachment trial of Andrew Johnson, and an unruly Congress was incapable of filling the vacuum. Loud but inconclusive debates raged over patronage and reform, the money question, and tariffs. People remained passionate about politics, voting in unprecedented numbers, but presidential campaigns often revolved around personalities and scandal while avoiding discussion of a host of unresolved national issues.

One of the most pressing "unresolved" issues concerned the plight of farmers in the South and Midwest. Increased production brought a dramatic decrease in prices for farm products and a declining standard of living for many farmers. Convinced that greedy railroad and grain elevator operators were at fault, farmers created the Grange movement in the 1860s. By the 1880s Granges gave way to the formidable Farmers' Alliance Movement, which articulated an ambitious program, including government ownership of the railroads, an inflated money supply, and direct democracy measures. When the major parties failed to respond to their agenda, farmers moved into electoral politics by forming the Populist Party. In 1892, the high point of the agrarian experiment, the Populist presidential candidate scored twenty-two electoral votes, and the party won a number of Senate and House seats.

Beginning in 1893 a severe economic depression provided momentum to the Populist challenge. With more than 3 million workers unemployed, many Americans feared widespread social unrest. Those fears seemed confirmed when "armies" of the unemployed marched on Washington calling for federal assistance, and when violent labor disputes shook Andrew Carnegie's steel plant in Homestead, Pennsylvania, and the Pullman Palace Car Company in Chicago.

Many of the social tensions of the decade found expression in the 1896 presidential election, which mirrored the continuing sectional divisions in America. The Democrats co-opted the Populist platform and nominated William Jennings Bryan. The Republicans selected William McKinley, who stood firmly on the gold standard. Bryan's message of reform resonated with struggling farmers in the Midwest and South, while McKinley's steadfast support for the gold standard endeared him to business interests in the East and Midwest and to urban workers wary of Populism's Protestant moralism. The decisive Republican triumph ended the politics of stalemate and inaugurated a new era of Republican dominance. The Populist challenge had failed, but the Republican administrations to come would open a new round of experimentation in national government.

Annotated Suggested Readings

Several excellent overviews of the Gilded Age discuss the period's politics and political culture. Sean Dennis Cashman's *America and the Gilded Age: From the Death of Lincoln to the Rise of Theodore Roosevelt* (1984) and Mark Wahlgren Summers's *The Gilded Age: or, The Hazard of New Functions* (1997) are both highly readable surveys. *The Gilded Age: Essays on the Origins of Modern America* (1996), edited by Charles Calhoun, is a collection of essays on a wide range of topics. Samuel Hays's *The Response to Industrialism, 1885–1914* (1957) and Robert Wiebe's *The Search for Order, 1877–1920* (1967) remain standard texts.

H. Wayne Morgan's *From Hayes to McKinley: National Party Politics, 1877–1896* (1969) is a good overview that corrects previous interpretations of Gilded Age politics as devoid of real issues or party differences. David J. Rothman's *Politics and Power: The United States Senate, 1869–1901* (1966) views the emergence of modern politics in the Gilded Age through the lens of the Senate. A synthesis of the pivotal election of 1896 is provided in Paul Glad's *McKinley, Bryan and the People* (1964).

Good political biographies of the major political figures of the period include Lewis Gould's *The Presidency of William McKinley* (1980). Gould updates his profile of McKinley in *The Modern American Presidency* (2003). Other useful biographies include Ari Hoogenboom's *Rutherford B. Hayes: Warrior and President* (1995) and Louis W. Koenig's *Bryan: A Political Biography of William Jennings Bryan* (1971). Three recent books reevaluate the presidency of Grover Cleveland: Henry F. Graff, *Grover Cleveland* (2002); H. Paul Jeffers, *An Honest President* (2000); and Alyn Brodsky, *Grover Cleveland: A Study in Character* (2000).

Several studies have tackled the major issues of the Gilded Age. Civil service reform is covered by John G. Sproat in *"The Best Men": Liberal Reformers in the Gilded Age* (1968). Tom Terrill examines the tariff issue in *The Tariff, Politics, and American Foreign Policy, 1874–1901* (1973). The currency issue is treated by Irwin Unger in *The Greenback Era: A Social and Political History of American Finance, 1865–1879* (1964) and by Walter Nugent in *Money and American Society, 1865–1880* (1968).

In the past thirty years historians have uncovered a fascinating and vibrant political culture in the Gilded Age. Robert Cherny provides a synthesis of recent interpretations in *American Politics in the Gilded Age, 1868–1900* (1997). Morton Keller's *Affairs of State: Public Life in Late Nineteenth Century America* (1977) is a comprehensive study. In *The*

Third Electoral System, 1853–1892: Parties, Voters and Political Cultures (1979), Paul Klepp-ner studies American voting behavior. The 1884 election is the subject of Mark Summers' *Rum, Romanism, and Rebellion* (2000). Michael McGerr, *The Decline of Popular Politics* (1986), argues that even while popular participation reached its zenith during this time, political reform had already begun eroding it with measures that reduced the communal nature of partisan politics. Alexander Keyssar looks at efforts to restrict the franchise in *The Right to Vote: The Contested History of Democracy in the United States* (2000).

More specific aspects of the political culture are covered by several commendable works. Rebecca Edwards offers a fascinating look at the gender dimension of political culture during this time in *Angels in the Machinery: Gender in American Party Politics from the Civil War to the Progressive Era* (1997). Robert Kelley's *The Transatlantic Persuasion* (1969) puts Gilded Age political culture in international perspective. In *Cross of Culture: A Social Analysis of Midwestern Politics, 1850–1900* (1970), Paul Kleppner finds that eth-nicity and religion mattered more than class in party affiliation. Richard Jensen comes to a similar conclusion in *The Winning of the Midwest: Social and Political Conflict, 1888–1896* (1971).

The economics behind the Panic of 1893 are examined by Charles Hoffman in *The Depression of the Nineties: An Economic History* (1970). Samuel McSeveney examines the political ramifications of the depression in *The Politics of Depression: Political Behavior in the Northeast, 1893–1896* (1972). Several excellent books have been written on the social unrest that accompanied the depression. Carlos Schwantes's *Coxey's Army: An American Odyssey* (1985) is a highly readable narrative on the experiences of the men who marched on Washington. Paul Krause examines the larger issues involved in the Home-stead strike in *The Battle for Homestead, 1880–1892: Politics, Culture and Steel*. Stanley Buder offers a wonderful examination of the Pullman strike in *Pullman: An Experiment in Industrial Order and Community Planning* (1967).

Richard Hofstadter's classic work, *The Age of Reform* (1955), focused on the reac-tionary aspect of the Populist movement. Since the fifties this perception has been chal-lenged by a number of works, most notably Lawrence Goodwyn in *Democratic Promise: The Populist Movement in America* (1976). Gene Clanton also stresses the genuine reform content of the movement in *Populism: The Humane Preference in America* (1991). In *The Populist Response to Industrial America* (1962), Norman Pollack likewise views Populism as a broad "social gospel" movement until the currency issue superseded all others and killed the movement. Robert Durden stresses the importance of organization over ideol-ogy in *The Climax of Populism: The Election of 1896* (1965). In *American Populism: A Social History, 1877–1898* (1993), Robert McMath takes a grassroots approach to the move-ment. For a good local study, see Jeffrey Ostler's *Prairie Populism: The Fate of Agrarian Rad-icalism in Kansas, Nebraska, and Iowa, 1880-1892* (1993).

The *History Companion*

Populism and Its Critics

The Populist Party Platform

On July 4, 1892, the People's Party unveiled its platform at its first national convention in Omaha, Nebraska. The preamble, written by Minnesota Populist leader Ignatius Donnelly, crystallized the basic ideals and discontents of the Populist movement, including its demand for the coinage of silver.

The conditions which surround us best justify our co-operation; we meet in the midst of a nation brought to the verge of moral, political, and material ruin. Corruption dominates the ballot-box, the Legislatures, the Congress, and touches even the ermine of the bench. The people are demoralized. . . . The newspapers are largely subsidized or muzzled, public opinion silenced, business prostrated, homes covered with mortgages, labor impoverished, and the land concentrating in the hands of capitalists. . . . The fruits of the toil of the millions are boldly stolen to build up the colossal fortunes of the few, unprecedented in the history of mankind; and the possessors of these, in turn, despise the Republic and endanger liberty. From the same prolific womb of governmental injustice we breed the two great classes—tramps and millionaires.

The national power to create money is appropriated to enrich bond-holders; a vast public debt payable in legal-tender currency has been funded into gold-bearing bonds, thereby adding millions to the burdens of the people.

Silver, which has been accepted as coin since the dawn of history, has been demonetized to add to the purchasing power of gold by decreasing the value of all forms of property as well as human labor, and the supply of currency is purposely abridged to fatten usurers, bankrupt enterprise, and enslave industry. A vast conspiracy against mankind has been organized on two continents, and it is rapidly taking possession of the world. If not met and overthrown at once, it forebodes terrible social convulsions, the destruction of civilization, or the establishment of an absolute despotism.

We have witnessed for more than a quarter of a century the struggles of the two great political parties for power and plunder, while grievous wrongs have been inflicted upon the suffering people. . . . Neither do they now promise us any substantial reform. . . . They propose to drown the outcries of a plundered people with the uproar of a sham battle over the tariff, so that capitalists, corporations, national banks, rings, trusts, watered stock, the demonetization of silver and the oppressions of the usurers may all be lost sight of. . . .

We seek to restore the government of the Republic to the hands of the "plain people," with which class it originated. We assert our purposes to be identical with the purposes of the National Constitution. . . .

Our country finds itself confronted by conditions for which there is no precedent in the history of the world; our annual agricultural productions amount to billions of dollars in value, which must, within a few weeks or months, be exchanged for billions of dollars' worth of commodities consumed in their production; the existing currency supply is wholly inadequate to make the exchange; the results are falling prices, the formation of combines and rings, the impoverishment of the producing class. We pledge ourselves that if given power we will labor to correct these evils by wise and reasonable legislation, in accordance with the terms of our platform.

We believe the powers of the government—in other words, of the people—should be expanded . . . as rapidly and as far as the good sense of intelligent people and the teachings of experience shall justify, to the end that oppression, injustice, and poverty shall eventually cease in the land.

William Allen White Criticizes the Kansas Populists

Not everyone shared the Populist enthusiasm for reform. In 1896 William Allen White, the editor of a small Kansas newspaper, the *Emporia Gazette,* wrote a scathing critique of populism and its impact on his home state. The essay, which was published during the heat of the 1896 presidential campaign, was widely reprinted in Republican newspapers.

If there had been a high brick wall around the state eight years ago, and not a soul had been admitted or permitted to leave, Kansas would be half a million souls better off than she is today. . . . In five years ten million people have been added to the national population, yet instead of gaining a share of this—say, half a million—Kansas has apparently been a plague spot and, in the very garden of the world, has lost population by ten thousands every year.

Not only has she lost population, but she has lost money. Every moneyed man in the state who could get out without loss has gone. Every month in every community sees someone who has a little money pack up and leave the state. This has been going on for eight years. Money has been drained out all the time. In towns where ten years ago there were three or four or half a dozen money-lending concerns, stimulating industry by furnishing capital, there is now none, or one or two that are looking after the interest and principal already outstanding. . . .

Go east and you hear them laugh at Kansas; go west and they sneer at her; go south and they "cuss" her; go north and they have forgotten her. Go into any crowd of intelligent people gathered anywhere on the globe, and you will find the Kansas man on the defensive. The newspaper columns and magazines once devoted to praise of her, to boastful facts and startling figures concerning her resources, are now filled with cartoons. . . .

"There are two ideas of government," said our noble [William Jennings] Bryan at Chicago. "There are those who believe that if you legislate to make the well-to-do prosperous, this prosperity will leak through on those below. The Democratic idea has been that if you legislate to make the masses prosperous, their prosperity will find its way up through every class and rest upon them."

That's the stuff! Give the prosperous man the dickens! Legislate the thriftless man into ease, whack the stuffing out of the creditors and tell the debtors who borrowed the money five years ago when money "per capita" was greater than it is now, that the contraction of currency gives him a right to repudiate.

Whoop it up for the ragged trousers; put the lazy, greasy fizzle, who can't pay his debts on the altar, and bow down and worship him. Let the state ideal be high.

What we need is not the respect of our fellow men, but the chance to get something for nothing.

Oh, yes, Kansas is a great state. Here are people fleeing from it by the score every day, capital going out of the state by the hundreds of dollars; and every industry but farming paralyzed, and that crippled, because its products have to go across the ocean before they can find a laboring man at work who can afford to buy them. Let's don't stop this year. Let's drive all the decent, self-respecting men out of the state. Let's keep the old clodhoppers who know it all.

The Populist Party grew out of widespread rural discontent over falling farm product prices, rising costs due to high tariffs, high rates for rail contracts and grain elevators, and exorbitant credit terms. Gradually, farmers' complaints evolved into a broader critique of American society and the financial underpinnings of the new industrial order. Tapping into a rich rhetorical tradition that pitted the noble aspiration of the "common man" against greedy concerns of the elite, the Populists charged that a cabal of eastern capitalists had manipulated the money supply and cheated the "producing class" out of their fair share. They looked to the federal government for assistance, proposing a host of solutions, including greater democracy, regulation of the railroads, easier credit, and an expanded currency through the coinage of silver. For many struggling farmers, free coinage of silver emerged as a panacea for all the ills of the new industrial order. Expanding the currency would allow farmers to pay off debts with inflated money and raise the price of farm products.

Not everyone accepted the Populists' critique of current conditions or their ambitious program for reform. Many middle-class and business groups complained that the Populist commitment to silver, seething hostility to business, and unquestioned faith in the "common man" would lead to economic calamity. Urban workers, who shared the Populist anger toward big business and were equally frustrated with the established political parties, feared that expanding the currency would produce rampant inflation and lower living standards. Populists may have possessed good intentions, these critics charged, but their efforts to use government power to help the poor would strangle business and choke off prosperity. White viewed the economic crisis in Kansas as evidence that the siren call of Populism would lead to disastrous consequences. Republicans successfully used these arguments against William Jennings Bryan in the 1896 presidential campaign.

QUESTIONS FOR ANALYSIS

1. Whom do the Populists blame for the nation's moral and economic crisis?

2. Why is the silver issue so significant for the Populists?

3. Why do Populists see a need for a third party?

4. What are the Populists' views of government?

5. What is White's grievance with the Populists, and why does he blame them for Kansas's economic misery? Is his judgment fair?

6. How does White's view of government differ from the Populist view?

21

The Progressive Era

1889–1916

For solutions to many of the problems plaguing America's cities, Addams and other progressive reformers believed that only government could provide the services and the regulation that were necessary for future progress.

On September 18, 1889, Jane Addams, the thirty-year-old daughter of a prosperous Quaker from Cedarville, Illinois, and her college friend, Ellen Gates Starr, rented a rundown mansion at the corner of Halstead and Polk Streets on Chicago's West Side and began the first settlement house, or neighborhood center, in the Midwest. "Probably no young matron ever placed her own things in her own house with more pleasure than that with which we first furnished Hull House," Addams reflected.

Like a growing number of other educated, middle-class women, Addams was dissatisfied with the traditional options available to women. For most of the previous decade she had searched for a constructive outlet for her humanitarian instincts. The idea of creating a settlement house came to her when she visited Toynbee Hall in London, the world's first settlement house, which had been founded by students from Oxford University. "It is so free of 'professional doing good,' so unaffectedly sincere and so productive of good results in its classes and libraries so that it seems perfectly ideal," she wrote.

Addams returned to America determined to start her own Toynbee Hall. She would need determination and more to overcome many daunting obstacles. Chicago, the second-largest city in the country, was bursting at the seams with new immigrants from Europe. The area surrounding Hull House was one of the city's dirtiest and poorest neighborhoods. Most immigrants lived in crowded tenements; raw sewage flowed through the foul-smelling streets outside. Tuberculosis and smallpox ran rampant. Well-fed rats patrolled the neighborhood. Journalist Lincoln Steffens described the neighborhood as "first in violence, deepest in dirt, loud, lawless, unlovely, ill-smelling, criminally wide open, commercially brazen, socially thoughtless and raw."

Addams wanted to help her new neighbors, but she lacked a detailed blueprint of how to accomplish that goal. "We had no definite idea what we were there to do," she recalled. "But we hoped, by living among the people, to learn what was needed and to help out." She started by establishing a nursery for the children of working women, then expanded to include a kindergarten and a boys club for older youths. By the turn of the century the settlement covered an entire city block; included a gymnasium, auditorium, and library; and offered a wide range of services: a health clinic, vocational training, English classes, and music and art education. The "social experiment on Halstead Street" evolved into a workshop for urban progressivism—a collection of reform movements that focused on using government to tame the excesses of industrialization and urbanization.

Like many other progressive reformers who grew up in comfortable middle-class Protestant families, Addams believed that urban problems such as crime and poverty resulted not from individual failures, but from an unhealthy environment. Addams also shared contemporary fears that the massive influx of immigrants, combined with the evils of industrialization, would widen class and cultural differences in America. For solutions to many of the problems plaguing America's cities, Addams and other progressive reformers believed that only government could provide the services and the regulation that were necessary for future progress. To convince officials to take action, Hull House staff made elaborate studies of child labor, tenement conditions, and wage rates in the neighborhood. They joined coalitions with other progressive groups to advocate protective labor legislation for working women and children. They led the way in enacting legislation to regulate the sale of narcotics and initiated an investigation into the city's impure milk supply, thereby helping lower the infant mortality rate.

Jane Addams represented just one part of a new reform spirit that gathered momentum in the last decade of the nineteenth century and began to affect nearly every aspect of American life between 1900 and 1916. People living at the time felt excitement in the air. One reformer declared in 1913 that "one of the most inspiring movements in human history is now in progress." Millions of people called themselves progressives, although they did not always agree on the proper pace or the critical focus of reform. While social justice advocates like Jane Addams sought to make society more compassionate, other progressives concentrated on making it more efficient. Still others focused on improving social morality, which they hoped to do by prohibiting the sale of alcohol, outlawing prostitution, and limiting immigration.

For all of their differences, progressives spoke a common language of discontent, which emphasized the dangers of monopoly power, stressed the importance of community, and articulated a passion for social efficiency. In addition, progressives borrowed some of this language and many of their ideas from thinkers in Europe who were confronting many of the same social problems. Finally, when they agreed on an issue, progressives formed alliances with other groups. But the coalitions were usually short-lived, and allies one day might be opponents the next. All of the activity made the Progressive Era one of the most confusing in American history, but also one of the most exciting eras of experimentation in local and federal government.

- What was progressivism, and what groups in society tended to join in progressive reform movements?

- What new roles did progressives expect government to play in correcting America's problems?

- What was the difference between radicals and progressives?

- How did progressivism manifest itself in national politics and in actions by the federal government?

This chapter will address these questions.

THE RISE OF PROGRESSIVISM

A number of groups played important roles in laying the foundation of the progressive movement. Intellectuals challenged the assumptions of Social Darwinists, who argued that immutable laws of nature shaped society, while many middle-class women contributed to the reform spirit by campaigning for social justice. A new breed of investigative journalists, called muckrakers, aroused public anger with their graphic depictions of corruption in America. The new middle class, fascinated with social efficiency and scientific management, searched for ways to create a more orderly society. These various reform elements were united by a common desire to use activist government to limit the power of corporations and improve society.

The Challenge to Social Darwinism   Gilded Age intellectuals like William Graham Sumner had argued that Charles Darwin's theories of evolution could be applied to contemporary society. Reform was unnecessary, even counterproductive, they argued, because nature dictated the rules of the game and guaranteed the "survival of the fittest." By 1900 a number of intellectuals had initiated a spirited assault on Sumner's ideas. In the process they laid the intellectual foundation for the Progressive Era.

The new intellectuals showed less interest in how society was supposed to function than in how it really did. They differed widely in their views, but they shared the basic belief that people could improve society through reason and intelligence. Psychologist William James, older brother of novelist Henry James, laid the groundwork for much progressive social thought in *Principles of Psychology* (1890). James challenged the determinism and pessimism of Social Darwinism by arguing that human beings could control the process of their own evolution. His philosophy of pragmatism argued that modern society must rely for guidance less on old ideals and moral principles and more on the test of scientific inquiry. No idea was valid, he claimed, unless it worked. "Pragmatism," he wrote, "is willing to take anything, to follow either logic or the senses, and to count the humblest and most personal experiences."

An expanding network of social scientists brought this same concern for scientific inquiry into other areas of thought. Lester Frank Ward, a Brown University

CHRONOLOGY

1889	Addams founds Hull House
1892	Wells-Barnett begins antilynching campaign
1895	Anti-Saloon League founded
1900	Hurricane hits Galveston, Texas, which adopts city commission government
1901	Roosevelt becomes president after McKinley's assassination
1902	TR intervenes in the coal strike
1903	Holmes appointed to Supreme Court
1904	TR elected president Northern Securities Company dissolved as a railroad trust
1905	Industrial Workers of the World founded Pure Food and Drug Act passed
1906	Hepburn Act passed Sinclair publishes *The Jungle*
1908	Taft elected president Staunton, Virginia, hires first city manager in United States
1910	NAACP founded
1911	Triangle Shirtwaist fire
1912	TR bolts Republican Party Wilson elected president
1913	Seventeenth Amendment (direct election of senators) ratified Federal Reserve Act passed Underwood-Simmons Tariff lowered overall average duty on imports
1914	Sanger indicted for obscenity Clayton Anti-Trust Act passed
1916	Brandeis appointed to Supreme Court
1919	Eighteenth Amendment (Prohibition) ratified
1920	Nineteenth Amendment (women's suffrage) ratified

sociologist, argued that human intelligence allowed people to plan and to order their worlds as they saw fit. In his book *Dynamic Sociology* (1883), Ward argued that the Social Darwinists had underestimated the capability of human intelligence to alter the environment and improve society. Economist Thorstein Veblen added his influential voice to the chorus of social critics in two important works, *A Theory of the Leisure Class* (1899) and *The Theory of Business Enterprise* (1904). Veblen poked fun at the industrial tycoons of the late nineteenth century to show that greed, not natural laws, governed economic relations in America. As an antidote to laissez-faire, he called for a new class of government experts to develop policies for managing the economy. In *Economic Interpretation of the Constitution* (1913), the progressive historian Charles A. Beard set out to show that greed and self-interest, not divine inspiration, had influenced the creation of the Constitution. It was, he argued, a human document that could be changed to address new circumstances.

Others called for the new faith in scientific reasoning to be applied to education. In books such as *The School and Society* (1902) and *Democracy and Education* (1916), philosopher-educator John Dewey emphasized the value of a creative, flexible approach to education that would enable students to acquire practical knowledge. Dewey rejected the rote memorization of traditional education and instead tried to "make each one of our schools an embryonic community life, active with the types of occupations that reflect the life of the larger society." The scientific method, he believed, would be the governing principle of this new "instrumental" education.

Progressive legal thinkers such as Oliver Wendell Holmes, Jr., who was appointed to the Supreme Court in 1903, and Louis D. Brandeis, appointed in 1916, hoped to transform the law from a bulwark of the status quo into a vehicle for change. Although the two justices would not always line up on the same side of an issue, Holmes and Brandeis shared a similar conception of the relationship of law to society. "The life of the law has not been logic; it has been experience," Holmes argued in *The Common Law* (1881). Brandeis agreed, writing that the law must "guide by the light of reason." As a lawyer, Brandeis used mounds of statistical evidence showing that long working hours contributed to poor health to convince the courts to accept legislation establishing a ten-hour workday for women (*Muller* v. *Oregon* 1908). The law, he argued, must consider actual working conditions and not just legal precedent. It was a rare victory: Holmes and Brandeis seldom convinced a majority on the court, but their views influenced a generation of legal thinkers.

Church workers challenged the prevailing belief in Social Darwinism by appealing to religious conviction. Proponents of the Social Gospel argued that the main teachings of Christianity—social justice and sacrifice—should form the foundation of modern society. In his popular book *In His Steps* (1896) Charles Sheldon urged readers to ask "What would Jesus do?" as they made choices in their daily lives. Walter Rauschenbusch, a Protestant theologian from Rochester, New York, was the leading proponent of this new Social Gospel, a theology rooted in his own grim experience in New York's Hell's Kitchen, where he encountered the harsh realities of poverty and misery. In his most important works, *Christianity and the Social Crisis* (1907) and *Christianity and the Social Order* (1915), Rauschenbusch argued that all people should work toward creating the Kingdom of God on earth.

The growing presence of the Salvation Army in many cities was the most visible sign of the desire to proclaim the message of Christian social responsibility to an industrial society. The Salvation Army boasted a corps of three thousand officers and twenty thousand privates by 1900. Along with ministering to spiritual needs, the organization provided material aid—food pantries, employment bureaus, and day-care centers—to the urban poor.

Women and Social Justice

Excluded from formal participation in politics and from most male-dominated trade unions and fraternal organizations, women created separate organizations to shape legislation and protect their interests. Middle-class reformers expanded the nineteenth-century cult of domesticity to support women's expanding role in influencing public policy. "Woman's place is in the Home," wrote the suffragist Rheta Childe Dorr in 1910, "but Home is not contained within the four walls of an individual home. Home is the community." Reformers broadened the dominant belief in the moral superiority of women, and their special responsibility for dealing with the family and protecting children, into a "maternalist" vision of gender-specific reform.

To realize that vision, women reformers created a host of voluntary associations. The Woman's Christian Temperance Union (WCTU), founded in 1874, organized women in campaigns to enforce sobriety and defend the home. The National Congress of Mothers (1897), which promoted "all those characteristics which shall elevate and ennoble," sponsored playgrounds and kindergartens in a number of cities. The Women's Trade Union League (1903) attempted to organize women workers. The Young Women's Christian Association played an active role in local communities.

African-American women, barred from white clubs, organized their own groups to improve community life. The Women's Convention of the Black Baptist Church raised money for black women to attend college. In 1896 members of three dozen black clubs came together to create the National Association of Colored Women (NACW). Led by Mary Church Terrell, a graduate of the old abolitionist stronghold Oberlin College, the NACW offered self-help classes, homes for the elderly and for working girls, and public health information.

Paralleling the settlement house movement, female reformers used their voluntary associations to develop social welfare programs for working-class women and their children. One of the most successful advocates of social legislation was Florence Kelley. Born into a wealthy Philadelphia family, Kelley graduated from Cornell University in 1882. Refused admittance to the University of Pennsylvania for graduate studies because she was a woman, Kelley traveled to Switzerland. There she attended school, married, and gave birth to three children. In 1886 she returned to the United States and, after her marriage fell apart in 1891, became a resident at Hull House. Over the next few years she emerged as an outspoken and tireless champion for legislation to protect children and women. She published numerous studies documenting the ill effects of long working hours on women and children, and in 1893 convinced the Illinois legislature to pass an eight-hour workday law for women. When the state supreme court invalidated the legislation, Kelley took her cause to Washington. In 1899 she became the secretary of the National Consumers League, which attempted to mobilize public opinion in favor of new social legislation. After her death in 1932 Supreme Court Justice Felix Frankfurter wrote that Kelley "had probably the largest single share in shaping the social history of the United States during the first thirty years of this century."

More militant members of the social justice movement looked to class action. Among these were young female labor organizers who challenged the craft unionism of the AFL by trying to organize unskilled workers. In November 1909 the

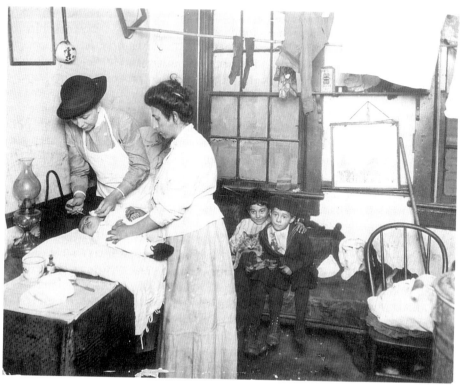

Nurse Visits a Tenement   Progressive reformers were greatly concerned about the poor conditions in which the urban working classes lived. Social workers and nurses, like the one attending the baby in this photograph, went door to door in tenement buildings, assessing the living conditions, teaching residents better sanitation and home economics, and administering medication. Most of these visiting professionals were educated, middle-class women; the work gave them a respectable outlet for their talents. (*Chicago Historical Society.*)

New York Women's Trade Union League and a local of the International Ladies Garment Workers Union held a massive and emotional rally in New York City's Cooper Union. After listening to impassioned speeches emphasizing their common struggle as exploited working women, thousands of garment workers voted to strike, demanding union recognition, higher wages, and better working conditions. Raising their right hands high in the air, the women sealed their commitment to strike with an oath: "If I turn traitor to the cause I now pledge, may this hand wither from the arm I now raise."

Over the next three months the strikers were arrested by police and beaten by thugs. But their spirits remained high. As one observer noted, "Neither the police, nor the hooligan hirelings of the bosses nor the biting frost and chilling snow of December and January damped their willingness to picket the shops from early morn till late at night." The strikers returned to work without union recognition, but their efforts had forced major concessions from management, including a fifty-hour workweek, wage increases, and preferential hiring for union members.

Some of the strikers worked at the Triangle Shirtwaist Company in downtown New York City, which caught fire on March 25, 1911. As the flames spread through the top three floors of the ten-story building, many workers, mostly young Jewish women, found themselves trapped by exit doors that had been locked from the outside to prevent workers from slipping out for breaks. Forty-seven women leaped to their deaths attempting to escape the flames. "They hit the pavement just like hail," reported a fireman. "We could hear the thuds faster than we could [see] the bodies fall." Another ninety-nine victims were consumed by flames and smoke. The tragedy led to the creation of the New York State Factory Commission, which recommended laws for improving working conditions and regulating hours and wages for women and children.

The Muckrakers

A small army of investigative reporters made important contributions to the progressive reform spirit's sense of moral indignation and idealistic purpose. Theodore Roosevelt branded these new journalists "muckrakers," after the "Man with the Muckrake" in John Bunyan's *Pilgrim's Progress:* "the man who could look no way but downward with the muckrake in his hands." Muckrakers combined factual reporting with heavy moralizing to expose dishonesty, greed, and corruption in American society and to arouse the indignation of middle-class readers.

Technological innovations allowed the muckrakers to reach a wider readership. Inexpensive popular newspapers and eye-catching specialty magazines proliferated thanks to new developments in printing. To sell more magazines, publishers began to replace political prose with news and feature articles. In 1902 *McClure's* ran a series of articles by Ida Tarbell that described the unfair business practices of John D. Rockefeller's Standard Oil trust. Tarbell described Standard Oil as "a big hand [that] reached out from nobody knew where, to steal" the oil entrepreneurs' accomplishments "and throttle their future." In another series, Lincoln Steffens described municipal corruption in several large eastern and midwestern cities. Other journalists jumped on the muckraking bandwagon. Ray Standard Baker exposed the brutal labor practices of railroad and mine owners. David Graham Phillip depicted the U.S. Senate as a playground for rich and powerful interests. These stories, often published later as books, reached millions of Americans. The most famous muckraker was a young radical novelist, Upton Sinclair, whose realistic novel *The Jungle* (1906) presented all-too-vivid descriptions of filth and confusion in "Packingtown" as beleaguered workers processed tainted and sometimes spoiled meat for public consumption.

The New Professions

Industrial society created a new layer of middle-class workers who kept it running smoothly and efficiently. At the same time the growth of scientific knowledge increased the power and prestige of physicians, lawyers, and others with advanced education. The new middle class and the interest groups its members formed were a powerful force for reform during the Progressive Era.

Many members of the new middle class shared a fear of social disorder and a passion for efficiency. They worried that the extraordinary forces transforming American society at the end of the nineteenth century—massive waves of immigrants flowing into congested cities, new factories forcing people to work long hours in dangerous conditions, powerful corporations that widened the gap between rich and poor and corrupted democratic institutions—offered a recipe for violent strikes and social unrest. In its search for order, the middle class was at the vanguard of a bureaucratic revolution that valued scientific procedures, centralized management, and social planning. "There are two gospels I always want to preach to reformers," Theodore Roosevelt said. "The first is the gospel of morality, the next is the gospel of efficiency." As an example of how to remedy the problem of disorder, many progressives pointed to the modern corporation, which, for all its faults, offered a model of organization and efficiency that could be extended to the larger society. "The trust," remarked Jane Addams, "is the educator of us all." Addams did not like trusts, and she certainly did not want to see their power expanded, but she, like most progressives, admired their efficiency.

Not surprisingly, members of the new middle class created a host of professional organizations both to protect their interests and to implement their ideas of social order. By 1916 lawyers had established professional bar associations in all forty-eight states. Teachers created the National Education Association in 1905. Social workers formed the National Federation of Settlements (1911). Business established some of the most powerful and effective organizations, including the National Association of Manufacturers (1895) and the United States Chamber of Commerce (1912). The most successful and influential new professional association emerged in medicine. In 1901 doctors reorganized the American Medical Association (AMA) into a modern institution. In that year only 8,400 doctors were members of the AMA. Ten years later the AMA claimed over 70,000 members, nearly 50 percent of the nation's physicians. The AMA organized the nation's doctors to upgrade standards and restrict the number of new physicians. Increased scrutiny forced many less rigorous medical schools to close their doors and slashed the number of new physicians entering practice.

As the political parties began to lose their grip on voter loyalties, these interest groups exercised greater political clout. Civil service reform during the 1870s and 1880s, combined with the widespread use of the secret ballot in the 1890s, weakened the power of party bosses and provided voters with more freedom to choose candidates. The new middle-class interest groups moved to fill the political void, encouraging voters to split their tickets and support reform candidates.

The Appeal of Progressivism

"Slowly as the new century came into its first decade I saw the Great Light," observed Kansas editor William Allen White. The "Great Light" brightening the horizon was progressivism—the collective effort of various reformers to tame the consequences of industrialism and urbanization. Their goals were different, sometimes even contradictory. Labor wanted better wages and hours; female reformers wanted the alleviation of poverty and better public education; temperance workers demanded laws to protect the family against saloons; farmers wanted debt relief and lower railroad rates. Ironically, many businessmen jumped on the progressive bandwagon, hoping heightened government involvement might stabilize the economy and restore competition.

For all their differences, progressives shared a common belief that government could be used as a powerful tool for social betterment. The depression of the mid-1890s added urgency to calls for activist government. By aggravating the festering social problems in the nation's cities and accelerating the trend toward corporate consolidation, the depression pushed the questions of how to regulate trusts and how to maintain social order to the top of the political agenda.

The progressives' temperament and agenda borrowed heavily from Populism, although the two movements were hardly identical. Progressives tended to be educated and middle class, based largely in the eastern and midwestern states. Populists, on the other hand, were largely uneducated farmers living in the South and West. But the Populists ceded to their urbane cousins both a moralistic world-view, which saw political issues as a clash between right and wrong, and an agenda for using government to rein in the trusts and empower the people. William White observed that the progressives "caught the Populists in swimming and stole all of their clothing except the frayed underdrawers of free silver."

In addition to a shared desire to expand government, progressives articulated a common social philosophy. First, they believed that people were essentially rational, and when confronted by evidence of corruption and inefficiency, they would respond by demanding changes to make government more responsive to the public will. Second, whether they were attacking the trusts or advocating for municipal ownership of utilities, progressives tapped into a deep-seated fear of monopoly power. Third, they challenged the notion that in a modern industrialized society individuals could live independently of one another. Progressives hoped to purge society of its individualistic excesses by stressing cooperation and emphasizing social responsibility. Finally, progressives shared a passion for social efficiency. Certain that most social problems resulted from a poor environment, progressives planned to employ experts and professionals to alter social conditions and improve society. "Those who have studied the causes of poverty and social evils have discovered that nine-tenths of the world's misery is preventable," said a reform-minded mayor. "Science has countless treasures yet to be revealed."

American progressives joined with reformers in Europe and Australia, who were struggling with many of the same social problems, to form a remarkable international conversation that focused on the central issue of the time: how to use government power to address the unwanted consequences of urbanization and industrialization. "America no longer teaches democracy to an expectant world," Walter Weyl observed in *The New Democracy* (1912), "but herself goes to school to Europe and Australia." Through travel and study abroad, international seminars, and professional journals, American progressives joined forces with like-minded reformers in England, Germany, and France to develop strategies for using public power to tame the excesses of industrialization. European reformers relied heavily on federal power, passing legislation guaranteeing national health insurance, unemployment insurance, and old-age pensions. Reflecting the traditional American fear of centralized power, progressives walked a tightrope between state control and laissez faire, creating a patchwork of local, state, and federal regulations. In doing so, they established the intellectual scaffolding for Franklin Roosevelt's New Deal.

POLITICAL REFORM

The progressive faith in reform through government intervention first found expression at the local level, where reformers mobilized to restructure city governments and pass new social justice measures. After conquering city hall, they carried their agenda to the statehouse; inspired by Robert La Follette's "Wisconsin Idea," progressives enacted a number of structural reforms to give voters a greater voice in policymaking. These reforms reduced the power of political parties and helped interest groups make their influence felt. Tapping into the reform spirit, suffragists pushed for enactment of a constitutional amendment granting women the right to vote. There was, however, a darker side to reform, as many progressives used government power to regulate morality as they saw it.

Reforming the City American cities continued to experience spectacular growth in the Progressive Era. Between 1900 and 1920 New York's population exploded from 3.4 million to 5.6 million; Chicago's from 1.7 million to 2.7 million. Immigrants made up 40 percent of New York's population in 1910. Including American-born children of immigrants, the figure soared to 80 percent! As detailed in Chapter 19, the influx of millions of immigrants strained the ability of cities to provide adequate housing, transportation, and municipal services.

The many native-born Americans who viewed the cities as threats to American democracy believed that local bosses built powerful political machines by preying on the ignorance of new immigrants. "Saloons and gambling houses and brothels," one Baltimore reformer charged, "are the nurseries of urban statesmen." Many reformers, ignoring the inherent difficulties of managing the exploding urban growth, blamed machine politicians and poor administration for urban problems such as unpaved streets, poor sanitation, corruption, and mismanagement. Using the corporation as a model, they promised to make government more efficient, honest, and responsive to the public interest.

During the 1890s reformers built a broad-based coalition to demand structural reform and policy changes in city government. Muckrakers aroused public indignation with exposés of municipal corruption to help reformers seize control of city halls. Once in power, progressives pushed for initiatives designed to undermine the power of urban bosses. To dilute the power of local immigrant machines, they switched from ward elections to citywide elections in which candidates needed to appeal to a broad spectrum of voters, not just to those in the neighborhoods they represented.

Some cities experimented with a commission form of government that was initially developed as an emergency measure. On a hot summer night in 1900 a giant tidal wave killed one out of every six people in Galveston, Texas. The tidal wave also overwhelmed the local government, which proved incapable of dealing with the massive destruction. To meet the crisis, reformers replaced the old system with a special commission of five men to run the government. Rather than dividing executive and legislative authority between a mayor and city council, the new system vested all power in a handful of commissioners, each of whom headed a particular city department. Galveston began to recover, and within a few years Houston, Dallas, and Austin had adopted the commission form. By 1911 nineteen states had granted their cities authority to establish commission government, and within five years the idea had spread to more than four hundred municipalities.

A third approach involved hiring a city manager to take charge of local government. In 1908 Staunton, Virginia, became the first municipality to hire a city manager—an appointed professional administrator who ran the government under the direction of the elected city council and mayor. Five years later Dayton, Ohio, attracted wider attention to the scheme when it adopted the new system after a major flood. The city manager system was borrowed directly from the corporate model, and the city manager served as the chief executive officer of the city. The ideal city, observed a Dayton reformer, was "a great business enterprise whose stockholders are the people."

The commission and city manager systems appealed to the business community and to the middle class by promoting efficiency and undermining the patronage power of big-city bosses and their immigrant machines. The new system replaced the older, decentralized system of city services, which benefited the working class, with a more centralized government controlled by the new professionals. Urban areas that adopted citywide elections, for example, saw a dramatic decrease in working-class and minority representatives. In Los Angeles the change prevented blacks and Hispanics from winning election to the city council. In Pittsburgh the reform allowed upper-class businessmen and professionals to gain control of the city council and the school committee.

The most successful efforts at urban reform came from mayors who won election calling for an end to corruption and advocating an ambitious agenda for social reform. The first progressive mayor was Hazen Pingree, mayor of Detroit from 1889 to 1896, who won election with the support of the city's conservative business community. Once in office, however, he implemented a program of administrative efficiency and broad social justice. He reduced the cost of utilities, slashing streetcar fares and gas rates, and exposed corruption in city government. During the depression of the 1890s he started work-relief programs for Detroit's unemployed, built schools and parks, and required the wealthy to pay higher taxes to finance the programs. In time he brought his reform agenda to the state level after winning election as governor in 1896.

Ohio produced two of the most active reform mayors. In Toledo, Samuel Jones, who served as mayor from 1897 to 1903, earned the nickname "Golden Rule" because he gave city workers an eight-hour workday, provided paid vacations, and barred child labor. Tom Johnson, mayor of Cleveland from 1901 to 1909, lowered fares on local trains, improved the police force, and provided free bathhouses and recreational facilities. He outraged business interests by advocating city ownership of utilities. "Only through municipal ownership," he argued, "can the gulf which divides the community into a small dominant class on one side and the unorganized people on the other be bridged."

Though they succeeded in capturing city hall, the reformers failed to fulfill many of the expectations they had raised. In most cases they helped make the cities cleaner and healthier, but they were more successful at arousing indignation than at creating responsive government. Efficient administration and modest social justice measures were no match for the enormous problems created by the flood of new immigrants and the consequences of industrialization.

Reform in the States   Progressives discovered that the road to reforming the city led inevitably to the statehouse. The states wrote the charters that spelled out city government powers. "Whenever we try to do anything, we run up against the charter," complained the progressive mayor of Schenectady, New York. "It is an oak charter, fixed and immovable." States also set the requirements for suffrage and voting procedures, regulated business and labor conditions, and legislated to enforce morality. Progressives understood that city governments did not have a monopoly on corruption and intransigence. "The legislature met biennially," William Allen White wrote of Missouri in a 1903 issue of *McClure's*, "and enacted such laws as the corporations paid for, and such others as were necessary to fool the people, and only such laws were enforced as party expediency demanded."

The most successful progressive reformer on the state level was Wisconsin Governor Robert M. La Follette. Born in Primrose, Wisconsin, in meager circumstances, La Follette worked his way through the University of Wisconsin law school before deciding to enter politics. He won a seat in Congress before his thirtieth birthday and then earned election as governor in 1900. A superb orator with a combative style who vowed "never to know defeat in a good cause," La Follette emerged as a national symbol of progressivism. During his two terms as governor—he won election to the Senate in 1906—"Fighting Bob" modernized the state government, turning Wisconsin into what reformers across the nation praised as a "laboratory of democracy." His state reform program included laws to establish a direct primary— which allowed voters a voice in the process of selecting a party nominee—to improve the civil service, and to create a graduated state income tax. He cracked down on corporations, forcing them to pay higher taxes and face tougher regulation. "Selfish interests," he proclaimed, "may resist every inch of ground, may threaten, malign and corrupt, [but] they cannot escape the final issues. That which is so plain, so simple, and so just will surely triumph."

The "Wisconsin Idea" quickly spread to other states. New York attorney Charles Evans Hughes, elected Republican governor in 1906, established stricter supervision of insurance companies and created a state public service commission to regulate utilities. In New Jersey, former Princeton University president Woodrow Wilson initiated a program of progressive reforms following his election as governor in 1910. In California, attorney Hiram Johnson campaigned against the Southern Pacific Railroad and its dominance of state government and entered the governor's mansion in 1911 with a slate of reforms.

What was the progressive agenda for the states? Rhetorically, the progressives promoted democracy as the antidote to corruption. "The voice of the people," proclaimed White, "is indeed the will of God." But before enacting their agendas, progressives "purged" the electorate of voters they considered unqualified. In the South this meant disfranchising blacks. In the North it meant eliminating newly

"Battling Bob" La Follette   Wisconsin governor Robert La Follette became famous for his progressive reforms, such as the direct primary, the regulation of railroads, and the use of statistics to research problems and draw up legislation. Other states and cities soon imitated the "Wisconsin Idea," and eventually it became a model for reforms on the national level. In 1906 La Follette was elected to the U.S. Senate, where he continued to work on the forefront of the progressive crusade.   *(Library of Congress.)*

arrived immigrant voters through increased residency requirements, thereby restricting suffrage to native-born or fully naturalized citizens.

After removing what they viewed as undesirable elements from the election rolls, progressives enacted a number of "direct democracy" measures. These measures represented an assault on the power of political parties, which reformers believed had become captive to powerful corporate interests. "The people have come to see," editorialized the *Saturday Evening Post* in 1905, "that parties are to a great extent the tools of the unscrupulous who make of politics a profession." Progressives proposed a number of measures designed to transfer power from organized parties to the people. The initiative allowed reformers to bypass legislatures by petitioning to submit proposed legislation directly to the voters in a referendum. In 1902 Oregon became the first state to enact such reforms. By 1918 nineteen other states had followed. To improve the quality and responsiveness of elected officials, progressives created the direct primary and the recall. The recall allowed voters to call a special election to remove an elected official. Progressive reformers achieved a major political victory in 1913 when the states ratified the Seventeenth Amendment, which provided for direct election of senators by popular vote rather than by state legislatures.

Progressives argued that the democratic reforms gave "to the people direct and continuous control over all the branches of government," so that they could "direct their attention more profitably to the problems connected with the prevention and relief of social and economic distress." Their efforts were aided by an influential group of college-educated female social workers such as Hull House residents Jane Addams, Grace Abbott, and Florence Kelley, who used their positions on state boards of charity and local welfare agencies to create the scaffolding of the modern welfare state. Women reformers lobbied state legislatures for passage of laws providing a monthly stipend to single mothers. In 1911 Illinois enacted the first statewide measure. By 1919 thirty-nine states had enacted mothers' pensions.

Progressive women were responsible for much other important social legislation as well. Drawing on their experience at settlement houses, reformers helped establish juvenile courts with probation officers, secured laws establishing an age limit on the employment of children, and led the drive for workers' compensation for laborers injured on the job. By 1916 every state had laws protecting children and nearly two-thirds had established workers' compensation.

Progressives also placed great hope in the power of independent commissions, such as the New York Factory Commission, to regulate business. They created state commissions to regulate railroads, utilities, and insurance companies. Progressives viewed the commissions as a moderate alternative to unrestrained competition on one hand and government ownership of industry on the other. The commissions were empowered to examine corporate records, hold public hearings, and establish prices and rates. In practice, however, they often lacked a clear sense of the public interest and lacked the authority to compel powerful groups to accept their demands. In many cases the commissions were dominated by the very interests they were created to regulate.

Women's Suffrage

Suffrage supporters had been struggling to gain the right to vote since before the Civil War (see page 624). During the Progressive Era, they slowly gained ground. They received a boost when Carrie Chapman Catt took over the leadership of the National American Woman Suffrage Association in 1900. A shrewd political strategist, Catt developed a grass-roots campaign at the state level that she called "the winning plan." She found many allies among middle-class women and the nexus of voluntary associations they had created. By 1910 nine states, all of them in the West, had granted women the vote. Fearing that the Supreme Court would invalidate their gains, suffrage supporters pressed for passage of a constitutional amendment granting women the right to vote.

Suffrage advocates refined and extended their arguments to win over reluctant male legislators. To appeal to other reformers, they argued that women would expand the universe of educated middle-class voters and battle against corrupt party politicians. Suffragists toned down appeals for equal rights and justice and instead emphasized the positive qualities that women would bring to politics from their domestic experience. Tragedies such as the Triangle Shirtwaist fire convinced many women that they needed the vote to protect their interests as mothers and as workers. They argued that the vote would better enable them to carry out their traditional role in the family. How could a mother teach her children about citizenship, they asked, if she was unable to exercise those rights herself?

Like other progressive reformers, supporters of women's suffrage sometimes based their appeal on nativism and racism. Suffragists from the South opposed voting by blacks, favoring the imposition of a literacy test to "abolish the ignorant vote." The southern suffragist Belle Kearney boldly predicted in 1903 that "The enfranchisement of women would insure immediate and durable white supremacy, honestly attained." In the North many advocates of women's suffrage suggested that middle-class Protestant women would dilute the immigrant vote in large cities. "Cut off the vote of the slums and give it to women," advised Carrie Chapman Catt.

Opponents charged that suffrage would in fact undermine traditional gender roles by blurring the line separating the male and female realms. A woman's place was in the home; men were responsible for the affairs of state. Giving women the right to vote, complained a congressman, "would disrupt the family, which is the unit of society, and when you disrupt the family, you destroy the home, which is the foundation of the republic." A senator insisted that their "milder, gentler nature" made women unprepared "for the turmoil and battle of public life."

When the Progressive Party splintered from the Republican Party in 1912, it endorsed the cause of women's suffrage. To signify its support, party leaders invited

Suffragettes in New York City, 1912   Women had been agitating for the right to vote for over half a century, but during the Progressive Era, they finally began to see tangible progress. In 1915 Carrie Chapman Catt reorganized the efforts of the National American Woman Suffrage Association, integrating state campaigns with the Washington headquarters, compiling information on every congressman and senator, and launching crusades in every electoral district. As this photograph seems to indicate, most American women, including the suffragettes themselves, maintained a traditional, family-centered outlook.   *(Library of Congress.)*

Jane Addams to make a major seconding speech for nominee Theodore Roosevelt. When the Progressive Party dissolved after the election, Republican and Democratic politicians began promoting the suffrage cause in hopes of gathering former members to their side. The sense of shared sacrifice during World War I aided the cause. By 1919 thirty-nine states had granted women the right to vote in at least some elections; fifteen allowed them full participation (see map below). That same year, the Senate adopted the Nineteenth Amendment with barely a two-thirds majority. It was ratified by its passage in the Tennessee legislature on August 21, 1920.

Controlling the Masses   Many progressive reformers were determined not only to improve institutions, but also to improve human behavior. To mold an America that reflected their values, they set out to purge society of drinking and prostitution and to cut off the influx of new immigrants.

By 1900 prohibitionists battling to outlaw alcohol consumption won support from many progressives who viewed the urban saloon as the most striking symbol of

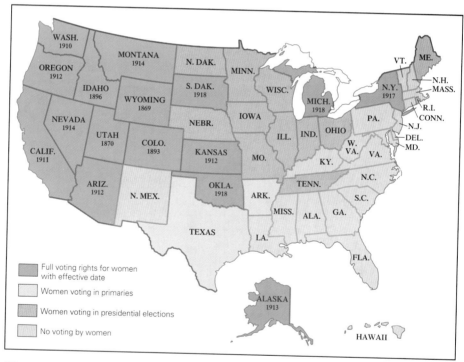

Women's Suffrage Before the Nineteenth Amendment   As Americans migrated West after the Civil War, the issue of women's suffrage traveled with them, finding fertile ground in frontier territories. Some western states granted women the right to vote even before being admitted as a state, as was the case with Alaska and Utah. Some states, like Wyoming and Arizona, granted women full voting rights in their original state constitutions, but most western states added constitutional amendments during the Progressive Era. Other states farther east provided limited suffrage in presidential elections or primaries, but women in the South and in New England would have to wait for passage of the Nineteenth Amendment before being granted the right to vote in any elections.

urban dissipation and disorder. The Reverend Mark Matthews, pastor of the largest Presbyterian congregation in the world, called the saloon "the most fiendish, corrupt and hell-soaked institution that ever crawled out of the slime of the eternal pit." Prohibitionists denounced liquor interests for polluting the political system, ruining families, eroding worker efficiency, and forcing taxpayers to fund new poorhouses and prisons. To members of the new urban middle class, the elimination of alcohol from American life was a necessary step in restoring order to society.

As late as 1900 the issue of prohibition was too hot for either political party to handle. Democrats were reluctant to pursue the issue because they depended heavily on Catholic immigrants; Republicans also counted many urban voters in their coalition. With the parties unwilling to alienate an important constituency group, prohibition supporters were forced to create an independent political pressure group—the Anti-Saloon League. Founded in Ohio in the 1890s the league started on the local level by supporting "local option" laws, which allowed a community's citizens to vote on whether to license saloons. Through this method reformers were able to isolate "wet" areas. In 1900 only 18 million of the nation's 76 million people were living in saloon-free cities and towns. By 1906 about 35 million, or 40 percent of the population, were living in "dry" territory, most of them under local option.

The league then moved to the state level. Since many elected representatives were unwilling to support prohibition, prohibition supporters used a number of direct democracy measures, especially the initiative and referendum. The strategy worked. Between 1906 and 1909 a dozen states went dry. Having established a strong foothold in many local areas and in over two dozen states, the Anti-Saloon League moved to the national level in 1913 by lobbying for a constitutional amendment to prohibit the "sale, manufacture for sale and importation for sale of beverages containing alcohol."

Aided by America's entrance into World War I in 1917 and emphasizing the need to protect the nation's soldiers and conserve grain supplies, progressive advocates of prohibition would finally steer a constitutional amendment embodying their demands through Congress. Two years later, after ratification by every state except Connecticut and Rhode Island, the Eighteenth Amendment became law, to take effect in January 1920.

Crusades against the saloons often spread to prostitution. Muckrakers exposed the operations of "white slavery" rings that kidnapped young women and forced them into prostitution. Between 1910 and 1915 at least thirty-five cities and states conducted major studies of prostitution. To the tools of investigation and publicity, anti-vice crusaders added marches and outdoor prayer meetings held in the heart of red-light districts. Convinced that poor living and working conditions were at the root of prostitution, reformers supported such progressive reforms as wage-and-hour laws and factory safety legislation. "Is it any wonder," asked the Chicago Vice Commission, "that a tempted girl who receives only six dollars per week working with her hands sells her body for twenty-five dollars per week when she learns there is a demand for it and men are willing to pay the price?" In 1910 Congress enacted the Mann Act, which prohibited transporting women across state lines "for immoral purposes." By 1915 every state had outlawed brothels and the public solicitation of sex.

Many progressives also pushed for legislation limiting immigration. Support came from many quarters. Rural Protestants wanted to dry up the cities' source of new voters. Labor leaders saw how employers exploited ethnic tensions to prevent effective union drives. Others based their appeal on simple prejudice. Sociologist Edward A. Ross painted new immigrants as "beaten members of beaten breeds" with "sugar loaf heads, moon faces, and goose-bill noses" who "lack the ancestral foundations of American character." Twice Congress passed laws imposing restrictions on immigration. Both times the president, William Howard Taft in 1913 and Woodrow Wilson in 1915, vetoed the legislation. In 1917 though, following America's entry into World War I, Congress overrode Wilson's second veto.

Some of the bitterest battles over immigration were fought on the state level. Many progressives in California crusaded against Japanese immigrants. Between 1901 and 1908 more than 125,000 Japanese immigrants came to the United States to work on the railroads, in mines, and in logging camps. After 1900 a wave of anti-Japanese hysteria swept through the state. Labor organizations and patriotic societies charged that Japanese immigrants lowered America's standard of living, refused to assimilate into American culture, and represented a threat to American security. Newspaper headlines blared warnings about the Japanese threat: "Brown Man an Evil in the Public Schools" and "The Yellow Peril—How the Japanese Crowd Out the White Race."

In 1906 the San Francisco School Board began segregating Japanese schoolchildren. When the Japanese government protested the decision, President Theodore Roosevelt intervened, forcing the school board to rescind the order. Two years later, Roosevelt negotiated an agreement with Japan—the Gentlemen's Agreement of 1908—limiting Japanese immigration to the United States. The agreement could not stem the tide of anti-Japanese feeling. The California Senate approved by a wide margin a 1913 bill denying Japanese immigrants the right to buy land. Over the next few years, twelve other states passed similar laws.

SOCIAL TENSIONS IN AN AGE OF REFORM

The spirit of reform was not confined to the white middle class; in fact, some of those advocating change proposed social and governmental reforms that challenged the traditional values of most Americans. The progressive period witnessed growing activism among African-Americans who found creative ways to protest injustice. Though excluded from most progressive organizations, blacks were invited to join the Socialist Party and militant labor groups, both of which gathered momentum during the period and called for radical changes in American society. An articulate feminist movement also emerged in the Progressive Era and looked beyond suffrage to challenge the prevailing gender assumptions of the time.

African-American Activism in the Progressive Era

Most progressives were blind to the contradiction between their rhetoric about helping ordinary Americans and their conscious discrimination against racial minorities. Beginning in the 1890s southern whites, fearful of a developing interracial alliance under populism, began the systematic disfranchisement of blacks and poor whites. Progressives continued the process. Progressive governors who supported social reform, such as James K. Vardaman of Mississippi, saw little irony in their vicious racism. While championing a number of progressive measures, including increased spending for education and tougher regulations of railroads, banks, and insurance companies, Vardaman denied that blacks had the right to vote. The African-American, he sneered, was "a lazy, lying, lustful animal which no conceivable amount of training can transform into a tolerable citizen."

Not all progressives endorsed discrimination against African-Americans. Members of the Niagara Movement—formed by activist black leaders in 1910 to protest lynchings, disfranchisement, and segregation—joined with a handful of whites to form the National Association for the Advancement of Colored People (NAACP). The new organization committed its energy and resources to ending racial segregation, guaranteeing equal education, and extending the franchise to all African-Americans. Over the next decade NAACP attorneys scored significant legal victories. In *Guinn* v. *United States* (1915), the Supreme Court ruled that Maryland and Oklahoma laws excluding blacks from voting were unconstitutional. Two years later, in *Buchanan* v. *Worley,* the justices struck down a Louisville, Kentucky, ordinance that required blacks and whites to live in separate communities.

Though black Americans were largely excluded from the progressive movement, they found creative ways to organize and to improve their lot. One way was to "vote with their feet." Between 1890 and 1920 over half a million black southerners moved to northern cities in search of better wages and freedom from the oppressive racial code of the South. Blacks not only went north; they also traveled west, establishing predominately black towns.

Those blacks who remained in the South did not passively endure segregation. In 1891, when Georgia passed a law allowing segregation on streetcars, blacks launched a massive boycott that crippled transportation companies in Atlanta, Savannah, and Augusta. Southern blacks also boycotted segregated banks and steamship lines. Black industrial workers, most of whom lived in the South, unionized. When barred from white unions, as was often the case, blacks formed their own.

Sometimes white racism led to violence. During the 1890s and 1900s major race riots broke out in a number of cities, including Memphis and Atlanta. In the 1906 Atlanta riot, African-Americans opened fire when a violent white mob, incited by a newspaper story accusing black men of raping white women, invaded their town. Race riots were not confined to the South. A white mob attacked the black community of Springfield, Illinois, in 1908, destroying numerous businesses and lynching three black men. In *United States v. Shipps* (1909), the Supreme Court attempted to intervene in the growing number of lynchings when they found a sheriff and several deputies guilty of contempt of court after they allowed a mob to break into a Tennessee jail and lynch a black man whose execution had been stayed by the Court. It was the only criminal case ever tried before the Supreme Court.

For African-Americans education symbolized freedom and autonomy, so when southern states withheld funds for black schools, they found alternative ways to educate their children. A black woman in South Carolina recalled that "there was no school for ten miles in no direction," so her father constructed a "small log house" and used it as a school. By 1915 blacks in Georgia had established 1,544 schools serving more than 11,500 students. Local Alabama communities joined forces with northern philanthropist Julius Rosenwald to create ninety-two schools between 1914 and 1916.

Black activists fought racial prejudice in the North as well. Ida Wells-Barnett, one of the most famous black activists of this period, began a massive antilynching campaign in 1892 after white vandals destroyed the office of her Memphis paper, *Free Speech*. Forced to flee to the North, she founded black women's clubs, such as the Women's Loyal Union in New York, and taught racial improvement and self-help. The club's motto, "Lifting as We Climb," expressed a hopeful spirit of racial progress and solidarity.

Southern educator Booker T. Washington remained the most prominent spokesman for African-Americans during the Progressive Era (see page 647). The black intellectual W. E. B. Du Bois disagreed with Washington's cautious message. The first African-American to earn a Ph.D. at Harvard, Du Bois taught at Atlanta University from 1897 to 1910 and articulated his views in *Souls of Black Folks* (1903). In a direct attack on the accommodationist philosophy of Washington's Atlanta Compromise, Du Bois said that blacks could not sit in "courteous and dumb self-forgetting silence" until whites chose to rescue them. Du Bois based his hopes for change on what he called the "Talented Tenth" of black leaders who would lead the struggle for civil rights.

Du Bois demonstrated the limits of Washington's strategy of accommodation, but his approach, too, was ineffective. His faith in a "Talented Tenth" had little impact on the vast majority of African-Americans who lacked basic social and political rights. "This faith in a black elite," observed one historian, "failed to recognize that there were few blacks as well educated as he, few white liberals who could be counted upon, and few judges who were willing to challenge white attitudes."

Radical Reformers   The enormous changes occurring in the United States in the late nineteenth century provided a breeding ground for radicalism. Like progressive reformers, radicals were troubled by the immense disparity of wealth, the deplorable condition of the urban poor, and the increasing power of huge corporations. Unlike reformers, however, radicals believed that altering society on the surface was not enough, and they instead called for fundamental changes—public ownership of industry, for example—in the structure of American society. The leading proponents of radical reform during the Progressive Era were the Socialist Party and the Industrial Workers of the World (IWW).

Though deeply divided by rival factions, the Socialist Party emerged as a significant political force after 1900. It held special appeal for urban workers, intellectuals, migrant laborers, and tenant farmers of the southern plains who felt displaced in the new industrial order. While socialists of every stripe agreed on the inherent inequities of capitalism, they were too divided ideologically to agree on a common agenda. They were united, however, in their passionate support for one man: Eugene Debs. A fiery and flamboyant speaker who had little patience for the ideological hair-splitting that consumed most socialists, Debs spoke passionately about the needs of society's outcasts. "While there is a lower class I am of it, while there is a criminal class I am of it, while there is a soul in prison I am not free." In 1904 Debs received just over four hundred thousand votes as the party's presidential candidate, and almost 1 million when he ran eight years later (see Competing Voices, page 842).

Debs's national support was not enough to win elections, but local support put many socialists in office. By 1912 the party held 1,200 public offices in 340 cities,

SOUTHERN HORRORS.
LYNCH LAW
IN ALL
ITS PHASES

Miss IDA B. WELLS.

Price,   ·   ·   ·   Fifteen Cents.

THE NEW YORK AGE PRINT.
1892.

Ida B. Wells Anti-lynching Campaign   Ida B. Wells, born a slave in Mississippi, embodied the belief that African-Americans should be social, economic, and political equals with whites. After a white mob lynched a friend, Ida turned her attention to researching and writing about the rising incidents of lynching in the south. Her findings, printed in pamphlets like the one shown here, argued that whites lynched blacks in retaliation for economic and social progress being made in black communities across the South. Wells spent her life leading the anti-lynching effort and at her death in 1931, W. E. B. DuBois described Wells as the woman who "began the awakening of the conscience of the nation." *(Manuscripts, Archives & Rare Books Division, Schomberg Center for Research in Black Culture, The New York Public Library, Astor, Lenox and Tilden Foundations.)*

including seventy-nine mayors in twenty-four states. Once in office, these radicals pursued a moderate agenda, building coalitions with progressive reformers on social justice and direct democracy measures, but opposing progressives on prohibition and immigration restriction.

The most radical group during this period was the Industrial Workers of the World (IWW), or "Wobblies," as they were often called. Founded in Chicago in 1905 by a zealous partnership of radical unionists and political leaders and led by the dynamic William (Big Bill) Haywood, the IWW envisioned a utopian state run by workers. "The final aim is revolution," said a Wobbly organizer. Unlike progressives who looked for common ground between workers and industry, the IWW sided exclusively with labor. "The working class and the employing class have nothing in common," Haywood declared. While the more conservative American Federation of Labor (AFL) denied membership to African-Americans and favored immigration restrictions, the Wobblies embraced society's outcasts, welcoming blacks, immigrants, and women into their ranks.

The Wobblies achieved a few significant victories, but overall their influence was marginal. In 1912 they joined forces with progressives to win higher wages for textile workers in Lawrence, Massachusetts. Progressives also fought to protect the IWW's right to free speech when police in California used force to prevent Wobblies from speaking on street corners. For the most part, however, the IWW's small membership—never exceeding a hundred thousand—and their uncompromising radical stance prevented them from building broad-based coalitions with other reform-minded groups. Most Americans, including workers, rejected the emphasis on class warfare. Whereas Debs and his party obtained respectability from middle-class Americans, the IWW earned only their suspicion.

Ultimately, both the IWW and the Socialist Party suffered from the incompatibility of their twin goals: immediate gains for workers and the long-term overhaul of society. The former necessitated working within the very system the latter sought to destroy. Socialists were more successful because they focused on immediate reforms, but in doing so, they compromised their role as a revolutionary organization. Wobblies never compromised their radical principles, but as a result, they failed to achieve the mass support of American workers, who were more concerned with improving their daily existence than with overthrowing the industrial order.

Feminism   While suffragists gathered momentum by adapting their arguments to traditional gender notions, a new generation of feminists called for liberation from all forms of sexual discrimination and demanded the freedom that men took for granted. Most were unmarried, college-educated, self-supporting, and eager to challenge the restraints of women's "separate sphere." "All feminists are suffragists," said one advocate, "but not all suffragists are feminists."

Among the outspoken leaders of this new feminist perspective was Emma Goldman, a Russian-Jewish immigrant who fled to America in 1885. Voicing her views in the journal *Mother Earth*, Goldman attacked the "conventional lie" of marriage and woman's role as "sex commodity." Women, she said, "must no longer keep their mouths shut and their wombs open." Frequently jailed for her radical activities in support of women's and workers' rights, she was ultimately deported to Russia in 1919.

Feminists fought for both economic and sexual liberation. Charlotte Perkins Gilman, in *Women and Economics* (1898), challenged domesticity. "Only as we live, think, feel, and work outside the home," she wrote, "do we become humanly developed, civilized, and socialized." Gilman argued that women must have the same opportunities as men to find freedom and satisfaction through meaningful work. Gilman crusaded for a form of communalism featuring large housing units, day nurseries, central kitchens, and maid service to relieve women of domestic chores. Margaret Sanger, a visiting nurse in New York's East Side, hoped to give women greater control over their lives by distributing information about contraception. Her advocacy of birth control aroused the wrath of traditionalists, who viewed the movement as a threat to family and morality. In 1914 the government indicted Sanger on nine counts of obscenity. The charges were later dropped, and in 1918 the courts permitted doctors to distribute birth control information.

THE PROGRESSIVE PRESIDENTS

In 1901 the progressive reform agenda moved to the national level when Theodore Roosevelt assumed the presidency. Viewing the office as a "bully pulpit," the immensely popular Roosevelt expanded the regulatory power of the national government and supported a wide range of progressive reforms. Progressives, however, rarely spoke with a single voice and, following the failure of his handpicked successor, William Howard Taft, Roosevelt had to contend with the growing popularity of New Jersey Governor Woodrow Wilson. The 1912 presidential campaign displayed two competing progressive reform agendas. Roosevelt's "New Nationalism" insisted that only a powerful federal government could regulate the economy and guarantee social justice. Wilson, on the other hand, appealed to traditional public distrust of centralized power by calling for a "New Freedom." This tension between the public's desire to use government to solve social problems and its deep-seated fear of ceding too much power to Washington would remain a dominant theme in American political discourse for the rest of the century.

TR On September 6, 1901, in Buffalo, New York, President McKinley was shot by a lone anarchist, Leon Czolgosz. McKinley lingered for eight days before dying from internal bleeding and infection. At his death, Vice President Theodore Roosevelt, only forty-two years old, became the youngest man ever to assume the office of chief executive.

Born into a distinguished New York family, Roosevelt had plunged into New York politics in 1880, winning election as a Republican state assemblyman after his graduation from Harvard. A profound personal tragedy struck in 1884 when his wife and mother died on the same day. Roosevelt sought refuge in the Dakota Badlands, where he worked as a rancher before returning to New York and resuming his climb up the political ladder. In 1889 he became a member of the state Civil Service Commission and in 1895 president of the New York City Police Board. In 1897 President McKinley appointed him assistant secretary of the navy. He resigned his office to fight in the Spanish-American War. As commander of a volunteer regiment known as the "Rough Riders," the young officer led a heroic charge that helped secure strategic San Juan Hill. "The only trouble" with the conflict, he said later, "was that there was not enough war to go around." In 1898 he returned from that war a hero and was elected governor of New York. In his spare time, Roosevelt managed to read voraciously and to write ten books, including five works of history.

Campaigning as a war hero, Roosevelt chose a conventional route to political power, but he was anything but a conventional politician. While police commissioner, he went on nighttime journeys through New York's slums to get a firsthand view of crime. He impressed settlement workers with his compassion for the poor and his willingness to learn new ideas. His youthful exuberance and dynamic personality impressed nearly everyone he met. "You go into Roosevelt's presence," a journalist wrote, "you feel his eyes upon you, you listen to him, and you go home and wring the personality out of your clothes."

During his two years as governor Roosevelt angered party bosses with his public criticism of powerful trusts and his strong support of land conservation. In 1900, hoping to remove him from the limelight, Republican leaders nominated the upstart to be McKinley's running mate. It was a risky strategy, as Republican power broker Mark Hanna understood when he wrote McKinley that "your duty to the Country is to live for four years from next March." Roosevelt complained that he would "a great deal rather be anything, say professor of history, than Vice-President." Despite his reservations, he accepted the offer.

McKinley's assassination upset the plans of party leaders. Hanna regretted bitterly that "that damned cowboy" had become president. Roosevelt assured worried Republicans that he would continue McKinley's policies, but it was only a matter of time before he made his mark on the office. He understood the power of the presidency to mold public opinion, and from the "bully pulpit" he cultivated the press to enhance his popularity and to gather support for his policies. He maintained public interest by feeding reporters a steady diet of colorful antics. He became the first president to ride in an automobile, fly in an airplane, and be submerged in a submarine. On one occasion he went swimming naked in the Potomac River. The public responded to Roosevelt's exuberance. People called him "Teddy," and when a toy manufacturer heard the story of the president protecting a bear cub, he introduced the "Teddy bear" to his line of stuffed animals.

Roosevelt brought more than just style to the presidency; he carried with him a well-developed political philosophy. Fearing both the excessive power of corporate wealth and the dangers of working-class radicalism, Roosevelt planned to use the presidency to mediate disputes and uphold the public interest. "The unscrupulous rich man who seeks to exploit and oppress those who are less well off is in spirit not opposed to, but identical with, the unscrupulous poor man who desires to plunder and oppress those who are better off," he said.

His approach revealed itself in his answer to one of the central questions of the time: how should government deal with the trusts? The process of corporate consolidation, which began in the late nineteenth century, picked up steam in the early twentieth century. By 1904, 1 percent of American companies produced 38 percent of all manufactured goods. A few corporate giants dominated the industrial landscape. J. P. Morgan's U.S. Steel controlled 80 percent of the market, while his International Harvester Company monopolized 85 percent of the farm-equipment business.

Roosevelt regarded centralization as a fact of modern economic life. "This is an age of combination," he said in 1905. However, he made the distinction between "good" trusts—those that did not abuse their power and that contributed to economic growth—and "bad" trusts—those few companies that used their market lever-age to raise prices and exploit consumers. He earned a reputation as a "trustbuster" largely because of his prosecution of J. P. Morgan's Northern Securities Company, which controlled nearly all the long-distance railroads west of Chicago, eliminated competition, and created the threat of higher rates. Morgan tried to bargain, telling the president to "send your man to my man and they can fix it up." Roosevelt resisted, and in 1904 the Supreme Court, siding with the president, ordered the combination dissolved. During his administration the president used the Sherman Anti-Trust Act twenty-five times, prosecuting some of the country's largest corporations, including Standard Oil of New Jersey and the American Tobacco Company.

Imbued with the progressive faith in scientific management and committed to enlarging presidential power, Roosevelt sponsored legislation that expanded the administrative power of the federal government. In 1903 Congress passed the Expedition Act, which required courts to give higher priority to antitrust suits. The same year Congress created the Department of Commerce and Labor, which included a

Theodore Roosevelt Making Use of His "Bully Pulpit"   A vigorous public speaker, Roosevelt fascinated the press and garnered widespread popularity with the American people. His exploits took him on numerous hunting trips, to Panama to view the construction of the canal, even skinny-dipping in the Potomac with a foreign diplomat. His exuberance for life translated into an active presidency that permanently expanded the powers and expectations of the executive branch. In speeches, Roosevelt outlined his plan for a strong America to the people, resulting in his reorganization of the army, build up of the navy, modernization of the diplomatic corps, and development of a more efficient and energetic federal government. *(© Collection of The New-York Historical Society. Neg. # 69991.)*

Bureau of Corporations to investigate firms involved in interstate commerce. Finally, the Elkins Act (also 1903) made it illegal for the railroads to give, or shippers to receive, rebates.

A similar faith in the regulatory power of the federal government shaped Roosevelt's approach to labor. In 1902 the president intervened with much fanfare to support striking Pennsylvania coal miners who were demanding a 20 percent wage increase, an eight-hour day, and recognition of their union. Roosevelt spoke out publicly in support of the miners and summoned both sides to the White House, where he asked them to accept impartial federal arbitration. When the mine owners refused to compromise, Roosevelt lashed out at their "arrogant stupidity" and threatened to send in ten thousand federal troops to seize the mines and resume coal production. The operators finally relented. Arbitrators awarded the strikers a 10 percent wage increase and reduced the workday to nine hours, but they refused to grant recognition to the union. Afterward, Roosevelt boasted that he had offered both sides a "square deal." The phrase stuck and became a familiar label for his policies as president.

Roosevelt's colorful style and progressive policies made him the most popular president since Andrew Jackson. He easily won his party's nomination in 1904. The Democrats passed over two-time loser William Jennings Bryan and selected a lackluster New York judge, Alton B. Parker, as their nominee. On election day Roosevelt won 7,628,461 popular votes (57.4 percent) to Parker's 5,084,223 (37.6 percent) and carried thirty-three of the forty-five states. His 336 electoral votes were the most ever won by a candidate up to that time. All his opponent's 140 electoral votes came from a handful of southern states. The breadth of TR's victory stunned even his supporters. "What are we going to do with our victory?" asked a Republican senator.

Roosevelt had no doubts about the significance of the election. "Tomorrow," he cried the day before his inauguration, "I shall come into my office in my own right. Then watch out for me." With public desire for bolder federal action increasing, Roosevelt announced his support for an ambitious social agenda including regulation of the railroads, increased federal power to regulate commerce, and passage of a range of legislation to improve working conditions. In 1906 he pushed through Congress the Hepburn Railroad Regulation Act, which authorized the Interstate Commerce Commission to set aside railroad rates on the complaint of a shipper and to establish lower rates. With Roosevelt's support Congress passed the Pure Food and Drug Act of 1905. The legislation made it a crime to sell adulterated foods or medicines and provided for correct and complete labeling of ingredients. Capitalizing on publication of Upton Sinclair's powerful novel *The Jungle* (1906), Roosevelt won passage of the Meat Inspection Act, which led to more effective supervision of meat processing.

Roosevelt's agenda on behalf of ordinary Americans produced mixed results for African-Americans. TR made a number of symbolic gestures toward blacks, including meeting with Booker T. Washington at the White House. But he shared the prevailing view that blacks were intellectually inferior. "[A]s a race and in the mass," he declared, "they are altogether inferior to the whites." In 1906, angered by unsubstantiated reports that black soldiers had killed a man in Brownsville, Texas, he discharged without honor 160 blacks from the army, including six Medal of Honor recipients. It took more than sixty years for the army to rectify Roosevelt's unjust punishment. In 1972 the secretary of the army granted the men, many of whom were by then dead, honorable discharges.

As president, Roosevelt was committed to using his office to bolster the American conservation movement. While western business interests advocated unrestrained exploitation of the nation's natural resources, the growth of congested cities and the closing of the frontier raised public concern about the environment. Essayist John Muir, the founder of the modern environmental movement, emerged as the most passionate and forceful proponent of the inherent value of the modern wilderness.

By temperament Roosevelt sided with Muir and the preservationists, but he understood the political power of western business interests and their representatives in Congress. Blending idealism and self-interest, he claimed that sound conservation and management were necessary for future development and for preserving America's natural heritage for future generations. A democratic tone echoed in his credo that natural resources should be reserved for all citizens, not just "for the very rich who can control private reserves." He was not a strict preservationist, but he sought to balance the needs of economic development with the desire to preserve the nation's wilderness heritage.

To carry out his policies, Roosevelt appointed Gifford Pinchot to head the new U.S. Forest Service. Like Roosevelt, Pinchot championed a "wise use" philosophy of public management. Following Pinchot's recommendation, Roosevelt used his executive authority to add 150 million acres of western virgin forest lands to the national forests and to preserve vast areas of water and coal from private development. The president also provided federal funds for the construction of huge dams, reservoirs, and canals in the West. By 1915 the government had invested $80 million in twenty-five projects to open new lands for cultivation and provide cheap electric power. It also strengthened the national park system. By 1916 the government had established thirteen national parks, which the writer Wallace Stegner called the nation's "crown jewels."

Taft and the Divided Republicans

Having promised in 1904 not to seek reelection, Roosevelt decided to back his good friend and political ally, Secretary of War William Howard Taft, as his successor. Taft had been a restrained and moderate jurist, the solicitor general of the United States, a federal circuit court judge, and governor of the Philippines. Roosevelt was confident that Taft would continue his reform efforts. "Things will be all right," he had assured people when he took vacations from Pennsylvania Avenue. "I have left Taft sitting on the lid."

The Democrats nominated William Jennings Bryan for the third time. Bryan adopted a broad progressive platform that embraced a strict antitrust policy, railroad regulation, and a host of social justice measures. "Shall the people rule?" he asked, framing the election as a choice between a government devoted to people's rights and a government by privilege. Taft counterattacked, charging that Bryan's economic views would produce "a paralysis of business." With the support of both Roosevelt and much of the Republican Old Guard, Taft easily won the election, although his popular margin was smaller than Roosevelt's in 1904. Taft took 51.6 percent (7,675,320) of the votes to 43.1 percent (6,412,294) for Bryan. His electoral margin was a comfortable 321 to 162.

In style and temperament William Howard Taft was a much different man than Roosevelt. Physically, Roosevelt was dynamic and charismatic; Taft was lazy and ponderous. Politically, Roosevelt had taken an expansive view of presidential power; Taft was more cautious, insisting that the president must observe the strict letter of the law. Taft sought to rein in the expanding social and economic role of the government by incorporating Roosevelt's bold reforms into the legal system. Taft was, in journalist Mark Sullivan's words, "a placid man in a restless time."

A major rift soon developed between Taft and progressive Republicans that would eventually destroy his presidency. On March 15, 1909, just eleven days after his inauguration, Taft called Congress into special session to lower tariff rates. A bill favored by progressives sailed quickly through the House but ran into tough opposition from Senate conservatives headed by Nelson W. Aldrich. For weeks a spirited battle raged on the Senate floor. Fearful of a party split, Taft retreated and threw his support behind the conservatives, who succeeded in gutting the House bill and passing the Payne-Aldrich Tariff, which actually raised tariffs on many important imports. Progressives led by Robert La Follette felt betrayed by the president, even more so when Taft described the new law as "the best tariff the Republican Party ever passed."

The president's efforts to reform the House of Representatives further divided Taft from the Republican progressives. Initially, Taft supported progressive efforts to diminish the almost dictatorial power of House Speaker Joseph Cannon, a sixty-five-year-old tyrant who used his power to frustrate reform efforts. "I am god-damned tired," Cannon said, "of listening to all this babble for reform." However, when Taft realized that he needed Cannon's support to pass tariff reform in the House, the president backed off, and support for the rebellion fell short. The following year progressives succeeded in stripping the Speaker of the power to make committee assignments. But once again they felt betrayed by a president who had raised their hopes and failed to deliver.

Taft also alienated progressive conservationists. This struggle stemmed from charges by chief forester Gifford Pinchot that Richard Ballinger, Taft's secretary of the interior, had conspired to turn over Alaska coalfields to a group of wealthy businessmen. Taft examined the charges and concluded that Ballinger had done nothing wrong. When Pinchot continued his attack, Taft fired him for insubordination. Progressives viewed Pinchot's dismissal as an ominous sign that Taft was betraying the conservationist cause, but Taft was certainly no enemy of conservation. He had used his executive power to remove more public land from private use than Roosevelt had in a comparable period of time.

During most of Taft's first year in office, Theodore Roosevelt was far from the political fray. He embarked on a long hunting safari in Africa. When he returned to New York in 1910, Roosevelt claimed that he would stay out of internal party squabbling, but within a month he announced that he would embark on a national speaking tour. He lashed out at Taft, complaining that the president had "completely twisted around the policies I advocated and acted upon."

A final break between Taft and Roosevelt occurred in October 1911, when the president ordered an antitrust suit against U.S. Steel, forcing the giant company to sell off its Tennessee Coal and Iron Company. Roosevelt, who had approved U.S. Steel's acquisition of the Tennessee Company in 1907, feared that Taft's action would create a panic on Wall Street. "To attempt to meet the whole problem by a succession of lawsuits," Roosevelt snapped, "is hopeless." Taft disagreed with TR's regulatory approach, arguing that the Sherman Act was a "good law that ought to be enforced, and I propose to enforce it." As a result, Taft filed more antitrust suits in four years than Roosevelt had in seven and a half.

Whose Progressivism? The Presidential Campaign of 1912

For Roosevelt the antitrust suit against U.S. Steel was the final straw. In February 1912 he announced that he would challenge Taft for the Republican nomination. "My hat is in the ring!" he declared with typical exuberance. "The fight is on and I am stripped to the buff!" Though Taft was a bigger trustbuster than Roosevelt, progressives alienated by his compromise on the tariff remained solidly in Roosevelt's corner. The campaign for the Republican nomination had now become a battle between Roosevelt, the champion of the progressives, and Taft, the candidate of the conservatives. In the months that followed, Roosevelt, clearly the favorite of the rank and file, scored overwhelming victories in the direct presidential primaries now held in thirteen states. Nevertheless, Taft controlled the party machinery, which chose most of the delegates at the convention, and narrowly secured renomination on the first ballot.

Roosevelt, outraged by the back-room methods Taft employed to deny him the party nomination, decided to run for president as the head of a third-party organization. On August 6 in Chicago, ten thousand frenzied supporters singing "Onward Christian Soldiers" formed the Progressive Party and nominated Theodore Roosevelt as its presidential candidate. In his acceptance speech, Roosevelt, pronouncing himself "as strong as a bull moose," delivered a spirited "Confession of Faith" in which he criticized Democrats and Republicans for protecting "the interests of the rich few."

In his speech, Roosevelt gave the fullest accounting of his political philosophy, which he called the New Nationalism (see Competing Voices, page 842). TR urged progressives to recognize that only a strong federal government could protect the public's interest. Democracy was not incompatible with increased government; indeed, only government could guarantee true freedom and democracy. Rather than breaking up the great corporations, Roosevelt wanted to increase the power of government to regulate industry. In many ways, TR envisioned the modern broker state that his cousin, Franklin D. Roosevelt, would create with his New Deal programs in the 1930s. In keeping with the New Nationalism philosophy, the Progressive Party platform, called a "Covenant with the People," advocated a bold list of new reforms, including strict regulation of corporations, a national presidential primary, the elimination of child labor, a minimum wage, and universal women's suffrage.

With the Republicans divided, the Democrats were confident of victory. They nominated New Jersey Governor Woodrow Wilson to lead the party. Born in Virginia and raised in Confederate Georgia, Wilson graduated from Princeton in 1879, studied law at the University of Virginia, and earned a Ph.D. in political science at

THE LATEST ARRIVAL AT THE POLITICAL ZOO

DRAWN BY E. W. KEMBLE

The Arrival of the "Bull Moose" This cartoon from the 1912 presidential campaign depicts a bewildered Democratic donkey and Republican elephant observing a strange new creature, the Progressive Party Bull Moose (so called because as he accepted the nomination, TR exclaimed he felt "as strong as a bull moose"). TR bolted the Republican Party after it failed to give him its nomination over President Taft. Roosevelt ran an energetic campaign, even completing a speaking engagement after being shot by a crazed man in Milwaukee. (New York Herald, *July 1912, Culver Pictures.*)

Johns Hopkins University in 1886. He then taught at the elite colleges Bryn Mawr and Wesleyan before returning to Princeton in 1890. Twelve years later Princeton named him president. In 1910, after a bruising battle with the dean of the graduate school, Wilson left the Ivy League to run a successful campaign for governor of New Jersey. The Democratic machine thought that Wilson would be a "safe" candidate who would not pursue radical change, but over the next two years the "scholar turned statesman" compiled an impressive record of progressive legislation that earned him a national reputation.

Like Roosevelt, Wilson possessed a strong intellect, a commitment to expansive presidential leadership, and a penchant for moralizing. A brilliant speaker and a shrewd political tactician, Wilson revealed an uncanny ability to sway an audience and a keen sense of public opinion. Tall, lean, and stiff, he could be aloof and self-righteous. A devoutly religious man, Wilson was certain that he had been placed on earth to do God's work. One politician noted that Wilson "said something to me, and I didn't know whether God or him was talking." Sometimes Wilson himself had trouble telling the difference. Medical historians speculate that health problems, including a possible stroke in 1906, may have affected his personality, accentuating his intolerance of opposing points of view.

Wilson responded to Roosevelt's call for a New Nationalism by developing his own reform program, which he called the "New Freedom." Wilson's program borrowed heavily from the brilliant progressive lawyer Louis D. Brandeis, who believed that concentrations of economic power threatened liberty and foreclosed economic opportunity. Echoing Brandeis, Wilson warned that regulatory agencies would become captive to the industries they were designed to control. He spoke in evangelical tones of the need to emancipate the American economy from the power of the trusts. "What this country needs above everything else," he said, "is a body of laws which will look after the men who are on the make rather than the men who are already made." Where Roosevelt envisioned a powerful federal government using its powers to regulate large corporations, Wilson wanted Washington to use its limited powers to break up large concentrations and promote free competition.

The duel between "nationalism" and "freedom" that the 1912 campaign slogans touted was more than a contest between Roosevelt and Wilson; it was part of a dilemma that American society would continue to face for the remainder of the century. Wilson, firmly rooted in the Jeffersonian tradition of individualism and limited government, believed that government should allow independent individuals to prosper free from both large corporations and a powerful government. Roosevelt, persuaded that concentration of power was inevitable, believed that Americans should discard their outworn faith in rugged individualism and adjust to the realities of an industrialized nation. Though Roosevelt recognized the inevitability of big government, he failed to appreciate how deeply wedded Americans were to their Jeffersonian roots.

From another perspective, newspaper editor William Allen White dismissed the differences between the two men: "Between the New Nationalism and the New Freedom was that fantastic imaginary gulf that always had existed between Tweedledum and Tweedle-dee." Many people agreed with White, and they turned to a more radical alternative—Socialist Party candidate Eugene Debs, who told audiences that workers had created the Socialist Party "as a means of wrestling control of government and industry from the capitalists and making the working class the ruling class of the nation and the world."

The campaign soon developed into a two-way contest between the moralizing Wilson and the crusading Roosevelt. Realizing he had little chance of winning, Taft refused to campaign. "I think I might as well give up so far as being a candidate is concerned," he wrote his wife in July. "There are so many people in the country who don't like me." Wilson held the lead as the campaign entered its final months. Roosevelt, who loved the thrill of battle, continued his crusade. Nothing, not even a would-be assassin's bullet, could stop him from campaigning. On October 14, as he entered an automobile in Milwaukee, a lone attacker fired a single bullet into Roosevelt's chest. It fractured a rib and lodged below his right lung. Roosevelt first ordered the crowd not to harm his assailant, then insisted on attending a previously scheduled rally, where he spoke to a stunned crowd for more than an hour. "It takes more than that to kill a Bull Moose," he told them.

The Republican split allowed Wilson to win the election. Though he won only 41.9 percent of the popular vote, he captured forty states and 435 electoral votes—beating TR's 1904 record. Roosevelt got 27.4 percent of the popular vote, carrying six states with 88 electoral votes. Taft finished a distant third with 23.2 percent of the vote and 8 electoral votes. Socialist Debs received nearly 1 million ballots, about 6 percent of the total (see map below). The Democrats also won control of both houses of Congress, and the new president planned to use his position as party leader to secure passage of his New Freedom legislation.

Woodrow Wilson and the New Freedom

Only the second Democrat to occupy the White House since the Civil War (the other, Cleveland, had been elected twice), Wilson continued the expansion of presidential power that had begun under Roosevelt. Using every device at his disposal to corral supporters, he conferred regularly with legislative leaders and enforced party discipline by dispensing patronage. He cultivated the press, holding weekly press conferences during his first two years in office. Wilson became the first president since Jefferson to deliver his annual State of the Union messages in person before joint sessions of Congress.

The president's tactics worked. Within a year and a half of Wilson's inauguration, Congress had passed a number of new initiatives. The Underwood Tariff Act (1913) reduced import taxes on most goods and levied a graduated income tax to replace the lost income, an option made possible by the recent ratification of the Sixteenth Amendment. Incomes under $4,000 per year were excluded, which exempted over 90 percent of American families in 1914, the first year the tax was in effect.

Wilson kept Congress in session through the summer to pass the most important progressive measure of his presidency—the Federal Reserve Act of 1913. The

The Election of 1912   The 1912 campaign proved to be one of the more interesting in American history, with Theodore Roosevelt, the third-party candidate, coming in second. Roosevelt's calls for a "New Nationalism" drew Republican supporters to his Progressive Party. Socialist Eugene Debs did not win a single state, but over 900,000 American voted in favor of that party's more radical agenda. Taft, the sitting president, won only two states, but the split within the Republican Party was enough to give the election to Woodrow Wilson, who gathered support from across the nation for his "New Freedom."

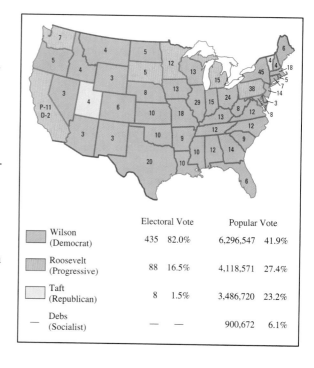

		Electoral Vote		Popular Vote	
Wilson (Democrat)		435	82.0%	6,296,547	41.9%
Roosevelt (Progressive)		88	16.5%	4,118,571	27.4%
Taft (Republican)		8	1.5%	3,486,720	23.2%
Debs (Socialist)		—	—	900,672	6.1%

law created the nation's first centralized banking system since Andrew Jackson had destroyed the Second Bank of the United States in the 1830s. Brokering a compromise between eastern conservatives, who argued for a privately owned central bank, and southern and western farming interests, who wanted the government to control the bank, the legislation reflected the progressive desire to regulate the economy by creating twelve regional banks to hold the cash reserves of member banks throughout the nation. These district banks had authority to lend money to member banks at a low rate of interest called the discount rate. By adjusting the discount rate, the regional banks could adjust the amount of money a bank could borrow and thereby increase or decrease the amount of money in circulation.

Wilson, influenced by Brandeis, was also the guiding force behind two initiatives that increased the government's power to regulate powerful trusts. In September 1914 Congress created the Federal Trade Commission with authority to investigate corporate operations and outlaw unfair practices. Three weeks later Congress passed the Clayton Anti-Trust Act, which amended the Sherman Anti-Trust Act by outlawing monopolistic practices. The Clayton Act exempted trade unions and agricultural organizations from antitrust laws, and it curtailed the use of court injunctions during strikes. Future court decisions weakened the legislation, but at the time it promised a new age in labor–management relations. AFL head Samuel Gompers called it the "Magna Carta of Labor."

Convinced that reform had gone far enough, Wilson wanted to go no farther. The New Freedom was complete, he wrote in late 1914; the future would be a "time of healing." Two years later political circumstances forced Wilson to reassess his position. Democrats fared poorly in the 1914 midterm elections, losing two dozen seats in the House and giving up the governorships of New York, New Jersey, Illinois, and Pennsylvania. Wilson realized that to win reelection he needed to reach out to the progressives who had supported Roosevelt in 1912. As a first step, he nominated Brandeis to the Supreme Court. The nomination thrilled progressives, who waged a successful battle in the Senate to confirm Brandeis's elevation to the bench, and he became the first Jewish member of the Court.

To make further inroads in Roosevelt's old constituency, Wilson advocated several measures he had resisted during his first two years in the White House. He supported passage of the Federal Farm Loan Act, which created banks to lend money at low interest rates to farmers. Faced with a railroad strike, he signed the Adamson Act, establishing an eight-hour workday for railway workers and guaranteeing them time-and-a-half overtime pay. The Keating-Owen Act outlawed child labor in businesses engaged in interstate commerce. The Workman's Compensation Act established an insurance program for federal workers. The president endorsed, and Congress passed, the Federal Highway Act of 1916, which appropriated $5 million to the states for road construction.

However, to African-Americans looking for support from Washington in their struggle for civil rights, Wilson was a bitter disappointment. A product of the segregated South, Wilson sanctioned the spread of discrimination against blacks in the government bureaucracy. In Georgia a federal official announced, "There are no government positions for Negroes in the South. A Negro's place is in the cornfield." The NAACP complained that federal agencies, such as the U.S. Post Office and the

Treasury Department, had separate shops, offices, and lunchrooms for their black employees. But Wilson was unconcerned: "I sincerely believe it to be in their [the blacks'] best interests."

Wilson, who came to the presidency promising to restore an older version of democracy, wound up continuing the trend toward greater concentration of power in Washington. By the end of his first term in office, Wilson had for all intents and purposes abandoned the New Freedom and embraced the New Nationalism. In 1901 there were 239,000 government employees. By the end of Wilson's first term in office, the number had grown to 349,000. The federal budget, which totaled $587,685,000 when Roosevelt became president, had swollen to $782,535,000. Together, Roosevelt and Wilson dramatically increased the stature and power of the president. All future presidents would build on their example.

Wilson, like Roosevelt, contributed to and reflected an important shift in public attitudes toward government. During the progressive period the American people, viewing the government as a positive force for social change, created laws and regulatory agencies that established the government's responsibility to protect the public interest. The change in attitudes toward government should not be exaggerated, however. Progressives may have enlarged the capacity of government, but they did not shed deeply held notions of individualism, limited government, and self-help.

CONCLUSION

A number of reform streams flowed together in the first years of the twentieth century to create the Progressive Era. Intellectuals challenged the nineteenth-century notion that immutable rules of nature governed society. Middle-class women such as Jane Addams campaigned for social justice while muckrakers reminded people of the problems that needed to be addressed. The middle class, fearful of the social disorder provoked by urbanization and industrialization—and infatuated by social efficiency and scientific management—joined the chorus calling for change. The various groups did not campaign for the same causes. Some people worked to improve the quality of life for working people, especially women and children; others concerned themselves with making society more efficient; and still others wanted to uplift the nation's soul through moral reform. Despite the different agendas, these disparate reform efforts were united in their belief that government at all levels—local, state, and federal—needed to limit the power of large corporations and improve social conditions in the nation's urban areas. They were also committed to gradual change, working through the established institutions of government. Progressives were reformers, not revolutionaries.

Initially, progressives focused their efforts on the cities, where they believed the combination of explosive population growth and political corruption threatened social order. Reformers experimented with new forms of city government, including the commissioner and city manager models. Progressives modeled their reforms at the state level on the "Wisconsin Idea" of Robert La Follette, which included initiatives designed to make government more responsive to the public will. Progressive reform also possessed a dark side. When in power, progressives systematically disfranchised many segments of the population, particularly blacks in the South and immigrants in the North. In their drive to improve human behavior along with human institutions, progressives tried to outlaw the consumption of alcohol and succeeded in many states and counties.

Not all activists accepted the progressive faith that change should occur gradually and in cooperation with established institutions. African-Americans, who were largely excluded from mainstream political life in the South, developed alternative ways to improve their lives, including boycotts and protests. Socialists and Wobblies struggled to build a class-based reform movement that challenged the very foundation of capitalism. Feminists, meanwhile, advocated an end to all forms of sexual discrimination.

The progressive movement moved to the national stage when Theodore Roosevelt assumed the presidency in 1901. Roosevelt helped expand the power of the federal government. He regulated some trusts and broke up others, occasionally sided with the labor movement in its battles with management, and allied himself with the fledgling conservation movement. William Howard Taft, Roosevelt's handpicked successor, won the 1908 election, but Roosevelt quickly became dissatisfied with what he saw as Taft's half-hearted commitment to reform. In 1912 TR bolted the Republican Party and ran as a third-party candidate.

Roosevelt's was not the only articulate voice for reform on the national stage. The 1912 presidential contest witnessed two competing visions of progressivism: Roosevelt's New Nationalism and former New Jersey Governor Woodrow Wilson's New Freedom. Calling for smaller government and less regulation, Wilson won the election, but over the next few years he implemented many of the ideas of the New Nationalism.

Like the urge to reform at home, the drive to expand America's influence overseas required greater government intervention and experimentation in international affairs. Here too the progressive impulse would color America's role with an optimistic view of human nature and a faith in the possibilities of reform through American influence. By 1916 a brutal conflict in Europe threatened those assumptions. America's entrance into World War I in 1917 would twist the progressive agenda in ways that most reformers never imagined.

Annotated Suggested Readings

The Progressive Era has one of the most robust bodies of literature of any period in American history. Richard Hofstadter's *Age of Reform* (1955) remains one of the classic surveys of the progressive movement. Robert Wiebe provided the seminal study of the new professional middle class and its response to industrialization and urbanization in *The Search for Order, 1877–1920* (1967). Both Steven J. Diner's *A Very Different Age* (1998) and Michael McGerr's *A Fierce Discontent* (2003) offer thoughtful analysis that includes social and political topics. Alan Dawley's *Struggles for Justice* (1991) is another recent survey of the era, with particular emphasis on the origins of the new activist state.

Several scholars have tried to highlight the various distinct strains of thought that fed into the progressive movement. Robert Crunden examines the religious and moral traditions of the middle-class Protestants in the movement in *Ministers of Reform* (1982). In his *New Radicalism in America* (1965), Christopher Lasch portrays progressivism as a cultural revolt. The intellectual supports of progressive reform are outlined in Morton White's crucial work, *Social Thought in America: The Revolt Against Formalism* (1975). Charles Forcey focuses on the political thought of these intellectuals in *The Crossroads of Liberalism* (1961). James Kloppenberg's *Uncertain Victory* (1986) and Daniel Rodgers's *Atlantic Crossings* (1998) examine the growth of progressive thought from a transatlantic perspective.

The women reformers in the movement are the subjects of Nancy Woloch's *Women and the American Experience* (1984), while Allen F. Davis's *Spearheads of Reform* (1967) focuses on the settlement houses. More recently, Mina Carson's *Settlement Folk* (1990) and Ruth Hutchinson Crocker's *Social Work and Social Order* (1992) examine the settlement house movement. Editors Alan Sadovnik and Susan Semel provide insight on female educational reformers in *Founding Mothers and Others* (2002). Robyn Muncy, *Creating a Female Dominion in American Reform, 1890–1935* (1991), argues that during this period women created a network of reform institutions that thrived into the 1930s. A good starting point on women in the labor movement is Susan Glenn's *Daughters of the Shtetl* (1990). Nancy Dye's *As Equals and Sisters* (1980) examines the connection between working-class women reformers and upper-class women progressives.

Fewer works have focused on the rising middle class, but John Buenker's *Urban Liberalism and Progressive Reform* (1973) covers the basics. Oliver Zunz's *Making America Corporate* (1990) shows how white-collar employees established a corporate work environment. James Weinstein explains the appeal of progressivism's "efficiency" in *The Corporate Ideal in the Liberal State* (1969). David Chalmers's *The Social and Political Ideas of the Muckrakers* (1964) is a useful introduction to the muckrakers.

John Teaford's *City and Suburb* (1979) offers a broad survey of urban reform efforts. Bradley Rice critiques the rise of the commission government in *Progressive Cities* (1972). Jack Tager evaluates the impact of the elite intrusion into municipal government in *The Intellectual as Urban Reformer* (1968). Steven Piott's *Giving Voters a Voice* (2003) looks at the evolution of the initiative and referendum. Kenneth Finegold's *Experts and Politicians* (1995) examines the reform challenge to machine politics. Camilla Stivers's *Bureau Men, Settlement Women* (2000) also explores municipal reform, with an emphasis on the issue of gender.

For reform in the states, Wisconsin is the natural starting point. The premiere study of the state is David Thelen's *The New Citizenship* (1972). A more recent biography of La Follette is Carl Burgchardt's *Robert M. La Follette, Sr.: The Voice of Conscience* (1992). Other insightful examinations of progressivism on the state level include Thomas Pegram's *Partisans and Progressives* (1992) on Illinois, David Thelen's *Paths of Resistance* (1986) on Missouri, and William Link's *The Paradox of Southern Progressivism* (1992).

The women's suffrage movement is studied in Aileen Kraditor's *The Ideas of the Woman Suffrage Movement* (1965). For feminism in the Progressive Era, Rosalind Rosenberg's *Beyond Separate Spheres* (1982) is essential. For works on progressivism as social control, see Paul Boyer's *Urban Masses and Moral Order in America* (1978). The world of prostitution in the Progressive Era is examined from both sides in Ruth Rosen's *The Lost Sisterhood* (1982). Norman Clark's *Deliver Us from Evil* (1976) covers the prohibition reform movement, as does a recent synthesis on the movement, *Battling Demon Rum* (1998) by Thomas Pegram. The nativist movement is the subject of John Higham's *Strangers in the Land* (1955). Several books explore the relationship between government and business during this time, including Louis Galambos and James Pratt's *The Rise of the Corporate Commonwealth* (1988) and Martin Sklar's *The Corporate Reconstruction of American Capitalism* (1992). Two books by Morton Keller, *Regulating a New Society* (1994) and *Regulating a New Economy* (1990), are essential for understanding progressive public policy.

Two of the best introductions to African-American activism in this period are Louis Harlan's *Booker T. Washington* (1983) and Stephen R. Fox's *The Guardian of Boston:*

William Monroe Trotter (1971), which emphasizes the revival of black protest. Also see August Meier's *Negro Thought in America* (1963) for the intellectual underpinnings of black activism in this period. A valuable book on the Great Migration is James Grossman's *Land of Hope* (1989), in which he portrays the migration as a grass-roots effort for greater freedom. William Cohen's *At Freedom's Edge* (1991) examines the issue of black mobility as a whole and southern efforts to contain it. In *Contempt of Court* (1999) Mark Curriden and Leroy Phillips analyze the importance of the Supreme Court's decision to intervene in the state criminal trial of Ed Johnson and the subsequent contempt charges against the law enforcement agents who allowed his lynching.

The material available on the socialists and other radicals of this era is immense. James R. Green's *The World of the Worker* (1980) provides a thorough introductory overview. Melvyn Dubofsky's *We Shall Be All* (1969) is the best history of the Wobblies, while Nick Salvatore's *Eugene V. Debs* (1982) is the most acclaimed biography of that important socialist leader.

Two of the most readable accounts of the progressive presidents were both written by John Morton Blum: *The Republican Roosevelt* (1954) and *Woodrow Wilson and the Politics of Morality* (1956). John Milton Cooper's *The Warrior and the Priest* (1983) is an excellent comparative biography of Wilson and Roosevelt. Arthur Link's *Woodrow Wilson and the Progressive Era* (1954) is still a good choice. A recent survey of politics in this time period is Sean Dennis Cashman's *America Ascendant: From Theodore Roosevelt to FDR* (1998).

The **istory** **ompanion**

Managing Modern Society

The New Nationalism, 1910

On August 31, 1910, Theodore Roosevelt launched his campaign to return to the White House in a speech before a group of Civil War veterans in Osawatomie, Kansas. Calling for a "New Nationalism," Roosevelt argued that the national government retained the right to regulate the use of property "to whatever degree the public welfare may require."

I stand for the square deal. But when I say that I am for the square deal, I mean not merely that I stand for fair play under the present rules of the game, but that I stand for having those rules changed so as to work for a more substantial equality of opportunity and of reward for equally good service.

. . . The citizens of the United States must effectively control the mighty commercial forces which they have themselves called into being. There can be no effective control of corporations while their political activity remains. To put an end to it will be neither a short nor an easy task, but it can be done.

Combinations [trusts] in industry are the result of an imperative economic law which cannot be repealed by political legislation. The effort at prohibiting all combination has substantially failed. The way out lies, not in attempting to prevent such combinations, but in completely controlling them in the interest of the public welfare. . . .

The absence of effective State, and especially national, restraint upon unfair money-getting has tended to create a small class of enormously wealthy and economically powerful men . . . we should permit [such fortunes] only so long as the gaining represents benefit to the community. This, I know, implies a policy of a far more active government interference with social and economic conditions in this country than we have yet had, but I think we have got to face the fact that such an increase in governmental control is now necessary. . . .

This New Nationalism regards the executive power as the steward of the public welfare.

The New Freedom, 1912

In October 1912 Democratic presidential candidate Woodrow Wilson laid out an alternative vision of the role of government in modern society. In a series of speeches he called for a "New Freedom," through which Americans could live free of interference from both large corporations and big government.

Gentlemen have been saying for a long time that trusts are inevitable. . . . I am not willing to be under the patronage of the trusts, no matter how providential a government presides over the process of their control of my life. My thought about both Mr. Taft and Mr. Roosevelt is that of entire respect, but these gentlemen have been so intimately associated with the powers that have been determining the policy of this government . . . [that] their thought is in close, habitual association with those who have framed the policies of the country during all our lifetime. Those men have coordinated and ordered all the great economic forces of this country in such a way that nothing but an outside force breaking in can disturb their domination and control.

The hands that are being stretched out to monopolize our forests, to prevent the use of our great power-producing streams—the hands that are being stretched into the bowels of the earth to take possession of the great riches that lie hidden [there] . . . are the hands of monopoly. Are these men to continue to stand at the elbow of government and tell us how we are going to save ourselves—from themselves? You can not settle the question while monopoly is close to the ears of those who govern.

I take my stand absolutely, where every progressive ought to take his stand, on the proposition that private monopoly is indefensible and intolerable. And there I will fight my battle.

Eugene Debs's Address of Acceptance, 1912

Eugene V. Debs, jailed leader of the Pullman Strike, became the Socialist Party's leading spokesman and five-time presidential candidate. In October 1912 Debs accepted the Socialist Party nomination and explained why the party was "fundamentally different from all other parties."

The world's workers have always been and still are the world's slaves. . . . The workers in the mills and factories, in the mines and on the farms and railways never had a party of their own until the Socialist Party was organized. They divided their votes between the parties of their political masters. They did not realize that they were using their ballots to forge their own fetters. . . .

The infallible test of a political party is the private ownership of wealth and the means of life. Apply that test to the Republican, Democratic and Progressive parties and upon that basic, fundamental issue you will find them essentially one and the same. They differ according to the conflicting interests of the privileged classes, but at bottom they are alike and stand for capitalist class rule and working class slavery. . . .

Social reorganization is the imperative demand of the world-wide revolutionary movement. The Socialist Party's mission is not only to destroy capitalist despotism but to establish industrial and social democracy.

Theodore Roosevelt, Woodrow Wilson, and Eugene Debs couched the 1912 election in terms of "the struggle of free men to gain and hold the right of self-government as against the special interests." While Debs focused on liberating the working class, Wilson and Roosevelt sought to free both working people and small businessmen. All three men recognized a specific group of special interests—modern industrial corporations. Yet in their competing visions of how government could help free men "to gain and hold" rights, the 1912 presidential candidates struggled with a question that is as old as the federal government itself: when is it right for government to intervene in society to protect some individuals from the depredations of others?

The founders of the republic had not initially worried about this question. They were concerned with limiting the abusive power of government, and to that end they tried to limit its activities as much as possible. Within a few years, however, politicians had begun to take sides over which government actions were abusive. On one side were Alexander Hamilton and his allies, who argued that government had a responsibility to encourage industry and protect the financiers who provided the capital for economic growth. On the other side stood Jefferson and his supporters, who saw Hamilton's policies as favoritism to the rich and called for a limited government that allowed the common man—ideally, the "yeoman farmer"—to prosper.

Though the players changed over the years—as Federalists begot Whigs and Republicans, and the Democratic-Republicans spawned the Democrats and Populists—the terms of the argument did not. The two options available in the political mainstream were a powerful government that supported the holders of wealth and capital and a limited government that, in a pinch, sided with the working people or the petite bourgeoisie. The election of 1912 was important because Theodore Roosevelt changed the terms of the debate. He brought a new argument from the fringes to the mainstream of political thought: a strong, activist government was a good thing, provided it worked for the weak as well as the strong. In his 1910 speech on the New Nationalism, he claimed that the old division between Hamilton and Jefferson was irrelevant to a modern, industrial society. Americans should develop a new concept of government that borrowed the strengths of both of the old arguments.

Rising discontent with the status quo, as attested to in the growing numbers of people joining the Socialist Party, made Roosevelt's ideas even more poignant. While Debs did not call for a violent overthrow of the American government, he brought together disparate groups who felt there was something seriously wrong with the political system and demanded reform. Like Roosevelt, Debs envisioned a stronger federal government in his call for government ownership of utilities, mines, banks, and railroads, as well as federal unemployment insurance and old-age pensions.

Woodrow Wilson's New Freedom argued for the old Jeffersonian ideals of free competition and individual liberty, insisting that they were still relevant in the modern world. Unlike Roosevelt, who was willing to accept large concentrations of wealth and power and wanted to regulate them for the common good, Wilson wanted to dismantle the trusts, which would ultimately require less government intervention in society.

Though Wilson's ideas won the campaign, Roosevelt's seemed to win the war, and Debs's plan stirred debate for decades to come. During his two terms in office, Wilson came to enact many of the reforms that Roosevelt had proposed. In the new age of activist government, though, Wilson's "conversion" did not amount to the betrayal it might have been had it occurred in the nineteenth century. The activist government of the twentieth century held out promises to both sides of the old debate: government could both encourage industry and protect the common man.

QUESTIONS FOR ANALYSIS

1. What are the "present rules of the game" that Roosevelt refers to in his opening?

2. How does Roosevelt propose to employ an activist government?

3. According to Wilson, why is Roosevelt wrong to claim that trusts are inevitable?

4. How does Wilson propose to deal with trusts?

5. Why does Debs believe that workers cannot trust the other three parties in the 1912 election?

6. How does each presidential candidate appeal to the common man?

7. Are the New Nationalism and the New Freedom incompatible? Why?

8. Are Roosevelt's, Wilson's, and Debs's ideas still applicable to today's society? If so, which candidate would you choose in an election? Why?

The Age of Reform

The so-called Progressive Era has generated more disagreement among historians than perhaps any other period in American history. Scholars do not even agree on the era's chronological parameters. Some see this age of reform beginning around 1890, others at the turn of the century; some mark its terminus as early as 1914, while others point to 1920, and still others emphasize the reformist impulses of the 1920s. The very term *Progressivism* is not an agreed-on descriptor for the period, partly because the term has fallen out of favor in the wake of the failures of the liberal reform efforts of the 1960s and because many of the late nineteenth and early twentieth century reform impulses—including prohibition, immigration restriction, eugenics, and segregation, all of which had much more to do with social control than with social justice—hardly seem progressive a century later.

The first scholars to examine Progressivism, such as Charles Beard, wrote in the early twentieth century, when the reform impulse was still very much alive, and considered themselves Progressive historians. They viewed the period in clear dualistic terms as a struggle between the people, represented by the reformers, and the interests, a sinister conglomeration of big business owners and corrupt politicians who profited at the people's expense. But such assessments of Progressivism accepted at face value the reformers' rhetoric.

By the 1950s, historians were offering a more skeptical assessment of the reformers' goals and motivations. Richard Hofstadter in *The Age of Reform* (1955) argued that the Progressives were members of the old middle class, the long-established social elite who felt their social prominence was being eclipsed by the rise of a new and superwealthy business class. Suffering from status anxiety, members of this old middle class sought to reform America to recreate the social world that they had previously dominated.

Robert Wiebe's *The Search for Order* (1967) offered a rather different explanation for the reform impulse and the clearest articulation of what is known as the organizational synthesis. Emphasizing the nation's shift, in the late nineteenth and early twentieth centuries, from a world of separate island communities to a more organized and integrated society, Wiebe highlighted the efforts of a new middle class, a professionally trained elite of doctors, lawyers, economists, engineers, and so on, to establish a more rationally structured and efficient society.

Gabriel Kolko in *The Triumph of Conservatism* (1963) offered another striking assessment of the goals and motivations of the Progressive Era. Kolko argued that reform of big business was initiated by the business class itself, which feared the consequences of internecine competition and understood that regulatory legislation would maximize profits.

The Hofstadter, Wiebe, and Kolko arguments all assessed Progressivism cynically, emphasizing the self-interest of the reformers, whether they hailed from the old middle class, the new middle class, or the business class, not their altruism. Others, such as J. Joseph Huthmacher in his 1962 study, also stressed self-interest, but at the same time gave agency to the people, arguing that the reform impulse came from the working class, and particularly from new immigrants, who pressed for work safety legislation, higher pay, and shorter working days.

By the 1970s and 1980s, the horizons of scholarship had broadened considerably as historians paid increasing attention to the roles of women reformers, African-American reformers, immigrant associations, working-class activists, and religion. In the 1990s, the parameters of Progressivism became even more expansive, and even the most basic assumptions about the era were called into question. For example, Elizabeth Sanders countered the commonly accepted notion that Progressive reform was a largely urban phenomenon in her study *Roots of Reform* (1999), arguing that Progressive leaders generally hailed from rural backgrounds and built their reform agenda on the foundation of the Populist Party platforms of the 1890s.

Like other subfields within American history, the study of late nineteenth and early twentieth century reform has been broadened in scope geographically, too. The most significant example of this internationalization of American historical scholarship is Daniel T. Rodgers's study *Atlantic Crossings* (1998), which examines the currents of reform in six European countries and Australia, as well as the United States, thus deexceptionalizing American Progressivism. Recent scholarship has also paid increasing attention to U.S. imperialism during the age of reform. Gail Bederman in *Manliness and Civilization* (1995) viewed the imperialist impulses of the Progressive Era as partly a manifestation of fears over declining American manhood and emphasized Theodore Roosevelt's dedication to "the millennial struggle for Americans to perfect civilization by becoming the most manly, civilized, and powerful race in the world." Glenda Elizabeth Gilmore in her study of the South during the Progressive Era, *Gender and Jim Crow* (1996), also explores the intersection of race and gender.

Michael McGerr's important recent study, *A Fierce Discontent,* (2003) emphasizes the middle-class origins of Progressive reformers and their passion, dedication, and radicalism. McGerr's picture, though, is complicated by his examination of the dedication or at least acquiescence of most Progressives to racial segregation—of African-Americans in the North as well as in the South, of Native Americans in the West, and of southern and eastern European immigrants in the cities of the Northeast and Midwest. The reformers' fierce discontent, when it came to the central issue of race, turned out to be a muted fury at best, an accommodation to racism, an acceptance of segregation because of fear of the violence that might accompany close social relations between white Americans and Americans of color.

The first historians of Progressivism paid comparatively little attention to the issue of race beyond the South. Historians up until the 1970s tended to view southern Progressivism's mix of reformist and racist impulses as an anomaly. They generally assumed that Progressives outside of the South largely ignored issues of race in their effort to get on with the task of reforming society. One thing that most historians would now agree on, looking back on the Progressive Era from the vantage point of the twenty-first century, is that our current understanding, informed as it is by recent scholarship on the intersections of race, gender, and reform, is considerably more complex and inclusive than that in the first waves of writing on the period.

22

The Experiment in American Empire

1865–1917

It took the U.S. Army Corps of Engineers eight years to finish the 50-mile-long canal, which a British observer called "the greatest liberty Man has ever taken with Nature."

On November 9, 1906, President Theodore Roosevelt set sail on the new sixteen-thousand-ton *Louisiana*, the largest battleship in the growing U.S. Navy. The first president ever to leave the country during his term in office, Roosevelt was headed for Panama to examine progress on the construction of a new U.S. canal—the most daring and ambitious engineering marvel of the time. Convinced that the United States needed a gateway between the Atlantic and Pacific Oceans, Roosevelt had maneuvered to purchase the rights to the canal from Panama in 1904. Not even the fierce rainstorm that greeted Roosevelt's arrival on November 15 could dampen his enthusiasm for the project. Over the next two days the president leaped into ditches, inspected the complicated gears used to operate the great locks, and steered the gigantic steam shovel that moved mountains of earth and rock. Afterward, Roosevelt wrote to his son that the canal was "the greatest engineering feat of the ages. . . . I went over everything that I could possibly go over."

The canal was made possible by the marriage of imagination with industrial might and technological know-how. Engineers slashed through mountains, carved out ditches, fabricated locks wide enough to float the world's biggest ships, and constructed the largest dam ever built. "Everything is on a colossal scale," noted *Scientific American*. How colossal? Manufacturers poured millions of tons of concrete to erect the mammoth canal walls—enough concrete to build a wall 8 feet thick, 12 feet high, and 133 miles long. American factories churned out the hardware—special bearings, gears, wheels, and struts—that opened and closed the immense locks. Ironically, the greatest threat to success came from the tiniest of enemies, the mosquito. Carriers of malaria and yellow fever, mosquitoes had helped doom an earlier French effort to build a canal, wiping out more than twenty thousand workers. U.S. Army doctors, however, developed effective countermeasures, destroyed the mosquito population, and reduced the incidence of disease.

The U.S. government had never undertaken a project as big, complex, and expensive as the Panama Canal. It took the U.S. Army Corps of Engineers eight years to finish the 50-mile-long canal, which a British observer called "the greatest liberty Man has ever taken with Nature." When opened in August 1914 the canal shortened the distance between New York and San Francisco by boat from 15,615 miles to 5,300 miles. U.S. merchants and warships now moved easily between the Atlantic and Pacific Oceans.

The experiment in canal building was an outgrowth of America's growing global ambitions, its desire to quicken the pace of commerce and to project military power abroad. In the two decades following the Civil War Americans remained too absorbed in westward expansion and industrialization to devote serious attention to foreign policy. By the 1880s, however, a new spirit of imperialism gripped the major Western powers. In a scramble for new markets, England, France, and Germany established economic, and in most cases political, control over vast regions of Africa and Southeast Asia, seizing 10 million square miles and subjugating half a billion people. In 1898 the United States went to war with Spain to assert its influence in the Western Hemisphere. It also extended its power in the Pacific by annexing the Hawaiian Islands and establishing a protectorate over the Philippines.

Despite their differences, the Progressive Era presidents—Roosevelt, Taft, and Wilson—shared an expansive view of the nation's global interests and showed a new willingness to flex U.S. military muscle. Projecting the reform impulse outward, they sought to extend American values through the experiment in empire building. Theodore Roosevelt established American dominance in the Caribbean and worked to maintain open markets in China. His decision to build the Panama Canal was the most dramatic expression of America's muscular foreign policy. Woodrow Wilson came to office promising a foreign policy based on morality, not self-interest. But his active intervention in the Caribbean, especially Mexico, demonstrated that his policies differed little from the militaristic Roosevelt's.

- Why did America abandon its traditional isolationism at the end of the nineteenth century?

- In what way was the war with Spain a critical turning point in U.S. foreign policy?

- What was Theodore Roosevelt's view of America's world role, and how successful was he in implementing it?

- How did Wilson's foreign policy differ from Roosevelt's? What did their policies have in common?

This chapter will address these questions.

THE ROOTS OF EXPANSION, 1865–1898

For most of the nineteenth century, Americans focused their expansionist ambitions on the West. Except for a handful of imperialist thinkers such as Secretary of State William Seward, few Americans expressed interest in foreign policy in the years following the Civil War. By the end of the nineteenth century, however, a number of forces—the search for new markets, the popularity of Social Darwinism, social anxieties bred by the end of the frontier, and the emergence of influential advocates of expansion—were pushing the United States to experiment with a more aggressive role in the world. America's involvement in Hawaii and Samoa revealed a growing interest in distant markets and lands.

Gilded Age Diplomacy, 1865–1889

During the 1860s and 1870s few Americans cared about foreign policy. Isolationists dominated Congress, and public sentiment favored internal improvement and development westward over external expansion. The *Chicago Tribune* noted soon after the Civil War that "we already have more territory than we can people in fifty years." Americans lacked any sense of imminent threat from abroad. Geographical distance continued to protect America from what Jefferson had called "the broils of Europe." Moreover, a stable balance of power had preserved international peace in Europe for most of the nineteenth century after the defeat of Napoleon III in the Franco-Prussian War in 1870. The waves of new immigrants seeking opportunity on the nation's shores reaffirmed Americans' fears about the corruption of the "Old World" and reinforced the desire to avoid entangling alliances with European powers. Even if Americans had wanted to get involved in world affairs, they lacked the means to do so. The State Department consisted of only sixty full-time staff members. In the 1880s the United States was represented abroad by twenty-five ministers, but no ambassadors. In 1883 the U.S. Navy was a pitiful collection of ninety woeful ships, fifty-eight made of wood. Representative John D. Long of Massachusetts described it as "an alphabet of floating washtubs." Foreign policy was impulsive rather than systematic. American leaders responded to individual crises but lacked a global strategy or a coordinated vision of America's role in the world.

During these years the United States nevertheless made its first steps toward world power. Leading the charge were bold expansionists, in particular Secretary of State William H. Seward (served 1861–1869). Seward's belief that the United States should hold a "commanding sway in the world" foreshadowed American foreign policy in the next century. Believing that "empire has, for the last three hundred years . . . made its way constantly westward," Seward wanted the United States to establish dominance over Latin America and extend its reach into Asian markets, especially China, which he called "the chief theatre of events in the world's great hereafter."

Acting on his expansionist impulses, Seward negotiated a treaty with Nicaragua in 1867 giving the United States rights to build a canal from the Atlantic to the Pacific at a later date. Two months later he annexed the Midway Islands west of Hawaii, which opened up a commercial route to Korea, Japan, and China. The Senate, however, which was consumed by the impeachment of President Andrew Johnson, rejected Seward's efforts to buy the Virgin Islands—St. Thomas and St. John in the Caribbean—from Denmark for $7.5 million.

In his most significant and controversial acquisition, Seward purchased Alaska from Russia in March 1867. Critics, who called the deal "Seward's Folly," complained that the United States had little need for "a barren, worthless, God-forsaken region." Supporters emphasized Alaska's rich mineral resources and suggested that acquiring Alaska would lead to the possible annexation of Canada. Although the Senate

CHRONOLOGY

1867	Seward purchases Alaska
1872	*Alabama* claims settled
1889	U.S. enters tripartite protectorate over Samoan Islands
1890	Naval Act passed
1895	Venezuelan border dispute
1896	McKinley elected president
1898	Spanish-American War begins and ends Hawaii becomes a U.S. territory U.S. annexes part of Samoa and Wake Island Anti-Imperialist League formed
1899	U.S. sovereignty established over the Philippines and Puerto Rico Philippine insurrection begins Hay's Open Door notes Boxer Rebellion in China
1901	Roosevelt becomes president Emilio Aguinaldo surrenders
1904	Senate approves Panama Canal treaty Roosevelt Corollary
1905	Portsmouth peace conference
1907	Great White Fleet sails around the world
1908	Root-Takahira Agreement Taft elected president
1909	Taft unveils dollar diplomacy
1912	Marines invade Nicaragua Lodge Corollary Wilson elected president
1914	World War I begins in Europe Panama Canal opens American troops invade Mexico
1915	Marines invade Haiti

approved the purchase on April 6, Congress did not appropriate the purchase money of $7.5 million until 1870, and then only after the Russian minister had spent some of it in advance to bribe influential congressmen. Seward thus added 586,000 square miles, or an area more than twice the size of Texas, to the Union.

In 1869 newly elected President Ulysses Grant appointed Hamilton Fish to replace Seward as secretary of state. Like Seward, Fish struggled against strong isolationist forces. The administration's attempt to annex Santo Domingo for $1.5 million aroused a storm of public protest. In June 1870 the Senate fell ten votes short of ratification and the treaty died. Americans were opposed to annexing more territory in the Caribbean, but they were willing to go to war to defend America's national honor. A major crisis arose in 1875 when a Spanish gunboat seized the *Virginius,* a Cuban-owned ship that was carrying weapons to rebels on its home island, in international waters. The crew members, including eight Americans, were later tried and executed. Cries went up in the United States for revenge. Fish, after discovering that the ship was not legally registered in the United States, negotiated a settlement by which Spain agreed to pay $80,000 for the lives of the crew members.

More pressing than acquiring additional territory was settling disputes with Great Britain left over from the Civil War. Many in the North wanted the British to pay reparations for the damage inflicted on the Union by English-built Confederate ships. Most controversial of all were the *Alabama* claims, stemming from the destruction wrought by a single British-based raider. Charles Sumner, chairman of the Senate Foreign Relations Committee, claimed that such ships had prolonged the war by two years and demanded that Britain bear half the total cost of the war. His bill totaled $2.1 billion, but Sumner suggested that the United States would be happy to accept Canada instead of cash. After protracted negotiations, a joint Anglo-American–appointed judicial commission ruled that Britain had been negligent in allowing the *Alabama* and the other cruisers to participate in the war. In September 1872 it awarded the United States $15.5 million in compensation.

The New Manifest Destiny

As the last quarter of the nineteenth century unfolded, a number of forces were pushing the United States to assume a more aggressive posture toward the world. Developments in transportation and communication were shrinking the world economically and militarily. Steam-powered ships made travel between nations easier. In 1886 an underwater transatlantic cable linked the United States and Europe, cutting the transmission time for messages from weeks to hours. The U.S. telegraph system allowed direct communication with Brazil and Chile. "Commerce follows the cables," Henry Cabot Lodge observed in 1898, pointing out the link between communications and business. After devoting a generation to conquering the West and creating an industrial giant, many Americans turned their attention to new opportunities beyond the border.

Among the leading proponents of expansion were businessmen who believed that continued economic growth required tapping new markets abroad. Business did not speak with a single voice on the issue of overseas markets, however. Many business leaders, fearing that economic ties would inevitably entangle the United States in costly political struggles abroad, emphasized the importance of cultivating markets at home. Other businessmen saw the possibility of unlimited profits in untapped markets in Asia and Latin America. These regions also offered abundant raw materials such as sugar, coffee, oil, rubber, and minerals. In 1896 the newly formed National Association of Manufacturers declared "that the trade centres of Central and South America are natural markets for American products."

Advances in communication and growing competition to acquire new lands and new markets transformed the international order and established the foundation of globalization. According to British Prime Minister Lord Salisbury, the late nineteenth century was a time of "living" powers (Germany, Japan, and the United States) and "dying" powers (Great Britain, Spain, and China). These nations were engaged in global competition to establish economic dominance. According to many American businessmen, the nation would have to assert itself in this new age of imperialism and possibly acquire new territory if it was going to compete economically with its global rivals.

The decline in domestic consumption during the depression of the 1890s helped spread the conviction that the United States needed to aggressively cultivate markets abroad. "A policy of isolation did well enough when we were an embryo nation, but today things are different," Senator Orville Platt of Connecticut said in 1893. "We are sixty-five million of people, the most advanced and powerful on earth, and regard to our future welfare demands an abandonment of the doctrines of isolation."

Regardless of the debate over foreign markets, the last quarter of the nineteenth century witnessed an explosion of American economic involvement in the world. Between 1865 and 1898 the value of American exports jumped from $281 million to $1.3 billion, while imports rose from $259 million to $616 million. The young iron and steel industry exported 15 percent of its goods by the turn of the century. Almost 50 percent of copper mined in the United States was sold abroad. The Singer Company sold as many of its sewing machines overseas as it did at home. Over half of the petroleum refined in the United States ended up in Europe. Though most of the products flowed to Europe and Canada, American producers were also reaching into other areas. U.S. exports to Latin American, for example, increased from $50 million in the 1870s to over $120 million in 1900. By the 1890s the United States purchased 75 percent of Mexico's exports and was responsible for 50 percent of its imports. Exports represented a small percentage of the gross national product (GNP)—between 6 and 7 percent—but Americans were looking more and more to foreign markets for future growth (see figure on page 854.)

Many expansionists argued that it was America's destiny to expand not only to promote prosperity at home, but also to extend American blessings of liberty and democracy to the rest of the world. Americans had always believed that they possessed a special mission to reshape the world in their own image. Senator Albert Beveridge of Indiana explained in 1900 that God "has marked the American people as his chosen nation to lead in the regeneration of the world." After the Civil War, most evangelical Protestant denominations formed missionary societies that funded and trained workers who felt called to Christianize the people of foreign lands. Josiah Strong, a Congregational minister and author of the influential book *Our Country* (1885), promised that God was "preparing mankind to receive our impress." The United States, he charged, was "divinely commissioned" to spread Protestant Christianity and civilized values to the rest of the world. "As America goes, so goes the world." The missionaries heightened public awareness and interest

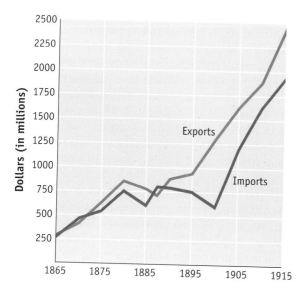

Imports and Exports, 1865–1915   The rapid expansion of American industry after the Civil War spurred America's involvement in the international economy. While America maintained a favorable balance of trade for most of the period, the rise in imported goods paralleled the advancements made in the export market.

in places such as China and Hawaii, as they laid the groundwork in those regions for further American incursions.

The growing popularity of Social Darwinism (see page 806) added force to the notion of an expansionist mission. Extending the notion that only the "fit" survive to be nations and societies, some expansionists argued that the United States needed to compete vigorously with other nations, or perish. "The rule of the survival of the fittest applies to nations as well as to the animal kingdom," an American diplomat noted in 1898.

The idea of natural selection also engendered a clear sense of racial hierarchy. New pseudoscientific studies suggested that people of Anglo-Saxon origin, namely Britons, Germans, Scandinavians, and Americans of those heritages, were superior to members of other races. By all standards of measure according to these theorists—industrial progress, military might, wealth, and influence—Anglo-Saxons were clearly at the pinnacle of the racial pyramid. This conviction of racial superiority encouraged a belief that the United States had an obligation to take part in instructing the world's less developed peoples in the superior ways of Anglo-Saxon civilization, but it also raised fears of racial mixing that would dilute the "pure" Anglo-Saxon stock.

Social anxieties born of the shrinkage in open land and opportunity in the West fed the expansionist appetite. For most of their history Americans had entertained the comforting belief that the constant movement westward acted as an escape valve for social tension. In 1893 Frederick Jackson Turner pronounced the frontier closed. Never again, he argued, would the frontier provide "a gate of escape from the bondage of the past." With the West settled, many people believed that Americans needed to find new outlets to absorb their dynamic energy. Turner observed that the frontier's disappearance created "demands for a vigorous foreign policy . . . and for the extension of American influence to outlying islands and adjoining countries."

Finally, in the mid-1890s a small group of influential men challenged traditional isolationist sentiment and advocated an expansionist foreign policy. Led by Assistant Secretary of the Navy Theodore Roosevelt and Republican Senator Henry Cabot Lodge of Massachusetts, these intensely nationalistic young men formed a close-knit circle of influence. Meeting regularly at private homes in Washington, they developed plans and lobbied aggressively for commercial and territorial expansion. They promised to replace the graying veterans of the Civil War who, chastened by their suffering during that war, had resisted the temptation of military adventure. As Teddy Roosevelt told a Civil War veteran, "You and your generation have had your chance from 1861 to 1865. Now let us of this generation have ours!"

This foreign policy elite exercised considerable influence because, except on occasions when they believed American honor was at stake, the "people" remained largely disinterested in debates about America's role in the world. Made up of educated upper- and middle-income groups, the "foreign-policy public" encompassed about 10 to 20 percent of the electorate. "After all, public opinion is made and controlled by the thoughtful men of the country," Secretary of State Walter Q. Gresham noted in 1893.

The new foreign policy elite found inspiration in the writings of Alfred Thayer Mahan, a naval strategist and prolific author who taught at the Naval War College. Mahan insisted in books such as *The Influence of Sea Power upon History* (1890) that control over international communications was the key to success in modern war. Believing that national power depended on sea power, Mahan supported U.S. colonies in both the Caribbean and the Pacific, linked by a canal built across Central America. In a Darwinian world, powerful nations had an obligation to dominate weak ones. If the United States was to be a great power, he argued, it must have a navy capable of carrying the battle to the enemy and not just defending the coastline (see map on page 856).

Mahan's followers lobbied Congress to build a new fleet of ships outfitted with the most modern weapons. A nation without a navy, they warned, could make little headway in world affairs in an age of sea power. "The sea will be the future seat of empire," observed Secretary of the Navy Benjamin F. Tracy. "And we shall rule it as certainly as the sun doth rise." The appeal found broad support in Congress, which in 1883 commissioned three steel-hulled, steam-powered cruisers, and in 1886 two battleships, the *Maine* and the *Texas*. The Naval Act of 1890 authorized the building of "three sea-going coastline battleships designed to carry the heaviest armor and most powerful ordnance." In 1880 the American navy was ranked the twelfth most powerful in the world. By 1900 it was third, with seventeen battleships and six armored cruisers.

Seeds of Empire   In diplomatic policy the new expansionism was evident in the administration of Benjamin Harrison, who came into office in March 1889. His secretary of state James G. Blaine, the "Plumed Knight from Maine" (see page 777) said that the goal of foreign policy must be to bring peace and trade to Latin America. "Our great demand is expansion," he stated. "I mean expansion of trade with countries where we can find profitable exchanges." Apprehensive about European influence in Latin America, he called the First International American Conference in 1889 and invited delegates from seventeen Latin American nations to discuss the creation of an inter-American common market. The conference failed to achieve that lofty goal, but it did lead to the building of the first Pan-American highway system. The following year Congress passed a new "reciprocity" tariff that allowed certain Latin American products (especially coffee, hides, and sugar) to enter the United States freely as long as the nations that produced them allowed U.S. exports into their countries equally free from tariff restrictions. Under the 1890 reciprocity treaties, trade immediately boomed with Cuba and Brazil, among others.

The goodwill generated by the conference was short-lived, however. In October 1891 more than a hundred drunken American sailors on shore leave from the U.S.S. *Baltimore* fought with anti-American Chileans in the port town of Valparaiso, Chile. Two sailors were killed and seventeen badly hurt. President Harrison insisted on a

Imperialism in Asia and the Pacific, 1914 As American businessmen turned their attention overseas to new markets they faced stiff competition from Europeans who were already establishing spheres of influence in Asia as part of their efforts to win trade routes to China. Few nations along the Pacific Rim remained independent by 1914 as Western industrialized nations formalized control of territories. Japan, following the western economic model, also began expansion in the region, acquiring Korea from the Russians and Formosa from the Chinese. Although China remained an independent nation, European, American and Japanese businesses dominated its economy and controlled several of its key port cities.

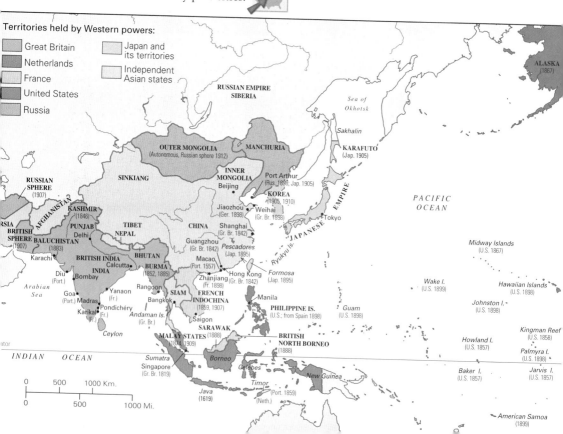

"prompt and full reparation," but the Chilean government scorned the demand. Harrison threatened war, and in January a new Chilean government apologized for the incident and paid a $75,000 indemnity.

While extending American influence in Latin America, continuing tensions with Great Britain centered on the question of U.S. fishing rights in Canadian waters. By 1886, after a number of attempts to reach a settlement, Canadians were seizing American fishing vessels, and Congress responded by giving President Grover Cleveland the power to ban Canadian ships from American waters. Soon thereafter, the United States began seizing Canadian ships hunting seals in the Bering Sea off Alaska, and in 1889 Congress declared the Bering Sea closed to foreign shipping. The British, refusing to accept America's claim, sent warships into the region. Cooler heads prevailed, however, and both nations agreed to submit the case to international arbitration, which eventually ruled against the United States and ordered the government to pay damages to Canada.

Less easily resolved was a fifty-year-old dispute over the boundary between Venezuela and British Guiana. Tensions between the two countries flared in 1895 when prospectors discovered gold in the disputed area. When Venezuela suspended diplomatic relations with Britain, the United States offered to arbitrate. But neither side was prepared to settle, and the dispute lingered on. In an effort to force an end to the conflict, President Cleveland instructed his secretary of state, Richard L. Olney, to draft a note that invoked the Monroe Doctrine to warn the British against interference in the Western Hemisphere. "Today, the United States is practically sovereign on this continent, and its fiat is law upon the subjects to which it confines its interposition . . . because, in addition to all other grounds, its infinite resources combined with its isolated position render it master of the situation and practically invulnerable as against any or all other powers."

Britain rejected both the American offer for arbitration and Olney's broad and pompous expression of the Monroe Doctrine. "The disputed frontier of Venezuela has nothing to do with any of the questions dealt with by President Monroe," declared the prime minister. Cleveland, who pronounced himself "mad clear through," made it plain in a message of December 17, 1895, that if Britain would not accept arbitration, he would impose a settlement. The British, distracted by a new crisis with Germany and fearing a conflict with the United States, agreed in the Treaty of Washington to accept arbitration by an independent commission. On October 3, 1899, the commission upheld most of the British claims. The peaceful resolution of the border dispute foreshadowed a new spirit of cooperation and goodwill that would characterize Anglo-American relations in the next century.

Hawaii and Samoa   By the 1870s the growing U.S. interest in Hawaii and Samoa revealed how American attitudes toward the world were changing. The Hawaiian (or Sandwich) Islands lay 2,300 miles southwest of California and served as the "Crossroads of the Pacific." After 1820 American missionaries arrived on the islands; by 1840 the capital, Honolulu, was an established port of call for American merchant ships and whalers.

In 1875 the United States and Hawaii signed a reciprocal trade agreement that allowed Hawaiian sugar to enter the United States duty-free and prevented the island monarchy from making treaties with other powers. With the rich U.S. market at their disposal, white planters forced a new constitution, which gave them dominance over Hawaii's economic and political life. Between 1876 and 1885 they raised their sugar production from 26 million pounds to 171 million pounds. Both sides renewed the reciprocal trade treaty in 1887, adding a provision giving the United States exclusive rights to a naval base at Pearl Harbor. In 1890, 99 percent of Hawaiian sugar exports went to the United States. Secretary of State James Blaine called the islands "a part of the productive and commercial system of the American states."

Not everyone on the islands welcomed the growing American presence. Native Hawaiians believed that increasing American involvement would result in annexation. In 1890 the McKinley Tariff Act ended the special status for Hawaii sugar. The new law sent the Hawaiian economy into a tailspin; unemployment rose and property values plummeted, along with the planters' profits. The following year a strong-minded nationalist, Queen Liliuokalani, assumed the throne. Tapping into deep resentment against the white minority, she abolished the constitution—the "Bayonet Constitution," she called it—and increased the power of native Hawaiians.

Seeing the Hawaiian nationalists as a threat to their predominance, the white plantation owners fought back, turning to the United States for help. They found a ready ally in John L. Stevens, the American minister in Honolulu. In 1893 plantation owners launched an armed revolt to unseat the Hawaiian government, and Stevens, acting on his own authority, ordered 150 marines from the offshore U.S.S. *Boston* to guard locations in Honolulu. After three days of fighting, Queen Liliuokalani surrendered, and the white minority established a provisional government. Stevens declared an American protectorate over Hawaii and raised the U.S. flag. "The Hawaiian pear is now fully ripe, and this is the golden hour for the United States to pluck it," he wrote. In February a committee for the new government signed a treaty of annexation with the United States.

By the time the Senate began considering the treaty, the Harrison administration, which favored annexation, had left office. The new president, Grover Cleveland, withdrew the treaty and dispatched a special commissioner, James H. Blount, to Hawaii. In July 1893 Blount reported that the "undoubted sentiment of the people is for the Queen, against the provisional Government and against annexation." Cleveland proposed restoring the queen to the throne, but the new government refused. In August Cleveland reluctantly recognized the independent Republic of Hawaii. The debate over annexation, however, continued through the 1890s.

Hawaii was not the only island in the Pacific that piqued American interest. The secretary of state during Cleveland's first term, Thomas F. Bayard, saw Samoa, a group of fourteen volcanic islands located 4,100 miles from the coast of California, as a valuable strategic asset in the South Pacific. On January 17, 1878, the Senate approved a treaty establishing U.S. trading rights and authorizing construction of a coaling station at Pago Pago on the island of Tutuila. Over the next few years the United States, Great Britain, and Germany jockeyed for power in the island chain. German Foreign Office officials angrily muttered that Bayard was extending the principles of "the Monroe Doctrine as though the Pacific Ocean were to be treated as an American lake."

Negotiations eventually eased tensions, and on June 14, 1889, the United States entered into a tripartite protectorate with Britain and Germany over the

Queen Liliuokalani (1838–1917)
Though Hawaiians had resented the growing influence of American sugar planters since the 1870s, not until Queen Liliuokalani assumed the throne in 1891 did they actively resist American imperialism. The indomitable monarch scrapped the Hawaiian constitution, drafted under the pressure of white planters, and declared "Hawaii for the Hawaiians." Her efforts, however, were no match for U.S. military might, which supported a planter coup in 1893. Hawaii officially became part of the United States during the Spanish-American War thanks to a joint resolution by Congress.
(Hawaii State Archives.)

Samoan Islands, which was ratified by the Senate on February 4, 1890. Secretary of State Walter Q. Gresham (served 1893–1895) observed later that the treaty represented "the first departure from our traditional and well-established policy of avoiding entangling alliances with foreign powers in relation to objects remote from this hemisphere."

WAR AND WORLD RESPONSIBILITIES, 1898–1901

The United States had been experimenting haphazardly with greater world involvement, but a series of events was about to propel the nation into a position of world power. In 1898 the United States found itself involved in a simmering revolt against Spanish policy in Cuba. The American public, aroused by sensationalized newspaper reports, sided with the Cuban rebels in their fight for independence. In April 1898, smarting from perceived provocations, the United States declared war on Spain. The war lasted only a few months, but the United States reaped great benefits from victory. For the first time Americans debated questions of empire and its role in the American experiment. While trying to quell an insurrection in the Philippines and establish stable governments in Cuba and Puerto Rico, the United States struggled to open new markets in China through a series of "Open Door" notes.

Origins of the Spanish-American War

For most of the previous quarter-century, Cubans had been revolting against Spanish colonialism. In February 1895 a new insurrection threatened Spanish rule on the island. Rebels established a provisional government and waged a guerrilla war against Spain. Both sides kept a cautious eye on the United States, which had investments totaling more than $50 million, much of that in sugar exports. "The sugar industry of Cuba is as vital to our people as are the wheat and cotton of India and Egypt to Great Britain," declared the American minister to Spain.

The Spanish dispatched 150,000 soldiers who, under the command of General Valeriano Weyler, known as "the Butcher," tried to destroy the rebels' base of popular support by instituting the brutal reconcentration program. Weyler's soldiers forced peasants into armed camps and then turned the Cuban countryside into a desert, burning crops, killing animals, and poisoning wells. About four hundred thousand *reconcentrados*, nearly a quarter of the Cuban population, perished in the camps. The revolution nevertheless continued to spread, and the insurgents responded with a scorched-earth strategy of their own, burning cane fields, blowing up mills, and disrupting railroads in an effort to make Cuba an economic liability to Spain. "The chains of Cuba have been forged by her own richness," declared the rebel leader.

Events in Cuba attracted the attention of the American press, which played on strong American sentiment in favor of the rebels. William Randolph Hearst's *New York Journal* and Joseph Pulitzer's *New York World* were locked in a battle for readers. Fiercely competitive, they experimented with new methods to attract readers, including using bold print that covered the front page and adding illustrations and an expanded Sunday edition with color comics. They fed the public a steady diet of titillating articles such as "Strange Things Women Do for Love." Both papers also carried a cartoon character, "The Yellow Kid," and became known as "yellow journals." Pulitzer and Hearst sent correspondents to Cuba to cover the grim story of the revolt. They sent back ghastly reports, often exaggerated, that inflamed the passions of Americans already inclined to view the Cuban insurrection in light of their own revolution against England.

Public and business pressure for action mounted. The combination of altruism and self-interest provided a powerful argument for intervention. Outraged Americans held public meetings in major cities to protest Spain's actions. Congress responded in April 1896, passing resolutions endorsing recognition of Cuban rebels and urging the president to support Cuban independence. President Cleveland, however, resisted public pressure and insisted on maintaining a policy of neutrality. The president believed the Cubans incapable of self-government and supported Spanish control, but he urged Spain to initiate modest political reforms to appease some of the rebels and neutralize the rebellion.

William McKinley came to office in early 1897 calling for a strong navy and demanding "the eventual withdrawal of the European powers from this hemisphere." But McKinley had little enthusiasm for war. As an eighteen-year-old volunteer, he had fought in the Civil War's bloodiest battles. "I have been through one war," he told a friend. "I have seen the dead piled up, and I do not want to see another." At first McKinley tried to walk a fine line between preserving American honor and avoiding armed intervention in Cuba.

Immediately after assuming office in March, he sent an aide to investigate conditions in Cuba. The aide returned with a horrifying account of Spanish atrocities that had wrapped Cuba "in the stillness of death and the silence of desolation." In June 1897 McKinley demanded an end to the "uncivilized and inhumane conduct." He pressed Spain to end the fighting and to grant reforms, indicating that otherwise the United States might intervene. A new government in Madrid offered a few concessions, removing "Butcher" Weyler, suspending its reconcentration camps, and offering the first steps toward Cuban autonomy.

Spain's action produced a temporary lull in the crisis, but two unpredictable events pushed the nations closer to war. On February 9 Hearst's *New York Journal* published a private letter from Spain's minister in Washington, Enrique Dupuy de Lôme, to a senior Spanish politician touring Cuba. The letter poked fun at McKinley, calling him "weak," a "bidder for the admiration of the crowd," and a "would-be politician." Along with insulting McKinley, the letter suggested that the promised Cuban reforms were not being carried out in good faith. The *Journal*, in a screaming headline, called the letter the "Worst Insult to the United States in History!" The little trust that Americans had in the Spanish evaporated.

Six days later, on February 15, an explosion destroyed the *Maine*, one of the U.S. Navy's most modern and imposing battleships, while it sat in Cuba's Havana harbor. The United States lost 260 sailors in the explosion. Though the cause of the explosion remained uncertain, Americans blamed Spain. Headlines clamored for vengeance. The *New York World* roared: "Remember the *Maine*! To hell with Spain!" Assistant Secretary of the Navy Theodore Roosevelt called the sinking "an act of dirty treachery on the part of the Spaniards."

After the *Maine*'s destruction, McKinley asked Congress for $50 million to begin mobilization for war. On March 9 Congress granted his request. On March 17 Republican Senator Redfield Proctor of Vermont, widely recognized as a sober and judicious man, stood on the Senate floor and delivered a powerful speech denouncing Spain's policy in Cuba. "That speech means war," a fellow senator declared; "that speech will stir the people of the United States from Maine to California, and no power on earth can longer keep them back."

But McKinley still hoped for peace. Between March 20 and 28 he sent a series of demands to Spain. The Spanish would have to pay an indemnity for the *Maine*, promise not to use the reconcentration camps, declare a truce in fighting with the rebels, and negotiate for Cuban independence, through U.S. mediation if necessary. The Spanish government, hoping to avoid a confrontation with the United States, surrendered to all the demands except the last.

McKinley's peace overtures, however, incurred the wrath of a nation intent on war. The *Journal* declared that the "whole country thrills with the war fever." The *World* commented on "the warlike spirit of the multitude." Theodore Roosevelt, banging his war drums, called McKinley "a white-livered cur." "The President," Roosevelt jeered, "has no more backbone than a chocolate eclair." The taunts and abuse took their toll on McKinley who, according to a friend, "broke down and cried like a boy of thirteen."

Remembering the *Maine*

The combination of an explosion on the U.S.S. *Maine* and an exploitative press created a public clamor for war so loud a reluctant McKinley could not ignore it. The explosion that sent the ship to the bottom of Havana harbor was never fully explained, but the press immediately accused Spain of orchestrating the tragedy, despite Spain's efforts to avoid war with the United States. This sheet of music demonstrates how the event became a part of American popular culture, as well as an effective propaganda tool for war supporters, calling for the nation to avenge the deaths on the *Maine.* *(John Hay Library, Brown University.)*

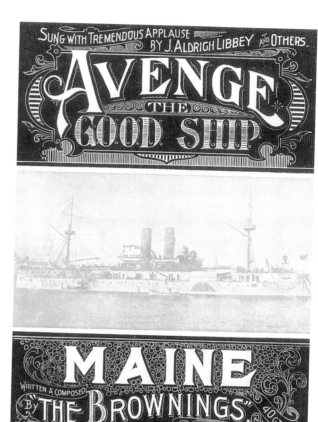

Reluctantly, McKinley prepared his war message. On April 11, 1898, in a long, tempered address, the president declared that the three-year struggle on the island had caused "very serious injury to the commerce, trade, and business of our people, and the wanton destruction of property." McKinley's war message triggered a spirited debate in Congress. Administration allies fought off attempts to include recognition of Cuban independence as part of the war declaration. Congress did, however, include the Teller Amendment, which disclaimed "any disposition or intention to exercise sovereignty, jurisdiction, or control over" Cuba and announced American intent "to leave the government and control of the island to its people." On April 21 Spain severed diplomatic relations with the United States. The following day American ships blockaded Cuba. On April 24 Spain declared war. The next day Congress declared that a state of war had existed since April 21.

A variety of motives pushed the nation into war. Moralism inspired many religious leaders to march in the war parade. Lyman Abbott, pastor of Plymouth Church in Brooklyn, thought war the "answer to America to the question of its own conscience: Am I my brother's keeper?" Emotional nationalism infused with notions of American superiority played a role. The de Lôme and *Maine* incidents, combined with the sensationalized accounts of Spanish atrocities, provoked widespread anger and convinced many Americans that intervention was both right and just. "At last, God's hour has struck. The American people go forth in a warfare holier than liberty—holy as humanity," noted a partisan. Business leaders, who had originally feared that conflict would disrupt commerce and endanger U.S. investment in Cuba, now saw war as a way to open trade doors by eliminating a colonial power from the hemisphere. Imperialists rallied around the prospect of the war's extending America's empire and serving as justification for an enlarged navy. Even many Americans who opposed empire hoped the war would halt the killing and restore order to a troubled nation.

"A Splendid Little War" The U.S. Army was ill-prepared for battle. The regular army consisted of only twenty-eight thousand officers and men scattered in small detachments around the country. The only officers with experience commanding troops in battle were aging veterans of the Civil War and Indian conflicts. The president called into service two hundred thousand volunteers, who flocked to army camps in Tampa, Florida, the base for the Cuban expedition. The army owned no accurate maps of Cuba. Essential equipment was in short supply. Ultimately, soldiers would be sent off to fight in a tropical climate with uniforms made of heavy wool, flannel, and cowhide. The food supplies sent with them rotted in the tropical heat. One food that did not, canned beef, contained so many chemical preservatives that soldiers called it "embalmed beef." Climate, combined with poor sanitation and limited medical care, produced widespread disease. For each soldier killed in combat, more than seven died from disease, usually typhoid fever or malaria.

Among the units ordered to Florida were four African-American army regiments that had been serving in the northern Great Plains and on the Mexican border. These black soldiers eventually made up almost one-fourth of the invasion force that sailed for Cuba. As they moved eastward by train, they were greeted by cheering crowds, but the cheering stopped when the trains entered the South. Sergeant Frank W. Pullen wrote, "We were 'niggers' as they called us and treated us with contempt." Once they arrived in Florida, black soldiers stationed near segregated towns endured constant indignities. In one town a sign read, "Dogs and niggers not allowed." At times tensions exploded into violence. In Tampa a confrontation led to a night of rioting in which three whites and twenty-seven black soldiers were wounded. A black chaplain asked, "Talk about fighting and freeing poor Cuba and of Spain's brutality; of Cuba's murdered thousands, and starving *reconcentrados*. Is America any better than Spain?"

Even before the declaration of war, Assistant Secretary of the Navy Theodore Roosevelt had been plotting American strategy. Believing that U.S. naval forces could cripple the Spanish fleet with a surprise attack in the Pacific, he had ordered Commodore George Dewey to head for Spain's colony in the Philippines and be ready to engage the Spanish there in case of war. On April 30, just one week after war was declared, Dewey arrived in Manila with four cruisers and two gunboats. After four hours of cannon fire, the Spanish fleet lay in ruins, having lost almost four hundred men. No U.S. ship was badly hit, and only eight U.S. sailors were

Two Faces of War Never were image and reality so starkly contrasted as during the Spanish-American War. In the public mind, it was a "splendid little war," short, painless, and heroic. The lithography above by W. G. Read conveys the image of a bombastic Teddy Roosevelt and his masculine band of Rough Riders taking San Juan Hill, imagining the men charging into battle on horseback rather than the less-than-romantic reality of running up the hill on foot. The dangers of the war did not end on the battlefield as disease, disorganization, and death proved all too real, as sketched by William Glackens of *McClure's*. This artistic rendition of the war depicts the dead and wounded at the Guamas River after Spanish snipers attacked. (*Library of Congress*.)

wounded. Every American ship in Manila harbor, declared Connecticut Senator Orville Platt, was "a new *Mayflower* . . . the harbinger and agent of a new civilization." After defeating the Spanish fleet, Dewey waited for reinforcements before leading a land assault. On August 13 the strengthened U.S. force, with the help of Filipino rebels, gained control of Manila and accepted Spain's surrender of the Philippines.

While Dewey gained control of the Philippines, a force of marines seized Cuba's Guantanamo Bay. On June 21 the main American invasion party of seventeen thousand men landed at Daiquiri in southeastern Cuba. The first major battle took place on July 1 when American troops, joined by experienced Cuban rebels, captured the fortified town of El Caney and drove the Spanish from San Juan Hill.

At the same time Theodore Roosevelt led a smaller unit in supporting an assault on nearby Kettle Hill. Hoping to get "in on the fun," Roosevelt had quit his position in the Navy Department and volunteered for service in Cuba. Determined to fight in style, he ordered a custom-fitted uniform from Brooks Brothers and organized a volunteer regiment that he called the "Rough Riders." Wanting his regiment to represent the best elements in American life, Roosevelt recruited other wealthy and educated men from Ivy League schools. But it was the cowboys he had met while living in the West who were the backbone of the regiment. No one was more eager for battle than Roosevelt. At Kettle Hill he charged directly at the Spanish guns. "I waved my hat and we went up the hill with a rush," he recalled in his autobiography. The Rough Riders stormed the slope, joined by black troopers from the Ninth and Tenth Cavalry. After a day of fierce fighting, the Spanish troops withdrew, but only after inflicting heavy casualties on the Americans.

Victory gave the Americans control of the strategic high ground overlooking the city of Santiago, where a fleet of Spanish ships was bottled up by an American blockade. As U.S. troops moved into Santiago by land, the Spanish ships in the harbor tried to escape. On the morning of July 3 the Spanish squadron ran directly into the path of twelve American vessels waiting in ambush. As the Americans engaged in what amounted to target practice, one U.S. officer felt moved to shout the order, "Don't cheer, men! Those poor devils are dying." On July 17 the Spanish in Santiago surrendered. The following week an American force seized control of Spanish-held Puerto Rico.

On August 12 representatives from the United States and Spain met at the White House to sign an armistice. The war had lasted four months. According to the terms of the treaty, Spain gave up control of Cuba, and the United States annexed Puerto Rico and occupied Manila until the two nations reached a final agreement on the Philippines. It all seemed so easy. At the cost of 2,900 lives (all but 400 the victims of disease, not enemy gunfire) and only $250 million, the United States became a great world power. John Hay, a future secretary of state, wrote his friend Theodore Roosevelt: "It has been a splendid little war; begun with the highest motives, carried on with magnificent intelligence and spirit, favored by that fortune which loves the brave."

The war with Spain marked a critical turning point in America's role in world affairs. The United States emerged from the conflict as a global power with overseas land and hopes of creating its own empire. The nation had moved "from a position of comparative freedom from entanglements into the position of what is commonly called a world power," Assistant Secretary of State John Bassett Moore observed. "Where formerly we had only commercial interests, we now have territorial and political interests as well."

Managing the New American Empire

For many Americans the euphoria of victory spawned dreams of empire. Much attention focused on the Philippines—more than seven thousand islands and 7 million people, stretched over 115,000 square miles. Businessmen saw commercial possibilities. The San Francisco Chamber of Commerce asked the president to keep the islands "with a view to strengthening our trade relations with the orient." Most Americans, reflecting prevailing racial attitudes, believed that the Filipinos were incapable of self-government. The United States, they maintained, had an obligation to teach Spain's former subjects the wonders of democracy.

America's control of the Philippines raised new interest in Hawaii, which provided a base for ships headed to Manila. Two days after learning of Dewey's victory in Manila, McKinley asked the Senate for Hawaiian annexation, declaring, "We need Hawaii just as much and a good deal more than we did California." McKinley still did not have the two-thirds vote needed for Senate ratification, so he resorted to the device of annexation through joint resolution of the House and Senate. The majorities needed for passing the joint resolution were easily secured in both houses, and on August 12, 1898, Hawaii became a U.S. territory. The United States also reached an agreement with Germany that each would annex part of the Samoan Islands. The United States also laid claim to Wake Island, located between Guam and the Hawaiian Islands.

Not everyone agreed with the new territorial ambitions. An anti-imperialist movement had grown rapidly during 1898 to oppose McKinley's policy on the Philippines (see Competing Voices, page 885). To build public support for their position, anti-imperialists formed the Anti-Imperialist League in November. The league organized mass meetings and published pamphlets calling on those "who believe in the republic against Empire." Within a few months the organization boasted nearly half a million members, including former Presidents Grover Cleveland and Benjamin Harrison, reformer Jane Addams, labor leader Samuel Gompers, and industrialist Andrew Carnegie.

The anti-imperialists' powerful arguments against empire would echo through the next century. Many took racial attitudes of the time a step farther than the imperialists, arguing that dark-skinned peoples were incapable of participating in a self-governing democracy. A South Carolina senator warned against "the incorporation of a mongrel and semi-barbarous population into our body politic." Others feared that imperialism abroad would erode freedom at home—that the acquisition of new lands would burden the United States, requiring a large defense buildup to protect far-flung, vulnerable possessions. Besides, they argued, the Constitution did not give the federal government the power to acquire foreign territory. "The power to conquer alien people and hold them in subjugation is nowhere expressly granted" to Washington by the Constitution, and "is nowhere implied," noted Senator George Hoar.

Above all, anti-imperialists argued, an aggressive foreign policy was incompatible with American liberty. Charles Sumner predicted ominously that "adventurous policies of conquest or ambition" would transform the American experiment in democracy into "another empire just after the fashion of all the old ones." Empire, he charged, would enlarge the power of the state, concentrate power in Washington, and produce factions that would vie for state favors.

McKinley, on the other hand, demanded U.S. sovereignty over the Philippines and Puerto Rico. Spain capitulated to all the American demands, and in return the United States offered a payment of $20 million. On December 10, 1898, the two nations signed the Treaty of Paris. Senate ratification provoked a bitter clash between imperialists and anti-imperialists. On February 6, 1899, the Senate voted in favor of the treaty after engaging in what Senator Lodge described as the "closest, most bitter, and most exciting struggle I have ever known, or ever expect to see in the Senate."

Filipinos were outraged by the treaty. The rebel forces that had fought alongside American troops to defeat the Spanish now began fighting the better-armed American troops. "War without quarter to the false Americans who have deceived us!" the rebel leader Emilio Aguinaldo ordered his troops. "Either independence or death!" During the first days of fighting, U.S. troops overwhelmed Aguinaldo's poorly equipped army of eighty thousand men. Shooting Filipinos, an American solider wrote, was "more fun than a turkey shoot." U.S. troops drove the insurrectionists into the hills, burned villages, and confined villagers in reconcentration camps similar to those used by the Spanish in Cuba. "We are destroying down to the root every germ of a healthy national life in these unfortunate people," admonished philosopher William James.

Unable to defeat the Americans using conventional tactics, the rebels turned to guerrilla warfare to frustrate American hopes of a quick victory. They raided supply lines, cut communications, and ambushed small detachments. After massacring an American regiment, Filipinos stuffed the corpses with molasses to attract ants. In March 1901 American soldiers penetrated a rebel camp and captured Aguinaldo. On April 19 he asked his troops to stop fighting. "There has been enough blood, enough tears, enough desolation," he said. The resistance soon faded. It had taken American troops three years to quell the rebellion. More than 5,000 Americans and 200,000 Filipinos died. Nearly 130,000 U.S. troops served in the war, which cost the United States at least $160 million.

On July 4, 1901, the United States transferred authority on the island from the military to a new civilian governor, William Howard Taft, then a prominent Ohio judge. His mission, he lectured the Filipinos, was to create a government "which shall teach those people individual liberty, which shall lift them up to a point of civilization . . . , and which shall make them rise to call the name of the United States blessed." Over the next few years Taft jailed dissenters and suppressed calls for independence at the same time that he expanded educational opportunities, built bridges and roads, and restructured the tax system. Not until July 4, 1946, however, would the United States grant the Philippines independence.

As events in the Philippines unfolded, the United States also debated the future of the other nations it had liberated from Spain—Cuba and Puerto Rico. Should

Dead Filipino Insurgents   Emilio Aguinaldo, the Filipino leader exiled for insisting a nationalist revolt in 1896, returned to the Philippines with Commodore Dewey during the Spanish-American War. Once Spain had been defeated, Aguinaldo and his revolutionary supporters proclaimed the Philippines an independent nation in January 1899. Senate ratification of the Treaty of Paris negated this declaration, resulting in a war between American forces and Aguinaldo's insurgents. This picture captures the carnage after one of the first battles between American forces and the Filipino insurgents near Santa Ana on February 7, 1899.   *(Corbis.)*

Cuba be granted independence or annexed by the United States? Most American leaders considered the Cubans incapable of independence. Asked when Cuban self-government might be possible, a U.S. general responded, "Why those people are no more fit for self-government than gun-powder is for hell." But McKinley, fearful of racial mixing, also ruled out annexation. Instead he opted for a middle ground. Because Cuba was so close to U.S. shores, he argued, the United States could control it without having to annex it. He appointed General Leonard Wood as military commander of the island, telling Wood, "I want you to go down there to get the people ready for a republican form of government."

Wood established a democratic procedure for the election of delegates to a Cuban constitutional convention. The convention adopted a new constitution modeled after the U.S. Constitution. Under intense pressure from Wood, the delegates, by a vote of fifteen to eleven, also accepted the conditions set forth in the Platt

Amendment. Passed by Congress in 1901, the Platt Amendment gave the United States the right to intervene in Cuban affairs, required the Cuban government to limit its debt with European nations, and prohibited the Cuban government from negotiating a treaty with a foreign power. The amendment also gave the United States a ninety-nine-year lease on the naval base at the island's Guantanamo Bay. The Platt Amendment continued to be the basis of U.S. policy in Cuba until 1934.

Puerto Rico also raised fundamental questions about how America would govern its distant territories. Shortly after conquering the country, the U.S. military commander announced that the United States intended to give Puerto Ricans "the immunities and blessings of the liberal institutions of our government." But instead of granting such blessings, Congress passed the Foraker Act of 1900, which made Puerto Rico an "unincorporated territory" subject to the laws of Congress but governed by the War Department. Residents could elect a Lower House, but the U.S. president would appoint the governor, the heads of executive departments, and members of the Upper House. Critics challenged the premise of the Foraker Act, asserting that "the Constitution followed the flag." Nevertheless, in a series of decisions known as the *Insular* cases, the U.S. Supreme Court upheld the procedure. The justices ruled that the United States could annex an area, make it an "unincorporated" territory, and refuse to grant its people citizenship.

The Open Door to China

Americans debated questions of empire amid growing national and international attention toward China. American attitudes about China were shaped by a mix of paternalism and profit. For years missionaries had enthralled Americans with stories of their work in the Far East, creating deep sympathy for the Chinese people. China accounted for only 2 percent of U.S. foreign trade, but American businessmen had high hopes for the vast Asian market. An astute secretary of state, John Hay, noted in 1900 that whoever understood China "has the key to world politics for the next five centuries." A group of New York businessmen agreed with Hay and in 1896 formed the American Asiatic Association to promote trade and development.

Many U.S. business interests feared being squeezed out of the China market. By the late 1890s Japan, Russia, Germany, France, and England had already carved out spheres of influence in China, which had been rendered helpless following its defeat in the Sino-Japanese War. "The various powers," observed a Chinese leader, "cast upon us looks of tiger-like voracity, hustling each other in their endeavors to be the first to seize upon our inner-most territories." Hay responded to this threatening situation by sending a series of notes to America's rivals in China. In these "Open Door" notes, Hay asked the other powers to guarantee that ports would remain open to all nations and to avoid offering special privileges to any group. The other nations sent ambiguous replies, but Hay announced agreement of all powers as "final and definitive."

Just as Hay was declaring victory, a new, more ominous threat to American interests emerged in China. In 1899 a radical antiforeign and militaristic society, the "Righteous and Harmonious Fists" (called "Boxers" by journalists), began murdering foreigners. By June Boxers controlled the capital and were besieging areas where most foreigners lived. In 1900 the United States sent 2,500 troops to join an international delegation to lift the siege. In addition, Hay dispatched a second series of notes in which he asked all powers to preserve "Chinese territorial and administrative integrity." Russia, Japan, Germany, and Britain accepted Hay's second Open Door notes.

This second round extended America's involvement in the Far East. Not only did the United States endorse and demand open commercial dealings in China, but it now also obligated itself to maintaining the political integrity of an endangered empire. But although Hay committed the nation to defending China, he knew that the United States lacked the will and the military might to abide by that commitment. The United States, Hay wrote, was "not prepared . . . to enforce these views on the east by any demonstration which could present a character of hostility to any other power." It was not until the 1930s, when an aggressive Japan threatened the balance of power in the region, that the United States would invoke the Open Door notes.

THEODORE ROOSEVELT AND THE "BIG STICK," 1901–1912

No one was more eager to assume the responsibilities of world power than Theodore Roosevelt, who asserted that only the president could conduct foreign policy. "Occasionally great national crises arise which call for immediate and vigorous executive action," he said. He came to the presidency with strong convictions about America's role in the world. A student of the writings of Captain Mahan, he was committed to establishing American control in the Western Hemisphere and opening new trade routes to Asia. He oversaw the building of the Panama Canal and established the Roosevelt Corollary to the Monroe Doctrine. His successor, William Howard Taft, lacked Roosevelt's skill and vision in foreign policy, and he failed in his effort to flex American economic might.

"I Took the Canal" Roosevelt hoped to use American influence to ensure order and stability in the hemisphere. When diplomacy would not achieve that result, Roosevelt was willing to use force. "There is a homely adage that runs 'speak softly and carry a big stick; you will go far,'" he noted in 1901. Although he could be forceful in dealing with other nations, Roosevelt was careful not to overextend American commitments, and his diplomatic experiments were characterized by restraint and by a firm grasp of the realities of international power politics.

Roosevelt believed that the emergence of new powers—especially Germany, Russia, and Japan—threatened the stability of the nineteenth-century world order. He was also motivated by a belief that the "civilized" nations had the obligation to uplift people in less developed countries. "More and more," he lectured Congress in 1902, "the increasing interdependence and complexity of international political and economic relations render it incumbent on all civilized and orderly powers to insist on the proper policing of the world." He urged Americans to take an active role in foreign affairs. "If we shrink from the hard contests," he warned, "then the bolder and stronger people will pass us by. . . . Let us therefore boldly face the life of strife." To prepare America for the challenge of world responsibility, Roosevelt centralized foreign policy decision making in the White House, doubled the size of the navy, reorganized the army and National Guard, and established several army war colleges to train new officers.

In keeping with the tenets Mahan espoused, Roosevelt's top priority was to build an American-controlled canal in the Caribbean. An initial obstacle was the 1850 Clayton-Bulwer Treaty with the British, which required joint Anglo-American control of any Central American canal. By November 1901, however, Secretary of State Hay and the British ambassador to Washington had negotiated the Hay-Pauncefote Treaty, which allowed the United States to build and control a canal of its own.

Now the United States needed to decide where to build the canal. Panama, a province of Colombia, offered one possibility. An isthmus of only 50 miles separated the Atlantic and Pacific Oceans along this route. But the New Panama Canal Company, a French-chartered firm that held the canal rights, was asking for an inflated sum of $109 million to sell its holdings. Another possible route crossed Nicaragua. It was 200 miles long, but it would be an easier challenge because it traversed Lake Nicaragua and other natural waterways. In 1902 Congress authorized a canal through Nicaragua, citing cost as the chief reason. After the decision, the New Panama Canal Company's American lawyer, William Nelson Cromwell, agreed to drop his price and began an intense lobbying campaign to get the decision reversed. On January 22, 1903, Hay negotiated a treaty with Thomas Herran, the Colombian chargé d'affaires. By its terms, the United States received a ninety-nine-year lease on a 6-mile-wide zone across the isthmus of Panama; in return the United States granted an initial payment of $10 million to Colombia and $250,000 annual rental.

But on August 12, 1903, the Colombian senate unanimously rejected the Hay-Herran treaty because the senators wanted more money and because the agreement, which severely infringed on Colombian sovereignty, was unpopular with the Colombian people. The senators demanded an initial payment of $15 million from the United States, and they also tried to extract $10 million from the New Panama Canal Company.

Further negotiations could have achieved an agreement with the Colombians, who were eager to have the United States build the canal. Instead, the imperious president lashed out at "those contemptible little creatures in Bogota." Roosevelt complained that "you could no more make an agreement with the Colombian rulers than you could nail currant jelly to the wall." The president planted stories in the press that he would not be displeased if Panama revolted against Colombia. The Panamanians, whose strong nationalist movement had repeatedly organized uprisings, needed little encouragement.

With American warships within view to prevent Colombian troops from interfering, the Panamanians revolted in November 1903. "The Americans are against us. What can we do against the American Navy?" asked a Colombian diplomat. Roosevelt recognized the new nation two days after the rebellion started. He soon signed a treaty by which Panama accepted the original offer of $10 million plus $250,000 a year for U.S. rights to a 10-mile-wide strip that cut the country in half.

The treaty granted the United States "power and authority" within the zone "in perpetuity" as "if it were the sovereign of the territory."

While the American public overwhelmingly approved the new treaty and the means required to achieve it, many major newspapers were critical of Roosevelt's actions. The "Panama foray is nefarious," thundered a Hearst newspaper. The *New York Times* declared that the United States had followed "the path of scandal, disgrace, and dishonor." Some Senate Democrats disapproved of the president's ruthless measures to gain control of the canal, but the complaints left Roosevelt unfazed. "I took the Canal Zone and let Congress debate," he bragged. On February 24, 1904, the U.S. Senate overwhelmingly approved the new treaty.

The Roosevelt Corollary   Now that the United States possessed the ability to project its military power in the region, securing the canal was but part of Roosevelt's broader vision for the Caribbean. He also wanted to exclude other powers from the area. In December 1902, when Venezuela refused payments on bonds held by European investors, Britain and Germany bombarded ports, seized ships, and imposed an economic blockade on Venezuela. Initially Roosevelt acquiesced to the action, but he soon began to worry that such limited military actions could lead to permanent occupation. "These wretched republics cause me a great deal of trouble," he complained. In January 1903 he ordered the navy to conduct maneuvers in the Caribbean to underscore his call for a quick end to the dispute. Both Britain and Germany immediately lifted the blockade and submitted their claims to the Permanent Court of World Justice at The Hague.

When a crisis threatened the stability of the Dominican Republic, Roosevelt announced a new American approach to the Caribbean. In 1904 the leaders of that financially strapped island pleaded with Roosevelt "to establish some kind of protectorate" to keep their European creditors from intervening. Roosevelt claimed to have as much interest in taking over the islands as "a gorged boa constrictor might have to swallow a porcupine wrong-end to." He did, however, want to prevent further European involvement in the Western Hemisphere. His new policy, which became known as the Roosevelt Corollary to the Monroe Doctrine, asserted that "chronic wrong-doing" or "impotence" by a nation of the Western Hemisphere could "force the United States, however reluctantly, in flagrant cases of such wrongdoing or impotence, to the exercise of an international police power." Roosevelt claimed that the ensuing American intervention would free the people of Santo Domingo "from the curse of interminable revolutionary disturbance" and give them "the same chance to move onward which we have already given the people of Cuba."

The Roosevelt Corollary marked a historic break from the Monroe Doctrine and shaped U.S. policy toward Central America for the rest of the twentieth century. The Monroe Doctrine had urged a policy of nonintervention in local revolutions in Latin America. Roosevelt, however, asserted America's right to intervene in any situation that threatened the order and stability of the region. Monroe believed that mutual economic ties, not U.S. military or economic power, would shape U.S. relations with Latin America. Roosevelt used the tools Monroe had shunned, U.S. economic and military might, to transform the Caribbean into an "American lake."

Roosevelt applied his new policy, taking charge of the Dominican Republic's revenue system, which, as in most small Caribbean countries, consisted primarily of customs revenues. Within two years Roosevelt had also established protectorates in Cuba and Panama. In 1905 the United States took over the customs and debt management of the Dominican Republic. The Roosevelt Corollary would guide American policy until the 1930s, when Franklin Roosevelt instituted the "Good Neighbor Policy."

Japan and the Open Door

Roosevelt was less successful in the Far East, where American influence was limited. Roosevelt remained committed to the Open Door in China, but he recognized that the United States lacked the military muscle to enforce the treaty. The Open Door policy was "an excellent thing" on paper, he conceded, but it "completely disappears as soon as a powerful nation determines to disregard it, and is willing to run the risk of war." The United States had to be careful not to offend traditional Asian powers such as Japan because they could easily overrun the Philippines, which he called "our heel of Achilles." Lacking a strong military option, Roosevelt hoped to protect American commitments in Asia by maintaining a delicate balance of power among the other powers in the region.

Russian and Japanese ambitions in Manchuria threatened that balance. When Russia stationed 175,000 troops in Manchuria and demanded exclusive commercial rights over the region, Tokyo decided to launch a preemptive strike, destroying Russia's Asian fleet in a surprise attack in 1904. Initially, Roosevelt cheered the Japanese attack, claiming that the war would enhance American interests by destroying the potential for "either a yellow peril or a Slav peril." However, he grew concerned when Japan scored a series of resounding military successes that threatened to drive Russia out of the region. Roosevelt agreed that Japanese victory might signify a "real shifting of equilibrium as far as the white races are concerned." He then inaugurated a series of secret maneuvers that culminated with both Japan and Russia agreeing to attend a peace conference in Portsmouth, New Hampshire, in the summer of 1905. By that time both nations were exhausted by the conflict and receptive to Roosevelt's diplomacy. In the resulting settlement Japan received control over Korea and in return promised an Open Door in Manchuria for the United States and the other powers. The Japanese also obtained key Russian bases in Manchuria, vital parts of the Chinese Eastern Railway running through Manchuria, and the southern half of the strategic island of Sakhalin. For his efforts, Roosevelt became the first American to win the Nobel Peace Prize.

The promise of the Open Door, however, soon proved empty. Such major American exporters as Standard Oil, Swift and Company meatpacking, and the British-American Tobacco Company found themselves being driven out of Manchuria by Japan. Tokyo capped its policy in 1907 when Japan and Russia, bloody enemies just twenty-four months before, agreed to divide Manchuria, with the Japanese exploiting the south and the Russians the north.

A temporary calm set in, but TR knew that he was confronting an aggressive Japan. To show America's naval strength, he decided to send sixteen American battleships on a cruise to the western Pacific. They were, he said, "sixteen messengers

TR Reviews the "Great White Fleet"   No one personified the new, activist American foreign policy better than Theodore Roosevelt. Roosevelt directed diplomacy more closely than any president before him, energetically maneuvering the United States into a strong position on the world stage. One of his methods was to build the American military, especially the navy, which he felt was the key to national power. On December 16, 1907, Roosevelt sent sixteen battleships of the newly expanded Atlantic fleet on a fourteen-month world tour to show off the United States' might. *(Theodore Roosevelt Birthplace, National Park Service.)*

of peace" on a "good will cruise" around the world. As Roosevelt expected, the visit of the Great White Fleet to Japan in 1907 impressed the Japanese and produced effusions of friendship on both sides, but it resoundingly failed to persuade Tokyo officials to retreat in Manchuria. In November 1908 the United States and Japan signed the Root-Takahira agreement, which affirmed the pledge to the Open Door but accepted Japan's control of South Manchuria. The agreement represented Roosevelt's attempt to balance America's ambition in East Asia with its real interests and its ability to defend them.

Dollar Diplomacy

William Howard Taft came to the presidency with extensive experience in foreign affairs. He had served not only as the first civil governor of the Philippines, but also as secretary of war, in which capacity he had conducted delicate negotiations with Japan and dealt successfully with Panama and Cuba. Pledging to continue Roosevelt's popular foreign policies, Taft chose Philander C. Knox, Roosevelt's attorney general, as his secretary of state. Unfortunately, Taft and Knox lacked the flexibility, energy, and forcefulness to adapt to a changing international environment.

Taft planned to add a new dimension to Roosevelt's policies. He described his approach as "substituting dollars for bullets." In 1910 Taft explained that he would engage in "active intervention to secure for our merchandise and our capitalists opportunity for profitable investment." America's burgeoning financial power, not armed troops, would be his main foreign policy instrument. To justify his policy, Taft pointed out that American overseas investments had increased from about $800 million in 1898 to more than $2.5 billion in 1909. Taft believed that the United States could reorder the world by marketplace supremacy. In the Caribbean, Taft believed the greatest threat to American security lay in the possibility that European powers would intervene to collect defaulted debts. To address the problem he moved to replace European loans with American money. Overall American investment in Central America increased from $41 million in 1908 to $93 million in 1914. In 1909 the president asked American bankers to assume the debt in Honduras to ward off European interest. A year later, he persuaded them to stabilize the finances of Haiti by investing in the National Bank of Haiti.

Taft used the marines to protect his new investments. When a new government in Nicaragua resisted American demands that it pay off long-standing claims to Great Britain by borrowing large sums from American bankers, the president withheld recognition and dispatched a warship to pressure the government into acceding to American demands. The Nicaraguans quickly signed the agreement. But the threat of intervention had lit the fires of Nicaraguan nationalism and imperiled the American-controlled government. In 1912 Taft, who vowed to maintain order in Central America even if he had to "knock their heads together," sent more than two thousand marines to protect American lives and property and to prevent European powers from intervening to shield the interests of their own citizens. The forces remained, reduced in number, until 1925, and then had to return in 1926 for another seven-year stay.

While the president dispatched troops to Central America, the U.S. Senate also tried to protect American interests in the area. In 1912 the Senate added the so-called Lodge Corollary to the Monroe Doctrine in reaction to the threat that a private Japanese company would obtain land in Mexico. The Lodge resolution stated that no "corporation or association which has such a relation to another government, not American" could obtain strategic areas in the hemisphere. This greatly extended the compass of the Monroe Doctrine, which had previously applied only to foreign governments, not companies. The State Department used the resolution during the next quarter-century to stop the transfer of lands, particularly in Mexico, to Japanese concerns (see map on page 876).

America's relations with its neighbor to the north, Canada, also suffered during Taft's administration. In 1911 the United States and Canada signed a reciprocity trade agreement. Canadian officials were initially pleased, believing that the pact opened the mammoth American market to their country's raw material producers. But the agreement also made these producers an integral part of the U.S. industrial complex. Careless U.S. politicians, who likened the move to "another Louisiana Purchase," raised fears north of the border that the new treaty would make Canada an American colony. Angry and frightened Canadian conservatives killed the agreement. A new government came to power, repudiated the reciprocity pact, and passed higher tariffs against U.S. goods.

In China, Taft reversed Roosevelt's policy of appeasing Japan. The president hoped that dollar diplomacy would strengthen Chinese nationalism, block Japanese aggression, and open new markets to American industry. "The more civilized

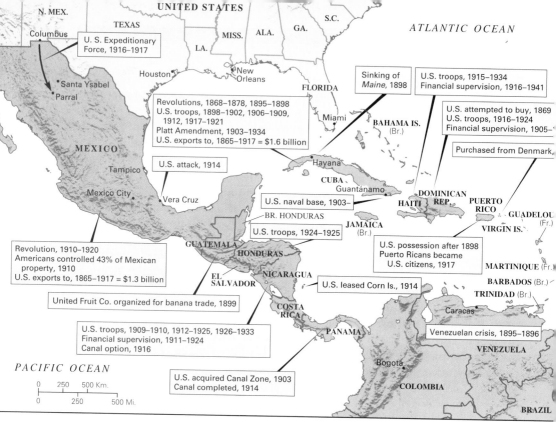

U.S. Presence in Latin America, 1895–1945 Basing their decisions on the Roosevelt Corollary and America's growing economic needs, government officials intervened in Latin America to promote capitalism and to protect American interests. The United States sent troops to suppress national opposition when they threatened America's goals in the region.

they become, the more active their industries, the wealthier they become, and the better market they will become for us." His efforts to apply financial leverage failed. Waving the Open Door principle, Secretary of State Knox proposed a "neutralization" scheme designed to break the Japanese-Russian hold on Manchuria. According to the plan, Americans and Europeans would pool their money to offer an international loan to China so it could buy back the key railroads in Manchuria from the Russians and Japanese. The Russians and Japanese were not receptive to the idea and moved closer together to fend off Knox. A Japanese official complained that the United States was "asking us to internationalize what is our property acquired by us at the cost of much treasure and many lives." On July 4, 1910, the two nations signed a fresh treaty of friendship. Seven weeks later Japan formally annexed Korea.

THE NEW FREEDOM ABROAD, 1912–1917

Woodrow Wilson came to the presidency promising a change from the imperial experimentation of Roosevelt and Taft. In practice, however, Wilson's approach differed little from that of his predecessors. In Asia, circumstances forced Wilson to abandon the principles of the Open Door and recognize Japan's predominance in the region. Wilson's response to the Mexican revolution highlighted the weaknesses of his new experiment in moralistic foreign policy.

Woodrow Wilson and World Power

When he took office in 1913, Woodrow Wilson knew little about foreign affairs. "It would be the irony of fate if my administration had to deal chiefly with foreign affairs," he told a friend in 1912. Though he possessed no expertise in foreign policy, Wilson was supremely confident of his ability to manage world affairs. Like Roosevelt, he took an expansive view of presidential power. "He *exercises* the power, and *we obey*," he once wrote.

Wilson shared contemporary views about the superiority of American values. Democracy, Wilson believed, offered the best possibility for stability and order. "When properly directed, there is no people not fitted for self-government," he noted. The American experience also highlighted the importance of slow, gradual change, and, by contrast to the European example, exposed the dangers of revolution. He also assumed it necessary to search for new economic markets abroad. U.S. producers, Wilson told the Democratic national convention in 1912, "have expanded to such a point that they will burst their jackets if they cannot find a free outlet to the markets of the world. Our domestic markets no longer suffice. We need foreign markets." Taft's dollar diplomacy, declared an administration official, tried to "till the field of foreign investment with a pen knife; President Wilson intends to cultivate it with a spade."

The new president promised to usher in a new idealistic foreign policy based more on morality than self-interest. "We dare not turn from the principle that morality and not expediency is the thing that must guide us," he declared in 1913. To demonstrate his break with the policies of Roosevelt and Taft, Wilson appointed William Jennings Bryan, an outspoken opponent of imperialism and militarism, as his secretary of state. Bryan launched an aggressive effort to convince other nations to settle disputes through mediation, not war. He signed "cooling off" treaties with over two dozen leaders. The treaties required nations to subject all disputes to an international commission.

The new president undertook a number of other initiatives to signal his break with the past. He pledged the United States to withdraw from the Philippines "as soon as a stable government can be established." In 1914 Bryan negotiated a treaty with Colombia, which was still smarting from Roosevelt's peremptory actions in Panama. The United States expressed "sincere regret" for its actions and paid an indemnity of $25 million.

The Far East

In his first major diplomatic action, Wilson scrapped Taft's dollar diplomacy in Asia. Wilson wanted to go it alone in China, using growing U.S. economic power in an effort to build China to the point where Japan and Russia could no longer exploit it at will. The Chinese revolution, which erupted in 1911 against both the Manchu dynasty and foreign interests, made a shamble of his policies, and the approach collapsed completely when World War I began in August 1914. Suddenly the British, French, Germans, and Russians—who Wilson assumed would check each other and the Japanese in China—were absorbed in Europe.

Virtually unchallenged, Japan swiftly moved to seize German possessions, including the strategic Shantung Peninsula. "When there is a fire in a jeweller's shop," a Japanese diplomat explained, "the neighbours cannot be expected to refrain from helping themselves." In January 1915 Tokyo tried to impose the so-called Twenty-one Demands on the Chinese. If China had acquiesced, these demands would not only have consolidated the Japanese hold on Manchuria, but would also have given Japan a protectorate over all of China. Wilson strongly protested the demands, but it was British pressure and Chinese resistance, not Wilson's strong words, that finally forced the Japanese to withdraw them.

In November 1917 the secretary of state negotiated the Lansing-Ishii Agreement. The United States recognized that "territorial propinquity creates special relations between countries," meaning it accepted Japanese dominance in such areas as southern Manchuria. In return, the Japanese secretly promised that they would not take advantage of the world war to seek privileges in China that would abridge the rights or property of Americans and citizens of the Allied powers.

Central America and the Caribbean

In Latin America Wilson and Bryan pledged to replace Taft's emphasis on the "pursuit of material interest" with the pursuit of "human rights" and "national integrity." A few months after his inauguration, Wilson promised that the United States would "never again seek one additional foot of territory by conquest." In the end, however, he continued Roosevelt's nationalistic policies, intervening more than either Taft or Roosevelt and for essentially the same reasons. In 1916, when the Dominican Republic threatened to default on its debt, Wilson sent in the marines. The following year U.S. troops entered Cuba once again, remaining until 1921 in order to protect American-controlled sugar plantations, particularly from attacks by armed Cubans.

Wilson's most controversial intervention in the Caribbean came in Haiti. A small nation sharing the island of Hispaniola with the Dominican Republic, Haiti had become the world's first black republic in 1804 when its black, largely slave majority defeated the ruling French colonials. Until 1910 the United States had displayed relatively little interest in Haiti. But then the nation's central bank fell into the hands of New York City bankers. Soon afterward, political turmoil threatened to destabilize the bank. In 1915, when a mob brutally killed the Haitian president, Wilson ordered more than three hundred marines to the island. A new government signed a treaty in August 1915 that granted the United States control over the country's foreign and financial affairs. It also granted the United States the right to intervene whenever Washington officials thought it necessary. The marines remained for nineteen years.

The Mexican Revolution

Three weeks before Wilson took office in 1913, the forces of General Victoriano Huerta gained control of Mexico's government and murdered Francisco Madero, an idealistic reformer who had gained power in 1911. Wilson saw Mexico as an opportunity for moral instruction. "I am going to teach the South Americans to elect good men," he declared. In a break with the American tradition of recognizing established governments, Wilson announced: "I will not recognize a government of butchers." Denouncing Huerta as a "diverting brute! . . . seldom sober and always impossible," the president demanded that Mexico hold democratic elections and institute broad land reform, insisting that the Mexican government "be founded on a moral basis." Business interests clamored for the United States to recognize the new government, but Wilson claimed that he was "not the servant of those who wish to enhance the value of their Mexican investments." Morality, not economic self-interest, would guide American policy.

Wilson searched for the opportunity to intervene. He threw his support behind Venustiano Carranza, the rival leader of the "Constitutionalist" faction. The president also tried to turn a minor clash between U.S. sailors and Mexican soldiers into a major international dispute and a justification for intervention. In April 1914 Huerta's agents arrested seven U.S. sailors who, while on shore leave, had strayed beyond the restricted area. Huerta quickly apologized and released the sailors, but he rejected Wilson's demands for concessions to satisfy American "honor," which included a twenty-one-gun salute to the United States flag. Two days later Wilson asked Congress for the authority to use military force in Mexico "to obtain from General Huerta and his adherents the fullest recognition of the rights and dignity of the United States."

While Congress debated the president's request, Wilson learned that a German ship planned to unload arms for Huerta at Vera Cruz on Mexico's Caribbean coast. Wilson ordered the navy to land troops and occupy the port. The next day, on April 22, 1914, firing broke out that killed 19 Americans and over 126 Mexicans. Although the U.S. invasion was intended to overthrow General Huerta, it offended Mexicans of all political persuasions, who viewed the U.S. actions as an affront to their nationalism and a threat to their independence. A humbled Wilson avoided war when he accepted an offer of mediation from other Latin American countries.

During the summer of 1914 Carranza's forces drove Huerta from power. Wilson hoped the new government would accede to his plans for Mexico. An ardent nationalist, Carranza refused to bargain with Wilson. Instead, he announced plans for agrarian reform and asserted Mexico's claim to all its subsoil mineral rights. The revolution had turned sharply to the left and threatened U.S. oil companies, which had invested over $2 billion in oil exploration and production.

The frustrated president again withheld recognition and now turned to aiding anti-Carranza forces, including Francisco "Pancho" Villa. Wilson saw Villa as a Robin Hood who had spent "a not uneventful life in robbing the rich in order to give to the poor." This was a serious miscalculation, for Carranza's forces were too strong for Villa. In 1915, distracted by growing tensions in Europe and realizing that Villa had been all but defeated, Wilson abandoned his Mexican crusade and reluctantly recognized Carranza's government. "Carranza will somehow have to be digested," he said. Villa responded by terrorizing Americans, hoping to force Wilson into military retaliation that would undermine Carranza's popularity. On March 9, 1916, Villa led a force of fifteen hundred revolutionaries across the border to burn the town of Columbus, New Mexico. The bloody battle left seventeen Americans and more than a hundred Mexicans dead.

Outraged by the attack, Wilson dispatched a punitive expedition into Mexico under the command of General John J. Pershing. His mission was to capture Villa

Pancho Villa and His Men   Francisco "Pancho" Villa became a legendary hero robbing from dictator Porfiriato Diaz's local government officials and giving to the poor. He joined the revolutionary forces of Francisco Madero in 1910 and after Madero's death continued to fight against the repressive Huerta and Carranza regimes. When Villa began raiding American border towns, many in Mexico saw Villa as an avenger, striking fear in the hearts of Americans who had economically dominated Northern Mexico for decades. President Wilson considered Villa a criminal, sending General Pershing to track down Villa, ultimately without success. Villa eventually made his peace with the Mexican government, which provided him with a general's pension until his assassination in 1923. *(Corbis-Bettmann.)*

and bring him back to the United States to stand trial. But Villa's force, seeming to blend into the country's wooded ravines, eluded the Americans. In vain pursuit, Pershing expanded his army to 11,600 men and moved them more than 300 miles into central Mexico. Carranza, agitated at the growing size and scope of the American military operation, ordered Pershing to stop his advance. On June 21 Mexican troops loyal to Carranza clashed with the Americans near Carrizal. Twelve Americans were killed and another twenty-four were captured.

War with Mexico now seemed inevitable. At this point, however, American soldiers admitted that they had started the Carrizal incident. Pacifists deluged Wilson with appeals for restraint, but an outraged public demanded a tough response. Carranza released the prisoners. Negotiations between the two countries then deadlocked over the sensitive issue of Pershing's troops, which Carranza demanded be withdrawn, and which Wilson, facing reelection, did not dare to remove. With the election safely behind him and with the prospect of having to fight in Europe looming dead ahead, Wilson knew he had to retreat. In January 1917 he ordered the withdrawal to begin, and in March, almost three years after Carranza had taken power, Wilson finally offered him official recognition.

In early 1917 the last American troops left Mexico. Carranza issued a new constitution several months later. Wilson had utterly failed to control the Mexican revolution. His motives and methods were condescending and heavy-handed. Wilson tried to impose gradual, progressive reform on a society sharply divided by race and class. The chief legacy of Wilson's meddling would be lingering Mexican resentment and mistrust of the United States. In 1917, however, with war threatening in Europe, most Americas remained oblivious to the festering resentment of their southern neighbors.

CONCLUSION

The last quarter of the nineteenth century witnessed a transformation in America's role in the world as a number of forces pushed the nation to experiment with an expansionist posture. A revolution in communications was bringing the world closer together. Many Americans believed that the closing of the frontier made foreign markets essential to ensuring future prosperity. A missionary zeal combined with deeply ingrained racial attitudes fed the belief that the United States had an obligation to spread American values and culture to "backward nations." Military strategists like Alfred Thayer Mahan argued that survival in a competitive world required a large navy and global possessions.

In the first decades after the Civil War the United States took its first tentative steps toward world power. In 1867 the United States purchased Alaska from Russia. Next America extended its influence in Latin America, asserting its right to mediate a border dispute between Great Britain and Venezuela. In a clear break with tradition, the United States developed close economic ties in Asia and the Pacific and debated whether to annex the Hawaiian Islands.

The war with Spain in 1898 represented an important turning point in America's role in the world. The war, fought to free Cuba from an oppressive Spanish rule, ended quickly and with few casualties. But the victory forced the United States to confront new responsibilities. What relationship should it have to the former Spanish colonies? While expansionists cried for the annexation of the Philippines, a vocal group of anti-imperialists argued against U.S. control. In the end, President McKinley sided with the expansionists. The result was a heated debate at home and a bloody struggle with independent-minded rebels in the Philippines. With the annexation of the Philippines, the acquisition of the Hawaiian Islands, and the declared commitment to an Open Door in China, the United States embarked on its experiment with the responsibilities of a world power.

For all of their differences in style and temperament, the progressive presidents—Roosevelt, Taft, and Wilson—shared the belief that the United States needed to play a major role on the world stage. Reflecting the general ethos of the Progressive Era, all three wanted the federal government to shake off its isolationist inertia and begin to spread American values and institutions abroad. Just as reformers at home tried to assimilate immigrants, the progressive presidents hoped to Americanize other societies, teaching them the benefits of democracy and the rule of law.

Theodore Roosevelt proved the most skilled at the art of international diplomacy. Along with fulfilling his goal of constructing the Panama Canal, Roosevelt expanded U.S. control over Latin America while balancing America's global ambitions with its limited power in the Far East. Taft's foreign policy, which stressed the primacy of economics, floundered because of a lack of imagination and energy. Despite his professions of idealism and morality, Wilson used force more often than any of his predecessors. By 1916 the United States had assumed the mantle of world power while angering many of its Latin American neighbors. It was only a matter of time before America's global experiment would draw the nation into a growing conflict in Europe.

Annotated Suggested Readings

Robert Beisner provides a concise and helpful synthesis on this period in *From the Old Diplomacy to the New, 1865–1900* (2d ed., 1986). Walter LaFeber's *The New Empire: An Interpretation of American Expansion, 1860–1898* (1983) and *The American Age* (1989) serve as examples of the economic school of interpretation, arguing that the drive for foreign markets was behind the development of U.S. foreign policy. LaFeber's work builds on the anti-imperialist views of William Appleman Williams' influential works: *Tragedy of American Diplomacy* (1988) and *Empire as a Way of Life* (2000). Robert Rydell examines the use of international fairs to promote the nationalistic and expansionist sentiment of elite America in *All the World's a Fair* (1984). Thomas Paterson et al. provide a useful and readable synthesis in *American Foreign Relations: A History* (1995).

For the intellectual roots of empire, Richard Hofstadter's *Social Darwinism in American Thought, 1860–1915* (1945) and Robert Bannister's *Social Darwinism: Science and Myth in Anglo-American Social Thought* (1979) are very informative. Milton Plesur also emphasizes intellectual forces over economic ones in the emergence of American world power in *America's Outward Thrust, 1865–1900* (1971). The impact of imperial expansion on American culture is carefully analyzed by Amy Kaplan in *The Anarchy of Empire in the Making of U.S. Culture* (2003). On the 1860s, Ernest Paolino's *Foundations of the American Empire: William Henry Seward and U.S. Foreign Policy* (1973) is informative. David Pletcher also sees the roots of imperialism in the policies of Secretaries of State Blaine and Frelinghuysen in *The Awkward Years: American Foreign Policy under Garfield and Arthur* (1962). Michael Hunt offers a provocative thesis about the roots of American expansion in *Ideology and U.S. Foreign Policy* (1987). Several good studies have been done on specific events during the 1865–1890 period, including Adrian Cook's *The Alabama Claims: American Politics and Anglo-American Relations* (1975) and Richard Bradford's *The Virginius Affair* (1980).

Ernest May examines changing European opinion of the United States in the 1890s and the "mass hysteria" that forced McKinley into war in *Imperial Democracy: The Emergence of America as a Great Power* (1961). David Healy's *U.S. Expansion: Imperialist Urge in the 1890's* (1970) covers a wide range of issues in the attempt to understand the "expansionist mystique." For the global roots of American expansionism see Thomas Schoonover's *Uncle Sam's War of 1898* (2003). Emily Rosenberg's *Spreading the American Dream: American Economic and Cultural Expansion, 1890–1945* (1982) and *Financial Missionaries to the World* (1999) demonstrate how business interests, missionaries, journalists, and others established in the 1890s a pattern of American cultural expansion that influenced foreign policy for decades to come.

Several regional studies shed light on late nineteenth-century American foreign policy. Michael Hunt's *The Making of a Special Relationship* (1983) is an essential overview of U.S. involvement with China. Also on China are Warren Cohen's *America's Response to China* (2d ed., 1980), which looks at the background and impact of the Open Door notes; and Marilyn Young's *The Rhetoric of Empire: America's China Policy, 1893–1901* (1968), which sees the efforts of business interests and missionaries as causative in the new diplomatic focus on China in the 1890s. The debate over the annexation of Hawaii is the subject of Thomas Osborne's *"Empire Can Wait": American Opposition to Hawaiian Annexation, 1893–1898* (1981).

The central event of the 1890s, and what most historians see as the culmination of growing trends in foreign policy, was the Spanish-American War. Historians have offered quite differing views on the reasons behind the war and McKinley's role in it. John Dobson's *Reticent Expansionism: The Foreign Policy of William McKinley* (1988) portrays McKinley as following public opinion into war rather than his own particular vision. Lewis Gould comes to the exact opposite conclusion in *The Spanish American War and President McKinley* (1982). In *America's Road to Empire: The War with Spain and Overseas Expansion* (1965), H. Wayne Morgan claims that McKinley was following established U.S. policy. John Offner blames the war on the inflexible Cuban rebels in *An Unwanted War: The Diplomacy of the United States and Spain over Cuba, 1895–1898* (1981). Gerald Linderman's *The Mirror of War: American Society and the Spanish-American War* (1974) examines the rationale behind the American people's clamor for war.

On the war itself, David Trask's *The War with Spain in 1898* (1981) is the most comprehensive account. For a shorter version from the perspective of the ordinary soldier, see Frank Friedel's *The Splendid Little War* (1958). Philip Foner's two-volume *The Spanish-Cuban-American War and the Birth of American Imperialism, 1895–1902* (1972) argues that the Cuban rebels neither needed nor wanted American help in defeating Spain. Vincent J. Cirillo looks at the impact of war on medicine in *Bullets and Bacilli* (2004).

Several impressive works have been written on American imperialism in the Philippines. Kenton Clymer's *Protestant Missionaries in the Philippines* (1986) analyzes the religious attitudes and work that shaped the missionary experience. Stuart Creighton Miller's *"Benevolent Assimilation": The American Conquest of the Philippines, 1899–1903* (1982) and Richard Welch's *Response to Imperialism: The United States and the Philippine-American War, 1899–1902* (1979) both examine McKinley's decision on annexation, the anti-imperialist protest, and the guerrilla war. Another helpful book on that subject is Robert Beisner's *Twelve Against Empire: The Anti-Imperialists, 1898–1900* (1975). A sweeping and engrossing examination of the entire history of American influence in the Philippines is Stanley Karnow's Pulitzer Prize–winning book *In Our Image: America's Empire in the Philippines* (1989). America's actions in the Philippines and their lasting impact on the island nation are examined in *Vestiges of War* (2002), edited by Angel Shaw and Luis Francia.

Howard Beale's *Theodore Roosevelt and the Rise of America to World Power* (1956) portrays the president as gifted, but too heavily influenced by the distorted ideas of Kipling and Mahan. Frederick Marks II, *Velvet on Iron: The Diplomacy of Theodore Roosevelt* (1979), is more favorable. Charles Neu also sees Roosevelt as a skilled diplomat in *An Uncertain Friendship: Theodore Roosevelt and Japan, 1906–1909* (1967). David McCullough's *The Path Between the Seas: The Creation of the Panama Canal, 1870–1914* (1977) views Roosevelt's actions with regard to the canal as part of a larger pattern of U.S. policy in Central America. William Tilcin's *Theodore Roosevelt and the British Empire* (1997) examines TR's approach to Europe. John Milton Cooper offers an insightful dual biography of Roosevelt and Wilson in *The Warrior and the Priest* (1983).

Arthur Link's *Woodrow Wilson and the Progressive Era* (1954) is a survey of all aspects of Wilson's presidency and has several informative chapters on his foreign policy. Frederick Calhoun's *Power and Principle: Armed Intervention in the Wilsonian Foreign Policy* (1986) and Frank Ninkovich's *The Wilsonian Century* (1999) examine the president's long-term impact on American foreign policy. Robert Quirk's *An Affair with Honor: Woodrow Wilson and the Occupation of Vera Cruz* (1962) is less favorable toward the president. P. Edward Haley looks at the differing responses of Taft and Wilson to unrest in Mexico in *Revolution and Intervention: The Diplomacy of Taft and Wilson with Mexico* (1970).

The **istory** **ompanion**

American Imperialism

McKinley Justifies U.S. Acquisition of Spanish Territories

President McKinley was a devout Christian, committed to the idea that the United States needed to serve as a moral beacon, promoting democracy and liberty around the world. In this speech given in Atlanta in December 1898, he seeks to reconcile this idealistic vision of America's virtuous role in the world with his support for the war with Spain and the acquisition of overseas territories that had belonged to Spain.

The peace we have won is not a selfish truce of arms, but one whose conditions presage good to humanity. The domains secured under the treaty yet to be acted upon by the Senate came to us not as the result of a crusade or conquest, but as the reward of temperate, faithful, and fearless response to the call of conscience, which could not be disregarded by a liberty-loving and Christian people. . . .

New conditions can be met only by new methods. . . . Without abandoning past limitations, traditions and principles, by meeting present opportunities and obligations, we shall show ourselves worthy of the great trusts which civilization has imposed upon us. . . .

[B]efore Manila and Santiago our armies fought, not for gain or revenge, but for human rights. They contended for the freedom of the oppressed, for whose welfare the United States has never failed to lend a helping hand to establish and uphold . . . the result will be incomplete and unworthy of us unless supplemented by civil victories, harder possibly to win, but in their way no less indispensable.

We will have our difficulties and embarrassments. They follow all victories and accompany all great responsibility. . . . But American capacity has triumphed over all in the past . . . our own history shows that progress has come so naturally and steadily on the heels of the new and grave responsibilities that as we look back upon the acquisitions of territory by our fathers, we are filled with wonder that any doubt could have existed or any apprehension could have been felt. . . .

Forever in the right, following the best impulses and clinging to high purposes, using properly and within right limits our power and opportunities, honorable reward must inevitable follow. . . . If we had blinded ourselves to the conditions so near our shores, and turned a deaf ear to our suffering neighbors, the issue of territorial expansion in the Antilles and the East Indies would not have been raised. . . .

With less humanity and less courage on our part, the Spanish flag, instead of the Stars and Stripes, would still be floating in Cavite, at Ponce, and at Santiago, and a "chance in the race of life" would be wanting to millions of human beings who to-day call this nation noble, and who, I trust, will live to call it blessed.

Thus far we have done our supreme duty. Shall we now, when the victory won in war is written in the treaty of peace, and the civilized world applauds and waits in expectation, turn timidly away from the duties imposed upon the country by its own great deeds?

Carl Schurz Opposes U.S. Expansion

Schurz was a German immigrant who became a brigadier general in the Union army and later served a term as a U.S. senator and as secretary of interior under President Hayes. Here, in a convocation address at the University of Chicago in 1899, he vigorously opposes the U.S. acquisition of Spanish possessions.

According to the solemn proclamation of our government, the [Spanish-American] war had been undertaken solely for the liberation of Cuba, as a war of humanity and not of conquest. But our easy victories had put conquest within our reach, and when our arms occupied foreign territory, a loud demand arose that . . . the conquests should be kept. . . .

The advocates of annexation answer cheerily, that when they belong to us, we shall soon "Americanize" them. . . . This is a delusion of the first magnitude. We shall, indeed, be able, if we go honestly about it, to accomplish several salutary things in those countries. But one thing we cannot do. We cannot strip the tropical climate of those qualities which have at all times deterred men of the northern races, to which we belong, from migrating to such countries in mass, and to make their homes there, as they have migrated and are still migrating to countries in the temperate zone. . . .

If we [rule territories as subject provinces], then we shall, for the first time since the abolition of slavery, again have two kinds of Americans: Americans of the first class, who enjoy the privilege of taking part in the government in accordance with our old constitutional principles, and Americans of the second class, who are to be ruled in a substantially arbitrary fashion by the Americans of the first class. . . .

If we do, we shall transform the government of the people, for the people and by the people . . . into a government of one part of the people, the strong, over another part, the weak. Such an abandonment of a fundamental principle as a permanent policy may at first seem to bear only upon more or less distant dependencies, but it can hardly fail in its ultimate effect to disturb the rule of the same principle in the conduct of democratic government at home. . . .

Nothing could be more irrational than all the talk about losing commercial or other opportunities which "will never come back if we fail to grasp them now." Why, we are so rapidly growing in all the elements of power ahead of all other nations that, not many decades hence, unless we demoralize ourselves by a reckless policy of adventure, not one of them will be able to resist our will if we choose to enforce it. . . .

"But we must civilize those poor people!" Are we not ingenious and charitable enough to do much for their civilization without subjugating and ruling them by criminal aggression? . . .

Whatever our duties to them may be, our duties to our own country and people stand first; and from this standpoint we have, as sane men and patriotic citizens, to regard our obligation to take care of the future of those islands and their people. . . .

Thus we shall be their best friends without being their foreign rulers. . . . However imperfect their own governments may still remain, they will at least be their own. . . .

If this democracy, after all the intoxication of triumph in war, conscientiously remembers its professions and pledges, and soberly reflects on its duties to itself and others, and then deliberately resists the temptation of conquest, it will achieve the grandest triumph of the democratic idea that history knows of.

The United States entered the war against Spain with the battle cry "Cuba Libre!" Fighting for Cuba's independence from Spain seemed consistent with American democratic ideals of promoting democracy and freedom. In addition, Cuba's proximity qualified it as part of the American sphere of influence under the Monroe Doctrine. Although the war had its critics, the case could be made that it had been both a noble mission and in the national interest.

But no sooner did the war conclude than the prospect of U.S. colonization reared its ugly head. American statesmen and intellectuals in the late nineteenth century subscribed to the ideas of Social Darwinism, a fanciful application of evolutionary biology to people and nations, which argued that strong countries would by nature dominate the weak. They were also influenced by Alfred T. Mahan, a historian who believed that the nations that controlled the seas ruled the world. With European powers already carving out places for themselves in world trade and establishing overseas colonies, many members of the "power elite" pushed for the United States to do the same. But the American public remained instinctively isolationist, unconvinced by lofty ideas and global strategy, and reluctant to involve the nation in foreign affairs. McKinley, who sincerely believed in American expansion, sought to convince his fellow citizens that foreign involvement and the acquisition of new territory were consistent with traditional American principles. He claimed that the United States was actually doing the people of the Philippines and other territories a favor by exposing them to Protestant Christianity, democratic government, Western education, and American business.

But others saw deep contradictions in the American presence in the Philippines in particular, a concern heightened by a bloody resistance to U.S. rule that lasted from 1899 until 1902. Although many anti-imperialists were motivated by isolationism and racism, idealism also played a role, as seen in Carl Schurz's comments. As with many of the new phenomena of the emerging modern America, imperialism raised deep concerns over the safety of the traditional values that Americans held so dear.

QUESTIONS FOR ANALYSIS

1. How does McKinley defend the Spanish-American War?

2. How does the president apply this defense to acquiring territory from Spain in the war's aftermath? What contradictions, if any, do you find in his rationale?

3. Why doesn't he mention the economic advantage that might come from U.S. colonies?

4. Why does Schurz so vehemently oppose overseas acquisitions?

5. What problems does Schurz see in attempting to "Americanize" other cultures?

6. What comparisons does Schurz make between American imperialism and slavery? What is his point?

23

Making the World Safe for Democracy: America and World War I

1914–1920

The American military helped ensure an Allied victory in World War I, but Wilson failed to secure a just peace.

A large crowd assembled at the White House on the rainy evening of April 2, 1917. Thousands more lined Pennsylvania Avenue. While waiting to get a glimpse of President Wilson as he made his way to the Capitol, they sang patriotic songs, including "The Star-Spangled Banner" and "Yankee Doodle." The city was decorated in red, white, and blue and overflowing with nationalistic fervor as the president's entourage left the White House shortly before 8:00 P.M. At 8:30 the Speaker of the House announced the arrival of the president to a joint session of Congress. As Wilson walked down the center aisle to the Speaker's platform, members of Congress, both Democrats and Republicans, erupted in thunderous applause. For two minutes they stood waving their tiny American flags, clapping their hands, and shouting their support. Wilson waited for the ovation to die down. Then, holding his typed address firmly with both hands, the president began talking in a subdued, conversational tone, outlining German violations of American neutrality. "International law had its origin in the attempt to set up some law which would be respected and observed upon the seas, where no nation had right of dominion. . . . This minimum of right the German Government has swept aside under the plea of retaliation and necessity and because it had no weapons which it could use at sea except these which it is impossible to employ as it is employing them without throwing to the winds all scruples of humanity. "

The suspense increased as Wilson moved closer to the critical part of his address. "I advise," he declared in a stern voice, that Congress "formally accept the status of belligerent which has thus been thrust upon it; and that it take immediate steps not only to put the country in a more thorough state of defense but also to exert all its power and employ all its resources to bring the government of the German Empire to terms and end the war." Before he finished the sentence, the packed chamber erupted into wild cheering. Wilson continued, intending to ensure the world understood idealism, not selfish gain, had propelled America into war. "The world," he declared, "must be made safe for democracy."

As the president walked out of the hall, the audience stood in applause. Those who were carrying flags waved them high in the air. Those who had been wearing them in their lapels tore them off and waved with the rest. Only a few dared dissent from Wilson's noble vision. One of the president's most vocal critics, Senator Robert La Follette of Wisconsin (see page 816), stood motionless, his arms folded tight to register his disapproval.

Although some progressives opposed U.S. entry into the war, fearing that it would sap momentum from the reform effort, many others believed that by joining the Allies America could shape the peace and therefore create a new liberal world order. At home, the war would promote collective action, patriotic sacrifice, and national unity—all critical ingredients in the progressive formula for social progress. The editors of the liberal *New Republic* observed that the "extension of government power during wartime was an opportunity to secure that radical reconstruction of American society which had long been advocated."

In the end, however, these hopes would not be realized. The American military helped ensure an Allied victory in World War I, but Wilson failed to secure a just peace. The belligerents agreed to create a League of Nations to mediate future disputes, but the U.S. Senate rejected any experiment in internationalism and failed to approve America's participation in the new organization. At home, progressive hopes for the postwar world turned quickly to bitterness and strife. The drive for national unity produced labor strikes, social unrest, and a postwar Red Scare that resulted in widespread violations of civil liberties and civil rights. By 1920 Americans, disillusioned with the war and with Wilson, looked to the Republicans to restore order.

- What traditions and values made Americans reluctant to enter World War I, and what events overcame that reluctance?

- What impact did the war have on individual rights and social reform at home? How did the demands of war mobilization change the scope of government power?

- What were the key ingredients in Wilson's peace plan, and what obstacles did he face in selling it abroad and at home?

- What social and cultural tensions contributed to the civil unrest and the Red Scare at the end of World War I?

This chapter will address these questions.

THE ROAD TO WAR, 1914–1917

When fighting broke out in Europe, Wilson pledged that the United States would remain neutral. But genuine neutrality proved difficult to sustain. As a global economic power, the United States depended heavily on trade from Great Britain.

When German submarines attacked unarmed ships, killing Americans, Wilson announced a policy of "strict accountability." The policy reflected a deep undercurrent of isolationist feeling. Most Americans hoped to protect American honor but also to avoid getting entangled in European affairs. When Germany announced that it would sink all neutral ships trading with England, Wilson felt he had no other recourse than war.

American Neutrality

On June 28, 1914, a Serbian youth assassinated Archduke Franz Ferdinand, heir to the throne of the Austro-Hungarian Empire. The assassination shattered the delicate balance of power that had maintained a fragile international peace in Europe since 1815. Protecting their economic and colonial interests, European diplomats had established an alliance system: the Triple Alliance (or Central Powers) of Germany, Turkey, Italy, and Austria-Hungary; and the Triple Entente (or Allied) powers of Great Britain, France, and Russia. These nations also promised protection to weaker European nations. Great Britain's treaty with Belgium, for example, guaranteed the neutrality of this small country wedged between powerful neighbors France and Germany (see map on page 911).

Three weeks after the assassination of its heir, Austria sent eleven demands to the Serbian government, and when Serbia refused to accept one of the conditions, Austria declared war on Serbia. Russia, fulfilling a promise to protect Serbian independence, began mobilizing its troops. Germany, traditionally fearful of an attack by Russia and its ally, France, declared war on Russia on August 1. Following military plans devised a decade earlier to weaken France, Germany invaded Belgium on August 4, leading Great Britain to declare war on Germany. By the end of 1914 the war had spread globally as Turkey attacked Russia and Japan invaded Germany's Far East possessions.

By September 1914 the Allied and Central Powers were locked in a deadly war of attrition—glaring at each other across trenches that stretched from the English Channel to the Alps. Everyone believed this would be a short war, but new technology hindered the prospects of a quick victory and led to bloodshed on a level never before seen in combat. Barbed-wire, machine-gun nests, and heavy artillery guns dominated the landscape, preventing either side from launching successful charges against the enemy. Airplanes provided officers with information about the enemy's positions and on occasion were used to drop grenades and target artillery. Soldiers used poison gas, introduced in 1915, to neutralize soldiers in the enemy's trenches during an attack. Both sides launched giant offensives, only to gain a few square miles of territory at the cost of tens of thousands of lives. At the Battle of Verdun in 1916, for example, over seven hundred thousand men perished as a result of the modern military arsenal.

When the war began, nearly all Americans assumed that the United States would never become involved. "I thank Heaven for many things—first the Atlantic Ocean," the American ambassador in London wrote the president, reflecting the popular belief that geography would isolate the United States from the conflict. On August 14 President Wilson urged Americans to "be neutral in fact as well as in name during these days that are to try men's souls. We must be impartial in

CHRONOLOGY

1914	Archduke Franz Ferdinand of Austria assassinated World War I begins; President Wilson announces American neutrality
1915	British liner *Lusitania* sunk by German U-boat Bryan resigns and Lansing becomes secretary of state U-boat sinks *Arabic*
1916	Germany issues *Sussex* pledge Wilson reelected
1917	Germany resumes unrestricted U-boat warfare U.S. enters the war Selective Service Act sets up national draft Race riot in East St. Louis, Illinois National Civil Liberties Union founded
1918	Wilson outlines Fourteen Points for peace Debs imprisoned for speaking against the war Alien and Sedition Acts passed Armistice signed
1919	Peace treaty signed at Versailles May Day bombings help stimulate Red Scare Communist party of the United States of America founded Versailles Treaty rejected by Senate
1920	Palmer raids organized by Justice Department American Civil Liberties Union created Harding elected president

thought as well as in action." Newspaper accounts, illustrated with battlefield photographs, of the miserable conditions of trench warfare reinforced America's desire to stay out of the conflict. The title of a popular song expressed the feeling of most Americans: "Don't Take My Darling Boy Away."

However, genuine neutrality proved impossible. America's large immigrant population had roots on both sides of the conflict. While Irish and German immigrants were strongly anti-British, cultural links and commercial contacts tied many Protestant Americans to the Allies. British propagandists cleverly manipulated American support by swamping the United States with sensationalized stories of German soldiers mutilating children and raping women. Despite their professed desire not to choose sides, Wilson and nearly all his leading advisers believed that American interests and ideals would fare better if Britain prevailed over Germany. Wilson confessed at one point that a German victory "will be fatal to our form of Government and American ideals." Secretary of State William Jennings Bryan, who did not want the United States to enter the war on either side, was perhaps the only genuinely neutral member of the cabinet.

Battlefield of Passchendale, 1917   New technology created even more devastating battlefields during the Great War, destroying all forms of life in its wake. For four years, soldiers on both sides suffered in the trenches—digging deep to protect themselves from incoming ordnance, living with lice and rats, and struggling through hot summers and cold wet winters. In this picture, Allied soldiers sit in the craters created by artillery shells after the Battle of Passchendale, the third major battle in the region around Ypres, Belgium, in three years.   *(©Hulton-Deutsch Collection/Corbis.)*

In fact, America's long-standing economic ties with the Allies made neutrality impossible. Even before the outbreak of hostilities, England was America's primary trading partner, and the war only intensified that relationship. In 1914 U.S. exports to the Allies totaled $753 million. By 1916 trade soared to nearly $3 billion. During that same period trade with Germany tumbled from $345 million to a paltry $29 million. Initially, the administration banned private banks from making loans to the cash-strapped Allies. Bryan protested that such loans, though legal, were "inconsistent with the true spirit of neutrality." In 1915 Wilson, worried that the prohibition would stifle profitable wartime trade, reversed course and lifted the ban, ending any pretense of financial neutrality. Bankers, who had close ties to England, immediately floated over $500 million. "Our firm had never for one moment been neutral," a Morgan partner recalled. "From the very start we did everything we could to contribute to the cause of the Allies." By 1917 America had loaned $2.2 billion to the Allies, but only $27 million to Germany.

America's relationship with the belligerents was further complicated by British control of the ocean. To strangle Germany, Britain took liberties with international law, expanding the definition of contraband of war to include nearly every possible item, including food. The Royal Navy forced neutral ships into port for inspection and halted trade to Germany's neutral neighbors, Holland and Denmark. The British, observed a critic, "ruled the waves and waived the rules." The British navy frequently intercepted American ships, causing long delays and confiscating some or all of their cargoes. When Wilson protested, the British government temporarily eased the blockade or offered to pay American companies for seized goods. Despite occasional complaints, Washington acquiesced to the British maritime system. The British managed to sever American trade with the Central Powers without rupturing Anglo-American relations.

In an effort to challenge British control of the seas, the Germans launched a frightening new weapon, the U-boat (short for *Unterseeboot*, or "undersea boat"). On February 4, 1915, the German foreign minister announced that waters around Great Britain and Ireland would become a war zone in which German submarines would seek "to destroy every enemy merchant ship." "Neutrals," he continued, "are therefore warned against further entrusting crews, passengers, and wares to such ships." Not only did the German submarines threaten Allied shipping, but they also muddied the waters of international maritime law. The fragile U-boat, vulnerable to gunfire on the surface and dependent on the element of surprise, ignored laws requiring belligerent ships to allow civilian passengers and crew to disembark before attacking.

The German announcement set the stage for a major confrontation with the United States. Wilson told German leaders that if any American property or lives were lost in the war zone, Germany would be held to "strict accountability." His message amounted to an ultimatum, threatening war if German attacks killed Americans. Because the Germans promised not to attack American ships in the war zone, the issue became the right of Americans to sail and work on the ships of belligerents.

The issue came to a head on May 7, off the southern Irish coast, when a German submarine torpedoed the British luxury liner *Lusitania*. The ship, whose cargo included 4.2 million rounds of rifle ammunition, sank in eighteen minutes, carrying 1,198 people to their deaths, 128 Americans among them. Most Americans were horrified by the attack. "The Torpedo which sank the *Lusitania*" *The Nation* editorialized, "also sank Germany in the opinion of mankind." Theodore Roosevelt, beating his war drums, called it "an act of piracy."

The sinking narrowed Wilson's options. In an attempt to calm public outrage, he declared that "There is such a thing as a man being too proud to fight. There is such a thing as a nation being so right that it does not need to convince others by force that it is right." At the same time, he sent the Germans stiff notes demanding the payment of reparations for injuries and a pledge to cease submarine attacks on passenger liners. Berlin did not want to antagonize America, but it was unwilling to abandon one of its most effective weapons against British control of the seas. Eventually, Germany expressed "regret" over the American deaths and agreed to pay an indemnity.

The sinking of the *Lusitania* incited a debate at home over Wilson's liberal application of neutrality law, which he claimed gave Americans the right to travel safely on the ships of belligerent nations. Critics of Wilson's "strict accountability" policy wanted the president to require American passengers who wished to traverse the war zone to travel on American ships. In February Congress began debate on the Gore-McLemore resolutions, which warned American citizens not to travel on armed belligerent ships. The resolutions generated widespread public support, but Wilson opposed any compromise of American neutral rights, and the resolutions went down to defeat. Clinging to a rigid definition of neutrality, Wilson refused to respond to the complications created by the submarine or to appreciate how his policy clearly benefited the British. To prevent American passage on ships, he declared, would produce national humiliation and the destruction of the "whole fine fabric of international law." The British may have been violating U.S. commercial rights, he reasoned, but the Germans were violating human rights.

Wilson's strong stand on American neutrality rights led to the resignation of Secretary of State Bryan, who feared that the president's policy would lead inevitably to war. "He is absolutely sincere," Bryan said of Wilson. "That is what makes him dangerous." Bryan's replacement, Robert Lansing, an international lawyer and conservative Democrat with pro-British leanings, supported Wilson's position. Years later, Lansing recalled that after the *Lusitania*, he was convinced "that we would ultimately become an ally of Great Britain."

Events in the summer of 1915 supported Lansing's prediction. On August 30, 1915, a German submarine torpedoed another British liner, the *Arabic*, killing two Americans. Lansing warned Germany that if it continued attacking passenger liners the United States, "would certainly declare war." Berlin responded with the so-called *Arabic* pledge, promising never again to attack a passenger ship without warning. However, in March 1916 a German submarine attacked a French channel steamer, the *Sussex*. Four Americans were injured. The submarine claimed to have mistaken the *Sussex* for a minesweeper, but the attack was an overt violation of the *Arabic* pledge. On April 18, 1916, an angry Wilson instructed the Germans that unless they abandoned their "present methods of submarine warfare against passenger and freight-carrying vessels," he would move to sever diplomatic relations. The Germans, unwilling to risk war with the United States, again promised (the *Sussex* pledge) not to attack merchant ships without warning. Germany also pleaded with Washington to stop British violations of international law—a request that Wilson ignored.

Peace, Preparedness, and the 1916 Election

With a presidential election year approaching, Republicans charged that Wilson's "strict neutrality" policy failed to protect American interests. The Germans, one critic said, were "standing by their torpedoes, the British by their guns, and Wilson by strict accountability." Theodore Roosevelt, more militaristic than ever, called the president a "peace prattler" who had "done more to emasculate American manhood and weaken its fiber than anyone else I can think of."

Though many of these critics stopped short of advocating war, they called for an aggressive campaign to build up the military in case of war. Initially, Wilson opposed a preparedness campaign, but as tension mounted, he gradually switched positions. In the fall of 1915 he endorsed an ambitious proposal to increase the size of the armed forces. Calling for a "navy second to none," he supported the Naval Construction Act of 1916, which proposed an aggressive expansion of the navy, including the construction of ten battleships, ten cruisers, fifty destroyers, and one hundred submarines. The president also supported passage of the National Defense Act of 1916, which increased the size of the regular army from 90,000 to 223,000 and expanded the National Guard. During the winter of 1916 he went on a whirl-wind two-week speaking tour to rally public support for the measures. Wilson's strong endorsement secured passage of both measures despite stiff opposition from peace advocates in Congress.

His outspoken support for preparedness damaged Wilson's relationship with progressive peace advocates. In 1915 feminists Jane Addams and Carrie Chapman Catt formed the Women's Peace Party. Their platform demanded that "as human beings and the mother half of humanity," they must have a say in national affairs. Peace sentiment was strong in the Plains states and the Midwest, which had weaker commercial and sentimental ties to the Allies and (in some cases) were home to rel-atively large numbers of German-Americans. Progressive Republican senators, such as Wisconsin's La Follette and George Norris of Nebraska, feared the abridgement of individual liberties and the growth of close government–business ties that would result from a war. The Socialist Party and its leader Eugene Debs condemned the war as "unjustifiable," fomented largely by big business.

In the 1916 presidential campaign Republicans attempted to capitalize on Wil-son's difficulties. By 1916 many of the insurgents who fled the party four years ear-lier to support Roosevelt's Progressive Party had returned to the fold. At their convention they nominated Supreme Court Justice Charles Evans Hughes, formerly a progressive governor of New York. Hughes tried unsuccessfully to focus public attention on the failure of Wilson's diplomacy while avoiding a clear stand that might divide elements of his own party. Unable to excite even traditional Republi-can audiences, he tried to play to both sides on the peace issue. He told German-American audiences in the Midwest that he favored neutrality. When campaigning in the East, he criticized Wilson for not supporting the Allies more strongly. Teddy Roosevelt frustrated Hughes's effort to reach out to the peace groups by publicly pressuring him to take an unequivocal position in favor of a more aggressive pro-Allied policy.

While Hughes floundered, Wilson and the Democrats managed to harness the peace issue. The Democratic Party campaigned on the slogan "He kept us out of war." A Democratic handbill reminded voters, "You Are Working—Not Fighting! Alive and Happy—Not Cannon Fodder!" Even while campaigning on a peace plat-form, Wilson recognized a potential danger in his policy of strict accountability: it depended on German restraint. "I can't keep the country out of war," he observed privately. "Any little German lieutenant can put us into war at any time by some calculated outrage."

The election was too close to call when voters went to the polls on November 7. First returns, which showed Hughes winning in the Northeast and Midwest, sug-gested a big Republican victory. But results trickled in during the night showing

Wilson scoring well in the West. Not until two days later, when votes from California were counted, was Wilson declared the winner. A difference of fewer than four thousand votes in California would have removed Wilson from the White House. Final returns gave him 277 electoral votes from thirty states to Hughes's 254 from eighteen states. Wilson won with less than 50 percent of the popular vote (see map below). The Democratic strength continued to be based in the South and West. The Republican stronghold remained the Northeast and Midwest. The Democrats retained narrow majorities in the Senate and the House.

"Peace Without Victory"   Looking to end the stalemate of trench warfare, Germany announced that it would resume unrestricted submarine warfare on February 1, 1917. The German government warned that all ships, including unarmed American merchant ships, would be attacked on sight in the war zone. The Germans realized that this action would provoke the United States to enter the war, but they hoped to starve the Allies into defeat before American troops could be mobilized. "England will lie on the ground in six months, before a single American has set foot on the continent," boasted a German naval commander.

While Germany prepared to unleash its submarines, Wilson attempted to bring both sides to the negotiating table. On December 18, 1916, Wilson urged them to make public their war aims in hopes of finding a compromise that would end the war. Their response was not promising. Germany did not want a nonbelligerent like the United States involved in the negotiations, while the Allies claimed they would continue fighting until Germany was no longer ruled by an imperialistic monarch. On January 22, 1917, in an eloquent speech before the Senate, the president called for "a peace without victory," in which nations would guarantee the fundamental rights of all people. He attacked the European balance of power, which had repeat-

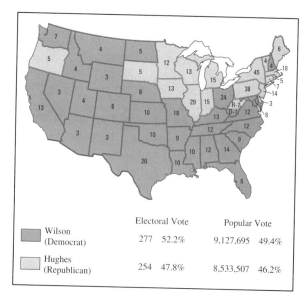

The Election of 1916   Rejecting Theodore Roosevelt for his beliefs that Americans should take a more active stand on the war raging in Europe, the Republican Party turned to Charles Evans Hughes, a Supreme Court Justice since 1910. While Hughes managed to win eastern states with large electoral votes, Woodrow Wilson's pledge to keep America out of the war won him the West and the South—enough to win the election.

	Electoral Vote	Popular Vote
Wilson (Democrat)	277 52.2%	9,127,695 49.4%
Hughes (Republican)	254 47.8%	8,533,507 46.2%

edly failed to prevent war. "There must be not a balance of power, but a community of power; not organized rivalries, but an organized common peace." Such a peace, he insisted, needed to be based on self-determination for all nations, freedom of the seas, and an end to "entangling alliances." "These are American principles, American policies," he declared in a final effort to convince the combatants to abandon their destructive ways and embrace a more enlightened approach to the world.

The speech scored well with Congress and the public, but it fell on deaf ears in Europe. A French writer compared Wilson's "peace without victory" to "bread without yeast, . . . love without quarrels, a camel without humps, night without moon, roof without smoke, town without brothel." Germany responded by fulfilling its pledge to initiate total submarine warfare on February 1. Two days later Wilson broke diplomatic relations with Germany. It was, he told Congress, the only "alternative consistent with the dignity and honor of the United States."

Wilson still hoped to avoid war with Germany. Only "actual overt acts," he said, would convince him that Berlin intended to carry out its threats. On February 26 he asked Congress to grant him authority to arm merchant vessels. The bill passed the House but got bogged down in the Senate, where a group of noninterventionist senators led by La Follette filibustered it to death. Furious, Wilson excoriated them as a "little group of willful men, representing no opinion but their own, who have rendered this great nation helpless and contemptible." After consulting with the attorney general, Wilson declared that his executive authority gave him the right to arm the ships without congressional consent.

Meanwhile, an unforeseen event had pushed America closer to war. On February 24 the British had given Wilson an intercepted telegram sent by Arthur Zimmermann, the German foreign secretary, to the Mexican government. The message, dated January 16, 1917, proposed a military alliance with Mexico if the United States entered the war against the Central Powers. In return, Germany promised Mexico the "lost territory in Texas, New Mexico, and Arizona." For millions of Americans the threat of Mexican involvement brought what had been a distant conflict desperately close to home. On February 26 Germany provided the "overt act" that the president had been waiting for by sinking the American merchant ship *Laconia*, killing two Americans. Armed neutrality did little to protect American ships from German torpedoes. In March several more went down, and newspaper headlines screamed with the sinking of each. The assault on American shipping produced a wave of emotion in favor of war. Six hundred Republicans met at the Union League Club in New York to demand intervention. Aroused citizens held mass public rallies in New York, Philadelphia, Chicago, Boston, and Denver. The Russian Revolution of March 1917, which replaced Russia's totalitarian monarchy with a constitutional monarch and democracy, added to the momentum for war by making it easier for Americans to view the Allied cause as a democratic crusade.

Increasingly, Wilson felt he had no options other than war. German aggression had to be resisted and American neutrality defended. Moreover, the president believed that the United States would have more influence in shaping the peace if it entered the war. On March 20 his previously divided cabinet unanimously favored war with Germany. Wilson delivered his war message on the evening of April 2.

Over the next four days Congress debated the president's war resolution. Emotions ran high. Opposition to the war was strongest in the agricultural Midwest. Nebraska's populist senator, George Norris, denounced the resolution as a conspiracy engineered by Wall Street. "We are going into war upon the command of gold," he thundered. "We are about to put the dollar sign upon the American flag." Six senators and fifty representatives ultimately voted against American entry into the war, more than opposed any other war resolution in American history. "I want to stand by my country," declared Representative Jeannette Rankin, the first woman elected to Congress, "but I cannot vote for war." Opponents, however, were outnumbered in Congress, their voices drowned in a patriotic tidal wave. After the vote a newspaper headline proclaimed: "The Yanks Are Coming!" For the first time in its history, the United States was to enter a war on another continent.

WAR, MOBILIZATION, AND PROGRESSIVE REFORM, 1916–1919

A few weeks after Wilson's war message, journalist Walter Lippmann declared that the nation stood "at the threshold of a collectivism which is greater than any as yet planned by the Socialist party." How would Americans balance the need for collective action with the respect for individual rights and small government? In facing the challenges of mobilization—creating an army, regulating the economy, forging a sense of national unity—the administration relied on a combination of patriotic appeals and government coercion. Often, concern for individual rights fell by the wayside, sometimes a victim of ethnic prejudice. The war did, however, produce gains for many Americans. It also gave momentum to the Progressive Era drive to pass constitutional amendments to prevent the sale of alcohol and to grant women the right to vote.

Creating an Army   On April 1, 1917, the U.S. Army, which numbered only 5,791 officers and 121,797 enlisted men, ranked seventeenth in the world. In comparison, Germany had two hundred divisions massed on the western front, and in the next two months the British army alone lost 177,000 men in a single offensive. The War Department still relied on a table of organization devised by John C. Calhoun in 1817. The military significance of the United States, scoffed a German official, was "zero, zero, zero."

To mobilize armed manpower as quickly as possible, Wilson proposed a draft requiring all men between the ages of twenty and thirty to register. The draft raised widespread fears in a nation that valued individual freedom and disliked distant and impersonal government. Memories of Civil War conscription, which had created offensive disparities and led to bloody rioting in New York City, soured many Americans on the idea. Some objected to the restriction of personal freedom. House Speaker Champ Clark declared that "there is precious little difference between a conscript and a convict."

The administration diffused these objections through a massive public relations campaign. The worst feature of the Civil War draft, declared one official, was that it "bared the teeth of the Federal Government in every home within the loyal states." Calling its program "selective service" rather than "conscription," the administration tried to remove the stigma of a distant and impersonal government by allowing local citizens to administer the draft through draft boards, which became "buffers between the individual citizen and the federal Government." The president reassured the nation, declaring that the draft was "in no sense a conscription of the unwilling," but rather "selection from a nation which has volunteered in mass."

Wilson designated June 5, 1917, as the first day of national registration. Many people predicted violent protest, but the administration's use of patriotic appeals blunted any hint of rebellion. Local officials joined in massive celebrations of patriotic fervor to encourage men to register. The recruits were, according to an observer, "exhorted by their mayors, prayed for by their clergymen, and wept over by sundry females." By the end of the day, nearly 10 million Americans between the ages of twenty-one and thirty-five registered for the draft. (In 1918 the ages for draftees changed to between eighteen and forty-five years of age.)

Recruiting an Army   The Selective Service Act created an army of almost 5 million by the war's end. Local draft boards had discretion in selecting which drafted men in their community would serve. Most married men with dependents, along with those who worked in essential industries, were eligible for exemptions. The enthusiasm shown by the soldiers in this photograph reveals how patriotic appeals encouraged many men to serve.   *(Brown Bros.)*

By war's end 24 million men, or 44 percent of American males, had registered for the draft. Almost 5 million were drafted into the service, and 2 million had been sent to fight in France. More than 1.5 million Americans enlisted in the army. Another 520,000 signed up for service in the navy and the marines. Over 20,000 women served in the armed forces. Almost 5,000 went to France, where they worked as army nurses, but most served as clerks and secretaries. The military awarded deferments to millions of draft-age men because they worked in war industries or had dependents. Men were at the mercy of local draft boards, each with its own interpretation of what was required for deferment and vulnerable to local political pressure and prejudices. Over 340,000 men—11 percent of candidates—evaded the draft by refusing to register or by not responding when called. Almost 65,000 declared themselves conscientious objectors, mostly based on religious beliefs.

Proponents of military training viewed the army as an ideal vehicle for forging a common sense of identity. "The military tent where they all sleep side by side," observed Teddy Roosevelt, "will rank next to the public schools among the great agents of democratization." In fact, the army reflected the divisions within American society. The armed forces remained rigidly segregated. The marines excluded blacks; the navy assigned them to mess duty. Blacks, relegated to separate areas in training camps, received inferior equipment and training. The War Department made no provision for commissioning or training black recruits as officers until protests by the NAACP led to the establishment of one officer candidate program in June 1917. Its graduates always worked under white supervision. "Under capable white officers and with sufficient training," declared John J. Pershing, "negro soldiers have always acquitted themselves creditably."

Blacks made up about 1 percent of the officer corps of an army with 13 percent black enlisted men. When the United States entered the war, the highest-ranking black officer was Colonel Charles Young of the Tenth Cavalry Division. The third black graduate of the United States Military Academy, Young had acquired a distinguished service record in the war with Spain and later in fighting Pancho Villa's guerrillas in Mexico. Despite his record, a number of white officers refused to serve under him. Four of them complained to their senators, who then lobbied the secretary of war to remove Young from his command. Shortly afterward, the army forced Young to retire. Other black officers suffered similar indignities. An investigator reported that at one army camp, nearly 90 percent of the whites refused to salute black officers.

Given such attitudes, it is unsurprising that the armed forces were not exempt from the racial violence that plagued civilian society. In 1917 black troops stationed at Houston, Texas, angered by the constant humiliation of that city's Jim Crow laws, exploded in violence. On the night of August 23 they shot to death seventeen white civilians. The army, under intense pressure from southern congressmen, dealt harshly with the troops. More than a hundred blacks, denied benefit of an appeal to the War Department, were court-martialed, and thirteen were executed. After the riot, the War Department dispersed black recruits throughout its camps, maintaining a two-to-one ratio of white to black trainees.

The draft and voluntary enlistments solved America's manpower needs. Now the army had to build camps to train the new recruits, provide them with arms, and transport them overseas. The army had to construct from scratch thirty-two training camps, each equipped to handle forty thousand men. According to one estimate, the army used enough wood in the construction to build a boardwalk 12 inches wide and 1 inch thick to the moon and halfway back! After creating the small cities, the military had to supply them with medical equipment, food, clothing, weapons, and ammunition. "The supply situation was," in the words of one official, "as nearly a perfect mess as can be imagined." Recruits frequently trained in civilian clothes for weeks before receiving uniforms. The army owned only three thousand transport trucks and six hundred thousand rifles. As of July 1917 the navy owned only seven troop and cargo ships. For most of the war effort, American troops used equipment furnished by Britain and France.

In staffing and assigning military personnel, the army made use of a new psychological tool—the intelligence quotient, or IQ test. The scientists who administered the test concluded that 31 percent of recruits were illiterate. Minorities and whites from rural regions scored especially low. Questions such as "Who wrote 'The Raven'?" (a poem by nineteenth-century author Edgar Allan Poe) revealed a great deal about the class backgrounds and cultural assumptions of the university-trained scientists who created the test but offered little insight into the ability of the enlistees who took it.

The army also initiated an ambitious program of sex education to limit the threat from sexually transmitted diseases. By 1917 over a million French troops had contracted either syphilis or gonorrhea. Because researchers had not yet developed antibiotics, these venereal diseases could sap the strength of fighting forces. The War Department established a Committee on Training Camp Activities (CTCA) to shut down red-light districts near its training camps. The CTCA turned out lurid films and issued pamphlets that taught trainees how to keep "fit to fight." The messages were often explicit. "You wouldn't use another fellow's toothbrush. Why use his whore?" The army even issued condoms to soldiers.

For many young men the war seemed to offer an exciting opportunity to go "Over There," as a patriotic song of the time put it. Sustained by the belief that theirs was a noble cause, they embarked on what Theodore Roosevelt called the "Great Adventure." The harsh realities of mud, poison gas, and mangled bodies would soon dim many of these expectations. "How I wish the whole business was over," Lieutenant Frederick T. Edwards wrote his family in 1917, "and that we could pick up the things we did and dropped last Spring . . . for the war is like a Winter, chilling and freezing the soul."

Regulating the Economy   The U.S. economy was wholly unprepared for war in April 1916. The government lacked any mechanism for coordinating the war effort: for making decisions about what the Allies would need and how to apportion material between military and civilian use. Transporting millions of troops and vast quantities of war supplies overwhelmed the nation's railroad system. At one point, railroad cars destined for the East Coast were backed up as far west as Chicago. Military demand for food and fuel produced shortages, raising the prospect of civilians going cold and hungry.

With the mobilization effort a shambles, Congress passed the Lever Food and Fuel Control Act in August 1917. The legislation, one of the most sweeping grants of executive power in American history, authorized the president to regulate the output, distribution, and price of food and to control every product that was used in food production. Exercising his new powers, Wilson created a Fuel Administration and a Food Administration, charging the new agencies with expanding output and restricting civilian consumption. The head of the Food Administration, Herbert Hoover, rejected coercive rationing and price-fixing and instead depended on "the spirit of self-sacrifice." Hoover mobilized huge publicity campaigns to promote "wheatless Mondays," "meatless Tuesdays," and "porkless Thursdays and Saturdays." At the same time he encouraged increased production by arranging for the government to buy crops at high prices, enticing farmers to plant more. The Fuel Administration, headed by Williams College president Harry Garfield, following Hoover's example, instituted fuel "holidays." Garfield introduced daylight savings time to conserve energy and set high prices on coal so that even inefficient mines could make a profit.

In December 1917 the government moved to ease the transportation crisis by taking control of most of the country's railroads. The president created a Railroad Administration, naming Treasury Secretary William Gibbs McAdoo as its director-general. McAdoo quickly took charge of nearly 400,000 miles of track, including railroad terminals and warehouses. He suspended unessential traffic, poured in money to improve track conditions, consolidated ticket offices, and gave railroad workers a generous pay raise to improve morale. His actions showed immediate results: the logjam disappeared, trains ran more efficiently, and the railroad system benefited from the infusion of resources.

Along with running the nation's railway system, McAdoo had to deal with the daunting task of developing ways to finance the war. Before it entered the war, the federal government spent almost $1 billion a year. By 1920 annual expenditures had soared to $19 billion. How to pay for the war became a central question in the White House and on Capitol Hill. Conservatives called for higher taxes on consumer goods, which would be distributed broadly. Progressives wanted wealthy individuals and corporations to bear the heaviest burden. McAdoo recognized that higher taxes were inevitable, but he also believed that patriotic appeals could help the government pay for the war. The administration launched a drive to solicit loans by selling so-called Liberty Bonds to the American people. "Every person who refuses to subscribe," McAdoo asserted, ". . . is a friend of Germany." By 1920 sales of Liberty Bonds produced $23 billion of the $32 billion spent on the war. In the end, taxes paid for about one-third of the war expense.

Despite its modest nature, the tax program produced a fiscal revolution in America. In part, the revolution was psychological. The war introduced the principle of progression—the idea that the tax burden should fall on those most able to pay—into the nation's tax system. The 77.7 percent of taxpayers whose income was less than $3,000 paid less than 3.6 percent of all tax receipts; corporations and the wealthy paid the rest. The war also built on the foundation constructed by the income tax amendment of 1913 to dramatically enlarge the tax base. The number of tax returns filed jumped from 437,036 in 1916 to 3,472,890 in 1917 and then doubled again in 1920. "Never before," observed the historian Bruce D. Porter, "had federal taxation affected so many Americans so directly."

The keystone of the wartime mobilization effort was the War Industries Board (WIB), which coordinated the government's purchases of military supplies, helped convert plants to military production, and arranged for the construction of new factories. In March 1918 Wilson appointed Wall Street businessman Bernard Baruch to take control of the board. Assuming extraordinary new powers, Baruch set production schedules, mediated disputes between industries, and standardized procedures. Whenever possible, Baruch avoided using coercion. Instead, he used lucrative contracts to persuade manufacturers to shift to war goods, and he promised to cover all costs and guarantee a profit. Coercion remained an available method, however. When one executive refused WIB requests, Baruch threatened to turn public opinion against him and make him "such an object of contempt and scorn in your home town that you will not dare to show your face there." When auto companies refused to cut back on the production of passenger cars, Baruch threatened to cut off coal and steel supplies, with swift results.

Workers and the War   Samuel Gompers, the head of the AFL (see page 722), hoped to translate support for the war into tangible gains for organized labor. An intense labor shortage provided both government and business with a strong incentive to develop a partnership with organized labor. By July 1918 thirty-four states faced serious shortages of unskilled workers. In 1917 more than a million workers took part in 4,200 strikes in war-related industries.

In September 1917 Wilson established the Mediation Commission to further "the development of a better understanding between laborers and employers." The commission consisted of two business and two labor representatives. The group and its secretary, Harvard law school professor Felix Frankfurter, visited strike-plagued areas and made recommendations for improving labor–management relations.

In April 1918 the president established the National War Labor Board (WLB) as a kind of supreme court for labor controversies. When Gompers and the AFL executive committee offered a "no strike" pledge, Wilson instructed the board to protect the right of workers to organize and bargain collectively—the first time a federal agency had wielded a prolabor policy. The administration backed up the pledge with muscle. When the management at the Smith and Wesson arms plant in Springfield, Massachusetts, and the Western Union telegraph company violated WIB rules, Wilson sent federal agents to take over the plants. The board also attempted to guarantee all workers under their jurisdiction a "living wage"—an income sufficient to provide a minimum of health and decency—and it compelled the adoption of the eight-hour workday. Federal support for organizing efforts helped union membership rise from 2.7 million in 1916 to over 4 million in 1919.

With the war consuming material needed to build new homes, the nation faced a severe housing shortage, especially in the areas around booming factories. Many workers who moved to take jobs in wartime plants found themselves without a place to live. To remedy the problem, the Labor Department formed the United States Housing Corporation (USHC) and the Emergency Fleet Corporation (EFC) in 1917. The USHC built low-cost housing for nearly six thousand families and over seven thousand individuals. In some cases, the government constructed model communities, such as Union Park Gardens in Wilmington, Delaware, which included schools, a playground, and a community center.

Wartime spending produced a tremendous economic boom. America's gross national product increased from $62.5 billion in 1916 to $73.6 billion in 1919. But the benefits were not equally distributed. Though wages increased during the war, inflation eroded most of the gains. The great mass of workers saw their purchasing power drop by more than 20 percent between 1916 and 1919. Not surprisingly, business gained the most from the war. Corporate profits, even after higher taxes, jumped 30 percent between 1914 and 1920. The profits of U.S. Steel skyrocketed from $76 million to $478 million between 1914 and 1917.

Many women hoped the wartime need for labor would break down traditional barriers that had barred them from employment. "At last, after centuries of disabilities and discrimination," declared a feminist, "women are coming into the labor and festival of life on equal terms with men." To a limited extent, the optimism was warranted. About a million women joined the work force for the first time during the war. Many of the 8 million women who already worked in low-paying positions switched to higher-paying industrial jobs. Between 1910 and 1920 the number of female clerical workers more than doubled, while the number of female domestic servants declined. The number of female railroad workers tripled during the war. A survey of 690 plants in Cincinnati, Ohio, found a 22.7 percent increase in the number of women employed between 1917 and 1918.

For most women the opportunities proved limited and brief, ending with the war. During the war women were paid less than men for the same work. In milling companies in Cincinnati, men earned between $15 and $20 per week; women performing the same work averaged between $6 and $10. Trade unions remained hostile to women workers and assumed, like most people, that women would return to the home at the end of the war. A union official bluntly suggested that "the same patriotism which induced women to enter industry during the war should induce them to vacate their positions after the war." Most women, willingly or not, followed the advice.

The war also raised the expectations of African-Americans, who hoped both to prove their loyalty and to benefit from the labor shortage. W. E. B. Du Bois (see page 824) urged blacks "to seize the opportunity to emphasize their American citizenship" because "out of this war will rise, too, an American Negro with the right to live without insult." The search for better-paying jobs in war-related industries accelerated a massive migration of blacks from the rural South to the industrial Northeast and Midwest. Between 1910 and 1920 about 330,000 blacks fled poverty and oppression in the South, heading north for Detroit, Chicago, and New York City. The black population of Chicago swelled from 44,000 to 109,000; New York's grew from 92,000 to over 153,000.

Most African-Americans found work in heavy industry—steel, auto, shipbuilding, meatpacking, and mining—where they were relegated to unskilled jobs at low wages. In some cases the increase in African-American employment was pronounced. The Westinghouse Company employed only 25 blacks in 1916; by 1918 it employed 1,500. The number of black shipyard workers rose from about 37,000 to over 100,000 in the same period. Many black women moved from domestic work

The Home Front   Women, such as these riveters in Puget Sound, Washington, filled in for men absent from the work force. The war offered new job opportunities and better wages for women, but these gains did not persist after the war's conclusion. Women's work greatly aided the war effort, as did their role as managers of the family economy. *(National Archives.)*

into factories. The number of African-American women in manufacturing rose from over 67,000 in 1910 to almost 105,000 in 1920.

Ḁ The war offered African-Americans economic opportunity in the North, but it did not provide sanctuary from racism. Northerners, alarmed by the "invasion," retaliated by imposing discriminatory residential requirements that ghettoized the new migrants. Mobs beat blacks who strayed out of their neighborhoods and stoned black families who dared to move into white areas of the cities. Racial tensions erupted in riots in twenty-six cities during 1917, including a riot in East St. Louis that killed thirty-nine blacks and nine whites. The NAACP responded by staging a protest in New York. One of the banners asked, "Mr. President, why not make America safe for Democracy?"

Ḁ Southerners also viewed the migration to the North with alarm. "We must have the Negro in the South," declared the *Macon* (Georgia) *Telegraph.* "It is the only labor we have, it is the best we possibly could have—if we lose it, we go bankrupt!" Many whites in the South used violence and intimidation to stem the tide fleeing North. Lynching increased from thirty-four cases in 1917 to sixty in 1918, and to more than seventy in 1919.

In the Southwest Mexicans benefited from the wartime labor shortage. Growers needing labor to run their farms pressured the government into relaxing immigration restriction and exempting Mexican workers from the draft. Between 1917 and 1920 a hundred thousand Mexicans migrated across the border into Texas, California, Arizona, and Colorado. Like African-Americans, Mexicans confronted segregated communities, schools, and restaurants. Although they found employment, Mexicans were paid less than Anglos who worked with them.

The Search for National Unity   Many progressives believed that the war would promote national unity by ending class and ethnic divisions. The struggle would infuse the nation's citizens with a new sense of patriotism and thus undermine dangerous radicalism. A new moral purpose would replace selfish individualism. The war, they believed, could represent the culmination of decades of progressive efforts to forge a sense of social bonding. In its search for public unity, the Wilson administration authorized a massive propaganda campaign. On April 14, 1917, eight days after the declaration of war, Wilson asked George Creel, a progressive journalist from Denver, to head the Committee on Public Information. Creel remarked that his goal was to mold Americans into "one white-hot mass . . . with fraternity, devotion, courage, and deathless determination." Before the war had ended he had mobilized 150,000 lecturers, writers, artists, actors, and scholars in what Creel called "the world's greatest adventure in advertising." Officially titled "Four-Minute Men," the volunteers appeared in front of movie screens and on stages at schools, lodges, and union halls to give brief speeches on topics such as "why we are fighting" and "maintaining morals and morale." The committee placed illustrated advertisements in magazines such as the *Saturday Evening Post*, exhorting readers to report to the Justice Department "the man who spreads pessimistic stories . . . , cries for peace, or belittles our efforts to win the war." It produced upbeat films such as *Pershing's Crusaders* and *The Beast of Berlin*. Fears of disloyalty among the foreign-born prompted the CPI to organize "loyalty leagues" in ethnic communities.

When persuasion failed, the government resorted to coercion. The Espionage Act, enacted in June 1917, specified imprisonment and heavy fines for persons who engaged in spying or sabotage. But other repressed activities were less clearly criminal or treasonous. The act made illegal any public criticism that could be considered detrimental to the war effort. The Trading with the Enemy Act (1917) forbade trade with the enemy and empowered the postmaster general to deny use of the mails for any printed matter that, in his opinion, advocated treason, insurrection, or forcible resistance to the laws of the United States. The Alien Act (1918) gave the government broad power to deport noncitizen residents suspected of disloyalty. Finally, the Sedition Act, enacted in 1918, made it a crime to obstruct the sale of war bonds or to use "disloyal, profane, scurrilous, or abusive" language against the government, the Constitution, the flag, or military uniforms. It made almost any publicly voiced criticism of government policy or the war effort a crime punishable by fines, imprisonment, or both. Dissent, a protected right, had become a crime.

Postmaster General Albert Burleson and Attorney General Thomas W. Gregory made full use of their new arsenal to crush dissent. "May God have mercy on them," Gregory said of war opponents, "for they need expect none from an outraged people and an avenging government." Burleson used his new power to prevent the mailing of most socialist publications. Max Eastman, editor of a leading socialist journal, *The Masses*, ironically invoked the Bill of Rights guarantee of peaceful assembly when he complained, "You can't even collect your thoughts without being arrested for unlawful assembly."

While the post office tried to weed out literature critical of the war effort, law enforcement officials moved against suspected opponents of the war. Gregory's Justice Department initiated nearly 2,200 prosecutions and secured 1,055 convictions under the Espionage and Sedition Acts, and used threats to bully many more people into silence. Like Burleson, Gregory made socialists the main target of his assaults. Among socialist leaders prosecuted under the Espionage Act were Victor Berger of Milwaukee, who was twice denied his seat in Congress as a result of his conviction. The most famous victim of wartime repression was Eugene Debs, the Socialist Party leader who had received nearly 1 million votes for president in 1912 (see page 835). He was arrested and sentenced to ten years in federal prison for telling listeners, "You need to know that you are fit for something better than slavery and cannon fodder." The Justice Department took aim at other radical unionists who threatened to disrupt wartime production. In September 1917 federal agents arrested 133 leaders of the Industrial Workers of the World (Wobblies) for interfering with the war effort.

To help track down potential subversives, the Justice Department supported the creation of a quasi-vigilante organization called the American Protective League (APL). Carrying "Secret Service Division" cards, APL agents spied on, slandered, and arrested other Americans. They opened mail, intercepted telegrams, and organized raids against draft evaders. The APL was, according to one scholar, "a force for outrageous vigilantism blessed with the seal and sanction of the federal government." The government looked the other way when ultra-patriotic groups—bearing such names as the American Defense Society, the Sedition Slammers, and the Boy Spies of America—engaged in similar illegal activities.

State and local authorities joined with the federal government to stifle antiwar attitudes. Nine states outlawed opposition to the war effort. Local communities created committees, often called "councils of defense," to help the federal government rouse patriotic feeling and fight dissent. By 1918, 184,000 local chapters policed opinion across the country. The councils encouraged Americans to spy on one another and to report evidence of disloyalty. In Washington a state-sponsored group called the "Minute Men" planted spies in schools and colleges to report on instructors who taught the German language. The *Tulsa* (Oklahoma) *Daily World* advised its readers, "Watch your neighbor. If he is not doing everything in his power to help the nation in this crisis, see that he is reported to the authorities."

Most of these groups hoped to use civic fervor to exclude aliens and immigrants and to preserve older ways of life. The *Saturday Evening Post* voiced their sentiments when it demanded the removal of "the scum of the melting pot." German-Americans were the most frequent targets, but anyone who questioned the war effort was a potential victim. In April 1918 a Missouri mob seized Robert Prager, a young man whose only crime was that he had been born in Germany. He was bound in an American flag, paraded through town, and then lynched. A jury acquitted his killers on the grounds that they had acted in self-defense. By the summer of 1918 almost half the states forbade the teaching of German or church services conducted in German. Even everyday language was cleansed. Sauerkraut was renamed "liberty cabbage," and German measles became "liberty measles." A well-meaning motion picture producer was sentenced to ten years in jail for his movie *The Spirit of '76* because it allegedly aroused hostility to Britain, America's wartime ally. Perhaps the height of absurdity came when Cincinnati removed pretzels from saloon lunch counters.

In response to government repression, a young social worker named Roger Baldwin founded the National Civil Liberties Union in 1917. Raised in a wealthy Protestant family, Baldwin challenged both the government's refusal to grant conscientious objector status to opponents of the war and the increasing censorship. Critics dismissed Baldwin and his followers as a "little group of malcontents." "Jails are waiting for them," the *New York Times* warned. The organization increased in size and in 1920 became the American Civil Liberties Union (ACLU).

In 1919 the Supreme Court catered to illiberal feelings by sustaining the wartime statutes. The Espionage Act, Justice Oliver Wendell Holmes held in *Schenck* v. *U.S.* (1919), was justified (see Competing Voices, page 926). "The question in every case," he ruled, "is whether the words are used in such circumstances and are of such a nature as to create a clear and present danger that they will bring about the substantial evils that Congress has a right to prevent." To illustrate his point, Holmes used the analogy of shouting "Fire!" in a crowded theater. Authorities could, he argued, restrict speech under such conditions of "clear and present danger."

Holmes later rethought his position on the First Amendment. In August 1918 the government arrested six anarchists protesting the deployment of U.S. troops in the new Soviet Union. "Workers, our reply to the barbaric intervention has to be a general strike!" read one of their leaflets. Charged with violating the Espionage Act, the anarchists were convicted and given sentences of up to twenty years. By a seven to two vote, the U.S. Supreme Court in *Abrams* v. *U.S.* upheld their convictions, with Holmes and Justice Louis Brandeis dissenting. Holmes's reversal stunned the legal community. Tightening the "clear and present danger" standard, Holmes argued that the government had to prove "imminent danger" to the war effort to justify curtailing free speech. Advocating resistance, he said, should have to mean urging "some forcible act of opposition to some proceeding of the United States in pursuance of the war." Although Holmes's argument failed to convince the Court in 1918, it would eventually form the foundation on which Supreme Court decisions favoring free speech would rest.

Prohibition and Suffrage

The war added a powerful new weapon to the prohibitionists' arsenal—patriotism. Since grain supplies were limited, Congress prohibited the use of grain for distilling and brewing. The Anti-Saloon League (see page 821) forced adoption of an amendment to the Selective Service Act of 1917 forbidding the sale of alcoholic beverages at or near army camps and naval bases. The league charged that brewers, most of whom had German names, were sabotaging the war effort: "The worst of all our German enemies, the most treacherous, the most menacing are Pabst, Schlitz, Baltz, and Miller."

Emboldened by their success, prohibitionists made the final push for a constitutional amendment to forbid the manufacture, sale, and consumption of alcoholic beverages. In December 1917 their appeals to patriotic idealism convinced Congress to approve the amendment and pass it on to the states for ratification. Since twenty-seven states were already dry, prohibitionists needed the support of only nine additional states to win. The thirty-sixth state ratified on January 14, 1919. Only New Jersey, Rhode Island, and Connecticut—all states with large immigrant populations—rejected the amendment. After the war Congress passed the National Prohibition Act, called the Volstead Act, which established the enforcement procedures for the amendment.

The war also helped progressives win the battle for women's suffrage. By the time the United States entered the war, women had gained the vote in eleven states, but the suffrage engine seemed stalled. Suffragists revived the movement by wrapping themselves in the flag. They downplayed the earlier opposition of prominent feminists to American entry into the war and emphasized the incongruity of fighting a war for democracy while denying the vote to half the population. Before the war suffrage advocates argued that the vote could help women reform American society; now they contended that enfranchised women would help America reform the world. The moderate National American Woman Suffrage Association, under the leadership of Carrie Chapman Catt, orchestrated an effective lobbying campaign on Capitol Hill and in state capitals. While appealing largely to principle, the suffragists were not above tapping into public prejudice. "Every slacker has a vote," Catt told audiences. "Every newly made citizen will have a vote. Every pro-German . . . will have a vote. . . . It is a risk, a danger to a country like ours to send 1,000,000 men out of the country who are loyal and not replace those men by the loyal votes of women they have left at home."

At the same time, more radical feminists led by the Quaker activist Alice Paul formed the National Woman's Party (NWP). In January 1917 the NWP began picketing outside the White House. Over the next eighteen months thousands of women marched silently past the gates carrying banners that read, "How Long Must Women Wait for Liberty?" When police arrested the marchers, the protesters insisted on being treated as political prisoners and went on hunger strikes in jail. Wilson complained that the Women's Party seemed "bent on making their cause as obnoxious as possible." But the pressure worked. "My God," cried a New York politician, "we'd better do something to satisfy those hellions."

The combination of Paul's aggressive tactics, which generated a great deal of publicity, and Catt's lobbying, which won new converts, helped secure victory. The amendment sailed through the House in January 1918, but then languished in the Senate. During the summer of 1918 Wilson actively lobbied Senate Democrats, calling suffrage "an essential psychological element in the conduct of the war for democracy." In June 1919 the Senate narrowly passed the amendment. The following year, in August 1920, three-fourths of the states approved it. With the Nineteenth Amendment in place, women voted in a presidential election for the first time in 1920.

MAKING WAR AND PEACE, 1917–1919

While American soldiers helped secure victory on the battlefield, the president had a difficult time convincing both the Allies and the U.S. Senate to accept his liberal peace plan. At Versailles Wilson had to contend with the conservative agenda of French and British leaders determined to preserve their empires and to impose a harsh peace on Germany, and he also had to prevent Russian communism from threatening his liberal program. At home the bitter debate over U.S. entry into the League of Nations underscored the tension between internationalism and nationalism that shaped America's view of its role in the world.

"Days of Hell" The belief that U.S. involvement would be brief and limited encouraged American enthusiasm for the war. "They don't need more warriors," said the *New York Morning Telegraph* in April 1917; "they want money and food, and munitions of war." American leaders soon learned, however, that the plight of the Allies required a greater commitment. In April an Allied delegation to Washington outlined the desperate conditions. By 1917 Britain was on the verge of exhaustion. The Italian army was disintegrating. The Russians, who had suffered over 9 million casualties, appeared ready to quit the war effort.

In desperation the French and British asked Wilson to rush fresh troops to Europe to bolster Allied spirits and demoralize the enemy. "We want men, men, men," French Marshall Joseph Joffre begged. Responding to the request, the American First Division departed for combat in June 1917. By December two hundred thousand American soldiers were in Europe, stationed in "quiet" zones where they could train for future battles.

In March 1918 the Germans forced Russia out of the war, imposing a harsh peace in the Brest-Litovsk Treaty. In the south the Italians suffered a disastrous defeat at Caporetto, a village in Yugoslavia. With its eastern front secure, Germany launched a major western offensive, smashing through Allied lines. In shock and fear the Allies pleaded for American troops to cut short their training and enter combat. Wilson directed General John J. Pershing, the leader of the American Expeditionary Force (AEF), to allow American troops to be used as replacements in British and French units until Americans arrived in sufficient numbers to form an independent force.

In May Americans participated in a series of bloody battles at Belleau Wood to first blunt, and then repel, the German offensive. For twenty days, in what Private Hiram B. Pottinger called "days of hell," American marines stopped the German advance and slowly pushed the enemy back, all the time enduring withering machine-gun fire, exploding artillery shells, and deadly poison gas. In one day of fighting the Americans lost 1,087 men. Of the 8,000 marines who participated in the battle to recapture Belleau Wood, over 5,000 were killed or wounded. By July the Germans were retreating, their offensive quashed. "On the Eighteenth, even the most optimistic among us knew that all was lost," observed the German chancellor.

The American troops had helped turn the tide, but the war was not over. Between September 12 and 16 the American First Army, grown to six hundred thousand troops and fighting in concert with French forces, retook a strategically important rail junction south of Verdun. In two days they captured fifteen thousand prisoners at a cost of fewer than eight thousand casualties. Two weeks later 1.2 million American soldiers drove into the Argonne Forest. In forty days and nights of heavy fighting, they fought their way through the forest and the formidable defenses of the Hindenburg Line. To the west French and British forces staged similar drives. On November 1 the Allies broke through the German center and raced forward (see map below). As the western front crumbled, the German High Command pleaded for peace. "Open armistice negotiations as soon as possible," a general told Kaiser Wilhelm, the German monarch. The stalemate was over.

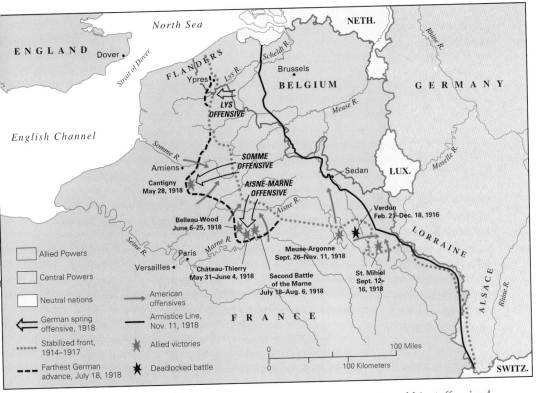

World War I, the Western Front   Although General John J. Pershing and his staff arrived in France June 13, 1917, American troops were not deployed into the heart of battle in large numbers until early 1918. The American battle at Cantigny proved the AEF could carry out its own operations and provided American troops across the western front a much-needed boost of confidence. American forces at the battles of Belleau Wood and Chateau-Thierry experienced the heavy casualties to which the other Allies had already become accustomed. Beginning with the Second Battle of the Marne, the Allies began to push the Germans back, with the final offensive at Meuse-Argonne.

American soldiers on the front were unprepared for the hardships of battle. They were forced to spend weeks in water-soaked trenches surrounded by decaying bodies and body parts and human and animal waste. Lice crawled on their bodies and rats patrolled the trenches, often nibbling on the toes and fingers of sleeping men. Many soldiers were traumatized by the sight of mangled, decaying bodies, the odors of poison gas and human excrement, and the cries of wounded comrades. Perhaps the most terrifying moments came with the prolonged head-splitting concussions of bombs. "To be shelled is the worst thing in the world," recalled a soldier. "There is a faraway moan that grows to a scream and then a roar like a train, followed by a ground-shaking smash and a diabolical red light."

How decisive was American involvement in World War I? In the nick of time, Winston Churchill later reflected, the Allies had gained "a new giant in the West to replace the dying titan of the East." The arrival of significant numbers of fresh American soldiers starting in mid-1918 tipped the balance decisively toward the Allies. On April 1, 1918, the Germans had a superiority of 324,000 infantrymen on the western front. By June American reinforcements had given the Allies a manpower majority. And by November the Allied preponderance was more than 600,000 men, enough to overwhelm the German defenses. "The American infantry in the Argonne [Forest] won the war," commented German Marshal Paul von Hindenburg.

Women at War   Thousands of American women traveled to France to serve the men in uniform as nurses and physicians with the Red Cross and the YMCA. In June 1918, two American mobile hospital units comprised of only women physicians and nurses landed in France to assist as well. While these women rarely worked on the front lines, their efforts in field hospitals provided vital services to Allied soldiers. This woman, with the Salvation Army, writes a letter home for a wounded American soldier. (*National Archives.*)

Negotiating the Peace Treaty

Wilson led the nation into war promising that a stable peace and a renewed international commitment to democracy would follow. The postwar settlement, he had declared, should be based on moral principle, not selfish interest. On January 8, 1918, Wilson outlined his vision of the postwar settlement in his Fourteen Points address to a joint session of Congress. Among his specific recommendations were calls for self-determination, freedom of the seas, open covenants (an end to secret agreements) among nations, free trade, and reduced spending on the military. The final and, for Wilson, most important point outlined "a general association of nations . . . [to guarantee] political independence and territorial integrity to great and small states alike."

An armistice that virtually disarmed Germany ended the fighting at the eleventh hour of the eleventh day of the eleventh month of 1918. The Americans had lost 48,909 men killed, with another 230,000 wounded. Losses to disease, mainly influenza, eventually ran the death total to over 112,000. The loss was small compared to the 1,700,000 Russians, 1,357,000 French, and 900,000 Britons who died.

In the final weeks of the war Wilson lured the Germans into overthrowing the kaiser and surrendering by promising them a peace based on the Fourteen Points. He then pressured the Allies into accepting the Fourteen Points, somewhat modified, as the basis for conducting the impending peace conference. Relishing his role as world leader, Wilson decided to head the American delegation to the treaty negotiations in Paris. On December 4, 1918, Wilson sailed from New York aboard the U.S.S. *George Washington*. Except for a few days in March 1919, he would remain abroad for almost six months. Enthusiastic crowds greeted the president and his call for a just peace when he arrived in Paris on December 13. "No one ever heard such cheers," observed a journalist.

The crowds loved him, but Wilson faced serious obstacles in his effort to create a new, stable world order based on American values. First, support for his peace program had eroded at home, at least in Congress, owing to a number of political blunders. During the 1918 congressional campaign Wilson asked the voters to elect Democrats who would support him in his global mission. The voters, concerned with domestic issues, particularly inflation, promptly elected Republican majorities to both houses of Congress. The outcome of the 1918 elections meant that any treaty Wilson brought back from Paris would have to be ratified by a Republican-controlled Senate. Wilson compounded his error by not including a prominent Republican in the five-man peace delegation he brought to France.

Second, the European leaders who greeted him in Paris shared little enthusiasm for Wilson's plan. Twenty-seven nations assembled in Paris, but most matters were decided among the leaders of four nations—the United States, Britain, France, and Italy. The European leaders, determined to punish the Germans and committed to maintaining control of their colonies, had little patience with Wilson's pleas for a just peace and self-determination. Referring to Wilson's peace plan, French Premier Georges Clemenceau said, "President Wilson and his Fourteen Points bore me. Even God Almighty has only ten!" Clemenceau and Prime Minister David Lloyd George of Britain were immovable in their resolve to impose a harsh settlement on Germany, securing punitive economic and territorial aims that they had secretly mapped out early in the war. The Italian delegate, Prime Minister Vittorio Orlando, was concerned primarily with gaining disputed territory for his country. The Japanese exerted pressure for further concessions in East Asia.

The specter of Bolshevism, or communism, also haunted the conference. While battling with the conservative ambitions of French and British allies who hoped to return Europe to its pre-1914 status—absent a powerful Germany—Wilson had to contend with the radical message of class revolution coming from the Soviet Union. In November 1917 V. I. Lenin led his Bolsheviks, or radical socialists, in toppling the Russian government. After seizing power, the Bolsheviks made peace with Germany, nationalized banks, placed factories under worker control, confiscated private property, and launched an attack on organized religion. Secretary of State Lansing observed that the Bolsheviks fundamentally challenged Western "political institutions as they now exist." The president feared that communism would appeal to millions of war-weary people around the globe, providing a radical alternative to his liberal agenda. "Bolshevism is gaining ground everywhere," a close White House adviser noted in his diary. "We are sitting upon an open powder magazine and some day a spark may ignite it."

The question facing the Allies in 1918 was how to deal with the Soviet threat. Wilson's friend, Ray Stannard Baker, observed that "Paris cannot be understood without Moscow." Even before the war was over, France and Britain favored military force to overthrow Lenin. Wilson, who privately complained about the "poison of Bolshevism," suggested that the only way to deal with the Soviets was "to open all the doors to commerce." Only after repeated requests from the Allies did the president choose, however reluctantly, to send American forces to northern Russia in the summer of 1918 to guard Allied military supplies sent before Russia had pulled out of the war. Despite Wilson's stated desire to avoid mingling in Soviet internal affairs, the troops provided assistance to an unsuccessful effort to overthrow the Bolshevik regime. The Western powers also imposed a strict economic blockade in an effort to cripple the Soviet government. The tactics ultimately backfired. After crushing their opposition, the Bolsheviks used the Allied intervention to arouse nationalist feelings in Russia.

The weight of the obstacles at home and abroad overwhelmed Wilson and prevented him from achieving the type of peace treaty he had envisioned. Throughout the long negotiating sessions, he compromised away parts of his Fourteen Points. He fought hard for decolonization and for self-determination, but he had to make many concessions to imperialism. The Versailles Treaty placed former German colonies in the Middle East and Africa in a mandate system that gave the French, British, and Japanese access to their resources. Japan assumed responsibility for Germany's holdings in China as well as many of its former Pacific island colonies. France occupied Germany's Rhineland, which abutted the French border. The treaty said nothing about freedom of the seas or lowering international economic barriers. The secret negotiating sessions at Versailles made a mockery of Wilson's call for "open covenants of peace openly arrived at." Most serious of all, the victors imposed a severe, vindictive penalty on Germany, forcing it to agree to pay reparations that would total $33 billion. The debates over reparations, noted American adviser Bernard Baruch, revealed the "blood-raw passions still pulsing through people's veins." By crippling the German economy, the treaty designed to end one great war planted the seeds of a second.

Wilson did not leave the conference empty-handed, however. The president achieved his central goal—a League of Nations for the postwar world. The heart of the League's covenant was Article X, the collective security provision. It provided for League members to "respect and preserve as against external aggression the territorial integrity and existing political independence" of all members. To enforce Article X, the delegates agreed to a security arrangement whereby all member nations were bound to defend each other against aggression.

The Fight over Ratification

While the peace conference was still in session, Republican Senator Henry Cabot Lodge of Massachusetts, a Harvard-educated patrician who chaired the Foreign Relations Committee, circulated a resolution signed by thirty-nine senators, more than enough votes to block ratification, stating that the League charter did not protect American national interests. Wilson responded by writing language into the League covenant that exempted the Monroe Doctrine (see page 318) and U.S. internal matters from League jurisdiction. The additions failed to satisfy Lodge, who introduced fourteen reservations, modifications that he wanted made in the League charter before he would approve the treaty. These reservations, designed to protect American sovereignty, included exempting U.S. immigration policy from League decisions and giving Congress the right to approve any League resolution that implemented Article X.

Wilson returned home with the flawed Versailles Treaty on July 8, 1919. Initially, the public responded favorably to the treaty. Thirty-two state legislatures and thirty-three governors endorsed the League, while a poll indicated that an overwhelming majority of the nation's newspapers held a similar opinion. Critics soon gained the upper hand, however. Many progressives attacked Wilson's betrayal of his Fourteen Points. "How in our consciences are we to square the results with the promises?" asked journalist Walter Lippmann. Senator La Follette said the treaty's provisions confirmed his view that World War I was nothing more than a struggle between rival imperialists. Isolationists feared that Article X would obligate the United States to provide armed forces to preserve collective security in every corner of the postwar world.

Senate Republicans presented Wilson with his biggest obstacle. The forty-nine Republican senators who opposed the treaty formed two distinct factions. The first group earned the name "Irreconcilables" because they opposed the treaty in any form and were determined to oppose it with or without reservations. They were joined by a second group of "Reservationists," led by Lodge, who were willing to support the treaty if Wilson included the added amendments. Both groups were troubled by the same questions. As Lodge asked, "Are you willing to put your soldiers and your sailors at the disposition of other nations?" Republicans also asked whether the terms of the treaty would require the United States to intervene to repress democratic movements in the British and French empires. "I am opposed to American boys policing Europe and quelling riots in every new nation's back yard," explained California progressive Hiram Johnson.

Wilson began to realize that the situation was passing out of his control, and he decided on bold steps. In September he set out on a cross-country speaking tour to rally public support for the treaty. He traveled more than 8,000 miles through the Midwest and Far West for three weeks and delivered some thirty-seven addresses. The strain began to take a toll on Wilson even before the tour was half over. He began to have blinding headaches and to show signs of exhaustion. Finally, after one

The Fate of the League of Nations   This cartoon reflects on the short life of Wilsonian ideals. Although the Treaty of Versailles on the whole disappointed Wilson, it did include one major victory, the creation of the League of Nations. However, on Wilson's return home, the Republican-dominated Senate burst even that "bubble" by revising the treaty to weaken the United States' role in the League. Wilson refused to support the amended treaty, and it went down to defeat.   *(National Archives.)*

of his longest and most important speeches at Pueblo, Colorado, on September 25, he collapsed. His physician then canceled the remaining speeches and ordered the presidential train to return to Washington. On October 2 Wilson suffered a stroke that paralyzed the left side of his face and body. For days his life hung in the balance.

In November 1919, shortly after Wilson suffered his stroke, Lodge reported out the treaty with fourteen reservations. Most Democratic supporters of the League seemed willing to accept Lodge's version. Most of the reservations made little difference, they pointed out, and even the modification of Article X was acceptable to the European powers. Had Wilson followed their advice, it is possible that the treaty would have passed. But Wilson, his concentration hampered and his stubbornness accentuated by the stroke, refused to compromise. Lodge's reservations, he insisted, removed America's all-important moral obligation. Before the votes were taken, the Senate Democratic floor leader, Gilbert Hitchcock, told the president that the treaty could not pass without reservations. He suggested that "It might be wise to compromise." Wilson responded curtly, "Let Lodge compromise!" Obstinately, he instructed his Democratic followers to hold firm, and on November 19 they joined the Irreconcilables in voting fifty-five to thirty-nine against the treaty with reservations. In March 1920 the treaty came up for another vote. A number of Democrats broke ranks and supported the revised treaty, but the vote, forty-nine to thirty-five, fell short of the necessary two-thirds majority needed for passage. "It is dead," Wilson told his cabinet.

The debate over American entry into the League exposed an old tension about America's role in the world. Wilson believed that America's long-term interests could best be protected through international collective security. Lodge and other opponents of the treaty tapped into both a strong sense of nationalism and a deep-seated American isolationism. Neither perspective, Wilson's nor Lodge's, offered the American people a realistic framework for understanding America's role in the twentieth-century world. Wilson may have appreciated the need to join forces with other nations, but his vision was hopelessly naive and self-righteous. Lodge expounded on the dangers of collective security but failed to offer a realistic alternative for defining and protecting American national interests. That unresolved debate between nationalism and internationalism would remain at the core of American experiments in foreign policy for the rest of the century. Unable to achieve a consensus, the United States lurched into the 1920s without a definitive foreign policy.

AN UNCERTAIN PEACE, 1919–1920

The summer and fall of 1919 were a tense, anxious time for many Americans. During the war Americans sanctioned a degree of government control over the economy that deviated from traditional economic individualism. "Never did the crust of civilization seem so thin," reflected a disillusioned progressive. "There is so much unrest. So much unreason, so much violence; so little sense!" Shocked by seeming threats to their social and economic traditions, Americans reacted to the turmoil by searching for scapegoats. Fear of social unrest combined with a growing concern about communist revolution produced one of the most repressive periods in American history. By 1920 progressivism had run its course. Americans, tired of Wilsonian idealism abroad and progressive reform at home, turned to the Republican Party, which promised a return to "normalcy."

Unsettled Times   As wounded soldiers returned home in 1918, they brought with them a deadly influenza epidemic that had already killed tens of thousands in Europe. By September the flu spread to the civilian population. About 20 million Americans fell ill during the winter of 1918–1919; over half a million died. More American soldiers died from the flu than were killed by enemy bullets. The flu created fear and panic in American cities, where many people resorted to wearing surgical masks to avoid the germs. Public facilities that could spread the flu—dance halls, phone booths, theaters, even some churches—were closed.

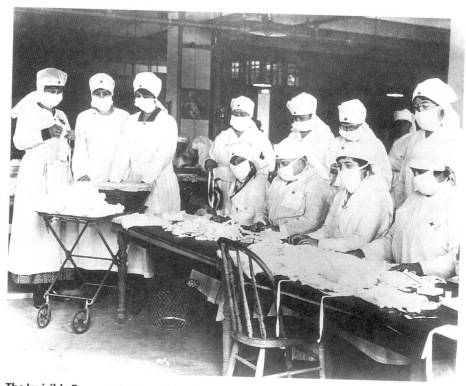

The Invisible Enemy   Of the 112,000 American soldiers who died in World War I, half were casualties of disease. Influenza was a particularly deadly killer; epidemics in 1918 on both sides of the Atlantic and at sea killed thousands of American soldiers and afflicted even more. Though some believed the German had introduced the disease as a form of warfare, the 186,000 German victims of the virus indicate otherwise. The epidemic did not just target soldiers—an estimated 20 million died worldwide from the disease. Here American Red Cross nurses make gauze masks for distribution, not only for soldiers but for members of their own communities. Health departments in cities across the country passed ordinances requiring citizens to wear the masks in public. *(Brown Bros.)*

An epidemic of racial violence also infected the United States following the war. African-American soldiers returned to their homes in the South emboldened by their experience in Europe. The two hundred thousand African-Americans who served overseas had tasted an equality unknown in their native South. "I'm glad I went," declared a black veteran. "I done my part and I'm going to fight right here till Uncle Sam does his." Du Bois observed a "new, radical Negro spirit" among veterans. The attitude of the "New Negro," he said, was "I ain't looking for trouble, but if it comes my way I ain't dodging." NAACP membership reached ten thousand by 1918 and was over sixty-two thousand by 1919.

Southerners viewed the new activism with alarm and moved to crush it. Ten black veterans, several of them still in uniform, were lynched in 1919; fourteen blacks were burned at the stake. Southern white terrorism also found expression in the rapid spread of the newly revived Ku Klux Klan.

The clash between African-American pride and white hostility was explosive. Beginning in July 1919 the nation experienced an outbreak of the most fearful race riots in American history. The first riot began in Longview, Texas, and a week later violence erupted in the nation's capital, where mobs composed principally of white servicemen pillaged the black section. The worst riot broke out in Chicago after an altercation between whites and blacks on a Lake Michigan beach. Mobs roamed the slum areas of the city for thirteen days, burning, pillaging, and killing. When it was all over, 15 whites and 23 blacks were dead; 178 whites and 342 blacks were injured; and more than 1,000 families were homeless. During the next two months, major riots broke out in Knoxville, Tennessee, Omaha, Nebraska, and Elaine, Arkansas. The final count by the end of 1919 revealed some twenty-five riots, with hundreds dead and injured and property damage running in the millions.

In addition to social and economic tensions, basic values seemed under assault. In September 1919, when the favored Chicago White Sox lost the World Series to the Cincinnati Reds, rumors circulated that Chicago players had thrown the game, taking payoffs from professional gamblers. A jury refused to convict them, but the commissioner of baseball banned the eight from the game for the rest of their lives. "Say it ain't so, Joe," a young fan pleaded with Chicago's star center fielder "Shoeless Joe" Jackson. "Yes, kid, I'm afraid it is," Jackson replied.

The rising cost of living added to postwar anxiety. The war ended before the administration could devise a plan for reconversion to a peacetime economy. Wilson lifted all price controls as soon as the war ended, but with contracts for war orders running until 1920, the supply of goods fell far short of the demand. Prices shot up as consumers scrambled for scarce products. In 1919 the consumer price index rose by 77 percent over the 1916 level. In August 1919 the *Washington Post* called rising prices "the burning domestic issue."

Released from their no-strike pledges, labor leaders fought to make sure that wages kept up with the spiraling inflation. There were more strikes in 1919 than in any other year in American history: more than 4 million workers—about 20 percent of the industrial work force—walked off their jobs in 2,665 strikes. In January 1919 shipyard workers in Seattle went on strike. When laborers in other trades joined them, it appeared for a few days that a general strike of a hundred thousand people might paralyze the region. The mayor denounced the general strike as an attempt "to duplicate the anarchy of Russia." Public reaction was hostile. "The strike is Marxian," cried the *Los Angeles Times*. The strike collapsed in nine days.

Fears of public disorder rose again in September 1919 when three-quarters of Boston's fifteen hundred policemen went on strike. Wilson called the walkout a "crime against civilization." For a few days, the streets of Boston belonged to rioters and looters. Boston newspapers branded the striking policemen as "agents of Lenin." The governor of Massachusetts, an obscure Republican politician named Calvin Coolidge, called out the Massachusetts National Guard, which restored order and broke the strike. "There is no right to strike against the public safety by anyone, anytime, any where," Coolidge declared.

The Red Scare   To many Americans, the greatest threat seemed to come from Russia, where the Bolsheviks had proclaimed their dedication to worldwide revolution. In 1919 the Soviets established the Comintern to promote world revolution, and in the same year radical socialists formed two Communist parties in the United States. Communist uprisings occurred and failed in Hungary and Germany. Nervous Americans, aware that a small, disciplined band of revolutionaries had come to power in Russia, worried that revolution might find a foothold in the United States.

Thus many Americans were certain that revolution was at hand when more than thirty-six homemade bombs, timed to go off on May Day, were delivered to unsuspecting targets. Among the intended victims were John D. Rockefeller, Postmaster General Burleson, and Seattle's mayor Ole Hanson. "Reds Planned May Day Murders," headlines screamed. On June 2 bombs exploded in eight American cities at the same hour; one damaged the home of Attorney General A. Mitchell Palmer.

Although only a small number of radicals were involved in these plots, the bombings unnerved Americans, who responded by lashing out at potential enemies. Sensational newspaper reports magnified the events and stimulated widespread public alarm. In May 1919 an enraged sailor shot and killed a man for not standing during the playing of "The Star-Spangled Banner." According to press reports, "The crowd burst into cheering and handclapping" following the shooting. In February a jury in Hammond, Indiana, deliberated for two minutes before acquitting a man for killing an alien who had shouted, "To Hell with the United States." Some four hundred soldiers and sailors invaded the offices of the *New York Call*, a Socialist daily, and beat up several May Day celebrants. In other parts of New York, and in Boston and Cleveland, May Day paraders clashed with servicemen and police.

A. Mitchell Palmer, who had been appointed attorney general in March 1919, stepped forward to save America from communist revolution. A former congressman from Pennsylvania with solid progressive credentials, Palmer had opposed wartime repression of civil liberties. But he also possessed a genuine fear of Bolshevism and planned to ride the red tide into the White House in 1920. Claiming that America was in imminent peril of revolution, Palmer hired a young lawyer named J. Edgar Hoover to direct a new Bureau of Investigation. Hoover placed thousands of people in many organizations under surveillance.

In November, using information provided by Hoover, Palmer staged raids on radicals in twelve cities, seizing files, breaking up machines and furniture, and arresting 250 people. In December the government deported 249 aliens, including the veteran anarchist Emma Goldman (see page 826), to Russia. A month later Palmer's men arrested more than 4,000 alleged communists in one night of raids in thirty-three cities. Many of the suspects were held in filthy, overcrowded jail cells without food or water. They were prevented from talking with family or lawyers. The raids were justified, Palmer said, because the country was infested with the "moral perverts and hysterical neurasthenic women who abound in communism."

The Red Scare subsided almost as quickly as it had started. In April 1920 Palmer warned of a series of radical activities planned for the anniversary of the 1919 mail bombings. When the day passed without incident, newspapers ridiculed Palmer, dismissing him as a modern-day Chicken Little squawking that the sky was falling. By midsummer 1920 most of the conditions that fed the fear of radicalism had dissipated. Labor agitation had been quashed, and American radicals had split into warring factions of socialists, communists, and communist laborites. Most important, Americans relaxed as the threat of Bolshevism in Europe subsided. By September Americans refused to respond to Palmer's proclamation of impending revolution even after a wagonload of bombs exploded on Wall Street, killing thirty-three and injuring two hundred. Presidential candidate Warren Harding, no radical, pronounced the epitaph: "Too much has been said about Bolshevism in America."

The cruel and high-handed treatment of dissenters during 1919 and 1920 marked the most widespread peacetime attack on civil liberties in American history. And it profoundly discouraged people who might otherwise have worked for reform. Frederic Howe, the immigration commissioner who fought deportations, confessed that his faith in public power as an agent of reform had been misplaced. "My attitude toward the state," he wrote later, "was changed as a result of these experiences. I have never been able to bring it back. I became distrustful of the state."

The Election of 1920

The presidential campaign of 1920 revealed America's disenchantment with progressive reforms and Wilsonian idealism. Over the previous eight years Wilson had managed to alienate large groups of voters. Irish-Americans and German-Americans resented his support of the British. Industrialists and businessmen rebelled against higher taxes and government regulation. Meanwhile, die-hard reform-minded progressives were angry over the Palmer raids and the harsh peace treaty. "The country," said the *New York Tribune*, "was weary of Wilsonianism in all its manifestations."

With Wilson no longer a viable candidate, Democrats struggled over which new face should lead the party. At the convention, forces of Wilson's son-in-law and secretary of the treasury, William G. McAdoo, and Attorney General Palmer fought to a standstill for thirty-seven wearying ballots before Ohio Governor James M. Cox was nominated on the forty-fourth roll call on July 5. As his running mate, Cox chose the assistant secretary of the navy and prominent Wilsonian, Franklin D. Roosevelt of New York. Wilson wanted his party to make the election a "solemn referendum" on the League of Nations. Party leaders, showing more sensitivity to public opinion, only reluctantly embraced the League.

The eager Republicans smelled victory in 1920. The front-runner, General Leonard Wood, inherited most of the following of Theodore Roosevelt, who had died in 1919. Other candidates were Governor Frank O. Lowden of Illinois, Senator Hiram W. Johnson of California, Herbert Hoover, and a number of favorite sons, including the nondescript Senator Warren G. Harding of Ohio. When the Wood and Lowden forces deadlocked at the Republican convention in June 1920, the party's Old Guard selected Harding. For vice president, the convention nominated Governor Calvin Coolidge of Massachusetts police strike fame. The platform roundly repudiated Wilsonianism. It condemned Wilson's League but approved membership in the World Court and international agreements to preserve peace. It promised a return to traditional GOP domestic policies—high tariffs and low taxes—and an end to further federal social legislation. Finally, it pledged to support restrictions on immigration and aid to farmers.

Harding captured the mood of the times when he told a Boston audience, "America's present need is not heroics, but healing; not nostrums, but normalcy; not revolution, but restoration; not agitation, but adjustment; not surgery, but serenity; not the dramatic, but the dispassionate; not experiment, but equipoise; not submergence in internationality, but sustainment in triumphant nationality." A critic sniped that Harding's speeches "left the impression of an army of pompous phrases moving over the landscape in search of an idea."

Harding's speeches may not have impressed critics, but his call for a "return to normalcy" struck a chord with voters. The result was a smashing electoral triumph. "It wasn't just a landslide," said a politician, "it was an earthquake." Harding won all the states outside the South, for an electoral vote of 404; and he even broke the Solid South by carrying Tennessee. Cox came away with only 127 electoral votes (see map below). The Republicans' sweep in the senatorial and congressional contests gave them a commanding majority of 22 seats in the Senate and 167 in the House.

The election signaled an important shift in the public mood. The war disillusioned a generation of progressives who had shared Wilson's idealistic dream of

The Election of 1920   With World War I and the fierce battle over the Treaty of Versailles behind them, many Americans agreed with Republican candidate Warren G. Harding's call for a return to "normalcy." Republicans spent most of the campaign attacking the policies of Woodrow Wilson rather tan attacking the platform of the Democratic candidate, James Cox, who failed to emerge from the ailing president's shadows, even losing the traditionally Democratic stronghold of Tennessee.

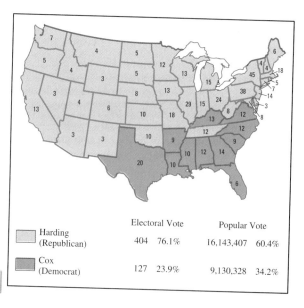

	Electoral Vote		Popular Vote	
Harding (Republican)	404	76.1%	16,143,407	60.4%
Cox (Democrat)	127	23.9%	9,130,328	34.2%

"making the world safe for democracy." The war had exposed progressivism's vulnerability. In the words of William Allen White, Americans in 1920 were "tired of issues, sick at heart of ideals, and weary of being noble."

CONCLUSION

When war broke out in Europe in 1914, America still embraced its traditional isolationism, and many Americans hoped the country would remain neutral. Many progressives feared entry into the war would set back reform efforts, and Americans of German and Irish heritage felt little sympathy for Britain. Most important, America's global role made true neutrality impossible. The United States had close cultural and commercial ties to the Allies, and a number of key members of the Wilson administration made clear they preferred a British victory. The British navy's domination of the seaways strangled U.S. trade with Germany, belying U.S. claims of neutrality. German use of U-boats to attack civilian ships further tested the limits of American neutrality.

Through it all, Wilson called for a policy of "strict neutrality," insisting that Americans had the right to travel safely on the passenger ships of belligerent nations. When Germany, convinced it could score a decisive blow against the Allies before the United States could mobilize, announced that it would begin unrestricted submarine warfare in the Atlantic, Wilson's policy left him no choice but to ask Congress for a declaration of war.

Once war was declared, Congress gave the president broad powers to regulate the economy and restrict individual liberty. Washington seized control of the railroads, regulated the production and distribution of food, dramatically increased the tax base, and created the War Industries Board (WIB) to coordinate the conversion to military production. To forge a sense of national unity, the administration created the Committee on Public Information (CPI). When propaganda failed, Wilson resorted to coercive measures to compel loyalty. Armed with wartime legislation banning dissent, Postmaster General Albert Burleson led a crusade to identify and imprison suspected subversives. Patriotic appeals also helped progressives achieve two major victories: passage of constitutional amendments to ban alcohol and give women the right to vote. World War I succeeded, where the progressive experiment had failed, in broadening the scope of government.

Having entered the war to shape the peace, Wilson offered the world a liberal plan based on his Fourteen Points, which included self-determination for all people, open covenants among nations, free trade, demilitarization, and a League of Nations. The president proposed his plan as an alternative both to the traditional European balance of power politics and to the new radical ideas emanating from the Soviet Union. Wilson had to compromise most of the Fourteen Points during the writing of the Versailles Treaty. In a stunning blow to Wilson's ambition to shape the postwar world, the Senate refused to approve U.S. entry into the League of Nations. The United States returned to the isolationism it had practiced before the war.

War's end found little peace at home. A massive influenza epidemic swept across the country. As the economy slowed and inflation soared, millions of workers struck for better labor conditions. African-Americans, encouraged by their employment gains and military service during the war, called for fair treatment—to which the white mainstream reacted with a series of bloody race riots. Fearful of the new "red" menace in the Soviet Union, government officials expanded the wartime restrictions on individual rights.

By 1920 many Americans were tired of the unrest and upheaval that had characterized the Wilson years. Disenchanted with social and international experimentation, the public gave a landslide victory to Republican Warren G. Harding, who called for a return to "normalcy." As the war experience faded, Americans turned away from the affairs of other nations and hoped to find peace and stability through their traditional political and social values.

Annotated Suggested Readings

Niall Ferguson's *The Pity of War* (2000) offers a provocative revisionist interpretation of the European origins of the war. John Ellis offers the most in-depth analysis of the horrors of trench warfare in *Eye Deep in Hell* (1989). From the American perspective, David M. Kennedy's *Over Here* (1980) is the most comprehensive one-volume study of the war's impact on domestic life. Ronald Schaffer argues in *America in the Great War* (1991) that America's involvement in World War I sparked the rise of the welfare state and promoted progressive reforms. Robert Ferrell's *Woodrow Wilson and World War I* (1985) provides a detailed survey of the war at home and abroad. Meirion and Susie Harries's *Last Days of Innocence* (1997) details the relationship between the war and American society. Neil A. Wynn's *From Progressivism to Prosperity* (1986) links the war years with currents from the Progressive Era and developments in the 1920s. Ellis W. Hawley argues that World War I was a turning point for modern societies in *The Great War and the Search for Modern Order* (1979).

Ernest R. May's *The World War and American Isolation* (1966) chronicles the shift from neutrality to intervention. John Coogan examines the shift in popular attitudes toward intervention in *The End to Neutrality* (1981). In *Spreading the American Dream* (1982), Emily Rosenberg focuses on the ideological support for American intervention. Ross Gregory's *The Origins of American Intervention in the First World War* (1971) is a detailed one-volume survey of the forces pushing for intervention. John Whiteclay Chambers, Jr., details the history of the draft in *To Raise an Army* (1987). Paul Chapman covers the rise of intellectual testing in *Schools as Sorters* (1988), while Allan Brandt describes the campaign against venereal disease in *No Magic Bullet* (1985). The work of the Commission on Training Camp Activities in providing wholesome recreation for conscripted troops is the focus of Nancy Bristow's *Making Men Moral* (1996).

Robert D. Cuff's *The War Industries Board* (1973) provides a representative study of war mobilization. Kathleen Burk studies the industrial cooperation across the Atlantic in *Britain, America and the Sinews of War* (1985). Valerie Jean Conner explores the government's policies toward labor in *The National War Labor Board* (1983). The effects of World War I on publicists and journals that promoted the progressive movement is the theme of John A. Thompson's *Reformers and War* (1987).

Maurine W. Greenwald's *Women, War and Work* (1980) analyzes the war's impact on women in the economy. Susan Zeiger's *In Uncle Sam's Service* (2004) explores the reasons why women joined the war effort. Barbara Steinson evaluates women's social and political contributions to the war effort in *American Women's Activism in World War I* (1982).

The work of women in traditionally male occupations is compared to that of women during World War II in Carrie Brown's *Rosie's Mom* (2002). The role of women in protesting the war is examined in Kathleen Kennedy's *Disloyal Mothers and Scurrilous Citizens* (1999). The best sources on the suffragist movement are David Morgan's *Suffragists and Democrats* (1972) and Rebecca J. Mead's *How the Vote Was Won* (2004). Joe William Trotter, Jr., collects several essays on the African-American experience of World War I in *The Great Migration in Historical Perspective* (1991).

Stephen Vaughan examines the efforts to promote national unity in *Holding Fast the Inner Lines* (1980). Alfred E. Cornbise focuses on the "Four-Minute Men" in *War as Advertised* (1984). Michael Pearlman explores the vigilante preparedness committees in *To Make Democracy Safe for America* (1984). The plight of German-Americans during the war is covered in Frederick Luebke's *Bonds of Loyalty* (1974). The civil liberties issues raised by mobilization are examined in Paul L. Murphy's *World War I and the Origin of Civil Liberties* (1979).

Edward M. Coffman's *The War to End All Wars* (1968) is a solid overview of the World War I armed forces, as is the more recent work of John Keegan, *The First World War* (2000). Laurence Stallings focuses on the battlefront experience in *The Doughboys* (1963), which is also the foundation of Byron Farwell's *Over There* (1999). Mark Meigs's *Optimism at Armageddon* (1997) describes the war through the words of American soldiers. Dorothy Schneider and Carl J. Schneider document the work of American women who served in the war in *Into the Breach* (1991), while A. E. Barbeau and Florette Henri chronicle the experience of black soldiers in *The Unknown Soldiers* (1974).

N. Gordon Levin, Jr., *Woodrow Wilson and World Politics* (1968), documents Woodrow Wilson's reaction to the Bolshevik revolution and his role at Versailles. Arthur Link's *Woodrow Wilson: Revolution, War, and Peace* (1979) and Arthur Walworth's *Wilson and His Peacemakers* (1986) describe Wilson's efforts to create world order around principles of self-determination and democracy. Ralph A. Stone provides a blow-by-blow account of the Senate fight over the League of Nations in *The Irreconcilables* (1970). Thomas Knock's *To End All Wars* (1992) emphasizes the role of ideology in Wilson's approach to peacemaking. A more recent work that studies the failure of the Senate to ratify the treaty is Herbert Margulies's *The Mild Reservationists and the League of Nations* (1989). The Russian intervention is covered in Peter Filene's *Americans and the Soviet Experiment* (1967); and more recently in *Russian Sideshow* (2003) by Robert Willett.

William M. Tuttle, Jr., *Race Riot* (1970), offers a tragic account of the Chicago race riot of 1919. James R. Grossman's *Land of Hope* (1989) also has good material on postwar race relations. The strikes of 1919 and antilabor sentiment are the subjects of Burl Nogle's *Into the Twenties* (1974). Robert K. Murray's *Red Scare* (1955) is still the best study of the Bolshevik revolution's impact on domestic politics.

The History Companion

National Security Versus Individual Liberty

Schenck v. U.S., 1919

In 1917 Charles Schenck, the general secretary of the Socialist Party, mailed fifteen thousand leaflets to conscription-age men, urging them to resist the draft. Shortly thereafter, he was arrested and charged with obstructing the war effort in violation of the Espionage Act of 1917. Schenck appealed his conviction, arguing that the act violated the freedoms of speech and the press protected by the First Amendment. In a unanimous decision, the Court upheld both Schenck's conviction and the constitutionality of the Espionage and Sedition Acts. Writing the Court's decision, Justice Oliver Wendell Holmes outlined the "clear and present danger" clause: individual rights could be constrained, he argued, when their exercise posed a direct and unmistakable threat to national survival.

The document in question upon its first printed side recited the first section of the Thirteenth Amendment, said that the idea embodied in it was violated by the Conscription Act and that a conscript is little better than a convict. In impassioned language it intimated that conscription was despotism in its worse form and a monstrous wrong against humanity in the interest of Wall Street's chosen few. It said, "Do not submit to intimidation" but, in form at least, confined itself to peaceful measures such as a petition for the repeal of the act. The other and later-printed side of the sheet was headed "Assert Your Rights." It stated reasons for alleging that any one violated the Constitution when he refused to recognize "your right to assert your opposition to the draft.". . . Of course the document would not have been sent unless it had been intended to have some effect, and we do not see what effect it could be expected to have upon persons subject to the draft except to influence them to obstruct the carrying of it out. . . .

But it is said, suppose that that was the tendency of this circular, it is protected by the First Amendment to the Constitution. . . . We admit that in many places and in ordinary times the defendants in saying all that was said in the circular would have been within their constitutional rights. But the character of every act depends upon the circumstances in which it is done. . . . The most stringent protection of free speech would not protect a man in falsely shouting fire in a theatre and causing a panic. . . . The question in every case is whether the words used are used in such circumstances and are of such a nature as to create a clear and present danger that they will bring about the substantive evils that Congress has a right to prevent. It is a question of proximity and degree. When a nation is at war, many things that might be said in time of peace are such a hindrance to its effort that their utterance will not be endured so long as men fight and that no Court could regard them as protected by any constitutional right. . . . The statute of 1917 in §4 punishes conspiracies to obstruct as well as actual obstruction. If the act, . . . its tendency and the intent with which it is done are the same, we perceive no ground for saying that success alone warrants making the act a crime. . . . Judgments affirmed.

Address to the Jury, 1917

On June 15, 1917, federal marshals raided the joint offices of Emma Goldman's *Mother Earth* magazine and Alexander Berkman's labor newspaper, *The Blast.* Goldman and Berkman were charged with conspiring to obstruct the conscription effort. After President Wilson signed the Draft Bill in May 1917, Berkman and Goldman printed and distributed a hundred thousand copies of a "No-Conscription Manifesto." Goldman and Berkman acted as their own attorneys during their trial. In her summation to the jury, Goldman pleaded with the jury to remember that speaking in opposition to the war effort did not by itself make one a conspirator.

Gentlemen of the jury, we respect your patriotism. . . . But may there not be different kinds of patriotism as there are different kinds of liberty? I for one cannot believe that love of one's country must consist in blindness to its social faults . . . neither can I believe that the mere accident of birth in a certain country or the mere scrap of a citizen's paper constitutes the love of country.

I know many people—I am one of them—who were not born here, nor have they applied for citizenship, and who yet love America with deeper passion and greater intensity than many natives whose patriotism manifests itself by pulling, kicking, and insulting those who do not rise when the national anthem is played. Our patriotism is that of the man who loves a woman with open eyes. He is enchanted by her beauty, yet he sees her faults. So we, too, who know America, love her beauty, her richness, her great possibilities—above all we love the people that have produced her wealth, her artists who have created beauty, her great apostles who dream and work for liberty— but with the same passionate emotion we hate her superficiality, her cant, her corruption, her mad, unscrupulous worship at the altar of the Golden Calf.

We say that if America has entered the war to make the world safe for democracy, she must first make democracy safe in America. How else is the world to take America seriously, when democracy at home is daily being outraged, free speech suppressed, peaceable assemblies broken up by overbearing and brutal gangsters in uniform; when free press is curtailed and every independent opinion gagged. Verily, poor as we are in democracy, how can we give of it to the world? . . .

The District Attorney has dragged in our Manifesto, and he has emphasized the passage, "Resist conscription." [A]dmitting that the Manifesto contains [that] expression . . . is there only one kind of resistance? Is there only the resistance which means the gun, the bayonet, the bomb or flying machine? Is there not another kind of resistance? May not the people simply fold their hands and declare, "We will not fight when we do not believe in the necessity of war"? May not the people who believe in the repeal of the Conscription law, because it is unconstitutional, express their opposition in word and by pen, in meetings and in other ways?

Total war was a new thing to America in 1917. Not even the Civil War had required the degree of mobilization that seemed necessary to fight in World War I. Americans had watched the fighting in Europe for three years and had seen the massive, intrusive government agencies that the combatants had made to oversee the war effort. The Wilson administration was determined not to create such an apparatus. Instead, Wilson decided to persuade Americans to voluntarily contribute work and money for the mobilization. Ironically, it was this effort to avoid government coercion that gave birth to the massive violations of civil liberties.

Through the propaganda of the Committee on Public Information, the Wilson administration stressed the need for unity and national security. Yet because the system Wilson devised was not coercive, it had no way to prevent the excesses of patriotic citizens. The federal government did not have to work hard to violate people's rights; in the mania that gripped the country during the war, private citizens were happy to do the violating themselves.

Justice Holmes's opinion in the *Schenck* case can be interpreted in light of these feelings. The "clear and present danger" clause Holmes outlined is not itself a threat to civil liberties. Its application to Schenck, however, was controversial. Was Schenck shouting "Fire!" in a crowded theater? Or was he rather standing outside a theater, telling people not to enter because of a fire inside? Such criticism, though, missed the more fundamental argument in Holmes's decision: the standard by which we judge threats to national security is different in war than in peacetime.

Emma Goldman never accepted Holmes's argument. Goldman questioned whether total national unity was necessary even to fight a major war. The damage done by Wilson's repression to American democratic institutions, she argued, would be far greater than that done to the war effort. Was the United States willing to make that sacrifice?

National security and individual liberty are often opposed to each other and usually exist in delicate balance. In 1917 Wilson upset the balance between these two values. The government restricted rights as though America's survival was threatened, but America had not been attacked. The Wilson administration treated skepticism and public dissent like threats to national safety.

While the Committee on Public Information demanded total unity, Emma Goldman and other thinkers developed a more nuanced conception of loyalty and love of country. Goldman placed love of a people above loyalty to a government and suggested that following government orders, if they were against the public interest, was foolish. In such a case, she said, it is one's patriotic duty to oppose the government.

Both Holmes's new, intensified conception of loyalty and Goldman's new, subtler defense of disloyalty have become features of American politics. Their clash of ideals presaged the Red Scares of the 1920s and the 1950s. The public hysteria of World War I offers a lesson about national emergencies: perception of a threat can be more important than actual danger in shaping public behavior.

QUESTIONS FOR ANALYSIS

1. Why does Schenck cite the Thirteenth Amendment in his leaflet?

2. According to Holmes, why are Schenck's actions not protected under the First Amendment?

3. What constitutes a conspiracy for Holmes?

4. How does Goldman define love of country?

5. What does Goldman find lacking in American democracy?

6. How does Goldman propose to resist the government?

7. Goldman spoke almost two years before Holmes's decision. Did she anticipate any of his arguments?

8. Is Holmes justified in restricting rights in wartime? To what degree?

24

The New Era

1920–1928

Many Americans marveled at the benefits of a modern industrialized society that made transatlantic flights and other amusements possible, even as they clung tenaciously to the values of rugged individualism deeply rooted in the nation's agricultural past.

On May 20, 1927, an early morning fog had settled over Long Island's Roosevelt Field, but the weather did little to dampen the spirits of the hundreds of spectators lining the runway, who had gathered in the predawn hours to witness aviation history. At 7:42 A.M. Charles Lindbergh, a twenty-five-year-old airmail pilot, climbed into his cramped single-engine plane, the *Spirit of St. Louis*. Equipped with the latest in aviation technology and burdened with 450 gallons of gasoline, the plane lurched down the muddy runway. It hopped into the air only to bounce back to the ground. With only a few thousand feet of runway left, the plane finally climbed into the sky, clearing telephone wires at the end of the runway by a few feet. Lindbergh's destination: Paris.

Lindbergh would not be the first person to fly across the Atlantic, but his flight from New York to Paris would be 400 miles longer than any before and, most important, he was doing it alone. Shortly after sunrise on the twenty-sixth hour of his flight he spotted a fishing boat. "Which way to Ireland?" he shouted to the men below. Next came the coast of England, and finally, France, "like an outstretched hand to meet me." It was 10 P.M. in Paris when Lindbergh picked out the floodlights showing the edge of a runway at Le Bourget airport. Thirty-three and a half hours after leaving New York, he circled the Eiffel Tower and set the *Spirit of St. Louis* down as an enthusiastic crowd of a hundred thousand rushed to greet him.

America erupted in celebration on hearing the news that Lindbergh had safely completed the 3,610-mile journey. President Coolidge decorated him with the Distinguished Flying Cross and awarded him the rank of colonel in the army reserves.

Several days later in New York City more than 4 million people lined the streets to shower their hero with confetti and ticker tape. Advertisers offered him hundreds of thousands of dollars to endorse their new consumer products.

The outpouring of affection and adulation that Lindbergh's feat inspired highlighted the intense cultural conflict of the decade. Many Americans marveled at the benefits of a modern industrialized society that made transatlantic flights and other amusements possible, even as they clung tenaciously to the values of rugged individualism deeply rooted in the nation's agricultural past. Lindbergh was a product of the new machine age, but the plainspoken, clean-cut aviator also seemed to represent a simpler America. Americans refused to see his flight as a triumph of technology. Rather it was a pioneering personal accomplishment, affirming the importance of traditional values from which Americans drew their identity—individualism, hard work, and self-sacrifice—that seemed suddenly vulnerable in a more complex and mechanized world. Charles Lindbergh, observed a contemporary, "has shown us that we are not rotten at the core, but morally sound and sweet and good."

The same confused reaction characterized America's response to other changes in the 1920s. Technological breakthroughs led to the production of a host of new products and the beginning of a consumer society. Many young urbanites rebelled against the older order of things. Young men and women challenged Victorian values. African-Americans trumpeted a sense of nationalism and pride in their heritage. Confronted by these and other extraordinary changes, many Americans tightened their grips on the past. The growth of the Ku Klux Klan, the rise of fundamentalism, and support for immigration restriction and Prohibition revealed traditional America's desire to preserve the past against the onslaught of social experimentation.

- Why is the decade of the twenties called the "New Era"?

- What was at issue in the cultural clash that characterized the 1920s?

- Who were the contestants in the struggle?

- What trends in national politics reflected the era's tensions?

This chapter will address these questions.

THE MODERN AGE

People living during the 1920s marveled at the extraordinary changes they witnessed. Experimentation and drive led to advances in technology and the development of new consumer goods that fueled a growing economy, though not everyone shared equally in the prosperity. The communications revolution, which began breaking down regional and class barriers, helped erect the scaffolding of a national culture. Little wonder that contemporaries referred to the 1920s as the "New Era."

The New Economy   World War I had inspired a brief business boom, which was then followed by a recession that lasted until 1921, when the economy again began to heat up. Between 1922 and 1929 every index of economic growth measured impressive gains. Not even a

CHRONOLOGY

1915	Ku Klux Klan revived
1917	Garvey founds Universal Negro Improvement Association
1920	KDKA covers presidential race in nation's first radio broadcast League of Women Voters organized Fitzgerald publishes *This Side of Paradise* Prohibition begins Harding elected president
1921	Farm bloc organized in Congress National Woman's Party founded Washington Conference on naval disarmament
1922	Lewis publishes *Babbitt*
1923	Harding dies; Coolidge becomes president
1924	Green becomes AFL president Johnson-Reed Immigration Act passed Coolidge elected president Dawes Plan rescues postwar Germany
1925	Scopes trial
1926	Hemingway publishes *The Sun Also Rises*
1927	Lindbergh flies nonstop to Paris Sacco and Vanzetti executed
1928	Kellogg-Briand Pact Hoover elected president

mild recession in 1924 could stem the remarkable surge. The national income rose from $63.1 billion to $87.8 billion. The gross national product grew from $74.1 billion to $103.1 billion. The nation's manufacturing output increased by more than 60 percent. Unemployment remained below 4 percent while inflation never topped 1 percent. By the end of the decade, most Americans were working fewer hours, producing more goods, and earning fatter paychecks. Between 1920 and 1930 factory workers saw their hours decrease from 47.4 per week to 42.1, and their wages increase by about 11 percent.

A number of changes contributed to the new prosperity. Technological innovations improved manufacturing efficiency and yielded new products. Advances in technology allowed for the mass production of manufactured goods at reduced cost. In 1913 Henry Ford had opened the first moving assembly line for manufacturing his Model T automobile, known affectionately as the Tin Lizzie. In 1927 he perfected the assembly line at his River Rouge plant in Michigan. The assembly line, which succeeded by "taking the work to the men instead of the men to the work," emphasized uniformity, speed, and precision that produced high profits for manufacturers and low prices for consumers. The assembly line cut the amount of time it took Ford workers to build a car from twelve and a half hours to sixty seconds. Soon the assembly line became a standard feature in American factories and the key to American industrial supremacy.

Streamlined factories began to run on new power sources and to produce new products. During the decade the electric motor replaced the steam engine as the chief source of power. By the end of the decade almost half of the nation's manufacturing plants were powered by electricity. In 1912 only 16 percent of U.S. households had access to electricity; by 1927 that figure had soared to 63 percent. Electricity, in turn, opened up a vast market for home appliances. Americans were bombarded with new devices and gadgets that changed the daily habits of millions: refrigerators, radios, washing machines, automatic ovens, vacuum cleaners, electric toasters. The number of telephones doubled to over 20 million between 1915 and 1929. "What an age," declared a journalist. "Machines that think. Lights that pierce fog. . . . Vending machines to replace salesmen. . . . The list of modern marvels is practically endless."

It was the phenomenal growth of the automobile industry, however, that provided the keystone for the prosperity of the 1920s. The automobile's impact on the economy was similar to the railroad's impact in the late nineteenth century. By the end of the decade more than half of all American families owned a car. New York City alone had more cars than the entire continent of Europe. One of every eight U.S. workers was employed in an automobile-related job. According to one estimate, the industry was responsible for the employment of nearly 4 million workers in 1929. Fifteen percent of all steel and 80 percent of all rubber went into the production of automobiles. By 1925 local and state governments were spending over $1 billion on roads, parkways, bridges, and tunnels to handle the explosion in traffic—the second-highest public expenditure after education. When asked to explain the changes taking place in Muncie, Indiana, during the 1920s, an older resident responded, "I can tell you what's happening in just four letters: A-U-T-O!"

The car gave Americans new mobility. Paved roads helped establish a wider sense of community, connecting small towns with larger cities, bringing people who had lived in geographic isolation in touch with a larger universe. By the end of the decade about one-fifth of America's 3 million miles of roads were paved. Florida built the Tamiami Trail through the swampy Everglades; Arizona paved a road through the desert west of Phoenix; and Massachusetts carved the Mohawk Trail out of the Hoosac mountain range. By 1928 a driver could travel on hard-surfaced roads from New York to Kansas. The nation witnessed a number of "firsts" as the landscape changed to accommodate the new technology: the first "mo-tel" (in San Luis Obispo, California, 1925), the first traffic lights (New York City, 1922), the first road atlas (1924), and the first parking garage (Detroit, 1929).

The automobile allowed people to escape crowded cities for the more spacious suburbs. For the first time, suburbs (defined as residential areas outside the core city but within the larger metropolitan region) grew at a faster pace than the nation's central cities. The borough of Queens, across the East River from New York City's business district on Manhattan Island, doubled its population in the 1920s. Suburbs

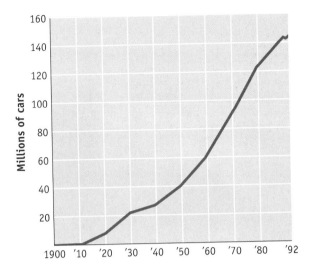

The Automobile Age In the 1920s, mass production decreased the price of cars and enabled increasing numbers of Americans to purchase their own. The chart, which traces the tremendous rise of registered passenger cars in the United States, also suggests the growing significance of the automobile in American's daily lives.

surrounding Detroit and Chicago grew by over 700 percent in ten years. By 1930 nearly one in six Americans lived in the suburbs. Most Americans applauded the suburban trend, which made attractive neighborhoods available to ordinary citizens. Signs of future trouble, however, began to simmer: the suburbs drained talent and resources from the inner cities, intensified race and class divisions, and wreaked havoc on the local environment.

The suburban boom was part of an unprecedented demand for new housing that followed World War I as returning veterans swarmed to the cities. Between 1920 and 1930 the population of Miami, Florida, ballooned from 29,571 to 110,637. To accommodate the new demand, cities had to grow both vertically and horizontally. Architects used steel-skeleton construction to build skyscrapers. In 1931 workers completed New York's Empire State Building, which towered eighty-six stories in the sky, making it the tallest building in the world. Big cities were not the only communities building skyscrapers: Tulsa, Oklahoma City, Houston, Cleveland, and dozens of other medium-sized cities boasted skylines. Cities also spread outward, spilling over into the surrounding countryside. Los Angeles, a sprawling metropolis connected by multilane highways, saw its population increase from around 100,000 in 1900 to over 1 million by 1930.

The automobile industry also showed the power of advertising as automobile corporations and many others turned to advertising to stimulate consumer demand. Advertising income increased from $1.3 billion in 1915 to $3.4 billion in 1929. Advertising, Calvin Coolidge proclaimed in 1926, "is the most potent influence in adopting and changing the habits and modes of life, affecting what we eat, what we wear, and the work and play of the whole nation." The makers of Listerine mouthwash used fear of what their ads called halitosis (bad breath) to increase sales from $100,000 in 1920 to over $4 million in 1927. Public relations man Ivy Lee came up with the slogan "Breakfast of Champions" to sell Wheaties and created Betty Crocker as the symbol for General Mills products. Curtiss Candy Company

Los Angeles Suburb, 1924 This photograph of Whittier Boulevard demonstrates the interconnections in the new economy. Electricity allowed the cheap manufacture of cars and other consumer products, while the automobile fueled the construction of suburbs, and suburbs provided new markets and helped drive a new consumer culture. These advancements also changed the way Americans lived. Cars gave them mobility and freedom, while electricity filled suburban homes with new appliances and other conveniences. *(Seaver Center for Western History Research, Los Angeles County Museum of Natural History.)*

promoted its Baby Ruth candy bar—"a center of caramel filled with peanuts enrobed in chocolate"—by dropping free samples from an airplane.

For the first time many companies allowed customers to purchase products on credit. Time payment schemes, reported a special commission on social trends during the decade, allowed people "to telescope the future into the present." A family could purchase a $97.50 washing machine for just $5 down and $8 a month. "A dollar down and a dollar forever," a critic remarked. By the end of the 1920s Americans were buying over 60 percent of their cars and 80 percent of their radios and furniture on the installment plan. Between 1925 and 1929 the amount of money Americans owed creditors doubled to $3 billion.

Paralleling the new techniques in manufacturing and marketing, corporations redesigned their management techniques to make them more effective and efficient. The spread of "scientific management" (see page 713), pioneered by Frederick W. Taylor before the war, encouraged this trend. Corporations also increased their commitment to research and development and reorganized into divisions organized by function—sales, marketing, production—and created a top tier of management to oversee the entire operation. As corporations grew larger and their stock ownership became more diverse, professional business administrators began to appear in boardrooms. By the end of the decade, a "managerial revolution" had transformed the modern corporation as plant managers and corporate executives, rather than owners, made key decisions.

The businessman bathed in the warm glow of public adulation. A poll of college students early in the decade named Henry Ford the third-greatest figure of all time, trailing Jesus Christ and Napoleon. "The man who builds a factory builds a temple," President Coolidge declared. "The man who works there worships there." In a 1925 book entitled *The Man Nobody Knows*, advertising executive Bruce Barton claimed that Jesus Christ was the "founder of modern business." Jesus, he argued, was a great executive who "picked up twelve men from the bottom rank of business and forged them into an organization that conquered the world." The book became an instant bestseller. "Presumably," observed historian Michael Parish, "one served God not only by following a calling but also by taking advantage of the installment plan."

The reorganized corporations accomplished a consolidation of American business. By 1929 the leading two hundred corporations controlled 49 percent of all corporate wealth and received 43 percent of corporate income. Before 1910 two hundred firms had made cars, but by 1930 the Big Three—Ford, General Motors, and Chrysler—had established their control of the industry with 83 percent of sales. Chain stores, with large inventories and low prices, took the place of smaller, less-efficient stores. A&P, the most successful of the new chains, expanded from 400 grocery outlets in 1912 to 15,500 in 1932.

Mass Communications and Mass Culture

The proliferation of chain stores was part of a larger move toward greater standardization in American life. New advances in communications led the way, promoting many of the new consumer products while also nationalizing standards of taste and style. For the first time millions of Americans shared identical experiences: they watched the same newsreels and films, listened to the same radio broadcasts, and read similar newspapers.

Movies emerged as the most popular form of public entertainment. By 1925 twenty thousand theaters dotted the nation. For fifty cents people could watch a silent movie along with a live stage show. In 1929 Chicago theaters had enough seats for half of the city's population to attend a movie each day. By 1930 the average weekly attendance was 90 million. Moviegoers in small towns and big cities flocked to see stars such as Douglas Fairbanks, Charlie Chaplin, Clara Bow, and Joan Crawford. Perhaps Hollywood's most famous silent-screen actor was Rudolph Valentino, an Italian gardener from Long Island, New York, who became the sex symbol of the decade after he abducted the swooning damsel in *The Sheik*. When he died suddenly in 1926 his funeral drew more than thirty thousand female mourners. The movies taught people how to dress, talk, and appear "sexy." Young women imitated Clara Bow's sexual gestures; men copied Valentino's baggy trousers.

Movies were not the only popular form of entertainment shaping a national culture. The growth and influence of radio were equally impressive. Pittsburgh-based Westinghouse station KDKA provided the nation's first public radio broadcast when it reported the presidential election of 1920. The first commercial radio station was licensed in 1921. Within a year 570 stations vied for air space, and hundreds of companies were manufacturing stylish new sets. Broadcasting created a national community of listeners. Early in the decade local topics dominated the radio airwaves. In Chicago, radio broadcasters included a "Polish Hour," an "Irish Hour," and a "Chicago Federation of Labor Hour." By 1926 two radio giants began consolidating stations into nationwide networks—the National Broadcasting Company (NBC) and Columbia Broadcasting Systems (CBS). Network radio created a new phenomenon: the shared national experience. Millions of Americans in big cities, small towns, and isolated farms listened to *The Maxwell House Hour* and *The General Motors Family.*

Changes in print journalism contributed as well to the emergence of national culture. Though the literacy rate was rising rapidly during the 1920s, fewer and fewer sources of information were servicing larger and larger groups of people. The number of local newspapers was shrinking. Chicago boasted seven morning dailies at the beginning of the decade; only two by the end. More than 600 newspapers died between 1914 and 1926. Many that survived were becoming parts of national chains. By 1927 fifty-five chains controlled 230 major newspapers. By the early 1930s the massive Hearst organization owned one of every four Sunday papers sold in America.

Spectator Sports and the Cult of Individualism

Mass communications made possible another cultural phenomenon of the 1920s: the sports hero. The nineteenth century had admired its sporting heroes, but the mass media extended their reach, transforming local idols into national celebrities. A cultural dimension magnified the nation's fascination with athletic achievement. As society became more urban and collective, nostalgia for the free-spirited, untamed individual became more pronounced. Americans transformed the sports field into a new frontier and the athlete into a pioneer. In athletic competition, as on the frontier, men confronted physical obstacles and overcame them with talent and determination. Victory was the result of superior ability and courageous perseverance.

Millions of Americans crowded into halls to watch boxers slug it out in the ring. No boxer received more adulation than Jack Dempsey, who embodied the nation's frontier past. Raised in Manassas, Colorado, he learned to fight in local bars against miners, cowboys, and anyone else foolish enough to challenge him. "Jack Dempsey hit like a sledgehammer and absorbed punishment like a sponge," wrote historian Michael Parrish. "He was not a boxer, but an earthquake that left blood, flesh, and bone scattered in its wake." During the twenties his two grueling championship bouts with Gene Tunney proved enormously popular. In 1926 Tunney defeated Dempsey in their first fight before a rain-soaked crowd in Philadelphia. While as many as 150,000 people paid to see their rematch the following year in Chicago, some 50 million listened to it on radio. The referee's famous "long count" may have cost Dempsey the second fight when he knocked Tunney to the canvas but failed to go immediately to a neutral corner.

Having gained momentum during the late nineteenth century, baseball earned its reputation as the national pastime during the 1920s. Rooted in the nation's rural past, the game was now played in front of largely urban audiences. While talented players such as Lou Gehrig, Rogers Hornsby, Dazzy Vance, Walter Johnson, and Grover Alexander kept the myth of individualism alive, the game became big business during the corporate era of the 1920s.

No one did more for the game than the "Bambino," Babe Ruth, who single-handedly transformed a contest of pitching and defense into a game of sluggers. Raised in an orphanage, Ruth showed that the American dream of rags to riches still existed in an industrial age. The New York Yankees, with Ruth clobbering home runs, won the American League pennant three consecutive years from 1926 to 1928 and the World Series twice. In 1927 he hit sixty home runs in a season of 154 games, establishing one of sports' most enduring records. Three years later the growing gate receipts enabled the Yankees to open a grand new stadium in the Bronx, "the house that Ruth built." Ruth embraced his role as celebrity. The first professional athlete to hire a press agent, Ruth used his star status to sell a host of new consumer products, everything from fishing equipment to alligator shoes.

Barred from segregated professional baseball, African-Americans developed the Negro League, which featured their own stars, during the 1920s. In 1923 four hundred thousand black fans turned out to watch Negro League pitchers "Smokey Joe" Williams and "Bullet" Joe Rogan intimidate opposing hitters and to marvel at the speed and power of Oscar Charleston. While the mainstream media ignored black baseball players, they became popular figures in black communities across the United States.

The exploits of Ruth and Dempsey filled newspapers and airwaves but never exhausted the appetite of American consumers for sports heroes and heroines, who reaffirmed the value of individualism in a corporate, collectivized society. In his

Babe Ruth and His Fans The rise of mass culture in the 1920s created national celebrities in sports and entertainment. The radio, the growth of leisure time, the automobile, and other aspects of modern culture made such fame possible and drew in a national audience. Here, Babe Ruth, the well-known and well-loved Yankee slugger, is seen in Syracuse, New York, engulfed by admirers, most of them young boys. *(Corbis-Bettmann.)*

final college football season, Harold Edward "Red" Grange, the Galloping Ghost, rushed for over 360 yards against Pennsylvania. After college he signed with the Chicago Bears, who paid him the then astonishing sum of $12,000 a game. In addition to his successful football career, Grange had a lucrative business off the field endorsing products, selling chocolate bars, and even acting in a Hollywood movie. In 1923 seventeen-year-old Helen Wills became the youngest woman to that time to win the singles tennis title at the U.S. Open. That same year Johnny Weissmuller swam the 200-yard freestyle in one minute fifty-nine seconds, then the fastest time in history. He won two gold medals in the 1924 Olympic games in Paris, and a third gold medal four years later at Amsterdam. He went on to become a Hollywood star.

The Limits of Prosperity

Not everyone benefited from the extraordinary changes transforming American society. Some older industries, unable to satisfy changing consumer tastes, suffered during the decade. Railroads were unable to compete with the emerging trucking industry. Mine owners abandoned some coalfields, along with the mine workers, as more Americans used petroleum and electricity as sources of energy. The development of synthetic fibers for textiles turned New England cotton mill communities into ghost towns. Despite the postwar construction boom, lumber companies from Washington to Georgia showed only modest gains as builders turned to substitute materials such as concrete. While millions of Americans benefited from the booming economy, class barriers remained firmly entrenched. Sociologists Robert and Helen Lynd spent years studying the daily habits of residents of Muncie, Indiana. The "division into working class and business class" constituted "the outstanding cleavage" in the community, noted the Lynds, determining everything from the schools people attended to the quality and variety of food they ate.

Small farmers suffered the most during the decade. During World War I government purchases of farm products, combined with European demands, had inflated prices for many crops. Between 1916 and 1919 net farm income more than doubled from $4 billion to $10 billion. Convinced the prosperity would continue into the next decade, farmers took out loans to buy land and expand operations with new machinery. But the bubble burst in 1920 when the U.S. government stopped buying wheat and European farms recovered from the war. Prices plummeted as the market flooded with surplus crops. In just a few months in 1920, farmers watched the price of a bushel of wheat plunge from $2.50 to less than $1. The value of cotton, hogs, and cattle suffered similar declines. During the decade, both farm net income and real purchasing power fell by 25 percent. By the end of the decade, as they watched their share of the national income drop from 16 percent in 1919 to 8.8 percent, hundreds of thousands of farmers quit the land and looked for jobs in mills and factories.

In May 1921 a group of congressmen from agricultural states organized the farm bloc to fight for laws to aid beleaguered farmers. The new group managed to push a number of measures through Congress, but it was unable to address the basic problem of low farm prices. On four separate occasions Congress debated legislation that would have established federal price supports for agricultural products. Under the proposals the government would purchase surplus crops according to "a fair exchange formula" that would protect farmers from wild fluctuations in the market. In the first two attempts the bills languished in Congress, but in 1926 and again in 1927 Congress managed to pass the legislation. Both times President Coolidge vetoed the experiment in government intervention.

Industrial workers fared better than farmers. Most workers saw their standard of living increase during the decade. Some workers benefited from a new paternalism among many employers, an experiment that came to be called "welfare capitalism." The term applied to a broad range of programs designed to inspire worker loyalty and to promote efficiency. "We must find ways and means to help our workers get their worries out of their minds, so they can get on the job rarin' to go," said E. K. Hall, president of American Telephone and Telegraph Company. A few of the country's largest corporations hoped to avoid labor disputes and limit the growth of unions by establishing grievance committees, group life insurance, old-age pensions, "employee representation" or company unions, and stock ownership plans. Henry Ford, for example, raised wages, shortened the workweek, and offered paid vacations.

Corporate paternalism failed to alter the gross inequities between labor and management, however. Most workers earned less than the $1,800 a year needed to maintain a decent standard of living. Welfare capitalism also affected only a small number of employees who happened to work in large corporations. It did nothing for teenage girls who worked long hours in cotton mills for sixteen to eighteen cents an hour, or for miners who enjoyed neither regular work nor basic civil liberties, such as freedom of speech. "We work in *his* mine," one complained. "We live in *his* house. Our children go to *his* school. On Sunday we're preached at by *his* preacher. When we die we're buried in *his* cemetery."

The combination of corporate assertiveness, political resistance, and labor timidity produced a decline in union membership from 5 million in 1920 to less than 3 million by 1929. In the wake of the reaction against suspected radicals during the Red Scare of 1919–1920, corporations exploited the fear of radicalism to push for open shop laws by which workers could choose *not* to join a local union. The National Association of Manufacturers called the open shop the "American Plan." The Supreme Court sanctioned many of the anti-union efforts, especially after the appointment of William Howard Taft as chief justice in 1921. Between 1921 and 1925 the Court issued a series of rulings that restricted the right to strike and limited the effectiveness of child labor and minimum wage laws.

Workers who tried fighting against the conservative tide by unionizing faced numerous obstacles during the decade. The Red Scare had marginalized radical labor leaders, giving added power to the conservative leadership of the American Federation of Labor (AFL), which concentrated on working with business to maintain benefits for its skilled workers. Some people hoped that the death of cigar-chomping Samuel Gompers in 1924 would breathe new life into the AFL. But the new president, William Green of the United Mine Workers, did not alter the AFL's basic philosophy or tactics. Like Gompers, Green was more interested in maintaining the economic privileges of the craft unions' skilled members than in extending unionism to the 90 percent of the work force that remained unorganized. The AFL was also determined to convince the public that it was a respectable organization. Consequently, the number of strikes declined dramatically from one hundred a year in 1919–1920 to only eighteen by the end of the decade.

Women found new opportunities as the business expansion increased the need for office clerks, typists, telephone operators, and salespeople. Two million women went to work during the decade, driving the total to 10.8 million, a fivefold increase since 1914. The number of married women in the work force jumped from 15 percent of working women in 1900 to 29 percent in 1930. During that period, the number of women working in the professions increased by 50 percent. While impressive, the gains did little to challenge male domination of the workplace. Most working-class women clustered in the low-paying areas already defined as "women's work"—typing, stenography, bookkeeping, and sales. Three of four professional women entered traditional "women's fields" such as education and social work. The vast majority of working wives were African-Americans who were pushed by poverty into employment. "The woman," a reformer noted in 1929, "is nearly always the cheap or marginal worker, and . . . she is expected by the public and the employer to remain one."

The decade's prosperity also eluded the overwhelming majority of nonwhite Americans. Despite the movement of nearly 2.5 million blacks to northern cities by the end of the 1920s, most black Americans continued to labor in the South as tenant farmers, sharecroppers, and farm workers. In 1930 about 3 million blacks—25 percent of the nation's total black population—lived in the three Deep South states of Georgia, Mississippi, and Alabama, and 80 percent of these lived in rural poverty. Even in the North blacks were systematically excluded from the work force, barred from joining most unions, and forced to live in segregated neighborhoods.

Mexicans, by far the largest minority group in the Southwest, suffered similar social and economic discrimination. According to the U.S. Immigration Service, an estimated 459,000 Mexicans entered the United States between 1921 and 1930. In the area from Texas, New Mexico, and Colorado to California, Mexicans provided much of the labor that transformed the desert landscape into rich agricultural farmland. Seventy-five percent of California's farm laborers, for example, were Mexican. Many Mexican-Americans gravitated toward the cities. By the end of the 1920s Hispanics made up more than half the population of El Paso, slightly less than half of San Antonio, and one-fifth of Los Angeles.

THE CULTURE OF DISSENT

In *Preface to Morals* (1929), journalist Walter Lippmann referred to the "acids of modernity" to describe the forces that were corroding the stability and certainty of contemporary life. Among the most corrosive acids were, first, a new morality that was eating away at Victorian notions of womanhood and, second, a chorus of intellectuals who questioned tradition and criticized the crass materialism of modern society. At the same time, African-Americans startled white America with new cultural and political institutions to articulate a sense of racial pride and to explore the dilemmas of race.

The New Morality and the New Woman

During the 1920s many young women in large urban areas challenged traditional assumptions and experimented with new expressions of freedom. Teenage girls adopted the flapper image: The flapper wore cosmetics, cut her hair short, threw away the restrictive corset, and hemmed her skirts above the knee. She drank openly, played golf on public courses, and practiced the latest dances, which, according to one minister, brought "the bodies of men and women in unusual relations to each other." The liberated women of the 1920s considered cigarette smoking a symbol of emancipation. "Cigarette in hand, shimmying to the music of the masses, the New Woman and the New Morality have made their theatric debut upon the modern scene," observed a journalist. These youthful women and their male counterparts created for the first time in American history a unique youth culture removed from the traditional style and moral norms of their parents.

Changing sexual practices were among the most obvious manifestations of the "new morality." Middle-class girls led the way in replacing old courtship rules by which male suitors would "call" on them at home—under the watchful eye of a parent—with a new "dating" system in which a couple would go out unsupervised. The automobile, which replaced the front porch, contributed to the new dating ritual by providing young couples with an escape from their parents' scrutiny. Dating and the automobile contributed to another innovation—petting. Traditionalists suggested that a woman not allow a man to kiss her unless he intended to marry her. One study of college youth during the 1920s found that 92 percent of coeds had engaged in kissing. A judge in Muncie declared that of thirty girls brought before his court for "sex crimes," nineteen had committed their crimes in a car.

The virtual legalization of birth control information and devices in many states permitted a substantial number of Americans to put into practice the radical idea that sex could be a source of pleasure detached from procreation. Birth control, wrote Walter Lippmann, "is the most revolutionary practice in the history of sexual

Clara Bow, 1928   One product of modernity was the "New Woman," characterized by her greater personal freedom. Movie stars conveyed this image on the screen, wearing skimpy costumes and exuding a more overtly sexual image than their counterparts the previous decade, who had epitomized the girl next door. Clara Bow was nicknamed the "It" girl for her 1927 movie of that title, which told the story of a young flapper looking for love. Though Bow became one of America's first sex symbols, even the "It" girl had sexual boundaries—in the movie, she slapped her boss when he tried to kiss her at the end of the night.
(Kobal Collection.)

morals." It legitimized female sexuality, promoted sexual experimentation, and transformed marital ideals. Use of the diaphragm became commonplace among middle-class women. A survey in 1925 showed that 60 percent of women used contraceptives; for middle-class women the figures were even higher. Family size declined during the 1920s as the birthrate fell from near twenty-four per thousand in 1920 to less than nineteen per thousand in 1930.

By separating sex from procreation, birth control liberated women from "involuntary motherhood," raising expectations that marriage could be based on companionship and shared interest. Women now envisioned "sharing joys and sorrows with a mate who will be not merely a protector and provider but an all round companion." Sexuality was central to the marriage of the 1920s. In her manual *Happiness in Marriage,* birth control advocate Margaret Sanger wrote that both partners must realize "the importance of complete fulfillment of love through the expression of sex." The changed expectations may have contributed to a rising divorce rate. By 1928 one of every seven marriages ended in divorce.

To many Americans, recently publicized Freudian psychology seemed to support the new morality. Freud, the famous Viennese physician, had visited the United States briefly in 1909, but his theories about unconscious sexual urges failed to reach a larger audience until the 1920s. *Webster's Dictionary* added the word *Freudian,* and terms such as *id* and *superego* became familiar. Numerous Americans became obsessed with Freud's psychosexual theories, but the public, misunderstanding the complexities of the irrational and the unconscious, grossly simplified them. Popular interpreters suggested that Freud called for abandoning all sexual inhibition and advocated unrestrained self-gratification. "Are you shackled by repressed desires?" asked an ad in a popular magazine. "Psychoanalysis, the new miracle science, proves that most people live only half-power lives because of repressed sex instincts."

Popular culture reinforced the emphasis on sex. People turned on the radio to hear songs with titles such as "Hot Lips," "I Need Lovin'," and "Burning Kisses." Popular movies included *Sinners in Silk, Women Who Give,* and *Rouged Lips.* Advertisers emphasized youth and beauty to sell their products. A clothing advertisement pictured a middle-aged woman and acknowledged that "within this woman's soul burns still the flame of her desire for charm and beauty." Many women responded to the new sales pitch. The number of beauty shops expanded from five thousand to forty thousand during the decade. Between 1914 and 1925 sales of cosmetics exploded from $17 to $141 million. It was during the 1920s that Miss America beauty contests became an annual ritual. The focus was exclusively on physical beauty. Contestants might have talent, noted one of the organizers, but "things would be better if they kept it to themselves."

The movement for sexual freedom was not as threatening to the family as many contemporaries feared. Despite their suggestive titles, most movies featured the wife returning to her husband and the young woman marrying the boy next door. Sexual liberation had little impact on the lives of working-class and minority women, who struggled with the more mundane problems of earning a living and supporting a family. Even the liberated attitudes of young urbanites were wedded to old-fashioned aspirations. Few young women were willing to sacrifice marriage for career but hoped rather to attain "a richer and fuller life" with "an all round companion." Progressive women's colleges, such as Smith, Vassar, and Bryn Mawr, taught the value of domesticity. By the middle of the 1920s Vassar offered courses in "Husband and Wife," "Motherhood," and the "Family as an Economic Unit." The college also founded a School of Euthenics whose purpose was to educate women "along the lines of their chief interest and responsibilities, motherhood and the home." Most of the Vassar women polled as early as 1923 believed that marriage was "the biggest of all careers."

The decade's preoccupation with private behavior prevented women from making significant gains in the public sphere. The achievement of suffrage removed the central issue that had given cohesion to the disparate forces of female reform activism. In the first few years of the decade Congress responded to the possibility of an organized women's vote by passing the Sheppard-Towner Act of 1921. The first federal health care act, Sheppard-Towner provided states with matching federal funds to establish centers for mothers and children. Within a few years, however, much of the energy of the suffrage campaign had dissipated as young women showed little interest in organized feminism. "'Feminism' has become a term of opprobrium to the modern young woman," writer Dorothy Dunbar Bromley told the readers of *Harper's* in 1927.

Not only were young women less interested in the cause, but mainstream reformers split into rival camps at the end of the war. On one side stood the National American Woman Suffrage Association, which reorganized itself as the League of Women Voters (LWV) in 1920. About one-tenth of its former size, the league fought to democratize political parties, abolish child labor, and support protective legislation for women and children. On the other side of the debate, the National Woman's Party (NWP), founded in 1921, planned to fight for full legal and civil equality by working "to remove all the remaining forms of the subjection of women." In 1923 the NWP proposed a brief Equal Rights Amendment to the Constitution, which declared that "Men and women shall have equal rights throughout the United States and every place subject to its jurisdiction." Many social reformers complained that the NWP's agenda of outlawing legal discrimination ignored the concerns of working-class women, who were the chief beneficiaries of protective laws. "Women cannot be made men" by constitutional amendment, Florence Kelly charged. The conflict over equality and protection dominated women's politics during the decade, dividing the movement and decreasing its influence.

Discontent of the Intellectuals

The literature of the 1920s rebelled against the standardization of American life that resulted from mass production and large-scale industrialization. Disillusionment in the aftermath of World War I's seemingly senseless slaughter increased the tone of despair among young European authors who had suffered through four years of war and had witnessed massive casualties. This anguish made its way into the works of young American writers, prompting Gertrude Stein to describe them as "a lost generation." Although a diverse group, these writers all explored the problems of life in an age of machines and mass culture and a time of uncertainty and skepticism.

The theme of rootlessness and cynicism pervades the writing of the most famous writers of the Lost Generation. Ernest Hemingway, perhaps the most celebrated American writer of the twenties, captured the sense of loss following World War I. His characters are interested in simple pleasures, not lofty ideals. In *The Sun Also Rises* (1926) a hopelessly lost pack of friends travels from Paris to Pamplona in an alcoholic stupor, their adventures chronicled by Jake Barnes, whom the war left both physically and emotionally impotent. In his first novel of the decade, *This Side of Paradise* (1920), F. Scott Fitzgerald depicted a world occupied by a generation "grown up to find all Gods dead, all wars fought, all faith in man shaken."

While Hemingway and Fitzgerald focused on personal alienation, others launched a wider attack on the sterility of American culture, inveighing against the materialism and provincialism of contemporary life. In the pages of his magazines, first *The Smart Set* and later *The American Mercury,* Henry Louis Mencken ridiculed small-town and rural America. "Civilized life," he charged, was not "possible under a democracy" because it placed government in the hands of common people. Sinclair Lewis's *Main Street* (1920) described the complacency and narrow-mindedness that seemed to symbolize all small American communities. His most famous novel, *Babbitt* (1922), told the story of a small-town real-estate agent whose "symbols of truth and beauty" are mechanical contraptions. Lewis received wide acclaim for his penetrating portraits of national life and in 1930 became the first American to win a Nobel Prize in literature.

Many artists experimented with new modes of expression to capture the chaos of life in the machine age. Poets Hart Crane, E. E. Cummings, and William Carlos Williams displayed new rhythms and challenged traditional lyric forms. Cummings, for example, underscored the irrationality of contemporary society by ignoring rules of capitalization and using inventive punctuation. In his powerful trilogy, *U.S.A.*, the novelist John Dos Passos used unconventional methods— "Newsreel" and "Camera Eye"—to break up the narrative and convey the fragmentation of modern life.

Intellectuals in other disciplines contributed to the critique of contemporary society. The Lynds' *Middletown: A Study in American Culture* emerged as the most influential sociological study of the decade. The authors exposed a wide gulf between the theory and practice of American democracy. Franz Boas, the father of modern anthropology, questioned traditional ideas about racial inferiority. He used the data from measurements of black skulls and brain cavities to help disprove the myth that low scores by blacks on intelligence tests were due to smaller, inferior brains. In a series of books beginning with *The Mind of Primitive Man* (1911), he demonstrated that environment, not heredity, played a major role in determining ability. Other anthropologists used similar scientific methods to question the superiority of Western culture. After studying Indian cultures in the Southwest, Ruth Benedict praised the noncompetitive and nonmaterialistic Zuñi tribe of Pueblo Indians. She published her findings in an influential book, *Patterns of Culture.*

New Visions in Black America

The northward migration of African-Americans stimulated by the war continued into the 1920s, when as many as 600,000 migrated from the South. By 1920, 2 million of the nation's 11 million blacks lived in the North. During the decade New York City's black population climbed from 152,000 to 328,000 and Chicago's from 109,000 to 233,000. In New York's Harlem and

Chicago's South Side, growing numbers of African-Americans crowded into grimy tenements. In 1927 a housing commission reported of Harlem that "the State would not allow cows to live in some of these apartments."

African-Americans faced rigid discrimination in employment. Most blacks could find jobs only as menial or unskilled workers, and even then took home less pay than their white counterparts. Most black men who found jobs worked as porters, waiters, and janitors; black women served as cooks, domestics, and washerwomen. There were two kinds of businesses in New York, the sociologist E. Franklin Frazier commented, "those that employ Negroes in menial positions, and those that employ no Negroes at all." Poverty produced chronic ill health: the syphilis rate in Harlem was nine times higher than in white Manhattan; the tuberculosis rate was five times higher; and the pneumonia and typhoid rates were twice as high. The concentration of blacks in the industrial cities of the North increased racial tension that occasionally flared into violence. In the early 1920s riots exploded in Knoxville, Tennessee; Tulsa, Oklahoma; and Omaha, Nebraska.

These conditions made possible the spectacular success of Marcus Garvey. Born and raised in Jamaica, Garvey arrived in the United States in 1916 at the age of twenty-eight. In 1917 he established the United Negro Improvement Association (UNIA) in order to promote "the spirit of race pride and love." The following year he founded a weekly newspaper, *Negro World,* which exhorted blacks to build independent social and economic institutions and look toward Africa as a future homeland. He took as his colors red (for slave blood), black (for skin color), and green (for African fertility). "The world has made being black a crime," he said. "I hope to make it a virtue." His flamboyance, together with the pride in color that he evoked, gave his movement an unprecedented mass appeal in Harlem in the early 1920s. The UNIA claimed more than seven hundred branches in thirty-eight states, while his newspaper had a weekly circulation of between fifty thousand and two hundred thousand.

Garvey tapped into a deep undercurrent of black nationalism, a desire to build and sustain African-American institutions. "We have a beautiful history," he declared, "and we shall create another one in the future." He established the Negro Factories Corporation, which operated grocery stores, restaurants, and a clothing factory. He sold stock to followers to create the Black Star Line, which owned three ships for transporting passengers between the United States, the West Indies, and Africa. All the employees—over one thousand at its peak—were black. "Girls who could only be washerwomen in your homes, we made clerks and stenographers," Garvey told white businessmen. There was, however, a darker side to Garvey's racial views. He championed the notion of "a pure black race" and opposed race mixing. He attacked moderate black leaders who tried to build alliances with white moderates.

Garvey's ideas were controversial among other black leaders. Many middle-class blacks rejected his separatist ideas, while the leaders of other activist groups complained that Garvey distracted people from the real battle for economic equality. A. Philip Randolph, a socialist and cofounder of the *Messenger* (subtitled the *Only Radical Negro Magazine in America*), was one of Garvey's toughest critics. Randolph tried to forge an interracial coalition of low-income people. In 1925 he started the Brotherhood of Sleeping Car Porters in an effort to develop working-class consciousness among African-Americans. Throughout the decade he campaigned for the interracial organization of workers and called for militant demonstrations aimed at breaking the power of corporate elites.

When Garvey's steamship line fell on hard financial times, many prominent black businessmen alerted J. Edgar Hoover, director of the Justice Department's general intelligence division, who was about to become head of the FBI. Hoover's agents infiltrated the UNIA, combing through its records for incriminating evidence. Poor record keeping made an indictment easy, and in 1922 the government charged Garvey with using the mail to defraud investors. The following year he was convicted and sentenced to five years in prison. Late in 1927 President Coolidge commuted his sentence, and the government deported him as an undesirable alien. He would spend the remaining twelve years of his life in exile in Jamaica and London.

The expressions of black nationalism were not confined to politics. The decade witnessed an extraordinary outburst of African-American writing, unprecedented both in the amount of poetry and fiction produced and in its racial assertiveness. The literary renaissance was based in New York's Harlem, which became a mecca for aspiring African-American artists during the 1920s. "We younger Negro artists," wrote Langston Hughes, the poet laureate of Harlem, "intend to express our individual dark-skinned selves without fear or shame." The person who did most to publicize the movement was Alaine Locke, a Phi Beta Kappa graduate of Harvard and the first black awarded a prestigious Rhodes scholarship at England's Oxford University. "In Harlem," he wrote, "Negro life is seizing upon its first chances for group expression and self-determination."

Despite its intense poverty, Harlem emerged during the 1920s as a bubbling caldron of creativity. People gathered in small cafés and clubs to listen to the jazz musicians Louis Armstrong and Edward "Duke" Ellington. Painters such as Aaron Douglas and Archibald Motley, Jr., translated the jazz aesthetic onto canvas by using a new visual language of bold colors and improvised compositions. Singers such as Florence Mills and Ethel Waters performed in the growing circuit of black nightclubs, theaters, and vaudeville houses. African-American artists, writers, and musicians also initiated an international cultural exchange as Europeans embraced their creative style. The cultural capital of Europe, the city of Paris, became home to hundreds of African-Americans seeking greater artistic and racial freedom.

Many black artists who gathered in Harlem used their poetry, novels, and short stories to give expression to the pain of racism and to examine what it meant to be black in America. "I, too, sing America," Hughes wrote. "I am the darker brother. / They send me to eat in the kitchen / When the company comes, / But I laugh, / And eat well, / And grow strong." Questions of black identity were at the heart of much of the work produced in the Harlem Renaissance: What did it mean to be black in America during the 1920s? While some African-American artists emphasized the similarities between black and white cultures, most tried to build on the distinctiveness of the black experience in America.

THE GUARDIANS

Many of the New Era's instruments of mass culture—the automobile, the radio, and movies—forced a renewed confrontation between traditional Protestant values associated with the rural past and the new urban culture. At stake, some believed, was

Small's Paradise Club Small's Paradise opened its doors in 1925 and was one of the three big clubs in Harlem during the 1920s and 1930s. The club was known for its exotic floor shows and big band sessions that trained a whole new generation of jazz musicians, as well as an entertaining wait staff that did the Charleston and spun their trays as they navigated around the tables. While not as racially segregated as the Cotton Club, where blacks could only enter through the back and serve as staff or entertainers, Small's Paradise did cater to a predominately white clientele who found the club a safe place to dabble in black night life among the thousands of clubs, cafes, and speakeasies in Harlem. *(© Bettmann-Corbis.)*

the essence of what it meant to be American. "Americanism still has a mission to the world," declared Henry Ford's *Dearborn Independent,* but "we shall have to save ourselves before we can hope to save anyone else." Salvation, self-proclaimed guardians of American tradition believed, required an assault on foreign immigrants, a revival of fundamentalist Christianity, and the enforcement of Prohibition.

The Revival of Nativism World War I all but halted the influx of immigrants to the United States, but the flood resumed immediately afterward. In 1919, 110,000 immigrants arrived; in 1921 the figure shot up to 805,000, of whom two-thirds were from southern and eastern Europe. The new wave of immigration rekindled widespread concern that "inferior" immigrants of southern and eastern European stock along with blacks and other undesirables would overwhelm white Protestant America. "The welfare of the United States demands that the door should be closed to immigrants for a time," observed an influential congressman in 1920. "We are being made a dumping-ground for the human wreckage of the [world] war." The fears were widespread. Journalists complained that in cities such as New York, where three out of every four persons were foreigners or the children of foreigners, immigrants were responsible for rising crime rates. Prominent scientists, infatuated by new theories of eugenics, claimed that recent immigrants from southern Europe and Asia possessed more "inborn socially inadequate qualities" and were therefore unable to assimilate. Business leaders fretted that the newcomers would swell the ranks of organized labor.

In 1924 Congress responded to these fears by passing the Johnson-Reed Immigration Act (see Competing Voices, Chapter 19, page 762). Under the law, the government allocated visas to Eastern Hemisphere nations in ratios determined by the number of persons of each nationality in the United States in 1890. Not surprisingly, Europe consumed 98 percent of the quota, leaving only 2 percent for the rest of the world. Three countries—Ireland, Great Britain, and Germany—accounted for nearly 70 percent of the total. In addition to dramatically cutting immigration rates from southern Europe—Italians and Greeks were especially hard hit—the law almost completely excluded Asians. The quota did not apply to spouses or minor children of U.S. citizens or to residents of the Western Hemisphere, who could immigrate without restriction. In 1929 Congress legislated an even more draconian measure that set the yearly immigration quota at 150,000, with the proportion of entering nationals based on the 1920 census. Italy, for example, could send 6,000 immigrants under this law, although hundreds of thousands wished to enter.

Many intellectuals who opposed nativism viewed the sensational trial of two Italian immigrants, Nicola Sacco and Bartolomeo Vanzetti, as evidence of the decade's intolerance of foreigners. In 1920 Sacco and Vanzetti were arrested and charged with the murders of a paymaster and guard in South Braintree, Massachusetts. Both were convicted and sentenced to death after a trial marked by gross prejudice. Presiding Judge Webster Thayer, for example, referred to the defendants as "anarchistic bastards" and "damned dagos." Their cause won worldwide sympathy. Prominent writers such as John Dos Passos, liberal jurists such as Felix Frankfurter of the Harvard Law School, and socialist Eugene Debs rallied around the convicted men. The verdict pleased some, such as evangelist Billy Sunday, who stormed, "Give 'em the juice. Burn them if they're guilty. That's the way to handle it. I'm tired of hearing these foreigners, these radicals, coming over here and telling us what we should do." On August 23, 1927, after years of protest and appeals, Sacco and Vanzetti died in the electric chair. After the executions, many in the funeral cortege wore armbands emblazoned, "Remember—Justice Crucified— August 23, 1927."

The "New" Klan   The revival of the Ku Klux Klan represented the most dramatic example of the rise of nativist and racist sentiment. In the years following the Civil War white southerners had organized the Ku Klux Klan to terrorize blacks and prevent them from voting. This early organization passed away with the end of Reconstruction. The modern Klan was organized in 1915 by William J. Simmons, a onetime Methodist minister. On Stone Mountain outside Atlanta, Georgia, before an American flag and a burning cross, the faithful swore allegiance to the new Klan. The ceremony coincided with the appearance in Atlanta of the popular motion picture *The Birth of a Nation,* which depicted heroic Klansmen redeeming the South from the grip of Radical Reconstruction. In the early 1920s millions of Americans joined the hooded order, although membership probably never exceeded 1.5 million at any one time.

The new Klan was not simply a reincarnation of the old. The Klan of the 1920s, although strong in the South, was stronger still in Indiana, Illinois, and Ohio. Perhaps three of every five members lived outside the South or Southwest. The new Klan also was not as heavily rural, but enlisted members in Chicago, Detroit, Atlanta, Denver, and other cities. One of every three Klansmen lived in a city with a population of over a hundred thousand. Finally, the Klan was no longer primarily a white supremacist group. The Invisible Empire gained legitimacy by fashioning itself as a middle-class Protestant populist movement crusading for social purity and against vice, crime, and deteriorating morality. To symbolize its role as the inspired guardian of social and religious tradition, the Klan carried ritual, pageantry, and secrecy to the extreme. Klansmen met in a Klavern, held Klonklaves, carried on Klonversations, and even sang Klodes. They followed a Kalendar in which 1867 was the year 1. The white gowns and hoods they wore during ritualistic meetings stood for a purity of life now under siege from alien elements. To preserve that purity the Klan resorted to threats, cross-burnings, beatings, kidnappings, mutilations, and murders.

In many states women counted for nearly half of all Klan members. One-third of white native-born women in Indiana joined the Klan. What attracted so many women to the group? For many native-born white Protestant women, the Klan provided a social setting to celebrate their racial and religious privileges. Viewing the Klan as a powerful force for protecting their communities from corruption and immorality, Klanswomen mixed support for white Protestant women's rights with racist, anti-Semitic, and anti-Catholic politics. Women dramatically extended the reach of the Klan by orchestrating consumer boycotts through "whisper" campaigns, which encouraged people to avoid merchants who failed the test of whiteness and Protestantism.

The boycotts served as a powerful economic weapon, allowing the Klan to become a potent political force in California, Ohio, Indiana, and Oregon, as well as in the South. It showed considerable strength in northern cities, especially those to which blacks and immigrants had streamed during recent years. In Texas it helped elect a senator, held a majority in the state legislature for a time, and controlled the city governments in Dallas, Fort Worth, and Wichita Falls. The Indiana Klan, under David Stephenson, built a machine that dominated state politics. In Denver a Klansman was named manager of public safety. On August 8, 1925, in a brazen demonstration of strength, more than fifty thousand Klan members marched down Pennsylvania Avenue in Washington, D.C.

After 1925 a series of internal power struggles and sordid scandals eroded support for the Klan. By 1930 the organization was in disarray. A fitting symbol of the organization's fall from grace occurred in Atlanta, where the Catholic Church took over the Klan's national offices and turned the building into the official residence of the archbishop.

KKK Women Marching in Washington   The revived Ku Klux Klan of the 1920s differed from its predecessor in its greater religious intolerance and its wider geographical spread. It also included large numbers of women for the first time. The presence of women was important to the Klan's claim to the role of guardian of traditional morality. The women who joined did so for the feeling of importance and power the Klan offered its members.   *(Library of Congress.)*

Fundamentalism   Apparent disparities between modern science and religion became another focus for the cultural conflicts of the 1920s. The main dispute centered around Darwinism versus biblical beliefs. Charles Darwin's *Origin of Species* (1859) posited a gradual evolution of species over a period of several million years, a theory at odds with God's seven-day creation of the world described in the biblical book of Genesis. Many modern Christians had reconciled the differences by accepting the Bible as divinely inspired but not literally true. Many others, however, rejected any compromise with Darwinism. These fundamentalists clung to the view that the truths of Scripture were absolute and all one needed to know. Fundamentalists were numerous during the 1920s, especially in the rural South. As the celebrated journalist H. L. Mencken noted, you could "heave an egg out of a Pullman and you will hit a Fundamentalist almost everywhere in the United States."

In the early 1920s fundamentalists crusaded for laws that would prohibit the teaching of Darwinism in public schools. More than twenty states debated such laws, but they became law in only five—Oklahoma, Florida, Tennessee, Mississippi, and Arkansas. The Tennessee bill barred the teaching of "any theory that denies the Story of the Divine Creation of Man as taught in the Bible, and [holds] instead that man has descended from a lower order of animals." In 1925 a group of citizens in

Dayton, Tennessee, contacted part-time teacher John Scopes, who agreed to challenge the law, and a local official who promised to prosecute. The publicity stunt proved a dramatic success: press from around the world flooded into Dayton to cover "the trial of the century." Clarence Darrow agreed to defend Scopes and former Democratic Party presidential nominee William Jennings Bryan joined the prosecution (see Competing Voices, page 966).

At the trial, Bryan defended the state's anti-evolution law by insisting that "it is better to trust in the Rock of Ages than to know the age of rocks; it is better for one to know that he is close to the Heavenly Father than to know how far the stars in the heavens are apart." But Bryan wilted under Darrow's intense cross-examination. He admitted that religious dogma was subject to more than one interpretation, and he conceded that the "day" of creation might mean a million years. For many members of the press, Bryan's poor performance on the witness stand symbolized the triumph of modernist scientific thinking over religious fundamentalism, a sentiment they conveyed through the media to people across the country. The victory, however, was not so clear-cut. Not only was Scopes found guilty (his conviction was later overturned on a technicality), but anti-evolution laws remained on the books for forty-two more years. By 1930, 70 percent of high schools in the United States omitted any reference to evolution. Despite press ridicule of Bryan, who died two weeks after the trial ended, religious fundamentalism would remain a power in American life for decades to come.

Fundamentalism held the allegiance of millions of Americans thanks in part to the work of extraordinary revivalists who used fire-and-brimstone sermons to warn their followers of the evils of modern life. The athletic Billy Sunday strode back and forth across the stage, often stomping and jumping to emphasize his points. Perhaps the most popular evangelist was the Canadian-born Aimee Semple McPherson. The flamboyant McPherson, dressed in white satin robes, proclaimed the gospel from her huge lakefront temple outside Los Angeles. Preaching with the help of three bands, two orchestras, three choirs, and six quartets, she combined Hollywood showmanship, New York advertising, and old-fashioned religion to become the nation's most famous revivalist by the end of the decade. McPherson was as effective at raising money as she was at saving souls. A year after the temple was opened, Sister Aimee began broadcasting "The Sunshine Hour" every morning over Los Angeles radio station KFSG, which stood for Kalling Foursquare Gospel, the name of her church.

The Unintended Consequences of Prohibition

The progressive fascination with social efficiency and scientific management had helped secure passage of the Eighteenth Amendment banning the sale of alcohol. By the time it became law in 1920, however, Prohibition had become a rallying cry for Americans who were fearful of the changes transforming the nation and hopeful of returning to a simpler past. At an emotional rally in Virginia on January 16, 1920, a zealous Billy Sunday captured the feeling of millions when he proclaimed that Prohibition would cleanse the nation's soul. "Men will walk upright now, women will smile, and the children will laugh," he told the audience. "Hell will be forever for rent."

It quickly became evident that Prohibition would not fulfill these expectations. The amendment did cut down on alcohol consumption. Rural areas went completely dry, and many working-class immigrants in the city, who could not afford the high prices of bootlegged beer, changed their drinking habits. But Prohibition made drinking fashionable among the middle class, and alcohol easy to obtain. Bootleggers produced dozens of new concoctions. Their inviting names—Soda Pop Moon and Yack Yack Bourbon—were deceptive. Many of the drinks were poisonous. According to one story, a patron sent a sample of his ill-gotten alcohol to be analyzed by a chemist, who replied, "Dear Sir, your horse has diabetes."

Though intended to create a more orderly society, Prohibition had the opposite effect. It stimulated organized crime, encouraging smuggling and bootlegging and producing widespread disregard for the law. Illegal saloons, called "speakeasies" sprang up in most major cities. By the end of the decade New Yorkers could choose from among thirty-two thousand, which was double the number of bars that had existed before Prohibition. In 1926 *Time* printed a recipe for making gin. A Prohibition agent conducted a survey to see how long it took to buy a drink in a number of cities: Atlanta, seventeen minutes; Chicago, twenty-one minutes; New Orleans, thirty-five seconds. In Washington, D.C., the agent searched for an hour before a policeman pointed him toward a local bootlegger.

Prohibition turned local mobsters into national celebrities. The tabloids were filled with the exploits of Al "Scarface" Capone, "Machine Gun" Jack McGurn, and George "Bugsy" Moran. "Prohibition is a business," Chicago gangster Al Capone insisted. "All I do is supply a public demand. I do it in the best and least harmful way I can." In fact, Capone presided over a vast criminal empire and was responsible for as many as three hundred murders. Most of the city's politicians and judges were on his payroll. In the age of the automobile he drove around in the biggest car of all—a seven-ton, armor-plated Cadillac equipped with bulletproof glass and a special compartment for machine guns.

Despite evidence that the Prohibition experiment was a failure, many provincial, largely rural, Protestant Americans continued to defend it. In their minds, Prohibition had always been about more than alcohol. It represented an effort to defend traditional American values against the growing influence of an urban, cosmopolitan culture. Throughout the decade, "wets" and "drys" battled to define America.

REPUBLICANS IN POWER

The battles over the League of Nations and the social unrest that followed the end of World War I left many Americans longing for political stability during the 1920s. The Republicans controlled the White House and Congress by appealing to the tradition of smaller government and swearing off the preceding decade's experiments in centralization. They scaled back government regulations and promised to promote business expansion. Opening foreign markets and limiting the possibility of war dominated the Republican approach to the world. The demoralized Democrats, torn by divisive social issues that reflected the tensions of the era, failed to offer a compelling alternative during most of the decade. The party showed signs of recovery in 1928, however, when it nominated New York governor Al Smith for president.

The "21" Club During Prohibition   Although the Eighteenth Amendment banned the sale of alcohol, the "speakeasies" in many cities outnumbered the saloons of the pre-Prohibition years. But unlike the old saloons, speakeasies were fashionable establishments, frequented by patrons with the means to pay for illegal spirits. Working-class speakeasies could generally be found in allies or basements, while more upscale speakeasies, like the famous "21" in New York (which featured a restaurant, two bars, and a secret chute for disposing of liquor bottles in case of a raid), catered to the wealthy. The social elite of New York—debutantes, stockbrokers, movie and Broadway stars—packed "21" night after night for business dealings and socializing.   *(Courtesy "21" Club.)*

**Republican
Ascendancy**

Warren G. Harding won a landslide victory in the 1920 election. A senator from Ohio since 1914, Harding was the first man ever to move directly from the Senate to the White House. Reflecting the contemporary mood, Harding promised a return to "normalcy" (he meant to say *normality*).

Harding was a modest man who worked hard at the job of being president. "I am a man of limited talents from a small town," Harding confessed to friends. His personal style was always warm and gracious. He opened the White House every day so he could greet visitors and often stayed up late at night to answer routine mail from citizens. "It is," he lamented, "really the only fun I have." Despite his self-professed limitations, Harding tried to perform his responsibilities with distinction. He approved a new budget system, advocated a federal antilynching law, called for a Department of Public Welfare, intervened to end the twelve-hour work-day in steel mills, and approved legislation assisting farm cooperatives and liberalizing farm credit. His tolerant approach to civil liberties brought Americans a necessary respite from postwar acrimony. Harding not only let socialist Eugene Debs out of jail; he received him in the White House.

His chief defect was that he believed in rewarding old friends with federal jobs. He appointed many party hacks, members of the "Ohio Gang," to important offices. They gathered with Harding at the famous "Little Green House" on K Street, where they drank illegal alcohol (delivered courtesy of a corrupt Prohibition officer), played poker, and entertained attractive women. Many of them abused the president's trust by swindling the government. Charles R. Forbes, the director of the Veterans Bureau, stole nearly $250 million before fleeing the country to avoid arrest. Jesse Smith, a Justice Department official, accepted thousands of dollars in bribes for protecting criminals from prosecution. The attorney general resigned when charged with authorizing the sale of alcohol from government warehouses to bootleggers. The most infamous scandal centered around allegations that Harding's secretary of the interior, Albert Fall, had leased government oil reserves in Teapot Dome, Wyoming, to private owners in order to line his own pockets. Fall resigned in disgrace and later served a one-year prison sentence.

By the summer of 1923 Harding had learned of the corruption within his administration. "My God, this is a hell of a job," he lamented to a journalist. "I have no trouble with my enemies. . . . But my damned friends, my God-damned friends . . . they're the ones that keep me walking the floor nights!" That summer, tired and depressed, Harding traveled to Seattle and San Francisco, where on August 2 he died of a massive heart attack.

Vice President Calvin Coolidge was in Vermont when he received word of Harding's death. His father, a local justice of the peace, administered the oath of office. In personality Coolidge and Harding could not have been more different. Harding was gregarious and warm; Coolidge was dour and cold. In the weeks following Harding's death, Coolidge held twice-weekly press conferences and regular radio addresses both to reassure the nation and to consolidate power.

A progressive Republican and supporter of Theodore Roosevelt's New Nationalism, Coolidge had won election as governor of Massachusetts in 1919 campaigning on a platform supporting women's suffrage, government regulation to protect the environment, and higher salaries for teachers and other public employees. Despite his early progressive record, Coolidge adopted a hands-off approach once in the White House. In an era of peace and prosperity, Coolidge felt little need to flex federal power. His outlook may well have been conditioned by the tragic loss early in his term of his sixteen-year-old son, who died when a blister he developed while playing tennis became infected. When Calvin Jr. died, Coolidge recalled, "the power and the glory of the Presidency went with him." Coolidge had always been a man of few words, but only after his son's death did he become "Silent Cal."

Americans' hostility toward federal power reflected long-held and deep-seated fears that became especially pronounced during the 1920s. During the war the general public experienced the long arm of federal power: millions of young men were conscripted into the service; Washington's regulation of food and fuel touched every home; and government at every level restricted individual liberties. Before the war, progressives such as Jane Addams had argued that government power could expand individual opportunity by taming the excess of industrialism, but critics in the 1920s believed that intrusive federal power restricted individual freedom and local control. The "remorseless urge of centralization, the insatiable maw of bureaucracy," wrote a progressive senator, "are depriving more and more the people of all voice, all rights touching home and hearthstone, of family and neighbor."

Both Harding and Coolidge believed that Washington's primary goal was to foster business enterprise. This meant a hands-off policy in areas where businessmen wanted freedom of action and intervention in areas where they needed help. "Never before," observed the *Wall Street Journal*, "has a government been so completely fused with business." The emphasis on close business–government cooperation found expression in the regulatory commissions. Harding and Coolidge filled them with businessmen who believed their role was not to regulate but to assist business. Under Attorney General Harry Daugherty, the Justice Department refused to enforce antitrust statutes. "So long as I am Attorney General," Daugherty declared, "I am not going unnecessarily to harass men who have unwittingly run counter with the statutes." The Interstate Commerce Commission helped railroad companies negotiate lucrative contracts with shippers. In 1925, when Coolidge appointed William Humphrey to head the Federal Trade Commission (FTC), big business seized control of the agency. Humphrey, who denounced the FTC as "an instrument of oppression" created to "spread socialistic propaganda," used the organization to help businessmen set prices and limit production costs.

Secretary of the Treasury Andrew Mellon, who resigned from the boards of directors of fifty-one corporations on assuming office, feared that if high taxes deprived the businessman of a fair share of his earnings, then "he will no longer exert himself and the country will be deprived of the energy on which its continued greatness depends." Mellon fought successfully to reduce taxes on inheritances, corporate profits, and the well-to-do. By 1926 Congress had cut the tax rate on income of $1 million from 66 percent to 20 percent. These policies helped widen the gulf between rich and poor and concentrate capital in relatively few hands.

Secretary of Commerce Herbert Hoover, who dominated the cabinets of Harding and Coolidge before becoming president himself in 1928, believed that enlightened businessmen should play an important role in government. He called for the creation of an "associative state" in which government and business would work together to promote the public interest. Government must refrain from using coercive power, he argued; its role should be limited to authorizing studies and collecting data. Implementing his philosophy of government as information gatherer, Hoover transformed the Bureau of Standards into a national research center that encouraged businesses to adopt common standards of production.

Divided Democrats

A divided and demoralized Democratic Party offered little opposition to the revitalized Republicans. For most of the previous quarter-century, the Democratic Party's roots had been firmly planted in the rural South and West. In recent years, however, many of the immigrants flooding the nation's cities had joined the party, often as part of powerful urban machines. During the 1920s the two factions fought for control of the party.

WHAT A FRIEND
WE HAVE IN COOLIDGE!

THE CASH REGISTER CHORUS.

"The Cash Register Chorus"   The chief feature of the Harding and Coolidge administrations was a very favorable stance toward big business. Coolidge, who once said that "the chief business of the American people is business," believed that everyone benefitted when business interests prospered, and government's chief function was to ensure that they did. This cartoon features a quartet of businessmen singing the president's praises, accompanied by a ringing cash register.   (*State Historical Society of Missouri, Columbia.*)

The tension between these two constituencies played out at the party's 1924 convention. The convention assembled on June 24 in New York City's Madison Square Garden. In the midst of a terrible heat wave, the delegates battled for seventeen days. The party's urban wing rallied behind New York Governor Al Smith, whom Franklin Roosevelt called the "happy warrior of the political battlefield." Smith, a product of boss-led Tammany Hall, identified with the immigrant culture of the city. He wore the symbol of Tammany Hall—a brown derby hat set at a slight angle. A Catholic and former altar boy, he hung a portrait of the pope in his office. He drank openly in defiance of Prohibition, earning the nickname "Alcohol Al." The rural Protestant faction supported William Gibbs McAdoo of California, a strict prohibitionist, former secretary of the treasury, and son-in-law of Woodrow Wilson.

A fierce debate over a resolution to condemn the Klan exposed the deep cultural divide within the party and made futile any attempt to broker a compromise. The Smith forces hoped to embarrass McAdoo supporters by including a plank in the platform that condemned the Klan for its violations of civil liberties. William Jennings Bryan took the floor to oppose the amendment, which he claimed would tear the party apart. Smith delegates booed the former presidential nominee. During the balloting delegates engaged in fistfights. The mayor called out an additional thousand policemen to patrol the convention floor. Finally, after hours of debate, the convention voted 542 to 541 not to mention the Klan by name.

The debate over the Klan polarized the convention. In ballot after ballot neither Smith nor McAdoo received the two-thirds vote needed for nomination. Finally, after 102 ballots, both candidates withdrew their names. The nomination went to the obscure John Davis—a West Virginian by birth and a Wall Street lawyer. In order to add geographic and political balance to the ticket, the convention chose Governor Charles W. Bryan of Nebraska—the younger brother of William Jennings Bryan—as its vice-presidential nominee.

The Republicans had little difficulty deciding on incumbent Calvin Coolidge. As his running mate they chose former budget director Charles Dawes. The Republican platform, reflecting Coolidge's conservative views, stressed limited government, immigration restriction, and support for Prohibition.

In July progressives, dissatisfied with both nominees, held their own convention in Cleveland to organize a farmer–labor party to "break the power of the private monopolistic system over the economic and political life of the American people." They called on sixty-nine-year-old Robert M. La Follette ("Battling Bob") of Wisconsin to head their ticket (see page 816). Opponents branded La Follette a dangerous radical, the candidate of "the Reds, the Pinks, the Blues, and the Yellows." The Progressives, moreover, faced many of the same obstacles that traditionally hamper third parties: lack of funds, absence of grass-roots organization, inability to get on the ballot in every state.

On election day most voters decided to "Keep Cool with Coolidge." The Republican nominee won 54 percent of the popular vote, carried thirty-five states, and took 382 electoral votes. Davis received only 28.8 percent of the popular vote, twelve states, and 136 electoral votes. He carried only one state outside the South, Oklahoma. In four states—California, North Dakota, Wisconsin, and Minnesota—he carried less than 10 percent of the total vote. La Follette obtained 4.8 million votes—under 17 percent of the total—and captured only Wisconsin's thirteen electoral votes (see map on page 958). "In a fat and happy world, Coolidge is the man of the hour," observed William Allen White.

Commercial Diplomacy

The United States emerged from the war as a major power. During the 1920s American diplomats tried to reconcile the nation's new status as an economic and military power with its persistent isolationist streak. The nation's approach to the world was characterized less by a strict isolationism than by an "independent internationalism." The goal was to limit the likelihood of future wars by emphasizing nonmilitary means—treaties, conferences, and disarmament—to achieve world stability, preserve the freedom to act independently to protect the national interest, and extend

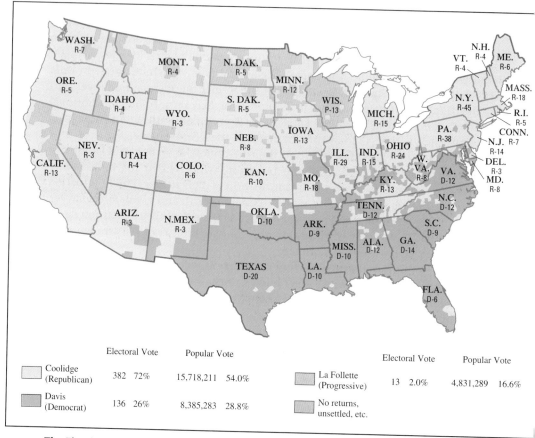

	Electoral Vote		Popular Vote			Electoral Vote		Popular Vote	
Coolidge (Republican)	382	72%	15,718,211	54.0%	La Follette (Progressive)	13	2.0%	4,831,289	16.6%
Davis (Democrat)	136	26%	8,385,283	28.8%	No returns, unsettled, etc.				

The Election of 1924   The majority of Americans chose to "keep cool with Coolidge" in the 1924 election, but obvious signs of political discontent were present. Robert M. La Follette led a third party of farmers suffering from declining crop prices, but the party's platform failed to stir urban voters. Disaffection also plagued the Democratic Party, whose internal rifts prevented it from gaining many votes outside the rural South.

American economic influence. The nation, observed a diplomat, championed a "commercial and non-military stabilization of the world."

Since neither Harding nor Coolidge had much interest in foreign policy, they delegated most of the responsibility to their secretaries of state. When a reporter asked Harding his views on Europe, the president responded, "I don't know anything about this European stuff." To run his foreign policy establishment Harding chose Charles Evans Hughes, a distinguished jurist, former governor of New York, and the 1916 Republican nominee for president. A patient and pragmatic diplomat, Hughes placed a premium on using international law and treaties to attain world order. The United States could not retreat from its world responsibilities. Instead, it must seek "to establish a *Pax Americana* maintained not by arms but by mutual respect and good will and the tranquilizing processes of reason." America, he maintained, needed to build a new international system, constructed and dominated by U.S. economic power.

That power was immense. After World War I the United States produced 70 percent of the world's petroleum and 40 percent of its coal. Between 1925 and 1929 it accounted for half of all industrial goods produced in the world. American private investment abroad grew fivefold, from $3.5 billion in 1914 to $17.2 billion in 1930. American culture also began its worldwide expansion as U.S. communications giants International Telephone and Telegraph (ITT), Radio Corporation of America (RCA), and Associated Press (AP) emerged as global giants. Hollywood as well extended its reach beyond the border. One critic observed that the sun "never sets on the British Empire and the American motion picture." The economic success fed the belief in the superiority of American values and the need to spread them to other nations. "There is only one first-class civilization in the world today, the *Ladies Home Journal* trumpeted. "It is right here in the United States."

The first step toward defusing international tensions was to stop growing military competition. The United States feared a new arms race with western Europe and Japan. Money spent on rifles was better invested in automobiles so standards of living could rise. The Far East remained a troubled spot. Policymakers worried that the alliance between Japan and a revitalized Britain would limit American influence and commerce in the region. In late 1921 Hughes invited eight leading powers (Britain, France, Italy, Japan, China, Belgium, the Netherlands, and Portugal) to Washington to discuss the naval arms race and competition in Asia.

In his opening speech at the Washington Conference, the bewhiskered Hughes startled the delegates by announcing that the United States would scrap thirty ships. He then turned to the British and Japanese delegates and challenged them to make similar cuts. "Secretary Hughes sank in 35 minutes more ships than all the admirals of the world have sunk in centuries," a British observer noted. Despite grumbling from naval officers, the diplomats successfully negotiated three agreements. In signing the Five-Power Treaty the leading powers agreed to achieve real disarmament by scrapping existing naval vessels. They accepted ratios for tonnage of battleships, battle cruisers, and aircraft carriers (smaller vessels were not covered) of approximately 5 for the United States and Great Britain, to 3 for Japan, and 1.75 for France and Italy. The Four-Power Treaty (United States, Britain, France, and Japan) declared that each nation would respect the others' rights in the Pacific. Finally, the Nine-Power Treaty (signed by the four powers plus Italy, China, Belgium, the Netherlands, and Portugal) politely endorsed the ideals of the Open Door toward China.

Avoiding military entanglements with other nations became a preoccupation of American policymakers during the decade. In 1928, when the French foreign minister Aristide Briand pressed the United States to join an alliance against Germany, Secretary of State Frank Kellogg (who had replaced Hughes in 1925) transformed the request into an agreement to "condemn recourse to war for the solution of international controversies, and renounce it as an instrument of national policy." The Kellogg-Briand Pact, later laughed at as nothing more than an "international kiss," was signed by most nations in the world.

With the arms race under control, the Republican administrations focused their energy on the global economic system that was still reeling from the impact of World War I. The United States planned to use its economic might to create a new world economic order. "Our international problems tend to become mainly economic problems," Hughes proclaimed in 1922. In Europe, Germany remained the critical problem. "There can be no economic recuperation in Europe unless Germany recuperates," Hughes declared. But the German economy was in shambles. In 1922, burdened with a $33 billion bill for war reparations, uncontrolled inflation, and a crippled economy, the Germans defaulted on their loans. France and Belgium, hoping to keep the Germans in debt and therefore unable to threaten their neighbors, refused to abrogate the harsh terms. In 1923 the French sent troops into the rich Ruhr Valley to pressure the German government into maintaining its payments. With the European economic system threatened with catastrophe, Washington negotiated a new agreement called the Dawes Plan, after Chicago banker and later vice president of the United States Charles G. Dawes. The plan reduced German reparations to $250 million annually and offered generous private loans to Germany.

The government aggressively flexed American economic muscle in Latin America. A 1924 survey revealed that of the twenty Latin American nations, only six were free of some kind of U.S. "management." During the 1920s the United States relied on economic might and political subversion to maintain its control. U.S. investments in Latin America jumped from $1.26 billion in 1914 to $3.52 billion in 1929. American corporations such as United Fruit Company and ITT invested millions in the region, aided by the government programs that helped build highways, communications systems, and utilities needed to attract private capital. Nor did America reject all use of military force. In 1926, when political instability threatened U.S. investment in Nicaragua, President Coolidge sent in the marines to restore order. The following year Washington negotiated the Peace of Tipitapa, which resulted in a U.S. supervised election in 1928.

Most Americans celebrated the economic and diplomatic achievements of the decade, but serious foreign policy problems remained. Nationalist leaders in Latin America resented U.S. dominance of the region. An Argentine writer called America the "new Rome," which enjoyed the "essentials of domination" without the "deadweight of areas to administrate and multitudes to govern." Many of the treaties negotiated contained potentially fatal flaws. The Washington Naval Treaty did not limit submarines, destroyers, or cruisers. None of the armament treaties provided means for verification or enforcement. Since the major powers were trying to isolate the Bolsheviks, they excluded Russia from the conference. The Dawes Plan may have averted a crisis, but it created a rickety financial structure that depended on a vigorous expansion of world trade and a constant stream of American dollars flowing into Germany.

Al Smith and the 1928 Election   In August 1927 President Coolidge handed reporters a slip of paper containing a simple, twelve-word sentence: "I do not choose to run for President in nineteen twenty-eight." The announcement shocked the nation and forced Republican leaders to find a nominee. It did not take long. Nearly everyone agreed that Secretary of Commerce Herbert Hoover was the most qualified prospect. A skilled engineer, a successful administrator, and a shrewd businessman, he seemed the perfect candidate for the new corporate age. In accepting the party's nomination, Hoover said, "We in America today are nearer to the final triumph over poverty than ever before in the history of the land." Hoover stressed the American system of free enterprise as the source of prosperity, promising a "chicken in every pot and two cars in every garage."

The Democrats managed to avoid the turmoil that had marred their 1924 convention. The death of William Jennings Bryan, and William McAdoo's announcement that "in the interest of party unity" he would not run, left the rural faction of the party without a visible leader. It also left the nomination to Al Smith. To balance the ticket Democrats selected Senator Joseph G. Robinson of Arkansas, a Protestant prohibitionist, to run for vice president. The platform avoided discussion of the social issues that had divided the party and instead took aim at Republican economic policies, which it charged had left the country with "its industry depressed, its agriculture prostrate."

Prosperity made a Republican victory almost certain, but social issues dominated the campaign. The two candidates highlighted the cultural clash of the decade. Smith opposed Prohibition; Hoover supported it. Smith hailed from the city; Hoover was from the country. Smith was Catholic; Hoover was Protestant. "If you vote for Al Smith," cried a preacher, "you're voting against Christ and you'll be damned." In radio broadcasts one preacher equated Smith with the urban evils of "card playing, cocktail drinking, poodle dogs, divorces, novels, stuffy rooms, dancing, evolution, Clarence Darrow, overeating, nude art, prize-fighting, actors, greyhound racing, and modernism."

On November 6 Hoover rolled to an overwhelming victory. No Democrat could have defeated the Great Engineer in the fall of 1928. As Mencken observed ruefully, "I incline to believe that Hoover could have beaten Thomas Jefferson quite as decisively as he beat Al." Hoover garnered 21.4 million popular votes (58.2 percent of those cast) to 15 million for Smith and 330,725 for socialist Norman Thomas and other minor party candidates. In the electoral college Hoover's margin was even more crushing. He carried forty-two of the forty-eight states, including New York, for 444 votes to Smith's 87 (see map on page 962). For the first time since Reconstruction, the party of Lincoln broke the Democratic hold on the South, capturing Virginia, North Carolina, Texas, Florida, and Tennessee. The victor's coattails gave Republicans big majorities in both houses of Congress.

Though Smith lost the election, his candidacy had an important impact on the future of the Democratic Party. Smith brought millions of ethnic voters to the polls for the first time in a national election. He defeated Hoover by two to one in Boston. He won previously Republican cities such as New Haven, Albany, Scranton, and St. Louis. In 1920 Harding had carried all twenty-seven of the nation's major cities outside the South. In 1928 Smith captured eight of those and registered gains in all the rest. In 1924 Republicans carried the largest twelve cities by a plurality of 1.3 million. In 1928 the Democrats carried these same cities by thirty thousand votes. The 1928 election saw a dramatic increase in voter turnout, with many people voting for the first time. Almost 25 percent more people voted in 1928 than in the previous presidential election. In 1928 most people contented themselves with

The Election of 1928

Herbert Hoover emphasized the Republican prosperity of the 1920s and his accomplishments as secretary of commerce under Harding and Coolidge in his bid for the White House. His opponent, New York Governor Alfred E. Smith, the son of Irish immigrants, fought to combat his stereotyped image as an urbanite, a "wet," and a Catholic. In November, only the Deep South remained wedded to the Democratic Party.

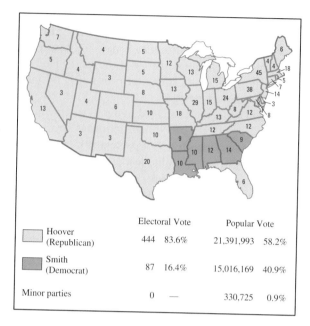

	Electoral Vote		Popular Vote	
Hoover (Republican)	444	83.6%	21,391,993	58.2%
Smith (Democrat)	87	16.4%	15,016,169	40.9%
Minor parties	0	—	330,725	0.9%

fulfilling the new president's promise of continued prosperity. Little did they realize that the world of the twenties was about to come crashing to an end. Only after the economic collapse would Americans slowly begin to realize that the cracks in the nation's economy had appeared long before the end of the roaring twenties.

CONCLUSION

Many trends and experiments from the previous decades—urbanization, industrialization, mechanization—combined to produce great changes in American society during the 1920s. The innovations in industrial technology, corporate organization, and mass culture have earned the decade the moniker "the New Era." During this period, new technologies such as electricity and electrical appliances reached millions of homes. The automobile provided Americans with a new freedom of mobility, helping spawn the suburban boom that would radically transform living patterns and the natural landscape in the second half of the century. With the rise of advertising, consumer culture became an integral part of American life. Though the prosperity of the decade was by no means universal, many groups— such as industrial workers and the growing number of clerical workers—did see their standards of living improve.

The development of mass entertainment established the groundwork for a new national culture. For the first time, Americans in different parts of the country were watching the same movies, listening to the same radio stations, and reading the same popular magazines. Mass culture intensified the cultural conflict of the decade by bringing previously isolated groups into contact with one another. The "combatants" in this clash of cultures took several sides. One group consisted of those who embraced the New Era and its experiments: young women who chose to assert their sexuality and independence, young men who embraced the automobile and the freedom it provided, advertisers who worked to sell modern age to consumers, urban workers who drank illegal liquor, jazz music *afficionados*, moviegoers, sports fans, and countless others. On the other side were people who distrusted modern society and disliked the new morality, viewing them as threats to the traditional values that set Americans apart in the world. This group included many white Protestants, prohibitionists, religious fundamentalists, Klansmen (and women), and nativists. Disenchanted intellectuals, often influenced by European writers, formed a third group that criticized both the provincialism of the traditionalists and the crass materialism of the modern enthusiasts.

Amidst these cultural upheavals politicians in the 1920s recoiled from the Progressive Era's reformist experimentation. Conservative Republican Presidents Warren G. Harding and Calvin Coolidge focused on limiting government regulation, promoting business expansion, and opening foreign markets. In the wake of social agitation, reform, and war, the Republicans emphasized the theme of "normalcy." Abroad, they stressed free trade and commercial expansion, while working for international disarmament and trying to avoid military entanglements with foreign powers. An experiment in adapting traditional isolationism to its new global role, the "independent internationalism" allowed the United States to assume a prominent place in world affairs without fielding a large peacetime military.

National politics was not immune to the cultural conflicts of the decade, however. The clash of cultures played out at the 1924 Democratic convention, where the party's urban and rural factions battled to a standstill. Four years later the cultural conflict found expression in the presidential contest. The Democrats nominated New York Governor Al Smith, a city-bred Catholic and outspoken critic of Prohibition. The Republicans chose Commerce Secretary Herbert Hoover, a Protestant from small-town Iowa and a supporter of Prohibition. Hoover soundly defeated Smith in the 1928 election, but Smith's campaign mobilized new voter groups—primarily immigrants and urban voters—and the Democrats captured the nation's large cities. This outcome presaged the alliance between the party's new urban wing and its traditional rural supporters that would become the New Deal coalition of the next decade.

Annotated Suggested Readings

Robert and Helen Lynd's *Middletown* (1929) provides a superb survey of American life and thought in the period. Frederick Lewis Allen's *Only Yesterday* (1931) appraises the so-called Roaring Twenties from the depths of the Great Depression. *Calvin Coolidge and the Coolidge Era* (1998), edited by John Earl Haynes, is a more recent collection of essays on a wide range of topics pertaining to the politics, diplomacy, economy, and culture of the period. Ellis Hawley examines the 1920s as a development of the First World War in *The Great War and the Search for a Modern Order* (1979). William Leuchtenburg's *The Perils of Prosperity* (1958) studies the economic weaknesses of the decade. Michael Parrish's *Anxious Decades* (1992) artfully connects the insecurities of the 1920s with the crises of the 1930s. Recent surveys of the social and political history of the 1920s are Lynn Dumenil's *The Modern Temper* (1995) and David Goldberg's *Discontented America* (1999). David

Montgomery's *The Fall of the House of Labor* (1987) provides information on industrial workers and the decline of the labor movement in the decade.

Jim Potter's *The American Economy Between the Wars* (1974) offers an introduction to the new economy of the 1920s. The best history of the rise of the automobile is James Flink's *The Car Culture* (1975). The history of the suburbs is the focus of Kenneth Jackson's *Crabgrass Frontier* (1985), while John Teaford studies the cities in *The Twentieth-Century American City* (1986). The growth of the advertising industry is chronicled in Ronald Marchand's *Advertising the American Dream* (1985) and Daniel Pope's *The Making of Modern Advertising* (1983). Alfred Chandler, Jr.'s two works, *Strategy and Structure* (1962) and *The Visible Hand* (1977), cover the corporate revolution. James Gilbert's *Designing the Industrial State* (1972) examines the cooperation between business and government in the 1920s.

Daniel Boorstin traces the emergence of mass culture in *The Democratic Experience* (1973). In *Daily Life in the United States* (2003), David Kyvig studies how people adjusted to the new technological and urban culture. The burgeoning movie industry is the subject of Robert Sklar's *Movie-Made America* (1976). Erik Barnouw studies the early development of radio in *A Tower of Babel* (1966). For sports in the 1920s, Elliott Gorn and Warren Goldstein's *A Brief History of American Sports* (1993) is a good starting point. Lizabeth Cohen's *Making a New Deal* (1990) describes how working people and immigrants adapted mass culture to fit their lives.

The "New Woman" and the new morality are the subjects of Sara Evans's *Born for Liberty* (1989). Beth Bailey studies the youth of the 1920s in *From Front Porch to Back Seat* (1988), while Susan Strasser examines middle-class women and popular culture in *Never Done* (1982). Angela Latham introduces women performers and the redefinition of sexual standards in *Posing a Threat* (2000). Alice Kessler-Harris focuses on wage-earning women in *Out to Work: A History of Wage-Earning Women in the United States* (1982). Sharon Strom Hartman's *Beyond the Typewriter* (1992) explores the gender and class hierarchy of the office culture. The contradictions in organized feminism during the decade are outlined in Nancy Woloch's *Women and the American Experience* (1984). Also see Nancy Cott's *The Grounding of Modern Feminism* (1987). Kenneth Rose studies the role of women's groups in the campaigns for Prohibition and repeal in *American Women and the Repeal of Prohibition* (1996).

For material on the Lost Generation, begin with Henry May's *The Discontent of the Intellectuals* (1963). Nathan Miller uses F. Scott Fitzgerald as the foundational character in *New World Coming* (2003). Stanley Coben examines the role of intellectuals in the assault on traditional morality in *Rebellion Against Victorianism* (1992). Edmund Wilson's *The Twenties* (1975) also covers intellectuals during the 1920s, as does Roderick Nash's *The Nervous Generation* (1969). David Cronin's *Black Moses* (1962) is a helpful introduction to Marcus Garvey; Theodore Vincent's *Black Power and the Garvey Movement* (1970) places Garvey in the broader African-American struggle. The Harlem Renaissance has been the subject of many wonderful books; Nathan Huggins's *Harlem Renaissance* (1971) and Gloria Hull's *Color, Sex, and Poetry: Three Women Writers of the Harlem Renaissance* (1987) are two of the best. Mark Robert Schneider emphasizes the role of the NAACP in *We Return Righting* (2001), while Tim Madigan looks at the Tulsa race riot of 1921 in *The Burning* (2001).

Maldwyn Jones's *American Immigration* (1960) contains some excellent material on immigration restriction. Paul Avrich's *Sacco and Vanzetti: The Anarchist Background* (1991) is a cultural history of the immigrant world of the 1920s. For the "new Klan," Kenneth Jackson's *The Ku Klux Klan in the City* (1967) is classic; also see Richard Tucker's *The Dragon and the Cross: The Rise and Fall of the Ku Klux Klan in Middle America* (1991). Nancy MacLean's *Behind the Mask of Chivalry* (1994) studies the world-view of Klan members.

Kathleen Blee's *Women of the Klan* (1991) explores the role women played in the group.

Edward Larson provides the most insightful analysis of the Scopes trial and its meaning in *Summer for the Gods* (1997). For the intellectual development of fundamentalism, see George Marsden's *Fundamentalism and American Culture* (1980). Prohibition has been studied at length. A good introduction is Andrew Sinclair's *Prohibition: The Era of Excess* (1962). Thomas Pegram's *Battling Demon Rum* (1998) is a survey of the entire temperance/prohibition movement, including repeal.

The Republican presidents of the 1920s were studied by John Hicks in *Republican Ascendancy* (1960) and by Robert Murray in *The Politics of Normalcy* (1973). Donald McCoy's *Calvin Coolidge* (1967) and David Burner's *Herbert Hoover* (1979) are two excellent biographies of the presidents. Robert Ferrell's *The Presidency of Calvin Coolidge* (1998) and *The Strange Deaths of President Harding* (1996) are recent assessments of the two presidencies. Emily Rosenberg studied the international expansion of American commerce and culture in *Spreading the American Dream* (1982). David Burner's *The Politics of Provincialism* (1967) is still the classic for the Democratic Party of the 1920s. Also see Kristi Andersen's *The Creation of a Democratic Majority, 1928–1936* (1979) for material on the Democrats and the 1928 campaign.

The **H**istory **C**ompanion

The Church and State

"For the Defense," 1925

Clarence Darrow was one of the country's most famous trial lawyers when he agreed to join John Thomas Scopes's legal team in 1925. He had won a reputation for fighting for progressive causes, defending the rights of labor, and opposing the death penalty. Since Scopes admitted he had violated the Tennessee law that prohibited teaching evolution in the state's public schools, Darrow had to challenge the constitutionally of the law, claiming that it violated the boundaries between church and state.

That is what was foisted on the people of this State . . . that it should be a crime in the State of Tennessee to teach any theory . . . except that contained in the divine account as recorded in the Bible.

But the State of Tennessee, under an honest and fair interpretation of the Constitution, has no more right to teach the Bible as the Divine Book than that the Koran is one, or the Book of Mormon, or the Book of Confucius, or the Buddha, or the Essays of Emerson. . . .

I know there are millions of people in the world who derive consolation in their times of distress from the Bible . . . but what is it? . . . The Bible is made up of sixty-six books written over a period of about 1,000 years, some of them very early and some of them comparatively late. It is a book primarily of religion and morals. It is not a book of science—never was and was never meant to be.

Who is the chief mogul that can tell us what the Bible means? . . . There are in America at least 500 different sects or churches, all of which quarrel with each other on the importance and non-importance of certain things or the construction of certain passages. All along the line they do not agree among themselves and cannot agree among themselves. They never have and they never will. . . . Who is it that can tell us that John Scopes taught certain theories that denied the . . . divine story of creation as recorded in the Bible? How did he know?

If today you can take a thing like evolution and make it a crime to teach it in the public schools, tomorrow you can make it a crime to teach it in the private schools . . . at the next session you may ban books and the newspapers. Soon you may set Catholic against Protestant, and Protestant against Protestant, and try to foist your own religion upon the minds of men.

"For the Prosecution," 1925

A celebrity also graced the ranks of the prosecution: William Jennings Bryan, the midwestern Populist who had three times been the Democratic nominee for president. A strict fundamentalist, Bryan accepted the Bible as literal truth and argued for strict enforcement of the law. He contended that the people of Tennessee had a right to decide what to teach in their schools and that Mr. Scopes had an obligation to comply with the people's will. The speech would be Bryan's swan song; he died only a few days after his famous cross-examination by Clarence Darrow.

Our position is that the statute is sufficient. The statute defines exactly what the people of Tennessee decided and intended and did declare unlawful, and it needs no interpretation.

The caption [of the statute] speaks of the evolutionary theory, and the statute specifically states that teachers are forbidden to teach in the schools supported by taxation in this State any theory of creation of man that denies the Divine record of man's creation as found in the Bible. . . .

The people of this State knew what they were doing when they passed the law, and they knew the dangers of the doctrine that they did not want it taught to their children.

The question is, Can a minority in this State come in and compel a teacher to teach that the Bible is not true and make the parents of these children pay the expenses of the teacher to tell their children what these people believe is false and dangerous?

Has it come to a time when the minority can take charge of a state like Tennessee and compel the majority to pay their teachers while they take religion out of the heart of the children of the parents who pay the teachers? Shall we be detached from the throne of God and be compelled to link their ancestors with the jungle,— tell that to these children? This is the doctrine that they . . . would force upon the schools, that they will not let the Bible be read!

Your Honor, we believe that [the defense's] evidence is not competent. This is not a mock trial. This is not a convocation brought here to allow these men to come and stand for a time in the limelight and speak to the world. . . . The facts are simple, the case is plain, and if these gentlemen want to enter upon a larger field of educational work in the subject of evolution, let us get through with this case and then convene a mock court, or it will deserve the title of mock court if its purpose is to banish from the hearts of the people the Word of God as revealed.

It had all begun simply enough. In 1924 the State of Tennessee passed a statute prohibiting the teaching of evolution in the state's schools. The American Civil Liberties Union, which saw the statute as an unacceptable infringement on academic freedom, offered to pay the legal expenses of any teacher who was willing to challenge the statute in court.

In Dayton, Tennessee, a group of townspeople read the ACLU's offer in the newspaper and decided that the trial could bring some much-needed publicity to their rundown steel town. They met with John Scopes, a math teacher and part-time football coach who had been teaching biology while the regular instructor was out sick. They explained that, by teaching evolution, he had been in violation of the new law. Then they asked: "John, would you be willing to stand for a test case?"

Everything seemed to be going according to the ACLU's plan. The plotters had failed to take into account, though, the larger debate that had been raging across the country. As Darwinian theory gained scientific credibility around the turn of the century, fundamentalist Christians began a campaign to keep the new scientific teachings out of the classroom. After several unsuccessful attempts in Kentucky and Georgia in 1921 and 1922, the anti-evolution crusade scored its first victory in Tennessee.

By the time of the ACLU test case in 1925, both sides of the debate were itching for a fight. Champions for both sides volunteered quickly. William Jennings Bryan had personally campaigned for the Tennessee statute and offered to help prosecute Scopes. Clarence Darrow had been a critic of Christianity his entire life and jumped at the chance to match wits with Bryan in court. A narrow test of a state law expanded into a national debate about evolution itself.

Yet the Scopes monkey trial was about more than just evolution. Many people were suspicious of where the decade's scientific "progress" was leading the country. If science and God had become incompatible, as Bryan argued, which should be retained? Many people also resented the Progressive Era's reliance on elites for reform. To many Tennesseans the ACLU lawsuit was yet another example of self-appointed "experts" overriding the popular will in service of the "public good." For the prosecution and its supporters the teaching of evolution signified more than simply an assault on traditional beliefs; it symbolized the contempt the nation's educated elite had for the "common people."

Clarence Darrow, however, did not question whether the majority of Tennesseans wanted evolution driven from the schools. Instead, he reminded the court of the harmful potential of majority rule. When the will of the majority interfered with the individual rights of the minority, he argued, the majority could and should be overridden. And when Tennesseans tried to enshrine religious dogma in the public school biology classes, they were violating the individual rights of teachers, who would not be able to teach what they thought was the truth.

The Scopes monkey trial had been treated more as a showcase than a serious legal proceeding. Accordingly, the trial did not resolve this cultural conflict. If anything, it clearly defined the growing chasm between progress and traditional belief.

QUESTIONS FOR ANALYSIS

1. Why does Darrow say that the Tennessee statute requires the teaching of religion?

2. Why does Darrow think teaching religion is impossible?

3. What dangerous consequences does Darrow see in the statute?

4. On what grounds does Bryan call the defense's case inappropriate?

5. According to Bryan, why is it just for Tennessee to pass such a statute?

6. Is Bryan's argument antidemocratic? Why?

7. Is evolution really at the heart of this debate? If not, what is?

8. Why do you think religion and education have been at the heart of so many controversies in American history?

25

"Fear Itself": Crash, Depression, and the New Deal

1929–1938

"Never in modern times, I should think, has there been so widespread unemployment and such moving distress from cold and hunger."

On March 4, 1933, in Washington, D.C., standing hatless and coatless on a dreary, windswept inauguration day, Franklin D. Roosevelt placed his hand on an old family Bible open at Paul's First Epistle to the Corinthians: "And now abideth faith, hope, charity, these three; but the greatest of these is charity." After reciting the oath of office, the new president turned to face the hundred thousand spectators somberly gathered in front of the Capitol. Despite the festive music and waving flags, the faces that greeted him were lined with despair. A journalist had compared the preinaugural atmosphere in Washington to "that which might be found in a beleaguered capital in wartime." But in the winter of 1933, it was not war that threatened the American democratic experiment. It was a deep and relentless economic depression.

The four-month interval between Roosevelt's election in November 1932 and his inauguration in March 1933 proved to be the most painful winter of the Great Depression. One in four Americans was without a job. Each month, thousands of farmers and business owners went bankrupt. As people lost faith in the economy, they withdrew funds from local banks. By March 3, the day before Roosevelt took office, thirty-eight states had shut down all their banks, and the remaining ten states were moving to close theirs. Normal business and commerce ground to a halt. A Roosevelt adviser, Rexford Guy Tugwell, wrote in his diary, "Never in modern times, I should think, has there been so widespread unemployment and such moving distress from cold and hunger."

On inauguration day, as he glanced out from behind the Great Seal of the United States, Roosevelt knew that his first task as president was to restore a sense of hope for the future and confidence in government. "Let me first assert my firm belief that the only thing we have to fear is fear itself—nameless, unreasoning, unjustified terror which paralyzes needed efforts to convert retreat into advance." In a firm and confident voice, he promised to ask Congress for "broad executive power to wage a war against the emergency, as great as the power that would be given to me if we were invaded by a foreign foe." For twenty minutes Roosevelt held the audience under his spell. When he finished, the crowd responded with cheers and thunderous applause. A few days later, a man who had listened to the address on the radio wrote a short note to the president that summed up the nation's reaction to the speech. "It seemed to give the people, as well as myself," he wrote, "a new hold upon life."

Roosevelt's words offered reassurance to a nation traumatized by the depression, but it would take more than words to ease the public's suffering. Beginning in 1933 the American people witnessed a frenzy of activity in Washington as Roosevelt launched a host of new programs and created myriad government agencies in the battle for recovery. The New Deal experiment built on the foundation of government activism laid during the Progressive Era to dramatically expand federal power. Despite the extraordinary changes, American social values and culture showed remarkable resilience. Most Americans endured the depression without losing faith in the capitalist system or their belief in the traditional notions of individualism and self-help at the core of the American experiment.

- What factors contributed to the economic collapse of the early 1930s?

- What was the New Deal, and how did it expand the role of government? How successful were New Deal programs at pulling the nation through the depression?

- How did American culture respond to the depression?

- What groups benefited the most from Roosevelt's policies? Why?

This chapter will address these questions.

THE GREAT DEPRESSION

The prosperity of the twenties had been built on a foundation of quicksand. The stock market crash in October 1929 exposed those weaknesses and signaled a steep descent into depression. The economic collapse imposed extraordinary hardships on almost all Americans. Conventional wisdom and past practice suggested that Washington maintain a hands-off approach to the collapse. Only slowly and reluctantly did President Herbert Hoover try to use the federal government to pull the nation from depression; his modest efforts were too little, too late. By 1932 Americans looked desperately for new leadership and greater government involvement to guide them through the troubled times.

The Crash The first signs that the fragile prosperity of the 1920s was about to shatter came on Wednesday, October 23, 1929. For the previous five years Wall Street investors had come to expect healthy profits as stock prices, in the words of a contemporary observer, "soared . . . into the blue and cloudless empyrean." The value of all stocks on the New York Stock Exchange

CHRONOLOGY

1929	Stock market crashes
1930	New York's Bank of the United States closes
1931	Reconstruction Finance Corporation created
1932	Bonus Army and the "Battle of Anacostia Flats" Franklin D. Roosevelt elected president
1933	Emergency Banking Act First Fireside Chat Prohibition repealed Public Works Administration and Civil Works Administration established Agricultural Adjustment Act and National Industrial Recovery Act Tennessee Valley Authority created Disney produces *Three Little Pigs*
1934	Indian Reorganization Act
1935	National Labor Relations Act, or Wagner Act Social Security Act guarantees old-age pensions Works Progress Administration formed from Emergency Relief Appropriation Congress of Industrial Organization formed *Schechter* v. *U.S.*
1936	Roosevelt wins reelection Keynes publishes *The General Theory of Employment, Interest, and Money* *Butler* v. *U.S.*
1937	United Automobile Workers strike in Flint, Michigan Roosevelt attempts to "pack" the Supreme Court Economy slides into deep recession
1938	O. Wells broadcasts H. G. Wells's *The War of the Worlds*
1939	Steinbeck publishes *The Grapes of Wrath*

almost doubled between 1925 and 1929, rising from $34 billion to $64 billion. The laws of economic gravity suggested that the market could not continue its upward spiral. No one, however, expected the fall to be so sudden or so steep. On October 23, however, a wave of panic selling gripped investors, who dumped more than $4 billion in stocks. By noon the next day, a day known as "Black Thursday," the market had lost another $9 billion.

Leading bankers assembled in an emergency meeting to develop a strategy to stem the collapse. They decided that all the nation needed was a show of confidence. "It's going to be all right," exclaimed the head of the nation's largest bank, who orchestrated a $20 million buying binge among leading investors. The reassuring words and the infusion of new money failed to slow the market's fall. The following Tuesday, October 29, in what the economist John Kenneth Galbraith called "the most devastating day in the history of the New York Stock Market," panicked investors sold more than 16.4 million shares—a record that would stand until 1968. By the end of the day the market had lost $32 billion. An October 30 newspaper headline declared "Wall St. Lays an Egg." The slide continued for three more weeks. By the time it ended in mid-November, the stock market had lost nearly one-third of its value.

The market collapse had little direct impact on the overall economy. Only a handful of wealthy Americans—about 2.5 percent of the population—owned stock. No companies went bankrupt. Most economists, who blamed the crash on reckless speculation, saw the drop as a necessary correction and predicted a complete recovery. "The great task of the next few months," wrote the editors of the left-leaning *Nation*, "is the restoration of confidence—confidence in the fundamental strength of the financial structure . . . confidence in the essential soundness of legitimate industry and trade."

Had the economy been sound and healthy, public confidence could have been restored. But the economy was neither. The nation's haphazard banking system was the weakest link in the economic chain. Only one-third of the twenty-five thousand banks operating in 1929 were members of the Federal Reserve System, which had been created by President Woodrow Wilson in 1913 to bring financial stability and standardized practice to banks. Most banks were small, independent, and grossly undercapitalized. Beginning in 1930 American depositors and foreign investors, worried about the economy and spooked by Wall Street, began withdrawing funds. Caught with huge outstanding liabilities and dwindling deposits, banks called in mortgage and loan repayments. When people could not come up with the cash, the banks foreclosed on homes and property before going under themselves, leaving investors empty-handed. Initially, the panic was confined to rural areas, but on December 11, 1930, it struck at the heart of the U.S. banking system, forcing New York's Bank of the United States, which held the savings of some four hundred thousand persons totaling nearly $286 million, to close its doors.

The combination of the stock market collapse and the bank failures killed any attempt to revive public confidence. Consumer spending, often on credit, had stoked the economic fires during the 1920s. In 1930, with many Americans shaken by the events on Wall Street and concerned about their jobs and bank accounts, consumer spending dropped by 10 percent, driving down the sales of new cars, homes, and household items. This in turn led companies to cut production and lay off workers.

By 1929 Americans' purchasing power was too feeble to keep the financial boat afloat. Most of the decade's economic gains had gone to a handful of wealthy people whose spending habits could not sustain economic growth. By the end of the decade, the richest 1 percent of the population owned 60 percent of the nation's wealth. Industrial output had soared by 40 percent and corporate profits increased by 80 percent, but workers' wages grew by only 8 percent. Farmers, who had been plagued by falling prices for most of the decade (see page 938), had little money.

It also became clear by 1930 that the expansion rested on a flimsy framework of speculative buying and unregulated practices. There was no effective regulation of the securities market, and investment bankers, lawyers, and accountants allowed investors to borrow heavily and to purchase stock on margin, putting down as little as 10 percent of a stock's value. As long as the value of the stock increased, as it had for most of the decade, everyone was happy: investors made money and brokers reaped large commissions. The phantom prosperity evaporated when the market crashed. Brokers called in their loans, leaving individual investors with huge bills.

Finally, the frailties in the international economic system began to take their toll. World War I had left England and France heavily in debt to America. The Allies tried to fund repayment by squeezing Germany for reparations (see page 960). Until 1928 American investors helped prevent catastrophe by pouring loans into Germany, but the market crash choked off foreign loans. In addition, high U.S. tariffs stifled international trade, which fell by nearly $1.2 billion in 1930. Cut off from American credit and markets, Europe's economy crumbled. By September 1930 England was burdened with 25 percent unemployment. Rising joblessness in Europe, in turn, dried up markets for American goods and agricultural products. In the first three years of the depression, the value of American foreign trade fell from $9 billion to $3 billion. The precarious economic conditions caused an unprecedented decline in the national income from $88 billion in 1929 to $40 billion four years later. In 1930 twenty-six thousand businesses failed; the following year another twenty-eight thousand collapsed. Corporate profits fell from $10 billion to less than $1 billion. The gross national product dropped from $80 billion to $42 billion as the economy shrank to half its former size. As one observer put it, "People felt the ground give way beneath their feet."

Hard Times   As the collapse constricted the economy, corporations slashed jobs and wages. Workers, who on average earned a weekly wage of $25 in 1929, received only $16.73 in 1933. And they were the lucky ones. Nearly a quarter of the work force was unemployed in 1933. That year in Ohio 50 percent of the labor force in Cleveland and 80 percent of workers in Toledo were without work. More than a million people were jobless in New York. Unemployed office workers sold apples on street corners for five cents apiece. *Fortune* magazine estimated that 27.5 million Americans had no regular income at all. Without paychecks many Americans were unable to make mortgage payments on their homes. By 1933 nearly six hundred thousand homeowners had lost their property.

Unable to pay rents or mortgages, people and families without work either lived off the generosity of relatives or became part of the sea of the homeless. By 1932 between 1 and 2 million people were homeless in America. In parts of Arkansas, families lived in caves; in Oakland, California, they sought refuge in sewer pipes. More than a million of the jobless roamed the country as hobos. The situation in Washington, D.C., was terrifying. "I come home from [Capitol] Hill every night filled with gloom," a newsman wrote. "I see on the streets filthy, ragged, desperate-looking men such as I have never seen before."

The growing waves of misery overwhelmed relief efforts, which existed only at the local level. Bread lines and soup kitchens staffed by local charities proliferated but failed to stem the tide of suffering. In the winter of 1931–1932 New York City families on relief received $2.39 per week. In Houston city officials stopped processing relief applications from black and Hispanic families. Philadelphia, Detroit, and St. Louis dropped families from relief roles because of a lack of money. More than a hundred cities provided no relief at all. In 1932 total public and private expenditures on relief amounted to only $317 million, less than $27 for the entire year for each of the 12 million jobless.

For many people, finding food became a daily struggle. One of five children attending school in New York City suffered from malnutrition. In depressed coal-mining areas of Illinois, Kentucky, Ohio, Pennsylvania, and West Virginia, more than 90 percent of children went hungry. In cities across the country, children and adults dug through garbage cans for rotten food. In Chicago, according to one report, after a trash truck dumped its cargo, a waiting crowd "started digging with sticks, some with their hands, grabbing bits of food and vegetables." When a teacher in West Virginia told a young girl to go home and eat, the child replied: " I can't. This is my sister's day to eat."

The majority of American families maintained at least some source of income during the depression, but it was often sharply reduced, and the average family struggled to adapt. Many families tried to cut costs by sharing living space with other families. Young couples, worried about earning a living, delayed marriage. The year 1932 saw 250,000 fewer marriages than 1929. For the first time in Ameri-

Hard Times   The bread line, like this one at a Chicago soup kitchen in 1931, was a familiar sight during the depths of the depression. In some cities, the ranks of the unemployed comprised 40 percent of the population, including many middle-class men who normally would have been too proud to accept charity. Such conditions to some degree broke the American spirit of individualism that had historically proved hostile to the idea of public assistance. *(National Archives.)*

can history, the birthrate dropped below the replacement level. Divorce rates also declined, a trend that inspired some observers to suggest that the depression strengthened families. A Muncie, Indiana, newspaper editorialized, "Many a family that has lost its car has found its soul."

This optimistic pronouncement did not take into account the tremendous strains the economic collapse imposed on families. Divorce declined, but desertion soared. By 1940 more than 1.5 million married women lived apart from their husbands. The number of neglected or abandoned children placed in institutions increased by 50 percent during the first two years of the depression. More than two hundred thousand vagrant children, victims of broken families, roamed the nation's streets. The Children's Bureau reported that many children found themselves "going for days at a time without taking off their clothes to sleep at night, becoming dirty, unkempt, a host to vermin. They may go for days with nothing to eat but coffee, bread and beans."

The depression blurred gender roles within the family. Many men were overwhelmed by guilt because they could not support their loved ones. "I haven't had a steady job in more than two years," moaned one father. "Sometimes I feel like a murderer. What's wrong with me, that I can't protect my children?" The father's diminished role increased the mother's role as provider. Homemakers watched household budgets with a close eye. In towns and cities flowerbeds became vegetable gardens. Despite widespread hostility, many women entered the workplace. In most cases the opportunities were limited to traditional "women's work." But there were exceptions. In Mississippi two-thirds of all female textile workers were married. In black families the economic contributions of married women were great. Forty percent of black women were in the labor force at any time, compared to 20 percent of white women. A government study, noting that nearly half of black women workers had lost their jobs as compared to three out of ten white women, concluded that the economic hardship of the depression had fallen "with double harshness upon Negro women."

In both the North and the South the depression pushed African-Americans deeper into poverty. In 1930 the majority of blacks still lived below the Mason-Dixon Line, most growing cotton as sharecroppers and tenant farmers. Their livelihoods crumpled even before the stock market: cotton prices had dropped sharply through the twenties from eighteen cents per pound in 1919 to six cents in 1933. That year, two-thirds of the African-Americans cultivating cotton had no earnings after paying their debts. Moving to southern cities in search of work, blacks encountered angry unemployed whites shouting slogans such as "No Jobs for Niggers Until Every White Man Has a Job!" By 1931 more than 50 percent of blacks living in southern cities were unemployed.

Competition for scarce resources inflamed racial tensions. The Ku Klux Klan reported an upsurge in membership, and the number of lynchings tripled between 1932 and 1933. In 1935 alone, white mobs lynched nearly two dozen blacks. One of the most notorious cases of racial injustice revolved around the plight of the "Scottsboro boys." In 1931 authorities arrested nine black teenagers and charged them with raping two white women on a train bound for Scottsboro, Alabama. Twelve days after their arrest, an all-white jury sentenced them to the electric chair.

The Supreme Court overturned the conviction the following year, on the grounds that the young men had not received a proper defense. A second trial demolished the prosecution's case: there was no physical evidence of rape and one of the women recanted her testimony. Still, another all-white jury found the youths guilty, only to have the Supreme Court once again reverse the decision, claiming the defendants had been denied due process. In 1935 state officials dropped charges against four of the "Scottsboro boys." The other five served long prison terms.

In northern cities unemployment rates among blacks soared to levels similar to those in the South. In 1931 sociologist Kelley Miller described the black worker as "the surplus man, the last to be hired and the first to be fired." The statistics told the story of hardship and hunger. In a survey of 106 cities, the Urban League found that "with a few notable exceptions . . . the proportion of Negroes unemployed was from 30 to 60 percent greater than for whites." Discriminated against by both employers and unions, adult black males faced bleak alternatives.

Other ethnic minorities faced similar hardships. During the 1920s hundreds of thousands of Mexicans had moved to California and the Southwest. Mexican-Americans reacted to hard times by forming unions and engaging in strikes for better wages. The Immigration Service supported the efforts of powerful growers to break the strikes by deporting workers who joined unions. Aiding the growers was an influx of three hundred thousand white migrants who arrived in California's Central Valley desperate for work in the fields between 1935 and 1938. Growers were happy to hire them as strikebreakers and replacements for the Mexicans, many of whom were forcibly taken to Mexico or went voluntarily. An estimated five hundred thousand Hispanic workers, many of them legal residents or American citizens by birth, crossed into Mexico during the decade. By the late 1930s poor whites made up 90 percent of the state's migrant farm workers. Most had come from the Great Plains states.

Residents of the Great Plains had to contend with the dual impact of depression and drought. Searing summer heat killed thousands of people, cattle, fish, and birds. By 1930 years of land mismanagement and below-normal rainfall were destroying whole communities on the Great Plains as the topsoil dried up and blew away. Each year between 1929 and 1933 scores of dust storms howled across the land. These black blizzards transformed western Kansas, eastern Colorado, western Oklahoma, the Texas Panhandle, and eastern New Mexico into an ecological wasteland. "This is the ultimate darkness," wrote a Kansas victim. A journalist traveling across the southern plains coined the phrase "Dust Bowl" to describe the tragic conditions he witnessed. "The impact is like a shovelful of fine sand flung against the face," reported an observer. "People caught in their own yards grope for the doorstep. Cars come to a standstill, for no light in the world can penetrate that swirling murk."

Millions of people fled the stricken region. Nearly a million Dust Bowl refugees, collectively called "Okies," took to the nation's highways and railroads. Railroad officials in Kansas City observed 1,500 transients a day hitching rides on freight trains. In 1936 seven counties in southeastern Colorado reported only 2,078 houses occupied; 2,811 houses were abandoned and another 1,522 homes had disappeared. Most of the migrants made their way to California, where they hoped to

Dust Storm in Springfield   Exploitative farming practices and overgrazing combined with natural phenomena to create the Dust Bowl, one of the worst ecological disasters in American history, affecting vast portions of the western Great Plains. The dry and windy conditions sent hundreds of millions of tons of topsoil into the air, creating storms like this one in Springfield, Colorado. The storm snuffed out sunlight and seeped through the cracks in people's homes to cover them and their possessions in a fine layer of dust. When the storm passed, residents emerged to find streets, cars, and sometimes even small buildings buried in dirt.   *(Corbis.)*

find new opportunity. But in the words of one journalist, "To the vast majority of the refugees the promised land proved to be a place of new and cruel tragedy." A migrant family earned about $450 a year on average, less than half the subsistence level. One of the characters in John Steinbeck's novel chronicling a family's migration, *The Grapes of Wrath* (1939), lamented, "Oakie use' ta mean you was from Oklahoma. Now it means you're scum."

Hoover Faces the Depression

Few people were better prepared to confront the growing crisis than President Herbert Hoover. After saving Belgium and Russia from starvation as the head of the American Relief Administration at the end of World War I, Hoover spent eight years as commerce secretary. Along the way, he earned high marks for his progressive ideas and efficient administration. A journalist noted that Hoover "gave the effect of having thoroughly anticipated the debacle and mapped out the shortest road to recovery."

Most economists and many leading politicians argued that government should refrain from interfering with the market and allow the depression to run its course. The United States had experienced steep declines in the past, one as recently as 1921, and the economy had always rebounded without help from Washington. "You might just as well try to prevent the human race from having a disease as to prevent economic grief of this sort," advised Oklahoma's Democratic senator, Thomas Gore.

Hoover, however, was unwilling to abide by the conventional wisdom. Like most Americans in 1929 and 1930 he assumed that the crash marked a temporary dip in the business cycle. "The fundamental business of the country is on a sound and prosperous basis," Hoover said the day after Black Thursday. But he also believed that the national government needed to take active steps to end the deflationary spiral and restore public confidence in business. In November 1929, during the Wall Street selloff, he summoned business leaders to the White House and pressured them to agree to maintain wages and employment. He goaded the Federal Reserve System to ease credit by lowering its discount rate to member banks. In December he asked Congress to appropriate $140 million for new public buildings.

The president's unprecedented response incurred the wrath of both the business community and many conservative Democrats and Republicans, but it failed to revive the economy. By the end of 1930, 26,355 business had failed, the gross national product had slumped more than 12 percent, and production in steel mills and automobile factories had dropped by 38 percent. When his efforts to revive domestic spending failed, Hoover turned his attention to stabilizing failing international economic markets. Claiming that "the major forces of the depression now lie outside of the United States," Hoover moved to balance the federal budget and raise taxes in 1931. A balanced budget, he contended, would reassure foreign investors, produce lower interest rates, and encourage business borrowing. In his boldest move, Hoover approved creation of the Reconstruction Finance Corporation (RFC), which lent money to financial institutions. By July the RFC had pumped $1.2 billion into the economy. Later that year, he signed legislation allowing the RFC to lend money directly to state and local governments. However, the RFC also faced intense criticism for its suspected favoritism toward certain banks. These suspicions seemed confirmed by a $90 million loan to a Chicago bank owned by the RFC's first chairman, Charles G. Dawes, shortly after his resignation from the RFC. Hoover also asked Congress to pass the Federal Home Loan Bank Act and to increase funding for federal land banks. The Glass-Steagall Act of February 1932 added $1 billion of gold to the money supply.

Hoover's experiments in economic intervention were far from timid, but nothing seemed to work. He, like the rest of the nation, was overwhelmed by the severity of the crisis. Critics, most of whom offered no viable alternatives to halting the suffering, pilloried the hapless Hoover, accusing him of being callous and indifferent to the despair around him. Democrats labeled the crisis the "Hoover Depression." The tarpaper-and-cardboard shacks housing the nation's homeless became known as "Hoovervilles." As public hostility increased, Hoover withdrew into himself, communicating with the American public through press releases. According to one story, Hoover asked Treasury Secretary Andrew Mellon, "Can you lend me a nickel to call a friend?" Mellon responded, "Here's a dime. Call all of them."

His reaction to the Bonus Army sealed Hoover's doom. The "army" was made up of veterans of World War I who descended on Washington to lobby for immediate payment of bonuses due them (in 1945) for their service. Many brought wives and children along. When the Senate rejected the bonus bill, most of the veterans left for home. About eight thousand, however, camped in ramshackle quarters on Anacostia Flats across the river from the Capitol, promising to squat there "until 1945" if necessary to receive their money. When a scuffle between some veterans and police resulted in gunfire, Hoover called in the army to maintain order. Army Chief of Staff General Douglas MacArthur, exceeding his orders, decided instead to forcibly remove the protesters. At dusk on July 28, 1932, MacArthur charged into the Flats with tanks and a column of infantry, tossing tear gas canisters into tents and plunging with bayonets drawn into crowds of men, women, and children. The image of armed soldiers with tanks routing citizens outraged many Americans. The so-called Battle of Anacostia Flats marked the low point of the Hoover presidency.

THE NEW DEAL EXPERIMENT, 1933–1938

When Franklin Roosevelt assumed the presidency, a desperate public looked to him for action. "Yours is the first opportunity to carve a name in the halls of immortals beside Jesus," a citizen wrote in a letter to the White House. Roosevelt responded with a bold program of measures to provide relief for the unemployed and recovery for the economy. The unprecedented experiment called the New Deal did not end the depression or silence critics, but it did win the support of millions of Americans who now swore allegiance to the Democratic Party. It also earned Roosevelt the lasting enmity of tradition-minded conservatives who opposed the New Deal's expansion of government size and influence. By 1938 the New Deal had lost momentum, but not before Roosevelt had dramatically altered the role of government and established himself as one of the most influential presidents in American history.

FDR and the 1932 Election

Franklin Delano Roosevelt was born on January 30, 1882, in Hyde Park, New York. His patrician family provided him with all the comforts of wealth. He received his early education from private tutors and enjoyed life on his family's 187-acre Hyde Park estate. In 1896 he enrolled in Groton, a distinguished prep school near Boston. Four years later he entered Harvard. While at Harvard he fell in love with his distant cousin Eleanor, who charmed him with her sincerity and intelligence. They were married in 1905. That same year Roosevelt enrolled in Columbia University Law School. Although he left without earning his degree, he passed the bar exam and entered a prestigious Wall Street law firm. But corporate law could never satisfy his ambition. He yearned for a larger arena and found it in politics.

Choosing the Democratic Party, Roosevelt began his political career in 1910 when he won election as a New York state senator. In 1913 he became Wilson's assistant secretary of the navy, and in 1920 he was the party's popular choice to run for vice president in the losing campaign of James Cox. The following year, Roosevelt's bright political life nearly ended when, at the age of thirty-nine, he was stricken with poliomyelitis. The disease left Roosevelt paralyzed from the waist down. Usually depending on a wheelchair, he managed to walk only with the aid of heavy steel braces and crutches. Roosevelt emerged from the ordeal with greater character, patience, and empathy for the less fortunate. He once told a friend that the hardest thing he ever tried to do was to wiggle his big toe after polio had destroyed his legs. After that struggle, he said, all else was easy.

In 1928 Roosevelt withstood the Republican landslide that swept Hoover into office and won election as the governor of New York. As governor he advanced many ideas that were to mark his early presidency—repeal of the Prohibition amendment, government regulation of electric utilities, unemployment insurance, and the use of public works to provide jobs. His political success made him a leading contender for president. Despite opposition from conservative Democrats, Roosevelt gained the party's nomination on the fourth ballot. To mollify the rural, southern wing of the party, he asked Speaker of the House John Nance Garner of Texas to join the ticket as the party's vice-presidential nominee.

The depression had crippled Hoover's presidency and made a Democratic victory almost certain. "All you have to do," Garner told FDR, "is to stay alive until election day." But Roosevelt waged an energetic campaign, traveling by train on a 13,000-mile whistle-stop trip to the West Coast, giving nearly a hundred speeches along the way. His addresses failed to present a coherent agenda, and often his proposals for expanded public works seemed to contradict his pleas for lower taxes and reduced government spending. Though vague on specifics, however, Roosevelt managed to

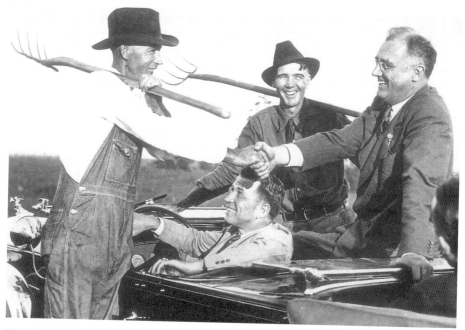

FDR, the Candidate   Though he gave no specifics during the campaign, Roosevelt's promise of a "new deal for the American people" and the spirit of optimism he projected accounted for his enormous appeal in 1932. This photograph of Roosevelt greeting farmers in Georgia speaks to another of his assets, a common touch that belied his aristocratic background. Notice too that FDR is campaigning from his car; for most of his presidency, he managed to disguise the paralysis that confined him to a wheelchair. *(Hulton Getty/Liaison.)*

convey to most Americans that he planned to use the power of the federal government to lift the nation out of depression and aid those in need. In his acceptance speech at the Democratic convention, Roosevelt told the delegates, "I pledge you, I pledge myself, to a New Deal for the American people." He promised to look after the "forgotten men, the unorganized but indispensable units of economic power."

As expected, on election day the voters repudiated Hoover and the Republicans by decisive majorities. Roosevelt received almost 23 million votes to Hoover's almost 15.8 million. He carried forty-two of forty-eight states and gained 472 electoral votes to Hoover's 59 (see map below). The Democrats attained their largest majorities in both houses of Congress since before the Civil War, winning the House with 312 seats to 123 seats and the Senate with 59 seats to 37 seats.

The First Hundred Days

In the months between Roosevelt's election in November 1932 and his inauguration in March 1933, the nation slid deeper into the trough of the depression. "When we arrived in Washington on the night of March 2," wrote a Roosevelt adviser, "terror held the country in grip." How would the new president respond to the crisis?

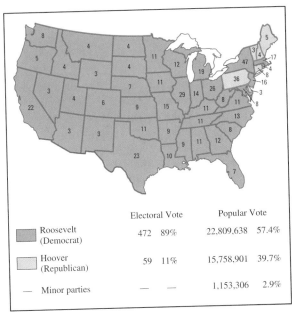

	Electoral Vote		Popular Vote	
■ Roosevelt (Democrat)	472	89%	22,809,638	57.4%
□ Hoover (Republican)	59	11%	15,758,901	39.7%
— Minor parties	—	—	1,153,306	2.9%

The Election of 1932   After narrowly winning his party's nomination, Franklin Roosevelt spent the campaign season touring the country, uniting traditional southern Democrats and the northern working class with frustrated western farmers. Americans were looking for someone who could end the economic crisis, but few were willing to stray from the two major parties. Third parties such as the Socialists, who polled only 882,000 votes, were no match for the charismatic Franklin Roosevelt, whose campaign song "Happy Days Are Here Again" exemplified his campaign's hopeful vision for the future.

The first order of business was to save the nation's banks, which had been bleeding money as panicked investors withdrew their life's savings. On March 5 Roosevelt proclaimed a nationwide "bank holiday" to last until he could push a recovery bill through Congress. With the banks closed, Roosevelt hurried through Congress the Emergency Banking Act, which provided expanded federal credit for banks and authorized the reopening of banks under strict new guidelines. The day before the banks were scheduled to reopen, Roosevelt addressed the nation in the first of his "Fireside Chats" over the radio (see Competing Voices, page 1007). In a commanding yet intimate voice, he reassured his 60 million listeners, explaining in simple terms "that it is safer to keep your money in a reopened bank than under the mattress." The public responded to Roosevelt's calming message. By March 15 deposits were exceeding withdrawals, and by the end of the month nearly $1 billion had flowed back into the system. Later that spring, Congress passed a second Glass-Steagall Banking Act, which prevented commercial banks from engaging in risky investments and created the Federal Deposit Insurance Corporation (FDIC) to insure individual bank deposits up to $2,500. The administration also sought to shore up confidence in the stock and bond markets with passage of the Federal Securities Act in May. This legislation, which required issuers of securities to provide full public disclosure, led to the creation of the Securities and Exchange Commission (SEC) in 1934.

On March 10 Roosevelt sent his second emergency proposal to Congress. The Economy Act fulfilled the president's pledge to reduce government spending, cutting $400 million from veterans' payments and $100 million from the salaries of federal employees. Congress approved the measure on March 20 and two days later passed the Beer-Wine Revenue Act, signaling an end to Prohibition. On April 7 beer was legally sold in America for the first time since 1919.

After the initial flurry of activity, the administration turned its attention to its two top priorities: relief for the millions of Americans left jobless by the collapse, and recovery for the ailing economy. The government offered relief to the unemployed by providing jobs in the new Civilian Conservation Corps (CCC). One of the most popular New Deal programs, the CCC provided jobs for more than 2 million men in army-style camps in national parks and forests. For $30 a month, they planted trees, cleared campsites, built bridges, constructed dams, and blazed fire trails. Congress appropriated $3.3 billion for a new Public Works Administration (PWA) to undertake an ambitious public construction program. The PWA's impact was limited by the cautious, penny-pinching ways of its head, Interior Secretary Harold Ickes. "He still has to learn," complained one of his assistants, "that the Administrator of a $3 billion fund hasn't time to check every typewriter acquisition."

Congress also approved creation of the Federal Emergency Relief Administration (FERA), headed by former social worker Harry Hopkins, to allocate $500 million to state and local governments to dispense to needy families. Half the money went to the states on a matching basis of one federal dollar for three state dollars. Hopkins had discretion to distribute the remaining $250 million on the basis of "need." In a flurry of executive action, Hopkins distributed over $5 million during his first two hours in office.

With FERA the New Deal took its first tentative steps toward the welfare state. But FERA's brief history underscored the problems Roosevelt faced by challenging

The Civilian Conservation Corps The CCC, one of the most successful New Deal programs, pumped millions of dollars into the nation's economy. The government required that $25 of all CCC employees' monthly paychecks be sent home to their families, while another $5 a month went directly to the workers, who spent the money in communities near their work sites. Their efforts also furthered the field of conservation across the country. They planted almost three million trees before the program ended in 1942, as well as creating reservoirs and irrigation systems, and building roads and campgrounds in national parks. These CCC workers are returning to camp after a hard day in Yosemite National Park. *(National Archives.)*

ingrained notions of self-help and limited government. Since FERA's staff was small, never numbering more than a few hundred people, Hopkins had to rely on state and county officials to screen applicants and distribute benefits. Even so, and even though most states had exhausted their own limited funds for dealing with the needy, many complained about federal intrusion into what had traditionally been a local function. More important, the whole idea of government relief ran counter to cherished American faith in self-sufficiency. A reporter noted that the state relief committee in North Dakota was dominated by officials who "think there is something wrong with a man who cannot make a living." The attitude was shared by the unemployed, who were reluctant and often embarrassed to seek relief. "I have seen thousands of these defeated, discouraged, hopeless men and women, cringing and fawning as they come to ask for public aid," said the mayor of Toledo, Ohio. "It is a spectacle of national degeneration."

By October 1933 Hopkins, having grown frustrated with the inherent problems of public relief, convinced Roosevelt to set up a temporary program that coupled relief with work, the Civil Works Administration (CWA). Within a month Hopkins had put 2.6 million people on his payroll. CWA workers refurbished 500,000 miles of roads and 40,000 schools, and they built 150,000 outdoor privies throughout the

South. Hopkins hired actors to give free shows and librarians to catalog archives. He even paid researchers to study the history of the safety pin. Jobs in the CWA gave hope and a sense of pride to the unemployed and the distressed. "When I got that [CWA] card it was the biggest day of my whole life," recalled a CWA participant. "At last I could say, 'I've got a job.'"

Developing programs to revive the economy proved more difficult. The administration realized that recovery would not be possible without an aggressive policy to aid the nation's ailing farmers. For most of the previous decade, farmers had produced more crops than the market could absorb. With supply outpacing demand, the prices farmers received for their commodities plummeted. A bushel of wheat that sold in Chicago for $2.94 in 1920 sold for $1 by 1929 and for thirty cents by 1932. To remedy the supply problem, Roosevelt pushed the Agricultural Adjustment Act (AAA) through Congress in May 1933. The law provided farmers with subsidies for letting acreage lie fallow or shifting its use to nonsurplus crops. Corn producers, for example, received thirty cents a bushel for corn not raised. The AAA also created a "commodity loan" program designed to keep crops that had already been harvested from reaching the market.

Secretary of Agriculture Henry A. Wallace was charged with the distasteful task of ordering farmers to plow up millions of acres of cotton, corn, and wheat and to slaughter millions of baby hogs to be eligible for the subsidy payments. Over the next two years, farmers took more than 30 million acres out of production and received over $1.1 billion in government subsidies. These drastic actions, taken at a time when many Americans were starving, provoked angry disapproval. A critic noted that Roosevelt solved the paradox of want amid plenty by doing away with plenty. But the policies achieved their desired goals. The price of a bushel of wheat almost tripled between 1932 and 1936, and the price of hogs increased from $3.34 per hundredweight to $9.37. During the same period, farm income surged from $1.8 billion to $5 billion.

Not everyone benefited from the rising incomes. To make the AAA as democratic as possible, Roosevelt allowed local farmers to decide what lands to leave fallow. In most cases, large landowners cut the acreage of tenants and sharecroppers or forced them off the land altogether. African-Americans, who made up the vast majority of sharecroppers, suffered the most. As many as two hundred thousand black tenant farmers were displaced. In 1934 ousted tenants and sharecroppers in Arkansas and Alabama organized unions to stem the evictions and increase their bargaining power. The landlords struck back, using violence to crush the union drive. Few blacks shed a tear when the Supreme Court, in *Butler* v. *U.S.* (1936), ruled the AAA unconstitutional.

A month after passing the AAA program for agriculture, Congress enacted a comprehensive program for industrial recovery called the National Industrial Recovery Act (NIRA), which set up a planning agency called the National Recovery Administration (NRA). Roosevelt called the NRA "the most important and far-reaching legislation ever passed by the American Congress." Under NRA supervision, competing businesses within a given industry met with union leaders and consumer groups to draft codes of fair competition that limited production and stabilized prices. Section 7(a) of the NRA guaranteed workers' rights to join unions and engage in collective bargaining. It also established minimum wages and maximum hours for workers. As a symbol of the program, the NRA adopted a blue eagle with the legend "We Do Our Part." Blue Eagle badges soon appeared on store windows, theater marquees, and delivery trucks.

From the beginning the NRA ran into a host of problems that would ultimately erode public support and lead to its premature death. In many industries, especially steel and automobile manufacturing, the largest producers dominated the code-making bodies, generating cries of unfair treatment from small operators, labor, and consumer groups. In addition, developing codes for nearly every industry proved overwhelming. Almost overnight the NRA mushroomed into a bureaucratic giant. In its first two years the NRA drafted thirteen thousand pages of codes and issued eleven thousand rulings. Even gravediggers and striptease artists had codes. Many businesses simply ignored or artfully evaded the codes. The public also turned against the Blue Eagle icon, which journalist Walter Lippmann now slammed as a symbol of "excessive centralization" and "the dictatorial spirit." The final blow came in May 1935 when the Supreme Court, in *Schechter* v. *U.S.*, ruled the NIRA unconstitutional.

Along with boosting farm prices and reviving industrial production, the New Deal embarked on a number of public electric power and water projects that both offered jobs to the unemployed and dramatically altered the environment to improve the quality of life in some rural areas. In 1935 the government completed work on the Boulder Dam, later called the Hoover Dam, which was designed to harness the power of the Colorado River to generate electricity for Los Angeles and southern Arizona and to provide drinking water for southern California. In 1938 it completed the 80-mile All-American Canal. Connecting the Colorado River to California's Imperial Valley, the canal opened up an additional 1 million acres of desert land. The West's largest power and irrigation project was the Grand Coulee Dam on the Columbia River northwest of Spokane, Washington. Completed in 1941 Grand Coulee was the largest concrete structure built up to that time. It towered 550 feet in the air and created a reservoir 150 miles wide. The construction of Grand Coulee, and a number of other smaller projects, successfully converted the power of the Columbia River into cheap electricity, irrigated previously uncultivated land, and stimulated the economic development of the Pacific Northwest. It also reduced the majestic Columbia River to a series of lakes.

In May 1933 Congress created the Tennessee Valley Authority (TVA), one of the great achievements of the New Deal. The TVA spent billions in federal money constructing dams for flood control and the generation of hydroelectric power for one of the poorest, most depressed areas of the nation. It provided power for farms and made possible the development of industry in the region. Other TVA projects reclaimed and reforested land and fought soil erosion. The TVA also provided thousands of jobs for poor residents, both black and white, of the region. Critics condemned the TVA as "socialism," but it proved enormously popular among people living in the region.

No other New Deal measure improved the quality of rural life as much as the federally funded Rural Electrification Administration (REA). Until 1935 rural America lacked electrical power. Kerosene lamps illuminated homes after dark, and farms lacked washing machines, refrigerators, vacuum cleaners, and radios. In 1935 fewer than 10 percent of rural homes had electricity. By 1940, 40 percent were electrified, and by 1950, 90 percent.

Other significant early New Deal measures included the new Home Owners Loan Corporation (HOLC), which provided loans of up to $14,000 at 5 percent interest. By the end of Roosevelt's first term, the HOLC had made more than a million loans totaling $3 billion. Roosevelt also took the nation off the international gold standard in order to inflate the currency to complement his efforts to raise domestic price levels through the AAA and the NRA.

Recovery remained elusive for most Americans, but they were grateful to Roosevelt for having done so much to help. Voters showed their appreciation in the 1934 elections, giving the Democrats an additional 13 seats in the House and 9 in the Senate. The party now enjoyed massive majorities in Congress, holding 322 seats in the House and 69 in the Senate. Forty-one of the forty-eight states elected Democratic governors. Confirming that the political balance of power in the party was migrating away from the rural South and toward the industrial North and West, Democrats again scored well with urban voters, especially Catholic and Jewish immigrants and African-Americans living in the North. Arthur Krock of the *New York Times* exclaimed that the New Deal had won "the most overwhelming victory in the history of American politics." The victory provided FDR with the opportunity to push another round of New Deal legislation through Congress.

Attacks from the Left and Right

Roosevelt's actions angered conservatives, who charged that he was trying to assume dictatorial powers and extinguish individual rights. H. L. Mencken complained about the emerging welfare state, calling the Roosevelt administration "a milch cow with 125,000,000 teats." However, Roosevelt's greatest challenge came not from the right but from demagogues on the left who appealed to the dissatisfactions and frustrations of many Americans. Father Charles Coughlin, "the radio priest," developed a following of millions with his weekly radio program from the Shrine of the Little Flower. A masterful performer, Coughlin blamed the depression on wealthy bankers and rallied his large radio audience in support of Roosevelt's New Deal. By 1934, however, he turned against the president, denouncing him as a "liar" and a tool of the moneyed elite. He dismissed the New Deal, which he once referred to as "Christ's Deal," as a "Pagan Deal."

Dr. Francis E. Townsend, a retired dentist, proposed that all people over sixty receive $200 per month on the condition that they spend the money during the same month they got it. The money for the pensions would be raised by a "transaction tax," a sales tax levied each time goods were sold. He claimed his plan would both provide for the elderly and end the depression by pumping billions of dollars of purchasing power into the economy. Dr. Townsend's scheme attracted a huge following. He was offering seniors $200 a month at a time when only twenty-eight states provided old-age pensions, and those ranged from $8 to $30 a month. When a bill modeled after his plan was introduced in Congress in 1935, Townsend secured 20 million signatures calling for its passage.

The most significant challenge to the New Deal came from Huey Long, a charismatic, ambitious, and shrewd politician. A gifted speaker, Long became governor of Louisiana in 1929 and U.S. senator in 1932. His program of imposing heavy taxes on big business to pay for public works made him immensely popular with Louisiana's workers and farmers. On that foundation, he built a powerful political machine, dominated the legislature, and restricted the press.

At first Long supported the New Deal, but he soon turned against Roosevelt. By 1935, fashioning himself as a modern-day Robin Hood, Long announced his "Share Our Wealth" plan, which promised to "soak" the rich and make "every man a king." The government, he insisted, must "limit the size of the big men's fortune and guarantee some minimum to the fortune and comfort of the little man's family." Share Our Wealth proposed using the government's tax power to confiscate all incomes over $1 million and all estates over $5 million. The money raised would go to farmers and industrial workers, furnishing each family with $5,000 for buying a farm or home, an annual income of $2,000, a free college education for their children, a radio, and other benefits. By 1935 twenty-seven thousand Share Our Wealth clubs claimed 4.7 million members eager to reverse their fortunes.

Long's scheme appealed to the aspirations of poor people during the depression, to their resentment of the rich, and to their disappointment with New Deal efforts. Like Coughlin, he tapped into a strong populist undercurrent by portraying politics as a struggle between the noble intentions of "the people" and the greedy interests of elites. The message had special appeal to middle-class Americans who had enjoyed a degree of independence and autonomy in the past, but who now felt threatened by the many changes around them. They lashed out at those groups—bankers, Jews, communists, and Washington bureaucrats—who they considered responsible for the depression.

Roosevelt feared that a Long challenge in 1936 could siphon off needed support in key states. Polls showed Long running strong in a handful of states and likely to garner about 12 percent of the popular vote. An assassin ended the threat of a Long candidacy in September 1935. Gerald L. K. Smith assumed control of the Share Our Wealth clubs, but without Long's charismatic leadership the movement quickly disintegrated.

Many other left-wing critics also railed against the New Deal. Both the Communist and Socialist parties attacked it as too conservative. In California socialist muckraker Upton Sinclair (see page 811) captured the 1934 Democratic Party gubernatorial nomination, campaigning on a program he called End Poverty in California (EPIC). Although he lost to a conservative Republican, Sinclair attracted over eight hundred thousand votes. Minnesota governor Floyd Olson confessed, "I hope the present system of government goes right down to hell." Communism proved an attractive ideology for many. Membership in the Communist Party increased from eight thousand to seventy-five thousand between 1928 and 1938. During the thirties the movement made inroads in labor and among intellectuals and leading Hollywood figures, but it never developed a mass following.

The Second New Deal

"I am fighting Communism, Huey Longism, Coughlinism, Townsendism," Roosevelt blustered in 1935. Attacks from the left combined with growing resistance of business groups convinced Roosevelt to move leftward. His rhetoric became bolder as he attacked the "unjust concentration of wealth and economic power," and his agenda became more expansive as he declared that "social justice, no longer a distant ideal, has become a definite goal." His new agenda found expression in landmark legislation that would profoundly alter the relationship between the American people and the government: the National Labor Relations (or Wagner) Act, the Social Security Act, and the Emergency Relief Appropriation Act (ERA).

Roosevelt's fingerprints were all over the National Labor Relations Act (NLRA), which legislated the right of workers to unionize and to bargain collectively, reaffirming the guarantee in section 7(a) of the National Recovery Administration. Supporters called the NLRA "labor's Magna Carta." The brainchild of New York Senator Robert Wagner, the NLRA created the National Labor Relations Board (NLRB) to supervise union elections and to issue "cease and desist" orders against companies that committed unfair labor practices. In the long term, the legislation made the federal government the arbitrator between labor and management.

In August 1935, after lengthy hearings and intense bargaining, Congress approved Roosevelt's ambitious plan for social security. Virtually alone among industrialized countries, the United States faced the depression without a national system to aid the unemployed and elderly. Nearly half of all Americans over sixty-five were on relief in 1935. The Social Security Act remedied that problem, promising to provide "security against the hazards and vicissitudes of life." The new law featured three forms of aid: pensions for people over sixty-five, unemployment compensation for people temporarily out of work, and "categorical assistance" for specific groups that could not qualify for WPA work or find other forms of employment, such as the blind, dependent children, and the disabled.

Compared with social insurance programs implemented by European nations, social security appeared skimpy. Because the old-age pensions did not extend to workers who held low-wage positions, the act excluded many minorities and women. Funding for the unemployment and categorical assistance programs depended on cooperation between the federal government and the states, and wide disparities emerged among states in funding and compensation levels. With all its faults, however, the social security law was a major step forward in assistance to the "forgotten man." As one social worker exulted, "During the years between 1929 and 1939 more progress was made in public welfare than in the hundred years after this country was founded."

In April 1935 Roosevelt proposed and Congress passed the Emergency Relief Appropriation Act (ERA). The ERA asked for the largest peacetime appropriation to date in American history—$4 billion in new funds to be used for work relief and public works construction. In explaining the bill to Congress, Roosevelt, learning from the experience with FERA, drew a sharp distinction between "relief" and "work relief." Doling out cash, he claimed, "induces a spiritual and moral disintegration fundamentally destructive to the national fibre." Work, on the other hand, nurtured "self-respect . . . self-reliance and courage and determination."

The most important program in the ERA was the Works Progress Administration (WPA). The WPA became the nation's biggest employer, hiring more than 3 million people in its first year. During its eight years of operation it created jobs for 8.5 million Americans at a cost of $11 billion. WPA workers built over 650,000 miles of roads, 125,000 public buildings, 8,000 parks, and hundreds of bridges. The WPA created New York City's La Guardia Airport, restored the riverfront of St. Louis,

Missouri, excavated Indian burial grounds in New Mexico, and operated the bankrupt city of Key West, Florida.

Encouraged by Eleanor Roosevelt, the WPA established projects for thousands of artists, musicians, actors, and writers. "Hell, they've got to eat just like other people," WPA head Harry Hopkins told critics. Artists on WPA payrolls painted murals in post offices and other public buildings. The Federal Music and Theater Projects sponsored symphony orchestras and jazz groups and brought dramas, comedies, and variety shows to cities and towns across the nation. Some young artists who acted and directed in the Theater Project—John Houseman and Orson Welles, for example—would later achieve nationwide fame. At its height, the Federal Writers Project employed five thousand writers, including Richard Wright, John Steinbeck, and John Cheever. Most notably, it produced the *American Guide Series*, a popular set of guidebooks to each of the states, their major cities, and highway routes. The 150-volume *Life in America* series included valuable oral histories of former slaves, studies of ethnic cultures and Indians, and pioneering collections of American songs and folktales.

The 1936 Election   With public opinion polls taken in 1936 showing that his New Deal programs enjoyed broad popular support in all regions of the nation, Roosevelt turned his reelection campaign into a great nonpartisan liberal crusade, a clash between the "haves" and

WPA Artist at Work   The Works Progress Administration employed millions of Americans for a variety of construction projects, such as bridges, airports, and road improvements. In addition, the agency sponsored writers, artists, musicians, and actors. This Michigan artist sketches other WPA workers, including blacks who took advantage of the WPA's anti-discrimination policy. The lasting results of the WPA include state guides, murals, and the Historical Records Survey. The agency was also a forerunner of the National Endowment for the Arts.   *(National Archives.)*

"have-nots." His opening speech attacked "economic royalists" who took "other people's money" to impose a "new industrial dictatorship." The forces of "organized money are unanimous in their hate for me," he told a cheering crowd in New York's Madison Square Garden, "and I welcome their hatred."

To oppose the popular president, the GOP turned to Alfred M. "Alf" Landon, a former follower of Theodore Roosevelt and then the progressive Republican governor of Kansas. Landon campaigned as a moderate, expressing support for New Deal goals but claiming he could achieve the same results more efficiently and with less bureaucracy.

Roosevelt and the Democrats swept to a landslide victory. Roosevelt received 27.8 million votes to Landon's 16.7 million. The Union Party, a third-party challenge made up of followers of Long, Coughlin, and Townsend, managed to draw only 882,479 votes. The president swept every state but Maine and Vermont, and carried with him unprecedented Democratic margins of 331 to 89 in the House and 76 to 16 in the Senate. Six million more people voted in 1936 than in 1932, and the bulk of these new voters cast their ballots for Roosevelt. Most were recruited from the ranks of the poor, people on relief, the unemployed, and the working classes, and these groups expressed their solidarity with the man who created the New Deal.

By 1936 Roosevelt and the Democrats had forged a new political coalition firmly based on the mass of voters living in large northern cities. The ethnic groups and black voters in the cities had benefited from New Deal programs and were delighted at the attention New Dealers gave them. Hard times and New Deal programs had also attracted the votes of most farmers and of the elderly. Organized labor, as an integral part of the New Deal coalition, fused the interests of millions of workers, skilled and unskilled, native-born and foreign-born, white and nonwhite, male and female. Many formerly Republican progressive middle-class voters and thousands of former socialists also joined the Roosevelt coalition. By 1936 few besides business leaders and conservative, old-stock Americans in small towns and cities clung to the GOP.

The commanding personality of Franklin Roosevelt was the core of the new Democratic coalition. His smashing electoral victory confirmed his popularity and the political success of New Deal programs. "Every house I visited," a social worker reported after a tour in South Carolina, "had a picture of the President. These ranged from newspaper clippings (in destitute houses) to large colored prints, framed in gilt cardboard. The portrait holds the place of honor over the mantel; I can only compare this to the peasant's Madonna."

The Decline of the New Deal

Uplifted by his electoral landslide, Roosevelt began his second term by raising hopes that new, perhaps even bolder initiatives lay ahead. "I see one-third of a nation ill-housed, ill-clad, ill-nourished," the president declared in his second inaugural address. Instead of reform, however, Roosevelt's second term produced stalemate and eventual retrenchment.

Two weeks after his inauguration, Roosevelt announced a misconceived plan to reform the Supreme Court. The plan called for the addition of a new judge to the Supreme Court whenever an incumbent refused to retire at the age of seventy. The

Supreme Court, which then had six judges (of the nine total) over seventy, could be expanded to a maximum of fifteen. Publicly the president defended the change by suggesting that the Court had fallen behind in its work. In fact, as far as Roosevelt was concerned, the problem was that the Court was performing too efficiently. It had already overturned the NRA and the AAA. FDR worried that new initiatives, especially the Social Security Act and the Wagner Act, would suffer similar fates unless he could add some supportive justices to the bench.

As expected, conservatives attacked the plan, accusing Roosevelt of trying to "pack" the Court. Much to the president's surprise, his reform plan also angered the public, which held the Court in high esteem and valued the independence of the judiciary. Many congressional Democrats, including the president's staunch liberal supporters, hotly denounced the plan.

Ironically, the Court itself undermined any support for the plan by suddenly reversing course. In two critical decisions, the justices sustained a minimum wage law and upheld the sweeping terms of the Wagner Act. The Court decided both decisions by a five to four margin with Justice Owen Roberts, until then a member of the conservative bloc, switching sides to give liberal justices the majority. The turnabout led one observer to suggest that "a switch in time saves Nine." Why Roberts switched is unclear, but his decision permitted Roosevelt to brag late in 1938, "We obtained 98 percent of all the objectives intended by the Court plan." What some scholars have called "The Constitutional Revolution of 1937" secured the New Deal's achievements and cleared the constitutional path for further reforms.

However, Roosevelt had expended a considerable amount of political capital on the Court fight, squandering the momentum from the 1936 election. The battle exposed deep wounds in the Democratic Party, and conservatives prepared to revolt against a weakened president. "What we have to do," North Carolina's Senator Josiah Bailey wrote, "is to preserve, if we can, the Democratic Party against his efforts to make it the Roosevelt party." The Court battle energized the conservative coalition of Republicans and southern Democrats into an organized legislative force determined to block future New Deal legislation.

A dramatic downturn in the economy further eroded Roosevelt's stature. Early in 1937 the economy seemed to be making steady progress toward recovery. Between 1933 and 1937 the gross national product grew at a yearly rate of 10 percent. Industrial output had increased and unemployment had declined. Believing the economy sound and worried about the $4 billion budget deficit, Roosevelt reduced federal spending by cutting relief. But the president had overestimated the strength of the economy and underestimated the importance of continued government spending. Roosevelt's actions precipitated a severe recession that lasted from fall 1937 to spring 1938. The rate of decline was sharper than in 1929. Nearly 4 million people lost their jobs, boosting total unemployment to 11.5 million. "We are headed right into another Depression," an adviser warned the president.

An intense battle erupted within the administration over how to respond to the crisis. White House advisers rehashed familiar debates between Theodore Roosevelt's New Nationalism and Woodrow Wilson's New Freedom. Should the president reassure business by cutting spending and limiting regulation? Or should he expand federal power through new regulations? Roosevelt equivocated for months before cautiously siding with advisers who suggested a third direction: using consumer spending to lift the nation out of depression. This policy adopted the ideas of British economist John Maynard Keynes who, in *The General Theory of Employment, Interest, and Money* (1936), proposed that government spend its way out of depression. Keynes argued that during economic downturns, governments needed to abandon their faith in balanced budgets and pump money into the economy. In the spring of 1938 Roosevelt proposed a $3.75 billion package for public works and WPA programs. Congress passed a revised AAA, removing the tax declared unconstitutional by the Supreme Court. The revised legislation once again allowed the government to assist farmers in reducing surplus and raising prices. That same year, Congress enacted the Fair Labor Standards Act, which required businesses involved in interstate trade to pay their employees a minimum wage. The new legislation, combined with increased public spending, eased the recession, but the pace of recovery remained slow.

People blamed Roosevelt and his party for the recession, and they expressed their anger toward the Democrats in the 1938 midterm elections. Roosevelt added to the Democrats' problems by announcing his plan to "purge" the party by campaigning in the primaries against conservatives who had opposed New Deal measures. The effort backfired. Most people resented the president's active involvement in local politics. Republicans, taking full advantage of the opportunity, picked up eighty-one seats in the House and eight seats in the Senate, and they gained thirteen governorships. Since all Democratic losses took place in the North and West, Southern conservatives emerged in a much stronger position. For the first time Roosevelt could not form a majority in Congress without the help of some Republicans or southern Democrats. The mountain of political capital that Roosevelt had amassed in 1936 had been leveled in just two years.

By the end of 1939 the New Deal was for all practical purposes dead. A decidedly more conservative Congress abruptly cut off funds for the Federal Theater Project, repealed a New Deal tax measure, and refused to increase expenditures for public housing. Public attitudes had also shifted. Polls taken after 1937 indicated that a sizable majority of people, including Democrats, wanted the Roosevelt administration to follow a more conservative course. Recognizing how far the pendulum had swung, Roosevelt became more cautious. He refused to endorse new legislation to strengthen social security and provide extended health care. Increasingly, foreign policy issues, especially events in Europe, occupied his attention.

DEPRESSION CULTURE, 1929–1938

The declining fortunes of Roosevelt's reform agenda at the end of the decade revealed the resiliency of conservative attitudes about government. American culture demonstrated a similar elasticity. The most striking feature of American culture during the depression was how quickly it adapted to crisis. Helen and Robert Lynd, the chroniclers of "Middletown," commented that "a Rip Van Winkle, fallen asleep in 1925 while addressing Rotary or the Central Labor Union, could have awakened in 1935 and gone right on with his interrupted address to the same people with much the same ideas." A few artists documented the pain and anguish of the "depression decade." Some, by suggesting that the economic collapse represented a failure of institutions, challenged traditional American individualistic values. Most Americans, however, searched for affirmation of older verities or looked for escape from the drudgery of daily life.

Social Realism and Social Escape During the 1930s

Novels of social realism, depicting a stark and unforgiving society, were popular with Americans trying to understand the depression. John Dos Passos's *Big Money* (1936), the concluding volume of his massive trilogy *U.S.A.*, describes the pernicious effect of materialism on characters cast as ordinary Americans. James T. Farrell's *Studs Lonigan* trilogy (1932–1938) depicts the harsh urban realities of his native Chicago. The trilogy ends when Lonigan, alone and unemployed, dies of tuberculosis. Richard Wright's *Native Son* (1940), set in Chicago's black belt, features the evils of racism and capitalism. Clifford Odets's *Waiting for Lefty* uses the struggle of a group of taxi drivers to highlight the limits of individualism and the need for collective action. William Faulkner's *As I Lay Dying* (1930) and *Light in August* (1932) paint vivid portraits of life in rural Mississippi. John Steinbeck's *The Grapes of Wrath* (1939) tells the story of an uprooted Dust Bowl family, the Joads, making their way along Route 66 to California.

Social realism was not limited to literature. Jacob Lawrence drew directly on his own experience growing up in Harlem in a series of sixty paintings entitled *The Migration of the Negro*. Together the paintings told the story of dispossessed blacks during the 1930s. Painters Reginald Marsh and Edward Hopper, members of the so-called Fourteenth Street School of New York, tried to capture the vitality of urban life on their canvases.

Many artists experimented with the camera to document the searing pain of the depression and to accentuate the valiant struggle of people fighting to preserve their dignity. Photography took on new vitality. "The image has become the queen of our age," noted a publisher. "We are no longer content to know, we must see." New photojournalism magazines, including *Life* (1936) and *Look* (1937), reflected the new documentary impulse. Poet-screenwriter James Agee and photographer Walker Evans documented the life of poor white tenant farmers in the South in *Let Us Now Praise Famous Men* (1941), capturing the tenants' transcendent sense of pride among their small wooden shacks and meager furnishings. Photojournalists such as Dorothea Lange and Marion Post Wolcott recorded the plight of migrant farm workers for the Farm Security Administration in a number of memorable images.

The best-selling books were not chronicles of contemporary pain and hardship but stories that offered readers a respite from the hardship of depression life. Margaret Mitchell's *Gone With the Wind* (1936) sold 178,000 copies within its first three weeks of publication. It remained on the best-seller lists for twenty-one consecutive months and sold 2 million copies. The panoramic love story paints a nostalgic picture of southern culture and white paternalism during the Civil War and Reconstruction.

Gone With the Wind revealed another depression trend in the arts: a renewed appreciation of small-town and rural ways of life. Because of hard times, some Americans romanticized the virtues of living close to the soil. Regionalist painters, led by John Steuart Curry, Grant Wood, and Thomas Hart Benton were among the most widely reproduced and popular artists of the decade. They revolted against European fashions in art and focused on pastoral scenes of the American Plains and Midwest. In 1930 a group of southern historians, novelists, and poets published *I'll Take My Stand*, which contrasted the harmony of life in the Old South (including slavery) with the impersonal and chaotic fate of modern society.

Entertaining the Masses

To cope with idleness, millions of unemployed Americans read more and took up stamp collecting, games, and fads. Dance marathons, roller derbies, six-day bicycle races, and flagpole-sitting contests became popular. The first All-American Soapbox Derby was held in Dayton, Ohio, in 1934. Millions of cash-strapped Americans tried to "make a killing" by accumulating make-believe fortunes in a new game called Monopoly.

Escapism and images of a better future scored well with the American public during the decade. Superman, who fought "a never-ending battle for truth, justice, and the American way," appeared in *Action Comics* in June 1938. Women's magazines, which claimed a readership of 13 million, offered a steady diet of love stories. *Reader's Digest*, the most popular periodical of the decade with a circulation of more than 7 million, carried upbeat articles about personal and business success. At the depth of the depression in 1933 and 1934, 20 million people marveled at the possibilities of science at the "Century of Progress" exposition in Chicago. In 1939 New York's World's Fair attracted nearly 50 million people who admired a 180-foot globe that symbolized "The World of Tomorrow."

Millions of Americans remained enthusiastic sports fans during the depression. The most popular sport continued to be baseball, the "national pastime." Each year millions of Americans clustered around their radios to listen to the World Series. In 1938 heavyweight boxing champ Joe Louis, "the Brown Bomber," pounded German Max Schmelling in New York's Madison Square Garden. The novelist Richard Wright wrote that in Louis's victory "blacks took strength, and in that moment all fear, all obstacles were wiped out, drowned." Another African-American athlete, sprinter Jesse Owens, "the Ebony Antelope," won four gold metals in the 1936 Olympic games held in Berlin. Despite the success of Louis and Owens, black athletes faced many obstacles in competing in popular sports. Big Ten basketball barred black players. Hall of Fame baseball players such as Satchel Paige and Josh Gibson played in the Negro baseball league of the 1930s, but few white Americans paid attention to the all-black Homestead Grays or Pittsburgh Crawfords.

In 1930 an estimated 110 million people attended movie theaters each week. Three years later, with the economy at rock bottom, 60 to 80 million managed to find the twenty-five cents for admission. Over 60 percent of Americans attended one of the nation's twenty thousand movie houses each week. Throughout the depression, the movie industry, fast becoming dominated by a small number of large studios, produced more than five hundred movies a year. The major studios tended to serve up escapist fare that steered clear of depression realities and avoided raising serious social issues. Horror pictures such as *Frankenstein* and gangster films such as *The Public Enemy*, both made in 1931, were popular. Outstanding comedians, among them W. C. Fields, Laurel and Hardy, Charlie Chaplin, Will Rogers, and the Marx Brothers, brought laughter to millions of Americans. Movie musicals offered plots that were usually upbeat, revolving around stories of rags to riches, or poor chorus girls marrying wealthy bluebloods. But reality often intruded. *Gold Diggers* opened with Ginger Rogers and sixty showgirls singing "We're in the Money," but ended with local authorities closing down the show because the producer failed to pay his bills.

Walt Disney and Frank Capra emerged as the decade's most successful directors. Disney's *Three Little Pigs* (1933) featuring the hit song "Who's Afraid of the Big Bad Wolf?" reminded many people of Roosevelt's assertion that Americans had nothing to fear but fear itself. Capra's films, including *Mr. Smith Goes to Washington* (1939), reaffirmed faith in individual initiative and suggested that old-fashioned values of kindness, loyalty, and charity could solve most of the nation's ills. One observer noted in 1934 that "no medium has contributed more greatly than film to the maintenance of the national morale during a period featured by revolution, riot and political turmoil in other countries."

A few iconoclasts used movies to challenge conventional thinking. Perhaps no one was more successful at defying traditional values than actress Mae West, whose liberated spirit and appetite for pleasure defied sexual mores. "Is that a gun in your pocket, big boy," she asked of her leading men, "or are you just glad to see

Hollywood Escapism   In difficult times, Americans looked to the entertainment industry to help them forget their troubles. The 1930s saw over 50 million Americans attending the movies every week. Films such as *Gold Diggers* of 1933, featured in this photograph, employed themes of wealth and optimism that starkly contrasted with the reality of the day. *Gold Diggers'* major musical number buoyantly declared, "We're in the money / We're in the money / We've got a lot of what / It takes to get along / We never see a headline / About a breadline / Today." *(Photofest.)*

me?" Traditionalists responded angrily to West's films, and others viewed them as licentious. In 1933 the Catholic Church created the Legion of Decency and pressured Hollywood to establish strict guidelines of behavior on the screen. The new code banned kissing, nudity, and "sympathetic treatment of wrongdoing."

The Golden Age of Radio

Although many radio stations banned Mae West from the airwaves, film actors often took parts in radio dramas and variety programs. The 1930s became the golden age of radio. The number of Americans who owned radios increased from 10 million in 1929 to 27.5 million a decade later, at which time 90 percent of the nation's homes had at least one radio. Each radio, one survey found in 1937, was used for an average of four and a quarter hours a day.

Music and variety shows dominated radio broadcasting during the decade. Millions gathered around their Philco or Stromberg-Carlson radios to hear the songs of Bing Crosby and Frank Sinatra or the big band sounds Benny Goodman. Many others delighted in the wisecracks of Bob Hope and Jack Benny. Popular ongoing daytime stories were called soap operas because they were sponsored by soap companies. The plots were usually simple, appealing to the romantic fantasies of middle-class women. *Mary Noble, Backstage Wife* was the story of "an Iowa stenographer who fell in love with and married Broadway matinee idol Larry Noble."

Soaps about crime fighting were also popular with depression audiences searching for reassurance that the old rules of right and wrong still applied. In *The Shadow,* crime-fighter Lamont Cranston, reassured audiences that "Crime does not pay . . . the Shadow knows!" By 1939 *The Lone Ranger* was being heard three times a week on 140 stations. The hero, a mysterious masked man aided by a faithful Indian companion, Tonto, brought justice to the Wild West. *The Green Hornet* sought to capture "public enemies that even the G-Men cannot catch."

By 1940 radio had supplanted newspapers as the public's primary source of information. Millions of Americans huddled next to the radio to listen to Roosevelt's Fireside Chats. In 1935 radio provided extensive coverage of the trial of Bruno Hauptmann, who stood accused of kidnapping and murdering Charles Lindbergh's infant son. In May 1937 Herb Morrison of Chicago's WLS radio station unexpectedly and emotionally covered the explosion of the *Hindenburg* passenger blimp as it attempted to dock in Lakehurst, New Jersey. Sometimes radio made it difficult to distinguish fact from fiction. A popular weekly news show, *The March of Time,* embellished news events with dramatization. In 1938 Orson Welles and his Mercury Theater broadcast H. G. Wells's classic science fiction tale, *The War of the Worlds.* "Ladies and gentlemen, this is the most terrifying thing I have ever witnessed . . . ," the "correspondent" sobbed as he described a Martian invasion of New Jersey. Hundreds of thousands of listeners believed every word, and terrified people jammed New Jersey roads trying to avoid the advancing aliens.

THE NEW DEAL AND SOCIETY, 1933–1938

The theme of continuity and change that characterized the depression's impact on cultural values also applies to the New Deal's influence on society. In many ways, the New Deal accepted and reinforced traditional divisions based on race, class, and gender. But in significant ways it challenged existing power structures, offering support to previously marginalized social groups. The New Deal enhanced the bargaining power of organized labor, which witnessed extraordinary gains during the decade. Minorities and women also received benefits from New Deal programs designed to help the poor and unemployed. On balance, New Deal reforms had a lasting impact on American society, but the New Deal experiment did not end the depression or threaten the basic tenets of capitalism.

The Rise of Organized Labor

Perhaps no group benefited more from the New Deal than organized labor, which made tremendous gains during the depression decade. Union membership jumped from 3.6 million in 1930 to nearly 10.5 million in 1941. Roosevelt's support for the Wagner Act, which created an atmosphere hospitable to labor, contributed to the growth. But the grass-roots activity of militant workers produced the greatest gains. Many of these workers, who labored in large-scale, mass-production industries such as automobiles, steel, rubber, electrical goods, and textiles, engaged in a number of successful strikes. The number of workers involved in walkouts rose from 324,210 in 1932 to 1.6 million in 1933. In 1934 working-class militancy reached new heights as violent industrial conflicts paralyzed cities in Ohio, California, and Minnesota. The strikes spurred increases in membership. The United Mine Workers grew from about 60,000 to over 500,000. The International Ladies' Garment Workers' Union (ILGWU) increased fourfold, and the United Textile Workers tripled its membership.

The AFL continued to show little interest in organizing unskilled workers in mass-production industries other than coal mining and clothing. Following enactment of the Wagner Act, a group within the AFL, led by the forceful and articulate John L. Lewis of the United Mine Workers, demanded that the AFL commit itself to the "industrial organization of mass production workers." At the AFL convention in 1935 delegates, mostly from craft unions, rejected Lewis's proposal. At the end of the convention an angry Lewis signaled his break with the AFL by punching carpenters' union head "Big Bill" Hutcheson, bloodying his face and leaving him to be carried from the platform. "With this historic punch," observed a labor historian, "Lewis signified the formal beginning of the industrial-union rebellion within the House of Labor and made himself the leading rebel."

Three weeks later, on November 10, 1935, Lewis and the heads of seven other AFL unions announced the formation of the Committee for Industrial Organization, later called the Congress of Industrial Organization (CIO). The CIO launched major organizing drives in mass-production industries in the late 1930s. In 1937 a total of 4.7 million workers were involved in 4,740 strikes that affected all of the nation's key industries—steel, coal, auto, rubber, and electricity (see figure on page 998).

In January 1937 in Flint, Michigan, the United Automobile Workers (UAW), a CIO affiliate, began a strike against General Motors, seeking union recognition. If Flint autoworkers could beat General Motors, the world's largest industrial corporation, their victory would galvanize workers in auto and other basic industries. Their grievances were common to auto plants of the 1930s: frequent layoffs, arbitrary

Labor Union Membership

The New Deal's inclusion of Section 7A in the National Labor Recovery Act and the 1935 Wagner Act opened the doorway to union membership by guaranteeing workers the right to organize. Leaders of the American Federation of Labor and the newly created Congress of Industrial Organizations worked diligently recruiting workers, and membership in both organizations soared.

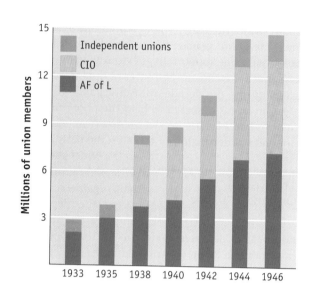

management decisions, and poor working conditions. The strikers used a novel tactic, the "sit-down" strike, against the giant automaker. Participants refused to work but stayed in the factory to prevent nonunion workers from keeping the plants going.

The sit-down strike was highly controversial, but it worked. Company guards turned off the heat and barred strikers from bringing in food, but the strikers refused to budge. On January 11 sheriff's deputies and police stormed the plant. Strikers drove them back, deluging police with fire hoses and pelting them with car hinges, stones, and anything else they could get their hands on. Ten thousand people turned out the next day at UAW headquarters, voicing support for the striking workers with the traditional union anthem "Solidarity Forever." During the first eight months of 1937 UAW membership increased from eighty-eight thousand to four hundred thousand. Unable to dislodge the Flint strikers, in February 1937 the General Motors company became the first major manufacturer to recognize the UAW. All the other auto manufacturers followed suit, except Ford, which held out until 1941.

A few weeks after the settlement with General Motors, United States Steel agreed to recognize the CIO, increased wages by 10 percent, established a forty-hour workweek, and provided seniority rights and paid vacations. The lesser steel companies (known as "Little Steel") were far less ready to give in, however. On Memorial Day 1937 police attacked strikers picketing Republic Steel in Chicago, firing into a crowd, killing ten, and wounding dozens more. The "Memorial Day massacre" created widespread sympathy for the strikers, but Little Steel broke the strike and defeated the CIO's organizing effort. The companies did not officially recognize the steelworkers' union until 1941.

By the end of 1937 the new CIO unions claimed 4 million members. The number of women in CIO unions tripled to eight hundred thousand in 1940. The AFL, revitalized by the CIO challenge, also experienced unprecedented membership gains. Still, the triumph of industrial unionism in the 1930s was far from complete.

In 1939 the Supreme Court outlawed the sit-down strike. As late as 1940 American unions embraced only 28 percent of nonagricultural workers. Most of the unskilled remained unrepresented and relatively powerless.

A New Deal for Minorities?

Among the unorganized and powerless were millions of African-Americans, many of whom now looked to the White House for assistance. They were often disappointed. Unwilling to risk alienating southern whites and their conservative congressmen, Roosevelt never endorsed two key political initiatives of the 1930s: demands for a federal antilynching law and abolition of the poll tax. Neither effort succeeded.

African-Americans had other grievances against the administration. New Deal programs routinely accepted and practiced discrimination. The AAA forced thousands of black sharecroppers and farm laborers off the land and offered white farmers and workers higher rates of support than their black counterparts received. The National Recovery Administration failed to protect black workers from discrimination in employment and wages. Blacks denounced the NRA as "Negroes Ruined Again" and "Negro Removal Act" because the codes led many businesses to lay off black employees. The CCC was racially segregated, as was the TVA, which constructed all-white towns and confined black workers to low-paying job categories. Millions of African-Americans were excluded both from social security coverage and from the minimum wage provisions of the Fair Labor Standards Act. Relief agencies paid black clients less than whites. In Atlanta African-Americans received $19.29 per month, compared with $32.66 for whites.

Yet blacks made some limited gains during the decade. By some estimates, nearly 30 percent of African-Americans received some form of New Deal assistance. In 1935 Roosevelt issued an executive order banning discrimination in WPA projects. Blacks, who accounted for 10 percent of the nation's population, held 18 percent of WPA jobs. The Public Works Administration employed black workers to construct a number of integrated housing complexes. The Farm Security Administration helped relocate fourteen hundred black families to "homesteads."

The New Deal also offered African-Americans a number of symbolic, but nevertheless significant gains. Roosevelt invited many black visitors to the White House and appointed an unofficial "black cabinet" to advise him on issues important to African-Americans. At the 1936 convention Democrats seated blacks for the first time as delegates, and an African-American gave a seconding speech on behalf of the president. In 1937 Roosevelt appointed the first black judge to the federal bench, William Hastie. Two years later, in an effort to challenge discriminatory voting practices in the South, FDR encouraged the attorney general to create the Civil Rights Division in the Department of Justice.

Within the administration, Eleanor Roosevelt emerged as the most powerful voice for combating discrimination in New Deal programs and elsewhere. She visited black churches and colleges and invited black leaders to the White House. She helped the NAACP raise money, and she added her name to fundraising ventures by other black groups. In 1939 the Daughters of the American Revolution denied renowned African-American opera singer Marian Anderson use of Constitution Hall for a planned Easter concert. At Eleanor's urging, the administration suggested an alternative site: the steps of the Lincoln Memorial. On Easter Sunday 1939 more than seventy-five thousand people gathered to hear the recital. Seated in the front row with Eleanor Roosevelt were senators, congressmen, and Supreme Court justices.

Despite the shortcomings of the New Deal for African-Americans, they supported it enthusiastically. When black voters joined the Roosevelt coalition, they abandoned their historical allegiance to the Republicans—the party of Lincoln. "Go turn Lincoln's picture to the wall," said one writer. "That debt has been paid in full." Two-thirds of black voters had voted for Hoover in 1932. In 1936 two-thirds voted for Roosevelt. By 1938 Democratic candidates received 85 percent of the vote in African-American communities in New York's Harlem and Chicago's South Side.

Perhaps no minority group gained more from the New Deal than Native Americans. Ravaged by infant mortality, alcoholism, tuberculosis, and many other ail-

Marian Anderson Performs at the Lincoln Memorial   When the Daughters of the American Revolution barred Anderson from using their Constitution Hall for a concert, Eleanor Roosevelt resigned her membership, then helped organize the Lincoln Memorial venue for Anderson. Mrs. Roosevelt's actions were typical of the Roosevelt administration's record on civil rights in two respects. First, FDR did not involve himself in the incident, instead leaving the matter to his wife and his subordinates; and second, the Anderson concert was largely a symbolic gesture. Although the importance of these gestures should not be underestimated, on the whole the New Deal did little to advance the economic and political rights of minorities. *(Thomas McAvoy/LIFE Magazine © Time, Inc.)*

ments, Indians suffered from the worst poverty of any group in the nation. In 1933 President Roosevelt appointed John Collier to reform the Bureau of Indian Affairs (BIA). Collier's greatest accomplishment was securing congressional passage of the Indian Reorganization Act in 1934. The "Indian New Deal" reversed the emphasis on assimilation that had been codified into law by the Dawes General Allotment Act (see page 670). The old land allotment system had worked to transfer much Indian land to white ranchers, miners, and farmers. Since 1887 Indian landholdings had dropped from 138 million acres to 48 million. The Indian Reorganization Act restored lands to tribal ownership and protected Native American religious practices and traditional culture. It provided for Indian self-government on reservations, new loans for economic development, and expanded medical and educational services. Many of the new tribal constitutions written under Collier's supervision promoted gender equality by giving women the right to vote in tribal elections and to hold office. Collier also made sure that the BIA offered native women training both in agriculture and animal husbandry and in nursing and secretarial work.

Women During the 1930s

The depression reinforced the belief that a woman's place was in the home. A Gallup poll revealed that 82 percent of Americans, including 75 percent of women, agreed that wives should not work if their husbands were employed. Federal regulations prohibited more than one member of a family from holding a civil service job. Three-quarters of those forced to resign were women. Most states passed laws excluding married women—whom one politician called "undeserving parasites"—from public employment. The AFL joined the effort, claiming that married women with working husbands "should be discriminated against in the hiring of employees."

Family need, however, triumphed over traditional attitudes. The proportion of married women serving in the work force, often as temporary or part-time help, actually increased from 11.7 percent to 15.3 percent during the decade. The overall female proportion of the work force rose from 22 percent to 25 percent. But discrimination still routinely forced women into low-paying and low-status jobs. Between 1930 and 1940 the percentage of women in the professions declined from 14.2 percent to 12.3 percent. Not surprisingly, the average woman worker earned about half the yearly income of a working man—$525 compared with $1,027.

Women did benefit from many New Deal programs, however. In 1933 Harry Hopkins sent an order to all state FERA directors to "pay particular attention that women are employed whenever possible." By 1934 more than three hundred thousand women—more than half of those qualified for relief—were working on various CWA projects. The WPA hired nearly half a million women in 1936, nearly 15 percent of all its workers. Three-fourths of the NRA codes included provisions for equal pay to women workers. The National Youth Administration, which provided part-time employment to college students and assistance to jobless youth, also included programs for young women. Women wage earners, especially those employed in the garment industry and textile production, benefited from the New Deal's support of organized labor.

Women held a number of appointive positions in New Deal agencies. Concentrated in the Labor Department, the FERA and WPA, and the Social Security Board, they worked together to maximize their influence on government policy. FDR appointed Frances Perkins secretary of labor, the first woman cabinet member in U.S. history. Grace Abbott, a veteran of Hull House (see page 804), joined a handful of women reformers to write the welfare provisions of the Social Security Act. Eleanor Roosevelt was the central figure in the increase in women's political influence, working both in public and behind the scenes with a wide network of women professionals. Her closest political ally was Molly Dewson, who served as director of the Women's Division of the national Democratic Party. Under her leadership women became an important part of the Democratic Party machinery. "Those of us who worked to put together the New Deal," Frances Perkins reflected, "are bound by spiritual ties that no one else can understand."

New Deal Legacies The New Deal transformed the relationship between the people and the federal government. First, it dramatically increased the size and scope of government. In 1932 there were 605,000 federal employees; by 1939 there were nearly a million. Before FDR few Americans felt that Washington had, or should have had, much influence on

Women Reporters with Eleanor Roosevelt Although the New Deal's record on women's issues was mixed, the Roosevelt administration appointed the first female cabinet member, Labor Secretary Frances Perkins; the first women ambassador, and an Appeals Court judge. Mrs. Roosevelt deserves a great deal of the credit for these advances. She not only influenced her husband, she worked with Perkins and others in the administration to study and address issues important to women. In addition, she held regular press conferences, to which she invited only female reporters. *(Stock Montage.)*

their lives. During the New Deal era the federal government became the focal point for civic life. People who had once turned to local and state governments now looked to Washington for solutions to problems. A British observer noted in 1939, "Just as in 1929 the whole country was 'Wall Street conscious,' now it is 'Washington conscious.'"

Second, the New Deal altered the distribution of political power. By empowering new groups—farmers, labor, and the urban working class—the New Deal political coalition forced business to share political power. The coalition, which would endure for a generation, offered tangible benefits to groups that had long been excluded from the mainstream of American political life.

The shift in political power produced a modest redistribution of wealth. In 1929 the top 5 percent of the population received 30 percent of national income. In 1938, at the end of the New Deal, the top 5 percent's share had dropped to 26 percent. The income did not travel far. Middle- and upper-middle-class families were the chief beneficiaries. They saw their share increase from 33 percent in 1929 to 36 percent in 1938. The income share going to the poorest families rose only slightly, from 13.2 percent to 13.7 percent.

The New Deal experiment failed to remedy the fundamental economic ills caused by the Great Depression. As the New Deal ended in 1938, over 10 million men and women were still without jobs, and the unemployment rate hovered near 20 percent. New Dealers never solved the puzzle of unemployment. Underconsumption plagued efforts to boost production and sales. In 1929 new car sales totaled $6.5 billion. In 1938, at the end of the New Deal, the figure was $3.9 billion. Per capita national income did not regain 1929 levels until early 1940.

Still, by every measure, the New Deal had a profound and lasting impact on American society and politics. It preserved America's capitalistic system by rescuing it from collapse and continuing the Progressive Era faith in government's ability to improve people's lives. Roosevelt "saved capitalism," declared author Gore Vidal. Though programs like the NRA and AAA faded into history, many of Roosevelt's reforms—social security, stock market regulation, minimum wage, insured bank deposits—became accepted features of American life. Apart from specific programs, Roosevelt reinterpreted the Constitution's pledge to "promote the general welfare," expanding it to give the federal government the right to intervene in all substantive aspects of the nation's economic life. The debate between supporters of New Deal intervention and opponents who sought a limited role for the national government would be a part of the political experiment for the rest of the century.

CONCLUSION

The economic prosperity that characterized the 1920s began to fall apart in October 1929. The crash on Wall Street—resulting from years of speculation and unsavory trade practices—was the first domino to fall. The banking system, which had always been unregulated and prone to failures, was next, depriving millions of their savings and eroding public confidence in the economy. These events exposed serious structural flaws in the economy—a decade-long weakness in the agricultural market, more recent industrial overproduction, and a continuing fragile international economic system. Herbert Hoover, who had been elected as a champion of prosperity in 1928, seemed unable to devise a solution for the nation's economic woes. In 1932 a frustrated nation turned to Democrat Franklin Roosevelt.

When Franklin Roosevelt assumed the presidency in March 1933 unemployment had soared to record levels. Unable to support themselves in these grim economic times, millions of families found themselves homeless and forced to look to private charity—which was itself quickly swamped by the demand. Even families that maintained some source of income found their standards of living sharply reduced.

In his first hundred days in office Roosevelt proposed an ambitious federal experiment to revitalize the economy, aid the unemployed, and restore public faith. The New Deal dramatically extended the power of the federal government, creating a host of "alphabet agencies" that assumed responsibilities traditionally left to local government or private charity. The Civilian Conservation Corps (CCC) provided jobs to more than 2 million men, while the Federal Emergency Relief Administration (FERA) offered relief to needy families. Reviving the New Nationalism of his cousin Theodore, FDR created the Agricultural Adjustment Act (AAA) and the National Recovery Act (NRA) to help revive the struggling economy. With passage of the Social Security Act in 1935, Roosevelt created the scaffolding of the modern welfare state. The ambitious social agenda of the New Deal inaugurated the age of activist government.

Despite the broad popularity of Roosevelt and his reforms, the New Deal did not fundamentally change American values. Even as they took jobs in the new federal agencies and accepted federal relief, Americans still clung to their notions of individuality and self-support. American culture demonstrated a similar resiliency. While some artists, filmmakers, authors, and playwrights documented the pain and hardship suffered by Americans during the depression, most people sought refuge in more traditional entertainment and escapist fare that took them far from the drudgery of everyday life. Many people, disillusioned with contemporary life, looked back to idealized images of small towns and local solutions to problems.

Not everyone benefited from the New Deal; women, for example, were still largely confined to traditional, lower-wage occupations. Roosevelt also failed to take a bold stand on civil rights. Many poor farmers of all races were hurt by the New Deal's agricultural programs. The New Deal did, however, transform the American political landscape. By 1936 Roosevelt had dramatically expanded the traditional southern white base of the Democratic Party to include African-Americans, urban immigrants, and organized labor. This "Roosevelt coalition" would dominate American politics for the next thirty years, providing the political muscle for a more active federal government.

The Great Depression had confronted the United States with one of its most trying domestic challenges. By the end of the 1930s, however, a new and potentially more dangerous threat was rising in Europe, endangering the very existence of the American experiment.

Annotated Suggested Readings

Robert McElvaine's *The Great Depression* (1983) is an excellent one-volume survey of the 1930s; it has particularly strong material on the origins and early years of the depression, as does the more recent work by Gene Smiley, *Rethinking the Great Depression* (2002). David Kennedy's *Freedom from Fear* (1999) covers the entire period, paying extra attention to the later New Deal years and World War II. William E. Leuchtenburg's *Franklin D. Roosevelt and the New Deal, 1932–1940* (1963) is still the best single-volume study of the New Deal.

John K. Galbraith's *The Great Crash* (1955) is a landmark study of the stock market crash, its causes, and its implications. Milton Friedman and Anna J. Schwartz offer an opposing explanation of the crash in *A Monetary History of the United States* (1965). Michael Bernstein supplies a more recent interpretation in *The Great Depression* (1989). Several oral histories about the privations of the depression years have been compiled. Studs Terkel's *Hard Times* (1970) is the most famous.

Among the several studies of Herbert Hoover and his response to the depression, George Nash's two-volume *The Life of Herbert Hoover* (1983, 1988) is the most extensive. Joan Hoff Wilson highlights Hoover's progressive roots in *Herbert Hoover: Forgotten Progressive* (1992). Martin Fausold's *The Presidency of Herbert C. Hoover* (1985) examines the complexities of the man, how the office of the president developed during his term, and the ways he attempted to handle the growing crisis.

For biographies on Roosevelt, the starting place is Kenneth Davis's encyclopedic three-volume collection, *FDR* (1985, 1986, 1993). Frank Freidel offers a detailed one-volume survey of Roosevelt in *Franklin Roosevelt: Rendezvous with Destiny* (1990). Arthur Schlesinger, Jr.'s *The Coming of the New Deal* (1959) is the definitive treatment of FDR's first hundred days, and his *Politics of Upheaval* (1960) is a necessary accompaniment.

The literature on various New Deal reform measures is voluminous. Richard Polenberg offers a readable overview in *The Era of Franklin D. Roosevelt* (2000). Anthony Badger's *The New Deal* (1989) describes the extent of public need and Roosevelt's mixed attempt to address it. Jim Powell argues that the New Deal actually prolonged the depression in his work, *FDR's Folly* (2003). Jordan Schwarz argues in *The New Dealers* (1993) that the primary goal of agency leaders was the creation of self-sustaining regional economies, not relief measures. Linda Gordon gives readers a thoughtful study of gender and the origins of the welfare state in *Pitied but Not Entitled* (1995). Donald Worster studies the farm crisis in *Dust Bowl* (1979), as does Richard Lowitt in *The New Deal and the West* (1984). Janet Poppendieck examines the impact of food assistance on farmers and consumers in *Breadlines Knee-Deep in Wheat* (1986).

The premiere study of Father Coughlin and Huey Long is Alan Brinkley's *Voices of Protest* (1982), while Donald Warren's *Radio Priest* (1996) and William Hair's *The Kingfish and His Realm* (1991) deal with each protester individually. Mark Naison's *Communists in Harlem During the Depression* (1983) focuses on FDR's left-wing critics, as does Robin Kelley's *Hammer and Hoe* (1990). *Campaign of the Century* (1992) by Greg Mitchell looks at Upton Sinclair's gubernatorial race in California.

Roosevelt's second term has not been studied as intensely as his first, but James MacGregor Burns's *Roosevelt: The Lion and the Fox* (1956) contains an overview. Irving Bernstein's *Turbulent Years* (1969) has especially good material on the creation of the National Labor Relations Board. William Leuchtenburg's *The Supreme Court Reborn* (1995) chronicles the constitutional revolution in the Court during the 1930s. The opposition strategy pursued by the Republican Party is the focus of Clyde Weed's *The Nemesis of Reform* (1995). Alan Brinkley details the transformation and decline of the New Deal after the 1937 recession in *The End of Reform* (1996).

David Peeler's *Hope Among Us Yet* (1986) discusses the mixture of social criticism and spirit of hopefulness found in 1930s art. Richard Pells studies the growing radicalization of depression-era artists in *Radical Visions and American Dreams* (1973). Daniel Aaron's

Writers on the Left (1961) is a good starting point for information on authors of the 1930s. *The Genius of the System* (1988) by Thomas Schatz examines how working within the new studio system made good studios great. Andrew Bergman's *We're in the Money* (1971) stresses the escapist tenor of most depression-era cinema.

Lizabeth Cohen's masterful synthesis, *Making a New Deal* (1990), highlights Roosevelt's impact on organized labor. Irving Bernstein traces the history of labor in the 1930s in *A Caring Society* (1985). Melvyn Dubofsky and Warren Van Tine's *John L. Lewis* (1977) portrays one of the most influential labor leaders of the decade, while Steven Fraser's *Labor Will Rule* (1991) looks at the CIO's cofounder Sidney Hillman. Alice and Staughton Lynd's *Rank and File* (1973) contains oral histories by many labor organizers from the period. Joseph Cohen's *When the Old Left Was Young* (1993) chronicles the fortunes of the American Student Union during the depression.

Harvard Sitkoff's *A New Deal for Blacks* (1978) examines the bitter fruits many African-Americans reaped from the New Deal. It should be read in concert with Nancy Weiss's *Farewell to the Party of Lincoln* (1983), since the two works offer conflicting interpretations of the black experience. Dan Carter's *Scottsboro* (1969) is a moving account of this divisive case. It should be read along with James Goodman's *Stories of Scottsboro* (1995). Patricia Sullivan examines the relationship between the federal government, blacks, and whites in *Days of Hope* (1996). Laurence Kelly's *The Assault on Assimilation* (1983) is a detailed overview of the New Deal's impact on Native Americans. Abraham Hoffman's *Unwanted Mexican-Americans in the Great Depression* (1974) and Francisco Balerman's *In Defense of La Raza* (1982) evaluate the prejudices faced by Mexican-Americans during the depression.

Lois Scharf studies the movement of women into the 1930s work force in *To Work and to Wed* (1980). Susan Ware's *Holding Their Own* (1982) and *Beyond Suffrage* (1987) discuss the growing authority women assumed in many families during the depression. Blanche Wiesen Cook provides insight into the personality and influence of the First Lady in *Eleanor Roosevelt, 1884–1933* (1992) and *Eleanor Roosevelt, 1933–1938* (1999). From her voluminous correspondence, Robert Cohen has published letters from depression-era children in *Dear Mrs. Roosevelt* (2002).

The **H***istory* **C***ompanion*

Government and the New Deal

Roosevelt's Fireside Chat, 1934

In a series of radio broadcasts that he called Fireside Chats, Franklin Roosevelt spoke directly to the people, explaining his policies and asking for their support. In this address, the president articulated why it was necessary to launch his sweeping and comprehensive New Deal reforms. The grave economic crisis, he argued, required bold experimentation, including an unprecedented expansion of government power.

I am happy to report that after years of uncertainty, culminating in the collapse of the spring of 1933, we are bringing order out of the old chaos with a greater certainty of the employment of labor at a reasonable wage and of more business at a fair profit. These governmental and industrial developments hold promise of new achievements for the Nation.

Men may differ as to the particular form of governmental activity with respect to industry and business, but nearly all are agreed that private enterprise in times such as these cannot be left without assistance and without reasonable safeguards lest it destroy not only itself but also our process of civilization. . . .

In our efforts for recovery we have avoided, on the one hand, the theory that business should and must be taken over into an all-embracing Government. We have avoided, on the other hand, the equally untenable theory that it is an interference with liberty to offer reasonable help when private enterprise is in need of help. The course we have followed fits the American practice of Government, a practice of taking action step by step, or regulating only to meet concrete needs, a practice of courageous recognition of change. I believe with Abraham Lincoln, that "The Legitimate object of Government is to do for a community of people whatever they need to have done but cannot do at all or cannot do so well for themselves in their separate and individual capacities."

In meeting the problems of industrial recovery the chief agency of the Government has been the National Recovery Administration [NRA]. Under its guidance, trades and industries covering 90 percent of all industrial employees have adopted codes of fair competition, which have been approved by the President. . . . Closely allied to the NRA is the program of public works provided for in the same Act and designed to put more men back to work, both directly on the public works themselves, and indirectly in the industries supplying the materials for these public works. To those who say that our expenditures for public works and other means for recovery are a waste that we cannot afford, I answer that no country, however rich, can afford the waste of its human resources. Demoralization caused by vast unemployment is our greatest extravagance. Morally, it is the greatest menace to our social order. . . .

I am not for a return to that definition of liberty under which for many years a free people were being gradually regimented into the service of the privileged few. I prefer and I am sure you prefer that broader definition of liberty under which we are moving forward to greater freedom, to greater security for the average man than he has ever known before in the history of America.

"This Threat to Our Liberty," 1936

Herbert Hoover had dabbled in many of the ideas later realized in the New Deal, though in a much more limited form, while he was president. Hoover never adopted a truly activist conception of government, however, and he drifted rightward during Roosevelt's first term in office. By 1936 he had emerged as one of the New Deal's harshest conservative critics. In this October 30 speech, Hoover leveled the classic conservative accusation that government interference in the economy would lead to despotism. He claimed that government could create institutions that would stimulate the economy without interfering with the "economic liberty" of the individual citizen.

Through four years of experience this New Deal attack upon free institutions has emerged as the transcendent issue in America.

All the men who are seeking for mastery in the world today are using the same weapons. They sing the same songs. . . . But their philosophy is founded on the coercion and compulsory organization of men. True liberal government is founded upon the emancipation of men. This is the issue upon which men are imprisoned and dying in Europe right now. . . . Freedom does not die from frontal attack. It dies because men in power no longer believe in a system based on liberty. . . .

I gave the warning against this philosophy of government four years ago from a heart heavy with anxiety for the future of our country. It was born from many years' experience of the forces moving in the world which would weaken the vitality of American freedom. It grew in four years of battle as President to uphold the banner of free men.

And that warning was based on . . . my knowledge of the ideas that Mr. Roosevelt and his bosom colleagues had covertly embraced despite the Democratic platform. Those ideas were not new. Most of them had been urged upon me.

During my four years powerful groups thundered at the White House with these same ideas. Some were honest, some promising votes, most of them threatening reprisals, and all of them yelling "reactionary" at us. I rejected all these things because they would not only delay recovery but because I knew that in the end they would shackle free men.

The New Dealers say that all . . . that we propose is a worn-out system; that this machine age requires new measures for which we must sacrifice some part of the freedom of men. Men have lost their way with a confused idea that government should run machines.

Man-made machines cannot be of more worth than men themselves. Free men made these machines. Only free spirits can master them to their proper use. . . . Free government is the most difficult of all government. But it is everlastingly true that the plain people will make fewer mistakes than any group of men no matter how powerful. But free government implies vigilant thinking and courageous living and self-reliance in a people. Let me say to you that any measure which breaks our dikes of freedom will flood the land with misery.

Few events have shaken American society like the Great Depression. In the early 1930s the American economy seemed to be "broken." The failure of the economy to recover without government helped force Americans to confront deeply ingrained cultural notions. Though most Americans deeply valued self-reliance, millions were forced to seek relief aid; and though most people believed in private charity, the demands for aid quickly overwhelmed the capacity of private charity to respond. Where was an ill-paid, ill-fed, ill-housed nation to turn?

The idea that the federal government should marshal resources for public relief was not new. A number of groups including socialists, the Populists, and the progressives had argued that regulation of industry was necessary to protect the common people from the abuses of large businesses. They demanded a social safety net for those who were unable to provide for themselves. Franklin Roosevelt constructed his New Deal on the foundation created by previous generations of reformers. Only a democratically elected government, he argued, could protect the public welfare against the ravages of greed and industrial capitalism.

While his program won widespread popular support, skeptics on both sides attacked him for either doing too much or not doing enough to end the depression. Left-leaning critics such as Huey Long wanted the president to impose greater government controls on the economy by redistributing wealth from the rich to the poor. Conservatives such as Hoover argued that no crisis warranted the extent of government interference that Roosevelt proposed. FDR claimed to be searching for a middle ground between the extremism of the left and the right, reassuring the public that the New Deal's goal of providing the American people with security did not "indicate a change in values."

Ultimately, the debate between Roosevelt and Hoover revolved around competing notions of liberty. Roosevelt, always the political pragmatist, favored experimentation, arguing that the New Deal promoted liberty by freeing people from the shackles of poverty and depression. Hoover, reflecting America's deep-seated aversion to federal power, maintained that government coercion and individual liberty were incompatible. A powerful central government may be appropriate for European powers, he argued, but it clashed with the American faith in individualism and self-help.

QUESTIONS FOR ANALYSIS

1. What does Roosevelt mean when he calls for "a practice of courageous recognition of change"?

2. Why do you think Roosevelt quotes from Lincoln to justify his policies?

3. In his opening ("All the men who are seeking"), Hoover compares Roosevelt to totalitarian dictators Hitler (Germany), Mussolini (Italy), and Stalin (the Soviet Union). Why does he draw that parallel?

4. What does Hoover see as the greatest threat to American democracy?

5. Are liberty and freedom synonymous?

6. Why are Americans so skeptical about government activism?

26

War and Society

1933–1945

The Japanese surprise attack on Pearl Harbor, and the declaration of war that followed, shattered the illusion that the United States could remain detached from world events. World War II converted the nation from isolationism to internationalism.

At 7:55 A.M. on the morning of December 7, 1941, thirty-nine-year-old Japanese bomber pilot Mitsuo Fuchida, leader of a 353-plane armada, peered down at ninety-four U.S. Navy ships, including eight battleships and twenty-nine destroyers, lined up at the U.S. naval base at Pearl Harbor, Hawaii. "To-to-to," the first syllable of the Japanese word for "charge," he shouted into his radio. That was followed by an even more significant transmission: "Tora, tora, tora," meaning "tiger," the message confirming that the attack was catching the Americans by surprise. The waves of Japanese bombers and fighters swooped down, dropped their deadly bombs on American ships, and strafed planes parked wingtip-to-wingtip at nearby airbases. Fuchida set his sights on the U.S.S. *Arizona*, slamming a thousand-pound, armor-piercing bomb against its hull. "I saw a huge explosion almost reaching the sky," he recalled. The ship split in half and quickly sank, entombing over a thousand sailors onboard. When the attack ended two hours later, twenty-four hundred Americans lay dead. Japanese pilots disabled or destroyed eighteen ships—including all eight battleships, three light cruisers, three destroyers, and four auxiliary craft—and 188 aircraft. The Japanese lost 29 planes and ninety-six men.

The next day, more than 60 million Americans huddled by their radios to hear President Franklin Roosevelt ask a joint session of Congress for a declaration of war against Japan, swearing to fight until total victory was won. December 7, 1941, he declared was "a date which will live in infamy." For two years the same Congress had resisted the president's efforts to aid the Allies. Now it enthusiastically endorsed his call for war. The Senate approved a war resolution 89 to 0, the House 388 to 1. Congresswoman Jeanette Rankin of Montana, a pacifist and suffragist, was the lone dissenter. Three days later, Adolph Hitler declared war on the "half Judaized and the other half Negrified" American people.

The Japanese surprise attack on Pearl Harbor, and the declaration of war that followed, shattered the illusion that the United States could remain detached from world events. World War II converted the nation from isolationism to internationalism. It dramatically accelerated the preceding decade's growth in the size and scope of government, produced unprecedented economic expansion, and offered new opportunities to groups that had been excluded from the American mainstream. The conflict united the nation like no previous crisis and helped produce a national culture. These changes in the structure of American life did not, however, produce a rethinking of American values or attitudes toward government. In the face of new experiments in government power, Americans—as they had during the hardships of depression—remained deeply wedded to their faith in local democracy. The war-fueled economy offered new opportunities for minorities and women, but the United States remained a society deeply divided by race, class, and gender. The nation emerged from the struggle as the world's premier military and economic power. But despite the American experiment's now global proportions, most Americans were reluctant to accept the responsibility of power.

- How did isolationist sentiment shape American policy toward Europe and Asia during the 1930s?

- What was the Allied strategy for victory, and how did disagreements among the "Big Three" contribute to postwar tensions between the Soviets and the West?

- How did the war contribute to the development of a national culture? How did it contribute to social tensions?

- What impact did the war have on American attitudes toward government and world affairs?

This chapter will address these questions.

AMERICA AND THE WORLD CRISIS, 1933–1941

During the 1930s leaders in Germany, Italy, and Japan decided to use the cover of depression to realize their expansionist goals. How would America respond to the growing threat in Europe and Asia? Amid advancing aggression, Franklin Roosevelt tried to navigate between a peace movement that wanted Washington to remain neutral and a growing belief that the national interest required the United States to aid the Allies. Struggling with depression and conscious of the slaughter of World War I, Americans had little interest in international experimentation. As Hitler's army rampaged through Europe and Japan ransacked East Asia, Roosevelt nudged a reluctant nation closer to war.

The Gathering Storm   The first challenge to peace came in Asia, where Japan's army was on the march. Since the 1890s Japanese leaders had coveted the Manchurian region in northern China. Comprising an area as large as France and Germany, Manchuria served as a defensive buffer against Russia. More important, it was rich in the coal, iron, timber, and soybeans that the import-dependent Japanese desperately needed. In 1931 Tokyo seized Manchuria, established a puppet government, and dispatched colonists to settle the land. In 1937 Japan intensified and broadened its invasion, bombing Chinese cities and killing thousands of civilians. Japanese troops slaughtered one hundred thousand Chinese in Nanking. In December, in the midst of a full-scale military attack against China, Japanese warplanes sank the American gunboat *Panay*, killing two American sailors and wounding thirty. Though Roosevelt privately considered responding with economic sanctions, he did nothing once Japan apologized.

While an emboldened Japan extended its reach into China, Italy attempted to realize its own territorial ambitions. Benito Mussolini, who had governed Italy since 1922, dreamed of creating an Italian empire in northern Africa. In October 1935 he tried to distract Italians from their economic woes at home by launching an invasion of the independent African state of Ethiopia. Within a year he had gained control of the lightly armed country.

The greatest threat came not from Japan or Italy, but from a revitalized Germany. In January 1933 Adolf Hitler bulled his way to power as Germany's chancellor. The charismatic and demented Hitler tapped into a deep well of resentment that Germans felt toward the West for imposing a punitive peace following World War I. He vowed to revive German economic and military power, to crush the Bolshevik threat, and to rid the German "race" of the "contamination" of Jewish influence, which he blamed for all of Germany's many severe problems. Once in office Hitler took the title of *Fuhrer* ("leader") and outlawed political parties other than his own National Socialists, or Nazis. As the Nazis consolidated power at home, they also asserted it abroad. Hitler, repudiating the Versailles Treaty, withdrew from the League of Nations in 1933 and unilaterally announced that Germany would rearm. On March 7, 1936, Hitler ordered German troops into the Rhineland, the strategic buffer that lay between France and Germany.

Hitler accurately predicted that the West would respond feebly to his aggression. European powers, he said, would "never act. They'll just protest. And they will always be too late." Traumatized by their experience in World War I and consumed with economic problems at home, the European powers settled on a policy of "appeasement," hoping to satisfy Hitler's and Mussolini's limited goals in order to avoid another war. Britain acquiesced to German plans to rebuild its navy; France registered only mild protest when Germany advanced on the Rhineland. When Hitler's ally Mussolini annexed Ethiopia, the League of Nations imposed an embargo on the shipment of war-related goods to Italy but excluded the most important item—oil. The French and British were willing to sacrifice Ethiopia to prevent a general war in Europe.

Encouraged by the timid response to their aggression, Hitler and Mussolini attempted to extend their influence in Europe by intervening in a civil war that

CHRONOLOGY

1931	Japan seizes Manchuria
1935	Italy invades Ethiopia
1936	Spanish Civil War begins
1937	Japan invades China
1938	Hitler forces the *Anschluss* and invades Sudetenland Munich Agreement
1939	Hitler invades Poland and war begins
1940	France surrenders to Germany Battle of Britain Roosevelt reelected
1941	Lend-Lease Act Pearl Harbor attacked
1942	Operation TORCH Battles of Coral Sea and Midway
1943	Allied invasion of Italy
1944	D-Day Roosevelt reelected
1945	Yalta Conference Roosevelt dies; Truman becomes president Germany surrenders Atomic bombs dropped; Japan surrenders

broke out in Spain. In the summer of 1936 General Francisco Franco led an armed revolt against Spain's democratically elected government. While Germany and Italy fortified Franco's cause with military aid, the West hid behind the veil of neutrality. Most Americans were indifferent, but a handful of impassioned idealists saw the struggle for Spain as a great moral confrontation between democracy and totalitarianism. American volunteers, many of them communist and calling themselves the Abraham Lincoln Battalion, went to Spain to fight for the republican cause. In early 1939 Franco prevailed, establishing an authoritarian government that lasted until his death in 1976.

American indifference to the Spanish Civil War seemed to confirm Hitler's belief that he had nothing to fear from the United States. America, he told an aide, "was incapable of conducting war." It was a "Jewish rubbish heap," incapacitated by depression and poor leadership. But Hitler underestimated Roosevelt's interest in world affairs. As a child, Roosevelt had traveled extensively throughout Europe, making his first trip at the age of three. While a student at the prestigious Groton

School and later at Harvard, he debated international issues and gloated over his cousin Theodore's exploits. As undersecretary of the navy during the Wilson administration, Roosevelt became firmly convinced that a great power such as the United States should play an important role in world affairs.

As president, Roosevelt acted on his internationalist impulses. He chose as his secretary of state Cordell Hull, a former Tennessee judge and congressman who believed that world trade was the key to international understanding. Under Hull's watchful eye, the president developed the Export-Import Bank, which helped U.S. businesspeople finance overseas sales, and the Reciprocal Trade Act (RTA), which gave the president new powers to bargain for foreign markets by automatically extending tariff preferences to favored nations. In November 1933 FDR overcame a decade of hostility and formally recognized the Soviet Union, hoping that diplomatic recognition would encourage the Soviets to pay their war debts and limit their propaganda in the United States. The Soviets also had the potential to be a lucrative trading partner—always a major consideration during the depression.

Along with recognizing the Soviets, Roosevelt moved to develop closer ties with other nations in the Western Hemisphere. In his inaugural address in 1933 Roosevelt announced a new "Good Neighbor" policy toward Latin America. At the Inter-American Conference at Montevideo, Uruguay, in 1933 the United States supported a declaration pledging nonintervention among Western Hemisphere states. The president underscored this policy by renouncing the Platt Amendment, which had given the United States the right to intervene in the affairs of Cuba. In a treaty with Panama in 1936 U.S. negotiators relinquished similar privileges. The president withdrew marines from Haiti in 1934 and joined with representatives of twenty other South American governments to ratify a Protocol of Non-Intervention at the Inter-American Conference in Buenos Aires, Argentina, in 1936. The following year, Mexico became the first country to test the U.S. commitment to nonintervention when it nationalized American oil companies. Despite heavy pressure from Hull to retaliate, Roosevelt refused to intervene.

A powerful wave of isolationism, however, limited Roosevelt's internationalist ambitions. Isolationist sentiment had deep roots in the American past. During the 1930s disillusion with World War I and concern about jobs at home intensified the hands-off attitude. Since the president's first priority was to resuscitate the American economy, international diplomacy necessarily took a back seat. Popular writers, who claimed that selfish business interests conspired to lead the United States into World War I, whipped disenchantment with World War I into a frenzy. A thesis represented by books such as Walter Millis's *Road to War* (1935) argued that America mobilized in 1917 not to preserve democracy but to protect Wall Street bankers. In 1934 a congressional committee headed by Gerald P. Nye of North Dakota added credibility to these charges. Despite flimsy evidence, the Nye Committee concluded that the bankers who had lent the Allies money and the "merchants of death" who had sold them ammunition had conspired with President Woodrow Wilson to take the country to war. "For the sake of profits, for dollars to protect the loans of certain commercial interests in this country, 50,000 boys now lie buried in France," declared Senator Homer Bone of Washington. By 1937, 60 percent of Americans believed that U.S. involvement in World War I had been a mistake.

The combination of depression and disillusion produced a powerful peace movement. Led by women, clergy, and college students, the cause claimed 12 million adherents by the middle of the decade. On April 6, 1935, the eighteenth anniversary of American entry into the First World War, 50,000 veterans held a "march for peace" in Washington. Three days later over 175,000 college students participated in a one-hour "strike for peace" on campuses across the country. "Schools, not battleships," they chanted. "Let us turn our eyes inward," exhorted a leading Democratic governor. "If the world is to become a wilderness of waste, hatred, and bitterness, let us all the more earnestly protect and preserve our own oasis of liberty."

Congress reflected the isolationist sentiment by passing restrictive neutrality legislation during the decade. As early as 1933 Congress refused to give Roosevelt discretionary power to apply arms embargoes against aggressor nations. It passed three major Neutrality Acts during the decade. In 1935 Congress imposed an automatic embargo on American arms and ammunition to all parties at war. The following year Congress added a ban on loans to belligerents. In May 1937 Congress, still preoccupied with learning lessons from 1914–1917, banned American ships from war zones, prohibited Americans from traveling on belligerent ships, and extended the embargo to include not just armaments, but also the oil, steel, and rubber needed for war machines. Foreign belligerents could buy such goods only if they paid for them in cash and carried them in their own ships. "With stout legal thread," observed historian David Kennedy, "Congress had spun a straitjacket that rendered the United States effectively powerless in the face of the global conflagration that was about to explode."

The Failure of Neutrality

Though alarmed by events in Europe and Asia, Roosevelt was distracted by the depression and restrained by the neutrality laws. In October 1937 he tested the depth of isolationist sentiment in a now famous speech in which he denounced the "reign of terror and international lawlessness" that threatened the peace. "When an epidemic of physical disease starts to spread, the community approves and joins in a quarantine of the patients in order to protect the health of the community." When public reaction proved mixed, Roosevelt backed away from the internationalist implications of his message. "It's a terrible thing," Roosevelt said, "to look over your shoulder when you are trying to lead—and find no one there."

In 1938, while America watched from the sidelines, Hitler pressed Europe to the brink of war, proclaiming the German nation's right to *lebensraum*, or living space. "Germany's problems could be solved only by means of force," he told his aides. In March he forced Austria into *Anschluss* (union) with Germany. In the fall Hitler threatened to invade Czechoslovakia when it refused to give him its Sudetenland, a mountainous region bordering Germany and inhabited mostly by ethnic Germans. British Prime Minister Neville Chamberlain and French Premier Edouard Daladier hastily scheduled meetings with Hitler in Munich on September 29–30, 1938. Hitler reassured them by promising, "This is the last territorial claim I have to make in Europe." Hoping to avoid confrontation, the West sacrificed the Sudetenland on the altar of appeasement, agreeing to a gradual transfer to German control.

Denied outside support, the Czechs surrendered, demobilized their army, and allowed Germany to shear off the Sudetenland. Huge crowds filled the streets of London to celebrate Chamberlain's announcement that Munich had secured "peace in our time." Future prime minister Winston Churchill revealed a better grasp of the situation. "Britain and France had to choose between war and dishonor," he said. "They chose dishonor. They will have war."

Six months later German troops swept down on the rest of Czechoslovakia, smashing Western illusions that Hitler could be appeased. Within weeks the British government reversed course, announcing that it was committed to the defense of Poland, Hitler's next possible target. The European situation grew more dangerous in August when the Germans and Russians concluded a nonaggression pact. Stalin was certain that Hitler would finish with Poland and invade the Soviet Union, and the Munich episode convinced him that the West would not come to his aid. His deal with Hitler would buy him time to rebuild his forces. The agreement provided for the partition of Poland and for Soviet absorption of the Baltic states as well as territory in Finland and Bessarabia. With his eastern flank secured, Hitler unleashed his fire and steel on the Polish people on September 1, 1939. In a brilliant display of military skill and power, the Germans conducted a *Blitzkrieg* (lightning war), sending 1.5 million men pouring over the Polish border. "Close your hearts to pity," Hitler told his generals. "Act brutally." Two days later, honoring their commitments to Poland, Britain and France declared war on Germany. World War II in Europe had begun.

By late 1939 American sympathy was clearly with the Allies, but most people continued to believe that Britain and France could defend Europe without U.S. assistance. The British, who claimed the largest navy in the world, would strangle the German economy. Many military strategists believed that France's eight-hundred-thousand-man standing army supporting the French Maginot Line of fortifications along the French-German border could resist any invasion. The calm that settled over Europe during the winter of 1939–1940 added to the detachment. Isolationist Senator William Borah sniffed, "There's something phony about this war."

The lull complicated Roosevelt's task of educating the American people about the dangers posed by the European situation. Roosevelt hoped to avoid war by providing assistance to the Allies, but the Neutrality Acts tied his hands. "It is, of course, obvious that if the Neutrality Act remains in its present form, France and England will be defeated rapidly," a diplomat informed the president. In November 1939 Roosevelt pressured Congress to pass a revised Neutrality Act that lifted the arms embargo against belligerents, but retained the cash-and-carry provision. The new law also forbade American merchant ships from entering a broad "danger zone" that included most of the major shipping lanes to Europe.

A German offensive in April 1940 shattered the false confidence that Hitler could be contained. On April 9 Hitler's *blitzkrieg* overran Denmark, and German troops swarmed over Norway, the Netherlands, Luxembourg, and Belgium, and on into France. In the chaos that followed the Allied retreat, Britain managed to rescue some 338,000 troops from the northern French port of Dunkirk, but the troops left behind ninety thousand rifles, seven thousand tons of ammunition, and 120,000 vehicles. On June 22, 1940, the French surrendered to Hitler in the same railcar in which the Germans had capitulated to the Allies in 1918. A reporter noted that Hitler was "afire with scorn, anger, hate, revenge, triumph." The Germans installed a puppet government in the town of Vichy. "The Battle of France is over," Churchill, who had become prime minister ten days earlier, told a somber Parliament. "I expect that the Battle of Britain is about to begin."

The fall of France changed the military calculus in Washington. Roosevelt had believed the combination of British sea and air power, French land forces, and American industrial might would stymie Hitler's advance. The question now was whether Britain could survive alone against Hitler's military juggernaut. Beginning in the summer of 1940 Hitler hurled his *Luftwaffe* (air force) at the British. Soon frustrated by the resistance of the Royal Air Force (RAF), Hitler ordered the terror bombing of London. From September to November, during the Battle of Britain, nearly 250 German bombers dropped their deadly cargo over London every night. The British people, though badly battered, refused to break.

Following the fall of France, Roosevelt abandoned any pretense of neutrality by committing the United States to a policy of "all aid to the Allies short of war." The president offered the British fifty World War I–vintage destroyers in exchange for leases to eight British military bases. Congress also approved Roosevelt's request for $8 billion in additional funds to rearm the nation, and it authorized a one-year draft, the first peacetime conscription in American history.

The 1940 Election Campaign

Questions of war and peace dominated the 1940 presidential campaign. Growing concern about the deteriorating situation in Europe pushed the Republican Party to abandon its isolationist moorings and nominate little-known Wendell Willkie, a forty-eight-year-old Wall Street lawyer and utilities executive.

Initially, Willkie expressed support for Roosevelt's defense policies and focused his attacks on the perceived failures of the New Deal. In August, trailing badly in the polls, Willkie shifted gears. Three days after publicly supporting Roosevelt's destroyers-for-bases deal, Willkie condemned the move as "the most arbitrary and dictatorial action ever taken by a President in the history of the United States." Over the next few months, he sharpened his attacks. Early in October, charging that the president was leading the country into war, Willkie vowed that he would not send "one American boy into the shambles of another war."

Roosevelt, who was seeking an unprecedented third term, feared that the peace issue would catch fire. By mid-October polls showed Willkie gaining ground in key states with large electoral votes, including Illinois, Indiana, and Michigan. The president decided to douse the flames with deception. In late October, in what became the most quoted statement of the campaign, Roosevelt told a crowd in Boston, "I have said this before, but I shall say it again and again and again: Your boys are not going to be sent into any foreign wars." By the fall of 1940 the president knew that his policies would likely lead the nation into war. Instead of engaging the American people in a thoughtful discussion of the issue, both Roosevelt and his internationalist-minded opponent told the American people what they most wanted to hear.

Roosevelt's reassurances worked. He fended off Willkie's late surge and won reelection handily. The president received 27 million votes to Willkie's 22 million.

Roosevelt carried thirty-eight states and 449 electoral votes to Willkie's ten states and 82 votes (see map below). Willkie, who received 5 million more votes than Landon had in 1936, gave Roosevelt a tough challenge, but the New Deal coalition remained intact.

To the Brink   The president interpreted the election as an endorsement of his policies. He moved quickly to push for more aid to Britain. Churchill privately warned Roosevelt that the war was draining money from the British Treasury and that the "moment approaches when we shall no longer be able to pay cash for shipping and other supplies." A few days after Christmas Roosevelt responded by unveiling a "Lend-Lease" proposal that would allow the United States to provide Britain with valuable war material. Roosevelt compared Lend-Lease to a garden hose one lends to a neighbor whose house is on fire—receiving it or a replacement when the fire is out. Aiding the British was the best way to keep America out of the war, he said, and he urged the United States to "be the great arsenal of democracy."

Isolationists in Congress battled to defeat Lend-Lease. "Lending war equipment is a good deal like lending chewing gum," Senator Taft grumbled. Lend-Lease, its enemies cried, was a grim reaper's AAA that would "plow under every fourth Amer-

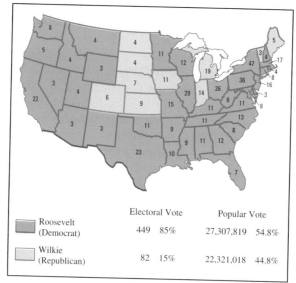

	Electoral Vote	Popular Vote
Roosevelt (Democrat)	449 85%	27,307,819 54.8%
Wilkie (Republican)	82 15%	22,321,018 44.8%

The Election of 1940   With war raging in Europe, Roosevelt spent most of the campaign season handling foreign affairs. Meanwhile, Republican candidate Wendell Willkie, a Midwestern native and World War I veteran, found Roosevelt's public support so strong that he was left with little to attack besides the threat of war and Roosevelt's violation of the two-term presidential tradition. The majority of Americans rejected the tradition and agreed with Roosevelt's slogan "Don't switch horses in the middle of the stream."

ican boy." Isolationists formed the America First Committee to organize opposition. Led by a diverse group that included Ohio Senator Robert Taft, aviator-hero Charles Lindbergh, and socialist Norman Thomas, committee members denied that Hitler posed a threat to American security.

However, the momentum of war was influencing American attitudes about the nation's role in the struggle for Europe. Polls showed over 60 percent of the American public supporting Lend-Lease. Internationalists organized the Committee to Defend America by Aiding the Allies, which called for unlimited aid to Britain. "Every time Hitler bombed London, we got a couple of votes," declared a supporter. The Lend-Lease proposal quickly passed in both the House and Senate.

As Roosevelt had hoped, Lend-Lease proved to be of vital assistance to the Allies. By 1945 it totaled some $50 billion, or four times the amount loaned to the Allies between 1917 and 1919. Passage of Lend-Lease marked a point of no return for America. The United States had committed itself to the survival of Great Britain with an economic aid program that amounted to a declaration of economic warfare on Germany. When Hitler turned on Stalin to launch a bold attack against the Soviet Union in June 1941, Roosevelt convinced Congress to include the Soviets in the Lend-Lease program.

Lend-Lease aggravated a growing controversy over escorts in the Atlantic. "The decision for 1941 lies upon the seas," Churchill warned Roosevelt. German U-boats (submarines) were sinking British ships at nearly five times the rate at which new construction could replace them. British ships needed better protection, which only the United States could provide, but Lend-Lease specifically barred the U.S. Navy from providing convoys.

In August Roosevelt and Churchill met at Placentia Bay in Newfoundland in the first of many conferences between the two leaders. The most famous product of the summit came in an eight-point statement of war aims called the Atlantic Charter. The two leaders pledged to honor the principles of self-determination, free trade, nonaggression, and freedom of the seas, promising a postwar world in which all people "may live out their lives in freedom from fear and want." More practical concerns were also addressed. Churchill pressed Roosevelt for a declaration of war against Germany. Roosevelt, believing that the public would not support such a bold move, promised "to wage war, but not declare it." He pledged the navy to protect British convoys as far east as Iceland while he looked for an "incident" to justify a more aggressive posture.

The president got his incident the following month. On September 4, 1941, a U-boat, after being chased for hours by a destroyer, U.S.S. *Greer*, turned and attacked the destroyer. The following month, a U-boat torpedoed the U.S. destroyer *Kearny*, killing eleven. "America has been attacked," Roosevelt blustered. On October 30 the *Reuben James* was hit, with the loss of ninety-six men. In response, Roosevelt ordered all ships engaged in escort duty to "shoot on sight" any German submarines appearing in waters west of Iceland.

Public anger at the sinking of American ships provided Roosevelt with the support he needed to repeal the neutrality legislation. On November 13, 1941, Congress voted by a narrow margin to permit American ships to sail through war zones to British and Russian ports. The last remaining restrictions on American actions had been removed. The *New York Times* editorialized, "The Battle of the Atlantic is on."

"This Is War" The story unfolded differently in the Pacific. Since 1931 the United States had criticized Japanese aggression in the Far East, refusing to recognize Tokyo's claim to territory in China. In reality, however, the United States lacked the power to challenge Japanese predominance in East Asia. The only effective weapon in the American arsenal was economic. Japan depended on the United States for a long list of strategic materials, especially oil. Throughout the decade, Roosevelt tried to use the economic leverage to tame Japanese aggression without triggering a confrontation that would distract attention and resources from the European theater. "I simply have not got enough Navy to go around—and every little episode in the Pacific means fewer ships in the Atlantic," Roosevelt complained.

Despite his worry, the logic of American policy moved the United States and Japan closer to confrontation. In 1939 Roosevelt threatened an economic embargo, hoping to shock the Japanese into tempering their action in the region. The threat did not deter the Japanese, who secured bases in Indochina on September 24. America responded immediately with an embargo on high-quality scrap iron and steel. Japan's answer to the tightened sanctions was to announce the Tripartite Pact with Germany and Italy on September 27. The pact pledged its signatories to come to one another's help in the event of an attack "by a power not already engaged in war." The treaty clearly aimed to dissuade the United States from either joining the British against the Germans or directly opposing Japan's efforts to carve out an empire in China and Southeast Asia. When Japanese forces overran the rest of Indochina in July, the administration reacted by freezing Japanese assets in the United States and by ending all shipments of oil. Japan now faced a difficult choice: either it could submit to American demands or conquer new territory to secure oil for its war machine. Since peace with the United States now seemed impossible, Japan planned for war.

In October the militant war minister, Hideki Tojo, who opposed compromise with the United States, gained control of Japan's imperial government. On November 5 Tojo decided he would continue diplomatic efforts to relax the embargo for three more weeks. If no agreement were reached by November 26, Japan would go to war. He set the date for attack: December 7, 1941.

American officials learned of Japan's intentions by intercepting messages between Tokyo and its embassy in the U.S. capital, but they did not know where the attack would come. Military leaders warned all American military installations in the Pacific of possible attack. Most Americans expected Japan to attack British Malaya or the Philippines. On the evening of December 6 American intelligence decoded a long message from Tokyo to its ambassador in Washington. Its final section announced there was no chance of reaching a diplomatic settlement "because of American attitudes." Roosevelt, after reading the message, concluded, "This is war." On December 7 Washington sent another warning about a possible Japanese attack. The warning came too late. On the morning of December 7

Japanese planes launched their attack against Pearl Harbor. The next day America entered World War II.

FIGHTING A GLOBAL WAR, 1941–1945

The declaration of war presented the administration with two monumental tasks. At home it needed to refit the economy for wartime production; abroad the challenge was to coordinate military strategy with Allied leaders to defeat Hitler's formidable army. The "Big Three"—Roosevelt, Churchill, and Stalin—shared the same goal, but they disagreed on strategy. The most important question was: when should the western allies launch a second front against Hitler to relieve pressure on Soviet troops battling in the east? Stalin insisted on an attack as early as 1942, but Churchill and Roosevelt stalled until 1944. The delay proved costly. It nurtured suspicion between Stalin and the West, making for a precarious peace at the end of the war.

The Arsenal of Democracy

The mobilization of the American economy for war was a staggering task full of confusion and chaos. It brought into conflict two competing forces: the need to coordinate a massive economy and build an army while preserving faith in volunteerism and local government. America's faith in democracy required that mobilization be conducted piecemeal. "If you are going to . . . go to war, . . . in a capitalist country," Secretary of War Henry L. Stimson observed, "you have got to let business make money out of the process." As much as possible, Roosevelt sought to elicit voluntary compliance from business, workers, farmers, and consumers.

Before the Japanese attack on Pearl Harbor, Roosevelt had rejected recommendations for a powerful administrator with government authority to limit supplies of important resources and force businesses to convert to war production. As a result of Roosevelt's indecision, the mobilization effort drifted. When in May 1940 Roosevelt issued a call for production of fifty thousand military aircraft, industry was capable of producing only half the needed aluminum. Steel shortages prevented the construction of ships needed to transport Lend-Lease supplies.

The mobilization effort shifted gears following Pearl Harbor. Congress granted the president extraordinary powers to reshuffle the domestic economy in any way necessary to guarantee the war effort. The president had to tackle four related but complicated issues: mobilizing industry to produce material for war, controlling wages and prices, financing the war, and raising an army.

In January 1942 Roosevelt created the War Production Board (WPB) to develop policies governing all aspects of production and to "exercise general responsibilities" over the nation's economy. To head the agency Roosevelt chose Donald Nelson, the former head of Sears, Roebuck and Company. Despite his broad mandate, Nelson took a limited view of his powers. He allowed "little czars" to retain considerable autonomy in dealing with petroleum, rubber, and labor, and he permitted both the army and the navy to maintain separate purchasing authority.

Perhaps most important, Nelson tried to gain the confidence of the business community by offering financial incentives. Government made war production attractive by underwriting the cost of expansion and by guaranteeing profits. The government granted generous "cost-plus" arrangements, promising repayment of all development and production costs as well as guaranteeing a percentage profit. The administration abandoned antitrust legislation, allowing large corporations to pool resources. Enticed by the incentives, manufacturers switched from making shirts to making mosquito netting, from making cars to making tanks.

The close government–business cooperation benefited large corporations that possessed the resources and workers to produce necessary materials. Two-thirds of military contracts went to 100 firms. Almost half went to three dozen major corporations. With large firms controlling most of the market, competing for the leftovers pushed many small firms into bankruptcy. In 1940, 175,000 companies accounted for 70 percent of the nation's manufacturing output. By March 1943 that number had dwindled to just 100 companies. Corporate after-tax profits climbed from $6.4 billion in 1940 to $10.8 billion in 1944.

Despite the incentives, the mobilization effort remained plagued with problems. Industry scrambled to obtain scarce vital resources, producing bottlenecks in the production process. One of the biggest shortages was rubber. By early 1942 Japan had blocked off 90 percent of America's crude rubber supply in the Dutch East Indies and Malaya. Every armored tank used a ton of rubber. The president, sensitive to public fears of intrusive government, resisted calls for strict rationing and instead called for a voluntary scrap drive. On June 12 he appealed to the people to turn in "old tires, old rubber raincoats, old garden hoses, rubber shoes, bathing caps, gloves—whatever you have that is made of rubber." In less than four weeks Americans donated 450,000 tons of scrap rubber. At the same time, the government spent $700 million to create a new synthetic rubber industry.

All the problems could not obscure the obvious conclusion that conversion to wartime production had been a dramatic success. Between 1941 and 1943 America realized more than an 800 percent increase in military production. By then more than half of all world manufacturing was taking place in the United States. By the end of the war the United States had produced 86,000 tanks, 295,000 airplanes, 12,000 ships, 15 million rifles and machine guns, and 40 billion bullets. At its productive peak the United States built a ship a day and an airplane every five minutes.

Fearful that so much demand chasing so few products would produce spiraling inflation, Roosevelt created the Office of Price Administration and Civilian Supply (OPA) in April 1940. The OPA established a system of rationing civilian purchases of tires, cars, gasoline, sugar, and later shoes, oil, and coffee. "Use it up, wear it out, make it do or do without," became the OPA slogan. The agency also imposed a cap on most prices and rents. Political controversies overwhelmed the OPA. Business lobbyists, farm-bloc politicians, and union leaders waged unceasing "guerrilla warfare" against the agency. Consumers chafed under rationing restrictions, particularly those on beef and gasoline.

To control inflation the administration needed to regulate wage increases as well as prices. To carry out that task, Roosevelt created the National War Labor Board in January 1942. In July the board adopted a formula that permitted wage increases in line with the 15 percent rise in the cost of living since January 1941. Organized labor objected to the check on their earning power and threatened to

Mobilizing the People   Although the American people were of divided opinion before the United States' entry into the war, the attack on Pearl Harbor instantaneously unified and mobilized public opinion. "Remember Pearl Harbor" remained a rallying cry throughout the war. These workers at a bicycle factory in Minnesota celebrate the New Year just weeks after the attack. While their patriotic fervor continued, more than likely their work was altered as war-related goods, like tanks, planes, and weapons, replaced bicycles on the production floor.   *(Myron H. Davis/LIFE Magazine © Time, Inc.)*

break the no-strike pledge they had given after Pearl Harbor. Work stoppages, though usually short-lived, increased from 2,968 in 1942 to 4,956 in 1944.

The most dramatic confrontation was a strike by four hundred thousand members of the United Mine Workers led by John L. Lewis in May 1943. "The coal miners of America are hungry," he charged. "They are ill-fed and undernourished." The president seized the coal mines and threatened to draft miners into the army. But in the end he negotiated a settlement that offered the miners substantial new benefits. Congress and the public were less understanding. Lewis became the most hated man in America in 1943. In June 1943 Congress responded to labor arrogance by passing the Smith-Connolly bill (also known as the War Labor Disputes Act), which empowered the president to seize any vital war plant shut down by strikes. Not wanting to alienate an important ally, Roosevelt vetoed the bill. Congress, however, mustered the necessary votes to override the veto and enact the legislation.

To help pay for the government's prodigious wartime expenditures, Congress broadened and deepened the tax structure. The Revenue Acts of 1942 and 1943 created the modern federal income tax system. Most Americans had never filed an income tax return before World War II because the income tax, on the books since 1913, had been a small tax on upper-income families. Starting with 1942, anyone earning $600 or more annually had to file a return. Income tax withholding from paychecks went into effect in 1943. Income tax revenues rose from $5 billion in 1940 to $44 billion in 1945.

Still, Congress refused to ask Americans to pay the full cost of the war. Only 40 percent of the total came from taxes. To fill the gap, Congress tried to entice Americans to support the effort through voluntary loans. War bonds, peddled by movie stars and professional athletes, added $100 billion to the war coffers. But taxes and bonds fell far short of paying the bills. By war's end the national debt had climbed to $280 billion, up from $40 billion when it began.

The ultimate challenge of mobilization was to build not ships and planes, but an army to fight the enemy. In the summer of 1940 the regular U.S. Army ranked eighteenth in the world, with barely 250,000 men, compared to Hitler's 6 million to 8 million. Following the Japanese attack on Pearl Harbor, Congress ordered the registration of all men between the ages of twenty (lowered to eighteen in 1942) and forty-four for war service. Recruits called themselves "GIs" because of the "Government Issue" stamp on their gear.

The nation committed itself to total war. "We must fight with everything we have," declared Herbert Hoover. Despite the commitment, the draft reflected the continuing strength of parochial interests. Reflecting America's faith in localism, the draft was administered by no fewer than 6,500 local draft boards. By 1944 the system had become a mess of special interests trying to avoid service despite the cries for total mobilization for total war. The farm lobby won deferments for farmers, including tobacco growers, whose crop Congress declared "essential." Despite all the deferments and disputes, the draft succeeded in achieving its original objective. During the war the nation peacefully registered 49 million men, selected 19 million, and inducted 10 million, twice the number who volunteered.

The Battle for Europe   The major Allied powers—Britain, Russia, the United States, and China—faced a bleak situation in 1942. The Axis powers—Germany, Italy, and Japan—possessed war-tested armies and the forced labor and resources of conquered peoples in Europe and Asia. On land the German *Panzer* divisions mobilized firepower unequaled by the West. German "wolf pack" submarines controlled the oceans. In the first eleven months of 1942 they sank a total of 8 million tons of shipping. But although staggered by the opening onslaught, the Allies were not defenseless. They had clear numerical superiority, a unified command structure, and enormous industrial capacity.

Victory required that the Allies develop a unified military strategy, but from the very beginning of the war clear differences emerged. The Soviets, fighting more than two hundred German divisions on the eastern front, desperately wanted Churchill and Roosevelt to relieve the pressure by opening a second front in western Europe. At first, the Americans responded favorably to the Russian request. But the British, who had lost a whole generation of young men through frontal attack in World War I, wanted to weaken the enemy by striking at the periphery of Axis power. They proposed instead Operation TORCH, a joint Anglo-American invasion of North Africa, where the British had been tied down in a struggle with Italian and German forces.

American military leaders vehemently disagreed with Churchill's plan, dismissing it as "strategically unsound." Roosevelt, however, felt he had little leverage in his discussions with Churchill since America had not fully mobilized and the British would be supplying most of the troops and ships. The decision to delay a second front infuriated Stalin and nourished the seeds of suspicion that would blossom in the postwar period. "I must state in the most emphatic manner," Stalin wrote Churchill, "that the Soviet Government cannot acquiesce in the postponement of a second front in Europe until 1943."

Anglo-American forces launched Operation TORCH on November 8, 1942. Under the command of General Dwight Eisenhower, they stormed ashore at points along the coasts of the French North African colonies of Morocco and French North Africa. At the same time, the British Eighth Army, under General Bernard Montgomery, pushed eastward from Egypt. After initial setbacks, the combined British-American forces trapped one of Hitler's best generals, Field Marshall Erwin Rommel (the "Desert Fox") in a giant pincer. On May 13, 1943, the Allied army captured a quarter of a million Axis troops, including 125,000 Germans (see map on page 1026).

While the Allies were winning the North African campaign, the Soviets launched a winter offensive against the Germans. In less than a month, Hitler's troops had advanced more than 300 miles into Soviet territory, but German soldiers lacked the clothing and equipment to sustain their attack through the harsh Russian winter. Stalin's army surrounded a large German force at Stalingrad. In February 1943, after four months of intense fighting, the Germans at Stalingrad, having lost three hundred thousand men, surrendered.

In January Roosevelt and Churchill met in the Moroccan city of Casablanca in northern Africa to discuss the next step in the European war. American military planners urged Roosevelt to push ahead with the second front both to aid the Soviets and to strike at the heart of the German forces. Once again, Churchill held sway, calling instead for a continuation of the Mediterranean campaign with an invasion of Sicily.

In July Allied troops assaulted the island. General George Patton sliced through weak Italian defenses and entered the city of Palermo on July 22. In the midst of the battle, Italy's King Victor Emmanuel II arrested and imprisoned Mussolini and then surrendered to the Allies. Overnight, Italy was transformed from a German ally to a German occupied country as Hitler poured sixteen divisions into the peninsula. In September three British and four American divisions glided onto the beaches of Salerno, beginning the long, bloody struggle for Italy.

In another major victory, scientific breakthroughs had given Allied naval power control of the Atlantic by the end of 1943. Centimeter radar allowed aircraft to track enemy submarines, and sonobuoys—sound-detecting radio transmitters dropped by plane—allowed destroyers to home in on the noise from U-boat engines. Allied destroyers and planes unleashed a deadly array of new, more powerful antisubmarine rockets and depth charges. In May 1943 the Germans ordered all but a handful of U-boats out of the Atlantic. "We had lost the battle of the Atlantic," noted a German commander.

The Allies also gained control of the sky, launching B-17 bombers, popularly known as the "Flying Fortress," against strategic German targets: submarine yards,

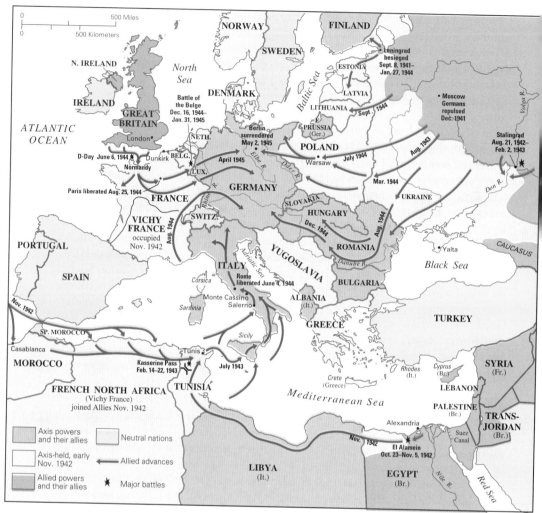

World War II in Europe and Africa   By 1942, the Axis powers in Europe, controlling Northern Africa, France, Poland, and Yugoslavia had reached the furthest extent of their power. In 1943 the tide began turning in favor of the Allies thanks to Operation TORCH and a Russian victory at Stalingrad. For the rest of the war, the Allies slowly strengthened their grip on the European continent, pushing and punishing Germany from all sides, working toward the goal of Germany's unconditional surrender.

munitions factories, and railroad lines. The bombers flew their first missions in August 1942, shielded by a swarm of Royal Air Force (RAF) spitfire fighters. From 1943 to war's end Allied planes dropped more than 2.5 million tons of explosives on occupied Europe and Germany. In a raid on the city of Dresden in February 1945, the RAF dropped 2,660 tons of bombs, creating a firestorm that killed more than a hundred thousand civilians.

With the momentum of war shifting toward the Allies, Roosevelt traveled to Tehran, Iran, to confer with Churchill and Stalin in late November 1943. The most pressing decision concerned the second front. Churchill continued to plead for delay, but this time he was overmatched by Roosevelt and Stalin. The three leaders formally approved an invasion across the English Channel to be launched in the spring of 1944. During four days of meetings, the heads of state also discussed the future of the postwar world. Stalin demanded a buffer zone—Soviet control over eastern Europe—to protect against another invasion. Notwithstanding the Atlantic Charter's stated support for self-determination, Roosevelt reassured Stalin that the United States would not interfere, but he said that for political reasons he could not "publicly take part in any such arrangements at the present time." With the 1944 presidential campaign looming, Roosevelt feared alienating the millions of Americans of Polish and Lithuanian heritage who wanted self-determination in their former homelands. Roosevelt also explained that, as at the end of World War I, the persistent strength of isolationist sentiment would make a lasting American military force in Germany unlikely. After the Tehran conference, Roosevelt assured the American people in a radio address that "we are going to get along very well with [Stalin] and the Russian people—very well indeed."

"D-Day" Reeling from the Soviet offensive in the east, the Germans prepared for an Anglo-American assault on the western flank. Knowing the invasion must come somewhere along the English Channel, Hitler reinforced heavily fortified bunkers on the French shoreline with three hundred thousand men. "The enemy must be annihilated before he reaches our main battlefield," General Rommel told his troops. "We must stop him in the water." While the Allies planned their assault for the French coast at Normandy, a complex deception operation, with fake radio signals, fooled the Germans into thinking that the attack would come farther north at Pas de Calais. Hitler stationed his finest troops, including six *Panzer* divisions, to wait for the phantom army.

In the early morning hours of June 6, 1944, the designated day, or "D-Day," the Allies under the supreme command of General Eisenhower launched the long-delayed second front. Operation Overlord was the greatest amphibious assault in recorded history, employing over five thousand ships and eleven thousand airplanes. The first wave of landing craft carried American, Canadian, and British troops onto code-named beaches. The British and Canadian troops, who landed on the beaches Gold, Juno, and Sword, and the Americans who stormed Utah beach, encountered light resistance. The U.S. soldiers who assaulted Omaha beach were not so lucky. A wall of German gunfire and artillery pinned down 14,000 American soldiers. More than 2,000 were killed or wounded in the first two hours of combat. "The surface of the water was covered with thousands and thousands of helmets floating upside down," recalled a participant. After three hours a few GIs managed to climb the beach cliffs and destroy the German positions. By nightfall the Allies controlled the five beaches, but not before losing 6,603 American, 3,000 British, and 946 Canadian soldiers.

In July, when General George Patton's Third Army broke through German defenses and moved inland through Brittany, Allied forces began their relentless

Hitting the Beach on D-Day   On June 6, 1944, the Allies launched the greatest amphibious invasion in military history, involving 175,000 men, over 5,000 sea craft, and 11,000 aircraft in the initial assault. The German army, fortified at the top of cliffs above the beaches, bombarded the Allied forces with artillery. Losses were particularly heavy on Omaha beach, where members of the U.S. First Army, including this soldier, attempted to disembark from landing crafts and swim to shore while Germans shot from cliffs 100 feet above.   *(Robert Capa/Magnum Photos, Inc.)*

drive to Berlin. They streaked across France and liberated Paris on August 25. In December, as Allied troops massed on the German border, Hitler masterminded one final assault. In the Battle of the Bulge, German tanks crashed through weakly fortified Allied troops in Belgium. Before American air power blunted the assault, more than eight thousand American soldiers were killed, another twenty-one thousand captured or missing. But after the battle, the German war machine was in complete and final retreat.

As Allied armies liberated Poland and conquered Germany, they discovered the death camps that revealed the full horror of the Nazi regime. The sight of charred skeletons and living corpses shocked the Western world. "The smell of death overwhelmed us," recalled General Omar Bradley, who toured the concentration camp in Ohrdruf after Allied occupation. Throughout the 1930s the Nazis persecuted Jews—organizing boycotts, limiting their civil rights, barring them from employment. In November 1938, after a Jewish man killed a German official, Nazi thugs had organized an orgy of arson and murder of Jews known as *Kristallnacht* (Crystal Night) for the pools of broken glass that littered German streets. A few days later German officials confiscated all Jewish assets and shipped fifty thousand Jews to concentration camps. The brutal policy foreshadowed Hitler's "final solution" of what he called the "Jewish problem." Beginning in 1941 German soldiers packed much of the Jewish population of eastern Europe and the Soviet Union into railroad freight cars and dumped them in death camps such as Buchenwald and Dachau. Another 3 million people—Poles and Russians, Slavs, gypsies, criminals, homosexuals, and resistance fighters—suffered the same fate.

The West failed to respond to the Holocaust. As the Nazis extended their reign of terror across Europe, Jews had flooded into immigration offices in an effort to escape persecution. Though outraged by Hitler's actions, Americans were unwilling to bend rigid immigration quotas to admit more European refugees—a view reinforced by anti-Semitism. Breckinridge Long, the State Department official responsible for refugee issues, blocked efforts to save Jews and later suppressed information about the death camps. In 1939 the U.S. government refused entry to 930 desperate Jewish refugees onboard the *St. Louis*, forcing the captain to return to Europe, where many of the refugees again suffered Nazi reprisals. "The cruise of the *St. Louis*," editorialized the *New York Times*, "cries to high heaven of man's inhumanity to man."

Hitler tried to keep the death camps secret, but by 1942 the United States had reliable information about their existence. The reaction was indifference, and the State Department continued its policy of refusing visas to European refugees trying to enter the United States. "It takes months and months to grant a visa and then it usually applies to a corpse," a 1943 government study concluded. In response to the desperate appeals, Roosevelt created the War Refugee Board, which used private funds to establish refugee camps abroad. The board saved over two hundred

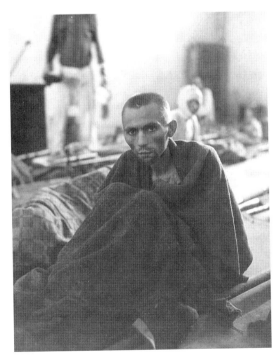

Uncovering the Holocaust

Although the U.S. government had received classified information on the Nazis' extermination of European Jews as early as 1942, the world did not realize its full extent until Allied armies stumbled upon the death camps as they marched toward Germany. What they found horrified them—mass graves, gas chambers, starving inmates, including this one at an Austrian camp, and the personal effects of millions of victims. History has been critical toward the Roosevelt administration for doing so little to rescue Europe's Jews, 6 million of whom died at the hands of the Nazis, along with 3 million other civilians that Hitler deemed unfit or a threat to his regime. *(National Archives.)*

thousand Jews, but for millions of refugees, it was too little, too late. Roosevelt's indifference to the Holocaust, concluded historian David Wyman, "emerges as the worst failure of his presidency."

Wartime Politics   At a press conference in 1943 President Roosevelt announced that "Dr. New Deal" had been replaced by "Dr. Win the War." During the 1940s Roosevelt backed away from liberal reform measures. Responding to new political realities, he agreed to drop several New Deal programs. The war and economic growth gave support to a growing conservative coalition in Congress, as people who were prosperous once more could afford to forget the assistance the Democrats had given them in the past. The resistance became clearly visible in 1942. With the war not yet going well militarily, Republicans made substantial inroads in the 1942 congressional elections. They gained 9 seats in the Senate and 44 in the House, giving them a total of 209 House seats—only 13 fewer than the Democrats' 222.

Compounding the effect of the Republican gains was the increased strength of conservative Democrats from the South. Democratic defeats in the North and Midwest continued to enhance southern influence. In the House, representatives from fifteen southern and border states claimed 120 of the 222 Democratic seats; in the Senate they held 29 of 57 seats. They also dominated the major committees. Thus, when Republicans and southern Democrats banded together, they constituted an insurmountable bloc.

The conservative coalition in Congress argued that the New Deal had gone too far. Conservatives wanted to cut back what they considered to be a bloated federal bureaucracy, to circumscribe the power of labor, and to end New Deal planning schemes that they contended impinged on free enterprise and individual initiative. They succeeded in virtually every sphere. Congress liquidated the Civilian Conservation Corps (CCC) and the Works Progress Administration (WPA). (Both faced declining enrollments anyway as better jobs became available in the massive war production effort.) In 1943 the National Youth Administration became another casualty. A whole range of other agencies suffered similar fates.

Conservatives hoped to make further gains in the 1944 election, the first wartime presidential contest since 1864. The Republicans nominated New York governor Thomas Dewey and chose John W. Bricker, the conservative governor of Ohio, as his running mate. Dewey accepted the broad outlines of Roosevelt's domestic and foreign policy. He supported social security, unemployment insurance, relief for the poor, and collective bargaining. But he attacked the bureaucratic inefficiency of the New Deal, complaining that the Democrats had "grown old in office," and had become "tired and quarrelsome."

Most of all, Republicans raised questions about Roosevelt's age and declining health. For most of the previous year, Roosevelt had been plagued with colds and bronchial problems. In March 1944 doctors learned that he suffered from heart disease and that his chronic high blood pressure had worsened, though they were careful to keep this information from the public. Reporters noted the president's haggard appearance—dark circles under the eyes, suits made baggy by excessive weight loss, a shaky hand—but they were unaware of the seriousness of his condition. Roosevelt was also breaking with tradition by becoming the first president to seek a fourth term in office.

Always the practical politician, Roosevelt coasted with the political currents. At the Democratic convention he wooed conservatives by dumping his outspoken and liberal vice president, Henry Wallace. At the request of party leaders, he asked Missouri Senator Harry S Truman to join the ticket. Truman had won national attention in the Senate as the head of a committee investigating corruption and graft in the defense program. Hailing from a border state, he was acceptable to party conservatives. As a protégé of party boss Tom Pendergast in Kansas City, he also had close ties to big city machines.

During most of the fall Roosevelt paid little attention to either his opponent or Republican rhetoric. Then, a month before the election, the president began to campaign energetically. Standing in drenching rain, riding in open-car motorcades, and speaking to huge crowds of supporters, FDR showed his stamina to rebut Republican charges that he was in poor health. Roosevelt could also count on the enthusiastic support of organized labor, which experienced remarkable growth during the war. Union membership increased from 9 million in 1940 to almost 15 million in 1945, a pace more rapid than at any other time in American history.

Many observers predicted a close election, but the 1944 results were nearly identical to those of 1940. The president carried thirty-six states and 432 electoral votes and won 3.5 million more popular votes than Dewey: 25,606,585 to 22,014,745. The labor vote in the big cities made the crucial difference for Roosevelt. In cities with population over one hundred thousand, Roosevelt received 60.7 percent of the vote (see map on page 1032).

The Yalta Conference

In February 1945, flush from his electoral victory at home, Roosevelt traveled to Yalta, a resort on the Black Sea coast, to meet with Churchill and Stalin. The Big Three had to address a number of thorny questions: the occupation of Germany, the creation of the United Nations, and the status of eastern Europe. From the beginning, differences emerged between Stalin and his western Allies. The Soviets' vision of world stability differed greatly from what the English and Americans had in mind. Roosevelt, and to a lesser extent Churchill, subscribed to the principles of the Atlantic Charter, with its emphasis on free elections and self-determination, but Stalin insisted on maintaining a sphere of influence in eastern Europe.

The leaders reached compromises on many issues. Stalin promised to declare war on Japan within a few months of Germany's surrender. In return, Roosevelt accepted Soviet claims to the Kurile Islands in the Far East. Stalin dropped his demands for $20 billion in German reparations, agreeing to discuss the issue further. Roosevelt achieved one of his major diplomatic goals by gaining Stalin's support for the creation of the United Nations. All three leaders approved plans for a United Nations Conference in San Francisco in April 1945.

The postwar political status of Poland, which Churchill counted as "the most urgent reason for the Yalta Conference," caused the most controversy. Two Polish governments demanded recognition. The British and Americans supported the exiled government located in London. Stalin recognized a communist-led provisional

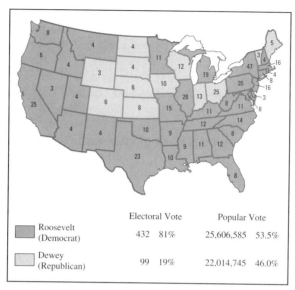

	Electoral Vote	Popular Vote
Roosevelt (Democrat)	432 81%	25,606,585 53.5%
Dewey (Republican)	99 19%	22,014,745 46.0%

The Election of 1944   Unable to attack Roosevelt's handling of the war effort, Thomas Dewey challenged the president's continuing New Deal programs and emphasized the need for new blood in the White House. Though Roosevelt at times showed signs of exhaustion, he proclaimed his willingness to continue serving "as a good soldier." Roosevelt did change vice presidents, selecting the more conservative Harry S Truman rather than continuing with liberal reformer Henry Wallace and thereby retaining the support of southern Democrats. Roosevelt won by the narrowest popular vote of his presidential career, but maintained an impressive electoral college victory.

government based in Lublin, Poland. To avoid letting arguments over Poland undermine conference harmony, the Allies worked out an agreement that papered over their significant differences with vague, elastic language. Stalin agreed to "free and unfettered elections" in Poland, but at a conveniently unspecified time in the future.

Roosevelt left Yalta convinced that he had laid the foundation for a peaceful postwar world. "We were absolutely certain that we had won the first great victory of the peace," Harry Hopkins remarked. Years later, critics would charge Roosevelt with selling out to the Russians by acquiescing in Soviet domination of eastern Europe. But military and political realities weakened Roosevelt's bargaining position. By the time of the Yalta Conference, the powerful Red Army already dominated most of Poland, Czechoslovakia, and Hungary, and Roosevelt desperately wanted Russian assistance in defeating the Japanese. Knowing that most Americans wanted an end to the hostilities and a return of U.S. servicemen, the president had little choice but to accept Soviet control and focus on building trust between the two nations.

Roosevelt returned home from Yalta a very ill man. On March 1 the president told Congress that Yalta had been "a great success," and he asked the American people to support the agreements reached there. Soon afterward, Roosevelt retreated to

The Big Three at Yalta   In February of 1945, Churchill, Roosevelt, and Stalin met amid the rubble in the Soviet city of Yalta to hammer out the details of peace. Bitter disagreements about Poland and war reparations led to a vaguely defined accord that only delayed a larger conflict between the Soviet Union and its Allies. Roosevelt, the one optimistic player, died two months later, leaving a more suspicious Truman to finish the war and handle the postwar threats to the Yalta agreement.   *(National Archives.)*

his vacation home in Warm Springs, Georgia, to try to recoup his energy. Around noon on April 12 he slumped in his chair. "I have a terrific headache," he muttered. A few hours later, he died of a cerebral hemorrhage. Roosevelt's death left his successor, Harry S Truman, with the task of seeing the war to its end and resolving the complicated and confusing questions of postwar global security.

On April 25 the western Allied armies rolled up to the Elbe River, where they joined hands with the Russians, who had been advancing from the east. A few days later, with Russian troops closing in on Berlin, Hitler married his mistress, Eva Braun, then carried out their suicide pact by killing her and himself. On May 7 the new German government signed an unconditional surrender in Allied headquarters, and Eisenhower dictated his final note of World War II: "The mission of this Allied force was fulfilled 0241 local time, May 7, 1945."

WAR AND NATIONAL CULTURE, 1941–1945

Since nearly all Americans supported the war effort, Roosevelt did not employ the coercive methods against dissent that Wilson used during World War I. For the most part, the media exercised self-censorship and voluntarily joined the war propaganda effort. The treatment of Japanese-Americans was the one major exception to this record of restraint. By bringing together groups that had lived in isolation, the war blended ethnic and social differences and accelerated the development of a national culture. The war also offered new opportunities to groups that had previously been excluded, especially women and minorities, inspiring many to assert their rights in American society. Despite the enormous changes, traditional attitudes persisted, limiting the political and personal gains and undermining experiments with new social roles.

Propaganda and Popular Culture   World War II was the most popular war in American history. Five million young men volunteered for military service, and more than one hundred thousand nurses joined the WACS, WAVES, and SPARS—the women's branches of the army, navy, and coast guard. After Pearl Harbor, volunteers flooded into recruiting offices. Victory gardens sprouted everywhere. In 1943 gardeners grew more than 8 million tons of produce on 20 million individual plots.

In December 1941 Roosevelt created the Office of Censorship, which examined all letters going overseas and worked with publishers to suppress information that might be damaging to the war effort. But since the war was so popular, Roosevelt felt little need to resort to more coercive propaganda and restraint of dissent. An executive order of June 1942 created the Office of War Information (OWI), headed by Elmer Davis and staffed by advertising executives, which sold the war to the public.

The war poster became the most effective weapon in the OWI's arsenal. Posters were everywhere, pushing prowar activities and attitudes: Buy bonds. Enlist. Work Harder. Plant a Victory Garden. They were the "weapons on the wall" designed to arouse fear of the enemy and intense patriotism for the American cause. One poster shouted, "Stay on the job until every murdering Japanese is wiped out!" Another showed a dead GI slumped over a machine gun with the caption, "What did you do today . . . for freedom?"

Roosevelt's efforts were aided by the influence of the national media, which made Americans aware of their common culture and shared values. World War II was the first war given on-the-scene radio coverage. Millions of Americans sat by the family radio listening in suspenseful anticipation as newscasters Edward R. Murrow, Charles Collingwood, Howard K. Smith, and other pioneers of modern radio described the march of German soldiers through Europe. Later they listened to morale-lifting programs such as "The Army Hour" and "Report to the Nation." The networks collaborated with the government to produce a thirteen-part series entitled *This Is War.*

The U.S. entertainment industry was an enthusiastic booster of the Allied cause. Washington understood the value of movies. OWI Director Elmer Davis said, "The easiest way to inject a propaganda idea into most people's minds is to let it go in through the medium of an entertainment picture when they do not realize that they are being propagandized." Hollywood released fifteen hundred films during the war; one-fourth of which were combat pictures. Box office receipts soared during from $735 million in 1940 to $1.4 billion in 1945. More than 60 million Americans attended movies weekly throughout the war. Moviegoers would have a complete war experience: an opening newsreel of war news, followed by a cartoon of Popeye fighting Japanese spies, ads for war bonds and enlistment, then a war movie. Afterward, patrons could buy a war bond at the booth set up in the lobby.

Music makers also joined the war effort. Patriotic songs became enormously popular. Millions of Americans played 78-rpm records of Kate Smith singing "God Bless America" on their RCA Victrolas. Sentimental tunes reflecting the loneliness of separations caused by the war also topped the charts. The most-played recording composed during the war was Irving Berlin's 1942 "White Christmas," sung by Bing Crosby, which became the mantra of homesick soldiers. Other sentimental songs were also big hits, including 1944's "I'll Be Seeing You" and "I'll Be Home for Christmas."

Not even children's entertainment avoided military service. Comic-book hero Captain Midnight, who tracked down Nazi spies, asked children to recite a pledge "to save my country from the dire peril it faces or perish in the attempt." If enemy agents escaped the grasp of Captain Midnight, other super heroes, such as Superman or Jack Armstrong, stood ready to swing into action. (The government had granted Superman a deferment because he failed his induction physical for the army. When asked to read from an eye chart, his x-ray vision mistakenly read from a chart in the next room!)

Japanese Internment

The major exception to the administration's restraint in sedition control measures was the removal and incarceration of immigrant and American-born Japanese living on the West Coast. Shortly after Pearl Harbor, wild stories circulated about plots among Japanese residents to aid an enemy landing on the coast of California. The press, patriotic organizations, and powerful business groups joined in a chorus against Japanese-Americans. "Don't kid yourselves and don't let someone tell you there are good Japs," Representative Alfred Elliot of California declared in Congress in early 1942. "A good solution to the Jap problem," the governor of Idaho suggested, "would be to send them all back to Japan, then sink the island. They live like rats, breed like rats and act like rats."

On March 21, 1942, Roosevelt signed Executive Order 9066 authorizing the forced evacuation of Japanese residents on the West Coast. The order required more than one hundred thousand people, many of them American citizens, to dispose of their property and move to government "relocation centers" scattered throughout the West. "Truthfully," wrote an internee sent to the Arizona desert, "I must say this scorching Hell is a place beyond description and beyond tears." By December 1944 the government declared the emergency over and allowed residents to return home. By the time the Supreme Court ruled that same month (*Korematsu* v. *U.S.*) that the evacuation was constitutional, the camps had already begun to empty.

The treatment of the Japanese-Americans was the worst violation of civil liberties on the American side of the struggle. By one estimate they suffered nearly $400 million in property damage, not to mention the humiliation of being accused of disloyalty. Authorities invoked military necessity and national security to justify their actions. In 1982 a government commission reviewing the internment criticized the Roosevelt administration for "race prejudice, war hysteria, and a failure of political leadership." In 1988, agreeing with the commission's shameful findings, Congress compensated Japanese-Americans interned during the war.

Japanese Internment: Mother and Children   One of the darkest chapters in American history involved the wartime internment of over one hundred thousand Japanese-Americans in desolate western camps. These Americans not only lived in stark, barrack-style conditions for several years, they also lost their property, their jobs, and most of their personal belongings. The government claimed the action was in the interest of national security, and very few Americans raised any objections in the emotional climate after Pearl Harbor. As General John DeWitt, the West Coast military commander, claimed, "A Jap is a Jap. It makes no difference whether he is an American citizen or not." *(Japanese American Citizens League.)*

The Breakdown of Provincialism

Increased geographic mobility added to the breakdown of regional differences in America. Fifteen million men and several hundred thousand women—one in nine Americans—moved because of military service. At least as many relocated to be near family members in the armed forces or to find new jobs in wartime industry. Lured by the surplus of wartime jobs, some 6 million people left farms to work in the cities. Nearly seven hundred thousand African-American civilians left the South during the war. By the end of the war, one in every five Americans had changed residence.

The development of war plants in the South and on the West Coast stimulated industrial development and reduced the economic uniqueness of both regions. Between 1941 and 1945 the federal government awarded more than $4 billion in war contracts to the South. By 1945 two-thirds of the nation's military bases and training camps were in a broad southern belt stretching from Washington, D.C., to

El Paso, Texas. The influx of money and resources led to rapid urbanization in the region. Of forty-eight metropolitan areas in the South, thirty-nine experienced rapid war-related growth. Savannah grew by 29 percent between 1940 and 1950, Charleston by 37 percent, Norfolk by 57 percent, and Mobile by 61 percent.

The war had a similar impact on the West. Domestic mobilization diversified the western economy and made it more self-sufficient and independent. In four years a region almost entirely dependent on the extraction of raw materials transformed into one producing ships and airplanes, aluminum, magnesium, and steel. As in the South, the war spurred the pace of urbanization in the West, where it also added to ethnic and racial diversity. San Diego doubled its population to 450,000. Los Angeles gained 30 percent in four years, as did San Francisco and Portland, Oregon. The state of California welcomed nearly 3 million new residents during the war, a 53 percent population growth.

The practical effect of the wartime experience enhanced national unity. For millions of young men and women service in the armed forces constituted a common rite of passage that created a sense of shared values. People who had lived all their lives in small, provincial communities suddenly found themselves, because of new jobs or wartime responsibilities, in new and unfamiliar places, meeting new and unfamiliar people. The intermixing of cultures diminished the strong ethnic differences that had shaped American society for the previous generation. The foreign-language press lost ground. Between 1940 and 1945 more than two hundred ethnic-language newspapers failed. The whole range of ethnic theaters, language schools, political organizations, and lodges declined as well. Before World War II "staying in America was something Italian-Americans did to make money. You didn't stay in America to lead a good life," explained an Italian-American veteran. "That happened after the war." Italian shops and basement wine cellars disappeared, and Italians started speaking English to one another. "We became respectable," he said.

While the war experience diminished ethnic identity, it increased the consciousness of other groups. Social mobility laid the foundation of the modern gay rights movement. "For many gay Americans," observed a historian, "World War II created something of a nationwide coming out experience." Hundreds of thousands of young men and women were given their first taste of freedom from parental supervision and from the social norms of their hometowns. After the war they migrated to large cities. In many large cities during the 1940s exclusively gay bars appeared for the first time. The bars became seedbeds of collective consciousness that would flower in the 1960s.

Rosie the Riveter   On the eve of Pearl Harbor nearly 14 million American women (26 percent of the total work force) were employed as wage earners. Most were segregated into traditional women's work: teaching, nursing, social work, and the civil service. The vast majority of wage-earning black and Hispanic women were domestic servants. Young, unmarried women made up the bulk of the female work force. Almost half of all single women were employed in 1940, but only 15 percent of the larger pool of married women and only 6 percent of women with children worked outside the home.

With men being drafted for the service, employers looked to women to maintain the mobilization at home. "In some communities," Roosevelt said in 1942, "employers dislike to employ women. In others they are reluctant to hire Negroes. . . . We can no longer afford to indulge such prejudices or practices." The government encouraged women to work in steel plants, shipyards, and airplane factories. "Rosie the Riveter" who, according to a popular song of the time, was "making history working for victory," became the media symbol of a woman at work. She could do a man's job without compromising her feminine qualities. On the cover of the *Saturday Evening Post,* Norman Rockwell depicted a defiantly muscular Rosie. *Life* magazine hailed her as "the heroine of a new order."

Over the next four years nearly 6 million women responded to the call. By the end of the war almost 19 million women (or 36 percent) were working, many at jobs from which they had previously been excluded. Nearly 2 million women— about 10 percent of female workers—took up jobs in defense plants. Almost 500,000 worked in the airplane industry; another 225,000 worked in shipbuilding. The percentage of black women who did paid housework declined from 69 percent to 35 percent, as many found work in industrial occupations.

Women at War   In the absence of so many American men, women enjoyed new opportunities performing work that under normal circumstances would have been deemed inappropriate. These women are helping assemble an aircraft, one of many factory positions that drew women's average weekly wages up to $31—still $23 less than a man working in a comparable position. The jobs also proved temporary. As the war wound down, the government, which had conjured up "Rosie the Riveter" to vigorously recruit women workers at the war's start, urged women to resume more traditional roles so returning soldiers could find jobs.   *(Lockheed-California Company.)*

Though Rosie the Riveter became a popular symbol of working women during the war, most women remained at home. In 1941 about 30 million women were homemakers. In 1944 seven of eight of these women were still engaged in homemaking. Polls showed that majorities of men and women disapproved of working wives, and most women of traditional childbearing age (twenty to thirty-four) remained at home. As a result, the war did little in the short run to challenge traditional notions that a woman's proper place was in the home raising the children. "The housewife, not the WAC or the riveter, was the model woman," observed historian D'Ann Campbell.

In the long run, however, the growth of female employment during the war widened the public sphere of women; the image of Rosie—strong and capable—challenged the older notions. As women ventured into the working world in ever-increasing numbers, they provided an economic and ideological underpinning to later movements for women's liberation. For many women, working in the factories represented "the first time we got a chance to show that we could do a lot of things that only men had done before."

**The War for
Racial Equality**

W. E. B. Du Bois defined World War II as a struggle for "democracy not only for white folks but for yellow, brown, and black." The war forced Americans to look critically at racism at home. "A nation making an all-out effort . . . on the side of democracy," the *New York Times* editorialized, "must leave open the doors of opportunity to all, regardless of race."

For African-Americans World War II offered economic opportunities marred by continuing discrimination. Twelve months after the bombing of Pearl Harbor, some half-million blacks had been inducted into a rigidly segregated army. Military attitudes had changed little since a 1925 Army War College study reported that blacks possessed a "smaller cranium, lighter brain [and] cowardly and immoral character." In 1940 the army had just five African-American officers, and three of them were chaplains. Black soldiers had to watch the army segregate the blood plasma of whites and blacks. Regulations restricted blacks to their own barracks, movie houses, and commissaries. Traveling through the South to military camps, officers ordered them to pull down their train shades so as not to be shot at by local whites. In the navy blacks were restricted to the minor roles of mess attendants or cooks. More than twenty riots or mutinies broke out on military bases, many of them ignited when northern blacks resisted the indignities of segregation.

Conditions on the home front were not much better. Management and labor joined forces to limit black access to the war boom. "We will not employ Negroes," declared the president of North American Aviation. "It is against company policy." Black migration from rural southern areas to the urban centers of war production caused terrible crowding and competition for scarce housing and schools in the cities. In 1942 a riot in Alexandria, Louisiana, left twenty-eight African-Americans wounded and nearly three thousand arrested. There were as many as 240 racial incidents in forty-seven cities in the summer of 1943. The worst riot erupted on a steamy June night in Detroit and left thirty-four people dead and more than seven hundred injured.

Faced with these conditions, black Americans launched a "double V" campaign: V for victory in the war against the dictators overseas and V for victory in their own

The Ninety-ninth Fighter Group   Because of racial prejudice, only a handful of the hundreds of thousands of African-Americans who served in the armed forces during the war ever saw combat. Among those who did were the famed "Tuskegee Airmen," black fighter pilots trained at segregated facilities near the school organized by Booker T. Washington in Alabama. These brave soldiers served their country with devotion and repeatedly distinguished themselves in battle.   *(© Gordon Parks.)*

struggle for fair treatment at home. In January 1941 A. Philip Randolph, head of the Brotherhood of Sleeping Car Porters, proposed a massive march on Washington to protest discrimination and segregation. FDR feared that such a demonstration would tarnish the nation's image in the eyes of the world. How could America lead a crusade against Nazi atrocities when it practiced discrimination at home? Unable to convince Randolph to cancel the march, the president agreed to his demands. On June 25, 1941, President Roosevelt signed Executive Order 8802, which declared, "There shall be no discrimination in the employment of workers in defense industries or government because of race, creed, color, or national origin." The order established a President's Fair Employment Practices Committee (FEPC), which, though underfunded and understaffed, conducted a number of highly visible hearings that focused public attention on discrimination in government agencies.

Randolph's activism reflected a growing militancy among African-Americans. As one black newspaper noted, it "demonstrated to the Doubting Thomases among us that only mass action can pry open the doors that have been erected against America's black minority." Existing civil rights organizations witnessed dramatic growth during the war. NAACP membership soared from 50,000 in 1940 to over 450,000 in 1946. New civil rights groups appeared. In 1942 the Congress of Racial Equality (CORE), founded by a group of pacifists in Chicago, orchestrated sit-in demonstrations and picketing campaigns to desegregate public facilities. In 1944 picketers outside a segregated Washington, D.C., restaurant carried signs that read: "Are you for Hitler's Way or the American Way?" and "We Die Together, Let's Eat Together."

African-Americans also challenged employment discrimination by taking advantage of shortages in the labor market. Black employment rose by over a million during the war. The number of unemployed blacks dropped from 937,000 to 151,000. Union membership doubled. The number of African-American employees increased from 6,000 to 14,000 in shipyards and from zero to 5,000 in aircraft plants. Most African-Americans labored as janitors and custodians; few gained opportunities as craftsmen or foremen. Nevertheless, World War II constituted what one historian called "more industrial and occupational diversification for Negroes than had occurred in the seventy-five preceding years."

Like blacks, Hispanics faced opportunity tempered by discrimination during World War II. In 1940 about 1.5 million Spanish-speaking people lived in the United States, some in eastern cities, many more in the West and Southwest. The war caused an acute shortage of farm labor, and the federal government looked to Mexicans to help meet the need, importing contract laborers, or *braceros*. By the end of the war, over 120,000 workers were part of the program.

But the need for workers did not dispel discrimination. Anglos segregated Chicanos by skin color, frequently lumping them with African-Americans. "For Coloreds and Mexicans," read a sign outside a Texas church. Large growers forced *braceros* to work and live in dismal conditions, overlooked them for supervisory or skilled jobs, and paid them lower wages than white workers. Hispanics living in major cities faced a different form of discrimination. By 1943 Anglo anger focused on gang members called *pachucos*, or "zoot-suiters," because of their distinctive clothing. In the summer of 1943 in Los Angeles, following rumors that a gang of Mexican youths had assaulted a sailor, thousands of servicemen took to the streets, assaulting any youth wearing a zoot suit.

Labor shortages also shaped the war experience of Native Americans. By 1945 half of all Native Americans on the home front had left Indian reservations for war industries. Before the war only 5 percent of Native Americans lived in cities; by 1950 the figure had grown to 20 percent. For Indians winning the war meant more than just defeating Hitler. "We want to win the war," an Indian said, "because victory will mean new hope for men and women who have no hope." The Commissioner of Indian Affairs reported that groups of Indians had shown up at his agency headquarters, "each man with his gun ready to register for Selective Service and to proceed immediately to the scene of the fighting." More than twenty-five thousand Native Americans served in the armed forces, including eight hundred women. Among their contributions was the valuable service of using native languages such as Navajo to create unbreakable codes for American military communication.

Despite continuing discrimination at home, the war offered African-Americans, Hispanics, and Native Americans á chance to "prove" their loyalty. "All we wanted," declared a Hispanic soldier, "was a chance to prove how loyal and American we were."

VICTORY, 1942–1945

Germany's surrender allowed the United States to focus its military might in the Pacific theater. After destroying the Japanese navy in two decisive contests, U.S. forces began advancing closer to the Japanese mainland in a series of bloody battles.

Meanwhile American scientists created a powerful new atomic weapon. In an experiment that tested American values, President Truman had few reservations about using the bomb to bring about a quick end to the conflict. By the time it ended in August 1945, however, the war had transformed American society.

War in the Pacific   For six months after Pearl Harbor, the Japanese ruled the Pacific. The advancing Japanese army conquered Guam, Hong Kong, and Java. In February they captured Singapore, the supposedly unconquerable "Gibraltar of the Pacific," forcing the surrender of eighty-five thousand British troops. As they pushed into the American-held Philippines, Roosevelt, knowing the islands were doomed, ordered General Douglas MacArthur to evacuate. "I shall return," MacArthur vowed. On May 6, more than seventy-five hundred American and Filipino soldiers surrendered. Many of the prisoners died as their Japanese captors forced them to march, without water or food, 65 miles in the broiling heat to concentration camps.

The Japanese next turned their attention to Australia, sending a naval force to secure bases on the north coast. American military planners deciphered the Japanese code and rushed a task force to intercept them. At the Battle of the Coral Sea, the first naval battle fought exclusively by carrier-based aircraft, the U.S. blunted the offensive.

One month later Japanese and American forces squared off again in the most important naval battle of the Pacific war—the Battle of Midway. Japan wanted control of the Midway Islands to launch air strikes against American installations in Hawaii. Knowing that this would force the Americans to defend the islands and hoping for a final decisive sea battle, Japan assigned four aircraft carriers equipped with its best planes and pilots to Midway. The American Navy, still battered from Pearl Harbor, could muster only three carriers for the battle, including one, the *Yorktown,* that had sustained severe damage during the Battle of the Coral Sea. It appeared that only a miracle could give the United States victory over vastly superior Japanese forces.

Once again American code breakers scored an intelligence coup, if not a miracle, when they decoded a Japanese message that enabled them to learn the exact date, time, and place of the impending attack and the composition of oncoming forces. Using this valuable information, Admiral Chester Nimitz, commander of the Pacific Fleet, was able to surprise the Japanese. Luck also played a part. On June 4, 1942, American fighter planes caught the Japanese carriers between launches of their aircraft, when they were most vulnerable. American dive-bombers sank all four Japanese aircraft carriers, destroying the heart of the enemy's mighty task force.

Following the victories in the Coral Sea and at Midway, American marines and army infantry began an "island-hopping" offensive in the South Pacific, inching closer to the Japanese mainland. After months of grueling combat in steamy jungles and rugged mountainous terrain, American troops gained control of the islands of Guadalcanal, Saipan, and Guam. In August 1944 Roosevelt approved a massive air, land, and sea campaign to liberate the Philippines. Before regaining the islands the U.S. met Japanese warships in the largest naval engagement in world history in the Battle of Leyte Gulf. The increasingly desperate Japanese used kamikazes, pilots trained to crash-dive their planes onto enemy aircraft carrier decks, for the first time. Though they inflicted heavy losses on U.S. naval forces, kamikazes could not prevent a crushing Japanese defeat that secured U.S. naval control of the Pacific. As he had promised General MacArthur then led U.S. troops in retaking the Philippines.

In February 1945 U.S. forces captured Iwo Jima, a speck of an island that cost 4,189 American lives. Two months later 11,260 U.S. soldiers died in the successful assault on Okinawa. The fanatical resistance of Japanese defenders on Iwo Jima and Okinawa foretold that the inevitable invasion of their home islands would be a long, bloody campaign. War planners estimated that the conquest of Japan, scheduled to begin on November 1, 1945, could take a year and could cost as many as a million American casualties.

The Bomb

An extraordinary new weapon radically altered the predicted scenario. In 1939 the noted scientist Albert Einstein had informed President Roosevelt that it might be possible to build "extremely powerful [atomic] bombs." Roosevelt, after conferences with scientific advisers, ordered work to begin to develop a nuclear weapon. Between 1941 and 1945 American and British scientists, engineers, and technicians, under the leadership of J. Robert Oppenheimer, labored on the secret, top-priority program, code-named the "Manhattan Project" (see Competing Voices, page 1050).

In July 1945 project scientists exploded the world's first atomic device at Alamogordo, New Mexico. The bomb weighed five tons. At its core was a package of uranium 235 about the size of a football. Within nine seconds of the explosion, the temperature at ground zero equaled that on the surface of the sun. An awed Dr. Oppenheimer, witnessing the enormous fireball created by the explosion, was reminded of a passage from Hindu scriptures: "I am become Death, destroyer of worlds."

On August 6, 1945, a B-29 named the *Enola Gay* dropped an atomic bomb on Hiroshima, Japan. The sky exploded: The world's first atomic bomb struck with the force of twelve thousand tons of TNT. It killed about 100,000 people instantly, and thousands more died later of burns, shock, and radiation poisoning. "What you remember most are the screams for water," recalled a survivor of the bomb. About 130,000 of the city's 250,000 inhabitants perished in the attack. On August 8 Red Army units invaded Manchuria and Korea. The day after Russia entered the war, the United States dropped a second atomic bomb on Nagasaki, incinerating 40,000 people and obliterating much of the city (see map on page 1044).

Even after the atomic bombings and the Soviet entry into the war, Japanese military leaders wanted to fight on. Only the personal intercession of Emperor Hirohito induced them to surrender. On August 10 the Japanese offered to surrender if they could keep their emperor. Truman would accept only unconditional surrender, which came on August 14, although he did allow the Japanese to retain their emperor. Surrender ceremonies took place on September 2.

The Legacy of War

The United States suffered fewer casualties during World War II than the other major warring nations. While just under four hundred thousand Americans lost their lives during the war, the struggle killed 2.8 million German soldiers. Combined military and civilian losses in Russia topped 20 million. Poland lost as much as 20 percent of

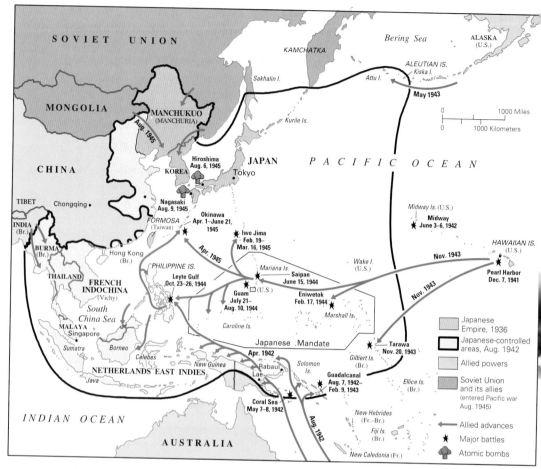

World War II in the Pacific The Battles of the Coral Sea and Midway Island in the late spring of 1942 ended the Japanese expansion in the Pacific Ocean. The Allies then began a strategy of island hopping—cutting supply lines to Japanese strongholds before moving on to the next island chain, all the time inching closer to the Japanese mainland.

its population. Throughout Europe the war's massive bombings left economies in ruins and millions homeless. Still, though U.S. cities were never bombed and civilian life continued with few interruptions, World War II served as a dramatic catalyst for change in American society.

The most obvious change was a dramatic increase in the size and scope of government power. The growing centralization of power in Washington, begun during the New Deal, accelerated during World War II. Between 1940 and 1945 the number of civilian employees in government posts rose from 1 million to 3.8 million. Federal expenditures rose from $9 billion in 1940 to $98.4 billion in 1945. The final bill for the war came to more than $330 billion, a sum ten times larger than the

The Remains of Hiroshima Strategists chose Hiroshima as the target for the first atomic bomb because the city's slight damage during the war made measuring the power of the bomb more accurate. Although scientists had tested an atomic bomb in the deserts of New Mexico, the destruction at Hiroshima stunned all involved. As seen in this photograph, the atomic bomb leveled the houses and buildings within a 1.5 square mile radius of the blast sight, killing over 130,000. *(National Archives.)*

direct expense of World War I and twice as large as the total of all government spending in the history of the United States to that point.

The dramatic increase in government spending produced prosperity that would have seemed unimaginable just a few years earlier. "The facts," Stuart Chase, a liberal economist, calculated, "show a better break for the common man than liberals in 1938 could have expected for a generation." National income jumped from $81 billion in 1940 to $181 billion five years later, or from $573 to $1,074 per capita. The war improved the distribution of income—an accomplishment that had eluded New Deal planners. The share of income owned by the richest 5 percent declined from 23.7 to 16.8 percent, while the average wages of workers employed full-time in manufacturing rose from $28 per week in 1940 to $48 in 1944. The enormous productivity of the war years fostered new confidence in government's ability to regulate the economy. Full employment was possible, liberal economists believed, and they now felt they knew how to use their tools to achieve that end.

The war altered the global balance of power. While Europe's power was diminished, America emerged from the struggle as the leading economic and military power in the world. Many leaders, including former isolationists, hoped to avoid the mistakes of the past. They argued that the United States needed to play a more active role in world affairs. "No more Munichs!" declared former isolationist leader

Senator Arthur Vandenberg. "America must behave like the number one world power which she is." The rhetoric of economic internationalism echoed through the halls of government as well. In 1944 delegates from forty-four nations met at Bretton Woods in New Hampshire to create the International Bank for Reconstruction and Development (the World Bank) and the International Monetary Fund (IMF). Staffed by Washington officials and floated with American money, both organizations promoted the American ideal of global economic growth and trade.

Americans also abandoned their deep-seated isolationism, reluctantly accepting the responsibilities of a global superpower. In 1944 representatives from the United States, Britain, the Soviet Union, and China met at Dumbarton Oaks in Washington, D.C., to hammer out the general charter of the new international organization. In April 1945, meeting in San Francisco, they agreed that the United Nations would represent a mix of balance-of-power and collective security arrangements. The charter gave every nation membership in a weak General Assembly, but only the five victorious allies from World War II—the United States, the Soviet Union, Britain, France, and China—retained permanent seats on the powerful twelve-member Security Council. The other seven seats rotated among member states. In sharp contrast to its actions after World War I, when it voted down American involvement in the League of Nations, the Senate approved the UN Charter by a lopsided vote of eighty-nine to two.

On issues of both international diplomacy and domestic government, the people and Congress now looked to the president for leadership. The entire twelve years that Roosevelt spent in the White House were a time of crisis. Whether fighting the depression or rallying the nation to global war, Roosevelt made the presidency the focus of the public's hopes and expectations. Recognizing the growing power of the office, Congress delegated enormous power to the president, who in turn delegated it to the sprawling bureaucracy he controlled.

By raising expectations, the war laid the foundation for social changes that would occur in the 1950s and 1960s. "The war changed our whole idea of how we wanted to live when we came back," explained a veteran. Americans who fought in the war felt they deserved "a good job, a respectable life." War-bred opportunities whetted the appetite of women, who planned to build on those gains in the postwar period. Organized labor hoped to reap the benefits of the new prosperity. The aroused expectations exercised their most profound impact on African-Americans, who looked for continued improvement in their economic conditions and opportunities once the war ended. But when peace came in 1945, poet Maya Angelou saw black soldiers returning home, treated "like forgotten laundry left on a back yard fence."

CONCLUSION

During the 1930s, convinced that American participation in World War I had been a mistake and consumed by economic problems at home, most Americans believed they should remain aloof from the conflagration that was consuming Europe and Asia. Congress reflected the public mood by passing restrictive neutrality legislation that prevented the internationalist-minded Roosevelt from aiding the Allies. As German forces overran most of Europe in 1940, Roosevelt abandoned any pretense of neutrality, offering Britain military and financial aid. With the Japanese attack on Pearl Harbor in December 1941, America could not avoid joining the war.

The Big Three—Roosevelt, Churchill, and Stalin—clashed repeatedly over the proper military strategy to defeat Hitler's army. Stalin insisted on a second front in western Europe to relieve pressure on the Soviet army fighting Hitler in the east, while Churchill argued for delaying a cross-Channel attack and instead engaging German and Italian troops in North Africa and Italy. Roosevelt was sympathetic to Stalin but acquiesced to Churchill's plan to attack the Axis on the periphery. The Allies finally opened a second front in the D-Day invasion in June 1944, but the nearly three-year delay had reinforced Stalin's suspicions of the West.

World War II was almost universally popular, and war experiences contributed to the developing national culture. The home-front mobilization brought people of diverse backgrounds together, blurring the differences among social groups. The war industries also offered new employment opportunities for minorities and women. Millions of Americans—prompted by military service or employment opportunities—moved around the country during the war years. The creation of defense-related industries in the South and West, in particular, foreshadowed a long-term population shift away from the Northeast. Not all moved of their own free will: the government, fearing subversion, sent thousands of Japanese-Americans to internment camps. The internment, along with continuing racial discrimination and riots pitting whites against African-Americans and Chicanos, starkly highlighted the limitations of the new sense of national unity.

In the Pacific the United States adopted a strategy of island-hopping. American forces steadily retook Japan's conquests and worked their way toward the Japanese home islands. Japan finally surrendered after the United States dropped atomic bombs on Hiroshima and Nagasaki.

The mobilization for total war and the growth of a national culture would have far-reaching consequences for American society. Ironically, at the same time that the war contributed to the growth of big government and the nationalization of culture, it reaffirmed Americans' faith in limited government and individualism. In all of the major initiatives of the war—building an army, mobilizing industry, controlling wages and prices—Americans experimented to balance the needs of war with the values of democracy. The brutality of Hitler's regime made Americans more skeptical of state power. In a war depicted as a struggle between good and evil, the victory over fascism seemed to confirm the continuing relevance of America's democratic experiment. Flush from victory and armed with enormous military might and confidence in the universality of American values, the United States prepared to launch a new crusade.

Annotated Suggested Readings

John Morton Blum's *V Was for Victory* (1976) is a colorful analysis of American culture and society during World War II. Richard Polenberg's *War and Society* (1972) surveys the home front. Geoffrey Perrett's *Days of Sadness, Years of Triumph* (1973) studies both the domestic and military aspects of the war. John Keegan's *The Second World War* (1990) is the best one-volume study of the military campaigns. William O'Neill's *A Democracy at*

War (1993) is a fascinating look at the impact of American political ideology on mobilizing the country for war. Studs Terkel's *The Good War* (1984) is a powerful oral history of the war. *The Best War Ever* (1994) offers a revisionist account by Michael Adams that dispels numerous "myths" about World War II.

Robert Dallek's *Franklin D. Roosevelt and American Foreign Policy, 1932–1945* (1995) remains the definitive account of FDR's approach to the world. Wayne S. Cole's *Roosevelt and the Isolationists* (1983) examines the battles over foreign policy in the 1930s and World War II. Robert Cohen discusses the peace movement of the 1930s in *When the Old Left Was Young* (1993). Patrick Heardon's *Roosevelt Confronts Hitler* (1987) focuses on the economic motivations for American entry into the war. The Atlantic Charter and the Anglo-American alliance is the subject of Theodore Wilson's *First Summit* (1991). Warren Kimball studies the Lend-Lease Act and its implications in *The Most Unsordid Act* (1969). Gordon Prange's *At Dawn We Slept* (1981) explores the events culminating in the U.S. entry.

Gordon Wright's *The Ordeal of Total War* (1968) is a standard account of America's military mobilization. George Q. Flynn's *The Mess in Washington* (1979) details the policy end of mobilizing, as does Bruce Catton's *War Lords of Washington* (1964). Nelson Lichtenstein covers the role of the CIO in fighting the war in *Labor's War at Home* (1983).

Gerald Linderman's *The World Within War* (1997) examines the life of the average soldier. Stephen E. Ambrose's *The Supreme Commander* (1970) is a portrait of Dwight Eisenhower as a military coordinator. Mark A. Stoler explores the diplomatic wrangling among the Allies in *The Politics of the Second Front* (1977). John Keegan covers the D-Day invasion in his *Six Armies in Normandy* (1982), while John Toland's *The Last Hundred Days* (1966) details the end of the fighting in Europe. America's treatment of European Jews before and during the war is the subject of David S. Wyman's *The Abandonment of the Jews* (1984).

Warren Kimball's *Forged in War* (1997) examines the unique relationship between FDR and Churchill and their attempts to deal with Stalin. Stephen Ambrose's *Rise to Globalism* (1988) chronicles the United States' ascension to world power. Russell Buhite explores the ramifications of the Yalta Conference in *Decision at Yalta* (1986). John L. Gaddis locates the roots of the Cold War in World War II diplomacy in *The United States and the Origins of the Cold War* (1972).

Allan Winkler offers a valuable study of the Office of War Information in *The Politics of Propaganda* (1978). Holly Cowan Shulman studies the propaganda produced by the entertainment industries in *The Voice of America* (1991). Thomas Doherty's *Projections of War* (1999) demonstrates World War II's impact on the relationship between Hollywood and American culture.

Roger Daniels offers perhaps the definitive account of the Japanese internment in *Concentration Camps USA* (1981). Michi Weglyn's *Years of Infamy* (1976) has valuable primary source material on the internment. Gerald D. Nash explores the new mobility and the rise of the Sunbelt during the war in *The American West Transformed* (1985). John D'Emilio's *Sexual Politics, Sexual Communities* (1983) studies the impact of the war on gay Americans. Allan Berube's *Coming Out Under Fire* (1991) details the plight of gays on the home front and in the military.

Sherna Berger Gluck's *Rosie the Riveter Revisited* (1987) is a compelling oral history of women workers during World War II. Karen Anderson's *Wartime Women* (1981) examines the broad social transformations of women's roles during the war. Susan M. Hartmann's *The Home Front and Beyond* (1982) includes material on women at the battlefront. Molly Merryman's *Clipped Wings* (1998) is a history of the Women's Airforce Service Pilots.

Richard M. Dalfiume's *Desegregation of the U.S. Armed Forces* (1969) analyzes wartime race relations in the military. Albert Russell Buchanan's *Black Americans in World War II*

(1977) is a moving account of the African-American struggle to challenge discrimination during the war. David Kryder's *Divided Arsenal* (2000) explores the government's dealings with the race issue as a whole. Mario T. Garcia's *Mexican-Americans* (1989) examines the Hispanic experience during the war. Kenneth Townsend addresses the impact of the war on Native Americans in *At the Crossroads* (2000). Dominic Capeci, Jr.'s *Race Relations in Wartime Detroit* (1984) and Mauricio Mazan's *The Zoot Suit Riots* (1984) explore the racial tensions of the period. Ronald Takaki's *Double Victory* (2000) is a general history of the wartime experiences of various segments of the American population.

The impact of the war and FDR's tenure on the presidency is the subject of Matthew Dickinson's *Bitter Harvest* (1997). James Atleson's *Labor and the Wartime State* (1998) argues that current policies toward and regulations of labor relations were formulated during World War II.

John Dower analyzes the racism among World War II Americans and Japanese in *War Without Mercy* (1986). Ronald H. Spector's *Eagle Against the Sun* (1984) is an in-depth account of the Pacific war. Akira Iriye studies the war from both sides in *Power and Culture: The Japanese-American War* (1981). Gordon Prange's *Miracle at Midway* (1982) chronicles this crucial battle.

There is extensive material on the atomic bomb. Gar Alperovitz studies the political aspects of the Manhattan Project in *Atomic Diplomacy* (1965). Herbert Feis's *The Atomic Bomb and the End of World War II* (1966) and Dennis D. Wainstock's *The Decision to Drop the Atomic Bomb* (1996) explore the development and decision to use the bomb on Japan. John Hersey's *Hiroshima* (2d ed., 1985) remains a powerful telling of the aftermath of the bombing. Paul Boyer's *By the Bomb's Early Light* (1985) investigates the intellectual culture behind the development of the bomb.

The **H**istory **C**ompanion

The Dropping of the Bomb

The Interim Committee, 1945

The Manhattan Project was so secret that not even Vice President Harry Truman had been informed of its existence. On April 25, 1945, thirteen days after Roosevelt's death, Secretary of War Henry Stimson briefed Truman on the bomb's development and the ongoing debate over whether to use it. Truman decided that he could not make such a decision by himself and appointed a committee of experts, drawn from the agencies working on the bomb, to advise him. Chaired by Office of War Mobilization Director James Byrnes, the so-called Interim Committee evaluated several scenarios for deploying the bomb. The following excerpts, describing the final deliberations before the committee decided to recommend using the bomb on a Japanese city, showcase the assumptions that dominated the decision-making process in the Truman administration. On May 31, Secretary of War Stimson refuted arguments for a demonstration of the bomb and called for a surprise bombing. Arthur H. Compton, a scientist on the committee, later related the session:

It was evident that everyone would suspect trickery. If a bomb were exploded in Japan with previous notice, the Japanese air power was still adequate to give serious interference. An atomic bomb was an intricate device, still in the development stage. . . . If during the final adjustments of the bomb the Japanese defenders should attack, a faulty move might easily result in some kind of failure. Such an end to an advertised demonstration of power would be much worse than if the attempt had not been made. It was now evident that when the time came for the bombs to be used we should have only one of them available, followed afterwards by others at all-too-long intervals. We could not afford the chance that one of them might be a dud. If the test were made on some neutral territory, it was hard to believe that Japan's determined and fanatical military men would be impressed. If such an open test were made first and failed to bring surrender, the chance would be gone to give the shock of surprise that proved so effective. On the contrary it would make the Japanese ready to interfere with the atomic attack if they could. Though the possibility of a demonstration that would not destroy human lives was attractive, no one could suggest a way in which it could be made so convincing that it would be likely to stop the war. . . .

After much discussion concerning various types of targets and the effects to be produced, the Secretary expressed the conclusion, on which there was general agreement, that we could not give the Japanese any warning; that we could not concentrate on a civilian area; but that we should seek to make a profound psychological impression on as many of the inhabitants as possible.

The Franck Report, 1945

When James Franck brought his report to the White House on June 11, he was unaware that Truman had already made the decision to drop the atomic bomb on a Japanese city. Franck, who chaired the Social and Political Implications Committee of the Metallurgical Laboratory at the University of Chicago, was among a handful of scientists who tried to convince the president not to drop the bomb on a civilian center. Like most of the scientists working on the Manhattan Project, Franck and his colleagues were not well briefed on the military situation in Japan. They focused on the longer-term strategic implications of the decision, not on the moral or ethical ramifications of dropping the bomb.

The development of nuclear power not only constitutes an important addition to the technological and military power of the United States, but also creates grave political and economic problems for the future of this country.

Nuclear bombs cannot possibly remain a "secret weapon" at the exclusive disposal of this country for more than a few years. The scientific facts on which their construction is based are well known to scientists of other countries. Unless an effective international control of nuclear explosives is instituted, a race for nuclear armaments is certain to ensue following the first revelation of our possession of nuclear weapons to the world. Within ten years other countries may have nuclear bombs, each of which, weighing less than a ton, could destroy an urban area of more than ten square miles. In the war to which such an armaments race is likely to lead, the United States, with its agglomeration of population and industry in comparatively few metropolitan districts, will be at a disadvantage compared to nations whose population and industry are scattered over large areas.

We believe that these considerations make the use of nuclear bombs for an early, unannounced attack against Japan inadvisable. If the United States were to be the first to release this new means of indiscriminate destruction upon mankind, she would sacrifice public support throughout the world, precipitate the race for armaments, and prejudice the possibility of reaching an international agreement on the future control of such weapons.

Much more favorable conditions for the eventual achievement of such an agreement could be created if nuclear bombs were first revealed to the world by a demonstration in an appropriately selected uninhabited area.

In case chances for the establishment of an effective international control of nuclear weapons should have to be considered slight at the present time, then not only the use of these weapons against Japan, but even their early demonstration, may be contrary to the interests of this country. A postponement of such a demonstration will have in this case the advantage of delaying the beginning of the nuclear armaments race as long as possible.

If the government should decide in favor of an early demonstration of nuclear weapons, it will then have the possibility of taking into account the public opinion of this country and of the other nations before deciding whether these weapons should be used against Japan. In this way, other nations may assume a share of responsibility for such a fateful decision.

Most historians agree that Truman decided to use the bomb in order to save American lives. "Until newly found documents show otherwise, the available evidence points to the unremarkable conclusion that Truman approved using the bombs for the reason he said he did: to end a bloody war that would have become far bloodier had an invasion proved necessary," historian Robert Maddox wrote in 1995. Truman realized that the public would have been outraged if it later discovered that he had a weapon that could have ended the war before an American invasion of Japan.

Though the thesis that Truman dropped the bomb solely to intimidate the Soviets (historian Charles L. Mee, Jr., writing in this vein, called the bombings "wanton murder") has been largely discredited, political concerns certainly motivated Truman. In his analysis of the bombing, former Smithsonian director Martin Harwit cites Henry Stimson's numerous diary entries and State Department reports concerning not the lives of GIs, but the Soviet Union. Stalin had pledged to enter the Pacific war within three months of the German surrender. Truman knew the Soviets were poised to dominate postwar developments in Manchuria and possibly Korea, and hoped the atomic bomb would force Japan to surrender before the Soviets could become involved there as well.

Several members of the Manhattan Project, though, had begun to have second thoughts about the bombing. Many of the scientists who helped develop the bomb had fled Europe and the Nazis. Certain that Germany was developing an atomic bomb, they thought the United States needed to counter this threat. When Germany surrendered in May 1945 some of those scientists were dismayed to learn that the military planned to use the bomb on Japan.

"By the end of July 1945, if not before," historian David Wainstock has written, "Japan was militarily defeated. Fire raids had ravaged its major cities; its best troops were killed or missing in East Asia and the South Pacific, and many were still fighting in China. Twenty-two million Japanese were homeless, and the U.S. naval and air blockade had cut off imports of fuel, food, and raw materials." The men behind the Manhattan Project had begun to think beyond the present fighting to the postwar consequences of such a bombing. When Truman finally decided to use the bomb on the city of Hiroshima, he was motivated by calculations of international prestige and influence as much as by estimations of human lives.

QUESTIONS FOR ANALYSIS

1. Why does the Interim Committee oppose giving Japan advance warning?

2. How does the Interim Committee picture the Japanese armed forces?

3. According to Franck, why would the United States be at a disadvantage in a nuclear war?

4. Why do Franck and his colleagues want to delay using the bomb?

5. Were their predictions accurate?

6. How did assumptions about the world shape the strategic recommendations of the Interim Committee and the Franck Report?

7. How did the atomic bomb change America's international image?

27

The Cold War

1945–1952

According to Kennan's analysis, the Soviets were solely to blame for international tensions; negotiations and compromise had reached an impasse; only military and economic pressure could tame the Russian bear.

On February 22, 1946, the State Department's telex machine began clattering with a secret eight-thousand-word telegram from Moscow. The cable, written by George Frost Kennan, a forty-two-year-old Soviet specialist in the U.S. embassy, tried to explain Soviet aggression to puzzled officials in Washington. Since the end of World War II, U.S. policymakers had grown increasingly alarmed as the Soviets violated wartime agreements and tightened their military grip over Eastern Europe. Worried officials were all asking the same questions: what were Soviet intentions, and how should the United States respond to them? They turned to Kennan for the answers.

Kennan laid out a frightening picture of an aggressive Soviet Union intent on world domination. The Soviets, he wired, were driven by a "neurotic view of world affairs" that emerged from an "instinctive Russian sense of insecurity." They compensated for their insecurity by going on the attack "in patient but deadly struggle for total destruction of rival power, never in compacts and compromises with it." Moscow, he suggested, was "highly sensitive to logic of force. For this reason it can easily withdraw—and usually does—when strong resistance is encountered at any point." According to Kennan's analysis, the Soviets were solely to blame for international tensions; negotiations and compromise had reached an impasse; only military and economic pressure could tame the Russian bear.

Kennan's telegram caused a sensation in Washington. "Splendid analysis," exclaimed Secretary of State James Byrnes. "Magnificent . . . to those of us here struggling with the problem," said H. Freeman Matthews, the head of the State Department's Office of European Affairs. The following year Kennan published an expanded public version of the telegram in an article written under the pseudonym

"Mr. X." The Soviets, he argued, saw the world divided into hostile capitalist and communist camps between which there could be no peace. He recommended a U.S. foreign policy based on the "long-term, patient, but firm and vigilant containment of Russian expansive tendencies." From Kennan's essay a word emerged to characterize a new experiment in American foreign policy: *containment*.

The so-called Long Telegram and the Mr. X article provided the ideological justification for a new "get tough" approach with the Soviets. The strategy of containment fundamentally transformed American foreign policy. It ripped the United States from its isolationist roots, imposed new international obligations on the American people, and created a massive national security state.

At first, Harry Truman seemed ill prepared to lead the nation in its new international experiment and its return to a peacetime economy. But during the 1948 presidential campaign Truman managed to find his voice, unite the New Deal coalition, and score a surprising victory. Truman hoped his election would signal a revival of liberalism, but a public weary of New Deal–type experimentation and a conservative coalition in Congress frustrated most of his "Fair Deal" agenda. A series of foreign policy setbacks inflicted the most devastating blow to Truman's reform hopes. News that the Soviets had acquired atomic weapons, the communist victory in China, and, most of all, the communist North Korean invasion of South Korea in June 1950 eroded public trust in the administration.

Foreign policy setbacks abroad intensified fears of communist subversion at home. Critics charged that leftist sympathizers had aided the communist cause by passing atomic secrets to the Soviets. Charges of espionage and subversion gripped the nation. The anticommunist hysteria created a fertile breeding ground for demagogues who used fear of communism as a blunt weapon against dissent, real or imagined. Wisconsin Senator Joseph McCarthy emerged as the leader of an unprecedented experiment in repression.

- What factors in the postwar period influenced Americans' attitudes toward government and reform? How did these attitudes affect Truman's domestic agenda?

- How did the Korean conflict manifest a new direction in foreign policy and military strategy?

- Why were Americans so fearful of communism, and how did that fear affect attitudes toward society and individual rights?

This chapter will address these questions.

FROM WORLD WAR TO COLD WAR, 1945–1949

World War II dramatically altered the global balance of power. Before 1939 Europe had dominated world affairs. After 1945 the United States and the Soviet Union emerged as superpowers that combined global political ambitions with massive military might. During World War II the need to sustain the Grand Alliance and defeat Nazi Germany forced the United States and the Soviet Union to down-

CHRONOLOGY

1945	Yalta Conference FDR's death; Truman becomes president United Nations created Potsdam Conference United States drops atomic bombs; World War II ends
1946	Kennan's "Long Telegram" Churchill's "iron curtain" speech Republicans win majority in both houses
1947	Truman Doctrine and Marshall Plan announced Stalin creates Cominform President's Committee on Civil Rights established Taft-Hartley Act Federal Employee Loyalty Program established HUAC investigations of Hollywood
1948	Communist coup in Czechoslovakia Congress passes National Security Act Soviet blockade of Berlin begins Israel founded Truman elected president Truman moves to end discrimination in the military
1949	NATO approved by Senate China falls to communists USSR explodes a nuclear weapon Hiss trial COMECON formed
1950	North Korea invades South Korea NSC-68 China enters Korean War McCarthy announces communists in State Department
1951	General MacArthur fired Rosenbergs sentenced to death for espionage
1952	U.S. explodes first H-bomb
1955	Warsaw Pact formed

play their differences. By the end of the war, however, serious questions had emerged about the future of the postwar world. As we saw in Chapter 26, Roosevelt at first tried to balance Soviet aims with American ambitions, but by 1945 Stalin's intransigence encouraged a tougher line with Moscow.

Harry Truman picked up where Roosevelt left off. The Truman Doctrine and the Marshall Plan signaled a basic shift in American foreign policy that challenged isolationism and helped institutionalize the new hostility. Fear of mutual annihilation prevented the hostility from exploding into open warfare, but it gave birth to the precarious new peace that contemporaries titled the Cold War.

Roots of the Cold War

Who started the Cold War? The question has inspired passionate debate among historians. Some scholars place most of the blame on the Soviet Union, charging that its aggressive foreign policy was the logical outgrowth of an ideological commitment to world revolution. Other scholars contend that Russian aggression reflected a legitimate fear of American economic imperialism.

In recent years historians studying the origins of the Cold War have emphasized that both nations shared responsibility for the conflict, though they differ greatly on how much responsibility to assign each side. Rather than seeing the Cold War as the product of conspiracies hatched in the Kremlin or in Washington, post–Cold War historians stress how history, ideology, and national interest created serious misperceptions, limited the range of options on both sides, and made confrontation nearly inevitable.

The Cold War between the Soviet Union and the United States had roots deep in the past. In 1917 relations between the two nations plummeted into the deep freeze when the Bolsheviks seized control of the Russian government. Under Lenin, the Soviets pulled out of World War I, leaving the West to fight the Central Powers alone. More important, the Soviets committed the new state to the goal of world revolution and the destruction of capitalism. Communism challenged the basic tenets of the American dream: it threatened democratic government, supported state power over individual freedom, cut off free markets, and eliminated religion altogether.

The brutality of the Soviet regime added to American hostility. Stalin, who seized control of the Soviet Union following Lenin's death in 1924, consolidated his power through a series of bloody purges that killed nearly 3 million citizens. He initiated a massive effort to collectivize agriculture that led to the deaths of 14 million peasants. In 1939, after Stalin signed the prewar nonaggression treaty with Hitler, he sent troops into Finland, Estonia, Latvia, and Lithuania. By then most Americans agreed with the *Wall Street Journal* that "the principal difference between Mr. Hitler and Mr. Stalin is the size of their respective mustaches."

The Soviets also had reason to distrust the United States. The rhetoric and actions of American policymakers lent credence to one of the principal teachings of Marxist-Leninist doctrine: the incompatibility of capitalism and communism. Western leaders, including President Woodrow Wilson, made no secret of their contempt for Lenin or their desire to see him ousted. Wilson's decision to send American troops on a confused mission to Siberia in 1918 confirmed Soviet suspicion of a Western conspiracy to topple their government. The United States did not extend diplomatic relations to the Soviets until 1933—sixteen years after the new government came to power.

Hitler's invasion of Russia in 1941 forced the United States and the Soviet Union into a brief alliance to defeat Germany. Wartime cooperation greatly improved the Soviet Union's image in America. Confronted with evidence that the Russian people were willing to fight for their government, many Americans jumped to the conclusion that the Soviet Union had suddenly become a democracy. In the best-selling book *Mission to Moscow* (1943), Joseph E. Davies proclaimed that "the Russia of Lenin and Trotsky—the Russia of the Bolshevik Revolution—no longer exists." *Life* magazine in 1943 declared that Russians "look like Americans, dress like Americans and think like Americans."

The war may have softened American public opinion, but it did little to ease the mistrust between leaders. Roosevelt, though hopeful about a postwar settlement, recognized that "a dictatorship as absolute as any . . . in the world" ruled Moscow. At the same time, Roosevelt's agreement with Churchill to delay a second front in Europe and his refusal to share information about the development and testing of the atomic bomb convinced Stalin that the Western allies could not be trusted.

As the war ground to an end, it became clear that the United States and the Soviet Union possessed fundamentally different visions of the postwar world. Since the early days of the republic, Americans believed in their mission to spread their revolutionary ideology of democracy, individual rights, and open markets, but they differed on how to fulfill that mission. Some Americans advocated a policy of active intervention in the affairs of other nations, while others suggested that America should keep to itself and lead by example. In the nineteenth century America's sense of mission translated into a "manifest destiny" to expand to the Pacific and to civilize the Indians. During World War I Woodrow Wilson expanded the notion to include spreading democracy and liberal capitalism around the globe. President Roosevelt extended that vision into the postwar world in the Atlantic Charter (1941), which affirmed the right of all peoples to choose their own form of government and assured all nations equal access to trade and raw materials.

America's vision of universal rights clashed with Stalin's insistence on maintaining a Soviet "sphere of influence" in Eastern Europe. Since historians have just begun to examine the documents in Soviet archives (opened for research in the 1990s after the Soviet Union's collapse), it is hard to know Stalin's intentions at the end of the war. Most of the available evidence, however, suggests that the Soviets had one overriding goal: to secure their borders from foreign invaders. Twice in the twentieth century German armies had swept over Russia like hungry locusts. In the most recent assault by Hitler's Nazis, as many as 20 million Soviets died. Six hundred thousand starved to death in the two-year battle and siege of Leningrad alone. Along with the millions of deaths the war caused enormous physical destruction. The Soviets, determined to head off another attack, insisted on defensible borders and friendly regimes on their western flank. As early as December 1941 Stalin asked the British and Americans to accept Soviet influence in Eastern Europe. "All we ask for," he told the British foreign minister, "is to restore our country to its former frontiers."

Europe emerged as the key battleground between these rival visions of the postwar world. The war had devastated Europe, weakened established powers, and created a power vacuum that the United States and the Soviets moved to fill. "The odor of death," recalled an American diplomat, "was everywhere." Fifty million people had perished. Great cities had been reduced to rubble. Tens of millions of people had no shelter. Everywhere farmlands had been despoiled and animals slaughtered. In Poland almost three-fourths of the horses and two-thirds of the cattle were gone.

The wretched conditions in Europe precipitated a historic shift in American foreign policy. The United States could not withdraw to its side of the Atlantic as it had after World War I. "We are for all time deisolated," wrote an observer. With the world's largest navy and air force, a monopoly on nuclear weapons, and a thriving economy, the United States seemed poised to fulfill its historic mission to spread the values of democracy and free enterprise to the rest of the world. "We are going forward to meet our destiny—which I think Almighty God intended us to have—and we are going to be the leaders," Harry Truman told his Missouri neighbors in 1945.

Yet despite its global military might, the United Sates was unable to control events in the Soviet "sphere of influence." In 1945, with the 10-million-man Red Army in control of most of Eastern Europe, the Soviets were in a position to impose their will by force. Within weeks of the Yalta Conference, at which he agreed to hold "free and unfettered elections," Stalin installed a pro-Soviet puppet government in Poland. With Poland firmly in his grasp, Stalin moved to strangle the rest of Eastern Europe. He appointed a communist-led government in Rumania and reoccupied Latvia, Estonia, and Lithuania.

American officials viewed Soviet actions as a real threat to U.S. interests. No policymaker worried about a direct Soviet assault on the United States, and few believed the Soviets could muster the resources—military, financial, or psychological—for an invasion of western Europe. The danger was that the Soviets would extend their influence politically by capitalizing on social and economic chaos in Europe, which created a fertile breeding ground for communism. In France, Italy, and Finland, 20 percent of the public voted Communist in elections after the war; in Belgium, Denmark, Norway, Holland, and Sweden, the figure was nearly 10 percent. If the trend continued, the Soviets could capture vital strategic resources and cut the United States off from potential markets.

By 1945 the battle lines were clearly drawn. Stalin interpreted U.S. calls for free elections and democratic reform in Eastern Europe as part of a capitalist plot to surround the Soviet Union. The Americans viewed the Soviet Union's effort to consolidate its control over Eastern Europe as the first step of a larger plan of global conquest. "We can't do business with Stalin," Roosevelt complained three weeks before his death. "He has broken every one of the promises he made at Yalta." Moscow and Washington became ensnarled in a "security dilemma": each step taken by one side to enhance its security appeared an act of provocation to the other.

Harry Truman Takes Charge

When he assumed the presidency in April 1945, Harry Truman knew little about Roosevelt's hardening line toward the Soviets. He learned quickly when he sought the recommendations of Roosevelt's advisers, most of whom favored a tougher policy. "We had better have a showdown with them now than later," declared Secretary of the Navy James Forrestal.

A combative posture fit Truman's temperament. Impulsive and decisive, he lacked Roosevelt's talent for ambiguity and compromise. "When I say I'm going to do something, I do it," he once wrote. On his desk he displayed his credo in a sign: "The Buck Stops Here." Truman viewed the Yalta Accords as contracts between East and West. He was committed to seeing that Stalin honored the agreements.

The new president, emboldened by America's monopoly on atomic weaponry and eager to show critics and the nation that he was in charge, matched Stalin's inflexibility with calls for self-determination and free elections in Eastern Europe. In office less than two weeks, he scolded the Soviet foreign minister Vyacheslav Molotov for Soviet aggression in Poland. When Molotov protested, "I have never been talked to like that in my life," Truman retorted, "Carry out your agreements and you won't get talked to like that."

The Russians interpreted Truman's tongue-lashing as proof that the new administration had abandoned Roosevelt's policy of cooperation. When a bureaucratic blunder led to the abrupt termination of Lend-Lease shipments to the Soviets, a bitter Stalin complained that the United States was trying to use economic pressure to force political concessions. Despite reassurances that the decision resulted from a bureaucratic error, the incident likely reinforced the Kremlin's deep suspicion of the West. In May former Undersecretary of State Sumner Welles charged, "Our Government now appears to the Russians as the spearhead of an apparent bloc of the western nations opposed to the Soviet Union."

Although Truman believed the United States needed to confront Soviet aggression, he also recognized that U.S.–Soviet cooperation was necessary to guarantee a lasting peace. In July 1945 Truman carried these conflicting goals to Potsdam, outside Berlin, for the final meeting of the Grand Alliance. Truman and Stalin squabbled over the sensitive issues of reparations and implementation of the Yalta Accords, but by the end of the meeting the leaders had reached tentative agreements. Russia would permit Anglo-American observers in Eastern Europe to monitor free elections and would withdraw its troops from oil-rich Azerbaijan in Iran. In return, the West reluctantly accepted Soviet occupation of eastern Germany and approved Russian annexation of eastern Poland. On the key issue of reparations the leaders agreed that each power would extract reparations from its own zone in occupied Germany, and that the Western powers would transfer 15 percent of the capital equipment in their zones to Russia in return for food, coal, and other raw materials. Despite their obvious differences, Truman left Potsdam hopeful that he could develop a working relationship with Stalin. "I can deal with Stalin," he wrote in his diary. "He is honest—but smart as hell."

The Iron Curtain Falls

Truman's optimism proved unfounded. With the Red Army occupying half of Europe at the end of the war, Stalin moved decisively to establish his control over Eastern Europe. Violating his pledge at Potsdam to allow free elections, Stalin tightened his grip over Poland, Bulgaria, Hungary, and Rumania. He denied western observers access to Eastern Europe and continued his occupation of Azerbaijan.

Soviet actions in Germany did little to ease U.S. suspicions about Soviet intentions. Yalta had divided Germany into four zones and Berlin into four sectors (U.S., USSR, British, and French). The Soviets, wanting to punish Germany for

Truman Tours Potsdam   The devastation of much of Germany was readily apparent when President Truman journeyed to Potsdam in July 1945 to meet with Stalin and Churchill. In this picture, Truman (seated in the back of the car on the far side with Secretary of State James Byrnes in the middle) views the ruins of the Reichschancellery, the scene of many of Hitler's public appearances. The ravaged city hosted another epic battle during the conference itself, one of the opening rounds of the Cold War. Truman, less patient than Roosevelt had been, clashed with Stalin over the Polish border, German reparations, and other matters crucial for the shape of the postwar world. *(US Army, Courtesy Harry S. Truman Library.)*

its aggression, planned to impose a harsh peace. By April 1946 the Soviets had stripped their zone of industry and started to make heavy demands for factories, power plants, and tools from the American and British zones. The Truman administration feared that the Soviets would cripple Germany, produce widespread famine, and require a massive infusion of American resources. Truman halted reparations for the Soviets in May 1946. In September Secretary of State James Byrnes stated that the United States would no longer seek agreement with the Soviets on the future of Germany.

Disputes over the control of nuclear technology further divided the former allies. In December 1945 the Big Three foreign ministers established an Atomic Energy Commission to deal with the question of nuclear weapons in the postwar world order. In June 1946 the Americans proposed a plan that allowed the United

States to retain its nuclear monopoly while the United Nations implemented a system of international control. The most controversial clause of the plan stipulated mandatory United Nations inspection of Soviet nuclear facilities—a condition the administration knew Stalin would never accept.

By the summer of 1946 neither Truman nor Stalin was interested in making a deal. Truman did not want to relinquish America's nuclear monopoly. We "should not under any circumstances," he declared, "throw away our guns until we are sure the rest of the world cannot arm against us." For his part Stalin wanted no place in an international scheme that would prevent the Soviets from developing their own atomic bomb. Unable to reach agreement the United States put aside plans for international cooperation. In 1946 Congress created the Atomic Energy Commission to control research and development of nuclear energy.

Both the Soviets and the Americans heightened tensions by engaging in a war of words. On February 9, 1946, Stalin delivered a rare public speech in which he explained the fundamental incompatibility of communism and capitalism. The American system, he stressed, needed war for raw materials and markets. The Second World War had been the most recent in a chain of conflicts that could be broken only when the world's economy made the transformation to communism. *Time* magazine concluded that the remarks were "the most warlike pronouncement uttered by any top-rank statesman" since the war had ended.

A few weeks later Winston Churchill returned the fire. Speaking in March 1946 in Fulton, Missouri, with Truman on the platform, the former prime minister declared of Europe that "from Stettin in the Baltic to Trieste in the Adriatic, an iron curtain has descended across the Continent." To counter the threat he called for an association of English-speaking peoples to remain vigilant at all times.

Polls suggested that the American public agreed with Churchill's assessment. Shortly after the speech a survey showed that 60 percent of the public believed that the United States was being "too soft" on the Russians. Soviet actions and hardening public attitudes pushed many isolationists into the internationalist camp. Most conservatives, distrusting European leaders and fearing that active involvement in world affairs would enlarge presidential power, had hoped to resurrect traditional isolationist sentiment after the war. By 1946, however, the threat of Soviet expansion forced many to reconsider their views. "I am more than ever convinced," said Senator Arthur Vandenberg, "that communism is on the march on a worldwide scale which only America can stop." For Vandenberg, fear of Soviet domination outweighed deeply held ideas about American self-reliance.

Americans supported a tougher line with the Soviets, but they remained deeply ambivalent about assuming the responsibility of world power. Many of the same people who feared Soviet aggression also clamored for the president to bring home American soldiers and convert to a peacetime economy. Congress delivered the contradictory message directly to the president. Legislators eager to reestablish their control over foreign policy called on Truman "to get tough with Russia." Yet they also pushed for lower taxes and for a rapid demobilization of the armed forces. By mid-1946 the total number of American forces on active duty had dropped from 12 million to fewer than 3 million.

Containing Communism: The Truman Doctrine and the Marshall Plan

Reflecting his growing impatience with the Russians, Truman replaced his secretary of state, James Byrnes, with General George C. Marshall in January 1947. While Byrnes was a largely ineffectual and absent leader, Marshall, who served as Army Chief of Staff during the war, had earned a well-deserved reputation as a distinguished military officer and skilled manager. As secretary of state, Marshall presided over the process that transformed America's approach to the world.

For advice Marshall turned to two State Department professionals who had long harbored deep suspicions of the Soviets: Undersecretary of State Dean Acheson and Moscow diplomat George Kennan. An elegant and arrogant man, Acheson rejected suggestions that morality should drive American policy and instead stressed that American power was essential to peace. By 1946 Acheson urged Truman to employ the full range of American power—economic, military, and diplomatic—to tame the Soviet bear. "I think it is a mistake to believe that you can, at any time, sit down with the Russians and solve questions," he told the Senate in 1947, echoing many of the ideas Kennan espoused.

By 1947 a communist insurgency was battling the right-wing monarchy in Greece. Stalin was also pressuring Turkey to share control of the strategic Dardanelles strait, the waterway linking the Black Sea and the Mediterranean. In February 1947 the British ambassador informed the American State Department that his country could no longer afford to support Greece and Turkey with economic and military aid. The Truman administration, fearful that the Soviet-backed insurgents might gain the upper hand, wanted to fill the vacuum. First, the administration needed to overcome deep-seated American fears of getting involved in European affairs. Senator Vandenberg suggested building support by "scaring hell out of the country."

The administration accepted the challenge. On March 12, 1947, Truman stood before a joint session of Congress to make his case for American aid to Greece and Turkey. "I believe that it must be the policy of the United States to support free peoples who are resisting attempted subjugation by armed minorities or by outside pressures," he declared. The future of the "free world," he insisted, rested in America's hands. After setting the stage Truman requested that Congress appropriate $400 million for Greek and Turkish military and economic aid. The American people rallied around the cause of freedom. Public opinion strongly supported the request, and Truman's poll ratings leaped ten points.

The Truman Doctrine represented a turning point in American foreign policy. By rooting America's response to a decidedly local conflict in traditional rhetoric of good and evil, free and unfree, Truman hoped to prepare the American people for their responsibility as a world power. Presidential aide Clark Clifford called it "the opening gun in a campaign to bring the people up to [the] realization that the war isn't over by any means."

The administration recognized that military assistance might deter the Soviets in Greece and Turkey, but it would not save war-torn western Europe from economic disaster. Europe, Churchill declared, had become "a rubble heap, a charnel house, a breeding ground of pestilence and hate." To challenge the strength of

Communist parties and Soviet influence, administration officials moved to shore up Europe's battered economy.

On June 5, 1947, Secretary of State George C. Marshall offered his prescription for recovery. He chose the Harvard University commencement ceremony to announce a bold new plan of economic assistance to Europe. Marshall explained that the aid program was "directed not against any country or doctrine but against hunger, poverty, desperation, and chaos." Marshall invited the participation of any country, including the Soviet Union, that was "willing to assist in the task of recovery." Truman realized that Stalin would never accept a plan that required him to share vital economic information with the United States while Western leaders controlled how funds would be distributed. In December 1947 Truman submitted the plan to Congress, with a recommendation that the United States spend $17 billion over four years.

At first congressional leaders were cool to the idea. Critics condemned the plan as a gigantic "international WPA," "a bold Socialist blueprint." Vandenberg led the bipartisan supporters, calling the plan a "calculated risk" to "help stop World War III before it starts." While Congress held hearings during the fall, Europe sank deeper into its economic abyss. England announced that it was cutting individual meat rations to twenty cents worth per week.

The Marshall Plan at Work in Austria
In the war's aftermath, the United States sent $17 billion to Europe in the form of money and supplies to bolster relief and rebuilding efforts. While Europeans had already begun to repair the physical and economic devastation by 1947, weaknesses remained and Americans feared that if these problems continued unchecked, a political and social vacuum could develop, making those nations ripe for communist exploitation. Secretary of State George Marshall and other policymakers believed that massive aid would enable European nations to resist communism and would build loyalty to the United States among the European people. They certainly won a friend in this little boy, who is obviously pleased with his new shoes, brought by American planes and distributed by the American Red Cross. *(American Red Cross.)*

Inadvertently, the Soviet Union provided the Marshall Plan with the boost it needed. During the summer of 1947 Stalin established the Communist Information Bureau (Cominform), which tightened his control in the Eastern bloc and within Russia. The Cominform also called upon communists in the underdeveloped world to accelerate "their struggle" for liberation. A U.S. diplomat called the creation of the Cominform "a declaration of political and economic war against the U.S. and everything the U.S. stands for in world affairs."

In February 1948 Communists staged a coup in Czechoslovakia, overthrowing a freely elected coalition government. Two weeks later the popular Czech foreign minister Jan Masaryk died in a fall from a bathroom window. The Soviets said it was suicide; critics said he was murdered. Western leaders interpreted the coup as part of an aggressive Soviet plan to conquer Europe before it could be revived. According to Kennan, a "real war scare" swept Washington. Opposition to the Marshall Plan wilted in the heated atmosphere. On April 2 the House approved the plan by the lopsided vote of 318 to 75. The Senate roared its approval by an overwhelming voice vote. As a program to revitalize Europe's troubled economy, the Marshall Plan was a dramatic success. Thanks in part to its provisions, European industrial production increased 200 percent between 1948 and 1952. The British foreign secretary called the Marshall Plan "a lifeline to sinking men" (see map on page 1065).

The Marshall Plan added to the mutual misperception that contributed to the Cold War. It reassured European allies, but it worried Stalin, who was convinced that the United States designed the aid program to lure Eastern European nations out of the Soviet orbit and to rebuild Germany. In response, the Kremlin cracked down on dissent in Poland, Romania, and Bulgaria, encouraged the coup in Czechoslovakia, and blockaded Berlin. "For Stalin," concluded two scholars familiar with newly obtained archival information in Moscow and Eastern Europe, "the Marshall Plan was a watershed."

The Soviet moves in turn magnified the threat in Washington, leading to a massive expansion of federal power in a nation traditionally against centralized government. In 1947 Congress institutionalized the Cold War with passage of the National Security Act. The legislation created the skeleton of what would become an overpowering national security apparatus. The act expanded executive power by centralizing previously dispersed responsibilities in the White House. It established the Department of Defense to oversee all branches of the armed services and formed the Joint Chiefs of Staff, which included the generals of the three services and the marines. The act also created the National Security Council (NSC), a cabinet-level body to coordinate military and foreign policy for the president. Led by the president the NSC included the head of the Joint Chiefs of Staff, the secretaries of state and defense, the vice president, and any other members the president chose to appoint. Finally, the legislation set up the Central Intelligence Agency (CIA), which carried out espionage operations directly under the authority of the National Security Council. Following the passage of the act, a journalist noted an ominous trend toward "militarization of [the] government and of the American state of mind." By blurring the line between peace and war, the Cold War led the government to adopt a constant state of readiness.

Mounting Tensions, Precarious Solutions

In June 1948 the West consolidated its hold on Germany. It fused the French zone with the British and American areas, creating "Trizonia," which contained Germany's richest industrial resources and a population of 50 million. The Western powers also invited the Germans to create a new government in West Germany and initiated financial reforms that produced a remarkable economic revival.

The Russians retaliated on June 24 by clamping a tight blockade around West Berlin, which lay 110 miles within the Soviet occupation zone. The Western powers had failed to write clear arrangements for land access to Berlin into their agreement with the Soviets. Taking advantage of the legal confusion, the Soviets blocked all surface transportation into West Berlin, depriving some 2.5 million people of food and fuel.

Cold War Europe   With the end of World War II, political ideologies divided Europe. The United States worked to maintain noncommunist governments in the West by means of the Marshall Plan and the North Atlantic Treaty Organization, but Western European leaders did not always agree with America's plans. Spain did not join NATO until 1982. France withdrew from NATO's integrated military system in 1966 and developed its own independent military strategy. Meanwhile, the Soviet Union supported a Communist Party coup in Czechoslovakia in 1948 and created the Warsaw Pact in 1955 to counter what it perceived as American aggression in Europe.

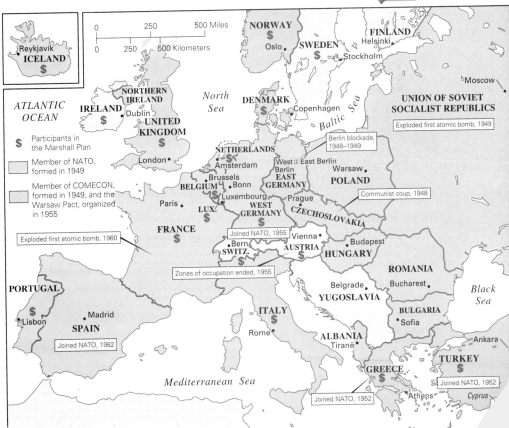

The action forced Truman to respond. A retreat from Berlin, Marshall warned, meant the "failure of the rest of our European policy." But an effort to break the blockade might lead to armed confrontation, and Truman searched for a safer response that would demonstrate American resolve. His answer was a massive airlift operation. For the next 324 days American and British planes dropped 2.5 million tons of provisions to sustain the ten thousand troops and 2 million civilians in West Berlin. Truman publicly threatened to use "the bomb" if the Soviets shot down the relief planes. He wrote in his diary that "we are very close to war." On May 12, 1949, however, the Russians swallowed defeat and ended the blockade.

The Berlin crisis further catalyzed Western leaders to present a unified front to the Soviets. Already Great Britain, France, Belgium, the Netherlands, and Luxembourg had signed the Brussels Treaty (1948), which provided for collective self-defense. In January 1949 Truman proposed expanding the alliance by committing the United States to the defense of Europe. In April he pledged American involvement in the North Atlantic Treaty Organization (NATO), a mutual defense pact that

The Berlin Airlift Greeted by German Children   When the Soviet Union sealed off the city of Berlin in June 1948, the United States and Great Britain launched Operation Vittles. The operation involved sending hundreds of planes loaded with supplies to Berlin every day, eventually totaling over 278,000 flights and resulting in the deaths of thirty-one Americans and thirty-nine Britains whose planes crashed during the missions. As with the Marshall Plan, the airlift not only allowed Western Berlin to remain free of Soviet domination, it created a psychological bond between West Germans and the United States. These children enthusiastically wave at an incoming plane. Notice they are standing on rubble, still plentiful in Europe three years after the war's end. *(Corbis-Bettmann.)*

bound twelve signatories to fight against aggression. Article 5 provided "that an armed attack against one or more . . . shall be considered an attack against them all."

The treaty still needed Senate approval, and Truman anticipated a heated debate. Since George Washington first warned against "entangling alliances" with Europe, the United States had avoided peacetime involvement in collective security agreements with other countries. But NATO supporters, led by Vandenberg, argued that the Soviet threat required the country to develop a new approach to the world. On July 21, 1949, in a clear indication of the shift in American thinking from isolationism to internationalism, the Senate approved the NATO treaty by a wide margin of eighty-two to thirteen. In 1950 Truman appointed General Dwight D. Eisenhower to serve as NATO supreme commander and ordered four American divisions stationed in Europe.

While challenging the Soviets claim to a "sphere of influence" in Europe, the United States consolidated its own sphere in the Western Hemisphere. In 1947 in the Rio Treaty, U.S. and Latin American signatories agreed that "any armed attack by any state against an American state shall be considered an attack against all the American states." The following year North and Latin American countries created the Organization of American States (OAS). Despite these professions of unity, U.S. relations with Latin America were based on suspicion. Most Latin American countries remained politically unstable, suffering from wide gaps between rich and poor and governed by repressive military dictatorships. For now, American policymakers were more concerned about preventing Soviet military influence from creeping into the hemisphere than in offering economic assistance to needy neighbors.

The Cold War also shaped American policy in the Middle East. After World War II many Jews who had survived Nazi concentration camps resettled in British-controlled Palestine. In 1947 the British, weakened by World War II, turned over control of Palestine to the United Nations, which voted to partition the region into separate Jewish and Arab states. Violence between Arabs and Jews escalated as each side tried to maximize its territorial position in advance of the British partition. The president's military advisers, including Secretary of State Marshall and Defense Secretary James V. Forrestal, feared that recognition of the Jewish state of Israel would anger Arab oil-producing nations. On an emotional level, however, the president empathized with the suffering of Jews during World War II. And as a practical matter, since Stalin had already announced his support for Israel, Truman worried about the possibility of a close Soviet–Israel relationship that would exclude the United States. Truman also respected the political clout of Jewish voters at home. "In all of my political experience," Truman remarked during the campaign of 1948, "I don't ever recall the Arab vote swinging a close election."

On May 14, 1948, Israel declared its independence. Within a few hours the United States recognized the new state. Less than a week later five Arab neighbors invaded Israel, which beat back the attack and expanded its control over territory designated for the Palestinian Arab State. Jordan and Egypt occupied the other parts of the territory. Over half the Palestinian population fled or was expelled. Between six hundred thousand and seven hundred thousand Palestinians became refugees, forced to live in squalid conditions in the West Bank and along the Gaza Strip. The "Palestinian issue" would remain a source of anger and frustration in the Middle East for years to come.

The Soviets matched Western initiatives by intensifying their domination of Eastern Europe. In October 1949 Stalin created a separate government in East Germany, the German Democratic Republic. Moscow tightened its economic grip by sponsoring the Council for Mutual Economic Assistance or COMECON (1949) and its military grip by forming the Warsaw Pact (1955). The Soviets poured massive aid into Poland, Czechoslovakia, and Bulgaria to accelerate industrialization and increase Soviet control. The only exception to Soviet domination was Yugoslavia, which stubbornly resisted Soviet influence and gradually managed to develop as an independent socialist state.

Debating Containment   The adoption of the containment policy thrust upon the United States political and military responsibilities as a "world policeman" that went far beyond anything ever contemplated by the American people. It also raised new and troubling questions that went to the heart of American identity. Could the nation adapt to the demands of total war without losing its democratic identity? Many conservatives feared that the new military bureaucracy threatened to regiment American life and take the nation down the same road as Nazi Germany. "We must not let our fear of Communism blind us to the danger of military domination," complained a Republican congressman. Conservatives also feared that an expansive foreign policy would distort national and international priorities. Powerful Republican Senator Robert Taft of Ohio observed that the traditional purpose of U.S. involvement in the world was "to maintain the liberty of our people" rather than "reform the entire world or spread sweetness and light and economic prosperity to peoples who have lived and worked out their own salvation for centuries."

A few voices on the left joined the chorus of criticism, though often for different reasons. In a series of newspaper columns later published in book form as *The Cold War*, journalist Walter Lippmann charged that containment would increase executive power at the expense of the other branches of government and divert energy and resources away from domestic needs. Most of all, he argued that it would militarize American foreign policy and force it to support corrupt dictators.

The administration argued that a new era of total war required the country to take unprecedented steps to defend its interests. Total war could not be confined to the battlefield, but required the full participation of the home front as well. All of the nation's resources had to be mobilized to defeat the enemy, blurring the line between civilian and military. Every citizen was a soldier, responsible for defending the American way of life. In an age of total war, Americans had to abandon traditional objections to a standing army and enlarged federal power. "Wars are no longer fought solely by armed forces," explained Admiral Ernest J. King. "Directly or indirectly, the whole citizenry and the entire resources of the nation go to war." Since the United States faced an enemy possessing a "messianic" ideology, it needed to be prepared to fight at any time. The greatest threat to American liberty lay not in the expansion of state power produced by national security needs, but in the threat from abroad.

IN THE SHADOW OF FDR, 1945–1948

Truman could not match his success in winning support for his Cold War policies abroad with similar achievements in domestic policy. Postwar prosperity, concern over the administration's anti-Soviet policies, and a divisive debate over civil rights exposed cracks in the Democratic coalition. Continuing currents of conservatism headed off Truman's liberal proposals. Truman managed to pull together the New Deal coalition to score a surprising victory in the 1948 election. But the Cold War drained reformist energy at home and prevented Truman from expanding Roosevelt's agenda.

The Economic Shock of Rapid Reconversion

"We are completely unprepared for a Japanese collapse," journalist I. F. Stone wrote in August 1945, a few weeks before the war ended, "and unless we act quickly and wisely [we] may face an economic collapse ourselves." As Stone had predicted, the sudden end of the war sent shock waves through the American economy. Within a month the government canceled $35 billion in war contracts and slashed war-related production by 60 percent. The cuts prompted massive layoffs. Within ten days of the Japanese surrender 2.7 million men and women lost their jobs. Economists predicted that more than 10 million Americans would be thrown out of work by peace. At the same time a flood of servicemen returned home looking for civilian jobs. The government released almost 7 million men and women from the armed forces by April 1946. The dislocations raised widespread fear that the nation was headed toward another depression.

Soaring inflation added to public anxiety. During the war, speculation had pushed property values and stock prices to new highs. Between 1941 and 1945 the national debt climbed from $61 billion to $253 billion; government spending rose from $9 billion to $98 billion. Savings accounts multiplied, increasing liquid assets of individuals and corporations to almost $200 billion. A postwar rush to spend the savings threatened to unleash a spiral of rising prices. In August 1945 Office of Price Administration (OPA) chief Chester Bowles said the nation was in "one of the most dangerous periods in our country's economic history."

Bowles and many other liberals wanted Truman to limit inflation damage by continuing wartime price controls. But a coalition of Republicans and conservative Democrats in Congress, eager to eliminate most wartime controls, slashed the OPA budget. Truman fought the effort, but he lacked the votes in Congress to keep the OPA alive. The first week after controls ended in July 1946, prices increased 16 percent. Steak increased in price from fifty-five cents to one dollar a pound. Staples such as milk, butter, and vegetables all showed huge increases overnight.

The combination of high prices and job losses squeezed organized labor. During the war labor unions had for the most part honored a voluntary no-strike pledge. With the war ended and prices rising, labor demanded steep wage increases. By October 1945 half a million workers went out on strike. In April 1946 John

L. Lewis (see page 1023) led four hundred thousand coal miners out of the pits. For forty days the strike cut off the nation's supply of fuel and threatened European recovery. On May 21 Truman ordered government troops to take over the mines. "Let Truman dig coal with his bayonets," Lewis snarled.

The Republicans, capitalizing on the pervasive dissatisfaction with rising prices, labor strikes, and Cold War anxieties, pounced on the hapless Democrats in the 1946 congressional elections. Their campaign slogan was as simple as it was effective: "Had enough?" The Republicans gained control of both houses of Congress for the first time since 1930. Among the new members of the class of '46 were Representative Richard Nixon of California and Senator Joseph McCarthy of Wisconsin.

Harry Truman and the Divided Democrats

Truman's plummeting popularity and the Republican success in the 1946 election left liberals sour and disillusioned. The Cold War with Russia and the conservative resurgence at home frustrated their hopes for the postwar world. Most blamed Truman for their plight, agreeing with the *Nation's* characterization of the president as a "weak, baffled, angry man." Columnists Joseph and Stewart Alsop, looking toward the 1948 election, predicted, "If Truman is nominated, he will be forced to wage the loneliest campaign in history."

Truman, the last American president to have not attended college, lacked the grace and magnetism liberals had come to expect from the White House. Born on May 8, 1884, in Lamar, Missouri, Truman spent most of his early years in the farm country of western Missouri. After high school he moved to Kansas City, where he worked as a banker. In 1906 he returned to help with the family farm. Over the next eleven years, while keeping the farm afloat, Truman devoted considerable effort to courting Bess Wallace, whom he later married.

After a stint in the army during World War I Truman set up a haberdashery and sold men's clothing in Kansas City until a steep recession in 1921 destroyed the business. A few years shy of his fortieth birthday, he confronted a bleak future: He had to contend with a failed business and the real threat of bankruptcy, and he had few career options. Then one day in the summer of 1921, a representative of the notorious Pendergast political machine, which dominated Kansas City politics, invited Truman to run for county judge. Truman won election in 1922 and served on the court for most of the next twelve years, struggling to satisfy his patron while also providing good government for his constituents.

In 1934 Truman won election to the U.S. Senate. Many people, including his fellow senators, treated him with contempt, dismissing him as the "Senator from Pendergast." Truman cast aside the criticism and threw himself into his work. With the nation mired in depression, Truman supported most of Franklin Roosevelt's New Deal agenda. It was during World War II, as head of a committee to investigate the national defense program, that Truman distinguished himself and caught the attention of party leaders. That exposure, along with his border-state background, helped gain him the vice-presidential nomination in 1944 when the Democrats were looking for a compromise choice.

In April 1945 a cerebral hemorrhage brought Franklin Roosevelt's life to a tragic end and elevated Truman to the presidency. "For a time," observed a journalist, "he walked in the long shadow of the dead President." Compared with his mythic predecessor's grace, dignity, and patrician vision, Truman seemed a provincial man who was incapable of transcending his modest roots. Compounding the problem, Truman frequently appointed to important government jobs his unremarkable political friends, who lacked the stature of the men who had served Roosevelt. The journalist I. F. Stone put it bluntly: "The Truman era was the era of the moocher. The place was full of Wimpys who could be had for a hamburger."

Most of these criticisms were unfair. Unlike Roosevelt, Truman had to contend with a Republican Congress determined to reverse liberal gains achieved since the 1930s. The Republican Eightieth Congress frustrated most of Truman's domestic agenda, rejecting his appeals for public housing, federal aid to education, and relaxed immigration quotas. Fearing continued Democratic dominance of the White House, it passed a constitutional amendment limiting the president to two terms. In 1948, after failing twice to override Truman vetoes, Congress finally mustered enough votes to pass a large tax cut on personal income. Most significant, Congress passed, over Truman's veto, the Labor-Management Relations Act of 1947, better known as the Taft-Hartley Act. The measure outlawed the closed shop, which had required that all hiring be done through a union hall; permitted states to pass so-called right-to-work laws allowing nonunion members to work in unionized plants; empowered authorities to issue federal injunctions against strikes that jeopardized public health or safety; and gave the president power to stave off strikes by imposing "cooling-off" periods of up to eighty days. The legislation also required union leaders to swear that they were not communists. "We have got to break with the corrupting idea that we can legislate prosperity, legislate equality, legislate opportunity," declared Senator Robert Taft, the chief spokesman for economic conservatism.

These political setbacks further frustrated liberals, who were unanimous in their disaffection with Truman's domestic leadership but divided over how to respond to Cold War tensions. Many liberals, who called themselves Progressives, believed that continued American–Soviet cooperation was essential to the preservation of the wartime antifascist alliance. Believing that legitimate security needs inspired Stalin's actions in Eastern Europe, they opposed Truman's growing hard line with the Soviets. Many Progressives also hoped to rebuild the left-of-center Popular Front of the mid-1930s by forging a powerful coalition that would include labor, small farmers, intellectuals, communists, and socialists. Only by combining to fight the forces of reaction, they argued, could liberals retain power in the postwar period.

Progressives looked to former Vice President Henry Wallace for leadership. In September 1946 Truman fired Wallace from his position as secretary of agriculture after Wallace criticized the administration's growing hard line with the Soviets. Two months later Wallace announced that he would run for president on a third-party Progressive ticket. Few people believed that Wallace could win the election, but many Democrats feared that he could siphon liberal votes away from Truman in key states. In an effort to keep liberal support Truman championed an aggressive domestic reform agenda, calling for a far-reaching housing program, stronger rent control, a sweeping enlargement of social security coverage, and federal aid to education. Before Congress had a chance to act, he went on the offensive, blaming Republicans for not supporting his program.

Truman made support for civil rights a centerpiece of his fighting liberal program. In 1946 Truman had established the President's Committee on Civil Rights, the first presidential committee ever created to investigate race relations in America. Later that year the committee released its report, *To Secure These Rights,* which called for an end to segregation and discrimination and advocated legislation to abolish lynching and the poll tax. In February 1948 Truman hailed the message as "an American charter of human freedom" and asked Congress to support the committee's recommendations. In July Truman signed Executive Order 9981, which set up procedures for ending racial discrimination in the military. Though not implemented until the Korean War, the order symbolized Truman's commitment to civil rights. The *Chicago Defender,* a black newspaper, called the order "unprecedented since the time of Lincoln." In July the Democratic party included a strong civil rights plank in its platform.

Truman's advocacy of civil rights in 1948 exposed the deep ideological and sectional strains in his party. The New Deal coalition consisted of groups that shared a common sense of class solidarity but were deeply divided on social issues such as race relations. During the 1930s, fearing a possible white backlash, Roosevelt avoided tackling sensitive civil rights issues. But the war had elevated racial tension in both the North and the South and had increased white anxiety about the future of race relations. Industrial expansion lured African-Americans to the North to fill the desperate labor shortage. During the 1940s Chicago experienced a 77 percent increase in its black population. In Detroit, where Ford, Chrysler, and General Motors served as the "arsenal of democracy," the African-American population doubled. To preserve the whiteness of their neighborhoods, many locals refused to sell goods to blacks, established restrictive covenants, and used intimidation to discourage their movement away from black enclaves. In June 1943 race riots in Harlem and Detroit devastated swaths of the urban landscape.

African-Americans—many of whom anticipated a "double victory" over fascism abroad and racism at home—grew less patient with rhetorical and symbolic actions. The National Association for the Advancement of Colored People (NAACP) railed against lynching and sought a federal law making it illegal. At the same time black veterans began to challenge the disfranchisement of African-Americans. In 1944 the Supreme Court in *Smith* v. *Allwright* struck down the white Democratic primary. Signs of growing black activism, combined with signs that the federal government would support the cause, produced a wave of anxiety and fear across the white South.

Rejected by the national party, southern delegates stormed out of the Democratic convention, formed the States' Rights Democratic, or "Dixiecrat" Party, and nominated Governor J. Strom Thurmond of South Carolina for the presidency. "We stand for the segregation of the races and the racial integrity of each race," the platform declared. For his part Thurmond avoided direct racial appeals and instead focused on states' rights. The civil rights program and the expansion of federal power that it required had "its origin in communist ideology" and sought "to excite race and class hatred" and thereby "create the chaos and confusion which leads to communism."

The 1948 Election   With little fanfare and even less debate, the Republicans nominated New York Governor Thomas E. Dewey, who had run a strong race against Roosevelt in 1944 and seemed certain to beat Truman. Their convention, which was the first ever televised, picked

California Governor Earl Warren for the second spot on the ticket and adopted a platform promising a foreign policy based on "friendly firmness which welcomes cooperation but spurns appeasement."

Confident of victory, Dewey spent much time campaigning for other Republican candidates in states that were not crucial to his own election. Ignoring Truman and avoiding specific issues, he concentrated on convincing voters that he was an efficient administrator who could bring unity to the country and effectiveness to its foreign policy. According to one observer, Dewey sought the presidency "with the humorless calculation of a Certified Public Accountant in pursuit of the Holy Grail."

While Dewey tried to stay above the partisan fray, Truman waged a tough, bareknuckled campaign. The president went on a whirlwind, transcontinental railroad trip in which he gave 351 speeches to an estimated 12 million people. He blamed the "do-nothing, good-for-nothing 80th Congress" for everything from high prices to poor health care. "If you send another Republican to Washington," he told audiences, "you're a bigger bunch of suckers than I think you are."

Truman on the Campaign Trail   Considered the underdog in 1948, President Truman ran an aggressive campaign, touring the country on a train called the *Ferdinand Magellan*. The train had 17 cars, room enough for Truman, his family, his political advisors, and journalists who documented the "whistle-stop" campaign. Truman covered 31,000 miles and spread his message to an estimated 12 million Americans. Surrounded by the press, Harry and Bess Truman prepare to pull out of Washington's Union Station in September 1948. *(Corbis.)*

Truman tied himself to Roosevelt's legacy, reminding voters that the Democratic Party had led the nation through depression and world war. He peppered his speeches with references to "Republican gluttons of privilege" who had "stuck a pitch fork in the farmer's back" and "begun to nail the American consumer to the wall with spikes of greed." His speeches pictured politics as a struggle between the "people," represented by the Democrats, and the "special interests," represented by Republicans. Enthusiastic crowds shouted, "Give 'em hell, Harry!" Truman responded, "I don't give 'em hell. I just tell the truth and they think it's hell."

Despite his energetic campaign, Truman lagged behind Dewey in the polls. The day before the election, the Gallup poll gave Dewey 49.5 percent of the popular vote and Truman 44.5 percent. On election night, long before the votes were in, the *Chicago Tribune* ran its front-page announcement: "DEWEY DEFEATS TRUMAN."

Instead, Truman scored the most dramatic upset victory in the history of presidential elections, winning 24.1 million votes to Dewey's 22 million (see map below). How did Truman pull off such a surprising victory? First, both Wallace and Thurmond were hurt by the public's reluctance to waste their votes on a third-party candidate with little chance of victory. At the same time, their campaigns actually helped Truman. Wallace was openly supported by the communists, and Truman denounced him, so the president was much less vulnerable than he might otherwise have been to charges of being "soft" on communism. The Dixiecrat rebellion against Truman's civil rights program encouraged the loyalty of liberals and most black voters, many of whom might otherwise have been attracted to Wallace or even to Dewey.

The Election of 1948

Thomas Dewey was the favorite in the polls, in large part due to the fracturing of the Democratic Party as Dixiecrats and Progressives rejected Truman's domestic and international policies. While several states in the Deep South supported J. Strom Thurmond's states' rights and segregationist platform, Progressive candidate Henry Wallace failed to win a single state. Truman's aggressive campaign, in which he castigated the "do-nothing" Republican Congress, helped him pull out the unlikely victory.

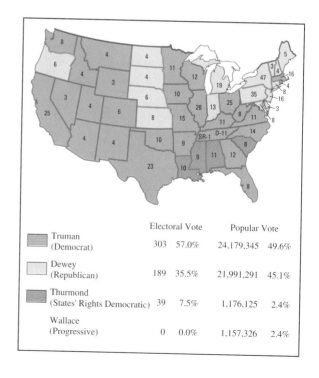

	Electoral Vote		Popular Vote	
Truman (Democrat)	303	57.0%	24,179,345	49.6%
Dewey (Republican)	189	35.5%	21,991,291	45.1%
Thurmond (States' Rights Democratic)	39	7.5%	1,176,125	2.4%
Wallace (Progressive)	0	0.0%	1,157,326	2.4%

Second, Dewey's bland campaign failed to excite voters. Dewey was vague and unclear on the issues, and he ignited little grass-roots enthusiasm. Fewer Republicans came to the polls in 1948 than in either 1940 or 1944.

Finally, the election demonstrated the enduring appeal of the New Deal. "I talked about voting for Dewey all summer, but when the time came I just couldn't do it," confessed one farmer. "I remembered the depression and all the other things that had come to me under the Democrats." The Democrats, by picking up nine seats in the Senate and seventy-five in the House, regained control of Congress. "[T]he party that Roosevelt formed has survived his death," Walter Lippmann observed, "and is without question the dominant force in American politics."

The Vital Center Although he won the election by a slim margin, Truman viewed his victory as a mandate for liberalism. The president outlined his ambitious social and economic program in his 1949 State of the Union message. "Every segment of our population and every individual," he declared, "has a right to expect from our Government a fair deal." In the most ambitious burst of reform since 1935, Congress increased the minimum wage from forty to seventy-five cents per hour, authorized the construction of low-income housing, extended rent controls, expanded social security coverage, and approved a displaced persons act admitting some four hundred thousand refugees to the United States. Congress, however, showed little desire to support Truman's calls for new programs that moved beyond the New Deal. It rejected the president's proposals for establishing federal aid to education, creating a civil rights division within the Justice Department, instituting national health insurance, and repealing Taft-Hartley.

To some extent, Truman's Fair Deal was a victim of the Cold War, which drained attention and resources away from domestic initiatives. The Cold War also strengthened the power of conservatives, whose support Truman needed to maintain his foreign and defense policies. At the same time, the promise of prosperity sapped public enthusiasm for government intervention.

Truman may have governed in the shadow of Roosevelt, but his administration produced a limited redefinition of America liberalism and marked an important shift in the evolution of the Democratic Party. The liberalism that emerged in America after World War II rested on a foundation of shared assumptions forged during the depression and World War II. Arthur Schlesinger, Jr., in a popular book published in 1949, referred to the new liberalism as *The Vital Center*, which he defined as a middle way between the tyranny of the left and the right.

Three basic assumptions informed the Vital Center. The "gospel of economic growth" formed the first pillar. By 1949 most Americans believed that economic growth would eliminate class division, guarantee social harmony, and provide a constant source of revenue for necessary social programs. This faith in capitalism marked an important shift from the New Deal. During the 1930s many liberals had been convinced that the Great Depression signaled the death of capitalism. They spent most of the decade experimenting with different plans for restructuring the economy. All included large-scale government planning and controls. But enormous productivity during the war, when the GNP doubled in four years, revitalized liberal faith in capitalism and fostered new confidence in government's ability to regulate the economy. Full employment was possible, liberal economists believed, and they now felt they knew how to use their tools to achieve that end.

Foreign policy issues had been largely absent from the New Deal agenda, but the question of America's role in the world was central to the Vital Center. Between 1946 and 1948 Truman shifted liberals and the Democratic Party toward an aggressive internationalism based on fear of Soviet expansion and an expansive definition of American interests. Truman's victory in the 1948 election signaled the triumph of liberal anticommunism.

Prosperity served as the third pillar of the Vital Center. Economic growth and the constant tax revenue that it provided would give the nation the resources it needed to fund necessary social programs at home while also paying for the military needs of the Cold War. The nation, in other words, could have both guns and butter. Prosperity also guaranteed social harmony by muting ideological differences and by blurring the lines of potential conflict. Everyone benefited from abundance: Business reaped high profits; labor received better wages; farmers earned larger incomes; and the poor—both black and white—gained the opportunity to lead better lives.

In the end, the Vital Center created unrealistic expectations about the possibilities of change and sowed the seeds of dissent in the 1960s. Though general prosperity increased the quality of life for most Americans, it did not produce meaningful redistribution of income. Economic growth not only failed to erase class division, but it was also unable to mute ideological conflict in America. At the same time, the promise of gradual reform failed to satisfy the rising expectations of African-Americans, who demanded an end to segregation in the South. The bipolar view of the world, born in the heat of the Cold War, quickly became obsolete as nationalist movements in the Third World complicated the global balance of power.

THE COLD WAR HEATS UP, 1950–1952

Just as U.S.–Soviet tension stabilized in Europe with the creation of NATO in 1949, the Cold War expanded to Asia. With the "fall" of China to the communists in 1949, American policymakers began rethinking U.S. defense priorities in Asia. The most dramatic policy decision occurred in June 1950, following the invasion of South Korea by communist North Korea. Viewing the attack as part of a larger Soviet design to challenge American interests around the globe, Truman reacted swiftly, sending American troops to repel the invasion. The U.S. response frustrated North Korean hopes of unifying the peninsula under communist rule. But a bitter dispute between Truman and General Douglas MacArthur raised troubling questions about America's containment experiment.

The Cold War Spreads to Asia   When World War II ended China was torn between Jiang Jieshi's (Chiang Kai-shek's) Nationalists in the south and Mao Zedong's (Mao Tse-tung's) Communists in the north. At first the Nationalists had the upper hand, but Jiang's corrupt and incompetent government failed to inspire public support or stem the tide of Chinese communism. In 1945 and 1946 Truman, anxious to work out a peaceful settlement between Jiang and Mao, sent General George C. Marshall to China in a failed attempt to negotiate a compromise. U.S. efforts continued, but by 1949 Truman had grown weary of Jiang's refusals to undertake necessary reforms or attack corruption in his government. The president wrote in his diary that Jiang's government "was one of the most corrupt and inefficient that ever made an attempt to govern a country."

Deciding there was little the United States could do to salvage the noncommunist government, Truman stopped all aid to Jiang in 1949. Shortly afterward, Jiang's forces collapsed, sending the Nationalist leader scurrying to the offshore island of Formosa (Taiwan), where Nationalists set up an independent Republic of China. The Soviet Union consolidated its power in Asia by extending diplomatic recognition to Mao's Communist government and signing a "mutual assistance" agreement.

The Communist victory precipitated a firestorm of criticism at home against those responsible for "losing China." Friends of Jiang in the Republican Party complained that Democrats had let the Communists win. Led by publisher Henry Luce, the "China Lobby," an influential group that advocated U.S. intervention in China, wondered aloud why the Truman administration had stopped supplying weapons to Jiang after the Marshall mission of 1946. Years later, John F. Kennedy and Lyndon Johnson, remembering the bruising assault Truman endured for "losing China," would determine never to lose another inch to the communists.

The emotional reaction to the Communist triumph in China focused U.S. attention on Asia. At the end of World War II the United States occupied Japan and, under the leadership of General Douglas MacArthur, transformed the vanquished country into a model Western democracy in which women could vote, trade unions were encouraged, and land was redistributed among the peasants. Wanting to make sure that Japan would never reemerge as a military threat, the United States wrote a constitution, adopted in 1946, that renounced war, promising that "land, sea and air forces, as well as other war potential, will never be maintained." The growing communist threat in Asia, however, forced a dramatic shift in American policy. Now viewing Japan as a potential military counterweight against China, policymakers negotiated a new treaty in 1951 that terminated the U.S. occupation and conceded to Japan "the inherent right of individual or collective self-defense."

The "fall" of China also transformed a local nationalist struggle against French rule in Indochina into a globally strategic battleground. During World War II Roosevelt had expressed support for Vietnamese nationalist forces led by Ho Chi Minh, a communist educated in Paris and Moscow, and called for an end to French colonial rule. After Jiang's collapse, American policy shifted. Fearing that a communist "victory" in Indochina would become a sweep of Southeast Asia and tilt the global balance of power, the United States abandoned its pretense of neutrality and openly endorsed French policy in Asia. In 1950, when the Soviet Union and China extended diplomatic recognition to Ho's government, Truman supplied military aid to the French. America had taken its first step into the Vietnam quagmire.

While debating the consequences of the "fall" of China, Americans experienced another Cold War setback. On September 23, 1949, Truman issued a terse press release: "We have evidence that within recent weeks an atomic explosion occurred in the U.S.S.R." Though the administration publicly downplayed the significance of the Soviet breakthrough, it realized that, in Vandenberg's words, "This is now a different world." Since the United States could not match the Soviets in manpower, military planners had depended on "the bomb" to deter Soviet aggression.

Together the "fall" of China and the Soviet nuclear test forced American policymakers to rethink U.S. strategic doctrine. A fierce debate erupted in the administration over the development of a hydrogen bomb, potentially a thousand times more powerful than the atomic weapons that had destroyed Hiroshima and Nagasaki. J. Robert Oppenheimer, the "father" of the atomic bomb, questioned the morality of such a powerful weapon and feared the consequences of an escalating arms race. "We may be likened to two scorpions in a bottle," he wrote, "each capable of killing the other, but only at the risk of his own life." In January 1950 Truman sided with German-born physicist Edward Teller, who argued that the Soviets would eventually develop the weapon and use it to blackmail the United States.

In April 1950 after months of deliberation, the National Security Council recommended that the president initiate a massive rebuilding of both nuclear and conventional military forces to confront the new Soviet nuclear threat. The report, National Security Council Memorandum 68 (NSC-68), presented a frightening portrait of a Soviet system driven by "a new fanatic faith" that "seeks to impose its absolute authority over the rest of the world." To intimidate the Russians and inspire confidence in America's allies, the report called for an extraordinary increase in the defense budget from $13 billion to $50 billion a year.

On November 1, 1952, the United States exploded the first H-bomb, obliterating an uninhabited island in the Pacific. The bomb blast created a fireball 5 miles high and 4 miles wide and left a hole in the Pacific floor a mile long and 175 feet deep. The following year the Russians exploded their first hydrogen bomb. Britain and France soon joined the nuclear club. The arms race had entered a frightening new phase.

The Korean War: From Invasion to Stalemate

In January 1950 Secretary of State Dean Acheson omitted any mention of Korea when he outlined the "defensive perimeter" that the United States would protect in Asia. At the end of the Second World War the United States and the Soviets had temporarily divided the Korean peninsula, previously dominated by Japan, at the thirty-eighth parallel. Cold War tensions, however, ended any hope of unification. The Russians installed Kim Il Sung to lead the communist north, while Syngman Rhee, a conservative nationalist, emerged as the American-sponsored ruler in the south. Korea was not a top American priority, however, and the United States withdrew its troops from Korea in June 1949.

The scenario changed on June 25, 1950, when 110,000 North Korean soldiers crossed the thirty-eighth parallel and overpowered South Korean forces within hours. The circumstances surrounding the invasion remain unclear, but documents in Soviet archives, made available to historians at the end of the Cold War, suggest that the North Koreans, not the Soviets, pushed for the invasion. Truman viewed the situation in a dramatically different light. He interpreted the invasion as a Soviet-engineered assault, the opening salvo in a broader Soviet attack on America's global allies. With memories of Western appeasement of Hitler fresh in his mind, Truman immediately ordered American air and naval forces to support the South

Koreans. "If this was allowed to go unchallenged," he wrote in his memoirs, "it would mean a third world war, just as similar incidents had brought on the second world war." Two days later, on Tuesday, June 27, 1950, Truman asked the United Nations Security Council to condemn North Korea as an aggressor and to send forces to South Korea. The resolution passed because the Soviet delegate, who could have used his veto to defeat the measure, was boycotting the meetings. The defense effort was theoretically a UN venture, but in the end the United States provided half the ground troops and most of the sea and air support.

In the first few weeks it appeared that the North Korean forces might win a decisive victory. They pushed the South Koreans and the entire U.S. Eighth Army all the way to the peninsula's tip near the port city of Pusan. Then, on September 15, General Douglas MacArthur turned the war around with a daring amphibious invasion behind enemy lines at Inchon, near the South Korean capital of Seoul. At the same time the American and South Korean armies counterattacked in force at Pusan. The dual tactic fooled the North Koreans, who suffered heavy losses and quickly retreated beyond the thirty-eighth parallel. By the end of the month American troops had liberated Seoul and reestablished Syngman Rhee's government in the south (see map on page 1080).

The dramatic victory on the ground raised hopes that U.S. forces could advance beyond the thirty-eighth parallel, overthrow Kim Il Sung, and unite Korea under a noncommunist government. On September 27 Truman authorized MacArthur to cross into North Korea. Within a few weeks, MacArthur's forces had advanced within fifty miles of the Yalu River, the boundary between Korea and the Chinese province of Manchuria.

When the Communist Chinese condemned the U.S. invasion of North Korea and threatened retaliation, Truman began to have second thoughts about his strategy. In October the president flew to Wake Island in the Pacific to consult with MacArthur. The general assured Truman that the Chinese Communists, despite their buildup of troops on the border and their loud warnings, would not intervene in the war, which MacArthur insisted was over. Acheson agreed with MacArthur's assessment. "I should think it would be sheer madness for the Chinese to intervene," he said. The president, uplifted by MacArthur's optimistic assessment and Acheson's unequivocal support, returned home confident that the war had been won.

MacArthur and Acheson were wrong. On November 27, 1950, a Chinese army of four hundred thousand men armed with Soviet tanks and aircraft attacked the American forces in North Korea. By Christmas the massive wave of Chinese troops had pushed MacArthur south of the thirty-eighth parallel again. Shaken, the general pressured Truman for permission to attack Chinese military bases in the north. This time Truman rejected MacArthur's strategy, fearing that direct attack on Chinese installations would antagonize the Russians and precipitate a global conflict. In January 1951 the U.S. Eighth Army halted the communist advance, and by March pushed back to the thirty-eighth parallel. The war then bogged down, with neither side able to gain the advantage.

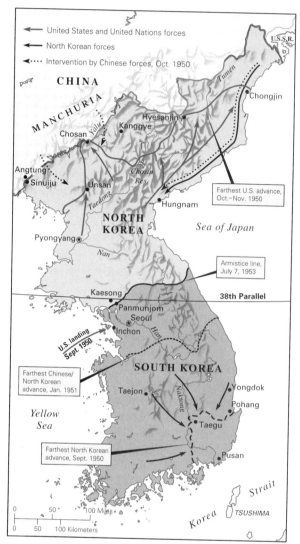

The Korean War, 1950–1953

After the initial wave of North Korean troops swept through the South in the summer of 1950, United Nations' forces under General Douglas MacArthur countered at Inchon and Pusan. By November, UN troops occupied most of Korea, but Chinese troops quickly repulsed the advance and pushed MacArthur's men south of the thirty-eighth parallel. Although talks to end the Korean War began in the summer of 1951, both sides agreed the fighting would continue until they signed the armistice—two years later.

The Truman-MacArthur Bout and the Trials of Containment

With the public growing weary of war and the threat of continued bloody fighting, Truman looked for a diplomatic solution to the conflict. MacArthur opposed a settlement and insisted that U.S. forces must attack Chinese bases north of the thirty-eighth parallel. He criticized his civilian commander-in-chief in the press, sabotaged Truman's efforts to achieve a negotiated settlement, and sent long-winded telegrams to veterans' groups outlining his own personal foreign policy for Asia. In April he wrote a letter to Republican House minority leader Joseph J. Martin of Massachusetts denouncing the stalemate. As MacArthur had hoped, Martin read the letter on the floor of the House. Truman, fed up with his general's insubordination, exploded. On April 11, 1951, he relieved MacArthur of his command.

Truman miscalculated the warrior's grip on the public imagination. Within twelve days the White House received over twenty-seven thousand angry letters protesting the firing. MacArthur returned from Korea to a hero's welcome in San Francisco, and millions crowded downtown Manhattan for one of New York's largest-ever ticker-tape parades. Republican leaders clamored for a congressional investigation and threatened to impeach Truman. On April 19 MacArthur gave an impassioned farewell address to a joint session of Congress. He concluded by repeating a line from a West Point ballad: "Old soldiers never die, they just fade away." The words moved many congressmen to tears.

The general's appeal transcended mere sentimentality. The response to MacArthur's critique of Washington's handling of the Korean conflict revealed the frustration and confusion of a nation struggling to adjust to the idea of a limited war. Seventy years old when the Korean War started, MacArthur had been trained in the military doctrine of total war. His experience in two world wars taught him that "In war, there is no substitute for victory."

Truman and his advisers argued that the Cold War forced America to develop a new strategy suited to fighting limited wars. MacArthur, they argued, failed to recognize that the real enemy was not North Korea but the Soviet Union. The fighting in Korea was a strategic diversion, a Russian maneuver to draw American strength away from Europe. Larger strategic goals, namely containing Moscow, required the United States to avoid squandering its resources on the pursuit of "victory" in proxy wars in remote places.

The administration won the debate with MacArthur, but the questions raised by the confrontation would continue to haunt policymakers. Americans accustomed to waging total war and reaping the benefits of total victory never fully adjusted to the demands of limited war. Containment required Americans to settle for fighting limited, protracted wars, seeking diplomatic solutions rather than military victory, and enduring the tribulation of an uncertain peace.

Consequences of Korea

The stalemated fighting in Korea would drag on, amid cease-fire talks, for more than a year, ending soon after Truman left office. Despite its limited nature, the war resulted in 36,940 American deaths and left 103,284 American soldiers wounded. It also brought significant change within the United States. It produced a huge escalation of defense spending from approximately $14 billion in 1949 to $44 billion in 1953. As government spending created millions of new jobs, unemployment dropped to its lowest level in years. Federal expenditures, together with special tax incentives, encouraged industries to expand production. From 1950 to 1954 steel capacity increased by 24 percent, electrical generating capacity by 50 percent, and aluminum capacity by 100 percent.

The Korean War accelerated the desegregation of the armed services. By mid-1950 the navy and air force had taken strides toward desegregation, but the army still maintained separate black and white units. Critics had complained that segregation, besides being morally wrong, was also wasteful and inefficient. Korea exposed another problem with segregation: assigning African-Americans to non-combat duty led whites to suffer a disproportionate share of casualties. When white troops experienced heavy losses in the early days of the war, field commanders in

Korea broke with existing policy and used black soldiers as replacements. In March 1951 the Pentagon announced the integration of all training facilities in the United States. By the end of the war nearly all African-American soldiers were serving in integrated units.

The war continued the expansion of presidential power begun under Roosevelt. When North Korea invaded, Truman made a unilateral decision to intervene, acting with neither Congress's approval nor its declaration of war. Only after he had authorized American force did Truman meet with Congress to inform members about what he had done.

THE POLITICS OF FEAR, 1945–1952

The Korean War intensified suspicions of communist subversion at home. Americans viewed communism as a double threat. Ideologically, communist doctrine challenged basic American notions of private property and individual rights. Strategically, its chief supporter, the Soviet Union, was engaged in a global struggle against the United States. Rumors that Soviet spies had infiltrated the upper echelons of American society, especially government, ignited a wildfire of fear and suspicion. Anxious Americans rushed to prove their loyalty and to punish potential subversives, who seemed to be un-American. Ferreting out disloyalty became a duty of both the citizenry and the government. No one exploited these fears more effectively than Wisconsin Senator Joseph McCarthy.

The Second Red Scare   In March 1945 government agents found numerous classified government documents in the Manhattan offices of the allegedly procommunist *Amerasia* magazine. A year later a Canadian investigation led to the arrest of twenty-two men and women for passing classified U.S. documents to the Soviets. Together the cases proved that Soviet spies had gained access to secret government documents. "The disloyalty of American Communists is no longer a matter of conjecture," declared FBI head J. Edgar Hoover.

Americans cried out for protection from communist influence in government. In an attempt to quell public concern, President Truman, in March 1947, issued Executive Order 9835, which established the Federal Employee Loyalty Program. The Truman program allowed dismissal of any federal employee whenever "reasonable grounds exist for belief that the person involved is disloyal." The question of loyalty and disloyalty touched on a recurring issue in American history: What does it mean to be an American? Most loyalty review boards imposed a narrow definition of loyal citizenship, using the fear of communism to intimidate people who had different ideas. Civil rights activists came under intense scrutiny, and homosexuals were automatically dismissed as security threats. The head of one government loyalty board noted, "The fact that a person believes in racial equality doesn't prove he's a Communist, but it certainly makes you look twice, doesn't it?"

Truman also used a high-profile court case to convince the public that his administration was tough on communism. In July 1948 the administration charged eleven top communists with violating the Smith Act of 1940, which made it a crime to conspire to "advocate and teach" the violent overthrow of government. After ten months of trial and deliberation, a lower court declared the Smith Act constitutional and the communists guilty. The Supreme Court, in *Dennis* v. *U.S.* (1951), upheld the conviction, clearing the way for prosecution of other communist leaders.

In perhaps the most talked-about loyalty case, in August 1948 Whittaker Chambers, an editor at *Time* magazine, accused Alger Hiss, who had served as a high-ranking aide to Franklin Roosevelt at Yalta, of having been a communist. Chambers claimed that in 1938 Hiss had given him microfilm of classified State Department documents. For many conservatives, Hiss was a symbol of the generation of young, idealistic, Ivy League liberals who had masterminded the New Deal. By attacking him they hoped to undermine faith in the Democratic Party and remove some of the luster from Roosevelt's memory.

To prove his charges Chambers produced microfilm of supposedly secret documents taken from a hollowed-out pumpkin on his Maryland farm. (The documents, quickly labeled the "Pumpkin Papers," were later revealed to contain information on navy life rafts and fire extinguishers.) Testifying before a grand jury in New York, Hiss denied Chambers's charges. Since the statute of limitations on espionage had expired, Hiss was indicted for perjury. After one mistrial Hiss was found guilty in a second trial and sentenced to five years in jail. More than any other event, the Hiss trial convinced many Americans that the Roosevelt and Truman administrations had been oblivious to the dangers of communist espionage. California Congressman Richard Nixon, among the most aggressive investigators of subversion, described the case as "the most treasonable conspiracy in American history."

Two weeks after Hiss's conviction, the British government announced the arrest of Klaus Fuchs, an atomic physicist who had worked at the Los Alamos atomic energy laboratory. Shortly afterward the FBI arrested Julius and Ethel Rosenberg for conspiring with Fuchs to pass secrets to the Russians. The Rosenbergs denied the allegations, insisting they were the victims of anticommunist hysteria and anti-Semitism. In 1951, after a two-week trial, a jury pronounced them guilty of espionage. Recent declassified documents suggest that the government knew Ethel to be innocent of espionage but charged her in an effort to squeeze a confession out of her husband. In June 1953, despite personal pleas from the pope and worldwide protests, the husband and wife were executed.

Well before this time, actions against communists and their sympathizers had spread into American culture. In 1947 the House Committee on Un-American Activities (HUAC) opened a series of investigations into the Hollywood entertainment industry. In September the committee subpoenaed forty-one witnesses. Most cooperated with the committee by offering names of suspected communists. A small group of screenwriters, the "Hollywood Ten," served prison terms for refusing to answer questions about their ties to the Communist party. Shaken by the hearings, the studios initiated a policy of blacklisting writers, directors, technicians, and actors who refused to denounce communism.

The fear of subversion produced a culture of suspicion and mistrust. In 1948 *Look* asked, "Could the Reds Seize Detroit?" The answer, which included "enacted" photos, was yes. "Many factors," the magazine claimed, "make Detroit a focal point of Communist activity." In the hysteria over communist subversion, many Americans went

Bogey and Bacall Attend the Hollywood Ten Trials   Anticommunist hysteria infiltrated all walks of American life, including the film industry, which the House Un-American Activities Committee (HUAC) began investigating in 1947. Actors, writers, and directors faced the difficult decision of cooperating with the investigation or risking their careers. When called before the committee, the Hollywood Ten refused to answer questions, claiming that, even if they were communists, the First Amendment gave them that right. Humphrey Bogart and Lauren Bacall, seen here leading a Hollywood contingent into the hearings, joined other stars to form the Committee for the First Amendment in support of those who refused to cooperate. However, most studio heads, fearing a public backlash against their films, blacklisted the Ten and over two hundred others.   *(Corbis-Bettmann.)*

to extreme lengths to prove their loyalty. Indiana required professional boxers and wrestlers to take a noncommunist oath before entering the ring. A small town in New York required residents to take a loyalty oath before getting a permit to fish in the local reservoir. The Cincinnati Reds baseball team proved its patriotism by changing its name to the Cincinnati Redlegs. The desire to prove one's Americanism often produced unusual responses. On July 4, 1951, a reporter in Madison, Wisconsin, asked people to sign a petition that contained the words of the Declaration of Independence and the Bill of Rights. More than a hundred people read the petition. Only one signed it. The others dismissed it as communist propaganda.

Congress responded to the hysteria by passing the Internal Security Act of 1950. Among other restrictions, the act required communist and communist-front organizations to register with the government and to identify as communist all of their official mail and literature. The act's most severe provisions authorized the government to place all communists in concentration camps whenever a national emergency should occur. Truman vetoed the bill, denouncing it as "the greatest danger to freedom of speech, press, and assembly, since the Alien and Sedition Laws of 1798." But Congress garnered enough votes to override the veto and enact the measure into law.

Was this fear of domestic communism justified? Previously secret American reports of decoded Soviet intelligence traffic during these years—called the Venona Intercepts—reveal that the Soviets had planted as many as a hundred spies in high-level government positions and offer incriminating evidence against Alger Hiss and Julius and Ethel Rosenberg. Declassified files from Soviet and Eastern European archives support these conclusions while also suggesting that the Communist Party in America took its orders directly from Moscow. "Not every American communist was a spy," noted the historian Harvey Klehr, "but almost every spy was a communist."

While a handful worked as spies, most communists and their liberal sympathizers did not threaten national security. The party was disintegrating in the wake of Cold War fears, evidence of Stalin's tyranny, and Truman's loyalty program. Party membership dropped from an estimated high of eighty thousand in 1944 to only forty thousand in 1949. Ironically, the anticommunist crusaders, in their reckless disregard for civil rights and liberties, posed a more serious threat to American society.

Joseph McCarthy

In the midst of this cultural Red Scare, Joseph McCarthy became the most feared demagogue of his time. Born in 1908 to poor Irish-American farmers in northeastern Wisconsin, McCarthy earned a degree in 1935 and entered politics in 1939, running successfully for circuit judge in Wisconsin's Tenth Circuit. With the outbreak of World War II McCarthy decided to join the glamorous marines. For three years he served as an intelligence officer, debriefing American pilots following raids over the Pacific. Not satisfied with his low-profile role but unwilling to risk injury in combat, McCarthy fabricated his military record for the folks back home. He bragged about his exploits as a tail gunner, flying dangerous missions and shooting down enemy planes. He claimed to have been injured when his plane crash-landed. During his Senate campaigns, he walked with a limp and complained about having "ten pounds of shrapnel" in his leg. In reality, he injured his leg not while flying on a dangerous mission, but during a hazing ceremony aboard a navy ship when he slipped as he was running a gauntlet of paddle-wielding sailors.

In 1946, armed with phony wartime press releases, McCarthy won election to the Senate. By 1950 McCarthy was searching for an issue that would grab the public's attention. He found it in Wheeling, West Virginia, where he had traveled to speak to the Republican Women's Club. His speech, standard Republican rhetoric of the time, charged that traitors and spies had infiltrated the State Department. What was different about the speech was McCarthy's claim to have proof. "I have here in my hand," he blustered, "a list of names that were known to the secretary of state and who nevertheless are still working and shaping the policy of the State Department." Though few people paid him much notice at first, he repeated, expanded, and varied his charges in succeeding speeches. By March he was front-page news across the country. McCarthy, observed a journalist, "was a political speculator who found his oil gusher in Communism."

Democrats tried to knock out McCarthy before he could do any damage to the president. Senate Democrats established a special committee to investigate McCarthy's charges and stacked it with administration loyalists. "Let me have him for three days in public hearings," boasted Maryland's powerful Millard Tydings, who chaired the committee, "and he'll never show his face in the Senate again." Tydings underestimated his opponent. McCarthy used the attention to make wild accusations. The hearings established to destroy McCarthy helped transform him into a towering national figure.

McCarthy shrewdly manipulated the press, which treated his sensational charges as page-one news. He held press conferences early in the morning to announce that he would soon release dramatic information on domestic spying. The nation's afternoon papers printed banner headlines, "McCarthy's New Revelations Expected Soon." When reporters hounded him for details, McCarthy announced that he would soon produce a key witness. Headlines the following day would read, "Delay in McCarthy Revelations: Mystery Witness Sought." McCarthy never produced the evidence to support his accusations. But his tactics gained him the publicity he needed and thus fueled his attacks. By the fall of 1950 McCarthy

McCarthy and His Fans   Senator Joseph McCarthy from Wisconsin went on a massive anti-communist witch-hunt in the early 1950s. His list of suspects, which included people at all levels and in all branches of the government, led many Americans to question the loyalty of the nation's politicians and diplomats. As this photograph indicates, McCarthy at first enjoyed widespread support from those who believed him to be a tireless crusader for national security. But when McCarthy launched televised investigations of top army officials, Americans saw firsthand how irrational and ruthless he was, and his popularity quickly evaporated.   *(AP/Wide World Photos, Inc.)*

was the most feared man in American politics. His face appeared on the cover of *Time* and *Newsweek*. A new word entered the language: *McCarthyism*.

McCarthy's appeal was largely a result of the way he capitalized on Cold War anxieties. McCarthy offered simple answers to complex questions. Strong faith in the righteousness of their position left Americans ill prepared to comprehend the foreign policy setbacks of the immediate postwar years. McCarthy reassured a troubled nation that the string of bad news resulted from the traitorous actions of a few individuals, not from a flawed view of the world or the strength of communist opponents. China turned communist, he explained, because traitors in the State Department had sold out American interests, not because of the internal weakness of the Nationalist regime. The Soviets developed the atomic bomb because spies sold them America's secrets, not because they had talented scientists capable of developing their own bomb.

McCarthy's charges against the established elite tapped into a deep populist impulse in the American character. McCarthy called Dean Acheson a "pompous diplomat in striped pants, with a phony British accent." He denounced the "egg-sucking phony liberals" who defended "communists and queers." In focusing on liberal thinkers, homosexuals, and others who did not fit with Americans' traditional view of themselves, McCarthy exploited America's unease with its new international stature and its discomfort with alien ideas and lifestyles. In this sense, McCarthyism was part of a recurring pattern in American history. In 1798 Federalists had tried to silence critics by introducing the Alien and Sedition Acts, targeting dissenters as traitors. Waves of prejudice against foreigners swept the country during the 1850s and again in the 1870s. Following World War I the United States tried to drown "radical" thoughts in a Red Scare wave of "100 percent Americanism."

Most of all, McCarthyism was the product of partisan politics at midcentury. McCarthy had the support of conservative Republicans, who saw him as a useful means to reassert their authority in the country. So long as McCarthy wielded his anticommunist club against Democrats, many Republicans were willing to overlook his offensive tactics. Many GOP members repeated the refrain, "I don't like some of McCarthy's methods but his goal is good."

CONCLUSION

The Cold War provided the dramatic backdrop for American politics and society at the end of World War II. The United States and the Soviet Union emerged from the war as the dominant military powers in the world. But the two nations, burdened by the weight of history and ideology, possessed fundamentally different visions of the postwar world. The Soviets, determined to prevent another invasion of their homeland, consolidated their control in eastern Europe. The United States, resolved to thwart potential aggression, insisted that the postwar structure must be based on universal principles of free elections and open markets. American policymakers interpreted Soviet actions as part of an aggressive plan to strangle markets and extinguish individual rights.

Cold War tensions forced the United States to take an active role in shaping the postwar peace. In assuming a prominent position in the peacetime affairs of

Europe, policymakers abandoned a tradition of isolationism and signaled an important shift in U.S. foreign policy. The Truman administration adopted a policy of containment, using economic assistance and military might to deter Soviet aggression. The new policy found expression in three key initiatives: the Truman Doctrine, which extended U.S. military aid to Greece and Turkey; the Marshall Plan, which provided economic assistance to Western Europe; and NSC-68, which dramatically expanded American defense capabilities.

The experiment in internationalism did not, however, mean that the United States had fundamentally altered the way it viewed the world. Most Americans interpreted the U.S. victory in World War II as an affirmation of their commitment to open markets and free elections. Since the founding days of the republic, Americans had believed fervently in their mission to remake the world in their own image. The Cold War added a new dimension to an old impulse. For the first time, the United States confronted a powerful enemy (the Soviet Union) that possessed an ideology (communism) to rival its own. Faced with the new challenge, American policymakers decided that the nation needed to play an active role to fulfill its mission.

While building public support for his containment policy abroad, Truman struggled to build on the New Deal legacy at home. He encountered numerous obstacles: a conservative Congress, a public weary of government controls and regulation, and a party deeply divided over the Cold War and civil rights. Despite these problems Truman managed to win a surprising victory in the 1948 presidential election. Emboldened by his triumph he called for a Fair Deal—an ambitious program of reform that would extend and enhance the New Deal.

The president's reform agenda fell victim to hardening Cold War tensions and growing fears of communist subversion. The "fall" of China, the Soviet explosion of an atomic bomb, and most of all the North Korean invasion of South Korea sent global relations into a deep freeze. With U.S. soldiers engaged in a bloody conflict on the Korean peninsula, many Americans turned their attention to the covert battle against Soviet spies at home. Stories of Soviet spies—some real, some imagined—swept across the country, raising paranoiac fears that communists had infiltrated American institutions and were sowing the seeds of an alien ideology. The poisoned atmosphere provided a fertile environment for demagogues such as Senator Joseph McCarthy.

In many ways America was a much different nation when Truman left office in 1952 than it had been when he assumed the presidency in 1945. The Cold War had ripped the nation from its isolationist moorings and thrust it into a position of global leadership. But Americans had not completely abandoned the past. Nor had they lost confidence in the future. After fighting a world war and securing an uncertain peace, many Americans looked forward to celebrating the triumph of American values and enjoying the material benefits of the consumer society.

Annotated Suggested Readings

Walter LaFeber's *America, Russia, and the Cold War* (6th ed., 1990) provides a good overview of Cold War–era politics, while Stephen Ambrose's *Rise to Globalism* (8th ed., 1997) focuses on Cold War foreign policy. John Diggins surveys U.S. culture and politics in the 1940s and 1950s in *The Proud Decades* (1989), as does *Cold War Constructions*

(2000), edited by Christian Appy. George Lipsitz studies popular culture during the era in *Class and Culture in Cold War America* (1981). Also useful is Stephen J. Whitfield's *The Culture of the Cold War* (1996). Melvyn Leffler's *A Preponderance of Power* (1992) is the most comprehensive history of the early Cold War, with John L. Gaddis providing the most up-to-date synthesis in *We Now Know* (1997). The Cold War from the Soviet Union's perspective, using recently declassified materials, is *Inside the Kremlin's Cold War* (1996) by Vladislav Zubok and Constantine Pleshakov.

Bernard Weisberger's *Cold War, Cold Peace* (1984) is a solid standard account of the immediate postwar period. *The Devil We Knew* (1993) by H. W. Brands examines how the Cold War mentality developed and its effect on American society. Daniel Yergin's *Shattered Peace* (1977) demonstrates both the American and Soviet motives that contributed to the arms race.

Lawrence Wittner focuses on the Greek civil war in *American Intervention in Greece* (1982). Gregg Herken critiques U.S. leaders' reliance on the bomb in *The Winning Weapon* (1980), and Richard Rhodes's *Dark Sun* (1995) traces the development of the hydrogen bomb. Michael Hogan's *The Marshall Plan* (1987) is a thorough one-volume history of that ambitious initiative. Imanuel Wexler's *The Marshall Plan Revisited* (1983) offers a more-critical analysis of the plan. Timothy P. Ireland examines the formation of NATO in *Creating the Entangling Alliance* (1981). Joyce and Gabriel Kolko's *The Limits of Power* (1972) discusses how the complexity of foreign affairs stymied American attempts to dictate world politics.

Bruce R. Kuniholm's *The Origins of the Cold War in the Near East* (1980) has interesting material on the formation of Israel, while the division of Germany is the foundation of Carolyn Eisenberg's *Drawing the Line* (1996). Richard Freeland's *The Truman Doctrine and the Origins of McCarthyism* (1972) links Truman's policies with the later Red Scare. George Kennan's *American Diplomacy, 1900–1950* (1952) and Dean Acheson's *Present at the Creation* (1970) offer intriguing insiders' accounts of the early Cold War, while John L. Harper compares these two men to FDR in *American Visions of Europe* (1994). Walter Isaacson and Evan Thomas's *The Wise Men* (1986) is a study of Truman's advisers' impact on American foreign policy.

Jack S. Ballard's *The Shock of Peace* (1983) recounts the economic trauma of demobilization at war's end. In *Beyond the New Deal* (1973), Alonzo L. Hamby assesses Truman's effort to preserve and expand the New Deal. Robert J. Donovan captures the 1940s feeling of upheaval in *Tumultuous Years* (1982). Elaine T. May's *Homeward Bound* (1988) captures the impact of the Cold War on domestic life. David G. McCullough's *Truman* (1992) is a generally uncritical appraisal of Truman's life and policies. Alonzo Hamby provides the best biographical treatment of Truman in *Man of the People* (1995).

The 1948 election is detailed in Zachary Karabell's *How Harry Truman Won the 1948 Election* (2000). William C. Berman's *The Politics of Civil Rights in the Truman Administration* (1970) covers the controversy within the Democratic Party. John C. Culver and John Hyde's *American Dreamer* (2000) traces the life of Henry Wallace. . Arthur Schlesinger, Jr., argues the virtues of Fair Deal liberalism in *The Vital Center* (1949). Susan Hartmann outlines Truman's first-term frustrations in *Truman and the 80th Congress* (1971). Monte S. Poen details the defeat of national health insurance in *Harry S Truman Versus the Medical Lobby* (1979).

Akira Iriye's *The Cold War in Asia* (1974) is a good introduction to developments on that continent. Russell D. Buhite's *Soviet-American Relations in Asia* (1982) details the superpowers' conflict over the region. Michael Schaller's *The American Occupation of Japan* (1985) and John Dower's *Embracing Defeat* (1999) both study the American role in postwar Japan. The fall of China and the domestic reaction is the subject of Kenneth Shewmaker's

Americans and the Chinese Communists (1971), while the widening ideological gulf between the two nations is the subject of *Useful Adversaries* (1996) by Thomas J. Christensen. Clay Blair's *The Forgotten War* (1988) offers a moving account of the first limited war and the people who fought it, while the best treatment of the causes and consequences of the conflict is William Stueck's *The Korean War* (1995). Rosemary Foot's *The Wrong War* (1985) explores America's unpreparedness to fight a war in Asia. Bruce Cummings's two-volume *Origins of the Korean War* (1981, 1990) is a detailed study of the politics around the conflict. AP reporters Sang-Hun Choe, Martha Mendoza, and Charles J. Hanley examine the Korean war through the eyes of civilian and military participants in *The Bridge at No Gun Ri* (2001). For General MacArthur, William Manchester's *American Caesar* (1979) is the classic work; Michael Schaller's *Douglas MacArthur* (1989) is also helpful.

E. J. Kahn, Jr., covers the *Amerasia* controversy in *The China Hands* (1975). Allen Weinstein's *Perjury* (1978) explores the Hiss case. John E. Haynes and Harvey Klehr's *Venona* (1999) offers a new interpretation of the case based on declassified Soviet documents. Walter and Miriam Schneir detail the Rosenberg trial in *Invitation to an Inquest* (1983). Victor S. Navasky surveys the world of informants and blacklists in *Naming Names* (1980). Larry Ceplair and Steven Englund's *The Inquisition in Hollywood* (1980) analyzes the Red Scare's impact on popular culture. Athan Theoharis and John S. Cox study the roles of J. Edgar Hoover and the FBI in the Red Scare in *The Boss* (1988).

Two of the most valuable studies of Joseph McCarthy are Richard Fried's *Nightmare in Red* (1990) and Stanley Kutler's *The American Inquisition* (1982). David M. Oshinsky's *A Conspiracy So Immense* (1983) portrays Joseph McCarthy as a product of the political conditions of the era. Ellen Schrecker's *The Age of McCarthyism* (1994) uses primary documents from the period to show how most politicians from both parties aided and abetted the Red Scare. Interviews with Ethel Rosenberg's brother, David Greenglass, are the basis of Sam Robert's *The Brother* (2001).

The *istory* *ompanion*

America's Role in the World

"Getting Tough with the Russians"

On July 12, 1946, while having drinks with a few aides in the White House, President Truman vented his frustrations with the Soviet Union. The president said that he was tired of being pushed around by the Russians, "here a little, there a little," and that it was time to stand up to Stalin. Why make new agreements, he asked, if the Kremlin refused to comply with the old ones? The president turned to Special Counsel Clark Clifford and asked him to produce a record of Soviet violations of international agreements.

Clifford and his assistant George Elsey decided to expand the scope of their project. In September 1946 Clifford sent President Truman a comprehensive statement on U.S.–Soviet relations. Written with the cooperation of senior administration officials, the report reflected America's growing hard line with the Soviet Union.

The most obvious Soviet threat to American security is the growing ability of the USSR to wage an offensive war against the United States. . . . Stalin has declared his intention of sparing no effort to build up the military strength of the Soviet Union. . . .

The primary objective of the United States policy toward the Soviet Union is to convince Soviet leaders that it is in their interest to participate in a system of world cooperation, that there are no fundamental causes for war between our two nations, and that the security and prosperity of the Soviet Union, and that of the rest of the world as well, are being jeopardized by the aggressive militaristic imperialism such as that in which the Soviet Union is now engaged.

However, these same leaders with whom we hope to achieve an understanding on the principles of international peace appear to believe that a war with the United States and the other leading capitalistic nations is inevitable. They are increasing their military power and the sphere of Soviet influence in preparation for the "inevitable" conflict, and they are trying to weaken and subvert their potential opponents by every means at their disposal. So long as these men adhere to these beliefs, it is highly dangerous to conclude that hope of international peace lies only in "accord," "mutual understanding," or "solidarity" with the Soviet Union.

Unless the United States is willing to sacrifice its future security for the sake of "accord" with the USSR now, this government must, as a first step toward world stabilization, seek to prevent additional Soviet aggression. . . .

The language of military power is the only language which disciples of power politics understand. The United States must use that language in order that Soviet leaders will realize that our government is determined to uphold the interests of its citizens and the rights of small nations. Compromise and concessions are considered, by the Soviets, to be evidences of weakness and they are encouraged by our "retreats" to make new and greater demands.

The main deterrent to Soviet attack on the United States, or to attack on areas of the world which are vital to our security, will be the military power of this country. It must be made apparent to the Soviet government that our strength will be sufficient to repel any attack and sufficient to defeat the USSR decisively if a war should start. The prospect of defeat is the only sure means of deterring the Soviet Union.

"The Last Chance for Peace"

Escalating Cold War tensions troubled many liberals who hoped to continue Roosevelt's policy of wartime cooperation with Stalin. In July 1946 Secretary of Commerce Henry Wallace sent President Truman a twelve-page, single-spaced letter asking him to reconsider his "get tough" policy.

I should list the factors which make for Russian distrust of the United States and of the Western world as follows. The first is Russian history, which we must take into account because it is the setting in which Russians see all actions and policies of the rest of the world. Russian history for over a thousand years has been a succession of attempts, often unsuccessful, to resist invasion and conquest. . . . The Russians, therefore, obviously see themselves as fighting for their existence in a hostile world.

Second, it follows that to the Russians all of the defense and security measures of the Western powers seem to have an aggressive intent. Our actions to expand our military security system . . . appear to them as going far beyond the requirements of defense. I think we might feel the same if the United States were the only capitalistic country in the world, and the principal socialistic countries were creating a level of armed strength far exceeding anything in their previous history.

Finally, our resistance to her attempts to obtain warm-water ports and her own security system in the form of "friendly" neighboring states seems, from the Russian point of view, to clinch the case. After twenty-five years of isolation and after having achieved the status of a major power, Russia believes that she is entitled to recognition of her new status. Our interest in establishing democracy in Eastern Europe, where democracy by and large has never existed, seems to her an attempt to re-establish the encirclement of unfriendly neighbors which was created after the last war, and which might serve as a springboard of still another effort to destroy her.

If this analysis is correct, and there is ample evidence to support it, the action to improve the situation is clearly indicated. The fundamental objective of such action should be to allay any reasonable Russian grounds for fear, suspicion and distrust. . . .

We should make an effort to counteract the irrational fear of Russia which is being systematically built up in the American people by certain individuals and publications. The slogan that communism and capitalism, regimentation and democracy, cannot continue to exist in the same world is, from a historical point of view, pure propaganda. . . .

. . . We are by far the most powerful nation in the world, the only Allied nation which came out of the war without devastation and much stronger than before the war. Any talk on our part about the need for strengthening our defenses further is bound to appear hypocritical to other nations.

"We agreed that Kennan's Long Telegram was brilliant," Clifford recalled, "but he had confined himself to analysis." Clifford and Elsey decided "to fill the gap between Kennan's analysis and policy recommendations" by making concrete suggestions for the president to follow.

Clifford had not spoken with Secretary of Commerce Henry A. Wallace, the lone voice in high government circles for resisting Kennan's interpretation of Soviet behavior. Wallace, who had served as Roosevelt's vice president until being dumped from the ticket in 1944, believed that Russian friendship was essential to preserve international peace and security. The administration's most outspoken liberal, Wallace watched nervously as the administration, swayed by Kennan's Long Telegram, adopted a "get tough" approach to the Soviets.

Wallace's letter outlining his grievances with the administration's evolving hard line angered Truman, who wanted to fire the secretary but feared that such a move would anger liberals. He complained to aides that Wallace was too idealistic and failed to understand the harsh realities of international power politics. "I do not understand a 'dreamer' like that," Truman wrote in his diary.

On September 12 Wallace delivered a major foreign policy speech at New York City's Madison Square Garden in which he repeated many of the points he had previously voiced in private. The press accurately reported Wallace's address as a stinging critique of administration policy. Secretary of State James Byrnes sent Truman an angry message threatening to resign if the president did not silence his commerce secretary. On September 20 Truman announced Wallace's resignation at a packed news conference. The last Cold War dissident had been forced out of the administration. After the reporters had left the room, Truman slumped into his chair, turned to his press secretary, and said, "Well, the die is cast."

Clifford's memorandum and Wallace's letter exposed a tension in the way Americans viewed their role in the postwar world. The struggle against fascism and the emerging battle against communism had convinced most Americans that the United States needed to play an active role in international affairs. But how would Americans define that role?

QUESTIONS FOR ANALYSIS

1. Why does Clifford believe the Soviet Union is to blame for the Cold War?

2. What does Clifford mean by the "inevitable" conflict between the United States and the Soviet Union?

3. How does Clifford propose the United States should respond?

4. On what grounds does Wallace reject Clifford's interpretation and recommendations?

5. What alternative explanation does he present to explain Soviet actions?

6. According to Wallace, how has the United States contributed to Cold War tensions?

7. Why did Truman consider Clifford a "realist" and Wallace an "idealist"?

8. If President Truman had asked you to analyze U.S.–Soviet relations, what would you have told him? What recommendations for action would you have made?

28

The Consumer Society

1945–1960

America's love affair with the material benefits of prosperity bred contentment, especially among the expanding white middle classes, and reinforced traditional American optimism about the future.

As shocked journalists looked on, Vice President Richard Nixon and Soviet Premier Nikita Khrushchev stood toe to toe in the hottest personal confrontation of the Cold War. The exchange took place in July 1959 as Nixon escorted the Soviet leader through the U.S. National Exhibition, a two-week exhibit in Moscow that celebrated American life. After playing with the new TV equipment and sipping soda from a bottle of Pepsi-Cola, they moved on to the most publicized display of American affluence: a six-room, model suburban ranch house filled with shining new furniture. "I want to show you this kitchen," Nixon said. "It is like those of our houses in California." "We have such things," Khrushchev retorted. But in the United States any worker could afford a $14,000 house, Nixon replied. When Nixon turned the topic to the new consumer devices making life easier in American homes, Khrushchev became enraged. "You Americans think that the Russian people will be astonished to see these things!" They were, he blustered, worthless gadgets.

Within minutes the conversation about television sets and washing machines escalated into an ideological clash between communism and capitalism. A defensive Khrushchev charged that the American military wanted to destroy the Soviet Union. Jamming his thumb into Nixon's chest to underscore his point, Khrushchev warned, "If you want to threaten, we will answer threat with threat." So as not to appear intimidated, Nixon brazenly waived his finger in Khrushchev's face and shot back that it was the Soviets, not the Americans, who threatened the world's peace. Later that evening at a state dinner, Nixon, still gloating over the display of American affluence, told his Soviet hosts that the United States had achieved "the ideal of prosperity for all in a classless society."

The "kitchen debate" captured the conflicting currents of the decade. Appropriately, the simulated kitchen of a suburban house hosted the Nixon–Khrushchev confrontation. During the 1950s the United States experienced a "consumer revolution" as millions of Americans scrambled to buy a new home in the suburbs and to fill it with the latest consumer gadgets. Television, the most popular of the new products, reinforced the celebration of traditional values by offering Americans a steady diet of shared images. America's love affair with the material benefits of prosperity bred contentment, especially among the expanding white middle classes, and reinforced traditional American optimism about the future. For many of these people, President Dwight Eisenhower was a reassuring symbol. At home he accepted the major outlines of the welfare state while promising to control its excesses. Abroad, despite some rhetorical excesses, caution guided his approach to the world.

But there was another side to the celebration of consumption during the 1950s. The decade was full of anxiety about the Cold War, fear of revolution in the Third World, and apprehension about the consequences of mass culture for American identity. It was a time when the celebration of family values limited opportunities for women and the signs of a booming economy obscured the growing gap between rich and poor. It was also a time when African-Americans established the foundation of a powerful social movement that would change forever the face of American society and the way Americans viewed one another.

- What were the roots of the "consumer revolution," and how did consumerism change American society?

- What were the manifestations of mass culture in the 1950s? Why were critics worried about the impact of consumerism and mass culture on American character, and were their fears justified?

- How did American values shape Eisenhower's policies? What limitations constrained his approach at home and abroad?

- How did social realities in the 1950s differ from the ideals portrayed in mass culture?

- By 1960 what factors undercut Americans' sense of satisfaction and security?

This chapter will address these questions.

THE CONSUMER REVOLUTION

The United States experienced an unprecedented economic boom following World War II. Between 1940 and 1960 the gross national product (GNP) more than doubled from $227 billion to $488 billion (see figure on page 1096). The median family income rose from $3,083 to $5,657, and real wages rose by almost 30 percent. By 1960 a record 66.5 million Americans held jobs. And unlike in earlier boom times, runaway prices did not eat up rising income: inflation averaged only 1.5 percent annually in the 1950s. "Never had so many people, anywhere, been so well off," the satisfied editors of *U.S. News and World Report* concluded in 1957, reaffirming the belief that the American experiment was a model for the rest of the world.

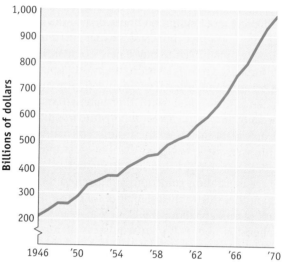

Gross National Product   A number of factors, including pent-up consumer demand and profuse military spending, spurred the GNP upward after World War II. The climbing GNP figures reflect the prosperity of the 1950s and 1960s, with the production rate of all Americans almost doubling between 1945 and 1960. An even more dramatic growth occurred in the 1960s as the GNP doubled again in a decade.

At the heart of the new prosperity was a dramatic increase in consumer spending. A postwar "baby boom" created enormous demand for new consumer goods that propelled the economy forward as Americans experimented with new ways of living and spending. To provide more room for growing families, millions of Americans moved to the new suburban communities sprouting up around major cities. The development of a consumer society produced important changes in the nature of work and confronted organized labor with new challenges.

The "Baby Boom" and the Rise of Mass Consumption   "It seems to me," observed a British visitor to America in 1958, "that every other young housewife I see is pregnant." Americans in the postwar period were marrying younger and having more children then ever before. Between 1940 and 1955 the United States experienced the largest population increase in its history—27 percent, from 130 million to 165 million. The so-called baby boom peaked in 1957, when 4.3 million babies were born, one every seven seconds (see figure on page 1098).

Why the rush to have babies? Several reasons can be identified. First, young couples who had delayed getting married during World War II decided to make up for lost time. Then, as the decade progressed, the median age of those getting married hit historic lows—20.1 years for women and 22.5 years for men. Young couples were starting families earlier and continuing to have children over a longer period of time.

CHRONOLOGY

1944	GI Bill
1947	First Levittown constructed on Long Island
1948	Kinsey's *Sexual Behavior in the Human Male*
1952	Eisenhower elected president Nixon's "Checkers" speech
1953	Korean War ends Stalin dies; Khrushchev comes to power Kinsey's *Sexual Behavior in the Human Female*
1954	Army–McCarthy hearings; Senate censures McCarthy Arbenz deposed in Guatemala Defeat of French forces at Dien Bien Phu Geneva Accords signed *Brown* v. *Board of Education*
1955	Ray Kroc establishes McDonald's chain Montgomery bus boycott
1956	Interstate Highway Act Elvis Presley hits it big with "Heartbreak Hotel" Eisenhower reelected; Democrats keep both houses Nasser seizes Suez Canal; Israel invades Sinai Peninsula
1957	Eisenhower Doctrine Little Rock crisis USSR launches *Sputnik*
1958	Galbraith publishes *The Affluent Society* National Defense Education Act
1959	"Kitchen debate" Castro overthrows Batista regime
1960	Kennedy elected president U-2 incident

Second, changing cultural attitudes toward sexuality and pregnancy created a "procreation ethic" that encouraged young couples to have children. Popular television shows and magazine stories celebrated the joys of pregnancy and motherhood, as did advertisers: "I'm Alice Cook," declared a suburban housewife in one aspirin commercial. "I have six children, and they come in all shapes and sizes. So do their colds."

Third, a general spirit of confidence about the future convinced young couples that they could afford the demands of parenthood. Government policies played a key role in promoting the new optimism. The Serviceman's Readjustment Act, popularly

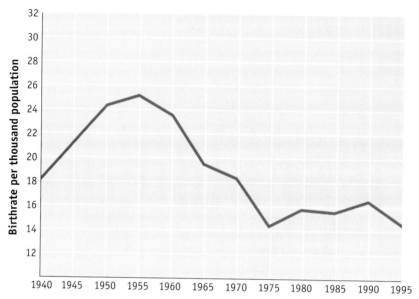

American Birthrate The bulge in the birthrate from the end of World War II to 1965 marks the extent of the generation known as the "baby boomers." By their sheer numbers, the members of this generation could not help but shape every aspect of American culture for the rest of the twentieth century. This generation did not choose to have as many children as their parents did, as seen in the precipitous decline in the birthrate in the early 1970s, followed by two decades of relatively similar numbers.

known as the GI Bill, which Congress passed in 1944, pumped millions of dollars into the economy by providing veterans with unemployment compensation, medical benefits, business loans, and tuition reimbursements for continuing education.

Fourth, modern science contributed to the fertility euphoria by conquering diseases that had plagued human beings for centuries. Antibiotics and other new drugs subdued diseases such as tuberculosis, diphtheria, whooping cough, and measles. The most significant achievement was the victory over poliomyelitis (polio), most of whose victims were children. Between 1947 and 1951 this crippling disease struck an annual average of thirty-nine thousand Americans. In 1955 Dr. Jonas Salk of the Pittsburgh Medical School developed the first effective vaccine against polio, and by 1960 vaccines had practically eliminated the disease in the United States.

Although the consumer revolution traced its roots back to the 1920s, postwar affluence and the baby boom allowed it to blossom in the years following World War II. In 1958 *Life* magazine called children the "Built-in Recession Cure," concluding that all babies were potential consumers who spearheaded "a brand-new market for food, clothing, and shelter." Parents purchased an endless number of products to raise their families. In 1957 Americans spent $50 million on diapers. Toy sales skyrocketed. By the end of the decade Americans were buying over two million bicycles a year. Many Americans turned to new discount stores to get the latest products at the lowest prices.

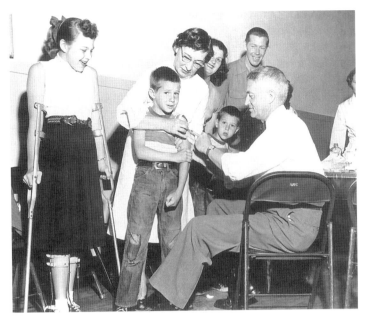

The End of Polio   By the 1950s, polio had killed or disabled thousands of children and young adults, and epidemics in the early 1950s led to 20,000 new cases a year and caused a nationwide panic. A massive effort by medical researchers and ordinary Americans who contributed to the March of Dimes finally yielded success on April 12, 1955—the tenth anniversary of polio-patient Franklin Roosevelt's death. On that day, Dr. Jonas Salk, himself a victim of the disease, announced his vaccine was effective. By the end of the decade, most children had been inoculated, and the disease was virtually eradicated in the United States. Here six-year-old Michael Urnezis of San Diego reluctantly receives his vaccine while his twelve-year-old sister and polio survivor, Joanne, joyfully looks on.   *(Corbis-Bettmann.)*

Many people used credit cards to pay for their accumulating merchandise. The credit card business began in 1950 with the introduction of the Diner's Club card. Its enormous success spurred oil firms, motel and hotel chains, and many other companies to introduce credit cards in the 1950s as well. By the end of the decade Sears Roebuck, a large national department store, had more than 10 million charge accounts. *Newsweek* announced in 1953: "Never before have so many owed so much to so many." As a result, total private debts in the United States increased nearly 300 percent during the 1950s, from $73 billion to $196 billion.

The Rise of the Suburbs   Many urban Americans looked to the suburbs to provide the additional space needed for their growing families, while rural residents and farmers moved to the sprawling suburbs in search of better jobs and more opportunity. In New York City 1.5 million people moved to the suburbs in the 1950s, while outside Los Angeles, Orange County more than tripled in population. Similar growth occurred around many other cities across the country, until by 1960 almost 60 million people, making up about one-third of the total population, resided in suburban areas.

Builders plowed under more than a million acres of farmland every year to make way for new communities. Of the 13 million homes built in the decade before 1958, 85 percent were built in the suburbs. Inexpensive housing in the suburbs led to a boom in home ownership, which by 1960 was double that of any other industrialized country in the world.

Builder William Levitt made the suburban dream a reality for millions of Americans. In 1949 Levitt bought four thousand acres of potato fields in Hempstead, Long Island. Using mass production methods he produced affordable suburban homes for young families. Every house was identical: one story high, with a 12-by-16-foot living room, a kitchen, two bedrooms, and a tiled bathroom. The price was $7,990, or $60 a month with no money down. Levitt produced as many as 150 homes a week. Builders throughout the country quickly followed his example.

Levitt built the houses, but government made the homes affordable for millions of young families. More than 3.75 million veterans bought homes under a Veterans Administration program that required only a token down payment and provided long-term, low-interest mortgages. The Federal Housing Administration financed 30 percent of all new houses in the 1950s.

The suburbs fed the consumer society's appetite for new products. The average suburban family earned 70 percent more income than the rest of the nation. "Suburbia," *Fortune* magazine observed in 1953, is "the cream of the market." But suburbanites were not the only Americans filling their homes with new furniture and the latest in electrical gadgetry. By 1960, 96 percent of the nation's families owned refrigerators, 87 percent their own TV sets, and 75 percent their own washing machines. The swimming pool, in the past affordable only by the rich, began to appear in the yards of more and more middle-class homeowners.

For all the opportunities opened up by the development of suburbia, it was not the dream come true for all Americans. Blacks were excluded from many of the new communities. Levitt banned African-Americans from Levittown. Suburban communities used a variety of formal and informal methods to exclude blacks. In many cases, local real estate agents refused to sell houses to blacks, and bankers rejected their mortgage applications. Some communities adopted zoning regulations designed to exclude lower-income groups. The methods proved effective: by the end of the decade African-Americans made up less than 5 percent of suburban residents.

The Changing World of Work

Meeting the demands of the new consumer society produced enormous changes in the economy and the nature of work. The 1950s witnessed an acceleration of the trend toward concentration of power in the hands of fewer corporations. By the end of the decade some 600 corporations, which made up only half a percent of all U.S. companies, accounted for 53 percent of total corporate income. In the Cold War defense buildup, the government contributed to the growth of big business by awarding military contracts to a handful of large corporations. Industrial giants used their vast resources to gobble up smaller competitors. From 1950 through 1961 the 500 largest American corporations merged with or acquired 3,404 smaller companies.

Corporations not only merged; they extended their reach by establishing roots abroad. Boosted by government programs such as the Marshall Plan, U.S. corporate investment abroad increased by nearly 300 percent during the decade. After World War II the most successful corporations developed new products and moved into new markets.

Expanding computer use represented the decade's most significant technological development. First developed to aid the defense effort during World War II, the original machines were massive: the Mark I, completed in 1944, stretched 50 feet in length and stood 8 feet high. In 1946 engineers at the University of Pennsylvania marketed the first commercial computer. International Business Machines (IBM), already a leader in the office equipment industry, produced its first computer in 1953. The new technology was at the forefront of a wave of automation that promised to boost productivity and cut labor costs. By 1957 more than 1,250 computers were being used to make airline reservations, forecast elections, and help banks process checks.

Important economic changes were also disrupting the lives of millions of Americans. From 1947 to 1957 the number of factory workers dropped 4 percent. Automation alone eliminated the jobs of an estimated 1.5 million blue-collar workers, most of them union members, between 1953 and 1959. Those jobs were replaced by new service-sector positions. In 1956, for the first time in U.S. history, white-collar workers outnumbered blue-collar workers. In the two decades after 1950, 9 million jobs opened up for secondary school teachers, hospital support staff, and local government office workers. Consumer demand spurred the creation of new department stores and supermarkets staffed by 3 million additional employees.

The consumer economy presented organized labor with new challenges. At first glance, unions appeared to make tremendous gains during the decade. The number of union members in the United States climbed from 14.7 million in 1945 to 18 million in the mid-1950s. In 1955 the two most powerful labor organizations, the American Federation of Labor headed by George Meany and the Congress of Industrial Organizations led by Walter Reuther, merged into one great federation (AFL-CIO). But unions faced serious problems in their attempt to make inroads into the fastest growing segment of the work force: white-collar employees. By 1960 unions had organized fewer than 184,000 of 5 million public employees and only 200,000 of 8.5 million office workers.

SHAPING NATIONAL CULTURE, 1945–1960

Television emerged as the most visible symbol of the new consumer society. TV transformed the cultural landscape in America by bringing people from diverse backgrounds together in a shared experience. Along with the automobile, which broke down the geographical distance separating rural and urban, television helped promote a national culture. Popular music and religious revivalism added momentum to a homogenizing trend that worried many intellectuals. How would the experiment in fashioning a more uniform national culture affect what it meant to be an American?

The Shared Images of Television

Although television had been invented in the 1920s, it did not gain widespread acceptance until the 1950s. In 1946 about one of every eighteen thousand people owned a TV set. By 1960 nine out of every ten American homes had a TV. Its appeal was universal: designed for a mass audience, television did not honor race or class divisions. Most shows avoided controversy and celebrated traditional American values. Families were intact; men worked during the day; women stayed at home. No one was ever sick. No one was poor. African-Americans were absent from TV's fictions. Americans watched together as Milton Berle, Jackie Gleason, and Arthur Godfrey introduced a parade of entertainers on their live variety shows. Millions of families gathered around the television set each week to watch as Superman, a comic book hero turned television star, fought for "truth, justice, and the American way." Shows such as *Ozzie and Harriet, Father Knows Best,* and *Leave It to Beaver* presented a glossy image of middle-class suburban life. Supportive wives spent their days minding the household and the clean-cut kids while their husbands provided for the family and solved the family crisis of the day. Only a few shows, such as Jackie Gleason's *The Honeymooners,* which described life in a bleak urban apartment, hinted at the world beyond suburbia.

Television transformed American social habits. Studies showed that the average household watched five hours of television a day. Most viewers confessed to reading fewer books and magazines after purchasing a TV set. Saturated by commercials, children recited the Pepsi-Cola theme song before they learned the national anthem and recognized the word *detergent* before they could read.

The combination of advertising, prosperity, and television produced overnight national fads. In 1954 the popular Disney show *Davy Crockett* produced the first fad of the decade. The "King of the Wild Frontier" became an instant hero among millions of children. Enterprising manufacturers flooded the market with Davy Crockett coonskin caps, knives, tents, and bow and arrow sets and records of the show's theme song, "The Ballad of Davy Crockett." Before the fad was over, more than $100 million worth of Crockett paraphernalia had been sold.

Professional sports flowered under the sympathetic eye of the camera. Television exposed more people to sports, making popular figures out of athletic heroes and pouring money into team coffers. The leading spectator sport was baseball: in 1953 the sixteen major league teams drew 14.3 million into their parks, while millions more watched on television. Thanks to television, professional football became a new super sport, the first true rival to major league baseball for the nation's affection. Attendance at professional football games rose steadily for eight straight years, going from 1.9 million in 1950 to 2.9 million in 1957.

As television absorbed millions of dollars of advertising money, it squeezed out other entertainment sources. Radio suffered the most, losing nearly half its audience between 1948 and 1956. Thousands of motion picture houses were forced to close their doors. "Why go to the movies," asked film executive Samuel Goldwyn in 1955, "when you can stay home and see nothing worse?" Many large-circulation magazines suffered a similar fate. General interest magazines such as *Life, Saturday Evening Post, Look,* and *Women's Home Companion* lost circulation and eventually ceased publication.

The Car Culture   Television nationalized culture by projecting a common set of images that Americans from coast to coast experienced in the comfort of their homes. At the same time, the dramatic increase in the number of automobiles and new highways narrowed the physical gap between rural and urban communities.

Manufacturers had halted the production of automobiles during World War II, but once the war was over, car sales boomed. Car registrations soared from 26 million in 1945 to 60 million in 1960. The number of two-car families doubled from 1951 to 1958. By 1956 an estimated 75 million cars and trucks sped along American roads, themselves expanded by the Interstate Highway Act of 1956. The largest public works project in American history, the Interstate Highway Act appropriated $32 billion to build 41,000 miles of highway.

The car had a profound impact on American life. By the end of the 1950s the automobile was directly or indirectly responsible for one-sixth of the gross national product and millions of jobs. In turn the auto industry spurred production in petroleum, steel, tourism and travel, service stations, and highway construction and maintenance. The automobile also promoted the decline of metropolitan areas by accelerating the move to the suburbs, contributed to the decay of public transportation, and produced higher levels of air pollution.

Cars and new roads contributed to a massive population shift from the Northeast to the South and West. Florida's population boomed, fed by the tourist industry, the influx of retirees, and the rapid expansion of the fruit industry. The fastest growth occurred in California, which added 3.1 million residents and accounted for an astounding 20 percent of the nation's population growth in the fifties. By 1963 California had moved past New York as the nation's most populous state. By 1960 half of the people living in the West were living in a state different from the one in which they were born.

By opening the development of suburban retail commerce, the automobile also made the United States a more homogeneous nation. In metropolitan areas across the country small mom-and-pop stores gave way to mammoth shopping malls housing national retail chains on the edges of the city. Interchangeable motels and fast-food chains materialized nearby. In 1955 an ambitious salesman, Ray Kroc, established a chain of burger joints called McDonald's, which would become the symbol of the fast-food industry.

The automobile boosted the travel industry and made possible new forms of entertainment. In July 1955 the vast Disneyland theme park opened in southern California. The park attracted more than a million visitors in its first six months. Over 40 percent of the guests came from outside California, most of them by car. Inside the park, Main Street USA recalled America's small town past; Frontierland brought back the thrill of pioneer life; and Tomorrowland suggested the future frontier of space. While enjoying the thrill of Disneyland's amusements, visitors shared in the celebration of common cultural images that reaffirmed the nation's mythic past and its promising future.

Religious Revival

"Today in the U.S.," *Time* magazine claimed in 1954, "the Christian faith is back in the center of things." Considerable evidence existed to support the claim. Church membership skyrocketed from 64 million in 1940 to 114 million in 1960. Sales of Bibles reached an all-time high. In 1954 Congress added the phrase "under God" to the Pledge of Allegiance and the next year mandated "In God We Trust" on all U.S. currency. The return to religion found expression in religious songs such as "I Believe" and in inspirational movies, among them *The Robe* and *The Ten Commandments*.

Opening Day at Disneyland On July 17, 1955, Walt Disney, producer of children's movies, opened his theme park in Anaheim, California. The park, covering one hundred sixty acres of former citrus groves, cost almost $17 million to build. At first, Disneyland was not much of an amusement park; there were far more exhibits than rides and some buildings, like Sleeping Beauty's castle shown here, were completely empty. However, for American families, who had more kids and more money than ever before, Disneyland was a modern marvel. Its combination of nostalgia for the past (Main Street) and excitement for the future (Tomorrowland), along with its emphasis on youth culture (Fantasyland, Adventureland, and Frontierland), provided postwar parents with the perfect family vacation spot. *(Bettemann-Corbis.)*

Television transformed religious preachers into overnight celebrities. The first clergyman to become a television star was the Most Reverend Fulton J. Sheen, who warned viewers that godless communism was infiltrating American institutions, especially government, and advised against making peace with the Soviets. At the height of his popularity, Sheen's *Life Is Worth Living* show played to a weekly audience of 10 million people.

Sheen competed for airtime with ordained Methodist minister Norman Vincent Peale, who reached millions of people every week with his television and radio show and his own magazine. Peale preached a gospel of reassurance and comfort by mixing religion with traditional American ideas of success. Published in 1952 and selling for $2.95, his book *The Power of Positive Thinking* stayed at the top of the nonfiction bestseller list for 112 consecutive weeks. In 1954 it sold more copies than any other book except the Bible.

The most popular evangelist of the 1950s was undoubtedly Billy Graham. Handsome and dynamic, Graham used the mass media to reach millions of people. Like other popular preachers of the day, he downplayed doctrinal differences, emphasized the common link between Christian teachings and American values, and warned of the evils of communism, which he called "a great sinister anti-Christian movement masterminded by Satan."

Graham's ecumenical message helped transform Christianity into a national religion. Church membership and professions of faith became popular methods of affirming "the American way of life" during the Cold War. However, in an influential 1955 study, theologian Will Herberg complained that modern religion was "without serious commitment, without real inner conviction, without genuine existential decision." Polls showed that a majority of Americans could not distinguish the New Testament from the Old or even name one of the gospels. Religion offered Americans what they needed most in the 1950s: a sense of belonging in a rapidly changing society and divine support for traditional American values in the battle with communism. As *The Christian Century* noted in 1954, it had become "un-American to be unreligious."

Teenagers and the Rise of Rock and Roll

During the 1950s there were more young people in America than at any previous time in history. The word *teenager* entered the American language, and parents and educators worried about the emergence of a national youth subculture. American teens now had the purchasing power to taste the fruits of abundance—without having to seek parental approval. Postwar prosperity provided America's 13 million teenagers with more money than ever before. In 1956 teenage income from allowances and part-time jobs reached $7 billion a year. Between 1944 and 1958 the average teenager's weekly income quadrupled from $2.50 to $10.55. The expansion of public education contributed to the development of a teenage culture. A high school education was supposed to inculcate middle class values. But by segregating young people with many others of the same age, universal education gave teenagers the opportunity to develop their own values.

Writers, directors, and advertisers appealed directly to the teenager's sense of alienation from the adult world. The 1951 publication of J. D. Salinger's *The Catcher in the Rye* marked the beginning of the youth culture. The novel traced the thoughts and actions of sixteen-year-old Holden Caulfield who roams around New York City recording his rejection of the phoniness and corruption of the adult world. In the movie *Rebel Without a Cause*, teen idol James Dean abandons the middle-class values of his parents for the excitement of a lower-class car culture. Television made its contribution to the youth culture in 1957 with the debut of *American Bandstand*. The daily show hosted by Dick Clark showed clean-cut teenagers dancing with each other while others watched from the bleachers.

These reassuring images of young men in jackets and ties and young women in dresses did little to ease adult concern about juvenile delinquency. Between 1948 and 1953 the number of teenagers charged with crimes increased by 45 percent.

Especially troubling were the organized gangs that roamed the streets in many larger cities. As early as 1953 the federal government's Children's Bureau predicted that the exploding teenage population would soon produce an increase of 24 percent in car thefts, 19 percent in burglaries, and 7 percent in rapes. "Younger and younger children commit more and more serious and violent acts," wrote psychiatrist Fredric Wertham in his popular book, *Seduction of the Innocent* (1953).

Perhaps the most obvious symbol of the new youth culture was the emergence of rock and roll. Young adults used their added purchasing power to change musical taste in America by propelling "rock 'n' roll" to the top of the charts. A mix of rhythm and blues, country, and white gospel music, rock and roll had gained enormous popularity among African-Americans in the late forties. Because of its association with blacks and its strong sexual overtones, most whites dismissed the new sound as "race music." At the beginning of the decade, it was being recorded only by small record companies and played only on African-American radio stations. In 1951 a white disc jockey named Alan Freed began playing "race music" on his popular Cleveland radio station, renaming it "rock and roll," an urban euphemism for dancing and sex. By bringing "race music" to a white teenage audience, Freed's "Moondog's Rock and Roll Party" shattered musical barriers and instigated a national music craze.

Initially, most white radio stations refused to play rock and roll music that was performed by black singers. Pressed by growing teenage demand, major record companies produced white versions of songs originally recorded by black singers. In 1955 twelve of the year's top fifty songs were rock and roll, including "Rock Around the Clock," written by two white songwriters and recorded by an all-white group, Bill Haley and the Comets.

The Comets' success opened the door for the most popular rock and roll star of the decade: Elvis Aaron Presley (1935–1977). A nineteen-year-old truck driver from Tupelo, Mississippi, Presley emerged in 1956 with his hit single, "Heartbreak Hotel." The young entertainer adapted the powerful rhythms and raw sexual energy of "race music" to create his own unique style and sound. The new white star enthralled screaming audiences of white teens. Between 1956 and 1958 Presley had ten number-one hit records, including "Heartbreak Hotel," "Hound Dog," "All Shook Up," and "Jailhouse Rock." Many parents were aghast when they saw "Elvis the Pelvis," with his sensual pout and tight pants, swing his hips while young female fans screamed in excitement.

By the end of the decade white audiences were rushing to record stores to buy the original black versions of songs. *Billboard* magazine noted that "race music" was "no longer identified as the music of a specific group, but can now enjoy a healthy following among all people, regardless of race and color." Radio stations and record companies now featured black artists. Little Richard (born Richard Wayne Penniman) sang, shouted, danced, gyrated, and sweated profusely through "Tutti Frutti." Antoine "Fats" Domino, less threatening to whites than Little Richard, belted out songs such as "Blueberry Hill" (1956) and "Whole Lotta Loving" (1958). Chuck Berry, who developed a famous "duck walk" across the stage, hit the charts with "Roll Over Beethoven" (1956) and "Johnny B. Goode" (1957). The emergence of rock and roll produced a boom in national record sales. In 1950 Americans pur-

Elvis on Stage in Las Vegas, 1956
Though not a Baby Boomer himself, Elvis Presley became that generation's first rock and roll icon. Growing up in Memphis, Elvis was influenced not just by the pop and country music he heard on the radio, but also by the gospel choruses in church and the R&B rhythms he encountered in black neighborhoods. While working as a delivery driver in the summer of 1954, Elvis recorded his first single, "That's All Right," at Sun Records. Within two years, Elvis was an international singing sensation, much to the consternation of many parents, who found his performances to be too suggestive, as evidenced in this picture from a Las Vegas show. (© *Elvis Presley Enterprises, Inc.*)

chased 189 million records; by the end of the decade that number had soared to over 600 million. Teenagers accounted for nearly 70 percent of all record sales. In 1956 alone, Elvis Presley sold over 3.75 million albums.

Mass Culture and Its Critics

Many writers during the 1950s began to complain that mass culture promoted conformity and contributed to the homogenization of American society. The emphasis on consumerism had created a nation of ugly shopping strips, mindless entertainment, and rampant commercialization. In his popular book *The Lonely Crowd* (1950), sociologist David Riesman suggested that consumerism had moved America from an "inner-directed" culture in which people developed individualized goals to an "other-directed" society molded by peer-group pressures. Other critics took aim at the new service economy, which emphasized teamwork and frowned on mavericks. "When white-collar people get jobs, they sell not only their time and energy but their personalities as well," wrote sociologist C. Wright Mills in *White Collar* (1951).

Television received much of the blame for debasing American culture. Scores of articles and books suggested that television promoted violence, stifled communication in families, and suppressed intellectual creativity and independence of thought. In 1955 a best-selling book, *Why Johnny Can't Read,* blamed television for high rates of child illiteracy.

These critics pointed to the suburbs as evidence of the harmful impact of mass culture on contemporary society. Suburban communities, with row after row of identical homes and well-manicured lawns, suggested that uniformity was valued over individualism. Everyone in the suburbs, a hostile observer noted, "buys the right car, keeps his lawn like his neighbor's, eats crunchy breakfast cereal, and votes Republican."

While these critics were correct in highlighting the importance of mass culture, they frequently overplayed their hand. The public was not as passive, nor the dominant culture as monolithic, as they suggested. Despite dire warnings that television would overshadow other forms of information, Americans enjoyed a greater variety of cultural resources than at any time before. Book sales doubled during the decade. A dramatic increase in the number of specialized magazines such as *Sports Illustrated* and the *New Yorker* compensated for the decline of general readership publications. Innovative newspapers increased circulation by playing to the changing taste of suburban readers.

It is also difficult to measure how viewers interpreted the images they saw on their TV screens. Americans tended to filter the "messages" of mass media through the prism of their own experiences. Italians in Boston's North End may have watched the same television show as African-Americans in rural Alabama, but they responded to the images in different ways. By depicting America as a satiated and affluent society, television may actually have served as an unwitting vehicle of social change. TV's nightly diet of product advertising whetted the appetite of groups excluded from the consumer cornucopia, namely the poor and minorities, and added momentum to their drive for inclusion.

Finally, suburbs, which appeared to some as manifestations of the growing conformity of modern life, were more diverse than critics recognized. Suburban communities included managers and assembly-line workers, Democrats and Republicans, as well as a variety of ethnic and religious groups.

THE POLITICS OF MODERATION, 1952–1956

In style and manner, President Dwight D. Eisenhower served as a political symbol of the age. As one historian commented, "If he sought not to arouse the people to new political challenges, he was suited to reassure them that their elemental convictions were safe from doubt and confusion." At home, Eisenhower's philosophy of "dynamic conservatism" was a policy experiment that attracted groups with differing views of government, reassuring conservatives at the same time that it consolidated New Deal programs. Abroad, despite Republican rhetoric about national "liberation," Eisenhower allowed caution to guide his policy. By the end of the decade, however, the rise of Third World nationalism exposed the limits of America's bipolar view of world affairs.

"I Like Ike": The Election of 1952 Eisenhower had not taken the typical route into politics. Born in Denison, Texas, on October 4, 1890, Eisenhower grew up in Abilene, Kansas, before becoming a career military officer. After leading the British-American military forces that defeated Germany in 1945, Eisenhower remained in the army as Chief of

Staff until 1948, when he accepted the presidency of Columbia University. Three years later he was called back to serve as the first supreme commander of NATO forces in Europe.

Eisenhower's status as a war hero made him a popular choice to run for president in 1952. Bumper stickers across the country cheerily proclaimed "I Like Ike." At first, Eisenhower expressed little interest, but he feared that if he did not run the Republican Party would nominate Ohio Senator Robert Taft. Though Taft enjoyed a large following among the party's Old Guard, his isolationist views and uninspiring manner dismayed Eisenhower and limited Taft's appeal to mainstream voters. When, in February 1952, Taft advocated bringing American troops home from Europe, Eisenhower decided to run. He resigned from NATO and entered his name for the Republican nomination.

After a bitter convention struggle, Eisenhower won the nomination. To appease the party's right wing he selected thirty-nine-year-old Senator Richard Nixon of California as his running mate. Besides hailing from an important western state, Nixon had close ties to party conservatives. He was also a ferocious, frequently unscrupulous campaigner who could keep the Democrats on the defensive while Eisenhower took the high road.

The Democrats faced a more difficult choice. In March a beleaguered President Harry Truman announced that he would not seek a second term. Recent investigations had linked appointees in Truman's administration to influence peddling and other corrupt practices. The scandals, added to the stalemate in Korea and McCarthy's persistent accusations that the administration was "soft on communism," drove Truman's popularity to an all-time low of 26 percent. With Truman out of the picture, many Democrats looked to popular Illinois Governor Adlai Stevenson. Along with being an incumbent governor of a large and powerful state, Stevenson had endeared himself to party loyalists by taking strong positions on civil rights and civil liberties. Like Eisenhower, Stevenson expressed little interest in the nomination, but he bowed to party leaders' insistence. To balance the ticket, Stevenson selected a segregationist senator, John Sparkman of Alabama, to round out the ticket.

The GOP campaign correctly identified Korea, communism, and corruption as key issues. The Republicans complained of "plunder at home, blunder abroad" and promised to "clean up the mess in Washington." Nixon referred to "Adlai the Appeaser" who was a "Ph.D. graduate of Dean Acheson's cowardly College of Communist Containment." Eisenhower, just ten days before the election, declared, "I shall go to Korea." Though he did not say what he would do when he got there, his pledge was a masterful stroke. In a break with most presidential elections, which are decided primarily on domestic issues, more than half the electorate regarded the war as the country's single most important problem, and most people believed that Eisenhower's military background made him the best candidate to end the conflict.

The Republicans did have to endure an embarrassing scandal of their own, however. In September the *New York Post* revealed that a group of wealthy California businessmen had provided Nixon with an $18,000 private "slush fund" to pay for personal campaign expenses. On September 23 Nixon went on national television to defend himself, citing the emotional and material needs of his family, not personal ambition, as his reason for accepting the money. Near the end of the talk

Nixon told the story of one special gift he had received—a "little cocker spaniel dog," which his daughter Tricia had named Checkers. He vowed his family would keep the dog "regardless of what they say about it." The address revealed the growing importance of television in politics. Over 9 million sets were tuned into Nixon's speech, and popular reaction was overwhelmingly favorable. Eisenhower, recognizing the positive response, assured Nixon, "You're my boy."

On election day Eisenhower won 55.1 percent of the popular vote and carried thirty-nine states. Stevenson won 44.4 percent of the popular vote and carried nine states, all southern. Most significant, Eisenhower offset Democratic strength in major urban areas by scoring well in the growing suburbs (see map below).

"Dynamic Conservatism" at Home

Eisenhower called his political philosophy "dynamic conservatism," which he defined as "conservative when it comes to money and liberal when it comes to human beings." Like many conservatives, Eisenhower believed that the executive branch had grown too strong under Roosevelt and Truman. Government regulation had strangled business, while the growth of executive power had disrupted the delicate constitutional balance among the branches of government. The solution, he argued, was to take a more restrained

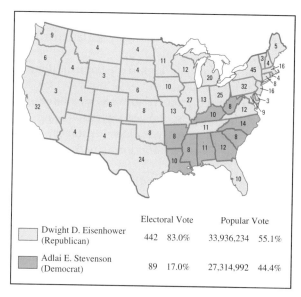

	Electoral Vote	Popular Vote
Dwight D. Eisenhower (Republican)	442 83.0%	33,936,234 55.1%
Adlai E. Stevenson (Democrat)	89 17.0%	27,314,992 44.4%

The Election of 1952   Though a political novice, Dwight D. Eisenhower's persona as a war hero and man of the people gave him the edge over his more experienced, yet less-well-known opponent, Adlai Stevenson. Stevenson won only eighty-nine electoral votes, all from traditionally Democratic southern states, while Eisenhower's popularity and his promise to end the Korean War swayed residents across the nation to vote for Ike. The 1956 election pitted the same two men against each other and again Eisenhower won—by an even greater margin of victory than in 1952.

approach to the presidency. "I am not one of those desk-pounding types that likes to stick out his jaw and look like he is bossing the show," he said.

The new president was determined to reverse the direction taken by the New Deal and Fair Deal or, in his words, to remove "the Left-Wingish, pinkish influence in our life." To help carry out his program, Eisenhower selected a conservative cabinet and gave it wide discretion. "The White House will stay out of your hair," he said.

Despite the hopes of many conservatives and the fears of liberals, Eisenhower did not undermine the foundation of the modern welfare state. Political and economic realities prevented such a drastic step. Congressional Democrats, who recaptured control of both houses in 1954 and retained it throughout the remainder of Eisenhower's presidency, would have blocked any attempt to repeal established programs. Also, sharp recessions in 1954 and 1958 led the president to abandon his budget-balancing efforts and to accelerate government spending.

Indeed, in the end, Eisenhower's policies consolidated and strengthened the New Deal's economic and social programs. The president and Congress agreed in 1954, and again in 1956, to increase social security benefits and to broaden the federal system to include an estimated 10 million new workers. In 1955 Congress and Eisenhower compromised on a new minimum wage law that increased the minimum from seventy-five cents to $1 an hour. Between 1953 and 1961 the federal government spent some $1.3 billion for slum clearance and public housing. In health and medical welfare, Eisenhower also carried forward the programs begun by Roosevelt and Truman. On April 1, 1953, Eisenhower signed a bill that raised the Federal Security Agency to cabinet rank as the Department of Health, Education, and Welfare.

While consolidating the New Deal, Eisenhower outflanked his party's right wing by intensifying the campaign against internal subversion. Soon after taking office, he toughened the government loyalty program. Under his new guidelines, almost ten thousand federal employees resigned or were dismissed. The administration also supported the Communist Control Act. Passed by Congress in 1954, the law prohibited communists from running for public office.

Eisenhower hoped that his aggressive loyalty program would steal the limelight from Joseph McCarthy. But McCarthy had other ideas. In October 1953 McCarthy blasted the administration for conducting a foreign policy of "whiny, whimpering appeasement." At the same time his subcommittee conducted seventeen hearings, including ten that focused on current subversion in government.

Eisenhower had had enough. In March 1954 the president leaked to the press an army report that documented attempts by McCarthy and his staff to win preferential treatment for a former staff member drafted into the army. The Senate, embarrassed by the army's accusations, decided to hold investigative public hearings carried live on national television. Beginning on April 27 as many as 20 million Americans watched the proceedings for thirty-five days. Toward the end, McCarthy savagely attacked a lawyer for having once belonged to a left-wing organization. Outraged, attorney Joseph Welch berated McCarthy, concluding, "Have you no sense of decency, sir, at long last? Have you left no sense of decency?" After watching McCarthy on television, a majority of Americans were asking the same question. As his appeal ebbed, the Senate roused itself against McCarthy, voting in

December 1954 to "condemn" him for bringing the Congress into disrepute. Three years later, at the age of forty-eight, Joseph McCarthy, once the most feared man in America, died of hepatitis and other health problems caused by alcoholism.

McCarthy's fall removed a major source of embarrassment and virtually guaranteed Eisenhower's reelection in 1956. Polls showed Ike leading all Democratic challengers by wide margins. The president's enormous popularity had as much to do with his style and personality as it did with his policies. Most people viewed Eisenhower as a strong leader and a likeable man who embodied traditional American values. He often spoke of old-fashioned virtues such as honor, duty, patriotism, and hard work. The White House seemed home to a traditional family, with First Lady Mamie Eisenhower playing the proper role of dutiful wife. "Ike took care of the office," she declared; "I ran the house."

Realizing that television allowed politicians to project themselves into the homes of millions of potential voters, Eisenhower hired movie star Robert Montgomery to help craft his media image. By 1955 Ike was so confident in his ability to perform for the cameras that he became the first president to allow television coverage of his press conferences.

After a spirited primary campaign, Democrats turned again to Adlai Stevenson to lead their party. Stevenson ran an energetic campaign for a "New America" where "poverty is abolished" and "freedom is made real for everybody." But he was no match for Eisenhower. On election day Ike polled 35,590,472 popular votes and carried forty-one states to Stevenson's meager 26,022,752 votes and seven states. It was an endorsement, however, of Eisenhower—not of his party. The Democrats actually increased their majorities in Congress and their governorships.

The "New Look" Abroad

Eisenhower came to the White House better prepared to handle foreign policy than any other twentieth-century president. He had toured the globe and served as supreme wartime commander of Allied forces and NATO. He already had a clear vision of America's role in world affairs. Like most Americans, Ike was convinced of the superiority of American values, committed to spreading the gospel of democracy and free enterprise around the globe, and determined to use American military might to limit Soviet expansion. But he was also a practical man who appreciated the dangers of excessive idealism and understood the need for compromise in the international arena.

Eisenhower delegated a great deal of authority to his secretary of state, John Foster Dulles, but he never relinquished control to Dulles. A leading Republican spokesman on foreign policy, Dulles possessed supreme confidence, faith in the righteousness of his position, and a domineering personality. Dulles, people said, carried foreign policy under his hat. He possessed deeply held convictions about America's role in the world. He believed in a monolithic "world Communist movement," the "unholy alliance of Marx's communism and Russia's imperialism." He came into office denouncing Truman's containment policy. The Eisenhower administration, he vowed, was committed to "liberation" of nations under communist rule. He favored a policy of "brinkmanship"—pushing the Soviet Union to the brink of war before considering negotiations.

Though Dulles dominated the rhetoric during the decade, Eisenhower maintained control of policy. Eisenhower's fiscal conservatism shaped his views of American foreign policy. The Korean conflict taught him that the United States could not afford to fight local wars with conventional troops. America, he believed, should instead take advantage of its overwhelming superiority in nuclear weapons, attacking enemy forces with small nuclear weapons or even striking at the source of the aggression—Moscow or Beijing. Being cheaper than conventional forces, nuclear weapons offered "more bang for the buck." The administration called its defense strategy the "New Look."

A number of features distinguished Eisenhower's New Look strategy. First, to make credible the threat to use atomic arms, the administration dramatically increased the nation's nuclear arsenal. Between 1952 and 1959 the number of nuclear weapons in the American arsenal grew from around fifteen hundred to over six thousand. The navy introduced submarine-based intermediate-range Polaris missiles. The Strategic Air Command (SAC) replaced its aging propeller-driven B-36 bombers with jet-propelled B-47s that could fly 600 miles an hour and hit targets in the Soviet heartland. Yet the New Look defense policy, coupled with the end of the Korean War, enabled Eisenhower to slash defense spending by some 20 percent in his first two years in office. Only the air force saw its budget rise from $15 billion to $19 billion between 1953 and 1959.

Second, in its efforts to surround the Soviet Union strategically, the Eisenhower administration negotiated a number of regional defense treaties. By the end of the 1950s the United States had signed agreements to defend forty-three different nations against "communist aggression."

Third, the administration dramatically expanded the role of the Central Intelligence Agency (CIA), which provided an inexpensive method of protecting American interests abroad. Headed by Allen Dulles, the brother of the secretary of state, by 1955 the CIA employed almost fifteen thousand people, triple its 1950 staff. Among the employees were thousands of covert agents stationed in so-called trouble spots around the world. The CIA expanded its role beyond intelligence gathering to a wide range of political activities, including the overthrow of foreign governments.

Rhetoric and Reality of Liberation

Despite the tough language about brinkmanship and liberation, Eisenhower and Dulles discovered that the realities of international power and domestic politics prevented a radical departure from past practices. The first indication of the continuity in their approach to the world came in Korea, where Eisenhower was determined to end American involvement. But on what terms? Dulles and conservative Republicans objected to any peace proposal that left the communists in control of North Korea and divided the nation into two societies—one free, the other communist. Eisenhower was more interested in ending the war and saving lives than in proving his fidelity to the Republican platform. As promised, he flew to Korea after the 1952 election to nudge the cease-fire talks. He also dropped hints to China that he was ready to use nuclear weapons in Korea. In July 1953 he agreed to terms that called for a division of Korea at approximately the same line that had marked the border in June 1950—the thirty-eighth parallel—with a demilitarized zone separating the two Koreas.

The president showed similar restraint in dealing with a potentially dangerous situation in China. During the fall of 1954, the Communist Chinese began to shell the offshore islands of Quemoy and Matsu, which were occupied by the Nationalist Chinese. Conservatives urged Eisenhower to respond forcefully, perhaps by bombing the mainland. Instead, Eisenhower signed a security agreement with the Nationalists that committed the United States to protect the strategically important island of Formosa (Taiwan), but left ambiguous America's commitment to Quemoy and Matsu. Again, he and Dulles issued public statements hinting at the possibility of using nuclear weapons to stem communist attacks. Chinese leaders, uncertain whether Eisenhower was bluffing, stopped the bombardment.

Eisenhower also pursued a moderate course in his dealings with the Soviet Union. In March 1953, shortly after Eisenhower's election, Soviet leader Joseph Stalin died, raising hopes of a thaw in relations between the two countries. Nikita Khrushchev became Soviet premier and secretary of the Communist Party in March 1958. A shrewd politician, Khrushchev planned to ease Cold War tensions so that his country could spend less money on the military and more on consumer goods.

We Like Ike   Dwight Eisenhower, with his illustrious military record and friendly personality, enjoyed enormous popularity as president. Here he is shown campaigning in New York during the 1952 presidential race. Traveling in an open car surrounded by a large crowd, Ike appears to be open and accessible to the public. Although Ike seemed to personify the blandness and simplicity of the decade, historians have since come to praise the president for his ability to work with the Democratic Congress behind the scenes, his ratification of the welfare state, and his caution in Cold War diplomacy. *(Corbis-Bettmann.)*

He also hoped that lowering the heat of the Cold War would weaken ties between the United States and its Western allies.

Eisenhower approached the new regime cautiously. In a major speech on April 16, 1953, he invited the Soviets to end the arms race. In a dramatic address to the United Nations on December 8 he proposed that the major scientific nations of the world jointly contribute to a United Nations pool of atomic power to be used solely for peaceful purposes. "Let no one think," he said, "that the expenditure of vast sums for systems and weapons of defense can guarantee absolute safety."

The Soviets responded by settling their differences with Germany over war prisoners, by establishing diplomatic relations with Greece, Israel, and Yugoslavia, and by withdrawing troops from neutral Austria. These initiatives led to the first U.S.–Soviet summit meeting in a decade. In July 1955 Eisenhower and Khrushchev, with their British and French counterparts, met in Geneva for the first top-level conference of the wartime Allies since the 1945 meeting at Potsdam. "The United States will never take part in an aggressive war," Eisenhower told the Soviets. Eisenhower also won a propaganda victory with his "Open Skies" proposal, which called for aerial surveillance of both countries' nuclear facilities. The suggestion was neither as bold nor as innovative as many at the time thought. Since American skies were already open, Eisenhower was asking the Soviets to make a unilateral concession—something they refused to do. Ignoring advice from Dulles that he maintain an "austere countenance" in all photographs taken at Geneva, Ike flashed his famous grin while posing with his Soviet counterpart. The cordial atmosphere produced a brief thaw in superpower tensions, which the press labeled "the spirit of Geneva."

The friendly words and smiling faces of Geneva could not mask the serious differences between the two countries. The thaw ended on October 29, 1956, when 200,000 Soviet soldiers and hundreds of tanks swept into Hungary to repress a popular uprising demanding democratic reforms. The Soviet juggernaut killed 40,000 Hungarian freedom fighters and forced 150,000 refugees to flee the country. Conservatives expected the administration to intervene to support the rebels. The CIA recommended parachuting arms and supplies to the Hungarian freedom fighters. But Eisenhower understood the military risks of attempting to intervene in a country so close to the Soviet border. Hungary, he observed sadly, was "as inaccessible to us as Tibet."

The Threat of Third World Nationalism

Hungarians were not alone in striving for independence. After World War II the major European colonial powers—Britain, France, and Portugal—were unable to maintain control of their far-flung empires. Between 1945 and 1960 almost forty nations with 800 million people fought nationalist struggles against colonial rulers. These newly independent nations in Asia, the Middle East, Latin America, and Africa became the new battlegrounds of the Cold War. Henry Cabot Lodge, U.S. ambassador to the United Nations, first asked the question that plagued American policymakers in the years following World War II: "The U.S. can win wars," but, he asked, "can we win revolutions?"

The Middle East confronted the administration with its first serious nationalist challenge. In 1954 Egyptian leader Colonel Gamal Abdel Nasser increased trade with the Soviet bloc and officially recognized China. Two years later, in an attempt to punish Egypt for its growing ties with communists, Dulles abruptly canceled American financing to build the Aswan Dam across the Nile. In response, Nasser seized control of the Suez Canal, the vital waterway between the Mediterranean and the Gulf of Suez, and used the revenue to complete the Aswan project. Arabs hailed Nasser as a hero for his bold stand against Western imperialism. The British, who had controlled the canal, and the French, angered by Nasser's aid to rebels defying French rule in Algeria, conspired to regain control of the canal and teach Nasser a lesson.

They got their chance on October 29, 1956, when, provoked by eight years of border attacks and fear of the Egyptian arms buildup, Israel invaded Egypt's Sinai Peninsula, advancing to within 10 miles of the Suez Canal. In an attack carefully coordinated with the Israelis, the British and French bombed Egyptian military targets and seized the northern third of the canal.

The Anglo-French military action angered Eisenhower, who feared it would alienate nationalist elements in the Middle East and drive the entire Arab world, and its lucrative oil fields, closer to the Russians. The president publicly condemned the attacks on Egypt and worked with the Soviets through the United Nations for a cease-fire and the creation of a special UN Emergency Force to supervise withdrawal of all outside forces from Egypt. By December 1956 the crisis was over, but the Suez affair had shaken the Western alliance to its foundations, provided the Russians with a foothold in the Middle East, and increased anti-Western sentiment in the region. In 1957 Eisenhower asked for, and both houses of Congress passed, a resolution that came to be called the Eisenhower Doctrine. The new plan provided the president with broad authority to provide economic and military assistance to defend any Middle East ally from "international communism."

The administration's foreign policy faced another test in Indochina, where Ho Chi Minh's nationalist movement controlled a part of northern Vietnam and continued to battle French colonial authority. Eisenhower, like Truman, viewed Ho as a communist puppet and believed that if southern Vietnam fell to the communists, all Southeast Asia would be at risk. He compared the nations of Southeast Asia to a row of dominoes: knock one over, and the rest would quickly fall. Eisenhower increased American military and economic aid to bolster the French, but in 1954 Vietnamese and Communist Chinese forces surrounded twelve thousand French troops at Dien Bien Phu, a remote jungle fortress. The French pleaded for direct American intervention to rescue their troops. For weeks the administration debated a course of action. Dulles wanted to take the nation to the "brink of war" by launching air strikes against the North Vietnamese. Vice President Nixon went farther, advocating the use of tactical nuclear weapons. But once again, Eisenhower preferred caution. The president had little faith in the military capability of the French, whom he called "a hopeless, helpless mass of protoplasm." European allies, especially the British, opposed American intervention. At home leading Democrats, including Senators Lyndon Johnson and John F. Kennedy, warned against using American soldiers in Indochina. Eisenhower also worried about the moral implications of using tactical nuclear weapons in Asia. "You boys must be crazy," Eisenhower said. "We can't use those awful things against Asians for the second time in ten years. My God." Without American support, the French garrison surrendered in May 1954.

In July the French government signed the Geneva Accords, which temporarily divided Indochina at the seventeenth parallel until free democratic elections were held in 1956. Realizing that the popular Ho Chi Minh would win in a free election, the administration installed Ngo Dinh Diem, an ardent Vietnamese nationalist who hated the French, as head of state in South Vietnam. Diem was also a staunch anticommunist and devout Catholic. The United States poured economic and military aid into the south in hopes of making Diem a viable leader. In 1954, in an effort to stem Soviet and Chinese influence in the area, Dulles set up yet another anticommunist military alliance, the Southeast Asia Treaty Organization (SEATO). The treaty pledged the United States to defend Australia, New Zealand, Thailand, Pakistan, and the Philippines against communist aggression.

In other regions of the world, the administration relied on the CIA to quell nationalist uprisings that appeared to threaten American interests. In Iran, when the government of Mohammed Mossadegha nationalized the Anglo-Iranian Oil Company in 1953, the CIA planned, financed, and orchestrated a coup to overthrow him. To replace him, the CIA worked with Iranian army officers to consolidate power behind the pro-Western Shah Reza Pahlavi.

In 1954 the administration used the CIA to topple the leftist government of Jacob Arbenz Guzman in Guatemala. In 1953 the Arbenz government had launched an ambitious land-reform program, which included seizing more than two hundred thousand acres controlled by the American-owned United Fruit Company. Warning that the country could become an outpost for communism in the Western Hemisphere, the CIA organized and financed an anti-Arbenz coup. A new government, approved by the CIA, took power and restored the appropriated lands to United Fruit.

Eisenhower's experiments in intervention revealed the flaws in America's approach to nationalist revolutions. Viewing local struggles as part of the superpower competition and as threats to U.S. security, Americans confused indigenous nationalist movements with Soviet-inspired aggression. America's attitude revealed an arrogance of strength, a belief that U.S. power could and should shape the internal affairs of distant nations. In time, America would pay a heavy price for its miscalculations.

AMERICAN IDEALS AND SOCIAL REALITIES, 1950–1960

Intellectuals, politicians, and a majority of Americans viewed postwar prosperity as a vindication of their faith in capitalism and individualism. At the same time, the Cold War sharpened the contrast between capitalism and communism, reinforcing the belief that America stood as a beacon of hope in a troubled world. Despite the popular belief that capitalism had eroded class differences, however, poverty remained a serious problem in the United States. A growing movement of women into the work force contradicted the popular veneration of traditional gender roles. Most striking of all was the continuing tension in the lives of

African-Americans between the promise of equal opportunity and the reality of racial discrimination. In response, black leaders undertook new experiments in pursuit of civil rights.

Intellectuals and the Celebration of Consensus

Postwar prosperity, the lure of suburbia, the stifling effects of McCarthyism, and the oppressive atmosphere of the Cold War discouraged critical social analysis and muted vigorous political debate in 1950s America. Intellectuals gave their scholarly blessing to the self-satisfied images that pervaded mass culture. In 1956 *Time* magazine observed that the intellectual "found himself feeling at home" in America.

Historians, sociologists, and political scientists heralded an "age of consensus," a time when prosperity, social programs, and fear of communism rendered social protest obsolete. At the end of the decade, the sociologist Daniel Bell declared all radical alternatives dead in *The End of Ideology* (1960). Historians such as Daniel Boorstin and Henry Steele Commager minimized the role of conflict and change in American history and stressed the importance of continuity and consensus. Surveys showing that 75 percent of Americans considered themselves part of the middle class contributed to the growing sense that the nation was evolving toward a classless society.

Liberals joined the celebration of consensus, abandoning or moderating their Great Depression arguments for sweeping changes in the nation's economic institutions. "American capitalism works," declared Harvard economist John Kenneth Galbraith early in the decade. Like earlier reformers, liberals in the 1950s believed that government needed to play a role in regulating the economy and guaranteeing social justice. But they also shared with many conservatives a reverence for the enormous potential of the free enterprise system and a fear of expansive federal power. Reflecting the broader Vital Center consensus, liberals believed that sustained economic growth, with a minimum of government regulation, would eliminate class divisions, create opportunity for all citizens, and ensure a stable society.

The New Poverty

The fanfare over a "classless society" fizzled. In spite of widening prosperity, the distribution of income remained uneven, and utopian hopes proved unfounded. In 1960 the top 1 percent of the population held 33 percent of the national wealth, while the bottom 20 percent held only 5 percent. In 1959 a quarter of the population had no liquid assets; over half the population had no savings accounts. "If we made an income pyramid out of child's blocks, with each portraying $1,000 of income," economist Paul Samuelson explained, "the peak would be far higher than the Eiffel Tower, but almost all of us would be within a foot of the ground."

Although poverty had declined significantly since the Great Depression, about 40 million Americans representing 25 percent of the population were poor in 1960. The elderly—people over sixty-five—made up one-fourth of the poor. A fifth were people of color, including 45 percent of African-Americans. The majority of these poor people received little help from the meager welfare system. About half of

America's poor families were not covered by social security in 1960. Only about 20 percent received assistance from the federal government. Money spent on them represented less than 1 percent of the gross national product.

What was new about poverty in the 1950s was that it had moved from the rural farm to the inner city. By 1960 some 55 percent of the poor lived in cities. African-Americans made up a majority of the new urban residents. Before World War II, 80 percent of African-Americans lived in the South. During the war, defense-related jobs lured almost 3 million southern workers to the nation's cities. In 1943 the mechanical cotton picker displaced perhaps 2.3 million family farm workers, many of whom traveled north looking for jobs. At one point in the 1950s the black population of Chicago swelled by more than 2,200 new arrivals each week. By 1960 half of all African-Americans lived in central cities.

Other minority groups joined African-Americans in the cities. During the 1940s the U.S. government encouraged the mechanization of Puerto Rico's sugar cane economy. As a consequence, rural employment plunged, and a large Puerto Rican migration to the mainland began. Between 1940 and 1960 the Puerto Rican population of New York City increased from 70,000 to 613,000. In the West between 1950 and 1960, the Mexican-American population of Los Angeles County doubled from 300,000 to more than 600,000. By 1960 Hispanics made up 16 percent of California's population. Nearly 80 percent of Hispanic-Americans lived in urban centers.

Minorities flooded the nation's cities just as the white middle class and many jobs were fleeing to the suburbs. As noted earlier, discrimination, prevented minorities from following the same route. The Federal Housing Administration, which financed 30 percent of all new homes in the 1950s, endorsed "restrictive covenants" prohibiting sales to minorities. It also contributed to the declining quality of urban housing by supporting redlining, the refusal to write mortgage loans to central city areas.

At the same time, many cities adopted ambitious urban renewal projects that demolished neighborhoods and displaced poor people in the name of progress. By 1963 urban renewal had uprooted 609,000 Americans, two-thirds of whom were minority group members. When planning the route of new superhighways to speed the commute between the suburbs and downtown, Los Angeles officials bypassed wealthy neighborhoods such as Beverly Hills and plowed through densely populated Chicano communities in East Los Angeles and Hollenbeck. In October 1957 the city displaced the Chicano community in Chavez Ravine to make room to build Dodger Stadium.

Women During the 1950s

A gap between popular perceptions and social realities also plagued women during the decade. In a special 1956 issue on American women, *Life* magazine concluded that the ideal modern woman married, cooked and cared for her family, and kept herself busy by joining the local Parent–Teachers Association and leading a troop of Campfire Girls. She entertained guests in her family's suburban house and worked out on the trampoline "to keep her size 12 figure." Television shows reinforced this message.

Life in Suburbia   The domestic wife was an important component of the new suburban culture. She kept a tidy home and garden, cooked delicious meals, raised numerous children, all while looking beautiful, fit, and trim. In keeping with these trends, the fitness craze had its beginnings in postwar America. Here, suburban housewives exercise in front of another sign of the times, the television.   *(Eve Arnold/Magnum Photos, Inc.)*

As the *Life* magazine article revealed, women faced enormous social pressure to conform to traditional gender roles. Many people viewed marriage and childbearing as keys to a stable society and a bulwark against communism. FBI director J. Edgar Hoover lectured that marriage and motherhood would help in the fight against "the twin enemies of freedom—crime and Communism." Popular culture often reinforced the message as Hollywood screen writers, still smarting from their confrontation with Red hunters, required career women to acknowledge marriage as their top priority. "Marriage is the most important thing in the world," Debbie Reynolds says in *The Tender Trap* (1955). "A woman isn't really a woman until she's been married and had children."

However, the decade's celebration of family life failed to account for important changes in women's lives. Between 1940 and 1960 the number of women in the work force doubled. By 1952, 2 million more women worked outside the home than during World War II. Many of the women who joined the work force were middle-aged wives looking for a second income to help their suburban families pay for their new consumer goods. By the early 1960s one worker in three was a woman, and three of five women workers were married.

At the same time the expanding economy provided jobs for women, it also relegated them to low-paying positions. A greater portion of women's jobs than men's jobs were not covered by minimum wage or social security. In 1960 women represented only 3.5 percent of lawyers and 6.1 percent of physicians. But they made up 97 percent of nurses and 85 percent of the librarians. Ninety percent of high school principals were male, whereas 85 percent of elementary school teachers were female.

Evidence of changing sexual behavior also challenged the celebration of traditional family life. Alfred Kinsey, an Indiana University zoologist who had previously studied bees, decided to turn his attention to human sexuality. His studies on *Sexual Behavior in the Human Male* (1948) and *Sexual Behavior in the Human Female* (1953) concluded that premarital sex was common and that married couples frequently engaged in extramarital affairs. His finding that over a third of adult males had homosexual experiences shocked people, and his suggestion that women were as sexually active as men outraged traditionalists, who liked to believe that women copulated only to give birth. *Life* magazine condemned Kinsey's results as an "assault on the family as a basic unit of society, a negation of moral law, and a celebration of licentiousness."

There was little desire to confront the contradictions in women's lives during the 1950s. When pollsters George Gallup and Evan Hill surveyed the views of "The American Woman" for the *Saturday Evening Post* in 1962, they had reason to conclude, after twenty-three hundred interviews, that "few people are as happy as a housewife." Indeed, 96 percent of the women surveyed declared themselves extremely happy or very happy, though most wished that their daughters would marry later and get more education.

The Struggle for Racial Equality

Nowhere was the contradiction between ideals and reality more striking than in the lives of African-Americans. The South's racially segregated schools formed only one piece in a vast mosaic of institutionalized racism. Wherever one looked in early postwar America, blacks were treated as second-class citizens.

Yet following World War II a combination of forces began undermining the pillars of racial segregation in the South. The war had dramatically changed the lives of many blacks, luring millions into armaments plants and labor unions in the North and West. Cold War concerns further eroded ingrained patterns of racism. The reality of racism proved embarrassing to a nation that denounced the Soviets for ignoring human rights and courted newly independent nations in Asia and Africa. It also became impossible to ignore when the mass media, especially television, revealed to the nation the violent white resistance that greeted civil rights activism in the South.

In 1954 the Supreme Court overturned the legal justification for one of the linchpins of white supremacy—the separate-but-equal doctrine—in a unanimous decision popularly known as *Brown v. Board of Education of Topeka, Kansas* (see Competing Voices, page 1134). The *Brown* decision declared segregation in public schools to be illegal. A year later the Supreme Court instructed federal district courts to require local authorities to show "good faith" and to move with "all deliberate speed" toward desegregation of all public schools.

The historic decision triggered massive resistance to ending Jim Crow among state and local politicians in the South. Nineteen southern senators and seventy-seven representatives signed a manifesto in 1956 that bound them to "use all lawful means to bring about a reversal of this decision which is contrary to the Court and to prevent the use of force in its implementation."

The first outright defiance of the federal courts occurred in Little Rock, Arkansas. Desegregation of Central High School was scheduled to begin in September 1957. But many whites wished to obstruct the plan, and the state's ambitious governor, Orville Faubus, believed that supporting desegregation would be political suicide. Faubus called out the National Guard to prevent black students from entering Central High. The guardsmen, with bayonets drawn, tuned back the nine young African-American students, impeding segregation for nearly three weeks until a federal judge ordered them removed. The students managed to enter the school, but only after a mob of unruly whites outside pelted and pushed the police who tried to protect the students. National television cameras recorded the ugly events. President Eisenhower, who privately deplored the *Brown* decision, responded by sending federal troops to uphold the Court order. For the first time since Radical Reconstruction, the federal government demonstrated that it would use military force to protect rights guaranteed to blacks by the Constitution. Troops patrolled the high school for months, but the controversy over desegregation convulsed the city for two more years.

The *Brown* decision and Eisenhower's forceful response in Little Rock offered hope that Washington had finally decided to join the black struggle for civil rights. African-Americans, however, were not going to wait for the federal government in their effort to end the daily humiliation of legal segregation. Even before *Brown*, African-Americans living in the South had laid the foundation of a powerful social movement that would challenge the edifice of white supremacy.

African Americans were not the only minority group challenging the fragile Cold War consensus. During the 1940s and 1950s the combination of technological innovation and a population explosion in Mexico propelled massive new waves of immigrants across America's southern border. When Puerto Rico mechanized its sugar cane production, many workers who lost their jobs migrated to the mainland. Between 1940 and 1960 the Puerto Rican population of New York City increased from 70,000 to 613,000.

At the same time the United States recruited millions of Mexican laborers through the *Bracero* program. Created to address the agriculture labor shortage during World War II, the program continued for more than two decades. At its peak in 1957, more than 450,000 Mexicans worked in U.S. agriculture, primarily in Texas and California. By 1960 Hispanics made up 16 percent of California's population. Nearly 80 percent of Hispanic-Americans lived in urban centers.

Hispanic veterans, inspired by their service in World War II and by the evolving African-American freedom struggle, spearheaded their own civil rights movement. "We had earned our credentials as American citizens," observed Hispanic veteran Sabine R. Ulibarri. "We had paid our dues on the counters of conviction and faith. We were not about to take any crap." In 1948, when a funeral home in Three Rivers, Texas, refused to conduct a burial service for a Mexican-American veteran, local leaders formed the American GI Forum (AGIF) to protest discrimination. Over the next decade, under the leadership of Dr. Hector Perez, a World War II combat surgeon with a distinguished service record, AGIF broadened its agenda. It led voter registration drives, filed lawsuits to end discrimination, and helped educate Mexican-American veterans about their rights under the GI Bill.

Native Americans faced renewed pressure after World War II to abandon their tribal associations and integrate into mainstream society. Leading politicians from both parties stressed the need to terminate the tradition of Indian self-rule on the reservation. In 1951 the Bureau of Indian Affairs, often with the support of local tribal councils, began relocating Indians from reservations to cities. The federal government recruited Indians, paid the cost of moving, and provided housing and jobs. By 1957 more than a hundred thousand Indians left the reservations to start new lives in places like Chicago, Los Angeles, and Denver. By the end of the decade more than six hundred thousand Indians, about one-third of the native population, were living in major cities.

The harsh realities of urban life often crushed hopes that burgeoning cities would offer better opportunities. Instead of integrating into American society, many Native Americans established small, often poor, enclaves in large cities. Most of the jobs were low-paying, entry-level positions that were the first cut when business slowed down. "You get placed on the job, and your first job don't work out, where are you?" asked a frustrated Indian. "Several thousand miles from your home and broke."

The Montgomery Bus Boycott

What would become one of the most dramatic symbols of the civil rights movement occurred in Mississippi in 1955. In September Emmett Till, a fourteen-year-old black youth from Chicago, visited relatives near Greenwood, Mississippi. After buying some candy at a rural store, Till allegedly said "Bye, baby" to the white female clerk. Three days later, after midnight, her husband and brother dragged Till from his relatives' home, shot him through the head, cut off his testicles, and dumped his body in the Tallahatchie River. Till's mother insisted on an open casket at the funeral so that, in her words, "All the world can see what they did to my boy." The image of Till's mutilated body, captured by television, seared itself into the consciousness of a generation of black leaders. Despite overwhelming evidence of guilt, an all-white, all-male jury found the two white suspects innocent of kidnapping.

The battered face of Emmett Till was fresh in people's minds when, on December 1, 1955, civil rights activist Rosa Parks intentionally violated Alabama law by refusing to give up her seat to a white person on a city bus in Montgomery. "I felt it was just something I had to do," Parks said. Her simple act of courage became a challenge to the edifice of racial injustice in the South. After police arrested Parks for her defiance, black leaders decided to boycott the city bus system and sought the support of black ministers, the traditional leaders of African-American communities.

Twenty-six-year-old Martin Luther King, Jr., pastor of the Dexter Baptist Church, agreed to head the Montgomery Improvement Association (MIA), created to promote and support the boycott. King had grown up in Atlanta, the son of a prosperous minister of one of the largest Baptist congregations in the country. After graduating from Atlanta's Morehouse College, he had attended Crozer Seminary in Pennsylvania and earned his doctorate at Boston University. King preached

Montgomery Bus Boycotters   In the 1950s, the civil rights movement evolved into a new, more determined phase dominated by ordinary people, such as seamstress Rosa Parks, who sparked the Montgomery bus boycott in 1955 by refusing to give up her seat on a segregated bus. For a little more than a year, African-Americans in the city refused to ride public buses, instead forming carpools and even walking miles to work each day. These black workers are waiting for their ride at a carpool pickup site. Their sacrifices reduced the profits on city buses by 65 percent and produced a Supreme Court decision that declared segregation on city buses unconstitutional.   *(Dan Weiner, Courtesy Sandra Weiner.)*

a philosophy of nonviolent resistance: "We must meet the forces of hate with the power of love; we must meet physical force with soul force."

To deal with their loss of public transportation, the bus boycotters organized a massive and complicated system of carpools that involved twenty-thousand people every day. Some preferred to walk, as far as twelve miles a day, to underline their determination and hope. One elderly woman, known as Mother Pollard, vowed to King that she would walk until it was over. "But aren't your feet tired?" he asked. "Yes," she said, "my feets is tired, but my soul is rested."

The city tried intimidation tactics to break the will of blacks. Policemen stopped carpool drivers and wrote tickets for imaginary violations of the law. The Ku Klux Klan (KKK) marched in full garb through black neighborhoods in an attempt to terrorize residents. Local prosecutors began mass arrests of MIA leaders, including King, under a 1921 statute prohibiting boycotts "without just cause and legal excuse."

The relentless harassment failed. In June 1956 a panel of federal judges struck down Montgomery's segregation ordinances. The state appealed to the Supreme

Court, which upheld the lower court decision. The Montgomery boycott demonstrated that intimidation, which had served for so long to repress black aspirations, would no longer work. In doing so, it laid the foundation for the civil rights struggle of the 1960s. It also established Martin Luther King, Jr., as a persuasive and articulate spokesman for the movement.

THE QUEST FOR NATIONAL PURPOSE, 1957–1960

As the 1950s drew to a close many Americans began to question their view of themselves as a prosperous, satisfied, and secure society. The Soviets' successful launch of a satellite to orbit the earth shocked the American public's confidence in Eisenhower's New Look. A combination of other events, at home and abroad, contributed to the sense that America had lost its way. The United States, many believed, had to muster a stronger resolve and dare a bolder experimentation to fulfill its mission. Echoing this conviction, the young senator from Massachusetts, John F. Kennedy, made the issue of national purpose the centerpiece of his 1960 campaign for president.

Atomic Anxieties   On October 4, 1957, the Soviet Union launched a 184-pound space satellite called *Sputnik,* or "Little Traveler." One month later, it launched a second satellite carrying a small dog, the first living creature to leave the earth's atmosphere. The Soviets gloated, claiming that the achievement demonstrated the superiority of their "socialist society." The Soviet success in space and earlier launch of an intercontinental ballistic missile (ICBM) dealt serious blows to American national pride and created widespread and unfounded fear of a "missile gap" between the United States and the Soviet Union. Asked by reporters what Americans would find should they ever reach the moon, Edward Teller, father of the hydrogen bomb, replied: "Russians."

With both sides armed with ICBMs, the world had been transformed into a global battlefield. At the end of World War II the United States did not have a plane capable of carrying an atomic bomb from the U.S. mainland to the Soviet Union. By 1960, however, it took less than forty-five minutes for an ICBM to travel from one continent to the other.

Sputnik brought to the surface America's underlying anxiety about atomic power. If the USSR had rockets powerful enough to launch satellites, it could also bombard the United States with nuclear weapons. Newspaper articles, books, and government studies reminded people that they were vulnerable to Soviet nuclear bombs. A generation of schoolchildren learned to "duck and cover" in classroom drills for a nuclear attack. A 1959 congressional study concluded that 28 percent of the population likely would be killed by such an attack. Many wealthy Americans responded by building private bomb shelters.

Americans also feared the by-products of the nuclear age, in particular the health consequences of radioactive fallout from bomb tests. The United States exploded 217 nuclear weapons over the Pacific and in Nevada between 1946 and

1962. The Russians conducted 122 tests in the 1950s, and the British at least 50. By the mid-1950s Americans were growing increasingly alarmed by radioactive substances turning up in the soil and in food.

The fears of atomic energy found creative outlet in popular culture. *Mad,* a favorite humor magazine among teens, fantasized that after a nuclear war the "Hit Parade" would include songs that lovers would sing as they "walk down moonlit lanes arm in arm in arm." Hollywood produced a series of monster and mutant movies suggesting that nuclear tests had either dislodged prehistoric monsters or created new, genetically altered creatures. Though universally panned for their cinematic quality, movies such as *The Creature from the Black Lagoon, The Blob,* and *Godzilla* played to public concern about life in the nuclear age.

Public sightings of unidentified flying objects (UFOs), or "flying saucers," also revealed America's atomic anxieties. The modern era of American UFO sightings began in 1947, when a pilot reported seeing nine aircraft resembling flying saucers moving across the sky at approximately 1,200 miles an hour. In these anxious days of the Cold War, Americans speculated that the saucers had either come from outer space or were a new Soviet weapon. Whatever the explanation, the number of UFO sightings skyrocketed during the decade. More than a thousand people reported seeing flying saucers in 1952.

Political and Economic Uncertainties

Sputnik was the first of a series of blows to Americans' pride and stature at the end of the decade. In May 1960 the Soviets shot down an American U-2 spy plane and its pilot, Gary Powers. Washington initially called the flight a weather-data–gathering mission that had strayed off course, but when the Soviets produced Powers and his espionage equipment, Eisenhower confessed responsibility for the U-2 flight. The incident took place two weeks before a scheduled summit meeting in Paris between Eisenhower and Khrushchev. An angry Khrushchev, who paraded the captured American pilot before the world media, canceled the summit and withdrew an invitation for Eisenhower to visit Moscow.

At home a persistent recession contributed to the sense of unease. Unemployment, which had held steady at 4 percent from 1955 to 1957, jumped to 8 percent in 1959. Since fewer people were working and paying taxes, the floundering economy produced huge budget deficits.

Potentially the greatest threat to American pride occurred 90 miles off the coast of Florida on the small island of Cuba. On January 1, 1959, a young lawyer turned revolutionary, Fidel Castro, led a successful insurrection against the American-supported dictatorship of Fulgencio Batista. American economic interests expressed concern when Castro began breaking up large cattle ranches and sugar plantations. When the United States threatened to cut off economic aid, Castro responded by declaring his support for communism and confiscating about $1 billion in U.S. property. In February 1960 the Cuban leader signed a trade agreement with the Soviet Union. In 1961 Eisenhower severed diplomatic relations with Cuba and authorized the CIA to train Cuban expatriates for an invasion of the island.

These blows to American pride spurred a debate about American identity—what it was becoming and what it should be. The poet Carl Sandberg expressed contempt for America's "fat-dripping prosperity." In 1958, in his best-selling book *The Affluent Society*, Harvard economist John Kenneth Galbraith complained that the consumer culture had produced a materialistic society that valued private wealth over public needs. The National Goals Commission, created by President Eisenhower to develop national objectives, supported the opinion of social critics that rampant consumerism had weakened America's moral fiber. By calling for increased government support for education and scientific research, the commission rejected Eisenhower's "dynamic conservatism" and signaled the dawn of more activist government.

Many people blamed the educational system for allowing the Soviets to pass America in the development of space-age rockets. To remedy the situation, Congress passed the National Defense Education Act (NDEA) of 1958. The legislation provided loan funds for college students and fellowships for advanced study, and it promised more resources to strengthen instruction in mathematics, the sciences, and foreign languages at the elementary and secondary school levels. Concern about Soviet missiles pushed Congress to accept the statehood applications of Alaska and Hawaii, areas positioned to provide an early warning system for potential Soviet rocket attacks.

Kennedy and the 1960 Presidential Election

Politically, Democrats planned to capitalize on the growing unease about national purpose. They sharpened their arguments in the 1958 congressional races, when they gained thirteen Senate seats and a massive majority in the House. Indicting a failure of leadership in Washington, Democratic congressional candidates won 56 percent of votes cast—the highest figure since 1936. They planned to continue the attack to capture the White House in 1960.

The Republicans, forced by the Twenty-second Amendment—which limited a president to two terms—to seek a new leader, turned to Vice President Richard Nixon to counter the Democratic offensive. At Nixon's request, Henry Cabot Lodge, ambassador to the United Nations, was drafted as his running mate.

After a tough primary campaign, the Democrats turned to the youthful and attractive Kennedy. The forty-two-year-old senator was the first Catholic to contend for the presidency since Al Smith in 1928. "Jack" Kennedy grew up in a conservative Boston Irish family. After graduating from Harvard he enlisted in the navy during World War II. When a Japanese destroyer rammed his patrol boat, *PT-109*, Kennedy spent hours swimming in shark-infested waters trying to save his crew. He returned from the war a hero, ready to fulfill the ambitions of his father, Joseph P. Kennedy, a wealthy businessman who had served under Roosevelt as ambassador to Great Britain. "It was like being drafted," Kennedy reflected. "My father wanted his eldest son in politics. 'Wanted' isn't the right word. He demanded it." The political journey began in 1946 when Kennedy won a congressional seat. He served three terms in the House before winning election to the Senate in 1954. Six years later voters reelected him to the Senate by the widest popular margin in Massachusetts history.

Kennedy attracted considerable media attention. With the help of his talented group of advisers, he carefully cultivated the image of a youthful, robust leader, hero of *PT-109* and the brilliant author of the Pulitzer Prize–winning book *Profiles in Courage* (1956). In later years, historians would discover that Kennedy had manufactured much of the image. In reality, he suffered from various illnesses, including Addison's disease, which required regular injections of cortisone. A speechwriter had written most of *Profiles in Courage,* and his father's intervention had secured him the Pulitzer Prize. Many liberals also complained that Kennedy's failure to vote with other Democrats to censure Joseph McCarthy revealed that he was long on profile and short on courage.

Whatever his shortcomings, Kennedy possessed considerable political skill and broad popular appeal. He revealed his shrewd political instincts at the 1960 Democratic convention. Realizing he needed a running mate who could provide regional balance and help diminish criticism of his religion, Kennedy asked Texas Senator Lyndon Johnson to join the ticket. The move startled the convention, especially liberals who felt that the selection of a conservative southerner betrayed the party's New Deal heritage. In fact, Kennedy's decision represented a brilliant political stroke that revealed both his pragmatism and his moderation.

Few substantive differences separated Kennedy and Nixon. Both candidates reflected the widespread belief that American institutions were fundamentally sound, that economic growth had alleviated the need for social conflict, and that Soviet

Kennedy Works a Crowd   The young and vibrant John F. Kennedy seemed to signify a new era in America. He challenged the country to reach higher and refuse to be satisfied with the status quo. His charismatic presence, clearly visible in this photograph of the Democratic candidate in South Dakota, helped turn the tide of the 1960 presidential election in his favor. In the first televised debate in American politics, Kennedy's physical appearance helped him emerge as the clear winner over the less exuberant Richard Nixon. *(George Tames/NYT Pictures.)*

aggression presented the greatest threat to American security. Kennedy, however, understood better than Nixon the public's desire for dynamic leadership. Throughout the campaign he struck the right tone with his calls for positive leadership, public sacrifice, and a bold effort to "get America moving again." "I run for the Presidency because I do not want it said that in the years when our generation held political power . . . America began to slip," Kennedy declared with a crisp Boston accent.

Despite Kennedy's appeal, the election remained close. Nixon skillfully played to public concern about Kennedy's inexperience, especially in foreign affairs. Most of all, many Americans were reluctant to vote for a Catholic for president. In a bold stroke Kennedy appeared on September 12 before the Protestant Ministerial Association of Houston, Texas, to emphasize that he placed his oath to the Constitution above the dictates of his church. "I am not the Catholic candidate for President," he said; "I am the Democratic Party's candidate for President who happens also to be a Catholic." Kennedy also energized the African-American community when he intervened to help secure Martin Luther King's release from a Montgomery jail.

The turning point in the campaign came in a series of four televised debates between September 26 and October 24. Kennedy used the debates—the first-ever televised face-off between presidential contenders—to demolish the Republican charge that he was inexperienced and badly informed. And he succeeded far better

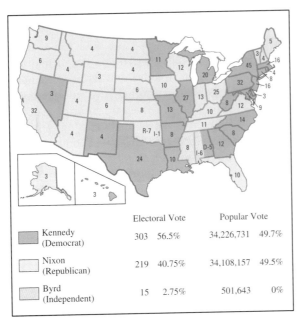

		Electoral Vote		Popular Vote	
Kennedy (Democrat)		303	56.5%	34,226,731	49.7%
Nixon (Republican)		219	40.75%	34,108,157	49.5%
Byrd (Independent)		15	2.75%	501,643	0%

The Election of 1960   The 1960 election was not only the closest presidential race in the twentieth century, it also had the highest voter turnout (63 percent). Yet the discontent of white southerners over the issue of civil rights was evident as all of Mississippi's delegates and some of Alabama's rejected both parties and voted for prosegregationist Senator Harry Byrd of Virginia.

than his opponent in communicating the qualities of boldness, imagination, and poise. Kennedy appeared alert, aggressive, and cool. Nixon, who perspired profusely, looked nervous and uncomfortable. Radio listeners divided evenly on who had won the debate. Television viewers, the overwhelming majority, gave Kennedy a decisive edge. The performance energized Kennedy's campaign, and the debates institutionalized television's role as a major force in American politics.

The momentum from the debate carried Kennedy to victory—though just barely. Of the nearly 68,500,000 popular votes cast, Kennedy won 34,226,731 and Nixon 34,108,157. Kennedy's popular majority of two-tenths of 1 percent was the smallest since 1880. His vote in the electoral college was only slightly more convincing: 303 to 219 (see map on page 1129).

Kennedy's victory signaled a desire for change, but the narrowness of his triumph reflected the caution with which Americans approached the challenges of the new decade. The consumer culture reinforced America's celebration of consensus at the same time that it whetted the appetite for change among groups that were excluded from the benefits of prosperity. During the campaign Kennedy managed to convey a message of change to Americans who questioned the complacency of the consumer culture at the same time that he reassured conservatives that he would not threaten existing arrangements. The tension between American ideals and social realities, which sharpened during the decade, foreshadowed the difficult balancing act that would confront the new president in the next decade.

CONCLUSION

Although the 1950s are generally viewed as a time when Americans rejected social or political experimentation, America and its people underwent enormous change between 1950 and 1960. A consumer revolution transformed American society in the years after World War II. Driven by an unprecedented baby boom, a growing economy, and the seductive appeal of advertising, Americans rushed to fill their new suburban homes with the latest consumer products. The demand for new consumer goods rippled through society, altering the way Americans earned a living, conducted business, and spent their leisure time.

The pervasive influence of the consumer society also altered America's cultural landscape. Television, the most effective purveyor of mass culture during the decade, projected shared images into millions of living rooms across the country. At the same time the boom in automobile sales and the construction of new highways broke down geographical barriers. Teenagers embraced the new culture, transforming rock and roll music into the language of youthful rebellion. Even the religious revivalism of the decade made effective use of mass culture. While some commentators charged that mass culture eroded traditional values and stifled individualism, most intellectuals reinforced the consumer culture's upbeat message.

President Dwight Eisenhower emerged as the most convincing political symbol of the consumer society. Making effective use of television, Eisenhower convinced most voters that he was a strong but amicable leader, the embodiment of traditional American values. A political moderate, Ike struggled to tame liberals who called for a more activist government and to appease conservatives who hoped to dismantle the welfare state. In the end, the president consolidated and strengthened New Deal programs but refused to support new federal initiatives. The public rewarded his effort in 1956, returning him to office in a landslide.

In foreign policy some rhetorical flourishes called for brinkmanship and liberation, and defense's New Look emphasized nuclear superiority, mutual assistance treaties, and covert intervention. But Eisenhower essentially continued his predecessor's containment policy. Like most Americans the president believed the United States had a mission to make the world safe for democracy and that international communism, spearheaded by the Soviet Union and China, represented the greatest threat to American security. But Eisenhower, the experienced soldier and diplomat, also understood that American idealism had to be tempered by political and military realities. He refused to intervene when Russian troops invaded Hungary in 1956 and attempted to lessen Cold War tensions by making peace overtures to the Soviets. The president's moderation did not extend to the Third World, where he unleashed the CIA to topple unfriendly governments and intervened in Indochina.

By portraying America as a prosperous and content society that had solved most of its pressing social and economic problems, the mass media blurred the line between American ideals and social realities. The pervasive image of prosperous white men and content suburban housewives disregarded the facts that nearly 25 percent of the population lived below the poverty line; that sexual discrimination limited opportunities for women; and that African-Americans, Hispanics, and Native Americans were denied the most basic political and civil rights.

Americans' view of themselves as a prosperous, stable people suited to world leadership was vulnerable to realities abroad as well as at home. The decade's placid public mood changed dramatically in October 1957 following the Soviets' successful launch of the space satellite *Sputnik*. Complacency yielded to anxiety as Americans fretted about the possibility of nuclear attack. A string of bad news—Soviet capture of an American spy plane, a communist revolution in Cuba, and a steep recession—led many Americans to believe that the nation had lost its sense of purpose. In the 1960 presidential campaign, Massachusetts Senator John F. Kennedy tapped into the public mood with his calls to "get the nation moving again" and scored a narrow victory over his Republican rival, Vice President Richard Nixon. But the close election suggested that Americans were very cautious about any experimentation that might alter the status quo.

Annotated Suggested Readings

John Diggins's *The Proud Decades* (1988) is a good one-volume survey of America in the 1950s. William E. Leuchtenberg's *A Troubled Feast* (rev. ed., 1983) highlights the contradictions and anxieties of American society during the period, while James T. Patterson focuses on the role of prosperity in *Grand Expectations* (1996). Lizabeth Cohen offers a critical assessment of the culture of consumption in *A Consumer's Republic* (2003). David Halberstam's *The Fifties* (1993) traces the major events and anxieties of the decade. The transformation of America's self-image is the focus of Tom Englehardt's *The End of Victory Culture* (1995).

Steve Gillon looks at the impact of the baby boom on American politics and culture in *Boomer Nation* (2004). Landon Y. Jones also tracks the largest generation through adolescence and early adulthood in *Great Expectations* (1980). Jane S. Smith recounts the development of the polio vaccine in *Patenting the Sun* (1990). Martin Campbell-Kelly and William Aspray study the rise of computers and automation in *Computer* (1996). Alfred D. Chandler chronicles the rise of the modern corporation in *The Visible Hand* (1977).

Kenneth T. Jackson's *Crabgrass Frontier* (1985) is a valuable survey of American suburbia. Dolores Hayden's *Redesigning the American Dream* (1984) discusses the social engineering behind the suburbs. Herbert Gans's *The Levittowners* (1967) is a nuanced study that focuses on the diversity of suburban communities. Tom Lewis's *Divided Highways* (1997) examines how the United States became an auto-oriented nation. The rise of the motel industry is told in Michael Witzel's *The American Motel* (2000), and Eric Schlosser traces the growth of fast-food chains and their impact on American diets in *Fast-Food Nation* (2001).

Erik Barnouw's *Tube of Plenty* (1982) tracks the rise of television, with emphasis on its impact on American culture and politics. Lynn Spigel's *Make Room for TV* (1992) considers the transformation wrought by television on family life, as does Karal A. Marling's *As Seen on TV* (1994). Biographies of influential religious leaders include Carol George's *God's Salesman* (1994) about Norman Vincent Peale and William Martin's *A Prophet with Honor* (1991), which examines the ministry of Billy Graham. The history of rock and roll is examined in James Miller's *Flowers in the Dustbin* (1999), and the role of teens in the Cold War era is examined by Grace Palladino in *Teenagers* (1996).

Stephen E. Ambrose's *Eisenhower* (2 vols., 1983, 1984) is a comprehensive scholarly biography of the president, as is Chester Pach, Jr., and Elmo Richardson's *The Presidency of Dwight D. Eisenhower* (rev. ed., 1991). Fred I. Greenstein's *The Hidden-Hand Presidency* (1982) has interesting material on Eisenhower's campaigns against Adlai Stevenson. In *Reevaluating Eisenhower* (1986), Richard Melanson and David Mayers, eds., explore Eisenhower's relationship with New Deal programs. Nicol Rae's *The Decline and Fall of the Liberal Republicans* (1989) chronicles the struggle between conservatives and moderates in the Republican Party.

In *Eisenhower and the Cold War* (1981), Robert Divine provides an excellent survey of U.S.–Soviet relations in the 1950s. Stephen E. Ambrose's *Ike's Spies* (1981) details the rise of the American intelligence establishment, and the impact of a daring few in the CIA's early years is examined in Evan Thomas's *The Very Best Men* (1995). Richard Immerman provides a valuable case study of the CIA's actions in *The CIA in Guatemala* (1982). Andrew Rotter focuses on America's early Indochina policy in *The Path to Vietnam* (1987), as does David L. Anderson in *Trapped by Success* (1991). Ray Takeyh's *The Origins of the Eisenhower Doctrine* (2000) examines Eisenhower's struggle to balance Cold War theory with the forces of nationalism in the Middle East.

Michael Harrington's *The Other America* (1962) is still a classic exposé of the hidden poverty of the 1950s. Thomas Sugrue's *The Origins of the Urban Crisis* (1996) focuses on inner-city Detroit. Nicholas Lemann covers postwar black migration in *The Promised Land* (1991). James T. Patterson's *America's Struggle Against Poverty* (1981) is a broad survey of the American underclass, as is Jacqueline Jones's tracing of interracial poverty in *The Dispossessed* (1992). Rodolfo Acuna's *Occupied America* (1988) has useful material on Hispanic poverty in the 1950s.

Glenna Matthews's *Just a Housewife* (1987) explores the world of 1950s homemakers, while Wini Brienes, in *Young, White, and Miserable* (1992), analyzes the conflicting sentiments of their daughters. Susan Strasser's *Never Done* (1982) paints a bleak picture of the demands placed on housewives. Betty Friedan's *The Feminine Mystique* (1963) is a critique of the myth of the fulfilled affluent housewife, while the essays in Joanne Meyerwitz's *Not June Cleaver* (1994) examine women who did not fit the domestic stereotype. Elaine Tyler May's *Homeward Bound* (1988) is a valuable study of the American family during the Cold War. The unrealistic image of the ideal family is the theme of Stephanie Coontz's *The Way We Never Were* (1992). The complexities and nontraditional images of the Cold War family structure are revealed in *To Have and to Hold* (2000) by Jessica Weiss.

Aldon D. Morris's *The Origins of the Civil Rights Movement* (1984) details the black community's organizing that presaged the upheaval of the 1960s. Mark Tushnet's *Making Civil Rights Law* (1994) examines the goals and legal work done by the NAACP. David Garrow provides a moving biography of Martin Luther King, Jr., in *Bearing the Cross* (1986). The death of Emmett Till and the subsequent trial and protest are the focus of Stephen Whitfield's *A Death in the Delta* (1991). Robert F. Burk evaluates Eisenhower's performance on race issues in *The Eisenhower Administration and Black Civil Rights* (1984).

Diane Ravitch describes the "crisis" in American education in *The Troubled Crusade* (1983). Robert Divine's *The Sputnik Challenge* (1993) examines Eisenhower's inability to suppress the American belief in a missile gap. Howard Ball's *Justice Downwind* (1986) studies the nuclear testing programs. Peter Wyden's *Bay of Pigs* (1980) details the American reaction to the Cuban revolution, while Thomas Paterson's *Contesting Castro* (1994) examines U.S.–Cuba relations during Castro's uprising and successful revolution.

The *History Companion*

The Politics of Race

Brown v. Board of Education, 1954

On May 17, 1954, Chief Justice Earl Warren read the Supreme Court's unanimous ruling in the case of *Brown* v. *Board of Education of Topeka.* The decision overturned the "separate-but-equal" doctrine established by the Court in 1896 in *Plessy* v. *Ferguson* (see page 646), which had provided the legal underpinning of the southern system of segregation.

The plaintiffs contend that segregated public schools are not "equal" and cannot be made "equal," and that hence they are deprived of the equal protection of the laws. . . .

In approaching this problem, we cannot turn the clock back to 1868 when the Amendment was adopted, or even to 1896 when *Plessy* was written. We must consider public education in light of its full development and its present place in American life throughout the Nation. Only in this way can it be determined if segregation in public schools deprives these plaintiffs of the equal protection of the laws. Today, education is perhaps the most important function of state and local governments. Compulsory school attendance laws and the great expenditures for education both demonstrate our recognition of the importance of education to our democratic society. . . . In these days, it is doubtful that any child may reasonably be expected to succeed in life if he is denied the opportunity of an education. Such an opportunity, where the state has undertaken to provide it, is a right which must be made available to all on equal terms.

We come then to the question presented: Does segregation of children in public schools solely on the basis of race, even though the physical facilities and other "tangible" factors may be equal, deprive the children of the minority group of equal educational opportunities? We believe that it does. . . .

To separate [children] from others of similar age and qualifications solely because of their race generates a feeling of inferiority as to their status in the community that may affect their hearts and minds in a way unlikely ever to be undone. The effect of this separation on their educational opportunities was well stated by a finding in the Kansas case by a court which nevertheless felt compelled to rule against the Negro plaintiffs: "Segregation of white and colored children in public schools has a detrimental effect upon the colored children. The impact is greater when it has the sanction of the law; for the policy of separating the races is usually interpreted as denoting the inferiority of the Negro group. . . . Segregation with the sanction of law, therefore, has a tendency to retard the educational and mental development of Negro children and to deprive them of some of the benefits they would receive in a [racially] integrated school system." Whatever may have been the extent of psychological knowledge at the time of *Plessy* v. *Ferguson,* this finding is amply supported by modern authority. . . .

We conclude that in the field of public education the doctrine of "separate but equal" has no place. Separate educational facilities are inherently unequal.

The Southern Manifesto, 1956

Angered by the *Brown* decision, many southern whites engaged in a campaign of massive resistance. Their defiance hardened after the Supreme Court ruled that local officials must move with "all deliberate speed" to implement desegregation. Prominent elected officials, such as Senator Harry Byrd of Virginia, helped orchestrate the resistance. Unable to secure the necessary votes for a congressional resolution denouncing *Brown*, Byrd issued the "Southern Manifesto" in March 1956. Signed by nineteen senators and eighty-two congressmen, the Manifesto sent a clear message of defiance to the rest of the nation.

We regard the decision of the Supreme Court in the school cases as clear abuse of judicial power. It climaxes a trend in the Federal judiciary undertaking to legislate, in derogation of the authority of Congress, and to encroach upon the reserved rights of the states and the people.

The original Constitution does not mention education. Neither does the Fourteenth Amendment nor any other amendment. The debates preceding the submission of the Fourteenth Amendment clearly show that there was no intent that it should affect the systems of education maintained by the states. . . .

When the amendment was adopted in 1868, there were thirty-seven states of the Union. Every one of the twenty-six states that had any substantial racial differences among its people either approved the operation of segregated schools already in existence or subsequently established such schools by action of the same lawmaking body which considered the Fourteenth Amendment. . . .

This unwarranted exercise of power by the court, contrary to the Constitution, is creating chaos and confusion in the states principally affected. It is destroying the amicable relations between the white and negro races that have been created through ninety years of patient effort by the good people of both races. It has planted hatred and suspicion where there has been heretofore friendship and understanding. . . .

With the gravest concern for the explosive and dangerous condition created by this decision and inflamed outside meddlers:

We reaffirm our reliance on the Constitution as the fundamental law of the land.

We decry the Supreme Court's encroachments on rights reserved to the states and to the people, contrary to established law and to the Constitution.

We commend the motives of those states which have declared the intention to resist forced integration by any lawful means.

We appeal to the states and people who are not directly affected by these decisions to consider the constitutional principles involved against the time when they too, on issues vital to them, may be the victims of judicial encroachments.

In 1951 the Reverend Oliver Brown tried to enroll his eight-year-old daughter Linda in an all-white elementary school in Topeka. School officials refused to admit her, citing a law in force in Kansas and sixteen other states requiring black children to attend segregated educational facilities. Instead of walking the four blocks to her neighborhood school, Linda had to board a bus every morning for the five-mile journey to an all-black school across town. With the help of a small team of skilled black lawyers from Howard University and the NAACP, led by Thurgood Marshall, the Reverend Brown took the case to court.

The suit claimed that refusal to admit Linda Brown violated the equal protection clause of the Fourteenth Amendment, according to which, "No State ... shall deprive any person of life, liberty, or property, without due process of law; nor deny to any person within its jurisdiction the equal protection of the laws." The case quietly worked its way up the appeal system and reached the Supreme Court in 1954.

The Supreme Court's unanimous decision in the *Brown* case represented a historic affirmation of the egalitarian ideals of American society. These ideals found expression in the preamble of the Declaration of Independence, which proclaims that "all men are created equal." America's commitment to equality has often been tested, but never more so than on issues of race. The nation's founders sanctioned slavery in the Constitution. The Civil War brought about the abolition of slavery. But for most of the next one hundred years, hopes for true equality in race relations were frustrated by deeply imbedded racial attitudes, government indifference, and a pervasive system of racial segregation. In 1954 the Warren Court stepped into the moral void and resurrected the American ideal of equality in race relations.

Opponents of the *Brown* ruling were not without their own ideological resources. They could tap into a competing strain of American political thought that stressed individual liberty and fear of centralized government. The nation's founders believed that government power was antithetical to individual liberty, and the Constitution limited federal power by delegating broad authority to the individual states. The belief in liberty and states' rights found full expression in the Southern Manifesto.

The *Brown* decision struck a fatal blow to the system of public segregation in the South. It added legitimacy to the civil rights movement and quickened the pace of change. But it left many issues unresolved. Would abolishing legal segregation alone be enough to guarantee blacks equal opportunity? The *Brown* case dealt with schools that legally mandated segregation between the races. What about schools that were segregated because they were in all-black or all-white neighborhoods? Should the Court also force them to integrate? These questions would continue to perplex Americans as they struggled to find common ground between the competing values of liberty and equality.

QUESTIONS FOR ANALYSIS

1. Why does the Court argue that segregated schools are "inherently unequal"?

2. Why is education regarded as fundamental to democratic society?

3. The *Chicago Defender,* a black newspaper, called *Brown* a "second emancipation proclamation." Is this assessment justified?

4. On what grounds does the Manifesto reject *Brown*?

5. Did the Court accept the NAACP's position, or did it find other reasons for overturning the doctrine of "separate but equal"?

6. How and why does the Manifesto's interpretation of the Fourteenth Amendment differ from the Supreme Court's?

7. What assumptions shape the Manifesto's view of race relations in the South? Does the Manifesto recognize that a problem existed?

29

Consensus and Confrontation

1960–1968

Mrs. Connally said, "Mr. President, you can't say Dallas doesn't love you." Kennedy answered, "That's obvious."

In November 1963 President John F. Kennedy began laying the foundation for his 1964 reelection campaign by visiting the key state of Texas. Shortly after noon on the twenty-second, his entourage arrived at Dallas's Love Field airport. Kennedy, handsomely attired in a gray suit and pinstriped shirt, exited the plane with his wife, Jacqueline, who wore a strawberry-pink wool outfit and matching pillbox hat and cradled a bouquet of red roses. After shaking a few hands, the president, the First Lady, and Texas Governor John Connally and his wife, Nellie, slid into the back of their open-top Lincoln limousine. Since it was a bright autumn day, Kennedy chose not to use the bulletproof bubble top.

Dense, friendly crowds greeted the president's motorcade of eighteen cars and three buses. When the cars turned westward onto Main Street, people were everywhere, waving from office buildings, filling the streets, cheering. As they rolled slowly through the crowds, Mrs. Connally said, "Mr. President, you can't say Dallas doesn't love you." Kennedy answered, "That's obvious." The time was 12:30 P.M.

Suddenly the sound of gunfire ripped through the air. "Oh no!" Mrs. Kennedy cried. The president clutched his neck with both hands and slumped down in his seat. One bullet had passed through his throat; another had shattered his skull. Governor Connally had also been hit, seriously but not mortally. The driver pulled the limousine out of the motorcade line and sped to Parkland Hospital's emergency entrance, arriving at 12:36 P.M. A Secret Service agent lifted Kennedy from his wife's arms, placed him on a stretcher, and rushed him into Trauma Room 1. Doctors were shocked by the extent of his wounds. "I looked at the President's head," recalled one physician. "A considerable portion of the skull, of the brain, was gone." As a grieving Mrs. Kennedy looked on, doctors worked feverishly to revive her husband. Their efforts were in vain. The president was pronounced dead at 1 P.M.

On the presidential plane carrying the slain president's body back to Washington, Judge Sarah T. Hughes of the Northern District of Texas administered the oath of office to Lyndon Johnson. A stunned and blood-soaked Mrs. Kennedy stood to the left of the new president. Within hours of the assassination, Dallas police arrested Lee Harvey Oswald and charged him with assassinating the president. Two days later, Jack Ruby, a Dallas nightclub owner, shot and killed Oswald as police were transferring him to another prison.

The trauma, played over seventy-five straight hours on television, burned into the national consciousness. On Monday, November 25, more than 100 million people watched as a horse-drawn caisson, the one that had brought home Abraham Lincoln's body in 1865, carried Kennedy's remains from the White House to the Capitol. Television viewing reached the highest level ever recorded up to that time—93 percent of homes with a television were tuned in.

For a generation of Americans, Kennedy's assassination served as a symbolic marker separating the confident consensus that marked the 1950s from the period of social conflict and radical experimentation that followed. The president's death was only one of a series of shocks that challenged the illusion of consensus. Domestic turmoil exposed profound race and class divisions in America and the persistence of conflict over America's purpose and image. The bitter debates over the Vietnam War raised anew differences about America's role in the world.

Kennedy's death also helped inspire the nation to accept the most ambitious liberal experiment since the New Deal of the 1930s. After winning a landslide election in 1964, Johnson pushed through Congress legislation broadening the federal government's social role. Ironically, at the same time that events were eroding the foundation of consensus, Johnson was constructing a reform agenda based on its assumptions.

● How did the liberal initiatives of Kennedy and Johnson underscore America's ambivalence toward larger government?

● How did African-Americans express their identity as Americans in the struggle for civil rights?"

● What does the youth revolt suggest about social divisions in America and differences over what it means to be an American?

● What impact did the Vietnam War have on Americans' view of themselves and their role in world affairs?

● Why did the liberal consensus prove illusory?

This chapter will address these questions.

THE KENNEDY PRESIDENCY, 1960–1963

Kennedy won election in 1960 by promising to "get the nation moving again." The new president's youthful style and soaring rhetoric inspired the nation and helped reinvigorate America's self-image, although his actions, especially on the home front, seemed timid by comparison. Reluctant to alienate conservatives, Kennedy chose to put off major experiments in social reform. Abroad, Kennedy's get-tough policies produced some of the tensest moments of the Cold War as he asserted America's role as the world's guardian against communist aggression.

CHRONOLOGY

1960	JFK elected president Sit-ins begin SNCC and SDS founded
1961	Bay of Pigs invasion Berlin Wall constructed CORE Freedom Rides begin
1962	Cuban missile crisis Meredith enrolls in University of Mississippi Port Huron Statement released
1963	Kennedy assassinated; Johnson becomes president Wallace stands in schoolhouse door March on Washington
1964	LBJ declares war on poverty LBJ elected president Civil Rights Act Freedom Summer in Mississippi Gulf of Tonkin Resolution passed Berkeley Free Speech Movement
1965	Medicare and Medicaid passed Voting Rights Act Watts riot Malcolm X assassinated Johnson commits American ground forces in Vietnam
1966	Carmichael coins phrase "Black Power"
1968	Tet Offensive LBJ drops out of presidential race King and Kennedy assassinated Democratic national convention erupts in violence Nixon elected president

JFK and the "New Frontier"

At the age of forty-three, John F. Kennedy was the youngest man ever elected president and the first American president born in the twentieth century. Kennedy's inaugural address, delivered on a cloudless and cold January day in 1961, captivated the nation's imagination and captured the hope and expectations of the decade. Calling for "a struggle against the common enemies of man: tyranny, poverty, disease, and war," he promised a "New Frontier" of opportunity and challenge.

Kennedy's youth and charm suited him to the new medium of television. "Memories of the Kennedy days are memories of television," recalled a prominent television producer. With the help of a media-conscious staff the administration produced a constant flow of endearing Kennedy images. His sophisticated and glamorous wife, Jacqueline, and two handsome children, Caroline and John, added to the Kennedy mystique.

Kennedy surrounded himself with bright young men who shared his faith in activist government. Foreign relations counselor McGeorge Bundy, a former Harvard dean, and Dean Rusk, a Rhodes scholar and former diplomat, typified "the best and the brightest." Critics complained that the president's choice for attorney general—his younger brother Robert—lacked legal experience, but Kennedy trusted Robert's shrewd political instincts, clear judgment, and firm support.

The Vital Center intellectuals who filled the White House shared the widely held belief that America had entered an age of consensus. Building on the ideas developed by liberals during the 1950s, they argued that economic growth, when combined with prudent government social programs, would provide every American with a minimum standard of living and boundless opportunity for success. Prosperity offered the added benefit of rendering ideological conflict and social

The King and Queen of Camelot   The Kennedys captivated the American people with their youth, style, and elegance. The First Lady in particular drew admiration; she served as the gracious hostess for lavish White House balls, wore beautiful designer gowns, worked tirelessly to restore the White House's interior, and of course took care of her two young children, themselves favorites of Americans. The fresh breath the Kennedys brought to the presidency earned the administration the nickname "Camelot," after the mythic reign of King Arthur. Here they leave a performance of Irving Berlin's "Mr. President" at Ford's Theater looking every bit American royalty. *(National Archives.)*

struggle obsolete. "Politics," Kennedy said in 1962, was to avoid "basic clashes of philosophy and ideology" and be directed to "ways and means of achieving goals." Proponents of consensus believed that international communism presented the greatest threat to American institutions and values. "The enemy," Kennedy declared with typical flourish, "is the Communist system itself—implacable, insatiable, increasing in its drive for world domination." Convinced that Eisenhower had failed to fight the Cold War with sufficient vigor, Kennedy moved to sharpen ideological differences and to increase military pressure on the Soviet Union.

Acting on the assumptions of the Vital Center, the new president focused much of his energy at home on revitalizing a stagnant economy. During the last two years of the Eisenhower administration, economic growth had slowed to about 2 percent, and unemployment had started creeping upward. At Kennedy's request Congress extended unemployment benefits, raised the minimum wage, broadened social security benefits, increased the defense budget by almost 20 percent, and approved over $4 billion in long-term spending on federally financed housing. It also approved the Area Redevelopment Act, which provided federal aid for poor regions, and the Manpower Retraining Bill, which appropriated $435 million for training workers. Kennedy prodded Congress to double the budget of the National Aeronautics and Space Administration (NASA) and approved a plan to put an American on the moon by 1970. Finally, Congress passed the Revenue Act of 1962, which granted $1 billion in tax breaks to business.

While using government spending to increase economic growth, Kennedy moved to keep the lid on price increases and control inflation by enlisting the aid of business leaders. When Roger Blough, the head of U.S. Steel, announced that he was raising prices $6 a ton in violation of a previous agreement with the White House, Kennedy complained about the "unjustifiable and irresponsible defiance of the public interest" by a "tiny handful of steel executives." After a well-orchestrated White House campaign, Blough retreated.

By 1963 a brief economic downturn convinced Kennedy that he needed to take bolder action. In January the president proposed a tax reduction of $13.5 billion that he hoped would stimulate consumer spending, create new jobs, and generate economic growth. His support of a tax cut revealed Kennedy's willingness to experiment with unconventional ideas. Many liberals, who wanted higher government spending, not more tax cuts, opposed the plan. Conservatives blustered at the idea of intentionally running a budget deficit. Ignoring criticisms from left and right, Kennedy submitted his proposal to Congress.

Kennedy faced many obstacles in his effort to fulfill his campaign promise to "get the country moving again." His narrow victory denied him a clear mandate. He presided over a divided party. Democrats controlled Congress, but conservative southern Democrats who were unsympathetic to Kennedy's liberal proposals controlled key congressional committees. Congress enacted only seven of twenty-three bills that the president submitted in his early months in office, Among the bills defeated was an ambitious health care plan for the elderly and a proposal for federal aid to education.

New Frontiers Abroad

Frustrated by a stubborn Congress at home, Kennedy was freer to express his activist instincts in foreign affairs. The president believed that instability in the Third World presented the greatest danger to American security in the 1960s. He took seriously Khrushchev's warning that the Soviets would continue support for "wars of national liberation" in Asia, Africa, and Latin America. The president and the men who surrounded him believed that Eisenhower's approach of threatening massive retaliation prevented the United States from responding to communist insurgents trying to topple pro-American governments.

The administration called its new defense strategy "flexible response" because it expanded the options for fighting the communist threat. The new strategy had three components. First, it called for a dramatic increase in America's strategic and tactical nuclear capability. In 1961 Kennedy increased the defense budget by 15 percent. By 1963 the United States had 275 major bases in thirty-one nations; sixty-five countries hosted U.S. forces; and the American military trained soldiers in seventy-two countries. In 1961 the United States had 63 intercontinental ballistic missiles (ICBMs); by 1963, 424. During the period 1961–1963, NATO's nuclear firepower increased 60 percent.

Second, it increased economic assistance in troubled parts of the Third World. The administration established the Agency for International Development (AID) to coordinate its foreign aid program. In 1962 the president created the Alliance for Progress, which called for a massive developmental program in Latin America. The most successful venture was the Peace Corps. Established by executive order in 1961, this volunteer group of mostly young Americans numbered five thousand by early 1963 and ten thousand a year later. The volunteers went into developing nations as teachers, agricultural advisers, and technicians.

Finally, to deter aggression, the Pentagon and the CIA increased the training of paramilitary forces. The Pentagon established the Jungle Warfare School, which taught Latin American police squads how to infiltrate leftist groups. Kennedy personally elevated the status of the American Special Forces units, or "Green Berets," who were trained to fight unconventional wars.

Escalating Tensions: Cuba and Berlin

Kennedy's instinctive activism and strong anticommunism led him into the first blunder of his presidency. As president-elect, Kennedy learned of a secret plan, approved by Eisenhower in spring 1960, for the invasion of Cuba by anti-Castro refugees. A few aides expressed doubts about the plan, but the CIA and most military advisers assured Kennedy that it was sound. Having criticized the Eisenhower administration for being soft on communism, Kennedy decided to support the plan.

The invasion on April 17, 1961, was a disaster. Castro's well-trained army anticipated the attack and lay in wait for the sixteen hundred American-trained Cuban exiles who landed at *Bahia de Cochinos* (Bay of Pigs). After three days of intense fighting, the invaders surrendered.

"How could I have been so stupid to let them go ahead?" Kennedy asked. In retrospect, the invasion's poor planning became obvious. American officials had hoped that as news of the rebel landing swept across the island, the Cuban people would rise up in rebellion. Instead, the invasion aroused Cuban nationalist sentiment, strengthened Castro's control over the nation, and pushed him closer to the Soviet Union. The United States suffered widespread international condemnation and humiliating loss of prestige in Latin America.

The public rallied behind the president, but Kennedy remained deeply shaken by the Bay of Pigs fiasco. Hoping to prove himself a leader on the world stage, the president agreed to a summit meeting in Vienna with Soviet premier Khrushchev in June 1961. The meeting did little to boost Kennedy's spirits. Khrushchev was especially militant about Berlin (see page 1059), a divided city deep in Soviet-controlled East Germany. The Soviet position in Germany had deteriorated in recent years. Thousands of skilled workers were pouring out of East Germany, seeking refuge and jobs in the more prosperous West. Khrushchev was determined to stop the exodus. Yet Kennedy was just as committed to maintaining the autonomy of West Berlin. The American public seemed to support taking a hard line. A poll showed 57 percent of Americans believed Berlin "worth risking total war."

Khrushchev continued to heighten the tension over access to Berlin, and by July a war of words and nerves had developed. Kennedy decided to make Berlin, in the words of a speechwriter, "a question of direct Soviet–American confrontation over a shift in the balance of power." On July 25 Kennedy announced that he was increasing draft calls, extending enlistments, and mobilizing some National Guard units.

Before dawn on August 13, 1961, the Soviets responded by starting construction of a wall separating East and West Berlin. American and Soviet tanks stared at each other across the rising barricade. A false move or miscalculation could lead to fighting, perhaps escalating to a nuclear confrontation. The troops managed to avoid an incident, and Khrushchev backed down from his threat to block American supply routes. Tensions between the superpowers eased—but only temporarily.

The Cuban Missile Crisis

On October 14, 1962, an American U-2 spy plane discovered offensive nuclear missile sites in Cuba. Khrushchev "can't do that to me!" Kennedy declared. Two days later, Kennedy met with his top advisers to consider how to respond to this audacious strategic move. The military warned that the missiles would soon be operational and able to strike cities up and down the East Coast of the United States.

Kennedy initially supported an air strike to destroy the missile sites, but an air strike alone could not destroy all the targets. Attorney General Robert Kennedy, who played an important role in the discussions, warned that the Soviet response to a military action "could be so severe as to lead to general nuclear war." He also worried that it would diminish America's moral position in the world.

On October 22 Kennedy decided on a more moderate course of action: he would impose a naval quarantine of the island. A blockade would provide more time for each side to contemplate the costs of its actions and possibly provide the Russians with a graceful way to back out of the crisis. Later that evening Kennedy delivered a nationwide television address to the American people. Declaring the Russian tactic in Cuba "deliberate, provocative, and unjustified," he insisted the United States must respond "if our courage and our commitments are ever again to be trusted by either friend or foe." Announcing establishment of a "strict quarantine of all offensive military equipment under shipment to Cuba," Kennedy asserted that the United States would demand "prompt dismantling and withdrawal" of all offensive missiles.

The nation, and the world, teetered on the edge of nuclear war. Tension mounted when Khrushchev denounced the blockade as "outright banditry" and accused Kennedy of driving the world to nuclear war. The crisis intensified as a dozen Soviet ships headed toward a possible confrontation with the U.S. Navy off the coast of Cuba. Raising the stakes, Kennedy ordered B-52 aircraft carrying nuclear weapons to stand ready and moved troops south to prepare for a possible invasion. Then he and his advisers waited for the Soviet response.

Khrushchev believed that Kennedy lacked the backbone to force a nuclear confrontation, but as the cargo ships pushed toward the American navy, his intelligence told him the Americans were holding firm. On October 28 Khrushchev retreated, ordering the Soviet ships to turn around. Secretary of State Rusk remarked, "We're eyeball to eyeball and I think the other fellow just blinked." Over the next few days the two superpowers hammered out an agreement to end the confrontation. The United States promised not to invade Cuba if the missiles were quickly withdrawn and if a number of Russian medium-range bombers were returned from Cuba to the USSR. Privately, Kennedy also agreed that American missiles in Turkey would be removed.

In the short run the missile crisis set the stage for a gradual improvement in U.S.–Soviet relations. Both nations, traumatized by their close brush with nuclear war, appeared ready to lessen tensions. Taking the initiative in a speech at American University in June 1963, Kennedy called for a reexamination of American attitudes toward the Soviet Union and the Cold War. He proposed a joint Soviet–American expedition to the moon and approved the sale of $250 million worth of surplus wheat to Russia. The White House and the Kremlin agreed to install a "hot line" to establish direct communications between the leaders of the world's two superpowers. Perhaps the most tangible evidence of the new thaw in relations was the nuclear test ban treaty. The treaty, initialed on July 25, banned atmospheric and underwater nuclear testing.

JFK and Vietnam   Kennedy had less success in dealing with a deteriorating situation in Vietnam. Between 1955 and 1961 the United States had provided over $1 billion in aid to South Vietnam and had sent more than fifteen hundred advisers to provide economic and military assistance. The American effort, however, focused on transforming Ngo Dinh Diem's government into an effective anticommunist fighting force, not on helping him establish a firm base of public support.

Diem had inherited from the French a crippled economy, a poorly trained army, and a corrupt and incompetent government bureaucracy. Ho Chi Minh, the nationalist leader of the communist forces in North Vietnam, added to Diem's problems by creating the communist National Liberation Front (NLF), called Vietcong, in the South to fight a guerrilla war against the Diem government. Diem's aloof personality and authoritarian style contributed to his failure to win his people's support. Indifferent to the concerns of peasants living in the countryside, he ruthlessly suppressed dissenters, including powerful Buddhist groups.

Kennedy had once described Vietnam as the "cornerstone of the free world in Southeast Asia." During the 1950s he publicly supported the Eisenhower administration's decision to maintain a noncommunist South by funneling aid to the Diem government. Yet Kennedy also harbored doubts about whether Diem could unite the country, and he questioned the wisdom of using American ground forces in the jungles of Southeast Asia.

His advisers offered conflicting advice. In 1961 the chairman of the Joint Chiefs of Staff, General Lyman L. Lemnitzer, urged Kennedy to "grind up the Vietcong with 40,000 American ground troops . . . grab 'em by the balls and their hearts and minds will follow." Undersecretary of State for Economic Affairs George Ball counseled caution, claiming that Vietnam was not a vital American interest. Caught in the middle, Kennedy initially tried taking a hard line with Diem, insisting that American aid was contingent on his willingness to reform his corrupt government and seek accommodation with dissident groups in South Vietnam. When Diem ignored the pressure, the administration backed down. Over the next three years Kennedy increased both economic aid and the number of American military advisers.

The infusion of American support did little to stabilize the Diem regime. The North Vietnamese–supplied Vietcong established control over large portions of the countryside. At the same time, American officials watched helplessly as Diem

Buddhist Monks Protest the Diem Government   From the beginning of American involvement in Vietnam, the United States found itself aiding less-than-democratic regimes in the South in order to thwart communism in the North. President Ngo Dinh Diem ruled autocratically, abolishing local elections, curbing the press, and harassing his enemies. In 1963, Diem's actions literally drew fire from devout Buddhist priests, who set themselves ablaze to protest his administration. Photographs such as this one horrified the American public, who questioned why the United States supported a government that provoked this kind of defiance. President Kennedy, also disturbed by the images, gave his tacit approval to a military coup that overthrew and assassinated Diem.   *(AP/Wide World Photos, Inc.)*

gradually lost control. The situation reached a boiling point in the summer of 1963 when Diem ordered his troops to fire on Buddhist leaders holding banned religious celebrations. Anti-Diem forces immediately rallied to the Buddhists, and civil war threatened within the principal cities. Several Buddhists responded by publicly burning themselves to death, an act that Diem's government ridiculed as a "barbecue show." The deaths, flashed on the evening news in the United States, dramatized the growing opposition, and forced Kennedy's hand.

Confronted by the possibility of a massive revolt against the Diem government, Kennedy reconsidered his support of the beleaguered ally. When South Vietnamese generals approached Washington with plans for a coup, Kennedy reluctantly agreed. On November 1, 1963, the generals seized key military and communications installations and demanded Diem's resignation. Later that day Diem was captured and, despite American assurances of safe passage, murdered.

During Kennedy's years in office, the United States spent nearly $1 billion in South Vietnam, increased the number of American military advisers to more than sixteen thousand, and witnessed the deaths of 108 U.S. soldiers. But the Vietcong were stronger than ever. Two weeks after the coup, Kennedy ordered a "complete and very profound review of how we got into this country, what we thought we were doing, and what we now think we can do." Kennedy would never see the report.

THE NEW LIBERAL EXPERIMENT, 1963–1966

Lyndon Johnson's vision of a "Great Society" was an experiment built on a foundation of shared assumptions. The president and many of his advisers believed that a rising tide of prosperity would ease the inherent tensions in American life— between equality and individualism, local control and national power—by forging a national consensus in favor of economic growth, anticommunism, and activist government. Johnson used his masterful political skills to push through a long list of legislation designed to achieve his goals.

Lyndon Johnson and the War on Poverty

Within months of Kennedy's assassination, polls showed a majority of Americans questioning whether Lee Harvey Oswald had acted alone. To quell the doubts, President Johnson appointed Chief Justice Earl Warren to chair an investigative commission of seven prominent public figures. On September 24, 1964, the President's Commission on the Assassination of President Kennedy, popularly known as the Warren Commission, reported that there was no conspiracy, foreign or domestic: Lee Harvey Oswald had acted alone.

The Warren Commission's findings failed to convince skeptics. A *Newsweek* poll taken in 1983, on the twentieth anniversary of the assassination, showed that 74 percent of Americans believed that "others were involved." Critics charged that the Warren Commission ignored evidence and witnesses suggesting another shooter and implicating groups with a motive to shoot the president. But while critics have poked holes in the Warren Commission's findings, they have failed to undermine its final conclusion that Oswald acted alone or to develop a convincing alternative interpretation of events on November 22, 1963.

Kennedy's death brought to the White House a man with a strikingly different background and temperament. Lyndon Baines Johnson was born in 1908 in Stonewall, Texas, and raised in that depressed rural area of the Texas hill country. After completing his education at Southwest Texas State Teachers College in nearby San Marcos, Johnson taught school for a few years. In 1931 he traveled to Washington, where he worked as a clerk to a Texas congressman.

As a young man in Washington during the Great Depression, Johnson developed deep admiration for Franklin Roosevelt, whom he described as "like a daddy to me." In 1937 he won election to Congress on a "Franklin D. and Lyndon B. ticket." He lost a Senate race in 1941, before serving as a lieutenant commander in the navy. In 1948 he earned the nickname "Landslide Lyndon" following his election to the Senate by a margin of eight votes.

Once in the Senate Johnson impressed powerful Democrats with his energy and ambition. As minority leader and then as majority leader, he became a master of parliamentary maneuver and a skillful behind-the-scenes negotiator. A tall, physically imposing man, Johnson was not afraid to twist arms to bend recalcitrant senators to his will. Two journalists described this process as the Johnson treatment. "He moved in close, his face a scant millimeter from his target, his eyes widening and narrowing, his eyebrows rising and falling." In 1955 Johnson suffered a near-fatal heart attack but recovered to seek the Democratic nomination in 1960. Overshadowed by the charismatic Kennedy, he reluctantly accepted second place on the ticket.

The new president displayed a quiet dignity in the traumatic days following Kennedy's assassination. On November 26 he addressed Congress, committing himself to fulfilling the slain president's agenda. "We would be untrue to the trust he reposed in us," he told a joint session of Congress, "if we did not remain true to the tasks he relinquished when God summoned him." Johnson used his political talent to push Congress into enacting a number of Kennedy's initiatives. In February 1964 Congress passed the Kennedy tax package, reducing personal income taxes by more than $10 billion. Many economists believe the tax cut contributed to an economic boom that saw the nation's GNP rise from $591 billion in 1963 to $977 billion in 1970. Johnson also steered through Congress Kennedy's stalled housing and food stamp programs.

Johnson was not content merely to pass Kennedy's agenda. He sought to create a program that would bear his personal brand. In January 1964, in his first State of the Union message, Johnson declared "unconditional war on poverty. . . . [W]e shall not rest until that war is won. The richest Nation on earth can afford to win it. We cannot afford to lose it."

The war on poverty actually had its roots in the Kennedy administration. Like many Americans, Kennedy took office believing that economic growth alone would solve the problems of poverty. In 1962 social activist Michael Harrington passionately challenged that notion in a popular book entitled *The Other America*. Estimating the ranks of the poor at 40 to 50 million, or as much as 25 percent of the U.S. population, Harrington argued that poverty resulted from long-term structural problems, such as unemployment and low wages, which only the federal government could address. On November 19, 1963, just three days before his death, Kennedy asked Walter Heller, the chairman of the Council of Economic Advisors, to design a legislative proposal for fighting poverty. The day after the assassination, Johnson enthusiastically endorsed the council's solution.

The poverty legislation, called the Economic Opportunity Act, authorized almost a billion dollars for a wide range of antipoverty programs including Head Start for preschoolers and the Job Corps for inner-city youth. Volunteers in Service to America (VISTA), a domestic version of the Peace Corps, provided volunteers with the opportunity to work in poor urban areas and depressed rural communities. The law authorized creation of the Office of Economic Opportunity (OEO) to coordinate the antipoverty battle. Johnson chose Peace Corps director R. Sargent Shriver, a Kennedy brother-in-law, to administer the OEO.

The centerpiece of the economic package was the community action program (CAP). The initiative, intended to stimulate sustained involvement among the poor,

Signing a Piece of the Great Society into Law Lyndon Johnson went farther than any previous president to employ the federal government to meet people's needs and solve social problems. Key to his program was ensuring that every American child had an adequate education, from preschool through high school. Johnson, raised in poor, rural Texas, justified his generous education package by claiming that "education is the only valid passport from poverty." Here he signs the Elementary and Secondary Education Act, accompanied by his first grade teacher at the site of the one-room schoolhouse he attended as a boy. *(AP/Wide World Photos, Inc.)*

called for the "maximum feasible participation" of local community members in shaping antipoverty programs. By 1967, however, local Democratic leaders complained that some community action programs had fallen into the hands of radicals. In response, Congress tightened the restrictions on allocating money, thus ending the brief experiment with "maximum feasible participation."

By some measures the various programs that made up the war on poverty succeeded. The proportion of Americans below the federal poverty line fell from 20 percent in 1963 to 13 percent in 1968. For African-Americans, who faced the most desperate conditions, the statistics were even more impressive. The percentage of blacks living below the poverty line dropped from 40 percent to 20 percent between 1960 and 1968. However, a booming economy contributed to these statistics as much as did the antipoverty efforts.

The larger goal of eradicating poverty altogether remained elusive, especially in inner cities. It was naive to believe that educational opportunities, job training, and a climate of hope could untangle the thicket of social problems that produced chronic poverty. But it was not politically feasible, nor did Johnson ever intend, to challenge the nation's basic socioeconomic structure by redistributing wealth. Despite the ambitious scope of the antipoverty agenda, funding proved modest. Average annual expenditures were about $1.7 billion—a small sum to care for the 25 to 35 million Americans who fell below the poverty line. One writer called the war on poverty "a classic instance of the American habit of substituting good intentions for cold hard cash."

By raising expectations in the inner cities and then failing to follow through, the war on poverty left a legacy of bitterness and frustration. The gap between the promise and the performance generated a cycle of disillusion that undermined public confidence in the program. "The program," a critic wrote, "was carried out in such a way as to produce a minimum of the social change its sponsors desired, and to bring about a maximum increase in the opposition to such change."

The 1964 Election and the Great Society

While launching his war on poverty, Johnson was laying the foundation for the 1964 presidential election. At the party's Atlantic City convention, Johnson won the nomination by acclamation. As his running mate, he chose Minnesota Senator Hubert Humphrey, a passionate proponent of civil rights and a leading liberal.

To oppose Johnson in November the Republicans nominated Arizona Senator Barry Goldwater. An outspoken critic of liberal reform, Goldwater hoped to rally millions of conservative voters in the South and West with his calls for smaller government and aggressive anticommunism.

Goldwater's extremism energized the party's vocal right wing but alienated Republican moderates and liberals. "Extremism in the defense of liberty is no vice," he orated. "Moderation in the pursuit of justice is no virtue." He suggested that nuclear weapons be used against Cuba, China, and North Vietnam if they failed to accede to American demands. "Our job, first and foremost," he wrote, "is to persuade the enemy that we would rather follow the world to Kingdom Come than consign it to Hell under communism." GOP campaign posters asserted, "In Your Heart You Know He's Right." (Democrats retorted, "In Your Guts You Know He's Nuts.")

By waging a campaign to court the right, Goldwater conceded the broad middle ground to Johnson, who brilliantly exploited the opportunity. He played the role of the fatherly figure committed to continuing the policies of the nation's fallen leader. Campaigning eighteen hours a day, he reminded voters of his party's past accomplishments and promised to carry the nation to new heights. The election was never close. Johnson's percentage of the popular vote, 61.1 percent, matched Roosevelt's in 1936. Congressional Democrats coasted to victory on the president's coattails, providing the administration with large majorities in both houses: 68 to 32 in the Senate and 295 to 140 in the House.

In spring 1964 Johnson coined a phrase meant to define his vision for the presidency, announcing that he hoped to build a "Great Society," "where men are more concerned with the quality of their goals than the quantity of their goods." At the heart of the Great Society was a belief that economic growth provided all Americans—rich and poor, urban blacks and rural whites, young and old—with the historic opportunity to forge a new national consensus that would shape a more inclusive American identity.

Not surprisingly, many observers viewed the Great Society as a second New Deal. The comparisons pleased Johnson who, on the day after the election, declared, "I am a Roosevelt New Dealer."

Following his victory over Goldwater in November, Johnson and the massive new majorities in both houses launched his Great Society. The administration's top priorities were to rescue two staples of the Democratic agenda since the Fair Deal that had been held hostage by congressional conservatives: medical insurance for the elderly and education funding for the young. Johnson and his new allies in Congress overwhelmed the opposition. Along with providing medical assistance to people on social security (Medicare), the legislation included a Medicaid program that would pay the medical expenses of the poor, regardless of age. "No longer will older Americans be denied the healing miracle of modern medicine," a triumphant Johnson declared. The president also managed to quiet opponents of federal aid to education and convince Congress to pass his Elementary and Secondary Education Act of 1965. Its heart was Title I, which provided more than $1 billion for textbooks, library materials, and special educational programs for poor children.

Mounting momentum enabled Johnson to push through a wide range of legislation. "The legislation rolled through the House and Senate in such profusion and so methodically," recalled one White House official, "that you seemed part of some vast, overpowering machinery, oiled to purr." Congress passed consumer protection acts and provided aid for mass transit, urban development, and slum clearance. The Immigration Act of 1965 eliminated discriminatory quotas and opened the door to an increased flow of immigrants from Asia and Latin America that would profoundly affect American life in the decades ahead.

Johnson made concern for the environment a central tenet of his Great Society. Prodded by the White House, Congress passed legislation mandating tougher regulation of water and air pollution. The Wilderness Act of 1964 set aside over 9 million acres of national forest to be preserved in their unspoiled state. A companion measure, the Wild and Scenic Rivers Act of 1968, similarly protected a number of rivers from the threat of development. The First Lady, Lady Bird Johnson, supported environmental awareness as an eloquent and effective leader of a campaign for national beautification.

Whether the Great Society programs were successful is a subject of heated scholarly debate. Supporters point out that programs such as Medicare and Medicaid provided essential medical benefits to the elderly and the poor. One scholar concluded that the combination of social insurance and public aid during the Great Society had a "highly egalitarian effect on income distribution." Critics, however, point out that the middle class, not the poor, were the chief beneficiaries of many Great Society programs. By refusing to impose restrictions on what doctors could charge patients, Medicare and Medicaid contributed to spiraling medical costs that benefited doctors. Medicare–Medicaid, observed the historian Alan Matusow, "primarily transferred income from middle-class taxpayers to middle-class health professionals." A similar complaint plagued Johnson's compensatory education program. To avoid raising fears of encroaching government power, Johnson gave local school districts authority for developing and implementing education programs. In a classic case of the "curse of localism," school officials skirted federal guidelines and redirected money toward middle-class students.

The Reforms of the Warren Court

The same activist spirit that guided the president and Congress infused the third branch of government—the courts. Under the leadership of Chief Justice Earl Warren the Supreme Court asserted its right to review and declare unconstitutional legislation that it believed infringed on individual rights. A group of liberal judges—especially William O. Douglas, Hugo Black, and William J. Brennan, Jr.—formed a powerful coalition in favor of liberal ideas. Kennedy's 1962 appointment of Secretary of Labor Arthur Goldberg to the Court guaranteed a liberal majority. Acting on its philosophy, the Court issued several landmark rulings.

On civil rights, liberal justices built on the foundation of *Brown* v. *Board of Education* (1954) by upholding the right of demonstrators to participate in public protests. The Court disallowed the use of the poll tax in state and local elections and in 1967 struck at the core of white supremacy doctrine by declaring laws prohibiting interracial marriages to be unconstitutional.

The Court extended its definition of individual rights to other explosive social issues. In the early 1960s twelve states required Bible reading in public schools. Children in New York State recited a nonsectarian Christian prayer: "Almighty God, we acknowledge our dependence upon Thee, and we beg Thy blessings upon us, our parents, our teachers and our country." The Supreme Court, in *Engel* v. *Vitale* (1962), ruled the New York prayer unconstitutional on the grounds that it was a religious activity that placed an "indirect coercive pressure upon religious minorities."

Nowhere did the Court break more decisively with the past than in the area of sexual freedom. In 1965, in *Griswold* v. *Connecticut*, the Court struck down a Connecticut statute banning the sale of contraceptives. In a ruling that would influence future debates about a woman's right to an abortion, Justice William O. Douglas wrote that the Constitution guaranteed "a right to privacy." In 1966 the Court ruled that states could not ban sexually explicit material unless "it is found to be utterly without redeeming social value." Under that standard, nearly all restrictions on the right of an adult to obtain sexually explicit material vanished.

A number of decisions overruled local electoral practices that had prevented full participation in the political process. In 1964, in *Reynolds* v. *Sims*, the Court established the principle of "one man, one vote." Legislative districts, the Court ruled, had to be apportioned so that they represented equal numbers of people. "Legislators represent people, not acres or trees," Warren reminded the country.

Perhaps the Court's most controversial decisions concerned criminal justice. In *Gideon* v. *Wainwright* (1963) the Court ruled that a pauper accused in state courts of a felony must be provided an attorney at public expense. The following year, in *Escobedo* v. *Illinois*, it voided the murder confession of a man who had been denied permission to see his lawyer. In the most controversial criminal rights case, *Miranda* v. *Arizona* (1966), a divided court required police to inform suspected criminals of their right to remain silent and to have an attorney present during interrogation.

The expansion of judicial activism touched a raw nerve among Americans fearful of encroaching federal power. One congressman claimed the justices were "a greater threat to this Union than the entire confines of Soviet Russia." Rulings on pornography, school prayer, and contraception outraged Catholics, fundamentalists, and other religious groups. The court's involvement in apportionment offended traditionalists who charged that questions of representation were best handled by elected leaders. The Court's rulings on criminal rights irked white middle-class Americans worried about rising crime. A 1966 poll showed that 65 percent of Americans opposed recent criminal rights decisions.

PROTEST, POLITICS, AND RACIAL EQUALITY

Racial tensions posed one of the gravest threats to Johnson's vision of a Great Society. By 1965 African-Americans' new, more confrontational strategy to challenge segregation in the South produced a number of notable achievements in securing blacks' rights as Americans.

The Movement Spreads   Late in the afternoon on Monday, February 1, 1960, four well-dressed black students sat down at a segregated lunch counter at a Woolworth's department store in Greensboro, North Carolina, and ordered coffee. "I'm sorry," the waitress said, "we don't serve you here." By the end of the week more than three hundred protesters occupied the Woolworth's lunch counter demanding service. As news of the sit-ins reached other cities, the protest spread "like a fever." By the end of 1960 over seventy thousand people in more than 150 southern cities and towns had participated in sit-ins.

The sit-in movement represented an important change in the strategy of civil rights protesters. It revealed the growing frustration of many younger blacks who were impatient with the slow pace of change and were convinced that more aggressive tactics could force the government to take bolder action to redress existing wrongs. In April 1960 these younger, more militant protesters formed the Student Nonviolent Coordinating Committee (SNCC). The sit-ins also underscored the decentralized, grass-roots approach of the civil rights movement. The success of national figures such as Martin Luther King, Jr., rested on a foundation forged by the courage and commitment of ordinary local people such as Fannie Lou Hamer, Robert Moses, Amelia Boynton, and Fred Shuttlesworth.

In 1961 members of the Congress of Racial Equality (CORE) decided to challenge another pillar of racial segregation. By 1960 the Supreme Court had barred racial segregation in bus and train stations, airport terminals, and other facilities related to interstate transit. But southerners widely ignored these decisions. In May 1961 seven black and six white "Freedom Riders" left Washington on two buses headed for Alabama and Mississippi. "Our intention," declared CORE national director James Farmer, "was to provoke the southern authorities into arresting us and thereby prod the Justice Department into enforcing the law of the land." As the vehicles moved into the Deep South white racists mobilized. At stops along the way the Freedom Riders were assaulted by gangs of thugs brandishing baseball bats, lead pipes, and bicycle chains. A white mob in Birmingham, Alabama, beat the riders so badly that an FBI informant reported that he "couldn't see their faces through the blood." President Kennedy, fearful that the violence would undermine American prestige abroad, negotiated a compromise with southern authorities: if local officials would guarantee the safety of the riders, the federal government would not protest their arrest. Over the next few months over three hundred Freedom Riders were arrested. In September 1961, after hundreds had risked their lives, the Interstate Commerce Commission banned segregation in interstate terminals.

In the fall of 1961 SNCC chose Albany, Georgia, as the site of the next campaign. Attempting to rally opposition to continuing segregation in bus and train terminals, schools, libraries, and parks, local leaders called in Martin Luther King. But wily local authorities avoided the overt violence King needed to arouse national indignation. By the summer of 1962 King left town and the movement had suffered its first defeat.

The Albany campaign had failed, but it left an important legacy to the movement. It was here that African-American spiritual and cultural power found its fullest expression. The sounds of freedom songs, which traced their roots to slave music of the nineteenth century, rocked black churches in Albany, inspiring spiritual commitment to the cause. One slave spiritual—"We Shall Overcome"—became the anthem of the movement. When congregations rose to sing it, recalled one participant, "nobody knew what kept the top of the church on its four walls. It was as if everyone had been lifted up on high."

From Albany the movement moved to Oxford, Mississippi, where James Meredith, a twenty-eight-year-old black air force veteran, attempted to register at the all-white University of Mississippi. When Governor Ross Barnett, a demagogic segregationist, personally blocked Meredith's attempt to register on September 20, 1962, Attorney General Robert Kennedy sent five hundred federal marshals to the university campus. "The eyes of the nation and all the world are upon you and upon all of us," President Kennedy admonished Mississippians. The federal presence failed to intimidate Barnett and his supporters. On September 30 a white mob attacked the federal marshals, killing two and injuring 375. Outraged by the violence, the president ordered thirty thousand regular army troops and federalized national guardsmen to Oxford to restore order. The massive show of force worked: Barnett backed down, and Meredith enrolled.

In March 1963 the civil rights struggle focused on Birmingham, Alabama, perhaps the most segregated city in the South. White terrorists had blown up so many buildings there that some called the town "Bombingham." In March, King decided to violate a state court injunction against protest marches. He and fifty others were promptly arrested and thrown into jail. He spent his weeks behind bars responding to criticism from white Alabama clergy that his tactics were too militant. The result was King's powerful argument for civil disobedience, "Letter from Birmingham Jail" (see Competing Voices, page 1179). King's passionate defense of nonviolence galvanized the Birmingham movement. In May, after his release from jail, King organized a peaceful march to City Hall. Police assaulted the crowd with fire hoses, nightsticks, and police dogs.

Television coverage of the clubbings aroused the indignation of the nation. Kennedy went on national television and called upon the citizens of Birmingham to "maintain standards of responsible conduct that will make outside intervention unnecessary." Eventually, the business community, stung by the national publicity and a black boycott, broke with the city government and agreed to most of King's demands.

In June 1963 the stage shifted to Alabama, where Governor George Wallace planned to fulfill his campaign promise to place himself in the doorway of any schoolhouse under court order to admit blacks. On the morning of June 11, under such a court order, two black students arrived to register at the Huntsville branch of the state university. With television cameras recording the drama, Wallace stood in the doorway, where a deputy attorney general confronted him. Having made his point, Wallace made a brief speech for the television cameras and then allowed the students to register.

The Civil Rights Act of 1964

That evening, Kennedy delivered one of the most eloquent, moving, and important speeches of his presidency. For the first time, he referred to civil rights as a moral issue, one that was, he said, "as old as the scriptures and as clear as the American constitution." Eight days later Kennedy sent his legislative proposals to Congress. He asked for laws to support voting rights, to provide assistance to school districts that were desegregating, to ban segregation of public facilities, and to empower the attorney general to initiate proceedings against the segregation of schools.

To build support for the legislation and to appeal to the conscience of the nation, black leaders organized a March on Washington for August 1963. On August 28 more than a quarter of a million people gathered under a cloudless sky at the Lincoln Memorial for the largest civil rights demonstration in the nation's history. The high point of the sweltering afternoon came when Martin Luther King took the speakers' podium. "Even though we face the difficulties of today and tomorrow," King intoned in his powerful cadence, "I still have a dream. It is a

The Birmingham Police Confront Marchers When civil rights demonstrators led by Martin Luther King, Jr., peacefully took to the streets of Birmingham in early May 1963, police met them with high-pressure fire hoses and trained attack dogs. In this photograph, a seventeen-year-old protester stoically marches ahead while a police dog viciously snaps at him. Images such as this one were displayed in newspapers and on television screens across the country, forcing all who saw them to rethink their positions on civil rights. One reader wrote in to his paper, "Never have I been so ashamed to be a member of the white race." *(Bill Hudson/AP/Wide World Photos, Inc.)*

dream chiefly rooted in the American dream . . . that my four little children will one day live in a nation where they will not be judged by the color of their skin but by the content of their character." For a brief moment the nation embraced King's vision of interracial brotherhood.

After Kennedy's death in November Lyndon Johnson, using the skills he had learned from years on Capitol Hill, assumed personal control of the fight to pass the civil rights package. He told legislators that he would not accept any compromise. In the House, opponents of the legislation attempted to divide liberal forces by adding a provision that would bar employment discrimination against women as well as blacks. But the measure backfired when Congress adopted the amendment without controversy.

The Civil Rights Act of 1964 was the most far-reaching law of its kind since Reconstruction. At its heart was a section guaranteeing equal access to public accommodations. It also strengthened existing machinery for preventing employment discrimination by government contractors and empowered the government to file school desegregation suits and cut off funds wherever racial discrimination was practiced in the application of federal programs.

Gaining Political Power

Many black leaders believed that racism would never be overcome until blacks exercised political power. In 1964 only 2 million of the South's 5 million voting-age blacks were registered to vote. In 1964 SNCC organized a voting rights campaign in Mississippi, where only 5 percent of blacks were registered to vote. The volunteer brigade working to help blacks register, which included many white college students, encountered fierce and sometimes fatal resistance. In June federal agents found the bodies of three workers who had been murdered.

Despite daily beatings and arrests, the volunteers expanded their program to challenge the state's lily-white Democratic organization. They formed their own Mississippi Freedom Democratic Party (MFDP) and elected a separate slate of delegates to the 1964 Democratic convention. When the regular all-white delegation threatened to walk out if the convention seated the protesters, Johnson offered the dissidents two at-large seats and agreed to bar from future conventions any state delegation that practiced discrimination. The Freedom Democrats rejected the compromise. "We didn't come all this way for no two seats," protested Fannie Lou Hamer, the daughter of sharecroppers who had lost her job and been evicted from her home because of her organizing efforts. In the end, however, Johnson and his liberal allies prevailed and the convention voted to accept the compromise.

The compromise at Atlantic City angered many blacks, who no longer felt they could achieve justice through the system. For others, however, it only intensified their efforts to gain the right to vote. In 1965 Martin Luther King chose Selma, Alabama, as the site of a renewed voting rights campaign. "We are not asking, we are demanding the ballot," he declared. Selma was home to 14,400 whites and 15,100 blacks, but its voting roles were 99 percent white and 1 percent black. SNCC workers had spent several frustrating months organizing local residents to vote. But their efforts had reaped few rewards. The chief obstacle was Sheriff Jim Clark, a bulldog-visaged segregationist who led a fearsome group of deputy volunteers, many of them Ku Klux Klan members.

Clark, however, fell prey to King's plan to provoke confrontation. The sheriff steadfastly turned away the waves of blacks who tried to register. During one week more than three thousand protesters were arrested. As police patience wore thin, their actions became more violent. In February a mob of state troopers assaulted a group of blacks, shooting twenty-six-year-old Jimmie Lee Jackson as he tried to protect his mother and grandmother.

Jackson's death inspired black leaders to organize a 54-mile march from Selma to Montgomery to petition Governor Wallace for protection of blacks registering to vote. On March 7, ignoring an order from the governor forbidding the march, 650 blacks and a few whites began walking through Selma. Conspicuously absent from the march was Martin Luther King who, after private pressure from the White House, returned to Atlanta.

On the other side of the Edmund Pettus Bridge, which crosses the Alabama River, a phalanx of sixty state policemen wearing helmets and gas masks awaited

A Former Slave Finally Gets the Vote   Although the Fifteenth Amendment gave African-Americans the right to vote in 1869, that right was effectively withheld from them through loopholes and discriminatory state legislation. The Voting Rights Act of 1965 authorized the attorney general to suspend local and state regulations that interfered with voter registration. The act transformed southern politics in particular, admitting hundreds of thousands of citizens into the political process for the first time. One hundred years after he was freed from slavery, this 106-year-old Mississippi man registers to vote in Batesville. He is escorted by members of the Mississippi Freedom Democratic Party.   *(Corbis-Bettmann.)*

the marchers. After a few tense minutes, the patrolmen moved on the protesters, swinging bullwhips and rubber tubing wrapped in barbed wire. The marchers stumbled over each other in retreat. The images, shown on the evening news, horrified the nation and catalyzed the administration into action.

On March 15 Johnson went before Congress to make his case for a powerful new voting rights bill. On August 6, 1965, after skillfully maneuvering the bill through Congress, Johnson signed into law the Voting Rights Act of 1965. The legislation authorized federal examiners to register voters, and it banned the use of literacy tests. The outcome permanently changed race relations in the South. The most dramatic result was in Mississippi. In 1965 just 28,500 blacks, a mere 7 percent of the voting age population, had been registered; three years later, 250,770 blacks were registered. In eleven southern states, black registration increased by 10 percent from 1964 to 1966, and by another 15 percent in the next four years.

VIETNAM: CONTAINMENT AND TRAGEDY, 1964–1968

Like Kennedy, Johnson was torn between his commitment to preventing a communist victory in Vietnam and his reluctance to get pulled into a major confrontation in Southeast Asia. But his doubts did not prevent him from dramatically enlarging America's involvement in the war. America's technological superiority and enormous firepower proved ineffective in the jungles of Southeast Asia. The young men who fought in Vietnam bore the brunt of a confused mission in an inhospitable environment, while Americans at home questioned the war's importance to U.S. global interests. Vietnam challenged the assumptions that had guided American foreign policy since the end of World War II, producing a passionate debate over America's role in the world.

The Decision to Escalate   The president's key advisers, all leftovers from the Kennedy administration, urged a strong U.S. military response to the deteriorating situation in Saigon. In March 1964 North Vietnam sent twenty-three thousand fresh recruits south to join forces with the National Liberation Front, swelling the ranks of the Vietcong. North Vietnam improved and extended the Ho Chi Minh trail, a network of trails and roads on which supplies flowed south. The increased military pressure added to the political instability in the South. Desertions in South Vietnam's military, the Army of the Republic of Vietnam (ARVN), reached epidemic levels, exceeding six thousand a month in 1964. The CIA estimated that the Vietcong controlled up to 40 percent of the territory of South Vietnam and more than 50 percent of the people.

The president's military advisers believed the war could not be won without severing the flow of supplies from North Vietnam. They recommended a campaign of strategic bombing both to shore up the government in the South and to send a clear signal of U.S. resolve to the North. Only Undersecretary of State George Ball refused to support a bombing mission. "Once on the tiger's back," he observed, "we can not be sure of picking the place to dismount."

Like Kennedy, Johnson dreaded getting mired in a protracted ground war in Southeast Asia. In private conversations he recorded on the White House taping system that were made public in 2001, the president describes himself as "depressed" and "scared to death" about the conflict. On the one hand he was convinced that the United States needed to expand the war to maintain its credibility, but on the other hand he doubted whether the nation could win a war in Vietnam. A wider war, he feared, would distract attention from his Great Society programs and provide critics with ammunition to scale back domestic spending. He told biographer Doris Kearns "that bitch of a war" would destroy "the woman I really loved—the Great Society." At the same time, he remembered the heavy political price Truman had paid for "losing China" (see page 1077), and he vowed not to become the president who "lost Vietnam." Like Kennedy, he accepted the major outlines of the containment policy: the United States had to maintain a strong presence in the world to thwart Soviet adventurism.

Despite his doubts, the president approved the recommendation of his military advisers calling for an incremental escalation in Vietnam. Before implementing the new tactics, Johnson wanted to neutralize potential critics by securing congressional support for a wider war. He needed a dramatic incident to convince the nation to support his plans. He did not have to wait long. On August 4, 1964, while operating in heavy seas about 60 miles off the North Vietnamese coast in the Tonkin Gulf, the U.S. destroyers *C. Turner Joy* and *Maddox* reported that they were under attack by North Vietnamese torpedo boats. Neither saw any enemy vessels, and afterward crew members speculated that poor weather conditions may have contributed to the confusion. Johnson expressed doubts. "For all I know, our navy might have been shooting at whales out there," he confided.

The reported attack nonetheless gave Johnson the opportunity he needed to establish congressional support for his actions in Vietnam. With little debate and strong public support, Congress overwhelmingly ratified the Tonkin Gulf Resolution, which authorized the president to take "all necessary measures to repel any armed attacks against the forces of the United States and to prevent further aggression." The resolution provided the legislative foundation for the Vietnam War. As Lyndon Johnson observed, it was "like Grandma's nightshirt, it covers everything."

Armed with congressional support for a wider war, Johnson launched "a carefully orchestrated bombing attack" against the North. The bombing accomplished neither of its objectives: the enemy intensified its efforts and the political situation in the South continued to deteriorate. In February 1965 the administration responded by launching operation Rolling Thunder, the sustained bombing of North Vietnam that would last until 1968. At first the president kept tight control of the bombing, claiming that the pilots "can't even bomb an outhouse without my approval." By spring he had loosened his control, authorized the use of napalm, and allowed pilots to drop their deadly cargo without prior approval.

Instead of intimidating the North Vietnamese, the bombing raids only stiffened their resolve, and the flow of arms into the South actually increased. In 1964, for the first time, regular North Vietnamese troops moved south to join the indigenous Vietcong. By the spring of 1965 more than sixty-five hundred northern-born regular troops were fighting in the South. The South Vietnamese government, weakened by corruption and constant political intrigue, seemed incapable of stemming the communist advance.

The deteriorating military situation frustrated Johnson, who complained that a "raggedy-ass, fourth-rate country like North Vietnam [could] be causing so much trouble." The Joint Chiefs of Staff pressed the commander-in-chief for both unlimited bombing of the North and the aggressive use of American ground troops in the South. "You must take the fight to the enemy," declared the chairman of the Joint Chiefs. "No one ever won a battle sitting on his ass." In mid-July Secretary of Defense Robert McNamara recommended sending a hundred thousand combat troops, more than doubling the number already there. Again Ball was the lone voice of dissent in the administration, telling the president that he had "serious doubt that an army of westerners can successfully fight Orientals in an Asian jungle."

In July 1965 Johnson made the fateful decision to commit American ground forces to offensive operations in Vietnam. He scaled back McNamara's request for a hundred thousand troops to fifty thousand, though privately he assured the military that he would commit another fifty thousand before the end of the year. Johnson made his decision without consulting Congress or the American people. Fearful of distracting attention from his Great Society programs, he refused to admit that he had dramatically increased America's involvement in Vietnam.

America's War

To lead the combat troops in Vietnam, Johnson chose General William Westmoreland, a veteran of World War II and former superintendent of West Point. Westmoreland planned to limit ground action to search-and-destroy missions launched from fortified bases in the countryside. Rather than confronting the enemy in large-scale ground assaults, he would depend on firepower from ground artillery, helicopter gunships, fighter aircraft, and B-52 bombers. "We'll just go on bleeding them," he said, "until Hanoi wakes up to the fact that they have bled their country to the point of national disaster for generations" (see map on page 1161).

Westmoreland's optimism proved premature. The air war failed to sever the flow of supplies between North and South. Thousands of peasants worked daily to rebuild parts of the Ho Chi Minh trail damaged by American bombs. By 1967 some six thousand tons of supplies arriving daily in North Vietnam from China and the Soviet Union diluted the effects of the bombing. Since the North had an agricultural economy with few industries vital to the war effort, aerial sorties against cities in North Vietnam had little impact on supplies. The civilian toll, however, was heavy. All told, U.S. bombs killed an estimated one hundred thousand North Vietnamese civilians.

Unable to win the war from the air, the administration gradually increased the number of ground troops from 184,000 in late 1965 to more than 500,000 in 1968 (see figure on page 1162). The Vietcong continued its guerrilla tactics, avoiding fixed positions and striking from ambush. By the end of 1967 more than 16,000 U.S. soldiers had lost their lives, with more than 10,000 killed in the previous twelve months. Hanoi's strategy was to fight a war of attrition, confident that American public opinion would sour on an inconclusive war. As the U.S. death count mounted, predicted North Vietnamese General Giap, "their mothers will want to know why. The war will not long survive their questions."

Along with trying to crush the enemy with its massive bombing and ground war, the United States launched a pacification and nation-building program in South Vietnam to build support for the noncommunist regime in Saigon. But the military effort directly undermined the political goals. By the end of 1968 almost 4 million South Vietnamese had lost their homes in aerial bombardments. Between 1965 and 1972 more than 1.4 million civilians died or were wounded by American forces. One American official observed, "It was as if we were trying to build a house with a bulldozer and wrecking crane."

The military's failure in Vietnam, despite its enormous advantages in firepower, underscored the fundamental problem with America's Vietnam policy. Blinded by rigid anticommunism, American policymakers rejected the nationalist impulse behind the Vietnamese revolution. Insisting on viewing Ho as a puppet of Soviet and Chinese aggression, the United States aided in the transformation of a local struggle into a superpower conflict. "We both overestimated the effect of South Vietnam's loss on the security of the West and failed to adhere to the fundamental principle that, in the final analysis, if the South Vietnamese were to be saved, they had to win the war themselves," the contrite former secretary of defense Robert McNamara reflected in 1995.

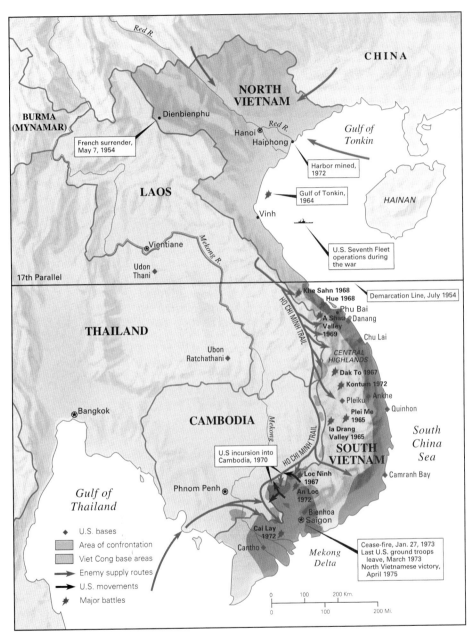

Vietnam, to 1968   Despite the number of soldiers and military bases in South Vietnam and Thailand, American troops could not confine and fight an enemy as mobile as the Vietcong. The Ho Chi Minh Trail, which bypassed the demarcation line by working through Laos and Cambodia, supplied the Vietcong with a steady stream of goods and soldiers from the North. Despite heavy bombing, American forces never completely closed the trail, but these attacks on Laos and Cambodia did spark intense criticism in America when they became public. The Tet Offensive of 1968 showed the effectiveness of the trail and perseverance of North Vietnam.

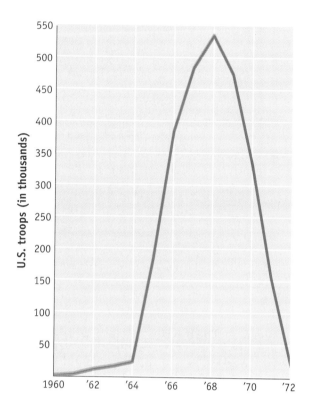

American Troop Levels in Vietnam   After Johnson's decision to send marines to Danang in March 1965, the American presence in Vietnam climbed precipitously. The troop levels reached their pinnacle in 1968, just at the time when the Tet Offensive caused many Americans to loudly demand an end to the war and a return home of the nation's soldiers. The outcry led to the election of Richard Nixon, whose plan of Vietnamization would rapidly reduce the number of ground forces in Vietnam.

The Soldier's War

Who fought in Vietnam? From 1964 to 1973, 2.2 million men were drafted, 8.7 million enlisted, and 16 million did not serve. The average age of American soldiers in Vietnam was nineteen. In World War II the average American solider was twenty-six years old. The estimated total of women who served in Vietnam, including those employed by private organizations such as the Red Cross, ranged from thirty-three thousand to over fifty thousand.

The majority of the young men who fought in Vietnam came from either poor or working-class backgrounds. Many youths from middle-class families used a liberal student deferment policy to avoid the draft. In 1969 *Newsday* traced the family backgrounds of four hundred men from Long Island who had been killed in Vietnam. "As a group," the newspaper concluded, "Long Island's war dead have been overwhelmingly white, working-class men. Their parents were typically blue collar or clerical workers, mailmen, factory workers, building tradesmen, and so on." Class was far more important than race in determining the overall social composition of American forces. Beginning in 1965, when African-Americans accounted for 24 percent of all army combat deaths, the Defense Department undertook a concerted campaign to reduce the minority share of the fighting. By 1970 blacks made up only 9 percent of combat troops in Vietnam.

For combat soldiers in the field, Vietnam could be hell. Climate and terrain imposed horrible conditions. Malaria, blackwater fever, and dysentery took their toll. "Our days were spent hacking through mountainous jungles," one marine remembered. "At night we squatted in muddy holes, picked off the leeches that sucked on our veins, and waited for an attack to come rushing at us from the blackness beyond the perimeter wire."

Combat involved constant patrolling, days and days of suspense waiting for an ambush or a booby trap, and then a short, intense firefight followed by more suspense. Units swept across the same area repeatedly, taking casualties each time, never seeming to achieve any lasting effect. One day they were trying to "win the hearts and minds" of local villagers; the next day they were ordered to destroy the village. A chopper pilot expressed typical bitterness: "Vietnam, man. Bomb 'em and feed 'em, bomb 'em and feed 'em."

In a war of attrition, the "body count" became the primary measure of success. It inflicted a terrible emotional toll on the nineteen-year-olds ordered to fight. "What am I doing here?" asked a young solider. "We don't take any land. We don't give it back. We just mutilate bodies." The tragic consequences of that policy played out in March 1968 when an American platoon led by Lieutenant William

On the Ground in Vietnam   For the "grunts" who faced the day-to-day reality of the Vietnam War, harrowing scenes such as this were all too common. These two GIs wait for a helicopter to carry them and their fallen comrade out of the jungle in Long Khanh province. The guerrilla tactics of the Vietcong, their frequent use of ambush attacks, and the difficulty distinguishing enemy soldiers from civilians made the war experience particularly frightful for American troops. Almost sixty thousand U.S. soldiers were lost in the war, and those who made it home often faced lingering psychological effects and an unsupportive public.   *(National Archives.)*

L. Calley descended on the tiny village of My Lai. Not a single shot was fired at the soldiers, and almost no men of military age were present in the village. Nonetheless, the American soldiers slaughtered more than 450 people and burned the village to the ground.

In the final years of the war, as American troop withdrawals increased, many soldiers refused to risk their lives in what they believed was a futile effort. Who wanted to be, asked Lieutenant John Kerry, "the last man to die in Vietnam"? Desertion and absent-without-leave (AWOL) rates skyrocketed. Violence against officers multiplied. Drug abuse reached epidemic proportions. In 1969 the Pentagon estimated that nearly two-thirds of combat soldiers had used marijuana, while one-third had tried heroin. "What the hell is going on?" asked a bewildered general. "Is this a goddamned army or a mental hospital?"

CHALLENGING THE CONSENSUS, 1960–1967

Vietnam became a catalyst in the passionate debates over American identity that polarized the nation in the late 1960s. Lyndon Johnson had built his vision of a Great Society on the Vital Center belief that America had forged a new national consensus around shared goals of economic growth, anticommunism, and activist government. A generation of young people on both the left and the right challenged the core of that belief, launching political and social experiments that defied American cultural traditions. At the same time, the violence that ripped through many American cities after 1965, and the white backlash that followed, served as powerful reminders of the limits of consensus and the persistence of racial divisions in America.

The Youth Culture Young Americans in the 1960s were not the first to speak against the injustice and hypocrisy of their elders, but social and demographic forces provided this generation with new clout. The postwar baby boom had dramatically increased the number of college-age students in America. In 1965, 41 percent of all Americans were under the age of twenty. College enrollments soared from 3.6 million in 1960 to almost 8 million in 1970. Because colleges contained the largest concentration of young people in the country, they became the seedbeds of youth protest.

In the 1950s "Beat" poets and artists had begun to decry American materialism and complacency. Writer Jack Kerouac, author of the best-selling novel *On the Road* (1957), coined the term *beat* to express the "weariness with all the forms of the modern industrial state." Poet Allen Ginsberg, in *Howl* (1955), railed against "Robot apartments! invincible suburbs! skeleton treasuries! blind capitals! demonic industries!" The Beats embraced open sexuality and free drug use as keys to spiritual liberation.

By the early 1960s the beat message, popularized in inexpensive paperback novels, television shows, and movies, had gained wide acceptance among young people and formed the backbone of the so-called counterculture movement. The movement lacked a coherent ideology, but participants shared a core of attitudes and beliefs. In search of a "higher consciousness," the counterculture rejected the tenets of modern industrial society: materialism, self-denial, sexual repression, individualism, and the work ethic. To the alarm of many older Americans, counterculture fashion promoted long hair for men, Eastern religious symbols, and clothes purchased from the Salvation Army.

Drug use was part of the message. The prophet of the new drug culture was Timothy Leary, a Harvard psychologist who preached to his students (and anyone else who would listen) about the wonders of magic mushrooms and LSD. "Tune in, turn on, drop out," he advised the young. According to *Life* magazine, by 1966 over a million people had experimented with LSD. But the drug of choice for the young remained marijuana. By 1969 more than 30 percent of all college students in the United States had smoked pot.

The counterculture defined itself through music. Bob Dylan's rapid rise to fame was emblematic of the new cultural sensibility. Dylan, born Robert Zimmerman, emerged on the New York folk scene in 1961. His hugely successful second album, *The Freewheelin' Bob Dylan* (1963), included calls to political and moral action in songs such as "A Hard Rain's Gonna Fall," "The Times They Are A-Changin'," and "Blowin' in the Wind" and sold two hundred thousand copies in two months.

After 1964 Dylan had to compete with a host of new rock bands from England. The most popular, the Beatles, captured the hearts of teenage America following a TV appearance on the popular Ed Sullivan television show in 1964. Initially, the Beatles, with ties, jackets, and well-kempt if long hair, hoped to reach a mass consumer market by avoiding a clear association with the counterculture. But their music, which seemed to mock the adult world, contained a message of freedom and excitement that belied their sometimes subdued lyrics. By 1967, however, with the release of *Sergeant Pepper's Lonely Hearts Club Band*, the Beatles were celebrating their new role as cultural antagonists. "When the Beatles told us to turn off our minds and float downstream," recalled one fan, "uncounted youngsters assumed that the key to this kind of mind-expansion could be found in a plant or a pill."

The Beatles changed their tune, in part, to keep ahead of other groups who were gaining widespread popularity by preaching a more potent message. In 1967 Mick Jagger, lead singer of the Rolling Stones, also a British import, was arousing young audiences with a mixture of anger and sexual prowess. During concerts Jagger would thrust the microphone between his legs and whip the floor with a leather belt in a deliberately ugly and blatantly erotic demonstration. "The Beatles want to hold your hand," said one critic, "the Stones want to burn your house."

New Left, New Right Many young people found more conventional means of expressing their discontent. In 1960 two University of Michigan students founded Students for a Democratic Society (SDS), which set forth its ideology in *The Port Huron Statement,* a founding text of the "New Left." While recognizing the need to address issues of poverty and racism, SDS suggested that the crisis of modern life was primarily moral. "A new left," SDS proclaimed, "must give form to the feelings of helplessness and indifference, so that people may see the political, social, and economic source of their personal troubles and organize to change society."

In 1963, 125 SDS members, mostly middle-class white men and women, set up chapters to organize poor whites and blacks in nine American cities. Other members traveled to Mississippi in 1964 as part of the SNCC Freedom Summer. The direct exposure to the brutality of southern justice radicalized many of the students, who returned to campus the following fall searching for an outlet for their fear and fury.

In October 1964 the administration of the University of California at Berkeley provided one. President Clark Kerr decided to enforce campus regulations prohibiting political demonstrations at the entrance of campus—a traditional site for student political expression. In response, student groups organized a Free Speech Movement (FSM). The movement soon broadened its focus to protest the "multiversity machine." The revolt quickly spread to other campuses and championed many causes, from opposing dress codes to fighting tenure decisions.

Mario Savio Speaks at Sproul Hall   When the University of California at Berkeley banned student organizations from setting up tables to promote political activism in front of the administration building (Sproul Hall), student groups banded together, under the leadership of Mario Savio, to form the Free Speech Movement. Though their grievances against the administration varied, undergraduate and graduate students worked together to organize a sit-in of Sproul Hall on December 2. Early the next morning, police began emptying the building, arresting eight hundred students who refused to leave voluntarily. By December 4, all but one of the arrested students had returned to Berkeley, where a noon rally was held, again on the steps of Sproul Hall. Five thousand students crammed into the plaza to hear Mario Savio, seen here, and others condemn the administration and police.   *(© Bettmann/Corbis.)*

While the public focused most of its attention on the Left, conservatives were healing old wounds and mobilizing new recruits. Until the 1950s conservatives had been divided into rival camps of Libertarians, who opposed all limitations on individual freedom, and Moralists, who believed that maintaining moral standards was more important than defending individual rights. By the end of the decade fear of communism and the growing threat from expanded government forced a fusion of the two strains of conservative thought. At the same time conservatives abandoned their traditional isolationism and advocated an aggressive internationalism.

With their ideological rift healed, conservatives presented a compelling alternative to the mainstream consensus. Like the New Left, the New Right attacked the moral relativism that blurred the distinction between right and wrong. Unlike their counterparts in SDS, however, the new conservatives called for an aggressive foreign policy, dramatic increases in military spending, and an end to most social welfare programs.

The Right also established an energetic presence on college campuses. In 1961 more than a hundred conservative students gathered at William Buckley's family estate in Sharon, Connecticut, to develop an agenda for conservative youth. "Now is the time for Conservative youth to take action to make their full force and influence felt," declared the invitation. The conference marked the birth of the Young Americans for Freedom (YAF). The students issued a statement of principles calling for restrictions on government power, for administration of justice and preservation of order to allow "the individual's use of his God-given free will," and for "victory over, rather than co-existence with" the Soviet Union. By 1961 YAF claimed twenty-four thousand members at 115 schools. Noting the proliferation of conservative clubs on college campuses, one conservative proclaimed a "new wave" of campus revolt. These new collegiate conservatives, he predicted, would be the "opinion-makers—the people who in ten, fifteen, and twenty-five years will begin to assume positions of power in America."

Black Power, White Backlash

In August 1965, five days after Johnson signed the Voting Rights Act into law, the Watts section of Los Angeles exploded in violence. Before the rioting ended, thirty-four were dead, nearly four thousand had been arrested, and property damage had reached $45 million. Fourteen thousand national guardsmen and several thousand local police needed six days to stop the arson, looting, and sniping.

The Watts explosion marked the first of four successive "long, hot summers." In the summer of 1966 thirty-eight disorders destroyed ghetto neighborhoods in cities from San Francisco to Providence, Rhode Island. The result was seven deaths, four hundred injuries, and $5 million in property damage. The following year, Newark erupted, leaving twenty-five dead and some twelve hundred wounded. In Detroit forty-three were killed, and more than four thousand fires burned large portions of the city.

At the root of the riots were deeply ingrained social problems. Blacks living in northern cities confronted overcrowding, unemployment, crime, and discrimination. In 1966, 41.7 percent of nonwhites in urban America lived below the federal poverty line. President Johnson's National Advisory Commission on Civil Disorders, created to investigate the causes of the riots, speculated that despair, black militancy, and white racism combined to create a combustible situation. Ominously, the commission warned: "Our nation is moving toward two societies, one black, one white—separate and unequal."

The urban riots precipitated a crisis in black leadership. Martin Luther King's strategy of passive resistance seemed ill equipped to deal with the issues that fueled the new violence. SNCC leader Stokely Carmichael captured the anger of many urban blacks when he coined the phrase "Black Power." Instead of integration, which he called "a subterfuge for the maintenance of white supremacy," Carmichael said that blacks needed to develop their own cultural heritage and become self-dependent. "We don't need white liberals," Carmichael told supporters. "We have to make integration irrelevant." Rejecting nonviolence, Carmichael said, "Black people should and must fight back."

In developing his message of black power, Carmichael drew on the writings of Malcolm X. A spellbinding preacher and a charismatic leader, Malcolm X offered a compelling alternative vision to King (see Competing Voices, page 1179). In 1946, while in prison for robbery, Malcolm Little converted to the Nation of Islam, or Black Muslims. On joining, Little abandoned his "slave name" in favor of Malcolm X; the X stood for his lost African name. Dismissing the aspirations of white civil rights leaders, he said that black nationalists did not want "to integrate into this corrupt society, but to separate from it, to a land of our own, where we can reform ourselves, lift up our moral standards, and try to be godly." In 1963 Malcolm X broke with the Nation of Islam, and after a 1964 pilgrimage to Mecca his ethical position shifted. He rejected racism, spoke of the common bond linking humanity, and suggested that blacks build alliances with like-minded whites. But he emphasized the need for blacks to unify themselves before they reached out for help from whites and liberals. His evolution remained incomplete. In February 1965 he was gunned down at a Harlem rally, apparently by Black Muslim loyalists.

Most whites responded to the riots and the new militancy with fear and anger. Millions angrily turned away from the civil rights movement and its liberal defenders. In 1966 whites sought revenge against the Democrats at the polls. In California second-rate movie actor Ronald Reagan won the governorship by blaming the Watts riot on liberal policymakers. Even his defeated opponent, liberal Pat Brown, declared in his concession speech that "whether we like it or not the people want separation of the races." The biggest change took place in Congress, where Republicans campaigning on a tough "law and order" platform gained 47 House seats and 3 in the Senate. The Democrats lost more seats in 1966 than they had won in 1964. After November 1966 there were 156 northern Democrats in the House, 62 short of a majority.

The Antiwar Movement   President Johnson's decision to escalate the conflict in Vietnam fanned the flames of student discontent. On March 24, 1965, students at the University of Michigan organized the first anti-Vietnam teach-in. Organizers planned lectures and discussions about the war in the hope of "educating" students to the dangers of American involvement in Vietnam. The restrained and respectable form of protest spread quickly to other college campuses.

Student anger reached a new level when, in January 1966, Johnson ended automatic draft deferments for college students. The threat of the draft persuaded young people to join demonstrations in which protesters burned draft cards and an occasional American flag. By highlighting the angriest confrontations between students and police, television contributed to a widespread public impression that the nation's campuses had been overrun by radicals. In fact, antiwar protest was largely confined to elite private colleges and large state universities. One study concluded that between 1965 and 1968 only 20 percent of college students participated in antiwar demonstrations.

Antiwar spirits were bolstered by establishment figures who joined the cause. In 1966 Democratic Senator J. W. Fulbright, the powerful chairman of the Senate Foreign Relations Committee, held nationally televised hearings on the war. The nation listened as George Kennan, the father of containment, complained that the administration's preoccupation with Vietnam was stretching America's power and prestige. In April 1967 Martin Luther King criticized the government for sending young black men "to guarantee liberties in Southeast Asia which they had not found in Southwest Georgia and East Harlem."

While the media publicized campus protests, it was not student ideology that turned the American public against the war. The student movement viewed the war as immoral, a reflection of fundamental problems in American society. To the great majority of Americans, however, the war was not immoral. It was a tragic mistake. They wanted to end the war because winning no longer seemed worth the price. Class resentment reinforced the ideological differences among war opponents. A large number of working-class Americans opposed the war, but they disliked privileged student protesters even more. "We can't understand," lamented a blue-collar worker, "how all those rich kids—the kids with the beads from the fancy suburbs—how they get off when my son has to go over there and maybe get his head shot off."

In the short run, the administration successfully exploited these divisions by appealing to ingrained habits of patriotism. As late as the summer of 1967 opinion surveys showed that a majority of Americans continued to support the president's Vietnam policy. In the long run, however, the antiwar protesters chipped away at one of the cornerstones of the postwar consensus: America's policy of global containment. Over time the Vietnam tragedy raised widespread doubts about the nation's anticommunist obsession and forced a rethinking of America's role in the world.

THE WATERSHED YEAR, 1968

All the conflicting currents of the decade converged in the presidential election year of 1968. The Vital Center found itself under assault from every direction. At issue was the very definition of American identity and of the role America should play in the world. As angry students protesting the administration's Vietnam policy flooded into the streets, many working-class whites, frustrated with social protest and urban riots, turned against the Democrats. The assassination of two political leaders seemed to confirm the nation's descent into political and social violence. A close November election suggested that voters had not abandoned the tattered Vital Center but hoped that their new president would experiment with the consensus in new ways.

Johnson Under Assault

On January 31, 1968, communist troops launched an offensive during the lunar New Year called Tet in Vietnam. The Vietcong invaded the U.S. embassy compound in Saigon and waged bloody battles in the capitals of most of South Vietnam's provinces. Sixty-seven thousand enemy troops invaded more than a hundred of South Vietnam's cities and towns. From a military perspective, the Tet Offensive was a failure for the North Vietnamese. They suffered heavy casualties and failed to gain new ground or incite a popular rebellion against the United States.

But Tet represented a striking psychological victory. The ferocity of the offensive belied the optimistic reports of General Westmoreland, who had proclaimed as recently as November 1967 that he had "never been more encouraged in my four years in Vietnam." Television pictures of marines defending the grounds of the American embassy in Saigon shocked the nation. "What the hell is going on?" blurted television news anchor Walter Cronkite, echoing many Americans. "I thought we were winning this war!"

The Tet Offensive dealt Johnson's credibility a crowning blow. At home, the chief political beneficiary was Senator Eugene McCarthy. The Minnesota senator had challenged Johnson in the New Hampshire primary, the first contest of the 1968 presidential campaign. The state's governor had predicted that Johnson would "murder" McCarthy in his state. Instead, McCarthy polled a stunning 42.2 percent of the Democratic vote to Johnson's 49.4 percent by galvanizing both "hawks" and "doves" who opposed Johnson's Vietnam policy. New Hampshire transformed McCarthy from a hopeless underdog into a serious challenger and demonstrated Johnson's vulnerability.

Four days after Johnson's embarrassment, Robert F. Kennedy, who had been a senator from New York since 1964, entered the race for the Democratic nomination. Many Democrats believed that Kennedy was the only politician in America who could pull together the fractured liberal coalition. On Vietnam, Kennedy, who had supported his brother's military escalation of the conflict, now called for a negotiated settlement. He focused most of his attention, however, on domestic issues. Kennedy believed that convincing poor people of all colors to pursue their shared class interests offered the only solution to the deep racial hostility that was tearing the nation apart. "We have to convince the Negroes and poor whites that they have common interests," Kennedy told a journalist. "If we can reconcile those two hostile groups, and then add the kids, you can really turn this country around."

Lyndon Johnson, meanwhile, seemed cornered by his own policies. Public support for his Vietnam policy dropped to 26 percent in the aftermath of Tet. His military advisers asked for an additional 206,000 troops, which would have brought the total to 750,000. His civilian advisers, led by veteran presidential consultant Clark Clifford, recommended a negotiated settlement. "We seem to have a sinkhole," Clifford said. Reluctantly, Johnson agreed.

On March 31 the president told a national television audience that he had ordered a temporary halt to the bombing and called for peace talks between the warring sides. At the end of the speech Johnson shocked the nation by announcing that he would not seek reelection. Three weeks later Vice President Hubert Humphrey announced that he would run in Johnson's place.

While Kennedy and McCarthy battled in the Democratic primaries, another outspoken critic of the administration was raising his voice in protest. By 1968 Martin Luther King had abandoned his previous emphasis on dramatic confrontations and accepted the SNCC strategy of community organizing in an effort to build a class-based, grass-roots alliance among the poor. King spent most of the winter organizing a "poor people's march on Washington." Like Kennedy, King argued that America's racial problems could not be solved without addressing the issue of class. "We must recognize," he said in 1967, "that we can't solve our problems now until there is a radical redistribution of economic and political power." King now considered himself a revolutionary, not a reformer.

In March 1968 King supported striking garbage workers in Memphis, Tennessee, hoping a peaceful, successful walkout would further his new, more aggressive message of redistribution of power and his enduring commitment to nonviolence. While in Memphis in April to encourage the strikers, he reaffirmed his faith in the possibility of racial justice: "I may not get there with you. But we as a people will get to the promised land." The following day, April 4, King died, shot to death by assassin James Earl Ray, a white ex-convict.

King's death touched off an orgy of racial violence. Rioters burned twenty blocks in Chicago, where Mayor Daley ordered embattled police to "shoot to kill." The worst violence occurred in Washington, D.C., where seven hundred fires burned and nine people lost their lives. For the first time since the Civil War, armed soldiers guarded the steps to the Capitol. Nationally, the death toll was forty-six. "Martin's memory is being desecrated," said one black leader.

With King dead, Kennedy became for many disaffected people, black and white, the only national leader who commanded respect and enthusiasm. Kennedy may have had the broadest base of support, but party leaders selected most convention delegates. A large majority of these delegates, remaining loyal to the administration, pledged their support to Humphrey. Kennedy's strategy was to sweep the remaining major primaries, showing such support at the polls that the convention delegates would have no choice but to nominate him.

Kennedy won a decisive victory over Humphrey and McCarthy in Indiana but lost in Oregon. The California primary on June 4 was critical, and Kennedy won. But that evening, after giving his victory speech, he was shot by Sirhan Sirhan, a Palestinian who opposed the senator's pro-Israel position. Twenty-five hours later, Robert Kennedy died, dimming Democrats' hopes of uniting their disparate coalition of blacks and whites, hawks and doves, young and old.

Robert Kennedy's death assured Humphrey of the nomination on the first ballot at the Democratic convention in Chicago. But it was preceded by a furor over the Vietnam plank of the party platform, which ultimately supported administration policy. And the real action was taking place outside the hall, where the police assaulted a group of peaceful demonstrators seeking to march on the convention headquarters. With no attempt to distinguish bystanders and peaceful protesters from lawbreakers, the police smashed people through plate-glass windows, fired tear-gas canisters indiscriminately, and brutalized anyone who got in their way. "These are our children," *New York Times* columnist Tom Wicker cried out as the violence swirled around him.

Television crews filmed the melee as it occurred, and footage of the violence was shown during the nomination speeches. The dramatic scenes overshadowed Humphrey's nomination on the first ballot and his selection of Maine Senator Edmund Muskie as his running mate.

The public's reaction to the police riot gave an indication of the American mood in 1968. Most Americans sympathized with the police. In a poll taken shortly after the Democratic convention, most blue-collar workers approved of the way the

Chicago, 1968 At the Democratic national convention, the tensions that had been building over the course of the decade came to a head. Twenty-eight thousand police, national guardsmen, federal troops, and secret service agents confronted a smaller contingent of protestors from over one hundred different anti-war organizations. The violence lasted throughout the convention as the city sought to remove protestors from parks where they congregated or to prevent their marches on the convention hall. Over one hundred police and about that same number of protestors were injured in the five days of riots, with the entire spectacle being broadcast on television to horrified Americans. *(Corbis-Bettmann.)*

Chicago police had handled the protesters; some of them thought the police were "not tough enough" on them. Bumper stickers declaring "We Support Mayor Daley and His Chicago Police," blossomed across the country.

The Center Holds: The Election of 1968

Two candidates were vying for the allegiance of these angry voters. The most direct appeal came from American Independence Party candidate George Wallace, whose symbolic stance in a university doorway had made him a hero to southern whites. In 1968 Wallace's antiestablishment populism also appealed to many northern Democrats angry over the party's association with protest and integration. Wallace moved up in the polls by catering to the resentments of his followers: "If a demonstrator ever lays down in front of my car," Wallace told large and enthusiastic crowds, "it'll be the last car he'll ever lay down in front of." Wallace's appeal was blatantly racist and anti-intellectual. One survey showed that more than half of the nation shared his view that "liberals, intellectuals, and long-hairs have run the country for too long."

Joining Wallace in pursuit of the hearts and minds of America's angry white voters was the Republican nominee, Richard Nixon. In the years following Goldwater's defeat in 1964, Nixon had emerged as a centrist who could appeal to both the liberal and conservative wings of the Republican Party. Nixon campaigned in 1968 as the candidate of unity, reflecting his belief that most Americans wanted an end to the civil discord. To capitalize on the yearning for tranquility, Nixon promised that he had a plan—never specified—to end the war in Vietnam. But his top priority, he declared, was the restoration of law and order. Nixon appealed to the "forgotten Americans" whose values of patriotism and stability had been violated by student protesters, urban riots, and arrogant intellectuals. His strategy for the campaign was to stay above the fray. He refused to debate Humphrey, and he limited his public appearances to televised question-and-answer sessions before audiences of partisan Republicans.

Humphrey emerged from the debacle in Chicago a badly damaged candidate. Antiwar protesters blamed him for LBJ's Vietnam policies, while many working-class Democrats associated him with the violent protest and civil unrest of the convention. On September 30 Humphrey discovered his independent voice and announced that he would "stop the bombing of North Vietnam as an acceptable risk for peace." On October 31, less than a week before election day, Johnson helped Humphrey's cause by announcing a bombing pause in Vietnam.

The weekend before the election Humphrey pulled even with Nixon in many polls. But on election day, Nixon won by a razor-thin majority in the popular vote, receiving 31,785,480 votes compared with Humphrey's 31,275,166. Less than seven-tenths of 1 percent separated the two candidates. Nixon took only 43.4 percent of the popular vote, the smallest share earned by a winning candidate since Woodrow Wilson in 1912. He scored a more decisive triumph in the electoral college, amassing 301 votes to Humphrey's 191. Wallace carried five states, receiving 46 electoral votes and 13.5 percent of the popular vote—the best showing for a third-party candidate in forty-four years (see map on page 1174).

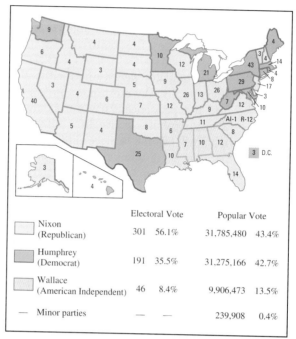

	Electoral Vote		Popular Vote	
Nixon (Republican)	301	56.1%	31,785,480	43.4%
Humphrey (Democrat)	191	35.5%	31,275,166	42.7%
Wallace (American Independent)	46	8.4%	9,906,473	13.5%
— Minor parties	—	—	239,908	0.4%

The Election of 1968 With Johnson out of the race and the assassination of Robert Kennedy, Hubert Humphrey became the Democratic presidential nominee. He steered away from Johnson's policy in Vietnam by calling for a halt to bombing, while Republican candidate Richard Nixon promised to end the war and appealed to the "silent majority" of Americans frustrated with the domestic turmoil. The popular vote was almost evenly split between the two major candidates, but Nixon's success in the West and key Midwestern states proved decisive in the Electoral College. Alabama Governor George Wallace, known for his support of segregation, showed the fissures within the Democratic Party over issues of race by winning the Deep South.

In a year that had witnessed almost unprecedented violence and turmoil, the voters produced a very conventional result. "Of all the extraordinary developments of 1968," observed one commentator, "perhaps least expected was the durability of characters and institutions in the face of defiant challenge." In a decade marked by challenges to established institutions, Americans looked to a familiar face and old values to guide them through the troubled days ahead.

CONCLUSION

In 1960 a common set of assumptions formed the foundation of American identity. Reflecting the broad outlines of the Vital Center, most Americans believed that economic growth, combined with finely tuned government programs, could solve most social problems, from poverty to civil rights. Abroad, Americans supported the continuing policy of global containment against a menacing Soviet Union.

No one captured the optimism of the consensus more eloquently than the new president, John F. Kennedy, who inspired the nation with his stirring rhetoric about national purpose. Restrained by a stubborn Congress from liberal experimentation at home, the young leader focused his energy on foreign policy, engaging in intense confrontations with the Soviets over Cuba and Berlin. Determined to prevent a Soviet advance in Southeast Asia, Kennedy increased support for America's beleaguered South Vietnamese ally.

Kennedy's death on November 22, 1963, stunned the nation, and his successor, Lyndon Johnson, invoked Kennedy's legacy and used his own political skills to advance an ambitious Great Society agenda. Under Johnson's watchful eye Congress passed the two most significant pieces of civil rights legislation since Reconstruction, banning segregation in public facilities and guaranteeing African-Americans the right to vote. The antipoverty programs, Medicare, and Medicaid expanded the social safety net and improved the quality of life for millions of Americans. Under Chief Justice Earl Warren the Supreme Court shared the activist temperament, issuing landmark rulings that expanded individual rights and freedom of the press.

Yet despite these notable accomplishments, the 1960s also revealed the fissures in the consensus and provoked a spirited debate about what it meant to be an American, about the proper role of government, and about America's place in the world. Popular fears of an intrusive national government limited the scope and effectiveness of Johnson's Great Society experiment. Antipoverty programs were plagued by modest funding and complicated administrative procedures that gave individual states control over funding. While many Americans supported legislation that banned segregation and provided African-Americans with basic political rights, they balked at more ambitious proposals for redressing economic inequality.

In many ways the much heralded consensus was an illusion. The black struggle for civil, political, and economic equality presented the most powerful challenge. In its early phase, moderate leaders like Martin Luther King, Jr., worked within the constraints of the consensus. King denounced violence, sought alliance with northern white liberals, and focused his efforts on banning segregation and achieving basic political rights. After 1965, however, the movement grew increasingly more radical as blacks pressed demands for economic as well as political equality.

While the civil rights movement exposed the limits of consensus at home, a costly war in Vietnam raised questions about America's policy of global containment. Confident in American power, Johnson escalated the conflict in Vietnam, transforming a local nationalist struggle into a superpower confrontation. Discontent and debate over the war exposed deep fault lines in American society between hawk and dove, between young and old, and between working-class families and middle-class students.

Young people, too, organized a powerful challenge to consensus. College campuses became seedbeds of political activity as students mobilized to support the civil rights movement in the South and, later, to protest the war in Vietnam. The divisive events of the decade polarized many middle-class college students, pushing them either to the left or to the right of the Vital Center. The rise of black nationalism and the orgy of riots that ripped through major cities between 1965 and 1968 underscored the deep racial divide in America and highlighted the frustration among many African-Americans at the slow pace of change.

Not all young people became politically active. Many turned to music and other forms of cultural expression to vent their frustration with contemporary society. Over a million people followed Timothy Leary's advice to "tune in, turn on, drop out."

By 1968 protest and police violence outside the Democratic convention in Chicago drove home how badly the consensus had splintered. Conservatives moved to fill the power vacuum. Richard Nixon's shrewd calls for unity and patriotism appealed to white voters angry with the Democratic Party's support for civil rights, frustrated with the situation in Vietnam, and exasperated by student protesters. This coalition of discontent gained control of the White House in 1968 and promised to flex its political muscle for years to come.

Annotated Suggested Readings

The 1960s were years conspicuous for the self-conscious commitment to social change they produced, a fact manifested in much of the gripping, often reflective writing produced by veterans of the period. Todd Gitlin, a former SDS president and war protester, combines memoir and critical analysis in *The Sixties* (1987). Allen Matusow's *The Unraveling of America* (1984) offers a more distanced account of the decade that centers on the crisis of liberalism. Michael Kazin and Maurice Isserman provide a compelling synthesis in *America Divided* (2000). David Burner captures the failed idealism of the decade in *Making Peace with the 60s* (1996). For a useful reference work on the 1960s, see David Farber and Beth Bailey, *The Columbia Guide to America in the 1960s* (2001).

John Kennedy is the focus of Theodore White's classic on the art of modern campaigning, *The Making of the President, 1960* (1961). Arthur Schlesinger's epic *A Thousand Days* (1965) provides a sympathetic insider's account. Robert Dallek's *An Unfinished Life: John F. Kennedy, 1917–1963* (2003) provides the most balanced assessment of Kennedy's life and legacy. Also valuable are Herbert Parmet's *JFK: The Presidency of John F. Kennedy* (1983) and James Giglio's *The Presidency of John F. Kennedy* (1991). Thomas Brown casts a skeptical eye on the use of the media to create an aura surrounding the Kennedy image in *JFK: The History of an Image* (1988). Robert Weisbrot analyzes the role of public perception and Kennedy's leadership qualities during the Cuban missile crisis in *Maximum Danger* (2001).

Irving Bernstein's comprehensive *Guns or Butter* (1996) chronicles the many significant accomplishments of Johnson's Great Society. John A. Andrew offers a brief overview in *Lyndon Johnson and the Great Society* (1998). Robert Caro's critical biographies—*The Years of Lyndon Johnson: Path to Power* (1982), *Means of Ascent* (1990), and *Master of the Senate* (2002)—need to be balanced with Robert Dallek's masterful volumes, *Lone Star Ris-*

ing (1991) and *Flawed Giant* (1998). James Patterson's *America's Struggle Against Poverty, 1900–1994* (1995) analyzes the fateful consequences of the Great Society's "welfare explosion." Michael Beschloss uses White House tape recordings to provide a rare glimpse inside the Johnson administration in *Taking Charge* (1997). In *Earl Warren* (1982) G. Edward White discusses the influential chief justice. Anthony Lewis brings to life the personal stakes of judicial activism in *Gideon's Trumpet* (1964).

In recent years historians have emphasized the grass-roots nature of the civil rights movement. John Dittmer's history of the civil rights movement in Mississippi, *Local People* (1994), reveals the commitment and grit of ordinary people that sustained an extraordinary social movement. Clayborne Carson's *In Struggle* (1981) provides the definitive history of SNCC. Doug McAdam's *Freedom Summer* (1988) studies the impact of SNCC's watershed moment on a generation of activists. In *Ella Baker and the Black Freedom Movement* (2003) Barbara Ransby chronicles the life and political activities of one of the movements most influential women. Important primary sources on civil rights include King's *Why We Can't Wait* (1964); James Baldwin's *The Fire Next Time* (1962); the Kerner Commission's *Report of the National Advisory Commission on Civil Disorders* (1968); and Stokely Carmichael and Charles Hamilton's *Black Power* (1967). Thomas Sugrue examines the roots of protest in Detroit in his *The Origins of the Urban Crisis* (1998).

The literature on the Vietnam War is immense. George Herring's *America's Longest War* (1986) and Stanley Karnow's *Vietnam* (1983) are good starting points. On the fateful decision to send troops, see Larry Berman's *Planning a Tragedy* (1982). Neil Sheehan captures the tragic dimensions of Americans' commitment to winning the war in his elegantly written *A Bright Shining Lie* (1988). David Halberstam, who made his name reporting from Vietnam, reveals in *The Best and the Brightest* (1972) the atmosphere of brash optimism that led to the U.S. commitment. *In Retrospect* (1995) offers Robert McNamara's reflections on mistakes made and lessons learned. David Maraniss offers a compelling account of the war at home and on the battlefield in *They Marched into Sunlight* (2003).

Godfrey Hodgson traces liberalism's cathartic passage through the 1960s in his masterful synthesis, *America in Our Time* (1976). Steven Gillon views the crisis within liberalism through the prism of Americans for Democratic Action in *Politics and Vision* (1987). John Diggins, *The Rise and Fall of the American Left* (1992), discusses the evolution of the American Left's troubled legacy. Maurice Isserman's *If I Had a Hammer* (1987) draws more sanguine connections between the Old Left and the New Left, although his account remains ambivalent. Jeff Shesol offers insight into the rivalry between Robert Kennedy and Lyndon Johnson in *Mutual Contempt* (1997). The political rift that dislocated liberalism in 1968 is nicely encapsulated in David Farber's *Chicago '68* (1988).

Much of the student activism that challenged centrist liberals in the 1960s was inspired by or patterned after the movement described by W. J. Rorabaugh in *Berkeley at War* (1989). Kirkpatrick Sales's *SDS* (1973) looks at the most influential radical group of the 1960s. Todd Gitlin unveils the opportunities and constraints the media posed for the New Left in *The Whole World Is Watching* (1980). Two especially good books on the antiwar movement are Charles DeBenedetti's *An American Ordeal* (1990) and Christian Appy's *Working-Class War* (1993). On Barry Goldwater and the rise of conservatism, see Robert Alan Goldberg's *Barry Goldwater* (1995) and Mary C. Brennan *Turning Right in the Sixties* (1995). John A. Andrew's *The Other Side of the Sixties* (1997) chronicles the growth of the conservative Young Americans for Freedom on college campuses.

The tendency to see the student protest movements as harbingers of a profound awakening of political activism was influenced early on by Theodore Roszak's *The Making of a Counter-Culture* (1969) and Charles Reich's *The Greening of America* (1971). Terry Anderson's *The Movement and the Sixties* (1995) provides a good overview of the politics and protest of the decade. David Caute's *The Year of the Barricades* (1988) identifies 1968 as a important turning point. George Katsiaficas's *The Imagination of the New Left* (1987) views the unrest as part of a global movement. Martin Lee and Bruce Shlain emphasize the distance between the counterculture and establishment in *Acid Dreams: The CIA, LSD, and the Sixties Rebellion* (1985). For a gripping, dizzying journey into the lives of some pioneers of the counterculture, see Tom Wolfe's *The Electric Kool-Aid Acid Test* (1968).

The istory ompanion

Martin Luther King, Jr., and Malcolm X

Letter from Birmingham Jail

On Good Friday, April 16, 1963, the Reverend Dr. Martin Luther King, Jr., was arrested and jailed for participating in a nonviolent protest in Birmingham, Alabama. While King sat imprisoned in a dark cell, cut off from the demonstrations he had helped mastermind, eight Birmingham clergymen released a statement criticizing the protest and asking King to leave Birmingham. The plea, published in the local newspaper, called King "an outsider," attacked the demonstrations as "unwise and untimely," and praised the police for keeping "order" and "preventing violence." King believed that the comments could not go unanswered. His response, written on scraps of paper using a pen smuggled into his cell, explained the religious and philosophical underpinnings of his strategy of nonviolence.

At first I was rather disappointed that fellow clergymen would see my nonviolent efforts as those of an extremist. I began thinking about the fact that I stand in the middle of two opposing forces in the Negro community. One is a force of complacency, made up in part of Negroes who, as a result of long years of oppression, are so drained of self-respect and a sense of "somebodiness" that they have adjusted to segregation; and in part of a few middle-class Negroes who, because of a degree of academic and economic security and because in some ways they profit by segregation, have become insensitive to the problems of the masses. The other force is one of bitterness and hatred, and it comes perilously close to advocating violence. It is expressed in the various black nationalist groups that are springing up across the nation, the largest and best-known being Elijah Muhammad's Muslim movement. Nourished by the Negro's frustration over the continued existence of racial discrimination, this movement is made up of people who have lost faith in America, who have absolutely repudiated Christianity, and who have concluded that the white man is an incorrigible "devil."

I have tried to stand between these two forces, saying that we need emulate neither the "do-nothingism" of the complacent nor the hatred and despair of the black nationalist. For there is the more excellent way of love and nonviolent protest. I am grateful to God that, through the influence of the Negro church, the way of nonviolence became an integral part of our struggle.

If this philosophy had not emerged, by now many streets of the South would, I am convinced, be flowing with blood. And I am further convinced that if our white brothers dismiss as "rabble-rousers" and "outside agitators" those of us who employ nonviolent direct action, and if they refuse to support our nonviolent efforts, millions of Negroes will, out of frustration and despair, seek solace and security in black-nationalist ideologies—a development that would inevitably lead to a frightening racial nightmare. . . .

I had hoped that the white moderate would see this need. Perhaps I was too optimistic; perhaps I expected too much. I suppose I should have realized that few members of the oppressor race can understand the deep groans and passionate yearnings of the oppressed race, and still fewer have the vision to see that injustice must be rooted out by strong, persistent and determined action. . . .

. . . We will reach the goal of freedom in Birmingham and all over the nation, because the goal of America is freedom. Abused and scorned though we may be, our destiny is tied up with America's destiny. . . . We will win our freedom because the sacred heritage of our nation and the eternal will of God are embodied in our echoing demands.

The Autobiography of Malcolm X

King's message of integration and nonviolence appealed to the largely southern, middle-class African-Americans who dominated the leadership of the early phase of the civil rights movement. As the decade progressed, however, the movement shifted northward, where it was forced to address the seething anger of an urban underclass trapped in poverty. Malcolm X, a leader of the Black Muslims, emerged as the most forceful and charismatic spokesman of the new militancy of poor urban blacks. In his autobiography, published in 1964, Malcolm X questioned King's strategy of nonviolence and offered black nationalism as an alternative. ___

I don't go for non-violence if it also means a delayed solution. To me a delayed solution is a non-solution. Or I'll say it another way: If it must take violence to get the black man his human rights in this country, I'm *for* violence exactly as you know the Irish, Poles, or Jews would be if they were flagrantly discriminated against. I am just as they would be in that case, and they would be for violence—no matter what the consequences, no matter who was hurt by the violence.

White society *hates* to hear anybody, especially a black man, talk about the crime the white man has perpetrated on the black man. I have always understood that's why I have been so frequently called "a revolutionist." It sounds as if I have done some crime! Well, it may be the American black man does need to become involved in a *real* revolution. . . . So how does anybody sound talking about the Negro in America waging some "revolution"? Yes, he is condemning a system—but he's not trying to overturn the system, or to destroy it. The Negro's so-called "revolt" is merely an asking to be *accepted* into the existing system! A *true* Negro revolt might entail, for instance, fighting for separate black states within this country—which several groups and individuals have advocated, long before Elijah Muhammad came along.

Does white America have the capacity to repent—and to atone? Does the capacity to repent, to atone, exist in a majority, in one-half, in even one-third of American white society?

Many black men, the victims—in fact most black men—would like to be able to forgive, to forget, the crimes.

But most American white people seem not to have it in them to make any serious atonement—to do justice to the black man.

Indeed, how *can* white society atone for enslaving, for raping, for unmanning, for otherwise brutalizing millions of human beings, for centuries? What atonement would the God of Justice demand for the robbery of the black people's labor, their lives, their true identities, their culture, their history—and even their human dignity?

A desegregated cup of coffee, a theater, public toilets—the whole range of hypocritical "integration"—these are not atonement. . . .

I kept having all kinds of troubles trying to develop the kind of Black National-ist organization I wanted to build for the American Negro. Why Black Nationalism? Well, in the competitive American society, how can there ever be any white–black solidarity before there is first some black solidarity?

. . . I mean nothing against any sincere whites when I say that as members of black organizations, generally whites' very presence subtly renders the black organ-ization automatically less effective. . . .

I tell sincere white people, "Work in conjunction with us—each of us working among our own kind." Let sincere white individuals find all other white people they can who feel as they do—and let them form their own all-white groups, to work trying to convert other white people who are thinking and acting as racist. Let sincere whites go and teach non-violence to white people!

Nearly a hundred years after the Civil War, America remained a society deeply divided by race. The South enforced a rigid system of legal segregation by violence and intimidation. But the South did not have a monopoly on racism. In 1966, after spending months fighting for inte-grated housing in Chicago, an exasperated Martin Luther King exclaimed, "I have never seen such hate." In the North racism relegated African-Americans to second-class citizenship, forc-ing them to live in communities plagued by crime, low employment, and poor public facilities.

Black leaders divided over the best strategy for confronting this racism and for improving the quality of life for most African-Americans. Like previous leaders such as the educator W. E. B. Du Bois (1868–1963), King viewed confrontation as a means of achieving integration and equal rights. Conscious of their minority status, leaders such as Du Bois and King hoped to build coalitions with white liberals. The challenge, Du Bois wrote, was to find a way "to be both a Negro and an American." Malcolm X, on the other hand, shared more in common with lead-ers such as Marcus Garvey, who, during the 1920s, urged blacks to reject everything white and crusaded for black economic self-sufficiency.

It is interesting to note, however, that both King and Malcolm were evolving, their views converging. By 1964 Malcolm rejected racism and spoke of the common bonds that linked all humanity. King was growing more radical as he came to appreciate the need for fundamental economic reforms. Tragically, neither man had the opportunity to finish his spiritual and intel-lectual journey.

QUESTIONS FOR ANALYSIS

1. Why was King confident about the ultimate success of the struggle for civil rights?

2. Why does Malcolm X oppose King's strategy of nonviolence?

3. What does Malcolm X offer as an alternative?

4. What does King have to say about black nationalism?

5. How do King's and Malcolm's views of Americans differ?

6. In your opinion, which leader offered the best strategy for helping black Amer-ica? Why?

The Civil Rights Movement and Martin Luther King, Jr.

Much of the historical writing on the African-American civil rights movement has centered on Martin Luther King, Jr. But there is an enormously varied scholarship on civil rights, including books on lesser-known activists and on particular episodes, such as the Emmett Till murder, school desegregation in Little Rock, Arkansas, the Freedom Rides, and Freedom Summer. In addition, there are studies of particular southern states and cities, of white southerners who bitterly opposed the movement, and of others who supported it. Many of these community studies tell the story of civil rights from the bottom up, rather than from the top down. Instead of focusing on a single civil rights leader or a handful of leaders or on policymakers at the national level, they tell the story of grassroots activism at the local level.

There is a growing body of scholarship that tries to place the civil rights movement in a global context. An excellent example is Mary Dzudziak's *Cold War Civil Rights* (2000). Dzudziak examines how civil rights activists in the 1950s and early 1960s emphasized the gulf between the United States' cold war rhetoric, which underscored the differences between U.S. democracy and Soviet totalitarianism, and the denial of freedom to millions of American citizens because of their race. Images of southern police and citizen brutality against African-Americans were printed and broadcast around the world, tarnishing the nation's reputation and forcing policymakers to push a civil rights agenda more quickly than they might otherwise have done.

Civil rights scholarship tells a complex and messy story. But how does the nation remember that story? In 1986 the first Pulitzer Prize–winning biography of King, David Garrow's *Bearing the Cross*, appeared and PBS broadcast the superb documentary *Eyes on the Prize*. Two years later Taylor Branch's King biography, *Parting the Waters*, was published; it also received a Pulitzer Prize. The year 1988 also saw the release of the movie *Mississippi Burning*, about the federal investigation of the 1964 murders of civil rights activists James Cheney, Andrew Goodman, and Michael Schwerner. 1989 saw the publication of Garrow's important *Martin Luther King Jr. and the Civil Rights Movement*, an 18-volume reprinting of important scholarship which has proven vital to those working on civil rights topics.

Why was there a surge of interest in King and civil rights in the mid- to late 1980s? Offering a controversial explanation in a 1991 article, historian Steven F. Lawson, insisted that "images of civil rights heroes and heroines making great sacrifices to transform their country and their lives contrasted sharply with the prevailing Reagan-era mentality that glorified the attainment of personal wealth and ignored community health. Returning to civil rights yesteryears made many Americans feel better about themselves and what they might accomplish once again in the future."

Yet it was President Reagan, who on January 20, 1986, proclaimed Martin Luther King, Jr., Day as a national holiday and declared in his speech that "Dr. King's activism was rooted in the true patriotism that cherishes American ideals and strives to narrow the gap between those ideals and reality." Reagan told the familiar story of the March on Washington where "King... held up his dream for America like a bright banner:'I have a dream....'"

But Vincent Gordon Harding, a friend of King and director of the Martin Luther King, Jr., Center for Nonviolent Social Change in Atlanta, had these words to say in a 1987 article in response to Reagan's proclamation:

"It appears as if the price for the first national holiday honoring a black man is the development of a massive case of national amnesia concerning who that black man really was....I would suggest that we Americans have chosen amnesia rather than continue King's painful, uncharted, and often disruptive struggle toward a more perfect union."

Harding urged American historians to "move beyond the static March-on-Washington, integrationist, civil-rights-leader image" and examine King's words from 1966 and after as a vital part of his legacy. In Chicago in 1966, during the Poor People's Campaign, King declared:"I choose to identify with the underprivileged. I choose to identify with the poor. I choose to give my life for the hungry. I choose to give my life for those who have been left out of the sunlight of opportunity."

King's commitment to the poor, his growing opposition to the war in Vietnam, and his growing awareness of the plight of peoples of color in South Africa and Central America, as well as Vietnam, led him to a more radical assessment of American society, one that centered on what he called the triple evils—racism, war, and economic exploitation. He proclaimed that "a nation that continues year after year to spend more money on military defense than on programs of social uplift is approaching spiritual death." Harding, in his assessment of the public memory of King, concluded:"For those who seek a gentle, non-abrasive hero whose recorded speeches can be used as inspirational resources for rocking our memories to sleep, Martin Luther King Jr. is surely the wrong man." Like Harding, Steven Lawson emphasized the gap between the angry, disenchanted King of 1966 to 1968 and "the King who emerges from public celebrations ... a perennial dreamer, frozen in time at his most famous address [in] 1963."

There is quite a gap between the diverse and complex scholarship of the last two decades on King and on the broader civil rights movement on the one hand and the public memory of King on the other. Some scholars, Lawson noted, have subscribed to "the notion of two King's—the reformer and the revolutionary"—to explain the shift in King's thinking. Why has America chosen to remember only the noncontroversial King, the reformer? Is it that King's criticisms of the Vietnam War, U.S. colonialism, and the presence of mass poverty in an affluent society are too bitter, too revolutionary a set of pills for the American memory to swallow and metabolize? Is it that the optimistic King of 1963, having a dream, provides us with a triumphal story of race in the United States to remember, one cleansed of the complexities of the black power movement and the urban riots of the mid- to late 1960s? How would King want us to remember him?

30

The Politics of Polarization

1969–1979

"My God, they're killing us!"

At noon on Monday, May 4, 1970, students at Kent State University in Ohio organized for an antiwar rally on the Commons, a grassy campus gathering spot. For the previous three days the lush lawns and green elms and maple trees of this 790-acre campus had been the site of violent confrontation between students and police. What ignited the protest was President Nixon's announcement on April 30 of his decision to widen the war in Vietnam by sending American ground troops into neighboring Cambodia. The surprise announcement came as a shock to a nation lulled into complacency by troop withdrawals and declining body counts.

National Guard jeeps drove onto the Commons, and an officer ordered the crowd to disperse. A platoon of guardsmen armed with M-1 rifles and tear-gas equipment followed, moving methodically across the green and over the crest of a hill, chasing the protesters. The crowd taunted the poorly trained guardsmen, chanting "Pigs Off Campus" and hurling stones and bricks. The troops, most of them local townspeople—accountants, bankers, barbers—responded by firing volleys of tear gas into the crowd.

Suddenly the crackle of gunfire cut through the tear-gas-laced air. A girl screamed, "My God, they're killing us!" Some students fled; others fell to the ground. The turmoil lasted only a few seconds, but by the time the shooting stopped, four students lay dead and another eleven were seriously wounded. None of those hit at Kent State had broken any law, and none was a campus radical; among them were two women who had never been part of the protest but were simply walking to class. An investigation by the Federal Bureau of Investigation agreed, calling the shootings "unnecessary, unwarranted, and inexcusable."

After the Kent State killings, in what Columbia University president William J. McGill called "the most disastrous month of May in the history of American higher education," over 400 colleges had to cancel some classes and 250 campuses were closed altogether as young people expressed their outrage. Not everyone was sympathetic to the students. One poll indicated that 58 percent of the public blamed the students for the Kent State deaths. A local resident told the town newspaper that the guardsmen "should have fired sooner and longer."

These responses revealed deep divisions in American society. During the 1970s Americans struggled to reconcile traditional beliefs and institutions with significant challenges to mainstream culture and politics. Abroad, the nation remained mired in a conflict it could neither win nor end. At home, minority demands for equal rights were met with growing resistance and anger from "middle America." Richard Nixon was elected on a promise to bring harmony to American politics. Despite his willingness to experiment in both foreign and domestic policy, his efforts to create a durable base of political support only clarified and hardened the divisions separating Americans and their visions of what the country should be both at home and abroad.

Later in the decade Americans were faced with a series of puzzling public problems that no one seemed able to solve. More than two decades of postwar economic growth came to a halt. Revelations of misconduct by high elected officials undermined public faith in political institutions. By the end of the decade an American president wondered at the cumulative effect of these shocks and warned the nation about its "crisis of confidence."

- How did the failure in Vietnam force Americans to reconsider their approach to the world?

- What was the "silent majority," and what accounted for its attitudes toward government and society?

- Why did so many groups mobilize to demand their rights during the 1970s?

- How did popular culture reflect the social conflicts of the decade? How did America's political institutions cope with the conflicting demands?

This chapter will address these questions.

EXPERIMENTS IN PEACEMAKING, 1969–1974

Nixon assumed the presidency confident in his ability to handle foreign affairs. He and his close aide Henry Kissinger believed that realism needed to replace the excessive moralism that often characterized American foreign policy and Americans' view of their role in the world. Consolidating enormous power in the White House, they launched aggressive experiments to secure "peace with honor" in Vietnam and to lessen tensions between the superpowers.

Nixon's War The Vietnam War was the most pressing issue confronting the new administration. In developing his strategy for dealing with the conflict, Nixon relied heavily on his national security adviser, Henry Kissinger, who became secretary of state in October 1973. Born in Germany in 1923, Kissinger traveled to the United States in 1938. After serving in World War II, he attended Harvard, earned a Ph.D. in government, and joined the faculty.

Nixon and Kissinger shared both a personal style and a similar view of America's role in the world. They possessed a desire for power and a penchant for secrecy and intrigue. Together, they concentrated decision making in the White House and excluded even close aides from sensitive diplomatic initiatives. An observer suggested that Kissinger's aides were like mushrooms: "They're kept in the dark, get a lot of manure piled on them, and then get canned." For his part, Nixon, who took great pride in his knowledge of international relations, functioned as his own secretary of state. The man who actually occupied the position, William Rogers, had little foreign policy experience and no influence in the White House. Nixon and Kissinger also shared an essentially pessimistic view of the behavior of nations, known as *Realpolitik*. Power, they believed, not ideals or moral suasion, counted in international affairs. Their approach emphasized "realism" over "idealism," arguing that nations could be expected to act in their own narrowly defined interest, not on "idealistic" humanitarian concerns.

Nixon understood that his administration's success hinged on diffusing the crisis in Vietnam. The president believed that by reducing the number of combat troops, which stood at 545,000 in 1969, he could cut the casualties that fueled home-front protest. In May 1969 he announced a new policy that he called Vietnamization: South Vietnamese forces would gradually be strengthened so that American troops could be withdrawn from the war. As promised, Nixon rapidly reduced the number of ground troops to thirty thousand by September 1972. In

Nixon and Kissinger   In one of many private conversations, Richard Nixon discusses foreign policy with special assistant for national security affairs, Henry Kissinger. Kissinger, a Harvard professor of international relations and part-time foreign policy advisor to Kennedy and Johnson, served as Nixon's national security advisor until 1973 when he became secretary of state. *(Camera Press/Retna Ltd.)*

CHRONOLOGY

1962	Chavez founds National Farm Workers Association
1966	NOW founded
1968	Nixon elected president
1969	Nixon announces Vietnamization Stonewall Inn riot
1970	Kent State University massacre Nixon orders ground troops into Cambodia Clean Air and Water Acts
1971	*Pentagon Papers* published Environmental Protection Agency created
1972	Nixon goes to China and Soviet Union Watergate break-in Nixon reelected Congress passes ERA
1973	Paris Peace Accords signed Allende overthrown and killed in Chile Yom Kippur War begins; OPEC imposes oil embargo on United States Watergate hearings Wounded Knee occupied *Roe* v. *Wade* War Powers Act
1974	Nixon resigns; Ford becomes president
1976	Carter elected president
1977	Panama Canal treaties
1978	*Bakke* v. *University of California* United States recognizes China Camp David Accords
1979	Iran hostage crisis Soviets invade Afghanistan Nuclear accident at Three Mile Island

December 1969 Nixon announced a draft lottery system that eliminated many of the inequities of the older system. By 1973 troop withdrawals would allow him to end the draft and create an all-volunteer army.

This did not mean, however, that Nixon intended to give up in Vietnam. Like Johnson, Nixon was committed to preserving an independent, noncommunist

South Vietnam. While official announcements focused on troop withdrawals, the president dramatically enlarged the bombing campaign. Nixon explained his approach as "the Madman Theory." "I want the North Vietnamese to believe I've reached the point where I might do anything to stop the war," he confided in 1968. In his first month in office Nixon authorized Operation Menu—the secret bombing of North Vietnamese bases and supply routes in Cambodia. Over the next fifteen months American B-52 bombers served up a deadly diet of explosives. By 1971 the United States had dropped more bombs on Indochina than it had in all the European and Pacific theaters during World War II. "I refuse to believe that a little fourth-rate power like North Vietnam does not have a breaking point," Kissinger told his staff.

The bombings not only failed to intimidate the North Vietnamese, but also did little to stem the losses on the ground in South Vietnam. The South's government was failing miserably in its efforts to win popular legitimacy and to build an effective military force. Its army suffered from massive desertions and poor, often corrupt and brutal leadership. In 1970 a senior army official questioned whether the South Vietnamese army could develop "the offensive and aggressive spirit that will be necessary to counter either the VC [Vietcong] or the NVA [North Vietnamese Army]."

American military officials believed that the NVA, despite aerial bombing, was still using Cambodia as a staging ground for attacks on South Vietnam. In April 1970 Nixon ordered American ground troops into the neutral country. Claiming that an American defeat in Vietnam would unleash the forces of totalitarianism around the globe, he insisted that the invasion of Cambodia was a guarantee of American "credibility." "The most powerful nation in the world," he said, could not afford to act "like a pitiful helpless giant."

The raids achieved some of the short-term goals set by military planners. American units seized large caches of Vietnamese weapons and disrupted some North Vietnamese bases. But on the whole the invasion was a failure. The NVA survived intact, while the raids destabilized Cambodian society and undermined the Cambodian government. American bombing raids produced more than 1 million refugees, who fled the countryside and jammed already overcrowded cities. In this atmosphere of chaos a small group of dedicated communists—the Khmer Rouge—seized control of the country and began a deadly purge that killed millions more. At home, the invasion reinflamed antiwar sentiment and eroded support for Nixon's policy. Anger swept like wildfire across the nation and revived the fledgling peace movement, which had been lulled into complacency by news of troop withdrawals. Within days of the Kent State killings, about a fifth of the nation's college campuses were forced to cancel classes. More than a hundred thousand people gathered in Washington to protest the Cambodian invasion and the student deaths. In San Diego a student holding a placard reading "In the name of God, end the war," doused himself with gasoline, then set himself on fire.

By the summer of 1971 over 70 percent questioned in one poll called American involvement in Vietnam a mistake, and only 31 percent approved of Nixon's handling of the war. Even in the heartland, people were turning against the war. "I don't think you could find a hawk around here if you combed the place and set traps," declared a small-town Kansas journalist.

Congress turned up the heat on the president. South Dakota's Democratic Senator George McGovern censured his colleagues for their part in the war: "This chamber reeks of blood." The Senate Foreign Relations Committee denounced the "constitutionally unauthorized, Presidential war in Indochina." In June Congress repealed the Tonkin Gulf Resolution of 1964 and considered amendments to cut off funds for all American military operations in Cambodia.

In public Nixon appeared unconcerned about the growing signs of discontent with his policies. He made a point of telling reporters that he watched the Washington Redskins football game while one large demonstration clamored for attention outside the White House. In February 1971, to prove that he had not been intimidated by the protests, Nixon used American air cover to support an invasion of neutral Laos. Once again the invasion produced no military advantage but resulted in thousands of civilian deaths and a sea of refugees.

Behind the confident façade, Nixon was growing increasingly isolated and embattled, paranoid that his enemies in the Congress, the press, and the antiwar movement were conspiring to destroy him. "Within the iron gates of the White House, quite unknowingly, a siege mentality was setting in," a Nixon aide recalled. "It was now 'us' against 'them.' Gradually, as we drew the circle closer around us, the ranks of 'them' began to swell."

The circle tightened in June 1971 when the *New York Times* began publishing the *Pentagon Papers*, a secret Defense Department study of American decision making in Vietnam before 1967. Leaked to the press by a former Pentagon official, Daniel Ellsberg, the report showed that Kennedy and Johnson had consistently misled the public about their intentions in Vietnam. Nixon tried to block further publication, claiming it would damage national security. The Supreme Court, by a vote of six to three, ruled against the administration, citing the First Amendment freedoms of speech and the press. The decision enraged Nixon.

Nixon's Vietnam strategy also failed to intimidate the North Vietnamese. In March 1972 North Vietnam's forces launched a massive invasion of the South. In April the U.S. ambassador in Vietnam cabled Nixon: "ARVN forces are on the verge of collapse." Nixon, refusing to allow South Vietnam to fall, initiated a risky plan to use American airpower to give the North a "bloody nose." In May the president announced the most drastic escalation of the war since 1968: the mining of Haiphong harbor, a naval blockade of North Vietnam, and massive, sustained bombing attacks. Johnson lacked the will to launch such an aggressive operation, Nixon boasted. I "have the will in spades." By approving the campaign, codenamed Linebacker, Nixon ran the risk of inflaming public opinion at home and jeopardizing a planned summit with the Russians. The gamble succeeded. The Soviets offered only tepid protest, and most Americans believed the North's invasion required a tough American response.

Peace with Honor? The North Vietnamese invasion and Nixon's forceful counterthrust created an opportunity for negotiations. Both sides had reason to seek accommodation. The North Vietnamese wanted to end the punishing American bombings; the United States needed to end the war quickly. Since early in 1971 Kissinger had been holding private meetings in a suburb of Paris with his North Vietnamese counterpart, Le Duc Tho. The key stumbling block had been Tho's insistence that South Vietnam's president Nguyen Van Thieu be removed from power and that North Vietnamese troops be allowed to remain in the South. For a year neither side budged. The only thing they had agreed on was the shape of the negotiating table.

In September 1972 Kissinger made the first move by agreeing to allow North Vietnamese soldiers to remain in South Vietnam. Tho responded by dropping the long-standing demands that Thieu resign and a coalition government be created. A settlement appeared imminent, and Kissinger announced that "peace is at hand." He had not anticipated, however, the fierce opposition of President Thieu, who adamantly opposed North Vietnamese troops in the South. When Nixon supported Thieu, Kissinger returned to the negotiating table armed with new demands. Feeling betrayed, Tho suspended negotiations and returned to Hanoi.

Nixon decided that only a dramatic demonstration of American power could reassure the South Vietnamese and intimidate the North. On December 18, 1972, he ordered Operation Linebacker II, a massive eleven-day bombing campaign over North Vietnam. "This is your chance to use military power to win this war," the president told the chairman of the Joint Chiefs of Staff, "and if you don't, I'll consider you responsible." The raids were directed at military targets, but inevitably bombs also fell on schools, hospitals, and prisoner-of-war camps. The American costs were also heavy: the loss of fifteen B-52 planes and the capture of ninety-eight American airmen. During the previous seven years, only one of these high-flying bombers had been downed.

The resumption of bombing, along with pressure from China and the Soviet Union, pushed North Vietnam back to the negotiating table. It did not, however, change the terms for peace. The stumbling block remained the same: Thieu refused to accept a settlement that would allow the North Vietnamese to keep troops in the South. With polls showing overwhelming public support for ending the war and with Congress threatening to cut off funding for the effort, Nixon needed an agreement. This time he privately warned Thieu of grave consequences if he rejected the agreement. He matched the threat with a promise to "respond with full force should the settlement be violated by North Vietnam."

The Paris Peace Accords, signed on January 27, 1973, officially ended U.S. involvement in the Vietnam War. The treaty required the United States to remove its remaining 23,700 troops and the North Vietnamese to return all American prisoners of war. As a face-saving measure for the United States, the accords also called for "free and democratic general elections" to choose a government for a unified Vietnam. More important, however, was the American and South Vietnamese concession that North Vietnamese troops could remain in the South.

Nixon told a national television audience that the United States had achieved "peace with honor." In fact, it had achieved neither peace nor honor. The North Vietnamese had no intention of abandoning their dream of unification. Kissinger hoped that the treaty would provide only for a "decent interval" between the U.S. military withdrawal and the North's complete military conquest of the South. As Kissinger predicted, the North violated the cease-fire within a few months and continued its relentless drive South. Thieu appealed to the United States for help, but a war-weary Congress refused to provide assistance. By April 1975, when the North's troops captured the South Vietnamese capital of Saigon, America had already turned its attention away from the nation's longest war.

The battles had ended, but the war left deep scars. Among the dead were 57,000 Americans, 5,200 allied soldiers, 184,000 South Vietnamese, and perhaps as many as 925,000 North Vietnamese troops. Five times as many were wounded. The nations of Indochina were devastated by years of bloody battles and heavy bombing. Millions of civilians died in Vietnam, Cambodia, and Laos. American veterans returned home to a nation deeply divided by the war and to a public that was indifferent to their suffering.

The war shattered the myth of American invincibility and rocked the foundation of postwar American foreign policy. "The United States entered the Vietnam

U.S. Embassy in Saigon, April 1975 With North Vietnamese forces closing in on Saigon, the U.S. military initiated evacuation plan "Frequent Wind," the airlift of American personnel and some South Vietnamese to ships in the South China Sea. At the American embassy in the heart of Saigon, the final airlift began on April 29. The sight of marines guarding the perimeter and helicopters landing on the roof signaled to the Vietnamese that their ally was leaving, prompting a panic as refugees tried to gain entrance to the embassy and thereby make it on one of the last flights out. Marines were ordered not to fire on those trying to scale the walls, but to use pepper spray to deter their climb. Early on the morning of April 30, the ambassador and his staff boarded one of the helicopters, followed several hours later by the last of the marines. *(AP/Wide World Photos, Inc.)*

War with the breezy self-confidence of a young warrior," remarked a journalist. "It limped away doubting itself and its powers." The broad consensus in favor of an activist, anticommunist foreign policy, which had shaped American foreign policy since the end of World War II, was replaced by acrimonious debates over the "lessons of Vietnam." Those on the left believed that the war exposed the fallacy of containment and the limits of American power. "We should emerge from the tragedy of Vietnam with a clearer understanding of this nation's world role and a healthier realism about the limits of American power," declared Congressman Lee Hamilton of Indiana. Conservatives learned different lessons, charging that a failure of political will had led to America's defeat. According to this view, American Cold War assumptions were valid and the war winnable, but timid politicians, caving into pressure from a liberal media and a student rabble, imposed too many restrictions on the military. David Christin, a decorated veteran of the war, declared, "If we had fought to win, we would have won the war." The "ghosts of Vietnam" would haunt the American psyche for years after the conflict ended.

Détente   For Nixon and Kissinger, achieving "peace with honor" in Vietnam represented only one piece in the larger puzzle of global politics. The key players, they argued, were the Soviet Union and China. Because they believed that the United States and the Soviet Union had reached a rough military parity, Nixon and Kissinger wanted to abandon the costly pursuit of weapons superiority and instead focus on peaceful economic competition. Nixon and Kissinger hoped that such a relationship, which they called *détente*, would lessen the threat of nuclear war, encourage the Soviets to pressure the North Vietnamese into a peace settlement, and diminish the possibility of another war like Vietnam beginning elsewhere in the Third World.

Détente was more than an abstract proposition. Circumstances had provided the administration both an urgent need and a historic opportunity to thaw the Cold War between the United States and the Soviet Union. The American public, weary of foreign involvement, seemed unwilling to provide the emotional or financial resources necessary to sustain the Cold War. The Soviets also had reasons to seek closer ties with the United States. Soviet leader Leonid Brezhnev presided over a struggling economy in desperate need of Western goods and capital. Like his American counterpart, he hoped to divert resources from the arms race to domestic use. The Soviets were also worried about the growing military power of China. Ancient animosities between the Russian and Chinese empires reached a new level of tension in 1964, when the Chinese exploded their first atomic bomb. In the spring of 1969 long-standing border disputes flared into skirmishes between Russian and Chinese regulars.

Shrewdly, Nixon and Kissinger began working to improve relations with Communist China, using the Sino–Soviet tension to America's strategic advantage. As an incentive Nixon offered the Chinese access to American technology, capital goods, and foodstuffs. With a solid groundwork established, Nixon made a historic trip to China in February 1972, becoming the first sitting American president to visit that nation and reversing more than twenty years of Sino–American hostility. At the end of the meeting Nixon and China's Premier Zhou Enlai issued a joint communiqué calling for increased contacts between the two nations.

The Soviets watched nervously as anticommunist Richard Nixon embraced the world's largest communist country. Fearing closer ties between the United States and China, they pushed for their own deal with the Americans. Four months after his historic trip to China, Nixon boarded Air Force One for Moscow. "There must be room in this world for two great nations with different systems to live together and work together," Nixon declared. Nixon and Brezhnev signed trade and technology agreements, plus a statement of "Basic Principles" that called on both sides to avoid both military confrontations and "efforts to obtain unilateral advantage at the expense of the other."

More important, Nixon reached an agreement with the Soviets on the terms of the Strategic Arms Limitation Talks (SALT), an unprecedented breakthrough in Soviet–American relations. Thereafter, the aim of American nuclear doctrine shifted from achieving "superiority" to maintaining "sufficiency." The SALT I agreement limited the building of antiballistic missile systems (ABMs) and froze for five years the number of strategic offensive weapons in both arsenals, including intercontinental ballistic missiles (ICBMs) and submarine-launched missiles. And for the first time, improvements in spy satellites made it possible to monitor an arms limitation agreement.

The Limits of Realism

Because he believed that a communist victory anywhere in the world tipped the global balance of power away from the United States, Nixon supplied arms to a number of repressive regimes willing to oppose the regional interests of the Soviet Union. Among others, Nixon sent aid and approved arms sales to the shah of Iran, President Ferdinand Marcos in the Philippines, and Balthazar Vorster's white-supremacist government of South Africa. He also intervened more actively to douse potential hot spots. When a Marxist, Salvador Allende, won election as president of Chile, Nixon directed the CIA to support Allende's opponents. "I don't see why we need to stand by and watch a country go communist due to the irresponsibility of its own people," Kissinger declared. The president cut off economic aid and prevented private banks from granting loans to Chilean concerns. Convinced by Washington's actions that the United States would support them, Chilean military leaders staged a successful coup and killed Allende in September 1973. The new anticommunist regime, under General Augusto Pinochet, was one of the most repressive in the hemisphere, but it was quickly recognized by the United States and warmly supported.

Nixon-Kissinger diplomacy faced a tough challenge in the Middle East. The region represented a tangle of competing interest: the United States supplied military and economic aid to ensure Israel's survival, but it was also heavily dependent on oil from the Arab states. Complicating the picture, the Mideast had become a Cold War battleground between Washington and Moscow. In 1967 Arab nations, which had never conceded Israel's right to exist, prepared to invade their neighbor. Forewarned, Israel attacked first, and in six days of fighting the Israeli army captured the Gaza Strip and the Sinai Peninsula from Egypt, the West Bank and East Jerusalem from Jordan, and the Golan Heights from Syria.

On October 6, 1973—the most sacred Jewish holy day, Yom Kippur—Syria and Egypt attacked Israel. In the first three days of fighting, Egyptian troops advanced into the Sinai and crossed the Suez Canal, while Syria's army in the north threatened to cut Israel in half by penetrating through the Golan Heights. With Israel's survival at stake, the United States ordered a massive supply of arms to its ally. The American aid proved decisive. Israel recovered and took the offensive before the fighting ended in late October. Over the next two years Kissinger pursued "shuttle diplomacy," traveling between capitals in the Middle East to promote peace. He made progress with Egypt, but the other Arab states, bruised by America's pivotal intervention, imposed an oil embargo against the United States, Europe, and Japan. The embargo, which lasted from October 17, 1973, to March 18, 1974, produced dramatically higher energy costs. Thereafter, the OPEC nations continued to raise oil prices, which increased 400 percent in 1974 alone, with devastating consequences for the oil-dependent U.S. economy.

Kissinger also made little progress in addressing the thorny issue of a Palestinian homeland. In 1964 Palestinian Arabs created the Palestine Liberation Organization (PLO), which called for an end to the Jewish state and the creation of a Palestinian homeland. Under the aggressive leadership of Yasir Arafat, PLO factions launched a series of terrorist attacks against Israeli targets, including the murder of eleven Israeli athletes at the 1972 Olympic games in Munich. In 1975, after Arafat offered to settle the Palestinian homeland issue peacefully through the United Nations, the United States acknowledged that "the legitimate interests of the Palestinian Arabs must be taken into account in the negotiating of an Arab-Israeli peace." The issue of "land for peace" would prove a source of continuing friction in the region.

RICHARD NIXON AND THE TWO AMERICAS, 1969–1974

Richard Nixon began his administration by extending an olive branch to his liberal critics, proposing innovative domestic programs and promising to bring the Vietnam War to a quick end. By 1970 Nixon abandoned his moderate tone and pursued an aggressive experiment in political power. Over the next few years, courting the "silent majority," he expanded the war, viciously attacked his opponents, and consolidated power in the White House. His strategy resulted in a landslide victory in the 1972 presidential election. But his paranoia precipitated his downfall and eventual resignation.

The Search for Stability at Home   By the time he took the oath of office in January 1969, Richard Nixon had been a part of American political life for more than twenty years. Born on January 9, 1913, in Yorba Linda, California, Nixon worked his way through Whittier College and Duke University Law School. In 1946 he won election to Congress, four years later moved to the Senate, and in 1952 became Dwight Eisenhower's vice president. In 1960 he ran for president and lost in a close election to John F. Kennedy.

Through it all, many people wondered who the real Richard Nixon was. He was a man of considerable intelligence and determination with an instinctive feel for public sentiment. At times he was capable of enormous acts of generosity. As a student at Duke Law School Nixon befriended a classmate crippled by polio. Every day he carried the student up the school's steep steps. As president, Nixon once wept while reading a Medal of Honor citation. Yet these insights into Nixon's inner self were rare. "His public self," wrote journalist Tom Wicker, "always has seemed palpably to be concealing a private self we do not know." What the public usually saw was a man who was haunted by self-doubt, poisoned by anger, and driven by ruthless ambition.

At the start of his administration, Nixon continued the message of unity that he had preached during the campaign. He told reporters that he planned to be a "consensus" president who would heal the deep wounds created during the 1960s. Acting on impulse, Nixon held a widely publicized meeting with his former rival Hubert Humphrey. He promised to do more for African-Americans than any other president in history. In his inaugural address he urged Americans to "speak quietly enough so that our words can be heard as well as our voices."

In his early years in office Nixon adopted moderately progressive positions. As the first elected president since 1849 forced to work with a Congress controlled by the opposition party, he favored cooperation over confrontation. In addition to signing Democratic bills raising social security benefits, Nixon increased federal funds for low-income public housing and even expanded the Job Corps. His first term saw steady increases in spending on mandated social welfare programs, especially social security, Medicare, and Medicaid. His most novel and surprising proposal was the Family Assistance Plan (FAP), which provided a guaranteed minimum income of $1,600 to every U.S. family. Although the proposal died in the Senate, it revealed Nixon's capacity for domestic innovation. Michael Harrington, whose *The Other America* had helped inspire the war on poverty, called it "the most radical idea since the New Deal."

At the same time that he advocated his bold new Family Assistance Plan, Nixon placated conservatives by proposing to limit the size of the federal government and provide local communities with greater power. His plan, which he called the "New Federalism," was designed to "start resources and power flowing back from Washington to the people." In 1972 he pushed through Congress the State and Local Fiscal Assistance Act, a revenue-sharing plan that distributed $30 billion in federal money to the states.

Public morale received a big boost in July 1969 when *Apollo 11* astronaut Neil Armstrong lifted his left foot off the landing pad of his spacecraft and pressed it into the soft powdery surface of the moon's Sea of Tranquility. Over 1 billion people watched as Armstrong and fellow astronaut Buzz Aldrin planted an American flag and a plaque reading in part, "We came in peace for all mankind." The next day headlines around the world shouted the news: "Man Walks on Moon."

For a brief time, Americans joined together to celebrate a triumph of the American spirit. The moon landing represented, glowed *Time* magazine, "a shining reaffirmation of the optimistic premise that whatever man imagines he can bring to pass." Many people hoped the sense of unity and accomplishment inspired by the moon landing would usher in a new decade of harmony and consensus. "For one priceless moment in the whole history of man," a hopeful Richard Nixon declared, "all the people of this earth are truly one."

Mobilizing the "Silent Majority"

Nixon shattered the delicate calm on April 30, 1970, when he announced the Cambodian invasion. Shocked by the public outcry, Nixon moved decidedly to the right, mobilizing the "silent majority" to build support for his policies. Nixon shrewdly played to the public's mood, which was growing increasingly hostile to protesters and reformers whose challenges often violated deeply held attitudes about patriotism and traditional values. Many began to worry about the fundamental stability of their society. "Everything is being attacked," declared a suburban housewife, "what you believe in, what you learned in school, in church, from your parents."

In the aftermath of the Kent State killings the "silent majority" lashed out at the most visible symbol of the challenge to authority—student protesters. When New York's liberal mayor, John Lindsay, lowered the American flag in mourning for the Kent State dead, angry construction workers chanting "All the way with the USA" waded into a pro-Lindsay crowd, swinging their tools and leaving seventy people wounded in their wake. "They went through those demonstrators like Sherman went through Atlanta," remarked one observer. Six days later the leader of the local construction workers' union traveled to the White House to present Nixon with an honorary hard hat. Nixon accepted it as a "symbol, along with our great flag, for freedom and patriotism to our beloved country."

The "silent majority" viewed student protesters as part of a larger threat to social stability. Sensationalized stories of radical bombings, mass murders, and a rising crime rate added to fears that the social fabric was unraveling. Between September 1969 and May 1970 radical groups claimed responsibility for 250 bombings—an average of almost one per day. In February 1970 bombs ripped through the New York headquarters of corporate giants IBM, General Telephone and Electronics, and Socony Mobil. Far more threatening, however, was the growth in violent crime in communities, big and small, across the country. The Justice Department reported that the crime rate grew by 60 percent between 1960 and 1966, then leaped by another 83 percent between 1966 and 1971.

Political calculations were at the heart of Nixon's appeal to the "silent majority." Nixon believed that his political future depended on adding to his core supporters those people who had voted for George Wallace in 1968. Wallace had won 10 million votes, or about 13.5 percent of the total vote cast in 1968. Most of these voters were, in the words of two political scientists, "unyoung, unpoor, and unblack." "These are my people," Nixon boasted. "We speak the same language." His strategy was to play on public fear of urban violence and social disorder. The party of FDR, he told wavering Democrats, had been hijacked by antiwar protesters and New Left radicals.

Nixon and his advisers developed a four-pronged approach to tap into the frustrations of the "silent majority." First, he appealed to working-class whites by trying to block congressional approval of the Voting Rights Act and by ordering the Justice Department to delay implementing school desegregation cases. "For the first time since Woodrow Wilson," the head of the NAACP protested, "we have a national administration that can be rightly characterized as anti-Negro."

Second, he championed the cause of "law and order" and attacked the Supreme Court's liberal views on crime. The Nixon Justice Department pursued high-profile prosecutions of antiwar activists, including the so-called Chicago Eight for their antics at the 1968 Democratic convention. Promising to "get tough on crime," Nixon called for granting judges and police expanded powers to jail suspects and to search houses without a warrant. The president unleashed the full powers of government against potential "enemies" of his administration. Among other illegal moves, Nixon instructed the Internal Revenue Service to audit tax returns of critics, authorized the FBI to wiretap phones and infiltrate leftist groups, and told the Small Business Administration to deny loans to prominent antiwar or civil rights activists.

For the third prong, Nixon nominated conservative southern judges to fill Court vacancies. In 1969 he successfully nominated conservative Warren Burger to replace departing Chief Justice Earl Warren. Later that year, when another vacancy opened on the Court, Nixon turned to South Carolina judge Clement Haynsworth. Though no one questioned Haynsworth's legal credentials, his strong opposition to desegregation angered Senate liberals and worried many moderate Republicans. For the first time since the administration of Herbert Hoover, the Senate rejected a Supreme Court nominee. Nixon responded by nominating Judge G. Harrold Carswell, an undistinguished jurist who had once declared his belief in white supremacy. The Senate again refused to confirm the president's nominee. Nixon lost the battle but he won the political war by skillfully using the Senate rejection to score political points in the South. "I understand the bitterness of millions of Americans who live in the South," he said.

Finally, Nixon unleashed vice president Spiro Agnew, who traveled the country denouncing the media, radical professors, student protesters, and liberals. "Will America be led by a President elected by a majority of the American people," he demanded, "or will it be intimidated and blackmailed into following the path dictated by a disruptive radical and militant minority—the pampered prodigies of the radical liberals in the United States Senate?" Agnew called the Kent State murders "predictable and avoidable" and attacked the "elitists" who regarded the Bill of Rights as a protection "for psychotic and criminal elements in our society."

The 1972 Election

In 1972 the Democratic Party nominated as its presidential candidate Senator George McGovern, an outspoken liberal critic of the Vietnam War who sought to win election by directly challenging Nixon's interpretation of American politics and culture. McGovern and the delegates at the Democratic Party convention adopted an aggressively liberal platform. Among its more controversial points were a call for the immediate withdrawal of U.S. troops from Vietnam, amnesty for those who had fled the draft, busing to achieve integration in the schools, and the abolition of capital punishment. The platform also included a vaguely worded statement— "Americans should be free to make their own choices of lifestyles and private habits without being subject to discrimination"—which many people interpreted as an endorsement of drug use and homosexuality.

This platform and McGovern's nomination reflected important changes stirring in the Democratic Party. New rules governing the selection of delegates to the party's convention guaranteed added representation to more liberal groups—minorities, women, and the young—at the expense of more conservative Democratic Party constituencies. "There is too much hair, and not enough cigars at this convention," one labor leader declared.

The progressive Democrats who had fought for rules changes thought they were making the party more representative of America and therefore more likely to win in November. They believed that most Americans did not support the status quo and would embrace sweeping changes in the political system. It was in this spirit that George McGovern portrayed the campaign as "a fundamental struggle between the little people of America and the big rich of America, between the average workingman and woman and the powerful elite."

The Democrats badly misread the mood of the electorate. In 1972 Nixon's foreign policy pleased many voters. American casualties in Vietnam had declined steadily during Nixon's first term, and the president's assurance that America would achieve a peace with honor in Vietnam was closer to what voters wanted than McGovern's call for immediate withdrawal. When a would-be assassin shot and critically wounded George Wallace during the 1972 primaries, Nixon inherited many of his angry white supporters. Most were former Democrats who disapproved of their party's liberal position on domestic issues. They saw McGovern not as their champion but as the candidate of a liberal, intellectual, Northeast establishment.

On election day Nixon scored a resounding victory, winning 60.7 percent (47,169,911) of the popular vote. McGovern received only 29,170,383 votes, or 37.5 percent. Nixon carried every state except Massachusetts and the District of Columbia, for a margin in the electoral college of 521 to 17 (see map on page 1199).

The Watergate Crisis

In the wake of this convincing victory, many expected that the second Nixon administration would consolidate its power and put its stamp on the nation. But a series of scandals almost immediately put the administration on the defensive. The trouble actually began before the election, on June 17, 1972, when a security guard foiled a break-in at the Democratic Party's national headquarters in the Watergate complex. One of those apprehended, James McCord, was also security coordinator for the Committee to Re-elect the President (CREEP). The committee immediately fired McCord, and the president reassured the American public that no one in his administration had been involved in this "bizarre incident."

At the burglars' trial, McCord at first testified that he had acted alone, confirming the president's version of the break-in. But under intense pressure from federal judge John Sirica, McCord admitted that high White House officials had both approved the break-in and pressured the defendants "to plead guilty and remain silent." President Nixon praised Sirica's courage and pledged, "I will do everything in my power to ensure that the guilty are brought to justice."

It was the Senate, however, that made the next move, in February 1973, by creating a bipartisan select committee to probe further into the Watergate affair. Over the next months the committee, headed by North Carolina Democrat Sam Ervin,

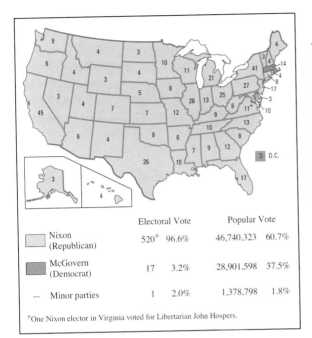

	Electoral Vote		Popular Vote	
Nixon (Republican)	520*	96.6%	46,740,323	60.7%
McGovern (Democrat)	17	3.2%	28,901,598	37.5%
— Minor parties	1	2.0%	1,378,798	1.8%

*One Nixon elector in Virginia voted for Libertarian John Hospers.

The Election of 1972   The assassination attempt on George Wallace and Edward Kennedy's personal crisis over Chappaquiddick removed two of the leading Democratic candidates for president, leaving Senator George McGovern of South Dakota to take the nomination. The apparent vacillations by McGovern on the campaign trail assisted Nixon in his reelection bid as he focused on his role as "global peacemaker." Nixon won by the largest majority of any Republican in American history.

uncovered a trail of corruption leading to higher and higher levels of the White House staff. Investigators learned, for example, that Nixon fundraisers had coerced corporations into "donating" millions of dollars to the president's reelection campaign. Following the publication of the *Pentagon Papers*, Nixon used the money to form a Special Investigations Unit, nicknamed "the plumbers," to plug leaks of sensitive information and to harass and demoralize the administration's "enemies." The plumbers, witnesses testified, were also behind the break-in at the Watergate.

Armed with these and other troubling revelations, the Ervin committee began to televise its hearings on May 17, 1973. A parade of witnesses confessed to criminal acts ranging from bribery to blackmail. Then, on June 25 White House counsel John Dean told the committee that the president had known about efforts to cover up the Watergate operation by September 1972 and had spoken to him about paying "hush money." Dean's proximity to the president and the concrete details he offered in his 245-page testimony made him a compelling witness. Even before he offered his testimony, a large majority of Americans believed that Richard Nixon had either planned or helped cover up the break-in at the Watergate. By June 1973 only 17 percent in one survey believed that Nixon was telling the truth. Still, there was no physical evidence to prove the president's guilt, and Nixon continued categorically to deny any wrongdoing. Exasperated, many despaired of ever finding the truth.

At this moment of uncertainty, a witness revealed that Nixon had installed a secret taping system to record, "for posterity," his private conversations in the White House and Executive Office Building. Ervin demanded that his committee be given access to the tapes. The special prosecutor, Harvard Law School Professor

Archibald Cox, asked the courts to order Nixon to release the tapes. Nixon refused. At issue, the president declared, was "the independence of the three branches of our Government." Ervin had a different definition of the question: "Whether the president is above the law."

When Cox persisted in his efforts to secure the tapes, Nixon ordered Attorney General Elliot Richardson to fire the special prosecutor. Richardson refused and was himself dismissed. His deputy, William Ruckelshaus, also refused, and he too was fired. On October 20, when Solicitor General Robert H. Bork finally carried out the president's order, a dramatic backlash ensued. The press referred to the firings as the "Saturday night massacre" and applauded Richardson and Ruckelshaus for their integrity. Members of Congress, citing an outraged public, demanded appointment of a new special prosecutor and release of the tapes. Compelled by this unified opposition, Nixon yielded some of the tapes and named a new special prosecutor, Leon Jaworski of Texas. Once again he declared his innocence, this time on television. "I am not a crook," he insisted.

The Saturday night massacre came in the midst of a series of scandals that kept the administration and the American public reeling. Just ten days earlier Vice President Spiro Agnew had pleaded no contest in federal court to charges of income tax evasion and admitted that he had accepted hundreds of thousands of dollars of bribes while governor of Maryland. Agnew resigned from the vice presidency, and Congress quickly confirmed Nixon's choice, Michigan Republican Gerald R. Ford, the House minority leader, to succeed Agnew under the terms of the Twenty-fifth Amendment. In late November Judge Sirica informed the public that eighteen minutes had been erased from a critical June 20, 1972, tape of a meeting between Nixon and his chief of staff, H. R. Haldeman. Nixon's secretary, Rosemary Woods, took responsibility, claiming that she had accidentally erased the tape while transcribing it. Experts testified, however, that the tapes had been deliberately tampered with by "manual" erasures. By December Nixon's own personal finances had come under increasingly critical scrutiny. The IRS disclosed that the president owed more than $400,000 in back taxes and penalties.

The air of scandal and uncertainty continued to hang over the capital until July 24, 1974, when a unanimous Supreme Court ordered President Nixon to turn over all relevant tapes. Just as Dean had contended, the tapes revealed that Nixon had personally intervened to stifle an FBI investigation into the Watergate break-in and that he had authorized payments of more than $460,000 in hush money to keep the Watergate burglars from implicating higher-ups in the administration. On August 8, 1974, facing certain impeachment, a disgraced Richard Nixon became the first American president to resign from office. At noon the next day, Vice President Gerald Ford was sworn in as the country's new chief executive. "Our long national nightmare," he declared, "is over."

Many forces conspired to create America's "national nightmare." The extraordinary growth of presidential power during the Cold War, the social upheaval and intense partisan divisions of the 1960s and early 1970s, and the emergence of a skeptical and assertive media all played important roles in Nixon's downfall. But it is impossible to understand Watergate without coming to terms with the ambitious, paranoid personality of Richard Nixon. Though he occupied the world's most pow-

Nixon's Goodbye On August 8, 1974, Richard Nixon became the first American president to resign from office after fellow Republicans made it clear that Nixon would be impeached and removed from office for his role in the Watergate cover-up. Gerald Ford, the House minority leader who had replaced Spiro Agnew as vice president the year before, was then sworn in as president. In this picture, Nixon and his family are saying their good-byes to Ford and his wife, Betty, before boarding the helicopter on the White House lawn for the last time. *(Nixon Presidential Materials Project, National Archives.)*

erful office, Nixon remained surprisingly insecure, fearful that his enemies in the establishment—liberals, media, and Congress—were out to destroy him. Since he equated his own political survival with the fate of the nation, Nixon felt justified in using whatever means necessary to destroy his opponents. "You were either for us or against us," recalled one aide, "and if you were against us, we were against you." In a chilling disregard for civil liberties, Nixon maintained that in curbing domestic dissent, "everything is valid, everything is possible." Perhaps Nixon offered the most insight into his own downfall in his farewell speech to the White House staff. "[N]ever be petty," he said, and "always remember, others may hate you, but those who hate you don't win unless you hate them, and then you destroy yourself."

OLD VALUES, NEW REALITIES, 1970–1979

The 1970s witnessed a continuation of the struggles over American identity that were unleashed during the previous decade. The civil rights struggle inspired an explosion in "rights consciousness," as other disadvantaged groups organized to fight for a broader, more inclusive vision of what it meant to be an American. On one level, many groups experienced unprecedented gains. Millions of African-Americans moved into the middle class, and black candidates won election to political offices. Other groups—women, gays, Hispanics, Native Americans—made important strides in their efforts to achieve equal rights. But the enormous material and political gains during the decade did little to eliminate race, class, and gender inequities in American society and culture. Many Americans, grown weary of the social struggles of the 1960s, turned inward in an attempt to make sense of the past and to find fulfillment in a confusing world.

African-Americans: Action Without Affirmation

As in the 1960s, racial relations continued to be the most divisive social issue with which Americans struggled. During the 1970s African-Americans made significant advances in the workplace and in politics. Many took white-collar jobs and held union memberships for the first time, earning higher incomes and enjoying greater job security. In the 1970s the earnings of between 35 and 45 percent of African-American families rose to middle-class levels. By 1980 the University of Michigan's National Opinion Research Center concluded that American society had "a truly visible black middle class" for the first time in its history.

With vigorous enforcement of the Voting Rights Act of 1965, African-Americans also began voting in unprecedented numbers and dramatically increased their representation in Congress and in state houses and town halls across the nation. The most impressive gains took place on the local level. In 1964 only 70 elected black officials served at all levels of government; by 1980 there were 4,600, including more than 170 mayors.

The civil rights movement also achieved a major victory in the Supreme Court, winning the Court's vigorous support for the desegregation of schools. Ever since the 1954 *Brown* decision (see page 1121), the Supreme Court had called for the desegregation of educational institutions. But it declined to specify remedies or insist on deadlines for implementation, and little progress occurred. Local school boards fiercely resisted local court orders and pleas from activists and parents. In Greensboro, North Carolina, when parents of three black children won a court order allowing their children to attend a predominantly white school, the local school board transferred all white students out of the school. In Boston, school board officials began busing white and black students out of their neighborhoods in the 1960s to keep schools segregated. Faced with such determined resistance, liberals and civil rights activists petitioned the Supreme Court to take a more forceful stand on the issue. In two unanimous cases—*Alexander* v. *Holmes County Board of Education* (1969) and *Swann* v. *Charlotte-Mecklenburg Board of Education* (1971)—the Supreme Court ordered a quick end to segregation, ruling that cities could be required to bus students if necessary to achieve integration. With the Supreme Court firmly behind busing as a remedy for school segregation, lower courts across the United States followed suit, ordering busing plans in numerous cities.

A divided Court also gave legal sanction to another controversial social policy: affirmative action programs that sought to achieve equality by reserving opportunities for minorities. In 1978 a white man, Allan Bakke, sued the University of California Medical School at Davis, claiming that the university had rejected him in favor of less-qualified minority candidates. A divided Supreme Court, in *Bakke* v.

University of California, ruled that the university's absolute quota for minorities was illegal, but it also agreed that schools could consider race as a "plus factor" in admissions so as to foster "diversity" in the classes.

Unfortunately, legal and economic gains took place against a backdrop of increasing misery for many African-Americans. In the 1970s black America increasingly divided into a two-class society. While some black families rose to middle-class income levels during the decade, about 30 percent slid deeper into poverty. African-Americans had long disproportionately suffered from poverty, but the impoverishment of the 1960s and 1970s was in many ways new, marked by a deeper isolation and hopelessness.

Tensions inherent in American political thought frustrated efforts to address racial injustice. Most whites supported racial equality as a general proposition. There was also broad support for African-American voting rights and the integration of public spaces. But minority leaders' and liberals' demands for affirmative action angered many whites. Such programs, many whites believed, elevated group remedies over individual rights and violated cherished notions of self-help. "Nobody ever gave me anything," said one frustrated man. "I worked hard to get a decent job to provide for my family. Now they want to change the rules and have everything given to them."

Many whites also resisted efforts to integrate schools and neighborhoods. By the 1970s the enforcement of segregation by law or informal covenant was no longer legal, but the segregation of housing actually increased during the decade. Busing plans, which frequently encountered fierce opposition from whites, failed to integrate the nation's schools. Worse, the plans were deeply flawed. In its 1974 *Milliken* v. *Bradley* decision, the Supreme Court prohibited the forced transfer of students between city and suburban schools. In many urban areas, the decision accelerated "white flight" to the suburbs, leaving urban schools more segregated than they had been before busing. Sixty-six percent of black students in the North and 50 percent in the South attended predominately black schools in 1979.

Voices of Protest: Hispanics, Native Americans, and Asian-Americans

In the 1970s Hispanic-Americans—a diverse group including immigrants from Mexico, Puerto Rico, and Cuba—were the fastest growing minority group in the country. Between 1960 and 1970 the documented Hispanic population in the United States nearly tripled, from 3 million to 9 million. During the 1970s the number of Hispanics increased to 14.6 million, or about 6 percent of the total population.

Hispanics remained one of the poorest groups in America. Before the 1960s nearly one-third of all Mexican-Americans worked long hours for low wages in the fields, picking crops. In 1962 the United Farm Workers (UFW) began a successful effort to organize them. Cesar Chavez, the UFW's charismatic leader, was the key figure in the organization's success. Chavez, a Mexican-American farm worker, echoed the religious themes and nonviolence of the early civil rights movement, framing the struggle between workers and growers as one of an oppressed minority seeking justice and simple dignity. "We hope that the people of God will respond to our call and join us," he declared, "just as they did with our Negro brothers in

Selma." Chavez's own religious faith and personal commitment inspired UFW members and supporters. By mid-1970 two-thirds of the grapes grown in California were harvested by workers under UFW contracts. The UFW also won passage of the 1975 California Agricultural Labor Relations Act, which gave farm workers the right to union elections with secret ballots.

In the 1960s and 1970s many younger Hispanics also challenged the value of assimilation, much as the black power movement did. For example, arguing that it was vital to preserve their traditions, some Mexican-Americans adopted the term *Chicano* to distinguish themselves from conservatives who wished to assimilate into Anglo culture. College courses in Hispanic culture were established in many universities. In 1968 Hispanic leaders and white liberals successfully lobbied the federal government to provide education in Spanish for children who had not learned English by the time they entered school. The government also recognized Hispanic-Americans as a distinct group and extended minority protection to them. In 1975 an amendment to the Voting Rights Act of 1965 extended to Hispanics the same federal protection that the law afforded to blacks.

Similar themes of control and ethnic pride animated the "red power" movement among American Indians. After John Collier resigned as head of the Bureau of

United Farm Workers on Strike Led by Cesar Chavez, Filipino farm workers in Delano, California, protested the horrible conditions of migrant labor camps, the corrupt labor contracts, and the intense racism of the San Joaquin region in 1965. By 1970, protests and boycotts forced twenty-six grape growers to the bargaining table, beginning the process of improving conditions for migrant workers in the West. *(George Ballis/Take Stock.)*

Indian Affairs in 1946, the federal government abandoned its New Deal–era experiments with tribal self-determination and sought instead to force tribes off reservations and into mainstream society. Fierce Indian resistance forced the government to cancel its plans.

The government's attempt to terminate federal protection for some tribes inspired Indians to take steps to improve conditions. In 1968 angry young Native Americans founded the American Indian Movement (AIM). In December 1972 AIM members orchestrated the seizure of the headquarters of the Bureau of Indian Affairs in Washington, D.C., and held it for a week. In February 1973, when local whites who had murdered a Sioux were lightly punished, two hundred AIM members occupied the town of Wounded Knee, South Dakota. They held the area for over two months, demanding that the government honor hundreds of broken treaties and calling for major changes in reservation government.

Other Native Americans used more traditional tactics to win a series of legal actions that reinstated treaties and extended legal rights. Armed with copies of abrogated treaties, Native Americans marched into courts and won the return of land wrongly taken from them. They also won legal battles to block strip mining and to preserve rights to fishing and mineral resources on reservation land.

Despite impressive gains, Native Americans faced overwhelming obstacles. Reservations, shrunken by treaty violations and far from employment opportunities, were dismal places. In 1971 unemployment among reservation Indians ranged from 40 to 75 percent, and annual family incomes averaged about $1,500. Life expectancy was only forty-six years, compared with the national average of seventy. Infant mortality rates were the highest in the nation.

The Asian-American experience was very different from that of most other minority groups. In the twenty years following the 1965 Immigration Act, the Asian population in the U.S. soared from 1 million to 5 million; nearly four times as many Asians entered the country during that period as had emigrated in the previous hundred years. Most came from the Philippines, China, Korea, and India.

Unlike the impoverished and often illiterate laborers who had once flocked to American shores, many of the new Asian immigrants were from middle-class backgrounds and had professional and technical skills. By 1974 Asian immigrants made up nearly one in five practicing physicians in the United States. The percentage was even higher in large urban areas. In some hospitals in New York City, Asian immigrants made up more than 80 percent of staff doctors.

Searching for an identity in a society that viewed race in terms of black and white, Asian-Americans convinced the U.S. Census Bureau to list Asian as a racial category on the 1980 census form. At the same time, third-generation Japanese-Americans, the Sansei, pressured Washington to establish a commission to investigate the internment of their parents during World War II. They also encouraged their parents—the Nisei—to speak out about their wartime experiences. In July 1980 the Commission on Wartime Relocation and Internment of Citizens (CWRIC) recommended that the government issue a formal apology for the internment and provide $20,000 in compensation to each survivor. Congress accepted the recommendation and enacted it into law in 1988.

The Modern Gay Rights Movement

Homosexuals, too, challenged prevailing ideas about their place in society. While small gay-rights organizations such as the Mattachine Society and the Daughters of Bilitis had been fighting for civil rights for years, the modern gay rights movement was born on Friday night, June 27, 1969, when a group of Manhattan police officers raided the Stonewall Inn, a gay bar in the heart of Greenwich Village. Such raids and the police abuse that frequently followed were routine affairs, but not this time. As one reporter noted, "Limp wrists were forgotten. Beer cans and bottles were heaved at the windows and a rain of coins descended on the cops."

The Stonewall Inn riot ignited a nationwide grass-roots "liberation" movement among gay men and women. Using confrontation tactics borrowed from the civil rights movement and the rhetoric of revolution employed by the New Left, the gay rights movement achieved a number of victories during the decade. The number of gay organizations in America grew from fewer than fifty to more than one thousand. In many large cities, gays and lesbians created support networks, newspapers, bars, and travel clubs. In less than a decade, noted an observer, American society had witnessed "an explosion of things gay." In 1973 the American Psychiatric Association reversed a century-old policy and stopped listing homosexuality as a mental disorder. More than half the states repealed their sodomy laws; the Civil Service Commission eliminated its ban against employment of homosexuals; and a number of politicians declared their support of gay rights.

Women's Liberation

Each of these groups—African-Americans, Hispanics, American Indians, and homosexuals—initiated significant changes in American society during the 1970s. But it was the women's liberation movement that emerged as the largest and most powerful social movement of the decade. Many date its beginnings to the publication in 1963 of Betty Friedan's best-selling book, *The Feminine Mystique*, which had sold 1.3 million copies by 1967.

A Smith College graduate, Friedan described the painful contradictions that she and many other educated women experienced. According to the most respected ideas of womanhood—promoted by the media, teachers, businessmen, social workers, and psychiatrists—women could find fulfillment only as wives and mothers and should leave careers for men. And yet, Friedan wrote, she and many of her peers found this life unsatisfying and confining. It gave them no chance to exercise their talents or develop their own identities. Suburbia was not the safe and secure haven they had been promised, but rather a "comfortable concentration camp" in which many felt trapped.

At the same time that *The Feminine Mystique* was released, the historic constituencies of American feminist movements—educated women and employed women—were growing dramatically. Although the percentage of women in American colleges had declined since the 1920s, the absolute number of women attending and graduating college had risen steadily. A booming economy attracted women to the work force in unprecedented numbers. Drawn by the desire for consumer goods, even many married women were working for pay for the first time; by 1968, 40 percent of married women with small children held at least a part-time job.

The women's movement took flight with two major wings. One group of feminists, led primarily by older professional women, sought to achieve change by working within the political system. The National Organization for Women (NOW) best exemplified this reform impulse. Formed in 1966 to lobby the government on behalf of issues of special concern to women and modeled after the NAACP, NOW announced that its purpose was to "take action to bring women into full participation in the mainstream of American society now, exercising all the privileges and responsibilities thereof in truly equal partnership with men." NOW called for an equal rights amendment (ERA) to the Constitution, which members believed would help them win other benefits: equal employment, maternity leave, child care, and the right to choose abortion.

Younger feminist leaders by and large rejected NOW's moderate approach and advocated bolder measures. Many had worked with the Student Nonviolent Coordinating Committee (SNCC) during the Freedom Summer of 1964 or in one of the student protest movements, frontline crucibles in which their beliefs about politics and protest were shaped. Like others in the New Left, these women's liberationists or radical feminists distrusted establishment political tactics and instead sought to change American culture and to build a society based on participatory democracy. Irreverent and eager to challenge prevailing beliefs, they used the tactics of mass protest, direct action, and political theater characteristic of the civil rights struggles.

The feminist movement won a number of impressive victories in the courts and legislatures during the 1970s. In 1972 Congress passed Title IX of the Higher Education Act, which banned discrimination "on the basis of sex" in "any education program or activity receiving federal financial assistance." The legislation set the stage for an explosion in women's athletics later in the decade. Also in 1972 Congress passed and sent to the states a constitutional amendment banning discrimination on the basis of sex—the ERA. By the end of the year all fifty states had enacted legislation to prevent sex discrimination in employment. Federal and state laws protecting victims of domestic violence and rape were strengthened. Congresswoman Bella Abzug declared 1972 "a watershed year. We put sex discrimination provisions into everything."

The most dramatic change came in the area of reproductive rights. On January 22, 1973, in the landmark case *Roe v. Wade*, the Supreme Court declared that a woman had a constitutional right to an abortion. Writing for the majority, Justice Lewis Blackmun asserted that the fourteenth amendment, which prohibited states from denying "liberty" to anyone without "due process," established a "right of privacy" that was "broad enough to encompass a woman's decision whether or not to terminate the pregnancy." The Court stated that during the first trimester the decision to abort a fetus should be left to the discretion of a woman and her doctor. Over the next three months, up until the point of fetal viability, the state could establish some limits on the right to an abortion. In the final trimester, the government could prohibit an abortion except where necessary to preserve the mother's life or health.

There were also signs of change in American culture. At the grass roots, feminist organizations flourished: feminist bookstores, rape crisis and domestic violence centers, and chapters of NOW formed across the nation. A feminist magazine, *Ms.*, attracted a large national circulation. And the proportion of women entering professional and graduate schools rose substantially. By the 1980s, 25 percent of new graduates of law, medical, and business schools were women, up from only 5 percent in the late 1960s. Opinion surveys recorded new attitudes about gender roles. "Women's liberation has changed the lives of many Americans and the ways they look at family, job and sexual equality," *Reader's Digest* concluded in 1976. Over two-thirds of the college women questioned by the magazine agreed that "the idea that a woman's place is in the home is nonsense."

Perhaps the most important accomplishment was the development of the women's health movement. What started as hippie "free clinics" in the 1960s grew into a national movement in the 1970s as female health activists disseminated biological knowledge, questioned doctors' control over reproductive decisions, and conducted "self-help gynecology" seminars. The publication of the popular *Our Bodies, Ourselves* (1973) marked an important shift in the women's movement. By emphasizing biological difference, the movement underscored the central paradox of postwar feminism: how to achieve equality while also honoring the difference between men and women.

Not everyone welcomed these changes in gender roles (see Competing Voices, page 1223). Traditionalists found a talented leader in Phyllis Schlafly, a conservative activist who campaigned tirelessly against the ERA. Tapping into traditional views

Dartmouth Tuck Graduates of 1970 The ideas that emerged from the feminist movement continued to influence women who demanded equal rights and opportunities. Growing numbers of women completed professional degrees in the late sixties and early seventies, including the woman in this photograph, Martha Fransson, who is shown with her fellow M.B.A. graduates at Dartmouth. In 1972, Congress passed the Educational Amendments Act, which required colleges to ensure equal opportunity for women like Fransson in the future. *(Courtesy Tuck School of Business Archives, Dartmouth Collage, Hanover, New Hampshire.)*

of womanhood, she complained that feminists had abandoned their God-given roles of wife and mother in favor of a radical political agenda that was "anti-family, anti-children, and pro-abortion." The affirmation of traditional gender roles struck a responsive chord with conservative men, but it also appealed to many working-class women who felt estranged from the largely middle-class leadership of the feminist movement. Schlafly's charges that the ERA would promote lesbianism, require women to serve in combat roles in the military, and roll back protective legislation that housewives and female workers cherished eroded public support and eventually killed the amendment.

Despite signs of progress, women still faced major discrimination in the workplace. In the 1970s jobs were still typically classified as "men's" or "women's" work, and as a consequence over 80 percent of all women workers were clustered in 20 of the 420 occupations listed by the Census Bureau. "Women's" jobs—secretary, waitress, sales clerk—typically offered low pay, little security, and no chance for advancement. When women did perform the same work as men, they received much lower wages. To compound these problems, unemployment rates among women consistently exceeded male averages by more than 20 percent.

This discrimination in the job market often had devastating consequences for women trying to live on their own. It was particularly hard on single women with children, who were increasingly numerous in the 1970s as divorce and out-of-wedlock births grew more common. During the 1970s the number of women heading families with children increased by 72 percent. A large proportion of their households, as many as one-third, fell below the poverty line. By 1980, 66 percent of all adults whom the government classified as poor were women. This new phenomenon, which sociologists called the "feminization of poverty," hit black women hardest of all. While the number of white families headed by women increased only marginally during the 1970s, the number of black families headed by women skyrocketed to 47 percent by 1980. One out of every three black children was born to a teenage mother, and 55 percent of all black babies were born out of wedlock. In inner-city ghettos, the figure for out-of-wedlock babies often climbed above 70 percent, and two-thirds of all black families living in poverty were headed by women.

The Me Decade "In the '70s, hardly anybody was a hippie, because everybody was," declared one observer. Emblems of sixties protest, such as long hair and ultracasual dress, gained mainstream appeal during the 1970s. Natural food stores sprouted from coast to coast. National supermarkets sold bean curd. The use of recreational drugs, especially marijuana, was commonplace. The proportion of Americans favoring the full legalization of marijuana doubled from 12 percent to 25 percent. Attitudes toward sex underwent a similar change. In 1969, 74 percent of women disapproved of sex before marriage. Four years later 53 percent of women saw nothing wrong with premarital sex.

Critics complained that these trends suggested that Americans had become more interested in personal pleasure than in social reform. One author called the 1970s the "Me Decade," and much evidence supported the unflattering label. The best-selling self-help book of the decade was *Looking Out for #1*. A health and fitness craze swept the nation as Americans by the millions started jogging. "If the emblem of the '60s was the angry banner of a protest marcher, the spirit of '79 was the jogger, absorbed in the sound of his own breathing—and wearing a smile button," observed *Newsweek*. Many Americans looked to Eastern religions "to get in touch with their feelings," taking up yoga, Zen Buddhism, and transcendental meditation (TM). The Korean missionary Sun Myung Moon, founder of the Unification Church, drew twenty thousand spectators to New York's Madison Square Garden. "I feel changed," exclaimed one convert. "I have much more of an inner peace."

Changing cultural fashions were most clearly evident in popular music. The protest songs of the 1960s were abandoned for the rhythmic beat of disco. Despite all the scorn heaped on it, disco preached a message of inclusion, a blurring of racial and gender differences that were hardening in other areas of American life. Disco was music made openly for and by gays as well as straights. Donna Summer and Gloria Gaynor became camp icons, and the Village People presented themselves as cartoon homosexual pinups—cowboy, construction worker, leather man, Native American, policeman, and soldier—and wiggled their way through hits such as "In the Navy," "YMCA," and "Macho Man."

The decade was not as shallow or as self-involved as critics suggested. The three major networks featured their share of mindless situation comedies, 1950s nostalgia, and sexual titillation. But the popular media also revealed the struggle of a culture attempting to reconcile new ideas with old realities. The popular ABC mini-series *Roots* (1976) provided audiences with a rich portrayal of the African-American experience. Norman Lear's popular sitcom *All in the Family* pitted Archie Bunker, who preferred an older, simpler America expressed in the theme song "Those Were the Days," against the progressive views of his liberal son-in-law, Michael. "Why fight it?" Michael asked Archie in the first episode. "The world's changing." But Archie, refusing to accept defeat, continued his fight against the forces of change, especially minorities, liberals, and radicals. "I'm against all the right things," Archie shouted, "welfare, busing, women's lib, and sex education."

A number of blockbuster movies also touched on sensitive issues and revealed the decade's conflicting social currents. In the 1976 Academy Award–winning film *Rocky*, Sylvester Stallone played a streetwise white roughneck named Rocky Balboa, "the Italian Stallion," who challenged the outspoken and black Apollo Creed for the heavyweight championship of the world. Movie audiences cheered for the white ethnic underdog, whom one movie critic called "the most romanticized Great White Hope in screen history." *Breaking Away* (1979), the story of blue-collar youth competing in a bicycle race in Bloomington, Indiana, offered a more nuanced and sensitive portrayal of working-class frustration.

Hollywood and the nation struggled during the decade to come to terms with Vietnam. The film *M*A*S*H* (1970), later made into a television sitcom, used the backdrop of an army field hospital during the Korean War to present a black comedy about Vietnam. In 1978 two Vietnam films, *Coming Home* and *The Deer Hunter*, swept the Oscars with their vivid portrayals of the war's traumatic impact on ordinary Americans. *Coming Home*, which starred peace activist Jane Fonda, was solidly antiwar. *The Deer Hunter* was more ambiguous. In tracing the tragic journey of three friends from a steel-mill town in western Pennsylvania who volunteered for the war, director Michael Cimino showed the tremendous price, both physical and psychological, that many Americans paid during the conflict. At the same time, critics charged, by depicting the Vietcong as "brutes and dolts" and the Americans as "innocents in a corrupt land," the movie took a subtle prowar position.

THE AGE OF LIMITS, 1974–1979

By the end of the decade Americans had reason to question their optimistic faith in the future of the American experiment. Recent events had challenged many of the pillars of American identity. Watergate eroded Americans' confidence in the nation's elected leaders and shook their faith in the nation's political institutions. Vietnam had forced the nation to question its role in world affairs. "Stagflation," a new and troubling combination of rising unemployment and soaring inflation, depressed the standard of living of millions of Americans and made them question whether they could pass on a better life to their children. Concern about limited resources also produced widespread fear of environmental disaster. Public leaders failed to offer convincing answers to the questions puzzling most Americans.

Congressional Resurgence and Public Mistrust

In the aftermath of Watergate and the Vietnam War, wrote Tom Wicker, many Americans had come to look on their government as "a fountain of lies." "All during Vietnam, the government lied to me," declared journalist Richard Cohen. "All the time. Watergate didn't help matters any. More lies . . . I've been shaped, formed by lies." Hoping to restore the public trust, the nation's political leaders undertook a series of political reforms. Most of the effort was directed at limiting the power of the presidency. In 1973 Congress passed the War Powers Act over President Nixon's veto. The act required a president to "consult with Congress" within forty-eight hours of committing American troops abroad and ordered him to withdraw them within sixty days unless Congress approved the mission. The Congress also enjoined the president from undertaking any military action in Vietnam after August 15, 1973.

Next, Congress moved to increase its influence over domestic policy. The Budget and Impoundment Control Act in 1974 streamlined the budgeting process in Congress and created the Congressional Budget Office, which produces an independent analysis of the president's budget each year. Congress expanded the personal staffs of individual senators and House members and committee staffs in both houses, and added to the research service of the Library of Congress. These steps, though little noticed, represented a significant change in the relationship between the two branches. Congress acquired new capability to evaluate and challenge programs sought by presidents.

Recognizing the strength of popular support for reform, House leaders also agreed to changes in the House structure that greatly diffused authority. The chairs of the twenty-two standing committees in the House, a small group of senior legislators, had long been able to decide which bills would receive consideration in their committees, and they could organize support or opposition to a bill that was almost always decisive. In 1974 House Democrats adopted "the subcommittee bill of rights," which parceled out the power of the original 22 committees to 172 subcommittees. Many complained that this redistribution of power made it difficult to build coalitions that could pass legislation.

Hoping to prevent another Watergate, Congress moved to limit the influence of money in politics, but the effort backfired. The Federal Election Campaign Act of 1974 placed caps on the amount of money that individuals could donate to political campaigns and provided some public funding for presidential campaigns. But loopholes in the act allowed new mechanisms of fundraising and donation that actually led to an increase in the flow of private money into elections. Political parties used direct mail to solicit huge numbers of small donations, which they then funneled into important campaigns. Political action committees (PACs) proliferated and dispersed campaign funds. In 1974 there were only 608 PACs; by 1984 the number had soared to over 4,000. Critics charged that well-financed PACs gave powerful interests inordinate influence in Congress. "What is at stake," cautioned journalist Elizabeth Drew, "is the idea of representative government, the soul of this country."

As the nation prepared to celebrate its two-hundredth birthday, polls showed that Americans had little confidence that their political leaders were dealing honestly with them. While faith in American political institutions remained firm, faith in Washington was languishing. A 1976 study revealed that 69 percent of respondents felt that "over the last ten years, this country's leaders have consistently lied to the people." What Americans were saying, declared two social scientists, was that "the system" works but "it is not performing well because the people in charge are inept and untrustworthy."

The Troubled Economy

A host of statistics revealed that the American economy had stalled during the 1970s. During the long postwar boom from 1947 to the mid-1960s the United States enjoyed average annual productivity increases of 3.2 percent. From 1965 to 1973, however, productivity growth averaged only 2.4 percent annually. By the end of the decade productivity was declining in absolute terms. As inflation exploded to nearly 10 percent and unemployment crept upward, Americans found that their discretionary income declined by 18 percent between 1973 and 1980. The average price of a single-family house more than doubled during the decade (see figure on page 1213).

The nation's economic difficulties had many causes. First, an inflationary trend began in the 1960s, when President Johnson and the Congress decided to expand defense and social spending without asking for higher taxes. Each year high government expenditures stimulated the economy more than taxes slowed it down, creating upward pressure on prices.

Second, in the 1970s America ran out of "easy oil," a serious challenge to the basic structures of the economy. The nation's expansion in the postwar era depended on the prodigious use of cheap energy. Americans living in sprawling suburban communities enjoyed driving powerful, energy-inefficient cars. Large single-family homes offered Americans more living space than people of any other country—but needed a great deal of oil to heat in the winter and of electricity to cool in summer. And as long as energy was cheap, American industry found it cost-efficient to use processes that were alarmingly wasteful.

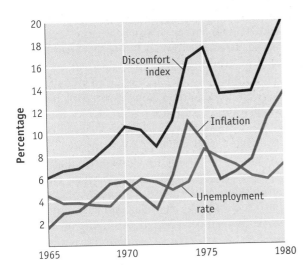

Discomfort Index During the 1970s the United States experienced both rising inflation and increased unemployment. During the 1976 presidential campaign Democrats developed the "discomfort" or "misery" index to measure the public impact of this destructive combination, and to attack their Republican opponents for their poor management of the economy. In 1980, however, Republicans used the same index to highlight Jimmy Carter's economic mismanagement.

In the early 1970s political turmoil in the Middle East led to dramatically higher oil prices and undermined the bedrock of this system. Between 1972 and 1979 the price of oil quintupled. Higher energy costs rippled through the economy. Inflation, which never exceeded 5 percent between 1955 and 1972 and was often as low as 2 or 3 percent, suddenly exploded to nearly 10 percent by the end of 1973.

A third cause for economic trouble lay abroad. For the first time since the end of World War II, American business faced stiff competition from other countries. The industrial economies of Western Europe and Japan, finally recovered from the war, began to win an increasing share of international trade. The U.S. share of world trade declined by 16 percent between 1960 and 1970 and dropped another 25 percent during the 1970s. What was even more troubling was that foreign competitors were winning a large share of the rich American market. With exports declining and imports rising, the United States posted its first balance of trade deficit in almost a century. The surge in foreign competition offered consumers quality products at lower prices. But it also threatened jobs that had for years provided high wages and dependable employment.

The decline of the American automobile industry was a clear example of this trend. In the 1950s and 1960s U.S. automakers ruled the domestic market. In the 1970s, with gasoline prices soaring and buying power pinched by inflation, car buyers welcomed affordable, more fuel-efficient imports such as Japan's Toyotas and Datsuns. Detroit, geared toward producing bulky six-passenger sedans, failed to convert in time, and part of its market drifted away. By 1980 imports had grabbed 34 percent of the U.S. auto market. The United Stares now imported 3.2 million foreign cars annually, about 60 percent of them from Japan.

In the midst of these crises, political leaders seemed unable to find solutions. Each presidential administration of the decade witnessed wild policy swings as leaders and economists sought to understand the profound changes shaking the American economy. Many of the experiments were based on short-term thinking; none seemed to improve the nation's economy very much. In combination they eroded the public's belief that the nation's leaders could manage the economy.

President Nixon, for example, began his administration by embracing the monetarist theories of Milton Friedman. The conservative Friedman claimed that prices could be lowered by reducing the quantity of money in the economy. If there was less money and borrowing was more expensive, reasoned Friedman, economic activity would ease and prices would stabilize. In practice, a reduced money supply did slow economic growth, but it did not stop prices from rising. This new and troubling phenomenon, dubbed "stagflation," haunted the economy for the rest of the decade.

Deeming monetarism a failure, Nixon tried other policies. In August 1971, faced with a combination of rising prices and high unemployment, Nixon shocked conservatives and delighted liberals by declaring, "I am now a Keynesian" (see page 992). Acting on his new faith, the president advocated traditionally liberal solutions, imposing wage and price controls, devaluing the dollar, and abandoning the gold standard. Fearing the political consequences of high unemployment in an election year, Nixon pressured the Federal Reserve Bank, the nation's central institution for setting interest rates and regulating the money supply, to turn on the money spigot. Commenting on Nixon's dramatic switch, a journalist quipped, "It's a little like a Christian crusader saying 'All things considered, I think Mohammed was right!'" Later that year Nixon announced a "new economic policy," imposing a 10 percent surcharge on U.S. imports. "My basic approach," said Secretary of Treasury John Connally, "is that the foreigners are out to screw us. Our job is to screw them first." The policies realized their short-term political and economic goals. During the 1972 election year the GNP grew by 7.2 percent and the unemployment rate plunged from 6 percent to 5.1 percent. In the long run, however, Nixon's policies proved disastrous. By ignoring clear signs of inflation and intentionally expanding the economy he contributed to a cycle of spiraling inflation that would soon cripple the economy.

These reverses assaulted Americans' optimistic faith in progress. For most of their history, Americans had believed that hard work and talent would be rewarded with upward mobility and greater economic opportunity. More, they had faith that the ingenuity of the American people and the continent's rich resources would lead to ever-increasing prosperity for all. Americans, Alexis de Tocqueville wrote as early as 1835, "consider society as a body in a state of improvement." By 1979, however, 55 percent of all Americans believed that "next year will be worse than this year." Nearly three out of four Americans polled agreed with the statement: "We are fast coming to a turning point in our history. The land of plenty is becoming the land of want."

The Environmental Movement

The obvious contribution of the oil shock to the nation's economic woes alerted many people to the possibility that their prosperity had been built on an unsustainable base, and a groundswell of environmentalism resulted. The birth of the modern environmental movement dated to the publication in 1962 of marine biologist Rachel Carson's book *Silent Spring*, which documented evidence that the widely used insecticide DDT was killing birds, fish, and other animals that ate insects. Sufficiently concentrated, DDT also posed significant health risks to humans. Chemical companies that manufactured DDT ridiculed Carson's book, but her eloquence and evidence won numerous allies. In 1972 the government banned the sale of DDT.

Highly publicized disasters fueled public concern about the costs of a technological society. When people living in the Love Canal housing development near Niagara Falls, New York, reported abnormally high rates of illness, miscarriages, and birth defects, investigators learned that the community had been built on top of an underground chemical waste disposal site. In March 1979 a frightening accident at the Three Mile Island nuclear power plant in Pennsylvania heightened public concern about the safety of nuclear power and led to calls for tighter regulation of the industry.

The government responded with several pieces of legislation. In 1971 Congress created the cabinet-level Environmental Protection Agency (EPA) to focus government efforts to protect the environment. Congress also passed legislation expanding the government's regulatory powers. The Water Quality Improvement Act and National Air Quality Standards Act strengthened controls against water and air pollution. The Resource Recovery Act provided $453 million for resource recovery and recycling systems. The National Environmental Policy Act required the government to consider in advance the impact of government programs on the environment.

Uneasiness about the state of the environment persisted and found expression in the popular culture of the 1970s. In best-selling books such as Hal Lindsey's *Late Great Planet Earth*, scientists were heard to predict the end of global supplies of oil and other natural resources. A popular movie, *The China Syndrome*, portrayed a fictitious nuclear power plant in which incompetence and greed threatened to lead to a nuclear meltdown. Other movies, such as *Soylent Green*, envisioned a world in which technological development and overpopulation had exhausted Earth's natural resources. Providing clear evidence of the broad-based, diverse support for environmentalism was the success of the first annual Earth Day celebration on April 22, 1970. Twenty million people gathered in local events across the country to hear speeches and see exhibits and demonstrations promoting environmental awareness.

The Vacuum of Leadership: Gerald Ford and Jimmy Carter

Faced with the delicate problem of succeeding Richard Nixon, Gerald Ford tried to present himself as a steady, sober leader whom the public could trust. With his friendly smile and reputation for honesty, Ford enjoyed wide respect. Within a month, however, he connected his administration to the Watergate scandal by granting Nixon "a full, free, and absolute pardon . . . for all his offenses against the United States." Overnight, Ford's approval ratings plunged from 71 percent to 50 percent.

Ford had a hard time overcoming this poor start. He fought constantly with Congress, vetoing more legislation than any president in history. Hoping to choke off the inflation that followed Nixon's relaxation of price controls, Ford drove interest rates to all-time highs and vetoed a tax cut designed to give consumers more money to spend. Though this brought inflation down to 5 percent by 1976, it also produced a serious contraction in 1975 as unemployment reached a post–Great Depression high of 9 percent.

Unemployed   During Gerald Ford's seventeen months as president, the United States slipped into its deepest recession since the Great Depression. Unemployment hit 9 percent in 1975, leaving millions of Americans with few options save filing for government relief. This was a choice few people, like this man at an unemployment agency in Cleveland, made easily. *(Settle/NYT Pictures.)*

During the 1976 Democratic primaries, one-term Georgia Governor Jimmy Carter emerged from a crowded pack of contenders by convincing voters that only he, an outsider, could clean up the mess in Washington. Deciding that most people were more interested in leadership and integrity than in issues, Carter avoided taking positions on controversial questions. The main issues of the campaign, he claimed, were two: "Can government work? And can government be decent, honest, truthful, fair, compassionate, and as filled with love as our people are?" To a public still smarting from Watergate, Carter said, "I will never lie to you." To balance the ticket and appeal to mainstream Democrats, Carter selected Minnesota Senator Walter F. Mondale, a protégé of Hubert Humphrey, as his running mate.

Although burdened by the legacy of Watergate, continuing bad economic news, and his own lack of charisma, Ford managed to keep the race close. Fewer than 2 percentage points separated the candidates in the popular vote—Carter won 40.8 million votes to Ford's 39.1 million. In the electoral college, Carter defeated Ford 297 to 240. It was the narrowest electoral victory since 1916, when Woodrow Wilson defeated Charles Evans Hughes by 23 electoral votes. Judging from the turnout, it was also one of the least compelling. A smaller percentage of Americans voted in 1976 than in any election since 1948 (see map on page 1217).

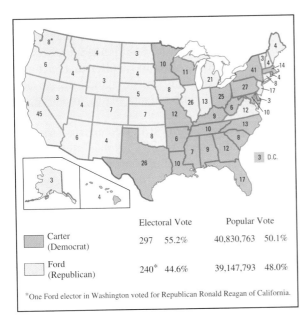

		Electoral Vote	Popular Vote	
Carter (Democrat)		297 55.2%	40,830,763 50.1%	
Ford (Republican)		240* 44.6%	39,147,793 48.0%	

*One Ford elector in Washington voted for Republican Ronald Reagan of California.

The Election of 1976 Ford's failure to solve the nation's economic problems led to doubts within his own party about his ability to lead the nation, culminating in a close race with Ronald Regan for the Republican Party nomination. Meanwhile, the Democrats selected Jimmy Carter of Georgia, who emphasized the need for a moral president after years of political corruption unearthed by the Watergate investigations. Fallout from the Watergate era could also be seen in the low voter turnout for the election, as almost half of eligible voters, alienated by the scandal, failed to vote.

The new president faced enormous obstacles in his effort to build a national consensus. His narrow electoral victory provided a shaky foundation for bold proposals. He presided over a party still torn by divisions over Vietnam and civil rights. A resurgent Congress, eager to reassert its authority after Watergate, and a public grown cynical about Washington and angry about rising unemployment and high inflation compounded his difficulties.

Much of Carter's presidency was marred by poor relations with Democratic congressional leaders. As a result, some of the administration's top legislative priorities were either gravely weakened or utterly abandoned. Carter also had significant trouble managing the economy. He began his presidency by raising government spending in an effort to rein in the spiraling unemployment generated by Ford's fiscal and monetary restrictions. In 1979, however, after OPEC announced another round of escalating oil prices that pushed inflation above 10 percent, Carter reversed course. He cut back public spending and appointed leading conservative Paul Volcker to head the Federal Reserve Board. Volcker, determined to wring inflation out of the economy, instituted a severe tight money policy. In 1980 this policy had devastating effects: unemployment shot up to more than 7.5 percent, but inflation remained above 12 percent, and interest rates topped out at the incredible figure of 20 percent.

In foreign policy, the president achieved a couple of notable successes. In December 1978 Carter completed the process initiated by Richard Nixon by formally recognizing the People's Republic of China. President Carter also convinced the Senate, in a very close vote, to ratify a treaty that promised to turn over the

Canal Zone to Panama by the year 2000. Carter moved to identify the United States with black African nationalism and to end the "last vestiges of colonialism" in Zimbabwe/Rhodesia and Namibia. Carter chided white South African rulers for apartheid—an official system of segregating nonwhites and whites that included removals of blacks to designated homelands, discriminatory wages based on race, the denial of voting rights and the absence of civil liberties for blacks, and arbitrary arrests of blacks.

For most of his four years in office, however, Carter struggled unsuccessfully to convince the American public that he could protect America's global interests from an aggressive Soviet Union. Carter came to power pledging to work for more amicable relations with the Soviet Union and to replace the Nixon-Kissinger commitment to realism with a concern for human rights. "We are now free of that inordinate fear of communism which once led us to embrace any dictator who joined us in our fear," Carter declared. He quickly opened a second round of arms limitations talks (SALT II) with the Soviet Union. But Carter was struggling to extend détente when many Americans were questioning its benefits. Since Nixon and Kissinger had announced their aim of achieving détente, the Soviet Union had repeatedly made clear its continuing support for "liberation" struggles in the Third World. It ordered Cuba to send troops to potential allies in Africa and worked to win influence among Arab nations sitting on the oil needed by Western nations.

1979: The Year of Crisis   In 1979 three events in the Middle East would have a dramatic impact on America's relationship with the world. First, in March, long-standing enemies Israel and Egypt signed a historic peace treaty. The Camp David Accords marked President Carter's most significant foreign policy success. In the treaty, Egypt recognized Israel's right to exist as a sovereign state and Israel agreed to return the Sinai Peninsula, seized in the 1967 war. The two nations also agreed to negotiate Palestinian autonomy in the Israeli-occupied West Bank and Gaza Strip, although little progress was made on the issue.

Second, revolutionaries ousted the pro-American regime of the shah of Iran, and Muslim fundamentalists loyal to religious leader Ayatollah Khomeini gained control of the country. When Carter agreed to let the deposed shah come to the United States for cancer treatment, many Iranians took the act as a direct insult. In retribution, Iranian nationalists seized fifty-three American soldiers and diplomats on November 4 and held them hostage in Tehran. With Carter unable to effect a release by threats or diplomacy, the hostages languished for week after week, then month after month.

Third, in December 1979 the Soviets invaded neighboring Afghanistan to prop up a bumbling regime. Outraged, Carter called the invasion the "most serious threat to world peace since World War II." He moved decisively away from détente, forbade U.S. athletes from participating in the 1980 Moscow Olympics, put an end to the SALT II negotiations, and ordered an embargo on U.S. grain exports to the Soviet Union. More important, he supplied military aid to the Afghan *mujahideen*— a coalition of radical Islamic rebels from throughout the world who resisted the Soviet occupation.

Camp David Accords   Carter's greatest foreign policy achievement was his brokering of a historic peace between Israel and Egypt. In the Camp David Accords, signed by Egyptian president Anwar Sadat (left) and Israeli prime minister Menachem Begin, Israel promised to return all land in the Sinai in return for Egypt's recognition of the Israeli state. Though it did not solve the issue of Palestinian refugees, the Accords did lessen the tensions in the region. *(Jimmy Carter Presidential Library.)*

Over time, the three events would polarize the region, feed the rise of Islamic radicalism, and present a serious threat to American global security. The Camp David Accords represented a major step in the development of moderate Arab regimes friendly to the United States and willing to live in peace with Israel. Yet the treaty also enraged the Arab militants who rejected Western influence in the region, opposed the state of Israel, and promised to overthrow the governments that made peace. They were emboldened by the success of the Iranian revolution, which replaced a repressive pro-American regime with an Islamic government ruled by clerics. Finally, the Soviet invasion of Afghanistan served as a rallying cry for Islamic fundamentalists determined to expel the secular invaders. For a brief period, America and Islamic fundamentalists shared a common agenda. After the defeat of the Soviets and the end of the Cold War, however, the militants would focus their hostility on the world's only superpower: the United States. "It's all very far away from you in America, isn't it?" a rebel leader told an American reporter in 1983. "But it is not as far as you think."

CONCLUSION

The aftershocks of the 1960s rumbled through the 1970s, producing angry recriminations, political polarization, and eventually stalemate. The decade witnessed a political and cultural clash between two powerful forces, each firmly rooted in American ideals and identity, neither willing to compromise. On one side stood social reformers who, inspired by the struggles of the 1960s, mobilized to force national leaders to confront the contradiction between the reality of discrimination and the American ideal of equality.

On the other side stood "angry white voters" who formed the backbone of Richard Nixon's "silent majority." Mobilized by a belief that student protests and racial riots threatened social stability, the silent majority organized an effective backlash against social reform. Like the advocates of social reform, the leaders of the silent majority appealed to American ideals, but their ideals were those of individual liberty and limited government. They viewed the demands for group remedy, preferential treatment, and activist government as a direct threat to the traditional individualism that defined Americans. Richard Nixon played to these concerns by emphasizing his commitment to law and order, by assailing his enemies as anti-American, and by stressing his commitment to small government. The silent majority rewarded him with a massive electoral landslide in the 1972 presidential election.

The two sides clashed repeatedly during the decade as they promoted conflicting experiments. Nixon's Cambodia incursion and the shootings at Kent State University underscored the intense divisions generated by the Vietnam War. America's defeat in Vietnam shattered the postwar foreign policy consensus and raised troubling new questions about America's role in the world. Controversial issues such as busing and affirmative action highlighted racial differences.

The decade witnessed an unprecedented ferment of reform among various minority groups—homosexuals, Hispanics, Native Americans, Asian-Americans—as well as a powerful women's movement. The "rights revolution" raised public awareness, developed a greater sense of group identity and pride, and, especially in the case of women, achieved notable legislative successes. For the most part, however, results fell far short of expectations.

The conflicting currents of the decade found expression in popular culture. Trends from the 1960s—drug use, liberal sexual attitudes, long hair, and casual dress—continued and gained broader support during the 1970s. Popular media articulated Vietnam's lessons of cynicism and tragedy. At the same time, people cheered Sylvester Stallone's celebration of traditional values in the blockbuster movie *Rocky* and laughed at the antics of the angry and intolerant Archie Bunker in the hit television show *All in the Family*. Many Americans turned to jogging, Eastern religions, and disco music in an effort to escape the decade's swirling passions.

Both sides looked to the federal government to reconcile the competing visions of America, but the government was experiencing its own crisis of authority in the 1970s. The Watergate scandal, which resulted in the first forced resignation of an American president, shook the foundations of government and eroded public confidence in national institutions. Congress passed a number of reforms designed to rebuild public faith in government. But public mistrust swelled as national leaders failed to stem the tide of rising unemployment, higher prices, and declining real income. Concern about limited resources produced a broad-based environmental movement.

In 1976 Jimmy Carter recaptured the presidency for the Democrats by promising to restore America's faith in government, but instead his administration became a casualty of the "Age of Limits," unable to establish control over a divided party and an unruly Congress. The most severe blow to Carter's leadership came from abroad, where the hostage crisis in Iran and the Soviet invasion of Afghanistan seemed to symbolize American impotence. Critical events in the Middle East in 1979 would have profound long-term consequences for America and its role in the world.

As the decade came to an end, Americans searched for experiments that might revitalize older notions of American identity, restore confidence in their governing institutions, and reestablish their dominance in world affairs.

Annotated Suggested Readings

Bruce Schulman offers the most insightful analysis of the decade in *The Seventies* (2001). David Frum offers a critical assessment of the social and cultural changes in *How We Got Here* (2000). Peter Carroll's *It Seemed Like Nothing Happened* (1983) is a lively collection of anecdotes about the decade and its frustrations.

Neil Sheehan's *A Bright Shining Lie* (1988) explores the government deception employed during the Vietnam War. William Shawcross indignantly describes Nixon and Kissinger's Cambodia policy in *Sideshow* (1979). Arnold Isaacs critiques Nixon's peace in *Without Honor* (1983), as does the more recent work by Larry Berman, *No Peace, No Honor* (2001). On the influence of the "Madman Theory" on Nixon's conduct of the war, see Jeffrey Kimball's *Nixon's Vietnam War* (1998). Lewis Sorley offers a revisionist account of the final days of the war in *A Better War* (1999).

Robert S. Litwak's *Detente and the Nixon Doctrine* (1984) is a good introduction to Nixon's foreign policy. Tad Szulc's *The Illusion of Peace* (1978) contrasts Nixon's domestic message with his international actions. Edy Kaufman's *Crisis in Allende's Chile* (1988) details the events leading to the 1973 coup. Stephen Rabe covers the crises in the Middle East in *The Road to OPEC* (1982).

In *The Declining Significance of Race* (1980), William J. Wilson describes the economic polarization of African-American society. Douglas Glasgow's *The Black Underclass* (1980) describes the black economic decline of the 1970s. Ronald Formisano explores the opposition to the busing movement in *Boston Against Busing* (1991). J. Anthony Lukas's *Common Ground* (1985) is a moving account of the Boston busing crisis through the eyes of three families.

Stan Steiner's *La Raza* (1970) looks at the early Hispanic protest movement. Matt Meier and Feliciano Rivera explore the generational conflicts among Hispanics in *The Chicanos* (1972). Vine DeLoria, Jr.'s *Custer Died for Your Sins* (1969) is an early document of Native American activism. Helen Hertzberg's *The Search for an American Indian Movement* (1971) chronicles the rise of the Red Power movement. John D'Emilio's *Sexual Politics, Sexual Communities* (1983) explores the formation of gay identity in the postwar years. Martin Duberman's *Stonewall* (1993) describes the birth of the modern gay liberation movement.

Sara Evans describes how the women's liberation movement evolved from the civil rights struggle in *Personal Politics* (1979). Jo Freeman's *The Politics of Women's Liberation* (1979) and Judith Hole and Ellen Levine's *The Rebirth of Feminism* (1971) describe the rise of the women's movement. The feminist movement also changed popular culture images of women in the 1970s, as evidenced in *Disco Divas* (2003), edited by Sherrie Inness. Susan Hartmann's *From Margin to Mainstream* (1989) has good material on economic sexual discrimination. Joel F. Handler's *We the Poor People* (1997) explores the feminization of poverty.

Christopher Lasch's *The Culture of Narcissism* (1978) is an influential description of the "Me Decade." Edwin Schur's *The Awareness Trap* (1976) describes the failure of social change and the rise of "awareness" movements.

Historians are still trying to come to terms with Richard Nixon and his presidency. For the best accounts see Melvin Small, *The Presidency of Richard Nixon* (1999); Joan Hoff, *Nixon Reconsidered* (1995); and Herbert Parmet, *Richard Nixon and His America* (1990). Allen Matusow offers a critical appraisal of the president's economic policy in *Nixon's Economy* (1998). David Greenberg uncovers the many competing images that Americans had of Richard Nixon in *Nixon's Shadow* (2003). Dan Carter examines George Wallace's impact on American politics and the Nixon administration in *The Politics of Rage* (1995). Thomas Edsall describes how Nixon helped mold public anger into a powerful conservative coalition in *Chain Reaction* (1992).

Stanley Kutler's *Abuse of Power* (1997) and *The Wars of Watergate* (1992) are essential reading for understanding Nixon's downfall. Bob Woodward and Carl Bernstein's *All the President's Men* (1974) and *The Final Days* (1976) are both captivating journalistic accounts. For an insightful look at how Americans have remembered the events that led to Nixon's resignation, see Michael Schudson, *Watergate in American Memory* (1992). Athan Theoharis's *Spying on Americans* (1978) details the illegal actions of the Nixon White House against dissidents. Tom Wells provides a biography of the man who stole the papers, Daniel Ellsberg, in *Wild Man* (2001). James I. Sundquist's *The Decline and Resurgence of Congress* (1981) tracks the changing balance of power between the branches of government. John P. Hoerr's tale of America's declining steel industry, *And the Wolf Finally Came* (1988), demonstrates the nation's industrial decline during the decade.

Rachel Carson's *Silent Spring* (1962) remains the eloquent first word of the environmental movement. Daniel F. Ford describes the nuclear power scare in *Three Mile Island* (1982), while Thomas Raymond Wellock looks at opposition to nuclear energy in California in *Critical Mass* (1998). Samuel P. Hays provides an overview of the movement in *Beauty, Health, and Permanence* (1987). Roderick Nash's *The Rights of Nature* (1989) outlines the environmentalist ethic.

John Robert Greene studies the Ford administration in *The Presidency of Gerald R. Ford* (1995). On the Carter presidency see Charles Jones's *The Trusteeship Presidency* (1988); Burton Kaufman, *The Presidency of James Earl Carter, Jr.* (1993); and the collection of essays by Gary M. Fink and Hugh Davis Graham, *The Carter Presidency* (1998). Gaddis Smith's readable *Morality, Reason, and Power* (1987) provides the best overview of Carter's erratic foreign policy, while Robert Strong offers a strong defense of Carter's foreign policy in *Working in the World* (2000). William Quandt describes the Egypt-Israeli peace accord in *Camp David* (1986). Barry Rubin's *Paved with Good Intentions* (1983) covers America's relations with Iran.

The Politics of Gender

The Feminist Perspective

A graduate of Smith College, Gloria Steinem was an aspiring journalist in the early 1960s, writing for popular journals such as *Esquire* and *Show* and the political satire magazine *Help!* Steinem established herself as an articulate and forceful proponent of a wide range of political causes—the peace movement, migrant farm workers, and civil rights. In 1970 her name began to be linked with women's liberation when she outlined a vision of what the country might look like if only women had equal power—though she didn't have the power to keep *Time* magazine from shortening "women's liberation" to "women's lib."

In Women's Lib Utopia, there will be free access to good jobs—and decent pay for the bad ones women have been performing all along, including housework. Increased skilled labor might lead to a four-hour workday, and higher wages would encourage further mechanization of repetitive jobs now kept alive by cheap labor.

With women as half the country's elected representatives, and a woman President once in a while, the country's *machismo* problems would be greatly reduced. The old-fashioned idea that manhood depends on violence and victory is, after all, an important part of our troubles in the streets, and in Vietnam. I'm not saying that women leaders would eliminate violence. We are not more moral than men; we are only uncorrupted by power so far.

Men will have to give up ruling-class privileges, but in return they will no longer be the only ones to support the family, get drafted, bear the strain of power and responsibility. Freud to the contrary, anatomy is not destiny, at least not for more than nine months at a time. In Israel, women are drafted, and some have gone to war. In England, more men type and run switchboards. In India and Israel, a woman rules. In Sweden, both parents take care of the children. In this country, come Utopia, men and women won't reverse roles; they will be free to choose according to individual talents and preferences.

Schools and universities will help to break down traditional sex roles, even when parents will not. Half the teachers will be men, a rarity now at preschool and elementary levels; girls will not necessarily serve cookies or boys hoist up the flag. Athletic teams will be picked only by strength and skill. Sexually segregated courses like auto mechanics and home economics will be taken by boys and girls together. New courses in sexual politics will explore female subjugation as the model for political oppression, and women's history will be an academic staple, along with black history, at least until the white-male-oriented textbooks are integrated and rewritten. . . .

As for the American child's classic problem—too much mother, too little father—that would be cured by an equalization of parental responsibility. . . .

Our marriage laws . . . are so reactionary that women's lib groups want couples to take a compulsory written exam on the law, as for a driver's license, before going through with the wedding. . . . [A] woman may lose so many of her civil rights that in the U.S. now, in important legal ways, she becomes a child again. . . .

Women's lib is not trying to destroy the American family. A look at the statistics on divorce—plus the way in which old people are farmed out with strangers and young people flee the home—shows the destruction that has already been done. Liberated women are just trying to point out the disaster, and build compassionate and practical alternatives from the ruins.

In Defense of Tradition

Steinem's chief antagonist was Phyllis Schlafly, a successful Illinois lawyer and an influential conservative activist in the Republican Party. After the Senate passed the Equal Rights Amendment in 1972, Schlafly entered the feminist fray. Called the "Sweetheart of the Silent Majority," Schlafly, the mother of six, accused feminists of being a radical fringe group out of touch with traditional values and intent on destroying the American family. In 1977 she published *The Power of the Positive Woman*, a forceful defense of traditional womanhood and a scathing attack on modern feminism.

If man is targeted as the enemy, and the ultimate goal of women's liberation is independence from men and the avoidance of pregnancy and its consequences, then lesbianism is logically the highest form in the ritual of women's liberation.

The Positive Woman will never travel that dead-end road. It is self-evident to the Positive Woman that the female body with its baby-producing organs was not designed by a conspiracy of men but by the Divine Architect of the human race. . . .

The Positive Woman looks upon her femaleness and her fertility as part of her purpose, her potential, and her power. She rejoices that she has a capability for creativity that men can never have. . . .

The women's liberationists are expending their time and energies erecting a make-believe world in which they hypothesize that *if* schooling were gender-free, and *if* the same money were spent on male and female sports programs, and *if* women were permitted to compete on equal terms, *then* they would prove themselves to be physically equal. Meanwhile, the Positive Woman has put the ineradicable physical differences into her mental computer, programmed her plan of action, and is already on the way to personal achievement. . . .

Despite the claims of the women's liberation movement, there are countless physical differences between men and women. . . . Males have a tendency to color blindness. Only 5 percent of persons who get gout are female. Boys are born bigger. Women live longer in most countries of the world, not only in the United States where we have a hard-driving competitive pace. Women excel in manual dexterity, verbal skills, and memory recall. . . .

The differences between men and women are also emotional and psychological. Without woman's innate maternal instinct, the human race would have died out centuries ago. . . . Even in the most primitive, uneducated societies, women have always cared for their newborn babies. . . .

Why? Because caring for a baby serves the natural maternal need of a woman. Although not nearly so total as the baby's need, the woman's need is nonetheless real. . . .

The woman's liberation movement complains that traditional stereotyped roles assume that women are "passive" and that men are "aggressive." The anomaly is that a woman's most fundamental emotional need is not passive at all, but active. A woman naturally seeks to love affirmatively and to show that love in an active way by caring for the object of her affections.

For most of American history, powerful cultural norms have established clear guidelines for male and female behavior. "The sum total of general belief of the most enlightened of both sexes," a speaker told the 1876 graduating class of Mount Holyoke College, "appears to be that there is a difference of kind in their natural endowments and that there is for each an appropriate field of development and action." Catharine Beecher, the author of a number of influential advice books in the 1860s and 1870s, urged women to gain the appropriate training for "her distinctive profession as housekeeper, nurse of infants and the sick, educator of childhood, trainer of servants and ministers of charities."

Numerous changes transformed women's role in American society in the hundred years between Catharine Beecher and Gloria Steinem. Perhaps the most dramatic was the movement into the workplace. In 1940 only one-quarter of American women worked for wages; by 1974, 46 percent did so. These economic changes dramatically altered women's role in the home. As late as the 1950s more than 70 percent of all American families consisted of a father who worked and a mother who stayed at home to take care of the children. By 1980 that description applied to only 15 percent of all families.

These economic changes, combined with the broader climate of protest during the 1970s, inspired feminists like Steinem to challenge the gap between America's professed faith in equal opportunity and the reality of gender discrimination. But Schlafly's successful campaign to defeat the ERA revealed that cultural values about gender roles proved more resistant to change. A poll taken in 1977 showed that two-thirds of Americans thought that preschool children were likely to suffer if their mothers worked for wages, 62 percent thought married women should not hold jobs when jobs were scarce and their husbands could support them, and a majority thought it more important for a woman to advance her husband's career than to have one of her own.

QUESTIONS FOR ANALYSIS

1. What does Steinem mean when she says "anatomy is not destiny"?

2. What changes would Steinem most like to see in her utopia?

3. What does Steinem identify as the chief obstacle to her vision?

4. What qualities does Schlafly associate with being female? With being male?

5. Why does Schlafly find women's liberation so threatening?

6. How are the women of Steinem's utopia different from Schlafly's "Positive Woman"?

7. Why have traditional values about gender roles proven so resistant to change?

8. Can you think of other times in American history when cultural values clashed with changing social realities?

31

The Reagan Experiment

1979–1988

"Everyone can't be the best."

New York real estate tycoon Donald Trump emerged as the most glaring symbol of a decade that celebrated ruthless competition and extravagant wealth. "There is no one my age who has accomplished more," he boasted after building the palatial Trump Tower skyscraper on New York City's fashionable Fifth Avenue. "Everyone can't be the best." With his empire estimated at more than $3 billion in 1987, Trump lived like a modern-day Gatsby, replete with a fleet of private jets, a $29 million yacht, a 110-room mansion in Florida, and a 10-acre, forty-five-room weekend getaway estate in Connecticut. With his name plastered on almost every building he owned and his face appearing on the cover of newsmagazines and daily gossip tabloids, Trump became one of the most recognizable men in America. He was, *Newsweek* reported, "the latest of a breed unique to the decade: the businessman who becomes larger than life, like a star athlete or popular actor."

During the 1980s Americans abandoned the previous decade's emphasis on limits and austerity and instead celebrated the culture of consumerism. "The man in the street, the little guy, digs the limo, the helicopter, the 727," Trump told a reporter. A rejuvenated economy fed the consumer society's appetite for money and wealth. Beneath the surface of prosperity, however, the American experiment was under stress. While much of the public debate focused on ways to obtain and display wealth, U.S. society suffered striking disparities between rich and poor, growing homelessness, and a stagnant middle class. The decade witnessed a spirited debate about the role of government in American society. The Reagan administration came to office promising to cut federal spending and reduce burdensome regulation while also reasserting U.S. power abroad. At the same time, a powerful coalition of religious conservatives precipitated a cultural civil war over controversial social issues such as abortion, gay rights, and immigration.

- What were the roots of public anger with government that fueled the conservative reaction in the 1980s?

- Describe the culture wars of the decade. How did they represent a clash of competing views of what it meant to be an American?

- How did Ronald Reagan tap into public discontent, and why was he so successful?

- What attitudes shaped Reagan's view of the world, and how realistic was his approach?

- Why were many Americans so fascinated with wealth and status, and how evenly distributed were the benefits from the economic boom in the 1980s?

This chapter will address these questions.

THE CONSERVATIVE REVIVAL, 1979–1980

Numerous forces conspired during the 1970s to undermine public support for government and to feed the conservative revival. The old New Deal coalition unraveled as evangelical Christians, middle-class property owners, and business and neoconservative intellectual leaders revolted against what they viewed as the twin big-government evils of social liberalism and high taxes. Promising a new experiment in conservative traditionalism, former California Governor Ronald Reagan rode the wave of discontent into the White House in 1980.

The Roots of Modern Conservatism

The conservative revival of the 1970s traced its roots to three sources. First, the decade witnessed a dramatic increase in the number of self-identified evangelical Christians who had experienced "born-again" conversions, believed in the literal interpretation of the Bible, and accepted Jesus Christ as their personal savior. The number of Americans who identified themselves as born-again increased from 24 percent in 1963 to nearly 40 percent in 1978. More than 45 million—one of every five Americans—considered themselves fundamentalists by the end of the decade. While mainstream church membership dropped between 1965 and 1980, the number of Southern Baptists rose from 10.8 million to 13.6 million.

Many fundamentalists were converted by television preachers who used mass media to preach a return to traditional values. The three most successful "televangelists"—Jerry Falwell, Pat Robertson, and Jim Bakker—reached an estimated 100 million Americans each week with fire and brimstone sermons about the evils of contemporary life (see Competing Voices, page 1259). Like traditional conservatives, the religious right believed in small government, low taxes, and free enterprise. Unlike the old Right, however, its members viewed politics through the prism of morality. America, they preached, confronted a crisis of the spirit brought on by the pervasive influence of "secular humanism," which stressed material well-being and personal gratification over religious conviction and devotion to traditional Christian values. In their minds, the federal government and the liberals who staffed it were responsible for America's moral decline. At the top of their agenda were overturning the 1962 Supreme Court decision to ban prayer in the public schools *(Engel* v. *Vitale)* and the 1973 *Roe* v. *Wade* decision that legalized abortion.

Second, a powerful anti-tax movement, ignited by passage of California's Proposition 13 in 1978, helped sweep conservatives into power and undermined support for liberal social programs. Proposition 13, a referendum that voters approved by a two-to-one margin, reduced assessments, limited property taxes to 1 percent of full value, and prevented the easy passage of new taxes. "This isn't just a tax revolt," insisted President Carter's pollster, Pat Caddell. "It's a revolution against government." The success in California emboldened tax reformers in other parts of the country. A dozen states followed California's lead, though most chose more moderate measures. Only two states—Idaho and Nevada—passed Proposition 13 look-alikes.

Two powerful currents carried the tax revolt. First, between 1960 and 1980 federal, state, and local taxes increased from less than 24 percent to more than 30 percent of the gross national product. The burden often was heaviest on the traditional Democratic constituencies of working-class families and elderly people on fixed incomes. Second, while taxes kept rising, Americans were losing faith in govern-

Jerry Falwell   In 1979, Reverend Jerry Falwell formed Moral Majority, Inc. to "promote morality in public life and to combat legislation that favors the legalization of immorality." The Moral Majority's political action group backed conservative candidates who supported prayer in school and the teaching of Creationism, while opposing the passage of the Equal Rights Amendment and abortion. Within two years of its founding, Falwell's organization had 4 million members. Falwell officially disbanded the group in 1989 as fundamentalists and other conservatives left the broad-based Moral Majority to focus on specific issues. *(Dennis Brack/Black Star/Sockphoto.com.)*

CHRONOLOGY

1978	California passes Proposition 13
1979	Falwell founds the Moral Majority
1980	Reagan elected president
1981	AIDS identified Attempted Reagan assassination O'Connor appointed to Supreme Court Economic Recovery Tax Act
1982	Reagan proposes Strategic Defense Initiative Contras infiltrate Nicaragua
1983	Marines invade Grenada U.S. barracks in Beirut bombed
1984	Reagan reelected Gorbachev comes to power in USSR Duarte elected in El Salvador Boland Amendment passed *Newsweek*'s "Year of the Yuppie"
1985	Secret arms sales to Iran
1986	Immigration Reform and Control Act Rehnquist becomes chief justice Reykjavik summit Iran-Contra exposed
1987	Intermediate Nuclear Forces Treaty
1988	Pan Am 103 bombed over Lockerbie

ment and the way it spent tax dollars. Poll after poll showed that a majority of Americans believed that government was wasteful and inefficient. By the 1970s many Democrats showed their anger by abandoning the party and joining forces with conservatives.

As the tax-cut wildfire spread through the states, Proposition 13's congressional cousin—the Kemp-Roth tax bill that called for a one-third slash in federal income taxes—gained converts in Washington. The idea was the brainchild of economist Arthur Laffer, who argued that hefty cuts in corporate and personal tax rates would stimulate investment and encourage production and consumption. Unlike the Keynesian principles that had guided policymakers since the 1930s (see page 992), Laffer's so-called supply-side theory argued that tax policy should reward the suppliers of wealth, not the consumers. By lowering taxes on the wealthiest Americans, the government would provide an incentive for them to reinvest, creating new business and more jobs. Even though tax rates would be lower, revenues would actually increase because more people would be paying taxes.

Many economists challenged the underlying assumptions of supply-side theory, but the idea was politically seductive. When conservative Barry Goldwater campaigned for president in 1964 on a platform calling for reduced taxes, he felt compelled to announce what government programs he would eliminate to balance the books. Supply-side theory allowed conservatives to have the best of both worlds: they campaigned as tax-reform crusaders but also claimed that they would be able to protect popular government entitlements such as social security.

Third, neoconservatives provided the intellectual scaffolding for the new conservatism. For most of the 1960s and early 1970s liberals were able to control the national agenda. During the 1970s conservative intellectuals began to dominate the public debate, ensuring that conservative ideas would receive respect and attention. With funding from wealthy individuals and foundations, conservative "think tanks" produced mounds of studies advocating the need for smaller government and a return to traditional values. These new organizations provided an intellectual home for a number of prominent neoconservatives, former liberals who had soured on government activism and who offered substantial intellectual ammunition to those seeking to reverse liberal "excesses." A neoconservative, observed social critic Irving Kristol, was a liberal who had been mugged by reality. Neoconservatives charged that many governmental programs of the sixties, which were designed to alleviate poverty and assist the working poor, had backfired. "Our efforts to deal with distress themselves increase distress," observed sociologist Nathan Glazer.

If neoconservatives provided the intellectual scaffolding for the conservative movement, corporate America provided the steel. During the 1970s corporate America established a powerful lobbying presence in Washington to advance its agenda, which included not only antiregulatory goals but tax cuts as well. Many corporations and trade associations opened Washington offices, hired Capitol Hill law firms, and retained legions of political consultants to keep track of pending legislation and to develop strategies for promoting favorable policies and killing those considered antibusiness. By 1980 nearly 500 corporations had Washington offices, up from 250 in 1970, and the number of lobbyists had tripled. Trade associations opened national headquarters at a rate of one per week, increasing from 1,200 to 1,739 during the decade.

The 1980 Presidential Campaign

By late 1979 President Carter's political stock hit rock bottom. During the summer, with inflation soaring into double digits, newly appointed Federal Reserve Chairman Paul Volcker applied the monetary brakes. The nation's major banks responded by raising their prime interest rates, first to 13 percent and then to 14.5 percent. With the prime rate reaching all-time highs, the economy began its inevitable slowdown. In October the Dow Jones index of industrial stocks lost nearly a hundred points, auto sales dropped 23 percent compared with the previous year, and rising mortgage rates strangled the housing industry. Carter seemed helpless in the face of problems both at home and abroad. The menacing Soviet army that had invaded Afghanistan raised fears that its next move would be to capture valuable Middle East oil supplies. Iranian militants continued to "hold America hostage," threatening to put their American captives on trial.

Carter's own party was in open revolt. With polls showing him leading the president by a three-to-one margin, Senator Edward Kennedy, the youngest brother of President John Kennedy and Senator Robert Kennedy and the keeper of the flickering liberal flame, announced in the fall of 1979 that he would challenge Carter for the nomination. The American people, however, instinctively rallied around the president during a time of international crisis. As Kennedy's campaign wilted in the patriotic afterglow, Carter secured his party's nomination on the first ballot.

Believing that the president's rise in the polls would be temporary, a revived Republican Party rallied around former Hollywood movie actor turned politician Ronald Reagan, who cruised to victory in the primaries, besting five challengers. An effective speaker and master of the media, Reagan articulated a simple but compelling message: love of country, fear of communism, and scorn of government. Preaching what economist Herbert Stein called the "economics of joy," Reagan repudiated the traditional Republican economic doctrine of tight fiscal policy and balanced budgets, and instead preached the wonders of supply-side economics. Responding to fears that America's stature in the world was in decline, Reagan called for a muscular foreign policy, including huge increases in military spending. Reflecting the influence of the religious right, the GOP platform also adopted a plank opposing abortion and the equal rights amendment (ERA). In an overture to moderate Republicans, Reagan selected the genial George H. W. Bush, a vanquished primary foe and former Central Intelligence Agency (CIA) head, as his running mate.

On election day, Reagan won 489 electoral votes to Carter's 49. In the popular vote, the Republican challenger received 43,904,153 million votes (50.7 percent) to Carter's 35,483,883 million (41 percent). Independent candidate John Anderson, a Republican congressman who bolted his party claiming that it had been hijacked by conservatives, won only 5,720,060 million popular votes (6.6 percent). The Democrats, moreover, lost thirty-four House seats and lost control of the Senate fifty-three to forty-seven, as the Republicans gained twelve seats. Ominously, almost 48 percent of eligible voters did not cast ballots, the lowest voter turnout since 1948 (see map on page 1232).

Most polling experts noted that the election represented "a strong call for moderate change." Though Reagan won a large margin in the electoral college, he captured only 51 percent of the voters, just 3 percent more than Ford had in losing in 1976. Reagan had assembled a disparate coalition, joining traditional Republicans who wanted to shrink government with the religious right, which wanted to use federal power to enforce its moral agenda. This coalition snared two groups that had been important Democratic voting blocs since the New Deal: southern whites, still smarting from their party's support for civil rights, and working-class whites in the Northeast and Midwest who were angry about high taxes and the sluggish economy. In reality, these groups had little in common other than frustration with the status quo. Yet because of his electoral college margin and his party's congressional gains, many observers viewed Reagan's election as a mandate for conservatism. As Democratic Senator Paul Tsongas observed, "Basically, the New Deal died yesterday." Reagan's task was to transform appearance into reality.

The Election of 1980 Economic woes and the continuing hostage crisis in Iran prompted the majority of Americans who voted in November 1980 to choose former actor and California governor Ronald Reagan. While Reagan also won a landslide in the electoral college, the number of popular voters and nonvoters provides a much more complex picture. Only 52.6 percent of eligible voters cast their ballots in the election, giving Reagan only 28 percent of the potential electorate and leading many to question why so many Americans chose not to vote.

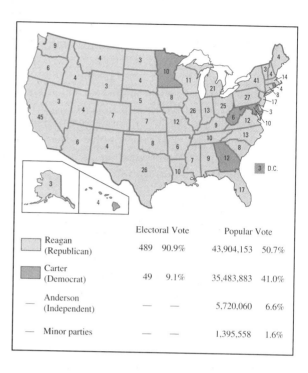

	Electoral Vote		Popular Vote	
Reagan (Republican)	489	90.9%	43,904,153	50.7%
Carter (Democrat)	49	9.1%	35,483,883	41.0%
Anderson (Independent)	—	—	5,720,060	6.6%
Minor parties	—	—	1,395,558	1.6%

THE CULTURE WARS, 1980–1988

During the 1980s politically active fundamentalists and evangelical Christians fought against a host of challenges to their traditional beliefs about how Americans should behave and think. They denounced what they viewed as threats to "family values," especially a woman's right to choose an abortion and equal rights for homosexuals. The massive wave of immigrants that flooded American cities also raised new questions about American racial and ethnic identity. Ultimately, the conflict over values and culture represented a struggle over national identity—over the meaning of America.

The Politics of Family Values

Religious and New Right conservatives traced the roots of most of America's social problems to the decline of the traditional family. The problem was real: during the 1980s a rising divorce rate accompanied the soaring numbers of illegitimate births, which doubled between 1975 and 1986. Conservatives blamed social liberalism and declining moral standards for the troubles plaguing the modern family. Paul Weyrich, a New Right political strategist, described the battle between the conservative "pro-family" forces and liberals as "the most significant battle of the age-old conflict between good and evil, between the forces of God and the forces against God, that we have seen in our country." In 1987 the Reagan administration released the *White House Task Force Report on the Family*, alleging that family life had been "frayed by the abrasive experiments of two liberal decades." Calling for a return to "traditional values," the religious right organized in local communities to challenge the teaching of evolution, ban books that disputed religious teachings, oppose sex education, and reinstate school prayer.

As the New Right pressed its case, liberals tried to redefine the debate over family values by focusing on economic issues—child care, tax credits for working families with children—that would lessen the burdens weighing on most Americans. They also touted individual rights and warned against unwarranted government intrusion into the lives of private citizens. In 1980 television producer Norman Lear founded People for the American Way to provide a political counterweight to the New Right. "First and foremost among our shared values is a celebration of diversity and respect for the beliefs of others," he declared.

Abortion   Debates over family values turned inevitably into a clash over abortion. Opponents of abortion and birth control found an ally in the White House. Reagan persuaded Congress to bar most public funding for birth control and to stop Medicare from funding abortions for poor women. An administration measure provided funding for religiously oriented "chastity clinics," where counselors advised teenage girls and women to "just say no" to avoid pregnancy.

Among activists, the debate over abortion revolved around different conceptions of motherhood. Abortion opponents believed in traditional sex roles and saw motherhood as a woman's highest mission in life. Viewing the conflict as a clash between "nurturance" and "selfish individualism," they saw abortion as one more assault on the last bastion of human tenderness in a cold and uncaring world. "We've accepted abortion because we're a very materialistic society and there is less time for caring," observed an antiabortion activist in Fargo, North Dakota.

The pro-choice activists, on the other hand, believed that motherhood was one of many roles women played. They argued that the best way to support families was to address gender inequalities that prevented women from competing equally against men. In the feminist strategy, the abortion option was indispensable: as the responsibility for children devolved to women, so must the choice as to when to bear them. Along with supporting a host of political and economic reforms—paid parental leave, flexible hours, child-care facilities—feminists trumpeted the value of individual liberty over government interference. Worried Planned Parenthood president Faye Wattleton, "The fundamental principles of individual privacy are under the most serious assault since the days of McCarthyism."

Activists on both sides represented a small proportion of opinions, however. Polls showed a public torn between the extremes of the abortion debate: overwhelming opposition to an absolute ban on abortion but discomfort with the absolute right to abortion. The public debate, however, obscured opportunity for consensus as both sides used powerful symbols to rally support for their cause. In 1984 antiabortion activists produced a graphic videotape, *The Silent Scream*, that showed abortion "from the point of view of the unborn child." As their own symbols pro-choice advocates often displayed coat hangers—grim reminders of the illegal and unsafe abortions that took place before the Supreme Court ruling.

Debate over Abortion As the religious right grew in political importance, so did the issue of a woman's right to an abortion, legalized by the 1973 Supreme Court decision in *Roe* v. *Wade*. Pro-life organizations held rallies and protested in front of abortion clinics, emphasizing that abortion was a form of infanticide. Though pro-choice advocates had the support of the courts, they continued to challenge the arguments made by pro-life advocates, pressing a woman's right to choose, as seen in this battle of protest signs in front of an abortion clinic in Boston. *(Evan Richman/The Boston Globe. Republished with permission of Globe Newspaper Company, Inc.)*

Class and religious beliefs served as the fault lines in the abortion debate. Polls showed that higher-income earners, college graduates, and the self-employed proved more likely to support a woman's right to choose. Only one-fourth of blacks and Latinos favored abortion, compared to more than a third of Anglos. Surprisingly, women and men divided equally on the issue. But people who deemed religion as "very important" in their lives opposed abortion by an overwhelming two-to-one margin.

Gay Rights and the AIDS Crisis

Perhaps with the exception of abortion, few issues during the 1980s generated more raw emotion than homosexuality. The gay rights movement, born at the Stonewall Inn in 1969, continued to gain momentum during the 1970s. Homosexuals flooded into cities such as San Francisco and New York, where they established a variety of support organizations. Between 1974 and 1978 more than twenty thousand homosexuals moved to San Francisco, many of them living in the city's Castro District. In response to the growing visibility of the gay community, a number of states repealed their sodomy statues, and a few enacted legislation preventing discrimination based on sexual orientation.

The movement took a tragic turn in 1981 when doctors in San Francisco and New York began reporting that young homosexual men were dying from rare diseases. As panic spread through the gay community, researchers at the Centers for Disease Control (CDC) discovered the villain: a deadly virus spread by bodily fluid that rendered the victim's immune system helpless against opportunistic infections. They named the mysterious disease Acquired Immune Deficiency Syndrome (AIDS).

Initially, the majority of American AIDS victims were homosexual men infected through sexual contact. During the 1970s many gay men associated freedom with sexual promiscuity. "The belief that was handed to me was that sex was liberating and more sex was more liberating," observed activist Michael Callen. "[Being gay] was tied to the right to have sex." As the death toll mounted gay leaders organized to educate the public and to pressure government to find a cure. In New York the Gay Men's Health Center spearheaded the effort, raising millions of dollars, offering services to the sick, and lobbying Washington. Gay writers—such as playwright Larry Kramer in *The Normal Heart* (1985) and journalist Randy Shilts in *And the Band Played On* (1987)—raised public awareness about the disease and about gay life. At the same time, radical groups such as the AIDS Coalition to Unleash Power (ACT UP), which was founded to protest a lack of commitment to finding a cure for AIDS, rattled politicians and drug companies with their colorful demonstrations. ACT UP's slogan, "Silence = Death," underscoring a pink triangle on black, became a trademark for late-1980s uncivil disobedience. In city after city, the gay community began exercising political muscle, demanding greater government support for AIDS research and protection against discrimination.

Conservatives reacted with horror, viewing gay rights as unnatural, contrary to God's will, and an assault on the traditional family. The gay rights movement represented "the most vicious attack on traditional family values that our society has seen in the history of our republic," declared a conservative congressman. White House adviser Pat Buchanan suggested that AIDS was God's revenge for violating natural law. "The poor homosexuals. They have declared war on nature and now nature is exacting an awful retribution."

By the end of the 1980s the AIDS epidemic had spread far beyond gay men. Thanks to grass-roots organizing and public education, the number of new AIDS cases among homosexuals had stabilized. In 1987, 50 percent of the deaths from AIDS in the United States were among intravenous drug users and their sexual partners, a group that was 90 percent African-American and Hispanic. Overall, blacks were three times more likely than whites to contract HIV, the precipitating virus. For Hispanics, the infection rate was twice as high. The disease was also spreading more rapidly among children than adults.

American Identities

The massive wave of immigrants that flooded American cities after 1965 raised new questions about the nation's racial and ethnic identity. "The nation is rapidly moving toward a multiethnic future," *Newsweek* reported. "Asians, Hispanics, Caribbean islanders, and many other immigrant groups compose a diverse and changing social mosaic that cannot be described by the old vocabulary of race relations." The immigration rate of the 1980s eclipsed the previous high set during the twentieth century's first decade as the new immigrants, mostly from Asia, Central and South America, and the Caribbean, sought new lives in the United States.

According to the Census Bureau the nation absorbed 8.9 million legal immigrants and, by most estimates, at least 2 million illegal ones, during the 1980s. In absolute numbers the decade saw more immigrants (legal and illegal) than any other decade in U.S. history. By the early 1990s over 1 million new legal immigrants were arriving in the U.S. every year, accounting for almost half of U.S. population growth. The vast majority of the new immigrants came from Asia and Latin America.

Most of these immigrants settled in large cities in a handful of states: New York, Illinois, and New Jersey, as well as Florida, Texas, and California. One of every three new immigrants entered the United States through California, making the nation's most populous state its unofficial Ellis Island. By 1990 the population of Los Angeles, the nation's second-largest city, was one-third foreign-born. Los Angeles was also home to the second-largest Spanish-speaking population (after Mexico City) on the North American continent. New York's foreign-born population, like that of Los Angeles, also approached 35 percent of its total populace in 1990, a level the city had last reached in 1910.

Most Americans saw daily reminders of the cultural impact of the new waves of immigrants. Urban streets were a babble of foreign tongues. In Miami three-quarters of residents spoke a language other than English at home; in New York City the figure was four out of ten, and of these, half could not speak fluent English (see map on page 1237). In kitchens across the country, salsa replaced ketchup as America's favorite condiment. In music, such Hispanic artists as Los Lobos, Lisa Lisa and Cult Jam, and the Miami Sound Machine topped the billboards with hit songs. Many white artists tried assimilating new cultural impulses into their music. David Byrne injected Talking Heads music with African, Latin, and other rhythms. Peter Gabriel and Paul Simon found similar success with African rhythms.

The new diversity provided fertile ground for bigotry. "The more diversity and burgeoning minority groups we have," the National Conference of Christians and Jews observed, "the more prejudice we must overcome." Blacks, Hispanics, and Asians often felt as much animosity toward one another as they did toward whites. In Florida Hispanics and blacks, who once considered themselves allies against the white power structure, battled each other for jobs and scarce resources. In many cities African-Americans and Korean immigrants engaged in heated confrontations. At the root of the conflict, exacerbated by language and cultural differences, was resentment of Korean immigrants' success in running small businesses in economically depressed black neighborhoods. In Spike Lee's movie *Do the Right Thing*, set in Brooklyn, a Korean shopkeeper averts a confrontation with black residents of the neighborhood by shouting in desperation, "Me no white. Me no white. Me black."

Many white Americans complained that the new immigrants stole jobs from native workers, and many whites worried about the cohesiveness of American culture and its ability to absorb and assimilate so many different cultural influences. "Is it really wise to allow the immigration of people who find it so difficult and painful to assimilate into the American majority?" asked conservative journalist

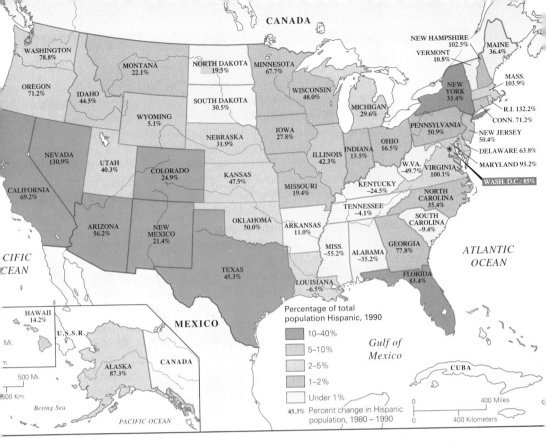

Percentage of total population Hispanic, 1990

- 10–40%
- 5–10%
- 2–5%
- 1–2%
- Under 1%

45.3% Percent change in Hispanic population, 1980 – 1990

Growth of Hispanic Population in the 1980s For the first time in American history, the majority of immigrants in the 1980s came from countries outside of Europe. The Hispanic population claimed the largest percentage of new immigrants. This influx altered the social and cultural dynamics of cities and states across the nation—most acutely in California, Nevada, and Florida—just as previous waves of immigration had done.

Peter Brimelow. In Miami cryptic bumper stickers appeared: "Will the last American out of Miami please take the flag." After years of debate on how to control illegal immigration, Congress passed the Immigration Reform and Control Act (IRCA) in 1986. It offered legal status to undocumented aliens who had lived and worked in the United States for a specified period, but imposed fines on employers who hired new undocumented workers.

Fears about the swelling foreign-language populations produced a powerful "English-only" movement. "The language of American government is English," said a Connecticut Republican. "The language of American business is English. We are not a dual-language society." In 1986 California spearheaded the English-only drive by voting overwhelmingly for a referendum outlawing bilingualism and defending "English as a unifying force in the United States." Representatives of Hispanic groups condemned the movement as "fundamentally racist in character," but before the end of the decade seventeen other states had joined California in passing English-only laws. "Language," the *Economist* noted, "symbolizes the United States' fear that the foreign body within its borders is growing too big ever to be digested."

A similar debate raged as colleges attempted to "increase sensitivity" to racial and cultural diversity in the university community. At Stanford reformers fought to change the Western civilization curriculum, which they claimed presented a "male, Eurocentric" view of the world. Many universities accommodated the pressure to diversify by expanding the range of programs in disciplines such as women's studies, African-American studies, Hispanic studies, and gay studies. In 1987 Allan Bloom led the conservative counterattack on changes in American higher education in *The Closing of the American Mind*. Subtitled *How Higher Education Has Failed Democracy and Impoverished the Souls of Today's Students*, the book asserted the primacy of "the great books" of Western civilization. "You can't talk about Chaucer without someone saying 'What's the woman's perspective?', 'What about the Third World perspective?'" he lamented. Bloom's volume remained at the top of the *New York Times* best-seller list for seven weeks, selling more than a million copies.

Historical experience suggests that concerns about the failure of immigrants to assimilate were misplaced; similar fears about past waves of immigrants proved unfounded. The public has always looked favorably on past generations of immigrants and unfavorably on contemporary newcomers. In the nineteenth-century Americans complained about the "lazy and hard-drinking Irish" who were "polluting" the cities; later waves of Italians and eastern Europeans confronted similarly hostile attitudes. Over time, however, those groups became acculturated and now swell the mainstream that fears the addition of new migrants from Mexico, Iran, and Haiti.

Increasingly strident affirmations of identity actually masked the waning of real ethnic differences; higher education, consumerism, movies and television, professional sports, and popular culture were working to make Americans more alike, whatever their ethnic origins. The rising rate of intermarriage between ethnic groups, especially Asian-Americans and non-Asians, also suggested that ethnic differences were softening over time. In the 1980s more than half of all Japanese-Americans and 40 percent of Chinese-Americans married outside their ethnic groups.

THE REAGAN PRESIDENCY, 1980–1988

The new president wasted little time in institutionalizing the new conservative creed. In 1981 he pushed his agenda of lower taxes and steep budget cuts through a reluctant Congress. At the same time, he appointed to his cabinet, and to the courts, conservatives who would carry out his vision of smaller government. Reagan's landslide in the 1984 presidential election underscored the political popularity of his conservative experiment. But the Reagan presidency exposed continuing tensions in American attitudes toward government. Americans applauded Reagan's rhetoric about reducing government power at the same time that they insisted on continuing, or in some cases expanding, popular federal programs.

The Reagan Agenda   At sixty-nine, Ronald Wilson Reagan was the oldest man ever elected president. Born in Tampico, Illinois, in 1911, Reagan graduated from Eureka College and worked briefly as a radio sports announcer before moving to California and signing a contract with Warner Brothers film studio in 1937. Over the next two decades he appeared in fifty-three movies but won little acclaim as an actor. The one exception was his role as George Gipp, Notre Dame's first All-American football player, in the 1940 classic *Knute Rockne, All American*. "Someday, when things are tough, maybe you can ask the boys to go in there and win just one for the Gipper," he pleads in a moving deathbed scene that brought tears to the eyes of millions.

Reagan made his political debut in 1964 when he delivered a moving tribute to Barry Goldwater. The speech established Reagan's conservative credentials and launched his successful bid for governor of California in 1966. After two successful terms, Reagan was ready for the national stage. With his telegenic features and extensive experience in front of a camera, Reagan was ideally suited for politics in a media age. Though intellectually unambitious and notoriously ignorant about the details of policies, Reagan brilliantly articulated the themes of patriotism, individualism, and limited government that resonated with countless Americans.

At the outset, the Reagan administration concentrated on reviving the slumping economy. The cost of living had increased by more than 12 percent in 1980; unemployment had risen to 7.4 percent; the prime lending rate was an astonishing

Ronald and Nancy A man who had spent the majority of his life in the eye of the camera, Ronald Reagan, pictured with his second wife, Nancy, exuded grace, poise, and opulence. Such characteristics typified the materialistic culture of the eighties and heightened the popularity of the president and first lady. (*Courtesy of Vanity Fair, June 1985/Conde Nast Publications, Inc. Photograph by Harry Benson.*)

20 percent; and the government was facing a projected budget deficit of $56 billion. "In this present crisis," Reagan said in his inaugural address, "government is not the solution to our problem; government *is* the problem." It was time, the new president declared, "to reawaken this industrial giant, to get government back within its means and to lighten our punitive tax burden."

The president's economic program consisted of three essential components. First, embracing the supply-side doctrine of the New Right, Reagan requested a 30 percent reduction in both personal and corporate income taxes over three years. Tax cuts, the administration reasoned, would stimulate the economy by providing incentives for individuals and businesses to work, save, and invest. Second, he planned to cut government spending for social programs by $41.4 billion in fiscal 1982. Reagan avoided trimming the politically sensitive, middle-class social security and Medicare entitlement programs, and instead cut programs that directly benefited the poor, such as Food Stamps, Aid to Families with Dependent Children, school lunches, housing assistance, and Medicaid. Finally, he planned to use a tight monetary policy to squeeze inflation out of the economy.

But in late March 1981, before Reagan could implement his economic program, a would-be assassin shot and seriously wounded the elderly president. Through the ordeal, Reagan showed courage and spirit. As he was wheeled into the operating room, he quipped to his wife, Nancy, "Honey, I forgot to duck." Reagan's behavior in adversity magnified his popularity. "The bullet meant to kill him," observed a journalist, "made him a hero instead, floating above the contentions of politics and the vagaries of good news or bad." In the long run, however, the assassination drained precious energy from an already diminished president. Reagan lost more than half his blood as doctors engaged in a dramatic struggle to save his life. The president's authorized biographer called the operation "a chilling physiological insult from which he would never fully recover."

Reagan used his enhanced stature to sway Congress into supporting his radical economic plan. Casting the debate in stark ideological language, Reagan called on Democrats to support his program; those who did not would be defending the "failed policies of the past." In May dispirited Democrats joined Republicans in passing a budget resolution that called for deep cuts in many social programs and increased spending for the military. "The Great Society, built and consolidated over fifteen years, was shrunk to size in just 26 hours and 12 minutes of floor debate," observed *Newsweek*. In August Congress rubber-stamped the administration's massive tax cut, providing for across-the-board reductions of 5 percent the first year and an additional 10 percent in each of the succeeding two years.

While the public gave the president credit for pushing his legislative program through Congress, it blamed him for the inevitable slowdown that resulted from his tight money policies. By limiting the amount of money in the economy, the Federal Reserve Board, with Reagan's implicit approval, incited a recession by making it difficult for businesses to borrow and expand. In 1982 and 1983 the "Reagan recession" forced some 10 million Americans out of work, and the 9.5 percent unemployment rate was the highest since 1941. The president urged Congress and the American people to "stay the course," predicting that the economy would rebound in 1983. He was right: the GNP increased an impressive 4.3 percent, and unemployment declined to 8 percent.

Attacking the Liberal State

As a presidential candidate Ronald Reagan pledged to shrink the scope of federal government by returning greater authority and responsibility to the states. He appointed to his cabinet conservatives determined to loosen federal regulation.

The most controversial of Reagan's administrators was Secretary of the Interior James G. Watt. Under Watt's leadership the Interior Department opened federal lands to coal and timber production, narrowed the scope of the wilderness preserves, and sought to make a million offshore acres with oil potential available for drilling. Watt's policies and provocative public statements kept him in the middle of controversy until he finally resigned in 1983.

The turbulent history of the savings and loan (S&L) industry during the 1980s exemplified the dangers of the Reagan passion for deregulation. Since the Great Depression, S&Ls (called thrifts) had been restricted to using investors' money for low-risk mortgage lending, whereas banks could offer checking accounts, trust services, and commercial and consumer loans. When interest rates soared in the 1970s, money bled out of the S&Ls and into higher-yielding money market accounts. Conservatives, arguing that deregulation was the key to saving the S&Ls and reviving the banking industry, loosened the rules governing S&L investments at the same time that they increased federal insurance on S&L deposits from $20,000 to $100,000. "This bill is the most important legislation for financial institutions in the last 50 years," President Reagan said in a ceremony announcing the new rules. "All in all, I think we hit the jackpot," he added.

Flush with money from investors trying to turn a quick profit, many S&Ls made risky loans on malls, apartment complexes, and office towers. Opportunists such as Charles Keating, owner of Lincoln Savings, turned their thrifts into giant casinos, using federally insured deposits to bet on high-risk corporate takeovers and junk bonds. It was a game of blackjack that only the consumers could lose. Instead of saving the S&Ls, the legislation produced a flood of bankruptcies by providing thrift owners with an incentive to engage in high-risk activity. Hundreds of thrifts folded, resulting in a $200 billion taxpayer-financed bailout that would cost $10 for every man, woman, and child in America.

Reagan Justice

As president, Reagan promised to appoint judges concerned with "protecting the rights of law-abiding citizens," defending "traditional values and the sanctity of human life," and maintaining "judicial restraint." Like many conservatives he believed that government should relax its efforts to ensure justice and equal opportunity for African-Americans and other minority groups.

To achieve the latter goals, the Reagan administration cut funding for the Equal Employment Opportunity Commission and for the civil rights division of the Justice Department. In 1981 the Justice Department supported a case brought by Bob Jones University against the Treasury Department, which had refused it tax-exempt status on the grounds that the university discriminated against blacks. Though the Supreme Court upheld the Treasury Department by an eight-to-one decision in 1983, the administration's support for the university made it abundantly clear that Reagan hoped to turn back the clock on civil rights.

The New Right especially welcomed Reagan's efforts to realign the Supreme Court. In 1981 Reagan appointed conservative Sandra Day O'Connor of Arizona as the first woman to serve on the High Court. When Chief Justice Warren Burger retired in 1986, Reagan elevated William Rehnquist, a strong advocate of law and order, to the chief justiceship. He offered the open seat to federal judge Antonin Scalia, a rigid advocate of executive power. In 1988 Reagan had sought to replace centrist Louis Powell with the conservative Robert Bork, but a coalition of civil rights and women's groups helped defeat the nomination. The seat was eventually filled by Anthony Kennedy, a federal appeals court judge from California.

The Reagan appointments yielded an aggressive conservative coalition of justices that took command of the court, issuing a series of decisions that reversed the direction of more than three decades of law on criminal procedures, individual liberties, and civil rights. Deciding most major cases by five-to-four margins, the Court ruled that under some circumstances police could submit confessions coerced from suspected criminals as evidence, and it curtailed the rights of immigrants to claim political asylum and limited the rights of death-row prisoners to challenge the death penalty. In their most significant civil rights ruling (*Wards Cove* v. *Atonio*, 1989), the justices shifted the burden of proof from those accused of practicing discrimination to its victims. But the justices were not always predictable. One surprise, much to conservatives' dismay, was the Court's decision that burning the American flag was political speech protected by the Constitution.

The 1984 Presidential Campaign

The improving economy of 1983–1984 revived Ronald Reagan's popularity. With polls showing the president enjoying a commanding lead against any potential Democratic opponent, many Republican strategists hoped for an electoral landslide that would herald Republican control of the White House for the rest of the century.

Reagan's challenger, former Vice President Walter Mondale, had won his party's nomination after a bruising primary fight against civil rights activist Jesse Jackson and Colorado Senator Gary Hart. Jackson, a former coworker of Martin Luther King, became the first African-American to win substantial support in his bid to receive a major party nomination. Mondale's challenge was to arouse the enthusiasm of the party's traditional constituencies—blacks, Jews, union members, urban residents—while reeling back into the party the "Reagan Democrats," the white middle class that had defected to the Republicans. As a first step in executing his strategy, Mondale tried to demonstrate that he was capable of bold leadership by selecting a woman vice presidential candidate, former Congresswoman Geraldine Ferraro of New York City. A few weeks later, in his acceptance speech at the Democratic convention, Mondale tried to prove he was fiscally responsible by proposing to raise taxes to help reduce the deficit.

Riding a wave of personal and organizational confidence, Reagan exhorted voters "to make America great again and let the eagle soar." In his speeches and commercials, the president promoted themes of small government, patriotism, and family. "We see an America," he declared, "where every day is independence day, the Fourth of July." At Republican rallies smothered in balloons and music, the president repeatedly invoked a booming economy and a safer world as evidence of the nation's success under his leadership.

On election day, voters returned Reagan to office with 58.8 percent (54,455,075) of the vote and the biggest electoral vote total in history—525. Mondale received 40.6 percent (37,577,185 popular votes) and 13 electoral votes. Reagan swept the entire nation except for Minnesota and the District of Columbia. The election, observed *Time* magazine, represented a collective "Thank You" to "a president who had made the country feel good about itself" (see map below).

REAGAN AND THE COLD WAR, 1980–1988

Reinvigorating the traditional conviction that the United States had a divinely ordained mission to spread American values around the globe, the Reagan administration came to office determined to reassert American power. A classic Cold Warrior, Reagan saw the Soviets at the heart of every international dispute, from revolution in Central America to international terrorism in the Middle East. While the public applauded the president's tough rhetoric, it divided on the wisdom of his specific policy experiments. Like previous administrations, Reagan's White House discovered the limits of American power, but it also inadvertently presided over a defusing of U.S.–Soviet tensions.

**Fighting the
"Evil Empire"**

After entering the White House Reagan denounced the Soviet Union as "the focus of evil in the modern world." In a sermon-like address to evangelical Christians, he declared that the United States was "enjoined by Scripture and the Lord Jesus" to oppose the Soviet Union. Most of the president's national security and foreign policy advisers—Secretary of State Alexander Haig, his successor George

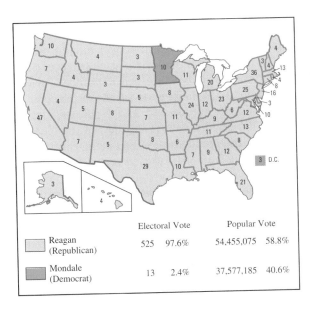

	Electoral Vote		Popular Vote	
Reagan (Republican)	525	97.6%	54,455,075	58.8%
Mondale (Democrat)	13	2.4%	37,577,185	40.6%

The Election of 1984 Americans, pleased with the improving economy and the administration's tough stand against communism, overwhelmingly supported President Reagan's bid for a second term in a office. Walter Mondale, a former senator and Jimmy Carter's vice president, failed to win electoral votes outside his home state of Minnesota and the District of Columbia.

Shultz, Secretary of Defense Caspar Weinberger, National Security Adviser Richard Allen, and Ambassador to the United Nations Jeanne Kirkpatrick—shared his exaggerated fear of Soviet power and his determination to assert American military might.

To thwart the Soviets Reagan called for the largest and most expensive peacetime military buildup in American history. "Defense is not a budget item," Ronald Reagan told his staff. "You spend what you need." Along with accelerating the development of existing weapons systems—both nuclear and conventional—the administration reincarnated programs canceled under Carter, including the trouble-plagued B-1 bomber and the controversial neutron bomb. By 1985 the Pentagon was spending more than $28 million an hour, every hour, seven days a week. Excluding veterans' affairs, the defense budget surged from $157 billion in 1981 to $273 billion in 1986. Corrected for inflation the increases averaged nearly 7 percent a year.

While strengthening America's strategic arsenal, Reagan declared that the United States stood ready to support anticommunist regimes anywhere in the world. In the Middle East, the Philippines, Chile, South Korea, and Angola, the Reagan administration supported repressive governments if they stood strongly against communism. This approach to world politics was especially clear with regard to South Africa, where the system of apartheid, which brutally excluded nonwhites from basic rights, threatened to provoke civil war. Committed to working with the South African whites-only government, the administration abandoned Carter's efforts to force change and adopted a policy known as "constructive engagement." Reagan resisted all calls by liberal and human rights groups to join other countries in coercing the government of South Africa into dismantling apartheid. South Africa, he believed, was a bulwark against the spread of communism. Congress repudiated his policy in 1986, demanding that Reagan take bold steps, including the imposition of economic sanctions, against the South African government.

The Escalating Arms Race

Reagan entered office with a deep-seated distaste for arms control, which he planned to subject to a period of "benign neglect" while the United States went about the business of "rearming." Thus he took a tough position in negotiations with the Soviets. As a goal for the Intermediate Nuclear Forces (INF) talks, initiated by the Carter administration to address the nuclear balance of power in Europe, Reagan embraced the "zero option," whereby the Soviets would agree to dismantle all intermediate-range missiles in Europe and Asia while the United States would agree only to deploy no new medium-range missiles. In the separate Strategic Arms Reduction Talks (START), the president proposed a one-third cut in nuclear warheads. The reductions, however, were structured in such a manner that the Soviets would have had to destroy a disproportionate share of their heavy land-based missiles. The proposals angered the Soviets, who grew increasingly distrustful of Reagan and his leading advisers.

U.S.–Soviet relations were already tense when in September 1983 a Soviet interceptor aircraft shot down a Korean Airlines plane, killing all 269 people on board, after the Boeing 747 strayed into Soviet air space on a flight from Anchorage to Seoul. American intelligence suggested the tragedy was the result of confusion and incompetence on the part of Soviet military officials who believed the civilian airliner to be a spy plane, but Reagan used the incident to bolster his contention that the Soviets were an "evil empire." Moscow, angered by Reagan's moralistic condemnation and frustrated with the stalemate on arms control, walked out of the INF talks. "The international situation" declared Politburo member Grigory Romanov, "is white hot, thoroughly white hot." The walkout left the superpowers with no ongoing arms control talks for the first time in fourteen years. The United States responded by deploying new missiles in West Germany, Britain, and Italy. The Soviets moved new rockets into Czechoslovakia and East Germany. "The second cold war has begun," shrilled an Italian newspaper.

Not all Americans agreed with the administration's hard-line approach. A nationwide poll in the spring of 1982 showed that 57 percent of the respondents favored an immediate freeze on the testing, production, and deployment of nuclear weapons. A wide variety of religious and academic leaders were questioning the wisdom of the administration's policies. "Cease this madness," implored George Kennan, the father of containment. The American Catholic bishops issued a pastoral letter on the moral and theological dimensions of nuclear deterrence. The message of the letter was clear: "We must continually say no to the idea of nuclear war." In 1984 over 100 million people anxiously watched a televised drama, *The Day After,* that portrayed the effects of nuclear war on Kansas.

Reagan tried to defuse the growing calls for arms limitation by proposing, in 1982, a space-based defensive shield that used laser beams to destroy incoming missiles. The Strategic Defense Initiative (SDI), nicknamed "Star Wars" by the media, reflected the administration's belief that improbable technological solutions could solve complex political problems. The administration's top military scientist pointed out that unless it was coupled with an offensive arms control agreement, the defensive system could certainly be overcome by Soviet weapons. "With unconstrained proliferation" of Soviet warheads, he said, "no defensive system will work." Despite the criticism, the administration pushed forward, spending $17 billion on SDI between 1983 and 1989.

By 1984, however, a number of developments were pushing Moscow and Washington closer together. Concerned about a possible backlash against his policies in the upcoming presidential campaign, Reagan called for a "constructive working relationship" with the Kremlin. He claimed that the massive military buildup during his first three years in office allowed the United States to negotiate from a position of strength. At the same time, a new leader, who seemed readier than his predecessors to renew détente with the United States, assumed leadership in the Soviet Union. Mikhail Gorbachev, fifty-four, the youngest head of the Soviet Communist Party since Josef Stalin, came to power determined to reform Soviet society. At home he advocated *perestroika,* or restructuring to relax government economic and social control. Abroad he championed a new policy of *glasnost,* or openness. Hoping to avoid an expensive arms race, Gorbachev declared a moratorium on deployment of medium-range missiles in Europe and asked the United States to do the same.

The result of these developments was a series of four Reagan–Gorbachev summits. In 1986 the two leaders met at Reykjavik, Iceland, and agreed on a first step to cut strategic nuclear forces in half. Gorbachev wanted to go farther, calling for the complete elimination of all nuclear weapons, but he insisted that the United States also abandon the SDI, something Reagan refused to do. The following year the United States and the Soviet Union agreed to the Intermediate Nuclear Forces Treaty (INF), which, for the first time, called for the destruction of existing missiles and allowed for on-site inspections to verify compliance. In December Gorbachev traveled to Washington to sign the treaty in a warm ceremony with Reagan. While in the United States the Soviet leader announced a unilateral reduction in Soviet military forces.

By the time Reagan left office, he and his counterpart in the Kremlin had toasted each other as "Ronnie and Mikhail." Opinion polls reported Americans feeling friendlier toward the Soviet Union than at any time since the end of World War II. When a reporter asked Reagan in 1987 if he still thought the Soviet Union was an evil empire, he responded, "No, I was talking about another time, another era."

Central America Before and during *glasnost*, Reagan's Cold War views shaped his approach to radical insurgencies in Latin America. Ignoring the complex social and political conditions that fostered revolution in the region, Reagan believed that Moscow was to blame for most of the trouble. "[L]et us not delude ourselves," he advised the American people. "The Soviet Union underlies all the unrest that is going on. If they weren't engaged in

Reagan in Moscow The thawing of Cold War tensions between the United States and the Soviet Union was evident in the signing of the Intermediate Nuclear Forces Treaty in December 1987, which eliminated intermediate-range nuclear missiles. This goodwill between the nations grew with Reagan's historic visit to Moscow in May 1988. Reagan and Mikhail Gorbachev toured Red Square and during this trip both men referred to each other as "friend." *(AP/Wide World Photos, Inc.)*

this game of dominos, there wouldn't be any hot spots in the world." For Reagan and his advisers, any leftist victory in Latin America would make possible another Cuba that could serve as a staging ground for Soviet expansion in the Western Hemisphere. The administration also worried that communist gains could produce a flood of political refugees who would pour over the U.S. border.

Since the administration viewed relations with Central America as an extension of the superpower conflict, it relied heavily on military aid and covert warfare to prop up friendly regimes and bring down unfriendly ones. In El Salvador, a poor country in which 2 percent of the people controlled nearly all the wealth, a coalition of leftist guerrillas had been attempting to topple the government. Reagan, convinced that rebels against the established regime represented Soviet influence, spent nearly $5 billion providing military and economic aid to the government. The army used the arms to wage a fierce campaign of repression against civilians suspected of sympathizing with the rebels or agitating for social change. Between 1979 and 1985 army death squads killed as many as forty thousand peasants, teachers, union organizers, and church workers. Despite the violence, Reagan certified that El Salvador was making "a concerted and significant effort" to protect human rights. In 1984 the moderate José Napoleon Duarte won a popular election and opened talks with rebel leaders, but the bloody civil war continued.

In Nicaragua Reagan committed the United States to overthrowing the Marxist-led Sandinistas, who had ousted repressive dictator Anastasio Somoza in 1979. Beginning in 1982 the CIA organized, trained, and financed the contras, a guerrilla army based in Honduras and Costa Rica. Infiltrating Nicaragua the contras sabotaged bridges, oil facilities, and crops. The CIA offered them training in how to assassinate and kidnap political leaders. Reagan praised the contras as "the moral equivalent of our Founding Fathers," but the Congress and the public disagreed. In December 1982 Congress, fearful of getting the nation involved in "another Vietnam," halted military aid to the contras for one year. In October 1984 the House passed the Boland Amendment, which forbade any direct aid to the contras.

Meanwhile, Reagan's fear of communism in the Caribbean found an outlet in the tiny nation of Grenada, a 133-square-mile island whose principal export was medical students. In 1983, when a leftist government friendly with Cuba assumed power in Grenada, Reagan ordered six thousand marines to invade the island and install a pro-American government. The administration claimed that the invasion was necessary to protect American students living on the island and to stop the construction of an airfield that would allegedly serve Cuban and Soviet interests. Critics asserted that the students were never in danger and the airfield was being built to boost the island's ailing tourist industry. World opinion condemned the invasion, but the first successful assertion of American military might since Vietnam renewed the pride and confidence of millions of Americans.

The Iran-Contra Scandal

Reagan came into office in 1980 on a groundswell of public outrage over Iran's seizure of American hostages. Believing that the Iranians had released the hostages on the day he was inaugurated because they feared his tough-minded approach, Reagan proudly emphasized that he would never negotiate with terrorists.

"The United States gives terrorists no rewards," he said in June 1985. "We make no concessions. We make no deals."

The administration's tough rhetoric did little to stem the tide of terrorism in the Middle East, where despite the Israeli–Egyptian treaty peace proved elusive. In 1983 Israeli forces attacked Palestine Liberation Organization (PLO) strongholds in southern Lebanon on Israel's northern border. The United States arranged for a withdrawal of both Israeli and PLO troops from Beirut and sent two thousand marines into the region as part of an international peacekeeping force. In October 1983 a radical Shiite Muslim terrorist drove a truck loaded with explosives into the U.S. barracks near the Beirut airport. The explosion killed 241 marines.

In 1985 terrorist attacks in the Middle East and Europe claimed the lives of more than 900 civilians, including 23 Americans. In June 1985 American television captured the ordeal of the 135 passengers aboard TWA flight 847. Hijacked over Greece they endured seventeen nightmarish days of captivity before being released. In 1986, when Libyan agents were implicated in the bombing of a Berlin nightclub frequented by American soldiers, Reagan, calling Libya's president Muammar Qaddafi the "mad dog of the Middle East," ordered a retaliatory air attack. The raid killed an estimated 37 Libyans, including Qaddafi's infant daughter. Americans applauded the flexing of U.S. military muscle, but the cycle of terrorism escalated. In December 1988 Libyan agents blew up a Pan Am jet en route from London to New York, killing all 259 aboard, including numerous Americans.

Despite the high-profile bombing of Libya, the administration believed that Iran presented the greatest threat to American interests in the region. In an effort to tame Iran's revolutionary fervor, Reagan supported Iraq in its eight-year war with Iran that began in 1980. The administration removed Iraq from its list of states that approved terrorism and restored diplomatic relations that had been severed in 1967. Over the objections of the Pentagon, Reagan shared critical intelligence with Iraq and approved the export of more than $700 million in sensitive technology.

At the same time, however, Reagan was negotiating behind the scenes with Iran to secure the release of American hostages taken in Beirut. In 1985 the president had approved a plan hatched by his national security adviser Robert McFarlane and CIA head William Casey. American agents would secretly try to curry favor with the radical regime in Iran by selling the Iranians high-tech U.S. arms, which they needed in their ongoing war against Iraq. The secretaries of defense and state had vigorously objected to the idea, dismissing it as "almost too absurd to comment on." The president, however, moved by the pleas of hostages' families to do something to bring their loved ones home, had approved the secret sale of state-of-the-art anti-tank missiles to Iran.

The plot had an added twist: U.S. operatives overcharged Iran for the weapons and diverted some of the profits to fund the contras in Nicaragua. The operation was carried out by National Security Council (NSC) aide Oliver North, who used various middlemen to funnel millions of dollars to the contras. It was in clear violation of the Boland Amendment, which expressly forbade aid to the contras. The flow of money continued through early autumn 1986 before a Lebanese newsmagazine exposed the scheme. At first, the administration denied that it had violated its own policy by offering incentives for the release of the hostages. Over the next few months, however, reporters exposed the sordid details of the arms sales and the funneling of money to the contras.

The scandal, which consumed Reagan's final two years in office, damaged the president's reputation as an effective leader. A congressional committee charged that the president had abdicated his "moral and legal responsibility to take care that the laws be faithfully executed," but stopped short of accusing him of intentionally breaking the law. Far more damaging was the report of independent counsel Lawrence E. Walsh, who concluded that the White House successfully constructed a "firewall" to protect the president, allowing lower-level officials—North along with two National Security Council officials, Robert McFarlane and John Poindexter—to take the blame for an illegal policy approved by the president. Walsh, however, never found conclusive evidence that linked Reagan directly to the illegal activities. And although troubled by the Iran-contra affair, the public, as with other scandals that plagued the Reagan administration, did not blame the president himself. Polls showed declining support for the administration, plus renewed questions about the president's casual leadership style, but Reagan remained immensely popular when he left office.

WEALTH AND POVERTY IN REAGAN'S AMERICA, 1980–1988

Reagan's attacks on the welfare state, his steep tax cuts, and his advocacy of small government struck a responsive chord with many young, affluent baby boomers who were entering their peak earning years. They helped lead the nation in a celebration of money-dominated American public life during the decade, but grimmer realities lay under the surface.

The Money Culture

Ronald and Nancy Reagan epitomized the new money culture of the 1980s. The public seemed fascinated by the air of unembarrassed extravagance that floated around the Reagans. The couple set the tone for the decade with an extravagant inaugural celebration that included two nights of show-business performances, an $800,000 fireworks display, and nine lavish inaugural balls. Once in the White House, First Lady Nancy Reagan unapologetically spent $209,508 for new White House china—a Lenox pattern with a raised gold presidential seal—while her husband was busy cutting welfare rolls.

The real nexus of the money culture, however, was Wall Street. Changes in the 1981 tax law, combined with the Reagan Justice Department's relaxed attitude toward enforcement of antitrust statutes, fueled a "merger mania" on Wall Street. Many of the nation's largest corporations, including R. J. Reynolds, Nabisco, Walt Disney, and Federated Department Stores, were the objects of leveraged buyouts. Between 1984 and 1987 Wall Street executed twenty-one mergers valued at over $1 billion each.

The money culture created lucrative opportunities for the battalions of bankers, investors, and venture capitalists who made money out of money. Among the very highest rollers was Ivan Boesky, who worked eighteen-hour days behind a three-hundred-line phone bank, lived like a feudal lord, and made $115 million in two huge oil company deals in 1984. "Greed is all right," he told a cheering University of California business school audience in 1985. "Everybody should be a little bit greedy." Greed, however, soon landed Boesky in jail. In late 1986 he pleaded guilty to using confidential information about corporate takeovers to trade stocks illegally. In 1987 *Fortune* magazine named him "Crook of the Year." Boesky was far from the only law-breaker. Between 1977 and 1989 Michael Milken raised more than $100 billion in funds for American business. In 1987 alone he earned more than $550 million in commissions. He later confessed to defrauding investors and rigging the bond market.

The emphasis on making money was a manifestation of the maturing of the baby boom generation—the 76 million men and women born from 1946 through 1964 who were entering high-earning, high-spending adulthood at the start of the 1980s. By mid-decade observers had coined the acronym "yuppie" to describe these ambitious young, urban professionals. *Newsweek* magazine named 1984 "The Year of the Yuppie." Yuppies aspired to become investment bankers, not social workers. In 1985, for example, one-third of the graduating class at Yale applied for jobs as financial analysts at First Boston Corporation. When college freshmen were asked in the late 1960s about personal goals, roughly 80 percent listed to "develop a meaningful philosophy of life," and only about 40 percent listed being "well off financially." By 1985, 71 percent listed being well off financially, and only 43 percent mentioned a philosophy of life.

Popular culture reinforced the Reagan era infatuation with wealth and status. *Dallas,* the most successful prime-time soap opera of the decade, chronicled the business intrigues and torrid sex life of Texas oilman J. R. Ewing. Robin Leach's *Lifestyles of the Rich and Famous* took viewers on shopping trips along exclusive Rodeo Drive and into the homes of the wealthy before ending with Leach's trade-mark sign-off, "May you have caviar wishes and champagne dreams." In Oliver Stone's film *Wall Street* , Gordon Gekko (played by Michael Douglas), a ruthless cor-porate raider who relies on insider information to swing deals, tells stockbrokers, "Greed, for lack of a better word, is good. Greed is right. Greed works."

The MTV Generation   As in other eras, technological changes during the eighties aided advertisers in their efforts to reach high-spending consumers. Over the decade, cable television grew from a flimsy presence in fewer than one in five homes to a favored medium in 56.4 percent of television homes. By the end of the decade, the average television household received more than twenty-seven channels. As viewers' choices grew and the three broadcast networks lost their automatic grip on the audience, the spoils increasingly went to the programmer who could cater to a special interest—and thereby offer advertisers a small but well-targeted cluster of consumers.

At the cutting edge of this new TV environment, the music television network known as MTV inspired a revolution in television broadcasting. "Ladies and Gentle-men," intoned a baritone voice at 12:01 A.M. on August 1, 1981, "Rock and roll!" MTV showed music videos around the clock, broken only by ads and bits of connective pat-ter from "veejays." From the beginning MTV was designed to appeal to young adults with lots of disposable income. "It was meant to drive a 55-year-old person crazy," said chairman Tom Freston. But that was simply MTV's shrewd twist on the key selling strategy of the decade: "narrowcasting," or niche marketing designed to "superserve" a narrowly defined viewer, or reader, or customer. In addition to MTV, networks pitched ads to children (Nickelodeon), to African-Americans (Black Entertainment Television), to news junkies (CNN), and to women between eighteen and forty-nine (Lifetime). Viewers willing to subscribe to premium services that charged an extra fee could choose all-sports, all-weather, all-movies, all-Spanish, all-sex, and more.

Television was only the most dramatic example of the culture's rearrangement into niches. Consumers could choose from hundreds of specialized magazines, among them twenty-nine new automotive magazines, twenty-five devoted to computers, nine food journals, thirteen gay magazines, and five bridal magazines. The splintering of the media reinforced and was fed by a splintering of the consumer market. Retailing saw a proliferation of stores that sold only coffee, or only socks. Within department stores merchandise was increasingly fractured into miniature enclaves sorted according to designer.

The success of MTV and other forms of niche marketing contributed to the fragmentation of public culture. During the 1940s and 1950s many technological changes helped create a sense of community and a more national culture. The advent of television, with just three networks, combined with the explosion in long-distance telephone service, the construction of interstate highways, and the expansion of air travel helped shrink distances and bring people closer together. Until the explosion in cable television and the proliferation of new networks, most of the viewing public watched the same television shows. As recently as the 1970s more than a third of U.S. homes tuned in weekly to watch *All in the Family.* "Television in the old days made it a smaller community," said producer Norman Lear. In the 1980s technology was transforming the mass culture into endless niche cultures. With so many shows to choose from, the audience splintered into smaller subsets of viewers. Studies showed, for example, that blacks and whites watched completely different shows.

The Hourglass Society

The public focus on the money culture during the Reagan era obscured the social reality affecting most Americans. Society in the 1980s assumed the appearance of an hourglass: bulging on the extremes and thin in the middle. "There are more and more affluent people, and more and more poor people," said Martin Holler, a Methodist minister who ran a food bank in Wichita, Kansas, "more people who have much more than they have ever had, and more people with nothing."

The number of millionaires doubled during the decade. The net worth of the four hundred richest Americans nearly tripled. By the end of the decade the top 1 percent of families owned 42 percent of the net wealth of all U.S. families, including 60 percent of all corporate stock and 80 percent of all family-owned trusts. Stated another way, the richest 2.5 million people had nearly as much income as the 100 million Americans with the lowest incomes.

The flurry of business mergers and acquisitions gave a handful of corporations increasing control over decision making in the private economy. The largest two hundred industrial corporations controlled roughly 60 percent of the assets of all industrial corporations, up from less than 50 percent in the early 1950s. And despite the continuing celebrations of "people's capitalism," the percentage of American households owning at least one share of stock fell from 25 percent in 1977 to 19 percent in 1983, while the wealthiest 1 percent of all American households controlled nearly three-fifths of all corporate stock.

While the rich got richer, the poor got poorer. The government classified about 26.1 million people (11.7 percent of the total population) as poor in 1979. By 1990 the number of poor had reached 33.6 million, making up 13.5 percent of the country. The aggregate numbers masked a major transformation in the nature of poverty. Government programs such as social security and Medicare had lifted most of the elderly and handicapped out of poverty, but they did little to alleviate the suffering of single mothers, young children, and young minority men, who made up the bulk of the poor population after 1980.

A marked jump in out-of-wedlock births, which doubled between 1975 and 1986, and in female-headed households, which did the same between 1970 and 1989, contributed to what analysts called the "feminization of poverty." By 1989 one of every four births in the United States was to an unwed woman. The feminization of poverty was also disproportionately black. By the early 1990s, 26 percent of all children under eighteen lived with a single parent; more than 60 percent of black children fell into that category. "With the exception of drugs and crime, the biggest crisis facing the black community today is the plight of the single mother," declared an NAACP publication.

By virtually any measure, the problems of society's poorest worsened during the 1980s. At any given time during the decade between 250,000 and 400,000 Americans were homeless. "Get off the subway in any American city," said the head of the National Coalition for Low Income Housing, "and you are stepping over people who live on the streets." Most of the homeless were unskilled workers, the chronically mentally ill, and women fleeing abusive spouses. Most had already been living in poverty before becoming homeless. During the 1980s high interest rates for construction coupled with tax law changes sharply cut commercial production of low-cost rental housing, leaving a shortage of affordable housing for low-income people. For many, the only choice was the streets. When Reagan's budget measures reduced funds available for homeless shelters, cities and states could not respond to the crisis.

As some of its members fell into poverty and others acquired wealth, the middle class shrank. According to some estimates, families making between $20,000 and $60,000 dwindled from 53 percent of the nation in 1973 to 49 percent in 1985. After doubling between 1947 and 1973, median family income stagnated. In 1985 the average middle-class family earned less money than it did in 1973. Hardest hit were younger families, who feared that the American Dream of rising prosperity would pass them by.

The New Economy

A number of factors led to the growing disparity of wealth and poverty in America. First, most of the new jobs created during the decade were lower-paying service jobs. By 1985 more people were flipping hamburgers at McDonald's for minimum wage

Homelessness During the 1980s the wealthiest Americans gained ground while the poorest segments saw their income decline. The homeless population skyrocketed, produced by a combination of an increase in the number of poor people, rising real estate prices, cuts in social programs, increased drug usage, and the deinstitutionalization of former mental patients. *(AP/Wide World Photos, Inc.)*

than were working in steel manufacturing—one of the cornerstones of America's industrial might. Between 1979 and 1984 six of ten jobs added to the U.S. labor market paid $7,000 a year or less. Most were such service-sector jobs as home health care attendant, sales clerk, food server, janitor, and office clerk. Besides low pay, these jobs offered few pension or health care benefits, were often part-time or temporary, and held out few opportunities for promotion. As a result, real hourly wages declined 0.5 percent per year from 1982 to 1987.

Second, government welfare programs were cut back or abandoned during the Reagan era. By 1989 state and local welfare payments dropped by an average of 40 percent from their 1973 levels. Job training programs were also sharply curtailed, and inflation stripped the minimum wage (frozen by the Reagan administration at 1981 levels) of some 44 percent of its real value.

Third, organized labor lost more than 3 million members over the course of the decade. By 1990 unions represented only 16 percent of the nation's 100 million workers. Not only were unions underrepresented in the fast-growing service sector of the economy, but the Reagan administration dealt labor a major blow in 1981 when it fired striking members of the Professional Air Traffic Controllers Organization (PATCO). The president's actions emboldened management and dispirited workers.

Fourth, Reagan's tax cuts worsened the skew toward an hourglass social structure by offering the largest breaks to the wealthy. At the same time, social security taxes roughly tripled. The blow fell most heavily on the middle and lower classes, since the social security tax exempts the portion of wage and salary income above $45,000 a year and all income from interest, dividends, and rent. The result was that only the top 10 percent of the population received a significant net tax cut between 1977 and 1988; most of the other 90 percent paid a higher share of their incomes to Washington. At the extremes, the richest 1 percent got a net tax savings of 25 percent; the poorest tenth of workers saw 20 percent more of their incomes swallowed by taxes.

While conditions restricted opportunities to make money for most people, expenses for basic necessities soared. A typical family home in 1984 absorbed 44 percent of the median family's yearly income, compared with 21 percent in 1973. Buying the average-priced car cost twenty-three weeks of pay in 1988. Ten years earlier it had cost eighteen weeks of pay.

The Reagan Legacy

The Iran-contra scandal cast a dark shadow over the final years of the Reagan administration and intensified debate about the president's legacy. Supporters argue that Reagan's economic policies produced a remarkable period of sustained growth. Between 1983 and 1990 unemployment fell to 5.2 percent, and the economy grew by a third and produced 19 million new jobs, while inflation remained stable at less than 4 percent. Abroad, Reagan's supporters contend that his tough rhetoric and increased military spending not only pushed the Soviets to the bargaining table, but also forced them to accept American terms. Reagan, they declared, was personally responsible for ending the Cold War.

The president's critics contend that his domestic policies imposed undue hardship on the poor and had little to do with the economic recovery. His income tax cut proved illusory for all except the wealthiest Americans. By the end of his administration, the average family was actually paying more in taxes than in 1980, thanks in large part to a sharp increase in social security taxes and hikes in state and local taxes to cover shortfalls from reduced federal outlays. Critics also challenge the notion that Reagan ended the Cold War; the Soviet Union they assert, collapsed under the weight of American's bipartisan policy of containment dating back to the Truman Doctrine and the Marshall Plan, and because of the inherent instability of communism.

It is difficult to reach conclusive answers on these questions. Until historians know more about the inner workings of Kremlin decision makers, it will be impossible to assess all the forces that contributed to Moscow's new openness to the West. Certainly Reagan's strident rhetoric and massive arms buildup intensified Cold War tensions, while many of his policies, especially those toward Latin America, overestimated Soviet influence and underplayed the role of local forces. Much to his credit, however, Reagan appreciated the need to soften his hard line with the Soviets, embracing Gorbachev and the new Soviet openness to the West.

On the home front, perhaps Reagan's chief legacy was a ballooning federal deficit. Reagan's inability to reconcile his tax-cutting policies with his spending priorities, especially the massive military increases, caused the federal deficit to soar. By the time Reagan left office, the federal government was spending $206 billion more per year than it was receiving in tax revenues. In just eight years the national debt rose from $908.5 billion to nearly $2.7 trillion. The mountain of red ink may have inadvertently furthered Reagan's agenda, since it focused public attention on cutting spending and dashed liberal hopes of funding new social programs (see figure on page 1255).

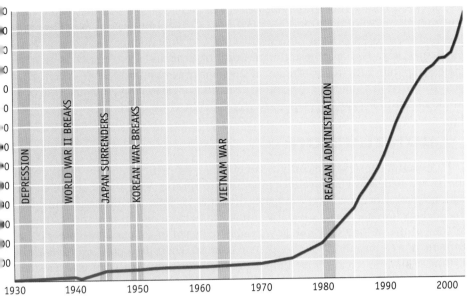

The National Debt, 1930–2003   Ending a pattern of static or slightly rising national debt, the Reagan era saw the deficit more than triple from $908 billion in 1980 to $2.9 trillion at the end of 1989. The reason: both Congress and the president refused to raise taxes or cut popular programs while spending billions for military expenditures. This trend in the deficit continued throughout the nineties and jumped sharply between 2000 and 2003 as government spending added another one trillion to the debt.

One Reagan legacy is little disputed, however. Reagan's skillful use of television transformed the style of presidential leadership. "Television in modern politics has been as revolutionary as the development of printing in the time of Gutenberg," journalist Teddy White observed. Television forced politicians to articulate themes that could appeal to a broad spectrum of the electorate at the same time that it personalized politics by allowing leaders to bypass parties and build a direct relationship with voters. President Reagan was a master craftsman of the new technology. Leaving the details of governing to aides, Reagan concentrated on the symbolic aspects of his presidency. Using television to emphasize resilient themes of self-help, individualism, and limited government, he rarely discussed specific policies. The president's advisers carefully orchestrated the media coverage. By limiting access to Reagan, the staff minimized the president's penchant for verbal miscues, prevented the press from asking tough questions, and guaranteed that the public saw him in brief visuals that served to enhance his stature. These images, designed around a daily message, allowed the White House to focus public attention on Reagan's accomplishments while ignoring his numerous failures. "So far, he's proving Lincoln was right," observed a veteran reporter. "You can fool all of the people some of the time."

Reagan's media savvy helped boost his personal popularity to record levels. Polls showed his approval rating at 68 percent in his final month in office—the highest ever recorded for a departing president. Reagan's appeal rubbed off on the rest of Washington. In 1980 only 22 percent of people polled said they could trust government "most of the time." After eight years of Republican rule the percentage had increased to 38 percent, and nearly half said they favored increased government spending. Perhaps the ultimate irony of Reagan's presidency was that he increased public faith in government at the same time that his massive deficits crippled Washington's ability to respond to demands for greater government services. It would be left to Reagan's successors to reconcile the contradiction.

CONCLUSION

Powerful conservative currents swept through American politics at the end of the 1970s. Religious conservatives mobilized to reverse what they considered the nation's moral decline; angry taxpayers revolted against an increased and often unequal tax burden; and conservative intellectuals launched an array of ideological missiles at the welfare state and government activism in general. The conservative currents flowed into the 1980 presidential contest, where the public, worried about soaring inflation, rising unemployment, and declining international prestige, rejected President Carter and elected former California Governor Ronald Reagan. The former actor combined telegenic features and a simple but compelling message to win the election.

The rise of the religious right inspired an angry debate over social values during the decade. At the heart of the culture wars was a dispute about American identity. Both sides were convinced that their values were "American" and best served the nation's traditional experiment in liberty. With the help of the Reagan administration, conservatives launched an assault against "liberal permissiveness," which they blamed for the decline of the family. While the Left and Right battled over abortion and gay rights, a massive tide of immigrants was changing the face of America. But the new immigration touched off another heated controversy over how newcomers should be integrated into the mainstream, or if indeed they should be welcomed at all.

As president, Ronald Reagan launched an assault on the welfare state, pushing Congress to pass ambitious tax and spending cuts. He attempted to rein in Washington's power by appointing cabinet members and Supreme Court justices who shared his disdain for bureaucracy and his disaffection with state power. The public appreciated Reagan's leadership style and in 1984 rewarded him with a resounding victory over his Democratic opponent, Walter Mondale.

Reagan came to office determined to reassert American power and tame the Soviet bear, which he believed was the instigator behind most trouble in the world. Convinced that the United States was losing its battle with the Soviet Union, the administration embarked on a massive armament program to build up the nation's stockpile of nuclear and conventional weapons. By 1986 the administration had retreated from its hard-line experiment with the Soviets. By the end of Reagan's second term, thanks in large part to new leadership in the Kremlin, the United States and the Soviets enjoyed the warmest relations since the end of World War II. That success was clouded by revelations that the White House had masterminded an illegal scheme to sell weapons to Iran and use the proceeds to fund anticommunist guerrillas in Nicaragua.

Americans in the 1980s seemed consumed with wealth and status. A Wall Street "merger mania" produced new opportunities to make money, advertisers eager to sell their goods, and a popular culture that glorified the pursuit of wealth. The benefits of the booming economy were not evenly distributed. The decade witnessed a widening gap between haves and have-nots, aggravated by Reagan's policies and rising prices of basic necessities. Economically, Reagan's policy experiments left a mixed legacy, including a huge federal deficit. His successor would confront the economic repercussions, as well as the diplomatic opportunities, that the Reagan era initiated.

Annotated Suggested Readings

The writing available on the 1980s is unusually polarized, but there are nonetheless some broad surveys of the period. Samuel Freedman's *The Inheritance* (1996) provides a good sense of the mood of many early Reagan voters. William Berman's *America's Right Turn* (1994) paints a broad picture of the rise of conservatism from Nixon to George H. W. Bush. Michael Schaller offers the first historical work on the 1980s in *Reckoning with Reagan* (1992). William Martin's *With God on Our Side* (1996) describes the changing politics of the religious right. Sidney Blumenthal's *The Rise of the Counter-Establishment* (1986) chronicles the emergence of the neoconservatives. Michael Lind, a defector from the conservative camp, critiques the New Right in *Up from Conservatism* (1996). Lisa McGirr roots the rise of conservatism in the fast-growing suburbs in *Suburban Warriors* (2002).

Most of the historical treatments of Reagan's presidency are sharply critical. In *Dutch* (1999) Edmund Morris, Reagan's authorized biographer, produces an idiosyncratic but useful portrait of the president. *The Reagan Presidency* (2003), edited by W. Elliot Brownlee and Hugh Graham, offers a balanced historical assessment. Gary Wills's *Reagan's America: Innocents at Home* (1987) is the classic treatment. Lou Cannon's *President Reagan: The Role of a Lifetime* (1991) stresses theatricality in Reagan's presidency. Haynes Johnson provides an overview of the country in *Sleepwalking Through History* (1991). Sidney Blumenthal and Thomas Edsall compile essays on Reagan's presidency in *The Reagan Legacy* (1988). It should be read with Larry Berman's *Looking Back on the Reagan Presidency* (1990). Peter Wallison, Reagan's White House counsel, provides an insider's perspective on Iran-Contra in *Ronald Reagan* (2002). For the more personal side of Reagan's leadership, see Ralph Weber's edited volume of Reagan's letters, *Dear Americans* (2003). Also useful, if uncritical, are Peggy Noonan's *What I Saw at the Revolution* (2003) and Michael Deaver's *A Different Drummer* (2003).

William Greider takes the Reagan economists to task in *The Education of David Stockman and Other Americans* (1982). E. J. Dionne's *Why Americans Hate Politics* (1991) captures the political mood of the 1984 campaign and the dilemma faced by the Democratic Party. Peter Goldman and Tony Fuller's *The Quest for the Presidency, 1984* (1985) recounts the strategies and actions of the two campaigners. Jack Germond and Jules Witcover express cynicism over Reagan's campaign of images in *Wake Us When It's Over* (1985). James Torr collected essays that offer a variety of glimpses into the decade in *The 1980s* (2000).

Richard Melanson argues in *Reconstructing Consensus* (1991) that the overarching foreign-policy goal of the Reagan administration was to rebuild the Cold War consensus that was destroyed during the Vietnam War. Seweryn Bialer and Michael Mandelbaum address the emerging détente between the superpowers in *Gorbachev's Russia and American Foreign Policy* (1988). Reagan's role in ending the Cold War is reassessed in *The Fall of the Berlin Wall* (2000), edited by Peter Schweizer. Broad introductions to Reagan's Central

American policies include Walter LaFeber's *Inevitable Revolutions* (1984) and Kenneth Coleman and George Herring's *The Central American Crisis* (1985). Robert Pastor surveys America's relations with Nicaragua in *Condemned to Repetition* (1987). The Nicaraguan operation fed directly into the Iran-contra scandal, which is covered by Jane Hunter et al. in *The Iran-Contra Connection* (1987). Bob Woodward reviews Reagan's secret operations in *Veil: The Secret Wars of the CIA* (1987). For a critical insider's account of Reagan's foreign policy see Constantine Menges, *Inside the National Security Council* (1998).

James Steward's *Den of Thieves* (1992) is an account of the shady dealings in the financial markets during the 1980s. Connie Bruck's *The Predators' Ball* (1988) details the world of the junk bond traders. Allan Murray's *Showdown at Gucci Gulch* (1987) explains the influence such financiers had on government during the decade. Nicolaus Mills's *Culture in an Age of Money* (1990) criticizes the influence of corporations and wealth on American culture during the 1980s. Barbara Ehrenreich studies the insecurities over wealth and status that preoccupied much of the middle class in her *Fear of Falling* (1989). Kevin Phillips attacks the growth of economic inequality in the 1980s in *The Politics of Rich and Poor* (1990). Thomas Edsall explains the political motivations for attacking the poor in *The New Politics of Inequality* (1984). Leslie Dunbar analyzes the impact of Reagan's economic policies on minorities in *Minority Report* (1984), while William Julius Wilson's *The Truly Disadvantaged* (1987) studies the effects of Reaganomics in the inner cities. The war on welfare is exposed in Michael Katz's *The Undeserving Poor* (1989).

James C. Mohr's *Abortion in America* (1978) is a good one-volume history of the abortion debate. Leslie Reagan reconstructs the situation for women before *Roe v. Wade* in *When Abortion Was a Crime* (1997). N. E. H. Hull and Peter Hoffer offer a balanced history of the abortion debate in America in *Roe v. Wade* (2001) The definitive discussion of the political campaign over abortion is found in Kristin Luker's *Abortion and the Politics of Motherhood* (1985). Works on gay rights range from broad surveys such as Eric Marcus's *Making History: The Struggle for Gay and Lesbian Equal Rights* (1992) to studies of specific issues, such as Randy Shilts's coverage of the early AIDS epidemic, *And the Band Played On* (1987).

David Reimers's *Still the Golden Door* (1985) is a good starting point for material on immigration. James Olson's *Equality Deferred* (2002), provides an overview of post-1945 immigration. Thomas Espenshade's *The Fourth Wave* (1985) describes the "New Asian" immigrants in California, while James Cockcroft's *Outlaws in the Promised Land* (1986) looks at the immigration experience of Hispanics. Peter Brimelow's *Alien Nation* (1995) offers a pessimistic analysis of the new wave of immigration.

The Role of Religion in American Life

Jerry Falwell, Return to Traditional Religious Values

The Reverend Jerry Falwell, worried about America's moral decline, decided that Christian fundamentalists had no choice but to get actively involved in public life. In 1979 he founded the Moral Majority to spearhead a crusade to change American culture. In his 1980 book *Listen America!* Falwell laid out the rationale and purpose of the new organization.

We must reverse the trend America finds herself in today. Young people between the ages of twenty-five and forty have been born and reared in a different world than Americans of the years past. The television set has been their primary babysitter. From the television sets they have learned situation ethics and immorality—They have learned a loss of respect for human life. They have learned disrespect for family as God has established it. They have been educated in a public school system that is permeated with secular humanism. They have been taught that the Bible is just another book of literature. They have been taught that there are no absolutes in our world today. They have been introduced to the drug culture. They have been reared by the family and by the public school in a society that is greatly void of discipline and character building. The same young people have been reared under the influence of a government that has taught them socialism and welfarism. They have been taught to believe that the world owes them a living whether they work or not. . . .

We must, from the highest office in the land right down to the shoeshine boy in the airport, have a return to biblical basics. If the Congress of the United States will take its stand on that which is right and wrong, and if our president, our judiciary system, and our state and local leaders will take their stand on holy living, we can turn this country around. . . .

I remember that time when it was positive to be patriotic, and as far as I am concerned, it still is. I remember as a boy, when the flag was raised, everyone stood proudly and put his hand upon his heart and pledged allegiance with gratitude. I remember when the band struck up "the Stars & Stripes forever," we stood and goose pimples would run all over me. . . . I believe that Americans want to see this country come back to basics, back to values, back to biblical morality, back to sensibility, and back to patriotism.

As a preacher of the gospel, I not only believe in prayer and preaching, I also believed in good citizenship. If a labor union in America has the right to organize and improve its working conditions, then I believe that the churches and the pastors, the priests, and the rabbis of America have the responsibility, not just the right, to see to it that the moral climate and conscience of Americans is such that this nation can be healed inwardly.

A. Bartlett Giamatti, "Letter to Yale Freshmen, 1981"

In remarks to Yale University students on August 31, 1981, university president A. Bartlett Giamatti challenged the growing influence of Jerry Falwell's Moral Majority. Championing the importance of liberal education and the pluralism of American society, Giamatti described the Moral Majority as a coercive organization attempting to destroy civil liberties in America. He argued that a liberal education was incompatible with the moral absolutism of religious fundamentalism.

I believe a liberal education is an education in the root meaning of "liberal"—"liber"—"free"—the liberty of the mind free to explore itself, to draw itself out, to connect with other minds and spirits in the quest for truth. . . . Its goal is to train the whole person to be at once intellectually discerning and humanly flexible, tough-minded and open-hearted; to be responsive to the new and responsible for values that make us civilized. It is to teach us to meet what is new and different with reasoned judgment and humanity. A liberal education is an education for freedom, the freedom to assert the liberty of the mind to make itself new for the others it cherishes. . . .

A self-proclaimed "Moral Majority," and its satellite or client groups, cunning in the use of a native blend of old intimidation and new technology, threaten the values I have named. Angry at change, rigid in the application of chauvinistic slogans, absolutistic in morality, they threaten through political pressure of public denunciation whoever dares to disagree with their authoritarian positions. Using television, direct mail and economic boycott, they would sweep before them anyone who holds a different opinion.

From the maw of this "morality" come those who presume to know what justice for all is; come those who presume to know which books are fit to read, which television programs are fit to watch, which textbooks will serve for all the young; come spilling those who presume to know what God alone knows, which is when human life begins. . . . There is no debate, no discussion, no dissent. They know. There is only one set of overarching political and spiritual and social beliefs; whatever view does not conform to these views, is by definition relativistic, negative, secular, immoral, against the family, anti-free enterprise, Un-American. What nonsense.

What dangerous, malicious nonsense. What a shame more of our captains of commerce have not seized the opportunity to speak up for free enterprise. . . .

What disgusts me so much about the "morality" seeping out of the ground around our feet is that it would deny the legitimacy of differentness. We should all be dismayed with the shredding of the spiritual fabric of our society, with the urging to selfishness and discrimination all around us. We should be concerned that so much of our political and religious leadership acts intimidated for the moment and will not say with clarity that this most recent denial of the legitimacy of differentness is a radical assault on the very pluralism—of peoples, political beliefs, values, forms of merit and systems of religion—our country was founded to welcome and foster.

Since the beginning of the republic, Americans have been torn between the belief in individual liberty, as expressed in the Declaration of Independence, and the quest to mold a morally righteous society, which found outlet in periodic religious "awakenings." The dramatic cultural changes since the 1960s intensified the conflict between individual expression and moral righteousness. Religious fundamentalists, who had avoided politics since the 1920s, decided they could no longer sit on the sidelines. Falwell claimed that God instructed him to bring together "the good people of America" in a Christian crusade against pornography, sex education, and abortion.

As a result, the political influence of activist fundamentalists and evangelical Christians increased dramatically during the 1980s. By 1989 over 1,300 religious radio stations turned airwaves into pulpits, and more than 330 Christian ministries broadcast regularly on television. In addition to these enterprises, Christians boasted a billion-dollar book industry that offered instruction on how to be a better Christian, how to raise children, and how faith could cure an ailing nation. Many Americans worried about the growing political clout of fundamentalists, fearing they would abolish the wall separating church and state and threaten hard-earned individual rights.

At the heart of the conflict were competing views of the meaning of American identity. Conservatives like Jerry Falwell emphasized the existence of a singular American cultural tradition and a shared national identity. Religion and the traditional values that it often embodied were central to their view of American identity. Many liberals like A. Bartlett Giamatti, however, spoke a language of cultural diversity, underscoring the importance of difference, and articulating a vision of a multicultural America. While not opposed to religious faith, they worried about using state power to impose the views of a particular faith.

QUESTIONS FOR ANALYSIS

1. How does Falwell believe that religion will solve America's social problems?

2. Do you accept Falwell's argument that religious leaders have a responsibility to be involved in public life?

3. Why does Giamatti believe that religion is such a threat to liberal education?

4. Why are schools so often at the center of the debate over controversial issues such as race and religion?

5. What role do you believe religion should play in American life?

32

America After the Cold War

1988–2000

The trial opened a window onto the conflicting social currents of post–Cold War America. . . . What role should America play in a post–Cold War world? Would the end of the Cold War alter Americans' attitude toward government?

On January 7, 1999, a cold, drizzly day in Washington, Chief Justice William Rehnquist, dressed in gold-striped black robes, entered the majestic nineteenth-century Senate chamber. The room was hushed, the galleries packed, and the hundred senators seated at rapt attention as the sergeant at arms opened the proceedings. "All persons are commanded to keep silence, on pain of imprisonment, while the House of Representatives is exhibiting to the Senate of the United States articles of impeachment against William Jefferson Clinton."

It was a historic event: the first impeachment trial of an elected U.S. president and only the second trial of a president in history. The House of Representatives had forwarded two charges against Clinton, the first two-term Democratic president since Franklin Roosevelt. The charges alleged that he had lied under oath and obstructed justice in an effort to hide his affair with Monica Lewinsky, a twenty-two-year-old former White House intern. Under the Constitution, if two-thirds of the Senate, or sixty-seven senators, voted for conviction on either of the two articles of impeachment, Clinton would be removed from office, and Vice President Al Gore would be sworn in to replace him.

After days of listening to Republican prosecutors from the House and to the president's defense lawyers, the senators closed the doors, turned off the television cameras, and deliberated. At the end of the fourth day of closed-door meetings, the doors opened. Curious onlookers packed the galleries and filled the aisles to hear the verdict. "Senators, how say you? Is the respondent, William Jefferson Clinton, guilty or not guilty?" Rehnquist asked after a clerk read the first charge of perjury. As the clerk called the senators' names one by one, each stood to announce his or her verdict. Ten Republicans joined a united Democratic Party in declaring the president "not guilty," making the final count forty-five to fifty-five. On the obstruction of justice charge, five GOP senators crossed over, resulting in a fifty-fifty vote. Clinton "hereby is acquitted of the charges," the chief justice proclaimed.

A subdued Clinton emerged from the Oval Office two hours later to apologize to the American people. "I want to say again to the American people how profoundly sorry I am for what I said and did to trigger these events and the great burden they have imposed on the Congress and the American people." The president could take solace, however, from the fact that neither of the two articles of impeachment attracted even a simple majority of senators' votes, and both fell far short of the two-thirds majority needed to convict and expel him.

The trial opened a window onto the conflicting social currents of post–Cold War America. With the country's mortal enemy, the Soviet Union, dissolved, Americans were forced to contend with questions that were central to national identity. What role should America play in a post–Cold War world? Would the end of the Cold War alter Americans' attitude toward government? Americans also engaged in a heated debate over the legacy of the 1960s. What was the proper balance between private behavior and public morality?

The shifting political winds caught President George Bush off guard and allowed Democrat Bill Clinton to capture the White House in 1992. Partisan divisions, which often had been kept in check by fear of a common enemy, intensified during the decade as Republicans gained a firm foothold in Congress and the Democrats controlled the presidency. No longer consumed by the global struggle against communism, American politicians felt they had the luxury to spend thirteen months debating the private life of a public official. The explosion of new media outlets, especially the Internet and twenty-four-hour news channels, fed the public a steady diet of salacious details. The American people, however, turned out to be more interested in the new prosperity generated by a booming stock market than in the president's sexual adventures. Still, the trial increased public cynicism about Washington and provided ammunition for the restless antigovernment groups that had sprung up during the decade.

- How did the end of the Cold War influence American attitudes toward government?

- How did U.S. actions toward Iraq and Yugoslavia reflect Americans' view of their national interests?

- What was the "information society," and how did it affect the economy?

- How did partisan divisions shape American politics during the decade?

- What social tensions characterized the decade? How were they expressed, and what did they say about Americans' view of themselves and their society?

This chapter will address these questions.

THE POST–COLD WAR EXPERIMENT, 1988–1992

When he assumed the reins of power from Ronald Reagan in 1989, George Bush confronted a world transformed by the dissolution of the Soviet Union and the end of the Cold War. The threat of a superpower conflict receded, but Iraq's Saddam Hussein reminded Americans that the post–Cold War world was not devoid of danger. While President Bush successfully rallied world opinion and American military might in the Gulf War, establishing U.S. leadership in the post–Cold War world, he failed to exercise similar leadership in confronting a host of problems at home. In 1992 the voters rejected Bush in favor of former Arkansas Governor Bill Clinton, who understood that after a generation of fighting communism, Americans were turning inward.

The Search for Reagan's Successor The Iran-contra affair had removed some of the luster from Reagan's star, but his conservative views remained popular with most Republicans, who now faced the difficult task of choosing a candidate to continue his policies. The logical choice was George H. W. Bush, who had served as Reagan's loyal vice president for the previous eight years. Bush, however, was not conservative enough for many party members, who rallied around two formidable primary opponents: televangelist Pat Robertson and Kansas Senator Robert Dole. After a slow start, Bush gathered endorsements from elected officials and votes in securing the nomination.

In his acceptance speech at the Republican convention in July 1988, Bush tried to energize the party's conservative faithful by promising to continue the fight against terrorism abroad and big government at home. The centerpiece of the speech was a dramatic and carefully scripted promise not to raise taxes. "Read my lips," he said. "No new taxes." The vice president also appealed to moderates by emphasizing his support for education and the environment. In a move that puzzled observers, as well as many of his closest advisers, Bush picked the untested and lightly regarded Dan Quayle, a conservative senator from Indiana, as his running mate.

The Democrats had a difficult time finding a nominee to challenge Bush. The party's front-runner, Colorado Senator Gary Hart, quit the race after reporters disclosed that he was having an extramarital affair. Michael Dukakis, the Greek-American governor of Massachusetts, moved to fill the void created by Hart's absence. Dukakis and Hart shared a belief that the Democratic Party had moved too far to the left since the 1960s. Dukakis warned that the party should "break with the past." During the primaries, Dukakis bragged about his success in creating jobs and lowering taxes in his home state, the so-called Massachusetts miracle. He promised "good jobs at good wages," clean air, child care, and increased federal support for education, but he never suggested how the additional spending would affect the deficit.

Dukakis faced a spirited challenge from African-American civil rights leader Jesse Jackson, who appealed to the party's traditional liberal base. Jackson won some important primaries, but in the end, Dukakis's moderate message and well-oiled organization won more. Nominated at the Democratic convention in August, Dukakis tried to skirt the sensitive social issues that had divided the party since the

CHRONOLOGY

1983	*Time* names PC "Machine of the Year"
1988	Bush elected president
1989	U.S. troops invade Panama Tiananmen Square demonstration in China
1990	Soviet regimes topple in Eastern Europe Berlin Wall comes down
1991	Soviet Union dissolves; Gorbachev resigns Gulf War Thomas–Hill controversy Civil war in Yugoslavia
1992	Clinton elected president Los Angeles riots
1993	Failure of Clinton health plan World Trade Center bombing
1994	Beginning of Whitewater investigation NAFTA and GATT Mandela elected president of South Africa
1995	Republican government shutdown O. J. Simpson acquitted of murder Oklahoma City bombing
1996	Welfare Reform Act Clinton reelected California voters pass Proposition 209
1998	Clinton impeached U.S. embassies in Kenya and Tanzania bombed
1999	NATO bombs Kosovo Clinton acquitted 40 to 60 million people worldwide on the Internet Columbine High School shootings

1960s by declaring that the campaign was about "competence, not ideology." To underscore his new centrist message, he chose conservative Texas Senator Lloyd Bentsen as his running mate.

The fall contest between Dukakis and Bush degenerated into one of the most negative campaigns in modern times. The Bush campaign concentrated on convincing the public that Dukakis was soft on crime, unpatriotically weak on defense, and an enemy of family values. The Republicans also exploited racial tensions.

Bush's most effective advertisement told voters about Willie Horton, an African-American who had raped a white woman while on weekend leave from a Massachusetts prison while Dukakis was governor.

Dukakis failed to respond to the Republican attacks, and by late October the Gallup polling organization reported a "stunning turnaround" in the polls. On election day Bush became the first sitting vice president since Martin Van Buren in 1836 to be elected directly to the presidency. He won 53.4 percent of the popular vote and carried forty states with 426 electoral votes. Dukakis won only ten states and the District of Columbia for a total of 111 electoral votes and 45.6 percent of the popular vote. (One Dukakis elector in West Virginia voted for Democratic vice-presidential nominee Lloyd Bentsen.) The Democrats, however, managed to increase their margins in Congress, where they held an eighty-nine-vote advantage in the House and fifty-six of a hundred seats in the Senate (see map below).

1989: "The Year of Miracles"

In 1989, as Bush was settling into office, a Polish shipyard electrician named Lech Walesa led the Solidarity trade union movement in a series of strikes that crippled Poland's Soviet-controlled government. Reformist Soviet leader Gorbachev refused to use the military to quell the uprising, and he instructed the puppet regime to negotiate with the reformers. The result was an agreement to hold free elections in 1990—the first free elections in Poland in sixty-eight years. The seed of revolution spread rapidly to other Soviet bloc countries. In Hungary reformers adopted a new constitution, called for elections, and disbanded the Communist Party. In Czechoslovakia playwright and populist Vaclav Havel helped orchestrate a "velvet revolution" that resulted in the resignation of the Soviet-installed regime and free elections that carried Havel to the presidency. The most dramatic events were occurring in East Germany. On November 9 the Communist

The Election of 1988 As vice president under Reagan, George H. W. Bush promised to continue the peace and prosperity he helped to create. At the same time he attacked his opponent, Massachusetts Governor Michael Dukakis, for releasing prisoners on furloughs, which left them free to commit more heinous crimes. For his part, Dukakis tried to reunite the divided Democratic Party, but failed to win any key electoral states besides New York.

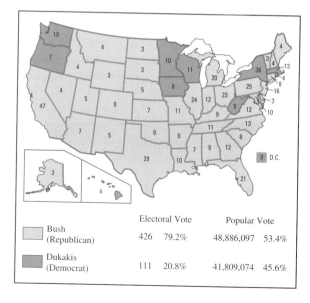

	Electoral Vote		Popular Vote	
Bush (Republican)	426	79.2%	48,886,097	53.4%
Dukakis (Democrat)	111	20.8%	41,809,074	45.6%

Party announced that residents of East Berlin were free to leave the country, rendering the Berlin Wall, the ultimate symbol of Cold War division, irrelevant. Jubilant Germans hung a banner on the wall—"Stalin Is Dead, Europe lives"—then dismantled the barrier piece by piece.

The revolutionary fervor was not confined to communist regimes in Eastern Europe, but soon swept into the Soviet Union itself. The Baltic states—Estonia, Latvia, and Lithuania—had lived under Soviet rule since 1939, when Stalin seized control as part of the Nazi–Soviet pact (see page 1016). In December 1989 the Lithuanian Communist Party formally broke ties with the Soviet Union. The following year Lithuania and Latvia declared their independence. Meanwhile, in March 1989 the Soviet Union held its first free elections since 1917. Voters turned hundreds of party officials out of office.

All these changes were too much for party hardliners in the Soviet hierarchy, who staged a coup in August 1991. With Gorbachev held under house arrest, a defiant Boris Yeltsin, the newly elected chairman of the Russian parliament, rallied protesters and faced down the powerful Russian army. Gorbachev survived the failed coup, but Yeltsin emerged as the most potent force for reform. By the end of the year Russia proclaimed its independence from Soviet control and, along with

Fall of the Berlin Wall   1989 was the year of revolutions in Europe as Poland, Romania, Czechoslovakia, and East Germany rebelled against communist rule. The most memorable act of tearing down the iron curtain came in Berlin where the wall that divided east and west came crashing down on November 9, 1989. As Berliners from both sides of the divide celebrated, people poured freely through the opening for the first time since the wall was built in 1961.   *(AP/Wide World Photos, Inc.)*

Ukraine and Byelorussia (now Belarus), formed the Commonwealth of Independent States. On Christmas Day 1991 a weary Gorbachev resigned as president of the Union of Soviet Socialist Republics that had ceased to exist.

The unraveling of the Soviet Union offered an opportunity to continue the progress in arms control that began in the final years of the Reagan administration. In 1989 Bush announced that it was time to "move beyond containment" by integrating the Soviet Union into "the community of nations." The following year NATO and the Warsaw Pact (see page 1068) agreed to the biggest weapons cut in history. The accord on conventional forces in Europe slashed Warsaw Pact weapons by more than 50 percent and NATO's by 10 percent. With the Soviet threat diminished, the Pentagon announced the largest U.S. troop cut in Europe since 1948, starting with an initial pullback of forty thousand personnel. Bush and Gorbachev signed agreements to open trade, expand cultural exchanges, and reduce chemical weapons. The two leaders signed the START I treaty, which cut their strategic nuclear forces in half—an agreement unimaginable just a few years earlier. Two years later Bush and Yeltsin came to terms on a START II agreement that called for further cuts and for the elimination of deadly multiple warhead (MIRV) intercontinental missiles by the year 2003. The Cold War was over.

The New World Order   President Bush declared that the end of the Cold War heralded a "New World Order" in which the United States was the only superpower, the rule of law must govern relations between nations, and the powerful must protect the weak. In some ways the optimism seemed justified. In a world no longer dominated by Cold War confrontations, the prospect for resolving local disputes brightened. In South Africa, U.S.-imposed economic sanctions pressured the newly elected president, F. W. de Klerk, to dismantle apartheid, by which whites had dominated the black majority for forty-two years. Along with lifting the government's ban on anti-apartheid organizations, de Klerk freed African National Conference deputy president Nelson Mandela, seventy-one, who was serving the twenty-seventh year of a life prison term. A symbol of resistance to apartheid, Mandela showed that imprisonment had not tempered his commitment to black majority rule. "Power! Power! Africa is ours!" he chanted in his first public appearance following his release. In April 1994 Mandela easily won election as South Africa's first black president.

In Latin America the end of the Cold War coincided with the demise of a number of authoritarian regimes. In Chile General Augusto Pinochet, the last military dictator in South America (see page 1193), turned over power to elected President Patricio Aylwin. In Brazil Fernando Collor de Mello took office as the first directly elected president since a 1964 military coup. In Haiti a leftist Roman Catholic priest, Father Jean-Bertrand Aristide, swept that nation's first fully free democratic election for president. Elsewhere in Latin America shaky experiments in democracy showed signs of growing stability. In Nicaragua newspaper publisher Violeta Barrios de Chamorro defeated Marxist president Daniel Ortega in a peaceful election, ending a decade of leftist Sandinista rule. In El Salvador the moderate government and opposition leaders signed a peace treaty early in 1992.

With the threat of Soviet influence in Latin America diminished, the Bush administration focused its attention on international drug sales, which the president referred to as "the gravest domestic threat facing our nation today." Though many nations were implicated in the drug trade, the administration identified Panamanian dictator General Manuel Noriega as the worst outlaw. During the 1980s American officials ignored Noriega's notorious cocaine trading because he was a CIA informer viewed as an ally in the larger battle to prevent communist infiltration. With that threat removed, American officials decided to move against him, cutting off aid and freezing Panamanian assets in the United States. When Noriega nullified the results of free elections in Panama, Bush urged the Panamanian people to overthrow him. The revolt failed to materialize, and soon after, when soldiers loyal to Noriega killed an American marine, Bush launched Operation Just Cause. On December 20, 1989, more than twenty-two thousand U.S. troops, backed by gunships and fighter planes, invaded Panama in the largest military operation since the Vietnam War. After two days of intense fighting, Noriega's resistance crumbled, and he sought asylum at the Vatican's diplomatic mission in Panama City. On January 3, 1990, he surrendered and was flown to Florida, where he faced trial for drug-related crimes and became the first former or current head of state to be convicted by an American jury.

The end of the Cold War also improved relations in the Middle East. No longer fearing Soviet influence in the region and less concerned about offending its ally Israel, the United States applied pressure on both Palestinian head Yasir Arafat and Israeli leader Yitzhak Rabin to work toward stability. Secretary of State James A. Baker III engaged in a new round of shuttle diplomacy, traveling to the Mideast eight times in 1991 to arrange negotiations in 1992. After more than a year of secret discussions, Arafat and Rabin traveled to Washington in September 1993 to sign a declaration of principles that allowed for eventual Palestinian self-rule in the Gaza Strip and the West Bank.

Only China seemed to buck the trend toward greater openness in the post–Cold War era. Bush, who had served briefly as ambassador to China under Nixon, came to office confident that he understood the Chinese leadership and could help promote closer economic ties while also encouraging the aging Chinese leadership to enact democratic reforms. His plan suffered a stunning setback in spring 1989 when the Chinese army brutally crushed a prodemocracy demonstration in Beijing's Tiananmen Square, killing an estimated four hundred to eight hundred young men and women. A wave of repression, arrests, and public executions followed. The assault, covered extensively by American television, outraged the public and exposed an underlying tension in America's attitude toward the post–Cold War world: Should the United States emphasize its moral leadership by taking action against nations that failed to live up to American standards of human rights, or should it restrict itself to more practical questions of national security?

An unusual coalition of liberals and conservatives wanted the administration to punish China for its repression by imposing economic sanctions and denying it special trading privileges that promoted economic relations. Many business groups warned that sanctions would be counterproductive, since they would alienate China, limit American influence, and allow Europeans to capture the lucrative and expanding Chinese market. Bush waffled on the question. Three days after the massacre, he suspended military sales to China and declared that normal relations could not be established until Chinese leaders "recognize the validity of the pro-democracy movement." Within weeks, however, he sent his national security adviser to China and began a gradual move toward normal relations.

War with Iraq

On August 2, 1990, elite Iraqi army troops smashed across the border of Kuwait and roared down a six-lane superhighway toward Kuwait City eighty miles away. Iraqi leader Saddam Hussein, who had just ended a bloody eight-year war with neighboring Iran, justified the invasion by claiming that Kuwait had been illegally stolen from Iraq by the British in the 1920s. The justification masked a more pressing concern, however. Hussein had nearly bankrupted his country in his war with Iran and now needed Kuwait's huge oil reserves to pay the bills.

President Bush saw the invasion as a direct challenge to U.S. leadership in the post–Cold War world. "This must be reversed," he announced after learning of the attack. His advisers spelled out how the invasion threatened American interests in the region: it would give the unpredictable Hussein control over vast quantities of valuable Kuwaiti oil reserves. Hussein could use the oil revenue to develop nuclear weapons to intimidate American allies in the region, especially Israel and Saudi Arabia. Over the next few months, in an impressive display of international diplomacy, Bush rallied world opinion against "Saddam." The United Nations Security Council passed resolutions to impose economic sanctions against Iraq in an effort to force it out of Kuwait. In November, after Hussein showed no signs of retreat, the Security Council authorized the use of force for the first time since the Korean War, giving Hussein a deadline of January 15, 1991, to pull out of Kuwait or face military action.

While rallying international opinion against Iraq, Bush confronted the difficult task of convincing the American people to go to war to expel Hussein from Kuwait. The administration faced an uphill battle. Polls showed that a majority of Americans opposed intervention; most wanted to continue to rely on economic sanctions even if they failed to prod the Iraqis out of Kuwait. In January, as the deadline for military action approached, the Senate and the House passed a resolution authorizing the use of military force (see Competing Voices, page 1297). Armed with congressional approval and bolstered by strong international support, the president started the war on January 16 with a massive and sustained air assault. On February 23, the Allies under the command of U.S. General H. Norman Schwarzkopf, launched a ground offensive that forced Iraqi forces out of Kuwait in less than one hundred hours. Only 140 U.S. troops died in the battle, while the Iraqi death toll topped 100,000. On February 27 coalition forces liberated Kuwait, and the president called off the attack, leaving a vanquished but defiant Saddam Hussein in power (see map on page 1271).

Problems on the Home Front

Ironically, Bush's success in the Gulf War may have contributed to his political problems at home, which had begun soon after he took office. With the Cold War over and with no clear foreign threat to distract them, Americans focused more attention on a stagnant economy. "We did not realize how much we had been

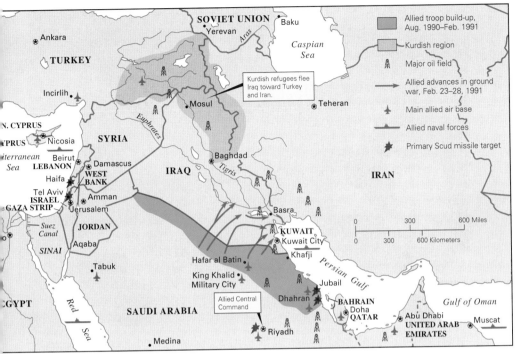

The Gulf War   On January 16, 1991, Allied planes stationed at bases across the Middle East and ships in the Persian Gulf began a six-week air assault on missile and anti-aircraft targets in Iraq, beginning the offensive known as Operation Desert Storm. On February 23, ground troops led by General H. Norman Schwarzkopf began pushing into Iraq and within three days of the ground assault's commencement Iraqi soldiers were in full retreat or surrender. The war resulted in the dismembering of the Iraqi army and the liberation of Kuwait, but left Saddam Hussein in power and did not protect the Kurds in the north.

leaning on the Berlin Wall until we tore it down," conceded one White House aide. While the president scored high marks for his adroit handling of the international scene, he never articulated a clear domestic agenda.

After only a few weeks in office, Bush angered voters and enraged conservatives by disavowing his "no new taxes" pledge. In 1990 Bush agreed to a deficit reduction compromise with congressional Democrats that included $133 billion in new taxes. Most observers agreed with the decision to raise taxes, but few were convinced that Bush learned of the need to do so only after the election. The *New York Post's* front page bellowed the reaction: "Read My Lips: I Lied."

The deficit package failed to stem the fiscal hemorrhaging. The federal deficit continued its upward spiral to $290 billion in 1992. The government was spending $200 billion per year—15 percent of all spending—to pay interest on the debt. The added spending weighed down the rest of the economy, which after seven booming years began to sputter. While the GNP increased at an anemic 2.2 percent,

Impact of War   After Iraq's invasion of Kuwait on August 2, 1990, President George H. W. Bush deployed more than 400,000 troops to Saudi Arabia in an attempt to force Iraq's withdrawal from its neighbor. Each American soldier sent to the Gulf left behind family and friends, as was the case with Army Specialist Hollie Vallance, seen here saying goodbye to her husband and seven-week-old daughter.   *(© Allen Horne, Courtesy of the Columbus Ledger, Columbus, Georgia.)*

unemployment crept upward, housing starts dropped, and consumer confidence hit new lows. By 1992 Bush's approval rating sagged to 34 percent, with fewer than 20 percent of the public approving his handling of the economy. The public clamored for the president to take decisive action to revive the ailing economy, but Bush and his advisers decided to take a hands-off approach. "I don't think it's the end of the world even if we have a recession," said Treasury Secretary Nicholas Brady. "We'll pull out of it again. No big deal."

Polls showed that Americans wanted more government involvement not only in economic matters but also in issues ranging from education to health care, but the president's hands were tied by the huge budget deficit left over from the Reagan years. Bush did sign one meaningful piece of legislation—the Americans with Disabilities Act (1990), which prohibited discrimination against the 40 million Americans who suffered from mental and physical disabilities.

Bush's handling of environmental issues underscored the difficult task he faced in trying to hold together a political coalition of moderates and conservatives during tough economic times. During the 1988 campaign Bush broke with Reagan's harsh approach to the environment, promising to be "the environmental president" who would champion tough new regulations to protect clean water and air and preserve public lands. Once in office, however, the president retreated when conservatives within the administration, led by Vice President Quayle, complained that new environmental initiatives would undermine American business competitiveness.

The debate sharpened in March 1989 when the giant oil tanker *Exxon Valdez* ran aground in Prince William Sound, Alaska, spilling 10.8 million gallons of crude oil that spoiled the pristine coastline and killed wildlife. Environmentalists called for an end to Alaskan oil drilling, but Bush disagreed, saying that the oil production was essential to meet the nation's energy needs. In the Pacific Northwest environmentalists clashed with loggers and timber companies over whether to preserve the delicate ecosystems of old-growth forest and their endangered inhabitant—the northern spotted owl. Once again Bush sided with business interests, saying that jobs and profits were a higher priority than preserving the environment. In 1992 the president attended a UN-sponsored "Earth Summit" in Rio de Janeiro, Brazil, but he refused to sign a sweeping but nonbinding resolution that would have pledged the nation's support for biodiversity. Environmentalists achieved a minor victory in 1990 when Bush signed a moderately progressive Clean Air Act, which forced gradual cutbacks on emissions from cars and power plants.

The abortion issue also complicated Bush's delicate political balancing act. In 1989 a divided Supreme Court upheld a Missouri law that restricted abortion *(Webster* v. *Reproductive Health Services)*. The law banned public facilities from performing abortions that were not necessary to save the mother's life, and the Court's decision seemed a step toward outlawing all abortions. Justice Harry Blackmun, who had written the original decision in *Roe* v. *Wade* sanctioning abortion, dissented: "The signs are evident and very ominous, and a chill wind blows." The decision, which encouraged other states to pass more restrictions on abortion, enraged many moderate Republicans. Polls showed a widening political gender gap as many women, including many Republicans, feared that more Republican judicial appointments could tip the Court's balance away from abortion rights. The justices calmed fears somewhat in 1992 when they struck down a Pennsylvania law restricting abortion on the grounds that it placed "undue burden" on women. More important, the majority stated that they were reluctant to overturn *Roe,* saying that doing so would cause "profound and unnecessary damage to the Court's legitimacy, and to the nation's commitment to the rule of law." That five-to-four decision, however, continued to underscore the precarious legal position of abortion rights.

Bush unintentionally widened the gender gap when he replaced the retiring liberal Justice Thurgood Marshall, the only African-American on the Court, with Clarence Thomas, a black conservative federal judge who had once served as head of Reagan's Equal Employment Opportunity Commission (EEOC) but was considered an undistinguished jurist. Civil rights and liberal groups howled in protest, but the nomination seemed certain until University of Oklahoma law professor Anita Hill stepped forward to charge that Thomas had sexually harassed her when he was her boss at the EEOC. Thomas denounced the televised Senate confirmation hearings as "a high-tech lynching for uppity blacks who in any way deign to think for themselves." Although many wavering senators believed Hill's testimony and voted against Thomas, his nomination survived by a fifty-two to forty-eight vote—the narrowest margin for a Supreme Court nominee in the twentieth century. But the public debate over Hill's charges raised awareness about sexual harassment in the workplace. The affair also alienated many moderate women, who were outraged by the way many senators dismissed and mocked Hill and angered by the administration's unwavering support for Thomas.

The serious social problems that plagued the nation and the president's lack of leadership came into sharp focus when riots tore through Los Angeles in April 1992. The riots commenced after a mostly white jury in a Los Angeles suburb acquitted four white police officers accused of savagely beating an African-American motorist, Rodney King, after stopping him for a traffic violation. The jury arrived at the verdict despite a videotape that showed the officers delivering numerous blows to a seemingly defenseless King. Shortly after the verdicts were announced, African-Americans in South Central Los Angeles erupted in the deadliest urban riot in over a century. By the time it ended three days later, fifty-eight people lay dead, over eight hundred buildings had been destroyed, and thousands more had been damaged or looted. The president's initial response was to blame the riots on failed liberal social programs from the 1960s. When that explanation did not convince people or reassure the nation, Bush traveled to the riot area and promised more federal aid. But for many people, the response was too little, too late.

The 1992 Presidential Campaign

Already politically vulnerable because of the struggling economy and sinking job approval, Bush had to fend off a revolt of angry conservatives, who rallied around former Reagan speechwriter Patrick Buchanan in the Republican primaries. Politically weaker than in 1988, Bush also faced a more formidable Democratic challenger in Arkansas Governor Bill Clinton. Born in 1946 in Hope, Arkansas, Clinton attended Georgetown University and went to Oxford on a Rhodes scholarship before returning to graduate from the Yale Law School. In 1978, at the age of thirty-two, he won election as governor of Arkansas. A party moderate, Clinton appealed to fellow baby boomers by casting himself as a "new Democrat" who understood the concerns of the struggling middle class. Campaigning as a cultural conservative, he professed his support for capital punishment and promised to "end welfare as we know it," to make the streets safer and the schools better, and to provide "basic health care to all Americans." For traditional Democrats he offered a message of economic populism, promising to raise taxes on the wealthy and fight to preserve popular social programs.

A charismatic personality and spellbinding speaker, Clinton emerged as the front-runner from a crowded pack of Democratic contenders. The road to the nomination, however, was strewn with questions about marital infidelity and draft dodging. His often evasive and unconvincing answers led to questions about whether Clinton possessed the strength of character to be a good president. The lingering doubts did not prevent him from winning the nomination earlier than any Democrat in more than two decades. At the party's convention in New York City, Clinton underscored the "new Democrat" theme by choosing fellow baby-boom southerner Al Gore, a senator from Tennessee, as his running mate. "There's a little Bubba in both of us," Clinton joked.

The fall race was complicated by the presence of an unpredictable third-party candidate, Texas billionaire Ross Perot. With a down-to-earth manner and a history of remarkable success in business, Perot tapped into public discontent with government and Washington by promising to balance the budget and cut the deficit. His position on most other issues remained a mystery, but by July he was leading both Clinton and Bush in the polls when he abruptly decided to leave the race. He returned just as unexpectedly in October, with only one month left, largely in the role of spoiler.

While Perot was on sabbatical from the campaign, Clinton moved to secure his followers and take the lead in the polls by focusing attention on the economy. He promised to "focus like a laser beam" on economic issues. A sign hanging in his campaign office summed up the Democratic strategy: "It's the economy, stupid." Clinton also proved an effective and unconventional campaigner, chatting with young voters on MTV, taking calls on the popular *Larry King Live* show, and playing the saxophone and discussing public policy with late-night talk show host Arsenio Hall. While Clinton climbed in the polls, Bush floundered. His greatest successes had been in dealing with Iraq and the Russians, but with the Cold War fading out of mind, the public showed little interest in foreign policy and instead directed its anger at the administration for the sluggish economy.

Voters rewarded Clinton on election night, giving him 43 percent of the popular vote, compared with 37.4 percent for Bush. Clinton's margin in the electoral college

Clinton Playing His Saxophone   Though a Yale Law School graduate and a Rhodes scholar, presidential nominee Bill Clinton was also a member of the baby boom generation, growing up listening to Elvis Presley and learning to play the saxophone. Working to increase his popularity with younger voters, Clinton appeared on MTV and on the Arsenio Hall show, where he sat in with the band for a rendition of "Heartbreak Hotel." *(AP/Wide World Photos, Inc.)*

was far more decisive. He won thirty-one states and 370 electoral votes. The public registered its disenchantment with both parties by giving Perot a bigger share of the vote—18.9 percent—than any third-party candidate since Teddy Roosevelt, who scored 27.4 percent in 1912. The Democrats retained control of both houses of Congress. Voters sent six women to the Senate and forty-eight to the House of Representatives. Observers triumphantly called 1992 "the year of the woman" (see map below).

THE CLINTON ADMINISTRATION, 1992–2000

William Jefferson Clinton, the first president born after World War II, came to office promising to experiment with policies to jump-start the economy and use government power to develop solutions to pressing social problems. Despite a number of legislative victories, he failed to fulfill many of his campaign promises, and Republicans molded public disillusion into a powerful political weapon to gain control of both houses of Congress in the 1994 congressional elections. A chastened Clinton responded by moving to the center, co-opting many Republican themes and trouncing his opponent in the 1996 presidential race. While hoping to focus most of his attention on domestic issues, Clinton faced the difficult task of readjusting American foreign policy for the post–Cold War era. An impeachment trial that grew out of a sordid affair with a White House intern tarnished Clinton's final years in office.

The Election of 1992 Despite America's victory in Operation Desert Storm, the stagnant economy affected President George H. W. Bush's chances of reelection. His broken pledge not to raise taxes made him vulnerable to attacks by Democrat Bill Clinton who pledged to work for national health care, welfare reform, and a strong economy. Dissatisfaction with Bush spilled over into the third party of H. Ross Perot who did not win any electoral votes in November, but who did gain 18.9 percent of the popular vote— the largest third party showing since the Bull Moose Party in 1912.

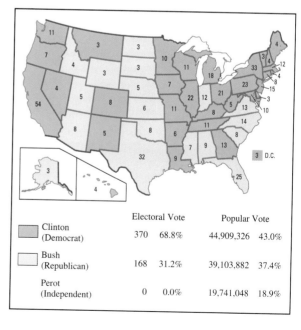

	Electoral Vote		Popular Vote	
Clinton (Democrat)	370	68.8%	44,909,326	43.0%
Bush (Republican)	168	31.2%	39,103,882	37.4%
Perot (Independent)	0	0.0%	19,741,048	18.9%

The Clinton Agenda

In February 1993 Clinton fulfilled his promise to "focus like a laser beam" on the economy by submitting an ambitious economic plan calling for a combination of spending cuts and tax increases to reduce the deficit to Congress. Both liberals and conservatives took aim at the plan. Liberals objected because it contained only one ambitious new social program—a national service corps by which college students could pay off federal education loans through community work. Conservatives opposed the tax hikes, which raised the top rate from 31 to 36 percent. After months of haggling, most Democrats fell in line with the president's proposal, and it passed the House by a one-vote margin. In an ominous warning of partisan confrontations to come, not a single House Republican voted for the Clinton program. It passed the Senate by a more comfortable margin.

Even before he submitted his economic package to Congress, Clinton created a political firestorm by proposing to lift the long-standing ban on homosexuals in the military. During the campaign Clinton had lobbied aggressively for gay votes, and once in office he moved on a number of fronts to open opportunities for homosexuals. He ended the federal policy of treating gays as security risks and invited gay activists to the White House for the first time. But his proposal to end discrimination in the military infuriated the Pentagon and aroused conservative opposition. Months of acrimonious public debate forced Clinton to retreat and agree to an unworkable "don't ask, don't tell" policy that angered both gay rights groups and conservatives. The debate over gays in the military was a political disaster for the new administration: it distracted public attention from Clinton's economic program and allowed conservatives to typecast the president as a social liberal, while the outcome disillusioned many of Clinton's liberal supporters.

After passage of his economic program, Clinton concentrated his energies on passing a complex health care proposal. In 1993 more than 37 million Americans lacked medical insurance, and millions more feared losing coverage. While coverage remained spotty, costs continued to escalate. From 1980 to 1992 Medicare and Medicaid payments jumped from $48 billion to $196 billion, consuming 14 percent of the federal budget. Shortly after the election the president asked First Lady Hillary Rodham Clinton, an accomplished lawyer with liberal leanings, to set up a health care task force. In October 1993 the administration unveiled its ambitious plan, which would guarantee Americans medical coverage and an array of preventive services. The plan proposed to limit Medicare and Medicaid payments, cap premiums, and foster competition among providers. The proposal, however, was dead on arrival on Capitol Hill, the victim of its own complexity and intense partisan wrangling.

More bad news followed the failure of the health care proposal. Congress asked a special prosecutor to investigate whether the Clintons had been involved in financial wrongdoing stemming from a bad land deal in which they invested in the 1970s. The investigation into the Whitewater development venture in northern Arkansas focused on whether the Clintons had received favorable treatment and been forgiven loans after the failure of the project. Around the same time, new reports surfaced that Arkansas state troopers procured women for Clinton when he was governor. Together, the questions over the land deal and the reports of womanizing tapped into larger public doubts about the president's character. By 1994 the news media featured more stories on Whitewater than on all facets of Clinton's domestic agenda combined.

Winning a Second Term

The failure of the health reform package, controversy over the measure to allow gays in the military, and the drumbeat of charges over Whitewater eroded public support for the Clinton presidency. After two years in office Clinton had the lowest poll ratings of any president since Watergate. Energized Republicans, led by Georgia fire-brand Newt Gingrich of the House, pounced on the helpless Democrats in the 1994 midterm elections. All three hundred Republican congressional candidates signed a ten-point "Contract with America," a political wish list polished by consultants and tested in focus groups, pledging to trim government waste, cap welfare payments, raise military spending, and lower taxes. On election day Republicans made major gains, seizing control of both houses for the first time in forty years and defeating thirty-five incumbent Democrats. "We got our butts kicked," said the chairman of the Democratic National Committee.

Clinton responded to the Republican triumph by moving to the center, co-opting Republican themes. By acting independently of both Republicans and Democrats, Clinton planned to occupy the high middle ground of American politics. Clinton's adviser, Dick Morris, called the strategy "triangulation." Clinton's first move was to accept the Republican goal of balancing the budget in ten years or less. "The era of Big Government is over," he announced in Reaganesque language. The president embraced other conservative proposals as well, including a crime bill that aimed to put a hundred thousand new police officers on the streets and stipulated manda-tory sentences for criminals convicted of felonies three times.

It was welfare reform, though, that was at the center of Clinton's new strat-egy. True to the terms of their "Contract with America," congressional Republi-cans passed the Personal Responsibility and Work Opportunity Reconciliation Act. Clinton objected to the original legislation, but later signed a bill that main-tained its central features. This 1996 welfare reform bill eliminated the federal guarantee of welfare as an entitlement, replacing it with a program that collapsed nearly forty federal programs, including Aid to Families with Dependent Chil-dren, into five block grants to the states, giving them authority to develop their own plans. The most striking provision of the new bill declared that the head of every family on assistance must work within two years, or the family would lose its benefits.

By 1996 the president's effort to rebuild public support by usurping Republican issues of welfare reform, crime, and a balanced budget had been remarkably suc-cessful. Aided by an expanding economy and declining unemployment, Clinton watched his job approval rating soar to over 60 percent—the highest rating of his presidency. Polls showed that many voters were willing to set aside concerns about Clinton's character in favor of their satisfaction with the humming economy and their general perception that the country was headed in the right direction.

Republicans chose Kansas Senator Robert Dole to challenge Clinton in the 1996 presidential contest. Dole, a seventy-three-year-old veteran of World War II and the

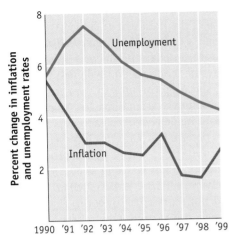

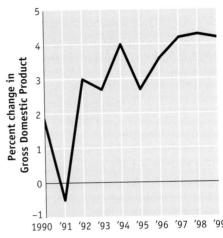

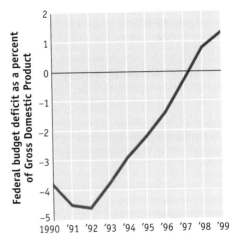

The Economic Boom of the 1990s   During the 1990s, Americans enjoyed the longest sustained period of economic growth since the end of the Second World War. Inflation remained steady, unemployment declined, and the gross domestic product rose. Beginning in 1998, the government also had a rosier economic outlook as the federal budget managed a surplus.

oldest man ever to seek the presidency, failed to excite voters. In an effort to reach out to younger voters, he chose former Buffalo Bills quarterback and ex-congressman Jack Kemp as his running mate. In the final weeks of the campaign, when all else had failed, Dole tried to exploit the "character" issue. Nothing seemed to work.

On election day Clinton became the first Democrat since Franklin Roosevelt to win a second term as president. Victories in thirty states and the District of Columbia gave him 379 electoral votes, 19 more than he had won in 1992. Dole and Jack Kemp carried fourteen states, primarily in the Deep South and the mountain states of the West, with a combined 159 electoral votes. Ross Perot, the Texas billionaire who ran on the ticket of the Reform Party, finished a distant third, drawing roughly half of the 18.9 percent he had won in 1992. "They have affirmed our cause and told us to go forward," Clinton said of the voters. But the election hardly represented a clear mandate. Clinton failed to produce coattails for other Democrats as the Republicans retained control of the House and gained a few seats in the Senate.

Impeachment

The year-long drama that consumed much of the nation's attention and led up to the trial of the president in January 1999 centered on an affair between Clinton and former White House intern Monica Lewinsky. When charges surfaced, a defiant president denied having had sexual relations with "that woman." After he made the same denials in a civil case and to a grand jury, Kenneth Starr, the special prosecutor in the case, recommended that the president be impeached and removed from office for "high crimes and misdemeanors." To support his conclusion, he delivered a steamy report to the House detailing the affair and offering eleven potential grounds for impeachment.

Clinton's attorneys raised a number of objections to the whole proceeding. Having an affair with an intern and then lying about it was wrong, they contended, but it did not rise to the level of an impeachable offense. Unlike Richard Nixon's actions in Watergate, Clinton's behavior did not represent a threat to the institutions of government. Moreover, they charged, the issue was being pushed by a highly partisan special prosecutor who seemed driven to destroy the president. House Republicans, however, were determined to press forward. After weeks of public hearings, the Judiciary Committee voted to send formal charges to the House, which in turn approved two counts—perjury and obstruction of justice—and sent them on to the Senate for trial.

In 1999 the Senate rang in the New Year by putting the president on trial. Over the next few weeks, the senators listened to often repetitive charges and countercharges by the House prosecutors (who were also called managers) and the White House defense team. The thirteen prosecutors, all Republicans, had to convince sixty-seven of one hundred senators both that the president's offenses were criminal and that they merited his removal from office. When the final votes were counted, the Senate failed to muster a majority on either count and fell far short of the constitutionally mandated two-thirds needed to convict the president.

In the end everyone came out of the affair with tarnished reputations. The president enjoyed high job approval ratings throughout the investigation, but the public gave him low marks for honesty and integrity. The GOP's pugnacious, partisan pursuit of impeachment backfired. In the 1998 congressional elections, the party not holding the White House lost seats in the House for only the second time in the century. The angry recriminations that followed led to the resignation of Republican Speaker Newt Gingrich. Republicans also appeared hypocritical when reports showed that some who condemned Clinton's behavior had checkered pasts of their own. Louisiana's Robert Livingston, for example, a harsh critic of the president's behavior whom Republicans chose to succeed Gingrich as House Speaker, resigned his seat after confessing that he had "on occasion strayed from my marriage."

The 2000 Presidential Election

Prosperity and impeachment provided the backdrop to the first presidential election of the new millennium. The Democrats rallied around Vice President Al Gore, who promised to sustain the Clinton-era economic growth. In August, at the party's convention in Los Angeles, Gore launched his "prosperity and progress" campaign, promising increased federal spending on health care, social security, and education. Striking a populist pose, he promised middle-class taxpayers that he would fight for "the people" and against "the powerful" special interests. Walking a political tightrope, Gore clung to Clinton's success while distancing himself from the president's scandals. "I stand here tonight as my own man," he told cheering delegates. As his running mate, Gore selected Joseph Lieberman, a centrist senator from Connecticut, who became the first Jewish-American vice presidential candidate nominated by a major party.

Eager to win back the White House, Republican leaders threw their support and money behind Texas Governor George W. Bush, the oldest son of the former president. After stumbling in the primaries against Vietnam War hero Senator John McCain, Bush regained his footing and captured his party's nomination. With federal coffers overflowing with revenue, Bush promised the nation "prosperity with a purpose." Calling for a "compassionate conservatism," the Republican nominee solidified his conservative base by advocating a massive tax cut while at the same time reaching out to independents with pledges to fund increased social spending for education and health care. Above all, he vowed to return honor and dignity to the White House. Ahead in the polls and confident of victory, Bush chose the uncharismatic former defense secretary Richard Cheney as his running mate.

Bush watched his once-sizable lead in the polls evaporate through the summer and fall. While Gore and Bush battled each other, consumer advocate Ralph Nader, running on the Green Party platform, mocked both candidates. Nader relished the role of spoiler, threatening to siphon enough votes in key states—California, Michigan, Oregon, and Washington—to deny Gore a victory. On election night Gore clung to a small margin in the popular vote, but with Florida and its crucial twenty-five electoral votes too close to call, the election remained deadlocked. After a series of counts and recounts, Florida's secretary of state certified Bush the winner on November 27—more than two weeks after the election. But the election did not end there. Gore contested the results, claiming that many ballots remained uncounted or were improperly counted, effectively disenfranchising thousands of voters. Republicans accused Gore of trying to steal the election; Democrats attacked the Republicans for thwarting the "will of the people." The nation braced for a constitutional crisis. On December 12, after weeks of legal maneuvering, a deeply divided Supreme Court ended the historic impasse. In a controversial five-to-four ruling in the case of *Bush* v. *Gore,* the justices blocked further manual recounts, which effectively named George Bush the winner. Bush became only the fourth president, and the first since 1888, to take office having lost the popular vote.

The election revealed that unprecedented prosperity had failed to mute deep social divisions in America. The public remained deeply troubled by the election outcome; the winner lacked a clear mandate; the Senate split fifty-fifty; and Republicans held only a razor-thin majority in the House. Included among the new class of senators was New York's Hillary Rodham Clinton, who became the only First Lady in history to seek and win elective office. Analysis of voting results revealed a deeply divided nation. By region Democrats did well in urban areas; Republicans won majorities in suburban and rural areas. By race African-Americans gave 95 percent of their votes to Gore; whites preferred Bush. By gender, women favored Democrats; men leaned toward the Republicans. Finally, by religion regular churchgoers voted Republican; the less religious supported the Democrats.

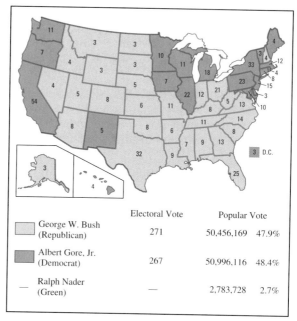

	Electoral Vote	Popular Vote	
George W. Bush (Republican)	271	50,456,169	47.9%
Albert Gore, Jr. (Democrat)	267	50,996,116	48.4%
Ralph Nader (Green)	—	2,783,728	2.7%

The Election of 2000   Early on the evening of the election (November 7), most of the major media outlets proclaimed Al Gore the winner in Florida, but as the night wore on and votes from the panhandle of the state trickled in, journalists recanted. By morning, George Bush's lead in Florida was so minimal that Gore did not publicly concede that he had lost that state's 25 electoral votes, and thereby the election. Questions concerning Florida ballots led to a month-long debate over whether the disputed ballots should be counted by hand, leaving the fate of the election undecided. The Supreme Court's decision on December 12 forced Gore to accept defeat, despite the fact that he had won the majority of popular votes.

GLOBALIZATION AND ITS DISCONTENTS

As the first president elected after the end of the Cold War, Clinton faced a variety of new and complex questions. As the only remaining superpower, what relationship should the United States have to the rest of the world? How would the communications revolution and the rise of the Internet change the way Americans viewed the world and their place in it? Many Americans celebrated the end of the Cold War, viewing it as a victory for the American ideals of freedom and democracy. But how would the nation define its vital interests in the post–Cold War era?

The Communications Revolution   Changes in communications spearheaded the emergence of the global economy in the 1990s. The most dramatic development was the widespread use of the Internet. Scientists launched the first phase of the computer revolution in 1946 when they turned the switch to start up the mammoth Electronic Numerical Integrator and Calculator (ENIAC). The mainframe computer weighed thirty tons, filled an enormous room at the University of Pennsylvania, consumed 150,000 watts of power, and used eighteen thousand vacuum tubes. The machine required so much power that it was rumored that the lights in the city of Philadelphia dimmed when the scientists turned it on. Over the next twenty years business adopted mainframe computers to handle basic tasks such as automating payroll, billing, and inventory controls.

In the 1970s a diverse collection of tinkerers working in garages in California's San Francisco Bay area were responsible for the second phase of the computing revolution—the birth of the personal computer (PC). In 1971 a small Silicon Valley company called Intel created the first microprocessor, an integrated circuit that put the power of a mainframe on a single chip. The microchip was to the modern information economy what the combustion engine was to the earlier industrialization of society. In 1977 a young entrepreneur, Steve Wozniak, used the chip to assemble the first Apple I computer in his garage. His invention would become the prototype of every desktop machine.

The shift from the mainframe to the PC during the 1980s was made possible by tremendous advances in technology. For example, Intel built its Pentium microprocessor on a piece of silicon the size of a thumbnail. Two decades of steady increases in the capacity of microprocessors drove down prices and put tremendous computing power in the hands of the average citizen. By the mid-1990s more than 90 percent of all businesses in the United States relied on personal computers for essential functions. More than one-third of families had a PC at home. In 1995, for the first time, the amount of money spent on PCs exceeded that spent on televisions.

The third phase of the computer revolution began with the birth of the Internet. Founded in the late 1960s by Defense Department scientists trying to develop a decentralized communications system, the Internet created a set of standards, or protocols, that enabled thousands of independent computer networks to communicate. The real explosion in Internet use took place during the early 1990s with the development of the World Wide Web, whereby almost any user with a telephone line and a modem could log on to a worldwide computer communications network. By 1999 between 40 and 60 million people worldwide were using the Internet annually, and those numbers were doubling almost every year.

The Web helped break down cultural and geographic borders by creating virtual communities of shared interests. E-mail emerged as the most visible and commonly used feature of the new information society. By 1999 Americans sent 2.2 billion e-mail messages a day, compared with 293 million pieces of first-class mail. People from all over the globe joined together in virtual town halls to discuss issues of mutual interest. Teenagers in San Diego could discuss music with peers in Boston and London; an AIDS patient in San Francisco could share treatment ideas with doctors in New York and Paris.

The information revolution was the cornerstone of American prosperity during the 1990s, accounting for 45 percent of industrial growth. From 1987 to 1994 the U.S. software industry grew 117 percent in real terms, while the rest of the economy grew only 17 percent. By the end of the decade computer companies based in and around the Silicon Valley possessed a market value of $450 billion. By comparison,

"Wiring" the Classroom   The computer revolution changed how Americans did almost everything, including how students learned. College classrooms became interactive, often linking students to other classrooms and teachers—not to mention other libraries, museums, and countless educational resources—across the country and around the world. In this cyber-lecture hall, Stanford students recline on beanbag chairs with their own laptop computers while a professor guides them on a projected computer screen.   *(William Mercer McLeod.)*

the auto companies and suppliers of Detroit—the cornerstone of America's previous Industrial Revolution—were worth about $100 billion. The U.S. software industry accounted for three-fourths of the world market, and nine of the world's ten biggest software companies were located in the United States.

By the end of the decade the gross domestic product (GDP), discounted for inflation, was growing at an annual rate of 4 percent, and unemployment had fallen to a quarter-century low of 4.7 percent. Wall Street was the most visible sign of the new prosperity. Between 1992 and 1998 the Dow Jones Industrial Average increased fourfold. The New York and NASDAQ stock exchanges added over $4 trillion in value—the largest single accumulation of wealth in history. With the tide rising rapidly for more than a decade, stock assets accounted for a larger share of household wealth than ever before: 24.2 percent in mid-1998.

The New Global Marketplace

The new technologies were a product of more open markets and reduced regulation. In 1990, $50 billion of private capital flowed into "emerging markets." By 1996 that figure had swelled to $336 billion. The Clinton administration made the promotion of open markets a centerpiece of its approach to the world. The president described the United States as "a big corporation competing in the global marketplace." In 1994 Clinton fought a tough legislative battle to win congressional approval of the North American Free Trade Agreement (NAFTA) negotiated during the Bush presidency. The agreement gradually abolished nearly all trade barriers between the United States, Mexico, and Canada. Later that year Clinton won another key free trade battle when the administration convinced Congress to approve the General Agreement on Tariffs and Trade (GATT), which allowed the United States to participate in a new worldwide trade agreement that would reduce tariffs over ten years.

While fighting for free trade in the hemisphere, the administration fought to open new markets to American goods. The president created a new agency—the National Economic Council—to coordinate domestic and foreign economic policies. In 1994 the United States made its peace with Vietnam by lifting its trade embargo and normalizing relations. American companies, which had been barred from doing business in Southeast Asia, rushed into the country. Within hours of the announcement Pepsi tried to get a jump-start on its arch-rival Coke by distributing over forty thousand free cans of its soft drink to the Vietnamese. During the 1992 campaign Clinton had criticized Bush for not punishing China for its human rights violations. Once in office, however, the president changed his tune. Emphasizing the importance of China as a trading partner, Clinton approved China's most favored nation status, which gave it the same privileges as America's closest allies, despite that nation's continued crackdown on dissent.

The 1990s also witnessed a trend toward globalization in culture. By 1996 international sales of American software and entertainment products totaled $60.2 billion, more than any other industry. The explosion in sales was spurred by the collapse of the Iron Curtain, rising prosperity, and the proliferation of TV sets, VCRs, stereos, personal computers, and satellite dishes. American corporations moved aggressively to tap into the new markets. The Blockbuster Entertainment Corporation video chain opened two thousand outlets in twenty-six foreign countries during the decade; Tower Records operated seventy stores in fifteen countries.

Foreigners were not only viewing and listening to U.S. culture; they also were eating American food, reading U.S. magazines, and wearing designer clothes produced in America. *Reader's Digest* circulated in nineteen languages; its forty-eight international editions, with a combined circulation of 28 million, dwarfed its U.S. circulation of 14.7 million. *Cosmopolitan* billed itself as the world's best-selling women's magazine, with international sales of 4.5 million from thirty-six foreign editions. McDonald's restaurants were opening at a rate of six a day around the world. In 1995 McDonald's served 30 million customers a day at twenty thousand restaurants in over a hundred countries. American fashion—baggy jeans and baseball caps—became the global teenage uniform. Globalization, an observer noted, has an "American face: It wears Mickey Mouse ears, it eats Big Macs, it drinks Coke or Pepsi and it does its computing on an IBM or Apple laptop, using Windows 98, with an Intel Pentium II processor and a network link from Cisco Systems."

The New Internationalism

The new global marketplace forced policymakers to rethink America's strategic interests in the world. For all of its peril, the Cold War had provided policymakers with a framework, though often a narrow one, for interpreting world events and for calculating the national interest. The United States had a grand concept—containment—to guide its approach to the world. The United States emerged from the Cold War as the world's only superpower, but whether the nation was prepared to bear the new burdens of internationalism remained unclear.

Although it lacked a clear organizing doctrine, the Clinton administration flexed American military muscle in a number of world hot spots. As the nexus of a thriving global economy, the United States assumed the role of guaranteeing stability, opening markets, and maintaining the peace. "What's the point of having this superb military that you're always talking about if we can't use it?" Secretary of State Madeline Albright asked General Colin Powell.

In the waning days of his administration, President Bush had sent the military on a humanitarian mission to help distribute food to starving Somalis. In October 1993 eighteen U.S. Army Rangers died in a bloody firefight in Somalia after President Clinton expanded their role to capture a powerful local warlord. A horrified nation watched television video of an American soldier being dragged through the streets of Mogadishu to the cheers of local crowds. The administration used the threat of military force more successfully closer to home in Haiti, where it forced the military rulers to allow the democratically elected government to return to power.

The most dramatic use of force took place in the Balkans, where the former Yugoslavia provinces of Slovenia, Croatia, and Bosnia-Herzegovina proclaimed their independence. The move infuriated the Serb-dominated federal government in Belgrade, headed by President Slobodan Milosevic. Determined to create a "Greater Serbia," Milosevic launched military attacks against Croats and Muslims living in areas dominated by ethnic Serbs. In Bosnia-Herzegovina Serbs shelled the capital of Sarejevo and murdered, raped, and imprisoned Muslims in a vicious campaign of "ethnic cleansing." By the end of 1992 more than 150,000 people had died. In 1995, under heavy pressure from the United States, the presidents of Bosnia, Croatia, and Serbia signed a peace agreement that solved territorial differences and brought an end to hostilities. As part of the agreement, Clinton committed American troops to Bosnia as members of a multinational peacekeeping force.

Boxed in by NATO troops in Bosnia, Milosevic turned his war machine against the province of Kosovo, where ethnic Albanians were struggling for independence. When Serb troops embarked on another campaign of "ethnic cleansing" in Kosovo, NATO tried to negotiate a peaceful settlement. But the Serbs remained defiant, refusing to sign the treaty and stepping up their campaign against innocent civilians. In March 1999 the United States and the NATO allies decided to use force to challenge the Serbs. In the clearest statement of American policy in the region, President Clinton told a skeptical public that Kosovo represented a vital interest that

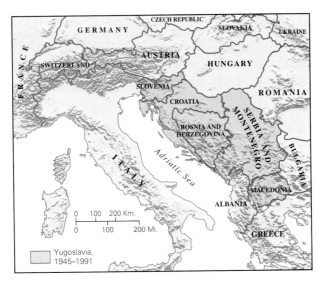

Division of Yugoslavia By 1990, Yugoslavia suffered from a heavy foreign debt, inflation, and unemployment, but nothing was more divisive than the growing nationalism and ethnic conflict long suppressed by communist dictators. When Serbian leaders blocked the election of a Croatian to the federal presidency in June 1991, Croatia declared its independence, followed by Macedonia, Slovenia, and Bosnia-Herzegovina. Bosnia immediately exploded into ethnic violence as Muslims, Croats, and Serbs sought to purge the country of each other. Montenegro and Serbia joined together in April 1992, under Serbian Slobodan Milosevic, who used his military to support ethnic cleansing and attempted to force the breakaway nations into accepting a reunified Yugoslavia, actions which led to international intervention.

the United States had to defend. It formed, he said, part of "the great battle between the forces of integration and the forces of disintegration; the forces of globalism versus tribalism; of oppression against empowerment."

Within hours U.S. warplanes, backed by cruise missiles and aircraft from other NATO allies, initiated a massive bombing campaign against the Serbs in Kosovo and Serbia itself. In May, after eighty days of intense bombardment that decimated his army and destroyed his country's fragile infrastructure, Milosevic gave in to NATO demands and withdrew his forces from Kosovo.

In attempting to define American national interests in the post–Cold War world the Clinton administration was forced to revisit the lingering threat posed by Saddam Hussein. Following Hussein's crushing defeat at the hands of the Allies in 1991, the Bush administration had assumed that opposition forces would mobilize to overthrow him. Instead, the cagey leader emerged from defeat as powerful as ever, crushing potential adversaries, threatening to destabilize the region, and playing a game of cat and mouse with UN inspectors assigned to root out his secret stockpiles of chemical and nuclear weapons. When Hussein made threatening moves toward Kuwait in 1994, the Clinton administration deployed fifty-four thousand troops and more warplanes to the Gulf. Two years later U.S. air units

struck Iraqi missile targets when Iraqi troops intensified their anti-insurgent operations in the northern part of the country. As Hussein grew more intransigent, the
U.S. position hardened. In December 1998 the United States and Britain launched
the largest bombardment of Iraq since the end of the Gulf War, unleashing cruise
missiles as well as fighters and bombers. The U.S. military declared the attack a success, but Hussein remained defiant.

Advances in military technology contributed to America's overwhelming military power. In just the few years since the end of the Gulf War, the air force had
developed a new generation of two thousand pound smart bombs, carried on B-2
stealth planes, which were guided to their target with deadly accuracy by satellite
technology. During the Gulf War only 9 percent of bombs were precision-guided. In
the Balkans over 60 percent were.

Globalization and Its Critics

In December 1999 thousands of protestors took to the
streets of Seattle, Washington, to disrupt the meeting of
the World Trade Organization. Vandals smashed the windows of multinational corporations—Starbucks, McDon-
ald's, and Old Navy. The size and anger of the crowd caught officials off-guard.
"How," asked the *Seattle Times*, "in a time of unprecedented economic growth,
could so many people be so angry about an organization designed to foster even
more prosperity?" The answer was that a global economy that allowed vast
amounts of capital to move around the globe with the click of a mouse and helped
sustain Clinton-era prosperity also produced considerable instability and hardship,
especially for unskilled workers.

The 1990s witnessed an increase in the number of workers who had been displaced from their former jobs. In the United States, at a time of low unemployment,
almost 30 percent of those employed were not in regular full-time jobs. Many
worked as day laborers, held temporary jobs, or were independent contractors. The
share of workers employed by agencies that supply temporary workers doubled
between 1989 and 1997. The vast majority of these workers were married women.
One estimate for 1995 placed the total number of contingent workers (part-time,
temporary, and contract workers) at close to 35 million, representing 28 percent of
the civilian labor force. Workers who lacked the education to adapt to the new
global economy fared worst. Salaries for college graduates, especially those with
training in computer technology, soared, while high school dropouts saw their
income drop by 22 percent between 1979 and 1993.

Despite low interest rates and strong job growth, the number of individuals filing for bankruptcy reached 1.3 million in 1998, up an astonishing 93 percent during the decade. Roughly one out of every seventy-five households filed for personal
bankruptcy in 1998. The reason? Especially among low-income households, the
desire for new consumer products outpaced income, encouraged by credit card
companies that begged people to use their cards.

Globalization also widened the gap between the haves and have-nots in the
world economy. North America, the European Union, and Japan accounted for
nearly 75 percent of all investment capital and 65 percent of world exports and
global gross domestic product (GDP). As the historian David Reynolds has pointed

out, two-thirds of the world's population accounted for only one-fifth of world trade and generated about 25 percent of GDP. Many places in the world also remained untouched by the communications revolution. In 1995 India averaged one phone line for every hundred people. While Americans wired their homes for cable television and Internet access, fewer than half the homes in India and Indonesia were wired for electricity.

There were limits to the power of capitalism to transform repressive governments. Old trouble spots like the Middle East proved to be immune to economic incentives. In some countries economic assistance and the opening of markets failed to produce the expected reforms. Russia received enormous sums of international aid but refused to phase out arms shipments to rogue nations. Many Third World nations viewed globalization as a rich country's game with rules rigged to favor industrialized nations.

At home opponents to globalization forged an unusual alliance of conservatives worried about the loss of American sovereignty and liberals concerned about the loss of high-paying jobs as businesses moved to take advantage of cheap Third World labor. "The sucking sound you hear is all the jobs heading south of the border," declared vanquished 1992 presidential candidate Ross Perot. They were joined by environmentalists and human rights activists who charged that American laws protecting workers and the environment would not be extended abroad. The coalition mobilized noisy protestors and organized opposition in Congress, which blocked Clinton's efforts to expand free trade to Africa and the Caribbean.

Global Terror

During the 1990s America's global dominance produced a backlash among Islamic fundamentalists who opposed continued U.S. military presence in the Middle East and rejected what they viewed as the corrupting influence of Western culture. The Islamic world was large and diverse, encompassing more than 1.2 billion Muslims living in sixty countries. A small number of militants organized a campaign of terror against the symbols of American military and economic power.

In February 1993 five people died and more than one thousand were injured when a bomb exploded in New York City's World Trade Center. Federal agents traced the bombing to a group of radical Muslims in New York. The same group, it turned out, planned to blow up other New York landmarks, including the United Nations headquarters and the George Washington Bridge. American targets outside the United Sates also found themselves vulnerable to attack. In 1996 a truck bomb exploded next to a military barracks in Saudi Arabia, killing nineteen U.S. servicemen. Two years later simultaneous bombs exploded in a crowded street in Nairobi, Kenya, and 450 miles away in front of the U.S. embassy in Tanzania. The bombs, said *Newsweek*, offered a dramatic but simple message: "don't forget the world's superpower still has enemies, secret, violent and determined."

The chief suspect in these bombings was an extremist Saudi millionaire, Osama bin Laden, who called on Muslims to declare war against Americans. Crafting a public image in the Islamic world as the leader of a religious struggle on behalf of the poor and the dispossessed, bin Laden led a worldwide network of supporters known in Arabic as *al Qaeda* ("the base"). Dubbed "Terror, Inc.," *al Qaeda* lacked a clear hierarchy with no lieutenants or generals, but maintained the sort of discipline found in well-trained armies. "It's a completely new phenomenon," said a British intelligence official. "You could call it disorganized-organized terrorism."

Ironically, the United States had supported bin Laden during the 1980s when both were fighting to expel the Soviet Union from Afghanistan. The CIA spent nearly $500 million a year to arm and train the Afghan and foreign rebels who ultimately forced the Soviets to withdraw. The United States considered its support of the insurgents one of the most successful examples of counterterrorism. But in a classic case of "blowback," the victory came back to haunt America. With the fall of the Soviet Union, many of the radical Arab rebels turned their jihad, or "holy war," against their former patron, the United States. "This is an insane instance of the chickens coming home to roost," said one U.S. diplomat in neighboring Pakistan.

In 1990, when the United States sent troops to Saudi Arabia during the Gulf War, bin Laden denounced the "occupation" of the Arab Holy Land by "American crusader forces," which he described as "the latest and greatest aggression" against the Islamic world since the death of the prophet Muhammad in 632. In the Sudan bin Laden financed several terrorist training camps and orchestrated attacks on American interests, including the 1993 attack on the World Trade Center. By 1996 he was in Afghanistan, where he provided financial support to the radical Taliban leaders who were fighting against the more moderate Northern Alliance for control of the capital of Kabul.

The United States responded to the attacks by bombing training camps in Afghanistan and a factory in Sudan that was suspected of producing chemical weapons. The Clinton administration warned Afghanistan's Taliban government that it risked further retaliation if it continued to give safe haven to bin Laden. The Taliban refused to turn him over, and the *al Qaeda* network continued its destructive ways. In October 2000 the USS *Cole*, a destroyer making a refueling stop in Yemen, was nearly sunk when a small boat loaded with explosives slammed into its side. "The destroyer represented the capital of the West," bin Laden said, "and the small boat represented Mohammed."

Not all terrorists were foreign extremists. Alienated Americans were among the most violent and determined enemies of the U.S. government. On April 19, 1995, Gulf War veteran Timothy McVeigh parked a rented truck packed with a mixture of ammonium nitrate and fuel oil in front of the Alfred P. Murrah Federal Building in Oklahoma City. At 9:02 A.M. the bomb exploded, and the blue-orange fireball ripped through the building, collapsing all nine floors on the building's north side. The blast killed 168 people, including 19 children. Prosecutors in the case disclosed that McVeigh was motivated by a paranoid hatred of the U.S. government.

SOCIAL TENSIONS IN THE NINETIES

During the 1990s the struggle over American identity found expression in popular culture and in the continuing debate about race. The huge increase in the number of new media outlets encouraged television executives to use sex and violence to attract audiences. The move produced an intense debate about popular culture's responsibility for the decline of traditional values and for a rash of school

Oklahoma City Memorial On the five-year anniversary of the day Timothy McVeigh detonated a bomb in front of the Alfred P. Murrah Federal Building, the Oklahoma City Memorial was dedicated on the site of the tragedy. The memorial includes a reflecting pool, a tree that survived the blast, and a museum dedicated to understanding terrorism. The most moving scene at the memorial is that of the 168 empty chairs, each inscribed with the name of a victim, which cover the ground where the building once stood. *(Steve Liss/TimeLife Pictures/Getty Images.)*

violence. The debate was intensified by the emergence of new musical tastes such as hip-hop. At the same time, the nation engaged in an angry debate over race that found expression in the public reaction to the sensational murder trial of former football great O. J. Simpson. The ongoing controversy over affirmation action, however, obscured the growing complexity of racial identity in America.

Sex, Violence, and the Debate over Popular Culture

Since the television networks needed to reach the broadest possible audience, they often tried to avoid controversial issues that would alienate potential viewers. The three major networks, which accounted for 90 percent of prime-time viewing in the 1970s, watched their audience share dip to 47 percent in 1998. By that time more than 75 percent of U.S. households received dozens of channels via cable or satellite dishes. The technology allowed new networks—Fox, CNN, the WB—to compete with the majors for prime-time ratings. In an effort to attract viewers, the three major networks relaxed rules limiting the airing of explicit sex and violence. At the same time, the courts placed severe limits on the ability of the Federal Communications Commission (FCC) to regulate shows that aired after 8:00 P.M.

The scramble for viewers and the looser regulations gave adventurous producers the opportunity to experiment with different themes and ideas. The *Ellen DeGeneres Show* featured an episode in which its central character, a lesbian, "came out" of the closet. ABC executives slapped *Ellen* with a parental warning label and eventually canceled the show because of poor ratings. But by the end of the decade more than a half-dozen prime-time shows featured gay characters. Television also attempted to tackle controversial social issues ranging from spousal abuse to teen pregnancy. The star of NBC's *The John Larroquette Show* played a recovering alcoholic; *Beverly Hills, 90210* featured a character dealing with drug addiction; an episode of *Murder One* dealt with three women who were raped by their doctor. Issues featured on the evening news one week turned up the next as plots in drama series like *NYPD Blue* and *The Practice*.

The most common competitive approach, however, was to lure in viewers with sex and violence. One study found that a sexual act or reference occurred every four minutes on average during prime time. *Dawson's Creek*, a popular weekly TV drama about a group of teenagers in the fictional small town of Capeside, Massachusetts, made recurring themes out of teenage sex and parental adultery. Daytime television was dominated by racy talk shows on which guests openly described their sex lives and family feuds. HBO's *Sex in the City* followed the lives of four young women who openly discussed every aspect of their sexual desires and habits.

Many Americans reacted in horror, arguing that mass culture was responsible for producing a generation of "selfish, dishonest, sexually promiscuous, and violent" children. A 1996 poll showed that two-thirds of the public believed that TV shows contributed to social problems like violence, divorce, teen pregnancy, and the decline of family values. A rash of school shootings in 1998 and 1999 intensified the public debate. The most deadly attack took place in April 1999 at Columbine High School in Littleton, Colorado. During the final week of classes, two disgruntled and heavily armed students killed twelve classmates and a popular teacher and planted thirty pipe bombs and other explosives before taking their own lives. Polls showed that a majority of Americans held Hollywood and television executives "at least partially" to blame for the killings, claiming that they helped create a culture that made violence acceptable. A minority found fault with the nation's lax gun laws, which allowed young people easy access to powerful weapons.

Hip-Hop Nation

Parents also worried about the appeal of new musical styles, especially hip-hop, among the young. Created by black artists on the mean streets of New York and Los Angeles, hip-hop used repetitive samples of musical tracks as background for the rhythmic poetry of rap singers. "We're marketing black culture to white people," claimed rap artist Doctor Dre. In the past African-American artists had softened their message to appeal to mainstream America. Hip-hop took a different approach, accentuating race and highlighting issues of the urban underclass. "Forget about watering down," claimed the cofounder of the group Public Enemy. "I think there's dehydration. Not only are we not going to add water, we're going to take water out." In 1998 rap surpassed country music as the nation's top selling format. "Hip-hop is the rebellious voice of the youth," boasted rapper Jay-Z. "It's what people want to hear."

By the end of the decade suburban whites purchased more than 70 percent of hip-hop albums.

Hip-hop was not only popular; it was also controversial. The glorification of violence, the relentless promotion of sex, and the derogatory treatment of homosexuals and women appealed to many suburban white youths, but it angered parents, the police, and many civic-minded groups. Police organizations complained about the song "Cop Killer," which included the lyrics "I'm 'bout to bust some shots off/I'm 'bout to dust some cops off" and a chant, "Die, Die, Die Pig, Die!"

Not all hip-hop artists promoted sex and violence. Artists such as DMX and Master P avoided controversy by writing songs that examined the pathologies of the black community but avoided encouraging social activism. Madison Avenue and Hollywood tried to tame hip-hop, making it less rebellious. Hollywood featured hip-hop artists Ice Cube, Queen Latifah, and Will Smith in movie releases. Designer Tommy Hilfiger turned inner-city clothing styles—oversized shirts and baggy, drooping pants—into a billion-dollar business, and advertising firms used a toned-down version of rap to sell a number of products to young people.

The Many Shades of Color in America

Sustained prosperity failed to bride the gap between the races. The disparity in world-views between blacks and whites became clear during the murder trial of former star football player O. J. Simpson, an African-American, who was charged in the 1994 murder of his ex-wife Nicole Brown Simpson and a friend, Ronald Goldman, at her posh Beverly Hills home. The ensuing televised trail, which lasted for nine months, transfixed the public, breathing new life into struggling cable news shows and tabloid newspapers desperate to attract an audience.

Most experts found the evidence against Simpson overwhelming. The jury of nine blacks, two whites, and one Hispanic disagreed. After only a few hours of deliberation, they delivered a verdict of not guilty on all counts. Polls showed that blacks and whites looked at the case through race-tinted glasses. By large majorities African-Americans believed in Simpson's innocence, convinced that the American justice system intentionally discriminated against minorities and that rogue cops often tilted the hand of justice. Their distrust of the police was so intense that even blacks who felt that Simpson was guilty believed that much of the evidence was tainted. "They framed a guilty man," observed one writer. Nearly 75 percent of whites rejected the suggestion that race played a role in the investigation and prosecution and assumed Simpson's guilt. Perhaps the American system of justice was the final victim of the trial. Blacks and whites seemed to agree on one thing: there was a different justice for those who have money and those who do not.

The racial divide exposed by the Simpson case revealed itself in the continuing controversy over affirmative action. In November 1996 California voters, by a 54 to 46 percent margin, passed Proposition 209, a ballot initiative that banned any preference based on race and sex in determining college admissions, contracting, and employment by the state. Men overwhelmingly supported the initiative (61 to 39 percent) while women disapproved (52 to 48 percent). Blacks and Latinos opposed it in large numbers.

At the same time Hispanics and Asians were dramatically altering a nation that had defined race in terms of black and white. Fueled by massive immigration and high birthrates, the nation's Hispanic population jumped by 38 percent during the decade, from 22.4 million to 35.3 million, while the overall population increased by only 9 percent. Demographers were predicting that Latinos would become the nation's largest minority by 2005, making up 25 percent of the U.S. population.

By 2000 Asian-American made up only 4 percent of the population, but they represented 5.4 percent of all college students, making them the only nonwhite group whose percentage of students was above its proportion of the national population. One in four undergraduates at Stanford was Asian; and one in five at Harvard, Northwestern, and the University of Pennsylvania. In California, where nearly 40 percent of Asians lived, they were the largest minority group among undergraduates at Berkeley, University of California at Los Angeles (UCLA), and UC Riverside. At many of these universities, Asian clubs organized around race rather than ethnicity. At UCLA, for example, about half of the sixty-five Asian-American student organizations were pan-Asian.

Although they shared a common identity as minorities in America, blacks, Latinos, and Asians did not always agree on a common agenda. They collaborated on mutual interests, such as defending affirmative action, fighting against police brutality, and seeking more government spending on education. In 1999 the National Latino Media Council, the NAACP, American Indians in Films and Television, and the National Asian-Pacific American Media united to demand greater minority representation in the major TV networks' programs. But African-Americans often opposed the efforts of Latinos to receive tax breaks for minority-owned businesses and or federal money to help students from disadvantaged backgrounds attend college. Some blacks joined whites in opposing immigration out of fear that immigrants would take away citizens' jobs. In the 1980s organized labor and segments of the black community supported tough immigration laws intended to reduce the influx of legal Hispanic immigrants. In 1994 a narrow majority of black voters in California supported Proposition 187, which would have barred any sort of state assistance to illegal aliens. Many Hispanic leaders, in turn, complained that blacks were overrepresented in the federal government, where they made up 17 percent of the civil work force, compared to 6 percent for Hispanics.

CONCLUSION

In 1988 George H. W. Bush won the presidency by promising to continue Reagan's conservative experiment. Following the break-up of the Soviet Union, however, Bush confronted a very different world both at home and abroad. The public applauded his handling of the Gulf War, the first major foreign policy crisis of the post–Cold war era. But Bush failed to appreciate that with the nation's mortal enemy gone, Americans' interest, and their expectations of government, had shifted toward solving problems closer to home. With the economy sputtering, voters in 1992 ignored Bush's foreign policy success and elected his Democratic opponent, Bill Clinton, who promised to focus like a "laser beam" on rejuvenating the economy.

Clinton came to office with high hopes and amid even higher expectations—expectations he was unable to fulfill. When Republicans scored major gains in the 1994 congressional races, capturing both houses of Congress, Clinton moved to the center, co-opting conservative themes at the same time that he demonized the Republican congressional leadership. The tactic worked: with his poll ratings rising, Clinton scored a resounding victory against Robert Dole in the 1996 presidential campaign. Although the nation experienced unprecedented economic growth during the decade, a messy impeachment struggle tainted Clinton's legacy, providing an opening for Republicans to win back the White House in a bitterly fought 2000 election.

In the post–Cold War era, globalization served as a loose new framework for defining America's interests in the world. The communication revolution and the growing interdependence of the world's largest economies convinced the Clinton administration that the United States needed to play a major role in preserving international stability and maintaining open markets for American products. Globalization, however, produced its own forms of instability both at home and around the world. By the end of the decade Americans were engaged in a loud debate about the consequences of globalization.

During the 1990s Americans also participated in vocal and often angry debates about American identity. The vigorous competition between the major television networks and new cable upstarts led many television executives to use sex and violence to lure viewers. The move outraged conservatives and worried parents who blamed popular culture for a variety of contemporary social problems. All television cameras were focused on the trial of African-American football hero O. J. Simpson. The public's reaction to the trial and the continuing controversy over affirmative action revealed that Americans were deeply divided about race.

Annotated Suggested Readings

Scholarship on the 1990s is limited and, for the most part, highly partisan. Arthur M. Schlesinger, Jr.'s *The Disuniting of America* (1991) is a good discussion about the conflicts and tensions of 1990s American society. Robert Bellah et al. discuss the continuing presence of a national culture through the 1990s in *The Good Society* (1991). Haynes Johnson examines the double-edge impact of prosperity in *The Best of Times* (2001).

Extensive material has been published on the end of the Cold War. Don Oberdorfer's *From the Cold War to a New Era* (1998) is a noteworthy introduction. Thomas G. Patterson's *On Every Front* (1992) details the American response to events in Russia. Francis Fukuyama's *The End of History and the Last Man* (1992) is an early and influential discussion of the post–Cold War world. Robert Tucker and David C. Hendricksen's *The Imperial Temptation* (1992) studies the emerging debates in American foreign policy after the Cold War. David Halberstam's *War in a Time of Peace* (2001) offers the best analysis of foreign and military policy in the 1990s. In *At The Highest Levels* (1993), Strobe Talbott et. al. tell the story of the end of the Cold War. President George Bush and National Security Advisor Brent Scrowcroft, two key players in the drama, reflect on events in *A World Transformed* (1998). Stephen R. Graubard's *Mr. Bush's War* (1992) discusses the behavior of the media during the war. Martin Yant's *Desert Mirage* (1991) is a sharply critical history of the war. Alberto Bin's *Desert Storm: A Forgotten War* (1998) discusses the dubious legacy of the conflict.

Arlene S. Skolnick's *Embattled Paradise* (1991) discusses the recession and budget crisis. Michael Meeropol's *Surrender* (1998) recounts how George Bush, and Bill Clinton after him, struggled to balance the budget. Patricia Albjerg-Graham's *SOS: Sustain Our Schools* (1992) studies the crisis in education. Alex Kotlowitz's *There Are No Children Here* (1991) is a searing depiction of urban poverty and violence in the 1990s. Roger Rosenblatt's *Life Itself* (1992) covers the abortion debate. Susan Faludi describes the growing gender gap in *Backlash* (1991). For competing views of the debate on multiculturalism, see Richard Bernstein, *Dictatorship of Virtue* (1994) and Lawrence W. Levine, *The Opening of the American Mind* (1996). Richard J. Herrnstein and Charles Murray's *The Bell Curve* (1996), though still hotly debated, is emblematic of the debate over affirmative action. Richard Abanes's *American Militias: Rebellion, Racism and Religion* (1996) and Philip Lamy's *Millennium Rage* (1996) are both good introductions to the antigovernment groups of the 1990s. Jeffery Toobin offers the most balanced assessment of the disputed 2000 election in *Too Close to Call* (2002).

Among the several character studies of Bill Clinton, David Maraniss's *First in His Class* (1996) is the leading biography. Also useful are Nigel Hamilton's *Bill Clinton: An American Journey* (2003); and Joe Klein's *The Natural* (2003). Former Clinton advisor George Stephanopoulos has written an insightful memoir, *All Too Human* (2000). Bob Woodward's *Agenda* (1994) is a detailed study of Clinton's first years in office. Sidney Blumenthal offers a spirited defense of the president in his insightful look at the political and culture wars of the 1990s in *The Clinton Wars* (2003). In *Living History* (2003) Hilary Clinton gives her unique perspective on events in the 1990s. Bill Clinton tells his side of the story in *My Life* (2004). Madeline Albright, the first woman to serve as secretary of state, tells her story in *Madam Secretary* (2003).

There is a small but growing body of literature on the impact of globalization. See, for example, Thomas L. Friedman's *The Lexus and the Olive Tree* (1999); Joseph Stiglitz, *Globalization and Its Critics* (2003); Michael Mandenbaum, *The Ideas That Conquered the World* (2002); and Amy Chua, *World on Fire* (2004). Michael Williams's *A History of Computing Technology* (1997) describes the development of the modern computer. In *The Politics of Cyberspace* (1997), Chris Toulouse and Timothy W. Luke explore the emerging information age. Juliet B. Schor's *The Overworked American* (1993) and *The Overspent American* (1998) both study the impact of globalization on American workers.

Popular culture in the 1990s has been exhaustively studied in popular books, though often without much historical perspective. Neal Gabler's *Life: The Movie* (1999) contains an excellent analysis of how entertainment has infiltrated and conquered reality. Lawrence M. Friedman's *The Horizontal Society* (1999) explores the democratization of modern popular culture. Todd Gitlin takes a critical look at changes in the media in *Media Unlimited* (2001).

The **History Companion**

Congress Debates War or Peace

Voices in Favor of War with Iraq

In January 1991 President George Bush asked both the House and the Senate to approve a resolution authorizing the use of military force to drive Iraqi troops from Kuwait. The authorization, which amounted to a vote for war, divided the nation and Congress. During three days of debate most Republicans and a few Democrats rose in support of the president's policy.

(*Representative Robert H. Michel, R-Illinois*) I speak from the prejudice of being a combat veteran of World War II. And those of our generation know from bloody experience that unchecked aggression against a small nation is a prelude to an international disaster.

Saddam Hussein today has more planes and tanks and, frankly, men under arms, than Hitler had at the time when Prime Minister Chamberlain came back from Munich with that miserable piece of paper—peace in our time. I'll never forget that replay of that movie in my life.

And I have an obligation, I guess, coming from that generation, to transmit those thoughts I had at the time to the younger generation who didn't experience what we did. Saddam Hussein not only invaded Kuwait, he occupied, terrorized, murdered civilians, systematically looted and turned a peaceful nation into a wasteland of horror. He seeks control over one of the world's vital resources, and he ultimately seeks to make himself the unchallenged anti-Western dictator of the Mideast.

Either we stop him now, and stop him permanently, or we won't stop him at all.

(*Senator Orrin G. Hatch, R-Utah*) Unless Saddam Hussein believes that the threat of war is real, he will not budge. I think we've learned that. The only way to avoid war, in my opinion in this particular situation, is to be prepared to go to war and to show that our resolve is for real. . . . Our actions should be decisive.

(*Senator William V. Roth Jr., R-Delaware*) One can only imagine what devastating consequence would fall should his dominance be allowed in the oil-rich Middle East. And this is the second reason why he must be stopped. When I speak of the danger that would result from his control of this region, I'm not talking about consequences to major oil companies—quite simply, I'm talking about jobs. I'm talking about the raw material of human endeavor.

Oil runs the economy of the world. It fuels our factories, heats our homes. Carries our products from manufacture to market. It's as basic to the economy as water is to life. And the free trade of international supplies is critical, not only for the industrial democracies, but the fragile third world nations that depend on this precious resource even more than we do.

Any attempt to disrupt these supplies will send a devastating quake to these economies, lengthening unemployment lines, boosting inflation in the industrial democracies and crushing the economies of developing countries where day to day existence depends on imported energy sources.

1297

Voices in Dissent

Leading Democrats opposed the authorization to use force, claiming that the United States should give economic sanctions more time to force Hussein to comply with the United Nations mandate to leave Kuwait.

(Senator George J. Mitchell, D-Maine) This is not a debate about American objectives in the current crisis. There is broad agreement in the Senate that Iraq must fully and unconditionally withdraw its forces from Kuwait. The issue is how best to achieve that goal. Most Americans and most members of Congress, myself included, supported the President's initial decision to deploy American forces to Saudi Arabia to deter further Iraqi aggression. We supported the President's effort in marshaling international diplomatic pressure and the most comprehensive embargo in history against Iraq.

Despite the fact that his own policy of international economic sanctions was having a significant effect upon the Iraqi economy, the President, without explanation, abandoned that approach and instead adopted a policy based first and foremost upon the use of American military force. As a result, this country has been placed on a course toward war. This has upset the balance of the President's initial policy, the balance between resources and responsibility, between interest and risk, between patience and strength.

(Senator Paul D. Wellstone, D-Minnesota) This is the most momentous decision that any political leader would ever have to make and decide we must. And let no one doubt that the Congress has the responsibility to make this decision. The Constitution is unambiguous on this point: Congress declares the war, not the President.

The policies that I am afraid the Administration is pursuing, the rush to war that I am afraid is so much of what is now happening in our country and the world, will not create a new order, Mr. President, it will create a new world disorder. What kind of victory will it be? What kind of victory will it be if we unleash forces of fanaticism in the Middle East and a chronically unstable region becomes even more unstable further jeopardizing Israel's security?

Some causes are worth fighting for. This cause is not worth fighting for right now. We must stay the course with economic sanctions, continue the pressure, continue the squeeze, move forward on the diplomatic front and Mr. President, we must not, we must not rush to war.

(Senator Edward M. Kennedy, D-Massachusetts) I urge the Senate to vote for peace, not war. . . . I reject the argument that says Congress must support the President, right or wrong. . . . War is not the only option left to us in the Persian Gulf. . . . Sanctions and diplomacy may still achieve our objectives, and Congress has the responsibility to insure that all peaceful options are exhausted before resort to war. . . .

Let there be no mistake about the cost of war. We have arrayed an impressive international coalition against Iraq, but when the bullets start flying, 90 percent of the casualties will be Americans. It is hardly a surprise that so many other nations are willing to fight to the last American to achieve the goals of the United Nations. It is not their sons and daughters who will do the dying. . . .

Not a single American life should be sacrificed in a war for the price of oil. Not a single drop of American blood should be spilled because American automobiles burn too many drops of oil a mile; not a single American soldier should lose his life in the Persian Gulf because America has no energy policy worthy of the name to reduce our dependence on foreign oil.

On January 12, 1991, Congress approved the resolution authorizing force in the Persian Gulf. Strong lobbying from the administration and a unified Republican Party pushed the resolution through the Senate by a narrow 52-to-47 margin, and by a more comfortable 250-to-183 margin in the House. A reporter noted that the votes "capped three days of the most intense, solemn and emotional debate seen in the Capitol in many years." The roll call marked the tenth time in history that Congress had supported sending American troops into battle. The president hailed the vote, claiming that it "unmistakably demonstrates the United States' commitment to the international demand for a complete and unconditional withdrawal of Iraq from Kuwait. This clear expression of the Congress represents the last, best chance for peace."

Despite their reservations about the war, Americans instinctively rallied around the troops once the fighting began. Unlike during coverage of Vietnam, Americans saw virtually no blood or death on their television screens. The Pentagon had imposed tough new restrictions on the press covering the war, forcing reporters to travel with escorts and exercising control over all reports from the Gulf. The victory produced an outpouring of patriotism and renewed faith in the military and its leaders that had been tarnished since Vietnam. It made heroes of military leaders, especially Norman Schwarzkopf and Colin Powell, the first African-American to serve as chairman of the Joint Chiefs of Staff. "By God, we've licked the Vietnam syndrome once and for all," Bush told a national television audience. The president reaped much of the credit for the operation. His approval rating shot to 89 percent—the highest ever recorded for a president.

QUESTIONS FOR ANALYSIS

1. Why did supporters of the president's policy believe that sanctions would not work?

2. What national interest did supporters believe was at stake in the Persian Gulf?

3. What arguments did opponents use to urge the Senate to reject the resolution?

4. How did different perceptions of national interest shape the debate over the use of force against Iraq?

5. How would you have voted?

Epilogue: The Challenges of the New Century

The debate over Iraq isolated the United States from most of Europe, exposing deep differences between the way Americans viewed their role in the world and the way most other nations saw the United States.

"My fellow citizens, at this hour American and coalition forces are in the early stages of military operations to disarm Iraq, to free its people and to defend the world from grave danger," President George W. Bush told the nation in a televised broadcast on March 19, 2003. The announcement that the United States, with a small "coalition of the willing," was going to war followed months of failed diplomacy as the administration tried to convince the United Nations to support a resolution to remove Saddam Hussein from power. Secretary of State Colin Powell told the UN Security Council that the United States had overwhelming evidence that Saddam Hussein was harboring stockpiles of chemical and biological weapons in clear violation of past UN mandates. Iraq had "shown utter contempt for the United Nations and the opinion of the world" by refusing to cooperate with the inspection process, he said.

Most of America's closest allies remained skeptical of U.S. claims that Hussein possessed weapons of mass destruction (WMD). They wanted to expand the inspection process to uncover clear evidence of Iraq's duplicity before using military force. French Foreign Minister Dominique de Villepin led the opposition. "The use of force against Iraq is not justified today," he declared. "There is an alternative to war, and that is to disarm Iraq through inspections." Secretary of State Powell responded for an administration still traumatized by the attacks on the World Trade Center and the Pentagon on September 11, 2001. "We cannot wait for one of these weapons [of mass destruction] to turn up in our cities. More inspections—I am sorry—are not the answer." On March 17 the administration, realizing that its efforts to build an international coalition had failed, withdrew its resolution and gave Hussein forty-eight hours to leave the country. Two days later, Bush launched the attack and addressed the nation.

The debate over Iraq isolated the United States from most of Europe, exposing deep differences between the way Americans viewed their role in the world and the way most other nations saw the United States. "America is virtually alone," observed *Newsweek.* "Never will it have waged a war in such isolation. Never have so many of its allies been so firmly opposed to its policies." The Cold War had provided a common bond uniting America with Europe by a shared sense of threat from the Soviet Union. The breakup of the Soviet Union, the emergence of the United States as the world's sole superpower, and the rise of radical terrorist groups had rearranged the global order. The changes also raised a new question: how would the new strategic environment change America's relationship with the world?

SEPTEMBER 11, 2001

At 8:45 A.M. on September 11, 2001, a hijacked passenger jet, American Airlines flight 11, crashed into the north tower of the World Trade Center. A few minutes later a second hijacked airliner rammed the south tower. The attacks on the World Trade Center were part of a well-coordinated terrorist assault on the symbols of American economic and military might. A third hijacked plane demolished the western part of the Pentagon. A fourth plane, possibly headed to the Capitol building or the White House, crashed in a field in western Pennsylvania after passengers struggled with hijackers. Before nightfall, 2,813 civilians were dead, making it the bloodiest day on American soil since September 17, 1862, when 6,300 Union and Confederate soldiers were killed or mortally wounded in the Civil War battle of Antietam.

The repercussions spread across the nation. The government closed borders. Major skyscrapers and other potential terrorist targets were evacuated. Global financial markets plunged into chaos. "IT'S WAR!" screamed the headline of the *New York Daily News.* Many observers believed that the threat of global terrorism would usher in a new era in international relations, reshuffling old alliances and reaffirming others in a struggle that would be as defining as the Cold War. "You recognize that something's changed forever in the way that the United States thinks about its security," observed national security adviser Condoleezza Rice.

The world community rallied around the United States in an unprecedented show of solidarity. In Germany more than two hundred thousand people marched under the Brandenburg gate to show their support. In London Buckingham Palace played the "Star-Spangled Banner" during the ceremonial changing of the guard. Paris-based *Le Monde* newspaper, often critical of American foreign policy, proclaimed: "We are all Americans now."

On the evening of the attacks a shaken President Bush declared war on global terrorism. Intelligence experts suspected that only Saudi billionaire Osama bin Laden possessed the resources to pull off such a daring and complicated operation. The United States took aim at bin Laden and the radical Taliban government of Afghanistan, which provided a safe haven for his operations. In the weeks leading up to the actual military assault on Afghanistan, the administration built an impressive

President Bush at Ground Zero
Three days after two planes crashed into the World Trade Towers, President George W. Bush visited ground zero, the eight-story plus pile of rubble and debris that remained when the two towers and several surrounding buildings collapsed. Standing on a burned out fire truck and using a bullhorn, Bush proclaimed to the crowd of rescue workers gathered near him, "I can hear you. The rest of the world hears you. And the people who knocked down these buildings will hear all of us soon." After his pronouncement, Bush comforted firefighter Bob Beckwith, seen here, while the crowd chanted "U.S.A., U.S.A.!" *(AP/Wide World Photos, Inc.)*

international coalition to bolster military action. As in the first Gulf War, America included a number of Arab states in its alliance to blunt bin Laden's effort to characterize the war as a battle between the Christian West and the Muslim East.

American military technology and airpower far overmatched the poorly equipped Taliban fighters. On October 7 the United States and Britain launched a series of punishing air strikes using long-range bombers and cruise missiles. Weakened by the air campaign, the Taliban regime gave up the capital of Kabul to opposition Northern Alliance forces in November. On December 6 Taliban forces surrendered the southern city of Kandahar, their last stronghold. Only pockets of Taliban forces continued to resist, launching hit-and-run attacks against Western troops. Many observers hailed the American campaign as "a masterpiece of military creativity and finesse," but it ended without the capture of Osama bin Laden or the leaders of the Taliban government.

WAR WITH IRAQ

Even while American troops were fighting in Afghanistan, the Bush administration began drawing up plans to send troops into Iraq. For the administration terrorism had replaced communism as the new ideological and military threat to American global interests in the post–Cold War era. The president and his advisers believed that new threats from terrorist networks and the states that sponsored them required a broader definition of American interests. "The greatest danger our nation faces lies in the crossroads of radicalism and technology," the president declared in September 2002. The proliferation of weapons of mass destruction—chemical, biological, and nuclear—had rendered irrelevant Cold War concepts such as deterrence and containment. Since deterrence cannot work against those who "seek martyrdom in death," the White House called for a new strategy of preemptive strikes. The United States would act decisively, and alone if necessary, to eliminate potential threats.

On March 19, 2003, U.S. forces launched a "shock and awe" military campaign. While cruise missiles and precision-guided bombs rained down on strategic targets in Baghdad, more than forty thousand troops rolled into southern Iraq. Despite fierce resistance, U.S. troops moved into Baghdad on April 9. On May 1 President Bush declared the end of "major combat operations" in Iraq, but the guerrilla-style war intensified over the next few months. On December 13 American soldiers pulled a disoriented Saddam Hussein from a "spider's hole" at a farm near his hometown of Tikrit, but his capture had little impact on the resistance. The administration discovered that maintaining the peace was more difficult than winning the war. U.S. soldiers were subject to daily deadly attacks, while sabotage weakened the already crippled Iraqi infrastructure. By September 2004 more than one thousand U.S. soldiers had been killed in Iraq.

Toppling of Saddam Hussein Statue As American troops moved into central Baghdad on April 9, 2003, Iraqis and American soldiers celebrated the occasion by bringing down a twenty-foot statue of Saddam Hussein in Fardus Square. While fighting continued in other parts of the city, an American armored vehicle and a chain were used to pull the statue down. In this picture, an Iraqi man throws stones at the statue before it is completely pulled from its pedestal. The event became a symbol of the collapse of the twenty-four year reign of Hussein, though the dictator himself would not be captured by Americans until December 14. (© *Reuters/Corbis.*)

Perhaps most damaging of all, the United States failed to uncover the promised stockpiles of chemical and biological weapons. In January 2004 David Kay, the former chief U.S. weapons inspector, told a Senate committee: "It turns out we were all wrong." In response, the administration justified the war on humanitarian grounds, claiming that the United States had rid the world of a repressive tyrant and had laid the foundation for democracy in the Middle East.

The threat of new attacks hardened the administration's desire to act unilaterally to protect American interests. Even before September 11 the administration

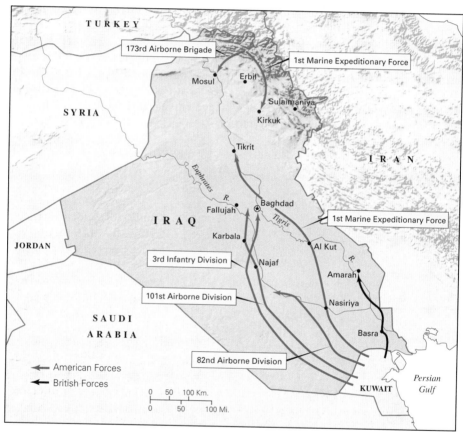

British and American Troop Movements, March–April 2003 Operation Iraqi Freedom began on March 19, 2003, with the launch of forty Tomahawk missiles from ships in the Persian Gulf and Red Sea. While bombings continued, American and British forces began heading into Southern Iraq from bases in Kuwait on March 21, with American troops targeting Najaf and Karbala on their way to Baghdad and the British moving on Basra and points along the Tigris River. American and Turkish forces joined with Kurdish fighters in northern Iraq, targeting the cities of Mosul and Kirkuk. On April 13, American marines entered the city of Tikrit, the birthplace of Saddam Hussein and the last major town not under the control of coalition forces.

ignored world opinion and abandoned the 1997 Kyoto Protocol, which required developed countries to reduce greenhouse gas emissions, and withdrew from a missile treaty with Russia so it could expand research on the Strategic Defense Initiative ("Star Wars") defense system.

Most Americans rallied around the administration and its evolving rationale for war. The September 11 terrorist attacks had left the nation feeling weak and vulnerable, and most Americans applauded the president's decisiveness and agreed with his tendency to see the world as divided between good and evil. Many people, especially religious conservatives who made up a major part of the Republican coalition, embraced the missionary goal of remaking the Middle East in the American image of democracy and individual rights.

Most of the world, however, rejected the nation's justifications for war. Europeans overwhelmingly disapproved: 87 percent in France, 85 percent in Germany, 83 percent in Russia, 79 percent in Spain, 76 percent in Italy, and 60 percent even in Britain, America's staunchest ally. While the United States believed that the terrorist threat justified a unilateral approach, most Europeans emphasized the need to build coalitions by using existing international institutions.

The new threat of global terrorism left Europe and the United States feeling insecure, but for different reasons. Americans felt vulnerable to another terrorist attack; Europeans, who had endured terrorist attacks of their own, worried about a unipolar world dominated by American military might. The difference in perception reflected the realities of power. In 2004 the United States spent as much on defense as the rest of the world (191 countries) combined. According to a NATO official, Europe was "a military pygmy" compared to the United States.

THE HOME FRONT

Despite the narrowness of his election victory, President Bush moved aggressively to pass key elements of his domestic agenda. First on the list was a $1.6 trillion, ten-year tax-cut package. The president's original proposal passed the Republican-dominated House, but ran into trouble in the Senate, where moderates trimmed roughly $450 billion from the proposal and added more spending than the president wanted. Passage of the trimmed-down tax cut, the largest since 1981, represented a major legislative victory for the new administration.

The September 11 terrorist attacks led to a major reordering of priorities for the Bush administration. Having won election promising to shrink the Washington bureaucracy and limit government spending, Bush presided over the largest expansion of federal power since the days of Lyndon Johnson's Great Society. Within the first few weeks of the crisis, the president approved $55 billion in federal spending, including a massive federal relief package for New York. He abandoned traditional conservative faith in deregulation and orchestrated a federal bailout of the airlines. In June 2002 Bush called for the creation of a new department of homeland security, which would include 169,000 employees from eight existing Cabinet departments and have a budget of $37.4 billion. The proposal represented the largest reorganization of the federal government since Harry Truman signed the National Security Act of 1947. In 2003 Bush added a new entitlement—prescription drug coverage—to Medicare. The new entitlement was expected to cost at least $400 billion over the next decade.

In its first three years in office, the administration watched a $236 billion federal budget surplus transform into a $400 billion annual deficit. Overall government spending increased by 16 percent. Although post–September 11 defense needs accounted for much of the increase, domestic spending also grew by 11 percent. For the first time since World War II, federal spending per household topped $20,000.

Perhaps the greatest expansion of federal power came in law enforcement. The administration claimed that a network of "sleeper agents" was operating in the United States and preparing a future attack. In the first few months after September 11, the FBI arrested over a thousand suspects, moved them to unknown locations, and monitored their communications with their lawyers. Attorney General John Ashcroft said that the policy was intended to stop inmates who had been involved in terrorism from passing messages to confederates through lawyers, their assistants, or translators. But critics asked how far the government would go in attempting to balance its need to protect the national welfare with its responsibility to protect civil liberties. A series of court decisions denied the government's efforts to detain terror suspects without filing formal charges or allowing them access to lawyers. "We call ourselves a nation of laws," a defense attorney said, "and the test of a nation of laws is whether it adheres to them in times of stress."

The administration appeared helpless, however, to tame the forces of globalization that drew a flood of white-collar jobs out of the United States. With the Internet and high-speed data networks increasing the speed and ease of communication over long distances, companies continued shipping "knowledge work" abroad. In 2003 Microsoft announced that it would invest $400 million in India over the next three years. That was in addition to the $750 million it was spending on outsourcing in China.

When combined with old-fashioned greed, globalization allowed rogue corporate managers to develop sophisticated methods for avoiding shareholder scrutiny. In many cases, they used the complexity of their worldwide operations to disguise corrupt practices. In 2003 five companies—Enron, WorldCom, Tyco, Qwest, and Global Crossing—were charged with squandering a combined $460 billion in shareholder value.

While many Americans worried about job security, much of the nation was embroiled in a heated debate over gay rights. The controversy was ignited by a Massachusetts court decision that extended marriage rights to same-sex couples. At issue was a basic question of American identity: could a minority be denied rights enjoyed by other Americans, and who—the courts, the states, or the federal government—should decide? Ironically, conservatives, who were traditionally skeptical of federal power, proposed a constitutional amendment that would define marriage as a union between a man and a woman. Liberals and gay rights supporters adopted the conservative states-rights mantra, while also claiming that the courts play a key role in the process. "It is fundamentally un-American for the tyranny of the majority to determine the rights of any minority," said a gay rights supporter. "That's what this country was raised on. You don't have popularity contests about who is equal under the law."

The American experiment will confront fresh challenges and new opportunities in the twenty-first century. Will popular attitudes toward government prove capable of reconciling the demands for greater services and security with the traditional fear of federal power? How will society adjust to the influence of its diverse population while maintaining its sense of a common identity? Can the government protect the national interest abroad without sacrificing democracy at home? The answers to those questions may prove elusive, but Americans will continue their search for a better society. "The idea of the search is what holds us together," noted the historian Daniel Boorstein. "The quest is the enduring American experiment. The meaning is in the seeking."

The **istory ompanion**

War in Modern America

In May 2004, Secretary of Defense Donald Rumsfeld, appearing before the Senate Foreign Relations Committee, noted that he had been reading a biography of Civil War general and later president Ulysses S. Grant (*Grant*, Jean Edward Smith, 2001). Paralleling the U.S. military effort in Iraq with that in its Civil War, Rumsfeld stated that "the casualties were high, the same kinds of concerns that we're expressing here were expressed then. [The people then] were despairing, they were hopeful, they were concerned, they were combative ...the carnage was horrendous, and it was worth it." Rumsfeld placed himself in a long line of historians, policymakers, and politicians in the twentieth and early twenty-first centuries who have compared ongoing or recently concluded wars with the nation's Civil War to illustrate whether those subsequent conflicts should have been fought or could have been avoided.

In the decades that followed the Civil War, most of the writing on the topic was done by northerners who viewed the war as a great moral conflict between the forces of freedom and those of slavery. After World War I, historians' thinking about the causes of the Civil War changed. While most Americans were relieved that the Allies had defeated the Central Powers, many were disappointed that the Treaty of Versailles had failed to secure President Woodrow Wilson's idealistic goal of making the world safe for democracy. A growing number of disillusioned historians in the postwar years blamed U.S. involvement in the war on bankers, seeking to secure loans they had made to the Allies, and munitions makers, aiming to profit from increased sales, and argued that the nation should have remained neutral.

Adopting a similarly skeptical perspective, Charles and Mary Beard, in their influential book *The Rise of American Civilization* (1927), downplayed slavery as the cause of the Civil War and emphasized the rise of industrial capitalism in the North and its unavoidable conflict with the plantation economy of the South. However, Civil War revisionists, as they came to be known, more commonly viewed that war not as an irrepressible conflict but as an avoidable one and blamed hotheaded abolitionists in the North and vocal proslavery advocates in the South for fueling the fires of sectional animosity. In addition, revisionist historians such as Avery Craven and James G. Randall tended to downplay the horrors of slavery and even argued that the system was dying out.

However, by the mid- to late 1940s, other American historians, influenced by the horrors of totalitarianism, most notably the Nazi Holocaust, began to offer a corrective to the revisionist argument. The first volume of Allen Nevins's *The Ordeal of the Union* (8 vols.) appeared in 1947 and emphasized that the problem of slavery was at the center of the cultural differences that precipitated the conflict between the North and South. Arthur Schlesinger, Jr., in an influential 1949 article, "The Causes of the Civil War," offered a stinging indictment of the revisionists. Schlesinger wrote: "To say there 'should' have been no abolitionists in America before the Civil War is about as sensible as to say that there 'should' have been no anti-Nazis in the nineteen-thirties or that there 'should' be no anti-Communists today." Recounting the scholarly debate in his autobiography *A Life in the Twentieth Century* (2000), Schlesinger implied that sometimes wars have to be fought, regardless of the cost in human lives, because some things are worth fighting for or against.

In the 1940s, many American intellectuals rejected the moral relativism that had prevailed in the post—World War I decades and moved toward a morally absolutist position. This absolutism emphasized the presence of clear moral differences in the world. World War II was characterized as the Good War, a struggle between the forces of light and the forces of darkness. Then, with the end of World War II and the onset of the Cold War, the Soviet Union, in the estimation of many Americans, replaced Fascist Germany and imperialist Japan as the great source of evil in the world. Within this intellectual climate, the Civil War was increasingly seen not as an avoidable tragedy but as a vital crusade against evil. Fascism and Communism, in the late 1940s, were both paralleled with slavery; and all three came to be viewed as cancers that had to be rooted out for the good of humanity.

In May 2004 Donald Rumsfeld sought to establish a moral high ground by paralleling the Civil War and the U.S. military effort in Iraq. The George W. Bush administration emphasized the liberation of the Iraqi people from Saddam Hussein's oppressive regime as the goal of the U.S. military effort. However, while the Civil War has served as a great moral barometer during the twentieth and early twenty-first centuries, America's longest war, the Vietnam War, has left an equally compelling legacy during the last generation. Immediately following the conclusion of military action in the First Gulf War, at the beginning of March 1991, President George H. W. Bush declared that "the specter of Vietnam has been buried forever in the sands of the Arabian Peninsula." The nation, the president hoped, had finally overcome its reluctance to risk casualties in important foreign military endeavors. But the critical public reaction to subsequent military ventures during the Clinton administration, in Somalia in 1993 and in Bosnia in 1994 and 1999, suggests that the ghosts of Vietnam have not been completely exorcised from the public consciousness. That reluctance to risk American lives overseas was also evident as the number of American casualties in Iraq grew in early 2004, after Saddam Hussein's regime had been dismantled by a U.S.-led coalition. As the media increasingly drew parallels with the war in Vietnam, it was not surprising that Rumsfeld sought to establish a more palatable point of comparison, the American Civil War. The matter of which of these parallels with the Iraq War—Vietnam or the Civil War—is more accurate or appropriate is highly debatable. What is clear is that our understanding of present wars and our remembrance of past ones are very much intertwined.

DOCUMENTS

DECLARATION OF INDEPENDENCE IN CONGRESS, JULY 4, 1776

When, in the course of human events, it becomes necessary for one people to dissolve the political bonds which have connected them with another, and to assume, among the powers of the earth, the separate and equal station to which the laws of nature and of nature's God entitle them, a decent respect to the opinions of mankind requires that they should declare the causes which impel them to the separation.

We hold these truths to be self-evident: That all men are created equal; that they are endowed by their Creator with certain unalienable rights; that among these are life, liberty, and the pursuit of happiness; that, to secure these rights, governments are instituted among men, deriving their just powers from the consent of the governed; that whenever any form of government becomes destructive of these ends, it is the right of the people to alter or to abolish it, and to institute new government, laying its foundation on such principles, and organizing its powers in such form, as to them shall seem most likely to effect their safety and happiness. Prudence, indeed, will dictate that governments long established should not be changed for light and transient causes; and accordingly all experience hath shown that mankind are more disposed to suffer, while evils are sufferable, than to right themselves by abolishing the forms to which they are accustomed. But when a long train of abuses and usurpations, pursuing invariably the same object, evinces a design to reduce them under absolute despotism, it is their right, it is their duty, to throw off such government, and to provide new guards for their future security. Such has been the patient sufferance of these colonies; and such is now the necessity which constrains them to alter their former systems of government. The history of the present King of Great Britain is a history of repeated injuries and usurpations, all having in direct object the establishment of an absolute tyranny over these states. To prove this, let facts be submitted to a candid world.

He has refused his assent to laws, the most wholesome and necessary for the public good.

He has forbidden his governors to pass laws of immediate and pressing importance, unless suspended in their operation till his assent should be obtained; and, when so suspended, he has utterly neglected to attend to them.

He has refused to pass other laws for the accommodation of large districts of people, unless those people would relinquish the right of representation in the legislature, a right inestimable to them, and formidable to tyrants only.

He has called together legislative bodies at places unusual, uncomfortable, and distant from the depository of their public records, for the sole purpose of fatiguing them into compliance with his measures.

He has dissolved representative houses repeatedly, for opposing, with manly firmness, his invasions on the rights of the people.

He has refused for a long time, after such dissolutions, to cause others to be elected; whereby the legislative powers, incapable of annihilation, have returned to the people at large for their exercise; the state remaining, in the mean time, exposed to all the dangers of invasions from without and convulsions within.

He has endeavored to prevent the population of these states; for that purpose obstructing the laws for naturalization of foreigners; refusing to pass others to encourage their migration hither, and raising the conditions of new appropriations of lands.

He has obstructed the administration of justice, by refusing his assent to laws for establishing judiciary powers.

He has made judges dependent on his will alone, for the tenure of their offices, and the amount and payment of their salaries.

He has erected a multitude of new offices, and sent hither swarms of officers to harass our people and eat out their substance.

He has kept among us, in times of peace, standing armies, without the consent of our legislatures.

He has affected to render the military independent of, and superior to, the civil power.

He has combined with others to subject us to a jurisdiction foreign to our constitution, and unacknowledged by our laws, giving his assent to their acts of pretended legislation:

For quartering large bodies of armed troops among us;

For protecting them, by a mock trial, from punishment for any murders which they should commit on the inhabitants of these states;

For cutting off our trade with all parts of the world;

For imposing taxes on us without our consent;

For depriving us, in many cases, of the benefits of trial by jury;

For transporting us beyond seas, to be tried for pretended offenses;

For abolishing the free system of English laws in a neighboring province, establishing therein an arbitrary government, and enlarging its boundaries, so as to render it at once an example and fit instrument for introducing the same absolute rule into these colonies;

For taking away our charters, abolishing our most valuable laws, and altering fundamentally the forms of our governments;

For suspending our own legislatures, and declaring themselves invested with power to legislate for us in all cases whatsoever.

He has abdicated government here, by declaring us out of his protection and waging war against us.

He has plundered our seas, ravaged our coasts, burned our towns, and destroyed the lives of our people.

He is at this time transporting large armies of foreign mercenaries to complete the works of death, desolation, and tyranny already begun with circumstances of cruelty and perfidy scarcely paralleled in the most barbarous ages, and totally unworthy the head of a civilized nation.

He has constrained our fellow-citizens, taken captive on the high seas, to bear arms against their country, to become the executioners of their friends and brethren, or to fall themselves by their hands.

He has excited domestic insurrection among us, and has endeavored to bring on the inhabitants of our frontiers the merciless Indian savages, whose known rule of warfare is an undistinguished destruction of all ages, sexes, and conditions.

In every stage of these oppressions we have petitioned for redress in the most humble terms; our repeated petitions have been answered only by repeated injury. A prince, whose character is thus marked by every act which may define a tyrant, is unfit to be the ruler of a free people.

Nor have we been wanting in our attentions to our British brethren. We have warned them, from time to time, of attempts by their legislature to extend an unwarrantable jurisdiction over us. We have reminded them of the circumstances of our emigration and settlement here. We have appealed to their native justice and magnanimity; and we have conjured them, by the ties of our common kindred, to disavow these usurpations, which would inevitably interrupt our connections and correspondence. They, too, have been deaf to the voice of justice and of consanguinity. We must, therefore, acquiesce in the necessity which denounces our separation, and hold them, as we hold the rest of mankind, enemies in war, in peace friends.

We, therefore, the representatives of the United States of America, in General Congress assembled, appealing to the Supreme Judge of the world for the rectitude of our intentions, do, in the name and by the authority of the good people of these colonies, solemnly publish and declare, that these United Colonies are, and of right ought to be, FREE AND INDEPENDENT STATES; that they are absolved from all allegiance to the British crown, and that all political connection between them and the state of Great Britain is, and ought to be, totally dissolved; and that, as free and independent states, they have full power to levy war, conclude peace, contract alliances, establish commerce, and do all other acts and things which independent states may of right do. And for the support of this declaration, with a firm reliance on the protection of Divine Providence, we mutually pledge to each other our lives, our fortunes, and our sacred honor.

ARTICLES OF CONFEDERATION

(The text of the Articles of Confederation can be found at http://college.hmco.com.)

CONSTITUTION OF THE UNITED STATES OF AMERICA AND AMENDMENTS*

Preamble

We the people of the United States, in order to form a more perfect union, establish justice, insure domestic tranquillity, provide for the common defense, promote the general welfare, and secure the blessings of liberty to ourselves and our posterity, do ordain and establish this Constitution for the United States of America.

Article I

SECTION 1 All legislative powers herein granted shall be vested in a Congress of the United States, which shall consist of a Senate and a House of Representatives.

SECTION 2 The House of Representatives shall be composed of members chosen every second year by the people of the several States, and the electors in each State shall have the qualifications requisite for electors of the most numerous branch of the State Legislature.

---

*Passages no longer in effect are printed in italic type.

No person shall be a Representative who shall not have attained to the age of twenty-five years, and been seven years a citizen of the United States, and who shall not, when elected, be an inhabitant of that State in which he shall be chosen.

Representatives and direct taxes shall be apportioned among the several States which may be included within this Union, according to their respective numbers, *which shall be determined by adding to the whole number of free persons, including those bound to service for a term of years and excluding Indians not taxed, three-fifths of all other persons.* The actual enumeration shall be made within three years after the first meeting of the Congress of the United States, and within every subsequent term of ten years, in such manner as they shall by law direct. The number of Representatives shall not exceed one for every thirty thousand, but each State shall have at least one Representative; *and until such enumeration shall be made, the State of New Hampshire shall be entitled to choose three, Massachusetts eight, Rhode Island and Providence Plantations one, Connecticut five, New York six, New Jersey four, Pennsylvania eight, Delaware one, Maryland six, Virginia ten, North Carolina five, South Carolina five, and Georgia three.*

When vacancies happen in the representation from any State, the Executive authority thereof shall issue writs of election to fill such vacancies.

The House of Representatives shall choose their Speaker and other officers; and shall have the sole power of impeachment.

SECTION 3 The Senate of the United States shall be composed of two Senators from each State, *chosen by the legislature thereof,* for six years; and each Senator shall have one vote.

Immediately after they shall be assembled in consequence of the first election, they shall be divided as equally as may be into three classes. The seats of the Senators of the first class shall be vacated at the expiration of the second year, of the second class at the expiration of the fourth year, and of the third class at the expiration of the sixth year, so that one-third may be chosen every second year; and if vacancies happen by resignation or otherwise, during the recess of the legislature of any State, the Executive thereof may make temporary appointments until the next meeting of the legislature, which shall then fill such vacancies.

No person shall be a Senator who shall not have attained to the age of thirty years, and been nine years a citizen of the United States, and who shall not, when elected, be an inhabitant of that State for which he shall be chosen.

The Vice-President of the United States shall be President of the Senate, but shall have no vote, unless they be equally divided.

The Senate shall choose their other officers, and also a President *pro tempore,* in the absence of the Vice-President, or when he shall exercise the office of President of the United States.

The Senate shall have the sole power to try all impeachments. When sitting for that purpose, they shall be on oath or affirmation. When the President of the United States is tried, the Chief Justice shall preside: and no person shall be convicted without the concurrence of two-thirds of the members present.

Judgment in cases of impeachment shall not extend further than to removal from the office, and disqualification to hold and enjoy any office of honor, trust or profit under the United States: but the party convicted shall nevertheless be liable and subject to indictment, trial, judgment and punishment, according to law.

SECTION 4 The times, places and manner of holding elections for Senators and Representatives shall be prescribed in each State by the legislature thereof; but the Congress may at any time by law make or alter such regulations, except as to the places of choosing Senators.

The Congress shall assemble at least once in every year, and such meeting *shall be on the first Monday in December, unless they shall by law appoint a different day.*

SECTION 5 Each house shall be the judge of the elections, returns and qualifications of its own members, and a majority of each shall constitute a quorum to do business; but a smaller number may adjourn from day to day, and may be authorized to compel the attendance of absent members, in such manner, and under such penalties, as each house may provide.

Each house may determine the rules of its proceedings, punish its members for disorderly behavior, and with the concurrence of two-thirds, expel a member.

Each house shall keep a journal of its proceedings, and from time to time publish the same, excepting such parts as may in their judgment require secrecy; and the yeas and nays of the members of either house on any question shall, at the desire of one-fifth of those present, be entered on the journal.

Neither house, during the session of Congress, shall, without the consent of the other, adjourn for more than three days, nor to any other place than that in which the two houses shall be sitting.

SECTION 6 The Senators and Representatives shall receive a compensation for their services, to be ascertained by law and paid out of the treasury of the United States. They shall in all cases except treason, felony and breach of the peace, be privileged from arrest during their attendance at the session of their respective houses, and in going to and returning from the same; and for any speech or debate in either house, they shall not be questioned in any other place.

No Senator or Representative shall, during the time for which he was elected, be appointed to any civil office under the authority of the United States, which shall have been created, or the emoluments whereof shall have been increased, during such time; and no person holding any office under the United States shall be a member of either house during his continuance in office.

SECTION 7 All bills for raising revenue shall originate in the House of Representatives; but the Senate may propose or concur with amendments as on other bills.

Every bill which shall have passed the House of Representatives and the Senate, shall, before it become a law, be presented to the President of the United States; if he approve he shall sign it, but if not he shall return it with objections to that house in which it originated, who shall enter the objections at large on their journal, and proceed to reconsider it. If after such reconsideration two-thirds of that house shall agree to pass the bill, it shall be sent, together with the objections, to the other house, by which it shall likewise be reconsidered, and, if approved by two-thirds of that house, it shall become a law. But in all such cases the votes of both houses shall be determined by yeas and nays, and the names of the persons voting for and against the bill shall be entered on the journal of each house respectively. If any bill shall not be returned by the President within ten days (Sundays excepted) after it shall have been presented to him, the same shall be a law, in like manner as if he had signed it, unless the Congress by their adjournment prevent its return, in which case it shall not be a law.

Every order, resolution, or vote to which the concurrence of the Senate and House of Representatives may be necessary (except on a question of adjournment) shall be presented to the President of the United States; and before the same shall take effect, shall be approved by him, or being disapproved by him, shall be repassed by two-thirds of the Senate and House of Representatives, according to the rules and limitations prescribed in the case of a bill.

SECTION 8 The Congress shall have power

To lay and collect taxes, duties, imposts, and excises, to pay the debts and provide for the common defense and general welfare of the United States; but all duties, imposts and excises shall be uniform throughout the United States;

To borrow money on the credit of the United States;

To regulate commerce with foreign nations, and among the several States, and with the Indian tribes;

To establish an uniform rule of naturalization, and uniform laws on the subject of bankruptcies throughout the United States;

To coin money, regulate the value thereof, and of foreign coin, and fix the standard of weights and measures;

To provide for the punishment of counterfeiting the securities and current coin of the United States;

To establish post offices and post roads;

To promote the progress of science and useful arts by securing for limited times to authors and inventors the exclusive right to their respective writings and discoveries;

To constitute tribunals inferior to the Supreme Court;

To define and punish piracies and felonies committed on the high seas and offenses against the law of nations;

To declare war, grant letters of marque and reprisal, and make rules concerning captures on land and water;

To raise and support armies, but no appropriation of money to that use shall be for a longer term than two years;

To provide and maintain a navy;

To make rules for the government and regulation of the land and naval forces;

To provide for calling forth the militia to execute the laws of the Union, suppress insurrections, and repel invasions;

To provide for organizing, arming, and disciplining the militia, and for governing such part of them as may be employed in the service of the United States, reserving to the States respectively the appointment of the officers, and the authority of training the militia according to the discipline prescribed by Congress;

To exercise exclusive legislation in all cases whatsoever, over such district (not exceeding ten miles square) as may, by cession of particular States, and the acceptance of Congress, become the seat of government of the United States, and to exercise like authority over all places purchased by the consent of the legislature of the State, in which the same shall be, for erection of forts, magazines, arsenals, dockyards, and other needful buildings; —and

To make all laws which shall be necessary and proper for carrying into execution the foregoing powers, and all other powers vested by this Constitution in the government of the United States, or in any department or officer thereof.

SECTION 9 *The migration or importation of such persons as any of the States now existing shall think proper to admit shall not be prohibited by the Congress prior to the year 1808; but a tax or duty may be imposed on such importation, not exceeding $10 for each person.*

The privilege of the writ of habeas corpus shall not be suspended, unless when in cases of rebellion or invasion the public safety may require it.

No bill of attainder or ex post facto law shall be passed.

No capitation, or other direct, tax shall be laid, unless in proportion to the census or enumeration herein before directed to be taken.

No tax or duty shall be laid on articles exported from any State.

No preference shall be given by any regulation of commerce or revenue to the ports of one State over those of another; nor shall vessels bound to, or from, one State, be obliged to enter, clear, or pay duties in another.

No money shall be drawn from the treasury, but in consequence of appropriations made by law; and a regular statement and account of the receipts and expenditures of all public money shall be published from time to time.

No title of nobility shall be granted by the United States: and no person holding any office of profit or trust under them, shall, without the consent of the Congress, accept of any present, emolument, office, or title, of any kind whatever, from any king, prince, or foreign state.

Section 10 No State shall enter into any treaty, alliance, or confederation; grant letters of marque and reprisal; coin money; emit bills of credit; make anything but gold and silver coin a tender in payment of debts; pass any bill of attainder, ex post facto law, or law impairing the obligation of contracts, or grant any title of nobility.

No State shall, without the consent of Congress, lay any imposts or duties on imports or exports, except what may be absolutely necessary for executing its inspection laws: and the net produce of all duties and imposts, laid by any State on imports or exports, shall be for the use of the treasury of the United States; and all such laws shall be subject to the revision and control of the Congress.

No State shall, without the consent of Congress, lay any duty of tonnage, keep troops or ships of war in time of peace, enter into any agreement or compact with another State, or with a foreign power, or engage in war, unless actually invaded, or in such imminent danger as will not admit of delay.

Article II

Section 1 The executive power shall be vested in a President of the United States of America. He shall hold his office during the term of four years, and, together with the Vice-President, chosen for the same term, be elected as follows:

Each State shall appoint, in such manner as the legislature thereof may direct, a number of electors, equal to the whole number of Senators and Representatives to which the State may be entitled in the Congress; but no Senator or Representative, or person holding an office of trust or profit under the United States, shall be appointed an elector.

The electors shall meet in their respective States, and vote by ballot for two persons, of whom one at least shall not be an inhabitant of the same State with themselves. And they shall make a list of all the persons voted for, and of the number of votes for each; which list they shall sign and certify, and transmit sealed to the seat of government of the United States, directed to the President of the Senate. The President of the Senate shall, in the presence of the Senate and House of Representatives, open all the certificates, and the votes shall then be counted. The person having the greatest number of votes shall be the President, if such number be a majority of the whole number of electors appointed; and if there be more than one who have such majority, and have an equal number of votes, then the House of Representatives shall immediately choose by ballot one of them for President; and if no person have a majority, then from the five highest on the list said house shall in like manner choose the President. But in choosing the President the votes shall be taken by States, the representation from each State having one vote; a quorum for this purpose shall consist of a member or members from two-thirds of the States, and a majority of all the States shall be necessary to a choice. In every case, after the choice of the President, the person having the greatest number of votes of the electors shall be the Vice-President. But if there should remain two or more who have equal votes, the Senate shall choose from them by ballot the Vice-President.

The Congress may determine the time of choosing the electors and the day on which they shall give their votes; which day shall be the same throughout the United States.

No person except a natural-born citizen, *or a citizen of the United States at the time of the adoption of this Constitution,* shall be eligible to the office of President; neither shall any person be eligible to that office who shall not have attained to the age of thirty-five years, and been fourteen years a resident within the United States.

In cases of the removal of the President from office or of his death, resignation, or inability to discharge the powers and duties of the said office, the same shall devolve on the Vice-President, and the Congress may by law provide for the case of removal, death, resignation, or inability, both of the President and Vice-President, declaring what officer shall then act as President, and such officer shall act accordingly, until the disability be removed, or a President shall be elected.

The President shall, at stated times, receive for his services a compensation, which shall neither be increased nor diminished during the period for which he shall have been elected, and he shall not receive within that period any other emolument from the United States, or any of them.

Before he enter on the execution of his office, he shall take the following oath or affirmation:—"I do solemnly swear (or affirm) that I will faithfully execute the office of the President of the United States, and will to the best of my ability preserve, protect and defend the Constitution of the United States."

SECTION 2   The President shall be commander in chief of the army and navy of the United States, and of the militia of the several States, when called into the actual service of the United States; he may require the opinion, in writing, of the principal officer in each of the executive departments, upon any subject relating to the duties of their respective offices, and he shall have power to grant reprieves and pardons for offenses against the United States, except in cases of impeachment.

He shall have power, by and with the advice and consent of the Senate, to make treaties, provided two-thirds of the Senators present concur; and he shall nominate, and by and with the advice and consent of the Senate, shall appoint ambassadors, other public ministers and consuls, judges of the Supreme Court, and all other officers of the United States, whose appointments are not herein otherwise provided for, and which shall be established by law: but Congress may by law vest the appointment of such inferior officers, as they think proper, in the President alone, in the courts of law, or in the heads of departments.

The President shall have power to fill up all vacancies that may happen during the recess of the Senate, by granting commissions which shall expire at the end of their next session.

SECTION 3   He shall from time to time give to the Congress information of the state of the Union, and recommend to their consideration such measures as he shall judge necessary and expedient; he may, on extraordinary occasions, convene both houses, or either of them, and in case of disagreement between them, with respect to the time of adjournment, he may adjourn them to such time as he shall think proper; he shall receive ambassadors and other public ministers; he shall take care that the laws be faithfully executed, and shall commission all the officers of the United States.

SECTION 4   The President, Vice-President and all civil officers of the United States shall be removed from office on impeachment for, and on conviction of, treason, bribery, or other high crimes and misdemeanors.

Article III

SECTION 1   The judicial power of the United States shall be vested in one Supreme Court, and in such inferior courts as the Congress may from time to time ordain and establish. The judges, both of the Supreme and inferior courts, shall hold their offices during good behavior, and shall, at stated times, receive for their services a compensation which shall not be diminished during their continuance in office.

SECTION 2   The judicial power shall extend to all cases, in law and equity, arising under this Constitution, the laws of the United States, and treaties made, or which shall be made, under their authority;—to all cases affecting ambassadors, other public ministers and consuls;—to all cases of admiralty and maritime jurisdiction;—to controversies to which the United States shall be a party;—to controversies between two or more States;—*between a State and citizens of another State;—between citizens of different States;*—between citizens of the same State claiming lands under grants of different States, and between a State, or the citizens thereof, and foreign states, citizens or subjects.

In all cases affecting ambassadors, other public ministers and consuls, and those in which a State shall be party, the Supreme Court shall have original jurisdiction. In all the other cases before mentioned, the Supreme Court shall have appellate jurisdiction, both as to law and fact, with such exceptions, and under such regulations, as the Congress shall make.

The trial of all crimes, except in cases of impeachment, shall be by jury; and such trial shall be held in the State where said crimes shall have been committed; but when not committed within any State, the trial shall be at such place or places as the Congress may by law have directed.

SECTION 3   Treason against the United States shall consist only in levying war against them, or in adhering to their enemies, giving them aid and comfort. No person shall be convicted of treason unless on the testimony of two witnesses to the same overt act, or on confession in open court.

The Congress shall have power to declare the punishment of treason, but no attainder of treason shall work corruption of blood, or forfeiture except during the life of the person attainted.

Article IV

SECTION 1   Full faith and credit shall be given in each State to the public acts, records, and judicial proceedings of every other State. And the Congress may by general laws prescribe the manner in which such acts, records, and proceedings shall be proved, and the effect thereof.

SECTION 2   The citizens of each State shall be entitled to all privileges and immunities of citizens in the several States.

A person charged in any State with treason, felony, or other crime, who shall flee from justice, and be found in another State, shall on demand of the executive authority of the State from which he fled, be delivered up, to be removed to the State having jurisdiction of the crime.

No person held to service or labor in one State, under the laws thereof, escaping into another, shall, in consequence of any law or regulation therein, be discharged from such service or labor, but shall be delivered up on claim of the party to whom such service or labor may be due.

SECTION 3   New States may be admitted by the Congress into this Union; but no new State shall be formed or erected within the jurisdiction of any other State; nor any State be formed by the junction of two or more States, or parts of States, without the consent of the legislatures of the States concerned as well as of the Congress.

The Congress shall have power to dispose of and make all needful rules and regulations respecting the territory or other property belonging to the United States; and nothing in this Constitution shall be so construed as to prejudice any claims of the United States, or of any particular State.

SECTION 4   The United States shall guarantee to every State in this Union a republican form of government, and shall protect each of them against invasion; and on application of the legislature, or of the executive (when the legislature cannot be convened), against domestic violence.

Article V

The Congress, whenever two-thirds of both houses shall deem it necessary, shall propose amendments to this Constitution, or, on the application of the legislatures of two-thirds of the several States, shall call a convention for proposing amendments, which, in either case, shall be valid to all intents and purposes, as part of this Constitution, when ratified by the legislatures of three-fourths of the several States, or by conventions in three-fourths thereof, as the one or the other mode of ratification may be proposed by the Congress; provided *that no amendments which may be made prior to the year one thousand eight hundred and eight shall in any manner affect the first and fourth clauses in the ninth section of the first article;* and that no State, without its consent, shall be deprived of its equal suffrage in the Senate.

Article VI

All debts contracted and engagements entered into, before the adoption of this Constitution, shall be as valid against the United States under this Constitution, as under the Confederation.

This Constitution, and the laws of the United States which shall be made in pursuance thereof; and all treaties made, or which shall be made, under the authority of the United States, shall be the supreme law of the land; and the judges in every State shall be bound thereby, anything in the Constitution or laws of any State to the contrary notwithstanding.

The Senators and Representatives before mentioned, and the members of the several State legislatures, and all executive and judicial officers, both of the United States and of the several States, shall be bound by oath or affirmation to support this Constitution; but no religious test shall ever be required as a qualification to any office or public trust under the United States.

Article VII

The ratification of the conventions of nine States shall be sufficient for the establishment of this Constitution between the States so ratifying the same.

Done in Convention by the unanimous consent of the States present, the seventeenth day of September in the year of our Lord one thousand seven hundred and eighty-seven and of the Independence of the United States of America the twelfth. In witness whereof we have hereunto subscribed our names.

AMENDMENTS TO THE CONSTITUTION*

Amendment I

Congress shall make no law respecting an establishment of religion, or prohibiting the free exercise thereof; or abridging the freedom of speech, or of the press; or the right of the people peaceably to assemble, and to petition the government for a redress of grievances.

Amendment II

A well-regulated militia being necessary to the security of a free State, the right of the people to keep and bear arms shall not be infringed.

Amendment III

No soldier shall, in time of peace, be quartered in any house without the consent of the owner, nor in time of war, but in a manner to be prescribed by law.

Amendment IV

The right of the people to be secure in their persons, houses, papers, and effects, against unreasonable searches and seizures, shall not be violated, and no warrants shall issue but upon probable cause, supported by oath or affirmation, and particularly describing the place to be searched, and the persons or things to be seized.

Amendment V

No person shall be held to answer for a capital, or otherwise infamous crime, unless on a presentment or indictment of a grand jury, except in cases arising in the land or naval forces, or in the militia, when in actual service in time of war or public danger; nor shall any person be subject for the same offense to be twice put in jeopardy of life or limb; nor shall be compelled in any criminal case to be a witness against himself, nor be deprived of life, liberty, or property, without due process of law; nor shall private property be taken for public use without just compensation.

Amendment VI

In all criminal prosecutions, the accused shall enjoy the right to a speedy and public trial, by an impartial jury of the State and district wherein the crime shall have been committed, which district shall have been previously ascertained by law, and to be informed of the nature and cause of the accusation; to be confronted with the witnesses against him; to have compulsory process for obtaining witnesses in his favor, and to have the assistance of counsel for his defense.

---

*The first ten Amendments (the Bill of Rights) were adopted in 1791.

Amendment VII

In suits at common law, where the value in controversy shall exceed twenty dollars, the right of trial by jury shall be preserved, and no fact tried by a jury shall be otherwise reexamined in any court of the United States, than according to the rules of the common law.

Amendment VIII

Excessive bail shall not be required, nor excessive fines imposed, nor cruel and unusual punishments inflicted.

Amendment IX

The enumeration in the Constitution, of certain rights, shall not be construed to deny or disparage others retained by the people.

Amendment X

The powers not delegated to the United States by the Constitution, nor prohibited by it to the States, are reserved to the States respectively, or to the people.

Amendment XI

[Adopted 1798]

The judicial power of the United States shall not be construed to extend to any suit in law or equity, commenced or prosecuted against one of the United States by citizens of another State, or by citizens or subjects of any foreign state.

Amendment XII

[Adopted 1804]

The electors shall meet in their respective States, and vote by ballot for President and Vice-President, one of whom, at least, shall not be an inhabitant of the same State with themselves; they shall name in their ballots the person voted for as President, and in distinct ballots the person voted for as Vice-President, and they shall make distinct lists of all persons voted for as President, and of all persons voted for as Vice-President, and of the number of votes for each, which lists they shall sign and certify, and transmit sealed to the seat of government of the United States, directed to the President of the Senate;—the President of the Senate shall, in the presence of the Senate and House of Representatives, open all the certificates and the votes shall then be counted;—the person having the greatest number of votes for President shall be the President, if such number be a majority of the whole number of electors appointed; and if no person have such majority, then from the persons having the highest numbers not exceeding three on the list of those voted for as President, the House of Representatives shall choose immediately, by ballot, the President. But in choosing the President, the votes shall be taken by States, the representation from each State having one vote; a quorum for this purpose shall consist of a member or members from two-thirds of the States, and a majority of all the States shall be necessary to a choice. And if the House of Representatives shall not choose a President whenever the right of choice shall devolve upon them, before *the fourth day of March* next following, then the Vice-President shall act as President, as in the case of the death or other constitutional disability of the President.

The person having the greatest number of votes as Vice-President shall be the Vice-President, if such number be a majority of the whole number of electors appointed; and if no person have a majority, then from the two highest numbers on the list the Senate shall choose the Vice-President; a quorum for the purpose shall consist of two-thirds of the whole number of Senators, and a majority of the whole number shall be necessary to a choice. But no person constitutionally ineligible to the office of President shall be eligible to that of Vice-President of the United States.

Amendment XIII

[Adopted 1865]

SECTION 1 Neither slavery nor involuntary servitude, except as a punishment for crime whereof the party shall have been duly convicted, shall exist within the United States, or any place subject to their jurisdiction.

SECTION 2 Congress shall have power to enforce this article by appropriate legislation.

Amendment XIV

[Adopted 1868]

SECTION 1 All persons born or naturalized in the United States, and subject to the jurisdiction thereof, are citizens of the United States and of the State wherein they reside. No State shall make or enforce any law which shall abridge the privileges or immunities of citizens of the United States; nor shall any State deprive any person of life, liberty, or property, without due process of law; nor deny to any person within its jurisdiction the equal protection of the laws.

SECTION 2 Representatives shall be apportioned among the several States according to their respective numbers, counting the whole number of persons in each State, excluding Indians not taxed. But when the right to vote at any election for the choice of Electors for President and Vice-President of the United States, Representatives in Congress, the executive and judicial officers of a State, or the members of the legislature thereof, is denied to any of the male inhabitants of such State, being twenty-one years of age and citizens of the United States, or in any way abridged, except for participation in rebellion, or other crime, the basis of representation therein shall be reduced in the proportion which the number of such male citizens shall bear to the whole number of male citizens twenty-one years of age in such State.

SECTION 3 No person shall be a Senator or Representative in Congress, or Elector of President and Vice-President, or hold any office, civil or military, under the United States, or under any State, who, having previously taken an oath, as a member of Congress, or as an officer of the United States, or as a member of any State legislature, or as an executive or judicial officer of any State, to support the Constitution of the United States, shall have engaged in insurrection or rebellion against the same, or given aid or comfort to the enemies thereof. Congress may, by a vote of two-thirds of each house, remove such disability.

SECTION 4   The validity of the public debt of the United States, authorized by law, including debts incurred for payment of pensions and bounties for services in suppressing insurrection or rebellion, shall not be questioned. But neither the United States nor any State shall assume or pay any debt or obligation incurred in aid of insurrection or rebellion against the United States, or any claim for the loss of emancipation of any slave; but all such debts, obligations, and claims shall be held illegal and void.

SECTION 5   The Congress shall have power to enforce, by appropriate legislation, the provisions of this article.

Amendment XV

[Adopted 1870]

SECTION 1   The right of citizens of the United States to vote shall not be denied or abridged by the United States or by any State on account of race, color, or previous condition of servitude.

SECTION 2   The Congress shall have power to enforce this article by appropriate legislation.

Amendment XVI

[Adopted 1913]

The Congress shall have power to lay and collect taxes on incomes, from whatever source derived, without apportionment among the several States, and without regard to any census or enumeration.

Amendment XVII

[Adopted 1913]

SECTION 1   The Senate of the United States shall be composed of two Senators from each State, elected by the people thereof, for six years; and each Senator shall have one vote. The electors in each State shall have the qualifications requisite for electors of [voters for] the most numerous branch of the State legislatures.

SECTION 2   When vacancies happen in the representation of any State in the Senate, the executive authority of such State shall issue writs of election to fill such vacancies: Provided, that the Legislature of any State may empower the executive thereof to make temporary appointments until the people fill the vacancies by election as the Legislature may direct.

SECTION 3   This amendment shall not be so construed as to affect the election or term of any Senator chosen before it becomes valid as part of the Constitution.

Amendment XVIII

[Adopted 1919; Repealed 1933]

SECTION 1   After one year from the ratification of this article the manufacture, sale, or transportation of intoxicating liquors within, the importation thereof into, or the exportation thereof from the United States and all territory subject to the jurisdiction thereof, for beverage purposes, is hereby prohibited.

SECTION 2   The Congress and the several States shall have concurrent power to enforce this article by appropriate legislation.

SECTION 3   This article shall be inoperative unless it shall have been ratified as an amendment to the Constitution by the legislatures of the several States, as provided by the Constitution, within seven years from the date of the submission thereof to the States by the Congress.

Amendment XIX

[Adopted 1920]

SECTION 1   The right of citizens of the United States to vote shall not be denied or abridged by the United States or by any State on account of sex.

SECTION 2   The Congress shall have power to enforce this article by appropriate legislation.

Amendment XX

[Adopted 1933]

SECTION 1   The terms of the President and Vice-President shall end at noon on the 20th day of January, and the terms of Senators and Representatives at noon on the 3rd day of January, of the years in which such terms would have ended if this article had not been ratified; and the terms of their successors shall then begin.

SECTION 2   The Congress shall assemble at least once in every year, and such meeting shall begin at noon on the 3d day of January, unless they shall by law appoint a different day.

SECTION 3   If, at the time fixed for the beginning of the term of the President, the President-elect shall have died, the Vice-President–elect shall become President. If a President shall not have been chosen before the time fixed for the beginning of his term, or if the President-elect shall have failed to qualify, then the Vice-President–elect shall act as President until a President shall have qualified; and the Congress may by law provide for the case wherein neither a President-elect nor a Vice-President–elect shall have qualified, declaring who shall then act as President, or the manner in which one who is to act shall be selected, and such persons shall act accordingly until a President or Vice-President shall have qualified.

SECTION 4   The Congress may by law provide for the case of the death of any of the persons from whom the House of Representatives may choose a President whenever the right of choice shall have devolved upon them, and for the case of the death of any of the persons from whom the Senate may choose a Vice-President whenever the right of choice shall have devolved upon them.

SECTION 5   Sections 1 and 2 shall take effect on the 15th day of October following the ratification of this article.

SECTION 6   This article shall be inoperative unless it shall have been ratified as an amendment to the Constitution by the Legislatures of three-fourths of the several States within seven years from the date of its submission.

Amendment XXI

[Adopted 1933]

SECTION 1   The eighteenth article of amendment to the Constitution of the United States is hereby repealed.

SECTION 2 The transportation or importation into any State, Territory, or Possession of the United States for delivery or use therein of intoxicating liquors, in violation of the laws thereof, is hereby prohibited.

SECTION 3 This article shall be inoperative unless it shall have been ratified as an amendment to the Constitution by conventions in the several States, as provided in the Constitution, within seven years from the date of submission thereof to the States by the Congress.

Amendment XXII

[Adopted 1951]

SECTION 1 No person shall be elected to the office of President more than twice, and no person who has held the office of President, or acted as President, for more than two years of a term to which some other person was elected President shall be elected to the office of President more than once. But this article shall not apply to any person holding the office of President when this article was proposed by the Congress, and shall not prevent any person who may be holding the office of President, or acting as President, during the term within which this article becomes operative from holding the office of President or acting as President during the remainder of such term.

SECTION 2 This article shall be inoperative unless it shall have been ratified as an amendment to the Constitution by the legislatures of three-fourths of the several States within seven years from the date of its submission to the States by the Congress.

Amendment XXIII

[Adopted 1961]

SECTION 1 The District constituting the seat of Government of the United States shall appoint in such manner as the Congress may direct:
    A number of electors of President and Vice-President equal to the whole number of Senators and Representatives in Congress to which the District would be entitled if it were a State, but in no event more than the least populous State; they shall be in addition to those appointed by the States, but they shall be considered for the purposes of the election of President and Vice-President, to be electors appointed by a State; and they shall meet in the District and perform such duties as provided by the twelfth article of amendment.

SECTION 2 The Congress shall have the power to enforce this article by appropriate legislation.

Amendment XXIV

[Adopted 1964]

SECTION 1 The right of citizens of the United States to vote in any primary or other election for President or Vice-President, for electors for President or Vice-President, or for Senator or Representative in Congress, shall not be denied or abridged by the United States or any State by reason of failure to pay any poll tax or other tax.

SECTION 2 The Congress shall have the power to enforce this article by appropriate legislation.

Amendment XXV

[Adopted 1967]

SECTION 1 In case of the removal of the President from office or of his death or resignation, the Vice-President shall become President.

SECTION 2 Whenever there is a vacancy in the office of the Vice-President, the President shall nominate a Vice-President who shall take office upon confirmation by a majority vote of both Houses of Congress.

SECTION 3 Whenever the President transmits to the President pro tempore of the Senate and the Speaker of the House of Representatives his written declaration that he is unable to discharge the powers and duties of his office, and until he transmits to them a written declaration to the contrary, such powers and duties shall be discharged by the Vice-President as Acting President.

SECTION 4 Whenever the Vice-President and a majority of either the principal officers of the executive departments or of such other body as Congress may by law provide, transmit to the President pro tempore of the Senate and the Speaker of the House of Representatives their written declaration that the President is unable to discharge the powers and duties of his office, the Vice-President shall immediately assume the powers and duties of the office as Acting President.

Thereafter, when the President transmits to the President pro tempore of the Senate and the Speaker of the House of Representatives his written declaration that no inability exists, he shall resume the powers and duties of his office unless the Vice-President and a majority of either the principal officers of the executive department[s] or of such other body as Congress may by law provide, transmit within four days to the President pro tempore of the Senate and the Speaker of the House of Representatives their written declaration that the President is unable to discharge the powers and duties of his office. Thereupon Congress shall decide the issue, assembling within forty-eight hours for that purpose if not in session. If the Congress, within twenty-one days after receipt of the latter written declaration, or, if Congress is not in session, within twenty-one days after Congress is required to assemble, determines by two-thirds vote of both Houses that the President is unable to discharge the powers and duties of his office, the Vice-President shall continue to discharge the same as Acting President; otherwise, the President shall resume the powers and duties of his office.

Amendment XXVI

[Adopted 1971]

SECTION 1 The right of citizens of the United States, who are eighteen years of age or older, to vote shall not be denied or abridged by the United States or by any State on account of age.

SECTION 2 The Congress shall have power to enforce this article by appropriate legislation.

Amendment XXVII

[Adopted 1992]

No law, varying the compensation for the services of the Senators and Representatives, shall take effect, until an election of Representatives shall have intervened.

POPULATION OF THE UNITED STATES

Year	Number of States	Population	Percent Increase	Population Per Square Mile	Percent Urban/Rural	Percent Male/Female	Percent White/Non-white	Persons Per House-hold	Median Age
1790	13	3,929,214		4.5	5.1/94.9	NA/NA	80.7/19.3	5.79	NA
1800	16	5,308,483	35.1	6.1	6.1/93.9	NA/NA	81.1/18.9	NA	NA
1810	17	7,239,881	36.4	4.3	7.3/92.7	NA/NA	81.0/19.0	NA	NA
1820	23	9,638,453	33.1	5.5	7.2/92.8	50.8/49.2	81.6/18.4	NA	16.7
1830	24	12,866,020	33.5	7.4	8.8/91.2	50.8/49.2	81.9/18.1	NA	17.2
1840	26	17,069,453	32.7	9.8	10.8/89.2	50.9/49.1	83.2/16.8	NA	17.8
1850	31	23,191,876	35.9	7.9	15.3/84.7	51.0/49.0	84.3/15.7	5.55	18.9
1860	33	31,443,321	35.6	10.6	19.8/80.2	51.2/48.8	85.6/14.4	5.28	19.4
1870	37	39,818,449	26.6	13.4	25.7/74.3	50.6/49.4	86.2/13.8	5.09	20.2
1880	38	50,155,783	26.0	16.9	28.2/71.8	50.9/49.1	86.5/13.5	5.04	20.9
1890	44	62,947,714	25.5	21.2	35.1/64.9	51.2/48.8	87.5/12.5	4.93	22.0
1900	45	75,994,575	20.7	25.6	39.6/60.4	51.1/48.9	87.9/12.1	4.76	22.9
1910	46	91,972,266	21.0	31.0	45.6/54.4	51.5/48.5	88.9/11.1	4.54	24.1
1920	48	105,710,620	14.9	35.6	51.2/48.8	51.0/49.0	89.7/10.3	4.34	25.3
1930	48	122,775,046	16.1	41.2	56.1/43.9	50.6/49.4	89.8/10.2	4.11	26.4
1940	48	131,669,275	7.2	44.2	56.5/43.5	50.2/49.8	89.8/10.2	3.67	29.0
1950	48	150,697,361	14.5	50.7	64.0/36.0	49.7/50.3	89.5/10.5	3.37	30.2
1960	50	179,323,175	18.5	50.6	69.9/30.1	49.3/50.7	88.6/11.4	3.33	29.5
1970	50	203,302,031	13.4	57.6	73.6/26.4	48.7/51.3	87.6/12.4	3.14	28.0
1980	50	226,542,199	11.4	64.1	73.7/26.3	48.6/51.4	85.9/14.1	2.75	30.0
1990	50	248,718,301	9.8	70.3	75.2/24.8	48.7/51.3	83.9/16.1	2.63	32.8
2000	50	281,421,906	13.1	79.6	80.3/19.7	49.1/50.9	77.1/22.9	2.59	35.3

NA = Not available.

IMMIGRANTS TO THE UNITED STATES

Immigration Totals by Decade

Years	Number
1820–1830	151,824
1831–1840	599,125
1841–1850	1,713,251
1851–1860	2,598,214
1861–1870	2,314,824
1871–1880	2,812,191
1881–1890	5,246,613
1891–1900	3,687,546
1901–1910	8,795,386
1911–1920	5,735,811
1921–1930	4,107,209
1931–1940	528,431
1941–1950	1,035,039
1951–1960	2,515,479
1961–1970	3,321,677
1971–1980	4,493,314
1981–1990	7,338,062
1991–2000	9,095,417
Total	66,089,413

THE AMERICAN WORKER

Year	Total Number of Workers	Males as Percent of Total Workers	Females as Percent of Total Workers	Married Women as Percent of Female Workers	Female Workers as Percent of Female Population	Percent of Labor Force Unemployed
1870	12,506,000	85	15	NA	NA	NA
1880	17,392,000	85	15	NA	NA	NA
1890	23,318,000	83	17	14	19	4 (1894 = 18)
1900	29,073,000	82	18	15	21	5
1910	38,167,000	79	21	25	25	6
1920	41,614,000	79	21	23	24	5 (1921 = 12)
1930	48,830,000	78	22	29	25	9 (1933 = 25)
1940	53,011,000	76	24	36	27	15 (1944 = 1)
1950	62,208,000	72	28	52	31	5.3
1960	69,628,000	67	33	55	38	5.5
1970	82,771,000	62	38	59	43	4.9
1980	106,940,000	58	42	55	52	7.1
1990	125,840,000	55	45	54	58	5.6
2000	138,734,064	54	46	NA	59	5.3

NA = Not available.

THE AMERICAN ECONOMY

Year	Gross National Product (GNP) and Gross Domestic Product (GDP)[a] (in $ billions)	Steel Production (in tons)	Corn Production (millions of bushels)	Automobiles Registered	New Housing Starts	Foreign Trade (in $ millions) Exports	Imports
1790	NA	NA	NA	NA	NA	20	23
1800	NA	NA	NA	NA	NA	71	91
1810	NA	NA	NA	NA	NA	67	85
1820	NA	NA	NA	NA	NA	70	74
1830	NA	NA	NA	NA	NA	74	71
1840	NA	NA	NA	NA	NA	132	107
1850	NA	NA	592[d]	NA	NA	152	178
1860	NA	13,000	839[e]	NA	NA	400	362
1870	7.4[b]	77,000	1,125	NA	NA	451	462
1880	11.2[c]	1,397,000	1,707	NA	NA	853	761
1890	13.1	4,779,000	1,650	NA	328,000	910	823
1900	18.7	11,227,000	2,662	8,000	189,000	1,499	930
1910	35.3	28,330,000	2,853	458,300	387,000 (1918 = 118,000)	1,919	1,646
1920	91.5	46,183,000	3,071	8,131,500	247,000 (1925 = 937,000)	8,664	5,784
1930	90.7	44,591,000	2,080	23,034,700	330,000 (1933 = 93,000)	4,013	3,500
1940	100.0	66,983,000	2,457	27,465,800	603,000 (1944 = 142,000)	4,030	7,433
1950	286.5	96,836,000	3,075	40,339,000	1,952,000	9,997	8,954
1960	506.5	99,282,000	4,314	61,682,300	1,365,000	19,659	15,093
1970	1,016.0	131,514,000	4,200	89,279,800	1,434,000	42,681	40,356
1980	2,819.5	111,835,000	6,600	121,601,000	1,292,000	220,626	244,871
1990	5,764.9	98,906,000	7,933	143,550,000	1,193,000	394,030	485,453
2000	9,926.6	112,200,000	9,968	217,028,000	1,575,000	771,994	1,224,408

[a] In December 1991 the Bureau of Economic Analysis of the U.S. government began featuring Gross Domestic Product rather than Gross National Product as the primary measure of U.S. production. [b] Figure is average for 1869–1878. [c] Figure is average for 1879–1888. [d] Figure for 1849. [e] Figure for 1859. NA = Not available.

PRESIDENTIAL ELECTIONS

Year	Number of States	Candidates	Parties	Popular Vote	% of Popular Vote	Electoral Vote	% Voter Participation[a]
1789	10	**George Washington**	No party			69	
		John Adams	designations			34	
		Other candidates				35	
1792	15	**George Washington**	No party			132	
		John Adams	designations			77	
		George Clinton				50	
		Other candidates				5	
1796	16	**John Adams**	Federalist			71	
		Thomas Jefferson	Democratic-Republican			68	
		Thomas Pinckney	Federalist			59	
		Aaron Burr	Democratic-Republican			30	
		Other candidates				48	
1800	16	**Thomas Jefferson**	Democratic-Republican			73	
		Aaron Burr	Democratic-Republican			73	
		John Adams	Federalist			65	
		Charles C. Pinckney	Federalist			64	
		John Jay	Federalist			1	
1804	17	**Thomas Jefferson**	Democratic-Republican			162	
		Charles C. Pinckney	Federalist			14	
1808	17	**James Madison**	Democratic-Republican			122	
		Charles C. Pinckney	Federalist			47	
		George Clinton	Democratic-Republican			6	
1812	18	**James Madison**	Democratic-Republican			128	
		De Witt Clinton	Federalist			89	
1816	19	**James Monroe**	Democratic-Republican			183	
		Rufus King	Federalist			34	
1820	24	**James Monroe**	Democratic-Republican			231	
		John Quincy Adams	Independent Republican			1	

PRESIDENTIAL ELECTIONS *(Continued)*

Year	Number of States	Candidates	Parties	Popular Vote	% of Popular Vote	Electoral Vote	% Voter Participation[a]
1824	24	John Quincy Adams	Democratic-Republican	108,740	30.5	84	26.9
		Andrew Jackson	Democratic-Republican	153,544	43.1	99	
		Henry Clay	Democratic-Republican	47,136	13.2	37	
		William H. Crawford	Democratic-Republican	46,618	13.1	41	
1828	24	Andrew Jackson	Democratic	647,286	56.0	178	57.6
		John Quincy Adams	National Republican	508,064	44.0	83	
1832	24	Andrew Jackson	Democratic	701,780	54.2	219	55.4
		Henry Clay	National Republican	484,205	37.4	49	
		Other candidates		107,988	8.0	18	
1836	26	Martin Van Buren	Democratic	764,176	50.8	170	57.8
		William H. Harrison	Whig	550,816	36.6	73	
		Hugh L. White	Whig	146,107	9.7	26	
1840	26	William H. Harrison	Whig	1,274,624	53.1	234	80.2
		Martin Van Buren	Democratic	1,127,781	46.9	60	
1844	26	James K. Polk	Democratic	1,338,464	49.6	170	78.9
		Henry Clay	Whig	1,300,097	48.1	105	
		James G. Birney	Liberty	62,300	2.3		
1848	30	Zachary Taylor	Whig	1,360,967	47.4	163	72.7
		Lewis Cass	Democratic	1,222,342	42.5	127	
		Martin Van Buren	Free Soil	291,263	10.1		
1852	31	Franklin Pierce	Democratic	1,601,117	50.9	254	69.6
		Winfield Scott	Whig	1,385,453	44.1	42	
		John P. Hale	Free-Soil	155,825	5.0		
1856	31	James Buchanan	Democratic	1,832,955	45.3	174	78.9
		John C. Frémont	Republican	1,339,932	33.1	114	
		Millard Fillmore	American	871,731	21.6	8	
1860	33	Abraham Lincoln	Republican	1,865,593	39.8	180	81.2
		Stephen A. Douglas	Democratic	1,382,713	29.5	12	
		John C. Breckinridge	Democratic	848,356	18.1	72	
		John Bell	Constitutional Union	592,906	12.6	39	
1864	36	Abraham Lincoln	Republican	2,206,938	55.0	212	73.8
		George B. McClellan	Democratic	1,803,787	45.0	21	
1868	37	Ulysses S. Grant	Republican	3,013,421	52.7	214	78.1
		Horatio Seymour	Democratic	2,706,829	47.3	80	

PRESIDENTIAL ELECTIONS *(Continued)*

Year	Number of States	Candidates	Parties	Popular Vote	% of Popular Vote	Electoral Vote	% Voter Partici-pation[a]
1872	37	**Ulysses S. Grant**	Republican	3,596,745	55.6	286	71.3
		Horace Greeley	Democratic	2,843,446	43.9	[b]	
1876	38	**Rutherford B. Hayes**	Republican	4,036,572	48.0	185	81.8
		Samuel J. Tilden	Democratic	4,284,020	51.0	184	
1880	38	**James A. Garfield**	Republican	4,453,295	48.5	214	79.4
		Winfield S. Hancock	Democratic	4,414,082	48.1	155	
		James B. Weaver	Greenback-Labor	308,578	3.4		
1884	38	**Grover Cleveland**	Democratic	4,879,507	48.5	219	77.5
		James G. Blaine	Republican	4,850,293	48.2	182	
		Benjamin F. Butler	Greenback-Labor	175,370	1.8		
		John P. St. John	Prohibition	150,369	1.5		
1888	38	**Benjamin Harrison**	Republican	5,447,129	47.9	233	79.3
		Grover Cleveland	Democratic	5,537,857	48.6	168	
		Clinton B. Fisk	Prohibition	249,506	2.2		
		Anson J. Streeter	Union Labor	146,935	1.3		
1892	44	**Grover Cleveland**	Democratic	5,555,426	46.1	277	74.7
		Benjamin Harrison	Republican	5,182,690	43.0	145	
		James B. Weaver	People's	1,029,846	8.5	22	
		John Bidwell	Prohibition	264,133	2.2		
1896	45	**William McKinley**	Republican	7,102,246	51.1	271	79.3
		William J. Bryan	Democratic	6,492,559	47.7	176	
1900	45	**William McKinley**	Republican	7,218,491	51.7	292	73.2
		William J. Bryan	Democratic; Populist	6,356,734	45.5	155	
		John C. Wooley	Prohibition	208,914	1.5		
1904	45	**Theodore Roosevelt**	Republican	7,628,461	57.4	336	65.2
		Alton B. Parker	Democratic	5,084,223	37.6	140	
		Eugene V. Debs	Socialist	402,283	3.0		
		Silas C. Swallow	Prohibition	v258,536	1.9		
1908	46	**William H. Taft**	Republican	7,675,320	51.6	321	65.4
		William J. Bryan	Democratic	6,412,294	43.1	162	
		Eugene V. Debs	Socialist	420,793	2.8		
		Eugene W. Chafin	Prohibition	253,840	1.7		
1912	48	**Woodrow Wilson**	Democratic	6,296,547	41.9	435	58.8
		Theodore Roosevelt	Progressive	4,118,571	27.4	88	
		William H. Taft	Republican	3,486,720	23.2	8	
		Eugene V. Debs	Socialist	900,672	6.0		
		Eugene W. Chafin	Prohibition	206,275	1.4		

PRESIDENTIAL ELECTIONS *(Continued)*

Year	Number of States	Candidates	Parties	Popular Vote	% of Popular Vote	Electoral Vote	% Voter Participation[a]
1916	48	Woodrow Wilson	Democratic	9,127,695	49.4	277	61.6
		Charles E. Hughes	Republican	8,533,507	46.2	254	
		A. L. Benson	Socialist	585,113	3.2		
		J. Frank Hanly	Prohibition	220,506	1.2		
1920	48	Warren G. Harding	Republican	16,143,407	60.4	404	49.2
		James M. Cox	Democratic	9,130,328	34.2	127	
		Eugene V. Debs	Socialist	919,799	3.4		
		P. P. Christensen	Farmer-Labor	265,411	1.0		
1924	48	Calvin Coolidge	Republican	15,718,211	54.0	382	48.9
		John W. Davis	Democratic	8,385,283	28.8	136	
		Robert M. La Follette	Progressive	4,831,289	16.6	13	
1928	48	Herbert C. Hoover	Republican	21,391,993	58.2	444	56.9
		Alfred E. Smith	Democratic	15,016,169	40.9	87	
1932	48	Franklin D. Roosevelt	Democratic	22,809,638	57.4	472	56.9
		Herbert C. Hoover	Republican	15,758,901	39.7	59	
		Norman Thomas	Socialist	881,951	2.2		
1936	48	Franklin D. Roosevelt	Democratic	27,752,869	60.8	523	61.0
		Alfred M. Landon	Republican	16,674,665	36.5	8	
		William Lemke	Union	882,479	1.9		
1940	48	Franklin D. Roosevelt	Democratic	27,307,819	54.8	449	62.5
		Wendell L. Wilkie	Republican	22,321,018	44.8	82	
1944	48	Franklin D. Roosevelt	Democratic	25,606,585	53.5	432	55.9
		Thomas E. Dewey	Republican	22,014,745	46.0	99	
1948	48	Harry S Truman	Democratic	24,179,345	49.6	303	53.0
		Thomas E. Dewey	Republican	21,991,291	45.1	189	
		J. Strom Thurmond	States' Rights	1,176,125	2.4	39	
		Henry A. Wallace	Progressive	1,157,326	2.4		
1952	48	Dwight D. Eisenhower	Republican	33,936,234	55.1	442	63.3
		Adlai E. Stevenson	Democratic	27,314,992	44.4	89	
1956	48	Dwight D. Eisenhower	Republican	35,590,472	57.6	457	60.6
		Adlai E. Stevenson	Democratic	26,022,752	42.1	73	
1960	50	John F. Kennedy	Democratic	34,226,731	49.7	303	62.8
		Richard M. Nixon	Republican	34,108,157	49.5	219	
1964	50	Lyndon B. Johnson	Democratic	43,129,566	61.1	486	61.7
		Barry M. Goldwater	Republican	27,178,188	38.5	52	
1968	50	Richard M. Nixon	Republican	31,785,480	43.4	301	60.6
		Hubert H. Humphrey	Democratic	31,275,166	42.7	191	
		George C. Wallace	American Independent	9,906,473	13.5	46	

PRESIDENTIAL ELECTIONS (Continued)

Year	Number of States	Candidates	Parties	Popular Vote	% of Popular Vote	Electoral Vote	% Voter Participation[a]
1972	50	Richard M. Nixon	Republican	47,169,911	60.7	520	55.2
		George S. McGovern	Democratic	29,170,383	37.5	17	
		John G. Schmitz	American	1,099,482	1.4		
1976	50	James E. Carter	Democratic	40,830,763	50.1	297	53.5
		Gerald R. Ford	Republican	39,147,793	48.0	240	
1980	50	Ronald W. Reagan	Republican	43,904,153	50.7	489	52.6
		James E. Carter	Democratic	35,483,883	41.0	49	
		John B. Anderson	Independent	5,720,060	6.6	0	
		Ed Clark	Libertarian	921,299	1.1	0	
1984	50	Ronald W. Reagan	Republican	54,455,075	58.8	525	53.3
		Walter F. Mondale	Democratic	37,577,185	40.6	13	
1988	50	George H. W. Bush	Republican	48,886,097	53.4	426	50.1
		Michael S. Dukakis	Democratic	41,809,074	45.6	111[c]	
1992	50	William J. Clinton	Democratic	44,909,326	43.0	370	55.2
		George H. W. Bush	Republican	39,103,882	37.4	168	
		H. Ross Perot	Independent	19,741,048	18.9	0	
1996	50	William J. Clinton	Democratic	47,402,357	49.2	379	49.1
		Robert J. Dole	Republican	39,196,755	40.7	159	
		H. Ross Perot	Reform	8,085,402	8.4	0	
		Ralph Nader	Green	684,902	0.7	0	
2000	50	George W. Bush	Republican	50,456,169	48.0	271	50.7
		Albert Gore	Democratic	50,996,116	49.0	267	
		Ralph Nader	Green	2,783,728	2.7	0	

Candidates receiving less than 1 percent of the popular vote have been omitted. Thus the percentage of popular vote given for any election year may not total 100 percent. Before the passage of the Twelfth Amendment in 1804, the Electoral College voted for two presidential candidates; the runner-up became vice president. Before 1824, most presidential electors were chosen by state legislatures, not by popular vote.

[a]Percent of voting-age population casting ballots. [b]Greeley died shortly after the election; the electors supporting him then divided their votes among minor candidates. [c]One elector from West Virginia cast her Electoral College presidential ballot for Lloyd Bentsen, the Democratic Party's vice-presidential candidate.

PRESIDENTS AND VICE PRESIDENTS

1.	President	**George Washington**	1789–1797
	Vice President	John Adams	1789–1797
2.	President	**John Adams**	1797–1801
	Vice President	Thomas Jefferson	1797–1801
3.	President	**Thomas Jefferson**	1801–1809
	Vice President	Aaron Burr	1801–1805
	Vice President	George Clinton	1805–1809
4.	President	**James Madison**	1809–1817
	Vice President	George Clinton	1809–1813
	Vice President	Elbridge Gerry	1813–1817
5.	President	**James Monroe**	1817–1825
	Vice President	Daniel Tompkins	1817–1825
6.	President	**John Quincy Adams**	1825–1829
	Vice President	John C. Calhoun	1825–1829
7.	President	**Andrew Jackson**	1829–1837
	Vice President	John C. Calhoun	1829–1833
	Vice President	Martin Van Buren	1833–1837
8.	President	**Martin Van Buren**	1837–1841
	Vice President	Richard M. Johnson	1837–1841
9.	President	**William H. Harrison**	1841
	Vice President	John Tyler	1841
10.	President	**John Tyler**	1841–1845
	Vice President	None	
11.	President	**James K. Polk**	1845–1849
	Vice President	George M. Dallas	1845–1849
12.	President	**Zachary Taylor**	1849–1850
	Vice President	Millard Fillmore	1849–1850
13.	President	**Millard Fillmore**	1850–1853
	Vice President	None	
14.	President	**Franklin Pierce**	1853–1857
	Vice President	William R. King	1853–1857
15.	President	**James Buchanan**	1857–1861
	Vice President	John C. Breckinridge	1857–1861
16.	President	**Abraham Lincoln**	1861–1865
	Vice President	Hannibal Hamlin	1861–1865
	Vice President	Andrew Johnson	1865
17.	President	**Andrew Johnson**	1865–1869
	Vice President	None	
18.	President	**Ulysses S. Grant**	1869–1877
	Vice President	Schuyler Colfax	1869–1873
	Vice President	Henry Wilson	1873–1877

PRESIDENTS AND VICE PRESIDENTS *(Continued)*

19.	President	**Rutherford B. Hayes**	1877–1881
	Vice President	William A. Wheeler	1877–1881
20.	President	**James A. Garfield**	1881
	Vice President	Chester A. Arthur	1881
21.	President	**Chester A. Arthur**	1881–1885
	Vice President	None	
22.	President	**Grover Cleveland**	1885–1889
	Vice President	Thomas A. Hendricks	1885–1889
23.	President	**Benjamin Harrison**	1889–1893
	Vice President	Levi P. Morton	1889–1893
24.	President	**Grover Cleveland**	1893–1897
	Vice President	Adlai E. Stevenson	1893–1897
25.	President	**William McKinley**	1897–1901
	Vice President	Garret A. Hobart	1897–1901
	Vice President	Theodore Roosevelt	1901
26.	President	**Theodore Roosevelt**	1901–1909
	Vice President	Charles Fairbanks	1905–1909
27.	President	**William H. Taft**	1909–1913
	Vice President	James S. Sherman	1909–1913
28.	President	**Woodrow Wilson**	1913–1921
	Vice President	Thomas R. Marshall	1913–1921
29.	President	**Warren G. Harding**	1921–1923
	Vice President	Calvin Coolidge	1921–1923
30.	President	**Calvin Coolidge**	1923–1929
	Vice President	Charles G. Dawes	1925–1929
31.	President	**Herbert C. Hoover**	1929–1933
	Vice President	Charles Curtis	1929–1933
32.	President	**Franklin D. Roosevelt**	1933–1945
	Vice President	John N. Garner	1933–1941
	Vice President	Henry A. Wallace	1941–1945
	Vice President	Harry S Truman	1945
33.	President	**Harry S Truman**	1945–1953
	Vice President	Alben W. Barkley	1949–1953
34.	President	**Dwight D. Eisenhower**	1953–1961
	Vice President	Richard M. Nixon	1953–1961
35.	President	**John F. Kennedy**	1961–1963
	Vice President	Lyndon B. Johnson	1961–1963
36.	President	**Lyndon B. Johnson**	1963–1969
	Vice President	Hubert H. Humphrey	1965–1969
37.	President	**Richard M. Nixon**	1969–1974
	Vice President	Spiro T. Agnew	1969–1973
	Vice President	Gerald R. Ford	1973–1974
38.	President	**Gerald R. Ford**	1974–1977
	Vice President	Nelson A. Rockefeller	1974–1977
39.	President	**James E. Carter**	1977–1981
	Vice President	Walter F. Mondale	1977–1981

PRESIDENTS AND VICE PRESIDENTS *(Continued)*

40. President	**Ronald W. Reagan**	1981–1989
Vice President	George H. W. Bush	1981–1989
41. President	**George H. W. Bush**	1989–1993
Vice President	J. Danforth Quayle	1989–1993
42. President	**William J. Clinton**	1993–2001
Vice President	Albert Gore	1993–2001
43. President	**George W. Bush**	2001–2008
Vice President	Richard Cheney	2001–2008

For a complete list of Presidents, Vice Presidents, and Cabinet Members, go to http://college.hmco.com.

TEXT CREDITS

page 700: Excerpt from "Bessemer Steel Production, 1867–1907" from *Triumphant Capitalism: Henry Clay Frick and the Industrial Transformation of America* by Kenneth Warren, © 1996 by University of Pittsburgh Press. Reprinted by permission of the University of Pittsburgh Press.

page 771: From *American Politics in the Gilded Age, 1868–1900* by Robert W. Cherny. Copyright © 1997 by Harlan Davidson, Inc. Used by permission.

page 946: 7 Lines from "I, Too, Sing America" from *The Collected Poems of Langston Hughes* by Langston Hughes, copyright © 1994 by The Estate of Langston Hughes. Used by permission of Alfred A. Knopf, a Division of Random House, Inc.

page 1008: Excerpts from Herbert Hoover's speech of October 30, 1936. Courtesy of the Hoover Presidential Library.

page 1179–1180: "Letter from Birmingham Jail" by Martin Luther King, Jr., is reprinted by arrangement with the Estate of Martin Luther King, Jr., c/o Writers House as agent for the proprietor New York, NY. Copyright 1963 Martin Luther King, Jr., copyright renewed 1991 Coretta Scott King.

page 1179: Excerpts from *The Autobiography of Malcolm X* by Malcolm X and Alex Haley, copyright © 1964 by Alex Haley and Malcolm X. Copyright 1965 by Alex Haley and Betty Shabazz. Used by permission of Random House, Inc.

pages 1223–1224: Gloria Steinem, "What it Would be Like if Women Win," *Time*, 31, August 1970, pp. 22 & 25. Reprinted by permission of Gloria Steinem, Consulting Editor, Ms. Magazine.

pages 1224–1225: Phyllis Schlafly, excerpt from *The Power of the Positive Woman* (1970), pp. 11–18. Reprinted by permission of the author.

page 1259: "Return to Traditional Religious Values, Jerry Falwell" from *Listen America* by Jerry Falwell, copyright © 1980 Jerry Falwell. Used by permission of Doubleday, a division of Random House, Inc.

page 1260: "Letter to Yale Freshman, 1981," text of A. Bartlett Giamatti. Letter to Yale Freshman as appeared in *New York Times*, September 6, 1981, p. 25. Reprint by permission of the estate of A. Bartlett Giamatti.

page 1279: "The Economic Boon of the 1990s," *New York Times*, News of the Week in Review, May 3, 1998. Copyright © 1998 by the New York Times Co. Reprinted by permission.

NDEX